P9-CQV-722

Writing America

Language and Composition in Context

AP* Edition

David A. Jolliffe
University of Arkansas

Hephzibah Roskelly
University of North Carolina at Greensboro

PEARSON

Boston • Columbus • Indianapolis • New York • San Francisco • Upper Saddle River
Amsterdam • Cape Town • Dubai • London • Madrid • Milan • Munich • Paris • Montreal • Toronto
Delhi • Mexico City • São Paulo • Sydney • Hong Kong • Seoul • Singapore • Taipei • Tokyo

Senior Sponsoring Editor: *Katharine Glynn*
Senior Development Editor: *Marion B. Castellucci*
Executive Market Development Manager: *Dona Kenly*
Product Manager: *Alicia Orlando*
Senior Marketing Manager: *Sandra McGuire*
Senior Supplements Editor: *Donna Campion*
Executive Digital Producer: *Stefanie A. Snajder*
Digital Editor: *Sarah Gordus*
Content Specialist: *Erin Reilly*
Production Manager: *Ellen MacElree*
Project Coordination and Text Design: *Electronic Publishing Services Inc., NYC*
Electronic Page Makeup: *Jouve*
Cover Designer/Manager: *Wendy Ann Fredericks*
Cover Photos: *© Fotolia*
Senior Manufacturing Buyer: *Roy L. Pickering, Jr.*
Printer and Binder: *RR DONNELLEY*
Cover Printer: *Lehigh-Phoenix*

This title is restricted to sales and distribution in North America only.

Credits and acknowledgments borrowed from other sources, and reproduced, with permission, in this textbook, appear on pages 1002–1005.

Library of Congress Cataloging-in-Publication Data

Jolliffe, David A.
Writing America : Language and Composition in Context / David Jolliffe and Hephzibah Roskelly.
pages cm
Includes index.
ISBN 978-0-13-274880-3
1. English language—Composition and exercises. 2. Readers (Secondary) 3. Language arts (Secondary)
I. Roskelly, Hephzibah. II. Title.
PE1408.J758 2013
808'.0427—dc23

2012046217

---

11 17

www.PearsonSchool.com/Advanced
ISBN 13: 978-0-13-274880-3 (High School Binding)
ISBN 10: 0-13-274880-0 (High School Binding)

Part Two An Anthology of Readings and Images 163

Unit 1 How Do We Become a Nation? Pre-colonial Times to 1789 164

Unit 3 How Do We Preserve a Nation? 1837–1865 416

Preface

We have designed *Writing America: Language and Composition in Context AP* Edition* so that it can be used as the foundational text in a course that emphasizes reading, writing, and analyzing texts. *Writing America* teaches reading as a dynamic, interactive process. It teaches writing as a craft, related to reading, that produces rich, purposeful, well-planned and well-executed texts. It teaches the structure and organization of texts, at the level of both the whole text and the sentence. It couches this instruction in an examination of vitally important works of American literature, art, and culture, accompanied by a study of contemporary pieces that unpack current thinking on the issues and themes raised by the historical works.

Above all else, we have designed *Writing America* so that it can be the central text in a course about *rhetoric,* in the very best sense of that word: the art of finding all the available means of persuasion in a given case, the art of crafting texts so that they accomplish a purpose, forge a meaning, and the art of reading texts with an understanding of how meanings and effects are crafted. No matter what the course is called—Rhetoric and Composition, Advanced Placement English Language and Composition, American Literature and Composition, or simply English—we believe that *Writing America* will serve students well as they learn to read, write, and understand the English language comprehensively in the twenty-first century. We believe that *Writing America* is a book that will serve teachers well as they work to help students become more skillful readers, writers, and thinkers.

Features and Benefits

Writing America addresses the interests of students and the Advanced Placement program.

We have tried our best to create a textbook that resonates with three interrelated interests. First, we believe *Writing America* will appeal to any student studying English—reading, writing, and language use—during the junior or senior (or perhaps even sophomore) year of high school. Second, as former Chief Readers for the Advanced Placement English Language and Composition Examination, we know that *Writing America* addresses directly the curricular and pedagogical "centers of gravity" that the AP course and examination incorporate. Third, we are convinced that the emphases in *Writing America* on close reading, strong, purposeful writing, and careful attention to language will make the book an ideal foundation for students to build upon as they advance in their studies.

Part One provides instruction on rhetorical reading and writing.

Writing America is divided into two major parts. The first is a seven-chapter text that explores rhetoric—in reading as well as writing. Chapters 1 and 2 introduce reading as meaning-making, focusing initially on the practice of reading in general and then on the roles that genre plays in helping students read critically, understanding the rhetoric of the texts they read. Chapter 3 introduces rhetoric as the art that links critical reading and effective writing, and then Chapters 4, 5, and 6 offer detailed instruction in the kinds of reading and writing that are involved when students engage in analysis, argument, and synthesis—three varieties of rhetorical activity that are incorporated in the Advanced Placement English Language and Composition course and are also central activities in most college and university courses. Chapter 7 concludes the first part of the book with principles of sentence construction that improve critical reading and writing. Features of this section of the text include:

- **Sample exam prompts and responses,** which give students the opportunity to preview aspects of the English Language and Composition Advanced Placement Examination.
- **Arrangement charts** to help students see the typical organization of types of essays.
- **Brief activities** throughout each chapter where students apply what they have just learned.
- **Chapter projects** to help students develop longer pieces of writing such as rhetorical analyses, arguments, and synthesis essays.
- **Chapter checklists** to give students a handy list of points to check when they are drafting and revising.

Part Two provides an anthology of American texts and visuals.

The second part of *Writing America* is a new kind of anthology. Organized by historical period, the anthology is first of all a collection of both readings and images, reflecting the fact that both verbal and visual texts have always shaped thought and culture in the United States. Second, each of the six units of the anthology is arranged around a central question that the readings and images respond to:

- How do we become a nation?
- How do we build a nation?
- How do we preserve a nation?
- How do we recover a nation?
- How should a nation change?
- How does a nation learn to live in the world?

Each anthology unit has a number of features that help students read and analyze the texts as well as make connections among them.

- A **contemporary visual text** provides an engaging introduction to the unit's major themes.
- A **brief overview of major events and issues** of the unit's historic period provides students with context for the readings and visuals.
- A **selection of the period's readings and visuals** shows students how writers and artists approached the key questions of their time.
- A **selection of contemporary readings** brings the central questions of the unit into current conversation for today's readers.
- **Readings are designed to resemble their genre** which not only provides visual interest, but calls students' attention to how genre shapes an author's aim as discussed in Chapter 2.
- **Post-reading question sets** consisting of Read, Write, and Connect items have students analyze the reading, write about aspects of the reading or its issues, and connect the reading to other readings in the text or to their own experiences.
- **End-of-unit writing assignments** give students the opportunity to write essays similar to those on the Advanced Placement Exam—rhetorical analyses, arguments, and synthesis essays.

Ideally, a high school English course can be a powerful agent of change for students. If students become in this kind of English course active meaning-makers as they read and write, they also, at least potentially, become better, more active citizens, understanding that, in the twenty-first century, they are surrounded by all kinds of texts that beg for critical meaning-making: political documents urging them to support or reject candidates, letters soliciting their applications to universities, fliers claiming to help with university costs with loans and credit cards, brochures detailing advantages of military service. If students in a course that uses *Writing America* become more capable in recognizing how texts of all kinds work to convince and persuade readers to action, how texts bond readers to communities of ideologies, beliefs, and practices, then the course, we believe, will have helped them become better citizens as well as better students.

Resources for Teachers and Students

An extensive package of supplements is available for the AP* Edition of *Writing America*. These resources were specifically designed to ensure that students are well supported as they approach the rigors of college-level language instruction by providing clear, accessible, and scaffolded instruction appropriate for today's high school classroom.

Instructor Resource Center

Many of the teacher supplements are available electronically at no charge to qualified adopters from the Instructor Resource Center (IRC).

To obtain Instructor Resource Center access, please go to www.PearsonSchool.com/Access_Request and select Instructor Resource Center. You will be required to complete a brief, one-time registration subject to verification of educator status. Upon verification, access information and instructions will be sent to you via email. Once logged into the IRC, enter your textbook ISBN (0-13-274880-0) in the Search Our Catalog box to locate your resources.

Your Pearson MyLab

Your Pearson MyLab delivers diagnostic and personalized writing instruction, practice, and assessments to ensure all students are well supported as they learn to craft rich, effective essays. From basic writing skill remediation through college readiness enrichment, your Pearson MyLab provides differentiated instruction and accessible support through multimedia tutorials, interactive exercises, sample essays, and multiple opportunities to practice and apply difficult concepts.

Your Pearson MyLab is an eminently flexible application that teachers can use in ways that best complement their students' needs and teaching styles. They can recommend it to students for self-study, track student progress, or leverage the power of administrative features to be more effective and save time. The composing space includes an assignment builder and commenting tools that bring teachers closer to their student writers, make managing assignments and evaluating papers more efficient, and put powerful assessments within reach. Students receive feedback within the context of their own writing, which encourages critical thinking and revision and helps them to develop skills based on their individual needs.

Online AP* Test Bank, exclusive to your Pearson MyLab, offers 500 AP-style multiple choice questions with instant feedback to test students' comprehension of the concepts in each chapter and many of the readings in the anthology section and prepare them for the rigors of the exam. The Test Bank items are also available as downloadable resources on the IRC.

Pearson eText, an interactive eText of *Writing America,* is available in your Pearson MyLab, coupling the many resources of your Pearson MyLab with the instructional content of the text to create an enhanced learning experience for students. Marginal icons in the Pearson eText link to a wealth of online resources:

Watch the Video on the Rhetorical Appeals at Your Pearson MyLab

Video tutorials illustrate key concepts, offering tips and guidance on critical reading, evaluating sources, avoiding plagiarism, and many other topics.

Analyze the Advertisement at Your Pearson MyLab

Sample documents illustrate the range of writing students do in composition classes, their other courses, the workplace, and the community.

Complete Additional Exercises on Twain's Essay at Your Pearson MyLab

Quizzes in your Pearson MyLab help students assess their understanding of concepts and readings, and give them practice with the types of questions they will encounter on the Advanced Placement Exam.

Free Teacher Preview Access

For FREE Teacher Preview Access: Register at www.PearsonSchool.com/Access_Request. Using Option #2, Teacher Preview Access, select Language Arts, select Jolliffe, *Writing America,* Pearson MyLab with eText. After following the registration prompts you will receive a confirmation email with login and access information.

Adoption Access

For Adoption Access for teachers and students, register at www.PearsonSchool.com/Access_Request. Using Option #3, Access for Textbook Adopters, select Language Arts, select Jolliffe, *Writing America,* Pearson MyLab with eText.

After following registration prompts, you will receive a confirmation email with login and access information for teacher and students within 48 hours. Accounts are good for one year from date of activation. Each year thereafter (in or around May), for the life of the adoption, the registered teacher will receive a new set of teacher and student access codes via email for the following school year. Teachers are responsible for distributing access codes to their students each year. Teachers may choose to "copy" their course from year to year or to create a new course each year. In the event of a personnel change in the school, the new teacher responsible for this course and textbook can follow the above instructions to receive access and register his or her email to receive the annual renewal registration for the balance of the adoption cycle.

For more information about your Pearson MyLab, visit: www.PearsonSchool.com/MyEnglishLabs.

100% Digital

A perfect solution for one-to-one or virtual learning environments, *Writing America* eText is available as a 100% digital option for one- or six-year access:

- Your Pearson MyLab with *Writing America* eText—Get all of the powerful resources of Pearson MyLab plus the full, interactive eText.
- CourseSmart for PearsonSchool CSPS —For eText access only, CSPS offers flexible features allowing students to search the text, bookmark passages, save their own notes, and print reading assignments that incorporate lecture notes.
- Android and iPad eTextbooks—Android and iPad versions of the eText provide the complete text and the electronic resources described above.

Contact your Account Executive for ordering information.

AP* Test Prep and Student Study Guide Workbook

This student study guide provides AP test-taking strategies and tips as well as sample multiple choice and essay questions. Student samples of AP essays representing all levels of writing scores (1–9) are annotated and backed by commentary to provide students with the insight and understanding they need to assess their and others' writing. These examples, coupled with scaffolded instructional support on how to approach reading, writing, and analyzing text, offer students a self-directed and accessible tool to help them succeed in the AP classroom.

AP* Teacher's Manual: Teaching Composition with *Writing America*

This AP* Teacher's Manual will help teachers present materials in the context of preparing for the AP Exam. It includes an overview of and teaching suggestions for each chapter, answers to all exercises and every study question in the anthology, plus a wealth of in-class activities, lesson planning tips, and classroom exercises.

In addition, the manual provides correlations to the AP Language and Composition objectives to better support teachers in meeting the rigorous demands of the AP course while ensuring ample coverage of college readiness outcomes. The included sample syllabi incorporates elements of an American Literature course with the AP English Language and Composition objectives to give teachers a foundation to address both standards and the flexibility to customize instruction based on their specific course needs.

PowerPoints to Accompany *Writing America*

The PowerPoints that accompany *Writing America* offer chapter-by-chapter classroom-ready lecture outline slides, lecture tips and classroom activities, and review questions. It is available for download from the Instructor Resource Center.

Test Bank

The *Writing America* Test Bank offers 500 questions that test student comprehension of the content of each chapter. The Test Bank, which resides in MyLab, serves as an assessment tool, allowing teachers the ability to measure each student's mastery of every topic covered in the book.

Acknowledgments

A great many colleagues, friends, and students helped us as we wrote this book, and to all of them we offer our thanks. First of all, we gratefully acknowledge the generosity of Bernard Phelan, who allowed us to use materials he has developed for teaching the essentials of English grammar. Chapter 7 of *Writing America* grows directly out of Bernie's approach. We recognize our many co-workers from high schools and colleges across the country—too many to mention by name—who have served with us over the years as readers, table leaders, and question leaders at the annual reading of the Advanced Placement English Language and Composition Examination. Their advice, and their friendship, have been invaluable. We both have been lucky to have a cadre of mentors and colleagues who over the years have shaped our thinking about the teaching of reading and writing: Lester Faigley, the late Maxine Hairston, the late James Kinneavy, and John Ruszkiewicz of the University of Texas; William Covino of California State University at Fresno; Ann Merle Feldman of the University of Illinois at Chicago; Roger Cherry and Marcia Farr of the Ohio State University; Darsie Bowden, Gerald Mulderig, Eileen Seifert, Craig Sirles, Christine Tardy, and Pete Vandenberg of DePaul University; Elias Dominguez Barajas, Sean Connors, Chris Goering, and Patrick Slattery of the University of Arkansas; Elizabeth Chiseri-Strater, Sara Littlejohn, and Karen Kilcup at the University of North Carolina at Greensboro; and Joe Comprone, Lucy Freibert, and Tom Byers at the University of Louisville. Through her work and example, Ann Berthoff continues to shape our thinking about reading and writing.

Finally, we offer abundant thanks to all our students, both undergraduate and graduate, who help us craft and improve our courses and our teaching. We particularly thank Michael Hensley and Alaina Rainey of the University of Arkansas, who were consistently ready to provide a student's perspective on teaching and learning that *Writing America* aims to support.

We are also grateful to and thankful for all the teachers and students we have worked with over the years, who have taught us so patiently how to be better readers, writers, and citizens, including:

James Butler, Kealakehe High School, Hawaii

Terry G. Caldwell, Loyola High School of Los Angeles, California

Dana Centeno, Paraclete High School, California

Marilyn Clanton, Martin High School, Texas

James T. Davis, Michigan State University

Norma Dejoy, Jamestown High School, New York

Carol Elsen, Valley Christian High School, Montana

Penny B. Ferguson, Maryville High School, Tennessee

Kenneth Hawkins, T.R. Robinson High School, Florida

Sheryl L. Miller Hosey, Council Rock High School South, Pennsylvania

Steven J. Jolliffe, St. Johnsbury Academy, Vermont

James Jordan, Sacred Heart Cathedral Preparatory, California

Gene Kahane, Encinal High School, California

Gail Langkusch, Carlmont High School, California

Tonji Lewis, Martin High School, Texas

Diane Derosier Mackie, Springfield Central High School, Massachusetts

Michelle Maiers, West Forsyth High School, Georgia

Susan Marion, Denver Center for International Studies, Pennsylvania

Kevin McDonald, Edmond Memorial High School, Oklahoma

Melissa Newport, The Master's Academy, Florida

Kathryn Pabst, Lovejoy High School, Texas

Jose Reyes, Marlborough High School, Massachusetts

Susan Sanchez, Alhambra High School, California

Joanne Steady, Melbourne High School, Florida

Theresa Stone, Newark Memorial High School, California

Becky Talk, Cushing High School, Texas

Louise Adair Taylor, Boulder High School, Colorado

Derek Thomas, H. B. Plant High School, Florida

Dianna Trang, Grapevine High School, Texas

Nora T. Tsoutsis, John D. O'Bryant High School, Massachusetts

Regina Tubbs, Riverview High School, Florida

Katherine Walden, Legacy High School, Nevada

Deon Youd, Spanish Fork High School, Utah

David A. Jolliffe
Hephzibah Roskelly

About the Authors

David A. Jolliffe is professor of English and curriculum and instruction at the University of Arkansas, where he holds the Brown Chair in English Literacy. A former high school English and drama teacher, Jolliffe taught at Bethany College, West Virginia University, the University of Illinois at Chicago, and DePaul University before moving to Arkansas. From 2002 through 2007 and again from 2010 to 2011, Jolliffe served as Chief Reader for the Advanced Placement English Language and Composition Examination. He is the author or editor of several books on rhetoric (including *Everyday Use: Rhetoric in Reading and Writing* with Hephzibah Roskelly), on the teaching of composition, and on the preparation of writing teachers.

Hephzibah Roskelly is professor of English at the University of North Carolina Greensboro, where she teaches courses in rhetoric, composition, American literature, and women's studies. She is a former Chief Reader of the English Language and Composition Advanced Placement Examination and test development member, and she now serves on the Advisory Board for the College Board. Professor Roskelly conducts institutes for high school teachers and students across the country on building academic skills in writing and interpretation. Her books include *Everyday Use: Rhetoric in Reading and Writing* with David A. Jolliffe (Pearson, 2010) and *Breaking Into the Circle: Groups for Gender and Racial Equity* (Heinemann, 2000).

part one

Reading and Writing

Readers and writers are always communicating—interpreting and creating ideas, evaluating and making arguments, analyzing and using language. Part One of this book is about how communication works when a reader reads a text and when a writer writes one.

The first two chapters explain how you can make meaning from what you read, using what you know and what you predict to interpret a text's purpose and evaluate its effectiveness. Readers have to invent as they read, and that suggests how closely writing and reading are connected. Chapters 3 through 7 develop that connection, showing how rhetoric—the art of communication—informs what you do when you write and when you read. Learning how to recognize and use the elements that affect communication, you'll strengthen your interpretive skill as a reader and your analytical, persuasive skill as a writer.

chapter 1

Reading as Inventing

What You Will Learn

- To build your reader experiences to help you interpret what you read
- To read for pleasure, for information, or for a combination of purposes
- To use the features of texts and authors to help interpret what you read

One has to be an inventor to read well.

—Ralph Waldo Emerson

The verb *to invent* suggests an awesome double meaning. On the one hand, its meaning is obvious: To invent something is to create something new. On the other hand, the verb hints at a wonderful act of breathing life into a process. Think "in + vent": Open the window, open the door, open your lungs, then breathe out, blow on the glowing ember, watch the life appear. This book, which is about learning to read and write successfully and well in school and beyond, begins with reading as inventing: reading as creating something new, reading as breathing new life into your world, your mind, and your studies.

The famous American author Ralph Waldo Emerson clearly understood this idea about reading. When Emerson wrote the sentence above, he was talking to a group of young Harvard University men who were preparing to be the leaders of a still-new country. Emerson felt that the country, though young, was old enough to make its own philosophy, in culture, and in art, not by copying the art and culture of the world the European colonists had left behind a hundred years before but by creating new ideas that would come from the experience of building a nation in a new world.

Emerson maintained that young people must create new ideas by observing and experiencing the world around them and by reading. For Emerson, reading, like experience, was more than simple decoding or memorizing—it was invention. To Emerson, readers must create and recreate what is on the page just as they "read" what is around them in the world.

We emphasize the same idea throughout this book. This is a book about

- How to read powerfully, thoughtfully, and critically
- How to write insightfully, effectively, and forcefully
- How to understand reading and writing in the context of several centuries of American culture, literature, and life

Reading Signs

It's true: The process of reading as inventing that Emerson urges is in fact ordinary. Everybody reads, even those who are not literate. We read signs and symbols that suggest meanings to us because all humans look for meaning around them. Consider some everyday instances of sign reading:

- The sky is overcast and the clouds are low. The day promises rain.
- You walk into a classroom, and the room is arranged in a circle instead of in rows. The class promises to be an open discussion.
- A person knows when a friend is angry or sad without a word spoken. Even a child reads a frown or an impatient gesture.

Just as we read the signs of nature, space, and facial expressions, we read images and words on the page, which in many ways should make reading easy. Reading an image or an essay—any text—is just a *kind* of reading, and reading is what people do all the time.

READING VISUAL TEXTS: An Example

Here are three visual images (Figures 1.1 through 1.3). How might they be read inventively? How can we use what we know and imagine to make the images make sense?

FIGURE 1.1 Ralph Waldo Emerson, 1838

FIGURE 1.2

Reading Rates in the United States, 1982–2002			
	1982	1992	2002
• 18–24-year-olds	59.8	53.3	42.8
• 25–34-year-olds	62.1	54.6	47.7
• 35–44-year-olds	59.7	58.9	46.6
• 45–54-year-olds	54.9	56.9	51.6
• 55–64-year-olds	52.8	52.9	48.9
• 65–74-year-olds	47.2	50.8	45.3

FIGURE 1.3

Reading the first paragraphs of this chapter gives you some **context**, a sense of time, place, and situation, to help you read the first image. This is a portrait of Emerson. What feeling do you get as you look at Emerson's picture? Does he appear kind or stern? Humorous or serious? Appealing or not? And more importantly, how do you make those decisions? Reading Emerson's expression and attitude by looking at elements of the portrait—Emerson's gaze, the shape of his mouth and other details—you might imagine something about him that contributes to your reading of his work. When you read Emerson's "The American Scholar," for example, his portrait might help you imagine his speech or his audience's reaction to him (see Unit 3).

Analyze a Venezuelan Mural at Your Pearson MyLab

How might you read the second image? Notice that it's a portrait of a sort as well. You probably assumed correctly, and without even stopping to consider it, that this image is a book cover. Its title, subtitle, and size provide clues, and your considerable experience with seeing book covers makes you able to identify it without conscious deliberation. Additionally, the shape of the words, the fact that the woman is drawn rather than photographed, and the background lines and swirls tell you something about the content of the book. It's about the world of comics, and the drawing reinforces the message of what's in the book.

And the last image? This chart depicts figures that force you to read both across the page and down in order to understand what the percentages and categories convey. It may be hard to tell what these figures mean without more context, knowing where the charts appear, reading the writer's introduction and follow-up to the figures provided, but you do make judgments even with the fragment. Both time and ages seem important. The statistics come from Mark Bauerlein's book *The Dumbest Generation,* a study and critique of both electronic communication and current education. Now that you know the title and the book's premise, you can read the negative message indicated by the numbers.

The Reader's Rhetorical Triangle

Throughout this book, we will use diagrams to help you conceptualize the points we're making about reading and writing. Here is the first, a triangle that captures the central idea of this chapter: As readers invent, they interact with texts, and the authors of those texts, to figure out what the author's **intention** or **purpose** was and to create a **meaning** for the text (see Figure 1.4).

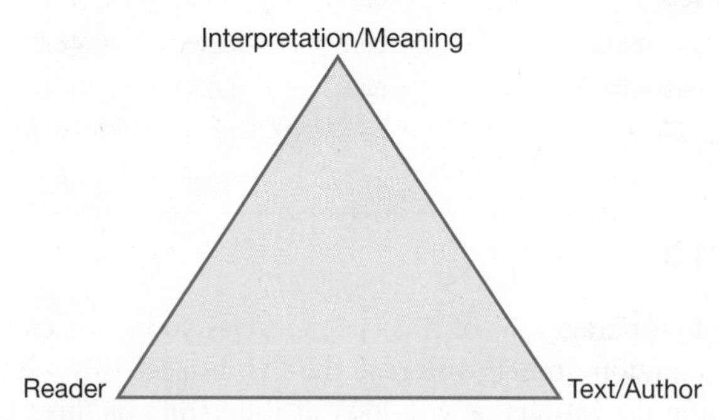

FIGURE 1.4 Reader's Rhetorical Triangle

We call this visual the **reader's rhetorical triangle**. Central to this label is the word **rhetoric**, which we define as "the way people produce texts to create and communicate meaning." With the reader's rhetorical triangle, we are depicting the reading-as-invention process: Readers bring what they know and what they can predict to the

Analyze an iPod Advertisement at Your Pearson MyLab

Analyze Information Graphics at Your Pearson MyLab

reading process. Texts use forms, language, and details to help guide the readers' predictions and to give focus to their decisions about what the text was written (or, in the case of a visual text, created) for—its intention or purpose—and what it might mean.

In the rest of this chapter, we will unpack the reader's role in this process, and we will examine part of the text's role.

The Reader's Role: Building Your Reader Experience

Good, inventive readers use everything they have at their disposal to make sense of what they read. They remember their own pasts. They test their own knowledge. They use what they know about the writer. They call upon their own beliefs and opinions. They compare texts they're familiar with to ones they're reading. All these resources together make up the **reader's experience**. We might even give it a fancy name: the **reader's repertoire**. In reading-as-invention, the more readers know—about reading, writing, authors, life, ideas, culture, and history—the richer the repertoire they can draw upon. The broader and deeper the repertoire, the more engaging and satisfying the reading experience.

How do you build your reader experience? Of course, a great deal of the building happens in school, where the activities are focused on developing understanding and knowledge in all kinds of subjects. But outside school, reading and generally living in the world build experience and information as well. To recognize how much a reader learns from life outside school is important, and that is why so many writers and thinkers keep journals describing and reflecting on experience and ideas. The **reading journal** might be a set of observations and then commentary—a **double-entry notebook** that, as writing teacher Ann Berthoff put it, helps writers "look and look again." In a double-entry notebook, you write your comments on one side of the page and then a comment on your comments on the other. This activity helps you realize how important your own observations and reflections are to the meaning of what you're reading. We will return to the reading journal in Chapter 3, showing what a valuable tool it is to prepare for a writing project.

There are, of course, other ways to build your repertoire to support effective reading. Here are some suggestions:

- **Take stock of what you already know.** When you begin to read a piece, think of what you may know about the author, the type of text, its apparent central idea, and your reason for reading it. Then decide what you think you need to know. Beginning this way will help you read efficiently, looking for material that reinforces what you know and material that provides new information.
- **Read around.** When reading a challenging piece, read related work. Investigate Internet sources. Read background summaries of the time period or author or

Analyze Understanding the Rhetorical Situation: The War Around Us at Your Pearson MyLab

topics that build your understanding. Doing this work for yourself will make your reading both more enjoyable and useful.

- **Talk to others.** One of the most important sources for broadening your own repertoire is accessing some of the repertoire of those around you. Ask questions in group meetings in school as you study a text. Talk to parents, friends, and acquaintances about their experiences and their reading. Listen well.
- **Read even if you know relatively little.** Realize that when you begin to read you may not know *everything* you need to know, but you'll almost always know *something* that will help you proceed. This is especially true when you read older literature, with contexts and language seemingly far away from contemporary life. You might not know much about Native American life in the seventeenth century, but you know about conflicts between parents and children or about the beauty of a forest, and that will help you understand what you don't yet know.
- **Read your own writing.** Get in the habit of reading what you write as a reader, noting how you respond to the cues the text you've written has offered, how you hear a style and voice, how you use the details to build an idea of intention. Really reading your own writing is the essential first step in making good revisions.

ACTIVITY Keeping a Double-Entry Journal

First of all, read the following brief excerpt, the opening two paragraphs of a newspaper article. (You can find the entire piece in Unit 6.)

Dave Barry
From "Independence Day"

This year, why not hold an old-fashioned Fourth of July picnic?

Food poisoning is one good reason. After a few hours in the sun, ordinary potato salad can develop bacteria the size of raccoons. But don't let the threat of agonizingly painful death prevent you from celebrating the birth of our nation, just as Americans have been doing ever since that historic first July Fourth when our Founding Fathers—George Washington, Benjamin Franklin, Thomas Jefferson, Bob Dole, and Tony Bennett—landed on Plymouth Rock.

[2003]

On the computer or in a notebook, create a two-columned page. Use the right-hand side of the page to record observations and details of an essay you're reading for class. After you read the essay, commenting as you go, go back to read your own comments. Use the left-hand side of the page to reflect on your comment. It might look something like this:

I quickly understood that Barry was mocking that type of article.	The text begins like a normal newspaper article, one that provides tips for throwing a successful party.

In a group or on your own, add two or three more paired entries, just for practice. We will return to the excerpt from Barry's essay later in this chapter.

Context: A Vital Part of Reader Experience

One very important clue that good readers use when they bring their experience into interaction with the text in an inventive reading is context, the time and place that a text was written or created and the situation, the circumstances, surrounding its creation and its reading. Sometimes the context is given. This chapter told you that Emerson was a nineteenth-century American author writing to students at Harvard University. You might know that Dave Barry is a writer whose humor column was published in U.S. newspapers and was the basis for the situation comedy, *Dave's World.* Sometimes, while reading, you have to figure out context just from clues in the text. Consider the following advertisement (Figure 1.5).

FIGURE 1.5

The ad appeared in a popular magazine. With both its words and its images, it asks the reader to use his or her experience in order to respond to the message. How do you read the signs in this text?

- Is the woman happy? How do you know?
- What is the time period? How do you know?
- What is important to the woman? To the artist? To the audience? How do you know?

Once you begin to look at the details of a text, visual or written, you begin the process of **analysis**, breaking down the general sense you have of what you're examining into smaller parts in order to find out how each contributes to the general impression and to account for your reactions and your interpretations. You make meaning of the text, using what you know from your experience as a thinker, and analysis is the record of how that meaning gets made. We will explain analysis, covering it in detail, in Chapter 4.

FIGURE 1.6

Above is another ad for a different product (Figure 1.6). Ask yourself the same questions as with the first ad:

- Is the woman happy? How do you know?
- What is the time period? How do you know?
- What is important to the woman? To the photographer? To the audience? How do you know?

When reading the ads, you use your experience with ad formats, with being a consumer, with relationships, and with the product as you respond. You use the context you infer—the time it's set in, the place, the situation—and your knowledge of the type of text to create your idea of what the ad is presenting and how it's persuading.

Sometimes readers don't have the right level of experience to create the context for certain texts, and then they feel unable to read those texts inventively and analytically. Think, for example, about trying to read specialized academic textbooks or complicated novels. Readers might know what they feel about the ideas they read but maybe don't have the tools required to discuss those ideas. Still, when we confront texts that at first seem too difficult to read, we tap into information we already know and terms we already use to help us interpret and analyze.

Juxtaposition: A Useful Tactic in Building Reader Experience

Advertisements are easy because they're so familiar. One of the problems with older texts or uncommon ones—texts far away from a person's experience or ideas—is that the reader doesn't have as much to bring and so has a harder time inventing. But when an older text is set against a contemporary one, as in the ads above, the context for the older one becomes easier, and understanding—reading—each of them can be deeper.

Juxtaposition, examining one thing in terms of another, engages a crucial principle of inventive reading. Observers (readers) don't just *see*; they always *see in terms of something.* Readers perceive or read with something in mind that helps them actually see what they're looking at, always using what they already know and believe to help them read or observe something new.

Consider what you discover when you put the two ads together, as shown in Figure 1.7: a change in tone between one and the other, different graphic styles,

FIGURE 1.7

similar attitudes, similar intentions? That comparison might suggest an idea, even the beginning of an argument, that you could explore using these ads. You might consider the desire of women to please the men they love, or the difference in written text and background information in the ads as well as the background information you use to make meaning from the ads' messages.

ACTIVITY Juxtaposing to Analyze the Ads

With a partner or in a group:

1. List five things that strike you about the two ads.
2. Discuss quickly what you think your lists tell you about the subject or the purpose or the audience of the ads. Then come up with a sentence that explains what you think the lists reveal.

Combined with more ads, histories, or research of other kinds, this quick activity might become the beginning of a fine analysis of visual texts and a fine argument about what those texts illuminate about art, advertising, economics, or gender roles over the course of time.

ACTIVITY Juxtaposing Multiple Texts

Choose one of the following topics (or select one of your own) and locate at least five visual texts that explore the topic from a variety of perspectives:

- The automobile
- The city
- The worker
- The holidays

You might choose advertisements or other visual art—sculpture, painting, photography, cartooning, for example. Select texts that you think demonstrate an attitude or an approach to the topic that you find interesting. Choose a variety—old and contemporary, abstract and realistic, serious and satirical, for example. Locate where there are patterns of similarity and difference in treatment of the subject.

Suppose you were asked to write an essay that discusses these artistic treatments of your subject, evaluating their effectiveness in conveying their message. (Your instructor, in fact, might direct you to write this essay.) You might choose photos of New York City, for example, arguing that the choice of light, color, and image presents conflicting views of the city.

To give you an idea of how you might proceed with this topic, here are two photographs of New York City from the turn of the century that show different perspectives on buildings and on the city itself (Figures 1.8 and 1.9).

FIGURE 1.8 **Alfred Steiglitz, *From the Back Window,* 1915**

From the Back Window, 291 (1915), Alfred Stieglitz. Platinum print, 25.1 x 20.2 cm (9 7/8 x 7 15/16 in.). Alfred Stieglitz Collection, 1949 (49.55.35). Image copyright © The Metropolitan Museum of Art/Licensed by Art Resource, NY.

FIGURE 1.9 **Jacob Riis, *New York Back-lot*, 1890**

New York, Old house on Bleeker Street, on a back lot between Mercer and Greene Streets (circa 1890), Jacob A. Riis. Photograph. Museum of the City of New York/Getty Images

1. How are the two photos alike?
2. How does their choice of light, image, and perspective alter the image of the city?
3. What do you read into these photos about the photographer's message?
4. Locate a painting of New York City online. Consider how the painting (another type of text) might compare to one of the photographs. Notice how color and shading give a **tone** (a descriptive feeling indicating the creator's attitude) to the image and how color, focus, and the choice of detail of roofs, lights, distance, and background make the tone of each photo vary. The choice of soft focus or brightly lit hard focus might be characteristic of these photographers, a **style** that each employs often as a defining feature of their art. The photographers have made choices to help us determine their intention and create a meaning, and juxtaposing the two photographs helps reveal those elements to you.

The Reader's Choice: Reading In, Reading Out

One decision that a reader needs to make—and perhaps continually to revise and remake—while doing an inventive reading is whether to **read in**, **read out**, or engage in a little bit of both. In other words, should the reader read the text for its beauty and for the experience of entering the world of the text (read in), or should the reader read the text to take away specific information from it (read out). Or should the reader do some of both?

Some texts make it clear how their authors/creators think they should be read. Others put the decision in the reader's lap. The following excerpt, the beginning of an essay by contemporary writer Amy Tan, illustrates the importance of the reader's thinking about this issue. You might know Tan as the author of the novel *The Joy Luck Club,* but this excerpt is from a nonfiction essay. (The full text of Amy Tan's "Mother Tongue" can be found in Unit 6). As you read these opening paragraphs, decide for yourself what argument you think Tan might be developing.

Amy Tan
Excerpt from "Mother Tongue"

I am not a scholar of English or literature. I cannot give you much more than personal opinions on the English language and its variations in this country or others.

> I am a writer. And by that definition, I am someone who has always loved language. I am fascinated by language in daily life. I spend a great deal of my time thinking about the power of language—the way it can evoke an emotion, a visual image, a complex idea, or a simple truth. Language is the tool of my trade. And I use them all—all the Englishes I grew up with.

As a reader, you invent as soon as you read the first lines of a text, speculating about the kind of text this might be, where and when it's written, why it opens the way it does. You might notice that Tan begins her piece by establishing her credentials and thus her credibility with the reader. The first sentence, that describes her in terms of what she is not, creates a kind of bond with readers who may not be scholars of English either but who, like her, enjoy language. She claims to be speaking personally, not as an expert. Still, as a writer, she says, she has a special interest in how language works. With this opening, Tan suggests that there might be both personal revelation in her story and new information as well.

Even in the first paragraph, you are making decisions about Tan, about the subject she's writing on, and about her effect on you.

- Do you like her voice?
- Do you agree with her about the power of language?
- Do you believe her when she says that she's not an expert?
- Do you understand what she means when she makes "English" plural?

As you answer questions like these, you create meaning from the text you're reading, and use the ideas you're gathering to create more meaning as you continue to read.

Now, here's a later paragraph:

> Recently, I was made keenly aware of the different Englishes I do use. I was giving a talk to a large group of people, the same talk I had already given to half a dozen other groups. The nature of the talk was about my writing, my life, and my book, *The Joy Luck Club*. The talk was going along well enough, until I remembered one major difference that made the whole talk sound wrong. My mother was in the room. And it was perhaps the first time she had heard me give a lengthy speech, using the kind of English I have never used with her. I was saying things like "The intersection of memory upon imagination" and "There is an aspect of my fiction that relates to thus-and-thus"—a speech filled with carefully wrought grammatical phrases, burdened, it seemed, with nominalized forms, past perfect tenses, conditional phrases, all the forms of standard English I had learned in school and through books, the forms of English I did not use at home with my mother.

From this later excerpt, we know that the essay is not just about the love of language but about Tan's mother and about the English she uses in public life and in life with her mother.

- Do we know about mother-daughter relationships in another story by Tan? Do we get a sense of the relationship between mother and daughter here?
- Do we know what "nominalizations" are? Do they seem negative?
- Do we wonder why Tan's mother is in the audience? Why she has never been before?

Readers still don't quite have Tan's complete argument, but recognize a conflict. Using experience with reading arguments, readers can speculate that Tan believes her "public speech" lacks something and that her mother has something to teach her about language. At the same time readers are connecting to Tan's experience as a daughter and speaker, we are learning something new about language.

Our experience with these two parts of the essay suggests that readers read in different ways with different purposes in mind—reading out for information, when they want to take ideas away to use them somehow, and reading in for experience, when they want to read to immerse themselves in the pleasure or interest of the reading itself.

If a reader began Amy Tan's piece hoping to gather information about second-language learning or even about Tan's relationship to the Chinese language, the reader would be reading out. On the other hand, if a reader read it with a desire to imagine the world the text presents or to listen for the beauty of the language, the reader would be reading in, for the experience of reading itself, bringing a wish to enter the situation the text presents. If a reader heard in Tan's language her anguish at her mother's experience with learning English, or appreciated Tan's use of dialect speech to symbolize the mother's difficulties, the reader would be reading in.

It's certainly possible to read and satisfy both purposes, as might be true in reading "Mother Tongue." In any case, our attitude or stance about what we read determines how we'll read it. Very often readers read *in* novels, poems, and cartoons, and read *out* essays, articles, and manuals. But that difference often comes less from the type of text than it does from the decision of the reader.

Why is this distinction important in your own reading in school? As you've probably already figured out, much of the reading you do seems to call for reading out. You read out in order to know something that you can use in a paper, an exam, a talk, or in classroom discussion. But in many cases, your ability to enter the text's world and its contexts and mysteries, to read in, dramatically improves your ability to interpret and analyze what you read out. To see, for example, that Tan's depiction of her mother both describes the situation of first-generation English learners and invites readers to sympathize in order to understand the complexities, is to find both reading-in and reading-out possibilities in Tan's essay. Identifying these two purposes for reading helps readers respond well to what they read, as well as helps them recognize their own power in making meaning from texts (see Figure 1.10).

Reader's Choice: Purposes for Reading		
	Reading In	**Reading Out**
What it is	Reading a text for its beauty, bringing your own experience into it	Reading a text to get information out of it
Why to do it	For pleasure, enjoyment, interest, knowledge	For knowledge and information
Typical texts	Novels, stories, poems, comics	Essays, articles, textbooks, manuals, diagrams

FIGURE 1.10

ACTIVITY **Practice Reading Out and Reading In**

Discuss with your group or write yourself a small list of texts that you think call for a reading-out response. (You might think of recipes as one, for example.) Then imagine how you might experience the same text by reading in. ("Drizzle chocolate liberally and swirl it. . . .") Reading out or reading in?

Practice the two kinds of reading from the alternate angle too. Pick texts you think ask you to respond by reading in (a beautiful poem or a stand-up routine perhaps). Then reimagine the text with a reading-out response.

Features of Texts and Authors

When readers are observing well—that is, making meaning from what they know and believe as well as what they see—they pick up the "moves" in the text they read: how the writer uses details, arranges ideas, chooses words, structures sentences, creates images, and how the writer uses all of these elements to heighten the meaning, purpose, and effect of the text. (From this list of writer's choices or maneuvers, you have an idea of what we mean by **rhetoric**. We will define it fully in Chapter 3.) In other words, they learn to tap into the features of the texts—and in doing so, understand something about the authors that created them—so that the *interaction* of reader with text and author kicks into full force.

Consider two texts to examine how elements in a piece of writing become effective moves for writers and strategies for readers in making meaning. We have seen the first already, the opening paragraphs of Dave Barry's essay, "Independence Day," from a collection of his humor columns called *Mirth of a Nation* (see Unit 6). (Have you already got a context? What are you reading *in* to the text before you ever start?)

How do you read this essay? How does Barry heighten his meaning, purpose, and effect? What helps you read it effectively? For example, you might ask how Barry uses a *chronological* organization to accomplish his purpose and how he uses features of the "how-to-organize-a-party" article to poke fun at that genre. Or you might ask how the statistics in the bullet points in the fourth paragraph contribute to the tone.

The second is an excerpt from an essay by Jennifer Price on a piece of popular art, the plastic pink flamingo.

Jennifer Price

Excerpt from "The Plastic Pink Flamingo: A Natural History"

When the pink flamingo splashed into the fifties market, it staked two major claims to boldness. First, it was a *flamingo.* Since the 1930s, vacationing Americans had been flocking to Florida and returning home with flamingo souvenirs. In the 1910s and 1920s, Miami Beach's first grand hotel, the Flamingo, had made the bird synonymous with wealth and pizzazz . . . [Later], developers built hundreds of more modest hotels to cater to an eager middle class served by new train lines—and in South Beach, especially, architects employed the playful Art Deco style, replete with bright pinks and flamingo motifs.

This was a little ironic, since Americans had hunted flamingos to extinction in Florida in the late 1800s, for plumes and meat. But no matter. In the 1950s, the new interstates would draw working-class tourists down, too. Back in New Jersey, the Union Products flamingo inscribed one's lawn emphatically with Florida's cachet of leisure and extravagance. The bird acquired an extra fillip of boldness, too, from the direction of Las Vegas—the flamboyant oasis of instant riches that the gangster Benjamin "Bugsy" Siegel had conjured from the desert in 1946 with his Flamingo Hotel. Anyone who has seen Las Vegas knows that a flamingo stands out in a desert even more strikingly than on a lawn. In the 1950s, namesake Flamingo motels, restaurants, and lounges cropped up across the country like a line of semiotic sprouts.

And the flamingo was *pink*—a second and commensurate claim to boldness. The plastics industries of the fifties favored flashy colors, which Tom Wolfe called "the new electrochemical pastels of the Florida littoral: tangerine, broiling magenta, livid pink, incarnadine, fuchsia demure, Congo ruby, methyl green." The hues were forward-looking rather than old-fashioned, just right for a generation, raised in the Depression, that was ready to celebrate its new affluence. And as Karal Ann Marling has written, the "sassy pinks" were "the hottest color of the decade." Washing machines, cars, and kitchen counters proliferated in passion pink, sunset pink, and Bermuda pink. In

1956, right after he signed his first recording contract, Elvis Presley bought a pink Cadillac.

Why, after all, call the birds "pink flamingos"—as if they could be blue or green? The plastic flamingo is a hotter pink than a real flamingo, and even a real flamingo is brighter than anything else around it. There are five species, all of which feed in flocks on algae and invertebrates in saline and alkaline lakes in mostly warm habitats around the world. The people who have lived near these places have always singled out the flamingo as special. Early Christians associated it with the red phoenix. In ancient Egypt, it symbolized the sun god Ra. In Mexico and the Caribbean, it remains a major motif in art, dance, and literature. No wonder that the subtropical species stood out so loudly when Americans in temperate New England reproduced it, brightened it, and sent it wading across an inland sea of grass.

[1999]

When you read Price's essay, what do you *read in*? That is, what experience do you bring with you as a reader that helps you understand and appreciate the story of the plastic pink flamingos? What associations with her examples and her tone do you draw upon as you read the text? Now, how do you *read out*? What do you think are the essential points of the text? How does she use evidence to prove her points? What do you think is the central argument?

You might hear the amused light and slightly critical tone, similar to that in the Jon Stewart parody above, even though the Price piece seems much less tongue-in-cheek—that is, facetious—than Stewart's. It's interesting to consider what they both are critical *of*, and how you know it.

What you have done with both texts is to tap into their specific features—their word choice, their sentences, their suggested meanings—and used that information, interacting with your reader's experience, to make decisions about the intention of the text and its possible meanings.

ACTIVITY Looking at a Text's Moves to Discover Tone

One aspect of a text that we will describe in detail in Chapter 3 is its **tone**, or the author's attitude about the subject matter, but let's offer a little preview of that material right now.

Write a short piece—two paragraphs or so—that describes the tone of the Price essay, first by indicating words or sentences or images that you think suggest the tone Price achieves and then explaining why you think the tone fits the writer's intention. What is she suggesting about Americans? About popular culture?

Understanding Tone

The excerpt from Price's essay was used in an Advanced Placement free response question for the English Language and Composition Exam in 2006. Read the prompt for the question, and begin to examine how your reading focuses its attention on features of the text and implications you might make about its author.

> The passage below is an excerpt from Jennifer Price's recent essay "The Plastic Pink Flamingo: A Natural History." The essay examines the popularity of the plastic pink flamingo in the 1950s. Read the passage carefully. Then write an essay in which you analyze how Price crafts the text to reveal her view of United States culture.

Notice that the prompt asks you to see the flamingo as a symbol for the view of culture that Price takes. It asks you as a writer to discuss craft as well, and your description of tone can help you discuss Price's choice of language and of example as evidence for the craft she uses to suggest her view of U.S. culture.

Your reading of Price helps you write about the tone of voice of the writer who describes pink flamingos. Your **close reading** of the AP prompt—that is, your perceiving the important nuances of what specifically the prompt tells you to do—helps you write with confidence about Price's view of American culture. Notice, for example, that the prompt directs writers to examine "how Price crafts the text." You need to consider the methods of crafting—the moves of the details, the diction, the evidence, and the tone—that contribute to your understanding of Price's view.

You might begin to analyze Price's piece as the prompt for the AP Exam directs by considering how your first response to the tone she adopts affects your interpretation of the text.

> Jennifer Price's ironic voice in her essay on "The Plastic Pink Flamingo: A Natural History" is established as soon as the reader reads the title. The irony is in every example and every story about America's obsession with the bright yard art, and the tone suggests that American culture is pretty shallow.

Or you might begin by establishing immediately what your careful reading revealed about Price's attitude toward flamingos and American culture.

> Jennifer Price uses the bright pink plastic flamingo to illustrate her claim that American culture is enamored of what's bold and what's fake.

However you begin, you see that the prompt directs you to get to your point fairly quickly and then to affirm it with your careful demonstration of how well you've read, and how creatively you've used your own reader experience to find the writer's strategies. Whether or not you emphasize directly the *effect* of the piece in your analysis, the reader's response is always key in this kind of critical examination. The reader is part of the writer's triangle. The exam question, which asks for your reader interpretation of writer choices, is a good way to see how the processes of reading and writing intertwine.

ACTIVITY **A First Pass at Writing that Analyzes Reading**

Now that you are seeing how your reader experience interacts with features of the text and implications about its author, you're ready to try your hand at describing this process.

In your group or on your own, write the paragraph that could follow either of the openings above for an essay on "The Plastic Pink Flamingo." See how clearly the opening leads you to find good examples, word choices, and lines from the text to begin to make your case. Or write a new opening that leads to similar, good examples and illustrations to strengthen your argument.

Understanding Style

To talk about style is in some ways to discuss all the elements that aid a reader in making meaning from writing, so it's a little hard to define. A writer's style is a combination of the type of text, sentence structure, context, word choice, tone, and detail that together create an individual style as well as a recognizable *kind* of style—professional, colloquial, narrative, academic, formal, terse—that readers respond to as they read.

Teachers of speaking and writing in classical times referred to style as **high**, **middle**, and **low**, which referred to the level of the language, its formality and elegance. One wasn't better than another; a writer used a style that fit the occasion and fit the audience's needs. As in classical times, appropriateness—what fits the audience and the occasion—remains the best guide for writers as they make choices about their vocabulary, their sentence structures, their punctuation, and their examples and images.

As readers, we understand style as the result of all these choices writers make. The ability to recognize a particular writer's style or a particular text type's style helps readers know the stance to take as they read and to be able to evaluate the effect of the piece they read.

ACTIVITY **Defining and Describing Style**

Following are a few examples of writers with interesting and varied styles. Read the lines and see how you might describe the style you read. Thinking of words to describe style will help you make decisions. Conversational, academic, reflective, meditative, formal, terse, flowing . . . are the sorts of adjectives that could describe a style you read.

Then examine the sentences closely to locate features—of word choice, punctuation, imagery, for example—that you think help determine the style of the sentence.

Bharati Mukherjee

This essay is about four narratives, those of expatriation, exile, immigration, and repatriation. From these subnarratives, I hope to weave a revisionist theory for contemporary residency and citizenship, or at least suggest new terms for the unresolved debate that threatens to grow louder and more rancorous in years to come.

David Sedaris

At the age of forty-one, I am returning to school and have to think of myself as what my French textbook calls "a true debutant." After paying my tuition, I was issued a student ID, which allows me a discounted entry fee at movie theaters, puppet shows, and Festyland, a far-flung amusement park that advertises with billboards picturing a cartoon stegosaurus sitting in a canoe and eating what appears to be a ham sandwich.

Judith Ortiz Cofer

At three or four o'clock in the afternoon, the hour of *café con leche,* the women of my family gathered in Mama's living room to speak of important things and retell familiar stories meant to be overheard by us young girls, their daughters. In Mama's house (everyone called my grandmother Mama) was a large parlor built by my grandfather to his wife's exact specifications so that it was always cool, facing away from the sun. The doorway was on the side of the house so that no one could walk directly into her living room.

Leslie Marmon Silko

You see that after a thing is dead, it dries up. It might take weeks or years, but eventually if you touch the thing, it crumbles under your fingers. It goes back to dust. The soul of the thing has long since departed. With the plants and wild game the soul may have already been borne back into bones and blood or thick green stalk and leaves. Nothing is wasted.

Mark Twain

Now when I had mastered the language of this water and had come to know every trifling feature that bordered the great river as familiarly as I knew the letters of the alphabet, I had made a valuable acquisition. But I had lost something, too. I had lost something which could never be restored to me while I lived. All the grace, the beauty, the poetry, had gone out of the majestic river! I still kept in mind a certain wonderful sunset which I witnessed when steamboating was new to me. A broad expanse of the river was turned to blood; in the middle distance the red hue brightened into gold, through which a solitary log came floating, black and conspicuous; in one place a long, slanting mark, was broken by boiling, tumbling rings, that were as many-tinted as an opal; where the ruddy flush was faintest, was a smooth spot that was covered with graceful circles and radiating lines, ever so delicately traced; the shore on our left was densely wooded and the somber ruffled trail that shone like silver; and high above the forest wall a clean-stemmed dead tree waved a single leafy bough that glowed like a flame in the unobstructed splendor that was flowing from the sun.

ACTIVITY Predicting Meaning

One way to build your ability to read inventively and rhetorically is to practice the craft of **prediction**, or anticipating what will come next in a text. The method many people use to practice prediction is called a **cloze test**, an example of which follows. Fill in the blanks with one word for each blank.

> Between me and the other world ____________ is ever an unasked question: ____________ by some through feelings of delicacy; ____________ others through the difficulty of ____________ framing it. All, nevertheless, flutter round ____________. They approach me in a half-hesitant ____________ of way, eye me curiously ____________ compassionately, and then, instead of saying ____________, How does it feel to be ____________ problem? They say, I know an ____________colored man in my town; or ____________ fought at Mechanicsville; or Do not ____________ Southern outrages make your blood boil?

Cloze tests show how readers read for meaning, always predicting in "chunks" or clusters of words and phrases rather than reading every word. The chunks comprise usually five to seven words, and that's what the cloze test mimics.

After you've filled these words in, see how others have responded. See if you can account for why you've chosen one word rather than another. Then consider the textual moves of the piece. What can you say about the speaker? About the context? About the aim and the audience? We'll study this piece at the end of Chapter 2.

CHAPTER ACTIVITY
Reader Experience and Text Features on Exams

Practicing with good, challenging multiple-choice tests can also help you develop your inventive reader's repertoire and your skill at prediction. When you read quickly, on a multiple-choice test for example, you're looking for the key phrases and ideas that will give you the best answers. The multiple-choice exam asks you to comprehend bits of texts quickly and accurately, and so your skills of prediction and completing, as in the cloze test above, become important.

To test the role of prediction and repertoire building with multiple-choice items, read the following exam prompt and passage and then on your own or in your group, answer the questions that follow it. As before with the cloze test, as you make decisions about one answer or another, discuss the reasons for your choices.

Read the following passage carefully before you choose your answers. *This passage is taken from a twentieth-century book.*

The town sits in a vale between two rounded-off, thickly wooded mountains. Hot mineral waters pour out of the mountainsides, and the hills for miles around erupt with springs, some of them famous and commercial, with bottled water for sale, others trickling under rotten leaves in deep woods and known only to the natives. From one spring the water gushes milky and sulphurous. From another it comes forth laced with arsenic. Here it will be heavy with the taste of rocky earth, there, as sweet as rainwater. Each spring possesses its magical healing properties and its devoted, believing imbibers. In 1541, on the journey that proved to be his last, Hernando de Soto encountered friendly tribes at these springs. For a thousand years before him the mound-building Indians who lived in the Mississippi Valley had come here to cure their rheumatism and activate their sluggish bowels.

The main street of town, cutting from northeast to southwest, is schizoid, lined on one side with plate-glass store fronts and on the other with splendid white stucco bathhouses, each with its noble portico and veranda, strung along the street like stones in an old-fashioned necklace. All but one of the bathhouses are closed down now. At the head of the street, on a plateau, stands the multistoried Arlington, a 1920s resort hotel and a veritable ducal palace in yellow sandstone. Opposite, fronted in mirrors and glittering chrome, is what once was a gambling casino and is now a wax museum. "The Southern Club," it was called in the days when the dice tumbled across the green baize and my father waited for the results from Saratoga to come in over Western Union. Lots of other horsebooks operated in that same neighborhood—the White Front, the Kentucky Club—some in back rooms and dives in which no respectable person would be seen. But the Southern was another thing. Gamblers from Chicago strolled in and out in their ice-cream suits and their two-tone shoes and nothing smaller than a C-note in their pockets. Packards pulled up to the door and let out wealthy men with showy canes and women in silk suits and alligator pumps who owned stables of thoroughbreds and next month would travel to Churchill Downs. I saw this alien world in glimpses as Mother and I sat at the curb in the green Chevrolet, waiting for the last race at Belmont or Hialeah to be over so that my father could figure the payoffs and come home to supper.

The other realm was the usual realm, Middletown, Everyplace. Then it was frame houses, none very new. Now it is brick ranches and splits, carports, inlaid nylon carpet, and draw-drapes. Now the roads are lined with a pre-fab forest of Pizza Huts, Bonanzas, ninety kinds of hamburger stand, and gas stations, some with an occasional Southern touch: a plaque, for example, that reads "Serve-U-Sef." In what I still remember as horse pasture now stands a windowless high school—windowless—where classes range up to one hundred, and the teacher may not be able to learn everybody's name. My old elementary school, a two-story brick thing that threatened to fall down, had windows that reached to the fourteen-foot ceiling. We kept them shut only from November to February, for in this pleasant land the willows turn green and the winds begin sweetening in March, and by April the iris and jonquils bloom so thickly in every yard that you can smell them on the schoolroom air. On an April afternoon, we listened to the creek rushing through the schoolyard and thought mostly about crawdads.

1. The passage as a whole is best described as
   (A) a dramatic monologue
   (B) a melodramatic episode
   (C) an evocation of a place
   (D) an objective historical commentary
   (E) an allegorical fable

2. The speaker's reference to Hernando de Soto's visit to the springs in 1541 (lines 9–10) serves primarily to
   (A) clarify the speaker's attitude toward the springs
   (B) exemplify the genuine benefits of the springs
   (C) document the history of the springs
   (D) specify the exact location of the springs
   (E) describe the origin of beliefs in the springs' magical properties

3. With which of the following pairs does the speaker illustrate what she means by "schizoid" in line 14?
   (A) "plate-glass store fronts" (line 14) and "splendid white stucco bathhouses" (line 15)
   (B) "stones in an old-fashioned necklace" (line 16) and "fronted in mirrors and glittering chrome" (lines 19–20)
   (C) "the multistoried Arlington" (line 18) and "The Southern Club" (line 21)
   (D) "once was a gambling casino" (line 20) and "now a wax museum" (lines 20–21)
   (E) "Chicago" (line 26) and "Churchill Downs" (line 31)

4. In describing the bathhouses and the Arlington hotel (lines 15–19), the speaker emphasizes their
   (A) isolation
   (B) mysteriousness
   (C) corruptness
   (D) magnificence
   (E) permanence

The first question is a general, overall question, and although you only had a part of this text to help you make decisions about the *kind* of text it is, you can form general impressions once you read the entire excerpt. Notice the descriptive details that both particularize the town and call up the writer's emotional response to it. These words and phrases lead you to conclude that the passage *evokes* a place (**C**).

The other questions direct you to look at specific, rather than general, features of the text, focusing your attention on language, logic, and detail, the very elements you examine when you're interpreting and writing about the texts you read. Question 2 asks you to look at the way a detail functions as support for the author's purpose. If you're reading closely, you use logic to connect "1514" to "history" in answer **C.** The third question is most dependent on outside knowledge, or at least the ability to predict meaning from context, with the word "schizoid" not directly defined in the text. Variations of the word are common enough in popular culture that even if you're not sure of the definition, you can figure out that the word has to do with contradiction and division, the qualities that mark the difference between store fronts and splendid bathhouses (**A**). The next question is perhaps the easiest of the group for you, in part because if follows so closely from the question before it, with the description of the bathhouses as splendid. You see that the question asks you to find the closest synonym to "splendid," and that's "magnificence" (**D**).

Other exercises to build reading skill and good predictions include many of the strategies you use as invention exercises to begin writing. Answering the journalist's questions of who, what, when, why, where (and how) is a quick method to get to analysis of the rhetoric of the text you read. Speculating or brainstorming in writing or in talk stimulates curiosity and gives more experience for reading. Good readers, like good writers, revise and rethink as they create texts.

CHAPTER CHECKLIST

Reading

- ☐ Have you used your reader experience—what you already know—to help you predict what you will be reading and interpret as you read?
- ☐ Have you decided your purpose for reading and whether you will read in, read out, or both?
- ☐ Have you examined the features of the text and the background of the author to help you understand and interpret what you are reading?

Complete the Chapter 1 Exercise at Your Pearson MyLab

chapter 2

Reading Genres

What You Will Learn

- How to use genre to make meaning as you read
- How to read nonfiction, fiction, poetry, film and drama, and visuals as genres
- How genre can help you read, respond, and write

On the 2005 Advanced Placement English Language and Composition Examination, test takers were presented with a text, clearly signaled as a mock press release from *The Onion,* a free newspaper devoted to humor and satire, about the benefits of a fictitious product called Magnasoles Shoe Inserts. The students were directed to "analyze the strategies used in the article to satirize how products are marketed to consumers." Of the thousands of students who took this examination, a substantial number read the text not as a satire, a mock press release, but instead as a *real* press release. They made a wrong decision about the *genre* they were asked to analyze and, therefore, were not able to analyze it correctly.

Genre is the term used to describe the specific form of a piece of writing or a visual artifact: a letter, short story, editorial, romantic comedy, advertisement, or news photograph, for example. The genre writers choose helps guide their decisions about the elements of the text they produce: format, evidence, diction, characters, speaker, and others. And because we understand common genres quite well, genre also guides us as readers.

The big categories of genre—poetry, drama, fiction, nonfiction—immediately suggest particular formats, language choices, examples, and other strategies. More narrow genres—the limerick, horror film, biography, academic essay, for example—suggest even more specifics about characters, voice, style, length, or use of details. New genres, such as the graphic narrative or the blog, develop their own conventions, and older genres add and modify theirs as readers and the culture changes.

In this chapter, we'll examine how knowing (or at least predicting) the genre of a text helps you read it. We'll suggest as well how you use your understanding of genre as you write texts of your own.

Identifying Genre

Read the following text carefully, listening for tone and observing the structure, and then decide what genre—what kind of text—it is.

Naomi Baron
Untitled

I've got this thing that logs all convos
Really?
Why's that?
I have every conversation I've had with anybody since the 16th
I got a mod for aim and it just does it 5
I'm not sure why
Lol
Cool

[2009]

- How do you read this text?
- Do you know the genre immediately?
- How is the genre made clear to you?
- What can you tell about tone or intention from the excerpt?

Like other genres, the instant message has characteristic language, a particular format, a clear voice, and a style that readers recognize immediately. Writers of instant messages are more successful when they use genre conventions rather than dismiss them. The message writer would be less effective and appropriate if he wrote, for example, "I've got a software program that records all conversations." Spelling out all the words or writing complete sentences would violate the genre and the aim. That aim, to get across a message quickly, is best conveyed using the tools the instant message (IM) genre has developed—abbreviations and slang.

In general, the genre of a text helps us know how to read, what approach we should take when we read, what we might expect as to length, form, diction, and syntax. That's why you recognized the instant message conversation above; its syntax and its word choice indicated the short electronic message characteristic of the genre.

The same is true with other genres. Look at these first lines and see if you can identify the genre.

- Once upon a time
- It was a dark and stormy night
- My life began in a small hospital on the outskirts
- Greetings and welcome
- Dear Friend
- Dear John

ACTIVITY **Responding to Genre Clues**

Write the next few sentences for each of the lines above, according to the genre you've predicted. Compare your compositions with a classmate's.

1. How did your identification of each line's genre help you write the next few sentences effectively?
2. What similarities clearly emerged in your own and your classmate's brief compositions?
3. What differences emerged?

Genres Readers Frequently Encounter in School

It would be a huge chore to try to inventory all of the genres you will encounter as you complete your education, but let's take a careful look at several of them that you read and write often in school. Each of these genres contains other genres—let's call them **subgenres**—and each of those subgenres has its own characteristic formats and styles. Knowing some of the characteristics of these genres, identifying them, and using what you identify as you respond and analyze as an active reader will improve your ability to enter the world of the text and to take ideas from it.

Nonfiction Prose

A great deal of what you have to read for your school work is **nonfiction prose**. But there's great variation within the nonfiction category: memoir, biography, editorial, news article, book, academic essay, lab report, just to name a few. An inventive reader, alert to how elements shift according to the type of text, is able to distinguish between popular nonfiction and academic nonfiction, between history and biography, research report and editorial, and can use those distinctions to interpret more effectively.

Read the following two excerpts to discover which appears to be popular and which academic:

1. Aside from the written documents of Central American natives, no other writing exists to provide North American perspectives. However, with the help of archaeological, ethnographical, and oral materials, much has been learned of the North American continent before and during the contact periods of European arrival. Such remaining traces of the indigenous civilizations and cultures have provided information about how these communities experienced colonization. Encounter-era treaty literature, Native American oral narratives and poetry, and descriptions of Native Americans in various explorer narratives and European captivity narratives suggest some of the Native response to the European invasion.

2. Everybody likes the "Jaywalking" segment on *The Tonight Show.* With mike in hand and camera ready, host Jay Leno leaves the studio and hits the sidewalks of L.A., grabbing pedestrians for a quick test of their factual knowledge. "How many stars on the American flag?" he asks. "Where was Jesus born? Who is Tony Blair?" Leno plays his role expertly, slipping into game-show patter and lightly mocking the "contestants." Sometimes he allows them to select the grade-level of the questions, offering a choice from eighth-grade, fourth-grade, and second-grade primers. A few of his best guests reappear on a mock quiz show presented on the *Tonight Show* stage.

The respondents tend toward the younger ages, a sign that their elders perform better at recall. It's the 20-year-olds who make the comedy, and keep "Jaywalking" a standard set piece on the air.

You probably have little trouble guessing which is the academic genre and which the popular nonfiction. But consider how you made the guess. One fairly clear predictor might be the popular culture references in the second piece, a characteristic of lighter, or entertaining, pieces. Other predictors include **syntax** (notice the difference in length and complexity of sentences), **punctuation** (notice the variety of punctuation in one and the limited variety in the other), **diction** (notice the vocabulary level and special terms), and **voice** (notice how syntax, punctuation, and diction help you hear a voice and how different the two voices are).

How do all those elements cue your decision about which is popular and which academic? In the first example, the series of words—*anthropological, ethnographical,* and *oral materials*—signals a seriousness of purpose and a desire to inform that are characteristic of academic writing. By contrast, the piled-on questions—"How many stars in the American flag? Where was Jesus born? Who is Tony

Blair?"—suggest both a lighter touch and an interested, rather than objective, observer. Details like these help you figure out genre without your being completely conscious that genre is guiding your responses and interpretations as you read.

The conventions of the genre, the use of specialized or common language to signal purpose, the degree of distance and authority in the author's voice, and the insertion of author's position—all these aid in making good predictions not only about what the genre is but also where each text will lead a reader. Do you have an idea about the intention in each of these texts based on the genre you infer? Your ability to read the text's elements closely in terms of genre helps you understand and analyze what you read.

Reading nonfiction effectively contributes to your being able to write it effectively. Since, as with reading, much of the writing you accomplish in school is nonfiction, and particular kinds of academic nonfiction, your reading of a variety of nonfiction texts will help you create your own persuasive and analytical nonfiction texts.

ACTIVITY Writing in Nonfiction Genres

Here are some details to use to develop a nonfiction text.

- Walt Disney developed the character of Mickey Mouse in the early 1920s.
- The first movie Mickey appeared in was *Steamboat Willie.*
- There have been millions of pairs of Mickey Mouse ears sold since they were introduced in the 1950s.
- The Mickey Mouse Club ran on TV for over twenty years.
- Walt Disney was born to a working class family in Chicago.
- The Magic Kingdom is said to be based on the Chicago World's Fair Exposition that his father helped build.
- The money people spend on visits to Disney World and Disneyland amounts to tens of millions of dollars a year.
- Mickey's girlfriend is named Minnie.

In a group or on your own, use any of the details to compose the first sentence of

1. A biography
2. An argument
3. A popular culture review
4. A letter or e-mail to the editor
5. A Facebook status update
6. An essay for English class

You'll see that as you produce these beginnings, you need to consider your writer's voice, which means your choice of words and sentence structure and length. You need to consider evidence and how and if you'll present it. And you need to consider how a reader will understand your intention based on the genre you're attempting to write.

Poetry

English critic John Stuart Mill defined poetry, in contrast to prose, as "feeling confessing itself to itself." The words and images of poetry symbolically represent the poet's feeling as precisely as possible. Mill's definition suggests that the poetic genre is not about the relationships among speaker, subject, and audience, but about a speaker and his feeling about a subject entirely. But although the poet's impression of experience is important, its oral qualities—the sound of syllables and words and lines—suggest it is also often meant to be heard; that is, with an audience. And the poems you read in this book carry more than emotional expression from the poet; they suggest an argument, or at least a message directed at a reader as well as at the experience itself. So often in this book we will ask you to analyze poetry much in the same way you analyze prose—looking at how the poem forges and develops its argument.

This short poem, a *haiku,* shows how the genre constraints of this shortest of poetry genres create effects on readers. This haiku was written by Matsuo Basho, a famous 17th century Japanese poet (1677–1694).

Matsuo Basho
Haiku

old pond
a frog jumps into
the sound of water.

The reader senses the contentment at the end of the day as the cat stretches. Short, evocative, detailed and descriptive, the poem uses the simplicity of line and image to suggest emotion and a message about how to value the small observation, the momentary pleasure.

You can go to dailyhaiku.org to find a haiku of the day.

ACTIVITY **Examining How a Poem Develops Its Central Idea**

This poem is by a former poet laureate of the United States.

Watch the Video on Reading a Poem at Your Pearson MyLab

Rita Dove
My Mother Enters the Workforce

The path to ABC Business School
was paid for by a lucky sign:
ALTERATIONS, QUALIFIED SEAMSTRESS INQUIRE WITHIN.
Tested on sleeves, hers
never puckered—puffed or sleek, 5
leg-o'-mutton or raglan—
they barely needed the damp cloth
to steam them perfect.

Those were the afternoons. Evenings
she took in piecework, the treadle machine 10
with its locomotive whir
traveling the lit path of the needle
through quicksand taffeta
or velvet deep as a forest.
And now and now sang the treadle, 15
I know, I know . . .

And then it was day again, all morning
at the office machines, their clack and chatter
another journey—rougher,
that would go on forever 20
until she could break a hundred words
with no errors—ah, and then

no more postponed groceries,
and that blue pair of shoes!

[1999]

After you've read the poem silently to yourself, read it aloud. Reading aloud will let you hear the rhythm and something about the tone of voice carried by the language. As you read, mark places that strike you, make you pause, or where you hear most emphasis. You might mark where you don't understand something because of a context it implies or where you read an unfamiliar word or image. Then develop a response that uses these questions.

1. What's the context for this poem? How do you know?
2. How does the narrator feel about the mother? How do you know?
3. Why the italics? Why the exclamation point?
4. How does the information given by the visual cues help your reading?

ACTIVITY Connecting One Poem to Another

Now read another poem.

Sandra Cisneros
Curtains

Rich people don't need them.
Poor people tie theirs into fists
or draw them tight as modest brides
up to the neck.

Inside they hide bright walls. 5
Turquoise or lipstick pink.
Good colors in another country.
Here they can't make you forget

the dinette set that isn't paid for,
floorboards the landlord needs to fix, 10
raw wood, linoleum roses,
the what you wanted but didn't get.

[1987]

Reread the Cisneros poem and mark where you find striking moments and where you feel some confusion. Then read it together with the Rita Dove poem.

1. Do the voices of narrators sound different? How? Find words and images to help you describe.
2. Does the structure of the poems (line lengths, rhymes, stanzas) contribute to your reading? Is it similar for both poems?
3. Are the marks you made about language or images similar in both poems?

Now, with your group, design a writing task—for a timed writing or for an out of class assignment—that would use these two poems as illustrations. Dove and

Cisneros use the same genre of poetry and take similar topics to create different portraits. As we explained in Chapter 1, juxtaposition, or understanding one thing *in terms of* another, helps readers read inventively.

Fiction

The famous author E. M. Forster claimed that fiction is all about the story—what happens and when and to whom. "It can only have one merit," he said, "that of making the audience want to know what happens next." Of course, Forster was being intentionally simplistic; novels and stories can do more than make a reader curious. Still, narrative, or storytelling, propels a reader forward, and in Forster's argument, it must if it is to be successful. When you read fiction, whether a fairy tale or a detective story, you expect characters to carry the story and a narrator to help explain the characters. But the writer uses all the elements of story—character, setting, dialogue, image, detail, action—to help readers realize the messages or themes the story suggests. Here's the opening to Toni Morrison's novel *Sula.*

Toni Morrison
Excerpt from *Sula*

In that place, where they tore the nightshade and blackberry patches from their roots to make room for the Medallion City Golf Course, there was once a neighborhood. It stood in the hills above the valley town of Medallion and spread all the way to the river. It is called the suburbs now, but when black people lived there it was called the Bottom. One road, shaded by beeches, oaks, maples and chestnuts, connected it to the valley. The beeches are gone now, and so are the pear trees where children sat and yelled down through the blossoms to the passersby. Generous funds have been allotted to level the stripped and faded buildings that clutter the road from Medallion up to the golf course. They are going to raze the Time and a Half Pool Hall, where feet in long tan shoes once pointed down from chair rungs. A steel ball will knock to dust Irene's Palace of Cosmetology, where women used to lean their heads back on sink trays and doze while Irene lathered Nu Nile into their hair. Men in khaki work clothes will pry loose the slats of Reba's Grill, where the owner cooked in her hat because she couldn't remember the ingredients without it.

Readers know at once and without thinking about it that they're reading a story. The setting is detailed, and the names the narrator mentions suggest that they're characters, people who readers are already interested in and expect to read about. The place is significant; notice the first phrase of the paragraph. Readers are already asking questions unconsciously that will direct their reading and their interpretations. Who are the people who lived here? Why was it called the Bottom? Where are the people now? The writer has already made us care.

Here are some other questions that can direct your reading and help you make good guesses about the piece:

- How do you characterize the speaker?
- How does the speaker feel about the Bottom ? How do you know?
- What is the speaker's aim or purpose? Why do you think so?
- How do you feel about the place and the passage? What words in the text contribute to your feeling?

Those questions become a beginning for an exploration of elements that guide your reading of the text. You might want to consider Morrison's sentences, their length and structure, as well as her word choice (why *blackberry*? Why *once*?). You might also want to think about how repetition reinforces the feeling of the place and the tone of the passage.

ACTIVITY Beginning an Analysis

Write a beginning of an essay that analyzes the maneuvers of the opening to Morrison's *Sula*. You might include strategies like use of images or syntax. Or write an essay examination question about the passage from *Sula*.

Film and Drama

Reading film and drama is similar to reading fiction, since they are all narratives, with characters who live out the story being told. But in film and drama, action—movement and sound—provide more avenues for the text to convey its message. When you read drama, rather than see it performed, you'll notice that language is heightened because there is little or no description to accompany the dialogue. As a reader, you need to pay close attention to the speech of the characters, since that is where the conflicts, and the playwright's aims, will be illuminated.

Susan Glaspell's 1916 play *Trifles* demonstrates how much readers must *read in* in order to gather the rhetorical aims of the playwright as well as the motives of the characters. Like many plays, this one begins with details of setting. The details of the setting seem significant as the reader reads them rather than simply observes them on the stage.

Susan Glaspell

Excerpt from *Trifles*

SCENE

The kitchen in the now abandoned farmhouse of John Wright, a gloomy kitchen, and left without having been put in order—unwashed pans under

Watch the Video on Reading a Story at Your Pearson MyLab

the sink, a loaf of bread outside the bread-box, a dish-towel on the table—other signs of incompleted work. At the rear the outer door opens and the sheriff comes in followed by the County Attorney and Hale. The Sheriff and Hale are in middle life, the County Attorney is a young man; all are much bundled up and go at once to the stove. They are followed by the two women—the Sheriff's wife first; she is a slight wiry woman, a thin nervous face. Mrs. Hale is larger and would ordinarily be called more comfortable looking, but she is disturbed now and looks fearfully about as she enters. The women have come in slowly, and stand close together near the door.

COUNTY ATTORNEY: [*rubbing his hands*] This feels good. Come up to the fire, ladies.

MRS. PETERS: [*after taking a step forward*] I'm not—cold.

SHERIFF: [*unbuttoning his overcoat and stepping away from the stove as if to mark the beginning of official business*] Now, Mr. Hale, before we move things about, you explain to Mr. Henderson just what you saw when you came here yesterday morning.

COUNTY ATTORNEY: By the way, has anything been moved? Are things just as you left them yesterday?

SHERIFF: [*looking about*] It's just the same. When it dropped below zero last night, I thought I better send Frank out this morning to make a fire for us—no use getting pneumonia with a big case on, but I told him not to touch anything except the stove—and you know Frank.

COUNTY ATTORNEY: Somebody should have been left here yesterday.

SHERIFF: Oh, yesterday. When I had to send Frank to Morris Center for that man who went crazy—I want you to know I had my hands full yesterday. I knew you could get back from Omaha by today and as long as I went over everything myself—

COUNTY ATTORNEY: Well, Mr. Hale, tell just what happened when you came by here yesterday morning.

HALE: Harry and I started to town with a load of potatoes. We came along by the road from my place and as I got here I said, "I'm going to see if I can get John Wright to go in with me on a party telephone." I spoke to Wright about it once before and he put me off, saying folks talked too much anyway, and all he asked was peace and quiet—I guess you know about how much he talked himself, but I thought maybe if I went to the house and talked about it before his wife, though I said to Harry that what his wife wanted made much difference to John—

COUNTY ATTORNEY: Let's talk about that later, Mr. Hale. I do want to talk about that, but tell now just what happened when you got to the house.

HALE: I didn't hear or see anything. I knocked at the door, and still it was all quiet inside. I knew they must be up, it was past eight o'clock. So I knocked again, and I thought I heard somebody, say, "Come in." I wasn't sure. I'm not sure yet, but I opened the door—this door [*indicating the door by which the two women are still standing*] and there in that rocker—[*pointing to it*] sat Mrs. Wright.

[1916]

Notice the gaps you must fill in as you read the opening to this drama. You ask why the people are there, you ask what the others are doing while some people are speaking, you ask what kind of play you're reading. You might need background that would tell you what a "party telephone" is or what rural life is like in winter. You're predicting as you read. The sheriff is there because there's been a crime; the house is the scene; the husband might be the victim. Will we discover who is the perpetrator? Is there a clue already?

The small details of language—Hale's going on about the telephone, the attorney's invitation to the women, Mrs. Peters's hesitation—are revealing, and they are the very details you might use to interpret the scene and the play, as well as to analyze as you write. Actions speak loudly in drama and film, so these will become part of the predictions you make, and the analysis you do. Hale's pointing, the women's standing, are potentially important moments as you uncover the playwright's methods and aim.

ACTIVITY **Writing Dialogue**

Create a small dialogue between two characters who are planning a trip to another country. One is afraid to travel; one is anxious to go. Set the scene. Give a few stage directions. Allow each character two or three speeches and see if you can suggest conflicts, motives, and possible outcomes.

Notice how much depends on the diction you choose for the characters and upon their movements.

Graphic Narratives

You've seen already in Chapter 1 how visuals work to persuade and affect readers. The details of design, color, light, and movement offer readers ways to analyze the working of a visual text that's similar to the way a novel or nonfiction essay might be interpreted and analyzed.

One recent development in visual texts is the graphic narrative, what some have called the serious comic book. Combining visual and linguistic elements, the graphic narrative invites readers to interpret and analyze in a variety of ways, observing closely and responding through the panels to the words on the page and the scene and symbols the visual elements suggest.

Here are opening panels from the graphic novel *La Perdida*, the narrative of a young woman who goes to Mexico to discover her Mexican roots.

Watch the Video on Conflict at Your Pearson MyLab

Jessica Abel

Excerpt from *La Perdida*

In graphic novels, the visual complements and completes the thought and dialogue of the characters. In the first panel, full page, the main character underscores her feeling of loss with the Mexican skeleton, an image used in Mexican feast and saints' days. Her flashback is reflective while the scene she recounts moves forward dynamically.

ACTIVITY **Connecting the Visual and the Linguistic**

In the first few panels of *La Perdida,* locate details that help develop the story the main character has begun to relate. Make a prediction by drawing your own visual about what will happen next.

Exam Questions

Exam questions are a genre that suggest particular strategies for effective reading and writing. They require close reading of both the prompt and the related text, if any; a direct response to the prompt's question or instructions; and clear, precise evidence citing appropriate elements in the text that support the response.

Here's a question from the 2003 AP exam in Language and Composition that shows how the genre works to help readers respond effectively as they read and write.

In his 1998 book *Life the Movie: How Entertainment Conquers Reality,* Neal Gabler wrote the following:

> One does not have to cluck in disapproval to admit that entertainment is all the things its detractors say it is: fun, effortless, sensational, mindless, formulaic, predictable, and subversive. In fact, one might argue that those are the very reasons so many people love it.
>
> At the same time, it is not hard to see why cultural aristocracy in the nineteenth century and intelligentsia in the twentieth hated entertainment and why they predicted, as one nineteenth century critic railed, that its eventual effect would be "to overturn all morality, to poison the essence of domestic happiness, to dissolve the ties of our social order, and to involve our country in ruin."

Write a thoughtful and carefully constructed essay in which you use specific evidence to defend, challenge or qualify the assertion that entertainment has the capacity to "ruin" society.

Because this is an exam question, readers know to look carefully at the prompt and the text as essential guides to how they'll write their essays. First, reading carefully, the reader recognizes that the text both creates an argument about entertainment and also refers to an earlier argument about its dangers. Both arguments are general: entertainment is pleasurable because it's sensational and predictable, and it is dangerous because of those things as well. How will a reader respond to the prompt that follows the excerpt, which asks for an argument that uses "specific evidence" to make some claim about the effect of entertainment?

In this question, readers are invited to use their own experiences, their knowledge and understanding about how entertainment works, in order to argue that entertainment is potentially ruinous, or that it's beneficial, or that some entertainment might be more beneficial or dangerous than others. Since the prompt directly asks for specifics, detailed, strong, and lively examples will be persuasive, as will a focused narrative or logical analogies. The focused approach to the task that the test question calls for is a signal to the writer to be focused too, and that precision is an advantage. Readers read with particular ideas in mind to use or to quote, and they quickly draw from their background knowledge examples that aid them in their argument.

Here are the beginning few lines of a student's response to this exam question.

> The gates of the transport unhinge, and with it comes a shower of bullets, mixed with tracer ammunition, a rainfall of death produced by German machine guns on courageous Americans in the Normandy invasion. As troops progress up the war-torn, bloodstained beach, a nearby explosion sends moviegoers to the backs of their seats. Yes, the scene described is from the opening scene of the famed Saving Private Ryan, one of the most visually spectacular war flicks of all time. Only entertainment? No.

This student opens with a visually compelling scene and with diction that helps evoke the scene's vividness. Readers are drawn in, already predicting that the scene itself will confront the question of entertainment and its capacity to affect audiences. The writer's syntax at the end of the paragraph—"Only entertainment? No."—dramatically asserts the writer's position. Visual, spectacular, entertaining film can be something other than entertaining. Readers predict that we'll learn what else a film like *Saving Private Ryan* might offer besides visual sensation.

ACTIVITY **Write the First Paragraph of an Exam Response**

Write your own first paragraph that responds to the contentions about entertainment that Gabler asserts in his essay. Consider the prompt carefully, use your repertoire of experience and observation, and locate an argument that clearly establishes whether you agree with the position, think it's fallacious, or believe there might be times when the contention is true and others when it isn't. Work toward establishing your own voice through the images and the word choices you make.

Responding to an Older Text

You have in this chapter read visual texts, instant messages, fiction, poetry, and nonfiction. You've examined how language affects your responses to what you read, and how genre and style help you understand writer's meanings.

Let's end the chapter by examining an older text. An older work often challenges your ability to predict meanings and respond to a text. But by using your reader experience, making predictions, revising and learning to hear style and argument, you learn to read all texts with confidence and skill.

The following is from W.E.B. DuBois's essay "Of Our Spiritual Striving." It was written in 1900. If your reader experience includes information about the author, you'll have an easy way into this text. But suppose you don't know that DuBois was an important philosopher and critic in the late nineteenth and early twentieth century, one of the first African Americans to graduate from Harvard University, and the author of a famous study of African American culture and people, *The Souls of Black Folk*. This essay is the opening to that work. You begin the text by reading a poem or a song that opens the essay. What does the poem tell? Its melancholy tone suggests a tone for the piece you are to read. But the title suggests that melancholy isn't the only emotion the writer will convey. Who is "our"? What does it mean to strive spiritually? These are questions that can guide you into the essay even if you know nothing of the author or his context.

Here is the first paragraph, the paragraph that was the example for the cloze test you completed at the end of Chapter 1. See how well you predicted.

W.E.B. DuBois
Excerpt from "Of Our Spiritual Striving"

Between me and the other world there is ever an unasked question: unasked by some through feelings of delicacy; by others through the difficulty of rightly framing it. All, nevertheless, flutter round it. They approach me in a half-hesitant sort of way, eye me curiously or compassionately, and then, instead of saying directly, How does it feel to be a problem? They say, I know an excellent colored man in my town; or, I fought at Mechanicsville; or, Do not these Southern outrages make your blood boil? At these, I smile, or am interested, or reduce the boiling to a simmer, as the occasion may require. To the real question, How does it feel to be a problem? I answer seldom a word.

But before this paragraph comes a poem and a line of music:

O water, voice of my heart, crying in the sand,
    All night long crying with a mournful cry,
As I lie and listen, and cannot understand
    The voice of my heart in my side or the voice of the sea,
O water, crying for rest, is it I, is it I? 5
    All night long the water is crying to me.

Unresting water, there shall never be rest
    Till the last moon droop and the last tide fall,
And the fire of the end begin to burn in the west:

And the heart shall be weary and wonder and cry like the sea.
All life long crying without avail,
As the water all night long is crying to me.

Arthur Symons

10

[1900]

The poem is a *lament*, an expression of woe about conditions as they are, and a reader can find the diction that makes the lament both vivid and sad. What does the line of music do? Perhaps it suggests the way that the group of people DuBois will write about, the "Black Folk" of the title, strive spiritually in poetry and in music.

Taken with the poem, the first paragraph constitutes DuBois's introduction to his book, the way he will draw the audience into his circle and explore his ideas, and perhaps ask the audience to consider something new or reconsider something familiar. Readers now recognize an essential fact of the point DuBois will make: a point about race from the perspective of the race that has been considered "a problem." Readers notice he repeats the point as a question and mark its significance.

There are things readers may not know as they read the paragraph.

- Where is Mechanicsville?
- Can you predict the significance of that word?
- Can you characterize the people who talk to him, those in what he calls "the other world"?
- Even if you hadn't known facts about the author, can you describe his level of education and sophistication from the language and style he chooses?
- Do you already have a sense of the aim of the piece?

CHAPTER ACTIVITY

Responding to a Text

Read the rest of DuBois's essay, which appears in Unit 3 of the Anthology, stopping to mark where you have questions about the text or where you think an important or interesting point is being made. Mark any features of style that stand out. Then on your own or in your group, respond to these questions.

1. What do you think caused the speaker's sudden awareness of his difference?
2. How is the "veil" a good metaphor for the condition he describes?
3. What is the effect on you as a reader of the rhetorical question the speaker asks in paragraph 2?
4. What kind of evidence is important to understanding the concept of "striving"?
5. How does Dubois use punctuation for effect? And what effect is he achieving?
6. Where do you hear irony in Dubois's voice in paragraphs 6 and 7? How does the message indented heighten the irony?
7. What do you feel Dubois is asking his audience?
8. How do you feel as a contemporary reader as you read his account?
9. Does the style remind you of any other reading you've done? Or something you've heard?
10. Is this high, middle, or low style? What makes you think so?

CHAPTER CHECKLIST

Reading Genres

- ☐ What is the genre of the piece you are about to read?
- ☐ How does your knowledge of genre help you predict what you will read?
- ☐ What elements of the genre can you identify in the piece?
- ☐ How effectively has the writer or artist used the conventions of the genre?
- ☐ How do your expectations of the genre help you understand and respond to the piece?

Complete the Chapter 2 Exercise at Your Pearson MyLab

chapter 3

Composing Rhetorically

What You Will Learn

- To define rhetoric
- To explain the rhetorical appeals of *logos, ethos,* and *pathos*
- To identify the elements of the rhetorical triangle
- To take a rhetorical approach to composing
- To analyze the rhetorical appeals in verbal and visual texts

Have you ever considered what a magical act *composition* is? If you're a painter, you take some oil or water colors, put them together on a canvas and, lo and behold, you have a work of art that people look at and say, "I wonder what that means," or "Aha, I see exactly what that means." If you're a musician, you take some notes, some harmonies, some rhythms and put them together on a score or play them on an instrument, and, lo and behold, you have a song, a sonata, a symphony that people listen to and say, "I can really feel the emotion in that number." If you're a film maker preparing to post on YouTube, you take a plot and characters, set them in action in a scene with sound effects, and, lo and behold, you have a video that people can view and say, "Wow, what an exciting story you told."

Notice what all of these acts share: Each of them involves creating something that invites people to read, to analyze and comprehend (and sometimes challenge) not only some central idea or point but also the impact that the piece they've experienced has on them and the impact you have on them as well. As the creator, you pull together and arrange different parts to create an idea, an impression, an attitude. Each part you design invites the audience—the people who look at the painting, hear the music, experience the video—to examine (and you hope admire) the way you have combined the parts so effectively.

Each of the genres above—the painting, the song, the film—is a **composition**, a common word in English that comes from the combination of the Latin prefix *com*, meaning "together," and *position*, meaning "a putting." It makes sense, doesn't it?

com + position = composition = a putting together

The chances are that if you're reading this book, you're taking a course that's teaching you *composition*. You may be taking a course called Advanced Placement English Language and Composition. You may be taking a course that's simply called "English" or "American Literature." But whatever it's called, the course is probably designed to teach you to do with *language* what painters do with color and form, what musicians do with tunes and harmonies and rhythms, what film makers do with dialog, video images, and sound effects. Your course teaches you to *put together* various "component parts" of language—patterns of organization, word choice, and sentence structure—to help you convey a compelling idea, produce an effect, achieve a purpose for your readers. You're learning to compose in ways that help readers trust your knowledge and your sincerity.

Rhetoric: A Good Thing for Composing

As the first two chapters made clear, when you read, you read inventively, capitalizing on how you, the reader, and the text and its author interact to make meaning. It makes sense, then, to understand that when you compose—in writing, in music, in art—you do so in the same way. In this chapter, we make clear that this way of writing—selecting and using the "component parts" of a text so that you accomplish a purpose and create meaning with a reader—is, in the very best sense of the word, **rhetorical**.

The word *rhetoric* has unfortunately been misused by critics sometimes, to suggest something empty, something that carries no authentic meaning, or even worse, something shady that obscures authentic meaning. It's too bad that some folks misunderstand the meaning of rhetoric. It doesn't mean empty words, dishonest communication, or overblown speechifying. Instead, rhetoric is an ancient and noble art that has been taught in schools for centuries, and it remains the most powerful tool for writers and readers as they interpret the world around them.

The ancient Greek philosopher Aristotle called rhetoric "the faculty of observing all the available means of persuasion in a given case." The Roman educator Quintilian described rhetoric simply as "the art of speaking well." (And we would add "writing well.")

Our definition builds on these classical concepts to define **rhetoric** as *the way people produce texts to create meaning*. The way we make meaning depends on whether we speak or write, read or listen. It depends on who is listening to us as we speak, what our backgrounds are as we read, and where in time and space we're located.

The Appeals: *Logos, Ethos,* and *Pathos*

When readers interpret, they predict main points or central themes, they respond to the character and knowledge of the writer they read, and they are moved by language and examples that touch an emotional chord. Similarly, when writers or speakers communicate, they

- Create a main point, a central argument, that seems logical and reasonable—what some people call *appealing to* ***logos;***
- Demonstrate knowledge as well as good character and good will—what some people call *appealing to* ***ethos;***
- Understand and speak to the emotional and the personal—what some people call *appealing to* **pathos.**

Aristotle developed these three categories of response that writers and speakers use to make connections with audiences and move them to agreement or action. These **appeals** are useful to consider for readers who are reacting to them as they read and for writers who are attempting to convey ideas effectively, provide evidence for analysis or for arguments or for evaluating the claims of a variety of positions or of several texts.

These three appeals are usually all in operation in any text, but depending on the rhetorical situation—the aim of the writer, the genre, the needs of an audience—one might be privileged over another.

- ***Logos:*** The emphasis in the use of *logos* is the reasoned and carefully constructed argument, with evidence that can be followed clearly and seems verifiable or rational. In much of the writing you do in school, for example, whether you're writing to analyze or to argue or claim or to evaluate, you likely privilege *logos* in the way you invent ideas, arrange them, and prove them.
- ***Ethos:*** The writer who appeals to an audience through *ethos* establishes credibility as the most telling or effective evidence for claims. If the writer can show superior knowledge, strength of character, understanding of situations, the audience might be convinced of the rightness of the position. Additionally, writers who use appeals to an audience's sense of ethical behavior—fair play, honesty, neighborliness—highlight this appeal.
- ***Pathos:*** The emotional appeal of *pathos* centers on the response from an audience and on a writer's focus on emotional effects of the claims made and evidence offered. The reactions of anger, pity, fear, sorrow, and others are elicited by careful choices of organization and word choice. *Pathos* is the most powerful appeal since it so often moves audiences to action; it is the most misused for that reason as well.

Writers who make use of the appeals consciously and appropriately are usually also readers who have been affected consciously by those appeals. Knowing how

Watch the Video on Rhetorical Appeals at Your Pearson MyLab

Watch the Video on Appeals to Reason: Logos at Your Pearson MyLab

Watch the Video on Appeals to Authority: Ethos at Your Pearson MyLab

Watch the Video on Appeals to Emotions: Pathos at Your Pearson MyLab

to respond and how to manipulate appeals is an important part of learning how to compose rhetorically.

The Writer's Rhetorical Triangle

Most important is the fact that the way we read and structure language is always *rhetorical*—always dependent on how speakers or writers, subjects, audiences, contexts and purposes interact to make communication work.

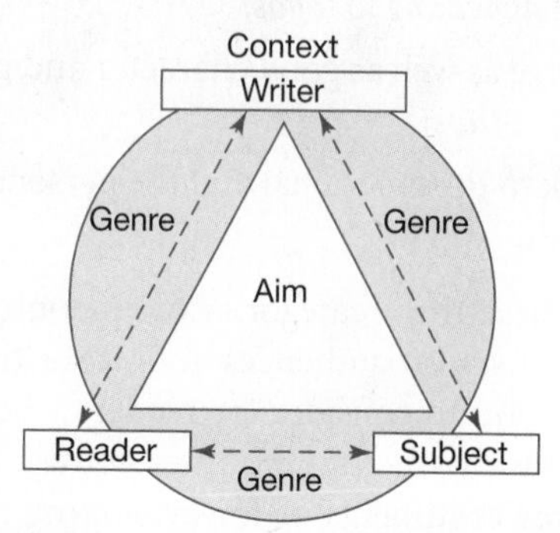

FIGURE 3.1 **The Writer's Rhetorical Triangle**

Figure 3.1 is a triangle showing rhetoric at work. The lines between speaker/writer—subject—audience illustrate the connections among those three elements. *Aim* (sometimes called "intention" or "purpose") is at the center of the triangle because it informs how the three components of the triangle will interact. Surrounding the triangle is the circle of *context,* the conditions of the interaction. And the space between triangle and circle is filled by *genre,* the characteristic forms and formats that are part of the interaction.

You'll notice that this triangle is similar to the reader's rhetorical triangle we examined in Chapter 1, and of course this similarity is intentional (see page 6). Not only do readers use the rhetorical triangle to analyze and interpret what they read, but also the act of reading itself involves a combination of elements—texts and the writers who make them, readers, aims, and effects. You can see that reading and writing require similar acts of thinking, similar strategies of connection. Above all, both are rhetorical acts, and the more you understand and practice rhetoric the more skillful and confident reader and writer you will be.

ACTIVITY Using the Rhetorical Triangle to Analyze a Text

On July 13, 1865, Horace Greeley, editor of the *New York Tribune,* wrote an editorial encouraging Civil War veterans to take advantage of the Homestead Act of 1862 and apply for ownership of a 160-acre "stake" of undeveloped land, owned by the U.S. Government, west of the Mississippi River. The editorial contained the following sentences:

> Washington is not a place to live in. The rents are high, the food is bad, the dust is disgusting and the morals are deplorable. Go West, young man, go West and grow up with the country.

With a classmate or in a group, refer to the Writer's Rhetorical Triangle diagram and discuss the following questions:

1. What is the context of Greeley's editorial and how does that context influence his aim?
2. Who is the primary audience for this editorial, and why might this audience be interested in the subject?
3. Judging just from this excerpt, what kind of personality do you think Greeley has?
4. What is the genre Greeley chooses to create, and why is it an appropriate one for the context and his aim?

Using Rhetoric to Compose

You may never have thought about writing, or composition, in this dynamic, rhetorical way before. Maybe you've thought of composing more in terms of fulfilling assignments, answering questions, producing the required number of pages, and making sure your grammar and spelling were correct. There's nothing wrong with thinking of writing that way: When a writer chooses to focus solely on correct form and conventions, it is a rhetorical decision—a choice to help achieve a purpose or create meaning—like any other strategy a writer might employ. But this book invites you to consider more interesting possibilities for yourself as a writer—to think of yourself as making meaning when you compose, not just following a guide to complete an assignment. As a meaning maker you use your growing rhetorical awareness, and you come to understand that *how* you decide to say something is as important as *what* you say. As you read and write, thinking about what you want to say and why, you might pause to ask yourself questions like these, questions that go beyond simply meeting the demands of an assignment.

Rhetorical Questions for Writers

- **What is my intention (or aim or purpose) in creating this composition?** Is it to convince people to think in a new way about my topic? To behave in a different way? Is my purpose to inform someone about something I know and they don't? Is my purpose to explain something to them? Is my purpose actually some combination of these?
- **Who is my audience?** Am I writing solely to my teacher? Am I writing to a community of people who are interested in the same things I am? Am I writing to other students in my course? Do I need to imagine an audience who'd like to hear what I'm saying?
- **What is my main point, my central argument?** Have I stated it directly? If not, could my audience infer it?

Watch the Video on Writing Purposes at Your Pearson MyLab

Watch the Video on Knowing Your Audience at Your Pearson MyLab

- **What kind of effect—emotional or psychological—do I want to have on my audience *(pathos)*?** How do my words or examples help achieve that effect?
- **What kind of person do I want my readers to perceive me to be *(ethos)*?** How do I want them, just from my writing, to characterize my personality? How do my words and ideas help to create this personality?
- **What tools of language will help me best communicate my argument, help me affect my audience's perceptions or opinions?** How can I create sentences, find words, craft images, and give examples that help persuade readers?

ACTIVITY **Analyzing a Brief Passage**

An op-ed column by Kyle Jarrard in the *International Herald-Tribune* titled "Those Were the Books" begins with this passage: "That's it, the world is truly coming to an end. Encyclopaedia Britannica is going online only, after 244 years of print publication. A sadness comes over me, as when I see a book, any paper book, tossed into the maw of the Internet."

Working just with this passage, discuss with a classmate Jarrard's aim, audience, and main point. In addition, discuss what kind of effect you think he wants to have on his audience and what kind of personality he hopes the audience will perceive him to have.

A Writer's Tools: Bringing the Appeals to Life

Good writers tap into the three related appeals—*logos, ethos,* and *pathos*—plus they also convey **tone**, the writer's attitude toward his or her subject, as they compose. They do so by selecting the best tools for the job. In other words, good writers make strategic choices about

- the organization or the **arrangement** of their texts,
- the words and phrases or the **diction** they employ,
- the shape and structure or the **syntax** of their sentences, and
- the images, allusions, metaphors or the **figurative language** they use.

Here is a basic list of the kinds of choices you as a good writer make as you flesh out your main idea, establish your credibility, influence your readers' emotions, and convey your attitude toward the subject.

Rhetorical Choices for Writers: Arrangement, Diction, Syntax, Voice, Persona

- **Arrangement: the organization and structure of your composition**—including, as we made clear in Chapter 2, its **genre** (an essay, a letter, an op-ed column, a brochure, a web page, a blog); its beginning, middle, and end; the order you choose for your details and evidence; transitional words and phrases; the incorporation of headings and subheadings.

- **Diction: your word choice**—the complexity of your words, whether multi-syllable and formal or single syllable and colloquial; your use of special terminology or everyday speech; your choice of emotional or nonemotional words.
- **Syntax: your sentence structure**—your use of long complex sentences or short simple ones; your use of active and passive verbs to change emphasis; your variation of sentence length and complexity.
- **Voice 1: your tone**—the attitude (serious, reverential, humorous, sarcastic, straightforward) you want to convey about your subject matter; your variation of tone for effect.
- **Voice 2: your stance**—the degree of your forcefulness or directness in the way you address an audience; your distance from the audience as a persona.
- **Persona: your personality, your character**—the way you come across as a person, a human being, to your readers.

Reading and Writing Rhetorically: An Example

Let's pull together everything we've unpacked so far about reading and writing as related acts of rhetorical composing by examining a text, tracing a rhetorical reading of it, and then planning a written response to it, a composition that might be published in a section of the same magazine where the original text appeared.

The anthology of this book introduces you to a broad array of themes that have dominated American thought and literature since the seventeenth century. A great many of those issues are still deeply embedded in the fabric of life in the United States today. One of these continuing central questions involves American ingenuity, especially in the area of technology. Americans value inventiveness, and Americans have faith in the power of technology to solve problems. In their time, the cotton gin, the sewing machine, the grain reaper, the assembly line—all invented by Americans—and the train, not invented but certainly exploited by Americans, were seen not only as advances but as problem solvers. Yet, in many cases, problems persist despite technology and our belief in it. In some cases new technologies might worsen rather than alleviate problems. So we confront a question: How much can we or should we rely on technology, especially to solve ongoing issues and problems of justice and equality?

In his essay for the *New Yorker,* Malcolm Gladwell writes of the problems with new technologies, and he links technology to community, another important theme for American literature and culture.

Malcolm Gladwell

Small Change

Why the revolution will not be tweeted

At four-thirty in the afternoon on Monday, February 1, 1960, four college students sat down at the lunch counter at the Woolworth's in downtown Greensboro, North Carolina. They were freshmen at North Carolina A&T, a black college a mile or so away.

"I'd like a cup of coffee, please," one of the four, Ezell Blair, said to the waitress.

"We don't serve Negroes here," she replied.

The Woolworth's lunch counter was a long L-shaped bar that could seat sixty-six people, with a standup snack bar at one end. The seats were for whites. The snack bar was for blacks. Another employee, a black woman who worked at the steam table, approached the students and tried to warn them away. "You're acting stupid, ignorant!" she said. They didn't move. Around five-thirty, the front doors to the store were locked. The four still didn't move. Finally, they left by a side door. Outside, a small crowd had gathered, including a photographer from the Greensboro *Record*. "I'll be back tomorrow with A&T College," one of the students said.

Now, let's stop at this opening, which functions as the setup for the argument Gladwell will make, as well as his method of drawing readers into that argument through the story he tells. As Chapter 4 will explain, this "drawing in" is called in rhetorical terms the **exordium**, the web a writer creates to prepare readers for what might come next and to stimulate their interest.

How does the reading of this small opening demonstrate how readers must be inventive with the text they're reading? First, as in writing, readers locate and make context. Gladwell tells us that the story takes place February 1, 1960, but his essay is written in 2010. We must write in our *own* context as we read the story. Maybe we're thinking about civil rights in 2010, perhaps how different the world seems now from that day. Maybe we're predicting that Gladwell is going to use that story somehow to make a point about 2010 issues since it doesn't seem to be simply a history given the essay's title.

As we read even these few lines, then, we are making meaning for ourselves, speculating about the reasons for the story, Gladwell's take on it, how it's going to be used, what it has to do with today, and, maybe most of all, what it has to do with Twitter. These questions, asked by us as readers, are the very ones we ask ourselves (mostly unconsciously) as we write. *Why should I use the quotes? How can I make the connection to my argument clear? Will people think what I'm saying is relevant to today? Will they get the reference to the title?*

There's more. You may know the story of the four North Carolina A&T students who walked from their university downtown to sit at the Woolworth's counter and changed history. You may have heard that the civil rights movement began that day, even if you also know that the movement had been active long before 1960. Maybe you live in North Carolina and know about A&T's homecoming weekends. Your background as a reader and your personal situation—where you live, the family stories you hear, how often you read the news—help you as you create, or write, the text you begin to read.

Gladwell continues:

> By next morning, the protest had grown to twenty-seven men and four women, most from the same dormitory as the original four. The men were dressed in suits and ties. The students had brought their schoolwork, and studied as they sat at the counter. On Wednesday, students from Greensboro's "Negro" secondary school, Dudley High, joined in, and the number of protesters swelled to eighty. By Thursday, the protesters numbered three hundred, including three white women, from the Greensboro campus of the University of North Carolina. By Saturday, the sit-in had reached six hundred. People spilled out onto the street. White teen-agers waved Confederate flags. Someone threw a firecracker. At noon, the A&T football team arrived. "Here comes the wrecking crew," one of the white students shouted. 5
>
> By the following Monday, sit-ins had spread to Winston-Salem, twenty-five miles away, and Durham, fifty miles away. The day after that, students at Fayetteville State Teachers College and at Johnson C. Smith College, in Charlotte, joined in, followed on Wednesday by students at St. Augustine's College and Shaw University, in Raleigh. On Thursday and Friday, the protest crossed state lines, surfacing in Hampton and Portsmouth, Virginia, in Rock Hill, South Carolina, and in Chattanooga, Tennessee. By the end of the month, there were sit-ins throughout the South, as far west as Texas. "I asked every student I met what the first day of the sitdowns had been like on his campus," the political theorist Michael Walzer wrote in *Dissent*. "The answer was always the same: 'It was like a fever. Everyone wanted to go.'" Some seventy thousand students eventually took part. Thousands were arrested and untold thousands more radicalized. . . .

Here is the end of the *exordium*.

> . . . These events in the early sixties became a civil-rights war that engulfed the South for the rest of the decade—and it happened without e-mail, texting, Facebook, or Twitter.

Now you can tell that Gladwell uses the Greensboro sit-ins as the first of a series that follows, and that the series of events taken together leads to the success of the civil rights movement in this country. You know it was a success because you mentally incorporate those events into what you know about life now. There are no more segregated lunch counters, no legal refusals to serve anyone on the basis of ethnicity or race. Gladwell's discussion of these events and the way he ends, by listing what the events did not depend on, tell the reader something important: Gladwell believes the civil rights movement was important and successful. And he doesn't believe new technology helps movements like this one occur.

Read the rest of this essay to see how Gladwell makes this connection. You may find yourself arguing with him or qualifying his conclusions. Maybe you have other evidence to offer. Or maybe you agree: community depends on factors that technology doesn't increase in significant ways.

As you read consider how you respond. Are you nodding or shaking your head? Are you coming up with rejoinders or more examples that make his point? Do you resist his implication about generational difference or find yourself asserting it? All these questions show how you're reading inventively—indeed, how you're writing—creating, interpreting, assigning value to—what you read.

The world, we are told, is in the midst of a revolution. The new tools of social media have reinvented social activism. With Facebook and Twitter and the like, the traditional relationship between political authority and popular will has been upended, making it easier for the powerless to collaborate, coordinate, and give voice to their concerns. When ten thousand protesters took to the streets in Moldova in the spring of 2009 to protest against their country's Communist government, the action was dubbed the Twitter Revolution, because of the means by which the demonstrators had been brought together. A few months after that, when student protests rocked Tehran, the State Department took the unusual step of asking Twitter to suspend scheduled maintenance of its Web site, because the Administration didn't want such a critical organizing tool out of service at the height of the demonstrations. "Without Twitter the people of Iran would not have felt empowered and confident to stand up for freedom and democracy," Mark Pfeifle, a former national-security adviser, later wrote, calling for Twitter to be nominated for the Nobel Peace Prize. Where activists were once defined by their causes, they are now defined by their tools. Facebook warriors go online to push for change. "You are the best hope for us all," James K. Glassman, a former senior State Department official, told a crowd of cyber activists at a recent conference sponsored by Facebook, AT&T, Howcast, MTV, and Google. Sites like Facebook, Glassman said, "give the U.S. a significant competitive advantage over terrorists. Some time ago, I said that Al Qaeda was 'eating our lunch on the Internet.' That is no longer the case. Al Qaeda is stuck in Web 1.0. The Internet is now about interactivity and conversation."

These are strong, and puzzling, claims. Why does it matter who is eating whose lunch on the Internet? Are people who log on to their Facebook page really the best hope for us all? As for Moldova's so-called Twitter Revolution, Evgeny Morozov, a scholar at Stanford who has been the most persistent of digital evangelism's critics, points out that Twitter had scant internal significance in Moldova, a country where very few Twitter accounts exist. Nor does it seem to have been a revolution, not least because the protests—as Anne Applebaum suggested in the *Washington Post*—may well have been a bit of stagecraft cooked up by the government. (In a country paranoid about Romanian revanchism, the protesters flew a Romanian flag over the Parliament building.) In the Iranian case, meanwhile, the people tweeting about the demonstrations were almost all in the West. "It is time to get Twitter's role in the events in Iran right," Golnaz Esfandiari wrote, this past summer, in *Foreign Policy.* "Simply put: There was no Twitter Revolution inside Iran." The cadre of prominent bloggers, like Andrew Sullivan, who championed the role of social media in Iran, Esfandiari continued, misunderstood the situation. "Western journalists who couldn't reach—or didn't bother reaching?—people on the ground in Iran simply scrolled through the English-language tweets posts with tag #iranelection," she wrote. "Through it all, no one seemed to wonder why people trying to coordinate protests in Iran would be writing in any language other than Farsi."

10 Some of this grandiosity is to be expected. Innovators tend to be solipsists. They often want to cram every stray fact and experience into their new model. As the historian Robert Darnton has written, "The marvels of communication technology in the present have produced a false consciousness about the past—even a sense that communication has no history, or had nothing of importance to consider before the days of television and the Internet." But there is something else at work here, in the outsized enthusiasm for social media. Fifty years after one of the most extraordinary episodes of social upheaval in American history, we seem to have forgotten what activism is.

Greensboro in the early nineteen-sixties was the kind of place where racial insubordination was routinely met with violence. The four students who first sat down at the lunch counter were terrified. "I suppose if anyone had come up behind me and yelled 'Boo,' I think I would have fallen off my seat," one of them said later. On the first day, the store manager notified the police chief, who immediately sent two officers to the store. On the third day, a gang of white toughs showed up at the lunch counter and stood ostentatiously behind the protesters, ominously muttering epithets such as "burr-head nigger." A local Ku Klux Klan leader made an appearance. On Saturday, as tensions grew, someone called in a bomb threat, and the entire store had to be evacuated.

The dangers were even clearer in the Mississippi Freedom Summer Project of 1964, another of the sentinel campaigns of the civil-rights movement. The Student Nonviolent Coordinating Committee recruited hundreds of Northern, largely white unpaid volunteers to run Freedom Schools, register black voters, and raise civil-rights awareness in the Deep South. "No one should go *anywhere* alone, but certainly not in an automobile and certainly not at night," they were instructed. Within days of arriving in Mississippi, three volunteers—Michael Schwerner, James Chaney, and Andrew Goodman—were kidnapped and killed, and, during the rest of the summer, thirty-seven black churches were set on fire and dozens of safe houses were bombed; volunteers were beaten, shot at, arrested, and trailed by pickup trucks full of armed men. A quarter of those in the program dropped out. Activism that challenges the status quo—that attacks deeply rooted problems—is not for the faint of heart.

What makes people capable of this kind of activism? The Stanford sociologist Doug McAdam compared the Freedom Summer dropouts with the participants who stayed, and discovered that the key difference wasn't, as might be expected, ideological fervor. "*All* of the applicants—participants and withdrawals alike—emerge as highly committed, articulate supporters of the goals and values of the summer program," he concluded. What mattered more was an applicant's degree of personal connection to the civil-rights movement. All the volunteers were required to provide a list of personal contacts—the people they wanted kept apprised of their activities—and participants were far more likely than dropouts to have close friends who were also going to Mississippi. High-risk activism, McAdam concluded, is a "strong-tie" phenomenon.

This pattern shows up again and again. One study of the Red Brigades, the Italian terrorist group of the nineteen-seventies, found that seventy per cent of recruits had at least one good friend already in the organization. The same is true of the men who joined the mujahideen in Afghanistan. Even revolutionary actions that look spontaneous, like the demonstrations in East Germany that led to the fall of the Berlin Wall, are, at core, strong-tie phenomena. The opposition movement in East Germany consisted of several hundred groups, each with roughly a dozen members. Each group was in limited contact with the others: at the time, only thirteen per cent of East Germans even had a phone. All they knew was that on Monday nights, outside St. Nicholas Church in downtown Leipzig, people gathered to voice their anger at the state. And the primary determinant of who showed up was "critical friends"—the more friends you had who were critical of the regime the more likely you were to join the protest.

15 So one crucial fact about the four freshmen at the Greensboro lunch counter—David Richmond, Franklin McCain, Ezell Blair, and Joseph McNeil—was their relationship with one another. McNeil was a roommate of Blair's in A&T's Scott Hall dormitory. Richmond roomed with McCain one floor up, and Blair, Richmond, and McCain had all gone to Dudley High

School. The four would smuggle beer into the dorm and talk late into the night in Blair and McNeil's room. They would all have remembered the murder of Emmett Till in 1955, the Montgomery bus boycott that same year, and the showdown in Little Rock in 1957. It was McNeil who brought up the idea of a sit-in at Woolworth's. They'd discussed it for nearly a month. Then McNeil came into the dorm room and asked the others if they were ready. There was a pause, and McCain said, in a way that works only with people who talk late into the night with one another, "Are you guys chicken or not?" Ezell Blair worked up the courage the next day to ask for a cup of coffee because he was flanked by his roommate and two good friends from high school.

The kind of activism associated with social media isn't like this at all. The platforms of social media are built around weak ties. Twitter is a way of following (or being followed by) people you may never have met. Facebook is a tool for efficiently managing your acquaintances, for keeping up with the people you would not otherwise be able to stay in touch with. That's why you can have a thousand "friends" on Facebook, as you never could in real life.

This is in many ways a wonderful thing. There is strength in weak ties, as the sociologist Mark Granovetter has observed. Our acquaintances—not our friends—are our greatest source of new ideas and information. The Internet lets us exploit the power of these kinds of distant connections with marvelous efficiency. It's terrific at the diffusion of innovation, interdisciplinary collaboration, seamlessly matching up buyers and sellers, and the logistical functions of the dating world. But weak ties seldom lead to high-risk activism.

In a new book called "The Dragonfly Effect: Quick, Effective, and Powerful Ways to Use Social Media to Drive Social Change," the business consultant Andy Smith and the Stanford Business School professor Jennifer Aaker tell the story of Sameer Bhatia, a young Silicon Valley entrepreneur who came down with acute myelogenous leukemia. It's a perfect illustration of social media's strengths. Bhatia needed a bone-marrow transplant, but he could not find a match among his relatives and friends. The odds were best with a donor of his ethnicity, and there were few South Asians in the national bone-marrow database. So Bhatia's business partner sent out an e-mail explaining Bhatia's plight to more than four hundred of their acquaintances, who forwarded the e-mail to their personal contacts; Facebook pages and YouTube videos were devoted to the Help Sameer campaign. Eventually, nearly twenty-five thousand new people were registered in the bone-marrow database, and Bhatia found a match.

But how did the campaign get so many people to sign up? By not asking too much of them. That's the only way you can get someone you don't really know to do something on your behalf. You can get thousands of people to sign up for a donor registry, because doing so is pretty easy. You have to send in a cheek swab and—in the highly unlikely event that your bone marrow is a good match for someone in need—spend a few hours at the hospital. Donating bone marrow isn't a trivial matter. But it doesn't involve financial or personal risk; it doesn't mean spending a summer being chased by armed men in pickup trucks. It doesn't require that you confront socially entrenched norms and practices. In fact, it's the kind of commitment that will bring only social acknowledgment and praise.

The evangelists of social media don't understand this distinction; they seem to believe that a Facebook friend is the same as a real friend and that signing up for a donor registry in Silicon Valley today is activism in the same sense as sitting at a segregated lunch counter in Greensboro in 1960. "Social networks are particularly effective at increasing motivation," Aaker and Smith write. But that's not true. Social networks are effective at increasing *participation*—by lessening the level of motivation that participation requires. The Facebook page of the Save Darfur Coalition has 1,282,339 members, who have donated an average of nine cents apiece. The next biggest Darfur charity on Facebook has 22,073 members, who have donated an average of thirty-five cents. Help Save Darfur has 2,797 members, who have given, on average, fifteen cents. A spokesperson for the Save Darfur Coalition told *Newsweek,* "We wouldn't necessarily gauge someone's value to the advocacy movement based on what they've given. This is a powerful mechanism to engage this critical population. They inform their community, attend events, volunteer. It's not something you can measure by looking at a ledger." In other words, Facebook activism succeeds not by motivating people to make a real sacrifice but by motivating them to do the things that people do when they are not motivated enough to make a real sacrifice. We are a long way from the lunch counters of Greensboro. 20

The students who joined the sit-ins across the South during the winter of 1960 described the movement as a "fever." But the civil-rights movement was more like a military campaign than like a contagion. In the late nineteen-fifties, there had been sixteen sit-ins in various cities throughout the South, fifteen of which were formally organized by civil-rights organizations like the N.A.A.C.P. and CORE. Possible locations for activism were scouted. Plans were drawn up. Movement activists held training sessions and retreats for would-be protesters. The Greensboro Four were a product of this groundwork: all were members of the N.A.A.C.P. Youth Council. They had close ties with the head of the local N.A.A.C.P. chapter. They had been briefed on the earlier wave of sit-ins in Durham, and had been part of a series of movement meetings in activist churches. When the sit-in movement spread from Greensboro throughout the South, it did not spread indiscriminately. It spread to those cities which had preexisting "movement centers"—a core of dedicated and trained activists ready to turn the "fever" into action.

The civil-rights movement was high-risk activism. It was also, crucially, strategic activism: a challenge to the establishment mounted with precision and discipline. The N.A.A.C.P. was a centralized organization, run from New York according to highly formalized operating procedures. At the Southern Christian Leadership Conference, Martin Luther King, Jr., was the unquestioned authority. At the center of the movement was the black church, which had, as Aldon D. Morris points out in his superb 1984 study, "The Origins of the Civil Rights Movement," a carefully demarcated division of labor, with various standing committees and disciplined groups. "Each group was task-oriented and coordinated its activities through authority structures," Morris writes. "Individuals were held accountable for their assigned duties, and important conflicts were resolved by the minister, who usually exercised ultimate authority over the congregation."

This is the second crucial distinction between traditional activism and its online variant: social media are not about this kind of hierarchical organization. Facebook and the like are tools for building *networks,* which are the opposite, in structure and character, of hierarchies. Unlike hierarchies, with their rules and procedures, networks aren't controlled by a single central authority. Decisions are made through consensus, and the ties that bind people to the group are loose.

This structure makes networks enormously resilient and adaptable in low-risk situations. Wikipedia is a perfect example. It doesn't have an editor, sitting in New York, who directs and corrects each entry. The effort of putting together each entry is self-organized. If every entry in Wikipedia were to be erased tomorrow, the content would swiftly be restored, because that's what happens when a network of thousands spontaneously devote their time to a task.

There are many things, though, that networks don't do well. Car companies sensibly use a network to organize their hundreds of suppliers, but not to design their cars. No one believes that the articulation of a coherent design philosophy is best handled by a sprawling, leaderless organizational system. Because networks don't have a centralized leadership structure and clear lines of authority, they have real difficulty reaching consensus and setting goals. They can't think strategically; they are chronically prone to conflict and error. How do you make difficult choices about tactics or strategy or philosophical direction when everyone has an equal say? 25

The Palestine Liberation Organization originated as a network, and the international-relations scholars Mette Eilstrup-Sangiovanni and Calvert Jones argue in a recent essay in *International Security* that this is why it ran into such trouble as it grew: "Structural features typical of networks—the absence of central authority, the unchecked autonomy of rival groups, and the inability to arbitrate quarrels through formal mechanisms—made the P.L.O. excessively vulnerable to outside manipulation and internal strife."

In Germany in the nineteen-seventies, they go on, "the far more unified and successful left-wing terrorists tended to organize hierarchically, with professional management and clear divisions of labor. They were concentrated geographically in universities, where they could establish central leadership, trust, and camaraderie through regular, face-to-face meetings." They seldom betrayed their comrades in arms during police interrogations. Their counterparts on the right were organized as decentralized networks, and had no such discipline. These groups were regularly infiltrated, and members, once arrested, easily gave up their comrades. Similarly, Al Qaeda was most dangerous when it was a unified hierarchy. Now that it has dissipated into a network, it has proved far less effective.

The drawbacks of networks scarcely matter if the network isn't interested in systemic change—if it just wants to frighten or humiliate or make a splash—or if it doesn't need to think strategically. But if you're taking on a powerful and organized establishment you have to be a hierarchy. The Montgomery bus boycott required the participation of tens of thousands of people who depended on public transit to get to and from work each day. It lasted a *year.* In order to persuade those people to stay true to the cause, the boycott's organizers tasked each local black church with maintaining morale, and put together a free alternative private carpool service, with forty-eight dispatchers and forty-two pickup stations. Even the White Citizens Council, King later said, conceded that the carpool system moved with "military precision." By the time King came to Birmingham, for the climactic showdown with Police Commissioner Eugene (Bull) Connor, he had a budget of a million dollars, and a hundred full-time staff members on the ground, divided into operational units. The operation itself was divided into steadily escalating phases, mapped out in advance. Support was maintained through consecutive mass meetings rotating from church to church around the city.

Boycotts and sit-ins and nonviolent confrontations—which were the weapons of choice for the civil-rights movement—are high-risk strategies. They leave little room for conflict and error. The moment even one protester deviates from the script and responds to provocation, the moral legitimacy of the entire protest is compromised. Enthusiasts for social media would no doubt have us believe that King's task in Birmingham would have been made infinitely easier had he been able to communicate with his followers through Facebook, and contented himself with tweets from a Birmingham jail. But networks are messy: think of the ceaseless pattern of correction and revision, amendment and debate, that characterizes Wikipedia. If Martin Luther King, Jr., had tried to do a wiki-boycott in Montgomery, he would have been steamrollered by the white power structure. And of what use would a digital communication tool be in a town where ninety-eight per cent of the black community could be reached every Sunday morning at church? The things that King needed in Birmingham—discipline and strategy—were things that online social media cannot provide.

30 The bible of the social-media movement is Clay Shirky's "Here Comes Everybody." Shirky, who teaches at New York University, sets out to demonstrate the organizing power of the Internet, and he begins with the story of Evan, who worked on Wall Street, and his friend Ivanna, after she left her smart phone, an expensive Sidekick, on the back seat of a New York City taxicab. The telephone company transferred the data on Ivanna's lost phone to a new phone,

whereupon she and Evan discovered that the Sidekick was now in the hands of a teen-ager from Queens, who was using it to take photographs of herself and her friends.

When Evan e-mailed the teen-ager, Sasha, asking for the phone back, she replied that his "white ass" didn't deserve to have it back. Miffed, he set up a Web page with her picture and a description of what had happened. He forwarded the link to his friends, and they forwarded it to their friends. Someone found the MySpace page of Sasha's boyfriend, and a link to it found its way onto the site. Someone found her address online and took a video of her home while driving by; Evan posted the video on the site. The story was picked up by the news filter Digg. Evan was now up to ten e-mails a minute. He created a bulletin board for his readers to share their stories, but it crashed under the weight of responses. Evan and Ivanna went to the police, but the police filed the report under "lost," rather than "stolen," which essentially closed the case. "By this point millions of readers were watching," Shirky writes, "and dozens of mainstream news outlets had covered the story." Bowing to the pressure, the N.Y.P.D. reclassified the item as "stolen." Sasha was arrested, and Evan got his friend's Sidekick back.

Shirky's argument is that this is the kind of thing that could never have happened in the pre-Internet age—and he's right. Evan could never have tracked down Sasha. The story of the Sidekick would never have been publicized. An army of people could never have been assembled to wage this fight. The police wouldn't have bowed to the pressure of a lone person who had misplaced something as trivial as a cell phone. The story, to Shirky, illustrates "the ease and speed with which a group can be mobilized for the right kind of cause" in the Internet age.

Shirky considers this model of activism an upgrade. But it is simply a form of organizing which favors the weak-tie connections that give us access to information over the strong-tie connections that help us persevere in the face of danger. It shifts our energies from organizations that promote strategic and disciplined activity and toward those which promote resilience and adaptability. It makes it easier for activists to express themselves, and harder for that expression to have any impact. The instruments of social media are well suited to making the existing social order more efficient. They are not a natural enemy of the status quo. If you are of the opinion that all the world needs is a little buffing around the edges, this should not trouble you. But if you think that there are still lunch counters out there that need integrating it ought to give you pause.

Shirky ends the story of the lost Sidekick by asking, portentously, "What happens next?"—no doubt imagining future waves of digital protesters. But he has already answered the question. What happens next is more of the same. A networked, weak-tie world is good at things like helping Wall Streeters get phones back from teen-age girls. *Viva la revolución.*

[2010]

Rhetorical Questions for Readers: Responding to Gladwell

The questions that follow help you make conscious what you do when you read rhetorically. A student has answered each question based on her reading of the Gladwell article. You may answer them differently; this is simply an example.

What do you predict about the text's central argument as you begin to read? What do you think the author wants you to take away after reading the text?
Community is something that happens face to face, as people know and respect one another to stand together. Twitter and other social network sites don't provoke that kind of mutual responsibility.

What specific material can you point to—literally, put your finger on in the text—that is evidence for your hypothesized central argument or main idea
The examples from the early civil rights movement are in the first three paragraphs. The Moldova example shows how technology was wrongly seen as responsible for the revolution there.

If someone were to ask you how this evidence supports the article's central claim, what would you say?
The movement was successful, and it still produces resounding effects. Something else, not the easy availability of information afforded by networks like Twitter, must be responsible for this kind of social action for justice.

What is the tone of the text? That is, what do you think is the author's attitude toward the subject matter he or she is writing about? How do you respond to it?
Gladwell is definite, maybe even defiant, about his position, which runs counter to what some claim about the wonders of the new technology where instant communication is possible. If I'm a reader who likes Twitter, I might be skeptical.

What specific evidence can you point to that supports your hypothesized tone?
His use of phrases like "we are told," as he calls into question the importance of instant message in the revolution in Moldova, carries a message that suggests the media's belief in technology is suspicious. He asks questions that put the Internet in its place: "Why does it matter who is eating whose lunch on the Internet?"

Does the author or speaker strike you as credible? Does he or she strike you as a person who is knowledgeable and who has his or her readers' best interests in mind?
He may not be in line with popular culture or popular ideas, but his facts seem straight and his voice clear.

These kinds of questions illustrate the kind of reading you do that keeps you actively making meaning as you read and reflect, and asking them helps you "write" or interpret what you think of the claims, the voice, the intention, and the effect of the piece. These sorts of rhetorical questions can guide you as a writer when you begin to analyze or respond to this piece in an essay of your own.

Other questions might concern the arrangement and genre of the essay and how it works to further the aim, the choice of diction and sentence structure that helps define the character of the speaker and the attitude toward the subject, the kinds of evidence presented and the strength of that evidence, and the way the piece ends. All these ideas strengthen the making of meaning with texts you read and write.

Writing Activities to Strengthen Reading

Before we get to the activity that calls on you to respond rhetorically, as a writer, to Gladwell's essay, let's consider two practices that will promote your development as a rhetorically savvy reader and writer.

Keeping a Journal

We introduced the reader's journal in Chapter 1 as a useful device for guiding your inventive reading. Let's return to it now, and tweak the label, calling it a "reader's/writer's journal." The journal, an ongoing record of how you're responding to a piece of reading, is also a powerful way to write your way into a text, and it can become the basis for more formal or researched essays on the text or its issues. It's just a bit more expansive than taking marginal notes because it gives a writer more space to comment (But marginal notes are good as well: they are the first and most important bits of interpretation a reader makes).

As you read, stop to comment where you are interested, perplexed or appreciative, or where you notice a particular rhetorical move, or where you see a pattern, or where you have a strong positive or negative reaction. Any of these moments can be the sites of your own interpretation developing, and any can help develop a piece of writing that might emerge from your reading. The Gladwell article occasioned marginal comments like these among some first year college readers:

What was Woolworth's?
I think I've seen a picture of this.
Can't believe the waitress would *say* that !!!

A beginning comment in a reader's journal might stop at the end of the exordium:

> So the writer is sort of telling us that we think it's not possible to connect without Facebook. Does he not trust networks or does he think the younger generation is lost?

When you reread these comments, you might see the beginning of an argument that would play off of Gladwell's position or a good analysis of how Gladwell communicates his contention about the need for what he calls "authentic" communication.

The reader's journal is one way that readers can locate the ways in which they are affected by what they read and how writers manipulate texts to achieve effects.

Writing Before You Read

One way to strengthen your ability to enter the world a text asks you to be a part of, whether it's a history or biography or textbook, is to write down ideas you have about the subject of the text or its time period or other elements before you read.

If you knew you were assigned the Gladwell article, for example, and you saw the title, a small beginning of your own would help you understand and be part of the argument Gladwell creates from the first. If you are on Facebook often, if you follow someone on Twitter or send many text messages during the day, you might begin by thinking through how these networks are useful to you. Do they help you know about other people? Do they make you feel part of a community? Writing like this builds your connections to the text and helps you find your own arguments and ideas as you're reading.

Some of the "big questions" we include as the beginning inquiry in each of the units in the Anthology might be ones that you could speculate on in writing before you read any texts in the unit. Writing in this way, you'll find yourself participating in the texts you read much more confidently and with much more pleasure.

ACTIVITY Responding to Gladwell

You've already read the article, so write a response to Gladwell, one that might go in the *Mail* column in the *New Yorker.* (To see samples from the *Mail* column go to the *New Yorker* Web site, click on "This Week's Issue" and then click on "The Mail.") How will you be persuasive? How will you provide your own claims, your own details to offer your own version of his argument, to agree with his position, to change his mind, or to take what he says in a new direction? Your letter shouldn't be too long—a page is all you'll be able to persuade the editors to publish—so you need to think how to get to your point efficiently and eloquently.

As you plan this composition, make notes in response to the following questions and discuss your ideas with a classmate or in a group.

1. What is your primary aim, intention, or purpose?
2. Who is your audience?
3. What main point do you intend to make?

4. What kind of effect do you want your response to have on your audience?
5. What kind of person/personality do you want your audience to perceive that you are/have?
6. How do you think you will organize and arrange your response?
7. What kinds of effective word choices do you think you will make?
8. How do you want your sentences to look and sound?
9. What do you want your audience to perceive your tone to be?
10. What do you want your audience to perceive your stance to be?

CHAPTER ACTIVITY
Analyzing the Appeals in Visual Texts

Images often carry great emotional appeal. They have their own logic as well, and their creators often have their own ethical personae and call up the audience's own ethics. In this book, you'll examine a fair number of visual texts—and perhaps be invited to produce some of your own.

As a way to begin considering how the visual text appeals to its viewers, examine the visuals below and on the next page (Figures 3.2 and 3.3).

These are images that reflect the Greensboro, North Carolina, civil rights sit-in protest on February 1, 1960. Figure 3.2 is a photograph taken that day of the four students who asked to be served at Woolworth's; Figure 3.3 is a statue commemorating the act that stands now on the campus of North Carolina A&T University.

FIGURE 3.2

FIGURE 3.3

Consider the images, your response to them, and their aim. Working with a classmate or in a group, use the rhetorical appeals—*logos, ethos,* and *pathos*—to characterize your reaction and your feeling about their intention. Then look back at Gladwell's essay. Does seeing the images affect your reading of Gladwell's text? As an option, return to the response to Gladwell you have already written and add a paragraph in which you incorporate your response to the images in your composition.

CHAPTER CHECKLIST
Composing Rhetorically

- ☐ Have you analyzed the use of the rhetorical appeals of *logos, ethos,* and *pathos* in your reading?
- ☐ Have you used the rhetorical appeals of *logos, ethos,* and *pathos* to make your writing more effective?
- ☐ Have you considered the use of arrangement, diction, syntax, tone, voice, and stance in what you read and write?
- ☐ Are you keeping a journal and writing before you read to improve the effectiveness of your reading?

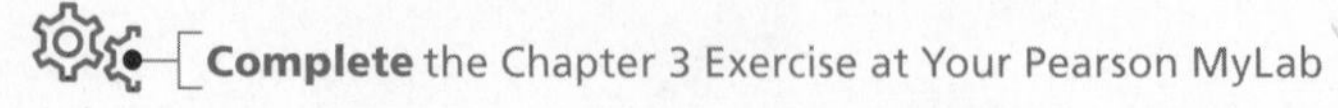

Complete the Chapter 3 Exercise at Your Pearson MyLab

chapter 4

Rhetoric and Analysis

What You Will Learn

- To determine the main idea, purpose, tone, author's credibility, and emotional effect of a text
- To analyze how a text's arrangement, diction, syntax, imagery and allusions, and figures of rhetoric support the main idea
- To write a rhetorical analysis essay

As the first three chapters suggest, we analyze nonstop while we read and write. But clearly analysis is not just a reading and writing activity. Consider the following ways you analyze in your daily lives.

- If you're thinking about going to college, you need to analyze the various factors involved in making a wise choice of institutions: How do people characterize the quality and reputation of the school? How much do tuition, fees, books, and room and board cost? Does the school have a good program in your proposed major? What is the social life like? Is the school close to your home—if you want to stay close?
- If you're working on a computer and you lose your connection to the Internet, you need to analyze what has gone wrong: Has the web site gone down? Has your location lost its Internet connection? Has something gone wrong with your particular computer? Did you do something to disconnect the Internet?
- If you're planning a major trip in a car, you need to analyze a range of options: Do you want simply to take the shortest route? Do you want to avoid congested traffic? Do you want to enjoy beautiful scenery? Do you want to stop off someplace—a shopping mall, a historic site, somebody's house—along the way?

In other words, you analyze all the time, and you analyze in similar ways no matter what the problem or plan. Notice what these situations share:

- They all have a big central question: Is this the best college or university for me? What has gone wrong with the Internet? What is the best route for our road trip?
- They all involve a series of smaller, more detailed speculations about the "component parts" that help answer the big, central issue: What's the cost? Is the computer plugged in? Will we stop on the trip?
- They all call on you to analyze.

Analysis is a term used so often that we seldom stop to think what exactly it means. It's helpful to return to the word's *etymology*, its origin. **Analysis** comes from an ancient Greek word meaning to unravel or loosen. For thinkers in the classical world of Greece and Rome, analysis referred to a systematic process of investigation, unraveling elements to see how they worked.

That's a pretty fair characterization of how the word is used today. When you analyze anything, whether for a specific assignment or for your everyday reading and homework, you think about the big question. Then you unravel it. You untie it. You divide it into its components to investigate it systematically, to see how its parts work, and to determine how the parts speak to the whole.

Think of all the opportunities you might have in school to engage in analysis during a typical semester. In economics, you analyze how stock market prices vary with unemployment statistics. In humanities, you analyze how Picasso's *Guernica* conveys an attitude about war. In health, you analyze the effects of diet on athletic performance. To begin the analysis in any of these classes, you confront the big, central question: In general, how does the stock market respond to unemployment rates? What is the central idea about war in *Guernica*? How important are proteins and carbohydrates in an athlete's diet? Then you unravel and loosen the object of analysis—the stock market, the painting, the diet—in order to formulate the "component parts" probes that collectively lead to an answer to the big central question.

In short, the keys to analysis—to the type of reading, thinking, and writing you must do in your everyday life, in many of your classes, and certainly on the Advanced Placement English Language and Composition examination—are two:

1. Determining and addressing the big central question of whatever you're being asked to analyze.
2. Probing how the component parts of the object at hand collectively answer the big central question.

There's an important idea related to this last point. Once you determine the components, the elements that make up the whole, you make decisions about which might be most important, which are less relevant, and you structure your analysis to reflect your evaluation of the elements you've examined.

In the rest of this chapter, we'll concentrate on how to do both these operations—find big ideas, examine and evaluate the parts that make them up—carefully and systematically in relation to a text. In short, we'll focus on how to do **rhetorical analysis**.

Three Texts for Our Analyses

Throughout this chapter, we'll need to refer specifically to whole texts and passages to make clear how you do a rhetorical analysis. So here are three pieces that we'll use: (1) the first chapter of a biography, in which Walter Isaacson examines the relevance of Benjamin Franklin's accomplishments for our own time; (2) the entire text of President Abraham Lincoln's Second Inaugural Address; and (3) a poem, "Indian Boarding School: The Runaways," by the contemporary writer Louise Erdrich.

Walter Isaacson

Benjamin Franklin and the Invention of America

His arrival in Philadelphia is one of the most famous scenes in autobiographical literature: the bedraggled 17-year-old runaway, cheeky yet with a pretense of humility, straggling off the boat and buying three puffy rolls as he wanders up Market Street. But wait a minute. There's something more. Peel back a layer and we can see him as a 65-year-old wry observer, sitting in an English country house, writing this scene, pretending it's part of a letter to his son, an illegitimate son who has become a royal governor with aristocratic pretensions and needs to be reminded of his humble roots.

A careful look at the manuscript peels back yet another layer. Inserted into the sentence about his pilgrim's progress up Market Street is a phrase, written in the margin, in which he notes that he passed by the house of his future wife, Deborah Read, and that "she, standing at the door, saw me and thought I made, as I certainly did, a most awkward ridiculous appearance." So here we have, in a brief paragraph, the multilayered character known so fondly to his author as Benjamin Franklin: as a young man, then seen through the eyes of his older self, and then through the memories later recounted by his wife. It's all topped off with the old man's deft little affirmation—"as I certainly did"—in which his self-deprecation barely cloaks the pride he felt regarding his remarkable rise in the world.

Benjamin Franklin is the founding father who winks at us. George Washington's colleagues found it hard to imagine touching the austere general on the shoulder, and we would find it even more so today. Jefferson and Adams are just as intimidating. But Ben Franklin, that ambitious urban entrepreneur, seems made of flesh rather than of marble, addressable by nickname, and he turns to us from history's stage with eyes that twinkle from behind those newfangled spectacles. He speaks to us, through his letters and hoaxes and autobiography, not with orotund rhetoric but with a chattiness and clever irony that is very contemporary, sometimes unnervingly so. We see his reflection in our own time.

He was, during his eighty-four-year-long life, America's best scientist, inventor, diplomat, writer, and business strategist, and he was also one of its most practical, though not most profound, political thinkers. He proved by flying a kite that lightning was electricity, and he invented a rod to tame it. He devised bifocal glasses and clean-burning stoves, charts of the Gulf Stream and theories about the contagious nature of the common cold. He launched various civic improvement schemes, such as a lending library, college, volunteer fire corps, insurance association, and matching grant fund-raiser. He helped invent America's unique style of homespun humor and philosophical pragmatism. In foreign policy, he created an approa.ch that wove together idealism with balance-of-power realism. And in politics, he proposed seminal plans for uniting the colonies and creating a federal model for a national government.

5 But the most interesting thing that Franklin invented, and continually reinvented, was himself. America's first great publicist, he was, in his life and in his writings, consciously trying to create a new American archetype. In the process, he carefully crafted his own persona, portrayed it in public, and polished it for posterity.

Partly, it was a matter of image. As a young printer in Philadelphia, he carted rolls of paper through the streets to give the appearance of being industrious. As an old diplomat in France, he wore a fur cap to portray the role of backwoods sage. In between, he created an image for himself as a simple yet striving tradesman, assiduously honing the virtues—diligence, frugality, honesty—of a good shopkeeper and beneficent member of his community.

But the image he created was rooted in reality. Born and bred a member of the leather-aproned class, Franklin was, at least for most of his life, more comfortable with artisans and thinkers than with the established elite, and he was allergic to the pomp and perks of a hereditary aristocracy. Throughout his life he would refer to himself as "B. Franklin, printer."

From these attitudes sprang what may be Franklin's most important vision: an American national identity based on the virtues and values of its middle class. Instinctively more comfortable with democracy than were some of his fellow founders, and devoid of the snobbery that later critics would feel toward his own shopkeeping values, he had faith in the wisdom of the common man and felt that a new nation would draw its strength from what he called "the middling people." Through his self-improvement tips for cultivating personal virtues and his civic-improvement schemes for furthering the common good, he helped to create, and to celebrate, a new ruling class of ordinary citizens.

The complex interplay among various facets of Franklin's character—his ingenuity and unreflective wisdom, his Protestant ethic divorced from dogma, the principles he held firm and those he was willing to compromise—means that each new look at him reflects and refracts the nation's changing values. He has been vilified in romantic periods and lionized in entrepreneurial ones. Each era appraises him anew, and in doing so reveals some assessments of itself.

Franklin has a particular resonance in twenty-first-century America. A successful publisher and consummate networker with an inventive curiosity, he would have felt right at home in the information revolution, and his unabashed striving to be part of an upwardly mobile meritocracy made him, in social critic David Brooks's phrase, "our founding Yuppie." We can easily imagine having a beer with him after work, showing him how to use the latest digital device, sharing the business plan for a new venture, and discussing the most recent political scandals or policy ideas. He would laugh at the latest joke about a priest and a rabbi, or about a farmer's daughter. We would admire both his earnestness and his self-aware irony. And we would relate to the way he tried to balance, sometimes uneasily, the pursuit of reputation, wealth, earthly virtues, and spiritual values.

Some who see the reflection of Franklin in the world today fret about a shallowness of soul and a spiritual complacency that seem to permeate a culture of materialism. They say that he teaches us how to live a practical and pecuniary life, but not an exalted existence. Others see the same reflection and admire the basic middle-class values and democratic sentiments that now seem under assault from elitists, radicals, reactionaries, and other bashers of the bourgeoisie. They regard Franklin as an exemplar of the personal character and civic virtue that are too often missing in modern America.

Much of the admiration is warranted, and so too are some of the qualms. But the lessons from Franklin's life are more complex than those usually drawn by either his fans or his foes. Both sides too often confuse him with the striving pilgrim he portrayed in his autobiography. They mistake his genial moral maxims for the fundamental faiths that motivated his actions.

His morality was built on a sincere belief in leading a virtuous life, serving the country he loved, and hoping to achieve salvation through good works. That led him to make the link between private virtue and civic virtue, and to suspect, based on the meager evidence he could muster about God's will, that these earthly virtues were linked to heavenly ones as well. As he put it in the motto for the library he founded, "To pour forth benefits for the common good is divine." In comparison to contemporaries such as Jonathan Edwards, who believed that men were sinners in the hands of an angry God and that salvation could come through grace alone, this outlook might seem somewhat complacent. In some ways it was, but it was also genuine.

Whatever view one takes, it is useful to engage anew with Franklin, for in doing so we are grappling with a fundamental issue: How does one live a life that is useful, virtuous, worthy, moral, and spiritually meaningful? For that matter, which of these attributes is most important? These are questions just as vital for a self-satisfied age as they were for a revolutionary one.

[2003]

Abraham Lincoln
Second Inaugural Address

Fellow-Countrymen:

At this second appearing to take the oath of the Presidential office there is less occasion for an extended address than there was at the first. Then a statement somewhat in detail of a course to be pursued seemed fitting and proper. Now, at the expiration of four years, during which public declarations have been constantly called forth on every point and phase of the great contest which still absorbs the attention and engrosses the energies of the nation, little that is new could be presented. The progress of our arms, upon which all else chiefly depends, is as well known to the public as to myself, and it is, I trust, reasonably satisfactory and encouraging to all. With high hope for the future, no prediction in regard to it is ventured.

On the occasion corresponding to this four years ago all thoughts were anxiously directed to an impending civil war. All dreaded it, all sought to avert it. While the inaugural address was being delivered from this place, devoted altogether to *saving* the Union without war, insurgent agents were in the city seeking to *destroy* it without war—seeking to dissolve the Union and divide effects by negotiation. Both parties deprecated war, but one of them would *make* war rather than let the nation survive, and the other would *accept* war rather than let it perish, and the war came.

One-eighth of the whole population were colored slaves, not distributed generally over the Union, but localized in the southern part of it. These slaves constituted a peculiar and powerful interest. All knew that this interest was somehow the cause of the war. To strengthen, perpetuate, and extend this interest was the object for which the insurgents would rend the Union even by war, while the Government claimed no right to do more than to restrict the territorial enlargement of it. Neither party expected for the war the magnitude or the duration which it has already attained. Neither anticipated that the *cause* of the conflict might cease with or even before the conflict itself should cease. Each looked for an easier triumph, and a result less fundamental and astounding. Both read the same Bible and pray to the same God, and each invokes His aid against the other. It may seem strange that any men should dare to ask a just God's assistance in wringing their bread from the sweat of other men's faces, but let us judge not, that we be not judged. The prayers of both could not be answered. That of neither has been answered fully. The Almighty has His own purposes. "Woe unto the world because of offenses; for it must needs be that offenses come, but woe to that man by whom the offense cometh." If we shall suppose that American slavery is one of those offenses which, in the providence of God, must needs come, but which, having continued through His appointed time, He now wills to remove, and that He gives to both North and South this terrible war as the woe due to those by whom the offense came, shall we discern therein any departure from those divine attributes which the believers in a living God always ascribe to Him? Fondly do we hope, fervently do we pray, that this mighty scourge of war may speedily pass away. Yet, if God wills that it continue until all the wealth piled by the bondsman's two hundred and fifty years of unrequited toil shall be sunk, and until every drop of blood drawn with the lash shall be paid by another drawn with the sword, as was said three thousand years ago, so still it must be said "the judgments of the Lord are true and righteous altogether."

[March 4, 1865]

Louise Erdrich
Indian Boarding School: The Runaways

Home's the place we head for in our sleep.
Boxcars stumbling north in dreams
don't wait for us. We catch them on the run.
The rails, old lacerations that we love,
shoot parallel across the face and break 5
just under Turtle Mountains. Riding scars
you can't get lost. Home is the place they cross.

The lame guard strikes a match and makes the dark
less tolerant. We watch through cracks in boards
as the land starts rolling, rolling till it hurts 10
to be here, cold in regulation clothes.
We know the sheriff's waiting at midrun

to take us back. His car is dumb and warm.
The highway doesn't rock, it only hums
like a wing of long insults. The worn-down welts 15
of ancient punishments lead back and forth.

All runaways wear dresses, long green ones,
the color you would think shame was. We scrub
the sidewalks down because it's shameful work.
Our brushes cut the stone in watered arcs 20
and in the soak frail outlines shiver clear
a moment, things us kids pressed on the dark
face before it hardened, pale, remembering
delicate old injuries, the spines of names and leaves.

[2003]

Before We Begin: Analysis of a Text *For Whom*?

Even before getting started with rhetorical analysis, we need to get one thing straight: When you analyze anything, you're always analyzing how it works *for someone*. So, while you analyze you need to hypothesize about what you think is the central idea, you need to think about what the author wants *readers* to take home, or what purpose the author wants to accomplish for *readers*, or what attitude about the subject the author wants *readers* to infer, or how the author wants *readers* to perceive the author's character, or how the author wants *readers* to respond emotionally—well, you get the idea.

Your analysis always must consider the text's audience, a potential set of readers or listeners—that's what makes it a *rhetorical* analysis, an examination of how a writer has crafted a text so that it conveys meaning, achieves a purpose, or creates an effect for an audience. Some tasks might ask you to analyze how a text works for an audience of yourself and your peers; others might require you to analyze how a text works for an audience of generally well-educated, curious adults; still others might expect you to analyze how a text works for readers of a particular journal or people with highly specialized knowledge about the subject matter.

It's not unusual for an analysis assignment to *omit* specific instructions about the audience for the text being analyzed. In that case, your first hypothesis has to identify these readers. Whom does the text seem to be addressing? How do you know? How does your analysis take these readers into consideration?

ACTIVITY **A Quick Look at Audience**

Having read Abraham Lincoln's Second Inaugural Address, discuss these two questions with a classmate or in a group: Whom does Lincoln's text seem to be addressing? How do you know?

Starting Rhetorical Analysis: Answering the Big Central Question and Four Related Questions

Writers always write to initiate the making of meaning. They create words that they know readers will encounter, interpret, and comprehend—in other words, readers will complete the making of meaning that the writers jump-start. The first step in writing analytically, therefore, requires you to be a "meaning-completing" reader, to take a leap of faith and *hypothesize* the big central question and a possible answer to it:

- **What is the central point, the major idea, that the author wants readers to understand about the subject?** In rhetorical terms, this idea would be the text's central **claim** or **thesis**. In this chapter, let's call it the "take-home idea."

In addition, you need to hypothesize about four other questions related to the take-home idea:

- **What is the author's primary purpose?** What does the author want to do *for* the readers: Inform them about something they need to know? Convince them to accept a proposition? Persuade them to think or act in a different way? Clarify an unclear concept? Amuse?
- **What attitude toward the subject matter does the author want readers to believe the author holds?** Serious about the subject at hand? Whimsical? Reverential? Ironic? Angry? This component of analysis is the **tone** of the piece.
- **How does the author convince the readers that the author is credible, trustworthy, worth listening to?** In rhetorical terms, how does the author establish his or her *ethos*?
- **What emotional effect does the author want to have on readers?** Does the author want to make readers happy? Angry? Satisfied or dissatisfied? Comfortable or uncomfortable? In rhetorical terms, how does the piece appeal to the readers' *pathos*?

Some people would argue that you can never know for certain what main point an author wants you to get in a text, what primary purpose the author wants to try to accomplish, what tone the author hopes to convey, how the author creates credibility, or what emotional effect the author wants to have on readers. You can't get

Watch the Video on Analyzing Texts at Your Pearson MyLab inside an author's head, these people argue, and, besides, even if an author did tell you about any of these things, he or she might not tell you the truth.

Fair enough. But the analyst must play the "what if" game: "*What if* I propose that X is the main idea of this text? *What if* I propose the author was trying to accomplish this purpose? *What if* I propose this is the tone the author was trying to convey? *What if* I argue that the author's credibility is established in ways that I specify? *What if* I maintain that the author was trying to have this emotional effect on the readers?" Once you make *hypotheses,* thoughtful speculations about what's being studied, rather than attempting to guess at what the author intended, you can generate good interpretations of big ideas and the elements that make them up. Notice that the word *I* is important. Other readers might find other big questions, and alternate elements that they regard as important. Analysis, like writing itself, is no exact science. It's an act of communication and thus an act of negotiation, what we think, what we read, how we put our thinking and our reading together.

ACTIVITY **A First Pass at Analysis**

Read the introductory chapter from Walter Isaacson's 2003 biography of Benjamin Franklin. Assume that Isaacson's primary audience consists of mostly well-educated adults who have a strong interest in contemporary political and social issues. Then, with a classmate, answer as specifically as you can the following questions:

1. What do you think is the big central question Isaacson is addressing in this piece? What is your hypothesized answer to that question?
2. What is the primary purpose Isaacson is trying to accomplish for his readers? What are some secondary purposes?
3. What tone is Isaacson trying to convey about his subject?
4. Why do you find Isaacson credible and trustworthy on the subject?
5. What emotional effect do you think Isaacson hopes his chapter will have on readers?

Hypothesizing about the Take-Home Idea

One big misperception that beginning analysts have is that the take-home idea is someplace on the page, in the text, and all you have to do is find it and underline it. That's generally not the case. There are often hints or clues about the main point in the text, but the actual construction of the take-home idea requires that you, the reader, participate in making meaning from the text as you read.

Let's assume that you and your classmates are interested in the political and social issues that Isaacson raises. Here's how you assist the text in *creating* the main idea:

1. **You ask yourself the big central question.** Why should we care about Benjamin Franklin now?

Watch the Video on Writing Rhetorical Analyses at Your Pearson MyLab

2. **You offer, as a hypothesis, your own answer to the big central question(s) that is full enough, robust enough to do justice to the text.** For example, simply quoting Isaacson and saying "Franklin has a particular resonance in twenty-first century America" doesn't represent the richness of Isaacson's thought. A better version would be this: "Franklin's character is particularly appealing to twenty-first-century thinkers, like my classmates and me, because of his emphasis on his own humble beginnings, his practical wisdom and inventiveness, his faith in 'the middling people,' and his belief that faith in the divine translates into doing good for his fellow humans."
3. **You find, in the text, specific pieces of evidence, examples, and reasons that support your answer to the big, central issue question.** You could mention, for instance, the anecdote he tells about his awkward first appearance to his eventual wife as demonstrating his humility. You could discuss his many discoveries and inventions—electricity in lightning, bifocal glasses, the lending library—as examples of his practical wisdom. You could examine how his list of virtues fostered religious and civic tolerance among his fellow citizens.
4. **You identify and explain (and this is the tricky part) the *unspoken* assumptions and ideas that come into play for the readers of the article when you connect your answer to the big, central issue question with the actual evidence, examples, and reasons you find in the text to support it.** In other words, you ask, "What do people like us think about when they consider subjects like the one at hand, and how does this text interact with that thinking?" So, for example, you might explain two sets of assumptions and ideas that come into play: (a) Some of us might think that true wisdom can only come from higher-level, specialized studies, rather than from interacting with humans and achieving a practical wisdom of human psychology. Franklin gives the lie to this assumption. (b) Most people genuinely trust a political figure who can convince them that he is truly altruistic, has their best interests in mind, and is just as "human" as they are. Franklin, of course, confirms that assumption.

Notice that, in this step, *you* participate in the making of meaning by drawing on these unspoken assumptions.

One way to characterize this four-part activity is shown in Figure 4.1:

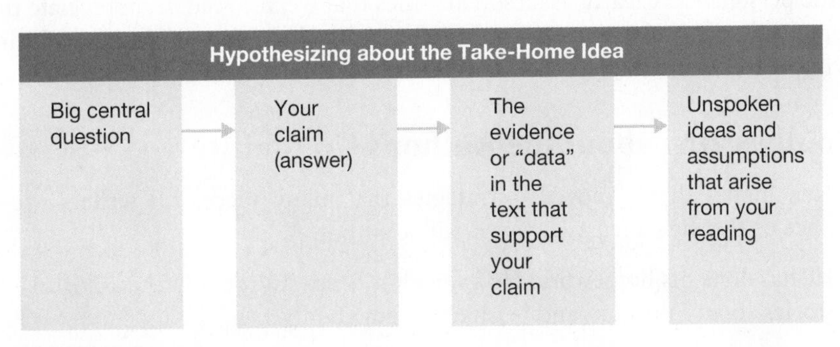

FIGURE 4.1

In short, to provide a basis for your analysis, you pose the big central question that you think the text is raising. Then you offer a *claim,* what you believe is a well-rounded answer to the big central question. You cite material that's actually in the text or on the page—called "data" in scare quotes, because it's not always "hard," empirical data such as scientists generate, but it is tangible evidence, examples, or reasons—that you believe supports your answer. Then you explain those sets of ideas, attitudes, and assumptions that are usually not on the page but that people generally believe about the topic at hand.

Hypothesizing about the Purpose

At first glance, offering a hypothesis about the author's purpose is considerably more straightforward than constructing the take-home idea. You ask yourself, "What do I think the author—Walter Isaacson in this instance—is trying to accomplish for us, his readers?" Hypothesizing about purpose is not as simple as it might sound, though. A good analyst looks at all the *possible* purposes the text might accomplish for its readers and then asks which one is, arguably, the *primary* purpose and which are *secondary.*

Look again at "Benjamin Franklin and the Invention of America." Certainly Isaacson knows some facts about Franklin and is trying to convey them to us, but is his primary purpose to inform us? Maybe Isaacson would like us—well-informed readers in the twenty-first century—to act more like Franklin, but it's not apparent from the text that he'd like us to change our behaviors. So is his primary purpose to persuade us to rethink what we might believe? A good hypothesis about the book's purpose might be something like this: "Primarily, Isaacson wants to convey an idea to us—that Franklin's attractiveness to twenty-first-century thinkers makes sense—and to convince us to accept that idea. So, the primary purpose of this excerpt would be to convince; its secondary purposes would be to inform and to rethink."

Hypothesizing about the Tone

This hypothesis is pretty simple. Isaacson clearly admires the daylights out of Franklin and wants us to share in his admiration. Notice the depth of detail Isaacson offers as he touts Franklin's many accomplishments and his outgoing, amiable, altruistic personality. Clearly, Isaacson assumes that we, his readers, appreciate those accomplishments and characteristics as much as he does. Thus, his tone is admiring and respectful.

Hypothesizing about the Author's Credibility

Isaacson makes three "moves"—strategies that many successful writers use—to convince us that he's a trustworthy, credible author.

1. He has done his homework: He *knows* lots of specific details and colorful stories about Franklin, and he shares them vividly.

2. He strikes us as having a good agenda: He seems to believe that the United States regularly needs to assess its political leaders' character traits and goals, and he apparently sees Franklin as a good role model for our leaders today.
3. He seems to share with us common sentiments about what makes a person a *good* person: hard work, humility, a sense of humor.

In short, Isaacson seems credible because he shows his intelligence, his good character, and his good will. Coincidentally, in his classic *Art of Rhetoric,* Aristotle in the fourth century B.C.E. noted these same three sources of an appeal to *ethos*: In his native Greek he called them *phronesis,* or practical intelligence; *arête,* or good character; and *eunoia,* or good will.

Hypothesizing about the Emotional Effect of the Text

Texts do more than convey a take-home idea, achieve purposes, convey tone, and establish credibility. They make readers *feel,* and having a hypothesis about what we think is the central emotion appeal of a text is as vital as having a hypothesis about its main idea, purpose, tone, and credibility. A text's establishment of emotional effect is clearly related to the author's tone, his or her attitude toward the subject matter. As we hinted above, Isaacson's tone might be characterized as *amused by* and *buoyant about* about Franklin's profile and its relevance for twenty-first-century life. Do you think Isaacson wants us to feel *uplifted* and *optimistic*? We do!

ACTIVITY **Trying Your Hand at the Big Central Question and the Four Related Ones**

Return to Abraham Lincoln's Second Inaugural Address. Reread it, if necessary. Then, with a classmate or in a group, discuss your hypothetical questions, and their answers, about Lincoln's take-home idea, his purpose, his tone, his credibility, and the emotional effect of his address.

"Going Deep" with One of the Elements: Analyzing Tone

Once you have learned to hypothesize about a text's take-home idea, purpose, tone, author's credibility, and the text's emotional effect, you can then choose in an analysis to "go deep" on any one of these features. Let's take a look at Louise Erdrich's poem, "Indian Boarding School: The Runaways," to learn how to delve more deeply into tone.

You may be asking, "Rhetorical analysis of a *poem*? We've considered a contemporary piece about Ben Franklin and an inaugural address by Abraham Lincoln, and we've studied how these texts craft their central idea, but does a poem have a central idea that we can analyze?" Most poems do: In an artistic way, they put forward a central idea that you can discern and analyze; they have a purpose and tone; they ask you to construct (and perhaps question) the narrator's credibility; they have an emotional effect on readers. In other words, we could do a full-fledged rhetorical analysis of many poems. In this case, however, let's just focus on tone.

In the first two chapters, we talk about how as a reader you make predictions and speculations about the tone of what you're reading. Understanding tone helps you *hear* the voice speaking and that helps you make decisions about the argument the writer might be making and about how the writer might want you to respond.

After you read Erdrich's poem, look back to see where you speculated about the tone—the narrator's attitude toward the subject matter—and write down three or four adjectives that you think describe that tone. Then take those adjectives and find places in the poem that directly illustrate the adjective you've chosen.

Here's an example: We might choose the adjective *tense* to describe the tone in the first nine lines of the poem. Then we might argue that the images in that section—boxcars that don't wait for the runaways, young children running to get into the boxcars in order to escape from the boarding school, a guard striking a match that pierces the darkness—have been deliberately crafted by Erdrich to convey her tone. Now, how would you follow this model with the adjective *pained* or the adjective *bitter*?

In completing this activity, you see how the general idea (what are adjectives that describe the tone of Erdrich's poem?) derives from particular moments in the text (what lines show how that adjective fits?). There might be tone shifts—a change in language that signals a change in attitude—or it might be that the tone you hypothesize at the beginning might get amplified as the writer moves through the lines of the poem. In any case, analyzing how tone works to establish aim and make connections to readers is a primary strategy for you to use when you are interpreting and analyzing what you read.

Taking the Next Step: Moving from the Starting Points to the Component Parts

Hypothesizing about what you think is the take-home idea, as well as the purpose, tone, credibility, and the emotional effect of a text, gives you a menu of possible *starting points* for reading and writing analytically. As the activities above suggest, you need to examine the moments or components of the text, see what its components are, and determine *how* those component parts work together to grasp the take-home idea, the purpose, and the emotional impact of the piece. Think about it this way: Every analysis *begins* with an argument: *You,* the analyst, *argue* that A is the take-home idea, B is the purpose, C is the tone, D is the credibility, and E is the emotional effect. You might discuss all or some of these factors. But whichever ones you include, you will look at the component parts of a text for evidence to support your arguments.

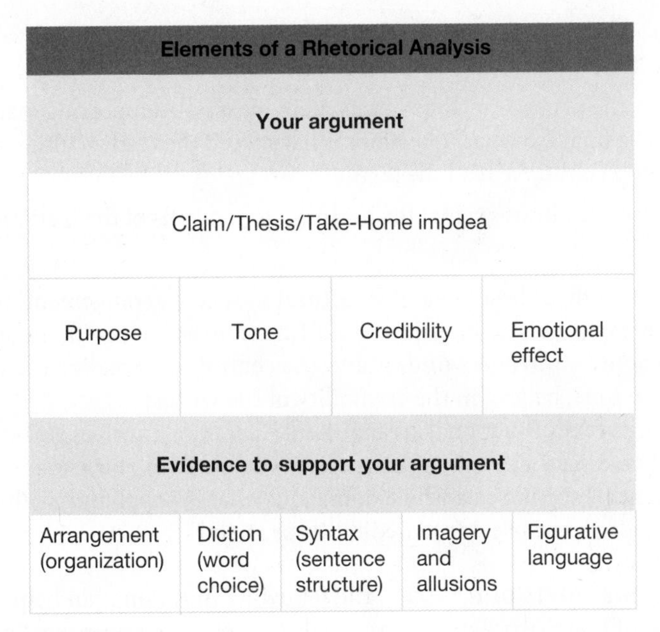

FIGURE 4.2

Working with written texts, you can divide these component parts into five categories: arrangement, diction, syntax, imagery and allusion, and figurative language (see Figure 4.2).

The key to a successful analysis, and a successful analytic paper, is not simply to point out interesting features of arrangement, diction, syntax, imagery, and figurative language. The key to a successful analysis is to understand, and show in your composition, *how* these features *bring to life* the main idea, purpose, tone, credibility, and effect. In the remainder of this chapter, let's examine how this connection happens.

Arrangement: The Shape of the Text

When you examine the arrangement of a text, you analyze how the shape of the text—its parts, its transitions, its beginning, middle, and end, help convey the writer's purpose and control the effect on readers. Pretty much every text you encounter can be described as having a beginning, a middle, and an end and points within it that signal shifts between these sections. Analyzing a text's *arrangement*, you can ask specific questions.

Questions for Analyzing a Text's Overall Arrangement

- Does the text state directly the central question it will answer, issue it will address, or argument it will develop? Where does the text suggest how its plan will proceed?

- How does the text offer support for its argument? Where does it develop these points with examples, illustrations, details, and reasons?
- How does the paper draw together its main ideas and supporting material to address the final "so what" question: What should the readers ultimately think or do now that they've read the text?
- What words or phrases signal the beginnings and ends of the sections of the text?

Once you've identified these general structural moves of arrangement, you begin to ask the important analytic question about function. What are these arrangement features *doing* to help readers understand the central idea, realize the purpose, be affected by the tone, believe in the credibility of the writer?

Analyzing a text's functional arrangement, therefore, involves two steps: (a) You divide a text into sections that make sense to you, and (b) you ask about each section, "What is this section as a whole doing and what is happening within it to convey the main idea, purpose, tone, credibility, or effect?"

Identifying the Parts of a Text The following questions can help you accomplish the first of these two steps. As you analyze a text, ask these questions, remembering that *not every text you examine is going to have all these parts.*

Questions for Identifying the Parts of a Text

- Is there a section that introduces the subject and writer's purpose in discussing it? Where does the section begin and end? Does the section indicate the text's central argument?
- Is there a part that gives readers background information? If so, where does this section begin and end?
- Is there some sentence or paragraph that focuses the readers' attention on some particular issue, aspect, or theme of the subject?
- Is there some section that purposefully supports the central question or argument? If so, where does this section begin and end?
- Is there a part that examines possible objections to the claims? If so, where does this section begin and end?
- Is there a section where the writer suggests what readers might or should think and do with what they've read?

Answering these questions, you get a sense of the parts of a text and how they work.

Analyzing the Arrangement of Each Part of a Text Now you can turn your attention to the second of the two steps and analyze how the arrangement of the text works *within* the parts. Keep in mind that with every question, you consider the response in terms of its effect on you as a reader.

Questions for Analyzing a Section about Subject and Purpose

- Are the subject and purpose directly stated or implied?
- Is some angle foregrounded and other material downplayed?
- Is there a statement that suggests the course that the remainder of the paper will take?

Questions for Analyzing a Section with Background Information

- Is there a statement about the direction the text will take or terms or phrases that signal how a reader moves from one section to another?
- Is background information arranged in some order—chronological (by time), spatial (by location), incremental (by importance)?
- Do words or phrases suggest that the writer is adding to the background material, or showing a consequence of it, or providing contrasting information?

Questions for Analyzing a Section That Supports the Central Claim

- Are there words or sentences that map out the direction this part of the paper will take?
- Does support include any of the following: telling stories, describing scenes and evoking sensory details, defining terms, dividing the whole into parts, categorizing the parts according to some principle, or providing cause-and-effect reasoning?

Questions for Analyzing a Section That Presents Objections to the Claim

- Is there language that suggests the writer wants to counter objections?
- Does some language suggest that the writer wants to concede the objections?

Questions for Analyzing a Section That Indicates What Readers Might Think or Do

- Is there a direct charge to readers to think or act in a new way after reading the piece, or does the writer imply new ways of thinking and acting? How does the degree to which these elements are revealed (or perhaps concealed) persuade you?
- What does the writer do with the words, phrases, and sentences in this work to give the text a sound of finality? What effect does this language have on you as a reader?

If you can generate good answers to these questions by referring to places in the text, you will have done a thorough analysis of arrangement.

ACTIVITY **Analyzing the Parts of Lincoln's Inaugural**

Take another careful look at Lincoln's Second Inaugural. Divide it into parts—as many as you think are sensible. Then, with a classmate or in a group, describe what each part does to contribute to the construction of the main idea, the achievement of a purpose, and the creation of an emotional effect.

Diction: Words That Make Meaning, Purpose Come to Life

Just as you can analyze how the arrangement of a text helps to develop its central meaning, purpose, tone, credibility, or effect, so you can investigate how specific words in a text make these features come to life for readers. Experienced analysts often use the term **diction**, from the classical Greek *dictio,* or "choice of words."

Analyzing diction offers you the opportunity to look carefully at several distinguishing features of words. But a word of caution: When you recognize something distinctive in a text's diction, you *always* need to ask yourself a "so what" question, such as "So what does this word choice *do* for the meaning or the effect?" It's not just "does the text use jargon?" or "are there formal and long words?" but *why* are those words used and *what* effect does it have on your reading?

General versus Specific Words Twentieth-century language expert S. I. Hayakawa describes a phenomenon he calls "the ladder of abstraction." At the top of the ladder he places abstract terms like *transportation* and *justice*; near the middle rungs slightly more specific terms like *automobiles* and *juvenile court*; and at the bottom of the ladder are specific, concrete terms like *my 2008 green Cobalt* and *the offender's five-year probation sentence for shoplifting.*

Ladder of Abstraction		
Abstract term	Transportation	Justice
More specific term	Automobiles	Juvenile court
Very specific, concrete term	My 2008 green Cobalt	Five-year probation for shoplifting

FIGURE 4.3

Not all texts need to employ specific diction—sometimes writers need to talk about abstract terms and concepts—but generally, the more concrete and specific a text's diction is, the more vivid the main idea, purpose, tone, credibility, and emotional effect are.

Denotation versus Connotation Intuitively, we all know that words can be loaded, carry attitudes and emotions as well as definitions. Careful readers are aware of how texts often capitalize on the multiple meanings of words—subtle, suggested meanings as well as obvious ones. Consider these two simple sentences:

> Benjamin Franklin was a perfect example of a statesman.
> Benjamin Franklin was a perfect example of a politician.

Even during his time, Franklin probably would have been pleased if someone said the first sentence about him, but likely not so happy with the second. *Statesman* suggests responsibility, intelligence, and high-mindedness; *politician* these days implies something less noble, more self-serving or even unprincipled. The differences in meaning in these two sentences illustrate what scholars of language refer to as denotation and connotation:

- **Denotation** refers to a literal meaning of a word.
- **Connotation** refers to an association, an effect, that the word provokes.

Both sentences above use words that might have the same *denotative* meaning—elected official—but carry quite different *connotations.*

Formal versus Informal Words The diction of a text might be compared to the way somebody dresses to go to a dance. If you're going to an informal party at a club, you dress down—jeans, comfortable shirt, flats. But for a formal dance like a prom, you dress up for the occasion—long skirt, high heels, tuxedo. The formality of a text's word choice is like dress; it gives some sense of the occasion—a comfortable casual "conversation" between the writer and readers, or a more formal presentation, with the writer "speaking" to the readers. Writers vary the formality of texts in a number of ways in their choice of words, sentences, and punctuation.

Contractions and Pronouns Two visible signals of formality are contractions and pronoun use. Contractions like "haven't" and "isn't" generally sound less formal than "have not" and "is not." First-person pronouns, with which the writer refers to himself (*I, me, my, mine, we, us, our,* and *ours*), sound less formal than words or phrases like "one" or "a person" or "he or she," which allow the writer to talk about a topic without personalizing it. Consider the following two sentences:

> I'm using my brain by playing on a team.
> A person develops multiple intelligences by participating in sports.

The first would be perfectly appropriate in a relatively informal essay, while the latter would be right at home in a more formal paper. Notice the other words that change to accommodate a more or less formal diction. "Brain" is a looser, more casual way to say "multiple intelligences." "Team" is a shorthand way to say "participating in sports."

Latinate versus Anglo-Saxon Words Historically, English is a mongrel language, a mix of many others. The ancestor of the English we speak and write today is Old English, a Germanic language. The variety of that language spoken in the

British Isles from around the fourth century to the eleventh century C.E. has been labeled Anglo-Saxon English because the two tribes who spoke it were the Angles and the Saxons. Around 1100 C.E., the language began to change. In 1066, England was invaded, and the English king was overthrown by a French king, William of Normandy. The Norman invasion opened Anglo-Saxon English to influence from the romance languages of French, Spanish, and Italian, called *romance* after the Latin language of Rome. Throughout the succeeding centuries, English acquired more and more words and phrases that had their origins in Latin. Because the people who brought this Latinate influence into the language tended to be the powerful nobility, the use of what is called **Latinate diction** has come to be associated with more formal writing, while the use of what is called **Anglo-Saxon diction** has come to be linked with more informal writing.

Here are some pairs of Latinate and Anglo-Saxon synonyms that show the difference in formality:

Formal versus Informal Diction

Formal Latinate term	Informal Anglo-Saxon term	Meaning
facilitate	help	to make easier
manufacture	make	to make
interrogate	ask	to question
maximize	grow	to make larger
minimize	shrink	to make smaller

FIGURE 4.4

Slang and Jargon Slang and jargon generally get a bad rap. Just look at how the Merriam-Webster Collegiate Dictionary defines the two terms. Slang is either "language peculiar to a particular group" or "an informal, nonstandard vocabulary composed of coinages, arbitrarily changed words, and extravagant, forced, or facetious figures of speech." Jargon is "confused, unintelligible language"; "a hybrid language or dialect simplified in vocabulary and grammar and used for communication between people of different speech"; "the technical terminology or characteristic idiom of a special activity or group"; or "obscure and often pretentious language marked by circumlocutions and long words."

Yikes! Given these definitions, who would ever use slang or jargon in a composition? The answer: lots of writers, depending on how informally they want to interact with their readers and how well they know their audience's background and interests. In a paper for a government class about how political figures try to reassure voters in a time of economic stress, a writer might use a sentence like this:

> The senator's speech was designed to calm voters' apprehensions about rising interest rates.

In an informal essay—or a personal piece, such as a commentary for a local newspaper—the writer might cast the same idea like this:

> The senator basically put it to the voters in these terms: Chill!

The same formal/informal depending-on-your-audience continuum prevails in analyses of the use of jargon. Suppose a writer was producing an account of how users of a new computer program were expected to operate. If the audience consisted of people familiar with computer terminology, the author might write:

> All beta testers know that they should clean up their orphans and then cold boot the machine.

On the other hand, for an audience not familiar with the world of computers, the following sentence would be more appropriate:

> All people who have agreed to test the new program know that they are expected to delete their unused file before they turn off the computer and turn it on again immediately.

Both slang and jargon seem like dangerous territory for a writer because both use language that might obscure a writer's message rather than clarify and simplify it. Savvy writers ought to be aware of the simpler, more direct, more common words they could use. But, as with all questions involving style, a writer's decision about whether to use slang or jargon depends on the situation in which he or she is writing. As always, the question is this: "Given this subject matter, this purpose, this audience, and this type of writing, is slang or jargon effective?" Sometimes the answer is yes. The use of slang or jargon can signal to readers that the writer is a member of their group, in solidarity with them, and that the author has done his or her homework about a particularly complicated topic that is important to the community.

Syntax

A third place to look for evidence to support claims about the main idea, purpose, tone, credibility, and effect of a text is **syntax**: the formation and structure of sentences in the text. Four specific features of syntax help you analyze sentences: length, type, structure, and voice and mode of verbs.

Sentence Length At the most basic level, an analyst can simply look at how long (or short) the sentences in a text are, how the writer varies (or doesn't vary) sentence length, and how sentence length affects reading. In general, long sentences give the writer a chance to develop a complicated thought for readers, but readers can get lost in the middle of them and lose the train of thought. In general, short sentences can be quite effective at the end of, or in the midst of, a series of long sentences. A well-placed short sentence can pull the reader up short and say, in essence, "Here's the point. Pay attention." A text with a variety of sentence lengths is usually more engaging than a text in which all the sentences are roughly the same length.

Look at the varied sentence length in this group of sentences in the first paragraph of Isaacson's chapter:

> But wait a minute. There's something more going on here. Peel back a layer and we can see him as a 65-year-old wry observer, sitting in an English country house, writing this scene, pretending it's part of a letter to his son, an illegitimate son who has become a Royal Governor with aristocratic pretensions and needs to be reminded of his humble roots.

Types of Sentences A slightly more challenging (and even more interesting) feature of syntax is sentence type. Traditional grammar describes four types. Notice how each of these four sentence types has a primary function.

- A **simple sentence** has one independent clause. Essentially, it expresses one idea:

  Abraham Lincoln struggled to save the nation.

- A **compound sentence** has two independent clauses, each of which can stand as a separate sentence. A compound sentence presents at least two ideas and suggests they are equal in importance:

  Abraham Lincoln struggled to save the nation, and Andrew Johnson assisted him.

- A **complex sentence** has one independent clause and at least one subordinate clause—a group of words with a subject and a verb that cannot stand by itself as a sentence. A complex sentence suggests that the idea in its independent (main) clause is more important than the idea in its subordinate clause (or clauses) and that the subordinate clause qualifies the main clause. In the following example, the independent clause is in boldface type:

  When the leaders of the Confederacy insisted that the rights of the states were more important than the maintenance of the union, **Abraham Lincoln struggled to save the nation**.

- A **compound-complex sentence** has two independent clauses and at least one subordinate clause. A compound-complex sentence combines the functions of the compound and the complex. In the following example, the two independent (main) clauses are in boldface type:

  When the leaders of the Confederacy insisted that the rights of the states were more important than the maintenance of the union, **Abraham Lincoln struggled to save the nation,** and **Andrew Johnson assisted him.**

Sentences are also characterized by type as "loose" or "periodic": A **loose sentence** is one that puts all its basic elements—subject, verb, and any complement—right at the beginning, and then adds any modifying elements:

> **Abraham Lincoln wept,** fearing the Union would not survive if the Southern states seceded.

A **periodic sentence** is one that delays completing its idea by putting its additional, modifying details in one of two positions, either before the basic sentence elements or in the middle of them:

> Alone in his study, lost in somber thoughts about his beloved country, dejected but not broken in spirit, **Abraham Lincoln wept.**
>
> **Abraham Lincoln**, alone in his study, lost in somber thoughts about his beloved country, dejected but not broken in spirit, **wept.**

Loose and periodic are not exclusive categories. A sentence can be more loose than periodic, but still have some periodic "feel" to it:

> Abraham Lincoln considered the Union an inviolable, almost eternally inspired, concept.

Similarly, a sentence can be more periodic than loose, but still have some "loose" feel to it:

> Abraham Lincoln, a self-taught philosopher, a political scientist even before there was such a field, considered the Union an inviolable, almost eternally inspired, concept.

When analysts look at sentences on the loose–periodic continuum, they notice how a writer either "fronts" essential information and then elaborates or delays essential information until as late as possible in the sentence.

Would you say this sentence in Isaacson's chapter is on the "loose" or the "periodic" end of the spectrum?

> Instinctively more comfortable with democracy than some of his fellow founders, and devoid of the snobbery that later critics would feel toward his shopkeeping values, he had faith in the wisdom of the common man and felt that a new nation would draw its strength from what he called 'the middling people.'

Verbs: Voice and Mode In English, the two most common categories of *voice* for verbs are active and passive. In a sentence that uses the **active voice**, the doer of the action is the subject, and the receiver of the action is the direct object:

In a sentence that uses the **passive voice**, the receiver of the action is the subject, the verb contains some form of *to be* as a helper and a participle, and the doer of the action is the object of a preposition in the prepositional phrase after the verb:

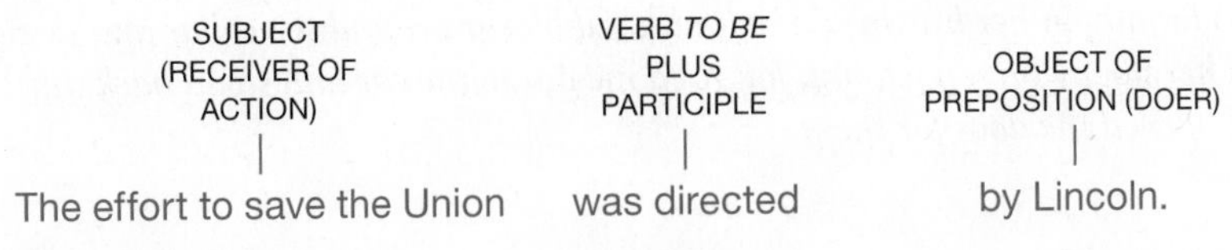

Guidebooks about effective writing often tell writers to "write in the active voice" and "avoid the passive voice." There are some good reasons to follow this advice. The passive voice requires more words than the active, and excessive use of the passive can cause a reader to feel the text is wordy. Also, the passive voice is *potentially* irresponsible because the writer can avoid mentioning the *doer. The effort to save the Union was directed* is a complete sentence, but it leaves out the actor, and that may be important if the actor might be culpable. The caution about passive voice however, is limited. A writer sometimes uses the passive voice purposefully to emphasize the action done, rather than the doer of the action. Consider this brilliant first paragraph of Lincoln's second inaugural address:

> At this second appearing to take the oath of the Presidential office there is less occasion for an extended address than there was at the first. Then a statement somewhat in detail of a course to be pursued seemed fitting and proper. Now, at the expiration of four years, during which public declarations have been constantly called forth on every point and phase of the great contest which still absorbs the attention and engrosses the energies of the nation, little that is new could be presented. The progress of our arms, upon which all else chiefly depends, is as well known to the public as to myself, and it is, I trust, reasonably satisfactory and encouraging to all. With high hope for the future, no prediction in regard to it is ventured.

Throughout the address, Lincoln keeps himself, as well as the armies of the North and the South, out of the "doer" position in sentence: *little that is new could be presented; no prediction in regard to it is ventured.* Let's concentrate on the action at hand, ending the long war, he seems to be saying. Let's not concentrate on who might be at fault.

A second good reason a writer uses the passive is to shift the doer of the action to the end of the sentence, where it will usually be most remembered. The sentence, *The effort to save the Union was directed by Lincoln,* emphasizes, rather than downplays, who is responsible.

Imagery and Allusions

When you read a particularly vivid text, its main idea, purpose, tone, credibility, and emotional impact are often heightened by the images it evokes and the allusions it makes. **Images** are generally sensory experiences: words, phrases, or clauses that lead you to visualize a scene, hear a sound, experience a feeling of touch, taste, or smell. Each of the five senses work to create images:

- **Visual (sight) image:** *Tante Lou, in her black overcoat and black rimless hat, and Miss Emma, in her brown coat with the rabbit fur around the collar and sleeves and her floppy brown felt hat, followed me out to the car and stood back until I had opened the door for them.*

- **Auditory (sound) image:** *The clackety-clack of the wheels on the track and steamy hiss of the engine made the sound of the Lincoln funeral train even more poignant.*
- **Tactile (touch) image:** *The weight of her father's strong arm around her shoulder comforted the mourning child.*
- **Gustatory (taste) image:** *The tang of the grapefruit slice made her mouth pucker.*
- **Olfactory (smell) image:** *The baking bread in the oven welcomed with its yeasty sweetness that filled the kitchen.*

Allusions are specific references to other texts or scenes outside the text that build readers' associations and deepen their understanding of the text. Sometimes these are clichés:

> Everybody has a cross to bear.

No matter what religious background you come from, you probably recognize that sentence as an allusion to the Biblical story of Jesus on his way to crucifixion. It tells you something about what the writer thinks about the burdens people carry. A writer might make an allusion to another text:

> "Ay, there's the rub."

The phrase is from Hamlet's famous "To be, or not to be" soliloquy in Shakespeare's play, and you recognize that the writer wants to suggest some kind of quandary or dilemma in using the phrase.

Figures of Rhetoric: Schemes and Tropes

To convey purpose and affect readers through the features of a text, writers almost always use **figures of rhetoric**, whether they do so consciously or not. Readers who analyze texts well recognize these figures and explain how the writer uses them in communicating and persuading.

People have been teaching and learning about the figures since ancient Greece and Rome, where rhetoric was first studied. Classical rhetoricians divided the figures into two broad categories: *schemes* and *tropes*. The definitions are simple:

- A **scheme** is any artful, that is, deliberate, variation from typical arrangements of words and sentences. For example, the following passage from Winston Churchill's famous Dunkirk speech during World War II is an example of the scheme of *anaphora,* the deliberate repetition of words, phrases, or clauses as the beginning of successive sentences:

  > We shall fight on the beaches, we shall fight on the landing-grounds, we shall fight in the fields and in the streets, we shall fight in the hills.

- A **trope** is any artful variation from the typical expressions of ideas or words. For example, this sentence contains an example of the trope of *metonymy,* in which a range of meanings and associations are packed into one word or phrase:

  > The top brass inspected the troops in the field.

In ancient Rome, and later in the European Middle Ages and Renaissance, scholars developed substantial lists of figures, categorizing them under these two general labels, and school children had to learn the definitions and find examples of the figures in literary works and public discourse. It would not have been unusual for a grammar school student in Renaissance England to be given a list of three hundred or so names of schemes and tropes and to be required to memorize the definitions and produce an example of any one of them on demand! Students undertook this task not simply to memorize or even to learn how to vary their own expression. Their lessons in schemes and tropes taught them something crucial about language, that a different way of *saying* something about the world was also a different way of *seeing* something about the world. In other words, classical instruction taught that using figurative language to express ideas helped to clarify and sharpen a person's thinking—not a bad lesson for students even today.

You don't have to memorize three hundred definitions to recognize and analyze the figures. (There are many excellent handbooks and Internet sites that list figures of rhetoric. One particularly helpful resource is Professor Gideon Burton's web site at Brigham Young University called *Silva Rhetoricae,* literally "the forest of rhetoric.") But you can learn to recognize schemes and tropes when you read them by how they work and their effect on readers. What follows are a few schemes and tropes in common use.

Schemes Involving Balance When a passage, a paragraph, or even a sentence has two or more similar ideas, a good writer will often express those ideas in the same grammatical form: words balance words, phrases balance phrases, clauses balance clauses. The writer is using parallel constructions to affect and balance readers' responses.

Abraham Lincoln was a master at creating parallel structure. His most famous work, the brief but eloquent Gettysburg Address, is a tour de force of parallelism. Here is its final paragraph. Notice how Lincoln both begins and ends this paragraph with a parallel structure:

> But, in a larger sense, we cannot dedicate—we cannot consecrate—we cannot hallow—this ground. The brave men, living and dead, who struggled here, have consecrated it, far above our poor power to add or detract. The world will little note, nor long remember what we say here, but it can never forget what they did here. It is for us the living, rather, to be dedicated here to the unfinished work which they who fought here have thus far so nobly advanced. It is rather for us to be here dedicated to the great task remaining before us—that from these honored dead we take increased devotion to that cause for which they gave the last full measure of devotion—that we here highly resolve that these dead shall not have died in vain—that this nation, under God, shall have a new birth of freedom—and that government of the people, by the people, for the people, shall not perish from the earth.

Three parallel, balanced clauses

Three parallel, balanced verbs

Three famous parallel phrases

What, in general, is the effect of parallel structure on the reader? The key concept is balance: A solid parallelism emphasizes the thoroughly trustworthy, balanced character of the speaker or writer. Because he or she is perceived as more credible, the readers adhere to the take-home idea more willingly.

One particular variety of parallelism is an **antithesis**, which emerges when the content of the clauses, phrases, or words being balanced in the parallel structure offer a striking contrast to the readers. A famous example of antithetical parallel structure can be found in President John F. Kennedy's inaugural address:

> Ask not what your country can do for you; ask what you can do for your country.

Another well-known example is the slogan from an anti-drug campaign in the late 1970s:

Up with hope, down with dope.

The parallelism in both cases emphasizes the writer's clever contrast.

And, of course, one of the most famous examples of antithesis in American literature comes from Lincoln's Second Inaugural Address:

> Both parties deprecated war, but one of them would *make* war rather than let the nation survive, and the other would *accept* war rather than let it perish, and the war came.

Parallelism uses the same grammatical structure for similar elements, and it helps readers understand the logical equivalence the writer gives to the parallel elements:

- **Parallelism of words:** Exercise physiologists argue that body-pump aerobics sessions benefit a person's heart and lungs, muscles and nerves, and joints and cartilage.
- **Parallelism of phrases:** Exercise physiologists argue that body-pump aerobics sessions help a person breathe more effectively, move with less discomfort, and avoid injury.
- **Parallelism of clauses:** Exercise physiologists argue that body-pump aerobics is the most efficient exercise class, that body-pump participants show greater gains in stamina than participants in comparable exercise programs, and that body-pump aerobics is less expensive in terms of equipment and training needed to lead or take classes.

Each of these three parallel schemes, by the way, is also called a **zeugma**, a figure in which more than one item in a sentence is governed by a single word, usually a verb. You see that the verb for these sentences is *argue*.

Antithesis points out to the reader differences between two juxtaposed ideas rather than similarities. Here are three antitheses (that's the plural spelling):

- **Antithesis of words:** When distance runners reach the state they call the zone, they find themselves mentally *engaged yet detached.*
- **Antithesis of phrases:** When distance runners reach the state they call the zone, they find themselves mentally engaged *with their physical surroundings yet detached from moment-to-moment concerns about their conditioning.*
- **Antithesis of clauses:** When distance runners reach the state they call the zone, they find *that they are empirically engaged with their physical surroundings, yet they are also completely detached from moment-to-moment concerns about their conditioning.*

A famous example of antithesis in clauses is "To err is human; to forgive, divine."

Another scheme like antithesis is an **antimetabole** (anti-muh-**TI**-boh-lee), in which words are repeated in different grammatical forms. Well-known examples of antimetabole are:

> When the going gets tough, the tough get going (adjective becomes noun; noun becomes verb)
>
> You can take the kid out of the country, but you can't take the country out of the kid.

Schemes Involving Interruption Sometimes a writer wants to interrupt the flow of a passage in order to provide information, give an insight, or make a comment to readers. Two schemes are especially useful for this purpose—parenthesis and appositive.

Parenthesis **Parenthesis** (the same word as the singular of parentheses, the punctuation marks) allows for this kind of interruption. Suppose you're writing a letter to a friend about your growing interest in sports. Here is a parenthesis embedded in a sentence from this letter:

> Sports night at the school always brings out the would-be jocks—who would expect any different?—ready to show that they're potentially as good as the varsity players.

Notice that this parenthesis is set off by dashes, the punctuation marks commonly used to set off an interruptive word, phrase, or clause. When you use dashes to set off an interruption, be sure to include them at the beginning and the end of the interruption. A parenthesis, however, can also be set off from the remainder of the sentences with parentheses:

> Sports night at the school always brings out the would-be jocks (who would expect any different?) ready to show that they're potentially as good as the varsity players.

Notice that a parenthesis in the form of a question, as in the example above, needs to be punctuated with a question mark. The same would hold true for an exclamatory word, phrase, or clause:

> When sports night is canceled—oh, sorrowful day!—all the would-be jocks get a case of show-off withdrawal.

but not for a simple declaratory sentence:

> Sports night supervisors have to stop people from trying to slam dunk—this is the ultimate showboat move—for fear that one of the would-be jocks might hurt himself.

Appositive A second scheme useful for setting off additional material is an appositive. An **appositive** is a construction in which two coordinating elements are set side by side, and the second explains or modifies the first.

> David Brooks calls Franklin, inventor, entrepreneur, and statesman, "our Founding Yuppie."

Schemes Involving Omission A writer occasionally needs to omit material from a sentence so that its rhythm is heightened or accelerated and so that the readers will pay close attention to the potentially dramatic effect. Two schemes useful for this purpose are ellipsis and asyndeton.

Ellipsis An **ellipsis** is any omission of words, the meaning of which is provided by the overall context of the passage:

> In times of conflict, if you talk to your friend, and he to you, you'll find a way around the fight.

The phrase *and he to you* omits "talk," and it highlights the connection by omitting the verb.

Asyndeton An **asyndeton** is an omission of conjunctions between related clauses. From Lincoln's Gettysburg Address: ". . . and that government of the people, by the people, for the people shall not perish from the earth."

Schemes Involving Repetition Writers are often warned not to be repetitive because saying something several times doesn't seem to advance a point. But repetition is not being repetitive. Repeating sounds or words can actually lead the reader to pay closer attention to the prose and to recognize the writer's purpose and respond to the writer's voice more clearly. You'll likely be familiar with some of the schemes involving the artful use of repetition.

- **Alliteration** is the repetition of consonant sounds at the beginning or in the middle of two or more adjacent words:

  > Fourscore and twenty years ago our forefathers brought forth upon this continent a new nation . . .

- **Assonance** is the repetition of vowel sounds in the stressed syllables of two or more adjacent words:

  > Ye shall say they all have passed away
  > That noble race and brave

- **Anaphora** (uh-**NA**-fuh-ruh) is the repetition of the same group of words at the beginning of successive clauses:

  We cannot dedicate, we cannot consecrate, we cannot hallow . . .

- **Epistrophe** (e-**PIS**-truh-fee) is the repetition of the same group of words at the end of successive clauses:

  Yes I am, I am Indian, Indian, I am.

- **Anadiplosis** (a-nuh-duh-**PLOH**-suhs) is the repetition of the last word of one clause at the beginning of the following clause:

  Watch your thoughts, they become words; watch your words, they become actions; watch your actions, they become habits.

- **Climax** is the repetition of words, phrases, or clauses in order of increasing number or importance:

  Excellent athletes need to be respectful of themselves, their teammates, their schools, and their communities.

Anadiplosis and climax are closely enough related that some teachers of the figures refer to the two schemes together as *climbing the ladder.*

Tropes Involving Comparisons The most important trope in this category, the one upon which all the others in this group are based, is **metaphor**, an implied comparison between two things that, on the surface, seem dissimilar but that, upon further examination, share common characteristics:

My life it stood, a loaded gun.

Clearly, a life and a gun are dissimilar. Yet the metaphor here suggests that life is awaiting and that it's potentially violent or tempestuous. A **simile** makes the comparison visible.

My life seemed like a loaded gun, waiting to be fired in some field.

Notice that this sentence, which begins with a simile, ends with an **implied metaphor**—it continues the metaphor by implying the consequences.

Other tropes involving comparison include the following:

- **Synecdoche** (suh-**NEK**-duh-kee): A part of something is used to refer to the whole.

  I would not keep in a cage

  A wing that would be free

- **Metonymy** (muh-**TAH**-nuh-mee): An entity is referred to by one of its attributes.

  I hear America singing.

- **Personification**: Inanimate objects are given human characteristics.

  You are loosed from your moorings, and are free.

- **Periphrasis** (puh-**RI**-frah-suhs): A descriptive word or phrase is used to refer to a proper name.

  Hog butcher to the world

Tropes Involving Word Play Some writers like to entertain (and even enlighten) their readers simply by playing with the sounds and meanings of words. The most common trope for doing so is the **pun**, a word that suggests two of its meanings or the meaning of a homonym. Puns have a bad reputation—and it's often well deserved. But sometimes a good pun can really attract a reader's attention:

> The tipped-but-caught third strike, ending a bases-loaded rally, was a foul most foul.

Two additional word-play tropes are:

- **Anthimeria** (an-thuh-**MEER**-ee-uh): One part of speech, usually a verb, substitutes for another, usually a noun.

  > When the Little Leaguers lost the championship, they needed just to have a good cry before they could feel okay about their season.

- **Onomatopoeia** (ahn-u-mah-tuh-**PEE**-uh): Sounds of the words used are related to their meaning.

  > Oh, the tintinnabulation of the bells

Tropes Involving Overstatement or Understatement A writer, ironically, can help readers see an idea or point clearly by overstating it or understating it. The trope of overstatement is called **hyperbole** (hye-**PUHR**-boh-lee):

> He couldn't make that shot again if he tried a million times.

while the trope for understatement is called **litotes** (**LYE**-tuh-tees):

> Shutting out the opponents for three straight games is no small feat for a goaltender.

Tropes Involving the Management of Meaning Some tropes can be seen as techniques that simply allow a writer to play with the meaning and development of ideas in strategic ways.

- **Irony**: Words are meant to convey the opposite of their literal meaning.

  > Their center is over seven feet tall—where do they come up with these little pipsqueaks?

When irony has a particularly biting or bitter tone, it is called **sarcasm**.

- **Oxymoron**: Words that have apparently contradictory meanings are placed near each other.

  > When you have to face your best friend in competition, whoever wins feels an aching pleasure.

- **Rhetorical question**: A question is designed not to secure an answer but to move the development of an idea forward and suggest a point.

  > Aren't I a woman?

ACTIVITY **Analyzing Figures of Rhetoric**

You've seen lots of examples of figures above, many of them coming from the literature you're reading in this book. See if you can find another example of a trope or scheme in either Lincoln's Second Inaugural or Isaacson's "Benjamin Franklin and the Invention of America" and explain how that figure produces an effect on your reading.

A Sample Rhetorical Analysis

What should a rhetorical analysis look like? An analytic essay is a relatively straightforward genre. It does not call for a very long introduction. Like most good answers on essay examinations, it calls on the writer to state clearly what he or she intends to demonstrate, to offer a map of how the development will proceed, to offer strong claims (specifically, claims about how the component parts of the text flesh out its take-home idea, purpose, and tone), to support those claims with specific evidence drawn from the text under consideration, and to conclude briefly and forcefully.

Let's return to Walter Isaacson's "Benjamin Franklin and the Invention of America" reprinted above. Consider the sample rhetorical analysis produced by the exemplary first-year college student Darcy Bell.

Darcy understands "rhetorical analysis for whom," and she will take Isaacson's audience into consideration.

Darcy introduces tone as a point of analysis.

Darcy summarizes what she sees as Isaacson's central idea.

Darcy has learned about the six-part oration for argumentative essays (see Chapter 5).

Darcy provides a map of her essay, laying out the analytic points she will unpack.

Darcy shows how Isaacson uses anecdote and detail to support each of the four points she listed in her summary of the main idea.

Darcy Bell

A Rhetorical Analysis of Walter Isaacson's
"Benjamin Franklin and the Invention of America"

Writing to an audience of readers interested in politics during an era when Americans might not have held their leaders in high esteem, Walter Isaacson in "Benjamin Franklin and the Invention of America" offers a glowing portrait of Benjamin Franklin, explaining that Franklin's character is particularly appealing to a twenty-first-century audience because of his emphasis on his own humble humanity, his practical wisdom and inventiveness, his faith in "the middling people," and his belief that faith in the divine translates into doing good for his fellow humans. Hinting that contemporary politicians might heed Franklin's model, Isaacson achieves his explanatory purpose by providing a rich store of vivid anecdotes, both real and hypothetical; by creating a sound model of a six-part essay; and by crafting his diction and syntax so that the admiring, almost reverential tone of the essay is inescapable.

Like all good writers, Isaacson does not merely tell his readers about his topic, the virtuous characteristics that Franklin embodied. He shows Franklin's qualities by providing lively stories from the past, inventing amusing scenarios that might exist today, and listing abundant concrete details. Isaacson shows Franklin's humble humility early in the essay, relating the story of his first encounter with Deborah Read, who would eventually become his wife. According to Franklin, Read "thought I made, as I most certainly did, a most awkward ridiculous appearance." Isaacson demonstrates Franklin's practical, wise, and innovative nature by offering a specific record of his inventions: a device to detect static electricity, bifocal glasses, the clean-burning stove, charts of the Gulf Stream, to name a few. Isaacson makes Franklin's faith in "the middling people" real with a humorous imagined scene from our own time: We are invited to consider ourselves (who, I maintain, are "the middling people") having a beverage with Franklin, showing him how to use a Palm Pilot (or maybe an I-Phone now), laughing at corny jokes with us. Isaacson makes a case that Franklin perceives his faith in the divine as requiring service to humankind by focusing on the most famous civic organization founded by Franklin: the public library. When we read, late in the excerpt, that Franklin's motto for the public library he founded was "[t]o pour forth benefits for the common good is divine," we can just nod in assent since we have encountered the evidence behind that claim.

The arrangement of Isaacson's essay is brilliantly designed both to demonstrate his central claim about Franklin and to anticipate and address any possible objections to it. Notice how Isaacson crafts the introduction. He begins not with general assertions but with details: Franklin's famous entry into Philadelphia carrying loaves of bread under each arm, his penning a fictitious letter to an illegitimate son, his first encounter with his eventual wife. We're drawn into this character before we even learn his full name, Benjamin Franklin, in the middle of the second paragraph. Isaacson then devotes several paragraphs to providing well-documented background information about Franklin's character and achievements, contrasting his approachability with the "austere" Washington and the potentially "intimidating" Jefferson and Adams, and

This paragraph explains the six "moves" that Isaacson makes: introduction, background, partition and thesis, confirmation, refutation, and conclusion.

listing the aforementioned inventions and initiatives that Franklin is responsible for. It's not until the beginning of the tenth paragraph that Isaacson sounds the note that will eventually become his thesis, by introducing the idea that "Franklin has a particular resonance in twentieth-century America." And while Isaacson hints that he clearly will have more details to offer in support of that claim as the essay proceeds, he pauses in the eleventh paragraph to anticipate and address possible objections, suggesting that some people might perceive in Franklin "a shallowness of soul and a spiritual complacency that seem to permeate a culture of complacency." But Isaacson quickly moves in the remainder of the chapter to dismiss those qualms, arguing that Franklin's critics "mistake his moral maxims for the fundamental faiths that motivated his actions." Such a clearly arranged and well-structured chapter builds Isaacson's ethos—we tend to trust people who lay out their cases so clearly. We're open to being convinced.

Darcy doesn't simply describe the arrangement. She also shows how it creates *ethos* or credibility.

Finally, one can drop into the excerpt almost anywhere and notice how Isaacson crafts his diction and syntax so that his admiration for Franklin and his own balanced persona shine through. Notice, for example, the reference in the second paragraph to Franklin's "pilgrim's progress," a direct allusion to John Bunyan's seventeenth-century British novel about the ideal Christian's path toward salvation. By equating Franklin with the central character, named Christian, Isaacson is hinting strongly that we should take note of Franklin's exemplary character.

The third paragraph is a particularly rich site to notice Isaacson's craft. We learn in the first sentence that "Franklin is the founding father that winks at us." What an evocative metaphor. Of course, Franklin does not *literally* wink at us, but the character Isaacson creates engages in lots of "winking" behavior, and someone who winks at you is probably saying, "I want to be your friend" or "we're on the same side here." While some winks might be troubling, Isaacson certainly suggests this is a warm, affectionate one. Further along

Darcy focuses on only a few paragraphs as a representative example of diction, making it easier for her own readers to follow her analysis.

in the paragraph, Isaacson characterizes Franklin as "a genial urban entrepreneur." Notice again the evocative language—"genial" meaning kind but also resonating with "genius," "urban" meaning "of the city" but also resonating with "urbane" or wise. Late in the paragraph, Isaacson contrasts "orotund rhetoric" with Franklin's "chattiness." We don't even have to know what "orotund" means (it means "pompous" or "pretentious") to perceive its similarity to the more common "rotund"—flabby, overweight, out of shape. As a speaker, Franklin was trim, fit, agile.

In this paragraph and the next two, Darcy shows how Isaacson's diction and syntax are not only impressive and precise but evocative of supporting thoughts.

The syntax of the eleventh paragraph suggests that Isaacson himself possesses the same stable, sensible character that he portrays Franklin as having. Notice the balance Isaacson creates in just these four sentences: "Some who see . . . . They say" (the critics' views); "Others see . . . His admirers" (the devotees' views).

We leave Isaacson's excerpt not only convinced of Franklin's admirable characters but also impressed by the writer's vivid, clear anecdotes and details and his rich, suggestive diction.

No elaborate conclusion is necessary. A strong sentence indicating the end is sufficient.

CHAPTER ACTIVITY

Rhetorical Analysis of Lincoln's Second Inaugural Address

Throughout this chapter, we have cited words, sentences, and passages from Abraham Lincoln's Second Inaugural Address to provide examples of his rhetorical skills as a writer. Now your task is to pull together everything you have learned in the chapter and produce a rhetorical analysis of the address on your own. Here's the task.

In his Second Inaugural Address, Abraham Lincoln, in his characteristically brief and eloquent fashion, makes an impassioned plea to the citizens of both the United States of America and the Confederate States of America. In a well-organized essay, analyze the rhetorical strategies Lincoln uses to make his central point about actions that need to happen or what states of mind need to prevail to bring the American Civil War to a conclusion.

CHAPTER CHECKLIST

Rhetorical Analysis

- [ ] Have you hypothesized about the text's take-home idea?
- [ ] Have you hypothesized about the author's purpose, tone, credibility, and the emotional effect of the text?
- [ ] Have you provided evidence from the text's arrangement, diction, syntax, imagery and allusions, and/or figurative language to support your claims?

Complete the Chapter 4 Exercise at Your Pearson MyLab

chapter 5

Argument

What You Will Learn

- To take a position on a topic
- To craft a good working thesis or take-home idea
- To build an argumentative position in four main ways—deductive, inductive, Toulmin, and Rogerian approaches
- To arrange an argument effectively
- To develop material that supports your thesis

What a confusing word *argument* is! Consider how the word is used in these two situations:

- Between classes in the hallway of your school, you can hear loud, angry shouting and the slamming of locker doors. You look in the direction of the noise and your friend tells you, "Oh, that's just Warren and Charlotte. They're having an argument."
- When you get to your Advanced Placement English Language and Composition course, you hear that students are expected to learn how to "create and sustain arguments based on readings, research, and/or personal experience."

Can these two examples possibly be referring to the same concept? In the first instance, argument stops communication. As stated in the second, argument is a *kind* of communication that's ongoing, sustained.

There are lots of the first kind of arguments that fascinate the general public—the magazines beside the grocery checkout are full of stories about Celebrity X arguing with Celebrity Y—but we're going to concentrate on the second kind in this chapter. (In fact, as you'll discover perhaps, knowing how to accomplish the second kind of argument can sometimes prevent the first from occurring.) As with *analysis,* the etymology, the origin, of *argument* suggests a path for our discussion. **Argument** comes from the Latin *argumentum,* meaning "evidence, ground, support, proof." By the time English came to use the term in the fourteenth century, it meant "statements and reasoning in support of a proposition." In academic settings, that meaning hasn't changed over the past seven centuries. That's what the second example above calls for. When you engage in an argument in school—when you produce an argumentative essay or, less formally, just argue a position—you focus on a specific, clear idea that you want your readers to consider carefully and finally adhere to: stick to, like a Band-Aid sticks to your skin. And you convince your readers to adhere to your central idea by offering details, explanations, and reasons, all arranged in an effective order and all well developed, that support your central idea.

Taking a Position

The most important step in engaging in academic argumentation and writing an argumentative essay is to construct your **position**, the central point you want to propose and develop—what we call the take-home idea in Chapter 4. You may not be completely certain about this main idea when you start working on an argumentative assignment—main ideas usually get developed while you're in the midst of considering them —but you should have a clear position formulated by the time you're producing the final draft to turn in.

How do you develop a main, take-home idea? Suppose you are constructing an argument in response to the following assignment, which actually appeared on the 2008 Advanced Placement English Language and Composition Examination:

> For years corporations have sponsored high school sports. Their ads are found on the outfield fence at baseball parks or on the walls of the gymnasium, the football stadium, or even the locker room. Corporate logos are even found on players' uniforms. But some schools have moved beyond corporate sponsorship of sports to allowing "corporate partners" to place their names and ads on all kinds of school facilities—libraries, music rooms, cafeterias. Some schools accept money to require students to watch Channel One, a news program that includes advertising. And schools often negotiate exclusive contracts with soft drink or clothing companies.
>
> Some people argue that corporate partnerships are a necessity for cash-strapped schools. Others argue that schools should provide an environment free from ads and corporate influence. Using appropriate evidence, write an essay in which you evaluate the pros and cons of corporate sponsorship for schools and indicate why you find one position more persuasive than the other.

After having considered both the pros and cons of corporate sponsorship for schools, let's say you want to argue in favor of allowing corporations to sponsor such school programs as library improvements (purchasing additional computers, more books), arts programs (paying for music, drama, and the visual arts), and clubs (providing funding for field trips). You decide on your position in part because of how you have reasoned through the situation as you read about it. In other words, while thinking as you read you already have begun to create arguments and reasons before you even begin to write. You might decide to support corporate sponsorships because there's an actual sponsorship in a school near you, or you might have read about schools' need for funds or heard people talking about other issues regarding corporations. Your consideration of reasons and ideas leads to your position—the controlling idea for your essay and the thesis of your argument.

Your Thesis: Developing a Take-Home Idea

Once you decide generally what position you think it best to take on an issue, or perhaps *while* you are deciding, you can begin to craft your take-home idea—the central proposition, or thesis. You formulate a thesis as you consider evidence, locate examples, conduct research, and talk to others about a topic. A reasoned, well thought-out argument does not simply preach a point. Instead, it treats the topic with respect, recognizing its complexity, acknowledging that more than one position could be offered. A good thesis will sustain the complexity of an issue, not oversimplify it. No intelligent audience will adhere to a take-home idea that essentially dumbs down the topic.

It's important, therefore, to think carefully and repeatedly about how you will word your thesis, your main point, your take-home idea. You may need to refine it more than once during the process of developing your argument.

Here are some characteristics of a good thesis:

- **It is *robust*:** It is rich, full, and strong enough to do justice to the complexity of the topic.
- **It is *finessed*:** It is carefully phrased to show the intricacy and subtlety of the thinking that will be involved in developing this main idea.
- **It is *nuanced*:** It is constructed to suggest careful distinctions that will emerge in the development.
- **It is *directive*:** It not only commits to a central idea but also suggests the way the idea will develop in the remainder of the essay.

What do these characteristics suggest about the actual construction of the thesis? Probably that a single, simple sentence will not suffice. Most effective thesis statements have more than one clause, and usually one of those clauses is subordinate to the other, allowing the writer to show the readers the complexity of his or her thinking. Sometimes, a writer needs more than one sentence to construct the position and suggest its direction to readers.

Watch the Video on Writing a Thesis Statement at Your Pearson MyLab

Let's say that you are writing on the role of women in a novel you're reading for class, *The Scarlet Letter*. You've decided that the women in the novel are the strongest characters, and you have some good evidence from events in the novel and dialogue between the characters to back up your position. Here's a possible thesis:

> Although it may seem that women in early America were assigned much weaker roles in the cultural and political life of the colonies, *The Scarlet Letter* suggests that may be a false assumption of twenty-first-century readers. Not only Hester, the main character in Hawthorne's novel, but others, including her daughter Pearl, effect changes in men's attitudes and in the entire culture of their small village through their strength and ability.

And what do these characteristics suggest about the nature of an *ineffective* thesis, the kind you want to avoid? Ineffective theses generally are blunt, shallow, and overbearing—the kinds of statements that suggest that you really don't want your readers to enter into a conversation with your position. Ineffective theses suggest that you simply want to lecture your readers, not to reason with them. Or they may be too vague and general, which leaves readers wondering what the idea is and why they should want to read about it. Here's a poorly designed thesis:

> Hester and Pearl stand up for themselves and so they are perfect examples of how women are often stronger than men in the novel.

ACTIVITY Forging a Good Thesis Statement

In a discussion with a classmate or a group, examine, compare, and contrast the following thesis statements on the issue of corporate sponsorship of schools.

1. Corporations should be allowed to support schools financially.
2. Corporations should be allowed to support schools financially, but their support should be monitored by schools, which are customers of the corporation. Corporations should not be permitted to display their advertisements on the school's property or on students' books and materials.
3. Although some critics might believe that corporate support for schools could interfere with students' academic success by distracting them from their studies, a carefully monitored program of corporate support could allow chronically underfunded parts of the school to flourish. In particular, corporate support could enable school libraries to upgrade their books and technology, arts programs to involve more students, and intramural clubs to engage in community service projects.
4. Corporations can bring needed resources to schools they support financially, but as with many gifts, strings may be attached. A school, therefore, should weigh carefully the potential benefits and losses that might come with corporate involvement in the classroom.

Extending Your Thesis Into a Full Argument: Four Paths

After thinking about the topic, perhaps discussing it with others or doing some reading about it, and crafting a version of your thesis that you're willing to refine as you proceed, you're ready to plot out the lines of your own argument. There are, of course, lots of ways to develop the idea you're beginning to shape as your thesis, and you may not decide on your method completely until you've gathered evidence from your reasoning and reading. But once you begin to write, systematic plans help you arrange ideas and make sure you've developed them well. Here are four possible avenues you might follow as you expand and deepen your thesis: deductive argument, inductive argument, Toulmin argument, and Rogerian argument.

1. The Deductive Argument

Deductive arguments work best when the issue at hand seems to be related to some general principle that you think most of your audience would agree with. When you argue **deductively**, you begin by describing this general principle, premise, or assertion. Then you cite a specific example that fits under this general premise and ultimately offer a conclusion that logically follows from the first two steps. For example:

General Premise: Corporations can become good citizens by taking some of their profits and supporting entities in their communities that do good work and need financial support.

Specific Example: Public schools do good work in the community and almost always need additional funding for libraries, the arts, and clubs.

Conclusion: Therefore, corporations should be encouraged to support libraries, the arts, and clubs in the schools that serve their communities.

2. The Inductive Argument

Inductive arguments are a good choice when you have access to lots of particular, specific pieces of evidence that you believe demonstrate a general point. When you argue **inductively**, you pull together a range of specific examples that collectively lead to a conclusion, the take-home idea that you finally argue for. For example:

Specific Example: Corporations sponsor school athletic teams.

Specific Example: Corporations sponsor local public libraries.

Specific Example: Corporations sponsor local public arts programs.

Specific Example: Corporations sponsor local citizens' service organizations.

Conclusion: Therefore, corporations should be permitted and also encouraged to support libraries, the arts, and clubs in the schools that serve their communities.

You are likely familiar with deductive and inductive reasoning from essays you've written and from work in other disciplines, like math and science. Arguments often proceed using one of these methods. You may be less familiar with the following two strategies for argument, though they're used often.

3. The Toulmin Argument

The **Toulmin argument** can be effective when you want to reason very carefully and specifically with your readers. In *The Uses of Argument,* the British philosopher Stephen Toulmin promoted a method of constructing and analyzing an argument that has come to be known simply as the Toulmin Model. Here's how it looks in a diagram, using a simple example as shown in Figure 5.1:

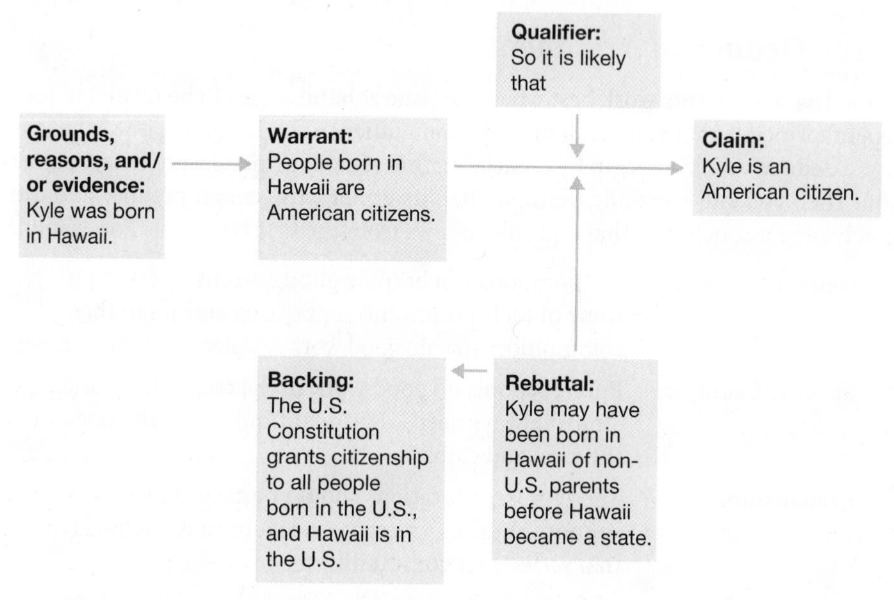

FIGURE 5.1 Toulmin Model of Argument

- The **claim** is the conclusion of the argument, the take-home idea.
- The **ground**, **reasons**, and/or **evidence** consist of specific examples and reasons that support the claim.
- The **warrant** is the general premise or line of reasoning that connects the grounds, reasons, and/or evidence to the claim.
- The **backing** comprises support, justification, or reasoning that "back up" the warrant.
- The **rebuttal** anticipates and addresses possible objections to the warrant and therefore leads to the **qualifier**, which specifies any possible limits to the claim.

Here is how our potential argument about corporate sponsorship might be mapped out with the Toulmin Model:

The claim:	Corporations should be permitted and also encouraged to support libraries, the arts, and clubs in the schools that serve their communities.
The grounds, reasons, and/or evidence:	Corporate contributions already support school athletics, plus community libraries, arts, and service organizations.
The warrant:	It is wise for corporations to find highly visible ways to support schools that do good work in the corporations' communities.
The backing:	Corporations can create good will and, therefore, do more profitable business in communities and schools that they serve financially.
The rebuttal:	Some may argue that corporate sponsorships in schools might encourage students to develop unhealthy consumer practices and spend money on products that they neither need nor can afford. However, we should assume that students have the good sense to monitor their own spending habits.
The qualifier:	If corporate sponsorship should somehow interfere with the best practices of teaching and learning in the schools, it should be stopped.

The Toulmin Model is not nearly as complicated as it might appear on first examination. The easiest way to understand it is to compare it to the deductive model. The warrant in the Toulmin Model corresponds to the *general premise* in the deductive argument. The grounds, reasons, and/or evidence in Toulmin corresponds to the *specific evidence* in the deductive, and the claim in Toulmin corresponds to the *conclusion* in the deductive. The other parts of the Toulmin Model—the backing, the rebuttal, and the qualifier—help you flesh out the reasoning of your argument in greater detail.

4. The Rogerian Argument

Rogerian argument, effective for situations in which you want to establish close, friendly contact with your readers from the outset, is named for the twentieth-century American psychologist Carl Rogers, who emphasized the need for arguments to be based on what he called "common grounds" that the writer shares with his or her audience. Rogerian argument is less concerned with winning the case than establishing a solution that will accommodate more than one position. The writer gives a fair statement of the position, but also fairly states the alternative. The writer consciously plays out instances where the alternate position might work and then discusses reasons for the position being advocated. Sometimes the aim is to reach a compromise or to leave open the possibility of change.

A Rogerian argumentative essay may or may not have a distinctive thesis statement. In essence, the writer offers points in support of a position and then asks the readers, "What can we agree upon?", "What might be the benefits of seeing the argument one way rather than another?"

Here are elements of Rogerian argument, using our sample topic:

- **Know your audience.** Let's assume the audience as members of the board of education and other citizens who want students to have the best education possible.
- **Establish common ground.** You, the writer, are a student in the school, and you realize that better libraries, arts programs, and clubs can benefit students, several of whom are the children and grandchildren of audience members.
- **Introduce the premises that underlie your position.** Corporations have a responsibility to support their communities. The schools are an important part of the community. Libraries, the arts, and clubs add value to a student's education. Students who have good libraries, arts organizations, and clubs are likely to become lifelong readers and learners and supporters of the arts and service organizations in the communities where they will eventually live.
- **Explain shared premises.** Parents, community members, and students have a vested interest in creating active, independent learners and citizens.
- **Introduce and develop your position.** Corporations should be permitted and also encouraged to support libraries, the arts, and clubs in the schools that serve their communities. Corporations are part of communities and act as citizens.
- **Consider possible objections.** Corporate support would limit the free expression of speech and thought in the schools, or encourage students to be unthinking consumers, buying items they neither need nor can afford.
- **Find places of agreement, compromise, contingency.** Explain how you and the audience can work together to be certain that these objections are observed, how alterations might occur if objections are observed, and how the benefits of your claim actually outweigh negative possible consequences.

Choosing an Argumentative Path

As a writer who has now developed a tentative thesis or main idea for your argument, read and thought through reasons and considered data, you decide on an argumentative path based on

- The strength of your opinion about the topic
- The knowledge, background, and attitude of your audience
- The amount or kind of data or reasons you have developed for your position
- The amount of space you have to devote to your discussion
- The persona you want to develop for persuasive effect

ACTIVITY **Try One or More of the Argumentative Paths**

With the assistance of your teacher or your classmates, focus on a topic and develop an argumentative position on an issue from the literature you are reading or from current local or national events. Experiment with one or all of these argumentative paths as you make decisions about your big ideas, your position, and the reasons you find the position persuasive. Make careful notes about your evolving argument.

Arrangement and the Argumentative Essay

Building your argumentative position by choosing one argumentative path or another is not the same as writing the argumentative essay, although lots of the thinking that goes into forging the main idea and considering how to develop it might eventually make its way into the essay. Choosing the appropriate arrangement for your argument helps move you into the writing of the essay and is key to your being most persuasive—you're choosing the right tool for the job.

As you move from developing your argumentative position—marshaling ideas and counter arguments, creating and refining your big idea—to drafting your argumentative essay, you have lots of choices for arranging ideas to deliver your message and persuade readers. What follows are three possibilities for arrangement. The first—the five-paragraph theme—is probably the most familiar to you, but we think it's actually the least effective in terms of writing a compelling argumentative essay. The other two offer you more opportunity to interact with and persuade your readers.

Five-Paragraph Theme

The familiar arrangement pattern is the **five-paragraph theme**, and its component parts are easy to describe. It begins with an opening paragraph to "hook" the reader and then offers a thesis statement. It then moves to three "body" paragraphs, each of which is supposed to have a topic sentence that grows out of your thesis statement. It then concludes with a paragraph where you "restate" and emphasize the importance of your thesis.

There is nothing especially wrong with the five-paragraph theme. It's a good genre to know. Imagine an examination question asked you to write a response to the following prompt:

> What were the major causes of the American Civil War?

You might begin with a paragraph that looks something like this:

> The American Civil War, 1861 to 1865, was tremendously destructive, both in terms of loss of life and devastation of property. Three major causes of this unfortunate event were disagreements about the rights of states versus those of the federal government, the controversy over the enslavement of African Americans, and the differences in ideology related to an agricultural economy in contrast to an industrial economy.

Watch the Video on Tests for Inductive and Deductive Reasoning at Your Pearson MyLab

Then each of your three body paragraphs would begin with a topic sentence about one of the three causes, and you would flesh out each of these paragraphs with facts, details, and explanations about the topic sentence. You might conclude the composition with the following:

> Given the complexity of the disagreements over states' rights, the intensity of ill feelings about slavery, and the conflicts between an industrial and an agrarian way of life, one might perceive that the American Civil War was inevitable. It's unfortunate that three such strong forces converged at the time and place they did.

The five-paragraph theme works well for many examination answers, but it does not lend itself well to writing an argumentative essay that really invites your readers to think deeply about your topic and, by interacting with you, the writer, come to the same thoughtful conclusion that your essay promotes. The five-paragraph essay does create a frame or box that establishes some signposts for your reader to notice. But there's little room in a five-paragraph theme for the reader to "talk back," to engage with the writer. Five-paragraph themes general don't make for interesting reading or persuasive writing.

Six-Part-Oration Model

A better arrangement pattern to use for an argumentative essay is the **six-part oration**, first taught by the first-century B.C.E. rhetorician, Marcus Tullius Cicero. He taught his students to create speeches by the model in Figure 5.2.

Notice how these six "moves"—they're not all necessarily paragraphs; some may take more than one paragraph to accomplish, some fewer—might structure an argumentative essay:

- You contextualize the issue at hand for your readers and let them know why your topic is an important one for them to consider.
- You provide background on your topic, sketching out what people generally talk about when the topic comes up or what compels you to discuss it.
- You divide your topic into smaller chunks, and then commit to developing one or more of them—your thesis—mapping out how you intend to do so.
- You generate points to support your thesis, and you make these points substantial by providing reasons, details, examples, and illustrations.
- You anticipate your readers' objections and address them, again with reasons, details, examples, and illustrations.

Arrangement of a Six-Part-Oration Argument	
Exordium (introduction)	Literally, the *web* that draws listeners into the speech; the speaker introduces the subject at hand and includes material that makes the audience both attentive and receptive to the argument.
Narration (background)	Background material or context on the topic or argument.
Partition (forecast and thesis)	Divides the topic into parts; makes clear which part or parts the speaker hopes to address, which parts might be omitted, and how parts will be arranged; and commits to a thesis.
Confirmation (development of points)	Offers points to develop and substantiate the thesis and provides reasons, details, illustrations, and examples in support of those points.
Refutation (consideration of opposing positions)	Considers possible objections to the thesis or its supporting points and tries to counter those objections.
Peroration (conclusion)	Draws together the entire argument as it makes the final persuasive case to the audience.

FIGURE 5.2

- You conclude by doing two things: (a) addressing the "so what" question—the implications of your thesis for further discussion or how readers might be better off for having read your essay and (b) *sounding* like a conclusion—giving your ending a rhythm and a finale, like the last chords in a song or symphony.

ACTIVITY Analyze a Sample Six-Part Argumentative Essay

The following is an argumentative essay submitted by student writer Alexandra Rooney in response to the corporate-sponsorship-of-schools prompt. Read it carefully and then identify the "moves" suggested by the six-part oration and evaluate how effectively the essay fulfills them.

Alexandra Rooney

Corporate Sponsorship in Today's Schools

Anyone who has sat at a hometown football game has seen the banners along the fence for local businesses. Look at the last few pages of an old yearbook and what does one find? Advertisements from restaurants to car shops to nail salons. Corporate sponsorship has grown from mom and pop shops donating $25 to a school for a business card sized advertisement in the school newspaper to things such as funding of new school buildings by businesses and exclusive contracts with companies such as Frito Lay in which only Frito Lay products would be sold in vending machines in exchange for large donations to the school. Corporate sponsorship involves a company giving money to a school in exchange for advertisement and/or exclusive distribution on school grounds.

Corporate sponsorship of schools is a very debatable topic. Many are strongly opposed to corporate funding, but is it really a bad thing? Each year there are growing needs in public education, which means more spending of public funds. As technology advances there are new demands for computer labs, smartboards, and even personal computers for students all the way down to the elementary level. With expanding immigrant populations there is a growing need for educators capable of working with ESL students. Often brand new programs are needed for these students. Technology and teachers cost money. As the list of needs grows from year to year the taxpayer's budget gets tighter and tighter. As America slowly recovers from a financial recession, people would like to hold onto their money, but at the same time they do not want to sacrifice the quality of their child's education.

In sweep corporate sponsorships to save the day! If a company supplies the funds for that new computer lab then the taxpayer can hold on to their money, and their children can still reap the benefits of the improved school facilities. Of course, things cannot be that easy. There are people who are swift to naysay.

Many argue that the majority of sponsorship funds go to school athletics, in particular football and/or basketball, only benefiting a minority of the students. First, there are several other extracurricular activities that benefit from corporate sponsorship, for example, the school newspaper. School newspapers are struggling to survive, and one way they can raise money is by selling advertisement space in the paper. It is not as glamorous as a brand new scoreboard funded by a large, local company, but it is necessary for the survival of the newspaper. Also, when outside funds are being used for athletics, it allows state funding, the actual taxpayer's dollar, to be used for educational purposes.

What about the influence a large corporation can have in a school's decisions due to the school's dependence on that corporation's support? Corporate sponsorship should never be the primary financial source of a public school and have that kind of power to dictate decisions down to what is taught in the classroom. A teacher should never be afraid to bring up the correlation between unhealthy junk food and obesity because a large soft drink producer has an exclusive contract with the school.

What about the pressure on children subjected to the advertising and limited resources as a result of certain contracts? If they see a Coca-Cola vending machine in every hallway are they not significantly more likely to drink Coca-Cola products? Issues, especially health-related issues such as obesity, are already bad enough. Should we encourage children to go ahead and drink soda despite the consequences of unhealthy eating? What if they do not want what is offered in the vending machine? What if they are missing out on other, better options? Children are subject to advertisements everywhere. Even if a Coca-Cola advertisement is not hanging in the gymnasium, chances are they will see other students carrying Coca-Cola products around campus. A logo may even be printed on another student's shirt. If students would like other options, they are welcome to bring a different drink in their backpacks. And, once again, corporate sponsorship should not provide a large enough percentage of funding to run a school. If students are being forced to look at advertisements on their textbooks each day or around every corner in every hallway, chances are there is too much dependence on a sponsor. When sponsorships have that much sway, schools have put too much emphasis on financial concerns and disregarded providing a quality education for students.

With growing needs and tight budgets, schools often have to be creative when it comes to improving facilities and opportunities for students. Corporate sponsorships can provide additional funding for new programs and improvements. State funding is not distributed evenly, and different districts have different needs. Local businesses and corporations can often provide for those specific needs the state cannot afford or chooses not to address.

Rogerian Argument

A third arrangement pattern is even more interactive than the six-part oration. Related to the argumentative paths for development of ideas we discussed earlier, Rogerian argument insists on alternative understandings of positions. An argumentative essay that grows out of Rogerian argument is shown in Figure 5.3.

Arrangement of a Rogerian Argument	
Introduction	Present your topic, and admit that people have differing views on it.
Benefit of discussing the topic	Explain why people who disagree about the topic should examine it together.
Thesis and objections	Present your main take-home idea briefly, and examine in detail the views of people who disagree with you.
Development of your argument	Explain your take-home idea more fully, and compare and contrast your ideas with those that differ from yours.
Common ground	Show where there is common ground between your views and the views of others.
Conclusion	Support your position, and call for continued discussion to produce even more common ground.

FIGURE 5.3

ACTIVITY Analyzing a Rogerian Argument

The following is an essay submitted by student writer Mitchell Hardaway in response to the corporate-sponsorship-of-schools prompt. Read it carefully and then describe and evaluate how effectively it constructs a Rogerian argument.

Mitchell Hardaway

Corporate Sponsorship in Schools: Finding Common Ground

Long has the topic of corporate sponsorship in schools been at the forefront of debate among parents, educators, and civic leaders. In recent years corporations have increased their role in schools by advertising in the cafeteria, sports field, and various other locations in exchange for a specific amount of money. The question becomes whether private enterprise warrants a place in the education domain; and countless interested parties have attempted to develop an answer. To be clear, the people waging this debate are acting on what they believe is in the best interest of the younger generation. Therein lies the problem. Some people glorify the boost in program funding that sponsorship provides, while others focus on the sometimes negatively influential effect advertising has on youth.

Since society has been unable to develop a clear resolution to the issue of sponsorship through the current process, cooperative collaboration should be considered. Everyone, from both sides of the argument, must begin by acknowledging that everyone is essentially on the same side, the side that benefits the whole of the students in America. Instead of looking at corporate sponsorship as a debate that can be won or lost, the issue must be approached with the goal to create a solution that works for the students. By working together, each side can present their unique perspective to the other side and combine to form a more perfect picture of what is occurring with corporate sponsorship in schools. The person who has experience with the negative effects of advertising and is therefore against sponsorship can open a dialogue with the veteran administrator of a cash-strapped school district who champions sponsorship because of the revenue it brings in.

Corporate sponsorship generates much angst among those people who idealize the innocent, undeveloped minds of students; however, financial conditions mandate that some schools resort to sponsorship in order to continue to provide adequate programming for their students. In the realistic best interest of today's students, the benefits of sponsorship outweigh any chance negative impact. But there are certainly some people who would disagree with this position. Although the financial rewards for sponsored schools carry an overwhelming amount of weight in the sponsorship debate, objections to the issue are definitely deserving of analysis because the more informed the decision, the better the decision. Many people see how young people can be easily influenced and quickly point out that advertising at school might prompt students to value certain ideas or items over others. Some would claim that schools that allow sponsorship are eliminating free choice, one of the great ideals of American individualism. Students have no choice in the advertising they are exposed to.

In an ideal world, schools are places free from any influences besides the positive pressures of education, social responsibility, and the like; however, the harsh conditions of the economy force schools to adopt alternative methods for generating operating funds, particularly corporate sponsorship. Sponsorship provides a means of revenue that is necessary but would otherwise be unavailable to the school, and costs only the space on the wall or a few seconds in the announcements. The school can gain an income that sustains important extracurricular programs by simply advertising for a specific company or product. As opposed to looking at the argument from a statistical viewpoint, consider the personal side of the debate. The student who is fascinated with drama, journalism, or golf is able to explore that interest because of corporate sponsorship, or possibly unable to due to a lack of sponsorship. To the aspiring journalist, viewing an advertisement at school every day is nothing compared to the fire that is fanned because a journalism class is being offered from funds generated by the marketing of a corporate sponsor. Young people have become accustomed to advertising through the mass-marketing tools employed on television during every broadcast, so a small amount of advertising media at school has relatively no effect. Claims that sponsorship has virtually no influence on students because they are immune to the vast amounts of media they are exposed to would immediately be met with resistance by those who emphasize the easily impressionable minds of youth that are guided by media, especially marketing media directed at them. Whereas those who are against sponsorship believe that advertising has a negative impact on young people, the pro-sponsorship side notes that students consume such a large amount of marketing they have built up a tolerance to it.

The ultimate goal of both sides of the debate has always been to provide for the well-being of our students. This patch of common ground is so substantial that all differences of opinion become insignificant. Everyone must acknowledge the revenue creation that corporate sponsorship provides, even if some of those people disagree with the trade-off for that money. And no one can deny the benefit of quality extracurricular programs, so to this point everyone is on the same page. Ultimately, each side agrees that schools need money to provide programs that enhance the education of students; however, the debate varies as to how best to generate those funds.

In today's ever-changing society, schools are called upon to give each child a complete education, and to do so with very limited resources; therefore, corporate sponsorship within schools provides the best avenue through which necessary funds become available. People who have a deep interest in the education of young people have long debated the ethics of sponsorship, but in the end finances always win out. The money that comes from sponsorship is vital to continuing that sports team that gives Johnny a reason to come to school every day or the school newspaper that allows Jennifer to express her complicated emotions. Without corporate sponsorship many schools would be forced to do without, and that is what would be unfair to the students. Adults making decisions, based on what they believe, affecting programs that students are actively involved in is dangerous territory that must be tread upon carefully. Everyone values a rich education, and corporate sponsorship is just a means to accomplish that shared goal.

Supporting, Developing, and Confirming Your Thesis

As we suggested earlier, a good writer learns how to craft the best arrangement for an argumentative essay. When you're successful at making a good argument, you know both the small component parts and the whole shape of the argumentative piece. Even more important, you know how the small parts work to reinforce and develop the whole shape. So you need to know what goes into these parts and how to put them into an effective order for your readers.

Once you have established your argumentative position, created a thesis, formulated a method for developing your argument, and decided the arrangement pattern you'll develop, you need to concentrate on figuring out which reasons, examples, data will best support and affirm your developing argument. You will have at this point been reading and considering claims and data, and some of what you've used to develop your thesis will become part of the supporting material you will use as support. There are two large categories that describe how you'll want to use these specifics to develop your thesis:

- **Details.** Facts or statistics, examples from reading or experience, and hypothetical cases are all strategies of detail that make your argument persuasive.
- **Reasons and Explanations.** Explanations offer logical guidance to readers making decisions about a topic. Comparisons that help readers understand your issue in other terms are helpful; *analogies* allow readers to make connections themselves and are also logically persuasive.

Watch the Video on Evidence for Argument at Your Pearson MyLab

And, of course, you can combine the two categories, offering a range of details, reasons, and explanations in support of your thesis.

Generating Supporting Material

How do you generate this good supporting material for your arguments, specific, appropriate details, reasons, and explanations? As we have argued throughout this book (using lots of details and reasons ourselves!), in general you need to be an avid, curious, active reader. You need to read not only books but also good newspapers and news magazines (most of which you can get free online or in your school's library). You need to watch high-quality current-affairs programs on television—the kind that allow people to express and explain their ideas fully, not the kind where people shout at each other and the host rudely interrupts their answers. You need to have conversations with your fellow students and with others—friends, parents, teachers, people in the community—who will listen to your ideas and respond to them and to whom you should listen and respond with equal attentiveness. Cicero wrote in his treatise *On the Orator* that the ideal statesman–rhetorician needs to know not only philosophy but also law, history, and psychology; needs to be able to move smoothly from the general to the specific and back to the general; needs a good sense of humor. In short, the best arguer is the one who has the widest, deepest education, the one who reads and writes a lot. You'll find details, reasons, and analogies from the world around you in school and outside it. And don't forget Cicero's advice about humor: your voice, your ability to play with words and ideas, is part of your sense of assurance and good humor that readers respond to. For the particular task of developing an argument, you begin the process of generating material by considering what you believe and know, by finding out more, by developing a beginning idea and considering more in order to confirm or alter it, and then by locating data that best makes the case you now believe you want to make.

Ordering Details and Explanations

In addition to knowing how to generate effective material to support, develop, and confirm your thesis, you also need to give considerable thought to how you order and introduce details and explanations. Too often writers simply insert specifics into the essay in the order it comes into their minds. Better by far is to make decisions about order by considering your argument and your readers. Which detail suggests another one? Which is easiest for a reader to understand or agree with? Which takes the longest to explain? Which is most interesting or fun? These questions suggest that you're thinking about your reader: what order works best to help readers believe me, understand me, stay attentive? If your topic has a chronological or historical dimension, you might order your supporting points by time: first this happened, then this, then this. If your topic has a geographical or spatial dimension, you can use location as your ordering device: here you see this point, there you see the other, and there you see yet another.

One common method of ordering the supporting material in an argument also comes from ancient Greek literature. The character of Nestor in *The Odyssey* chose to present supporting points in this order:

1. The second-to-most important point,
2. Any weaker point or points, and
3. The most important point.

This method of saving the strongest point for last has come to be known as **Nestorian order**.

Sometimes length is a good ordering strategy: varying short and long examples or explanations keeps readers interested. If your evidence or support uses both data and examples, you might alternate one and the other for interest as well. The point is that you want to understand your own order, have a reason that makes sense to you for the arrangement of ideas in your essay. The chances are your reader will understand the order too.

Using Transitions: Signal Words, Phrases, and Sentences

You can help the reader further by using phrases or sentences that point directly to how the supporting details are being used. Calling attention to the order helps readers follow the direction of your argument. Consider how introductory material like the following in the middle of an argumentative essay can orient your readers and help them follow your argument as it is developing:

- The first point a reader needs to notice is . . .
- The most important feature in this diagram is . . .
- The example of X compares to the main point of this essay: . . .
- Y offers a fascinating counter-example to what most critics say: . . .
- A small instance that may seem unrelated to the main argument but is actually directly connected to it is this: . . .

In short, feel free to *lead* your reader through the development of your argument. Don't simply assume your reader will "get it." Teach. Show. Develop. Argue.

ACTIVITY **Brainstorming for Support**

Return to the topic you (and perhaps your classmates) used to develop an argumentative position earlier in this chapter. Reconvene the group or form another one and collectively brainstorm about details, reasons, and explanations you could offer in support of any of the argumentative positions you developed.

ACTIVITY **Constructing Good Transitions**

Return to either of the sample argumentative essays in this chapter and revise them so that they include introductory and transitional phrases and sentences that guide the reader through the development and support of the take-home idea more effectively.

CHAPTER ACTIVITY

An Argument Project Rich with Possibilities

Your instructor will expose you to a wide range of assignments and projects that call upon you to write substantial arguments. Here is one of the most productive argument prompts ever used on the Advanced Placement English Language and Composition Examination:

> Contemporary life is marked by controversy. Choose a local, national, or global issue with which you are familiar. Then, using appropriate evidence, write an essay that carefully considers the opposing positions on this controversy and proposes a compromise or a solution.

For this activity, take this prompt a couple steps beyond what the exam required. Once you have settled on a controversial issue to write about, identify a specific audience whom you would sensibly write to about this topic. Then, using one of the argumentative paths described in this chapter, write an argumentative essay, using the arrangement pattern you think most appropriate, ordering your supporting material in the best way you can, and providing effective introductory and transition words, phrases, and clauses to guide your readers through the argument.

CHAPTER CHECKLIST

Argument

- ☐ Have you thought about your topic and developed a tentative, working thesis or take-home idea?
- ☐ Have you developed your argumentative position, using deductive, inductive, Toulmin, and Rogerian approaches as needed?
- ☐ Have you thought about your audience and purpose, your thesis, and your reasons and evidence?
- ☐ Have you arranged your argument effectively?
- ☐ Have you revised and finalized your thesis and decided what reasons and evidence best support it?
- ☐ Have you drafted your argument?
- ☐ Have you revised and proofread your argument?

Complete the Chapter 5 Exercise at Your Pearson MyLab

chapter 6

The Researched or Synthesis Essay

What You Will Learn

- To read and analyze several sources about the same issue
- To write a synthesis essay

Way back in 1581, the British poet Sir Philip Sidney captured a feeling that other writers had felt for centuries before him and have suffered with in the centuries since. In the first sonnet in a series called "Astrophel and Stella," Sidney describes how he felt when he failed to find the right words in the works of other writers to write a love poem to his beloved:

> Biting at my pen which disobeyed me, beating myself in anger,
> My Muse said to me 'Fool, look in your heart and write.'

Oh, if it were only that easy with the kinds of writing you have to do in school! Perhaps when you're writing a poem about love, or maybe a personal story about a life experience, you can simply "look into your heart and write." But when you're confronted with the writing tasks that a twenty-first-century student generally faces, you can't simply look inward—you have to look at others' texts, consider others' perspectives, weigh others' opinions and ideas.

Imagine, for example, that you've gotten these assignments:

- In a sociology class that's examining local food cultures and customs, you're required to investigate the growing movement called "locavorism," where people try to eat only food produced locally, within 150 miles of their homes.
- In a business class, you might be studying how not-for-profit organizations operate, and examining how museums negotiate tensions between the need to raise money and the need to respect artifacts in exhibits.

- In an American literature course, you could be comparing the social contexts and effects of two antislavery speeches delivered in the nineteenth century.

Whatever the class and assignment, you need to generate your own thesis—your perspective, your take-home idea, as we labeled it in Chapter 4. But in order to do the kind of work the examples above suggest, you also need, as Sidney put it, "to turn others' pages" to see how others' ideas might spark more of your own. Writing that asks for considered evaluation and opinion demands that the writer look outward as well as inward, to observe, evaluate, and rethink based on inquiry into a topic. As you write and read, your opinions emerge, and you evaluate the relevance and importance of information as your ideas develop.

Most of the writing students do in college courses, especially in the humanities and the social sciences, is writing about reading, about what you have read. This kind of writing about reading goes by different names. Some instructors assign what they call *research papers* or *term papers*. Some just label them *papers* or *essays*. Others call them *research-based arguments* or *documented essays*. In Advanced Placement English Language and Composition courses, a particular kind of writing about reading is called the *synthesis essay*.

But no matter what they're called, papers using a group of readings usually share these characteristics:

- They address a guiding question, issue, or problem that recurs in several of the texts students read in the course.
- They incorporate material from the course readings and perhaps other related sources.
- They demonstrate careful, perceptive use of sources, a focused thesis (the take-home idea), and appropriate citation form (usually MLA or APA formats; see Appendix 3 for citation forms), and they connect argument and thesis to supporting research with good reasons and examples.

As we'll explain below, these kinds of essays require you to enter into a "conversation" with the sources rather than to merely summarize them, and to use that conversation, which is a thoughtful assessment and evaluation, to develop the main argument. The rest of this chapter sets out four stages, four "moves" you can follow to define and generate the conversation you want to have with the readings you engage with as you're conducting research. The chapter concludes with a student paper, which provides a good example of how to incorporate the source-based conversation in a synthesis essay.

The Synthesis Essay as an Argumentative Essay

In almost all cases, a researched essay requiring several sources asks for an argument. The only real difference between the argumentative essays described in Chapter 5 and synthesis essays is this: In argumentative essays you usually tap into your general background knowledge of readings and experiences to develop your thesis/take-home idea, while in the researched essay or synthesis assignment, you incorporate specific sources as part of your thesis and the development of your paper.

Watch the Video on Synthesizing Sources at Your Pearson MyLab

In Chapter 5, we describe two approaches that writers often use to develop their arguments: the traditional argumentative essay based on the six-part oration and the Rogerian argumentative essay. Both of these work well in synthesis tasks too. Your arrangement of ideas in the synthesis essay might focus on pro and con positions you discover in your research, as a traditional argument proceeds, or you might read a variety of opinions about a topic and then mediate among them, as a Rogerian argument works.

Some of the assignments for synthesis essays may not look as though they directly call for argumentative writing. The local food synthesis assignment, for example, might include language like this:

> Using some or all of the sources you have read for this assignment, describe what you think are the major characteristics of locavorism and then explain the possible implications of these characteristics for a community that is considering initiating a locavore movement.

In this synthesis assignment, the requirement for the writer to produce an argument is implied in the direction to decide "what you think" and to "explain implications." The writer who responds to this assignment argues first that certain characteristics, and not some others, define locavore movements and then argues that these implications, and not some others, follow from putting a locavore movement into practice. The assignment asks writers to develop a strong thesis and create a robust argument based on careful reading of several sources.

In contrast, a more direct argument assignment might read something like this:

> Write an essay in which you take a position on whether the locavore movement is feasible and practical for a particular community. Support your position with evidence from the sources you have consulted.

Some synthesis assignments call on the writer to evaluate either the sources used or the possible outcomes of a proposed plan of action. Notice that evaluation is a kind of argument, a judgment about what you think might be better or worse, workable or unworkable.

A Sample Synthesis Project

So that we'll have some common ground for thinking about how to develop and write a synthesis essay, let us introduce you to a synthesis project and to a first-year college student, Don Worthington, who is completing the assignment. Don is taking an American Studies course that describes major cultural themes from the middle of the nineteenth century and explores how relevant those themes are in contemporary American culture. The instructor specializes in the history of railroads in the United States, so she offers the following prompt:

> Some writers and thinkers in nineteenth-century America saw the advent of the railroad and train travel as an unmistakable emblem of progress, while others at the time perceived this progress as having negative implications.

Similarly, in our own time, scholars and the general populace are wondering whether train travel, especially in the form of light rail, represents progress or problems for contemporary society. Read the following sources carefully. Then, in a well-developed essay that incorporates information and perspectives from at least four of the sources listed below, explain what you see as the most important sources of tension about the railroads and train travel, and then offer a reasoned, well-supported argument about the degree to which those tensions still prevail in contemporary discussions of rail and train travel.

The assignment directs Don to consider the following sources:

- Reilly, Megan. "Is Light Rail the Answer to Transit Woes?" published on March 15, 2010 (reprinted below)
- Thoreau, Henry David. From Chapter 2 of *Walden,* published in 1854 (reprinted below)
- Whitman, Walt. "To a Locomotive in Winter," composed around 1876 (reprinted in Unit 4 of this text's anthology)
- Hawthorne, Nathaniel. From *The House of the Seven Gables,* published in 1851 (reprinted in Unit 3)
- Melrose, Andrew. *Westward the* Star of Empire *Takes Its Way—Near Council Bluffs Iowa, 1867* (reprinted in Unit 4)
- Dickinson, Emily. "I like to see it lap the miles," composed around 1862 (reprinted in Unit 4)
- Krugman, Paul. "Stranded in Suburbia," from the *New York Times,* May 19, 2008 (reprinted in Unit 4)

In summary, the sources include two nineteenth-century poems, an excerpt from a nineteenth-century novel, an excerpt from a nineteenth-century essay, a reproduction of a nineteenth-century painting, and two contemporary essays about the themes and issues raised in the nineteenth-century sources. We reprint two of the sources here.

Megan Reilly

Is Light Rail the Answer to Transit Woes?

Light rail commuting may help with pollution issues and conserve resources, but at what cost?

Budget cuts. Who hasn't heard about those as of late? Even light rail systems aren't immune; with ridership down approximately 7%, they are cutting many a commuter's options. This is a stark contrast to when Salt Lake City hosted the Olympics in 2002; the two-line, 55-mile-per-hour, 16-station rail system was the talk of the town.

But, beyond the commute, environmental conservation is big enough to cause worry about the loss of popularity in the Salt Lake City line—a single light rail vehicle removes 60 to 125 cars from the road, according to LightRailNow.org. Breaking down the different eco-friendly benefits, every minute detail is mentioned, save the fact that seats are recycled (by reuse!). So, beyond all of the smoke and mirrors, here are some simple pros and cons for proving light rail transit.

Pros

Less traffic and wasted gas/energy: Light rail is much more fuel efficient than all of the cars that would be on the freeway. In a single hour, a freeway lane caries from 1,500 to 1,800 cars—and on average less than 2,200 people. A single light rail track can carry from 5,000–14,000 people per hour, saving two to seven freeway lanes of space and pollution.

4th Avenue in Tucson has been serviced by trolley cars for years. Is light rail now a better solution?

Reduced pollution: Electrified light rail does not pollute visually (no need to fear the bus stop trashcan!), because there simply aren't as many stops and the rail has better waste disposal options, according to LightRailNow.org's findings. Furthermore, according to those findings, this is a huge relief to home property values near those stations versus a traditional bus line.

The Big Con

Cost: Construction, construction, construction! It's all about money for cities that are struggling to pay for a new line, such as the $182-million light rail route considered in Tucson, AZ. When looking across the board at other cities, many hit just about that mark. Seattle, WA, for instance, undertook a $179-million price tag per mile for its light rail. According to a recent article in the *Arizona Reporter*, a route connecting downtown Tucson with the University of Arizona (totaling less than 5 miles) will cause a budget nightmare for Tucson that is expected to last into 2030. Though the city received a TIGER grant for $63 million and was already greenlighted for the Regional Transportation Authority tax and other federal grants, it is still struggling.

Still, supporters say that the light rail line is worth it not only from a transportation aspect, but also for the environmental benefits, while others question its commercial benefits. While cost will always be a factor, pollution and carbon emissions will be, too. It is likely to be a debate for quite some time. Luckily, the choice to ride right now or not is yours.

[2010]

Henry David Thoreau

From Chapter 2 of *Walden*

I went to the woods because I wished to live deliberately, to front only the essential facts of life, and see if I could not learn what it had to teach, and not, when I came to die, discover that I had not lived. I did not wish to live what was not life, living is so dear; nor did I wish to practice resignation, unless it was quite necessary. I wanted to live deep and suck out all the marrow of life, to live so sturdily and Spartan-like as to put to rout all that was not life, to cut a broad swath and shave close, to drive life into a corner, and reduce it to its lowest terms, and, if it proved to be mean, why then to get the whole and genuine meanness of it, and publish its meanness to the world; or if it were sublime, to know it by experience, and be able to give a true account of it in my next excursion. For most men, it appears to me, are in a strange uncertainty about it, whether it is of the devil or of God, and have somewhat hastily concluded that it is the chief end of man here to "glorify God and enjoy him forever."

Still we live meanly, like ants; though the fable tells us that we were long ago changed into men; like pygmies we fight with cranes; it is error upon error, and clout upon clout, and our best virtue has for its occasion a superfluous and evitable wretchedness. Our life is frittered away by detail. An honest man has hardly need to count more than his ten fingers, or in extreme cases he may add his ten toes, and lump the rest. Simplicity, simplicity, simplicity! I say, let your affairs be as two or three, and not a hundred or a thousand; instead of a million count half a dozen, and keep your accounts on your thumb-nail. In the midst of this chopping sea of civilized life, such are the clouds and storms and quicksands and thousand-and-one items to be allowed for, that a man has to live, if he would not founder and go to the bottom and not make his port at all, by dead reckoning, and he must be a great calculator indeed who succeeds. Simplify, simplify. Instead of three meals a day, if it be necessary eat but one; instead of a hundred dishes, five; and reduce other things in proportion. Our life is like a German Confederacy, made up of petty states, with its boundary forever fluctuating, so that even a German cannot tell you how it is bounded at any moment. The nation itself, with all its so-called internal improvements, which, by the way are all external and superficial, is just such an unwieldy and overgrown establishment, cluttered with furniture and tripped up by its own traps, ruined by luxury and heedless expense, by want of calculation and a worthy aim, as the million households in the land; and the only cure for it, as for them, is in a rigid economy, a stern and more than Spartan simplicity of life and elevation of purpose. It lives too fast. Men think that it is essential that the Nation have commerce, and export ice, and talk through a telegraph, and ride thirty miles an hour, without a doubt, whether they do or not; but whether we should live like baboons or like men, is a little uncertain. If we do not get out sleepers, and forge rails, and devote days and nights to the work, but go to tinkering upon our lives to improve them, who will build railroads? And if railroads are not built, how shall we get to heaven in season? But if we stay at home and mind our business, who will want railroads? We do not ride on the railroad; it rides upon us. Did you ever think what those sleepers are that underlie the railroad? Each one is a man, an Irishman, or a Yankee man. The rails are laid on them, and they are covered with sand, and the cars run smoothly over them. They are sound sleepers, I assure you. And every few years a new lot is laid down and run over; so that, if some have the pleasure of riding on a rail, others have the misfortune to be ridden upon. And when they run over a man that is walking in his sleep, a supernumerary sleeper in the wrong position, and wake him up, they suddenly stop the cars, and make a hue and cry about it, as if this were an exception. I am glad to know that it takes a gang of men for every five miles to keep the sleepers down and level in their beds as it is, for this is a sign that they may sometime get up again.

[1854]

Developing the Synthesis Essay: Four Steps to Success

The preparation for writing a synthesis essay might seem challenging given all the reading and thinking you need to do, but it's not overwhelming. Like many tasks, it's easier to accomplish if you break it into manageable chunks. Here are four such manageable chunks, procedural stages that help you develop your synthesis essay:

1. Read and analyze the sources.
2. Generate two or three potential theses.
3. Have a "conversation" with the authors/creators of the sources.
4. Refine the thesis, decide on sources, and plan the arrangement of your essay.

1. Read and analyze the sources.

Read the sources carefully and analyze how the writer develops a thesis or take-home idea. Take notes as you read each source and ask yourself questions about each one:

- What is its central point, its take-home idea, about the issue at hand—in this case about nineteenth-century or contemporary attitudes about the benefits of train travel? Where does it get stated? How do you respond to it?
- What is actually *in* the source—what specific details or data are presented on the page or in the image—that you might cite as evidence in support of what you believe is its thesis or central argument?
- How can you "show your work"? That is, how can you explain the connections that you make between the source's evidence and your take-home idea?

Here are notes that Don wrote as he completed this first move in his synthesis essay. Notice how Don makes a comment about

- the central idea,
- the evidence, and
- his reasoning and thinking that connects the evidence to the central idea.

Don's Notes on the Sources

Dickinson, "I Like to See It Lap the Miles"

- The main idea is that the locomotive is a marvelous, fun invention that amuses the speaker, who begins the poem by expressing her pleasure about the train.
- The speaker personifies the train, giving it a tongue that allows it to "lap the mile" and "lick the valleys," eyes to "peer in shanties by the sides of roads," and a boastful attitude that leads it to "complain" as it descends the hill and "neigh like Boanerges"—the nickname Jesus gave to his disciples James and John, who were fiery preachers.
- My thinking—Anyone who takes such pleasure in an invention and contends that it can, like a race horse, be both "docile and omnipotent," must see it as a boon to its culture, in this case the culture of nineteenth-century America.

Hawthorne, From <u>The House of the Seven Gables</u>

- Hawthorne creates a very strong spokesperson for the spiritual and material benefits of the railroad in Clifford Pyncheon.
- Clifford sees in train travel a means to escape home life, which he associates with "[m]orbid influences" that "pollute the life of households." As Clifford puts it, the trains "give us wings; they annihilate the toil and dust of

pilgrimage; they spiritualize travel." "Why should" a person "make himself a prisoner for life in brick, and stone, and worm-eaten timber," Clifford asks, "when he may just as easily dwell, in one sense, nowhere, —in a better sense, wherever the fit and beautiful shall offer him a home?"

- Clifford is a complex, strange character, but his redemption at the end of the novel, when we find out that he was actually framed and was innocent of the crime that imprisoned him for 30 years, suggests that his attitudes about the benefits of train travel might be those that Hawthorne himself shared.

Krugman, "Stranded in Suburbia"

- Krugman mostly talks about the need for Americans to buy and drive cars that get good gas mileage, but he also advises Americans: "Don't drive them too much." He means that Americans should take more public transportation, presumably trains. He acknowledges, though, that public transportation systems are generally not popular with Americans.
- Some public transit systems have seen their ridership increase by 5 to 10 percent recently, yet "fewer than 5 percent of Americans take public transit to work." Plus, it's hard to sell the high cost of public transportation systems to Americans unless they are living in high-population density areas, and most Americans associate high-density living with "poverty and personal danger."
- The high cost of gasoline, the poor mileage of most American cars, the tendency of Americans to want to live away from high-density populations, and the unpopularity of public transportation all, unfortunately, will lead Americans to be less affluent and "stranded in suburbia."

Melrose, <u>Westward the Star of Empire Takes Its Way—Near Council Bluffs Iowa, 1867</u>

- The train, known as "The Star of the Empire," is an unwelcome intruder, one that disrupts nature and calls into question the morality of "progress."
- The light of the train seems to come mysteriously out of nowhere, and it confronts the viewer almost like a menace. The wild deer scatter, their habitat disturbed, but the field they run into is desolate: a single, spare cabin, trees with their limbs stripped, stumps of removed trees still visible.
- Assuming that the viewer held to a romantic view of nature as the source of all life, this painting conveys a decidedly negative view of the progress wrought by the railroads in the nineteenth century.

Reilly, "Is Light Rail the Answer to Transit Woes?"

- Despite purporting to show both pros and cons of contemporary light rail, Reilly seems to come down strongly on the pro side: "[S]upporters say the

(continued)

light rail line is worth it not only from the transportation aspect, but also for the environmental benefits . . ."

- Pros—Less traffic, less wasted gas/energy, reduced pollution. Cons—There's really only one—construction costs. Reality—As cities have cut budgets for public transportation, ridership in some areas has gone down.
- Reilly seems to imply that the cities should buck up and pay the high cost of constructing light rail—it seems to be an investment in both the quality of life and the quality of the environment in cities.

Thoreau, from Walden

- Thoreau sees the railroads as part of the general move to dehumanize life in the nineteenth century, to clutter up our lives with unnecessary details, to speed up our lives when we should be content with moving more slowly.
- "We do not ride on the railroad; it rides on us." And so on.
- The passage about "sleepers" is a bit confusing. Thoreau seems to characterize as "sleepers" those people who are content to stay at home and live the simple life. He implies that the prevailing sentiment in the industrializing economy at the time is that these "sleepers" need to be roused so they can build the railroads that the new nation needs. Yet the railroads, he suggests, actually destroy these honest "sleepers" on whom the railroads are built.

Whitman, "To a Locomotive in Winter"

- Whitman's speaker enthusiastically endorses the idea that the railroad is a strong emblem of progress in nineteenth-century America.
- After a long string of vivid visual images, comes this line: "Type of the modern! Emblem of motion and power! Pulse of the continent!" The second stanza begins "Fierce-throated beauty" and later praises the "thrill of shrieks" as "unpent, and glad, and strong."
- All these enthusiastically positive, robust, muscular images must point to Whitman's love of the locomotive.

ACTIVITY **Reading and Analyzing Sources**

Choose two of Don's sources—Reilly, Thoreau, Dickinson, Whitman, Hawthorne, Krugman, or Melrose—and read them yourself. Take your own notes on each source.

Watch the Video on Taking Notes at Your Pearson MyLab

2. Generate two or three potential theses.

Look back over the sources and your notes and generate two or three possible arguments or positions—your own potential theses/take-home ideas.

You might wonder why we recommend that you consider more than one possible thesis/take-home idea for your synthesis essay. Keeping possibilities open allows you the leeway to ponder several potential paths and helps you resist the temptation to hone in on an obvious thesis immediately, perhaps oversimplifying your topic and argument. Following are three central ideas that Don decided he could develop well using the sources to create his argument.

Don's Potential Theses

- The growth of the railroads and train travel drew very mixed responses in the art and literature of nineteenth-century America, and these diverse responses are mirrored in contemporary attitudes about rail travel.
- The poetry of nineteenth-century America generally embraced the railroads as symbols of strength and success; today, however, rail travel seems to inspire no artistic, poetic responses.
- Nineteenth-century American writing and art saw in the railroads a threat of dehumanization and destruction, and some contemporary responses to the railroads echo that thought in their concern about clearing land and property to make way for the railroads.

ACTIVITY **Evaluating Potential Thesis Statements**

In a discussion with a classmate or in a group, evaluate which of the potential central ideas you find most approachable and appealing as a possible reader of Don's essay.

3. Have a "conversation" with the authors/creators of the sources.

Imagine that you need to present each of your possible theses to the authors/creators of the sources. Have an imaginary conversation with the authors/creators of the sources. Would the author/creator agree with your position? How do you know? After your "discussion" with the authors/creators, do you want to qualify your theses some way? How and why?

This vital step helps you look at your sources not simply as wells that you can dip into, but more as foundations for your critical inquiry. The point is to make the sources work for you and your developing position rather than just inserting a source's information into an essay. As you consider whether the writer or artist would think your argument fair or complete, you adjust your thinking, find new reasons, produce qualifications. If you can take the time to have these brief conversations with your sources, you will not only develop a thesis/take-home idea with a good argumentative edge (see Move 4), but you will also begin to develop strategies to synthesize and incorporate others' ideas into your own essay, not simply drop them in.

Here are Don's notes on his imaginary conversations with the sources' authors/creators about each of the possible theses.

Don's Notes on His "Conversations" with the Sources' Authors

Potential Thesis 1

The growth of the railroads and train travel drew very mixed responses in the art and literature of nineteenth-century America, and these diverse responses are mirrored in contemporary attitudes about rail travel.

- Dickinson: By and large, her response to railroads was positive and enthusiastic, although if you look closely at the poem, you might detect a note of concern about the trains, which "supercilious, peer/In shanties," or poor people's houses, and the train does bellow out a "horrid, hooting stanza."
- Hawthorne: Though Clifford Pyncheon welcomes the train as a means to escape the deadness of his old home, and while Hawthorne's speaker seems to embrace the idea that trains give new freedoms to travelers, Hawthorne does introduce the character of the old man who converses with Clifford and calls into question the need to stray far from home, an idea that echoes in the passage from "Walden" as well.
- Krugman: Krugman's attitude toward trains is quite positive, but he acknowledges the problems their promoters have today in a culture that seems to encourage living in low-density suburbs rather than high-density urban areas.
- Melrose: The artist sees lots to fear in the railroads—disruption of nature and destruction of property.
- Reilly: This is the better mixed-attitude piece of the two contemporary articles. The author consciously wants us to consider both the pros and cons of light rail.
- Thoreau: He has no use for the railroads at all and sees them as a dehumanizing influence.
- Whitman: Even more than in Dickinson's poem, the speaker here is spellbound by the train—completely taken in by it—so there's no mixed message whatsoever.

Potential Thesis 2

The poetry of nineteenth-century America generally embraced the railroads as symbols of strength and success; today, however, rail travel seems to inspire no artistic, poetic responses.

- Dickinson: Of course, nearly all of the poem's images of the train resonate with strength and the idea of success.
- Hawthorne: Since it's not poetry, it doesn't fit with this thesis.
- Krugman: Unless you consider small automobiles as varieties of contemporary art—and it wouldn't be too much of a stretch to do so—there's really no artistic response in Krugman to the contemporary transportation situation.
- Melrose: Well, this painting is almost Romantic in its imagery—look at the colors and the relatively "fuzzy" images of the deer, the misshapen trees, and the abandoned cottage. In a stretch, you could see this picture as a poetic symbol, but certainly not of strength and success.
- Reilly: The only connection to art and poetry in this piece rests in its references to environmentalism. The picture of a Tucson streetcar that accompanies the article is not particularly artistic or poetic.
- Thoreau: Since it's not poetry, it doesn't fit with the thesis—although the writing is downright poetic in places, and it doesn't sound completely like an expository essay. But whatever the case, Thoreau would not take to the idea that the railroads are symbols of strength and success.
- Whitman: But of course! The train is a strong, robust animal, forging its way through the growing nation and helping it prosper.

Potential Thesis 3

Nineteenth-century American writing and art saw in the railroads a threat of dehumanization and destruction, and some contemporary responses to the railroads echo that thought in their concern about clearing land and property to make way for the railroads.

- Dickinson: The speaker of this poem would not completely concur with this idea, though some images in the poem—of the train "paring" through a quarry, for example—could be read as destructive.
- Hawthorne: The old man with whom Clifford is speaking certainly suggests that a person needs to enjoy the comforts of home: "[W]hat can be better for a man than his own parlor and chimney?" So the old man sees Clifford's great enthusiasm for rail travel as inhumane and nonsensical.

(continued)

- Krugman: Krugman really doesn't speak to the issue of what property would need to be taken over (taken away from someone?) if light rail systems were to be built.
- Melrose: This picture speaks strongly to this potential thesis. Pretty much all the images in the picture are of impending death (the poor deer!) and destruction—the trees, the abandoned cottage—brought about by the approach of the train.
- Reilly: The "big con" in this article is "construction, construction, construction," which Reilly approaches only through the issue of cost. She doesn't mention the issue of clearing land and property to make way for light rail. She does, however, praise light rail systems for having a better track record for controlling garbage than bus stops.
- Thoreau: Wow. The excerpt from Walden speaks strongly to this thesis. The railroads force us to wake up the "sleepers," the common folk in the nation, and then the railroad companies exploit these people, getting them to build the railroads, but essentially killing the "sleepers" by building the railroad on them.
- Whitman: There's nothing destructive or dehumanizing here. The speaker casts the locomotive as a powerful, strong life force. There are no humans involved, but there's nothing dehumanizing either.

4. Refine the thesis, decide on sources, and plan the arrangement of your essay.

Refine and revise the thesis/take-home idea that you will develop in your synthesis essay. Consider which of the sources seems most helpful, how you'll integrate them into your big idea, and how you might arrange the evidence you've gathered from your reading.

After looking through his potential theses and his conversations with each of the seven sources, Don decided that his strongest synthesis essay could be constructed using the first potential thesis:

Potential Thesis 1

The growth of the railroads and train travel drew very mixed responses in the art and literature of nineteenth century America, and these diverse responses are mirrored in contemporary attitudes about rail travel.

Looking back over his notes about the conversations, however, he decided that the thesis wasn't quite clear enough: "mixed responses" and "diverse responses"

Watch Taking Notes at Your Pearson MyLab

bothered him because they seemed too vague and abstract. So he crafted a new thesis/take-home idea that he thought would be more forceful and direct:

Final Thesis

While nineteenth-century poets such as Emily Dickinson and Walt Whitman seemed to embrace train travel—especially its most visible emblem, the locomotive—as a powerful symbol of success and progress, one can detect some ambivalence about the power of the railroads in Dickinson's poetry and a great deal of it in other works of art and literature at the time, an ambivalence that still lurks behind the generally optimistic accounts of commentators in our own time.

ACTIVITY **Revising a Thesis**

Follow Don's example: Consider an argumentative paper that you're working on right now or that you have recently completed. Take a look back at your thesis—that part of the paper where you commit to develop a central idea. In a discussion with a classmate or in a group, evaluate the degree to which the thesis might benefit from some clarification, sharpening, and revision.

Before beginning to draft his essay, Don considered which of the two arrangement patterns described in Chapter 5, the six-part-oration model or the Rogerian model, would be more appropriate for this assignment.

Don's Notes on Arrangement

I think I should use the six-part-oration model. Unlike the topic used in the sample assignment in Chapter 5—whether corporations should be allowed to advertise in schools—the topic of writers' attitudes toward the railroads in the nineteenth century doesn't really invite the writer to find a common ground with the readers. This topic seems more like a straightforward academic argument, not a public policy one, and so I think the more direct six-part-oration model will work better.

A Draft Synthesis Essay

On the next page is a draft of the synthesis essay that Don wrote after carrying out the four steps described above, along with our comments about how Don crafts his argument in the composition.

Don Worthington

Railroads in the U.S., Then and Now:
Progress or Problems?

Don provides context and explains how the topic is still important.

This sentence provides background.

Don moves to break up the topic and focus on one idea.

It would be an understatement to say that the development of railroads radically altered both the economy and culture of the United States in the nineteenth century, and many people apparently hope that the development of new rail projects—notably light rail—will have a similarly transformative effect on the contemporary American scene. Rail transportation had such a high profile in the middle and late nineteenth century that it attracted the attention of poets, novelists, essayists, and painters; today it attracts the attention primarily of urban planners, economists, and journalists. While nineteenth-century poets such as Emily Dickinson and Walt Whitman seemed to embrace train travel—especially its most visible emblem, the locomotive—as a powerful symbol of success and progress, one can detect some ambivalence about the power of the railroads in Dickinson's poetry and a great deal of it in other works of art and literature at the time, an ambivalence that still lurks behind the generally optimistic accounts of commentators in our own time.

Don provides background about railroads in nineteenth-century America.

Following the boom period of railroad expansion, roughly from the 1830s through the 1860s, Americans could look back over an array of changes that train travel brought about. Just in terms of speed and efficiency, the railroads easily overtook the two modes of transportation that had dominated the American scene prior to 1830, the stagecoach and canals. Not only could people move from one location to another more quickly (and usually more safely and cleanly) but so could goods and services—everything from farm produce to textiles to the United States Mail. Commerce could grow more readily, and friends and families did not need to worry about having to say a final good-bye simply because someone moved to a distant locale. (See www.ushistory.org/us/25b.asp.) In the same spirit, some nineteenth-century writers embraced the railroads, seeing in them a kind of robust, muscular enterprise that was destined to help the nation and its people prosper.

What could possibly be wrong with such a rosy scenario? Two potential problems caused by the expansion of the railroads generally surfaced in literature and commentary from nineteenth-century American thinkers, and both had to do with disruption. Some artists and writers were obviously troubled by the fact that constructing railroad lines, especially through rural regions, damaged the physical and spiritual beauty of the country. On a more philosophical level, some people could not hide their concern that the construction of the railroads disrupted the calmness and sanctity of home life that prevailed in early American society. It is interesting to note that these two concerns still surface when thinkers in our own time consider the expansion of light rail travel.

Don shifts from *status quo* thinking to problems that he will address. He shows each writer's stance and then calls that stance into question.

Don develops his thesis by talking about the two meanings of *disruption* that he sees in works of literature and art.

Two nineteenth-century American poets seem to capture these schools of thought about the railroads. Composed around 1876, Walt Whitman's poem "To a Locomotive in Winter" exclusively embraces the optimistic view. Whitman's speaker enthusiastically endorses the idea that the railroad is a strong emblem of progress in nineteenth-century America. After a long string of vivid visual images, the speaker exclaims his praise for the locomotive: "Type of the modern! Emblem of motion and power! Pulse of the continent!" The second stanza amplifies this theme, calling the train a "[f]ierce-throated beauty" and praising the "thrill of shrieks" as "unpent, and glad, and strong." All these enthusiastically positive, robust, muscular images must point to Whitman's love of the locomotive.

Don uses direct evidence from the primary text (Whitman) with commentary to show how the cited material relates to the thesis.

Composed around 1862, Emily Dickinson's poem "The Railway Train"—also known by its first line, "I like to see it lap the miles"—is slightly more ambivalent. The poem embodies the idea that the locomotive is a marvelous, fun invention that amuses the speaker. The speaker personifies the train, giving it a tongue that allows it to "lap the miles" and "lick the valleys," eyes to "peer in shanties by the sides of roads," and a boastful attitude that leads it to "complain" as it descends the hill and "neigh like Boanerges"—the nickname Jesus gave to his disciples James and John, who

Don didn't know what "Boanerges" meant, so he looked it up.

were fiery preachers. One might think that any poet who takes such pleasure in an invention and contends that it can, like a race horse, be both "docile and omnipotent," must see it as a boon to its culture, in this case the culture of nineteenth-century America. Yet the speaker of "I like to see it lap the miles" also gives glimpses of an attitude of fear and apprehension at the sheer power of the train: The locomotive can "pare" a quarry "[t]o fit its sides." It screams in a "horrid, hooting stanza."

A transition contrasts the treatment of the railroad in the two poems with its treatment in other nineteenth-century literature and art.

The apprehension about the potential destructiveness of the railroads is played out more blatantly in other pieces of nineteenth-century art and literature. For example, Andrew Melrose's painting *Westward the* Star of Empire *Takes Its Way—Near Council Bluffs Iowa, 1867* depicts the train, known as "The Star of the Empire," as an unwelcome intruder, one that disrupts nature and calls into question the morality of "progress." The light of the train seems to come mysteriously out of nowhere, and it confronts the viewer like a menace. The wild deer scatter, their habitat disturbed, and scamper into a field, but it is desolate: a single, spare cabin, trees with their limbs stripped, stumps of removed trees still visible. To anyone adhering to a romantic view of nature as being the source of all life, this painting conveys a decidedly negative view of the progress wrought by the railroads in the nineteenth century.

Don's development pattern at work again: Evidence plus commentary.

A slightly different take on the destructiveness of the railroads is evident in Henry David Thoreau's *Walden,* published in 1854. Thoreau sees the railroads as part of the general move to dehumanize life in the nineteenth century, to clutter up our lives with unnecessary details, to speed up our lives when we should be content with moving more slowly. Shortly after Thoreau's famous quotation from this chapter—"Simplicity, simplicity, simplicity!"—he launches into a brief sermon about the railroads:

A transition contrasting the new Thoreau material with the material Don just finished describing.

> If we do not get out sleepers, and forge rails, and devote days and nights to the work, but go to tinkering upon our lives to improve them, who will build the railroads? And if railroads are not

built, how shall we get to heaven in season? But if we stay at home and mind our business, who will want railroads? We do not ride on the railroad; it rides on us.

In short, Thoreau questions whether the need for rail travel is actually more important than living a calm, simple life at home.

The development pattern again: direct evidence followed by commentary.

Ironically, this same tension between being able to travel inexpensively and efficiently versus choosing to live in a comfortable, uncluttered setting is played out in contemporary thinking about rail travel. For example, the prize-winning economist Paul Krugman, writing in 2008, argues that Americans should buy and drive cars that get good gas mileage, but he also adds that they should not "drive them too much"—by which he means that Americans should take more public transportation, presumably trains. He acknowledges, though, that public transportation systems are generally not popular with Americans. He notes that some public transit systems have seen their ridership increase by 5 to 10 percent recently, yet "fewer than 5 percent of Americans take public transit to work." Plus, it's hard to sell the high cost of public transportation systems to Americans unless they are living in high-population-density urban areas, and most Americans associate high-density living with "poverty and personal danger." Krugman concludes, therefore, that the high cost of gasoline, the poor mileage of most American cars, the tendency of Americans to want to live away from high-density populations, and the unpopularity of public transportation all, unfortunately, will lead Americans to be less affluent and "stranded in suburbia." So while Thoreau implicitly suggested that Americans should simplify their lives, stay home, and not take trains, Krugman notes that economic circumstances in our own times may actually force a simpler lifestyle on consumers because they do not want to live in regions where train travel is feasible and affordable.

Don uses the adverb *ironically* to signal his transition from the nineteenth-century material to the contemporary piece by Krugman: It's ironic that this issue from the nineteenth-century is still with us today.

Notice how Krugman's ideas are linked to those that Don focused on in Thoreau's work.

The essays and artworks about train travel from the nineteenth century and the present collectively show that

Don addresses the "so what" question by letting readers know that this issue will continue to be important, and offers a sound of finality.

any aspect of technology—any machine created to make the lives of human beings better—nearly always affects these human beings' lives in more ways than they might imagine. The choice of whether and why to support the expansion of rail travel is just as important for today's Americans as it was for our forebears over a century ago.

You can see that Don's draft uses sources thoroughly and well. In synthesis essays for an Advanced Placement Language and Composition course, sources are often provided by the teacher, and the student uses those sources with a minimal citation system (often indicating the source by author's name or a letter in parenthesis after quoted material).

If Don were writing a more formal essay, he would include a listing of Works Cited (if he was following the Modern Language Association [MLA] style) or References (if he was following the American Psychological Association [APA] style). Please consult Appendix 3 for a brief primer on using the MLA citation style in researched essays. Similarly, if Don were producing a more formal essay, he would take another step in his final revision and editing by making sure he had page numbers, quotations, and publication information complete and in correct order.

ACTIVITY Revising Don's Draft

In his draft, Don concentrates on his own argument and on developing it through the sources, rather than making the sources the primary focus, and that's a major strength of Don's essay. In a discussion with a classmate or a group, consider now how Don might go about making changes in his draft if he were continuing to work toward writing a very polished, finished essay rather than a timed or less formal essay. He wants to make sure his own argument is primary throughout the essay. He wants to write so that readers are interested in the argument and its development and that, by the end of the essay, they are persuaded that he has located useful, relevant material in his sources to support his position. Are there places where the reader gets lost? Would another quote be useful somewhere? Is there a place where more analysis of the text Don cites would make his argument more convincing?

CHAPTER WRITING ASSIGNMENT
A Synthesis Project

You've read Don's process and early ideas about how to create a good essay evaluating and analyzing a number of sources to come up with his own perspective on an issue. This kind of research process is one you will engage in often throughout a college career. Knowing how to assemble, analyze, and evaluate data, opinions, and experiences is useful in almost any occupation as well.

Here's a synthesis project to work with, following some of Don's methods of gathering, conversing, listing, and commenting that helped him locate evidence and create arguments. Like Don's project, this one is rooted in American history and literature and the continuing issues that concern American culture today.

From the time colonies were established in North America, people questioned and debated how to use the land they had begun to inhabit. Is the land a bounty to take and use? Should it be protected for others or for posterity? With environmental issues surfacing dramatically in the late twentieth century, the issue of land use and land ownership has become a subject of political debate and community concern.

Locate one land use issue in local, national, or international news during the past several years. (You might consider debates such as the Alaskan pipeline, offshore drilling in North Carolina and Texas, the oil spills off the coast of Louisiana, or governmental support for national parks as possibilities). Then evaluate the perspectives on the use of the land by examining the historical perspectives of at least four of the following writers, all located in the anthology in this text.

William Bradford
James Fenimore Cooper
Margaret Fuller
Rachel Carson
Andrew Jackson
William Apess
Alice Yang Murray
Franklin Roosevelt

Write a well-reasoned and well-researched essay that uses historical perspectives to evaluate the complexities of land use as you see those perspectives reflected in the current issue you investigate.

CHAPTER CHECKLIST
Synthesis Essay

- [ ] Have you read, analyzed, and taken notes on each of your sources?
- [ ] Have you developed two or three potential theses for your synthesis essay?
- [ ] Have you had an imaginary conversation with the author of each of your sources about your theses to develop your ideas further?
- [ ] Have you revised and finalized your thesis and decided which sources to use?
- [ ] Have you arranged your synthesis essay effectively?
- [ ] Have you drafted your essay?
- [ ] Have you revised and proofread your essay?

Complete the Chapter 6 Exercise at Your Pearson MyLab

chapter 7

Sentences

What You Will Learn

- To identify and analyze the elements, structure, and rhetorical effects of sentences
- To use the elements and structures of sentences rhetorically in your own writing

So far in this part of the book, we've met the challenge of some pretty complex questions:

- How do you read rhetorically?
- What is the traditional art of rhetoric, and how does knowing it well help you become a better reader and writer?
- How do you read and write analytically?
- How do you to write argumentatively?
- How do you synthesize sources into your own argument and write argumentative synthesis essays?

Now we come to a question that connects to all the others and, in some ways, represents the question students should concentrate on at every stage of learning to read and write effectively, from elementary school through graduation from college and beyond: How can I write excellent sentences?

Wait a minute! The *sentence,* you say? Haven't we been talking all along about reading essays, novels, stories, poems, and plays? Haven't we been concentrating on writing analytic papers, argumentative essays, and synthesis essays? Now we're going back to the *sentence?*

Indeed, we are. Even though we've completed six chapters about reading and writing, you know you're not "done" with learning to read and write well.

The late Supreme Court Justice Louis Brandeis was famous for this saying: "There is no great writing, only great rewriting." We might extend that aphorism: "There is good reading, but there's even better rereading." And we maintain that understanding how sentences work can help you rewrite your good sentences into great sentences and convert your good reading to a great rereading. As the basic unit of thought, the sentence packs a lot of power, and the more you concentrate on reading sentences well and writing them thoughtfully, the more you develop power as a "rhetorical composer," a creative and conscious thinker.

We'll begin this chapter by unpacking some basic principles of *sentence architecture,* how sentences work. Then we'll show you how to use these principles to write a variety of sentences for different kinds of texts and purposes and to read sentences analytically by examining the choices writers made when they composed them.

How Sentences Work: Eight Principles of Sentence Architecture

Principle 1

There are three basic sentence forms: subject-verb (S-V), subject-verb-object (S-V-O), and subject-linking verb-complement (S-LV-C).

Here's a simple experiment: Look around and describe what you perceive. Perhaps you're in the reading room of a library. Here is the scene:

A guy snores.

A girl does her homework.

Another guy seems confused.

What you have observed is not only a pretty accurate representation of what goes on in library reading rooms, but it also demonstrates that, in English, there are only three forms of sentences:

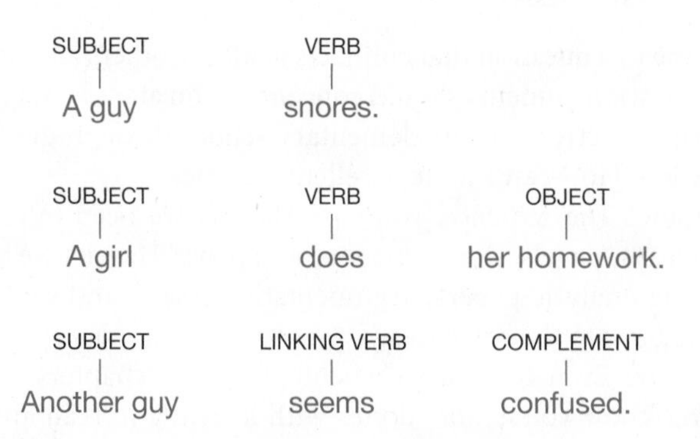

Let's call these three forms "core sentences." Here's bit more information about their component parts.

- The **subject** answers the question "who or what is doing something?"

  Albert Pujols is the first baseman.

- The **verb** is what the subject is doing, thinking, being, or becoming.

  Albert Pujols carried the glove.

- A special type of verb, a **linking verb**, expresses the last two items in that list, being or becoming.

  Albert Pujols is the first baseman.

- The **complement** is the thing or condition that the subject is being or becoming. Some complements are people or things:

  Albert Pujols is the first baseman. His equipment is a first-baseman's glove.

  Some complements are conditions:

  Albert Pujols will be delighted.

- The **object** is the answer to "who or what is having something done to him/her/it?"

  Albert Pujols carried the glove.

ACTIVITY **Writing Core Sentences**

As a "warm-up," write your own versions of the three types of core sentences described above. Keep them handy for building and practice throughout your work with this chapter.

Principle 2

The two major players in all sentences are nouns and verbs.

Subjects, objects, and complements—when they are people or things, not conditions—are generally **nouns**. Subjects do things. Objects have actions done to them. Complements essentially rename subjects. **Verbs** either express what these subjects do or link them to people, things, or conditions.

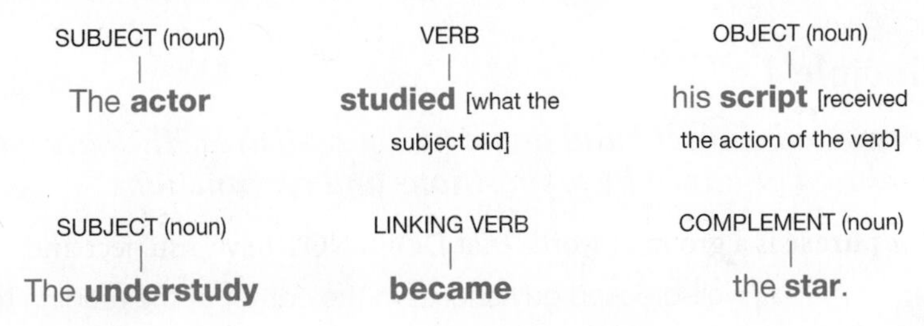

Therefore, in our system of sentence architecture, so far we have two "players": nouns and verbs. Pretty simple, eh?

Principle 3

Two modifiers—adjectives and adverbs—alter, change, or modify other components.

Now let's consider the elements of a sentence that affect other components in some way, the **modifiers**. Any component that modifies the subject, the complement when it is a person or thing and not a condition, or the object is an **adjective**.

Consider these sentences:

> A well-dressed guy snores. [*Well-dressed* is an adjective. It modifies *guy.*]
>
> A tall guy seems confused. [*Tall* is an adjective modifying *guy.*]
>
> A young girl does her calculus homework. [*Young* is an adjective modifying *girl. Calculus* is an adjective modifying *homework.*]

Any component that modifies the verb, the linking verb, or the complement when it is a condition and not a person or thing is an **adverb**. Now let's build these sentences a bit more with adverbs:

> A well-dressed guy snores loudly. [*Loudly* is an adverb modifying *snores.*]
>
> A tall guy apparently seems terribly confused. [*Apparently* is an adverb modifying *seems. Terribly* is an adverb modifying *confused.*]
>
> A young girl diligently does her calculus homework. [*Diligently* is an adverb modifying *does.*]

So now what do we have in our sentence architecture inventory? Two players, **nouns** and **verbs**; and two modifiers, **adjectives** and **adverbs** that change, alter, or modify other components.

ACTIVITY **Using Adjectives and Adverbs**

Return to the three core sentences you wrote. Add adjectives and adverbs to them and explain to a classmate or members of a group how your additions changed the sentences.

Principle 4

Phrases and clauses build and develop sentences. They are often introduced or joined by prepositions and conjunctions.

- A **phrase** is a group of words that DOES NOT have a subject and a verb.

> A well-dressed guy snores in the corner of the reading room.

- A **clause** is a group of words that DOES have a subject and a verb.

  After **she asks** her friend for advice, a young **girl** diligently **does** her calculus homework.

- A **preposition** is a word that introduces a phrase, called a **prepositional phrase**. Common prepositions are *of, to, from, for,* and *in*.

  A well-dressed guy snores **in** the corner **of** the reading room.

  Albert Pujols was the first baseman **for** the St. Louis Cardinals.

- A **conjunction** is a word that either joins together components in a sentence or introduces a clause. Common conjunctions are *and, but, yet, when, which, either, or, neither,* and *nor.*

  Albert Pujols was delighted **and** relieved **when** he signed a new contract.

  "When he signed a new contract" is a clause. It's called a **dependent clause** because it can't stand by itself. Say "when he signed a new contract" aloud. Can you hear that it's an incomplete expression, not a complete sentence? *When* at the beginning of that clause is a conjunction that introduces the dependent clause "when he signed a new contract." "Albert Pujols was delighted and relieved" is also a clause, but it's an **independent clause** since it can stand on its own as a complete sentence. *A dependent clause always needs an independent clause to hook onto.*

Let's summarize our system of sentence architecture so far. We have

- Two players, nouns and verbs
- Two modifiers, adjectives and adverbs
- Two building blocks, phrases and clauses
- Two introducers/joiners, prepositions and conjunctions

ACTIVITY **Using Prepositional Phrases and Dependent Clauses**

Return to the core sentences to which you added adjectives and adverbs. To each sentence, add either a prepositional phrase or a dependent clause and then explain to a classmate or a group how your additions change the sentences.

Principle 5

Three other types of phrases, infinitive, gerund, and participial, are introduced by verb forms.

Verbs can take several forms. Consider, for example, the regular verb *assist* and the irregular verbs *hide, ring,* and *burst,* as shown in Figure 7.1.

Infinitive	Simple Present	Simple Past	Present Participle	Past Participle
		Regular Verbs		
to assist	assist	assisted	assisting	assisted
		A Few Irregular Verbs		
to hide	hide	hid	hiding	hid
to ring	ring	rang	ringing	rung
to burst	burst	burst	bursting	burst

FIGURE 7.1

The infinitive, the present participle, and the past participle forms of verbs introduce three types of phrases:

- An **infinitive phrase** consists of *to + verb + optional other components,* usually a complement or an object.

  To daydream is considered by some as a waste of time.

  Keisha wanted her team to be ranked first nationally.

  He laughed to show his discomfort at the inappropriate remark.

- A **gerund** is the present participle form of a verb that serves as a noun. A **gerund phrase** consists of a *gerund + optional other elements,* usually a complement or an object.

  Daydreaming is considered by some as a waste of time.

  Keisha is good at daydreaming about her team's success.

- A **participial phrase** consists of *present participle or past participle + optional other components,* usually a complement or an object.

  He laughed loudly, showing his discomfort at the inappropriate remark.

  Shown the photographs of the crime scene, the witness broke down and cried.

  Being a perfectionist, Keisha practices several hours each day.

ACTIVITY **Using Infinitive, Gerund, and Participial Phrases**

Return to the original versions of the core sentences you wrote earlier. Rewrite one or more of the nouns as an infinitive phrase or a gerund phrase. Add a participial phrase to one or more of the sentences. Explain to a classmate or a group how your additions change the sentences.

Principle 6

Words, phrases, and clauses can be players, acting as nouns; and they can be modifiers, acting as adjectives or adverbs.

This principle is a little tricky. Both of the building blocks, phrases and clauses, can act as nouns, just as single words can. Consider the following sentences:

> He promised results. [A single word is acting as a noun acting as an object.]
>
> He promised to achieve results. [An infinitive phrase is acting as a noun acting as an object.]
>
> He promised that he would achieve results. [A clause is acting as a noun acting as an object.]

Here are three more sentences:

> His claims rubbed people the wrong way. [A single word is a noun acting as the subject.]
>
> Claiming victory over his opponents rubbed people the wrong way. [*Claiming victory* is a gerund phrase acting as a noun acting as the subject.]
>
> That he claimed victory over his opponents rubbed people the wrong way. [*That he claimed victory* is a dependent clause acting as a noun acting as the subject.]

Both of the building blocks, phrases and clauses, can act as adverbs and adjectives, just as single words can. Consider these sentences:

> Our guest arrived.
>
> Our guest arrived late. [*Late* is an adverb modifying *arrived.*]
>
> Our guest arrived after dinner. [*After dinner* is a prepositional phrase acting as an adverb modifying *arrived.*]
>
> Our guest arrived after we had eaten dinner. [*After we had eaten dinner* is a dependent clause acting as an adverb modifying *arrived.*]

Now consider four more examples of the same type of core sentence:

> Our guest arrived.
>
> Our honored guest arrived. [*Honored* is a single-word adjective modifying *guest.*]
>
> Our guest with a red cape arrived. [*With a red cape* is a prepositional phrase acting as an adjective modifying *guest.*]
>
> Our guest who was wearing a red cape arrived. [*Who was wearing a red cape* is a dependent clause acting as an adjective modifying *guest.*]

ACTIVITY **Using Phrases and Clauses as Nouns and Modifiers**

Return again to the original versions of your core sentences. For one of the nouns, rewrite it as a phrase and then rewrite it again as a clause. With one of your sentences, add modifiers in the form of a word, and then a phrase, and then a clause.

Principle 7

Pronouns stand in for nouns.

A **pronoun** is simply a word that can take the place of a noun or noun phrase.

A well-dressed guy snores loudly.

He snores loudly. [*He*, a pronoun, stands in for a *well-dressed guy.*]

We could say, "A young girl diligently does her calculus homework, hoping to complete *it*." *It* is a pronoun; saying *it* allows us not to have to repeat *calculus homework*.

For convenience of reference in our system of sentence architecture, let's tuck pronouns in beside nouns in our category of players.

Principle 8

The combining principle: All the elements in our system of sentence architecture can multiply and combine so that we can have core sentences with lots of modifying components, compound sentences with clauses that can themselves serve as complete sentences, complex sentences that have one independent and one dependent clause, or some combination of all these conditions.

English is a very constructive, generative language. The shortest sentence anyone can create would be two words—for example, *She tried*. Even the single word, *Surrender*, is a sentence, because the subject is the understood and unstated word *You*. The longest sentence possible in English is impossible to describe. So long as the creator of it introduced and joined the elements of the sentence correctly, there is no limit to how long such a sentence would be. It's easiest to see Principle 8, which we call the "combining principle," at work in actual samples of sentences, such as those we'll analyze, write, and rewrite in the activities that follow.

How Sentences Work: A Summary of the Eight Principles of Sentence Architecture

Let's summarize our system of the eight principles of sentence architecture. We have

1. Three core sentence types: subject–verb, subject–verb–object, and subject–linking verb–complement

2. Two players: nouns and verbs
3. Two modifiers: adjectives and adverbs
4. Two building blocks: phrases and clauses
5. Two introducers/joiners: prepositions and conjunctions
6. Phrases and clauses acting as nouns and modifiers
7. Pronouns standing in for nouns
8. The combining principle: an infinite number of ways to put together sentence elements

Putting the Principles to Work I: "Grammar Calisthenics"

If you've ever been an athlete, or even if you have taken a physical education class, you're probably familiar with calisthenics—a fancy name for exercises like push-ups, sit-ups, jumping jacks, and squat thrusts. If you had a good coach or a good teacher, he or she probably explained to you that no one does calisthenics just for the sake of doing exercises. On the contrary, one does calisthenics to build strength, agility, and endurance for other activities—such as playing a sport or simply living a longer, healthier life.

Equipped with the eight principles of sentence architecture, you as a growing, developing writer can do "grammar calisthenics," again not simply for the sake of doing the exercises but instead for this purpose: to see for yourself (and for others who might read your work) how manipulating the components of a sentence gives you the opportunity to ask (a) which version of a sentence actually seems to work best for you, and (b) which version of a sentence would seem to be most effective rhetorically—that is, which version would most effectively flesh out the meaning, accomplish a purpose, or achieve an effect for specific readers in a particular situation.

Here is just one of many one sample grammar calisthenics routines:

- Write one simple sentence in the **SUBJECT–VERB–OBJECT** form:

  Albert Pujols won the Most Valuable Player award.

- Add a prepositional phrase used as an adjective:

  Albert Pujols of the St. Louis Cardinals won the Most Valuable Player award.

- Add a prepositional phrase used as an adverb:

  Albert Pujols of the St. Louis Cardinals won the Most Valuable Player award for the third time.

- Add an adjective clause someplace in the middle of the sentence:

  Albert Pujols of the St. Louis Cardinals, who achieved the Central Division title in 2009, won the Most Valuable Player award for the third time.

- Add an adverbial clause:

  Albert Pujols of the St. Louis Cardinals, who achieved the Central Division title in 2009, won the Most Valuable Player award for the third time, even though his team did not make it to the World Series.

- Move either the adverbial prepositional phrase or the adverbial clause to another place in the sentence and see what difference it makes rhetorically:

  a. Moving the adverbial prepositional phrase:

  For the third time, Albert Pujols of the St. Louis Cardinals, who achieved the Central Division title in 2009, won the Most Valuable Player award, even though his team did not make it to the World Series.

  b. Moving the adverbial clause:

  Even though his team did not make it to the World Series, Albert Pujols of the St. Louis Cardinals, who achieved the Central Division title in 2009, won the Most Valuable Player award for the third time.

- Add an introductory participial phrase:

  Displaying superb skills as a hitter, fielder, and base runner, Albert Pujols of the St. Louis Cardinals, who achieved the Central Division title in 2009, won the Most Valuable Player award for the third time, even though his team did not make it to the World Series.

- Change one of the nouns to a gerund phrase or an infinitive phrase:

  Displaying superb skills in hitting, fielding, and running bases, Albert Pujols of the St. Louis Cardinals, who achieved the Central Division title in 2009, won the Most Valuable Player award for the third time, even though his team did not make it to the World Series.

ACTIVITY Grammar Calisthenics

Here's a set of instructions for a Grammar Calisthenics exercise you can do on your own, with a partner, or in a group. Try the exercise using a piece that you're writing or a text that you're reading.

1. Start with a SUBJECT–VERB sentence.
2. Write another SUBJECT–VERB sentence and combine the two sentences into one sentence.
3. Add a single-word ADJECTIVE.
4. Add a single-word ADVERB.
5. Add a dependent clause acting as an ADVERB. Try it at the beginning of the sentence and then try it in the middle of the sentence. Explain which version is more effective and why.

6. Remove the dependent clause and rewrite it as an independent clause. Explain where you would put it in relation to the rest of the material you've created if it were to stand on its own. Now put it back in the sentence as a dependent clause again.
7. Change one of the nouns to an infinitive phrase or a gerund phrase.
8. Add a participial phrase somewhere in the sentence. Then move it somewhere else in the sentence and explain which placement you believe is most effective.

Putting the Principles to Work II: Grammatical Analysis in Support of Rhetorical Analysis

A second way you can use the eight principles of sentence architecture is to deconstruct the grammar or syntax in the sentences of texts you read, analyzing the choices an author has made, and then evaluating how effective those choices are—that is, how effectively they create meaning, accomplish a purpose, or achieve an effect.

What follows are the first two paragraphs of Brent Staples's essay, "Black Men and Public Spaces," which is reprinted in its entirety in Unit 5 of this book. We have separated and numbered the sentences in the first paragraph so we can demonstrate how to analyze the grammatical choices as rhetorical choices. Then we provide you with the second paragraph so you can analyze it similarly on your own.

Brent Staples

Black Men and Public Spaces

[1] My first victim was a woman—white, well dressed, probably in her early twenties. [2] I came upon her late one evening on a deserted street in Hyde Park, a relatively affluent neighborhood in an otherwise mean, impoverished section of Chicago. [3] As I swung onto the avenue behind her, there seemed to be a discreet, uninflammatory distance between us. [4] Not so. [5] She cast back a worried glance. [6] To her, the youngish black man—a broad six feet two inches with a beard and billowing hair, both hands shoved into the pockets of a bulky military jacket—seemed menacingly close. [7] After a few more quick glimpses, she picked up her pace and was soon running in earnest. [8] Within seconds she disappeared into a cross street.

Sample Grammatical Analysis

Sentence one This sentence is an example of the SUBJECT–LINKING VERB–COMPLEMENT form, and it begins so simply. But Staples makes an interesting move after the dash: he adds three modifiers, all ADJECTIVES, describing the woman—one a single word, the second a two-word phrase, the third a five-word phrase. This gradual unfolding of modifying details—one word, then two words, then five words—not only builds an effect of gradually accelerating doom, but it also sounds an awful lot like the way police officers do when they write reports or the way characters playing police officers sound on television.

Sentence two This sentence is an example of the SUBJECT–VERB–OBJECT form, and it very effectively gets those three elements into the sentence quickly so that it can add a whole string of vivid modifiers at the end. Notice that we're treating "come upon"—used here the past tense, "came upon"—as a two-word verb that's really acting like a one-word verb. You could substitute a verb like "encounter" or "approach" for it. So, in essence the first three words in the sentence are "I encountered her": SUBJECT–VERB–OBJECT. But now look what Staples does next: five phrases, all acting as ADVERBS, all providing details about where and when he came upon this woman. Putting all that descriptive detail at the end of a sentence, rather than the beginning or elsewhere, leaves the graphic detail fresh in the readers' minds as they move on to the next sentence.

Sentence three Look how cleverly Staples links this sentence to the previous one by starting with a dependent clause acting as an ADVERB. The clause shows his movement in relation to the woman's. The independent clause is a special type of the SUBJECT–VERB type. In a sentence that begins with "There," that word is almost never the subject. "There" is what is called an "expletive," a place-holder. The grammatical subject of the sentence is "distance," and notice how Staples uses the "There" device to move that word to the end of the sentence, accompanied by two evocative ADJECTIVES, "discreet" and "uninflammatory," and a prepositional phrase acting as an ADVERB, "between us."

Sentence four Wow. A two-word, intentional sentence fragment. Staples thought the distance between himself and the woman was "discreet" and "uninflammatory." This fragment announces loudly that he realizes he was wrong.

Sentence five The language of this sentence cautiously moves away from the two-word fragment that precedes it. It's a simple SUBJECT–VERB–OBJECT sentence—"She cast . . . a . . . glance"—with a single-word ADVERB, "back," and a single-word ADJECTIVE, "worried." Look at how Staples is now using his language choices to get inside the mind of the woman.

Sentence six This sentence is a prime example of how Principle 8, the combining principle, works. The core of this sentence is a simple SUBJECT–LINKING VERB–COMPLEMENT form: "the . . . man . . . seemed close." But look at the modifiers that get added: At the beginning, a prepositional phrase acting as an ADVERB, "To her," allowing us to see Staples getting into her head. Then two ADJECTIVES that Staples uses about himself—"youngish" and "black." It's almost as if Staples is saying, "Who could be afraid of me? I'm just an ordinary, young African-American man." But look at the details he packs between the two dashes: a phrase describing his build, his hair, and his beard, and a dependent clause showing him with his hands not visible but "shoved into the pockets of a bulky military jacket." Suddenly we're inside the woman's mind ourselves: Why can't we see those hands? Does this man have a gun in his pocket? No wonder that Staples uses the evocative ADVERB "menacingly" to show the effect of his being so close to the woman.

Sentence seven Here's another great example of Principle 8. The main part of this sentence, "she picked up her pace and was soon running in earnest," could be written as two sentences: "She picked up her pace," a SUBJECT–VERB–OBJECT form, and "She was soon running in earnest," a SUBJECT–VERB form accompanied by a single-word ADVERB, "soon," and a prepositional phrase, "in earnest." But Staples combines them: The pace of his combined sentence emphasizes the hurry that the woman is in.

Sentence eight At its core, this is a simple SUBJECT–VERB form: "she disappeared." But Staples adds two little details to show how quickly this woman's panicked flight appeared and how shadowy the scene is. He begins with a prepositional phrase, acting as an ADVERB, and he ends with a prepositional phrase, also acting as an ADVERB.

ACTIVITY **Analyzing Grammar Rhetorically**

On your own or with a partner or in a group, do a grammatical analysis, leading to a rhetorical analysis, of each of the sentences in the second paragraph of Staples's essay.

> [1] That was more than a decade ago. [2] I was twenty-two years old, a graduate student newly arrived at the University of Chicago. [3] It was in the echo of that terrified woman's footfalls that I first began to know the unwieldy inheritance I'd come into—the ability to alter public space in ugly ways. [4] It was clear that she thought herself the quarry of a mugger, a rapist, or worse. [5] Suffering a bout of insomnia, however, I was stalking sleep, not defenseless wayfarers. [6] As a softy who is scarcely able to take a knife to a raw chicken—let alone hold it to a person's throat—I was surprised, embarrassed, and dismayed all at once. [7] Her flight made me feel like an accomplice in tyranny. [8] It also made it clear that I was indistinguishable from the muggers who occasionally seeped into the area from the surrounding ghetto. [9] That first encounter, and those that followed, signified that a vast, unnerving

gulf lay between nighttime pedestrians—particularly women—and me. [10] And I soon gathered that being perceived as dangerous is a hazard in itself. [11] I only needed to turn a corner into a dicey situation, or crowd some frightened, armed person in a foyer somewhere, or make an errant move after being pulled over by a policeman. [12] Where fear and weapons meet—and they often do in urban America—there is always the possibility of death.

CHAPTER ACTIVITY

Analyzing Grammar Rhetorically in a Text of Your Choice

Choose one of the essays, speeches, works of fiction, or poems in the units you've read so far, and find two or three sentences that are striking. Analyze the sentences as you've done above, pointing out the grammatical choices of the writer and discussing how and why those choices are effective.

CHAPTER CHECKLIST

Sentences

☐ Can you identify the eight principles of sentence architecture and use them in writing your own sentences?

- Three core sentence types: Subject–verb, subject–verb–object, and subject–linking verb–complement
- Two players: nouns and verbs
- Two modifiers: adjectives and adverbs
- Two building blocks: phrases and clauses
- Two introducers/joiners: prepositions and conjunctions
- Phrases and clauses acting as nouns and modifiers
- Pronouns standing in for nouns
- The combining principle: An infinite number of ways to combine sentence elements

☐ Have you analyzed a few sentences of a text you are reading to see how the author uses the elements of sentence architecture?

Complete the Chapter 7 Exercise at Your Pearson MyLab

part two

An Anthology of Readings and Images

This anthology is designed to follow a more or less chronological path from the beginnings of a literature of the American colonies to the literature of twenty-first-century texts, illustrating how ideas and forms shaped a dynamic American literature. Arranged in units, each group of texts confronts social, economic and cultural issues of the day and asks the big questions of land, people and policy that frames writers' rhetorical situations and strategies.

The texts you read represent an array of genres and are written by a wide variety of authors; civic leaders, preachers, statesmen, explorers, and women, people of color, indigenous people and others who claimed rhetorical space in the landscape.

The variety of voices and genres you find here—ancient and contemporary—helps you consider the essential questions that American literature continues to pose about individuals and communities, freedom and responsibility.

UNIT 1

This image is a digital creation that puts planet Earth on a background of binary numbers that ripple under the planet. The image comes from a web site called "dreamstime," which specializes in combining images of the stars and planets and digital data. It illustrates some of the technological advances in photography from space.

Read

1. What does the image suggest about the place of the United States in the world today?
2. What details contribute to the dream-like quality of the image?

Connect

1. What is the role of innovation as it is explored by texts in this unit?
2. How do the texts in the unit indicate a sense of the new nation's consciousness of itself in the world?

How Do We Become a Nation?

Pre-colonial Times to 1789

In the early European settlements in North America, people wondered about the future of the land as well as about the role of individuals and communities in creating that future. Indigenous Americans, many living in highly structured groups or nations, questioned their roles and their futures in the growing colonies. Colonists were forced to adjust to new circumstances in the small villages they built at the edges of the Wampanoag, Narragansett, Iroquois, and Croatan nations, questioning how to build and sustain a community.

For the first two centuries, the colonists in North America asked how they should go about building first a village, and then a colonial state, and finally a new country, just as indigenous peoples asked how they could sustain a nation, a village, and a people. Conflicting cultural, religious, economic, and social arrangements made relationships between the emerging nation and existing Indian nations difficult. The growing power of colonial states, backed by the nations in Europe, made their dominance almost a foregone conclusion. Still, the early encounters between Indians and settlers started a discussion of nationhood, civic responsibility among the citizenry, and the development of civic leadership that was to dominate actions and attitudes from the Colonial and Revolutionary War periods to early national government and expansion.

Keeping the big question in mind will help you give context to the plea of the Iroquois, the sermon of Winthrop, the speculation of Bradstreet, and the challenge of Franklin as you read their works. In one way or another, what was to become of the new land and its new—and ancient—peoples was a subject of wonder, hope, and fear for all.

GUIDING QUESTIONS

- How do we become a nation?
- Which experiments in living nurture the individual and the community?
- How does the land make a difference to experience?
- What is the role of religion in government?
- What does the community mean by freedom?

Texts and Visuals

Iroquois League

The Constitution of Five Nations of the Iroquois League, also known as the Great Binding Law, was formulated in the fifteenth century by five tribes—Cayuga, Mohawk, Oneida, Onondaga, and Seneca. It established laws and procedures for the large community in what is now the northeastern United States. Passed down orally for generations, the constitution was written in English language translation at the beginning of the twentieth century by Arthur Parker, a historian and ethnologist who is descended from the Iroquois. This excerpt gives 16 articles of the 117 that make up the document.

From *The Constitution of Five Nations*

The Council of the Great Peace

The Great Binding Law, Gayanashagowa

I am Dekanawidah and with the Five Nations' Confederate Lords I plant the Tree of the Great Peace. I plant it in your territory, Adodarhoh, and the Onondaga Nation, in the territory of you who are Firekeepers.

I name the tree the Tree of the Great Long Leaves. Under the shade of this Tree of the Great Peace we spread the soft white feathery down of the globe thistle as seats for you, Adodarhoh, and your cousin Lords.

We place you upon those seats, spread soft with the feathery down of the globe thistle, there beneath the shade of the spreading branches of the Tree of Peace. There shall you sit and watch the Council Fire of the Confederacy of the Five Nations, and all the affairs of the Five Nations shall be transacted at this place before you, Adodarhoh, and your cousin Lords, by the Confederate Lords of the Five Nations.

Roots have spread out from the Tree of the Great Peace, one to the north, one to the east, one to the south and one to the west. The name of these roots is The Great White Roots and their nature is Peace and Strength.

If any man or any nation outside the Five Nations shall obey the laws of the Great Peace and make known their disposition to the Lords of the Confederacy, they may trace the Roots to the Tree and if their minds are clean and they are obedient and promise to obey the wishes of the Confederate Council, they shall be welcomed to take shelter beneath the Tree of the Long Leaves. 5

We place at the top of the Tree of the Long Leaves an Eagle who is able to see afar. If he sees in the distance any evil approaching or any danger threatening he will at once warn the people of the Confederacy.

To you Adodarhoh, the Onondaga cousin Lords, I and the other Confederate Lords have entrusted the caretaking and the watching of the Five Nations Council Fire.

When there is any business to be transacted and the Confederate Council is not in session, a messenger shall be dispatched either to Adodarhoh, Honwirehtonh or Skanawatih, Fire Keepers, or to their War Chiefs with a full statement of the case desired to be considered. Then shall Adodarhoh call his cousin (associate) Lords together and consider whether or not the case is of sufficient importance to demand the attention of the Confederate Council. If so, Adodarhoh shall dispatch messengers to summon all the Confederate Lords to assemble beneath the Tree of the Long Leaves.

When the Lords are assembled the Council Fire shall be kindled, but not with chestnut wood, and Adodarhoh shall formally open the Council.

Then shall Adodarhoh and his cousin Lords, the Fire Keepers, announce the subject for discussion. 10

The Smoke of the Confederate Council Fire shall ever ascend and pierce the sky so that other nations who may be allies may see the Council Fire of the Great Peace.

Adodarhoh and his cousin Lords are entrusted with the Keeping of the Council Fire.

You, Adodarhoh, and your thirteen cousin Lords, shall faithfully keep the space about the Council Fire clean and you shall allow neither dust nor dirt to accumulate. I lay a Long Wing before you as a broom. As a weapon against a crawling creature I lay a staff with you so that you may thrust it away from the Council Fire. If you fail to cast it out then call the rest of the United Lords to your aid.

The Council of the Mohawk shall be divided into three parties as follows: Tekarihoken, Ayonhwhathah and Shadekariwade are the first party; Sharenhowaneh, Deyoenhegwenh and Oghrenghrehgowah are the second party, and Dehennakrineh, Aghstawenserenthah and Shoskoharowaneh are the third party. The third party is to listen only to the discussion of the first and second parties and if an error is made or the proceeding is irregular they are to call attention to it, and when the case is right and properly decided by the two parties they shall confirm the decision of the two parties and refer the case to the Seneca Lords for their decision. When the Seneca Lords have decided in accord with the Mohawk Lords, the case or question shall be referred to the Cayuga and Oneida Lords on the opposite side of the house.

I, Dekanawidah, appoint the Mohawk Lords the heads and the leaders of the Five Nations Confederacy. The Mohawk Lords are the foundation of the Great Peace and it shall, therefore, be against the Great Binding Law to pass measures in the Confederate Council after the Mohawk Lords have protested against them. 15

No council of the Confederate Lords shall be legal unless all the Mohawk Lords are present.

Whenever the Confederate Lords shall assemble for the purpose of holding a council, the Onondaga Lords shall open it by expressing their gratitude to their cousin Lords and greeting them, and they shall make an address and offer thanks to the earth where men dwell, to the streams of water, the pools, the springs and the lakes, to the maize and the fruits, to the medicinal herbs and trees, to the forest trees for their usefulness, to the animals that serve as food and give their pelts for clothing, to the great winds and the lesser winds, to the Thunderers, to the Sun, the mighty warrior, to the moon, to the messengers of the Creator who reveal his wishes and to the Great Creator who dwells in the heavens above, who gives all the things useful to men, and who is the source and the ruler of health and life.

Then shall the Onondaga Lords declare the council open.

The council shall not sit after darkness has set in.

The Firekeepers shall formally open and close all councils of the Confederate Lords, they shall pass upon all matters deliberated upon by the two sides and render their decision. 20

Every Onondaga Lord (or his deputy) must be present at every Confederate Council and must agree with the majority without unwarrantable dissent, so that a unanimous decision may be rendered.

If Adodarhoh or any of his cousin Lords are absent from a Confederate Council, any other Firekeeper may open and close the Council, but the Firekeepers present may not give any decisions, unless the matter is of small importance.

All the business of the Five Nations Confederate Council shall be conducted by the two combined bodies of Confederate Lords. First the question shall be passed upon by the Mohawk and Seneca Lords, then it shall be discussed and passed by the Oneida and Cayuga Lords. Their decisions shall then be referred to the Onondaga Lords (Fire Keepers) for final judgment.

The same process shall obtain when a question is brought before the council by an individual or a War Chief.

In all cases the procedure must be as follows: when the Mohawk and Seneca Lords have unanimously agreed upon a question, they shall report their decision to the Cayuga and Oneida Lords who shall deliberate upon the question and 25 report a unanimous decision to the Mohawk Lords. The Mohawk Lords will then report the standing of the case to the Firekeepers, who shall render a decision as they see fit in case of a disagreement by the two bodies, or confirm the decisions of the two bodies if they are identical. The Fire Keepers shall then report their decision to the Mohawk Lords who shall announce it to the open council.

If through any misunderstanding or obstinacy on the part of the Fire Keepers, they render a decision at variance with that of the Two Sides, the Two Sides shall reconsider the matter and if their decisions are jointly the same as before they shall report to the Fire Keepers who are then compelled to confirm their joint decision.

When a case comes before the Onondaga Lords (Fire Keepers) for discussion and decision, Adodarhoh shall introduce the matter to his comrade Lords who shall then discuss it in their two bodies. Every Onondaga Lord except Hononwiretonh shall deliberate and he shall listen only. When a unanimous decision shall have been reached by the two bodies of Fire Keepers, Adodarhoh shall notify Hononwiretonh of the fact when he shall confirm it. He shall refuse to confirm a decision if it is not unanimously agreed upon by both sides of the Fire Keepers.

No Lord shall ask a question of the body of Confederate Lords when they are discussing a case, question or proposition. He may only deliberate in a low tone with the separate body of which he is a member.

When the Council of the Five Nations Lords shall convene they shall appoint a speaker for the day. He shall be a Lord of either the Mohawk, Onondaga or Seneca Nation.

The next day the Council shall appoint another speaker, but the first speaker may be reappointed if there is no objection, but a speaker's term shall not be regarded more than for the day. 30

No individual or foreign nation interested in a case, question or proposition shall have any voice in the Confederate Council except to answer a question put to him or them by the speaker for the Lords.

If the conditions which shall arise at any future time call for an addition to or change of this law, the case shall be carefully considered and if a new beam seems necessary or beneficial, the proposed change shall be voted upon and if adopted it shall be called, "Added to the Rafters."

Read

1. How do the opening eight paragraphs (what we call in Chapter 3 the *exordium*) work to establish a primary goal of the document?
2. How does the speaker establish his authority in the council's constitution?
3. Why is the procedure for holding a council so important?
4. What is the significance of the name "Fire Keepers"?

Write

1. Discuss why you think the constitution goes to such lengths to prescribe behaviors at council meetings. Choose one or two procedures to help you as you consider possible reasons.
2. Write a reflection on the method of justice you see being established in the Iroquois League constitution.
3. Describe the style of this document, considering its use of language, images, and syntax, especially repetition.

Connect

1. How does the document's approach to audience, and its awareness of effect, seem similar to John Winthrop's sermon aboard the *Arbella* (p. 179)?
2. How does this piece draw connections to the natural world as part of the social and political world of the tribes?

John Smith

English explorer John Smith (1580–1631) sailed to North America and helped found the Jamestown (Virginia) colony in 1607. The record of his exploration, *A True Relation of Virginia,* was published in 1608. This journal and its sequel, including his experience with the leader Powhatan and his daughter Pocahontas, played a pivotal role in the early settling of the continent, though the famous rescue by Pocahontas is not mentioned in the original account. Smith's storytelling resulted in some discrepancies among the early accounts of relations with the Chesapeake and other tribes, but his adventures helped popularize the idea of settlement and helped the early colonizing efforts. Smith later explored the northeastern coast of the continent, which he named New England.

From *The Journal of John Smith*

Chapter II

What Happened till the First Supply

Being thus left to our fortunes, it fortuned that within ten days, scarce ten amongst us could either go or well stand, such extreme weakness and sickness oppressed us. And thereat none need marvel if they consider the cause and reason which was this: While the ships stayed, our allowance was somewhat bettered by a daily proportion of biscuit, which the sailors would pilfer to sell, give, or exchange with us for money, sassafras, furs, or love. But when they departed, there remained neither tavern, beer house, nor place of relief but the common kettle. Had we been as free from all sins as [we were free from] gluttony and drunkenness, we might have been canonized for saints; but our President would never had been admitted [to sainthood], for [he was guilty of] engrossing to his private,° oatmeal, sack,° oil, aqua vitae,° beef, eggs, or what not but the kettle; that indeed he allowed equally to be distributed, and that was half a pint of wheat and as much barley boiled with water for a man a day, and this, having fried some twenty-six weeks in the ship's hold, contained as many worms as grains so that we might truly call it rather so much bran than corn; our drink was water, our lodgings castles in the air.

With this lodging and diet, our extreme toil in bearing and planting palisades° so strained and bruised us, and our continual labor in the extremity of the heat had so weakened us, as were cause sufficient to have made us as miserable in our native country or any other place in the world. From May to September, those that escaped [death] lived upon sturgeon and sea crabs. Fifty in this time we buried; the rest [of us] seeing the President's projects to escape these miseries in our pinnace by flight (who all this time had neither felt want nor sickness) so moved our dead spirits as we deposed him and established Ratcliffe in his place (Gosnold being dead), Kendall [having been] deposed. Smith [being] newly recovered, Martin and Ratcliffe were by his care preserved and relieved, and the most of the soldiers recovered with the skillful diligence of Master Thomas Wotton our surgeon general. But now was all our provision spent, the sturgeon gone, all helps abandoned, each hour expecting the fury of the savages, when God, the patron of all good endeavors, in that desperate extremity so changed the heart of the savages that they brought such plenty of their fruits and provision as no man wanted.°

And now where some affirmed it was ill done of the [London] Council to send forth men so badly provided, this incontradictable reason will show them plainly they are too ill advised to nourish such ill conceits:° First, the

---

engrossing to his private: keeping for himself

sack: a dry white wine

aqua vitae: alcohol (brandy, whiskey, etc.; from Latin "water of life")

palisades: long narrow stakes to be used as fence

as no man wanted: that no one did without

conceits: ideas, notions

fault of our going was our own; what could be thought fitting or necessary we had, but [of] what we should find, or want, or where we should be, we were all ignorant; and supposing to make our passage in two months, with victual to live and the advantage of the spring to work, we were at sea five months, where we both spent our victual and lost the opportunity of the time and season to plant, by the unskillful presumption of our ignorant transporters that understood not at all what they undertook.

Such actions have ever since the world's beginning been subject to such accidents, and everything of worth is found full of difficulties, but nothing [is] so difficult as to establish a commonwealth so far remote from men and means and where men's minds are so untoward° as neither do well themselves nor suffer° others. But to proceed.

The new President [Ratcliffe] and Martin, being little beloved, of weak judgment in dangers, and less industry in peace, committed the managing of all things abroad° to Captain Smith, who, by his own example, good words, and fair promises, set some to mow, others to bind thatch, some to build houses, others to thatch them, himself always bearing the greatest task for his own share, so that in short time he provided most of them lodgings, neglecting any for himself. This done, seeing the savages' superfluity° begin to decrease, [Smith] (with some of his workmen) shipped himself in the shallop° to search the country for trade. The want of the language, [the want of] knowledge to manage his boat without sailors, the want of a sufficient power (knowing the multitude of the savages), [the want of] apparel for his men, and [the want of] other necessaries were infinite impediments yet no discouragement. 5

Being but six or seven in company he went down the river to Kecoughtan, where at first they [the Indians] scorned him as a famished man and would in derision offer him a handful of corn, a piece of bread, for their [the Englishmen's] swords and muskets, and such like proportions also for their apparel. But seeing by trade and courtesy there was nothing to be had, he made bold to try such conclusions° as necessity enforced; though contrary

untoward: perverse
suffer: allow, tolerate
abroad: out of doors
superfluity: overabundance (i.e., extra provisions)
shallop: small open boat
conclusions: actions

to his commission, [he] let fly his muskets [and] ran his boat on shore; whereat they all fled into the woods.

So marching towards their houses, they might see great heaps of corn; much ado he had to restrain his hungry soldiers from present taking of it, expecting as it happened that the savages would assault them, as not long after they did with a most hideous noise. Sixty or seventy of them, some black, some red, some white, some parti-colored, came in a square order, singing and dancing out of the woods with their Okee (which was an idol made of skins, stuffed with moss, all painted and hung with chains and copper) borne before them; and in this manner, being well armed with clubs, targets,° bows, and arrows, they charged the English that so kindly° received them with their muskets loaded with pistol shot that down fell their god, and divers° [Indians] lay sprawling on the ground; the rest fled again to the woods and ere long sent one of their Quiyoughcosucks to offer peace and redeem their Okee.

Smith told them if only six of them would come unarmed and load his boat, he would not only be their friend but restore them their Okee and give them beads, copper, and hatchets besides, which on both sides was to their contents° performed, and then they brought him venison, turkeys, wild fowl, bread, and what they had, singing and dancing in sign of friendship till they departed. In his return he discovered the town and country of Warraskoyack.

Thus God unboundless by his power,
Made them thus kind, would us devour.

Smith, perceiving (notwithstanding their late misery) not any regarded but from hand to mouth (the company being well recovered),° caused the pinnace° to be provided with things fitting to get provision for the year following, but in the interim he made three or four journeys and discovered the people of Chickahominy, yet what he carefully provided the rest carelessly spent.

The Spaniard never more greedily desired gold than he [Smith] victual, nor his soldiers more to abandon the country than he to keep it. But . . . he found] plenty of corn in the river of Chickahominy, where hundreds of savages 10

---

targets: small round shields

kindly: appropriately, in kind

divers: diverse, various

contents: content, satisfaction

perceiving . . . recovered: i.e., the men were using up their provisions and putting nothing aside for later

pinnace: a small sailing ship

in divers places stood with baskets expecting his coming. And now [with] the winter approaching, the rivers became so covered with swans, geese, ducks, and cranes that we daily feasted with good bread, Virginia peas, pumpkins, and persimmons, fish, fowl, and divers sorts of wild beasts as fat as we could eat them, so that none of our tuftaffaty° humorists° desired to go for England.

But our comedies never endured long without a tragedy; some idle exceptions° being muttered against Captain Smith for not discovering the head of [the] Chickahominy river and [being] taxed by the Council to be too slow in so worthy an attempt,° the next voyage he proceeded so far that with much labor by cutting of trees asunder he made his passage; but when his barge could pass no farther, he left her in a broad bay out of danger of shot, commanding [that] none should go ashore till his return; himself with two English and two savages went up higher in a canoe, but he was not long absent but his men [in the barge] went ashore, whose want of government° gave both occasion and opportunity to the savages to surprise one George Cassen, whom they slew, and [they] much failed not to have cut off the boat and all the rest.

Smith little dreaming of that accident,° being got to the marshes at the river's head twenty miles in the desert,° had his two men slain (as is supposed) sleeping by the canoe, while himself by fowling° sought them victual, who finding he was beset with 200 savages, two of them he slew, still defending himself with the aid of a savage his guide, whom he bound to his arm with his garters° and used him as a buckler,° yet he [Smith] was shot in his thigh a little, and had many arrows that stuck in his clothes but no great hurt, till at last they took him prisoner. . . .

The manner how they used and delivered him is as follows:

The savages having drawn from George Cassen whither Captain Smith was gone, prosecuting° that opportunity they followed him with 300

---

tuftaffaty: a taffeta (fabric) with a tufted pile
humorists: people subject to whims or caprices
exceptions: as in "I take exception to that"
so worthy an attempt: so vital an effort
government: discipline
accident: incident
desert: wilderness
fowling: hunting game birds
garters: leather bootstraps
buckler: shield
prosecuting: pursuing

bowmen, conducted by the King of Pamunkey, who in divisions searching the turnings of the river found Robinson and Emry by the fireside; those they shot full of arrows and slew. Then finding the Captain, as is said, who used the savage that was his guide as his shield (three of them being slain and divers others so galled) all the rest would not come near him. Thinking thus to have returned to his boat, regarding° them, as he marched, more than his way, [he] slipped up to the middle in an oozy creek and his savage with him, yet dared they not come to him till being near dead with cold he threw away his arms. Then according to their composition° they drew him forth and led him to the fire where his men were slain. Diligently they chafed his benumbed limbs.

He demanding for their captain, they showed him Opechancanough, King of Pamunkey, to whom he gave a round ivory double compass dial. Much they marveled at the playing of the fly° and needle, which they could see so plainly and yet not touch it because of the glass that covered them. But when he demonstrated by that globe-like jewel the roundness of the earth and skies, the sphere of the sun, moon, and stars, and how the sun did chase the night round about the world continually, the greatness of the land and sea, the diversity of nations, variety of complexions, and how we were to them antipodes,° and many other such like matters, they all stood as amazed with admiration. Notwithstanding, within an hour after, they tied him to a tree, and as many as could stand about him prepared to shoot him, but [seeing] the King holding up the compass in his hand, they all laid down their bows and arrows and in a triumphant manner led him to Orapaks, where he was after their manner kindly feasted and well used.

15

Their order in conducting him was thus: Drawing themselves all in file, the King in the midst had all their pieces and swords borne before him. Captain Smith was led after him by three great savages holding him fast by each arm, and on each side six went in file with their arrows nocked.° But arriving at the town (which was but only thirty or forty hunting houses made of mats, which they remove as they please, as we our tents), all the women

regarding: watching

composition: compact, agreement

fly: compass face

antipodes: opposites

nocked: fitted to the bowstring, ready to fire

and children staring to behold him, the soldiers first all in file performed the form of a bissom° so well as could be, and on each flank, officers as sergeants to see them keep their orders. A good time they continued this exercise and then cast themselves in a ring, dancing in such several postures and singing and yelling out such hellish notes and screeches; being strangely painted, every one [had] his quiver of arrows and at his back a club, on his arm a fox or an otter's skin or some such matter for his vambrace;° their heads and shoulders [were] painted red with oil and pocones° mingled together, which scarlet-like color made an exceeding handsome show; [each had] his bow in his hand and the skin of a bird with her wings [spread] abroad, dried, tied on his head, [with] a piece of copper, a white shell, a long feather with a small rattle growing at the tails of their snakes tied to it, or some such like toy.

. . .

At last they brought him to Werowocomoco, where was Powhatan, their Emperor. Here more than two hundred of those grim courtiers stood wondering at him, as [if] he had been a monster, till Powhatan and his train had put themselves in their greatest braveries.° Before a fire, upon a seat like a bedstead, he sat covered with a great robe made of raccoon skins and all the tails hanging by. On either hand did sit a young wench of sixteen or eighteen years and along on each side [of] the house, two rows of men and behind them as many women, with all their heads and shoulders painted red, many of their heads bedecked with the white down of birds, but every one with something, and a great chain of white beads about their necks.

At his entrance before the King, all the people gave a great shout. The Queen of Appomattoc was appointed to bring him water to wash his hands, and another brought him a bunch of feathers, instead of a towel, to dry them. Having feasted him after their best barbarous manner they could, a long consultation was held, but the conclusion was, two great stones were brought before Powhatan; then as many as could laid hands on him [Smith], dragged him to them, and thereon laid his head, and being ready with their clubs to beat out his brains, Pocahontas, the King's dearest daughter, when no entreaty could prevail, got his head in her arms and laid her own upon his to save him from death, whereat the Emperor was contented he should live

---

bissom: snakelike formation

vambrace: plate armor for the arm

pocones: puccoons, plants yielding a red pigment

braveries: splendors, finery

to make him hatchets, and her bells, beads, and copper, for they thought him as well [capable] of all occupations as themselves. For the King himself will make his own robes, shoes, bows, arrows, pots; plant; hunt; or do anything so well as the rest.

> They say he bore a pleasant show,
> But sure his heart was sad.
> For who can pleasant be, and rest,
> That lives in fear and dread:
> And having life suspected, doth
> It still suspected lead.

Two days after, Powhatan, having disguised himself in the most fearfulest manner he could, caused Captain Smith to be brought forth to a great house in the woods and there upon a mat by the fire to be left alone. Not long after, from behind a mat that divided the house, was made the most dolefulest noise he ever heard; then Powhatan, more like a devil than a man, with some two hundred more as black as himself, came unto him and told him now they were friends, and presently he should go to Jamestown to send him two great guns and a grindstone for which he would give him the country of Capahowasic and forever esteem him as his son Nantaquond.

So to Jamestown with twelve guides Powhatan sent him. That night they quartered in the woods, he still expecting (as he had done all this long time of his imprisonment) every hour to be put to one death or other, for all their feasting. But almighty God (by His divine providence) had mollified the hearts of those stern barbarians with compassion. The next morning betimes° they came to the fort, where Smith having used the savages with what kindness he could, he showed Rawhunt, Powhatan's trusty servant, two demiculverins° and a millstone to carry [to] Powhatan; they found them somewhat too heavy, but when they did see him discharge them, being loaded with stones, among the boughs of a great tree loaded with icicles, the ice and branches came so tumbling down that the poor savages ran away half dead with fear. But at last we regained some conference with them and gave them such toys° and sent to Powhatan, his women, and children such presents as gave them in general full content.

20

---

betimes: in good time, early
demiculverins: cannon
toys: trifles, things of little value

Powhatan's Discourse of Peace and War

Captain Smith, you may understand that I having seen the death of all my people thrice, and not anyone [is] living of those three generations but myself; I know the difference of peace and war better than any in my country. But now I am old and ere long must die; my brethren, namely Opitchapam, Opechancanough, and Kecoughtan, my two sisters, and their two daughters, are distinctly each other's successors. I wish their experience [with you to be] no less than mine, and your love to them no less than mine to you. But this bruit° from Nandsamund, that you are come to destroy my country, so much affrighteth all my people as they dare not visit you. What will it avail you to take that by force [which] you may quickly have by love, or to destroy them that provide you [with] food? What can you get by war, when we can hide our provisions and fly to the woods whereby you must famish° by wronging us your friends? And why are you thus jealous° of our love, seeing us unarmed, and [we] both do and are willing still to feed you with that [which] you cannot get but by our labors? Think you I am so simple [as] not to know it is better to eat good meat, lie well and sleep quietly with my women and children, laugh and be merry with you, have copper, hatchets, or what I want, being your friend, than be forced to fly from all, to lie cold in the woods, feed upon acorns, roots, and such trash, and be so hunted by you that I can neither rest, eat, nor sleep, but my tired men must watch, and if a twig but break, everyone cryeth, here commeth Captain Smith. Then I must fly I know not whither and thus, with miserable fear, end my miserable life, leaving my pleasures to such youths as you [are], who through your rash unadvisedness may quickly as miserably end [your own life] for lack of that [grain and meat] which you never know where to find. Let this therefore assure you of our love, and every year our friendly trade shall furnish you with corn, and [I would give you corn] now also, if you would come in [a] friendly manner to see us, and not [come] thus with your guns and swords as [if you intended] to invade your foes.

[1624]

---

bruit: rumor, report

famish: go hungry, starve

jealous: suspicious

Read

1. What images and language does Smith use to describe the condition of the men in Jamestown colony?
2. Why do you think Smith refers to himself in the third person?
3. What is the significance of the dance the tribe performs for Smith?
4. What does Smith mean by his "comedies" and "tragedies" (para. 11)?

Write

1. Describe how you think hunger shaped the events of Smith's narrative.
2. How does Smith feel about his fellow settlers? Find a few passages to explain your response.
3. How does Powhatan's "Discourse of Peace and War" create a dialogue with Smith's account of his adventure? Write a paragraph that reflects on the interaction of the two.
4. Do you think Smith makes himself the hero of his own story? Find some moments in the narrative, in its descriptions or reflections, to help you frame your response.

Complete Additional Exercises on Smith's Journal at Your Pearson MyLab

Connect

1. Consider journals or diaries you might have kept in the past or read. How is this journal like or unlike others you know about?
2. How does this account seem similar or unlike what you may have heard or seen in movies about the Pocahontas/John Smith tale?

John Winthrop

Born in England, the Puritan leader John Winthrop (1588–1649) came from a wealthy family and trained as a lawyer. He sailed for North America and arrived in Boston Harbor in 1630 on the ship the *Arbella,* where he delivered the sermon that is excerpted below. He became governor of Massachusetts Bay Colony soon after the settlement was established and served for twelve annual terms. His journal, entitled *The History of New England,* was first printed in 1790, and is one of the most important records of early Massachusetts history. Winthrop's conservative religious stance helped him emphasize duty, but he also stressed the need for Christian love and for logic as part of founding the new land.

From *A Modell of Christian Charity*

GOD ALMIGHTY in His most holy and wise providence, hath so disposed of the condition of mankind, as in all times some must be rich, some poor, some high and eminent in power and dignity; others mean° and in submission.

---

mean: low in rank or status

The Reason hereof:

1st Reason.

First to hold conformity with the rest of His world, being delighted to show forth the glory of his wisdom in the variety and difference of the creatures, and the glory of His power in ordering all these differences for the preservation and good of the whole, and the glory of His greatness, that as it is the glory of princes to have many officers, so this great king will have many stewards, counting himself more honored in dispensing his gifts to man by man, than if he did it by his own immediate hands.

2nd Reason.

Secondly, that He might have the more occasion to manifest the work of his Spirit: first upon the wicked in moderating and restraining them, so that the rich and mighty should not eat up the poor, nor the poor and despised rise up against and shake off their yoke. Secondly, in the regenerate,° in exercising His graces in them, as in the great ones, their love, mercy, gentleness, temperance etc., and in the poor and inferior sort, their faith, patience, obedience etc.

3rd Reason.

Thirdly, that every man might have need of others, and from hence they might be all knit more nearly together in the bonds of brotherly affection. From hence it appears plainly that no man is made more honorable than another or more wealthy etc., out of any particular and singular respect to himself, but for the glory of his Creator and the common good of the creature, Man. Therefore God still reserves the property of these gifts to Himself as Ezek. 16:17, He there calls wealth, His gold and His silver, and Prov. 3:9, He claims their service as His due, "Honor the Lord with thy riches," etc.—All men being thus (by divine providence) ranked into two sorts, rich and poor; under the first are comprehended all such as are able to live comfortably by their own means duly improved; and all others are poor according to the former distribution. 5

There are two rules whereby we are to walk one towards another: Justice and Mercy. These are always distinguished° in their act and in their object, yet may they both concur in the same subject in each respect; as sometimes there may be an occasion of showing mercy to a rich man in some sudden danger or distress, and also doing of mere justice to a poor man in regard of some particular contract, etc.

. . .

regenerate: reformed; spiritually reborn

distinguished: i.e., from one another

The definition which the Scripture gives us of love is this: Love is the bond of perfection. First it is a bond or ligament. Secondly, it makes the work perfect. There is no body but consists of parts and that which knits these parts together, gives the body its perfection, because it makes each part so contiguous to others as thereby they do mutually participate with each other, both in strength and infirmity, in pleasure and pain. To instance in the most perfect of all bodies: Christ and his Church make one body. The several parts of this body considered a part before they were united, were as disproportionate and as much disordering as so many contrary qualities or elements, but when Christ comes, and by his spirit and love knits all these parts to himself and each to other, it is become the most perfect and best proportioned body in the world (Eph. 4:15–16). Christ, by whom all the body being knit together by every joint for the furniture° thereof, according to the effectual power which is in the measure of every perfection of parts, a glorious body without spot or wrinkle; the ligaments hereof being Christ, or his love, for Christ is love (1 John 4:8). So this definition is right. Love is the bond of perfection.

From hence we may frame these conclusions:

First of all, true Christians are of one body in Christ (1 Cor. 12). Ye are the body of Christ and members of their part. All the parts of this body being thus united are made so contiguous in a special relation as they must needs partake of each other's strength and infirmity; joy and sorrow, weal and woe. If one member suffers, all suffer with it, if one be in honor, all rejoice with it.

Secondly, the ligaments of this body which knit together are love. 10

Thirdly, no body can be perfect which wants° its proper ligament.

Fourthly, all the parts of this body being thus united are made so contiguous in a special relation as they must needs partake of each other's strength and infirmity, joy and sorrow, weal and woe. (1 Cor. 12:26) If one member suffers, all suffer with it; if one be in honor, all rejoice with it.

Fifthly, this sensitivity and sympathy of each other's conditions will necessarily infuse into each part a native desire and endeavor, to strengthen, defend, preserve and comfort the other. To insist a little on this conclusion being the product of all the former, the truth hereof will appear both by precept and pattern. 1 John 3:16, "We ought to lay down our lives for the brethren." Gal. 6:2, "Bear ye one another's burdens and so fulfill the law of Christ."

. . .

furniture: furnishing

wants: lacks

From the former considerations arise these conclusions:

First, this love among Christians is a real thing, not imaginary. 15

Secondly, this love is as absolutely necessary to the being of the body of Christ, as the sinews and other ligaments of a natural body are to the being of that body.

Thirdly, this love is a divine, spiritual nature; free, active, strong, courageous, permanent; undervaluing all things beneath its proper object and of all the graces, this makes us nearer to resemble the virtues of our heavenly father.

Fourthly, it rests in the love and welfare of its beloved. For the full certain knowledge of those truths concerning the nature, use, and excellency of this grace, that which the holy ghost hath left recorded, 1 Cor. 13, may give full satisfaction, which is needful for every true member of this lovely body of the Lord Jesus, to work upon their hearts by prayer, meditation, continual exercise at least of the special influence of this grace, till Christ be formed in them and they in him, all in each other, knit together by this bond of love.

It rests now to make some application of this discourse, by the present design, which gave the occasion of writing of it. Herein are four things to be propounded; first the persons, secondly, the work, thirdly, the end, fourthly, the means.

First, for the persons. We are a company professing ourselves fellow members of Christ, in which respect only, though we were absent from each other many miles, and had our employments as far distant, yet we ought to account ourselves knit together by this bond of love and live in the exercise of it, if we would have comfort of our being in Christ. This was notorious° in the practice of the Christians in former times; as is testified of the Waldenses,° from the mouth of one of the adversaries Aeneas Sylvius° "*mutuo ament pene antequam norunt*"—they use to love any of their own religion even before they were acquainted with them. 20

Secondly, for the work we have in hand. It is by a mutual consent, through a special overvaluing providence and a more than ordinary approbation of the churches of Christ, to seek out a place of cohabitation and consortship° under a due form of government both civil and ecclesiastical. In such cases as this, the care of the public must oversway° all private respects, by which, not

---

notorious: notable, well-known (not necessarily in a pejorative sense)

Waldenses: members of a Christian movement of the later Middle Ages condemned as heretical by the Catholic Church

Aeneas Sylvius: Enea Silvio Piccolomini (1405–1464), Pope Pius II from 1458 until his death

consortship: fellowship, partnership

oversway: hold sway over

only conscience, but mere civil policy, doth bind us. For it is a true rule that particular° estates cannot subsist° in the ruin of the public.

Thirdly, the end is to improve our lives to do more service to the Lord; the comfort and increase of the body of Christ, whereof we are members, that ourselves and posterity may be the better preserved from the common corruptions of this evil world, to serve the Lord and work out our salvation under the power and purity of his holy ordinances.

Fourthly, for the means whereby this must be effected. They are twofold, a conformity with the work and end we aim at. These we see are extraordinary; therefore we must not content ourselves with usual ordinary means. Whatsoever we did, or ought to have done, when we lived in England, the same must we do, and more also, where we go. That which the most in their churches maintain as truth in profession only, we must bring into familiar and constant practice; as in this duty of love, we must love brotherly without dissimulation,° we must love one another with a pure heart fervently. We must bear one another's burdens. We must not look only on our own things, but also on the things of our brethren.

Neither must we think that the Lord will bear with such failings at our hands as he doth from those among whom we have lived; and that for these three reasons:

First, in regard of the more near bond of marriage between Him and us, wherein He hath taken us to be His, after a most strict and peculiar° manner, which will make Him the more jealous of our love and obedience. So He tells the people of Israel, you only have I known of all the families of the earth, therefore will I punish you for your transgressions.

25

Secondly, because the Lord will be sanctified in them that come near Him. We know that there were many that corrupted the service of the Lord; some setting up altars before his own; others offering both strange fire and strange sacrifices also; yet there came no fire from heaven, or other sudden judgment upon them, as did upon Nadab and Abihu,° whom yet we may think did not sin presumptuously.

---

particular: individual, private

subsist: exist, survive

dissimulation: pretense, hypocrisy

peculiar: distinctive, particular

Nadab and Abihu: the first two sons of Aaron, brother of Moses, they made an unsanctioned sacrifice of fire to God, and were consumed by God's own fire

Thirdly, when God gives a special commission He looks to have it strictly observed in every article; when He gave Saul a commission to destroy Amaleck,° He indented with him upon certain articles, and because he failed in one of the least, and that upon a fair pretense, it lost him the kingdom, which should have been his reward, if he had observed his commission.

Thus stands the cause between God and us. We are entered into covenant with Him for this work. We have taken out a commission. The Lord hath given us leave to draw our own articles. We have professed to enterprise these and those accounts, upon these and those ends. We have hereupon besought Him of favor and blessing. Now if the Lord shall please to hear us, and bring us in peace to the place we desire, then hath He ratified this covenant and sealed our commission, and will expect a strict performance of the articles contained in it; but if we shall neglect the observation of these articles which are the ends we have propounded, and, dissembling with our God, shall fail to embrace this present world and prosecute our carnal intentions,° seeking great things for ourselves and our posterity, the Lord will surely break out in wrath against us, and be revenged of such a people, and make us know the price of the breach of such a covenant.

Now, the only way to avoid this shipwreck, and to provide for our posterity, is to follow the counsel of Micah,° to do justly, to love mercy, to walk humbly with our God. For this end, we must be knit together, in this work, as one man. We must entertain° each other in brotherly affection. We must be willing to abridge° ourselves of our superfluities,° for the supply of others' necessities. We must uphold a familiar commerce together in all meekness, gentleness, patience, and liberality. We must delight in each other; make others' conditions our own; rejoice together, mourn together, labor and suffer together, always having before our eyes our commission and community in the work, as members of the same body. So shall we keep the unity of the spirit in the bond of peace. The Lord will be our God, and delight to dwell among us, as His own people, and will command a blessing upon us in all our ways, so that we shall see much more of His wisdom, power, goodness and truth, than formerly we have been acquainted with. We shall find that the God of Israel is among us, when ten of us shall be able to resist a thousand of our enemies; when He

---

a commission to destroy Amaleck: in 1 Samuel (Bible), Saul loses his kingship when he fails to complete the total destruction of the Amalekites and all their livestock commanded by God

prosecute our carnal intentions: strive to fulfill our earthly desires

Micah: prophet and author of the Book of Micah (Bible)

entertain: show hospitality to

abridge: deprive

superfluities: excess, luxuries

shall make us a praise and glory that men shall say of succeeding plantations,° "may the Lord make it like that of New England." *For we must consider that we shall be as a city upon a hill. The eyes of all people are upon us. So that if we shall deal falsely with our God in this work we have undertaken, and so cause Him to withdraw His present help from us, we shall be made a story and a by-word° through the world.* We shall open the mouths of enemies to speak evil of the ways of God, and all professors for God's sake. We shall shame the faces of many of God's worthy servants, and cause their prayers to be turned into curses upon us till we be consumed out of the good land whither we are going.

And to shut this discourse with that exhortation of Moses, that faithful servant of the Lord, in his last farewell to Israel, Deut. 30. "Beloved, there is now set before us life and death, good and evil," in that we are commanded this day to love the Lord our God, and to love one another, to walk in his ways and to keep his Commandments and his ordinance and his laws, and the articles of our Covenant with Him, that we may live and be multiplied, and that the Lord our God may bless us in the land whither we go to possess it. *But if our hearts shall turn away, so that we will not obey, but shall be seduced, and worship other Gods, our pleasure and profits, and serve them, it is propounded unto us this day, we shall surely perish out of the good land whither we pass over this vast sea to possess it.* 30

Therefore let us choose life,
that we, and our seed,
may live; by obeying His
voice and cleaving to Him,
for He is our life and
our prosperity.

[1630]

Read

1. What does the arrangement of the sermon (breaks, questions, punctuation) reveal about Winthrop's aim?
2. How does Winthrop explain the relationship between Christian duty and community?
3. How do the proofs Winthrop offers reflect his dual belief in faith and logic?
4. How does Winthrop define love?
5. What does the metaphor of the city on the hill suggest about the colonists' mission in New England?

---

plantations: colonies, settlements

a story and a by-word: i.e., an example

Write

1. Write a brief analysis of Winthrop's ideas about community as you see them expressed here.
2. Write a description of Winthrop's *persona* as you see it revealed in his choice of images, his approach to his listeners, and his choice of examples and evidence.
3. Do you think Winthrop was worried about the success of the enterprise? Find places in the text that support your perspective.

Connect

1. Write a reflection on this sermon from your perspective as a twenty-first century reader. Is it convincing? Interesting?
2. Now write a reflection imagining yourself in the audience aboard the ship. Consider what you might be wondering and how you might see Winthrop as a leader.

William Bradford

William Bradford (1590–1657) was born in Yorkshire, England. Following Separatist religious principles, he immigrated first to Holland and then to the New World aboard the *Mayflower* in 1620, hoping to reach the English settlement in Virginia. Only a few of the *Mayflower* Pilgrims were Separatists or "saints"; most came as secular colonists seeking opportunity rather than religious freedom. After 65 days aboard ship, the company sighted land at Cape Cod, Massachusetts, and decided to settle there. Bradford began to write *The History of Plymouth Plantation* in 1630 and it covered the early settlement until 1647. In his history, Bradford records daily struggles of the Pilgrims as well as attitudes toward the Indians who helped them survive.

From *A History of Plymouth Plantation*

from Chapter IX

Of their Voyage, and how they Passed the Sea; and of their Safe Arrival at Cape Cod

September 6. These troubles being blown over, and now all being compact together in one ship, they put to sea again with a prosperous wind, which continued divers° days together, which was some encouragement unto them;

---

divers: diverse, various

yet, according to the usual manner, many were afflicted with seasickness. And I may not omit here a special work of God's providence. There was a proud and very profane young man, one of the seamen, of a lusty, able body, which made him the more haughty; he would alway be contemning the poor people in their sickness and cursing them daily with grievous execrations; and did not let to tell them that he hoped to help to cast half of them overboard before they came to their journey's end, and to make merry with what they had; and if he were by any gently reproved, he would curse and swear most bitterly. But it pleased God before they came half seas over, to smite this young man with a grievous disease, of which he died in a desperate manner, and so was himself the first that was thrown overboard. Thus his curses light on his own head, and it was an astonishment to all his fellows for they noted it to be the just hand of God upon him. . . .

But to omit other things (that I may be brief) after long beating at sea they fell with that land which is called Cape Cod; the which being made and certainly known to be it, they were not a little joyful. After some deliberation had amongst themselves and with the master of the ship, they tacked about and resolved to stand for the southward (the wind and weather being fair) to find some place about Hudson's River for their habitation. But after they had sailed that course about half the day, they fell amongst dangerous shoals and roaring breakers, and they were so far entangled therewith as they conceived themselves in great danger; and the wind shrinking upon them withal, they resolved to bear up again for the Cape and thought themselves happy to get out of those dangers before night overtook them, as by God's good providence they did. And the next day they got into the Cape Harbor where they rid in safety. . . .

Being thus arrived in a good harbor, and brought safe to land, they fell upon their knees and blessed the God of Heaven who had brought them over the vast and furious ocean, and delivered them from all the perils and miseries thereof, again to set their feet on the firm and stable earth, their proper element. And no marvel if they were thus joyful, seeing wise Seneca was so affected with sailing a few miles on the coast of his own Italy, as he affirmed, that he had rather remain twenty years on his way by land than pass by sea to any place in a short time, so tedious and dreadful was the same unto him.

But here I cannot but stay and make a pause, and stand half amazed at this poor people's present condition; and so I think will the reader, too, when he well considers the same. Being thus passed the vast ocean, and a sea of troubles before in their preparation (as may be remembered by that which went before), they had now no friends to welcome them nor inns to entertain or refresh their weatherbeaten bodies; no houses or much less towns to repair° to, to seek for succour. It is recorded in Scripture as a mercy to the Apostle

repair: go

and his shipwrecked company, that the barbarians showed them no small kindness in refreshing them, but these savage barbarians, when they met with them (as after will appear) were readier to fill their sides full of arrows than otherwise. And for the season it was winter, and they that know the winters of that country know them to be sharp and violent, and subject to cruel and fierce storms, dangerous to travel to known places, much more to search an unknown coast. Besides, what could they see but a hideous and desolate wilderness, full of wild beasts and wild men—and what multitudes there might be of them they knew not. Neither could they, as it were, go up to the top of Pisgah to view from this wilderness a more goodly country to feed their hopes, for which way soever they turned their eyes (save upward to the heavens) they could have little solace or content° in respect of any outward objects. For summer being done, all things stand upon them with a weather-beaten face, and the whole country, full of woods and thickets, represented a wild and savage hue. If they looked behind them, there was the mighty ocean which they had passed and was now as a main bar and gulf to separate them from all the civil parts of the world. If it be said they had a ship, to succour them, it is true; but what heard they daily from the master and company? But that with speed they should look out a place (with their shallop)° where they would be, at some near distance; for the season was such as he would not stir from thence till a safe harbor was discovered by them, where they would be, and he might go without danger; and that victuals consumed apace but he must and would keep sufficient for themselves and their return. Yea, it was muttered by some that if they got not a place in time, they would turn them and their goods ashore and leave them. Let it also be considered what weak hopes of supply and succour they left behind them, that might bear up their minds in this sad condition and trials they were under; and they could not but be very small. It is true, indeed, the affections and love of their brethren at Leyden was cordial and entire towards them, but they had little power to help them or themselves; and how the case stood between them and the merchants at their coming away hath already been declared.

5 What could now sustain them but the Spirit of God and His grace? May not and ought not the children of these fathers rightly say: "Our fathers were Englishmen which came over this great ocean, and were ready to perish in this wilderness; but they cried unto the Lord, and He heard their voice and looked on their adversity," etc. "Let them therefore praise the Lord; because He is good: and His mercies endure forever." "Yea, let them which have been redeemed of the Lord, shew how He hath delivered them from the hand of

content: contentment, satisfaction

shallop: small open boat

the oppressor. When they wandered in the desert wilderness out of the way, and found no city to dwell in, both hungry and thirsty, their soul was overwhelmed in them. Let them confess before the Lord His lovingkindness and His wonderful works before the sons of men."

from Book II, Chapter XI

The Remainder of Anno 1620 [The Mayflower Compact]

I shall a little return back, and begin with a combination° made by them before they came ashore; being the first foundation of their government in this place. Occasioned partly by the discontented and mutinous speeches that some of the strangers° amongst them had let fall from them in the ship: That when they came ashore they would use their own liberty, for none had power to command them, the patent they had being for Virginia and not for New England, which belonged to another government, with which the Virginia Company had nothing to do. And partly that such an act by them done, this their condition considered, might be as firm as any patent, and in some respects more sure.

The form was as followeth

IN THE NAME OF GOD, AMEN

We whose names are underwritten, the loyal subjects of our dread Sovereign Lord King James, by the Grace of God of Great Britain, France, and Ireland King, Defender of the Faith, etc.

Having undertaken, for the Glory of God and advancement of the Christian Faith and Honour of our King and Country, a Voyage to plant the First Colony in the Northern Parts of Virginia, do by these presents° solemnly and mutually in the presence of God and one of another, Covenant and Combine ourselves together into a Civil Body Politic, for our better ordering and preservation and furtherance of the ends aforesaid; and by virtue hereof to enact, constitute and frame such just and equal Laws, Ordinances, Acts, Constitutions and Offices, from time to time, as shall be thought most meet and convenient for the general good of the Colony unto which we promise all due submission and obedience. In witness whereof we

5

combination: compact, covenant

strangers: those who were not members of the Pilgrims' congregation (the "Saints")

presents: legal term for "the present writings, this document" *have hereunder subscribed our names at Cape Cod, the 11th of November; in the year of the reign of our Sovereign Lord King James, of England, France and Ireland the eighteenth, and of Scotland the fifty-fourth. Anno Domini 1620.*

After this they chose, or rather confirmed, Mr. John Carver (a man godly and well approved amongst them) their Governor for that year. And after they had provided a place for their goods, or common store (which were long in unlading for want of boats, foulness of the winter weather and sickness of divers)° and begun some small cottages for their habitation; as time would admit, they met and consulted of laws and orders, both for their civil and military government as the necessity of their condition did require, still adding thereunto as urgent occasion in several times, and as cases did require.

In these hard and difficult beginnings they found some discontents and murmurings arise amongst some, and mutinous speeches and carriages° in other; but they were soon quelled and overcome by the wisdom, patience, and just and equal carriage of things, by the Governor and better part, which clave° faithfully together in the main.

[The Starving Time]

But that which was most sad and lamentable was, that in two or three months' time half of their company died, especially in January and February, being the depth of winter, and wanting° houses and other comforts; being infected with the scurvy and other diseases which this long voyage and their inaccommodate° condition had brought upon them. So as there died some times two or three of a day in the foresaid time, that of 100 and odd persons, scarce fifty remained. And of these, in the time of most distress, there was but six or seven sound persons who to their great commendations, be it spoken, spared no pains night nor day, but with abundance of toil and hazard of their own health, fetched them wood, made them fires, dressed them meat, made their beds, washed their loathsome clothes, clothed and unclothed them. In a word, did all the homely° and necessary offices° for them which dainty and queasy stomachs cannot endure to hear named; and all this willingly and cheerfully,° without any grudging in the least, showing herein their true love unto their friends and brethren; a rare example and worthy to be remembered. Two of these seven were Mr. William Brewster, their reverend Elder, and Myles Standish, their Captain and military commander, unto whom myself and many others

---

divers: various (diverse) people

carriages: behavior, deportment

clave: clung, adhered

wanting: lacking

inaccommodate: poorly provided for, inconvenient

homely: plain, unpretentious

offices: responsibilities, duties

cheerfully: heartily, ungrudgingly

were much beholden in our low and sick condition. And yet the Lord so upheld these persons as in the general calamity they were not at all infected either with sickness or lameness: And what I have said of these I may of many others who died in this general visitation,° and others yet living; that whilst they had health, yea, or any strength continuing, they were not wanting° to any that had need of them. And I doubt not but their recompense is with the Lord.

But I may not here pass by another remarkable passage not to be forgotten. As this calamity fell among the passengers that were to be left here to plant, and were hasted ashore and made to drink water that the seamen might have the more beer, and one in his sickness desiring but a small can of beer, it was answered that if he were their own father he should have none. The disease began to fall amongst them° also, so as almost half of their company died before they went away, and many of their officers and lustiest men, as the boatswain, gunner, three quartermasters, the cook and others. At which the Master was something strucken and sent to the sick ashore and told the Governor he should send for beer for them that had need of it, though he drunk water homeward bound.

But now amongst his company there was far another kind of carriage° in this misery than amongst the passengers. For they that before had been boon companions in drinking and jollity in the time of their health and welfare, began now to desert one another in this calamity, saying they would not hazard their lives for them, they should be infected by coming to help them in their cabins; and so, after they came to lie by it° would do little or nothing for them but, "if they died, let them die." But such of the passengers as were yet aboard showed them what mercy they could, which made some of their hearts relent, as the boatswain (and some others) who was a proud young man and would often curse and scoff at the passengers. But when he grew weak, they had compassion on him and helped him; then he confessed he did not deserve it at their hands, he had abused them in word and deed. "Oh!" (saith he) "you, I now see, show your love like Christians indeed one to another, but we let one another lie and die like dogs." Another lay cursing his wife, saying if it had not been for her he had never come this unlucky voyage, and anon° cursing his fellows, saying he had done this and that for some of them; he had spent so much and so much amongst them, and they were now weary of him and did not help him, having need. Another gave° his companion all he had, if he died, to help him in his weakness; he went and got a little spice and made him a mess of meat once or twice. And because he died not so soon as he expected; he went amongst his

10

---

visitation: of illness

wanting: lacking, deficient; failing to meet requirements or expectations

them: the crewmen

far another kind of carriage: a very different sort of behavior

came to lie by it: were felled by the illness

anon: at once; soon

gave: offered

fellows and swore the rogue would cozen° him, he would see him choked before he made him any more meat; and yet the poor fellow died before morning.

[Indian Relations]

All this while the Indians came skulking about them, and would sometimes show themselves aloof off, but when any approached near them, they would run away; and once they stole away their tools where they had been at work and were gone to dinner. But about the 16th of March, a certain Indian came boldly amongst them and spoke to them in broken English, which they could well understand but marveled at it. At length they understood by discourse with him, that he was not of these parts, but belonged to the eastern parts where some English ships came to fish, with whom he was acquainted and could name sundry° of them by their names, amongst whom he had got his language. He became profitable to them in acquainting them with many things concerning the state of the country in the east parts where he lived, which was afterwards profitable unto them; as also of the people here, of their names, number and strength, of their situation and distance from this place, and who was chief amongst them. His name was Samoset. He told them also of another Indian whose name was Squanto, a native of this place, who had been in England and could speak better English than himself.

Being, after some time of entertainment and gifts dismissed, a while after he came again, and five more with him, and they brought again all the tools that were stolen away before, and made way for the coming of their great Sachem, called Massasoit. Who, about four or five days after, came with the chief of his friends and other attendance, with the aforesaid Squanto. With whom, after friendly entertainment and some gifts given him, they made a peace with him (which hath now continued this 24 years) in these terms:

1. That neither he nor any of his should injure or do hurt to any of their people.
2. That if any of his did hurt any of theirs, he should send the offender, that they might punish him.
3. That if anything were taken away from any of theirs, he should cause it to be restored; and they should do the like to his.
4. If any did unjustly war against him, they would aid him; if any did war against them, he should aid them.
5. He should send to his neighbours confederates to certify them of this, that they might not wrong them, but might be likewise comprised in the conditions of peace.
6. That when their men came to them, they should leave their bows and arrows behind them.

After these things he returned to his place called Sowams, some 40 miles from this place, but Squanto continued with them and was their interpreter

cozen: cheat, trick

sundry: assorted, miscellaneous

and was a special instrument sent of God for their good beyond their expectation. He directed them how to set their corn, where to take fish, and to procure other commodities, and was also their pilot to bring them to unknown places for their profit, and never left them till he died. . . .

[1630]

Read

1. How does Bradford use images and detail to describe the explorers' attitude toward the Indians they encounter? How does he indicate the Indians' attitudes toward the white men?
2. How does Bradford justify the men's actions as they enter the Indian huts?
3. How does the Compact seek to resolve differences in the Pilgrims' mission?
4. What is the effect of Bradford's description of the first winter?

Write

1. Where do you see the conflict between individual and community desire in Bradford's account?
2. Write a reflection on the hardships faced by the Pilgrims the first years of the settlement. Why did they persist? How do you think they survived?
3. Do you hear any anger or regret in Bradford's account? Comment on where you find those emotions.

Connect

1. How does Bradford's description of the first year connect to what you have read or heard about the early days of Plymouth and relationships with the Indians there?
2. Does anything surprise you in this account? Write about something you learned that you didn't know before as you read the story of the Pilgrims as Bradford tells it.

Mary Rowlandson

Mary White Rowlandson (1637–1710) moved from England to Lancaster, Massachusetts, as a young child of a prosperous businessman. She married a Puritan minister and in 1676 survived an attack of Narragansett Indians who raided her village near the end of King Philip's War. Rowlandson was taken captive along with three of her children, one of whom died of wounds while traveling with the tribe. She became acquainted with the ways of the tribe, met Metacom, the Wampanoag chief, and his consort, and lived with the Indian tribes until she was ransomed and freed several months later. Her book became an immediate bestseller when it was published in 1682. It was the model for the great number of captivity narratives published during the next century. Rowlandson's Puritan faith is evident in her account; her use of experience that tests her faith is clear as well.

A Narrative of the Captivity and Restoration of Mrs. Mary Rowlandson

On the tenth of February 1675,° Came the Indians with great numbers upon Lancaster: Their first coming was about Sun-rising; hearing the noise of some Guns, we looked out; several Houses were burning, and the Smoke ascending to Heaven. There were five persons taken in one house; the Father, and the Mother and a suckling° Child, they knockt on the head; the other two they took and carried away alive. Their were two others, who being out of their Garrison upon some occasion were set upon; one was knockt on the head, the other escaped: Another there was who running along was shot and wounded, and fell down; he begged of them his life, promising them Money (as they told me) but they would not hearken to him but knockt him in head, and stript him naked, and split open his Bowels. Another seeing many of the Indians about his Barn, ventured and went out, but was quickly shot down. There were three others belonging to the same Garrison who were killed; the Indians getting up upon the roof of the Barn, had advantage to shoot down upon them over their Fortification. Thus these murtherous° wretches went on, burning and destroying before them.

At length they came and beset our own house, and quickly it was the dolefullest day that ever mine eyes saw. The House stood upon the edge of a hill; some of the Indians got behind the hill, others into the Barn, and others behind any thing that could shelter them; from all which places they shot against the House, so that the Bullets seemed to fly like hail; and quickly they wounded one man among us, then another, and then a third. About two hours (according to my observation, in that amazing° time) they had been about the house before they prevailed to fire it (which they did with Flax and Hemp, which they brought out of the Barn, and there being no defence about the House, only two Flankers° at two opposite corners and one of them not finished) they fired it once and one ventured out and quenched it, but they quickly fired it again, and that took. Now is the dreadfull hour come, that I

February 1675: Rowlandson gives dates according to the Julian calendar then in use; by the Gregorian calendar, used in Britain and America since 1752, these events took place on February 20, 1676

suckling: nursing

murtherous: murderous

amazing: astonishing

Flankers: fortified positions

have often heard of (in time of War, as it was the case of others) but now mine eyes see it. Some in our house were fighting for their lives, others wallowing in their blood, the House on fire over our heads, and the bloody Heathen ready to knock us on the head, if we stirred out. Now might we hear Mothers and Children crying out for themselves, and one another, Lord, What shall we do? Then I took my Children (and one of my sisters, hers) to go forth and leave the house: but as soon as we came to the door and appeared, the Indians shot so thick that the bulletts rattled against the House, as if one had taken an handfull of stones and threw them, so that we were fain to give back.° We had six stout Dogs belonging to our Garrison, but none of them would stir, though another time, if any Indian had come to the door, they were ready to fly upon him and tear him down. The Lord hereby would make us the more to acknowledge his hand, and to see that our help is always in him.° But out we must go, the fire increasing, and coming along behind us, roaring, and the Indians gaping before us with their Guns, Spears and Hatchets to devour us. No sooner were we out of the House, but my Brother in Law (being before wounded, in defending the house, in or near the throat) fell down dead, whereat the Indians scornfully shouted, and hallowed,° and were presently upon him, stripping off his cloaths, the bulletts flying thick, one went through my side, and the same (as would seem) through the bowels and hand of my dear Child in my arms. One of my elder Sister's Children, named William, had then his Leg broken, which the Indians perceiving, they knockt him on head. Thus were we butchered by those merciless Heathen, standing amazed, with the blood running down to our heels. My eldest Sister being yet in the House, and seeing those woefull sights, the Infidels hauling Mothers one way, and Children another, and some wallowing in their blood, and her elder Son telling her that her Son William was dead, and my self was wounded, she said, And, Lord, let me die with them; which was no sooner said, but she was struck with a Bullet, and fell down dead over the threshold. I hope she is reaping the fruit of her good labours, being faithfull to the service of God in her place. In her younger years she lay under much trouble upon spiritual accounts, till it pleased God to make that precious Scripture take hold of her heart, 2 Corinthians 12:9, *And he said unto me, my Grace is sufficient for thee.* More than twenty years after I have heard her tell how

---

fain to give back: compelled to go back

in him: from him (the Lord)

hallowed: shouted, hollered

sweet and comfortable that place was to her. But to return: The Indians laid hold of us, pulling me one way, and the Children another, and said, Come go along with us; I told them they would kill me: they answered, If I were willing to go along with them, they would not hurt me.

Oh the doleful sight that now was to behold at this House! *Come, behold the works of the Lord, what desolations he has made in the Earth.* Of thirty seven persons who were in this one House, none escaped either present death, or a bitter captivity, save only one, who might say as he, Job 1:15, *And I only am escaped alone to tell the News.* There were twelve killed, some shot, some stab'd with their Spears, some knock'd down with their Hatchets. When we are in prosperity, Oh the little that we think of such dreadfull sights, and to see our dear Friends, and Relations lie bleeding out their heart-blood upon the ground. There was one who was chopt into the head with a Hatchet, and stript naked, and yet was crawling up and down. It is a solemn sight to see so many Christians lying in their blood, some here, and some there, like a company of Sheep torn by Wolves, All of them stript naked by a company of hell-hounds, roaring, singing, ranting and insulting, as if they would have torn our very hearts out; yet the Lord by his Almighty power preserved a number of us from death, for there were twenty-four of us taken alive and carried Captive.

I had often before this said, that if the Indians should come, I should chuse rather to be killed by them than taken alive but when it came to the trial my mind changed; their glittering weapons so daunted my spirit, that I chose rather to go along with those (as I may say) ravenous Beasts, than that moment to end my days; and that I may the better declare what happened to me during that grievous Captivity, I shall particularly speak of the severall Removes° we had up and down the Wilderness.

The first Remove

Now away we must go with those Barbarous Creatures, with our bodies wounded and bleeding, and our hearts no less than our bodies. About a mile we went that night, up upon a hill within sight of the Town where they intended to lodge. There was hard by a vacant house (deserted by the English before, for fear of the Indians). I asked them whether I might not lodge in the house that night to which they answered, what will you love English men still? This was the dolefullest night that ever my eyes saw. Oh the roaring, and

5

---

removes: moves, relocations

singing and dancing, and yelling of those black creatures in the night, which made the place a lively resemblance of hell. And as miserable was the waste that was there made, of Horses, Cattle, Sheep, Swine, Calves, Lambs, Roasting Pigs, and Fowl (which they had plundered in the Town) some roasting, some lying and burning, and some boiling to feed our merciless Enemies; who were joyful enough though we were disconsolate. To add to the dolefulness of the former day, and the dismalness of the present night, my thoughts ran upon my losses and sad bereaved condition. All was gone, my Husband gone (at least separated from me, he being in the Bay;° and to add to my grief, the Indians told me they would kill him as he came homeward) my Children gone, my Relations and Friends gone, our House and home and all our comforts within door, and without, all was gone, (except my life) and I knew not but the next moment that might go too. There remained nothing to me but one poor wounded Babe, and it seemed at present worse than death that it was in such a pitiful condition, bespeaking° Compassion, and I had no refreshing° for it, nor suitable things to revive it. Little do many think what is the savageness and bruitishness of this barbarous Enemy, aye even those that seem to profess° more than others among them, when the English have fallen into their hands.

Those seven that were killed at Lancaster the summer before upon a Sabbath day, and the one that was afterward killed upon a week day, were slain and mangled in a barbarous manner, by one-ey'd John, and Marlborough's Praying Indians, which Capt. Mosely brought to Boston, as the Indians told me.

The second Remove

But now, the next morning, I must turn my back upon the Town, and travel with them into the vast and desolate Wilderness, I knew not whither. It is not my tongue, or pen can express the sorrows of my heart, and bitterness of my spirit, that I had at this departure; but God was with me, in a wonderfull manner, carrying me along, and bearing up my spirit, [so] that it did not quite fail. One of the Indians carried my poor wounded Babe upon a horse; it went moaning all along, I shall die, I shall die. I went on foot after it, with sorrow that cannot be exprest. At length I took it off the horse, and carried it in my armes till my strength failed, and I fell down with it: Then they set

---

the Bay: the Massachusetts Bay Colony
bespeaking: asking for
refreshing: food and/or drink
seem to profess: claim to be Christians

me upon a horse with my wounded Child in my lap, and there being no furniture° upon the horse back, as we were going down a steep hill, we both fell over the horse's head, at which they like inhumane creatures laught, and rejoiced to see it, though I thought we should there have ended our days, as overcome with so many difficulties. But the Lord renewed my strength still, and carried me along, [so] that I might see more of his Power, yea, so much that I could never have thought of, had I not experienced it.

After this it quickly began to snow, and when night came on, they stopt; and now down I must sit in the snow, by a little fire, and a few boughs behind me, with my sick Child in my lap; and calling much for water, being now (through the wound) fallen into a violent Fever. My own wound also growing so stiff, that I could scarce sit down or rise up; yet so it must be, that I must sit all this cold winter night upon the cold snowy ground, with my sick Child in my arms, looking that every hour would be the last of its life, and having no Christian friend near me, either to comfort or help me. Oh, I may see the wonderfull power of God, that my Spirit did not utterly sink under my affliction; still the Lord upheld me with his gracious and mercifull Spirit, and we were both alive to see the light of the next morning.

The third Remove

The morning being come, they prepared to go on their way. One of the Indians got up upon a horse, and they set me up behind him, with my poor sick Babe in my lap. A very wearisome and tedious day I had of it; what with my own wound, and my Child's being so exceeding sick, and in a lamentable condition with her wound. It may be easily judged what a poor feeble condition we were in, there being not the least crumb of refreshing that came within either of our mouths, from Wednesday night to Saturday night, except only a little cold water. This day in the afternoon, about an hour by Sun, we came to the place where they intended, *viz.*° an Indian Town, called Wenimesset, Northward of Quabaug. When we were come, Oh the number of Pagans (now merciless enemies) that there came about me, that I may say as David, Psalms 27:13, *I had fainted, unless I had believed,* etc. The next day was the Sabbath: I then remembered how careless I had been of God's holy time, how many Sabbaths I had lost and mispent, and how evily I had walked in God's sight, which lay so close unto my spirit, that it was easie for me to see how righteous it was with God to cut off the thread of my life and

---

furniture: equipment (i.e., saddle)

viz.: namely, that is to say (from Latin *videlicet*)

cast me out of his presence for ever. Yet the Lord still showed mercy to me, and upheld me; and as he wounded me with one hand, so he healed me with the other. This day there came to me one Robbert Pepper (a man belonging to Roxbury) who was taken in Captain Beers his° Fight, and had been now a considerable time with the Indians; and [he went] up with them almost as far as Albany, to see king Philip, as he told me, and was now very lately come into these parts. Hearing, I say, that I was in this Indian Town, he obtained leave to come and see me. He told me, he himself was wounded in the leg at Captain Beers his Fight, and was not able some time to go,° but as they carried him, and as he took Oaken leaves and laid to his wound, and through the blessing of God he was able to travel again. Then I took Oaken leaves and laid to my side, and with the blessing of God it cured me also; yet before the cure was wrought, I may say, as it is in Psalms 38:5,6, *My wounds stink and are corrupt, I am troubled, I am bowed down greatly, I go mourning all the day long.* I sat much alone with a poor wounded Child in my lap, which moaned night and day, having nothing to revive the body, or cheer the spirits of her, but in stead of that, sometimes one Indian would come and tell me one hour, that your Master will knock your Child in the head, and then a second, and then a third, your Master will quickly knock your Child in the head.

This was the comfort I had from them, miserable comforters° are ye all, as he said. Thus nine days I sat upon my knees, with my Babe in my lap, till my flesh was raw again; my Child being even ready to depart this sorrowfull world, they bade me carry it out to another Wigwam (I suppose because they would not be troubled with such spectacles) Whither I went with a very heavy heart, and down I sat with the picture of death in my lap. About two hours in the night, my sweet Babe like a Lamb departed this life, on Feb. 18, 1675. It being about six years, and five months old. It was nine days from the first wounding, in this miserable condition, without any refreshing of one nature or other, except a little cold water. I cannot, but take notice, how at another time I could not bear to be in the room where any dead person was, but now the case is changed; I must and could lie down by my dead Babe, side by side all the night after. I have thought since of the wonderfull goodness of God to me, in preserving me in the use of my reason and senses,

10

Beers his: Beers's; the reference is to a battle in King Philip's War fought near Deerfield, Massachusetts, in September 1675

go: walk, move

miserable comforters: a reference to the Book of Job (Bible), in which Job's three friends offer him poor comfort in the midst of his afflictions

in that distressed time, that I did not use wicked and violent means to end my own miserable life.

. . .

Now the Indians began to talk of removing from this place, some one way, and some another. There were now besides my self nine English Captives in this place (all of them Children, except one Woman). I got an opportunity to go and take my leave of them; they being to go one way, and I another. I asked them whether they were earnest with God for deliverance; they told me, they did as they were able, and it was some comfort to me, that the Lord stirred up Children to look to him. The Woman *viz.* Goodwife Joslin told me she should never see me again, and that she could find in her heart to run away; I wisht her not to run away by any means, for we were near thirty miles from any English Town, and she very big with Child, and had but one week to reckon,° and another Child in her Arms, two years old, and bad Rivers there were to go over, and we were feeble, with our poor and coarse entertainment.° I had my Bible with me, I pulled it out, and asked her whether she would read; we opened the Bible and lighted on Psalms 27, in which Psalm we especially took notice of that, *ver. ult.,*° *Wait on the Lord, Be of good courage, and he shall strengthen thine Heart, wait I say on the Lord.*

The fourth Remove

And now I must part with that little Company I had. Here I parted from my Daughter Mary, (whom I never saw again till I saw her in Dorchester, returned from Captivity), and from four little Cousins and Neighbours, some of which I never saw afterward; the Lord only knows the end of them. Amongst them also was that poor Woman before mentioned, who came to a sad end, as some of the company told me in my travel: She having much grief upon her Spirit, about her miserable condition, being so near her time, she would be often asking the Indians to let her go home; they not being willing to that, and yet vexed with her importunity,° gathered a great company together about her, and stript her naked, and set her in the midst of them; and when they had sung and danced about her (in their hellish manner) as long as they pleased, they knockt her on head, and the child in her arms with her: when they had done that, they made a fire and put them both into it,

---

to reckon: until her due date
entertainment: treatment in terms of nourishment and shelter
ver ult.: last verse (Latin: *versus ultimum*)
importunity: persistent pleading

and told the other Children that were with them, that if they attempted to go home, they would serve them in like manner: The Children said, she did not shed one tear, but prayed all the while. But to return to my own Journey; we travelled about half a day or little more, and came to a desolate place in the Wilderness, where there were no Wigwams or Inhabitants before; we came about the middle of the afternoon to this place, cold and wet, and snowy, and hungry, and weary, and no refreshing for man, but the cold ground to sit on, and our poor Indian cheer.°

Heart-aching thoughts here I had about my poor Children, who were scattered up and down among the wild beasts of the forrest: My head was light and dizzey (either through hunger or hard lodging, or trouble or altogether) my knees feeble, my body raw by sitting double° night and day, that I cannot express to man the affliction that lay upon my Spirit, but the Lord helped me at that time to express it to himself. I opened my Bible to read, and the Lord brought that precious Scripture to me, Jeremiah 31:16, *Thus saith the Lord, refrain thy voice from weeping, and thine eyes from tears, for thy work shall be rewarded, and they shall come again from the land of the Enemy.* This was a sweet Cordial° to me, when I was ready to faint, many and many a time have I sat down, and wept sweetly over this Scripture. At this place we continued about four days.

The fifth Remove

The occasion (as I thought) of their moving at this time, was, the English Army, it being near and following them: For they went, as if they had gone for their lives, for some considerable way, and then they made a stop, and chose some of their stoutest° men, and sent them back to hold the English Army in play° whilst the rest escaped....

The first week of my being among them, I hardly ate any thing; the second week, I found my stomach grow very faint for want of something; and yet it was very hard to get down their filthy trash; but the third week, though I could think how formerly my stomach would turn against this or that, and I could starve and die before I could eat such things, yet they were sweet and savoury to my taste. I was at this time knitting a pair of white

---

cheer: entertainment, especially with food and drink
sitting double: riding two on a horse
Cordial: restorative beverage
stoutest: boldest, most intrepid
in play: pinned down in combat

cotton stockings for my mistress; and had not yet wrought upon a Sabbath day; when the Sabbath came they bade me go to work; I told them it was the Sabbath-day, and desired them to let me rest, and told them I would do as much more to morrow; to which they answered me, they would break my face. And here I cannot but take notice of the strange providence of God in preserving the heathen: They were many hundreds, old and young, some sick, and some lame, many had Papooses at their backs, the greatest number at this time with us were Squaws, and they travelled with all they had, bag and baggage, and yet they got over this River aforesaid; and on Monday they set their Wigwams on fire, and away they went: On that very day came the English Army after them to this River, and saw the smoke of their Wigwams, and yet this River put a stop to them. God did not give them courage or activity to go over after us; we were not ready for so great a mercy as victory and deliverance; if we had been, God would have found out a way for the English to have passed this River, as well as for the Indians with their Squaws and Children, and all their Luggage. *Oh that my People had hearkened to me, and Israel had walked in my ways, I should soon have subdued their Enemies, and turned my hand against their Adversaries,* Psalms 81:13–14.

The sixth Remove

On Monday (as I said) they set their Wigwams on fire, and went away. It was a cold morning, and before us there was a great Brook with ice on it; some waded through it, up to the knees and higher, but others went till they came to a Beaver-dam, and I amongst them, where through the good providence of God, I did not wet my foot. I went along that day mourning and lamenting, leaving farther my own Country, and travelling into the vast and howling Wilderness, and I understood something of Lot's Wife's Temptation, when she looked back: we came that day to a great Swamp, by the side of which we took up our lodging that night. When I came to the brow of the hill, that looked toward the Swamp, I thought we had been come to a great Indian Town (though there were none but our own Company). The Indians were as thick as the trees: it seemed as if there had been a thousand Hatchets going at once: if one looked before one, there was nothing but Indians, and behind one, nothing but Indians, and so on either hand, I my self in the midst, and no Christian soul near me, and yet how hath the Lord preserved me in safety? Oh the experience that I have had of the goodness of God, to me and mine!

The seventh Remove

After a restless and hungry night there, we had a wearisome time of it the next day. The Swamp by which we lay, was, as it were, a deep Dungeon, and an exceeding high and steep hill before it. Before I got to the top of the hill, I thought my heart and legs and all would have broken, and failed me. What through faintness, and soreness of body, it was a grievous day of travel to me. As we went along, I saw a place where English Cattle had been; that was comfort to me, such as it was: Quickly after that we came to an English Path, which so took with° me, that I thought I could have freely lain down and died. That day, a little after noon, we came to Squaukheag, where the Indians quickly spread themselves over the deserted English Fields, gleaning what they could find; some pickt up ears of Wheat that were crickled° down, some found ears of Indian Corn, some found Ground-nuts, and others sheaves of Wheat that were frozen together in the shock, and went to threshing of them out. My self got two ears of Indian Corn, and whilst I did but turn my back, one of them was stolen from me, which much troubled me. There came an Indian to them at that time, with a basket of Horse-liver. I asked him to give me a piece: What, says he, can you eat Horse-liver? I told him, I would try, if he would give a piece, which he did, and I laid it on the coals to roast; but before it was half ready they got half of it away from me, so that I was fain° to take the rest and eat it as it was, with the blood about my mouth, and yet a savoury bit it was to me: *For to the hungry Soul every bitter thing is sweet.* A solemn sight methought it was, to see Fields of wheat and Indian Corn forsaken and spoiled; and the remainders of them to be food for our merciless Enemies. That night we had a mess of wheat for our Supper.

The eighth Remove

On the morrow morning we must go over the River, *i.e.* Connecticut, to meet with King Philip; two Canoes full, they had carried over, the next Turn I my self was to go; but as my foot was upon the Canoe to step in, there was a sudden out-cry among them, and I must step back; and instead of going over the River, I must go four or five miles up the River farther Northward. Some of the Indians ran one way, and some another. The cause of this rout was, as I thought, their espying some English Scouts, who were thereabout. In this travel up the River, about noon the Company made a stop, and sat

---

took with: affected
crickled: trampled
fain: compelled, obliged

down; some to eat, and others to rest them. As I sat amongst them, musing of things past, my Son Joseph unexpectedly came to me: we asked of each other's welfare, bemoaning our dolefull condition, and the change that had come upon us. We had Husband and Father, and Children, and Sisters, and Friends, and Relations, and House, and Home, and many Comforts of this Life: but now we may say, as Job, *Naked came I out of my Mother's Womb, and naked shall I return: The Lord gave, and the Lord hath taken away, Blessed be the Name of the Lord*.... We travelled on till night; and in the morning, we must go over the River to Philip's Crew. When I was in the Canoe, I could not but be amazed at the numerous crew of Pagans that were on the Bank on the other side. When I came ashore, they gathered all about me, I sitting alone in the midst: I observed they asked one another questions, and laughed, and rejoiced over their Gains and Victories. Then my heart began to fail; and I fell a weeping which was the first time, to my remembrance, that I wept before them. Although I had met with so much Affliction, and my heart was many times ready to break, yet could I not shed one tear in their sight, but rather had been all this while in a maze,° and like one astonished; but now I may say as, Psalms 137:1, *By the Rivers of Babylon, there we sat down: yea, we wept when we remembered Zion*. There one of them asked me, why I wept, I could hardly tell what to say; yet I answered, they would kill me: No, said he, none will hurt you. Then came one of them and gave me two spoon-fulls of Meal to comfort me, and another gave me half a pint of Peas, which was more worth than many Bushels at another time. Then I went to see King Philip; he bade me come in and sit down, and asked me whether I would smoke it (a usual Complement nowadays amongst Saints and Sinners) but this no way suited me. For though I had formerly used Tobacco, yet I had left it ever since I was first taken. It seems to be a Bait, the Devil lays to make men loose their precious time: I remember with shame, how formerly, when I had taken two or three pipes, I was presently ready for another, such a bewitching thing it is: But I thank God, he has now given me power over it; surely there are many who may be better employed than to lie sucking a stinking Tobacco-pipe.

. . .

The twelfth Remove

It was upon a Sabbath-day-morning, that they prepared for their Travel. This morning I asked my master whether he would sell me to my Husband; he answered me *Nux*, which did much to rejoice my spirit. My mistress, before we went, was gone to the burial of a Papoos, and returning, she found me

---

a maze: amazement, dazed condition

sitting and reading in my Bible; she snatched it hastily out of my hand, and threw it out of doors; I ran out and catcht it up, and put it into my pocket, and never let her see it afterward. Then they packed up their things to be gone, and gave me my load: I complained it was too heavy, whereupon she gave me a slap in the face, and bade me go; I lifted up my heart to God, hoping the Redemption was not far off, and the rather because their insolency grew worse and worse.

But the thoughts of my going homeward (for so we bent our course) much cheered my Spirit, and made my burden seem light, and almost nothing at all. 20

. . .

The eighteenth Remove

We took up our packs and along we went, but a wearisome day I had of it. As we went along I saw an English-man stript naked and lying dead upon the ground, but knew not who it was. Then we came to another Indian Town, where we stayed all night. In this Town there were four English Children, Captives; and one of them my own Sister's [child]. I went to see how she did, and she was well, considering her Captive-condition. I would have tarried that night with her, but they that owned her would not suffer° it. Then I went into another Wigwam, where they were boiling Corn and Beans, which was a lovely sight to see, but I could not get a taste thereof. Then I went to another Wigwam, where there were two of the English Children; the Squaw was boiling Horse's feet; then she cut me off a little piece, and gave one of the English Children a piece also. Being very hungry I had quickly eat up mine, but the Child could not bite it, it was so tough and sinewy, but lay sucking, gnawing, chewing and slabbering° of it in the mouth and hand; then I took it of the Child, and eat it my self, and savoury it was to my taste. Then I may say as Job, 6:7, *The things that my soul refused to touch, are as my sorrowfull meat*. Thus the Lord made that pleasant refreshing, which another time would have been an abomination. Then I went home to my mistress's Wigwam; and they told me I disgraced my master with begging, and if I did so any more, they would knock me in head: I told them, they had as good knock me in head as starve me to death.

The nineteenth Remove

They said, when we went out, that we must travel to Wachuset this day. But a bitter weary day I had of it, travelling now three days together, without resting any day between. At last, after many weary steps, I saw Wachuset hills, but

---

suffer: allow
slabbering: slobbering

many miles off. Then we came to a great Swamp; through which we travelled, up to the knees in mud and water, which was heavy going to one tired before.° Being almost spent,° I thought I should have sunk down at last, and never got out; but I may say, as in Psalms 94:18, *When my foot slipped, thy mercy, O Lord, held me up.* Going along, having indeed my life, but little spirit, Philip, who was in the Company, came up and took me by the hand, and said, Two weeks more and you shall be Mistress again. I asked him, if he spoke true? He answered, Yes, and quickly you shall come to your master again, who had been gone from us three weeks. After many weary steps we came to Wachuset, where he was; and glad I was to see him. He asked me, When I washt me? I told him not this month, then he fetcht me some water himself, and bid me wash, and gave me the Glass° to see how I lookt, and bid his Squaw give me something to eat; so she gave me a mess of Beans and meat, and a little Ground-nut Cake. I was wonderfully revived with this favour showed me, Psalms 106:46. *He made them also to be pittied, of all those that carried them Captives.*

My master had three Squaws, living sometimes with one, and sometimes with another one, this old Squaw, at whose Wigwam I was, and with whom my Master had been those three weeks. Another was Weetamoo with whom I had lived and served all this while: A severe and proud Dame she was, bestowing every day in dressing her self neat as much time as any of the Gentry of the land, powdering her hair, and painting her face, going with Neck-laces, with Jewels in her ears, and Bracelets upon her hands: When she had dressed her self, her work was to make Girdles° of Wampum and Beads. The third Squaw was a younger one, by whom he had two Papooses. By that time I was refresht by the old Squaw, with whom my master was, Weetamoo's Maid came to call me home, at which I fell a weeping. Then the old Squaw told me, to encourage me, that if I wanted victuals, I should come to her, and that I should lie there in her Wigwam. Then I went with the maid, and quickly came again and lodged there. The Squaw laid a Mat under me, and a good Rugg over me; the first time I had any such kindness showed me. I understood that Weetamoo thought, that if she should let me go and serve with the old Squaw, she would be in danger to lose, not only my service, but the redemption-pay° also. And I was not a little glad to hear this, being by

---

one tired before: one who was already tired

spent: worn out, exhausted

Glass: mirror

Girdles: belts, sashes

redemption-pay: ransom money

it raised in my hopes that in God's due time there would be an end of this sorrowfull hour. Then came an Indian, and asked me to knit him three pair of Stockings, for which I had a Hat, and a silk Handkerchief. Then another asked me to make her a shift,° for which she gave me an Apron.

Then came Tom and Peter, with the second Letter from the Council, about the Captives. Though they were Indians, I got them by the hand, and burst out into tears; my heart was so full that I could not speak to them; but recovering my self, I asked them how my husband did, and all my friends and acquaintances? They said, They are all very well but melancholy. They brought me two Biskets, and a pound of Tobacco. The Tobacco I quickly gave away; when it was all gone, one asked me to give him a pipe of Tobacco. I told him it was all gone; then began he to rant and threaten. I told him when my Husband came I would give him some: Hang him [as a] Rogue (says he) I will knock out his brains, if he comes here. And then again, in the same breath they would say that if there should come an hundred without Guns, they would do them no hurt. So unstable and like mad men they were. So that fearing the worst, I durst not send to my Husband, though there were some thoughts of his coming to Redeem and fetch me, not knowing what might follow. For there was little more trust to them than to the master they served. When the Letter was come, the Sagamores met to consult about the Captives, and called me to them to enquire how much my husband would give to redeem me, when I came I sat down among them, as I was wont° to do, as their manner is: Then they bade me stand up, and said, they were the General Court. They bade me speak what I thought he would give. Now knowing that all we had was destroyed by the Indians, I was in a great strait:° I thought if I should speak of but a little,° it would be slighted, and hinder the matter; if of a great sum, I knew not where it would be procured; yet at a venture, I said Twenty pounds, yet desired them to take less; but they would not hear of that, but sent that message to Boston, that for Twenty pounds I should be redeemed. It was a Praying-Indian° that wrote their Letter for them. There was another Praying Indian, who told me, that he had a brother that would not eat Horse, his conscience was so tender and scrupulous (though as large

---

shift: slip, underskirt
wont: accustomed
strait: difficult situation
but a little: only a small amount
Praying-Indian: i.e., a Christian convert

as hell, for the destruction of poor Christians). Then he said, he read that Scripture to him, 2 Kings 6:25, *There was a famine in Samaria, and behold they besieged it, untill an ass's head was sold for fourscore pieces of silver, and the fourth part of a kab° of dove's dung, for five pieces of silver.* He expounded this place to his brother, and showed him that it was lawfull to eat that in a Famine which is not at another time. And now, says he, he will eat Horse with any Indian of them all.

. . .

25 And now God hath granted me my desire. O the wonderfull power of God that I have seen, and the experience that I have had: I have been in the midst of those roaring Lions, and Savage Bears, that feared neither God, nor Man, nor the Devil, by night and day, alone and in company, sleeping all sorts together, and yet not one of them ever offered me the least abuse of unchastity to me, in word or action. Though some are ready to say [that] I speak it for my own credit; But I speak it in the presence of God, and to his Glory. God's Power is as great now, and as sufficient to save, as when he preserved Daniel in the Lions' Den; or the three Children in the fiery Furnace. I may well say as his Psalms 107:1, *Oh give thanks unto the Lord for he is good, for his mercy endureth for ever.* Let the Redeemed of the Lord say so, whom he hath redeemed from the hand of the Enemy, especially that I should come away in the midst of so many hundreds of Enemies quietly and peaceably, and not a Dog moving his tongue. So I took my leave of them, and in coming along my heart melted into tears, more than all the while I was with them, and I was almost swallowed up with the thoughts that ever I should go home again. About° the Sun going down, Mr. Hoar, and my self, and the two Indians came to Lancaster, and a solemn sight it was to me. There had I lived many comfortable years amongst my Relations and Neighbours, and now not one Christian to be seen, nor one house left standing. We went [farther] on to a Farm house that was yet standing, where we lay all night; and a comfortable lodging we had, though nothing but straw to lie on. The Lord preserved us in safety that night, and raised us up again in the morning, and carried us along, [so] that before noon we came to Concord. Now was I full of joy, and yet not without sorrow; joy to see such a lovely sight, so many Christians together, and some of them my Neighbours: There I met with my Brother, and my Brother in Law, who asked me, if

---

kab: a measure equal to about four pints

About: about the time of

I knew where his Wife was? Poor heart! He had helped to bury her, and knew it not. She, being shot down by the house, was partly burnt, so that those who were at Boston at [the time of] the desolation of the Town, and came back afterward, and buried the dead, did not know her. Yet I was not without sorrow, to think how many were looking and longing, and my own Children amongst the rest, to enjoy that deliverance that I had now received, and I did not know whether ever I should see them again. Being recruited° with food and raiment we went to Boston that day, where I met with my dear Husband, but the thoughts of our dear Children, one being dead, and the other we could not tell where, abated° our comfort each to other. I was not before so much hem'd in with the merciless and cruel Heathen, but now as much with pittiful, tender-hearted and compassionate Christians. In that poor, and distressed, and beggerly condition I was received in, I was kindly entertained° in severall Houses; so much love I received from several (some of whom I knew, and others I knew not) that I am not capable to declare it. But the Lord knows them all by name: The Lord reward them seven fold into their bosoms of his spirituals, for their temporals.°

. . .

I have seen the extreme vanity of this World: One hour I have been in health, and wealth, wanting nothing: But the next hour in sickness and wounds, and death, having nothing but sorrow and affliction.

Before I knew what affliction meant, I was ready sometimes to wish for it. When I lived in prosperity, having the comforts of the World about me, my relations by me, my Heart cheerfull, and taking little care for any thing; and yet seeing many, whom I preferred before my self, under many trials and afflictions, in sickness, weakness, poverty, losses, crosses, and cares of the World, I should be sometimes jealous lest I should not have my portion in this life, and that Scripture would come to my mind, Hebrews 12:6, *For whom the Lord loveth he chasteneth, and scourgeth every Son whom he receiveth*. But now I see the Lord had his time to scourge and chasten me. The portion of some is to have their afflictions by drops, now one drop and then another; but the dregs of the Cup, the Wine of astonishment, like a sweeping rain that leaveth no food, did the Lord prepare to be my portion. Affliction I wanted,

---

recruited: refreshed, restored

abated: diminished

entertained: shown hospitality

reward them . . . for their temporals: give them heavenly rewards for the earthly charity they displayed

and affliction I had, full measure (I thought) pressed down and running over; yet I see, when God calls a Person to any thing, and through ever so many difficulties, yet he is fully able to carry them through, and make them see, and say they have been gainers thereby. And I hope I can say in some measure, As David did, *It is good for me that I have been afflicted.* The Lord hath showed me the vanity of these outward things. That they are the Vanity of vanities, and vexation of spirit; that they are but a shadow, a blast,° a bubble, and things of no continuance. That we must rely on God himself, and our whole dependence must be upon him. If trouble from smaller matters begin to arise in me, I have something at hand to check my self with, and say, why am I troubled? It was but the other day that if I had had the world, I would have given it for my freedom, or to have been a Servant to a Christian. I have learned to look beyond present and smaller troubles, and to be quieted under them, as Moses said, Exodus 14:13, *Stand still and see the salvation of the Lord.*

[1682]

Read

1. How does Rowlandson use imagery to convey her terror during the attack on her house?
2. How would you characterize her reflections on her conditions and on her captors in the early "removes?"
3. What is the effect of the arrangement of the narrative into "removes?" Why are they called "removes?"
4. Where do you see a sense of Rowlandson's attitude toward the land and who might have rights to it?

Write

1. What is the role of faith for Rowlandson? How is the role made clear?
2. Write about the development of Rowlandson's understanding of her captors during her ordeal. How does her choice of language or image help you see a change in attitude?
3. Write a journal entry from the perspective of one of the Narragansett women who is traveling with the group. How might she see Rowlandson?

Connect

1. This narrative was a "best seller" in the colonies when it was published. Why do you think that was so?
2. Attempt to make connections to the two other journals you've read in this section: Smith and Bradford. Are the *personae* of the speakers at all alike? Do they have similar notions of audience? Are their purposes or aims connected?

---

a blast: of empty wind

Cyrus Dallin

Cyrus Dallin (1860–1943) was born to Utah territory pioneers who brought him up in Ute Indian territory. He knew the tribes well and became boyhood friends with the braves in the Crow and Ute tribes. He moved to Boston in 1879 to study sculpture and eventually to Paris to further develop his techniques. When the Buffalo Bill Wild West Show performed in Paris, Dallin discovered his first great subject in sculpture in the American Indian form. His sculpture, *Signal of Peace,* now standing in Lincoln Park in Chicago, taps into his memory of the Plains Indians with whom he grew up. He produced the statue of Massasoit as a commission by the Imperial Order of the Red Man as part of Plymouth's tri-centennial celebration of the founding of the colony.

Massasoit

Massasoit (1921), Cyrus E. Dallin. Bronze sculpture. Plymouth, Massachusetts. Photo by Patti McConville/Alamy

[1921]

Read

1. What specific details contribute to the sculpture's effect on the viewer?
2. How does the sculpture portray the attitude of the sculptor toward his audience?
3. How does the sculpture indicate an attitude toward Massasoit? Toward Indian tribes in general?

Write

1. Write a brief description of Massasoit's personality as you infer it from the sculpture.
2. The sculpture is placed near Plymouth Bay, where the Mayflower finally dropped anchor. How does this location affect the rhetorical effect of the sculpture?

Connect

1. How does Massasoit's sculpture connect to what you have learned about him in historical accounts, including Philbrick and Bradford?
2. How does the sculpture affirm stereotypes of Indians; how does it alter them?

Anne Bradstreet

Considered the first American poet, Anne Bradstreet (1612–1672) published the first book written by a woman of the colonies. Bradstreet was well educated in England and came to Massachusetts Bay Colony with her parents aboard Winthrop's ship the *Arbella.* She married John Bradstreet, who was a founder of Harvard University, moved to Andover, and began writing. Her collection of poems, *The Tenth Muse,* was published after her brother-in-law took her manuscript to England. Her poems document the struggles of Puritan life in North America and the roles of women within the colonial community. Bradstreet's earthly love for beauty, her husband, and children are as strongly evident in the poems as her Puritan faith and spiritual understanding.

The Author to Her Book

Thou ill-formed offspring of my feeble brain,
Who after birth did'st by my side remain,
Till snatcht from thence by friends, less wise than true,
Who thee abroad° exposed to public view,
Made thee in rags, halting° to th' press to trudge, 5
Where errors were not lessened (all may judge).
At thy return my blushing was not small,
My rambling brat (in print) should mother call.
I cast thee by as one unfit for light,
Thy visage° was so irksome in my sight, 10

---

abroad: far and wide; out in the world
halting: limping, lame
visage: face; appearance, aspect

Yet being mine own, at length affection would
Thy blemishes amend, if so I could.
I washed thy face, but more defects I saw,
And rubbing off a spot, still made a flaw.
I stretcht thy joints to make thee even feet, 15
Yet still thou run'st more hobbling than is meet.
In better dress to trim thee was my mind,
But nought save home-spun cloth, i' th' house I find.
In this array, 'mongst vulgars may'st thou roam.
In critic's hands, beware thou dost not come, 20
And take thy way where yet thou art not known.
If for thy father askt, say, thou hadst none;
And for thy mother, she alas is poor,
Which caused her thus to send thee out of door.

[1678]

Read

1. Where is the first indication to you that Bradstreet is talking about a piece of writing rather than a child?
2. What are three comparisons she makes between a child and the book?
3. How does language show her attitude toward her writing?

Write

1. Write about the persona Bradstreet creates in the poem. Does she seem strong or weak?
2. Rewrite at least five lines in contemporary English. See how close you can get to the rhythm of the poem.
3. Analyze the way Bradstreet uses audience in the poem to get across her point about her work.

Connect

1. Speculate about the reason for Bradstreet's apology for her "ill-formed" verse. Do you think she meant it?
2. Does Bradstreet strike you as a typical Puritan woman? Why or why not?

On the Burning of Her House

In silent night when rest I took,
For sorrow near I did not look,
I waken'd was with thund'ring noise

And piteous shrieks of dreadful voice.
That fearful sound of "fire" and "fire," 5
Let no man know is my Desire.°
I starting up, the light did spy,
And to my God my heart did cry
To straighten me in my Distress
And not to leave me succourless.° 10
Then coming out, behold a space°
The flame consume my dwelling place.
And when I could no longer look,
I blest his grace that gave and took,
That laid my goods now in the dust. 15
Yea, so it was, and so 'twas just.
It was his own; it was not mine.
Far be it that I should repine,°
He might of all justly bereft°
But yet sufficient for us left. 20
When by the Ruins oft I past
My sorrowing eyes aside did cast
And here and there the places spy
Where oft I sate° and long did lie.
Here stood that Trunk, and there that chest, 25
There lay that store° I counted best,
My pleasant things in ashes lie
And them behold no more shall I.
Under the roof no guest shall sit,
Nor at thy Table eat a bit. 30
No pleasant talk shall 'ere° be told
Nor things recounted done of old.
No Candle 'ere shall shine in Thee,

Let no man know is my Desire: Let no one imagine that I want to hear
succourless: without relief
a space: for a period of time
repine: complain, lament
He might of all justly bereft: He could by right have deprived us of everything
sate: sat
store: supply (of possessions)
'ere: e'er (ever)

Nor bridegroom's voice 'ere heard shall bee.
In silence ever shalt thou lie. 35
Adieu, Adieu, All's Vanity.
Then straight I 'gin° my heart to chide:
And did thy wealth on earth abide,
Didst fix thy hope on mouldring dust,
The arm of flesh didst make thy trust? 40
Raise up thy thoughts above the sky
That dunghill mists away may fly.
Thou hast a house on high erect
Fram'd by that mighty Architect,
With glory richly furnished 45
Stands permanent, though this be fled.
It's purchased and paid for too
By him who hath enough to do.
A price so vast as is unknown,
Yet by his gift is made thine own. 50
There's wealth enough; I need no more.
Farewell, my pelf;° farewell, my store.
The world no longer let me love;
My hope and Treasure lies above.

[1666]

Read

1. How does the poem suggest the relationship—or the conflict—between the spiritual and the earthly?
2. Where in this poem do you find Bradstreet to be more than a good Puritan woman?
3. How do you see logic finding a place in the poem?

Complete Additional Exercises on Bradstreet's Poem at Your Pearson MyLab

Write

1. Where do you see Bradstreet changing her attitude or her position in the poem? Write about why she makes this shift.
2. Comment on the use of the question in the poem. Who does she seem to be talking to?
3. Write a brief character description of the speaker of the poem, using examples from the poem's language and imagery to help you.

'gin: begin
pelf: money, wealth

Connect

1. What do the two poems reveal about the role of women in the new land?
2. How does Bradstreet suggest the adversity the Pilgrims faced and the perils of the land?

Anonymous

Next to the Bible, *The New England Primer* and the *Bay Psalm Book* were the most commonly owned books in the colonial household. Like the *Bay Psalm Book,* which translated Biblical psalms into common Puritan language, the *Primer* used common language and associations to teach Puritan values and ideas in "our English tongue." The *Primer* sold over five million copies in its various versions from 1683 to 1830, and it taught literacy and religious tenets to Puritan children. It demonstrated the community's belief in literacy as a way toward salvation and community order. It inculcated values so that each generation would learn the creeds while learning their letters.

From *The New England Primer*

Alphabet

A In *Adam's* Fall
We Sinned all.

B Thy Life to Mend
This *Book* Attend.

C The *Cat* doth play
And after slay.

D A *Dog* will bite
A Thief at night.

E The *Eagle's* flight
Is out of sight.

F The Idle *Fool*
Is whipt at School.

G As runs the *Glass*°
Man's life doth pass.

H My Book and *Heart*
Shall never part.

J *Job*° feels the Rod
Yet blesses GOD.

K Our *KING* the good
No man of blood

L The *Lion* bold
The *Lamb* doth hold.

M The *Moon* gives light
In time of night.

N *Nightengales* sing
In Time of Spring.

O The Royal *Oak*°
it was the Tree
That sav'd
His Royal Majesty.

Glass: hourglass

Job: afflicted but faithful servant of the Lord, in the Book of Job (Bible)

Royal Oak: tree in which King Charles II hid to escape from the victorious Puritan forces after the Battle of Worcester, the last battle of the English Civil War, in 1651

P *Peter* denies
His Lord and cries.

Q *Queen Esther*° comes
in Royal State
To Save the JEWS
from dismal Fate.

R *Rachel*° doth mourn
For her first born.

S *Samuel*° anoints
Whom God appoints.

T *Time* cuts down all
Both great and small.

U *Uriah's*° beauteous Wife
Made David seek his
Life.

W *Whales* in the Sea
God's Voice obey.

X *Xerxes*° the great did
die,
And so must you & I.

Y *Youth* forward slips
Death soonest nips.

Z *Zacheus*° he
Did climb the Tree
His Lord to see.

[1683]

Read

1. What tenets of Puritan thought are revealed in the *Primer*?
2. What life experiences are suggested?
3. How are the expectations for literacy demonstrated by the verses?
4. What do you think about the Puritan children's education after reading the verses?

Write

1. Categorize the alphabet verses into kinds of advice given in the verse. Religious and moral advice, warnings, history, for example. Then write a paragraph that analyzes what the categories reveal about Puritan ideas and thoughts according to the *Primer*.
2. How does the alphabet reveal Puritans' notions of duty and of life in the colonies?

Esther: Jewish wife of King Ahasuerus who saves her people from a massacre planned by the prince Haman, in the Book of Esther (Bible)

Rachel: wife of Jacob and mother of Joseph, in the Book of Genesis (Bible)

Samuel: a Hebrew judge and prophet, in the First Book of Samuel (Bible)

Uriah: Hittite captain sent to his death in battle by King David, who lusted after Uriah's wife, Bath-sheba, in the Second Book of Samuel (Bible)

Xerxes: king of Persia in the fifth century B.C.

Zacheus: Zacchaeus, a tax collector, who climbs a tree to see Jesus, and is moved to repentance of his corrupt ways by Jesus's kindness toward him, in the Gospel of Luke in the Bible

Connect

1. Write a primer for today's children using the Puritans' idea of the alphabet as a way to learn the lessons of the culture. Write at least five letters and share with your group.

Benjamin Franklin

Benjamin Franklin (1706–1790) was born in Boston of a poor family and became a printer, revolutionary, writer, and statesman. He is perhaps the most famous example of the American ideal of what the new country might offer individuals who strive. Moving to Philadelphia at 16, Franklin taught himself the printer's trade, began writing *Poor Richard's Almanac,* and served in the Pennsylvania Assembly. His pamphlets and tracts became influential in the move toward independence, and he served in the Continental Congress in 1775, becoming a primary editor of the Declaration of Independence. He was the new country's first Postmaster General and was the first ambassador to France. An inventor, scientist, and philosopher, Franklin was also one of the earliest advocates for the abolition of slavery and for the protection of rights for indigenous peoples. His views on American Indians are clear in his passionate "Notes Concerning the Savages."

Notes Concerning the Savages

Savages we call them, because their manners differ from ours, which we think the perfection of civility; they think the same of theirs.

Perhaps, if we could examine the manners of different nations with impartiality, we should find no people so rude,° as to be without any rules of politeness;° nor any so polite, as not to have some remains of rudeness.

The Indian men, when young, are hunters and warriors; when old, counselors; for all their government is by counsel of the sages; there is no force, there are no prisons, no officers to compel obedience, or inflict punishment. Hence they generally study oratory, the best speaker having the most influence. The Indian women till the ground, dress the food, nurse and bring up the children, and preserve and hand down to posterity the memory of public transactions. These employments of men and women are accounted natural and honorable. Having few artificial wants,° they have abundance of leisure for improvement by conversation. Our laborious manner of life, compared with theirs, they esteem slavish and base; and the learning, on which we value

---

rude: lacking refinement or culture
politeness: refinement, culture
wants: needs

ourselves, they regard as frivolous and useless. An instance of this occurred at the Treaty of Lancaster, in Pennsylvania, anno 1744, between the government of Virginia and the Six Nations. After the principal business was settled, the commissioners from Virginia acquainted the Indian by a speech, that there was at Williamsburg a college, with a fund for educating Indian youth; and that, if the Six Nations would send down half dozen of their young lads to that college, the government would take care that they should be well provided for, and instructed in all the learning of the white people. It is one of the Indian rules of politeness not to answer a public proposition the same day that it is made; they think it would be treating it as a light matter, and that they show it respect by taking time to consider it, as of a matter important.

They therefore deferred their answer till the day following; when their speaker began, by expressing their deep sense of the kindness of the Virginia government, in making them that offer; "for we know," says he, "that you highly esteem the kind of learning taught in those Colleges, and that the maintenance of our young men, while with you, would be very expensive to you. We are convinced, therefore, that you mean to do us good by your proposal; and we thank you heartily. But who are wise, must know that different nations have different conceptions of things; and you will therefore not take it amiss, if our ideas of this kind of education happen not to be the same with yours. We have had some experience of it; several of our young people were formerly brought up at the colleges of the northern provinces; they were instructed in all your sciences; but, when they came back to us, they were bad runners, ignorant of every means of living in the woods, unable to bear either cold or hunger, knew neither how to build a cabin, take a deer, or kill an enemy, spoke our language imperfectly, were therefore neither fit for hunters, warriors, nor counselors; they were totally good for nothing. We are however not the less obliged by your kind offer, though we decline accepting it; and, to show our grateful sense of it, if the gentlemen of Virginia will send us a dozen of their sons, we will take great care of their education, instruct them in all we know, and make men of them."

5 Having frequent occasions to hold public councils, they have acquired great order and decency in conducting them. The old men sit in the foremost ranks, the warriors in the next, and the women and children in the hindmost. The business of the women is to take exact notice of what passes, imprint it in their memories (for they have no writing), and communicate it to their children. They are the records of the council, and they preserve traditions of the stipulations in treaties 100 years back; which, when we compare with our writings, we always find exact. He that would speak, rises. The rest observe a profound silence. When he has finished and sits down, they leave him 5 or 6 minutes to recollect, that, if he has omitted anything he intended to say, or has anything to add, he may rise again and deliver it. To interrupt another, even in common conversation, is reckoned highly indecent. How different this from the conduct of a polite British House of Commons, where scarce a day passes without some confusion, that makes the speaker hoarse in calling to order;

and how different from the mode of conversation in many polite companies° of Europe, where, if you do not deliver your sentence with great rapidity, you are cut off in the middle of it by the impatient loquacity of those you converse with, and never suffered° to finish it.

The politeness of these savages in conversation is indeed carried to excess, since it does not permit them to contradict or deny the truth of what is asserted in their presence. By this means they indeed avoid disputes; but then it becomes difficult to know their minds, or what impression you make upon them. The missionaries who have attempted to convert them to Christianity all complain of this as one of the great difficulties of their mission. The Indians hear with patience the truths of the Gospel explained to them, and give their usual tokens of assent and approbation; you would think they were convinced. No such matter. It is mere civility.

A Swedish minister, having assembled the chiefs of the Susquehanah Indians, made a sermon to them, acquainting them with the principal historical facts on which our religion is founded; such as the fall of our first parents by eating an apple, the coming of Christ to repair the mischief,° His miracles and suffering, etc. When he had finished, an Indian orator stood up to thank him. "What you have told us," he says, "is all very good. It is indeed bad to eat apples. It is better to make them all into cider. We are much obliged by your kindness in coming so far, to tell us these things which you have heard from your mothers. In return, I will tell you some of those we have heard from ours. In the beginning, our fathers had only the flesh of animals to subsist on; and if their hunting was unsuccessful, they were starving. Two of our young hunters, having killed a deer, made a fire in the woods to broil some part of it. When they were about to satisfy their hunger, they beheld a beautiful young woman descend from the clouds, seat herself on that hill, which you see yonder among the blue mountains. They said to each other, it is a spirit that has smelled our broiling venison and wishes to eat of it; let us offer some to her. They presented her with the tongue; she was pleased with the taste of it, and said 'Your kindness shall be rewarded; come to this place after thirteen moons, and you shall find something that will be of great benefit in nourishing you and your children to the latest generations.' They did so, and, to their surprise, found plants they had never seen before; but which, from that ancient time, have constantly cultivated among us, to our great advantage. Where her right hand had touched the ground, they found maize; where her left hand had touched it, they found kidney-beans; and where her backside had sat on it, they found tobacco." The good missionary, disgusted with this idle tale, said, "What I delivered to you were sacred truths; but what you tell me is mere fable, fiction, and falsehood." The Indian, offended, replied "My brother, it seems your friends have not done you justice in your education; they have not well

---

companies: social gatherings
suffered: allowed
mischief: harm, damage

instructed you in the rules of common civility. You saw that we who understand and practice those rules, believed all your stories; you refuse to believe ours?"

When any of them come into our towns, our people are apt to crowd round them, gaze upon them, and incommode° them, where they desire to be private; this they esteem great rudeness, and the effect of the want° of instruction in the rules of civility and good manners. "We have," say they, "as much curiosity as you, and when you come into our towns, we wish for opportunities of looking at you, but for this purpose we hide ourselves behind bushes, where you are to pass, and never intrude ourselves into company."

Their manner of entering one another's village has likewise its rules. It is reckoned uncivil in traveling strangers to enter a village abruptly, without giving notice of their approach. Therefore, as soon as they arrive within hearing, they stop and hollow,° remaining there till invited to enter. Two old men usually come out to them, and lead them in. There is in every village a vacant dwelling, called the stranger's house. Here they are placed, while the old men go round from hut to hut, acquainting the inhabitants that strangers are arrived, who are probably hungry and weary; and every one sends them what he can spare of victuals, and skins to repose on. When the strangers are refreshed, pipes and tobacco are brought; and then, but not before, conversation begins, with inquiries who they are, whither° bound, what news, etc.; and it usually ends with offers of service, if the strangers have occasion of° guides, or any necessaries for continuing their journey; and nothing is exacted° for the entertainment.°

10

The same hospitality, esteemed among them as a principal virtue, is practiced by private persons; of which Conrad Weiser, our interpreter, gave the following instances. He had been naturalized among the Six Nations, and spoke well the Mohawk language. In going through the Indian country, to carry a message from our Governor to the Council at Onondaga, he called at the habitation of Canassatego, an old acquaintance, who embraced him, spread furs for him to sit on, placed before him some boiled beans and venison, and mixed some rum and water for his drink. When he was well refreshed, and had lit his pipe, Canassatego began to converse with him; asked how he had fared the many years since they had seen each other; whence he then came; what occasioned the journey, etc. Conrad answered all his questions; and when the discourse began to flag, the Indian, to continue it, said, "Conrad, you have lived long among the white people, and know something of their customs; I have been sometimes at Albany, and have observed, that once in seven days they shut up their shops, and assemble all in

---

incommode: inconvenience

want: lack

hollow: halloo (i.e., call out)

whither: where

occasion of: cause for

exacted: called for, demanded

entertainment: hospitality

the great house; tell me what it is for. What do they do there?" "They meet there," says Conrad, "to hear and learn good things." "I do not doubt," says the Indian, "that they tell you so; they have told me the same; but I doubt the truth of what they say, and I will tell you my reasons. I went lately to Albany to sell my skins and buy blankets, knives, powder, rum, etc. You know I used generally to deal with Hans Hanson; but I was a little inclined this time to try some other merchant. However, I called first upon Hans, and asked him what he would give for beaver. He said he could not give any more than four shillings a pound; 'but,' says he, 'I cannot talk on business now; this is the day when we meet together to learn good things, and I am going to the meeting.' So I thought to myself, 'Since we cannot do any business today, I may as well go to the meeting too,' and I went with him. There stood up a man in black, and began to talk to the people very angrily. I did not understand what he said; but, perceiving that he looked much at me and at Hanson, I imagined he was angry at seeing me there; so I went out, sat down near the house, struck fire, and lit my pipe, waiting till the meeting should break up. I thought too, that the man had mentioned something of beaver, and I suspected it might be the subject of their meeting. So, when they came out, I accosted my merchant. 'Well, Hans,' says I, 'I hope you have agreed to give more than four shillings a pound' 'No,' says he, 'I cannot give so much; I cannot give more than three shillings and sixpence.' I then spoke to several other dealers, but they all sung the same song—three and sixpence, three and sixpence. This made it clear to me, that my suspicion was right; and, that whatever they pretended of meeting to learn good things, the real purpose was to consult how to cheat Indians in the price of beaver. Consider but a little, Conrad, and you must be of my opinion. If they met so often to learn good things, they would certainly have learned some before this time. But they are still ignorant. You know our practice. If a white man, in traveling through our country, enters one of our cabins, we all treat him as I treat you; we dry him if he is wet, we warm him if he is cold, we give him meat and drink, that he may allay his thirst and hunger; and we spread soft furs for him to rest and sleep on; we demand nothing in return. But, if I go into a white man's house at Albany and ask for victuals and drink, they say, 'Where is your money?' and if I have none they say, 'Get out, you Indian dog.' You see they have not yet learned those little good things, that we need no meetings to be instructed in, because our Mothers taught them to us when we were children; and therefore it is impossible their meetings should be, as they say, for any such purpose, or have any such effect; they are only to contrive the cheating of Indians in the price of beaver."

[1784]

Read

1. Where do you see Franklin's belief in logic and reason demonstrated in his essay?
2. How does Franklin use the word "savage" for effect?
3. Where do you hear Franklin's emotional response in the essay?
4. How does the opening paragraph establish Franklin's position?

Write

1. Write a paragraph that describes Franklin's attitude about the religion practiced by the colonists. Use statements from the essay that you think convey his attitude.
2. Find two or three instances where Franklin uses irony and write a response to its effect on you as a reader.
3. Twenty-first century readers often think of Franklin as a reasonable, logical writer as well as practical. Explain how this essay fits into that characterization of his writing.

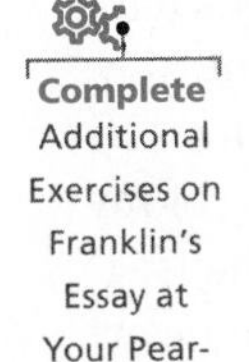

Complete Additional Exercises on Franklin's Essay at Your Pearson MyLab

Connect

1. What democratic values does Franklin use to make his argument? What do you think he wanted his audience to feel or to do?
2. How does the narrative Franklin describes connect with the document written by the Iroquois League in this unit?

Franklin's understanding of the American promise of equality of opportunity and of fairness of treatment extended to women. Here, in a fictional plea for justice from one Polly Baker, unmarried female of sullied reputation, Franklin uses the persona to call "American" ideals into question, thirty years before the Declaration of Independence was to make claims based upon those ideals.

The Speech of Polly Baker

The SPEECH of Miss Polly Baker, before a Court of Judicature,° at Connecticut in New England, where she was prosecuted the fifth Time for having a Bastard Child; which influenced the Court to dispense with her Punishment, and induced one of her Judges to marry her the next Day.

May it please the Honourable Bench to indulge me a few Words: I am a poor unhappy Woman; who have no Money to Fee Lawyers to plead for me, being hard put to it to get a tolerable Living. I shall not trouble your Honours with long Speeches; for I have not the presumption to expect, that you may, by any Means, be prevailed on to deviate in your Sentence from the Law, in my Favour. All I humbly hope is that your Honours would charitably move the Governor's Goodness on my Behalf, that my Fine may be remitted.° This is the Fifth Time, Gentlemen, that I have been dragg'd before your Courts on the same Account; twice I have paid heavy Fines, and twice have been brought to public Punishment, for want of Money to pay those Fines. This may have been agreeable to° the Laws; I do not dispute it: But since Laws are sometimes

Judicature: the administration of justice
remitted: excused
agreeable to: consistent with

unreasonable in themselves, and therefore repealed; and others bear too hard on the Subject in particular Circumstances; and therefore there is left a Power somewhere to dispense with the Execution of them; I take the Liberty to say, that I think this Law, by which I am punished, is both unreasonable in itself, and particularly severe with regard to me, who have always lived an inoffensive Life in the Neighbourhood where I was born, and defy my Enemies (if I have any) to say I ever wrong'd Man, Woman, or Child. Abstracted° from the Law, I cannot conceive (may it please your Honours) what the Nature of my Offence is. I have brought Five fine Children into the World, at the Risque° of my Life: I have maintained them well by my own Industry, without burthening° the Township, and could have done it better, if it had not been for the heavy Charges and Fines I have paid. Can it be a Crime (in the Nature of Things I mean) to add to the Number of the King's Subjects, in a new Country that really wants° People? I own I should think it rather a Praise worthy, than a Punishable Action. I have debauch'd° no other Woman's Husband, nor inticed any innocent Youth: These Things I never was charged with; nor has any one the least cause of Complaint against me, unless, perhaps the Minister, or the Justice, because I have had Children without being Married, by which they have miss'd a Wedding Fee. But, can even this be a Fault of mine? I appeal to your Honours. You are pleased to allow I don't want° Sense; but I must be stupid to the last Degree, not to prefer the honourable State of Wedlock, to the Condition I have lived in. I always was, and still am, willing to enter into it; I doubt not my Behaving well in it, having all the Industry, Frugality, Fertility, and Skill in economy, appertaining to a good Wife's Character. I defy any Person to say I ever Refused an Offer of that Sort: On the contrary, I readily Consented to the only Proposal of Marriage that ever was made me, which was when I was a Virgin; but too easily confiding° in the Person's Sincerity that made it, I unhappily lost my own Honour, by trusting to his; for he got me with Child, and then forsook me: That very Person you all know; he is now become a Magistrate of this County; and I had hopes he would have appeared this Day on the Bench, and have endeavoured to moderate the Court in my Favour; then I should have scorn'd to have mention'd it; but I must Complain of it as unjust and unequal, that my Betrayer and Undoer, the first Cause of all my Faults and Miscarriages (if they must be deemed such) should be advanced to Honour and Power, in the same Government that punishes my Misfortunes with Stripes°

Abstracted: removed, separated (i.e., apart)
Risque: risk
burthening: burdening
wants: lacks; needs
debauch'd: seduced, corrupted
want: lack
confiding: trusting
Stripes: lashes

and Infamy. I shall be told, 'tis like,° that were there no Act of Assembly in the Case, the Precepts of Religion are violated by my Transgressions. If mine, then, is a religious Offence, leave it, Gentlemen, to religious Punishments. You have already excluded me from all the Comforts of your Church Communion: Is not that sufficient? You believe I have offended Heaven, and must suffer eternal Fire: Will not that be sufficient? What need is there, then, of your additional Fines and Whippings? I own, I do not think as you do; for, if I thought, what you call a Sin, was really such, I would not presumptuously commit it. But how can it be believed, that Heaven is angry at my having Children, when, to the little done by me towards it, God has been pleased to add his divine Skill and admirable Workmanship in the Formation of their Bodies, and crown'd it by furnishing them with rational and immortal Souls? Forgive me Gentlemen, if I talk a little extravagantly on these Matters; I am no Divine: But if you, great Men, (*) must be making Laws, do not turn natural and useful Actions into Crimes, by your Prohibitions. Reflect a little on the horrid Consequences of this Law in particular: What Numbers of procur'd Abortions! and how many distress'd Mothers have been driven, by the Terror of Punishment and public Shame, to imbrue,° contrary to Nature, their own trembling Hands in the Blood of their helpless Offspring! Nature would have induc'd them to nurse it up with a Parent's Fondness. 'Tis the Law therefore, 'tis the Law itself that is guilty of all these Barbarities and Murders. Repeal it then, Gentlemen; let it be expung'd for ever from your Books: And on the other hand, take into your wise Consideration, the great and growing Number of Batchelors in the Country, many of whom, from the mean° Fear of the Expence of a Family, have never sincerely and honourably Courted a Woman in their Lives; and by their Manner of Living, leave unproduced (which I think is little better than Murder) Hundreds of their Posterity to the Thousandth Generation. Is not theirs a greater Offence against the Public Good, than mine? Compel them then, by a Law, either to Marry, or pay double the Fine of Fornication every Year. What must poor young Women do, whom Custom has forbid to sollicit the Men, and who cannot force themselves upon Husbands, when the Laws take no Care to provide them any, and yet severely punish if they do their Duty without them? Yes, Gentlemen, I venture to call it a Duty; 'tis the Duty of the first and great Command of Nature, and of Nature's God, *Increase and multiply*: A Duty, from the steady Performance of which nothing has ever been able to deter me; but for it's Sake, I have hazarded the Loss of the public Esteem, and frequently incurr'd public Disgrace and Punishment; and therefore ought, in my humble Opinion, instead of a Whipping, to have a Statue erected to my Memory.

[*The Maryland Gazette*, August 11, 1747; first printed April 15, 1747]

**Turning to some Gentlemen of the Assembly, then in Court.*

---

like: likely

imbrue: stain

mean: miserly; small-minded

Read

1. How does the speaker make use of *logos* in the speech?
2. How would you characterize the speaker's voice in the speech?
3. How does Franklin use humor to further his aim in the speech?
4. What do you think the purpose might be of giving the outcome of the "trial" at the beginning of the essay?

Write

1. Comment on a place in the essay where you begin to believe that the piece is not really a speech by Miss Polly Baker.
2. Why might Franklin choose to write from Miss Polly Baker's perspective?

Complete Additional Exercises on Franklin's Essay at Your Pearson MyLab

Connect

1. What do you find in this work that links to Franklin's approach in "Notes Concerning the Savages"?
2. How does Franklin reveal the position of women in colonial America in his essay?

Samson Occom

Samson Occom (1723–1792) was born into the Mohegan tribe and learned traditional customs as a young man. As part of the Great Awakening, a religious revival, Occom became a Christian at 16 and a leader of his tribe. His preaching made him famous and well respected, and in 1772 he became the first best-selling American Indian author with his "Sermon Preached by Samson Occom, Minister of the Gospel, and Missionary to the Indians; at the Execution of Moses Paul an Indian." The book went through 19 editions over the next 50 years. Occom's sermons, his poetry, and his autobiography reveal his belief in both Christianity and equality of native and colonist.

From *A Short Narrative of My Life*

From My Birth till I Received the Christian Religion

I was born a heathen and brought up in heathenism, till I was between 16 & 17 years of age, at a place called Mohegan, in New London, Connecticut, in New England. My parents lived a wandering life, for did all the Indians at Mohegan, they chiefly depended upon hunting, fishing, & fowling° for their living and had no connection with the English, excepting to traffic° with them in their

---

fowling: shooting or trapping birds
traffic: to carry on trade or commercial dealings

small trifles; and they strictly maintained and followed their heathenish ways, customs & religion, though there was some preaching among them: Once a fortnight, in ye summer season, a minister from New London used to come up, and the Indians to attend; not that they regarded° the Christian religion, but they had blankets given to them every fall of the year and for these things they would attend and there was a sort of school kept, when I was quite young, but I believe there never was one that ever learnt to read anything,—and when I was about 10 years of age there was a man who went about among the Indian wigwams, and wherever he could find the Indian children, would make them read; but the children used to take care to keep out of his way;—and he used to catch me sometimes and make me say over my letters; and I believe I learnt some of them. But this was soon over too; and all this time there was not one amongst us, that made a profession of Christianity.———Neither did we cultivate our land, nor kept any sort of creatures except dogs, which we used in hunting; and we dwelt in wigwams. These are a sort of tents, covered with mats, made of flags.° And to this Time we were unaquainted with the English tongue in general, though there were a few, who understood a little of it.

From the Time of Our Reformation till I Left Mr. Wheelock

When I was 16 years of age, we heard a strange rumor among the English, that there were extraordinary ministers preaching from place to place and a strange concern among the white people. This was in the spring of the year. But we saw nothing of these things, till sometime in the summer, when some Ministers began to visit us and preach the word of God; and the common people all came frequently and exhorted us to the things of God, which it pleased the Lord, as I humbly hope, to bless and accompany with divine influence to the conviction° and saving conversion of a number of us; amongst whom I was one that was imprest with the things we had heard. These preachers did not only come to us, but we frequently went to their meetings and churches. After I was awakened and converted, I went to all the meetings, I could come at; & continued under trouble of mind about six months; at which time I began to learn the English letters; got me a primer,° and used to go to my English neighbours frequently for assistance in reading, but went to no school. And when I was 17 years of age, I had, as I trust, a discovery of the way of salvation through Jesus Christ, and was

---

regarded: considered, showed interest in

flags: pieces of cloth

conviction: act of convincing, or state of being convinced

primer: an introductory text, often for instruction in reading

enabl'd to put my trust in him alone for life & salvation. From this time the distress and burden of my mind was removed, and I found serenity and pleasure of soul, in serving God. By this time I just began to read in the New Testament without spelling,°—and I had a stronger desire still to learn to read the Word of God, and at the same time had an uncommon pity and compassion to my poor brethren according to the flesh.° I used to wish I was capable of instructing my poor kindred. I used to think, if I could once learn to read I would Instruct the poor children in reading,—and used frequently to talk with our Indians concerning religion. This continued till I was in my 19th year: by this time I could read a little in the Bible. At this time my poor mother was going to Lebanon, and having had some knowledge of Mr. Wheelock and hearing he had a number of English youth under his tuition, I had a great inclination to go to him and be with him a week or a fortnight, and desired my mother to ask Mr. Wheelock whether he would take me a little while to instruct me in reading. Mother did so; and when she came back, she said Mr. Wheelock wanted to see me as soon as possible. So I went up, thinking I should be back again in a few days; when I got up there, he received me with kindness and compassion and instead of staying a forthnight or three weeks, I spent four years with him.—After I had been with him some time, he began to acquaint his friends of my being with him, and of his intentions of educating me, and my circumstances. And the good people began to give some assistance to Mr. Wheelock, and gave me some old and some new clothes. Then he represented the case to the Honorable Commissioners at Boston, who were commission'd by the Honorable Society in London for propagating the gospel among the Indians in New England and parts adjacent, and they allowed him 60 £ in old tender,° which was about 6 £ Sterling, and they Continu'd it two or three years, I can't tell exactly.—While I was at Mr. Wheelock's, I was very weakly and my health much impaired, and at the end of four years, I over strained my eyes to such a degree, I could not pursue my studies any longer; and out of these four years I lost just about one year;—And was obliged to quit my studies.

From the Time I Left Mr. Wheelock till I Went to Europe

As soon as I left Mr. Wheelock, I endeavored to find some employ among the Indians; went to Nahantuck, thinking they may want a schoolmaster, but

---

without spelling: without having to spell out the individual words
brethren according to the flesh: those related by blood (i.e., his fellow Indians)
tender: legal tender, currency

they had one; then went to Narraganset, and they were indifferent about a school, and went back to Mohegan, and heard a number of our Indians were going to Montauk, on Long Island, and I went with them, and the Indians there were very desirous to have me keep a school amongst them, and I consented, and went back a while to Mohegan and sometime in November I went on the island, I think it is 17 years ago last November. I agreed to keep school with them half a year, and left it with them to give me what they pleased; and they took turns to provide food for me. I had near 30 scholars this winter; I had an evening school too for those that could not attend the day school—and began to carry on their meetings, they had a minister, one Mr. Horton, the Scotch Society's missionary; but he Spent, I think two-thirds of his time at Sheenecock, 30 Miles from Montauk. We met together three times for Divine Worship every Sabbath and once on every Wednesday evening. I [used] to read the Scriptures to them and used to expound upon some particular passages in my own tongue.° Visited the sick and attended their burials.—When the half year expired, they desired me to continue with them, which I complied with, for another half year; when I had fulfilled that, they were urgent to have me stay longer, so I continued amongst them till I was married, which was about two years after I went there. And continued to instruct them in the same manner as I did before. After I was married a while, I found there was need of a support more than I needed while I was single,—and made my case known to Mr. Buell and to Mr. Wheelock, and also the needy circumstances and the desires of these Indians of my continuing amongst them, and the Commissioners were so good as to grant £ 15 a year Sterling——And I kept on in my service as usual, yea I had additional service; I kept school as I did before and carried on the religious meetings as often as ever, and attended the sick and their funerals, and did what writings they wanted, and often sat as a judge to reconcile and decide their matters between them, and had visitors of Indians from all quarters; and, as our custom is, we freely entertain all visitors. And was fetched often from my tribe and from others to see into their affairs both religious and temporal,—besides my domestic concerns. And it pleased the Lord to increase my family fast—and soon after I was married, Mr. Horton left these Indians and the Shenecock & after this I was [alone] and then I had the whole care of these Indians at Montauk, and visited the Shenecock Indians often. Used to set out Saturdays towards night and come back again Mondays. I have been obliged to set out from home after sunset, and ride 30 miles in the night, to preach to these Indians. And some Indians at Shenecock sent their children to my

---

tongue: language

school at Montauk; I kept one of them some time, and had a young man a half year from Mohegan, a lad from Nahantuck, who was with me almost a year; and had° little or nothing for keeping them.

My method in the school was, as soon as the children got together, and took their proper seats, I prayed with them, then began to hear them. I generally began [after some of them could spell and read] with those that were yet in their alphabets, so around, as they were properly seated till I got through and I obliged them to study their books, and to help one another. When they could not make out a hard word they brought it to me—and I usually heard them, in the summer season eight times a day four in the morning, and in the afternoon.—In the winter season six times a day, as soon as they could spell, they were obliged to spell whenever they wanted to go out. I concluded with prayer; I generally heard my evening scholars three times round, and as they go out the School, every one, that can spell, is obliged to spell a word, and to go out leisurely one after another. I catechised three or four times a week according to the assembly's shout or catechism, and many times proposed questions of my own, and in my own tongue. I found difficulty with some children, who were somewhat dull, most of these can soon learn to say over their letters, they distinguish the sounds by the ear, but their eyes can't distinguish the letters, and the way I took to cure them was by making an alphabet on small bits of paper, and glued them on small chips of cedar after this manner, A B & C. I would put these on letters in order on a bench then point to one letter and bid a child to take notice of it, and then I order the child to fetch me the letter from the bench; if he brings the letter, it is well; if not he must go again and again till he brings the right letter. When they can bring any letters this way, then I just jumble them together, and bid them to set them in alphabetical order, and it is a pleasure to them; and they soon learn their letters this way.—I frequently discussed or exhorted my scholars, in religious matters.—My method in our religious meetings was this; Sabbath morning we assemble together about 10 o'clock and begin with singing; we generally sung Dr. Watt's Psalms or hymns. I distinctly read the Psalm or hymn first, and then gave the meaning of it to them, after that sing, then pray, and sing again after prayer. Then proceed to read from suitable portion of Scripture, and so just give the plain sense of it in familiar discourse and apply it to them. So continued with prayer and singing. In the afternoon and evening we proceed in the same manner, and so in Wednesday evening. Some

---

had: received, was paid

time after Mr. Horton left these Indians, there was a remarkable revival of religion among these Indians, and many were hopefully converted to the saving knowledge of God in Jesus. It is to be observed before Mr. Horton left these Indians they had some prejudices infused in their minds, by some enthusiastical exhorters from New England, against Mr. Horton, and many of them had left him; by this means he was discouraged, and was disposed from these Indians. And being acquainted with the enthusiasts in New England and the make and the disposition of the Indians I took a mild way to reclaim them. I opposed them not openly but let them go on in their way, and whenever I had an opportunity, I would read such pages of the Scriptures, and I thought would confound their notions, and I would come to them with all authority, saying, "these Saith the Lord"; and by this means, the Lord was pleased to bless my poor endeavors, and they were reclaimed, and brought to hear almost any of the ministers.——I am now to give an account of my circumstances and manner of living. I dwelt in a wigwam, a small hut with small poles and covered with mats made of flags, and I was obliged to remove twice a year, about two miles distance, by reason of the scarcity of wood, for in one neck of land they planted their corn, and in another, they had their wood, and I was obliged to have my corn carted and my hay also,—and I got my ground plow'd every year, which cost me about 12 shillings an acre; and I kept a cow and a horse, for which I paid 21 shillings every year York currency, and went 18 miles to mill for every dust of meal we used in my family. I hired or joined with my neighbors to go to mill, with a horse or ox cart, or on horseback, and sometimes went myself. My family increasing fast, and my visitors also. I was obliged to contrive every way to support my family; I took all opportunities, to get something to feed my family daily. I Planted my own corn, potatoes, and beans; I used to be out hoeing my corn sometimes before sunrise and after my school is dismissed, and by this means I was able to raise my own pork, for I was allowed to keep five swine. Some mornings and evenings I would be out with my hook and line to catch fish, and in the fall of the year and in the spring, I used my gun, and fed my family with fowls. I could more than pay for my powder & shot with feathers. At other times I bound old books for Easthampton people, made wooden spoons and ladles, stocked guns, & worked on cedar to make pails, (piggins°), and churns etc. Besides all these difficulties I met with adverse Providence; I bought a Mare, had it but a little while, and she fell into the quicksand and died. After a while bought

---

piggins: small wooden buckets or tubs

another; I kept her about half year, and she was gone, and I never have heard of nor seen her from that day to this; it was supposed some rogue stole her. I got another and it died with a distemper, and last of all I bought a young mare, and kept her till she had one colt, and she broke her leg and died, and presently after the colt died also. In the whole I lost five horse kind; all these losses helped to pull me down; and by this time I got greatly in debt, and acquainted my circumstances to some of my friends, and they represented my case to the Commissioners of Boston, and interceded with them for me, and they were pleased to vote 15 £ for my Help, and soon after sent a letter to my good friend at New London, acquainting him that they had superseded their vote; and my friends were so good as to represent my needy circumstances still to them, and they were so good at last, as to vote £ 15 and sent it, for which I am very thankful; and the Revd Mr. Buell was so kind as to write in my behalf to the gentlemen of Boston; and he told me they were much displeased with him, and heard also once again that they blamed me for being extravagant; I can't conceive how these gentlemen would have me live. I am ready to (forgive) their ignorance, and I would wish they had changed circumstances with me but one month, that they may know, by experience what my case really was; but I am now fully convinced, that it was not ignorance, for I believe it can be proved to the world that these same gentlemen gave a young missionary, a single man, *one hundred pounds* for one year, and fifty pounds for an interpreter, and thirty pounds for an introducer; so it cost them one hundred & eighty pounds in one single year, and they sent him to where there was no need of a missionary.

5 Now you see what difference they made between me and other missionaries; they gave me 180 Pounds for 12 year's Service, which they gave for one year's services in another mission.—In my service (I speak like a fool, but I am constrained) I was my own interpreter. I was both a schoolmaster and minister to the Indians; yea I was their ear, eye & hand, as well as mouth. I leave it with the world, as wicked as it is, to judge, whether I ought not to have had half as much, as they gave a young man just mentioned, which would have been but £ 50 a year; and if they ought to have given me that, I am not under obligations to them; I owe them nothing at all; what can be the reason that they used me after this manner? I can't think of anything, but this, as a poor Indian boy said, who was bound out to an English family, and he used to drive plow for a young man, and he whipped and beat him allmost every day, and the young man found fault with him, and complained of him to his master and the poor boy was called to answer for himself before his master, and he was asked, what it was he did, that he was so complained of

and beat almost every day. He said, he did not know, but he supposed it was because he could not drive any better; but says he, I drive as well as I know how; and at other times he beats me, because he is of a mind to beat me; but says he believes he beats me for the most of the time "because I am an Indian."

So I am *ready* to say, they have used me thus, because I can't influence the Indians so well as other missionaries; but I can assure them I have endeavoured to teach them as well as I know how;—but I *must say,* "I believe it is because I am a poor Indian." I can't help that God has made me so; I did not make myself so.—

[1762]

Read

1. How does Occom describe his conversion to Christianity?
2. Why do you think he begins with his conversion?
3. How does Occom describe his methods as a teacher? How are those methods unusual?
4. What does Occom's narrative reveal about daily life in his time and how does the description become part of an argument?

Write

1. Using examples or lines from the narrative, write a brief analysis of the argument Occom makes.
2. Take a look at the last two paragraphs and describe how they differ in tone or form from the rest of the narrative. Why might Occom have made that decision?
3. What kinds of persuasive evidence does Occom present in support of his argument? Find several examples and comment on them.

Connect

1. How might Franklin have used Occom's narrative in support of his argument in "Notes Concerning the Savages"?
2. Comment on your response to Occom's narrative. What do you think it reveals about his character? About Indians?

John Singleton Copley

John Singleton Copley (1738–1815) was born in Boston. His stepfather was an artist, and unlike many of his peers in the colonies, Copley grew up surrounded by prints and paintings. He studied the art of the master portrait painters of the Renaissance and became one of the most renowned painters in the Colonies and well known in England as well. He was known for a realism and what the great English painter Joshua Reynolds called "hard detail." *Watson and the Shark* depicts a historical event, an attack on 14-year-old Brooks Watson in Havana Harbor in 1749, while he was serving onboard his uncle's trading ship. The shark attacked twice, severing Watson's foot, but the crew fought off the animal successfully. Watson led a full life afterward, becoming Lord Mayor of London. The story was famous when Copley retold it in painting.

Watson and the Shark

Watson and the Shark (1778), John Singleton Copley. Oil on canvas, overall: 182.1 x 229.7 cm (71 11/16 x 90 7/16 in.) framed: 241.3 x 264.2 x 10.1 cm (95 x 104 x 4 in.) Ferdinand Lammot Belin Fund 1963.6.1. Courtesy National Gallery of Art, Washington

[1778]

Read

1. Locate the painting on the Internet and describe how color contributes to the effect?
2. What images strike your eye first? What details contribute to your overall sense of the painting?
3. What might be a purpose for artistically rendering a popular narrative, as the story of Brooks Watson's attack was?
4. How do the individual characters in the boat and the one out of it suggest a theme or message of the painting?

Write

1. Write a paragraph that describes elements in the painting that make it feel heroic.
2. Comment on any techniques you observe that make the painting dynamic.

Connect

1. Write a narrative that explains the details in the painting. Give it a beginning and an ending.
2. Why do you think this painting might have been so popular?

Thomas Jefferson

Writer, farmer, statesman, and third President of the young United States, Thomas Jefferson (1743–1826) was also a powerful writer. The opening lines of the Declaration of Independence strike the chords of American ideals of opportunity, freedom, and justice that have resonated for over two centuries. He was a voracious reader and constant student of many subjects—technology, horticulture, astronomy, languages—and he donated his impressive library to the United States at his death, establishing what would become the Library of Congress. He laid out plans for a vigorous government, with support for education, inquiry, and individual liberty. His work shows the complexities of culture and the paradoxes inherent in his words "all men are created equal." His Declaration is an important statement of Enlightenment thought. He died, like his friend John Adams, on July 4, 1826.

Declaration of Independence

In Congress, July 4, 1776

The unanimous Declaration of the thirteen united States of America

When in the Course of human events it becomes necessary for one people to dissolve the political bands which have connected them with another and to assume among the powers of the earth, the separate and equal station to which the Laws of Nature and of Nature's God entitle them, a decent respect to the opinions of mankind requires that they should declare the causes which impel them to the separation.

We hold these truths to be self-evident, that all men are created equal, that they are endowed by their Creator with certain unalienable Rights, that among these are Life, Liberty and the pursuit of Happiness.—That to secure these rights, Governments are instituted among Men, deriving their just powers from the consent of the governed,—That whenever any Form of Government becomes destructive of these ends, it is the Right of the People to alter or to abolish it, and to institute new Government, laying its foundation on such principles and organizing its powers in such form, as to them shall seem most likely to effect their Safety and Happiness. Prudence, indeed, will dictate that Governments long established should not be changed for light and transient causes; and accordingly all experience hath shewn° that mankind are more disposed to suffer, while evils are sufferable than to right themselves by abolishing the forms to which they are accustomed. But when a long train of abuses and usurpations, pursuing invariably the same Object evinces a design to reduce them under absolute Despotism, it is their right, it is their duty, to throw off such Government, and to provide new Guards for their future security.—Such

shewn: shown

has been the patient sufferance of these Colonies; and such is now the necessity which constrains° them to alter their former Systems of Government. The history of the present King of Great Britain is a history of repeated injuries and usurpations, all having in direct object the establishment of an absolute Tyranny over these States. To prove this, let Facts be submitted to a candid° world.

He has refused his Assent to Laws, the most wholesome and necessary for the public good.

He has forbidden his Governors to pass Laws of immediate and pressing importance, unless suspended in their operation till his Assent should be obtained; and when so suspended, he has utterly neglected to attend to them.

He has refused to pass other Laws for the accommodation of large districts of people, unless those people would relinquish the right of Representation in the Legislature, a right inestimable° to them and formidable° to tyrants only. 5

He has called together legislative bodies at places unusual, uncomfortable, and distant from the depository of their Public Records, for the sole purpose of fatiguing them into compliance with his measures.

He has dissolved Representative Houses repeatedly, for opposing with manly firmness his invasions on the rights of the people.

He has refused for a long time, after such dissolutions, to cause others to be elected, whereby the Legislative Powers, incapable of Annihilation,° have returned to the People at large for their exercise; the State remaining in the mean time exposed to all the dangers of invasion from without, and convulsions within.

He has endeavoured to prevent the population° of these States; for that purpose obstructing the Laws for Naturalization of Foreigners; refusing to pass others to encourage their migrations hither, and raising the conditions of new Appropriations of Lands.

He has obstructed the Administration of Justice by refusing his Assent to Laws for establishing Judiciary Powers. 10

He has made Judges dependent on his Will alone for the tenure of their offices, and the amount and payment of their salaries.

He has erected a multitude of New Offices, and sent hither swarms of Officers to harass our people and eat out their substance.

He has kept among us, in times of peace, Standing Armies without the Consent of our legislatures.

He has affected to render the Military independent of and superior to the Civil Power.

---

constrains: compels

candid: honest, impartial

inestimable: invaluable

formidable: causing fear or apprehension

Legislative Powers, incapable of Annihilation: i.e., the king's disbanding of legislative bodies does not and cannot remove the necessity of making laws

prevent the population: i.e., from being increased

He has combined with others to subject us to a jurisdiction foreign to our constitution, and unacknowledged by our laws; giving his Assent to their Acts of pretended Legislation.

For quartering large bodies of armed troops among us:

For protecting them, by a mock Trial from punishment for any Murders which they should commit on the Inhabitants of these States:

For cutting off our Trade with all parts of the world:

For imposing Taxes on us without our Consent:

For depriving us in many cases, of the benefit of Trial by Jury:

For transporting us beyond Seas to be tried for pretended offences:

For abolishing the free System of English Laws in a neighbouring Province, establishing therein an Arbitrary government, and enlarging its Boundaries so as to render it at once an example and fit instrument for introducing the same absolute rule into these Colonies:

For taking away our Charters, abolishing our most valuable Laws and altering fundamentally the Forms of our Governments:

For suspending our own Legislatures, and declaring themselves invested with power to legislate for us in all cases whatsoever.

He has abdicated Government here, by declaring us out of his Protection and waging War against us.

He has plundered our seas, ravaged our coasts, burnt our towns, and destroyed the lives of our people.

He is at this time transporting large Armies of foreign Mercenaries to compleat the works of death, desolation, and tyranny, already begun with circumstances of Cruelty & Perfidy° scarcely paralleled in the most barbarous ages, and totally unworthy the Head of a civilized nation.

He has constrained our fellow Citizens taken Captive on the high Seas to bear Arms against their Country, to become the executioners of their friends and Brethren, or to fall themselves by their Hands.

He has excited domestic insurrections amongst us, and has endeavoured to bring on° the inhabitants of our frontiers, the merciless Indian Savages whose known rule of warfare, is an undistinguished destruction of all ages, sexes and conditions.°

In every stage of these Oppressions We have Petitioned for Redress in the most humble terms: Our repeated Petitions have been answered only by repeated injury. A Prince, whose character is thus marked by every act which may define a Tyrant, is unfit to be the ruler of a free people.

Nor have We been wanting in attentions to our British brethren. We have warned them from time to time of attempts by their legislature to extend an unwarrantable° jurisdiction over us. We have reminded them of the

---

Perfidy: faithlessness, betrayal
bring on: set upon
conditions: social positions
unwarrantable: unjustifiable

circumstances of our emigration and settlement here. We have appealed to their native justice and magnanimity, and we have conjured them by the ties of our common kindred to disavow these usurpations, which would inevitably interrupt our connections and correspondence. They too have been deaf to the voice of justice and of consanguinity.° We must, therefore, acquiesce in the necessity, which denounces° our Separation, and hold them, as we hold the rest of mankind, Enemies in War, in Peace Friends.

We, therefore, the Representatives of the united States of America, in General Congress, Assembled, appealing to the Supreme Judge of the world for the rectitude of our intentions, do, in the Name, and by Authority of the good People of these Colonies, solemnly publish and declare, That these united Colonies are, and of Right ought to be Free and Independent States, that they are Absolved from all Allegiance to the British Crown, and that all political connection between them and the State of Great Britain, is and ought to be totally dissolved; and that as Free and Independent States, they have full Power to levy War, conclude Peace, contract Alliances, establish Commerce, and to do all other Acts and Things which Independent States may of right do.—And for the support of this Declaration, with a firm reliance on the protection of Divine Providence, we mutually pledge to each other our Lives, our Fortunes, and our sacred Honor.

New Hampshire:
Josiah Bartlett, William Whipple, Matthew Thornton

Massachusetts:
John Hancock, Samuel Adams, John Adams, Robert Treat Paine, Elbridge Gerry

Rhode Island:
Stephen Hopkins, William Ellery

Connecticut:
Roger Sherman, Samuel Huntington, William Williams, Oliver Wolcott

New York:
William Floyd, Philip Livingston, Francis Lewis, Lewis Morris

New Jersey:
Richard Stockton, John Witherspoon, Francis Hopkinson, John Hart, Abraham Clark

Pennsylvania:
Robert Morris, Benjamin Rush, Benjamin Franklin, John Morton, George Clymer, James Smith, George Taylor, James Wilson, George Ross

---

consanguinity: kinship, blood relationship
denounces: announces, proclaims

Delaware:
Caesar Rodney, George Read, Thomas McKean

Maryland:
Samuel Chase, William Pace, Thomas Stone, Charles Carroll of Carrollton

Virginia:
George Wythe, Richard Henry Lee, Thomas Jefferson, Benjamin Harrison, Thomas Nelson, Jr., Francis Lightfoot Lee, Carter Braxton

North Carolina:
William Hooper, Joseph Hewes, John Penn

South Carolina:
Edward Rutledge, Thomas Heyward, Jr., Thomas Lynch, Jr., Arthur Middleton

Georgia:
Button Gwinnett, Lyman Hall, George Walton

[July 4, 1776]

Read

1. How do you define Jefferson's phrase "self-evident"? What does that suggest about Jefferson's argumentative strategy?
2. How does the arrangement of the Declaration help make it a persuasive document?
3. Reading the Declaration, how might a citizen characterize the nation that is about to be brought into being?
4. How do you see Jefferson's connection to the citizenry he speaks for?

Write

1. How would you characterize Jefferson's persona in this document? Find language or images and use them to help you describe his persona in the Declaration.
2. Write about some of the examples that Jefferson uses to establish the rightness of his cause. Are they convincing?

Complete Additional Exercises on the Declaration at Your Pearson MyLab

Connect

1. What phrases in the first few paragraphs of the Declaration are most familiar to you today?
2. Comment on what the familiar phrases mean in terms of today's government and today's citizens. How are meanings different? The same?

Anne Hutchinson

Anne Hutchinson (1591–1643) emigrated to the Massachusetts Bay Colony from Lincolnshire, England in 1634, after John Cotton, her mentor and minister, was banned from the pulpit in England. She was highly intelligent and well versed in the Bible, as well as skilled in medicine and midwifery. She quickly became a leader in the community in

Boston, eventually moving from explaining Cotton's sermons to others to preaching her own. Her sermons challenged the authority of church and government over individuals and came under criticism, especially after some of her supporters refused to take up arms against the Pequot tribe with whom the colonists were in conflict. In 1637, she was tried for sedition and heresy, when civic leaders brought charges. Prosecutors were also judges, and the outcome was not in doubt: she was excommunicated and departed for Rhode Island, where dissident Roger Williams had founded his own colony. She died in New York in an Indian raid.

From *The Examination of Mrs. Anne Hutchinson, at the Court of Newton, November 1637*

GOVERNOR JOHN WINTHROP: Mrs. Hutchinson, you are called here as one of those that have troubled the peace of the commonwealth and the churches here; you are known to be a woman that hath had a great share in the promoting and divulging of those opinions that are the cause of this trouble, and to be nearly joined not only in affinity and affection with some of those the court had taken notice of and passed censure upon, but you have spoken divers° things, as we have been informed, very prejudicial to the honor of the churches and ministers thereof, and you have maintained a meeting and an assembly in your house that hath been condemned by the general assembly as a thing not tolerable nor comely in the sight of God nor fitting for your sex, and notwithstanding that was cried down° you have continued the same. Therefore we have thought good to send for you to understand how things are, that if you be in an erroneous way we may reduce you° that so you may become a profitable member here among us. Otherwise if you be obstinate in your course that then the court may take such course that you may trouble us no further. Therefore I would entreat you to express whether you do assent and hold in practice to those opinions and factions that have been handled in court already, that is to say, whether you do not justify Mr. Wheelwright's sermon and the petition.

MRS. ANNE HUTCHINSON: I am called here to answer before you but I hear no things laid to my charge.

WINTHROP: I have told you some already and more I can tell you.

HUTCHINSON: Name one, Sir.

---

divers: diverse, various

cried down: complained of

reduce you: lead you back

WINTHROP: Have I not named some already?
HUTCHINSON: What have I said or done? 5
WINTHROP: Why for your doings, this you did harbor° and countenance° those that are parties in this faction that you have heard of.
HUTCHINSON: That's matter of conscience, Sir.
WINTHROP: Your conscience you must keep, or it must be kept for you.
HUTCHINSON: Must not I then entertain° the saints° because I must keep my conscience?
WINTHROP: Say that one brother should commit felony or treason and come to his brother's house, if he knows him guilty and conceals him he is guilty of the same. It is his conscience to entertain him, but if his conscience comes into act in giving countenance and entertainment to him that hath broken the law he is guilty too. So if you do countenance those that are transgressors of the law you are in the same fact. 10
HUTCHINSON: What law do they transgress?
WINTHROP: The law of God and of the state.
HUTCHINSON: In what particular?
WINTHROP: Why in this among the rest, whereas the Lord doth say honor thy father and thy mother.
HUTCHINSON: Aye, Sir, in the Lord. 15
WINTHROP: This honor you have broke in giving countenance to them.
HUTCHINSON: In entertaining those did I entertain them against any act (for there is the thing) or what God has appointed?
WINTHROP: You knew that Mr. Wheelwright did preach this sermon and those that countenance him in this do break a law.
HUTCHINSON: What law have I broken?
WINTHROP: Why the fifth commandment. 20
HUTCHINSON: I deny that for he [Mr. Wheelwright] saith in the Lord.°
WINTHROP: You have joined with them in the faction.
HUTCHINSON: In what faction have I joined with them?
WINTHROP: In presenting the petition.
HUTCHINSON: Suppose I had set my hand to the petition. What then? 25
WINTHROP: You saw that case tried before.
HUTCHINSON: But I had not my hand to [not signed] the petition.
WINTHROP: You have counseled them.
HUTCHINSON: Wherein?
WINTHROP: Why in entertaining them. 30

harbor: provide with shelter or lodging
countenance: support, encourage
entertain: show hospitality to
saints: members of the Puritan congregation
saith in the Lord: preaches with divine inspiration and/or in conformity with Christian doctrine

HUTCHINSON: What breach of law is that, Sir?

WINTHROP: Why dishonoring the commonwealth.

HUTCHINSON: But put the case, Sir, that I do fear the Lord and my parents. May not I entertain them that fear the Lord because my parents will not give me leave?

WINTHROP: If they be the fathers of the commonwealth, and they of another religion, if you entertain them then you dishonour your parents and are justly punishable.

HUTCHINSON: If I entertain them, as they have dishonored their parents I do. 35

WINTHROP: No but you by countenancing them above others put honor upon them.

HUTCHINSON: I may put honor upon them as the children of God and as they do honor the Lord.

WINTHROP: We do not mean to discourse with those of your sex but only this: you so adhere unto them and do endeavor to set forward this faction and so you do dishonor us.

HUTCHINSON: I do acknowledge no such thing. Neither do I think that I ever put any dishonor upon you.

WINTHROP: Why do you keep such a meeting at your house as you do every week upon a set day? 40

HUTCHINSON: It is lawful for me to do so, as it is all your practices, and can you find a warrant for yourself and condemn me for the same thing? The ground of my taking it up was, when I first came to this land because I did not go to such meetings as those were, it was presently reported that I did not allow of such meetings but held them unlawful and therefore in that regard they said I was proud and did despise all ordinances. Upon that a friend came unto me and told me of it and I to prevent such aspersions took it up, but it was in practice before I came. Therefore I was not the first.

WINTHROP: For this, that you appeal to our practice you need no confutation.° If your meeting had answered to the former it had not been offensive, but I will say that there was no meeting of women alone, but your meeting is of another sort for there are sometimes men among you.

HUTCHINSON: There was never any man with us.

WINTHROP: Well, admit there was no man at your meeting and that you was sorry for it, there is no warrant for your doings, and by what warrant do you continue such a course?

HUTCHINSON: I conceive there lies a clear rule in Titus that the elder women should instruct the younger and then I must have a time wherein I must do it. 45

---

confutation: argument or evidence to disprove the charge

WINTHROP: All this I grant you, I grant you a time for it, but what is this to the purpose that you Mrs. Hutchinson must call a company together from their callings° to come to be taught of you?

HUTCHINSON: Will it please you to answer me this and to give me a rule for them I will willingly submit to any truth. If any come to my house to be instructed in the ways of God what rule have I to put° them away?

WINTHROP: But suppose that a hundred men come to you to be instructed will you forbear to instruct them?

HUTCHINSON: As far as I conceive° I cross° a rule in it.

WINTHROP: Very well and do you not so here? 50

HUTCHINSON: No Sir for my ground is they are men.

WINTHROP: Men and women all is one for that, but suppose that a man should come and say Mrs. Hutchinson I hear that you are a woman that God hath given his grace unto and you have knowledge in the word of God I pray instruct me a little, ought you not to instruct this man?

HUTCHINSON: I think I may. Do you think it is not lawful for me to teach women, and why do you call me to teach the court?

WINTHROP: We do not call you to teach the court, but to lay yourself open.°

HUTCHINSON: I desire that you would then set me down a rule by which I may put them away that come unto me and so have peace in so doing. 55

WINTHROP: You must show your rule to receive them.

HUTCHINSON: I have done it.

WINTHROP: I deny it because I have brought more arguments than you have.

HUTCHINSON: I say, to me it is a rule. . . . If you look upon the rule in Titus it is a rule to me. If you convince me that it is no rule I shall yield.

WINTHROP: You know that there is no rule that crosses another, but this rule crosses that in the Corinthians. But you must take it in this sense that elder women must instruct the younger about their business and to love their husbands and not to make them to clash. 60

HUTCHINSON: I do not conceive but that is meant for some public times.

WINTHROP: Well, have you no more to say but this?

HUTCHINSON: I have said sufficient for my practice.°

WINTHROP: Your course is not to be suffered for.° Besides that we find such a course as this to be greatly prejudicial to the state. Besides the occasion that it is to seduce many honest persons that are called to those meetings 65

---

callings: professions, business

put: send

conceive: understand

cross: break, violate

lay yourself open: explain yourself

sufficient for my practice: enough to justify my actions

suffered for: tolerated

and your opinions and your opinions being known to be different from the word of God may seduce many simple souls that resort unto you. Besides that the occasion which hath come of late hath come from none but such as have frequented your meetings, so that now they are flown off from magistrates and ministers and since they have come to you. And besides that it will not well stand with the commonwealth that families should be neglected for so many neighbors and dames° and so much time spent. We see no rule of God for this. We see not that any should have authority to set up any other exercises besides what authority hath already set up and so what hurt comes of this you will be guilty of and we for suffering you.

HUTCHINSON: Sir, I do not believe that to be so.

WINTHROP: Well, we see how it is. We must therefore put it away from you or restrain you from maintaining this course.

HUTCHINSON: If you have a rule for it from God's word you may.

WINTHROP: We are your judges, and not you ours and we must compel you to it.

HUTCHINSON: If it please you by authority to put it down I will freely let you for I am subject to your authority. 70

. . .

WINTHROP: The court hath already declared themselves satisfied concerning the things you hear, and concerning the troublesomeness of her spirit and the danger of her course amongst us, which is not to be suffered. Therefore if it be the mind of the court that Mrs. Hutchinson for these things that appear before us is unfit for our society, and if it be the mind of the court that she shall be banished out of our liberties and imprisoned till she be sent away, let them hold up their hands.

[All but three hold up their hands.]

WINTHROP: Mrs. Hutchinson, the sentence of the court you hear is that you are banished from out of our jurisdiction as being a woman not fit for our society, and are to be imprisoned till the court shall send you away.

HUTCHINSON: I desire to know wherefore° I am banished?

WINTHROP: Say no more, the court knows wherefore and is satisfied.

[1637]

Read

1. How does Governor Winthrop's language suggest his reasons for bringing charges against Anne Hutchinson?
2. How does Hutchinson use logic to fight the charges?

---

dames: ladies, mistresses of households

wherefore: why

3. Where do you hear emotional responses from either of the participants in this exchange?
4. How is the Bible used by both sides to bolster the argument they make?

Write

1. How do you react to the last line of the text? Write a paragraph that describes its effect on you as a reader.
2. Characterize Winthrop and Hutchinson through their language to one another.
3. Describe what the trial document suggests about the reason for Hutchinson's being found guilty.

Complete Additional Exercises on Hutchinson's Trial at Your Pearson MyLab

Connect

1. What does the document suggest about the position of women in colonial times?
2. How does this trial connect to anything in the "trial" of Miss Polly Baker?

Anonymous (Hopi)

In this seventeenth century Hopi narrative of the coming of the Spanish to the American Southwest, centuries of time get compressed into one story. This oral tale paints an unflattering picture of the Spanish missionaries and shows the difference between the two cultures, especially the difference between the Hopi religion and the Catholicism of the colonizers. The Hopi, who revered the Kachina, the spirit ancestors of human beings, questioned how a God would ask them to abandon their faith. This is an excerpt from a 1936 book transcribed from the commentary of a Hopi named Edmund Nequatewa who was born in the 1880s.

From *The Coming of the Spanish and the Pueblo Revolt*

It may have taken quite a long time for these villages to be established. Anyway, every place was pretty well settled down when the Spanish came. The Spanish were first heard of at Zuni and then at Awatovi. They came on to Shung-opovi, passing Walpi. At First Mesa, Si-kyatki was the largest village then, and they were called Si-kyatki, not Walpi. The Walpi people were living below the present village on the west side. When the Spaniards came, the Hopi thought that they were the ones they were looking for—their white brother, the Bahana, their savior.

The Spaniards visited Shung-opovi several times before the missions were established. The people of Mishongovi welcomed them so the priest who was with the white men built the first Hopi mission at Mishongovi. The people of Shung-opovi were at first afraid of the priests but later they decided he was really the Bahana, the savior, and let him build a mission at Shung-opovi.

Well, about this time the Strap Clan were ruling at Shung-opovi and they were the ones that gave permission to establish the mission. The Spaniards, whom they called Castilla, told the people that they had much more power than all their chiefs and a whole lot more power than the witches. The people were very much afraid of them, particularly if they had much more power than the witches. They were so scared that they could do nothing but allow themselves to be made slaves. Whatever they wanted done must be done. Any man in power that was in this position the Hopi called *Tota-achi,* which means a grouchy person that will not do anything himself, like a child. They couldn't refuse, or they would be slashed to death or punished in some way. There were two *Tota-achi.*

The missionary did not like the ceremonies. He did not like the Kachinas° and he destroyed the altars and the customs. He called it idol worship and burned up all the ceremonial things in the plaza.

When the Priests started to build the mission, the men were sent away over near the San Francisco peaks to get the pine or spruce beams. These beams were cut and put into shape roughly and were then left till the next year when they had dried out. Beams of that size were hard to carry and the first few times they tried to carry these beams on their backs, twenty to thirty men walking side by side under the beam. But this was rather hard in rough places and one end had to swing around. So finally they figured out a way of carrying the beam in between them. They lined up two by two with the beam between the lines. In doing this, some of the Hopis were given authority by the missionary to look after these men and to see if they all did their duty. If any man gave out on the way he was simply left to die. There was great suffering. Some died for lack of food and water, while others developed scabs and sores on their bodies. 5

It took a good many years for them to get enough beams to Shung-opovi to build the mission. When this mission was finally built, all the people in the village had to come there to worship, and those that did not come were punished severely. In that way their own religion was altogether wiped out, because they were not allowed to worship in their own way. All this trouble was a heavy burden on them and they thought it was on account of this that they were having a heavy drought at this time. They thought their gods had given them up because they weren't worshiping the way they should.

Now during this time the men would go out pretending they were going on a hunting trip and they would go to some hiding place, to make their prayer offerings. So today, a good many of these places are still to be found where they left their little stone bowls in which they ground their copper ore to paint the prayer sticks. These places are called *Puwa-kiki,* cave places. If these men were caught they were severely punished.

Kachinas: wooden figures, or dolls, representing spirit beings

Now this man, *Tota-achi* (the Priest), was going from bad to worse. He was not doing the people any good and he was always figuring what he could do to harm them. So he thought out how the water from different springs or rivers would taste and he was always sending some man to these springs to get water for him to drink, but it was noticed that he always chose the men who had pretty wives. He tried to send them far away so that they would be gone two or three days, so it was not very long until they began to see what he was doing. The men were even sent to the Little Colorado River to get water for him, or to Moencopi. Finally, when a man was sent out he'd go out into the rocks and hide, and when the night came he would come home. Then, the priest, thinking the man was away, would come to visit his wife, but instead the man would be there when he came. Many men were punished for this.

All this time the priest, who had great power, wanted all the young girls to be brought to him when they were about thirteen or fourteen years old. They had to live with the priest. He told the people they would become better women if they lived with him for about three years. Now one of these girls told what the *Tota-achi* were doing and a brother of the girl heard of this and he asked his sister about it, and he was very angry. This brother went to the mission and wanted to kill the priest that very day, but the priest scared him and he did nothing. So the Shung-opovi people sent this boy, who was a good runner, to Awatovi to see if they were doing the same thing over there, which they were. So that was how they got all the evidence against the priest.

Then the chief at Awatovi sent word by this boy that all the priests would be killed on the fourth day after the full moon. They had no calendar and that was the best way they had of setting the date. In order to make sure that everyone would rise up and do this thing on the fourth day the boy was given a cotton string with knots in it and each day he was to untie one of these knots until they were all out and that would be the day for the attack. 10

Things were getting worse and worse so the chief of Shung-opovi went over to Mishongnovi and the two chiefs discussed their troubles. "He is not the savior and it is your duty to kill him," said the chief of Shung-opovi. The chief of Mishongnovi replied, "If I end his life, my own life is ended."

Now the priest would not let the people manufacture prayer offerings, so they had to make them among the rocks in the cliffs out of sight, so again one day the chief of Shung-opovi went to Mishongnovi with tobacco and materials to make prayer offerings. He was joined by the chief of Mishongnovi and the two went a mile north to a cave. For four days they lived there heartbroken in the cave, making pahos.° Then the chief of Mishongnovi took the prayer offerings and climbed to the top of the Corn Rock and deposited them in the shrine, for

pahos: prayer sticks

according to the ancient agreement with the Mishongnovi people it was their duty to do away with the enemy.

He then, with some of his best men, went to Shung-opovi, but he carried no weapons. He placed his men at every door of the priest's house. Then he knocked on the door and walked in. He asked the priest to come out but the priest was suspicious and would not come out. The chief asked the priest four times and each time the priest refused. Finally, the priest said, "I think you are up to something."

The chief said, "I have come to kill you." "You can't kill me," cried the priest, "you have no power to kill me. If you do, I will come to life and wipe out your whole tribe."

The chief returned, "If you have this power, then blow me out into the air; my gods have more power than you have. My gods have put a heart into me to enter your home. I have no weapons. You have your weapons handy, hanging on the wall. My gods have prevented you from getting your weapons." 15

The old priest made a rush and grabbed his sword from the wall. The chief of Mishongnovi yelled and the doors were broken open. The priest cut down the chief and fought right and left but was soon overpowered, and his sword taken from him.

They tied his hands behind his back. Out of the big beams outside they made a tripod. They hung him on the beams, kindled a fire and burned him.

Read

1. What are elements in the story that suggests its oral beginnings?
2. How would you characterize the attitude of the people toward the Spanish?
3. What words and images does the speaker use to describe the missionary priest?

Write

1. Find several places where religious conflict gets revealed in the narrative and comment on the effect of that conflict.
2. Why do the Pueblo allow the Spanish to build the mission? Speculate on their reasons in a paragraph.
3. How does the narrative create an argument? How would you describe the argument the story makes?

Connect

1. Compare this narrative with Franklin's "Notes Concerning the Savages" in terms of the story, its language, or the description of conflict.
2. What images of the land do you find in the narrative that connect to descriptions of the land in any other text in this unit?

Phillis Wheatley

Brought from Africa as a child, Phillis Wheatley (1753–1784) was sold to wealthy Boston resident Susanne Wheatley and raised in a strict Christian household. Her education and her ability to write well meant she escaped the worst of slavery, and she was freed by 1773. Wheatley was first published when she was about thirteen, and her volume of poetry in 1773 is the first volume of poetry known to have been published by an African American. She wrote about patriotism, Christianity, and racial consciousness.

On Being Brought from Africa to America

'Twas mercy brought me from my Pagan land,
Taught my benighted soul to understand
That there's a God, that there's a Saviour too:
Once I redemption neither sought nor knew.
Some view our sable° race with scornful eye, 5
"Their colour is a diabolic die."°
Remember, Christians, Negros, black as Cain,°
May be refin'd and join th'angelic train.

[1773]

Read

1. How does Wheatley use religion to explain her presence in America?
2. What word choices suggest to you Wheatley's position and the time period in which she is writing?
3. To whom is the poem addressed? How do you know?

Write

1. How does she call her new religion to account? Does she criticize it?
2. How do you characterize Wheatley's persona? Write a paragraph that describes her persona and if you find a difference from the beginning of the poem to its end.
3. How does the way the poem is set up, its lines and rhymes, contribute to its aim?

Connect

1. Does the tone of this poem seem similar to Franklin's tone in either of his pieces? Find some lines that suggest similarities.
2. How is Wheatley's use of religion in this poem like Occam's use of religion in his narrative?

---

sable: black, very dark

die: dye

black as Cain: After Cain had killed his brother, Abel, God placed a mark upon him, which some have interpreted to mean black skin.

Abigail Adams
John Adams

Both John Adams (1735–1826) and his wife, Abigail Adams (1744–1818), were highly educated Bostonians. Their marriage was an alliance of two strong minds and wills, as their letters show. Abigail pressed for real change to come from the Revolution in which both she and her husband played significant roles. She influenced her husband's career as an intellectual leader in Boston and in Congress as well as later when Adams served as second President of the United States from 1797 to 1801.

Letters

Abigail Adams to John Adams

Braintree, 31 March, 1776.

I wish you would ever write me a letter half as long as I write you, and tell me, if you may, where your fleet are gone; what sort of defense Virginia can make against our common enemy; whether it is so situated as to make an able defense. Are not the gentry lords, and the common people vassals?° Are they not like the uncivilized vassals Britain represents us to be? I hope their riflemen, who have shown themselves very savage and even blood-thirsty, are not a specimen of the generality° of the people. I am willing to allow the colony great merit for having produced a Washington; but they have been shamefully duped by a Dunmore.

I have sometimes been ready to think that the passion for liberty cannot be equally strong in the breasts of those who have been accustomed to deprive their fellow-creatures of theirs. Of this I am certain, that it is not founded upon that generous and Christian principle of doing to others as we would that others should do unto us.

Do not you want to see Boston? I am fearful of the small-pox, or I should have been in before this time. I got Mr. Crane to go to our house and see what state it was in. I find it has been occupied by one of the doctors of a regiment; very dirty, but no other damage has been done to it. The few things which were left in it are all gone. I look upon it as a new acquisition of property—a property which one month ago I did not value at a single shilling, and would with pleasure have seen it in flames.

---

vassals: subordinates; servants or slaves

generality: general run, majority

The town in general is left in a better state than we expected; more owing to a precipitate flight than any regard to° the inhabitants; though some individuals discovered a sense of honor and justice, and have left the rent of the houses in which they were, for the owners, and the furniture unhurt, or, if damaged, sufficient to make it good. Others have committed abominable ravages. The mansion-house of your President is safe, and the furniture unhurt; while the house and furniture of the Solicitor General have fallen a prey to their own merciless party. Surely the very fiends feel a reverential awe for virtue and patriotism, whilst they detest the parricide° and traitor.

I feel very differently at the approach of spring from what I did a month ago. We knew not then whether we could plant or sow with safety, whether where we had tilled we could reap the fruits of our own industry, whether we could rest in our own cottages or whether we should be driven from the seacoast to seek shelter in the wilderness; but now we feel a temporary peace, and the poor fugitives are returning to their deserted habitations. 5

Though we felicitate° ourselves, we sympathize with those who are trembling lest the lot of Boston should be theirs. But they cannot be in similar circumstances unless pusillanimity° and cowardice should take possession of them. They have time and warning given them to see the evil and shun it.

I long to hear that you have declared an independency. And, by the way, in the new code of laws which I suppose it will be necessary for you to make, I desire you would remember the ladies and be more generous and favorable to them than your ancestors. Do not put such unlimited power into the hands of the husbands. Remember, all men would be tyrants if they could. If particular care and attention is not paid to the ladies, we are determined to foment a rebellion, and will not hold ourselves bound by any laws in which we have no voice or representation.

That your sex are naturally tyrannical is a truth so thoroughly established as to admit of no dispute; but such of you as wish to be happy willingly give up the harsh title of master for the more tender and endearing one of friend. Why, then, not put it out of the power of the vicious and the lawless to use us with cruelty and indignity with impunity? Men of sense in all ages abhor those customs which treat us only as the vassals of your sex; regard us then as beings placed by Providence under your

---

regard to: concern for

parricide: one who kills a parent or other close relative

felicitate: congratulate

pusillanimity: timidity, lack of resolve

protection, and in imitation of the Supreme Being make use of that power only for our happiness.

John Adams to Abigail Adams

14 April, 1776.

You justly complain of my short letters, but the critical state of things and the multiplicity of avocations must plead my excuse. You ask where the fleet is? The inclosed papers will inform you. You ask what sort of defense Virginia can make? I believe they will make an able defense. Their militia and minute-men have been some time employed in training themselves, and they have nine battalions of regulars, as they call them, maintained among them, under good officers, at the Continental expense. They have set up a number of manufactories of fire-arms, which are busily employed. They are tolerably supplied with powder, and are successful and assiduous° in making saltpetre.° Their neighboring sister, or rather daughter colony of North Carolina, which is a warlike colony, and has several battalions at the Continental expense, as well as a pretty good militia, are ready to assist them, and they are in very good spirits and seem determined to make a brave resistance. The gentry are very rich, and the common people very poor. This inequality of property gives an aristocratical turn to all their proceedings, and occasions a strong aversion in their patricians to "Common Sense." But the spirit of these Barons is coming down, and it must submit. It is very true, as you observe, they have been duped by Dunmore. But this is a common case. All the colonies are duped, more or less, at one time and another. A more egregious° bubble was never blown up than the story of Commissioners coming to treat with the Congress, yet it has gained credit like a charm, not only with, but against the clearest evidence. I never shall forget the delusion which seized our best and most sagacious friends, the dear inhabitants of Boston, the winter before last. Credulity and the want of foresight are imperfections in the human character, that no politician can sufficiently guard against.

You give me some pleasure by your account of a certain house in Queen Street. I had burned it long ago in imagination. It rises now to my view like a phœnix. What shall I say of the Solicitor General? I pity his pretty children. I pity his father and his sisters. I wish I could be clear that it is 10

---

assiduous: tireless, persistent

saltpetre: a form of potassium nitrate used in making gunpowder

egregious: gross, outrageous

no moral evil to pity him and his lady. Upon repentance, they will certainly have a large share in the compassions of many. But let us take warning, and give it to our children. Whenever vanity and gayety, a love of pomp and dress, furniture, equipage,° buildings, great company, expensive diversions, and elegant entertainments get the better of the principles and judgments of men or women, there is no knowing where they will stop, nor into what evils, natural, moral, or political, they will lead us.

Your description of your own gaieté de coeur charms me. Thanks be to God, you have just cause to rejoice, and may the bright prospect be obscured by no cloud. As to declarations of independency, be patient. Read our privateering laws and our commercial laws. What signifies a word?

As to your extraordinary code of laws, I cannot but laugh. We have been told that our struggle has loosened the bonds of government everywhere; that children and apprentices were disobedient; that schools and colleges were grown turbulent; that Indians slighted their guardians, and negroes grew insolent to their masters. But your letter was the first intimation that another tribe, more numerous and powerful than all the rest, were grown discontented. This is rather too coarse a compliment, but you are so saucy, I won't blot it out. Depend upon it, we know better than to repeal our masculine systems. Although they are in full force, you know they are little more than theory. We dare not exert our power in its full latitude. We are obliged to go fair and softly, and, in practice, you know we are the subjects. We have only the name of masters, and rather than give up this, which would completely subject us to the despotism of the petticoat, I hope General Washington and all our brave heroes would fight; I am sure every good politician would plot, as long as he would against despotism, empire, monarchy, aristocracy, oligarchy,° or ochlocracy. A fine story, indeed! I begin to think the ministry as deep as they are wicked. After stirring up Tories, land-jobbers,° trimmers,° bigots, Canadians, Indians, negroes, Hanoverians, Hessians, Russians, Irish Roman Catholics, Scotch renegadoes, at last they have stimulated the ——— to demand new privileges and threaten to rebel.

---

equipage: can refer to a horse-drawn carriage and/or a group of servants or attendants

oligarchy: government by the few

jobbers: those who abuse a public office or trust for private profit

trimmers: those who change their views or positions out of expediency

Read

1. What word choices and images suggest to you the relationship between Adams and his wife?
2. How does Abigail convey her political astuteness in her letter? How does John convey his?
3. What kinds of appeals does Abigail use in her letter? What appeals does John use in his?

Write

1. Which writer has the stronger logic? What makes you think so?
2. Write a paragraph or so about what the letters reveal about the times in which they were written. Locate some lines or examples that suggest the context of the letters.

Connect

1. How does Abigail Adams seem to be a woman of her time? How does she seem to be unusual?
2. What links and differences do you observe between Abigail Adams and Anne Bradstreet?

Joseph Badger

Joseph Badger was a house painter in Boston during the early and mid eighteenth century. He painted his grandson James in 1760.

James Badger, age 3

Portrait of James Badger (1760), Joseph Badger. Oil on canvas, 42 1/2 x 33 1/8 in. (108 x 84.1 cm). Photo by Peter Horree/Alamy

[1760]

Read

1. What is the significance of the clothing of the boy in the portrait?
2. What details do you notice first?
3. How would you describe the stance of the figure?

Write

1. Comment on details of dress or props or background that suggest the activities of children.
2. How does the painter suggest the status of the child?
3. What age would you guess the child to be if you didn't know? Write the details that suggest the age to you.

Connect

1. What in *The New England Primer* makes a connection to this portrait?
2. How do you think the portrait suggests something about the changes in New England from the time of the Plymouth settlement to prerevolutionary Boston?

Contemporary Works

Nathaniel Philbrick

Writer and historian Nathaniel Philbrick (b. 1956) was born in Boston, Massachusetts. An expert in maritime and New England history, Philbrick published *In the Heart of the Sea: The Tragedy of the Whaleship Essex* in 2000, which won a National Book Award. In 2006, he published *Mayflower,* the story of the founding of the Plymouth colony. He now lives in Nantucket, Massachusetts, where he is writing a history of the early colony in Boston.

From *Mayflower*

They could not help but stare in fascination. He was so different from themselves. For one thing, he towered over them. He stood before them "a tall straight man," having not labored at a loom or a cobbler's bench for much of his life. His hair was black, short in front and long in back, and his face was hairless. Interestingly, the Pilgrims made no mention of his skin color.

What impressed them the most was that he was "stark naked," with just a fringed strap of leather around his waist. When a cold gust of wind kicked up, one of the Pilgrims was moved to throw his coat over the Indian's bare shoulders.

He was armed with a bow and just two arrows, "the one headed, the other unheaded." The Pilgrims do not seem to have attached any special significance to them, but the arrows may have represented the alternatives of war and peace. In any event, they soon began to warm to their impetuous guest and offered him something to eat. He immediately requested beer.

With their supplies running short, they offered him some "strong water"—perhaps the aqua vitae° they'd drunk during their first days on Cape Cod—as well as some biscuit, butter, cheese, pudding, and a slice of roasted duck, "all of which he liked well."

He introduced himself as Samoset—at least that was how the Pilgrims heard it—but he may actually have been telling them his English name, Somerset. He was not, he explained in broken English, from this part of new England. He was a sachem from Pemaquid Point in Maine, near Monhegan Island, a region frequented by English fishermen. It was from these fishermen, many of whom he named, that he'd learned to speak English. Despite occasional trouble understanding him, the Pilgrims hung on Samoset's every word as he told them about their new home. 5

He explained that the harbor's name was Patuxet, and that just about every person who had once lived there had "died of an extraordinary plague." The supreme leader of the region was named Massasoit, who lived in a place called Pokanoket about forty miles to the southwest at the head of Narragansett Bay. Samoset said that the Nausets controlled the part of Cape Cod where the Pilgrims had stolen the corn. The Nausets were "ill affected toward the English" after Hunt had abducted twenty or so of their men back in 1614. He also said that there was another Indian back in Pokanoket named Squanto, who spoke even better English than he did.

With darkness approaching, the Pilgrims were ready to see their voluble guest on his way. As a practical matter, they had nowhere for him to sleep; in addition, they were not yet sure whether they could trust him. But Samoset made it clear he wanted to spend the night. Perhaps because they assumed he'd fear abduction and quickly leave, they offered to take him out to the *Mayflower*. Samoset cheerfully called their bluff and climbed into the shallop.° Claiming that high winds and low tides prevented them from leaving shore, the Pilgrims finally allowed him to spend the night with Stephen Hopkins and his family. Samoset left the next morning, promising to return in a few days with some of Massasoit's men.

All that winter, Massasoit had watched and waited. From the Nausets he had learned of the Pilgrims' journey along the bay side of Cape Cod and their eventual arrival at Patuxet. His own warriors had kept him updated as to the progress of their various building projects, and despite their secret burials, he undoubtedly knew that many of the English had died over the winter.

---

aqua vitae: alcohol (brandy, whiskey, etc.; from Latin: "water of life")
shallop: small open boat

For as long as anyone could remember, European fishermen and explorers had been visiting New England, but these people were different. First of all, there were women and children—probably the first European women and children the Indians had ever seen. They were also behaving unusually. Instead of attempting to trade with the Indians, they kept to themselves and seemed much more interested in building a settlement. These English people were here to stay.

Massasoit was unsure of what to do next. A little over a year before, the sailors aboard an English vessel had killed a large number of his people without provocation. As a consequence, Massasoit had felt compelled to attack the explorer Thomas Dermer when he arrived the following summer with Squanto at his side, and most of Dermer's men had been killed in skirmishes on Cape Cod and Martha's Vineyard. Squanto had been taken prisoner on the Vineyard, but now he was with Massasoit in Pokanoket. The former Patuxet resident had told him of his years in Europe, and once the *Mayflower* appeared at Provincetown Harbor and made its way to Plymouth, he had offered his services as an interpreter. But Massasoit was not yet sure whose side Squanto was on. 10

Over the winter, as the Pilgrims continued to bury their dead surreptitiously, Massasoit gathered together the region's powwows, or shamans, for a three-day meeting "in a dark and dismal swamp." Swamps were where the Indians went in time of war: they provided a natural shelter for the sick and old; they were also a highly spiritual landscape, where the unseen currents of the spirits intermingled with the hoots of owls.

Massasoit's first impulse was not to embrace the English but to curse them. Bradford later learned that the powwows had attempted to "execrate° them with their conjurations." Powwows communed with the spirit world in an extremely physical manner, through what the English described as "horrible outcries, hollow bleatings, painful wrestlings, and smiting their own bodies." Massasoit's powwows were probably not the first and certainly not the last Native Americans to turn their magic on the English. To the north, at the mouth of the Merrimack River, lived Passaconaway, a sachem who was also a powwow—an unusual combination that endowed him with extraordinary powers. It was said he could "make the water burn, the rocks move, the trees dance, metamorphise himself into a flaming man." But not even Passaconaway was able to injure the English. In 1660, he admitted to his people, "I was as much an enemy to the English at their first coming into these parts, as anyone whatsoever, and did try all ways and means possible to have destroyed them, at least to have prevented them sitting down here, but I could in no way effect it; . . . therefore I advise you never to contend with the English, nor make war with them." At some point, Massasoit's powwows appear to have made a similar recommendation.

The powwows were not the only ones who weighed in on the issue of what to do with the Pilgrims. There was also Squanto. Ever since the appearance of the *Mayflower*, the former captive had begun to work his own kind of magic

---

execrate: curse

on Massasoit, insisting that the worst thing he could do was to attack the Pilgrims. Not only did they have muskets and cannons; they possessed the seventeenth-century equivalent of a weapon of mass destruction: the plague. At some point, Squanto began to insist that the Pilgrims had the ability to unleash disease on their enemies. If Massasoit became an ally to the Pilgrims, he would suddenly be in a position to break the Narragansetts' stranglehold on the Pokanokets. "[E]nemies that were [now] too strong for him," Squanto promised, "would be constrained to bow to him."

It was a suggestion that played on Massasoit's worst fears. The last three years had been a nightmare of pain and loss; to revisit that experience was inconceivable. Reluctantly, Massasoit determined that he must "make friendship" with the English. To do so, he must have an interpreter, and Squanto—the only one fluent in both English and Massachusett, the language of the Pokanoket—assumed that he was the man for the job. Though he'd been swayed by Squanto's advice, Massasoit was loath to place his faith in the former captive, whom he regarded as a conniving cultural mongrel with dubious motives. So he first sent Samoset, a visiting sachem with only a rudimentary command of English, to the Pilgrim settlement.

But now it was time for Massasoit to visit the English himself. He must turn to Squanto. 15

On March 22, five days after his initial visit, Samoset returned to Plymouth with four other Indians, Squanto among them. The Patuxet native spoke with an easy familiarity about places that now seemed a distant dream to the Pilgrims—besides spending time in Spain and Newfoundland, Squanto had lived in the Corn Hill section of London. The Indians had brought a few furs to trade, along with some fresh herring. But the real purpose of their visit was to inform the Pilgrims that Massasoit and his brother Quadequina were nearby. About an hour later, the sachem appeared on Watson's Hill with a large entourage of warriors.

The Pilgrims described him as "a very lusty [or strong] man, in his best years, an able body, grave of countenance, and spare of speech." Massasoit stood on the hill, his face painted dark red, his entire head glistening with bear grease. Draped around his neck was a wide necklace made of white shell beads and a long knife suspended from a string. His men's faces were also painted, "some black, some red, some yellow, and some white, some with crosses, and other antic works."° Some of them had furs draped over their shoulders; others were naked. But every one of them possessed a stout bow and a quiver of arrows. These were unmistakably warriors: "all strong, tall, all men in appearance." Moreover, there were sixty of them.

For the Pilgrims, who could not have mustered more than twenty adult males and whose own military leader was not even five and a half feet tall, it must have been a most intimidating display of physical strength and power. Squanto ventured over to Watson's Hill and returned with the message that

---

antic works: fantastic or grotesque decorations

the Pilgrims should send someone to speak to Massasoit. Edward Winslow's wife, Elizabeth, was so sick that she would be dead in just two days, but he agreed to act as Governor Carver's messenger. Clad in armor and with a sword at his side, he went with Squanto to greet the sachem.

First he presented Massasoit and his brother with a pair of knives, some copper chains, some alcohol, and a few biscuits, "which were all willingly accepted." Then he delivered a brief speech. King James of England saluted the sachem "with words of love and peace," Winslow proclaimed, and looked to him as a friend and ally. He also said that Governor Carver wished to speak and trade with him and hoped to establish a formal peace. Winslow was under the impression that Squanto "did not well express it," but enough of his meaning was apparently communicated to please Massasoit. The sachem ate the biscuits and drank the liquor, then asked if Winslow was willing to sell his sword and armor. The Pilgrim messenger politely declined. It was decided that Winslow would remain with Quadequina as a hostage while Massasoit went with twenty of his men, minus their bows, to meet the governor.

The Pilgrims were men of God, but they also knew their diplomatic protocol. Undoubtedly drawing on his experiences as an assistant to the English secretary of state, William Brewster appears to have orchestrated a surprisingly formal and impressive reception of the dignitary they called the "Indian King." A Pilgrim delegation including Standish and half a dozen men armed with muskets greeted Massasoit at the brook. They exchanged salutations, and after seven of the warriors were designated hostages, Standish accompanied Massasoit to a house, still under construction, where a green rug and several cushions had been spread out on the dirt floor. On cue, a drummer and trumpeter began to play as Governor Carver and a small procession of musketeers made their way to the house.

20

Upon his arrival, Carver kissed Massasoit's hand; the sachem did the same to Carver's, and the two leaders sat down on the green rug. It was now time for Massasoit to share in yet another ceremonial drink of liquor. Carver took a swig of aqua vitae and passed the cup to Massasoit, who took a large gulp and broke into a sweat. The Pilgrims assumed the aqua vitae was what made him perspire, but anxiety may also have been a factor. As the proceedings continued, during which the two groups worked out a six-point agreement, Massasoit was observed to tremble "for fear."

Instead of Carver and the Pilgrims, it may have been Massasoit's interpreter who caused the sachem to shake with trepidation. Squanto later claimed that the English kept the plague in barrels buried beneath their storehouse. The barrels actually contained gunpowder, but the Pilgrims undoubtedly guarded the storehouse with a diligence that lent credence to Squanto's claims. If the interpreter chose to inform Massasoit of the deadly contents of the buried stores during the negotiations on March 22 (and what better way to ensure that the sachem came to a swift and satisfactory agreement with the English?), it is little wonder Massasoit was seen to tremble.

Bradford and Winslow recorded the agreement with the Pokanoket sachem as follows:

1. That neither he nor any of his should injure or do hurt to any of our people.
2. And if any of his did hurt to any of ours, he should send the offender, that we might punish him.
3. That if any of our tools were taken away when our people were at work, he should cause them to be restored, and if ours did any harm to any of his, we would do the like to him.
4. If any did unjustly war against him, we would aid him; if any did war against us, he should aid us.
5. He should send to his neighbor confederates,° to certify them of this, that they might not wrong us, but might be likewise comprised in the conditions of peace.
6. That when their men came to us, they should leave their bows and arrows behind them, as we should do our pieces° when we came to them.

Once the agreement had been completed, Massasoit was escorted from the settlement, and his brother was given a similar reception. Quadequina quickly noticed a disparity that his higher-ranking brother had not chosen to comment on. Even though the Indians had been required to lay down their bows, the Pilgrims continued to carry their muskets—a clear violation of the treaty they had just signed with Massasoit. Quadequina "made signs of dislike, that [the guns] should be carried away." The English could not help but admit that the young Indian had a point, and the muskets were put aside.

Squanto and Samoset spent the night with the Pilgrims while Massasoit and his men, who had brought along their wives and children, slept in the woods, just a half mile away. Massasoit promised to return in a little more than a week to plant corn on the southern side of Town Brook. Squanto, it was agreed, would remain with the English. As a final gesture of friendship, the Pilgrims sent the sachem and his people a large kettle of English peas, "which pleased them well, and so they went their way." 25

After almost five months of uncertainty and fear, the Pilgrims had finally established diplomatic relations with the Native leader who, as far as they could tell, ruled this portion of New England. But as they were soon to find out, Massasoit's power was not as pervasive as they would have liked. The Pokanokets had decided to align themselves with the English, but many of Massasoit's allies had yet to be convinced that the Pilgrims were good for New England.

---

neighbor confederates: nearby allied
pieces: firearms

The next day, Squanto, who after a six-year hiatus was back to living on his native shore, left to fish for eels. At that time of year, the eels lay dormant in the mud, and after wading out into the cold water of a nearby tidal creek, he used his feet to "trod them out." By the end of the day, he returned with so many eels that he could barely lift them all with one hand. That night the Pilgrims ate the eels with relish, praising them as "fat and sweet," and Squanto was on his way to becoming the one person in New England they could not do without.

[2006]

Read

1. What is the first reaction of the Pilgrims to the Indians they see? What is the first reaction of the Indians to the Pilgrims?
2. Why does the Indian speak in English?
3. How does Philbrick characterize Massasoit?
4. What is Squanto's relationship with the Pilgrims?

Write

1. Write a journal entry from the perspective of a Pilgrim upon first landing at what was to be the Plymouth colony? What would you notice first? What would your emotions have been?
2. Find indications in the passage of the different attitudes of Pilgrims and Indians to the land. Write a comment on how these differing ideas might lead to conflict.

Connect

1. How does Philbrick's account add to what Bradford records in his history? Are there any conflicting pieces of information?
2. Comment on anything you read in this narrative that surprises you or that is new information for you about the founding of the settlement.
3. How does the account of the early relationship between colonist and Indian connect to the Thanksgiving story you might have heard?

Lerone Bennett, Jr.

Lerone Bennett (b. 1928), African American social historian, editor, and scholar, has written many books on African American history and culture, including *Before the Mayflower* in 1968. Revised and expanded in 1993, the book has been published in nine editions. Bennett traces the contributions of Africans and early black Americans to American life, uncovering little-known details about accomplishments, service, and community relationships that other histories have often overlooked. He was long-time executive editor of *Ebony Magazine.* In 2000, he published *Bound to Glory: Abraham Lincoln's White Dream.*

From *Before the Mayflower: A History of Black America*

A large proportion of the first generation of African-Americans entered America with Spanish names. For reasons that are not readily apparent, many black males were called Antonio, a name that quickly became Antoney or Anthony. Other popular names of the period included Michaela, Couchaxello, Mingo, Pedro, Francisco, Jibina, Maria, Wortello, Tomora, Angola, and Tony Kongo. Shortly after their arrival in America, many blacks discarded African and Spanish names and adopted English titles. Thus within the span of a generation the black soul moved from Africa to England to Spain to America—from the X of the severed African family tree to Antonio and the William X or the William? of the first native American black, who apparently had no surname at the time of his christening.

During the next forty-odd years, hundreds of Africans made that extraordinary cultural leap. In 1625 Brase, another victim of piracy, was brought into the colony. Four years later, in 1629, there was a substantial increase in the black population when the first ship from Africa arrived at Port Comfort, bringing blacks captured from a Portuguese ship off the coast of Africa. In the 1630s and 1640s approximately 160 blacks were imported. By 1649 colonial officials were able to report that "there are in *Virginia* about fifteen thousand English, and of *Negroes* brought thither, three hundred good servants."

The "good servants" came from different backgrounds with different experiences. Quite a few, as we have noted, came from England, where blacks had lived since the middle of the sixteenth century. Many came from Spain, Portugal and the West Indies. Significantly, many were Christians, baptized either in Spain or Portugal or on the high seas. In 1624 John Phillip testified in a Jamestown court and his testimony against a white man was admitted because he had been "christened in England twelve years since. . . ."

In a limited but nonetheless significant sense, then, the Jamestown experience was an open experience which provided unusual opportunities for individual blacks. This comes out most clearly in the life and times of Anthony Johnson, who came to America in 1621 or thereabouts from England. Like many other blacks of the period, Johnson quickly worked out his term of indenture and started accumulating property. In 1651, according to official records, he imported and paid for five servants, some of whom were white, and was granted 250 acres of land on the basis of the headright system, which permitted planters to claim fifty acres of land for each individual brought to the colony.

The abstract of the deed reads as follows: 5

> ANTHONY JOHNSON, 250 acs. Northampton Co., 24, July 1651, ... At great Naswattock Cr., being a neck of land bounded on the S.W. by the maine Cr. & on S.E. & N.W. by two small branches issueing out of the mayne Cr. Trans. of 5 pers: Tho. Bemrose, Peter Bughby, Antho. Cripps, Jno Gesorroro, Richard Johnson.

In the years that followed, Johnson and his relatives established one of America's first black communities on the banks of the Pungoteague River. In 1652 John Johnson, who was probably Anthony Johnson's son, imported eleven persons, most of them white males and females, and received headrights for 550 acres adjacent to Anthony Johnson. Two years later Richard Johnson imported two white indentured servants and received one hundred acres. Here are the records of the deeds:

> JOHN JOHNSON, 550 acs. Northampton Co., 10 May 1652 . . . At great Naswattocks Cr., adj. 200 acs. granted to Anthony Johnson. Trans. of 11 pers: John Edward, Wm. Routh, Tho. Yowell, Fra. Maland, William Price, John Owen, Dorothy Rily, Richard Hemstead, Law. Barnes, Row. Rith, Mary Johnson.
>
> RICH. Jnoson (Johnson—also given as John), Negro, 100 acs. Northampton Co., 21 Nov. 1654, . . . On S. Side of Pongoteague Riv., Ely. upon Pocomock Nly. upon land of John Jnoson., Negro, Wly. upon Anto. Jnoson., Negro, & Sly. upon Nich. Waddilow. Trans. of 2 pers: Wm. Ames, Wm. Vincent.

The Johnson settlement at its height included only a handful of blacks with large holdings. Other blacks lived in integrated communities in other areas of the colony. In 1656, for instance, Benjamin Doyle received a patent for three hundred acres in Surry County. In 1668 John Harris bought fifty acres in New Kent County; and Phillip Morgan, reflecting the optimism of the age, leased two hundred acres in York County for ninety-nine years.

One can hardly doubt, in the face of this clear evidence, that the first generation of blacks had, as J. H. Russell noted, "about the same industrial or economic opportunities as the free white servant." Additional evidence of the relatively high status of the first American blacks is to be found in colonial documents which indicate that they voted and participated in public life. It was not until 1723, in fact, that blacks were denied the right to vote in Virginia. According to Albert E. McKinley, blacks voted in South Carolina until 1701, in North Carolina until 1715, and in Georgia until 1754. Not only did pioneer blacks vote, but they also held public office. There was a black surety° in York County, Virginia, in the first decades of the seventeenth century, and a black beadle° in Lancaster County, Virginia.

Nor was this sort of thing confined to Virginia. The first blacks in Massachusetts—they arrived in 1638 on the *Desire,* America's first slave ship—were apparently assigned the status of indentured servants. In his classic work, *The Negro in Colonial New England,* Lorenzo J. Greene said that "until

---

surety: bondsman

beadle: parish sexton, or law-court messenger

almost the end of the seventeenth century the records refer to the Negroes as 'servants' not as 'slaves.' For some time no definite status could be assigned to incoming Negroes. Some were sold for a period of time only, and like the white indentured servants became free after their indenture."

10 The available evidence suggests that most of the first generation of African-Americans worked out their terms of servitude and were freed. A very interesting and instructive case in point is that of Richard Johnson, a black carpenter who came to Virginia in 1651 as a free man and signed a contract of indenture. Within two years Johnson was a free man. Within three years he was acquiring pounds and property and servants.

In addition to Johnson and other blacks who were freed as a matter of course, the record lists other cases in which colonial courts freed black servants. Such a case was that of Andrew Moore, who migrated to Virginia and bound himself out for a term of five years. In October, 1673, the General Court "ordered that the Said Moore bee free from his said master, and that the Said Mr. Light pay him Corne and Clothes according to the Custome of the Country and four hundred pounds tobac and Caske for his service done him Since he was free, and pay costs."

Looking back on that age from our own, one is struck by what can only be called equality of oppression. Not the least among the things that startle us in this period is that the colony's power structure made little or no distinction between black and white servants, who were assigned the same tasks and were held in equal contempt. This has caused no end of trouble for latter-day white historians, who have tried to explain away a record that is understandably astonishing in view of the later practices of some whites. It is interesting, for example, to observe that many white historians deny that white women worked in the fields. But contemporary witnesses tell us in no uncertain terms that white women not only worked in the fields but were also flogged at colonial whipping posts. There are also court records in which white women asked the courts to relieve them of this burden. Historian Philip A. Bruce conceded this point and commented with disapproval: "The class of white women who were required to work in the fields belonged to the lowest rank in point of character; not having been born in Virginia and not having thus acquired from birth a repugnance to associations with Africans upon a footing of social equality, they yielded to the temptations of the situations in which they were placed."

There is contradictory testimony which indicates that character, Bruce to the contrary notwithstanding, had little or nothing to do with the status of white servants. "They became in the eyes of the law," J. B. McMaster said, "a slave and in both the civil and criminal codes were classed with the Negro and the Indian. They were worked hard, were dressed in the cast off clothes of their owners, and might be flogged as often as the master and mistress thought necessary." There is also the testimony of T. J. Wertenbaker, who said that "the indentured servants . . . were practically slaves, being bound to the soil and forced to obey implicitly those whom they served."

Working together in the same fields, sharing the same huts, the same situation, and the same grievances, the first black and white Americans, aristocrats excepted, developed strong bonds of sympathy and mutuality. They ran away together, played together and revolted together. They mated and married, siring a sizeable mixed population. In the process the black and white servants—the majority of the colonial population—created a racial wonderland that seems somehow un-American in its lack of obsession about race and color. There was, to be sure, prejudice then, but it was largely English class prejudice which was distributed without regard to race, creed or color. There were also, needless to say, prejudiced *individuals* in the colony, but—and this is the fundamental difference between prejudice and racism—their personal quirks and obsessions were not focused and directed by the organized will of a community. The basic division at that juncture was between servants and free people, and there were whites and blacks on both sides of the line.

15

Of all the improbable aspects of this situation, the oddest—to modern blacks and whites—is that white people did not seem to know that they were white. It appears from surviving evidence that the first white colonists had no concept of themselves as *white* people. The legal documents identified whites as Englishmen and/or Christians. The word *white,* with its burden of arrogance and biological pride, developed late in the century, as a direct result of slavery and the organized debasement of blacks. The same point can be made from the other side of the line. For a long time in colonial America, there was no legal name to focus white anxiety. The first blacks were called Blackamoors, Moors, Negers and Negars. The word *Negro,* a Spanish and Portuguese term for black, did not come into general use in Virginia until the latter part of the century.

A similar course of development was roughly characteristic of New York, where the black settlement preceded the English and the name *New York.* There are records from 1626 identifying eleven blacks—about 5 per cent of the non-Indian population—who were servants of the Dutch West Indian Company. The eleven black pioneers were males. Responding to the pleas of these males, the Dutch imported three women, identified as "Angolans," in 1628.

In 1644, some eighteen years after their arrival, the "Dutch Negroes," as they were called, filed a petition for freedom, the first black legal protest in America. The petition was granted by the Council of New Netherlands, which freed the blacks because they had "served the Company seventeen or eighteen years" and had been "long since promised their freedom on the same footing as other free people in New Netherlands." The eleven blacks cited in the petition were Paul d'Angola, Big Manuel, Little Manuel, Manuel de Gerrit de Rens, Simon Congo, Anthony Portuguese, Gracia, Peter Santome, John

Francisco, Little Anthony and John Fort Orange. All received parcels of land in what is now Greenwich Village.

What is essential to grasp about the first blacks in New York is that they stood on the same footing as white indentured servants from the very beginning. "They had almost full freedom of motion and assembly," James Weldon Johnson wrote in *Black Manhattan*. "They were allowed to marry; wives and daughters had legal protection against the lechery of masters, and they had the right to acquire and hold property."

What has been outlined above with reference to New York and Virginia holds good also—though with minor variations—for other colonies, including Pennsylvania, where the system of black indentured servitude was so deeply rooted that black servants outnumbered black slaves at the time of the Revolution.

[1968]

Read

1. How does the writer draw comparisons between the early colonists both black and white?
2. How would you describe the writer's use of evidence to support his position?

Write

1. How would you describe the aim of this part of Bennett's history?
2. Write a paragraph that discusses Bennett's use of *logos* to convince his audience of his position.
3. Comment on the attitudes of white settlers toward the African population, using lines or examples from the excerpt to support your position.

Connect

1. How does the history Bennett tells alter or add to the history of colonial America you've found in reading other texts in this section?
2. How might you account for the change in attitudes of white America to black America from the time of the colonists to a later time in history?

Sarah Vowell

Sarah Vowell (b. 1969) has written books on history and contemporary culture and is a contributing editor for public radio's *This American Life.* Her account of the early lives of settlers in New England in *The Wordy Shipmates* draws on historical documents and current understandings to frame her account of the Puritans and the communities they created.

From *The Wordy Shipmates*

In September of 1637, one month after Henry Vane sailed away, the freemen meet to decide on matters Hutchinsonian. They resolve, writes Winthrop, "That though women might meet (some few together) to pray and edify one another," assemblies of "sixty or more" as were then taking place in Boston at the home of "one woman" who had had the gall to go about "resolving questions of doctrine and expounding scripture" are not allowed. The Bill of Rights, with its allowance for freedom of assembly, is a long way off.

Also, a member of a church's congregation "might ask a question publicly, after sermon, for information; yet this ought to be very wisely and sparingly done." In other words, no heckling the ministers allowed.

In November, Wheelwright appears before the court and, refusing to repent for his Fast Day sermon the previous January, is, Winthrop writes, "disenfranchised and banished." So are four other supporters of Hutchinson and Wheelwright, including John Underhill, hero of the Mystic Massacre.°

"The court also sent for Mrs. Hutchinson," writes Winthrop, "and charged her with . . . keeping two public lectures every week in her house," which were attended by "sixty to eighty persons." She is also accused of "reproaching most of the ministers," except for Cotton, "for not preaching a covenant of free grace, and that they had not the seal of the spirit."

Hutchinson's judges are Winthrop, Deputy Governor Thomas Dudley, five assistants, and five deputies. Various ministers, including John Cotton, are also present. As governor, Winthrop presides over the trial, for the most part stupidly. Hutchinson continually outwits him, even though she is, at the age of forty-six, pregnant yet again. 5

Winthrop explains to Hutchinson she has been "called here as one of those that have troubled the peace of the commonwealth." And, as is his policy toward all godly persons who repent their blunders, he offers the court's corrections, so that she "may become a profitable member here among us." If not, "the court may take such course that you may trouble us no further."

Hutchinson points out she has not been charged with anything. Winthrop says he just told her why she's here.

"What have I said or done?" she asks.

Winthrop answers that she "did harbor . . . parties in this faction that you have heard of." I.e., she invited troublemakers into her home.

Then he accuses her of being in favor of Wheelwright's Fast Day sermon,° and those in favor of the sermon "do break a law." 10

---

the Mystic Massacre: In May 1637, during the Pequot War, English forces and their Indian allies destroyed a Pequot village near present-day Mystic, Connecticut, killing more than 400 people, mostly women and children.

Wheelwright's Fast Day sermon: In January 1637, Rev. John Wheelwright had preached a sermon asserting grace through faith, in contrast to the Puritans' emphasis on grace through works.

"What law have I broken?" she asks.

"Why the fifth commandment," answers Winthrop. This is of course the favorite commandment of all ministers and magistrates, the one demanding a person should honor his father and mother, which for Winthrop includes all authority figures. Wheelwright's sermon was an affront to the fathers of the church and the fathers of the commonwealth.

A Ping-Pong match follows in which Winthrop accuses her of riling up Wheelwright's faction and she's, like, "What faction?" And he accuses her of having "counseled" this mysterious faction and she wonders how she did that and he answers, "Why in entertaining them."

She asks him to cite the law against having people over. And he lamely says she has broken the law of "dishonoring the commonwealth."

15 (Genealogy buffs might enjoy learning that this lopsided battle of the wits will be repeated between Winthrop and Hutchinson's descendants during the presidential debates of 2004. Winthrop's heir, John Kerry, debates Hutchinson's great-something grandson, George W. Bush. Only in this instance it's the Hutchinson who is flummoxed by his opponent's sensical answers. Bush's constant blinking appears on television as if he thinks the answers to the questions he's being asked are tattooed inside his own eyelids.)

Winthrop and Hutchinson go back and forth as to whether or not she's honoring her parents, and Winthrop is so flummoxed by the way she crushes his shaky arguments, he erupts, "We do not mean to discourse with those of your sex." Not a particularly good comeback, considering that they're the ones who have forced her into this discourse.

He then quizzes her on why she holds her commonwealth-dishonoring meetings at her house. She cites Paul's Epistle to Titus, in the New Testament, which calls for "the elder women" to "instruct the younger."

He tells her that what she's supposed to instruct the younger women on is "to love their husbands and not to make them clash."

She responds, "If any come to my house to be instructed in the ways of God what rule have I to put them away?"

20 "Your opinions," Winthrop claims, "may seduce many simple souls that resort unto you." Furthermore, with all these women at Hutchinson's house instead of their own, "Families should be neglected for so many neighbors and dames and so much time spent."

When she presses him once again to point out the Scripture that contradicts the Scripture she has quoted calling for elders to mentor younger women, Winthrop, flustered, barks, "We are your judges, and not you ours."

Winthrop really is no match for Hutchinson's logic. Most of his answers to her challenges boil down to "Because I said so."

In fact, before this trial started, the colony's elders had agreed to raise four hundred pounds to build a college but hadn't gotten around to doing anything about it. After Hutchinson's trial, they got cracking immediately and founded Harvard so as to prevent random, home-schooled female maniacs from outwitting magistrates in open court and seducing colonists, even male ones, into strange opinions. Thanks in part to Hutchinson, the young men of Massachusetts will receive a proper, orthodox theological education grounded in the rigorous study of Hebrew and Greek.

Moving along, Winthrop asks her of ministers preaching "a covenant of works, do they preach truth?"

"Yes sir," she answers, "but when they preach a covenant of works for salvation, that is not truth." In other words, it's fine to exhort people to good behavior, but good behavior is not going to save their souls. Which is in fact, what every person in the room, including Winthrop, believes. They are angry with her because she has accused all the ministers except for Cotton and her brother-in-law, Wheelwright, of preaching *only* a covenant of works, a Puritan put-down. Several ministers then gang up on her to claim that that's what she's been going around saying.

The trial resumes the next morning and John Cotton is called to testify, if the court can get the beloved Cotton, Hutchinson's highest-ranking friend, to rat her out for heresy or sedition, she's lost. He stands by her, though, more or less. He says he regrets that any comparison has been made between him and his colleagues, calling it "uncomfortable." But, he adds, "I must say that I did not find her saying that they were under a covenant of works, nor that she said they did preach a covenant of works."

Cotton has exonerated her. Now the court has to acquit her. And it would have except that one person stands up and gives the testimony that will get Anne Hutchinson banished from Massachusetts. And that person is: Anne Hutchinson.

"If you please to give me leave I shall give you the ground of what I know to be true," she says.

Music to John Winthrop's ears. He was about to step in and silence her. But, while the trial transcript proves that she's better debater than he, he's no idiot. He later recalls, "Perceiving whereabouts she went"—namely, self-incrimination—he "permitted her to proceed."

I wish I didn't understand why Hutchinson risks damning herself to exile and excommunication just for the thrill of shooting off her mouth and making other people listen up. But this here book is evidence that I have this confrontational, chatty bent myself. I got my first radio job when I was eighteen years old and I've been yakking on air or in print ever since. Hutchinson is about to have her life—and her poor family's—turned upside down just so she can indulge in the sort of smart-alecky diatribe for which I've gotten paid for the last twenty years.

Hutchinson starts by informing the court of her spiritual biography. She recalls that back home, she was disconcerted by the "falseness" of the Church of England and contemplated "turn[ing] Separatist." But after a "day of solemn humiliation," she had, like every man in the room, decided against separatism.

Unlike every man in the room, she claimed to hear the voice of God, who "let me see which was the clear ministry and which the wrong." Ever since, she continues, she has been hearing voices—Moses, John the Baptist, even "the voice of Antichrist."

To the men before her (and, by the way, to me) this is crazy talk. It might also be devil talk. An assistant asks her, "How do you know that was the spirit?"

Her answer couldn't be more uppity. She compares herself to the most exalted Hebrew patriarch facing the Bible's most famous spiritual dilemma: "How did Abraham know that it was God that bid him offer his son, being a breach of the sixth commandment?"

Dudley replies. "By an immediate voice."

Hutchinson: "So to me by an immediate revelation . . . by the voice of his own spirit to my soul." 35

This is blasphemous enough, but she's on a roll. She then dares them to mess with her, a woman who has the entire Holy Trinity on speed dial. "Look what you do," she warns. "You have power over my body but the Lord Jesus hath power over my body and soul." Their lies, she claims, "will bring a curse upon you and your posterity, and the mouth of the Lord hath spoken it."

Winthrop provokes her further. Since she is shameless enough to compare herself to Abraham, he seems to think it might be fun to find out if she is Daniel in the lion's den, too. "Daniel was delivered by miracle," he says. "Do you think to be delivered so too?"

Yep. "I do here speak it before the court," she responds helpfully, adding, "I look that the Lord should deliver me by his providence." She claims God told her, "'I am the same God that delivered Daniel out of the lion's den, I will also deliver thee.'"

She was quoting God. Not the Bible. Just something God said to her one day when they were hanging out.

A magistrate named William Bartholomew who had sailed to Massachusetts on the *Griffin* with Hutchinson pipes up that when Boston came into view she was alarmed by "the meanness° of the place" but then proclaimed that "if she had not a sure word that England should be destroyed, her heart would shake." Bartholomew recalls that "it seemed to me at that time very strange and witchlike that she should say so." 40

Hutchinson denies Bartholomew's claim. When Winthrop presses him further, Bartholomew says that back in England he heard her profess "that she had never had any great thing done about her but it was revealed to her beforehand." In other words, she claimed to be able to predict the future. Hutchinson denies this as well.

Now that her witchlike pronouncements are on the table, Deputy Governor Thomas Dudley shrewdly seizes the opportunity to challenge John Cotton as to whether "you approve of Mistress Hutchinson's revelations."

---

meanness: shabbiness

Cotton is stuck. Hutchinson has handily enumerated her shocking delusions of grandeur. She has claimed to hear the voice of God. Honorable men have testified that she boasts of being able to predict the future. The disquieting syllable "witch" has come up. On the one hand, this woman has been his friend and stalwart supporter for years. On the other hand, if he sticks up for her, he could end up like Wheelwright and Underhill and the other men who have defended her—banished. And Cotton already knows what that's like, remembers well his time back in England on the run from Bishop Laud,° hiding out in friends' houses, his wife being followed, unable to practice his calling. When he went underground, he was a man without a home or a church, which to an old preacher like Cotton is the same thing.

Dudley presses him: "Do you believe her revelations are true?"

Winthrop steps in, saying, "I am persuaded that the revelation she brings forth is delusion." There's a surprise. 45

Finally, in one sentence, Cotton sells out Hutchinson by recalling hearing another of her claims to predict the future. He says, "I remember she said she should be delivered by God's providence, whether now or at another time she knew not."

In this context, Cotton's concession is a smoking gun. He doesn't elaborate. He doesn't have to.

Winthrop is ready to take a vote:

> Mrs. Hutchinson for these things that appear before us is unfit for our society, and if it be the mind of the court that she shall be banished out of our liberties and imprisoned till she be sent away, let them hold up their hands.

Nine out of twelve hands go up, among them, of course, Winthrop's. He continues, "Mrs. Hutchinson, the sentence of the court you hear is that you are banished from out of our jurisdiction as being a woman not fit for our society, and are to be imprisoned till the court shall send you away."

She demands, "I desire to know wherefore I am banished?" 50

Winthrop waves her off. "Say no more," he commands. "The court knows wherefore and is satisfied."

In the *Short Story of the Rise, Reign, and Ruin of the Antinomians, and Libertines that Infected the Churches of New England,* a victory tract published in London in 1644 and almost certainly written by Winthrop, Hutchinson is famously described as "this American Jezebel" whose downfall came when "the hand of civil justice laid hold on her, and then she began evidently to decline, and the faithful to be freed from her forgeries."

Bishop Laud: William Laud, Archbishop of Canterbury, whose hostility to Puritanism exacerbated the tensions that led to the English Civil War; he was accused of treason and beheaded in January 1645.

After being banished by the court. Hutchinson is excommunicated by the church. Winthrop writes in his diary that though her banishment had left her "somewhat dejected," excommunication cheered her up. "She gloried in her sufferings, saying that it was the greatest happiness, next to Christ, that ever befell her." He adds that it's actually the churches of Massachusetts that are happiest, as the "poor souls who had been seduced by her" had "settled again in the truth."

[2008]

Read

1. How would you describe the style of this excerpt?
2. How does Vowell create a portrait of the antagonists Winthrop and Hutchinson?
3. Why has Hutchinson been called to court?
4. What is the major disagreement between the two antagonists?

Write

1. Write a discussion of the techniques Hutchinson uses to answer Winthrop. How does the author suggest she fares in the debate between the two?
2. Write about Vowell's use of humor to get across her aim in the description of the trial.

Connect

1. How does this account deepen or alter the trial account of Hutchinson in this unit?
2. How does this history suggest the roles of women and men in the Puritan community and Vowell's perspective on those roles?
3. How is Vowell's discussion made contemporary?

Mario Cuomo

Born in New York City in 1932 to Italian immigrant parents, Mario Cuomo was educated in New York schools and graduated first in his class from St. John's Law School. He was a trial attorney and later worked on urban housing issues for Mayor John Lindsay. Cuomo became governor of New York in 1982 and in 1984 gave the Keynote Address to the Democratic National Convention in San Francisco. Speculation followed for several years about Cuomo's own presidential ambitions, but he always declined to run. He was defeated in his fourth election for governor in part for his opposition to the death penalty, a position he has always held strongly. He speaks against the stereotyping of immigrants, especially Italian Americans, in his work as well. He has authored several books, including *Why Lincoln Matters* in 2004.

Keynote Address to the Democratic Convention, 1984

Thank you very much.

On behalf of the great Empire State and the whole family of New York, let me thank you for the great privilege of being able to address this convention. Please allow me to skip the stories and the poetry and the temptation to deal in nice but vague rhetoric. Let me instead use this valuable opportunity to deal immediately with the questions that should determine this election and that we all know are vital to the American people.

Ten days ago, President Reagan admitted that although some people in this country seemed to be doing well nowadays, others were unhappy, even worried, about themselves, their families, and their futures. The President said that he didn't understand that fear. He said, "Why, this country is a shining city on a hill." And the President is right. In many ways we are a shining city on a hill.

But the hard truth is that not everyone is sharing in this city's splendor and glory. A shining city is perhaps all the President sees from the portico of the White House and the veranda of his ranch, where everyone seems to be doing well. But there's another city; there's another part to the shining the city; the part where some people can't pay their mortgages, and most young people can't afford one; where students can't afford the education they need, and middle-class parents watch the dreams they hold for their children evaporate.

In this part of the city there are more poor than ever, more families in trouble, more and more people who need help but can't find it. Even worse: There are elderly people who tremble in the basements of the houses there. And there are people who sleep in the city streets, in the gutter, where the glitter doesn't show. There are ghettos where thousands of young people, without a job or an education, give their lives away to drug dealers every day. There is despair, Mr. President, in the faces that you don't see, in the places that you don't visit in your shining city. 5

In fact, Mr. President, this is a nation—Mr. President, you ought to know that this nation is more a "Tale of Two Cities" than it is just a "Shining City on a Hill."

Maybe, maybe, Mr. President, if you visited some more places; maybe if you went to Appalachia where some people still live in sheds; maybe if you went to Lackawanna where thousands of unemployed steel workers wonder why we subsidized foreign steel.

Maybe—Maybe, Mr. President, if you stopped in at a shelter in Chicago and spoke to the homeless there; maybe, Mr. President, if you asked a woman who had been denied the help she needed to feed her children because you said you needed the money for a tax break for a millionaire or for a missile we couldn't afford to use.

Maybe—Maybe, Mr. President. But I'm afraid not. Because the truth is, ladies and gentlemen, that this is how we were warned it would be. President Reagan told us from the very beginning that he believed in a kind of social Darwinism. Survival of the fittest. "Government can't do everything," we were told, so it should settle for taking care of the strong and hope that economic ambition and charity will do the rest. Make the rich richer, and what falls from the table will be enough for the middle class and those who are trying desperately to work their way into the middle class.

You know, the Republicans called it "trickle-down" when Hoover tried it. Now they call it "supply side." But it's the same shining city for those relative few who are lucky enough to live in its good neighborhoods. But for the people who are excluded, for the people who are locked out, all they can do is stare from a distance at that city's glimmering towers. 10

It's an old story. It's as old as our history. The difference between Democrats and Republicans has always been measured in courage and confidence. The Republicans—The Republicans believe that the wagon train will not make it to the frontier unless some of the old, some of the young, some of the weak are left behind by the side of the trail. "The strong"—"The strong," they tell us, "will inherit the land."

We Democrats believe in something else. We Democrats believe that we can make it all the way with the whole family intact, and we have more than once. Ever since Franklin Roosevelt lifted himself from his wheelchair to lift this nation from its knees—wagon train after wagon train—to new frontiers of education, housing, peace; the whole family aboard, constantly reaching out to extend and enlarge that family; lifting them up into the wagon on the way; blacks and Hispanics, and people of every ethnic group, and native Americans—all those struggling to build their families and claim some small share of America. For nearly 50 years we carried them all to new levels of comfort, and security, and dignity, even affluence. And remember this, some of us in this room today are here only because this nation had that kind of confidence. And it would be wrong to forget that.

So, here we are at this convention to remind ourselves where we come from and to claim the future for ourselves and for our children. Today our great Democratic Party, which has saved this nation from depression, from fascism, from racism, from corruption, is called upon to do it again—this time to save the nation from confusion and division, from the threat of eventual fiscal disaster, and most of all from the fear of a nuclear holocaust.

That's not going to be easy. Mo Udall° is exactly right—it won't be easy. And in order to succeed, we must answer our opponent's polished and appealing rhetoric with a more telling reasonableness and rationality.

15 We must win this case on the merits. We must get the American public to look past the glitter, beyond the showmanship to the reality, the hard substance of things. And we'll do it not so much with speeches that sound good as with speeches that are good and sound; not so much with speeches that will bring people to their feet as with speeches that will bring people to their senses. We must make—We must make the American people hear our "Tale of Two Cities." We must convince them that we don't have to settle for two cities, that we can have one city, indivisible, shining for all of its people.

Now, we will have no chance to do that if what comes out of this convention is a babel of arguing voices. If that's what's heard throughout the campaign, dissident sounds from all sides, we will have no chance to tell our message. To succeed we will have to surrender some small parts of our individual interests, to build a platform that we can all stand on, at once, and comfortably—proudly singing out. We need—We need a platform we can all agree to so that we can sing out the truth for the nation to hear, in chorus, its logic so clear and commanding that no slick Madison Avenue commercial, no amount of geniality, no martial music will be able to muffle the sound of the truth.

And we Democrats must unite. We Democrats must unite so that the entire nation can unite, because surely the Republicans won't bring this country together. Their policies divide the nation into the lucky and the left-out, into the royalty and the rabble. The Republicans are willing to treat that division as victory. They would cut this nation in half, into those temporarily better off and those worse off than before, and they would call that division recovery.

Now, we should not—we should not be embarrassed or dismayed or chagrined if the process of unifying is difficult, even wrenching at times. Remember that, unlike any other Party, we embrace men and women of every color, every creed, every orientation, every economic class. In our family are gathered everyone from the abject poor of Essex County in New York, to the enlightened affluent of the gold coasts at both ends of the nation. And in between is the heart of our constituency—the middle class, the people not rich enough to be worry-free, but not poor enough to be on welfare; the middle class—those

---

Mo Udall: Morris Udall (1922–1998), U.S. Congressman (D-AZ) from 1961 to 1991, introduced former President Jimmy Carter at the 1984 Democratic National Convention.

people who work for a living because they have to, not because some psychiatrist told them it was a convenient way to fill the interval between birth and eternity. White collar and blue collar. Young professionals. Men and women in small business desperate for the capital and contracts that they need to prove their worth.

We speak for the minorities who have not yet entered the mainstream. We speak for ethnics who want to add their culture to the magnificent mosaic that is America. We speak—We speak for women who are indignant that this nation refuses to etch into its governmental commandments the simple rule "thou shalt not sin against equality," a rule so simple—

I was going to say, and I perhaps dare not but I will. It's a commandment so simple it can be spelled in three letters: E.R.A. 20

We speak—We speak for young people demanding an education and a future. We speak for senior citizens. We speak for senior citizens who are terrorized by the idea that their only security, their Social Security, is being threatened. We speak for millions of reasoning people fighting to preserve our environment from greed and from stupidity. And we speak for reasonable people who are fighting to preserve our very existence from a macho intransigence that refuses to make intelligent attempts to discuss the possibility of nuclear holocaust with our enemy. They refuse. They refuse, because they believe we can pile missiles so high that they will pierce the clouds and the sight of them will frighten our enemies into submission.

Now we're proud of this diversity as Democrats. We're grateful for it. We don't have to manufacture it the way the Republicans will next month in Dallas, by propping up mannequin delegates on the convention floor. But we, while we're proud of this diversity, we pay a price for it. The different people that we represent have different points of view. And sometimes they compete and even debate, and even argue. That's what our primaries were all about. But now the primaries are over and it is time, when we pick our candidates and our platform here, to lock arms and move into this campaign together.

If you need any more inspiration to put some small part of your own difference aside to create this consensus, then all you need to do is to reflect on what the Republican policy of divide and cajole has done to this land since 1980. Now the President has asked the American people to judge him on whether or not he's fulfilled the promises he made four years ago. I believe, as Democrats, we ought to accept that challenge. And just for a moment let us consider what he has said and what he's done.

Inflation—Inflation is down since 1980, but not because of the supply-side miracle promised to us by the President. Inflation was reduced the old-fashioned way: with a recession, the worst since 1932. Now how did we—We could have brought inflation down that way. How did he do it? 55,000 bankruptcies; two years of massive unemployment; 200,000 farmers and ranchers forced off the land; more homeless—more homeless than at any time since the Great Depression in 1932; more hungry, in this world of enormous affluence, the United States of America, more hungry; more poor, most of them women. And—And he paid one other thing, a nearly 200 billion dollar deficit threatening our future.

Now, we must make the American people understand this deficit because they don't. The President's deficit is a direct and dramatic repudiation of his promise in 1980 to balance the budget by 1983. How large is it? The deficit is the largest in the history of the universe. It—President Carter's last budget had a deficit less than one-third of this deficit. It is a deficit that, according to the President's own fiscal adviser, may grow to as much 300 billion dollars a year for "as far as the eye can see." And, ladies and gentlemen, it is a debt so large—that is almost one-half of the money we collect from the personal income tax each year goes just to pay the interest. It is a mortgage on our children's future that can be paid only in pain and that could bring this nation to its knees. 25

Now don't take my word for it—I'm a Democrat. Ask the Republican investment bankers on Wall Street what they think the chances of this recovery being permanent are. You see, if they're not too embarrassed to tell you the truth, they'll say that they're appalled and frightened by the President's deficit. Ask them what they think of our economy, now that it's been driven by the distorted value of the dollar back to its colonial condition. Now we're exporting agricultural products and importing manufactured ones. Ask those Republican investment bankers what they expect the rate of interest to be a year from now. And ask them—if they dare tell you the truth—you'll learn from them, what they predict for the inflation rate a year from now, because of the deficit.

Now, how important is this question of the deficit. Think about it practically: What chance would the Republican candidate have had in 1980 if he had told the American people that he intended to pay for his so-called economic recovery with bankruptcies, unemployment, more homeless, more hungry, and the largest government debt known to humankind? If he had told the voters in 1980 that truth, would American voters have signed the loan certificate for him on Election Day? Of course not! That was an election won under false pretenses. It was won with smoke and mirrors and illusions. And that's the kind of recovery we have now as well.

But what about foreign policy? They said that they would make us and the whole world safer. They say they have. By creating the largest defense budget in history, one that even they now admit is excessive—by escalating to a frenzy the nuclear arms race; by incendiary rhetoric; by refusing to discuss peace with our enemies; by the loss of 279 young Americans in Lebanon in pursuit of a plan and a policy that no one can find or describe.

We give money to Latin American governments that murder nuns, and then we lie about it. We have been less than zealous in support of our only real friend—it seems to me, in the Middle East—the one democracy there, our flesh and blood ally, the state of Israel. Our—Our policy—Our foreign policy drifts with no real direction, other than an hysterical commitment to an arms race that leads nowhere—if we're lucky. And if we're not, it could lead us into bankruptcy or war.

Of course we must have a strong defense! Of course Democrats are for a strong defense. Of course Democrats believe that there are times that we must stand and fight. And we have. Thousands of us have paid for freedom with our lives. But always—when this country has been at its best—our purposes were clear. Now they're not. Now our allies are as confused as our enemies. Now we have no real commitment to our friends or to our ideals—not to human rights, not to the refuseniks, not to Sakharov, not to Bishop Tutu and the others struggling for freedom in South Africa. 30

We—We have in the last few years spent more than we can afford. We have pounded our chests and made bold speeches. But we lost 279 young Americans in Lebanon and we live behind sand bags in Washington. How can anyone say that we are safer, stronger, or better?

That—That is the Republican record. That its disastrous quality is not more fully understood by the American people I can only attribute to the President's amiability and the failure by some to separate the salesman from the product.

And, now—now—now it's up to us. Now it's up to you and to me to make the case to America. And to remind Americans that if they are not happy with all that the President has done so far, they should consider how much worse it will be if he is left to his radical proclivities for another four years unrestrained. Unrestrained.

Now, if—if July—if July brings back Ann Gorsuch Burford—what can we expect of December? Where would—Where would another four years take us? Where would four years more take us? How much larger will the deficit be? How much deeper the cuts in programs for the struggling middle class and the poor to limit that deficit? How high will the interest rates be? How much more acid rain killing our forests and fouling our lakes?

And, ladies and gentlemen, please think of this—the nation must think of this: What kind of Supreme Court will we have? 35

Please. [beckons audience to settle down]

We—We must ask ourselves what kind of court and country will be fashioned by the man who believes in having government mandate people's religion and morality; the man who believes that trees pollute the environment; the man that believes that—that the laws against discrimination against people go too far; a man who threatens Social Security and Medicaid and help for the disabled. How high will we pile the missiles? How much deeper will the gulf be between us and our enemies? And, ladies and gentlemen, will four years more make meaner the spirit of the American people? This election will measure the record of the past four years. But more than that, it will answer the question of what kind of people we want to be.

We Democrats still have a dream. We still believe in this nation's future. And this is our answer to the question. This is our credo:

We believe in only the government we need, but we insist on all the government we need.

We believe in a government that is characterized by fairness and reasonableness, a reasonableness that goes beyond labels, that doesn't distort or promise to do things that we know we can't do. 40

We believe in a government strong enough to use words like "love" and "compassion" and smart enough to convert our noblest aspirations into practical realities.

We believe in encouraging the talented, but we believe that while survival of the fittest may be a good working description of the process of evolution, a government of humans should elevate itself to a higher order.

We—Our—Our government—Our government should be able to rise to the level where it can fill the gaps that are left by chance or by a wisdom we don't fully understand. We would rather have laws written by the patron of this great city, the man called the "world's most sincere Democrat," St. Francis of Assisi, than laws written by Darwin.

We believe—We believe as Democrats, that a society as blessed as ours, the most affluent democracy in the world's history, one that can spend trillions on instruments of destruction, ought to be able to help the middle class in its struggle, ought to be able to find work for all who can do it, room at the table, shelter for the homeless, care for the elderly and infirm, and hope for the destitute. And we proclaim as loudly as we can the utter insanity of nuclear proliferation and the need for a nuclear freeze, if only to affirm the simple truth that peace is better than war because life is better than death.

We believe in firm—We believe in firm but fair law and order. 45

We believe proudly in the union movement.

We believe in a—We believe—We believe in privacy for people, openness by government.

We believe in civil rights, and we believe in human rights.

We believe in a single—We believe in a single fundamental idea that describes better than most textbooks and any speech that I could write what a proper government should be: the idea of family, mutuality, the sharing of benefits and burdens for the good of all, feeling one another's pain, sharing one another's blessings—reasonably, honestly, fairly, without respect to race, or sex, or geography, or political affiliation.

We believe we must be the family of America, recognizing that at the heart of the matter we are bound one to another, that the problems of a retired school teacher in Duluth are our problems; that the future of the child—that the future of the child in Buffalo is our future; that the struggle of a disabled man in Boston to survive and live decently is our struggle; that the hunger of a woman in Little Rock is our hunger; that the failure anywhere to provide what reasonably we might, to avoid pain, is our failure. 50

Now, for 50 years—for 50 years we Democrats created a better future for our children, using traditional Democratic principles as a fixed beacon, giving us direction and purpose, but constantly innovating, adapting to new realities: Roosevelt's alphabet programs;° Truman's NATO and the GI Bill of Rights; Kennedy's intelligent tax incentives and the Alliance for Progress; Johnson's civil rights; Carter's human rights and the nearly miraculous Camp David Peace Accord.

Democrats did it—Democrats did it and Democrats can do it again. We can build a future that deals with our deficit. Remember this, that 50 years of progress under our principles never cost us what the last four years of stagnation have. And we can deal with the deficit intelligently, by shared sacrifice, with all parts of the nation's family contributing, building partnerships with the private sector, providing a sound defense without depriving ourselves of what we need to feed our children and care for our people. We can have a future that provides for all the young of the present, by marrying common sense and compassion.

We know we can, because we did it for nearly 50 years before 1980. And we can do it again, if we do not forget—if we do not forget that this entire nation has profited by these progressive principles; that they helped lift up genera-

Roosevelt's alphabet programs: During the first term (1933–1937) of President Franklin Delano Roosevelt (1882–1945), the federal government enacted a number of programs to combat the Great Depression, such as the National Recovery Administration (NRA), the Civilian Conservation Corps (CCC), and the Works Progress Administration (WPA), that were popularly known by their acronyms.

tions to the middle class and higher; that they gave us a chance to work, to go to college, to raise a family, to own a house, to be secure in our old age and, before that, to reach heights that our own parents would not have dared dream of.

That struggle to live with dignity is the real story of the shining city. And it's a story, ladies and gentlemen, that I didn't read in a book, or learn in a classroom. I saw it and lived it, like many of you. I watched a small man with thick calluses on both his hands work 15 and 16 hours a day. I saw him once literally bleed from the bottoms of his feet, a man who came here uneducated, alone, unable to speak the language, who taught me all I needed to know about faith and hard work by the simple eloquence of his example. I learned about our kind of democracy from my father. And I learned about our obligation to each other from him and from my mother. They asked only for a chance to work and to make the world better for their children, and they—they asked to be protected in those moments when they would not be able to protect themselves. This nation and this nation's government did that for them.

And that they were able to build a family and live in dignity and see one of their children go from behind their little grocery store in South Jamaica on the other side of the tracks where he was born, to occupy the highest seat, in the greatest state, in the greatest nation, in the only world we would know, is an ineffably beautiful tribute to the democratic process. 55

And—And ladies and gentlemen, on January 20, 1985, it will happen again—only on a much, much grander scale. We will have a new President of the United States, a Democrat born not to the blood of kings but to the blood of pioneers and immigrants. And we will have America's first woman Vice President, the child of immigrants, and she—she—she will open with one magnificent stroke, a whole new frontier for the United States.

Now, it will happen. It will happen if we make it happen; if you and I make it happen. And I ask you now, ladies and gentlemen, brothers and sisters, for the good of all of us, for the love of this great nation, for the family of America, for the love of God: Please, make this nation remember how futures are built.

Thank you and God bless you.

[1984]

Read

1. What are some of the strategies Cuomo uses to characterize the problems the country faces early in his speech?
2. How does Cuomo create his own persona to draw in his audience?
3. How does the context for this speech—the Democratic convention—affect its arrangement and its argument?

Write

1. How does Cuomo envision the way the country should develop? Use examples and quotations from the speech to help frame your response.
2. Write a paragraph to discuss how Cuomo uses history and American idealism to make his speech persuasive.
3. Where do you hear emotional appeal most strongly? Write a few examples of Cuomo's use of *pathos* and comment on his success in using that appeal as a rhetorical strategy.

Complete Additional Exercises on Cuomo's Speech at Your Pearson MyLab

Connect

1. How do you read the shining city metaphor in comparison with Winthrop's use of the term? How does the allusion to Winthrop work?
2. Write a response to his speech from your perspective as a twenty-first-century reader.

UNIT ACTIVITIES

Rhetorical Analysis

1. Benjamin Franklin, inventor, Revolutionary War patriot, signer of the Declaration of Independence, and eminent eighteenth-century writer, wrote "Notes Concerning the Savages" in 1740. Read the excerpt from Franklin's essay and then write an essay that analyzes rhetorical strategies used by Franklin to call into question the "savagery" of the American Indians he describes.
2. Compare Benjamin Franklin's attitude toward the Indians in "Notes Concerning the Savages" to the attitudes evident in Mary Rowlandson's "Captivity Narrative." Include direct descriptions of the Indians from each of these pieces and your analysis of how these descriptions reveal their attitudes. Consider the context of the connection between colonist and Indian as you analyze attitudes, as well as the persona each writer creates through the use of language and evidence.

Argument

Examine Cyrus Dallin's 1921 sculpture of the Wampanoag leader Massasoit after reading William Bradford's account of the first year of life in the Plymouth colony. Then write a persuasive essay that accounts for the connections and the disparities between the visual depiction of the Wampanoag chief and Bradford's account of early encounters between Pilgrims and the Indians. Your argument might use whatever background information is appropriate but should clearly develop your own position about the disparities and connections you observe.

Synthesis

Locate at least three texts in the unit that you think describe the roles of and attitudes toward women in the early colonies. Using these sources, write an essay that characterizes women's roles and responsibilities in the colonies and the attitudes of the colonial culture toward them.

UNIT 2

The photo was taken by photographer Samantha Wagner at the 2012 Conservative Political Action Conference where attendees protested illegal immigration.

Read

1. Do you recognize the background setting in the photo? How does the background contribute to the effect?
2. How does the sign play with language to highlight its message?

Connect

1. How do any of the texts of explorers and settlers in this unit suggest an attitude toward immigration?
2. How does the photo demonstrate the ways in which attitudes about immigration have changed or remained constant?

How Do We Build a Nation?

1789–1837

As the group of colonies became a country, new questions arose in addition to the continuing questions of freedom and responsibility. How might people establish an identity for the new country's inhabitants? How would its day-to-day governing put into practice the ideals in the Declaration of Independence and the American Constitution? How should the country defend itself? How should it create borders?

Tension and Conflict The future was always in the minds of the former colonists who were now new Americans. The future was also in the minds of those whose land was now called America but who themselves were not "Americans"—the many tribal nations whose way of life and physical space were increasingly at risk. Population growth and new technologies, including better printing techniques and better transportation with the arrival of the train, increased the movements of people. The tensions between established settlements and new settlements, between the wilderness and the town, between the forest and the farm, were sometimes angry and violent. Indian tribes fought for the right to the land they inhabited, and European settlers fought for the right to possess it. What was considered the West moved farther and farther toward the Pacific Ocean on the other side of the continent.

Slavery Slavery's hold upon the economy in the Northern states weakened while it strengthened in the Southern states, and the tensions between North and South were evident decades before the Civil War. Treaties like the Missouri Compromise of 1820 tried to balance the interests of pro- and anti-slavery forces and put off the question of the growing rift between two sections of the country. Abolitionists, black and white, claimed the right of African slaves to be Americans and thus part of the promise expressed in the Declaration of Independence.

A Turning Point The year 1837 marked a serious financial panic whose effects were felt for years. It was also the year Ralph Waldo Emerson issued his call for a new literature that would reflect and inspire the new country. Fear and hope mingled in the country's writings and its politics. The new country was just learning how to be unified at the very time unity was being called into question.

GUIDING QUESTIONS

- How do we build a nation?
- Who can be called an American?

- How does economic growth change ideals?
- How far should our borders extend?
- What is the connection between individual and community morality?
- What is America's responsibility to its citizens? Its inhabitants?

Texts and Visuals

Red Jacket

Red Jacket (c. 1750–1830), also known as Sagoyewatha, was a Seneca chief born in New York State. His nickname comes from the many red coats he wore as an ally of the British during the Revolutionary War. After the war, the Iroquois confederation, of which the Seneca were part, faced enormous problems as white settlers continued to move into their territory. Red Jacket was the go-between for the new U.S. government and the Seneca; he met with George Washington in 1792 and received a peace medal for his efforts. In 1805, a Boston missionary society asked for Red Jacket's permission to preach among the Iroquois in New York State. Red Jacket presented a forceful defense of Iroquois religion in his response.

Then I Must Worship the Spirit in My Own Way

Friend and brother; it was the will of the Great Spirit that we should meet together this day. He orders all things, and he has given us a fine day for our council. He has taken his garment from before the sun,° and caused it to shine with brightness upon us; our eyes are opened, that we see clearly; our ears are unstopped, that we have been able to hear distinctly the words that you have spoken; for all these favors we thank the Great Spirit, and him only.

Brother, this council fire was kindled by you; it was at your request that we came together at this time; we have listened with attention to what you have said. You requested us to speak our minds freely; this gives us great joy, for we now consider that we stand upright before you, and can speak what we think; all have heard your voice, and all speak to you as one man; our minds are agreed.

Brother, you say you want an answer to your talk before you leave this place. It is right you should have one, as you are a great distance from home, and we do

---

taken his garment from before the sun: removed the darkness of night

not wish to detain you; but we will first look back a little, and tell you what our fathers have told us, and what we have heard from the white people.

Brother, listen to what we say. There was a time when our forefathers owned this great island. Their seats extended from the rising to the setting sun. The Great Spirit had made it for the use of Indians. He had created the buffalo, the deer, and other animals for food. He made the bear and the beaver, and their skins served us for clothing. He had scattered them over the country, and taught us how to take them. He had caused the earth to produce corn for bread. All this he had done for his red children because he loved them. If we had any disputes about hunting grounds, they were generally settled without the shedding of much blood. But an evil day came upon us; your forefathers crossed the great waters, and landed on this island. Their numbers were small; they found friends, and not enemies; they told us they had fled from their own country for fear of wicked men, and come here to enjoy their religion. They asked for a small seat; we took pity on them, granted their request, and they sat down amongst us; we gave them corn and meat; they gave us poison in return. The white people had now found our country; tidings were carried back, and more came amongst us; yet we did not fear them, we took them to be friends; they called us brothers; we believed them, and gave them a larger seat. At length, their numbers had greatly increased; they wanted more land; they wanted our country. Our eyes were opened, and our minds became uneasy. Wars took place; Indians were hired to fight against Indians, and many of our people were destroyed. They also brought strong liquor among us; it was strong and powerful, and has slain thousands.

5

Brother, our seats were once large, and yours were very small; you have now become a great people, and we have scarcely a place left to spread our blankets; you have got our country, but are not satisfied; you want to force your religion upon us.

Brother, continue to listen. You say you are sent to instruct us how to worship the Great Spirit agreeably to his mind, and if we do not take hold of the religion which you white people teach, we shall be unhappy hereafter. You say that you are right, and we are lost; how do we know this to be true? We understand that your religion is written in a book; if it was intended for us as well as you, why has not the Great Spirit given it to us, and not only to us, but why did he not give to our forefathers the knowledge of that book, with the means of understanding it rightly? We only know what you tell us about it. How shall we know when to believe, being so often deceived by the white people?

Brother, you say there is but one way to worship and serve the Great Spirit; if there is but one religion, why do you white people differ so much about it? Why not all agree, as you can all read the book?

Brother, we do not understand these things. We are told that your religion was given to your forefathers, and has been handed down from father to son. We also have a religion which was given to our forefathers, and has been handed down to us their children. We worship that way. It teacheth us to be thankful for all the favors we receive; to love each other, and to be united. We never quarrel about religion.

Brother, the Great Spirit has made us all; but he has made a great difference between his white and red children; he has given us a different complexion, and different customs; to you he has given the arts; to these he has not opened our eyes; we know these things to be true. Since he has made so great a difference between us in other things, why may we not conclude that he has given us a different religion according to our understanding. The Great Spirit does right; he knows what is best for his children; we are satisfied.

Brother, we do not wish to destroy your religion, or take it from you; we only want to enjoy our own. 10

Brother, you say you have not come to get our land or our money, but to enlighten our minds. I will now tell you that I have been at your meetings, and saw you collecting money from the meeting. I cannot tell what this money was intended for, but suppose it was for your minister; and if we should conform to your way of thinking, perhaps you may want some from us.

Brother, we are told that you have been preaching to the white people in this place. These people are our neighbors; we are acquainted with them; we will wait, a little while and see what effect your preaching has upon them. If we find it does them good, makes them honest and less disposed to cheat Indians, we will then consider again what you have said.

Brother, you have now heard our answer to your talk, and this is all we have to say at present. As we are going to part, we will come and take you by the hand, and hope the Great Spirit will protect you on your journey, and return you safe to your friends.

[1805]

Read

1. How does Red Jacket use "fire" symbolically?
2. How does the use of repetition suggest a purpose for Red Jacket's talk?
3. What effect does the concrete image have on you as a reader?
4. How does Red Jacket use logic and evidence as persuasive tools when he discusses the differences between the religion of the white man and that of his own people?

Write

1. Write a response to Red Jacket from your perspective as a twenty-first century reader.
2. Explain how Red Jacket uses narrative as argument to prove his case.
3. In a paragraph, describe the aim of the last paragraph and how you think that aim fits with Red Jacket's larger purpose.

Complete Additional Exercises on Red Jacket's Speech at Your Pearson MyLab

Connect

1. How does the description of the coming of the white man compare to portrayals in texts you read in Unit 1?
2. Compare the character of the Indian as described by Red Jacket to Mary Rowlandson's description in her captivity narrative in Unit 1.

Gilbert Stuart

Gilbert Stuart (1755–1828) is known as one of America's foremost portraitists. He painted over one thousand people during his career and received acclaim for his likenesses of private citizens and public figures, especially that of George Washington. Born in Rhode Island, Stuart showed early promise as an artist and studied in England during the Revolutionary War. He returned to Pennsylvania and opened a studio, where his paintings became sought after. His unfinished portrait of Washington is reproduced on the dollar bill, and he painted dozens of likenesses of the first president, including the portrait Dolley Madison saved from burning during the War of 1812, below.

George Washington

George Washington (Lansdowne portrait) (1796), Gilbert Stuart. Oil on canvas, 97 1/2 x 62 1/2 inches. National Portrait Gallery, Smithsonian Institution. Photo by AP Images

[1796]

Read

1. What do details contribute to the painting as a whole?
2. What might be the function of the background in the painting?
3. How is light important to the effect of the painting?

Write

1. How would you describe George Washington's persona in this painting?
2. What might be the artist's aim in this portrayal? Use a detail or two to help frame your response.

Connect

1. How does this view of George Washington connect to your knowledge of the first president?
2. Look at a quarter to see the depiction of Washington and compare it to the painting.
3. Find a piece in Unit 1 that seems to demonstrate or promote the qualities of character you think are suggested in the painting and discuss the connections.

Susannah Rowson

Susannah Rowson (1762–1824) was born in England and traveled to colonial Boston when she was five years old. She was brought up in a highly literate household and began writing stories and plays at a young age. She became a popular writer and remained popular for most her life, producing several bestselling novels, including *Charlotte Temple* (1794), excerpts from which are reprinted below. An early playwright in the colonies, she went on the stage with her husband in England and America and later established a well-regarded school for young ladies in Boston. When she died, she was one of the most famous women in America.

From *Charlotte Temple*

From Preface

For the perusal of the young and thoughtless of the fair sex, this Tale of Truth is designed; and I could wish my fair readers to consider it as not merely the effusion of Fancy, but as a reality. The circumstances on which I have founded this novel were related to me some little time since by an old lady who had personally known Charlotte, though she concealed the real names of the characters, and likewise the place where the unfortunate scenes were acted: yet as it was impossible to offer a relation° to the public in such an imperfect state, I have thrown

relation: relating of events, narration

over the whole a slight veil of fiction, and substituted names and places according to my own fancy. The principal characters in this little tale are now consigned to the silent tomb: it can therefore hurt the feelings of no one; and may, I flatter myself, be of service to some who are so unfortunate as to have neither friends to advise, or understanding to direct them, through the various and unexpected evils that attend a young and unprotected woman in her first entrance into life. . . .

Sensible as I am that a novel writer, at a time when such a variety of works are ushered into the world under that name, stands but a poor chance for fame in the annals of literature, but conscious that I wrote with a mind anxious for the happiness of that sex whose morals and conduct have so powerful an influence on mankind in general; and convinced that I have not wrote a line that conveys a wrong idea to the head or a corrupt wish to the heart, I shall rest satisfied in the purity of my own intentions, and if I merit not applause, I feel that I dread not censure.

If the following tale should save one hapless fair one° from the errors which ruined poor Charlotte, or rescue from impending misery the heart of one anxious parent, I shall feel a much higher gratification in reflecting on this trifling performance, than could possibly result from the applause which might attend the most elegant finished piece of literature whose tendency might deprave the heart or mislead the understanding.

From Chapter I

A Boarding School

"Are you for a walk," said Montraville to his companion, as they arose from table; "are you for a walk? or shall we order the chaise and proceed to Portsmouth?" Belcour preferred the former; and they sauntered out to view the town, and to make remarks on the inhabitants, as they returned from church.

Montraville was a Lieutenant in the army: Belcour was his brother officer: they had been to take leave of their friends previous to their departure for America, and were now returning to Portsmouth, where the troops waited orders for embarkation. They had stopped at Chichester to dine; and knowing they had sufficient time to reach the place of destination before dark, and yet allow them a walk, had resolved, it being Sunday afternoon, to take a survey of the Chichester ladies as they returned from their devotions.° 5

fair one: lovely young woman

devotions: religious observance, worship

They had gratified their curiosity, and were preparing to return to the inn without honouring any of the belles with particular notice, when Madame Du Pont, at the head of her school, descended from the church. Such an assemblage of youth and innocence naturally attracted the young soldiers: they stopped; and, as the little cavalcade passed, almost involuntarily pulled off their hats. A tall, elegant girl looked at Montraville and blushed: he instantly recollected the features of Charlotte Temple, whom he had once seen and danced with at a ball at Portsmouth. At that time he thought on her only as a very lovely child, she being then only thirteen; but the improvement two years had made in her person, and the blush of recollection which suffused her cheeks as she passed, awakened in his bosom new and pleasing ideas. Vanity led him to think that pleasure at again beholding him might have occasioned the emotion he had witnessed, and the same vanity led him to wish to see her again.

"She is the sweetest girl in the world," said he, as he entered the inn. Belcour stared. "Did you not notice her?" continued Montraville: "she had on a blue bonnet, and with a pair of lovely eyes of the same colour, has contrived to make me feel devilish odd about the heart."

"Pho,"° said Belcour, "a musket ball from our friends, the Americans, may in less than two months make you feel worse."

"I never think of the future," replied Montraville; "but am determined to make the most of the present, and would willingly compound° with any kind Familiar° who would inform me who the girl is, and how I might be likely to obtain an interview."

But no kind Familiar at that time appearing, and the chaise° which they had ordered, driving up to the door, Montraville and his companion were obliged to take leave of Chichester and its fair inhabitant, and proceed on their journey. 10

But Charlotte had made too great an impression on his mind to be easily eradicated: having therefore spent three whole days in thinking on her and in endeavouring to form some plan for seeing her, he determined to set off for Chichester, and trust to chance either to favour or frustrate his designs. Arriving at the verge of the town, he dismounted, and sending the servant forward with the horses, proceeded toward the place, where, in the midst of an extensive pleasure

Pho: an exclamation of annoyance
compound: make a bargain
Familiar: supernatural spirit
chaise: shay; an open, two-wheeled carriage, usually with a hood

ground, stood the mansion which contained the lovely Charlotte Temple. Montraville leaned on a broken gate, and looked earnestly at the house. The wall which surrounded it was high, and perhaps the Argus's° who guarded the Hesperian fruit within, were more watchful than those famed of old.

"'Tis a romantic attempt," said he; "and should I even succeed in seeing and conversing with her, it can be productive of no good: I must of necessity leave England in a few days, and probably may never return; why then should I endeavour to engage the affections of this lovely girl, only to leave her a prey to a thousand inquietudes,° of which at present she has no idea? I will return to Portsmouth and think no more about her."

The evening now was closed; a serene stillness reigned; and the chaste Queen of Night with her silver crescent faintly illuminated the hemisphere. The mind of Montraville was hushed into composure by the serenity of the surrounding objects. "I will think on her no more," said he, and turned with an intention to leave the place; but as he turned, he saw the gate which led to the pleasure grounds open, and two women come out, who walked arm-in-arm across the field.

"I will at least see who these are," said he. He overtook them, and giving them the compliments of the evening, begged leave to see them into the more frequented parts of the town: but how was he delighted, when, waiting for an answer, he discovered, under the concealment of a large bonnet, the face of Charlotte Temple.

He soon found means to ingratiate himself with her companion, who was a French teacher at the school, and, at parting, slipped a letter he had purposely written, into Charlotte's hand, and five guineas° into that of Mademoiselle, who promised she would endeavour to bring her young charge into the field again the next evening.

From Chapter VI

An Intriguing Teacher

Madame Du Pont was a woman every way calculated to take the care of young ladies, had that care entirely devolved on herself; but it was impossible to attend the education of a numerous school without

---

Argus's: Arguses (In Greek mythology, Argus was a many-eyed monster who guarded Zeus's favorite, Io, when she had been changed into a heifer.)

inquietudes: disturbances, anxieties

guinea: a British coin worth twenty-one shillings, replaced in 1816 by the pound

proper assistants; and those assistants were not always the kind of people whose conversation and morals were exactly such as parents of delicacy and refinement would wish a daughter to copy. Among the teachers at Madame Du Pont's school, was Mademoiselle La Rue, who added to a pleasing person° and insinuating° address,° a liberal education and the manners of a gentlewoman. She was recommended to the school by a lady whose humanity overstepped the bounds of discretion: for though she knew Miss La Rue had eloped from a convent with a young officer, and, on coming to England, had lived with several different men in open defiance of all moral and religious duties; yet, finding her reduced to the most abject want, and believing the penitence which she professed to be sincere, she took her into her own family, and from thence recommended her to Madame Du Pont, as thinking the situation more suitable for a woman of her abilities. But Mademoiselle possessed too much of the spirit of intrigue to remain long without adventures. At church, where she constantly appeared, her person attracted the attention of a young man who was upon a visit at a gentleman's seat° in the neighbourhood: she had met him several times clandestinely; and being invited to come out that evening, and eat some fruit and pastry in a summer-house belonging to the gentleman he was visiting, and requested to bring some of the ladies with her, Charlotte being her favourite, was fixed on to accompany her.

The mind of youth eagerly catches at promised pleasure: pure and innocent by nature, it thinks not of the dangers lurking beneath those pleasures, till too late to avoid them: when Mademoiselle asked Charlotte to go with her, she mentioned the gentleman as a relation, and spoke in such high terms of the elegance of his gardens, the sprightliness of his conversation, and the liberality with which he ever entertained his guests, that Charlotte thought only of the pleasure she should enjoy in the visit,—not on the imprudence of going without her governess's knowledge, or of the danger to which she exposed herself in visiting the house of a gay° young man of fashion.

Madame Du Pont was gone out for the evening, and the rest of the ladies retired to rest, when Charlotte and the teacher stole out at the back gate, and in crossing the field, were accosted by Montraville, as mentioned in the first chapter.

---

person: general appearance
insinuating: ingratiating
address: bearing, manner of speaking
seat: residence, country house
gay: lively, merry; given over to pleasure

Charlotte was disappointed in the pleasure she had promised herself from this visit. The levity of the gentlemen and the freedom of their conversation disgusted her. She was astonished at the liberties Mademoiselle permitted them to take; grew thoughtful and uneasy, and heartily wished herself at home again in her own chamber.

Perhaps one cause of that wish might be, an earnest desire to see the contents of the letter which had been put into her hand by Montraville. 20

Any reader who has the least knowledge of the world, will easily imagine the letter was made up of encomiums° on her beauty, and vows of everlasting love and constancy; nor will he be surprised that a heart open to every gentle, generous sentiment, should feel itself warmed by gratitude for a man who professed to feel so much for her; nor is it improbable but her mind might revert to the agreeable person and martial° appearance of Montraville.

In affairs of love, a young heart is never in more danger than when attempted° by a handsome young soldier. A man of an indifferent appearance, will, when arrayed in a military habit, shew° to advantage; but when beauty of person, elegance of manner, and an easy method of paying compliments, are united to the scarlet coat, smart cockade, and military sash, ah! well-a-day for the poor girl who gazes on him: she is in imminent danger; but if she listens to him with pleasure, 'tis all over with her, and from that moment she has neither eyes nor ears for any other object.

Now, my dear sober° matron, (if a sober matron should deign to turn over these pages, before she trusts them to the eye of a darling daughter), let me intreat you not to put on a grave face, and throw down the book in a passion and declare 'tis enough to turn the heads of half the girls in England; I do solemnly protest, my dear madam, I mean no more by what I have here advanced, than to ridicule those romantic girls, who foolishly imagine a red coat and silver epaulet constitute the fine gentleman; and should that fine gentleman make half a dozen fine speeches to them, they will imagine themselves so much in love as to fancy it a meritorious action to jump out of a two pair of stairs window, abandon their friends, and trust entirely to the honour of a man, who perhaps hardly knows the meaning of

---

encomiums: expressions of praise
martial: soldierly
attempted: assaulted with intent to subdue
shew: show
sober: serious-minded, levelheaded

the word, and if he does, will be too much the modern man of refinement, to practice it in their favour.

Gracious heaven! when I think on the miseries that must rend the heart of a doating parent, when he sees the darling of his age at first seduced from his protection, and afterwards abandoned, by the very wretch whose promises of love decoyed her from the paternal roof—when he sees her poor and wretched, her bosom torn between remorse for her crime and love for her vile betrayer—when fancy paints to me the good old man stooping to raise the weeping penitent, while every tear from her eye is numbered° by drops from his bleeding heart, my bosom glows with honest indignation, and I wish for power to extirpate those monsters of seduction from the earth.

Oh my dear girls—for to such only am I writing—listen not to the voice of love, unless sanctioned by paternal approbation: be assured, it is now past the days of romance:° no woman can be run away with contrary to her own inclination: then kneel down each morning, and request kind heaven to keep you free from temptation, or, should it please to suffer you to be tried,° pray for fortitude to resist the impulse of inclination when it runs counter to the precepts of religion and virtue. 25

From Chapter VII

Natural Sense of Propriety Inherent in the Female Bosom

"I cannot think we have done exactly right in going out this evening, Mademoiselle," said Charlotte, seating herself when she entered her apartment: "nay, I am sure it was not right; for I expected to be very happy, but was sadly disappointed."

"It was your own fault, then," replied Mademoiselle: "for I am sure my cousin omitted nothing that could serve to render the evening agreeable."

"True," said Charlotte: "but I thought the gentlemen were very free in their manner: I wonder you would suffer° them to behave as they did."

---

numbered: counted

romance: medieval chivalry, when women were presumably swept off their feet and carried off by their lovers

tried: tested, tempted

suffer: allow

"Prithee,° don't be such a foolish little prude," said the artful woman, affecting° anger: "I invited you to go in hopes it would divert you, and be an agreeable change of scene; however, if your delicacy was hurt by the behaviour of the gentlemen, you need not go again; so there let it rest."

"I do not intend to go again," said Charlotte, gravely taking off her bonnet, and beginning to prepare for bed: "I am sure, if Madame Du Pont knew we had been out to-night, she would be very angry; and it is ten to one but she hears of it by some means or other." 30

"Nay, Miss," said La Rue, "perhaps your mighty sense of propriety may lead you to tell her yourself: and in order to avoid the censure you would incur, should she hear of it by accident, throw the blame on me: but I confess I deserve it: it will be a very kind return for that partiality° which led me to prefer you before any of the rest of the ladies; but perhaps it will give you pleasure," continued she, letting fall some hypocritical tears, "to see me deprived of bread, and for an action which by the most rigid could only be esteemed an inadvertency, lose my place and character, and be driven again into the world, where I have already suffered all the evils attendant on poverty."

This was touching Charlotte in the most vulnerable part: she rose from her seat, and taking Mademoiselle's hand—"You know, my dear La Rue," said she, "I love you too well, to do anything that would injure you in my governess's opinion: I am only sorry we went out this evening."

"I don't believe it, Charlotte," said she, assuming a little vivacity; "for if you had not gone out, you would not have seen the gentleman who met us crossing the field; and I rather think you were pleased with his conversation."

"I had seen him once before," replied Charlotte, "and thought him an agreeable man; and you know one is always pleased to see a person with whom one has passed several cheerful hours. But," said she pausing, and drawing the letter from her pocket, while a gentle suffusion of vermillion tinged her neck and face, "he gave me this letter; what shall I do with it?"

"Read it, to be sure," returned Mademoiselle. 35

"I am afraid I ought not," said Charlotte: "my mother has often told me, I should never read a letter given me by a young man, without first giving it to her."

Prithee: pray thee; i.e., please

affecting: giving the appearance of, pretending

partiality: preference, favoritism

"Lord bless you, my dear girl," cried the teacher smiling, "have you a mind to be in leading strings° all your life time? Prithee open the letter, read it, and judge for yourself; if you show it your mother, the consequence will be, you will be taken from school, and a strict guard kept over you; so you will stand no chance of ever seeing the smart young officer again."

"I should not like to leave school yet," replied Charlotte, "till I have attained a greater proficiency in my Italian and music. But you can, if you please, Mademoiselle, take the letter back to Montraville, and tell him I wish him well, but cannot, with any propriety, enter into a clandestine correspondence with him." She laid the letter on the table, and began to undress herself.

"Well," said La Rue, "I vow you are an unaccountable girl: have you no curiosity to see the inside now? for my part I could no more let a letter addressed to me lie unopened so long, than I could work miracles: he writes a good hand," continued she, turning the letter, to look at the superscription.°

"'Tis well enough," said Charlotte, drawing it towards her. 40

"He is a genteel young fellow," said La Rue carelessly, folding up her apron at the same time; "but I think he is marked with the small pox."

"Oh you are greatly mistaken," said Charlotte eagerly; "he has a remarkable clear skin and fine complexion."

"His eyes, if I could judge by what I saw," said La Rue, "are grey and want expression."

"By no means," replied Charlotte; "they are the most expressive eyes I ever saw." "Well, child, whether they are grey or black is of no consequence: you have determined not to read his letter; so it is likely you will never either see or hear from him again."

Charlotte took up the letter, and Mademoiselle continued— 45

"He is most probably going to America; and if ever you should hear any account of him, it may possibly be that he is killed; and though he loved you ever so fervently, though his last breath should be spent in a prayer for your happiness, it can be nothing to you: you can feel nothing for the fate of the man, whose letters you will not open, and whose sufferings you will not alleviate, by permitting him to think you would remember him when absent, and pray for his safety."

Charlotte still held the letter in her hand: her heart swelled at the conclusion of Mademoiselle's speech, and a tear dropped upon the wafer° that closed it.

---

leading strings: straps and/or harness used with a child who is learning to walk

superscription: address on a letter

wafer: adhesive paper disk used to seal a letter

"The wafer is not dry yet," said she, "and sure there can be no great harm—" She hesitated. La Rue was silent. "I may read it, Mademoiselle, and return it afterwards."

"Certainly," replied Mademoiselle.

"At any rate I am determined not to answer it," continued Charlotte, as she opened the letter. 50

Here let me stop to make one remark, and trust me my very heart aches while I write it; but certain I am, that when once a woman has stifled the sense of shame in her own bosom, when once she has lost sight of the basis on which reputation, honour, every thing that should be dear to the female heart, rests, she grows hardened in guilt, and will spare no pains to bring down innocence and beauty to the shocking level with herself: and this proceeds from that diabolical spirit of envy, which repines° at seeing another in the full possession of that respect and esteem which she can no longer hope to enjoy.

Mademoiselle eyed the unsuspecting Charlotte, as she perused the letter, with a malignant pleasure. She saw, that the contents had awakened new emotions in her youthful bosom: she encouraged her hopes, calmed her fears, and before they parted for the night, it was determined that she should meet Montraville the ensuing evening. . . .

From Chapter XII

How Thou Art Fall'n!

. . . "Oh!" cried Charlotte . . . "let me reflect:—the irrevocable step is not yet taken: it is not too late to recede from the brink of a precipice, from which I can only behold the dark abyss of ruin, shame, and remorse!"

She arose from her seat, and flew to the apartment of La Rue. "Oh Mademoiselle!" said she, "I am snatched by a miracle from destruction! This letter has saved me: it has opened my eyes to the folly I was so near committing. I will not go, Mademoiselle; I will not wound the hearts of those dear parents who make my happiness the whole study of their lives."

"Well," said Mademoiselle, "do as you please, Miss; but pray understand that my resolution is taken, and it is not in your power to alter it. I shall meet the gentlemen at the appointed hour, and shall not be surprized at any outrage which Montraville may commit, when he finds himself disappointed. Indeed I should not be astonished, was he to come immediately here, and reproach you for your instability in the hearing of the whole school: and what will be the consequence? you will bear the odium of having formed the resolution of eloping, 55

---

repines: frets, complains

and every girl of spirit will laugh at your want of fortitude to put it in execution, while prudes and fools will load you with reproach and contempt. You will have lost the confidence of your parents, incurred their anger, and the scoffs of the world; and what fruit do you expect to reap from this piece of heroism, (for such no doubt you think it is?) you will have the pleasure to reflect, that you have deceived the man who adores you, and whom in your heart you prefer to all other men, and that you are separated from him for ever."

This eloquent harangue was given with such volubility,° that Charlotte could not find an opportunity to interrupt her, or to offer a single word till the whole was finished, and then found her ideas so confused, that she knew not what to say.

At length she determined that she would go with Mademoiselle to the place of assignation, convince Montraville of the necessity of adhering to the resolution of remaining behind; assure him of her affection, and bid him adieu.

Charlotte formed this plan in her mind, and exulted in the certainty of its success. "How shall I rejoice," said she, "in this triumph of reason over inclination, and, when in the arms of my affectionate parents, lift up my soul in gratitude to heaven as I look back on the dangers I have escaped!"

The hour of assignation arrived: Mademoiselle put what money and valuables she possessed in her pocket, and advised Charlotte to do the same; but she refused; "my resolution is fixed," said she; "I will sacrifice love to duty."

Mademoiselle smiled internally; and they proceeded softly down the back stairs and out of the garden gate. Montraville and Belcour were ready to receive them. 60

"Now," said Montraville, taking Charlotte in his arms, "you are mine for ever."

"No," said she, withdrawing from his embrace, "I am come to take an everlasting farewel."

It would be useless to repeat the conversation that here ensued, suffice it to say, that Montraville used every argument that had formerly been successful, Charlotte's resolution began to waver, and he drew her almost imperceptibly towards the chaise.

"I cannot go," said she: "cease, dear Montraville, to persuade. I must not: religion, duty, forbid."

"Cruel Charlotte," said he, "if you disappoint my ardent hopes, by all that is sacred, this hand shall put a period° to my existence. I cannot—will not live without you." 65

volubility: fluency

period: end

"Alas! my torn heart!" said Charlotte, "how shall I act?"

"Let me direct you," said Montraville, lifting her into the chaise.

"Oh! my dear forsaken parents!" cried Charlotte.

The chaise drove off. She shrieked, and fainted into the arms of her betrayer.

From Chapter XIV

Maternal Sorrow

. . . "Temple," said she, assuming a look of firmness and composure, "tell me the truth I beseech you. I cannot bear this dreadful suspense. What misfortune has befallen my child? Let me know the worst, and I will endeavour to bear it as I ought." 70

"Lucy," replied Mr. Temple, "imagine your daughter alive, and in no danger of death: what misfortune would you then dread?"

"There is one misfortune which is worse than death. But I know my child too well to suspect—"

"Be not too confident, Lucy."

"Oh heavens!" said she, "what horrid images do you start: is it possible she should forget—"

"She has forgot us all, my love; she has preferred the love of a stranger to the affectionate protection of her friends." 75

"Not eloped?" cried she eagerly.

Mr. Temple was silent.

"You cannot contradict it," said she. "I see my fate in those tearful eyes. Oh Charlotte! Charlotte! how ill have you requited° our tenderness! But, Father of Mercies," continued she, sinking on her knees, and raising her streaming eyes and clasped hands to heaven, "this once vouchsafe to hear a fond, a distracted° mother's prayer. Oh let thy bounteous Providence watch over and protect the dear thoughtless girl, save her from the miseries which I fear will be her portion, and oh! of thine infinite mercy, make her not a mother, lest she should one day feel what I now suffer.". . .

[1794]

Read

1. How does the preface work to help Rowson establish her voice as an author and give readers a sense of her message?
2. Where do you find the use of stock or stereotypical characters in the excerpt? How are they useful?
3. How does Rowson's narrator make use of the audience/reader in her text?

---

requited: returned, repaid

distracted: troubled, greatly disturbed

4. What does the excerpt suggest about cultural attitudes toward women at the time?

Write

1. Write a paragraph describing the character of Charlotte Temple, using a line of dialogue to support your characterization.
2. What do you think the primary conflict in the novel is? Find one or two details that provide evidence for your claim.
3. How or where do you find Rowson's persuasive message to her readers most evident?
4. Based on this excerpt, how would you say that Rowson defines "good" and "evil"?

Connect

1. How does Charlotte Temple's situation and character seem similar to other women in this unit or Unit 1?
2. Compare the differences you see in culture and society in the world of *Charlotte Temple* and one other text in Unit 1.

Maria Stewart

Maria Stewart (1803–1879) had a short but important career as a writer and speaker in Boston. She was a free black woman who worked as a servant in a clergyman's home and was part of Boston's small but vigorous African American middle class. Stewart was the first American woman to speak to a mixed—racially and by gender—audience. First published in William Lloyd Garrison's abolitionist newspaper, she later delivered four speeches, including the Lecture at Franklin Hall in 1832. The next year she disappeared from public life. She was a nurse in Washington, DC, during the Civil War. Her speeches were reprinted in 1879, the year she died.

Lecture Delivered at Franklin Hall

Why sit ye here and die? If we say we will go to a foreign land, the famine and the pestilence are there, and there we shall die. If we sit here, we shall die. Come let us plead our cause before the whites: if they save us alive, we shall live—and if they kill us, we shall but die.

Methinks I heard a spiritual interrogation—"Who shall go forward, and take off the reproach that is cast upon the people of color? Shall it be a woman?" And my heart made this reply—"If it is thy will, be it even so, Lord Jesus!"

I have heard much respecting the horrors of slavery; but may Heaven forbid that the generality° of my color throughout these United States should experience any more of its horrors than to be a servant of servants, or hewers of

---

generality: majority

wood° and drawers of water! Tell us no more of southern slavery; for with few exceptions, although I may be very erroneous in my opinion, yet I consider our condition but little better than that. Yet, after all, methinks there are no chains so galling as the chains of ignorance—no fetters so binding as those that bind the soul, and exclude it from the vast field of useful and scientific knowledge. O, had I received the advantages of early education, my ideas would, ere now, have expanded far and wide; but, alas! I possess nothing but moral capability—no teachings but the teachings of the Holy spirit.

I have asked several individuals of my sex, who transact business for themselves, if providing our girls were to give them the most satisfactory references, they would not be willing to grant them an equal opportunity with others? Their reply has been—for their own part, they had no objection; but as it was not the custom, were they to take them into their employ, they would be in danger of losing the public patronage.°

And such is the powerful force of prejudice. Let our girls possess what amiable qualities of soul they may; let their characters be fair and spotless as innocence itself; let their natural taste and ingenuity be what they may; it is impossible for scarce an individual of them to rise above the condition of servants. Ah! why is this cruel and unfeeling distinction? Is it merely because God has made our complexion to vary? If it be, O shame to soft, relenting humanity! "Tell it not in Gath! publish it not in the streets of Askelon!"° Yet, after all, methinks were the American free people of color to turn their attention more assiduously to moral worth and intellectual improvement, this would be the result: prejudice would gradually diminish, and the whites would be compelled to say, unloose those fetters! 5

Though black their skins as shades of night
Their hearts are pure, their souls are white.

Few white persons of either sex, who are calculated for any thing else, are willing to spend their lives and bury their talents in performing mean,° servile labor. And such is the horrible idea that I entertain respecting a life of servitude, that if I conceived of there being no possibility of my rising above the condition of a servant, I would gladly hail death as a welcome messenger. O, horrible idea, indeed! to possess noble souls aspiring after high and honorable acquirements, yet confined by the chains of ignorance and poverty to lives of continual drudgery and toil. Neither do I know of any who have enriched themselves by spending their lives as house-domestics, washing windows, shaking carpets, brushing boots, or tending upon gentlemen's tables. I can but die for expressing my sentiments; and I am

---

hewers of wood: woodcutters
patronage: business, custom (as in "customers")
Tell it not . . . Askelon: 2 Samuel 1:20 (Bible)
mean: lowly

as willing to die by the sword as the pestilence; for I and a true born American; your blood flows in my veins, and your spirit fires my breast.

I observed a piece in the *Liberator* a few months since, stating that the colonizationists° had published a work respecting us, asserting that we were lazy and idle. I confute them on that point. Take us generally as a people, we are neither lazy nor idle; and considering how little we have to excite or stimulate us, I am almost astonished that there are so many industrious and ambitious ones to be found; although I acknowledge, with extreme sorrow, that there are some who never were and never will be serviceable to society. And have you not a similar class among yourselves?

Again. It was asserted that we were "a ragged set, crying for liberty." I reply to it, the whites have so long and so loudly proclaimed the theme of equal rights and privileges, that our souls have caught the flame also, ragged as we are. As far as our merit deserves, we feel a common desire to rise above the condition of servants and drudges. I have learnt, by bitter experience, that continual hard labor deadens the energies of the soul, and benumbs the faculties of the mind; the ideas become confined, the mind barren, and, like the scorching sands of Arabia, produces nothing; or, like the uncultivated soil, brings forth thorns and thistles.

Again, continual hard labor irritates our tempers and sours our dispositions; the whole system becomes worn out with toil and failure; nature herself becomes almost exhausted, and we care but little whether we live or die. It is true, that the free people of color throughout these United States are neither bought nor sold, nor under the lash of the cruel driver;° many obtain a comfortable support; but few, if any, have an opportunity of becoming rich and independent; and the employments we most pursue are as unprofitable to us as the spider's web or the floating bubbles that vanish into air. As servants, we are respected; but let us presume to aspire any higher, our employer regards us no longer. And were it not that the King eternal has declared that Ethiopia shall stretch forth her hands unto God, I should indeed despair.

I do not consider it derogatory, my friends, for persons to live out to service. There are many whose inclination leads them to aspire no higher; and I would highly commend the performance of almost any thing for an honest livelihood; but where constitutional strength is wanting, labor of this kind, in its mildest form, is painful. And doubtless many are the prayers that have ascended to Heaven from Africa's daughters for strength to perform their work. Oh, many are the tears that have been shed for the want of that strength! Most of our color have dragged out a miserable existence of servitude from the cradle to the grave. And what literary acquirements can be made, or useful knowledge derived, from either maps, books or charm, by those who continually drudge from Monday morning until Sunday noon? O, ye fairer sisters, whose hands 10

---

colonizationists: those who favored relocating slaves and other African Americans in Africa

driver: slave driver

are never soiled, whose nerves and muscles are never strained, go learn by experience! Had we had the opportunity that you have had, to improve our moral and mental faculties, what would have hindered our intellects from being as bright, and our manners from being as dignified as yours? Had it been our lot to have been nursed in the lap of affluence and ease, and to have basked beneath the smiles and sunshine of fortune, should we not have naturally supposed that we were never made to toil? And why are not our forms as delicate, and our constitutions as slender, as yours? Is not the workmanship as curious and complete? Have pity upon us, have pity upon us, O ye who have hearts to feel for other's woes; for the hand of God has touched us. Owing to the disadvantages under which we labor, there are many flowers among us that are

> . . . born to bloom unseen
> And waste their fragrance on the desert air.°

My beloved brethren, as Christ has died in vain for those who will not accept of offered mercy, so will it be vain for the advocates of freedom to spend their breath in our behalf, unless with united hearts and souls you make some mighty efforts to raise your sons, and daughters from the horrible state of servitude and degradation in which they are placed. It is upon you that woman depends; she can do but little besides using her influence; and it is for her sake and yours that I have come forward and made myself a hissing and a reproach among the people;° for I am also one of the wretched and miserable daughters of the descendants of fallen Africa. Do you ask, why are you wretched and miserable? I reply, look at many of the most worthy and interesting of us doomed to spend our lives in gentlemen's kitchens. Look at our young men, smart, active and energetic, with souls filled with ambitious fire; if they look forward, alas! what are their prospects? They can be nothing but the humblest laborers, on account of their dark complexions; hence many of them lose their ambition, and become worthless. Look at our middle-aged men, clad in their rusty plaids and coats; in winter, every cent they earn goes to buy their wood° and pay their rents; their poor wives also toil beyond their strength, to help support their families. Look at our aged sires, whose heads are whitened with the front of seventy winters, with their old wood-saws on their backs. Alas, what keeps us so? Prejudice, ignorance and poverty. But ah! methinks our oppression is soon to come to an end; yes, before the Majesty of heaven, our groans and cries have reached the ears of the Lord of Sabaoth.° As the prayers and tears of Christians will avail the finally impenitent nothing; neither will the prayers and tears of the friends of humanity avail us any thing, unless we possess a

---

born to bloom . . . desert air: from "Elegy Written in a Country Churchyard" by British poet Thomas Gray (1716–1771)

made myself . . . among the people: Micah 6:16 (Bible)

wood: firewood

Lord of Sabaoth: translated in the Bible as "the Lord of Hosts"

spirit of virtuous emulation within our breasts. Did the pilgrims, when they first landed on these shores, quietly compose themselves, and say, "the Britons have all the money and all the power, and we must continue their servants forever?" Did they sluggishly sigh and say, "our lot is hard, the Indians own the soil, and we cannot cultivate it?" No; they first made powerful efforts to raise themselves and then God raised up those illustrious patriots WASHINGTON and LAFAYETTE, to assist and defend them. And, my brethren, have you made a powerful effort? Have you prayed the Legislature for mercy's sake to grant you all the rights and privileges of free citizens, that your daughters may raise to that degree of respectability which true merit deserves, and your sons above the servile situations which most of them fill?

[1832]

Read

1. How does Stewart use scripture to help make her points in the speech?
2. How does the opening of the speech—its *exordium*—create connections to the audience?
3. How would you describe the persona of the speaker? Locate words or images in the speech that help you characterize Stewart's persona.
4. What kinds of rhetorical appeals does Stewart use most in the speech as she persuades?

Write

1. How do you respond to the message Stewart delivers?
2. Write a brief analysis of one paragraph of Stewart's speech that you believe provides strong evidence for her claims.
3. Consider the effect of her speech at the time, and write a response from someone in her audience.

Connect

1. What comparisons can you draw between Stewart and Phillis Wheatley in Unit 1?
2. How does Stewart's talk conflict or connect with what you are learning of the position of women in her day?

Washington Irving

Born in New York City, Washington Irving (1783–1859) established himself as a writer early in his career, producing satirical articles for newspapers. In fact, he became one of the first Americans to make his living as a writer. His work often drew on the landscape of upstate New York (as in "Rip Van Winkle" and "The Legend of Sleepy Hollow") and on his Dutch roots, and he used humor and sentimentalism to tell his stories. He is among those credited with creating the short story as a genre. In later life he moved away from fiction and began to write biographies, writing about Columbus and George Washington.

The Legend of Sleepy Hollow

Found Among the Papers of the Late Diedrich Knickerbocker

A pleasing land of drowsy head it was,
  Of dreams that wave before the half-shut eye;
And of gay castles in the clouds that pass,
  For ever flushing round a summer sky.

Castle of Indolence°

In the bosom of one of those spacious coves which indent the eastern shore of the Hudson, at that broad expansion of the river denominated° by the ancient Dutch navigators the Tappan Zee, and where they always prudently shortened sail, and implored the protection of St. Nicholas when they crossed, there lies a small market-town or rural port, which by some is called Greensburgh, but which is more generally and properly known by the name of Tarry Town. This name was given, we are told, in former days, by the good housewives of the adjacent country,° from the inveterate° propensity of their husbands to linger about the village tavern on market days. Be that as it may, I do not vouch for the fact, but merely advert° to it, for the sake of being precise and authentic.° Not far from this village, perhaps about two miles, there is a little valley, or rather lap of land, among high hills, which is one of the quietest places in the whole world. A small brook glides through it, with just murmur enough to lull one to repose; and the occasional whistle of a quail, or tapping of a woodpecker, is almost the only sound that ever breaks in upon the uniform tranquillity.

I recollect that, when a stripling,° my first exploit in squirrel-shooting was in a grove of tall walnut-trees that shades one side of the valley. I had wandered into it at noon time, when all nature is peculiarly quiet, and was startled by the roar of my own gun, as it broke the Sabbath stillness around, and was prolonged and reverberated by the angry echoes. If ever I should wish for a retreat, whither I might steal from the world and its distractions, and dream quietly away the remnant of a troubled life, I know of none more promising than this little valley.

Castle of Indolence: *The Castle of Indolence* (1748), a long narrative poem by British author James Thomson (1700–1748)
denominated: named
country: area, countryside
inveterate: fixed, habitual
advert: refer
authentic: accurate
stripling: youth

From the listless repose of the place, and the peculiar° character of its inhabitants, who are descendants from the original Dutch settlers, this sequestered glen has long been known by the name of SLEEPY HOLLOW, and its rustic lads are called the Sleepy Hollow Boys throughout all the neighboring country. A drowsy, dreamy influence seems to hang over the land, and to pervade the very atmosphere. Some say that the place was bewitched by a high German doctor, during the early days of the settlement; others, that an old Indian chief, the prophet or wizard of his tribe, held his powwows there before the country was discovered by Master Hendrick Hudson. Certain it is, the place still continues under the sway of some witching power, that holds a spell over the minds of the good people, causing them to walk in a continual reverie. They are given to all kinds of marvellous° beliefs; are subject to trances and visions; and frequently see strange sights, and hear music and voices in the air. The whole neighborhood abounds with local tales, haunted spots, and twilight superstitions; stars shoot and meteors glare oftener across the valley than in any other part of the country, and the nightmare, with her whole nine fold,° seems to make it the favorite scene of her gambols.°

The dominant spirit, however, that haunts this enchanted region, and seems to be commander-in-chief of all the powers of the air, is the apparition of a figure on horseback without a head. It is said by some to be the ghost of a Hessian° trooper, whose head had been carried away by a cannon-ball, in some nameless battle during the revolutionary war; and who is ever and anon seen by the country folk, hurrying along in the gloom of night, as if on the wings of the wind. His haunts are not confined to the valley, but extend at times to the adjacent roads, and especially to the vicinity of a church at no great distance. Indeed, certain of the most authentic historians of those parts, who have been careful in collecting and collating the floating facts concerning this spectre, allege that the body of the trooper, having been buried in the church-yard, the ghost rides forth to the scene of battle in nightly quest of his head; and that the rushing speed with which he sometimes passes along the Hollow, like a midnight blast, is owing to his being belated,° and in a hurry to get back to the church-yard before daybreak.

---

peculiar: particular

marvellous: improbable, incredible

the nightmare, with her whole ninefold: a goblin and her host of followers

gambols: frolics, capers, romps

Hessian: German mercenary in the British Army during the American Revolution

belated: delayed, late

5

Such is the general purport° of this legendary superstition, which has furnished materials for many a wild story in that region of shadows; and the spectre is known, at all the country firesides, by the name of the Headless Horseman of Sleepy Hollow.

It is remarkable that the visionary propensity I have mentioned is not confined to the native inhabitants of the valley, but is unconsciously imbibed by every one who resides there for a time. However wide awake they may have been before they entered that sleepy region, they are sure, in a little time, to inhale the witching influence of the air, and begin to grow imaginative—to dream dreams, and see apparitions.

I mention this peaceful spot with all possible laud;° for it is in such little retired Dutch valleys, found here and there embosomed in the great State of New York, that population, manners, and customs, remain fixed; while the great torrent of migration and improvement, which is making such incessant changes in other parts of this restless country, sweeps by them unobserved. They are like those little nooks of still water which border a rapid stream; where we may see the straw and bubble riding quietly at anchor, or slowly revolving in their mimic harbor, undisturbed by the rush of the passing current. Though many years have elapsed since I trod the drowsy shades of Sleepy Hollow, yet I question whether I should not still find the same trees and the same families vegetating in its sheltered bosom.

In this by-place of nature, there abode,° in a remote period of American history, that is to say, some thirty years since, a worthy wight° of the name of Ichabod Crane; who sojourned, or, as he expressed it, "tarried," in Sleepy Hollow, for the purpose of instructing the children of the vicinity. He was a native of Connecticut; a State which supplies the Union with pioneers for the mind as well as for the forest, and sends forth yearly its legions of frontier woodsmen and country schoolmasters. The cognomen° of Crane was not inapplicable to his person. He was tall, but exceedingly lank, with narrow shoulders, long arms and legs, hands that dangled a mile out of his sleeves, feet that might have served for shovels, and his whole frame most loosely hung together. His head was small, and flat at top, with huge ears, large green glassy eyes, and a long snipe° nose, so that it looked like a weather-cock, perched upon his spindle neck, to tell which way the wind blew. To see him striding along the profile of a

---

purport: meaning
laud: praise
abode: lived (past tense of *abide*)
wight: person
cognomen: surname
snipe: long-billed game bird

hill on a windy day, with his clothes bagging and fluttering about him, one might have mistaken him for the genius° of famine descending upon the earth, or some scarecrow eloped° from a cornfield.

His school-house was a low building of one large room, rudely constructed of logs; the windows partly glazed, and partly patched with leaves of old copybooks. It was most ingeniously secured at vacant hours, by a withe° twisted in the handle of the door, and stakes set against the window shutters; so that, though a thief might get in with perfect ease, he would find some embarrassment in getting out; an idea most probably borrowed by the architect, Yost Van Houten, from the mystery of an eel-pot.° The school-house stood in a rather lonely but pleasant situation, just at the foot of a woody hill, with a brook running close by, and a formidable birch tree growing at one end of it. From hence the low murmur of his pupils' voices, conning° over their lessons, might be heard in a drowsy summer's day, like the hum of a bee-hive; interrupted now and then by the authoritative voice of the master, in the tone of menace or command; or, peradventure,° by the appalling sound of the birch,° as he urged some tardy loiterer along the flowery path of knowledge. Truth to say, he was a conscientious man, and ever bore in mind the golden maxim, "Spare the rod and spoil the child."—Ichabod Crane's scholars certainly were not spoiled.

10 I would not have it imagined, however, that he was one of those cruel potentates of the school, who joy in the smart° of their subjects; on the contrary, he administered justice with discrimination rather than severity; taking the burthen off the backs of the weak, and laying it on those of the strong. Your mere puny stripling, that winced at the least flourish of the rod, was passed by the indulgence; but the claims of justice were satisfied by inflicting a double portion on some little, tough, wrong-headed, broad-skirted Dutch urchin,° who sulked and swelled and grew dogged and sullen beneath the birch. All this he called "doing his duty by their parents;" and he never inflicted a chastisement without following it by the assurance, so consolatory to the smarting urchin, that "he would remember it, and thank him for it the longest day he had to live."

---

genius: demon or spirit
eloped: escaped, run away
withe: willow twig, or rope made of twisted twigs or stems
eel-pot: boxlike structure with funnel-shaped traps for catching eels
conning: learning, studying
peradventure: perhaps, possibly
birch: birch rod or bundle of twigs used for whipping
smart: pain
urchin: mischievous youngster

When school hours were over, he was even the companion and playmate of the larger boys; and on holiday afternoons would convoy some of the smaller ones home, who happened to have pretty sisters, or good housewives for mothers, noted for the comforts of the cupboard. Indeed it behooved him to keep on good terms with his pupils. The revenue arising from his school was small, and would have been scarcely sufficient to furnish him with daily bread, for he was a huge feeder, and though lank, had the dilating powers of an anaconda; but to help out his maintenance, he was, according to country custom in those parts, boarded and lodged at the houses of the farmers, whose children he instructed. With these he lived successively a week at a time; thus going the rounds of the neighborhood, with all his worldly effects tied up in a cotton handkerchief.

That all this might not be too onerous on the purses of his rustic patrons, who are apt to consider the costs of schooling a grievous burden, and schoolmasters as mere drones, he had various ways of rendering himself both useful and agreeable. He assisted the farmers occasionally in the lighter labors of their farms; helped to make hay; mended the fences; took the horses to water; drove the cows from pasture; and cut wood for the winter fire. He laid aside, too, all the dominant dignity and absolute sway with which he lorded it in his little empire, the school, and became wonderfully gentle and ingratiating. He found favor in the eyes of the mothers, by petting the children, particularly the youngest; and like the lion bold, which whilom° so magnanimously the lamb did hold, he would sit with a child on one knee, and rock a cradle with his foot for whole hours together.

In addition to his other vocations, he was the singing-master of the neighborhood, and picked up many bright shillings by instructing the young folks in psalmody.° It was a matter of no little vanity to him, on Sundays, to take his station in front of the church gallery, with a band of chosen singers; where, in his own mind, he completely carried away the palm from° the parson. Certain it is, his voice resounded far above all the rest of the congregation; and there are peculiar quavers still to be heard in that church, and which may even be heard half a mile off, quite to the opposite side of the mill-pond, on a still Sunday morning, which are said to be legitimately descended from the nose of Ichabod Crane. Thus, by divers° little make-shifts in that ingenious way which is commonly denominated "by hook and by crook," the worthy pedagogue got on tolerably enough, and was

---

whilom: once, formerly

psalmody: hymn-singing

carried away the palm from: outdid, outshone

divers: various

thought, by all who understood nothing of the labor of headwork, to have a wonderfully easy life of it.

The schoolmaster is generally a man of some importance in the female circle of a rural neighborhood; being considered a kind of idle gentlemanlike personage, of vastly superior taste and accomplishments to the rough country swains, and, indeed, inferior in learning only to the parson. His appearance, therefore, is apt to occasion some little stir at the tea-table of a farmhouse, and the addition of a supernumerary° dish of cakes or sweetmeats, or, peradventure, the parade of a silver tea-pot. Our man of letters, therefore, was peculiarly happy in the smiles of all the country damsels. How he would figure among them in the church-yard, between services on Sundays! gathering grapes for them from the wild vines that overrun the surrounding trees; reciting for their amusement all the epitaphs on the tombstones; or sauntering, with a whole bevy of them, along the banks of the adjacent mill-pond; while the more bashful country bumpkins hung sheepishly back, envying his superior elegance and address.°

From his half itinerant° life, also, he was a kind of travelling gazette, carrying the whole budget of local gossip from house to house; so that his appearance was always greeted with satisfaction. He was, moreover, esteemed by the women as a man of great erudition, for he had read several books quite through, and was a perfect master of Cotton Mather's history of New England Witchcraft, in which, by the way, he most firmly and potently believed. 15

He was, in fact, an odd mixture of small shrewdness and simple credulity. His appetite for the marvellous, and his powers of digesting it, were equally extraordinary; and both had been increased by his residence in this spellbound region. No tale was too gross or monstrous for his capacious swallow. It was often his delight, after his school was dismissed in the afternoon, to stretch himself on the rich bed of clover, bordering the little brook that whimpered by his schoolhouse, and there con over old Mather's direful tales, until the gathering dusk of the evening made the printed page a mere mist before his eyes. Then, as he wended his way, by swamp and stream and awful woodland, to the farmhouse where he happened to be quartered, every sound of nature, at that witching hour, fluttered his excited imagination: the moan of the whip-poor-will from the hill-side; the boding cry of the tree-toad, that harbinger° of storm; the dreary hooting of the screech-owl, or the sudden rustling in the thicket of birds frightened from their roost. The

---

supernumerary: additional, extra
address: manner of speaking
itinerant: wandering, migratory
harbinger: omen, foreshadowing

fire-flies, too, which sparkled most vividly in the darkest places, now and then startled him, as one of uncommon brightness would stream across his path; and if, by chance, a huge blockhead of a beetle came winging his blundering flight against him, the poor varlet° was ready to give up the ghost, with the idea that he was struck with a witch's token. His only resource on such occasions, either to drown thought, or drive away evil spirits, was to sing psalm tunes;—and the good people of Sleepy Hollow, as they sat by their doors of an evening, were often filled with awe, at hearing his nasal melody, "in linked sweetness long drawn out," floating from the distant hill, or along the dusky road.

Another of his sources of fearful pleasure was, to pass long winter evenings with the old Dutch wives, as they sat spinning by the fire, with a row of apples roasting and spluttering along the hearth, and listen to their marvellous tales of ghosts and goblins, and haunted fields, and haunted brooks, and haunted bridges, and haunted houses, and particularly of the headless horseman, or Galloping Hessian of the Hollow, as they sometimes called him. He would delight them equally by his anecdotes of witchcraft, and of the direful omens and portentous sights and sounds in the air, which prevailed in the earlier times of Connecticut; and would frighten them wofully with speculations upon comets and shooting stars; and with the alarming fact that the world did absolutely turn round, and that they were half the time topsy-turvy!

But if there was a pleasure in all this, while snugly cuddling in the chimney corner of a chamber that was all of a ruddy glow from the crackling wood fire, and where, of course, no spectre dared to show his face, it was dearly purchased by the terrors of his subsequent walk homewards. What fearful shapes and shadows beset his path amidst the dim and ghastly glare of a snowy night!—With what wistful look did he eye every trembling ray of light streaming across the waste fields from some distant window!—How often was he appalled by some shrub covered with snow, which, like a sheeted spectre, beset his very path!—How often did he shrink with curdling awe at the sound of his own steps on the frosty crust beneath his feet; and dread to look over his shoulder, lest he should behold some uncouth° being tramping close behind him!—and how often was he thrown into complete dismay by some rushing blast, howling among the trees, in the idea that it was the Galloping Hessian on one of his nightly scourings!

All these, however, were mere terrors of the night, phantoms of the mind that walk in darkness; and though he had seen many spectres in his time, and been more than once beset by Satan in divers shapes, in his lonely perambulations, yet daylight put an end to all

varlet: rascal

uncouth: unknown, unfamiliar

these evils; and he would have passed a pleasant life of it, in despite of the devil and all his works, if his path had not been crossed by a being that causes more perplexity to mortal man than ghosts, goblins, and the whole race of witches put together, and that was—a woman.

Among the musical disciples who assembled, one evening in each week, to receive his instructions in psalmody, was Katrina Van Tassel, the daughter and only child of a substantial Dutch farmer. She was a blooming lass of fresh eighteen; plump as a partridge; ripe and melting and rosy cheeked as one of her father's peaches, and universally famed, not merely for her beauty, but her vast expectations.° She was withal° a little of a coquette, as might be perceived even in her dress, which was a mixture of ancient and modern fashions, as most suited to set off her charms. She wore the ornaments of pure yellow gold, which her great-great-grandmother had brought over from Saardam;° the tempting stomacher° of the olden time; and withal a provokingly short petticoat, to display the prettiest foot and ankle in the country round. 20

Ichabod Crane had a soft and foolish heart towards the sex; and it is not to be wondered at, that so tempting a morsel soon found favor in his eyes; more especially after he had visited her in her paternal mansion. Old Baltus Van Tassel was a perfect picture of a thriving, contented, liberal-hearted farmer. He seldom, it is true, sent either his eyes or his thoughts beyond the boundaries of his own farm; but within those every thing was snug, happy, and well-conditioned. He was satisfied with his wealth, but not proud of it; and piqued° himself upon the hearty abundance, rather than the style in which he lived. His stronghold was situated on the banks of the Hudson, in one of those green, sheltered, fertile nooks, in which the Dutch farmers are so fond of nestling. A great elmtree spread its broad branches over it; at the foot of which bubbled up a spring of the softest and sweetest water, in a little well, formed of a barrel; and then stole sparkling away through the grass, to a neighboring brook, that bubbled along among alders and dwarf willows. Hard by the farmhouse was a vast barn, that might have served for a church; every window and crevice of which seemed bursting forth with the treasures of the farm; the flail° was busily resounding within it from morning to night; swallows and martins skimmed twittering about the eaves; and rows of pigeons, some with one eye turned up, as if watching the weather, some with

---

expectations: i.e., of inheritance

withal: besides

Saardam: Zaandam, a town in the Netherlands

stomacher: ornamented garment covering the breast and stomach

piqued: prided

flail: tool for threshing grain

their heads under their wings, or buried in their bosoms, and others swelling, and cooing, and bowing about their dames, were enjoying the sunshine on the roof. Sleek unwieldy porkers were grunting in the repose and abundance of their pens; whence sallied forth, now and then, troops of sucking pigs, as if to snuff the air. A stately squadron of snowy geese were riding in an adjoining pond, convoying whole fleets of ducks; regiments of turkeys were gobbling through the farmyard and guinea fowls fretting about it, like ill-tempered housewives, with their peevish discontented cry. Before the barn door strutted the gallant cock, that pattern of a husband, a warrior, and a fine gentleman, clapping his burnished wings, and crowing in the pride and gladness of his heart—sometimes tearing up the earth with his feet, and then generously calling his ever-hungry family of wives and children to enjoy the rich morsel which he had discovered.

The pedagogue's mouth watered, as he looked upon this sumptuous promise of luxurious winter fare. In his devouring mind's eye, he pictured to himself every roasting-pig running about with a pudding in his belly, and an apple in his mouth; the pigeons were snugly put to bed in a comfortable pie, and tucked in with a coverlet of crust; the geese were swimming in their own gravy; and the ducks pairing cosily in dishes, like snug married couples, with a decent competency° of onion sauce. In the porkers he saw carved out the future sleek side of bacon, and juicy relishing ham; not a turkey but he beheld daintily trussed up, with its gizzard under its wing, and, peradventure, a necklace of savory sausages; and even bright chanticleer° himself lay sprawling on his back, in a side-dish, with uplifted claws, as if craving that quarter° which his chivalrous spirit disdained to ask while living.

As the enraptured Ichabod fancied all this, and as he rolled his great green eyes over the fat meadow-lands, the rich fields of wheat, of rye, of buckwheat, and Indian corn, and the orchards burthened with ruddy fruit, which surrounded the warm tenement° of Van Tassel, his heart yearned after the damsel who was to inherit these domains, and his imagination expanded with the idea, how they might be readily turned into cash, and the money invested in immense tracts of wild land, and shingle palaces in the wilderness. Nay, his busy fancy already realized his hopes, and presented to him the blooming Katrina, with a whole family of children, mounted on the top of a wagon loaded with household trumpery,° with pots and kettles dangling beneath; and he

---

competency: sufficiency
chanticleer: rooster
quarter: mercy, pity
tenement: property
trumpery: trash

himself bestriding a pacing mare, with a colt at her heels, set-
...t for Kentucky, Tennessee, or the Lord knows where.

...hen he entered the house the conquest of his heart was complete. ...one of those spacious farmhouses, with high-ridged, but lowly-sloping roofs, built in the style handed down from the first Dutch settlers; the low projecting eaves forming a piazza along the front, capable of being closed up in bad weather. Under this were hung flails, harness, various utensils of husbandry,° and nets for fishing in the neighboring river. Benches were built along the sides for summer use; and a great spinning-wheel at one end, and a churn at the other, showed the various uses to which this important porch might be devoted. From this piazza the wondering Ichabod entered the hall, which formed the centre of the mansion and the place of usual residence. Here, rows of resplendent pewter,° ranged on a long dresser, dazzled his eyes. In one corner stood a huge bag of wool ready to be spun; in another a quantity of linsey-woolsey° just from the loom; ears of Indian corn, and strings of dried apples and peaches, hung in gay festoons° along the walls, mingled with the gaud of red peppers; and a door left ajar gave him a peep into the best parlor, where the claw-footed chairs, and dark mahogany tables, shone like mirrors; andirons, with their accompanying shovel and tongs, glistened from their covert of asparagus tops; mock-oranges and conch-shells decorated the mantelpiece; strings of various colored birds' eggs were suspended above it: a great ostrich egg was hung from the centre of the room, and a corner cupboard, knowingly left open, displayed immense treasures of old silver and well-mended china.

From the moment Ichabod laid his eyes upon these regions of delight, the peace of his mind was at an end, and his only study was how to gain the affections of the peerless daughter of Van Tassel. In this enterprise, however, he had more real difficulties than generally fell to the lot of a knight-errant of yore, who seldom had any thing but giants, enchanters, fiery dragons, and such like easily-conquered adversaries, to contend with; and had to make his way merely through gates of iron and brass, and walls of adamant,° to the castle keep, where the lady of his heart was confined; all which he achieved as easily as a man would carve his way to the centre of a Christmas pie; and then the lady gave him her hand as a matter of course. Ichabod, on the contrary, had to win his way to the heart of a country coquette, beset with a labyrinth of whims and caprices, which were for ever presenting new difficulties

---

husbandry: farming
pewter: plates and utensil of a tin and lead alloy
linsey-woolsey: rough linen warp
festoons: garlands hung in loops or curves
adamant: stone of great hardness

and impediments; and he had to encounter a host of fearful adversaries of real flesh and blood, the numerous rustic admirers, who beset every portal to her heart; keeping a watchful and angry eye upon each other, but ready to fly° out in the common cause against any new competitor.

Among these the most formidable was a burly, roaring, roistering° blade, of the name of Abraham, or, according to the Dutch abbreviation, Brom Van Brunt, the hero of the country round, which rang with his feats of strength and hardihood. He was broad-shouldered and double-jointed, with short curly black hair, and a bluff, but not unpleasant countenance, having a mingled air of fun and arrogance. From his Herculean frame and great powers of limb, he had received the nickname of BROM BONES, by which he was universally known. He was famed for great knowledge and skill in horsemanship, being as dexterous on horseback as a Tartar.° He was foremost at all races and cock-fights; and, with the ascendency which bodily strength acquires in rustic life, was the umpire in all disputes, setting his hat on one side, and giving his decisions with an air and tone admitting of no gainsay° or appeal. He was always ready for either a fight or a frolic; but had more mischief than ill-will in his composition; and, with all his overbearing roughness, there was a strong dash of waggish good humor at bottom. He had three or four boon companions, who regarded him as their model, and at the head of whom he scoured the country, attending every scene of feud or merriment for miles round. In cold weather he was distinguished by a fur cap, surmounted with a flaunting fox's tail; and when the folks at a country gathering descried° this well-known crest at a distance, whisking about among a squad of hard riders, they always stood by for a squall. Sometimes his crew would be heard dashing along past the farmhouses at midnight, with whoop and halloo, like a troop of Don Cossacks; and the old dames,° startled out of their sleep, would listen for a moment till the hurry-scurry had clattered by, and then exclaim, "Ay, there goes Brom Bones and his gang!" The neighbors looked upon him with a mixture of awe, admiration, and good will; and when any madcap prank, or rustic brawl, occurred in the vicinity, always shook their heads, and warranted Brom Bones was at the bottom of it.

This rantipole° hero had for some time singled out the blooming Katrina for the object of his uncouth gallantries, and though his

---

fly: hasten, rush
roistering: swaggering, boisterous
Tartar: Mongolian or Turkish tribesman
gainsay: deny
descried: saw, perceived
dames: mature women, usually married
rantipole: wild, rakish

us toyings were something like the gentle caresses and endear- of a bear, yet it was whispered that she did not altogether dis- e his hopes. Certain it is, his advances were signals for rival ates to retire, who felt no inclination to cross a lion in his amours; insomuch, that when his horse was seen tied to Van Tassel's paling,° on a Sunday night, a sure sign that his master was courting, or, as it is termed, "sparking," within, all other suitors passed by in despair, and carried the war into other quarters.

Such was the formidable rival with whom Ichabod Crane had to contend, and, considering all things, a stouter man than he would have shrunk from the competition, and a wiser man would have despaired. He had, however, a happy mixture of pliability and perseverance in his nature; he was in form and spirit like a supplejack—yielding, but tough; though he bent, he never broke; and though he bowed beneath the slightest pressure, yet, the moment it was away—jerk! he was as erect, and carried his head as high as ever.

To have taken the field openly against his rival would have been madness; for he was not a man to be thwarted in his amours, any more than that stormy lover, Achilles.° Ichabod, therefore, made his advances in a quiet and gently-insinuating manner. Under cover of his character of singing-master, he made frequent visits at the farm-house; not that he had any thing to apprehend° from the meddlesome interference of parents, which is so often a stumbling-block in the path of lovers. Balt Van Tassel was an easy indulgent soul; he loved his daughter better even than his pipe, and, like a reasonable man and an excellent father, let her have her way in every thing. His notable little wife, too, had enough to do to attend to her housekeeping and manage her poultry; for, as she sagely observed, ducks and geese are foolish things, and must be looked after, but girls can take care of themselves. Thus while the busy dame bustled about the house, or plied her spinning-wheel at one end of the piazza, honest Balt would sit smoking his evening pipe at the other, watching the achievements of a little wooden warrior, who, armed with a sword in each hand, was most valiantly fighting the wind on the pinnacle of the barn. In the mean time, Ichabod would carry on his suit with the daughter by the side of the spring under the great elm, or sauntering along in the twilight, that hour so favorable to the lover's eloquence.

30 I profess not to know how women's hearts are wooed and won. To me they have always been matters of riddle and admiration. Some seem to have but one vulnerable point, or door of access; while others

paling: stake or picket

Achilles: The Greek warrior and a central figure of Homer's *Iliad* is the subject of various legends involving women.

apprehend: fear

have a thousand avenues, and may be captured in a thousand different ways. It is a great triumph of skill to gain the former, but a still greater proof of generalship to maintain possession of the latter, for the man must battle for his fortress at every door and window. He who wins a thousand common hearts is therefore entitled to some renown; but he who keeps undisputed sway over the heart of a coquette, is indeed a hero. Certain it is, this was not the case with the redoubtable° Brom Bones; and from the moment Ichabod Crane made his advances, the interests of the former evidently declined; his horse was no longer seen tied at the palings on Sunday nights, and a deadly feud gradually arose between him and the preceptor° of Sleepy Hollow.

Brom, who had a degree of rough chivalry in his nature, would fain° have carried matters to open warfare, and have settled their pretensions° to the lady, according to the mode of those most concise and simple reasoners, the knights-errant of yore—by single combat; but Ichabod was too conscious of the superior might of his adversary to enter the lists° against him: he had overheard a boast of Bones, that he would "double the schoolmaster up, and lay him on a shelf of his own school-house;" and he was too wary to give him an opportunity. There was something extremely provoking in this obstinately pacific° system; it left Brom no alternative but to draw upon the funds of rustic waggery in his disposition, and to play off boorish practical jokes upon his rival. Ichabod became the object of whimsical persecution to Bones, and his gang of rough riders. They harried his hitherto peaceful domains; smoked out his singing school, by stopping up the chimney; broke into the school-house at night, in spite of its formidable fastenings of withe and window stakes, and turned every thing topsy-turvy: so that the poor schoolmaster began to think all the witches in the country held their meetings there. But what was still more annoying, Brom took all opportunities of turning him into ridicule in presence of his mistress,° and had a scoundrel dog whom he taught to whine in the most ludicrous manner, and introduced as a rival of Ichabod's to instruct her in psalmody.

In this way matters went on for some time, without producing any material effect on the relative situations of the contending powers. On a fine autumnal afternoon, Ichabod, in pensive mood, sat enthroned on the lofty stool whence he usually watched all the concerns of his little

---

redoubtable: formidable
preceptor: instructor, schoolmaster
fain: gladly
pretensions: claims
lists: enclosed arena for jousting
pacific: peaceful
mistress: sweetheart

° realm. In his hand he swayed a ferule,° that sceptre of domestic ; the birth of justice reposed on three nails, behind the throne, a nt terror to evil doers; while on the desk before him might be seen ° contraband articles and prohibited weapons, detected upon the persons of idle urchins; such as half-munched apples, popguns, whirligigs, fly-cages, and whole legions of rampant little paper gamecocks. Apparently there had been some appalling act of justice recently inflicted, for his scholars were all busily intent upon their books, or slyly whispering behind them with one eye kept upon the master; and a kind of buzzing stillness reigned throughout the school-room. It was suddenly interrupted by the appearance of a Negro, in tow-cloth jacket and trowsers, a round-crowned fragment of a hat, like the cap of Mercury, and mounted on the back of a ragged wild, half-broken colt, which he managed with a rope by way of halter. He came clattering up to the school door with an invitation to Ichabod to attend a merrymaking or "quilting frolic," to be held that evening at Mynheer° Van Tassel's; and having delivered his message with that air of importance, and effort at fine language, which a Negro is apt to display on petty embassies° of the kind, he dashed over the brook, and was seen scampering away up the hollow, full of the importance and hurry of his mission.

All was now bustle and hubbub in the late quiet school-room. The scholars were hurried through their lessons, without stopping at trifles; those who were nimble skipped over half with impunity,° and those who were tardy, had a smart application now and then in the rear, to quicken their speed, or help them over a tall word. Books were flung aside without being put away on the shelves, inkstands were overturned, benches thrown down, and the whole school was turned loose an hour before the usual time, bursting forth like a legion of young imps, yelping and racketing about the green, in joy at their early emancipation.

The gallant Ichabod now spent at least an extra hour at his toilet,° brushing and furbishing° up his best, and indeed only suit of rusty° black, and arranging his locks° by a bit of broken looking-glass, that

---

literary: concerning reading and writing

ferule: rod, cane, or flat piece of wood for striking on the open palm

sundry: various, diverse

Mynheer: Dutch term corresponding to "Mister"

embassies: missions undertaken by an agent or representative

impunity: freedom from punishment

toilet: act of dressing and preparing oneself

furbishing: freshening

rusty: faded, shabby

locks: hair

hung up in the school-house. That he might make his appearance before his mistress in the true style of a cavalier, he borrowed a horse from the farmer with whom he was domiciliated,° a choleric° old Dutchman, of the name of Hans Van Ripper, and, thus gallantly mounted, issued forth, like a knight-errant in quest of adventures. But it is meet° I should, in the true spirit of romantic story, give some account of the looks and equipments of my hero and his steed. The animal he bestrode was a broken-down plough-horse, that had outlived almost every thing but his viciousness. He was gaunt and shagged, with a ewe neck and a head like a hammer; his rusty mane and tail were tangled and knotted with burrs; one eye had lost its pupil, and was glaring and spectral; but the other had the gleam of a genuine devil in it. Still he must have had fire and mettle° in his day, if we may judge from the name he bore of Gunpowder. He had, in fact, been a favorite steed of his master's, the choleric Van Ripper, who was a furious rider, and had infused, very probably, some of his own spirit into the animal; for, old and broken-down as he looked, there was more of the lurking devil in him than in any young filly in the country.

Ichabod was a suitable figure for such a steed. He rode with short stirrups, which brought his knees nearly up to the pommel° of the saddle; his sharp elbows stuck out like grasshoppers'; he carried his whip perpendicularly in his hand, like a sceptre, and, as his horse jogged on, the motion of his arms was not unlike the flapping of a pair of wings. A small wool hat rested on the top of his nose, for so his scanty strip of forehead might be called; and the skirts of his black coat fluttered out almost to the horse's tail. Such was the appearance of Ichabod and his steed, as they shambled out of the gate of Hans Van Ripper, and it was altogether such an apparition as is seldom to be met with in broad daylight.

It was, as I have said, a fine autumnal day, the sky was clear and serene, and nature wore that rich and golden livery which we always associate with the idea of abundance. The forests had put on their sober brown and yellow, while some trees of the tenderer kind had been nipped by the frosts into brilliant dyes of orange, purple, and scarlet. Streaming files of wild ducks began to make their appearance high in the air; the bark of the squirrel might be heard from the groves

---

domiciliated: housed, quartered

choleric: irascible, testy

meet: proper

mettle: courage, fortitude

pommel: knob at the front and top of a saddle

n and hickory nuts, and the pensive whistle of the quail at in-
from the neighboring stubble-field.

e small birds were taking their farewell banquets. In the fulness revelry, they fluttered, chirping and frolicking, from bush to bush, and tree to tree, capricious from the very profusion and variety around them. There was the honest cock-robin, the favorite game of stripling sportsmen, with its loud querulous note; and the twittering blackbirds flying in sable clouds; and the golden-winged woodpecker, with his crimson crest, his broad black gorget,° and splendid plumage; and the cedar bird, with its red-tipt wings and yellow-tipt tail, and its little monteiro cap° of feathers; and the blue-jay, that noisy coxcomb,° in his gay light-blue coat and white under-clothes; screaming and chattering, nodding and bobbing and bowing, and pretending to be on good terms with every songster of the grove.

As Ichabod jogged slowly on his way, his eye, ever open to every symptom of culinary abundance, ranged with delight over the treasures of jolly autumn. On all sides he beheld vast store of apples; some hanging in oppressive opulence on the trees; some gathered into baskets and barrels for the market; others heaped up in rich piles for the cider-press. Farther on he beheld great fields of Indian corn, with its golden ears peeping from their leafy coverts, and holding out the promise of cakes and hasty pudding; and the yellow pumpkins lying beneath them, turning up their fair round bellies to the sun, and giving ample prospects of the most luxurious of pies; and anon° he passed the fragrant buckwheat fields, breathing the odor of the beehive, and as he beheld them, soft anticipations stole over his mind of dainty slapjacks,° well buttered, and garnished with honey or treacle, by the delicate little dimpled hand of Katrina Van Tassel.

Thus feeding his mind with many sweet thoughts and "sugared suppositions," he journeyed along the sides of a range of hills which look out upon some of the goodliest scenes of the mighty Hudson. The sun gradually wheeled his broad disk down into the west. The wide bosom of the Tappan Zee lay motionless and glassy, excepting that here and there a gentle undulation waved and prolonged the blue shadow of the distant mountain. A few amber clouds floated in the sky, without a breath of air to move them. The horizon was a fine golden tint, changing gradually into a pure apple green, and from that

---

gorget: patch on a bird's throat distinguished by its color

monteiro cap: hunter's cap, or a hat with a feather

coxcomb: fop, dandy

anon: soon, shortly

slapjacks: flapjacks, griddlecakes

into the deep blue of the mid-heaven. A slanting ray lingered on the woody crests of the precipices that overhung some parts of the river, giving greater depth of the dark-gray and purple of their rocky sides. A sloop was loitering in the distance, dropping slowly down with the tide, her sail hanging uselessly against the mast; and as the reflection of the sky gleamed along the still water, it seemed as if the vessel was suspended in the air.

It was toward evening that Ichabod arrived at the castle of the Heer Van Tassel, which he found thronged with the pride and flower of the adjacent country. Old farmers, a spare leathern-faced race, in homespun coats and breeches, blue stockings, huge shoes, and magnificent pewter buckles. Their brisk withered little dames, in close crimped caps, long-waisted short-gowns, homespun petticoats, with scissors and pincushions, and gay calico pockets hanging on the outside. Buxom lasses, almost as antiquated as their mothers, excepting where a straw hat, a fine ribbon, or perhaps a white frock, gave symptoms of city innovation. The sons, in short square-skirted coats with rows of stupendous brass buttons; and their hair generally queued° in the fashion of the times, especially if they could procure an eel-skin for the purpose, it being esteemed, throughout the country, as a potent nourisher and strengthener of the hair.

40

Brom Bones, however, was the hero of the scene, having come to the gathering on his favorite steed Daredevil, a creature, like himself, full of mettle and mischief, and which no one but himself could manage. He was, in fact, noted for preferring vicious animals, given to all kinds of tricks, which kept the rider in constant risk of his neck, for he held a tractable well-broken horse as unworthy of a lad of spirit.

Fain would I pause to dwell upon the world of charms that burst upon the enraptured gaze of my hero, as he entered the state parlor of Van Tassel's mansion. Not those of the bevy of buxom lasses, with their luxurious display of red and white; but the ample charms of a genuine Dutch country tea-table, in the sumptuous time of autumn. Such heaped-up platters of cakes of various and almost indescribable kinds, known only to experienced Dutch housewives! There was the doughty° dough-nut, the tenderer oly koek,° and the crisp and crumbling cruller; sweet cakes and short cakes, ginger cakes and honey cakes, and the whole family of cakes. And then there were apple pies and peach pies and pumpkin pies; besides slices of ham and smoked beef; and moreover delectable dishes of preserved plums,

---

queued: braided into pigtails

doughty: valiant

oly koek: precursor of the doughnut (Dutch for "oily cake")

and peaches, and pears, and quinces; not to mention broiled shad and roasted chickens; together with bowls of milk and cream, all mingled higgledy-piggledy, pretty much as I have enumerated them, with the motherly tea-pot sending up its clouds of vapor from the midst—Heaven bless the mark! I want breath and time to discuss this banquet as it deserves, and am too eager to get on with my story. Happily, Ichabod Crane was not in so great a hurry as his historian, but did ample justice to every dainty.

He was a kind of thankful creature, whose heart dilated in proportion as his skin was filled with good cheer; and whose spirit rose with eating as some men's do with drink. He could not help, too, rolling his large eyes round him as he ate, and chuckling with the possibility that he might one day be lord of all this scene of almost unimaginable luxury and splendor. Then, he thought, how soon he'd turn his back upon the old school-house; snap his fingers in the face of Hans Van Ripper, and every other niggardly° patron, and kick any itinerant pedagogue° out of doors that should dare to call him comrade!

Old Baltus Van Tassel moved about among his guests with a face dilated with content and good humor, round and jolly as the harvest moon. His hospitable attentions were brief, but expressive, being confined to a shake of the hand, a slap on the shoulder, a loud laugh, and a pressing invitation to "fall to, and help themselves."

And now the sound of the music from the common room, or hall, summoned to the dance. The musician was an old grayheaded Negro, who had been the itinerant orchestra of the neighborhood for more than half a century. His instrument was as old and battered as himself. The greater part of the time he scraped on two or three strings, accompanying every movement of the bow with a motion of the head; bowing almost to the ground, and stamping with his foot whenever a fresh couple were to start. 45

Ichabod prided himself upon his dancing as much as upon his vocal powers. Not a limb, not a fibre about him was idle; and to have seen his loosely hung frame in full motion, and clattering about the room, you would have thought Saint Vitus himself, that blessed patron of the dance, was figuring before you in person. He was the admiration of all the Negroes; who, having gathered, of all ages and sizes, from the farm and the neighborhood, stood forming a pyramid of shining black faces at every door and window, gazing with delight at the scene, rolling their white eye-balls, and showing grinning rows

---

niggardly: stingy

pedagogue: schoolteacher

of ivory from ear to ear. How could the flogger of urchins be otherwise than animated and joyous? the lady of his heart was his partner in the dance, and smiling graciously in reply to all his amorous oglings; while Brom Bones, sorely smitten with love and jealousy, sat brooding by himself in one corner.

When the dance was at an end, Ichabod was attracted to a knot of the sager° folks, who, with old Van Tassel, sat smoking at one end of the piazza, gossiping over former times, and drawling out long stories about the war.°

This neighborhood, at the time of which I am speaking, was one of those highly-favored places which abound with chronicle and great men. The British and American line had run near it during the war; it had, therefore, been the scene of marauding, and infested with refugees, cow-boys,° and all kinds of border chivalry. Just sufficient time had elapsed to enable each story-teller to dress up his tale with a little becoming fiction, and, in the indistinctness of his recollection, to make himself the hero of every exploit.

There was the story of Doffue Martling, a large blue-bearded Dutchman, who had nearly taken a British frigate with an old iron nine-pounder from a mud breast-work,° only that his gun burst at the sixth discharge. And there was an old gentleman who shall be nameless, being too rich a mynheer to be lightly mentioned, who, in the battle of White-plains, being an excellent master of defence, parried a musket ball with a small sword, insomuch that he absolutely felt it whiz round the blade, and glance off at the hilt: in proof of which, he was ready at any time to show the sword, with the hilt a little bent. There were several more that had been equally great in the field, not one of whom but was persuaded that he had a considerable hand in bringing the war to a happy termination.

But all these were nothing to the tales of ghosts, and apparitions that succeeded.° The neighborhood is rich in legendary treasures of the kind. Local tales and superstitions thrive best in these sheltered long-settled retreats; but are trampled under foot by the shifting throng that forms the population of most of our country places. Besides, there is no encouragement for ghosts in most of our villages, for they have scarcely had time to finish their first nap, and turn themselves in their graves, before their surviving friends have travelled 50

sager: wiser

the war: the American Revolution

cow-boys: members of pro-British guerilla bands during the Revolution

breast-work: fortification

succeeded: followed

away from the neighborhood; so that when they turn out at night to walk their rounds, they have no acquaintance left to call upon. This is perhaps the reason why we so seldom hear of ghosts except in our long-established Dutch communities.

The immediate cause, however, of the prevalence of supernatural stories in these parts, was doubtless owing to the vicinity of Sleepy Hollow. There was a contagion in the very air that blew from that haunted region; it breathed forth an atmosphere of dreams and fancies infecting all the land. Several of the Sleepy Hollow people were present at Van Tassel's, and, as usual, were doling out their wild and wonderful legends. Many dismal tales were told about funeral trains,° and mournful cries and wailings heard and seen about the great tree where the unfortunate Major André° was taken, and which stood in the neighborhood. Some mention was made also of the woman in white, that haunted the dark glen at Raven Rock, and was often heard to shriek on winter nights before a storm, having perished there in the snow. The chief part of the stories, however, turned upon the favorite spectre of Sleepy Hollow, the headless horseman, who had been heard several times of late, patrolling the country; and, it was said, tethered his horse nightly among the graves in the church-yard.

The sequestered situation of this church seems always to have made it a favorite haunt of troubled spirits. It stands on a knoll, surrounded by locust-trees and lofty elms, from among which its decent whitewashed walls shine modestly forth, like Christian purity beaming through the shades of retirement. A gentle slope descends from it to a silver sheet of water, bordered by high trees, between which, peeps may be caught at the blue hills of the Hudson. To look upon its grass-grown yard, where the sunbeams seem to sleep so quietly, one would think that there at least the dead might rest in peace. On one side of the church extends a wide woody dell, along which raves a large brook among broken rocks and trunks of fallen trees. Over a deep black part of the stream, not far from the church, was formerly thrown a wooden bridge; the road that led to it, and the bridge itself, were thickly shaded by overhanging trees, which cast a gloom about it, even in the daytime; but occasioned a fearful darkness at night. This was one of the favorite haunts of the headless horseman; and the place where he was most frequently encountered. The tale was told of old Brouwer, a most heretical disbeliever in ghosts, how he met the horseman returning from his foray into Sleepy Hollow, and was obliged to

---

trains: processions

Major André: John André (1750–1780), British officer and confederate of Benedict Arnold, captured by the Americans and hanged as a spy

get up behind him; how they galloped over bush and brake, over hill and swamp, until they reached the bridge; when the horseman suddenly turned into a skeleton, threw old Brouwer into the brook, and sprang away over the tree-tops with a clap of thunder.

This story was immediately matched by a thrice marvellous adventure of Brom Bones, who made light of the Galloping Hessian as an arrant° jockey. He affirmed that, on returning one night from the neighboring village of Sing Sing,° he had been overtaken by this midnight trooper; that he had offered to race with him for a bowl of punch, and should have won it too, for Daredevil beat the goblin horse all hollow, but just as they came to the church bridge, the Hessian bolted, and vanished in a flash of fire.

All these tales, told in that drowsy undertone with which men talk in the dark, the countenances of the listeners only now and then receiving a casual gleam from the glare of a pipe, sank deep in the mind of Ichabod. He repaid them in kind with large extracts from his invaluable author, Cotton Mather,° and added many marvellous events that had taken place in his native State of Connecticut, and fearful sights which he had seen in his nightly walks about Sleepy Hollow.

55

The revel now gradually broke up. The old farmers gathered together their families in their wagons, and were heard for some time rattling along the hollow roads, and over the distant hills. Some of the damsels mounted on pillions° behind their favorite swains, and their light-hearted laughter, mingling with the clatter of hoofs, echoed along the silent woodlands, sounding fainter and fainter until they gradually died away—and the late scene of noise and frolic was all silent and deserted. Ichabod only lingered behind according to the custom of country lovers, to have a tête-à-tête° with the heiress, fully convinced that he was now on the high road to success. What passed at this interview I will not pretend to say, for in fact I do not know. Something, however, I fear me, must have gone wrong, for he certainly sallied forth, after no very great interval, with an air quite desolate and chop-fallen.°—Oh these women! these women! Could that girl have been playing off any of her coquettish tricks?—Was her encouragement of the poor pedagogue all a mere sham to secure her

---

arrant: downright, thoroughgoing

Sing Sing: older name for the town of Ossining, New York

Cotton Mather: Puritan minister and author (1663–1728), whose *Wonders of the Invisible World* (1693) testified to his belief in witchcraft

pillions: pads or cushions attached behind saddles

tête-à-tête: private conversation (French for "head to head")

chop-fallen: dispirited, dejected

conquest of his rival?—Heaven only knows, not I!—Let it suffice to say, Ichabod stole forth with the air of one who had been sacking° a hen-roost, rather than a fair lady's heart. Without looking to the right or left to notice the scene of rural wealth, on which he had so often gloated, he went straight to the stable, and with several hearty cuffs and kicks, roused his steed most uncourteously from the comfortable quarters in which he was soundly sleeping, dreaming of mountains of corn and oats, and whole valleys of timothy° and clover.

It was the very witching time of night that Ichabod, heavy-hearted and crest-fallen, pursued his travel homewards, along the sides of the lofty hills which rise above Tarry Town, and which he had traversed so cheerily in the afternoon. The hour was as dismal as himself. Far below him, the Tappan Zee spread its dusky and indistinct waste of waters, with here and there the tall mast of a sloop, riding quietly at anchor under the land. In the dead hush of midnight, he could even hear the barking of the watch dog from the opposite shore of the Hudson; but it was so vague and faint as only to give an idea of his distance from this faithful companion of man. Now and then, too, the long-drawn crowing of a cock, accidentally awakened, would sound far, far off, from some farmhouse away among the hills—but it was like a dreaming sound in his ear. No signs of life occurred near him, but occasionally the melancholy chirp of a cricket, or perhaps the guttural° twang of a bull-frog, from a neighboring marsh, as if sleeping uncomfortably, and turning suddenly in his bed.

All the stories of ghosts and goblins that he had heard in the afternoon, now came crowding upon his recollection. The night grew darker and darker; the stars seemed to sink deeper in the sky, and driving clouds occasionally hid them from his sight. He had never felt so lonely and dismal. He was, moreover, approaching the very place where many of the scenes of the ghost stories had been laid. In the centre of the road stood an enormous tulip-tree, which towered like a giant above all the other trees of the neighborhood, and formed a kind of landmark. Its limbs were gnarled, and fantastic, large enough to form trunks for ordinary trees, twisting down almost to the earth, and rising again into the air. It was connected with the tragical story of the unfortunate André who had been taken prisoner hard by; and was universally known by the name of Major André's tree. The common people regarded it with a mixture of respect and superstition, partly out of sympathy for the fate of its ill-starred namesake, and

---

sacking: looting, plundering

timothy: a coarse grass used as fodder

guttural: harsh, croaking

partly from the tales of strange sights and doleful lamentations told concerning it.

As Ichabod approached this fearful tree, he began to whistle: he thought his whistle was answered—it was but a blast sweeping sharply through the dry branches. As he approached a little nearer, he thought he saw something white, hanging in the midst of the tree—he paused and ceased whistling; but on looking more narrowly, perceived that it was a place where the tree had been scathed by lightning, and the white wood laid bare. Suddenly he heard a groan—his teeth chattered and his knees smote against the saddle: it was but the rubbing of one huge bough upon another, as they were swayed about by the breeze. He passed the tree in safety, but new perils lay before him.

About two hundred yards from the tree a small brook crossed the road, and ran into a marshy and thickly-wooded glen, known by the name of Wiley's swamp. A few rough logs, laid side by side, served for a bridge over this stream. On that side of the road where the brook entered the wood, a group of oaks and chestnuts, matted thick with wild grapevines, threw a cavernous gloom over it. To pass this bridge was the severest trial. It was at this identical spot that the unfortunate André was captured, and under the covert of those chestnuts and vines were the sturdy yeomen° concealed who surprised° him. This has ever since been considered a haunted stream, and fearful are the feelings of the schoolboy who has to pass it alone after dark.

60

As he approached the stream his heart began to thump; he summoned up, however, all his resolution, gave his horse half a score of kicks in the ribs, and attempted to dash briskly across the bridge; but instead of starting forward, the perverse old animal made a lateral movement, and ran broadside against the fence. Ichabod, whose fears increased with the delay, jerked the reins on the other side, and kicked lustily with the contrary° foot: it was all in vain; his steed started, it is true, but it was only to plunge to the opposite side of the road into a thicket of brambles and alder bushes. The schoolmaster now bestowed both whip and heel upon the starveling° ribs of old Gunpowder, who dashed forward, snuffling and snorting, but came to a stand just by the bridge, with a suddenness that had nearly sent his rider sprawling over his head. Just at this moment a plashy° tramp° by the side

---

yeomen: dependable workmen, or farmers who cultivate their own land

surprised: came upon suddenly and unexpectedly

contrary: opposite

starveling: starving, undernourished

plashy: marshy, wet

tramp: firm, heavy tread

of the bridge caught the sensitive ear of Ichabod. In the dark shadow of the grove, on the margin of the brook, he beheld something huge, misshapen, black and towering. It stirred not, but seemed gathered up in the gloom, like some gigantic monster ready to spring upon the traveller.

The hair of the affrighted pedagogue rose upon his head with terror. What was to be done? To turn and fly was now too late; and besides, what chance was there of escaping ghost or goblin, if such it was, which could ride upon the wings of the wind? Summoning up, therefore, a show of courage, he demanded in stammering accents—"Who are you?" He received no reply. He repeated his demand in a still more agitated voice. Still there was no answer. Once more he cudgelled° the sides of the inflexible Gunpowder, and, shutting his eyes, broke forth with involuntary fervor into a psalm tune. Just then the shadowy object of alarm put itself in motion, and, with a scramble and a bound, stood at once in the middle of the road. Though the night was dark and dismal, yet the form of the unknown might now in some degree be ascertained. He appeared to be a horseman of large dimensions, and mounted on a black horse of powerful frame. He made no offer of molestation° or sociability, but kept aloof on one side of the road, jogging along on the blind side of old Gunpowder, who had now got over his fright and waywardness.

Ichabod, who had no relish for this strange midnight companion, and bethought himself of the adventure of Brom Bones with the Galloping Hessian, now quickened his steed, in hopes of leaving him behind. The stranger, however, quickened his horse to an equal pace. Ichabod pulled up, and fell into a walk, thinking to lag behind—the other did the same. His heart began to sink within him; he endeavored to resume his psalm tune, but his parched tongue clove to the roof of his mouth, and he could not utter a stave.° There was something in the moody and dogged silence of this pertinacious° companion, that was mysterious and appalling. It was soon fearfully accounted for. On mounting a rising ground, which brought the figure of his fellow-traveller in relief against the sky, gigantic in height, and muffled in a cloak, Ichabod was horror-struck, on perceiving that he was headless!—but his horror was still more increased, on observing that the head, which should have rested on his shoulders, was carried before him on the pommel of the saddle: his terror rose to desperation;

---

cudgelled: beat

molestation: assault, injury

stave: verse, stanza

pertinacious: persistent, tenacious

he rained a shower of kicks and blows upon Gunpowder, hoping, by a sudden movement, to give his companion the slip—but the spectre started full jump with him. Away then they dashed, through thick and thin; stones flying, and sparks flashing at every bound. Ichabod's flimsy garments fluttered in the air, as he stretched his long lank body away over his horse's head, in the eagerness of his flight.

They had now reached the road which turns off to Sleepy Hollow; but Gunpowder, who seemed possessed with a demon, instead of keeping up it, made an opposite turn, and plunged headlong down hill to the left. This road leads through a sandy hollow, shaded by trees for about a quarter of a mile, where it crosses the bridge famous in goblin story, and just beyond swells the green knoll on which stands the whitewashed church.

As yet the panic of the steed had given his unskillful rider an apparent advantage in the chase; but just as he had got half way through the hollow, the girths° of the saddle gave way, and he felt it slipping from under him. He seized it by the pommel, and endeavored to hold it firm, but in vain; and had just time to save himself by clasping old Gunpowder round the neck, when the saddle fell to the earth, and he heard it trampled under foot by his pursuer. For a moment the terror of Hans Van Ripper's wrath passed across his mind—for it was his Sunday saddle; but this was no time for petty fears; the goblin was hard on his haunches; and (unskillful rider that he was!) he had much ado to maintain his seat; sometimes slipping on one side, sometimes on another, and sometimes jolted on the high ridge of his horse's back-bone, with a violence that he verily feared would cleave him asunder.°

65 An opening in the trees now cheered him with the hopes that the church bridge was at hand. The wavering reflection of a silver star in the bosom of the brook told him that he was not mistaken. He saw the walls of the church dimly glaring under the trees beyond. He recollected the place where Brom Bones's ghostly competitor had disappeared. "If I can but reach that bridge," thought Ichabod, "I am safe." Just then he heard the black steed panting and blowing close behind him; he even fancied that he felt his hot breath. Another convulsive kick in the ribs, and old Gunpowder sprang upon the bridge; he thundered over the resounding planks; he gained the opposite side; and now Ichabod cast a look behind to see if his pursuer should vanish, according to rule, in a flash of fire and brimstone. Just then he saw the goblin rising in his stirrups, and in the very act of hurling his head at

---

girths: bands around a horse's belly that hold the saddle in position

cleave him asunder: split him apart

him. Ichabod endeavored to dodge the horrible missile, but too late. It encountered his cranium with a tremendous crash—he was tumbled headlong into the dust, and Gunpowder, the black steed, and the goblin rider, passed by like a whirlwind.

The next morning the old horse was found without his saddle, and with the bridle under his feet, soberly cropping° the grass at his master's gate. Ichabod did not make his appearance at breakfast—dinner-hour came, but no Ichabod. The boys assembled at the school-house, and strolled idly about the banks of the brook; but no schoolmaster. Hans Van Ripper now began to feel some uneasiness about the fate of poor Ichabod, and his saddle. An inquiry was set on foot, and after diligent investigation they came upon his traces. In one part of the road leading to the church was found the saddle trampled in the dirt; the tracks of horses' hoofs deeply dented in the road, and evidently at furious speed, were traced to the bridge, beyond which, on the bank of a broad part of the brook, where the water ran deep and black, was found the hat of the unfortunate Ichabod, and close beside it a shattered pumpkin.

The brook was searched, but the body of the schoolmaster was not to be discovered. Hans Van Ripper, as executor of his estate, examined the bundle which contained all his worldly effects. They consisted of two shirts and a half; two stocks for the neck; a pair or two of worsted° stockings; an old pair of corduroy small-clothes;° a rusty razor; a book of psalm tunes, full of dogs' ears;° and a broken pitchpipe. As to the books and furniture of the school-house, they belonged to the community, excepting Cotton Mather's History of Witchcraft, a New England Almanac, and a book of dreams and fortune-telling; in which last was a sheet of foolscap° much scribbled and blotted in several fruitless attempts to make a copy of verses in honor of the heiress of Van Tassel. These magic books and the poetic scrawl were forthwith consigned to the flames by Hans Van Ripper; who from that time forward determined to send his children no more to school; observing, that he never knew any good come of this same reading and writing. Whatever money the school-master possessed, and he had received his quarter's pay but a day or two before, he must have had about his person at the time of his disappearance.

---

cropping: biting off the tops or ends of; grazing on

worsted: wool cloth woven from twisted yarn or threads

small-clothes: knee breeches

dogs' ears: turned-down page corners

foolscap: inexpensive legal-sized writing paper

The mysterious event caused much speculation at the church on the following Sunday. Knots of gazers and gossips were collected in the church-yard, at the bridge, and at the spot where the hat and pumpkin had been found. The stories of Brouwer, of Bones, and a whole budget° of others, were called to mind; and when they had diligently considered them all, and compared them with the symptoms of the present case, they shook their heads, and came to the conclusion that Ichabod had been carried off by the galloping Hessian. As he was a bachelor, and in nobody's debt, nobody troubled his head any more about him. The school was removed to a different quarter of the hollow, and another pedagogue reigned in his stead.

It is true, an old farmer, who had been down to New York on a visit several years after, and from whom this account of the ghostly adventure was received, brought home the intelligence° that Ichabod Crane was still alive; that he had left the neighborhood, partly through fear of the goblin and Hans Van Ripper, and partly in mortification at having been suddenly dismissed by the heiress; that he had changed his quarters to a distant part of the country; had kept school and studied law at the same time, had been admitted to the bar, turned politician, electioneered, written for the newspapers, and finally had been made a justice of the Ten Pound Court.° Brom Bones too, who shortly after his rival's disappearance conducted the blooming Katrina in triumph to the altar, was observed to look exceedingly knowing whenever the story of Ichabod was related, and always burst into a hearty laugh at the mention of the pumpkin; which led some to suspect that he knew more about the matter than he chose to tell.

70

The old country wives, however, who are the best judges of these matters, maintain to this day that Ichabod was spirited away by supernatural means; and it is a favorite story often told about the neighborhood round the winter evening fire. The bridge became more than ever an object of superstitious awe, and that may be the reason why the road has been altered of late years, so as to approach the church by the border of the mill-pond. The school-house being deserted, soon fell to decay, and was reported to be haunted by the ghost of the unfortunate pedagogue; and the ploughboy, loitering homeward of a still summer evening, has often fancied his voice at a distance, chanting a melancholy psalm tune among the tranquil solitudes of Sleepy Hollow.

---

budget: quantity

intelligence: information, news

Ten Pound Court: small claims court (for disputes involving sums or goods worth ten pounds or less)

Postscript

Found in the Handwriting of Mr. Knickerbocker

THE preceding Tale is given, almost in the precise words in which I heard it related at a Corporation° meeting of the ancient city of the Manhattoes,° at which were present many of its sagest and most illustrious burghers.° The narrator was a pleasant, shabby, gentlemanly old fellow in pepper-and-salt clothes, with a sadly humorous face; and one whom I strongly suspected of being poor—he made such efforts to be entertaining. When his story was concluded there was much laughter and approbation,° particularly from two or three deputy aldermen,° who had been asleep the greater part of the time. There was, however, one tall, dry-looking old gentleman, with beetling eyebrows, who maintained a grave and rather severe face throughout; now and then folding his arms, inclining his head, and looking down upon the floor, as if turning a doubt over in his mind. He was one of your wary° men, who never laugh but upon good grounds—when they have reason and the law on their side. When the mirth of the rest of the company had subsided, and silence was restored, he leaned one arm on the elbow of his chair, and sticking the other akimbo,° demanded, with a slight but exceedingly sage motion of the head and contraction of the brow, what was the moral of the story, and what it went to prove.

The story-teller, who was just putting a glass of wine to his lips, as a refreshment after his toils, paused for a moment, looked at his inquirer with an air of infinite deference, and lowering the glass slowly to the table, observed that the story was intended most logically to prove:

"That there is no situation in life but has its advantages and pleasures—provided we will but take a joke as we find it;

"That, therefore, he that runs races with goblin troopers is likely to have rough riding of it;

"Ergo, for a country schoolmaster to be refused the hand of a Dutch heiress is a certain step to high preferment° in the State."

Corporation: the municipal authorities of a city or town
Manhattoes: Manhattan, New York City
burghers: town-dwellers, especially of the middle class; citizens
approbation: approval
aldermen: members of a municipal council
wary: cautious, watchful
akimbo: hand on hip and elbow bent outward
preferment: advancement or promotion

The cautious old gentleman knit his brows tenfold closer after this explanation, being sorely puzzled by the ratiocination° of the syllogism;° while, me-thought, the one in pepper-and-salt eyed him with something of a triumphant leer. At length he observed, that all this was very well, but still he thought the story a little on the extravagant—there were one or two points on which he had his doubts:

"Faith, sir," replied the story-teller, "as to that matter, I don't believe one-half of it myself."

D.K.

[1819]

Read

1. How does the perspective of the speaker of the story heighten the comic effect?
2. Where do you hear the speaker express an attitude toward his characters, especially the teacher Icabod Crane?
3. What effect does the humor have on the legend?
4. What does the tale reveal about daily life in the countryside in the eighteenth century?
5. Where is the story frightening? How does Irving use detail to create a thrill of fear in the reader?

Write

1. Write a sentence that describes the moral of the tale. Then use one example from the story to prove your point.
2. Comment on Icabod's relationship to the community and his students.
3. Have you read or seen any remakes of the story? Reflect on how more recent depictions (the Disney cartoon; the Johnny Depp movie) compare to the story you've read.
4. What does a "legend," a passed-down story, do for the people who pass it down and for those who hear it?

Connect

1. Write or talk about school or family stories that function as legends.
2. Find a text in Unit 1 or this unit where there's a conflict between an outsider and the community. How do situations, consequences and characters connect to "The Legend of Sleepy Hollow"? (Samson Occom's narrative makes a good comparison.)

---

ratiocination: process of logical reasoning

syllogism: piece of deductive reasoning

Meriwether Lewis and William Clark

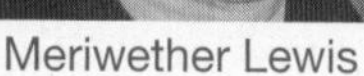

Meriwether Lewis

William Clark

Meriwether Lewis (1774–1809) and William Clark (1770–1838) led the famed expedition of the Corps of Discovery across the continent to reach the Pacific Ocean. They set out from Louisville in 1803 and traveled up the Missouri to what is now North Dakota to winter over with the Mandan tribe. They reached the Pacific in early 1806.

Meriwether Lewis was born in Virginia, the son of a Revolutionary War officer. He served in the Army, where he met William Clark. When Thomas Jefferson proposed the Western expedition Lewis's experience on the frontier and his study of routes and topography made him a natural choice to lead. After the expedition, Jefferson made him governor of the Louisiana Territory in 1808. He died the next year.

William Clark was a Virginian as well, the brother of Revolutionary War hero George Rogers Clark. He moved with his family to Kentucky and learned map drawing and navigating the wilderness. His journal entries show him interested in the Indians the Corps encountered, and his understanding of the vital role tribal people like the Shoshone guide Sacajawea played in the success of the expedition served him well in later years as Supervisor of Indian Affairs and Governor of the Missouri Territory. He named his son Meriwether Lewis Clark in honor of his friend and co-explorer.

From *Journal of the Expedition*

[Clark] 24th (23) of March Satturday 1805

after Brackfast Mr. La Rocke and Mr. McKinsey and the Cheifs & men of the Minetarras leave us. in the fore part in the evening a little rain & the first this winter.

25th (24th) of March Sunday 1805—

Saw Swans & Wild Gees flying N.E. this evening.

26th (25th) of March Monday 1805—

but fiew Inds. Visit us to day the Ice haveing broken up in Several places, The ice began to brake away this evening and was near destroying our Canoes as they were dec[e]nding to the fort,

30th (29) of March Sunday (Friday) 1805—

I observed extrodanary dexterity of the Indians in jumping from one cake of ice to another, for the purpose of Catching the buffalo as they float down many of the cakes of ice which they pass over are not two feet square. The Plains are on fire in View of the fort on both Sides of the River,

31st (30th) Saturday of March Monday— (Saturday) (Sunday) 1805—

all the party in high Sperits they pass but fiew nights without amuseing themselves danceing possessing perfect harmony and good understanding towards each other, Generally helthy except Venerials Complaints which is verry Common amongst the natives and the men Catch it from them

April the 3rd Thursday (Wednesday) 1805—

Mrs. La Rocke & McKinsey Clerk to the NW. Compy. Visit us. We are all day engaged packing up Sundery° articles to be sent to President of the U.S.

[Lewis] Fort Mandan April 7th. 1805.

Having on this day at 4. P.M. completed every arrangement necessary for our departure, we dismissed the barge and crew with orders to return without loss of time to St. Louis, a small canoe with two French hunters accompanyed the barge; these men had assended the missouri with us the last year as engages.° The barge crew consisted of six soldiers and two [blank space in MS.] Frenchmen; two Frenchmen and a Ricara Indian also take their passage in her as far as the Ricara Vilages, at which place we expect Mr. Tiebeau to embark with his peltry° who in that case will make an addition of two, perhaps four men to the crew of the barge. We gave Richard Warfington, a discharged Corpl., the charge of the Barge and crew, and confided to his care likewise our dispatches to the government, letters to our private friends and a number of articles to the President of the United States. One of the Frenchmen by the Name of Gravline an honest discrete man and an excellent boat-man is imployed to conduct the barge as a pilot; we have therefore every hope that the barge and with her our dispatches will arrive safe at St. Louis. Mr. Gravlin who speaks the Ricara language extreemly well, has been imployed to conduct a few of the Recara Chiefs to the seat of government who have promised us to decend in the barge to St: Liwis with that view.

Sundery: sundry (various)
engages: volunteers (from French, *engagé*)
peltry: collection of pelts

At the same moment that the Barge departed from Fort Mandan, Capt. Clark emba[r]ked with our party and proceeded up the River. as I had used no exercise for several weeks, I determined to walk on shore as far as our encampment of this evening.

Our vessels consisted of six small canoes, and two large perogues. This little fleet altho' not quite so rispectable as those of Columbus or Capt. Cook, were still viewed by us with as much pleasure as those deservedly famed adventurers ever beheld theirs; and I dare say with quite as much anxiety for their safety and preservation. we were now about to penetrate a country at least two thousand miles in width, on which the foot of civilized man had never trodden; the good or evil it had in store for us Was for experiment yet to determine, and these little vessells contained every article by which we were to expect to subsist or defend ourselves. However as the state of mind in which we are, generally gives the colouring to events, when the immagination is suffered to wander into futurity, the picture which now presented itself to me was a most pleasing one. enterta[in]ing as I do, the most confident hope of succeeding in a voyage which had formed a da[r]ling° project of mine for the last ten years, I could but esteem this moment of departure as among the most happy of my life. The party are in excellent health and sperits, zealously attached to the enterprise and anxious to proceed; not a whisper of murmur or discontent to be heard among them, but all act in unison, and with the most perfict harmony. Capt. Clark myself the two Interpretters and the woman and child sleep in a tent of dressed skins. this tent is in the Indian stile, formed of a number of dressed Buffaloe skins sewed together with sinues.° it is cut in such manner that when foalded double it forms the quarter of a circle, and is left open at one side here it may be attatched or loosened at pleasure by strings which are sewed to its sides for the purpose.

[Clark] Fort Mandan April 7th 1805.

(Sunday) at 4 oClock PM, the Boat, in which was 6 Soldiers 2 frenchmen & an Indian, all under the command of a corporal who, had the charge of dispatches, &c.—and a canoe with 2 french men, set out down the river for St. Louis. at the same time we Sout out on our voyage up the river in 2 perogues° and 6 canoes, and proceded on to the 1st villag. of Mandans & camped on the S.S. our party consisting of Sergts. Nathaniel Pryor, John 10

da[r]ling: favorite
sinues: sinews (tendons)
perogues: pirogues (dugout canoes)

Ordway, Patrick Gass, Pvts. William Bratton, John Colter, Joseph and Reuben Fields, John Shields, George Gibson, George Shannon, John Potts, John Collins, Joseph Whitehouse, Richard Windsor, Alexander Willard, Hugh Hall, Silas Goodrich, Robert Frazier, Peter Cruzatte, Baptiste Lepage, Francis Labiche, Hugh McNeal, William Werner, Thomas P. Howard, Peter Wiser, John B. Thompson and my servent York, George Drewyer who acts as a hunter & interpreter, Charbonneau and his Indian Squar to act as an Interpreter & interpretress for the snake Indians—one Mandan & Charbonneau's infant.

[Lewis] Tuesday April 9th

when we halted for dinner the squaw busied herself in serching for the wild artichokes which the mice collect and deposit in large hoards. this operation she performed by penetrating the earth with a sharp stick about some small collections of drift wood. Her labour soon proved successful, and she procured a good quantity of these roots. the flavor of this root resembles that of the Jerusalem Artichoke, and the stalk of the weed which produces it is also similar,

[Clark] 9th of April Tuesday 1805.—

I saw a Musquetor° to day great numbers of Brant° flying up the river, the Maple, & Elm has buded & cotton and arrow wood beginning to bud. But fiew resident birds or water fowls which I have Seen as yet Saw Great numbers of Gees° feedin in the Praries on the young grass, I saw flowers in the praries to day, juniper grows on the Sides of the hills, & runs on the ground

[Lewis] Wednesday April 10th 1805.

at the distance of 12 miles from our encampment of last night we arrived at the lower point of a bluff on the Lard° side; about 1½ miles down this bluff from this point, the bluff is now on fire and throws out considerable quantities of smoke which has a strong sulphurious smell at 1. P.M. we overtook three french hunters who had set out a few days before us with a view of traping beaver; they had taken 12 since they left Fort Mandan. these people avail themselves of the protection which our numbers will enable us to give them against the Assinniboins who sometimes hunt on the Missouri; and intend ascending with us as far as the mouth of the Yellow stone river

---

Musquetor: mosquito
Brant: small dark-colored geese
Gees: geese
Lard: leeward

and continue there hunt up that river. this is the first essay° of a beaver hunter of any discription on this river [above the villages]. the beaver these people have already taken is by far the best I have ever seen.

[Lewis] Saturday April 13th

The wind was in our favour after 9 A.M. and continued favourable untill three 3. P.M. we therefore hoisted both the sails in the White Perogue, consisting of a small squar sail, and spritsail, which carried her at a pretty good gate,° untill about 2 in the afternoon when a sudden squall of wind struck us and turned the perogue so much on the side as to allarm Sharbono who was steering at the time, in this state of alarm he threw the pirogue with her side to the wind, when the spritsail gibing° was as near overseting the perogue as it was possible to have missed. the wind however abating for an instant I ordered Drewyer to the helm and the sails to be taken in, which was instant executed and the pirogue being steered before the wind was agin plased in a state of security. this accedent was very near costing us dearly. beleiving this vessel to be the most steady and safe, we had embarked on board of it our instruments, Papers, medicine and the most valuable part of the merchandize which we had still in reserve as presents for the Indians. we had also embarked on board ourselves, with three men who could not swim and the squaw with the young child, all of whom, had the perogue overset,° would most probably have perished, as the waves were high, and the perogue upwards of 200 yards from the nearest shore; just above the entrance of the little Missouri the great Missouri is upwards of a mile in width, tho' immediately at the entrance of the former it is not more than 200 yards wide and so shallow that the canoes passed it with seting poles.

we found a number of carcases of the Buffaloe lying along shore, which had been drowned by falling through the ice in winter and lodged on shore by the high water when the river broke up about the first of this month. We saw also many tracks of the white bear of enormous size, along the river shore and about the carcases of the Buffaloe, on which I presume they feed. we have not as yet seen one of these anamals, tho' their tracks are so abundant and recent. the men as well as ourselves are anxious to meet with some of these bear. 15

---

essay: attempt, endeavor
gate: gait, pace
gibing: jibing (shifting side to side before the wind)
overset: overturned

the Indians give a very formidable account of the strength and ferocity of this anamal, which they never dare to attack but in parties of six eight or ten persons; and are even then frequently defeated with the loss of one or more of their party. The savages attack this anamal with their bows and arrows and the indifferent° guns with which the traders furnish them, with these they shoot with such uncertainty and at so short a distance, that (*unless shot thro' head or heart wound not mortal*) they frequently mis their aim & fall a sacrefice to the bear. this anamall is said more frequently to attack a man on meeting with him, than to flee from him. When the Indians are about to go in quest of the white bear, previous to their departure, they paint themselves and perform all those supersticious rights° commonly observed when they are about to make war uppon a neighbouring nation. Oserved more bald eagles on this part of the Missouri than we have previously seen. saw the small hawk, frequently called the sparrow hawk, which is common to most parts of the U. States. Great quantities of gees are seen feeding in the praries. saw a large flock of white brant or gees with black wings pass up the river; there were a number of gray brant with them.

Sunday April 14th 1805.

where the land is level, it is uniformly fertile consisting of a dark loam intermixed with a proportion of fine sand. it is generally covered with a short grass resembling very much the blue grass. the miniral appearances still continue; considerable quantities of bitumenous water, about the colour of strong lye trickles down the sides of the hills; this water partakes of the taste of glauber salts° and slightly of allumn. while the party halted to take dinner today Capt. Clark killed a buffaloe bull; it was meagre, and therefore took the marrow bones and a small proportion of the meat only. Passed an Island, above which two small creeks fall on the Lard. Side; the upper creek largest, which we called Sharbono's Creek, after our interpreter who encamped several weeks on It with a hunting party of Indians. this was the highest to which any whiteman had ever ascended, except two Frenchmen (one of whom Lapage was now with us) who having lost their way had straggled a few miles further tho' to what place precisely I could not learn.

---

indifferent: of poor or mediocre quality, inferior

rights: rites

glauber salts: water-soluble sodium sulfate crystals used as a laxative

[Clark] 18th of April Thursday 1805

after brackfast I assended a hill and observed that the river made a great bend to the South, I concluded to walk thro' the point about 2 miles and take Shabono, with me, he had taken a dost of Salts &c. his squar° followed on with her child, when I struck the next bend of the [river] could see nothing of the Party, left this man & his wife & child on the river bank and went out to hunt, Killed a young Buck Elk, & a Deer, the Elk was tolerable meat, the Deer verry pore, Butchered the meat and continued untill near Sunset before Capt Lewis and the party came up, they were detained by the wind, which rose soon after I left the boat from the N W. & blew verry hard untill verry late in the evening. Saw several old Indian camps, the game, such as Buffalow Elk, antelopes & Deer verry plenty

19th of April Friday 1805

the wind so hard from the N.W. that we were fearfull of ventering° our Canoes in the river, lay by all day on the S. Side in a good harber, the Praries appear to Green, the cotton trees bigin to leave, Saw some plumb bushes in full bloom, The beaver of this river is much larger than usual, Great deal of Sign of the large Bear,

20th of April Satturday 1805

we set out at 7 oClock proceeded on Soon after we set out a Bank fell in near one of the canoes which like to have filled her with water, the wind became hard and waves so rough that we proceeded with our little canoes with much risque, Our situation was such after setting out that we were obliged to pass round the 1st Point or lay exposed to the blustering winds & waves, in passing round the Point several canoes took in water as also our large Perogue but without injuring our stores &c. much a short distance below our Camp I saw some rafts on the S. S. near which, an Indian woman was scaffeled° in the Indian form of Deposing their Dead and fallen down She was or had been raised about 6 feet, inclosed in Several robes tightly laced around her, with her dog Slays,° her bag of Different coloured earths paint small bones of animals beaver nales and Several other little trinkets, also

---

squar: squaw
ventering: venturing
scaffeled: scaffolded
Slays: sleighs

a blue jay, her dog was killed and lay near her. Capt. Lewis joined me soon after I landed & informed me he had walked several miles higher, & in his walk killed 2 Deer & wounded an Elk & a Deer, our party shot in the river four beaver & cought two, which were verry fat and much admired by the men, after we landed they killed 3 Elk 4 Gees & 2 Deer we had some of our Provisions &c. which got a little wet aired, the wind continued so hard that we were compelled to delay all day. Saw several buffalow lodged in the drift wood which had been drouned in the winter in passing the river.

[Lewis] Monday April 22nd 1805.

Set out at an early hour this morning; proceeded pretty well untill breakfat, when the wind became so hard a head that we proceeded with difficulty even with the assistance of our toe° lines. the party halted and Cpt. Clark and myself walked to the white earth river which approaches the Missouri very near at this place, being about 4 miles above it's entrance. we found that it contained more water than streams of it's size generally do at this season. the water is much clearer than that of the Missouri. the banks of the river are steep and not more than ten or twelve feet high; the bed seems to be composed of mud altogether. the salts [alkali] which have been before mentioned as common on the Missouri, appears in great quantities along the banks of this river, which are in many places so thickly covered with it that they appear perfectly white. perhaps it has been from this white appearance of it's banks that the river has derived it's name. this river is said to be navigable nearly to it's source, which is at no great distance from the Saskashawan, and I think from it's size the direction which it seems to take, and the latitude of it's mouth, that there is very good ground to believe that it extends as far North as latitude 50° — this stream passes through an open country generally.

Coal or carbonated wood pumice stone lava and other mineral apearances still continue. the coal appears to be of better quality; I exposed a specimen of it to the fire and found that it birnt tolerably well, it afforded but little flame or smoke, but produced a hot and lasting fire. I asscended to the top of the cutt bluff this morning, from whence I had a most delightfull view of the country, the whole of which except the vally formed by the Missouri is void of timber or underbrush, exposing to the first glance of the spectator immence herds of Buffaloe, Elk, deer, & Antelopes feeding in one common and boundless pasture. we saw a number of bever feeding on the

---

toe: tow

bark of the trees alonge the verge of the river, several of which we shot, found them large and fat. walking on shore this evening I met with a buffaloe calf which attatched itself to me and continued to follow close at my heels untill I embarked and left it. it appeared allanned at my dog which was probably the cause of it's so readily attatching itself to me. Capt Clark informed me that he saw a large drove of buffaloe pursued by wolves today, that they at length caught a calf which was unable to keep up with the herd. the cows only defend their young so long as they are able to keep up with the herd, and seldom return any distance in surch of them.

Thursday April 25th 1805.

the water friezed on the oars this morning as the men rowed. about 10 oclock A.M. the wind began to blow so violently that we were obliged to lye too.° my dog had been absent during the last night, and I was fearfull we had lost him altogether, however, much to my satisfaction he joined us at 8 oclock this morning. Knowing that the river was crooked, from the report of the hunters who were out yesterday, and beleiving that we were at no very great distance from the Yellow stone River; I determined, in order as mush as possible to avoid detention,° to proceed by land with a few men to the entrance of that river and make the necessary observations to determine its position; accordingly I set out at 11 OCk. on the Lard. side, accompanyed by four men. when we had proceeded about four miles, I ascended the hills from whence I had a most pleasing view of the country, particularly of the wide and fertile vallies formed by the missouri and the Yellowstone rivers, which occasionally unmasked by the wood on their borders disclose their meanderings for many miles in their passage through these delightfull tracts of country. I determined to encamp on the bank of the Yellow stone river which made it's appearance about 2 miles South of me. the whol face of the country was covered with herds of Buffaloe, Elk & Antelopes; deer are also abundant, but keep themselves more concealed in the woodland, the buffaloe Elk and Antelope are so gentle that we pass near them while feeding, without appearing to excite any alarm among them; and when we attract their attention, they frequently approach us more nearly to discover what we are, and in some instances pursue us a considerable distance apparenly with that view. we encamped on the bank of the yellow stone river, 2 miles South of it's confluence with the Missouri.

---

lye too: lie to (remain stationary, with reference to a ship)
detention: being detained, forced delay

Read

1. How would you characterize the difference in details of observations in the entries of each man?
2. What do the journal entries reveal about the land they were encountering?
3. How do you see the explorers' attitudes toward the Indians?
4. What does the language demonstrate about the purpose of the record the men keep?

Write

1. In a paragraph, reflect on the purpose of the journey for Lewis or Clark as it's revealed in the men's journal entries.
2. Go online and find any images used by either of the men in the journal. Analyze how they help the reader understand the scene or the situation.
3. Write a sentence or two that speculates on who the audience for the journal might be.

Complete Additional Exercises on Lewis and Clark's Journal at Your Pearson MyLab

Connect

1. How might the Lewis and Clark journey remind you of Rowlandson's narrative? What are some differences?
2. Compare Lewis and Clark's depiction of the Indians they encounter with the characters or personae as you've understood them in two of the texts written by American Indians themselves.
3. How would Red Jacket react to the Lewis and Clark journey?

James Fenimore Cooper

James Fenimore Cooper (1789–1851) wrote popular stories and novels that could be called the first Westerns, although he never lived on the frontier. Raised in a rural setting in Cooperstown, New York, he seldom came in touch with Indians. But Leatherstocking, or Natty Bumppo, is the archetype of a Western cowboy hero and Chingachook, Leatherstocking's Mohican companion, is the archetype of the Western's loyal sidekick. Cooper was a seaman before he began writing the novels that would make him wealthy and world famous. His early novel *Spy* (1821) appealed to readers for its American setting and familiar events. *The Pioneers* (1823) was an immediate bestseller and was the first of five Leatherstocking Tales. Others are *The Last of the Mohicans* (1826), *The Prairie* (1827), *Pathfinder* (1840), and *Deerslayer* (1842). In all, Cooper wrote thirty-six novels as well as history and essays. Later criticized for stock plots and sentimental storylines, he was a pioneer in the development of American fiction.

The Slaughter of the Pigeons

From *The Pioneers*

From this time to the close of April, the weather continued to be a succession of great and rapid changes. One day, the soft airs of spring seemed to be stealing along the valley, and, in unison with an invigorating sun, attempting, covertly, to rouse the dormant powers of the vegetable world; while on the next, the surly blasts from the north would sweep across the lake, and erase every impression left by their gentle adversaries. The snow, however, finally disappeared, and the green wheat fields were seen in every direction, spotted with the dark and charred stumps that had, the preceding season, supported some of the proudest trees of the forest. Ploughs were in motion, wherever those useful implements could be used, and the smokes of the sugar-camps were no longer seen issuing from the woods of maple. The lake had lost the beauty of a field of ice, but still a dark and gloomy covering concealed its waters, for the absence of currents left them yet hid under a porous crust, which, saturated with the fluid, barely retained enough strength to preserve the contiguity of its parts. Large flocks of wild geese were seen passing over the country, which hovered, for a time, around the hidden sheet of water, apparently searching for a resting-place; and then, on finding themselves excluded by the chill covering, would soar away to the north, filling the air with discordant screams, as if venting their complaints at the tardy operations of nature.

For a week, the dark covering of the Otsego° was left to the undisturbed possession of two eagles, who alighted on the centre of its field, and sat eyeing their undisputed territory. During the presence of these monarchs of the air, the flocks of migrating birds avoided crossing the plain of ice, by turning into the hills, apparently seeking the protection of the forests, while the white and bald heads of the tenants of the lake were turned upward, with a look of contempt. But the time had come, when even these kings of birds were to be dispossessed. An opening had been gradually increasing, at the lower extremity of the lake, and around the dark spot where the current of the river prevented the formation of ice, during even the coldest weather; and the fresh southerly winds, that now breathed freely upon the valley, made an impression on the waters. Mimic waves begun to curl over the margin of the frozen field, which exhibited an outline of

Otsego: a small lake next to Cooperstown in upstate New York

crystallizations, that slowly receded towards the north. At each step the power of the winds and the waves increased, until, after a struggle of a few hours, the turbulent little billows succeeded in setting the whole field in motion, when it was driven beyond the reach of the eye, with a rapidity, that was as magical as the change produced in the scene by this expulsion of the lingering remnant of winter. Just as the last sheet of agitated ice was disappearing in the distance, the eagles rose, and soared with a wide sweep above the clouds, while the waves tossed their little caps of snow into the air, as if rioting° in their release from a thraldom° of five months' duration.

The following morning Elizabeth was awakened by the exhilarating sounds of the martens,° who were quarreling and chattering around the little boxes suspended above her windows, and the cries of Richard, who was calling, in tones animating as the signs of the season itself—

"Awake! awake! my fair lady! the gulls are hovering over the lake already, and the heavens are alive with pigeons. You may look an hour before you can find a hole, through which, to get a peep at the sun. Awake! awake! lazy ones! Benjamin is overhauling the ammunition, and we only wait for our breakfasts, and away for the mountains and pigeon-shooting."

There was no resisting this animated appeal, and in a few minutes Miss Temple and her friend descended to the parlour. The doors of the hall were thrown open, and the mild, balmy air of a clear spring morning was ventilating the apartment, where the vigilance of the ex-steward had been so long maintaining an artificial heat, with such unremitted diligence. The gentlemen were impatiently waiting for their morning's repast, each equipt in the garb of a sportsman. Mr. Jones made many visits to the southern door, and would cry— 5

"See, cousin Bess! see, 'Duke! the pigeon-roosts of the south have broken up! They are growing more thick every instant. Here is a flock that the eye cannot see the end of. There is food enough in it to keep the army of Xerxes for a month, and feathers enough to make beds for the whole country. Xerxes, Mr. Edwards, was a Grecian king, who—no, he was a Turk, or a Persian, who wanted to conquer Greece, just the same as these rascals will overrun our wheat-fields, when they come back in the fall. ——— Away! away! Bess; I long to pepper° them."

In this wish both Marmaduke and young Edwards seemed equally to participate, for the sight was exhilarating to a sportsman; and the ladies soon dismissed the party, after a hasty breakfast.

---

rioting: indulging in unrestrained revelry

thraldom: bondage, slavery

martens: weasel-like mammals, prized for their fur

pepper: i.e., with shot

If the heavens were alive with pigeons, the whole village seemed equally in motion, with men, women, and children. Every species of firearms, from the French duckinggun, with a barrel near six feet in length, to the common horseman's pistol, was to be seen in the hands of the men and boys; while bows and arrows, some made of the simple stick of a walnut sapling, and others in a rude imitation of the ancient cross-bows, were carried by many of the latter.

The houses, and the signs of life apparent in the village, drove the alarmed birds from the direct line of their flight, towards the mountains, along the sides and near the bases of which they were glancing in dense masses, equally wonderful° by the rapidity of their motion, and their incredible numbers.

10 We have already said, that across the inclined plane which fell from the steep ascent of the mountain to the banks of the Susquehanna, ran the highway, on either side of which a clearing of many acres had been made, at a very early day. Over those clearings, and up the eastern mountain, and along the dangerous path that was cut into its side, the different individuals posted themselves, and in a few moments the attack commenced.

Amongst the sportsmen was the tall, gaunt form of Leather-Stocking, walking over the field, with his rifle hanging on his arm, his dogs at his heels; the latter now scenting the dead or wounded birds, that were beginning to tumble from the flocks, and then crouching under the legs of their master, as if they participated in his feelings, at this wasteful and unsportsmanlike execution.

The reports° of the firearms became rapid, whole volleys rising from the plain, as flocks of more than ordinary numbers darted over the opening, shadowing the field, like a cloud; and then the light smoke of a single piece° would issue from among the leafless bushes on the mountain, as death was hurled on the retreat of the affrighted birds, who were rising from a volley, in a vain effort to escape. Arrows, and missiles of every kind, were in the midst of the flocks; and so numerous were the birds, and so low did they take their flight, that even long poles, in the hands of those on the sides of the mountain, were used to strike them to the earth.

During all this time, Mr. Jones, who disdained the humble and ordinary means of destruction used by his companions, was busily occupied, aided by Benjamin, in making arrangements for an assault of a more than ordinarily fatal character. Among the relics of the old military excursions,° that occasionally are discovered throughout the

---

wonderful: amazing, astonishing
reports: loud noises
piece: firearm
excursions: attacks, raids

different districts of the western part of New-York, there had been found in Templeton, at its settlement, a small swivel,° which would carry a ball of a pound weight. It was thought to have been deserted by a war-party of the whites, in one of their inroads into the Indian settlements, when, perhaps, convenience or their necessity induced them to leave such an encumbrance behind them in the woods. This miniature cannon had been released from the rust, and being mounted on little wheels, was now in a state for actual service. For several years, it was the sole organ° for extraordinary rejoicings used in those mountains. On the mornings of the Fourths of July, it would be heard ringing among the hills, and even Captain Hollister, who was the highest authority in that part of the country on all such occasions, affirmed that, considering its dimensions, it was no despicable gun for a salute. It was somewhat the worse for the service it had performed, it is true, there being but a trifling difference in size between the touch-hole and the muzzle. Still, the grand conceptions of Richard had suggested the importance of such an instrument, in hurling death at his nimble enemies. The swivel was dragged by a horse into a part of the open space, that the Sheriff thought most eligible for planting a battery of the kind, and Mr. Pump proceeded to load it. Several handfuls of duck-shot were placed on top of the powder, and the Major-domo° announced that his piece was ready for service.

The sight of such an implement collected all the idle spectators to the spot, who, being mostly boys, filled the air with cries of exultation and delight. The gun was pointed high, and Richard, holding a coal of fire in a pair of tongs, patiently took his seat on a stump, awaiting the appearance of a flock worthy of his notice.

So prodigious was the number of the birds, that the scattering fire of the guns, with the hurling of missiles, and the cries of the boys, had no other effect than to break off small flocks from the immense masses that continued to dart along the valley, as if the whole of the feathered tribe were pouring through that one pass. None pretended to collect the game, which lay scattered over the fields in such profusion, as to cover the very ground with the fluttering victims. 15

Leather-Stocking was a silent, but uneasy spectator of all these proceedings, but was able to keep his sentiments to himself until he saw the introduction of the swivel into the sports.

"This comes of settling a country!" he said—"here have I known the pigeons to fly for forty long years, and, till you made your clearings, there was nobody to skear° or to hurt them. I loved to see them come

---

swivel: small cannon mounted on a swivel

organ: instrument

Major-domo: chief steward or butler of a large household

skear: scare

into the woods, for they were company to a body; hurting nothing; being, as it was, as harmless as a garter-snake. But now it gives me sore thoughts when I hear the frighty things whizzing through the air, for I know it's only a motion to bring out all the brats in the village. Well! the Lord won't see the waste of his creaters for nothing, and right will be done to the pigeons, as well as others, by-and-by.—There's Mr. Oliver, as bad as the rest of them, firing into the flocks as if he was shooting down nothing but Mingo warriors."

Among the sportsmen was Billy Kirby, who, armed with an old musket, was loading, and, without even looking into the air, was firing, and shouting as his victims fell even on his own person. He heard the speech of Natty, and took upon himself to reply—

"What! old Leather-Stocking," he cried, "grumbling at the loss of a few pigeons! If you had to sow your wheat twice, and three times, as I have done, you wouldn't be so massyfully° feeling'd to'ards the divils.—Hurrah, boys! scatter the feathers. This is better than shooting at a turkey's head and neck, old fellow."

"It's better for you, maybe, Billy Kirby," replied the indignant old hunter, "and all them that don't know how to put a ball down a rifle-barrel, or how to bring it up ag'in with a true aim; but it's wicked to be shooting into flocks in this wastey° manner; and none do it, who know how to knock over a single bird. If a body has a craving for pigeon's flesh, why! it's made the same as all other creater's, for man's eating, but not to kill twenty and eat one. When I want such a thing, I go into the woods till I find one to my liking, and then I shoot him off the branches without touching a feather of another, though there might be a hundred on the same tree. You couldn't do such a thing, Billy Kirby—you couldn't do it if you tried." 20

"What's that, old corn-stalk! you sapless stub!" cried the wood-chopper. "You've grown wordy, since the affair of the turkey; but if you're for a single shot, here goes at that bird which comes on by himself."

The fire from the distant part of the field had driven a single pigeon below the flock to which it belonged, and, frightened with the constant reports of the muskets, it was approaching the spot where the disputants° stood, darting first from one side, and then to the other, cutting the air with the swiftness of lightning, and making a noise with its wings, not unlike the rushing of a bullet. Unfortunately for the wood-chopper, notwithstanding his vaunt,° he did not see this bird until it was too late to fire as it approached, and he pulled his

---

massyfully: mercifully

wastey: wasteful

disputants: people engaged in an argument

vaunt: boast

trigger at the unlucky moment when it was darting immediately over his head. The bird continued its course with the usual velocity.

Natty lowered the rifle from his arm, when the challenge was made, and, waiting a moment, until the terrified victim had got in a line with his eye, and had dropped near the bank of the lake, he raised it again with uncommon rapidity, and fired. It might have been chance, or it might have been skill, that produced the result; it was probably a union of both; but the pigeon whirled over in the air, and fell into the lake, with a broken wing. At the sound of his rifle, both his dogs started from his feet, and in a few minutes the "slut"° brought out the bird, still alive.

The wonderful exploit of Leather-Stocking was noised through the field with great rapidity, and the sportsmen gathered in to learn the truth of the report.

"What," said young Edwards, "have you really killed a pigeon on the wing, Natty, with a single ball?" 25

"Haven't I killed loons before now, lad, that dive at the flash?" returned the hunter. "It's much better to kill only such as you want, without wasting your powder and lead, than to be firing into God's creaters in this wicked manner. But I come out for a bird, and you know the reason why I like small game, Mr. Oliver, and now I have got one I will go home, for I don't relish to see these wasty ways that you are all practysing, as if the least thing was not made for use, and not to destroy."

"Thou sayest well, Leather-Stocking," cried Marmaduke, "and I begin to think it time to put an end to this work of destruction."

"Put an ind, Judge, to your clearings. An't the woods his work as well as the pigeons? Use, but don't waste. Wasn't the woods made for the beasts and birds to harbour in? and when man wanted their flesh, their skins, or their feathers, there's the place to seek them. But I'll go to the hut with my own game, for I wouldn't touch one of the harmless things that kiver the ground here, looking up with their eyes on me, as if they only wanted° tongues to say their thoughts."

With this sentiment in his mouth, Leather-Stocking threw his rifle over his arm, and, followed by his dogs, stepped across the clearing with great caution, taking care not to tread on one of the wounded birds in his path. He soon entered the bushes on the margin of the lake, and was hid from view.

Whatever impression the morality of Natty made on the Judge, it was utterly lost on Richard. He availed himself of the gathering of the sportsmen, to lay a plan for one "fell swoop" of destruction. The musketmen 30

"slut": female dog (archaic)
wanted: lacked

were drawn up in battle array, in a line extending on each side of his artillery, with orders to await the signal of firing from himself.

"Stand by, my lads," said Benjamin, who acted as an aide-de-camp,° on this occasion, "stand by, my hearties, and when Squire Dickens heaves out the signal to begin the firing, d'ye see, you may open upon them in a broadside. Take care and fire low, boys, and you'll be sure to hull° the flock."

"Fire low!" shouted Kirby—"hear the old fool! If we fire low, we may hit the stumps, but not ruffle a pigeon."

"How should you know, you lubber?" cried Benjamin, with a very unbecoming heat, for an officer on the eve of battle—"how should you know, you grampus? Havn't I sailed aboard of the Boadishy° for five years? and wasn't it a standing order to fire low, and to hull your enemy? Keep silence at your guns, boys, and mind the order that is passed."

The loud laughs of the musketmen were silenced by the more authoritative voice of Richard, who called for attention and obedience to his signals.

35 Some millions of pigeons were supposed to have already passed, that morning, over the valley of Templeton; but nothing like the flock that was now approaching had been seen before. It extended from mountain to mountain in one solid blue mass, and the eye looked in vain over the southern hills to find its termination. The front of this living column was distinctly marked by a line, but very slightly indented, so regular and even was the flight. Even Marmaduke forgot the morality of Leather-Stocking as it approached, and, in common with the rest, brought his musket to a poise.°

"Fire!" cried the Sheriff, clapping a coal to the priming of the cannon. As half of Benjamin's charge escaped through the touch-hole, the whole volley of the musketry preceded the report of the swivel. On receiving this united discharge of small-arms, the front of the flock darted upward, while, at the same instant, myriads of those in the rear rushed with amazing rapidity into their places, so that when the column of white smoke gushed from the mouth of the little cannon, an accumulated mass of objects was gliding over its point of direction. The roar of the gun echoed along the mountains, and died away to the north, like distant thunder, while the whole flock of alarmed birds seemed, for a moment, thrown into one disorderly and agitated mass. The air was filled with their irregular flight, layer rising above layer, far above the tops of the highest pines, none daring to advance beyond the dangerous pass; when, suddenly, some of the leaders of the feathered

---

aide-de-camp: personal assistant to a senior military officer

hull: pierce the hull of a vessel

Boadishy: *HMS Boadicea* was a 38-gun ship of the British Navy from 1797 to 1854

poise: state of readiness

tribe shot across the valley, taking their flight directly over the village, and hundreds of thousands in their rear followed the example, deserting the eastern side of the plain to their persecutors and the slain.

"Victory!" shouted Richard, "victory! we have driven the enemy from the field."

"Not so, Dickon," said Marmaduke; "the field is covered with them; and, like the Leather-Stocking, I see nothing but eyes, in every direction, as the innocent sufferers turn their heads in terror. Full one half of those that have fallen are yet alive: and I think it is time to end the sport; if sport it be."

"Sport!" cried the Sheriff; "it is princely sport. There are some thousands of the blue-coated boys on the ground, so that every old woman in the village may have a pot-pie for the asking."

"Well, we have happily frightened the birds from this side of the valley," said Marmaduke, "and the carnage must of necessity end, for the present.—Boys, I will give thee sixpence a hundred for the pigeons' heads only; so go to work, and bring them into the village." 40

This expedient° produced the desired effect, for every urchin on the ground went industriously to work to wring the necks of the wounded birds. Judge Temple retired towards his dwelling with that kind of feeling, that many a man has experienced before him, who discovers, after the excitement of the moment has passed, that he has purchased pleasure at the price of misery to others. Horses were loaded with the dead; and, after this first burst of sporting, the shooting of pigeons became a business, with a few idlers, for the remainder of the season. Richard, however, boasted for many a year, of his shot with the "cricket;" and Benjamin gravely asserted, that he thought they killed nearly as many pigeons on that day, as there were Frenchmen destroyed on the memorable occasion of Rodney's victory.°

[1823]

Read

1. How does Cooper set the scene for the events that will happen in the chapter? How does that opening comment on the later events?
2. What details or images give you a sense of the kind of character Leatherstocking is?
3. What effect does Leatherstocking's speech have on the crowd? What kinds of rhetorical appeals does Cooper make with it?
4. What elements of the genre of the Western do you find in this chapter?
5. How is language used to differentiate the characters?

---

expedient: means, stratagem

Rodney's victory: British admiral George Rodney (1718–1792) defeated a French fleet at the Battle of the Saintes, in the Caribbean, on April 12, 1782.

Write

1. Write a short paragraph describing the aim of this excerpt and include a line or two from the text that reinforces your thinking.
2. How does Cooper's language suggest his attitude toward the land?
3. Using Leatherstocking's persona and voice, write a brief scene that might follow this one.

Connect

1. How does the journal of Lewis and Clark compare with Cooper's tale?
2. How might you see Leatherstocking as symbolic of what people might claim is the "American character"?
3. Washington Irving set his story in New York State, as did Cooper. Do you find any similarities between the two stories?

Thomas Cole

English born, Thomas Cole (1801–1848) and his family moved to Ohio when he was five. He studied portraiture but quickly turned to landscape and began the art movement known as the Hudson River School, which captured the wilderness of the American landscape. The grandeur of nature and its awe-inspiring power were subjects for many of the Hudson River painters. He influenced artists such as Frederick Church and Asher Durand. Cole's romantic and naturalistic scenes included classical settings. This painting is based on a scene from James Fenimore Cooper's novel, *Last of the Mohicans*.

Last of the Mohicans

Scene from "The Last of the Mohicans," Cora Kneeling at the Feet of Tamenund (1827), Thomas Cole. Oil on canvas. 25 3/8 x 35 1/16 in. Bequest of Alfred Smith. 1868.31868.3. Wadsworth Atheneum Museum of Art, Hartford, CT/Licensed by Art Resource, NY

[1827]

Read

1. How does the use of light suggest the focus of the painting?
2. What is the rhetorical purpose of the backdrop to the scene?
3. How does knowing the title of the painting contribute to your "reading" of it?

Write

1. Write a sentence or two that describes the aim of the painter. Select details that support your description.
2. Speculate on the reasons for the relative sizes of figures and landscape. What might size suggest about Cole's attitude toward the land?

Connect

1. How does the painting's purpose connect to the aim you see in Cooper's excerpt in this unit?

George Catlin

George Catlin (1796–1872) was both an artist and a writer whose themes of Western scenes and American Indian life provoked enthusiasm and interest in frontier settlement. He grew up in Pennsylvania, where his mother told him stories of frontier life and Indian tribes, which fascinated him. He journeyed west in 1830, accompanying explorer William Clark, and spent months with various tribes in Western territories, recording daily life and painting. He first popularized his series of American Indian portraits in England. He wrote several works on various American Indian peoples including *Life Among the Indians* in 1867. His series of American Indian portraits hangs in the National Museum in Washington, DC.

Letter from the Yellowstone River

I arrived at this place yesterday in the steamer *Yellow Stone* after a voyage of nearly three months from St. Louis, a distance of 2,000 miles, the greater part of which has never before been navigated by steam; and the almost insurmountable difficulties which continually oppose the *voyageur* on this turbid stream, have been by degrees overcome by the indefatigable zeal of Mr. Chouteau, a gentleman of great perseverance, and part proprietor of the boat. To the politeness of this gentleman I am indebted for my passage from St. Louis to this place, and I had also the pleasure of his company, with that of Major Sanford, the government agent for the Missouri Indians.

The American Fur Company have erected here, for their protection against the savages, a very substantial fort, 300 feet square, with bastions° armed with ordnance;° and our approach to it under the continued roar of cannon for half an hour, and the shrill yells of the half-affrighted savages who lined the shores, presented a scene of the most thrilling and picturesque appearance. A voyage so full of incident, and furnishing so many novel scenes of the picturesque and romantic, as we have passed the numerous villages of the "astonished natives," saluting them with the puffing of steam and the thunder of artillery, would afford subject for many epistles; and I cannot deny myself the pleasure of occasionally giving you some little sketches of scenes that I have witnessed, and *am witnessing*; and of the singular feelings that are excited in the breast of the stranger travelling through this interesting country. Interesting (as I have said) and *luxurious,* for this is truly the land of epicures; we are invited by the savages to feasts of *dog's meat,* as the most honorable food that can be presented to a stranger, and glutted with the more delicious food of beavers' tails, and buffaloes' tongues.

You will, no doubt, be somewhat surprised on the receipt of a letter from me, so far strayed into the Western world; and still more startled when I tell you that I am here in the full enthusiasm and practice of my art. That enthusiasm alone has brought me into this remote region, 3,500 miles from my native soil, the last 2,000 of which have furnished me with almost unlimited models, both in landscape and the human figure, exactly those conditions on which alone I was induced to pursue the art as a profession; and in anticipation of which, alone, my admiration for the art could ever have been kindled into a pure flame. I mean the free use of nature's undisguised models, with the privilege of selecting for myself. If I am here losing the benefit of the fleeting fashions of the day, and neglecting that elegant polish, which the world say an artist should draw from a continual intercourse° with the polite world; yet have I this consolation—that in this country I am entirely divested of those dangerous steps and allurements which beset an artist in fashionable life, and have little to steal my thoughts away from the contemplation of the beautiful models that are about me. If, also, I have not here the benefit of that feeling of emulation,° which is the life and spur to the arts where artists are associates together, yet am I surrounded by living models of such elegance

bastions: projections in a fortification
ordnance: cannon or artillery
intercourse: dealings, communications
emulation: competition, desire to equal or excel

and beauty that I feel an unceasing excitement of a much higher order—the certainty that I am drawing knowledge from the true source.

My enthusiastic admiration of man in the honest and elegant simplicity of nature, has always fed the warmest feelings of my bosom, and shut half the avenues to my heart against the specious refinements of the accomplished world. This feeling, together with the desire to study my art, independently of the embarrassments which the ridiculous fashions of civilized society have thrown in its way, has led me to the wilderness for a while, as the true school of the arts.

I have for a long time been of opinion, that the wilderness of our country afforded models equal to those from which the Grecian sculptors transferred to the marble such inimitable grace and beauty; and I am now more confirmed in this opinion, since I have immersed myself in the midst of thousands and tens of thousands of these knights of the forest; whose whole lives are lives of chivalry, and whose daily feats, with their naked limbs, might vie with those of the Grecian youths in the beautiful rivalry of the Olympian games.°

No man's imagination, with all the aids of description that can be given to it, can ever picture the beauty and wildness of scenes that may be daily witnessed in this romantic country; of hundreds of these graceful youths, without a care to wrinkle, or a fear to disturb the full expression of pleasure and enjoyment that beams upon their faces—their long black hair mingling with their horses' tails, floating in the wind, while they are flying over the carpeted prairie, and dealing death with their spears and arrows, to a band of infuriated buffaloes; or their splendid procession in a war-parade, arrayed in all their gorgeous colors and trappings, moving with most exquisite grace and manly beauty, added to that bold defiance which man carries on his front,° who acknowledges no superior on earth, and who is amenable° to no laws except the laws of God and honor.

In addition to the knowledge of human nature and of my art, which I hope to acquire by this toilsome and expensive undertaking, I have another in view which, if it should not be of equal service to me, will be of no less interest and value to posterity. I have, for many years past, contemplated the noble races of red men who are now spread over these trackless forests and boundless prairies, melting away at the approach of civilization. Their rights invaded, their morals corrupted, their lands wrested from them, their

Olympian games: The reference is to the games of ancient Greece; the modern Olympics did not begin until 1896.

front: brow, forehead

amenable: submissive, answerable

customs changed, and therefore lost to the world; and they at last sunk into the earth, and the ploughshare turning the sod over their graves, and I have flown to their rescue—not of their lives or of their race (for they are *doomed* and must perish) but to the rescue of their looks and their modes, at which the acquisitive world may hurl their poison and every besom° of destruction, and trample them down and crush them to death; yet, phoenixlike, they may rise from the "stain on a painter's palette" and live again upon canvass, and stand forth for centuries yet to come, the living monuments of a noble race. For this purpose I have designed to visit every tribe of Indians on the continent, if my life should be spared; for the purpose of procuring portraits of distinguished Indians, of both sexes in each tribe, painted in their native costume; accompanied with pictures of their villages, domestic habits, games, mysteries, religious ceremonies, etc., with anecdotes, traditions, and history of their respective nations.

If I should live to accomplish my design, the result of my labors will doubtless be interesting to future ages, who will have little else left from which to judge of the original inhabitants of this simple race of beings, who require but a few years more of the march of civilization and death, to deprive them of all their native customs and character. I have been kindly supplied by the commander in chief of the army and the secretary of war, with letters to the commander of every military post and every Indian agent on the Western frontier, with instructions to render me all the facilities in their power, which will be of great service to me in so arduous an undertaking. The opportunity afforded me by familiarity with so many tribes of human beings in the simplicity of nature, devoid of the deformities of art,° of drawing fair conclusions in the interesting sciences of physiognomy and phrenology,° of manners and customs, rites, ceremonies, etc., and the opportunity of examining the geology and mineralogy of this Western, and yet unexplored country, will enable me occasionally to entertain you with much new and interesting information, which I shall take equal pleasure in communicating by an occasional letter in my clumsy way.

[1838]

---

besom: broom

deformities of art: the artificiality of sophisticated society

physiognomy and phrenology: Physiognomy is the practice of determining character and mental characteristics from facial features and bodily characteristics; phrenology is the practice of determining mental characteristics from the shape and size of the skull. Both of these pseudosciences were taken seriously by many in the nineteenth century.

Read

1. How would you describe Catlin's attitude toward his trip?
2. How does Catlin feel about the American landscape as a subject for art? The Indians?
3. What images and details does Catlin use to describe Indians? How do those images and details affect readers' reactions?
4. What is the purpose of Catlin's letter? What does he suggest is the purpose of his art?

Write

1. Write a short character description of Catlin, using some of his own words to develop your portrayal.
2. Respond to Catlin's description of the Western land and inhabitants, from your twenty-first-century perspective.
3. Try to respond from a nineteenth-century perspective!

Connect

1. Find one of Catlin's artworks and compare it to what he says about the function of art.
2. Compare Catlin's portrayal of Indians to any other writer's description of American Indians in this unit.

William Apess

The earliest major Indian nineteenth-century writer, William Apess (1798–?) was born in Massachusetts. He claimed descent from Metacomet, the Pequot chief called by the English King Philip. His mother may have been African American; she was owned as a slave before William was born. Bound out as a servant, Apess ran away, joined the army during the War of 1812 and later became a circuit preacher. His *Son of the Forest* (1829) is the first published autobiography by an Indian. He had a forceful style and was a strong advocate for Indian causes in the early part of the century. His writing helped the Mashpee tribe regain land in 1833, when most Indians were losing theirs.

From *A Son of the Forest*

Chapter I

William Apess, the author of the following narrative, was born in the town of Colrain, Massachusetts, on the thirty-first of January, in the year of our Lord seventeen hundred and ninety-eight. My grandfather was a white man and married a female attached to the royal family of Philip, king of the Pequot tribe of Indians, so well known in that part of American history which relates to the wars between the whites and natives. My grandmother was, if I am not misinformed, the king's granddaughter and a fair and beautiful woman. This statement is given not with a view of appearing great in the estimation of others—what, I would ask, is *royal* blood?—the blood of a king is no better than that of the subject. We are in fact but one family; we are all the descendants of one great progenitor—Adam. I would not boast of my extraction, as I consider myself nothing more than a worm of the earth.

I have given the above account of my origin with the simple view of narrating the truth as I have received it, and under the settled conviction that I must render an account at the last day, to the sovereign Judge of all men, for every word contained in this little book.

As the story of King Philip is perhaps generally known, and consequently the history of the Pequot tribe, over whom he reigned, it will suffice to say that he was overcome by treachery, and the goodly heritage occupied by this once happy, powerful, yet peaceful people was possessed in the process of time by their avowed enemies, the whites, who had been welcomed to their land in that spirit of kindness so peculiar to° the red men of the woods. But the violation of their inherent rights, by those to whom they had extended the hand of friendship, was not the only act of injustice which this oppressed and afflicted nation was called to suffer at the hands of their white neighbors—alas! They were subject to a more intense and heart-corroding affliction, that of having their daughters claimed by the conquerors, and however much subsequent efforts were made to soothe their sorrows, in this particular, they considered the glory of their nation as having departed.

From what I have already stated, it will appear that my father was of mixed blood, his father being a white man and his mother a native or, in other words, a red woman. On attaining a sufficient age to act for himself, he joined the Pequot tribe, to which he was maternally connected. He was well received, and in a short time afterward married a female of the tribe, in whose veins a single drop of the white man's blood never flowed. Not long after his marriage, he removed to what was then called the back settlements, directing his course first to the west and afterward to the northeast, where he pitched his tent in the woods of a town called Colrain, near the Connecticut River, in the state of Massachusetts. In this, the place of my birth, he continued some time and afterward

---

peculiar to: characteristic of

removed to Colchester, New London County, Connecticut. At the latter place, our little family lived for nearly three years in comparative comfort.

Circumstances, however, changed with us, as with many other people, in consequence of which I was taken together with my two brothers and sisters into my grandfather's family. One of my uncles dwelt in the same hut. Now my grandparents were not the best people in the world—like all others who are wedded to the beastly vice of intemperance, they would drink to excess whenever they could procure rum, and as usual in such cases, when under the influence of liquor, they would not only quarrel and fight with each other but would at times turn upon their unoffending grandchildren and beat them in a most cruel manner. It makes me shudder, even at this time, to think how frequent and how great have been our sufferings in consequence of the introduction of this "cursed stuff" into our family—and I could wish, in the sincerity of my soul, that it were banished from our land.

Our fare was of the poorest kind, and even of this we had not enough. Our clothing also was of the worst description: Literally speaking, we were clothed with rags, so far only as rags would suffice to cover our nakedness. We were always contented and happy to get a cold potato for our dinners—of this at times we were denied, and many a night have we gone supperless to rest, if stretching our limbs on a bundle of straw, without any covering against the weather, may be called rest. Truly, we were in a most deplorable condition—too young to obtain subsistence of ourselves, by the labor of our hands, and our wants almost totally disregarded by those who should have made every exertion to supply them. Some of our white neighbors, however, took pity on us and measurably administered to our wants, by bringing us frozen milk, with which we were glad to satisfy the calls of hunger. We lived in this way for some time, suffering both from cold and hunger. Once in particular, I remember that when it rained very hard my grandmother put us all down cellar, and when we complained of cold and hunger, she unfeelingly bid us dance and thereby warm ourselves—but we had no food of any kind; and one of my sisters almost died of hunger. Poor dear girl, she was quite overcome. Young as I was, my very heart bled for her. I merely relate this circumstance, without any embellishment or exaggeration, to show the reader how we were treated. The intensity of our sufferings I cannot tell. Happily, we did not continue in this very deplorable condition for a great length of time. Providence smiled on us, but in a particular manner.

Our parents quarreled, parted, and went off to a great distance, leaving their helpless children to the care of their grandparents. We lived at this time in an old house, divided into two apartments—one of which was occupied by my uncle. Shortly after my father left us, my grandmother, who had been out among the whites, returned in a state of intoxication and, without any provocation whatever on my part, began to belabor me most unmercifully with a club; she asked me if I hated her, and I very innocently answered in the affirmative as I did not then know what the word meant and thought all the while that I was answering aright; and so she continued asking me the same question, and I as often answered her in the same way, whereupon she continued beating me, by which means one of my arms was broken in three different places. I was then only four years of age and consequently could not take care of or defend myself—and I was equally unable to seek safety in flight. But my uncle who lived in the other part of the house, being alarmed for my safety, came down to take me away, when my grandfather made toward him with a firebrand,° but very fortunately he succeeded in rescuing me and thus saved my life, for had he not come at the time he did, I would most certainly have been killed. My grandparents who acted in this unfeeling and cruel manner were by my mother's side—those by my father's side were Christians, lived and died happy in the love of God; and if I continue faithful in improving that measure of grace with which God hath blessed me, I expect to meet them in a world of unmingled and ceaseless joys. But to return:—

The next morning, when it was discovered that I had been most dangerously injured, my uncle determined to make the whites acquainted with my condition. He accordingly went to a Mr. Furman, the person who had occasionally furnished us with milk, and the good man came immediately to see me. He found me dreadfully beaten, and the other children in a state of absolute suffering; and as he was extremely anxious that something should be done for our relief, he applied to the selectmen° of the town in our behalf, who after duly considering the application adjudged that we should be severally taken and bound out.° Being entirely disabled in consequence of the wounds I had received, I was supported at the expense of the town for about twelve months.

When the selectmen were called in, they ordered me to be carried to Mr. Furman's—where I received the attention of two surgeons. Some considerable time elapsed before my arm was set, which was consequently very sore, and during this painful operation I scarcely murmured. Now this dear man

---

firebrand: piece of burning wood

selectmen: members of a board of town officers (chiefly New England)

bound out: sent to work as an indentured servant

and family were sad on my account. Mrs. Furman was a kind, benevolent, and tenderhearted lady—from her I received the best possible care: Had it been otherwise I believe that I could not have lived. It pleased God, however, to support me. The great patience that I manifested I attribute mainly to my improved situation. Before, I was almost always naked, or cold, or hungry—now, I was comfortable, with the exception of my wounds.

In view of this treatment, I presume that the reader will exclaim, "What savages your grandparents were to treat unoffending, helpless children in this cruel manner." But this cruel and unnatural conduct was the effect of some cause. I attribute it in a great measure to the whites, inasmuch as they introduced among my countrymen that bane of comfort and happiness, ardent spirits—seduced them into a love of it and, when under its unhappy influence, wronged them out of their lawful possessions—that land, where reposed the ashes of their sires; and not only so, but they committed violence of the most revolting kind upon the persons of the female portion of the tribe who, previous to the introduction among them of the arts,° and vices, and debaucheries of the whites, were as unoffending and happy as they roamed over their goodly possessions as any people on whom the sun of heaven ever shone. The consequence was that they were scattered abroad.° Now many of them were seen reeling about intoxicated with liquor, neglecting to provide for themselves and families, who before were assiduously° engaged in supplying the necessities of those depending on them for support. I do not make this statement in order to justify those who had treated me so unkindly, but simply to show that, inasmuch as I was thus treated only when they were under the influence of spirituous liquor, that the whites were justly chargeable with at least some portion of my sufferings.

After I had been nursed for about twelve months, I had so far recovered that it was deemed expedient to bind me out, until I should attain the age of twenty-one years. Mr. Furman, the person with whom the selectmen had placed me was a poor man, a cooper° by trade, and obtained his living by the labor of his hands. As I was only five years old, he at first thought that his circumstances would not justify him in keeping me, as it would be some considerable time before I could render him much service. But such was the attachment of the family toward me that he came to the conclusion to keep

arts: schemes, wiles
abroad: far and wide
assiduously: diligently, industriously
cooper: one who makes or repairs barrels and casks

me until I was of age, and he further agreed to give me so much instruction as would enable me to read and write. Accordingly, when I attained my sixth year, I was sent to school, and continued for six successive winters. During this time I learned to read and write, though not so well as I could have wished. This was all the instruction of the kind I ever received. Small and imperfect as was the amount of the knowledge I obtained, yet in view of the advantages I have thus derived, I bless God for it.

Chapter II

I believe that it is assumed as a fact among divines° that the Spirit of Divine Truth, in the boundless diversity of its operations, visits the mind of every intelligent being born into the world—but the time when is only fully known to the Almighty and the soul which is the object of the Holy Spirit's enlightening influence. It is also conceded on all hands that the Spirit of Truth operates on different minds in a variety of ways—but always with the design of convincing man of sin and of a judgment to come. And, oh, that men would regard their real interests and yield to the illuminating influences of the Spirit of God—then wretchedness and misery would abound no longer, but everything of the kind give place to the pure principles of peace, godliness, brotherly kindness, meekness, charity, and love. These graces are spontaneously produced in the human heart and are exemplified in the Christian deportment of every soul under the mellowing and sanctifying influences of the Spirit of God. They are the peaceable fruits of a meek and quiet spirit.

The perverseness of man in this respect is one of the great and conclusive proofs of his apostasy,° and of the rebellious inclination of his unsanctified heart to the will and wisdom of his Creator and his Judge.

I have heard a great deal said respecting° infants feeling, as it were, the operations of the Holy Spirit on their minds, impressing them with a sense of their wickedness and the necessity of a preparation for a future state. Children at a very early age manifest in a strong degree two of the evil passions of our nature—*anger* and *pride.* We need not wonder, therefore, that persons in early life feel good impressions; indeed, it is a fact, too well established to admit of doubt or controversy, that many children have manifested a strength of intellect far

---

divines: clergymen, theologians
apostasy: abandonment of one's faith
respecting: concerning

above their years and have given ample evidence of a good work of grace manifest by the influence of the Spirit of God in their young and tender minds. But this is perhaps attributable to the care and attention bestowed upon them.

If constant and judicious means are used to impress upon their young and susceptible minds sentiments of truth, virtue, morality, and religion, and these efforts are sustained by a corresponding practice on the part of parents or those who strive to make these early impressions, we may rationally trust that as their young minds expand they will be led to act upon the wholesome principles they have received—and that at a very early period these good impressions will be more indelibly engraved on their hearts by the cooperating influences of that Spirit, who in the days of his glorious incarnation said, "Suffer little children to come unto me, and forbid them not, for of such is the kingdom of heaven."

But to my experience—and the reader knows full well that experience is the best schoolmaster, for what we have experienced, that we know, and all the world cannot possibly beat it out of us. I well remember the conversation that took place between Mrs. Furman and myself when I was about six years of age; she was attached to the Baptist church and was esteemed as a very pious woman. Of this I have not the shadow of a doubt, as her whole course of conduct was upright and exemplary. On this occasion, she spoke to me respecting a future state of existence and told me that I might die and enter upon it, to which I replied that I was too young—that old people only died. But she assured me that I was not too young, and in order to convince me of the truth of the observation, she referred me to the graveyard, where many younger and smaller persons than myself were laid to molder in the earth. I had of course nothing to say—but, notwithstanding, I could not fully comprehend the nature of death and the meaning of a future state. Yet I felt an indescribable sensation pass though my frame; I trembled and was sore afraid and for some time endeavored to hide myself from the destroying monster, but I could find no place of refuge. The conversation and pious admonitions of this good lady made a lasting impression upon my mind. At times, however, this impression appeared to be wearing away—then again I would become thoughtful, make serious inquiries, and seem anxious to know something more certain respecting myself and that state of existence beyond the grave, in which I was instructed to believe. About this time I was taken to meeting in order to hear the word of God and receive instruction in divine things. This was the first time I had ever entered a house of worship, and instead of attending to what the minister said, I was employed in gazing about the house or playing with the unruly boys with whom I was seated in the gallery. On my return home, Mr. Furman, who had been apprised° of my conduct, told me that I had acted very wrong. He did not, however, stop here. He went on to tell me how I ought to behave in church, and to this very day I bless God for such wholesome and timely instruction. In this particular I was not slow to learn, as I do not remember that I have from that day to this misbehaved in the house of God.

It may not be improper to remark, in this place, that a vast proportion of the misconduct of young people in church is chargeable to their parents and guardians. It is to be feared that there are too many professing Christians who feel satisfied if their children or those under their care enter on a Sabbath day within the walls of the sanctuary, without reference to their conduct while there. I would have such persons seriously ask themselves whether they think they discharge the duties obligatory on them by the relation in which they stand to their Maker, as well as those committed to their care, by so much negligence on their part. The Christian feels it a duty imposed on him to conduct his children to the house of God. But he rests not here. He must have an eye over them and, if they act well, approve and encourage them; if otherwise, point out to them their error and persuade them to observe a discreet and exemplary course of conduct while in church.

After a while I became very fond of attending on the word of God—then again I would meet the enemy of my soul, who would strive to lead me away, and in many instances he was but too successful, and to this day I remember that nothing scarcely grieved me so much, when my mind has been thus petted, than to be called by a nickname. If I was spoken to in the spirit of kindness, I would be instantly disarmed of my stubbornness and ready to perform anything required of me. I know of nothing so trying to a child as to be repeatedly called by an improper name. I thought it disgraceful to be called an Indian; it was considered as a slur upon an oppressed and scattered nation, and I have often been led to inquire where the whites received this word, which they so often threw as an opprobrious° epithet at the sons of the forest. I could not find it in the Bible and therefore concluded that it was a word imported for the special purpose of degrading us. At other times I thought it was derived from the term *in-gen-uity.* But the proper term which ought to be applied to our nation, to distinguish it from the rest of the human family, is that of "*Natives*"—and I humbly conceive that the natives of this country are the only people under heaven who have a just title to the name, inasmuch as we are the only people who retain the original complexion of our father Adam.

---

apprised: informed

opprobrious: abusive, contemptuous

Notwithstanding my thoughts on this matter, so completely was I weaned from the interests and affections of my brethren that a mere threat of being sent away among the Indians into the dreary woods had a much better effect in making me obedient to the commands of my superiors than any corporal punishment that they ever inflicted. I had received a lesson in the unnatural treatment of my own relations, which could not be effaced, and I thought that, if those who should have loved and protected me treated me with such unkindness, surely I had not reason to expect mercy or favor at the hands of those who knew me in no other relation than that of a cast-off member of the tribe. A threat, of the kind alluded to, invariably produced obedience on my part, so far as I understood the nature of the command.

I cannot perhaps give a better idea of the dread which pervaded my mind on seeing any of my brethren of the forest than by relating the following occurrence. One day several of the family went into the woods to gather berries, taking me with them. We had not been out long before we fell in with a company of white females, on the same errand—their complexion was, to say the least, as *dark* as that of the natives. This circumstance filled my mind with terror, and I broke from the party with my utmost speed, and I could not muster courage enough to look behind until I had reached home. By this time my imagination had pictured out a tale of blood, and as soon as I regained breath sufficient to answer the questions which my master asked, I informed him that we had met a body of the natives in the woods, but what had become of the party I could not tell. Notwithstanding the manifest incredibility of my tale of terror, Mr. Furman was agitated; my very appearance was sufficient to convince him that I had been terrified by something, and summoning the remainder of the family, he sallied out in quest of the absent party, whom he found searching for me among the bushes. The whole mystery was soon unraveled. It may be proper for me here to remark that the great fear I entertained of my brethren was occasioned by the many stories I had heard of their cruelty toward the whites—how they were in the habit of killing and scalping men, women, and children. But the whites did not tell me that they were in a great majority of instances the aggressors—that they had imbrued° their hands in the lifeblood of my brethren, driven them from their once peaceful and happy homes—that they introduced among them the fatal and exterminating diseases of civilized life. If the whites had told me how cruel they had been to the "poor Indian," I should have apprehended° as much harm from them.

---

imbrued: stained
apprehended: feared

Shortly after this occurrence I relapsed into my former bad habits—was fond of the company of boys—and in a short time lost in a great measure that spirit of obedience which had made me the favorite of my mistress. I was easily led astray, and, once in particular, I was induced by a boy (my senior by five or six years) to assist him in his depredations° on a watermelon patch belonging to one of the neighbors. But we were found out, and my companion in wickedness led me deeper in sin by persuading me to deny the crime laid to our charge. I obeyed him to the very letter and, when accused, flatly denied knowing anything of the matter. The boasted courage of the boy, however, began to fail as soon as he saw danger thicken, and he confessed it as strongly as he had denied it. The man from whom we had pillaged the melons threatened to send us to Newgate,° but he relented. The story shortly afterward reached the ears of the good Mrs. Furman, who talked seriously to me about it. She told me that I could be sent to prison for it, that I had done wrong, and gave me a great deal of wholesome advice. This had a much better effect than forty floggings—it sunk so deep into my mind that the impression can never be effaced. 20

I now went on without difficulty for a few months, when I was assailed by fresh and unexpected troubles. One of the girls belonging to the house had taken some offense at me and declared she would be revenged. The better to effect this end, she told Mr. Furman that I had not only threatened to kill her but had actually pursued her with a knife, whereupon he came to the place where I was working and began to whip me severely. I could not tell for what. I told him I had done no harm, to which he replied, "I will learn you, you Indian dog, how to chase people with a knife." I told him I had not, but he would not believe me and continued to whip me for a long while. But the poor man soon found out his error, as *after* he had flogged me he undertook to investigate the matter, when to his amazement he discovered it was nothing but fiction, as all the children assured him that I did no such thing. He regretted being so hasty—but I saw wherein the great difficulty consisted; if I had not denied the melon affair he would have believed me, but as I had uttered an untruth about that it was natural for him to think that the person who will tell one lie will not scruple at two. For a long while after this circumstance transpired, I did not associate with my companions.

[1829]

---

depredations: robberies, pillages

Newgate: a prison in East Granby, Connecticut, from 1773 to 1827

Read

1. What is the significance of the title of Apess's work for the audience?
2. How does Apess use logic to establish his claims?
3. Where do you get a sense of Apess's emotional connection to his description of Indian conditions and his discussion of why those conditions exist?
4. How does Apess use opposing views to help create his argument?

Write

1. Write about how you see Apess establishing a relationship with his audience and how he introduces the subject of his essay to them.
2. Reflect on why you think Apess is convincing or not.
3. How would you describe Apess's persona in this piece? Use Apess's diction to help you with your description.
4. Choose one or two sentences to analyze one important characteristic of Apess's style.

Connect

1. Why do you think the personal narrative often works as a persuasive tool? Find another narrative to help you consider.
2. How would you compare Apess's use of Christianity to Occom's, Stewart's, or others you've read?

William Travis

William Travis (1809–1836) was the commanding officer at the Alamo mission in Texas, where he led a group of Texas settlers who had demanded independence from Mexico. They were besieged at the mission by the Mexican commander Santa Anna. Along with legendary Jim Bowie and Davy Crockett, the troop held their posts for 12 days hoping for reinforcements from the U.S. government. Travis and his men were overcome by Mexican troops and all were killed. A few days later, Santa Anna's troops were defeated by Sam Houston at San Jacinto, whose battle cry became "Remember the Alamo!"

Message from the Alamo

Fellow Citizens and Compatriots:

I am besieged, by a thousand or more of the Mexicans under Santa Anna. I have sustained a continual bombardment for twenty-four hours and have not lost a man. The enemy have demanded a surrender at discretion;° otherwise the garrison are to be put to the sword if the place is

---

at discretion: unconditionally

taken. I have answered the summons with a cannon shot, and our flag still waves proudly from the walls.

I shall never surrender or retreat.

Then, I call on you in the name of liberty, of patriotism, and of everything dear to the American character to come to our aid with all dispatch. The enemy are receiving reinforcements daily and will no doubt increase to three or four thousand in four or five days. Though this call may be neglected, I am determined to sustain myself as long as possible and die like a soldier who never forgets what is due to his own honor and that of his country. Victory or Death!

W. Barret Travis
Lieutenant Colonel Commanding

P.S. The Lord is on our side. When the enemy appeared in sight we had not three bushels of corn. We have since found, in deserted houses, eighty or ninety bushels and got into the walls twenty or thirty head of beeves.°

[1836]

Read

1. How would you describe the audience for Travis's letter?
2. What tone does the letter take? What words especially seem to indicate it?
3. How does Travis present himself?
4. What details serve to describe the urgency of the message?

Write

1. Write a response to Travis's letter as though you were the audience for his letter.
2. Analyze Travis's choice of words that indicate his persona in the letter.

Connect

1. How does this letter reinforce the legend about the Alamo?
2. How does the voice in this letter compare with voice in another letter you've read? How does the genre of the letter affect purpose?

Andrew Jackson

The seventh president of the United States, Andrew Jackson (1767–1845) was born on the border of North and South Carolina. He served in the Revolutionary War when he was thirteen and was taken prisoner by the British. He became the first congressman from the new state of Tennessee and a senator. Later he served as a supreme court judge, governor of the Florida territory, and major general in the U.S. Army. In the War of 1812, he secured fame as he decisively defeated British troops in the Battle of New Orleans.

beeves: cattle, steers

He became president in 1828, the first president not to come from wealth and privilege. He was responsible for Indian removal to land beyond the Mississippi River, a decision that led in 1838 to the State of Georgia's removal of the Cherokee to Oklahoma.

On Indian Removal

It gives me pleasure to announce to Congress that the benevolent policy of the Government, steadily pursued for nearly thirty years, in relation to the removal of the Indians beyond the white settlements is approaching to a happy consummation. Two important tribes have accepted the provision made for their removal at the last session of Congress, and it is believed that their example will induce the remaining tribes also to seek the same obvious advantages.

The consequences of a speedy removal will be important to the United States, to individual States, and to the Indians themselves. The pecuniary advantages which it Promises to the Government are the least of its recommendations. It puts an end to all possible danger of collision between the authorities of the General and State Governments on account of the Indians. It will place a dense and civilized population in large tracts of country now occupied by a few savage hunters. By opening the whole territory between Tennessee on the north and Louisiana on the south to the settlement of the whites it will incalculably strengthen the southwestern frontier and render the adjacent States strong enough to repel future invasions without remote° aid. It will relieve the whole State of Mississippi and the western part of Alabama of Indian occupancy, and enable those States to advance rapidly in population, wealth, and power.

It will separate the Indians from immediate contact with settlements of whites; free them from the power of the States; enable them to pursue happiness in their own way and under their own rude° institutions; will retard the progress of decay,° which is lessening their numbers, and perhaps cause them gradually, under the protection of the Government and through the influence of good counsels, to cast off their savage habits and become an interesting, civilized, and Christian community. These consequences, some of them so certain and the rest so probable, make the complete execution of the plan sanctioned by Congress at their last session an object of much solicitude.°

Toward the aborigines of the country no one can indulge a more friendly feeling than myself, or would go further in attempting to reclaim them from their wandering habits and make them a happy, prosperous people. I have endeavored

remote: distant
rude: lacking culture and refinement
decay: decline in health, illness
solicitude: concern

to impress upon them my own solemn convictions of the duties and powers of the General Government in relation to the State authorities. For the justice of the laws passed by the States within the scope of their reserved powers they are not responsible to this Government. As individuals we may entertain and express our opinions of their acts, but as a Government we have as little right to control them as we have to prescribe laws for other nations.

With a full understanding of the subject, the Choctaw and the Chickasaw tribes have with great unanimity determined to avail themselves of the liberal offers presented by the act of Congress, and have agreed to remove beyond the Mississippi River. Treaties have been made with them, which in due season will be submitted for consideration. In negotiating these treaties they were made to understand their true condition, and they have preferred maintaining their independence in the Western forests to submitting to the laws of the States in which they now reside. These treaties, being probably the last which will ever be made with them, are characterized by great liberality on the part of the Government. They give the Indians a liberal sum in consideration of their removal, and comfortable subsistence on their arrival at their new homes. If it be their real interest to maintain a separate existence, they will there be at liberty to do so without the inconveniences and vexations to which they would unavoidably have been subject in Alabama and Mississippi. 5

Humanity has often wept over the fate of the aborigines of this country, and philanthropy has been long busily employed in devising means to avert it, but its progress has never for a moment been arrested, and one by one have many powerful tribes disappeared from the earth. To follow to the tomb the last of his race and to tread on the graves of extinct nations excite melancholy reflections. But true philanthropy reconciles the mind to these vicissitudes as it does to the extinction of one generation to make room for another. In the monuments and fortresses of an unknown people, spread over the extensive regions of the West, we behold the memorials of a once powerful race, which was exterminated or has disappeared to make room for the existing savage tribes. Nor is there anything in this which, upon a comprehensive view of the general interests of the human race, is to be regretted. Philanthropy could not wish to see this continent restored to the conditions in which it was found by our forefathers. What good man would prefer a country covered with forests and ranged by a few thousand savages to our extensive Republic, studded with cities, towns, and prosperous farms, embellished with all the improvements which art° can devise or industry execute, occupied by more than 12 million happy people, and filled with all the blessings of liberty, civilization, and religion?

The present policy of the Government is but a continuation of the same progressive change by a milder process. The tribes which occupied the countries now constituting the Eastern States were annihilated or have melted away to

art: exercise of skill (as opposed to the work of nature)

make room for the whites. The waves of population and civilization are rolling to the westward, and we now propose to acquire the countries occupied by the red men of the South and West by a fair exchange, and, at the expense of the United States, to send them to a land where their existence may be prolonged and perhaps made perpetual.

Doubtless it will be painful to leave the graves of their fathers; but what do they more than our ancestors did or than our children are now doing? To better their condition in an unknown land our forefathers left all that was dear in earthly objects. Our children by thousands yearly leave the land of their birth to seek new homes in distant regions. Does Humanity weep at these painful separations from everything, animate and inanimate, with which the young heart has become entwined? Far from it. It is rather a source of joy that our country affords scope where our young population may range unconstrained in body or in mind, developing the power and faculties of man in their highest perfection. These remove° hundreds and almost thousands of miles at their own expense, purchase the lands they occupy, and support themselves at their new homes from the moment of their arrival. Can it be cruel in this Government when, by events which it can not control, the Indian is made discontented in his ancient home to purchase his lands, to give him a new and extensive territory, to pay the expense of his removal, and support him a year in his new abode? How many thousands of our own people would gladly embrace the opportunity of removing to the West on such conditions! If the offers made to the Indians were extended to them, they would be hailed with gratitude and joy.

And is it supposed that the wandering savage has a stronger attachment to his home than the settled, civilized Christian? Is it more afflicting to him to leave the graves of his fathers than it is to our brothers and children? Rightly considered, the policy of the General Government toward the red man is not only liberal, but generous. He is unwilling to submit to the laws of the States and mingle with their population. To save him from this alternative, or perhaps utter annihilation, the General Government kindly offers him a new home, and proposes to pay the whole expense of his removal and settlement.

In the consummation of a policy originating at an early period, and steadily pursued by every administration within the present century—so just to the states and so generous to the Indians—the executive feels it has a right to expect the cooperation of Congress and of all good and disinterested men. The states, moreover, have a right to demand it. It was substantially a part of the compact which made them members of our Confederacy. With Georgia there is an express contract; with the new states an implied one of equal obligation. Why, in authorizing Ohio, Indiana, Illinois, Missouri, Mississippi, and Alabama to form constitutions and become separate states, did Congress include within their limits extensive tracts of Indian lands, and, in some instances, powerful Indian tribes? Was it 10

---

remove: move, relocate

not understood by both parties that the power of the states was to be coextensive with their limits, and that, with all convenient dispatch, the general government should extinguish the Indian title and remove every obstruction to the complete jurisdiction of the state governments over the soil? Probably not one of those states would have accepted a separate existence—certainly it would never have been granted by Congress—had it been understood that they were to be confined forever to those small portions of their nominal territory the Indian title to which had at the time been extinguished.

It is, therefore, a duty which this government owes to the new states to extinguish as soon as possible the Indian title to all lands which Congress themselves nave included within their limits. When this is done the duties of the general government in relation to the states and the Indians within their limits are at an end. The Indians may leave the state or not, as they choose. The purchase of their lands does not alter in the least their personal relations with the state government. No act of the general government has ever been deemed necessary to give the states jurisdiction over the persons of the Indians. That they possess by virtue of their sovereign power within their own limits in as full a manner before as after the purchase of the Indian lands; nor can this government add to or diminish it.

May we not hope, therefore, that all good citizens, and none more zealously than those who think the Indians oppressed by subjection to the laws of the States, will unite in attempting to open the eyes of those children of the forest to their true condition, and by a speedy removal to relieve them from all the evils, real or imaginary, present or prospective, with which they may be supposed to be threatened.

[1829]

Read

1. How does Jackson's characterization of the Indians contribute to his building of the case for their removal?
2. What details and evidence does Jackson use to justify his decision?
3. What appeals to the audience are evident in the decision?
4. How does word choice help provide an idea of Jackson's character and the persona he creates?

Write

1. Write about how Jackson's use of language and detail contribute to a sense of his authority as a speaker.
2. Do you find appeals to emotion or ethics in this discussion? Comment on them.
3. How do you respond to Jackson's claims from your perspective as a twenty-first-century reader?

4. Why do you think his claims were convincing to nineteenth-century readers?

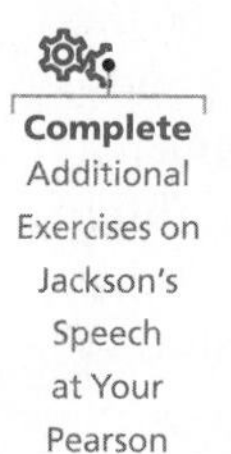

Connect

1. Find information on the Trail of Tears, the removal of the Cherokee from their homeland, and talk about the consequences of the presidential decision .
2. Compare Jackson's rationale for his decision to William Bradford's discussion of the development of the Plymouth settlement. How does each man justify his decisions?

William Cullen Bryant

William Cullen Bryant (1794–1878) was born in Massachusetts, and early in his life was considered a child prodigy as well as a fine poet. A poem criticizing Thomas Jefferson was published when he was 13. His most famous poem, "Thanatopsis," meditates on nature and death and anticipates the transcendental ideas of Ralph Waldo Emerson. Bryant became a journalist and the editor of the *New York Evening Post* in 1829 until his death. He backed populist causes including the Free Soil movement and was an avid supporter of Abraham Lincoln. His editorials were influential in shaping public opinion.

On the Right to Strike

Sentence was passed on Saturday on the twenty "men who had determined not to work." The punishment selected on due consideration by the judge was that officers appointed for the purpose should immediately demand from each of the delinquents a sum of money which was named in the sentence of the court. The amount demanded would not have fallen short of the savings of many years. Either the offenders had not parted with these savings, or their brother workmen raised the ransom money for them on the spot. The fine was paid over as required.

All is now well; justice has been satisfied. But if the expenses of their families had anticipated the law and left nothing in their hands, or if friends had not been ready to buy the freedom of their comrades, they would have been sent to prison, and there they would have stayed until their wives and children, besides earning their own bread, had saved enough to redeem the captives from their cells.

Such has been their punishment. What was their offense? They had committed the crime of unanimously declining to go to work at the wages offered to them by their masters. They had said to one another, "Let us come out from the meanness and misery of our caste. Let us begin to do what every order more privileged and more honored is doing every day. By the means which we believe to be the best, let us raise ourselves and our families above the humbleness of our condition. We may be wrong, but we cannot help believing that we might do much if we were true brothers to each other, and would resolve not to sell the only thing which is our own, the cunning° of our hands, for less than it is worth." What other things they may have done is nothing to the purpose; it was for this they were condemned; it is for this they are to endure the penalty of the law.

We call upon a candid° and generous community to mark that the punishment inflicted upon these twenty "men who had determined not to work" is not directed against the offense of conspiring to prevent others by force from working at low wages, but expressly against the offense of settling by preconcert° the compensation which they thought they were entitled to obtain. It is certainly superfluous to repeat that this journal would be the very last to oppose a law leveled at any attempt to molest the laborer who chooses to work for less than the prices settled by the union.

We have said, and to cut off cavil° we say it now again, that a conspiracy to deter, by threats of violence, a fellow workman from arranging his own terms with his employers is a conspiracy to commit a felony: a conspiracy which, being a crime against liberty, we should be the first to condemn; a conspiracy which no strike should, for its own sake, countenance for a moment; a conspiracy already punishable by the statute, and far easier to reach than the one of which "the twenty" stood accused; but a conspiracy, we must add, that has not a single feature in common with the base and barbarous prohibition under which the offenders were indicted and condemned. 5

They were condemned because they had determined not to work for the wages that were offered them! Can anything be imagined more abhorrent to every sentiment of generosity or justice than the law which arms the rich with the legal right to fix, by assize,° the wages of the poor? If this is not SLAVERY, we have forgotten its definition. Strike the right of associating for the sale of labor from the privileges of a freeman and you may as well at once bind him to a master or ascribe° him to the soil. If it be not in the color of his skin and in the poor franchise° of naming his own terms in a contract for his work, what advantage has the laborer of the North over the bondman of the South?

---

cunning: skill, craft

candid: honest, unbiased

preconcert: prior agreement

cavil: trivial objection

assize: judicial action, legal verdict

ascribe: assign

franchise: officially granted right or privilege

Punish by human laws a "determination not to work," make it penal by any other penalty than idleness inflicts, and it matters little whether the taskmasters be one or many, an individual or an order,° the hateful scheme of slavery will have gained a foothold in the land. And then the meanness of this law, which visits with its malice those who cling to it for protection, and shelters with all its fences those who are raised above its threats. A late solicitation for its aid against employers is treated with derision and contempt, but the moment the "masters" invoked its intervention, it came down from its high place with most indecent haste and has now discharged its fury upon the naked heads of wretches so forlorn that their worst faults multiply their titles to a liberty which they must learn to win from livelier sensibilities than the barren benevolence of Wealth, or the tardy magnanimity of Power.

Since the above was written we have read the report of Judge Edwards' address on sentencing the journeymen. It will be found in another part of this paper. We see in this address an apparent disposition to mix up the question of *combination,* which is a lawful act, with that of *violence,* which is allowed on all hands to be unlawful. We repeat that it was for the simple act of combining not to work under a certain rate of wages, and not for a disturbance of the peace, that the twenty journeymen were indicted, tried, convicted, and punished. It was expressly so stated in Judge Edwards' charge to the jury which brought in the verdict of guilty; and whoever will look at the address made by him in pronouncing the sentence will find that he still maintains and repeats, in various forms of expression, the doctrine that combinations to demand a fixed rate of wages are unlawful and punishable.

This tyrannical doctrine we affirm to be a forced construction° of the statute against conspiracies injurious to commerce—a construction which the makers of the law, we are sure, never contemplated. We are now told, however, that it will be insisted upon and enforced—let it be so—it is the very method by which either the courts of justice will be compelled to recede from their mistaken and arbitrary construction, or the legislature will interpose to declare that such is not the law. Carry it into effect impartially and without respect of persons° and there will not be people enough left without° the penitentiaries to furnish subsistence to those who are confined within them.

"Self-created societies," says Judge Edwards, "are unknown to the Constitution and laws, and will not be permitted to rear their crest° and extend their 10

order: organization

construction: interpretation

respect of persons: discrimination based on rank, power, wealth, etc.

without: outside of

crest: plume on a helmet or device on a coat of arms

baneful influence over any portion of the community." If there is any sense in this passage it means that self-created societies are unlawful and must be put down by the courts. Down then, with every literary, every religious, and every charitable association not incorporated! What nonsense is this! Self-created societies *are* known to the Constitution and laws, for they are not prohibited, and the laws which allow them will, if justly administered, protect them.

But suppose, in charity, that the reporter has put this absurdity into the mouth of Judge Edwards, and that he meant only those self-created societies which have an effect upon trade and commerce. Gather up then and sweep to the penitentiary all those who are confederated to carry on any business or trade in concert, by fixed rules, and see how many men you would leave at large in this city. The members of every partnership in the place will come under the penalties of the law, and not only these but every person pursuing any occupation whatever who governs himself by a mutual understanding with others that follow the same occupation.

The judge observes that "combinations which operate to the injury of the employers or of the trade, will, in the regular course of events, be found injurious to journeymen." We heartily wish that all the doctrines of the address had been as sound as this. Combinations to the injury of trade necessarily injure workmen, and in this lies the remedy. Workmen will not, any more than employers, do what is to their own injury. If they combine without good grounds, their error carries its own penalty along with it, and may be safely left to be chastised° by the suffering which is the natural consequence of such folly. The interposition of the law in that case is idle and presumptuous. You may as well make a law to prohibit people from going too thinly clad in cold weather.

"We have had in this country so little experience of these combinations," proceeds Judge Edwards, "that we are at a loss to know what degree of severity may be necessary to rid society of them." We wonder not at this embarrassment—the difficulties of which the judge speaks will be increased with every one of the penalties he threatens to impose. The severer the penalties, the more glaring will be the injustice of the law, the more it will be discussed, and the sooner will the legislature interfere.

England has had experience of these combinations, if we have not. England has had long, ample, and instructive experience, both of combinations and combination laws; and what is the lesson which this experience has taught her? She learned that "the attempts to enforce the provisions of the Combination Act," we quote the *Edinburgh Review,* "did infinitely more harm than good," and she accordingly, twelve years ago, blotted the combination laws from her

---

chastised: punished

statute book. She did this not with a Whig, or Radical, or reformed Parliament, but while the Tories were in power, and the realm was ruled by an aristocracy. Will not our own country be wise enough to profit by her experience without a taste of the evils by which it was acquired?

[1836]

Read

1. How does Bryant establish his case through his opening narrative?
2. What does Bryant show that he believes about his audience?
3. How does Bryant characterize the strikers and the reasons for the strike?
4. Where do you find appeals to logic? To ethics?
5 How does Bryant use analogy to make his case?

Write

1. Do you find Bryant's case convincing? Why or why not?
2. Bryant was known as a great orator. What elements in this piece suggest a reason for that reputation?
3. What images or language choices suggest Bryant's attitude toward workers?

Complete Additional Exercises on Bryant's Speech at Your Pearson MyLab

Connect

1. Find information on workers' rights and the union movement at the time and discuss how this context informs Bryant's piece.
2. Does Bryant's position seem relevant to worker-employee relations today as you've read about them or heard them discussed in the news?
3. Compare Bryant's use of logic to another writer's use of the same appeal in making an argument. (Consider Jackson, Apess, or Stewart as possibilities).

Ralph Waldo Emerson

Often called the father of American literature, Ralph Waldo Emerson (1803–1882) was a poet, minister, essayist, and lecturer, calling for a new literature and a new art to characterize the uniquely American experience. Born in Massachusetts, his minister father died when he was eight, and though he was of a genteel class, he was in poverty for much of his early life. He graduated from Harvard, became a minister, and began delivering sermons that soon brought him both acclaim and scorn for their nontraditional, romantic, and, some thought, sacrilegious content. His belief in the individual's original relationship to nature and the divine became the basis for the Transcendentalist movement in the early nineteenth century and made him world famous. Most of the writers and thinkers in nineteenth-century America were influenced by Emerson: Thoreau, Whitman, Hawthorne, Melville, Alcott, and others.

The American Scholar

An Oration Delivered Before the Phi Beta Kappa Society, at Cambridge, August 31, 1837

Mr. President and Gentlemen:

I greet you on the recommencement of our literary° year. Our anniversary is one of hope, and, perhaps, not enough of labor. We do not meet for games of strength or skill, for the recitation of histories, tragedies, and odes, like the ancient Greeks; for parliaments of love and poesy, like the Troubadours; nor for the advancement of science, like our contemporaries in the British and European capitals. Thus far, our holiday has been simply a friendly sign of the survival of the love of letters amongst a people too busy to give to letters any more. As such it is precious as the sign of an indestructible instinct. Perhaps the time is already come when it ought to be, and will be, something else; when the sluggard intellect of this continent will look from under its iron lids and fill the postponed expectation of the world with something better than the exertions of mechanical skill. Our day of dependence, our long apprenticeship to the learning of other lands, draws to a close. The millions that around us are rushing into life, cannot always be fed on the sere° remains of foreign harvests. Events, actions arise, that must be sung, that will sing themselves. Who can doubt that poetry will revive and lead in a new age, as the star in the constellation Harp,° which now flames in our zenith, astronomers announce, shall one day be the pole-star for a thousand years?

In this hope I accept the topic which not only usage but the nature of our association seem to prescribe to this day,—the American Scholar. Year by year we come up hither to read one more chapter of his biography. Let us inquire what light new days and events have thrown on his character and his hopes.

It is one of those fables which out of an unknown antiquity convey an unlooked-for wisdom, that the gods, in the beginning, divided Man into men, that he might be more helpful to himself; just as the hand was divided into fingers, the better to answer its end.°

The old fable covers a doctrine ever new and sublime; that there is One Man,—present to all particular men only partially, or through one faculty; and that

---

literary: academic

sere: dry, withered

the star in the constellation Harp: The star Vega of the constellation Lyra (or Harp) is the second-brightest star in the northern hemisphere and the fifth-brightest star in the night sky.

end: aim, purpose

you must take the whole society to find the whole man. Man is not a farmer, or a professor, or an engineer, but he is all. Man is priest, and scholar, and statesman, and producer, and soldier. In the *divided* or social state these functions are parcelled out to individuals, each of whom aims to do his stint of the joint work, whilst each other performs his. The fable implies that the individual, to possess himself, must sometimes return from his own labor to embrace all the other laborers. But, unfortunately, this original unit, this fountain of power, has been so distributed to multitudes, has been so minutely subdivided and peddled out, that it is spilled into drops, and cannot be gathered. The state of society is one in which the members have suffered amputation from the trunk, and strut about so many walking monsters,—a good finger, a neck, a stomach, an elbow, but never a man.

Man is thus metamorphosed into a thing, into many things. The planter, who is Man sent out into the field to gather food, is seldom cheered by any idea of the true dignity of his ministry. He sees his bushel and his cart, and nothing beyond, and sinks into the farmer, instead of Man on the farm. The tradesman scarcely ever gives an ideal worth to his work, but is ridden by the routine of his craft, and the soul is subject to dollars. The priest becomes a form; the attorney a statutebook; the mechanic a machine; the sailor a rope of the ship. 5

In this distribution of functions the scholar is the delegated intellect. In the right state he is *Man Thinking*. In the degenerate state, when the victim of society, he tends to become a mere thinker, or still worse, the parrot of other men's thinking.

In this view of him, as Man Thinking, the theory of his office° is contained. Him Nature solicits with all her placid, all her monitory° pictures; him the past instructs; him the future invites. Is not indeed every man a student, and do not all things exist for the student's behoof?° And, finally, is not the true scholar the only true master? But the old oracle said, "All things have two handles: beware of the wrong one." In life, too often, the scholar errs with mankind and forfeits his privilege. Let us see him in his school, and consider him in reference to the main influences he receives.

I. The first in time and the first in importance of the influences upon the mind is that of nature. Every day, the sun; and, after sunset, Night and her stars. Ever the winds blow; ever the grass grows. Every day, men and women, conversing—beholding and beholden. The scholar is he of all men whom this spectacle most engages. He must settle its value in his mind. What is nature to him? There is never a beginning, there is never an end, to the inexplicable continuity of

office: function, role
monitory: cautionary, warning
behoof: use, benefit, advantage

this web of God, but always circular power returning into itself. Therein it resembles his own spirit, whose beginning, whose ending, he never can find,—so entire, so boundless. Far too as her splendors shine, system on system shooting like rays, upward, downward, without centre, without circumference,—in the mass and in the particle, Nature hastens to render account of herself to the mind. Classification begins. To the young mind every thing is individual, stands by itself. By and by it finds how to join two things and see in them one nature; then three, then three thousand; and so, tyrannized over by its own unifying instinct, it goes on tying things together, diminishing anomalies,° discovering roots running under ground whereby contrary and remote things cohere and flower out from one stem. It presently learns that since the dawn of history there has been a constant accumulation and classifying of facts. But what is classification but the perceiving that these objects are not chaotic, and are not foreign, but have a law which is also a law of the human mind? The astronomer discovers that geometry, a pure abstraction of the human mind, is the measure of planetary motion. The chemist finds proportions and intelligible method throughout matter; and science is nothing but the finding of analogy, identity, in the most remote parts. The ambitious soul sits down before each refractory° fact; one after another reduces all strange constitutions, all new powers, to their class and their law, and goes on forever to animate the last fibre of organization, the outskirts of nature, by insight.

Thus to him, to this schoolboy under the bending dome of day, is suggested that he and it proceed from one root; one is leaf and one is flower; relation, sympathy, stirring in every vein. And what is that root? Is not that the soul of his soul? A thought too bold; a dream too wild. Yet when this spiritual light shall have revealed the law of more earthly natures,—when he has learned to worship the soul, and to see that the natural philosophy that now is, is only the first gropings of its gigantic hand, he shall look forward to an ever-expanding knowledge as to a becoming creator. He shall see that nature is the opposite of the soul, answering to it part for part. One is seal and one is print. Its beauty is the beauty of his own mind. Its laws are the laws of his own mind. Nature then becomes to him the measure of his attainments. So much of nature as he is ignorant of, so much of his own mind does he not yet possess. And, in fine, the ancient precept, "Know thyself," and the modern precept, "Study nature," become at last one maxim.

II. The next great influence into the spirit of the scholar is the mind of the Past,—in whatever form, whether of literature, of art, of institutions, that mind is inscribed. Books are the best type of influence of the past, and perhaps we shall get at the truth,—learn the amount of this influence more conveniently,—by considering their value alone. 10

anomalies: deviations, inconsistencies
refractory: stubborn, resistant

The theory of books is noble. The scholar of the first age received into him the world around; brooded thereon; gave it the new arrangement of his own mind, and uttered it again. It came into him life; it went out from him truth. It came to him short-lived actions; it went out from him immortal thoughts. It came to him business; it went from him poetry. It was dead fact; now, it is quick thought. It can stand, and it can go. It now endures, it now flies, it now inspires. Precisely in proportion to the depth of mind from which it issued, so high does it soar, so long does it sing.

Or, I might say, it depends on how far the process had gone, of transmuting life into truth. In proportion to the completeness of the distillation, so will the purity and imperishableness of the product be. But none is quite perfect. As no air-pump can by any means make a perfect vacuum, so neither can any artist entirely exclude the conventional, the local, the perishable from his book, or write a book of pure thought, that shall be as efficient, in all respects, to a remote posterity, as to contemporaries, or rather to the second age. Each age, it is found, must write its own books; or rather, each generation for the next succeeding. The books of an older period will not fit this.

Yet hence arises a grave mischief. The sacredness which attaches to the act of creation, the act of thought, is transferred to the record. The poet chanting was felt to be a divine man: henceforth the chant is divine also. The writer was a just and wise spirit: henceforward it is settled the book is perfect; as love of the hero corrupts into worship of his statue. Instantly the book becomes noxious: the guide is a tyrant. The sluggish and perverted mind of the multitude, slow to open to the incursions of Reason, having once so opened, having once received this book, stands upon it, and makes an outcry if it is disparaged. Colleges are built on it. Books are written on it by thinkers, not by Man Thinking; by men of talent, that is, who start wrong, who set out from accepted dogmas, not from their own sight of principles. Meek young men grow up in libraries, believing it their duty to accept the views which Cicero, which Locke, which Bacon, have given; forgetful that Cicero, Locke, and Bacon were only young men in libraries when they wrote these books.

Hence, instead of Man Thinking, we have the bookworm. Hence the book-learned class, who value books, as such; not as related to nature and the human constitution, but as making a sort of Third Estate with the world and the soul. Hence the restorers of readings, the emendators,° the bibliomaniacs of all degrees.

Books are the best of things, well used; abused, among the worst. What is the right use? What is the one end which all means go to effect?° They are for

15

emendators: correctors
effect: bring about, accomplish

nothing but to inspire. I had better never seen a book than to be warped by its attraction clean out of my own orbit, and made a satellite instead of a system. The one thing in the world, of value, is the active soul. This every man is entitled to; this every man contains within him, although in almost all men obstructed and as yet unborn. The soul active sees absolute truth and utters truth, or creates. In this action it is genius; not the privilege of here and there a favorite, but the sound estate of every man. In its essence it is progressive. The book, the college, the school of art, the institutions of any kind, stop with some past utterance of genius. This is good, say they,—let us hold by this. They pin me down. They look backward and not forward. But genius looks forward: the eyes of man are set in his forehead, not in his hindhead:° man hopes: genius creates. Whatever talents may be, if the man create not, the pure efflux° of the Deity is not his;—cinders and smoke there may be, but not yet flame. There are creative manners, there are creative actions, and creative words; manners, actions, words, that is, indicative of no custom or authority, but springing spontaneous from the mind's own sense of good and fair.

On the other part, instead of being its own seer, let it receive from another mind its truth, though it were in torrents of light, without periods of solitude, inquest,° and self-recovery, and a fatal disservice is done. Genius is always sufficiently the enemy of genius by over-influence. The literature of every nation bears me witness. The English dramatic poets have Shakspearized now for two hundred years.

Undoubtedly there is a right way of reading, so it be sternly subordinated. Man Thinking must not be subdued by his instruments. Books are for the scholar's idle times. When he can read God directly, the hour is too precious to be wasted in other men's transcripts of their readings. But when the intervals of darkness come, as come they must,—when the sun is hid and the stars withdraw their shining,—we repair° to the lamps which were kindled by their ray, to guide our steps to the East again, where the dawn is. We hear, that we may speak. The Arabian proverb says, "A fig tree, looking on a fig tree, becometh fruitful."

It is remarkable, the character of the pleasure we derive from the best books. They impress us with the conviction that one nature wrote and the same reads. We read the verses of one of the great English poets, of Chaucer, of Marvell, of Dryden, with the most modern joy,—with a pleasure, I mean, which is in great part caused by the abstraction of all *time* from their verses. There is some awe mixed with the joy of our surprise, when this poet, who lived in some past world, two or three hundred years ago, says that which lies close to my own

---

hindhead: i.e., the back of the head
efflux: outward flow
inquest: investigation
repair: go

soul, that which I also had well-nigh thought and said. But for the evidence thence afforded to the philosophical doctrine of the identity of all minds, we should suppose some pre-ëstablished harmony, some foresight of souls that were to be, and some preparation of stores° for their future wants,° like the fact observed in insects, who lay up food before death for the young grub they shall never see.

I would not be hurried by any love of system, by any exaggeration of instincts, to underrate the Book. We all know, that as the human body can be nourished on any food, though it were boiled grass and the broth of shoes, so the human mind can be fed by any knowledge. And great and heroic men have existed who had almost no other information than by the printed page. I only would say that it needs a strong head to bear that diet. One must be an inventor to read well. As the proverb says, "He that would bring home the wealth of the Indies, must carry out the wealth of the Indies." There is then creative reading as well as creative writing. When the mind is braced by labor invention, the page of whatever book we read becomes luminous with manifold allusion. Every sentence is doubly significant, and the sense of our author is as broad as the world. We then see, what is always true, that as the seer's hour of vision is short and rare among heavy days and months, so is its record, perchance, the least part of his volume. The discerning will read, in his Plato or Shakspeare, only that least part,—only the authentic utterances of the oracle;—all the rest he rejects, were it never so many times Plato's and Shakspeare's.

Of course there is a portion of reading quite indispensable to a wise man. History and exact science he must learn by laborious reading. Colleges, in like manner, have their indispensable office,—to teach elements. But they can only highly serve us when they aim not to drill, but to create; when they gather from far every ray of various genius to their hospitable halls, and by the concentrated fires, set the hearts of their youth on flame. Thought and knowledge are natures in which apparatus and pretension avail nothing. Gowns and pecuniary° foundations, though of towns of gold, can never contervail° the least sentence or syllable of wit.° Forget this, and our American colleges will recede in their public importance, whilst they grow richer every year. 20

III. There goes in the world a notion that the scholar should be a recluse, a valetudinarian,°—as unfit for any handiwork or public labor as a penknife for an axe. The so-called "practical men" sneer at speculative men, as if, because

stores: supplies
wants: needs
pecuniary: monetary, financial
countervail: counterbalance, offset
wit: understanding, intelligence
valetudinarian: invalid

they speculate or *see,* they could do nothing. I have heard it said that the clergy,—who are always, more universally than any other class, the scholars of their day,—are addressed as women; that the rough, spontaneous conversation of men they do not hear, but only a mincing and diluted speech. They are often virtually disfranchised; and indeed there are advocates for their celibacy. As far as this is true of the studious classes, it is not just and wise. Action is with the scholar subordinate, but it is essential. Without it he is not yet man. Without it thought can never ripen into truth. Whilst the world hangs before the eye as a cloud of beauty, we cannot even see its beauty. Inaction is cowardice, but there can be no scholar without the heroic mind. The preamble of thought, the transition through which it passes from the unconscious to the conscious, is action. Only so much do I know, as I have lived. Instantly we know whose words are loaded with life, and whose not.

The world,—this shadow of the soul, or *other me,*—lies wide around. Its attractions are the keys which unlock my thoughts and make me acquainted with myself. I run eagerly into this resounding tumult. I grasp the hands of those next to me, and take my place in the ring to suffer and to work, taught by an instinct that so shall the dumb abyss be vocal with speech. I pierce its order; I dissipate its fear; I dispose of it within the circuit of my expanding life. So much only of life as I know by experience, so much of the wilderness have I vanquished and planted, or so far have I extended my being, my dominion. I do not see how any man can afford, for the sake of his nerves and his nap, to spare any action in which he can partake. It is pearls and rubies to his discourse. Drudgery, calamity, exasperation, want, are instructors in eloquence and wisdom. The true scholar grudges every opportunity of action past by, as a loss of power. It is the raw material out of which the intellect moulds her splendid products. A strange process too, this by which experience is converted into thought, as a mulberry leaf is converted into satin. The manufacture goes forward at all hours.

The actions and events of our childhood and youth are now matters of calmest observation. They lie like fair pictures in the air. Not so with our recent actions,—with the business which we now have in hand. On this we are quite unable to speculate. Our affections as yet circulate through it. We no more feel or know it, than we feel the feet, or the hand, or the brain of our body. The new deed is yet a part of life,—remains for a time immersed in our unconscious life. In some contemplative hour, it detaches itself from the life like a ripe fruit, to become a thought of the mind. Instantly, it is raised, transfigured; the corruptible has put on incorruption. Always now it is an object of beauty, however base its origin and neighborhood. Observe, too, the impossibility of antedating this act. In its grub state, it cannot fly, it cannot shine,—it is a dull grub. But suddenly, without observation, the selfsame thing unfurls beautiful wings, and is an angel of wisdom. So is there no fact, no event, in our private history, which shall not, sooner or later, lose its adhesive inert form, and astonish us by soaring from our body into the empyrean.° Cradle and infancy, school and playground, the fear of boys, and dogs, and ferules,° the love of little maids and berries, and many another fact that once filled the whole sky, are gone already; friend and relative, profession and party, town and country, nation and world, must also soar and sing.

Of course, he who has put forth his total strength in fit actions, has the richest return of wisdom. I will not shut myself out of this globe of action and transplant an oak into a flower pot, there to hunger and pine; nor trust the revenue of some single faculty, and exhaust one vein of thought, much like those Savoyards,° who, getting their livelihood by carving shepherds, shepherdesses, and smoking Dutchmen, for all Europe, went out one day to the mountain to find stock, and discovered that they had whittled up the last of their pine trees. Authors we have in numbers, who have written out their vein, and who, moved by a commendable prudence, sail for Greece or Palestine, follow the trapper into the prairie, or ramble round Algiers to replenish their merchantable stock.

25 If it were only for a vocabulary the scholar would be covetous of action. Life is our dictionary. Years are well spent in country labors; in town; in the insight into trades and manufactures; in frank intercourse° with many men and women; in science; in art; to the one end of mastering in all their facts a language by which to illustrate and embody our perceptions. I learn immediately from any speaker how much he has already lived, through the poverty or the splendor of his speech. Life lies behind us as the quarry from whence we get tiles and copestones° for the masonry of to-day. This is the way to learn grammar. Colleges and books only copy the language which the field and the workyard made.

But the final value of action, like that of books, and better than books, is that it is a resource. That great principle of Undulation in nature, that shows itself in the inspiring and expiring of the breath; in desire and satiety;° in the ebb and flow of the sea; in day and night; in heat and cold; and, as yet more deeply ingrained in every atom and every fluid, is known to us under the name of Polarity,—these "fits of easy transmission and reflection," as Newton called them, are the law of nature because they are the law of spirit.

---

empyrean: heavens

ferules: wooden canes or paddles for punishing by striking on the palm

Savoyards: inhabitants of the Duchy of Savoy, in what is now southeastern France

intercourse: dealings, interactions

copestones: top stone of a building

satiety: the state of being satisfied

The mind now thinks, now acts, and each reproduces the other. When the artist has exhausted his materials, when the fancy no longer paints, when thoughts are no longer apprehended and books are a weariness,—he has always the resource *to live.* Character is higher than intellect. Thinking is the function. Living is the functionary. The stream retreats to its source. A great soul will be strong to live, as well as strong to think. Does he lack organ or medium to impart his truths? He can still fall back on this elemental force of living them. This is a total act. Thinking is a partial act. Let the grandeur of justice shine in his affairs. Let the beauty of affection cheer his lowly roof. Those "far from fame," who dwell and act with him, will feel the force of his constitution in the doings and passages of the day better than it can be measured by any public and designed display. Time shall teach him that the scholar loses no hour which the man lives. Herein he unfolds the sacred germ of his instinct, screened from influence. What is lost in seemliness is gained in strength. Not out of those on whom systems of education have exhausted their culture, comes the helpful giant to destroy the old or to build the new, but out of unhandselled° savage nature; out of terrible° Druids and Berserkers° come at last Alfred° and Shakspeare.

I hear therefore with joy whatever is beginning to be said of the dignity and necessity of labor to every citizen. There is virtue yet in the hoe and the spade, for learned as well as for unlearned hands. And labor is everywhere welcome; always we are invited to work; only be this limitation observed, that a man shall not for the sake of wider activity sacrifice any opinion to the popular judgments and modes of action.

I have now spoken of the education of the scholar by nature, by books, and by action. It remains to say somewhat of his duties.

They are such as become Man Thinking. They may all be comprised in self-trust. The office of the scholar is to cheer, to raise, and to guide men by showing them facts amidst appearances. He plies the slow, unhonored, and unpaid task of observation. Flamsteed° and Herschel,° in their glazed observatories, may catalogue the stars with the praise of all men, and the results being splendid and useful, honor is sure. But he, in his private observatory, cataloguing obscure and nebulous stars of the human mind, which as yet no man has thought of as such,—watching days and months sometimes for a few facts; correcting still his old records;—must relinquish display and immediate fame. 30

---

unhandselled: untouched, untamed

terrible: causing terror

Berserkers: ancient Norse warriors

Alfred: called "the Great" (849–899), king of the West Saxons (871–899)

Flamsteed: John Flamsteed (1646–1719), English astronomer

Herschel: Sir William Herschel (1738–1822), German-born English astronomer

In the long period of his preparation he must betray often an ignorance and shiftlessness in popular arts, incurring the disdain of the able who shoulder him aside. Long he must stammer in his speech; often forgo the living for the dead. Worse yet, he must accept—how often!—poverty and solitude. For the ease and pleasure of treading the old road, accepting the fashions, the education, the religion of society, he takes the cross of making his own, and, of course, the self-accusation, the faint heart, the frequent uncertainty and loss of time, which are the nettles and tangling vines in the way of the self-relying and self-directed; and the state of virtual hostility in which he seems to stand to society, and especially to educated society. For all this loss and scorn, what offset? He is to find consolation in exercising the highest functions of human nature. He is one who raises himself from private considerations and breathes and lives on public and illustrious thoughts. He is the world's eye. He is the world's heart. He is to resist the vulgar prosperity that retrogrades° ever to barbarism, by preserving and communicating heroic sentiments, noble biographies, melodious verse, and the conclusions of history. Whatsoever oracles the human heart, in all emergencies, in all solemn hours, has uttered as its commentary on the world of actions,—these he shall receive and impart. And whatsoever new verdict Reason from her inviolable seat pronounces on the passing men and events of to-day,—this he shall hear and promulgate.°

These being his functions, it becomes° him to feel all confidence in himself, and to defer never to the popular cry. He and he only knows the world. The world of any moment is the merest appearance. Some great decorum, some fetish of a government, some ephemeral trade, or war, or man, is cried up by half mankind and cried down by the other half, as if all depended on this particular up or down. The odds are that the whole question is not worth the poorest thought which the scholar has lost in listening to the controversy. Let him not quit his belief that a popgun is a popgun, though the ancient and honorable of the earth affirm it to be the crack of doom. In silence, in steadiness, in severe abstraction, let him hold by himself; add observation to observation, patient of neglect, patient of reproach, and bide his own time,—happy enough if he can satisfy himself alone that this day he has seen something truly. Success treads on every right step. For the instinct is sure, that prompts him to tell his brother what he thinks. He then learns that in going down into the secrets of his own mind he has descended into the secrets of all minds. He learns that he who has mastered any law in his private thoughts, is master to that extent of all men whose language he speaks, and of all into whose language his own can be translated. The poet, in utter solitude remembering his spontaneous thoughts and recording them, is found to have recorded that which men in crowded

---

retrogrades: moves backward, degenerates

promulgate: proclaim, advocate

becomes: suits, befits

cities find true for them also. The orator distrusts at first the fitness of his frank confessions, his want° of knowledge of the persons he addresses, until he finds that he is the complement of his hearers;—that they drink his words because he fulfils for them their own nature; the deeper he dives into his privatest, secretest presentiment, to his wonder he finds this is the most acceptable, most public, and universally true. The people delight in it; the better part of every man feels, This is my music; this is myself.

In self-trust all the virtues are comprehended. Free should the scholar be,—free and brave. Free even to the definition of freedom, "without any hindrance that does not arise out of his own constitution." Brave; for fear is a thing which a scholar by his very function puts behind him. Fear always springs from ignorance. It is a shame to him if his tranquillity, amid dangerous times, arise from the presumption that like children and women his is a protected class; or if he seek a temporary peace by the diversion of his thoughts from politics or vexed questions, hiding his head like an ostrich in the flowering bushes, peeping into microscopes, and turning rhymes, as a boy whistles to keep his courage up. So is the danger a danger still; so is the fear worse. Manlike let him turn and face it. Let him look into its eye and search its nature, inspect its origin,—see the whelping° of this lion,—which lies no great way back; he will then find in himself a perfect comprehension of its nature and extent; he will have made his hands meet on the other side, and can henceforth defy it and pass on superior. The world is his who can see through its pretension. What deafness, what stone-blind custom, what over-grown error you behold is there only by sufferance,°—by your sufferance. See it to be a lie, and you have already dealt it its mortal blow.

Yes, we are the cowed,—we the trustless. It is a mischievous notion that we are come late into nature; that the world was finished a long time ago. As the world was plastic° and fluid in the hands of God, so it is ever to so much of his attributes as we bring to it. To ignorance and sin, it is flint.° They adapt themselves to it as they may; but in proportion as a man has any thing in him divine, the firmament flows before him and takes his signet° and form. Not he is great who can alter matter, but he who can alter my state of mind. They are the kings of the world who give the color of their present thought to all nature and all art, and persuade men by the cheerful serenity of their carrying the matter, that this thing which they do is the apple which the ages have desired to pluck,

---

want: lack
whelping: birthing
sufferance: permission
plastic: moldable
flint: i.e., the material that lights a flame
signet: seal of identification or authentication

now at last ripe, and inviting nations to the harvest. The great man makes the great thing. Wherever Macdonald° sits, there is the head of the table. Linnæus° makes botany the most alluring of studies, and wins it from the farmer and the herb-woman; Davy,° chemistry, and Cuvier,° fossils. The day is always his who works in it with serenity and great aims. The unstable estimates of men crowd to him whose mind is filled with a truth, as the heaped waves of the Atlantic follow the moon.

For this self-trust, the reason is deeper than can be fathomed,—darker than can be enlightened. I might not carry with me the feeling of my audience in stating my own belief. But I have already shown the ground of my hope, in adverting to the doctrine that man is one. I believe man has been wronged; he has wronged himself. He has almost lost the light that can lead him back to his prerogatives. Men are become of no account. Men in history, men in the world of to-day, are bugs, are spawn, and are called "the mass" and "the herd." In a century, in a millennium, one or two men; that is to say, one or two approximations to the right state of every man. All the rest behold in the hero or the poet their own green and crude being,—ripened; yes, and are content to be less, so *that* may attain to its full stature. What a testimony, full of grandeur, full of pity, is borne to the demands of his own nature, by the poor clansman, the poor partisan, who rejoices in the glory of his chief. The poor and the low find some amends to their immense moral capacity, for their acquiescence in a political and social inferiority. They are content to be brushed like flies from the path of a great person, so that justice shall be done by him to that common nature which it is the dearest desire of all to see enlarged and glorified. They sun themselves in the great man's light, and feel it to be their own element. They cast the dignity of man from their down-trod selves upon the shoulders of a hero, and will perish to add one drop of blood to make that great heart beat, those giant sinews combat and conquer. He lives for us, and we live in him.

Men, such as they are, very naturally seek money or power; and power because it is as good as money,—the "spoils," so called, "of office." And why not? for they aspire to the highest, and this, in their sleep-walking, they dream is highest. Wake them and they shall quit the false good and leap to the true, and leave governments to clerks and desks. This revolution is to be wrought by the gradual domestication of the idea of Culture. The main enterprise of the world for splendor, for extent,° is the upbuilding of a man. Here are the materials strewn along the ground. The private life of one man shall be a more 35

Macdonald: head of the Scottish clan MacDonald

Linnæus: Carolus Linnaeus (1707–1778), Swedish botanist

Davy: Sir Humphry Davy (1778–1829), English chemist

Cuvier: Baron Georges Léopold Cuvier (1769–1832), French naturalist

extent: range, scope

illustrious monarchy, more formidable to its enemy, more sweet and serene in its influence to its friend, than any kingdom in history. For a man, rightly viewed, comprehendeth the particular natures of all men. Each philosopher, each bard, each actor has only done for me, as by a delegate, what one day I can do for myself. The books which once we valued more than the apple of the eye, we have quite exhausted. What is that but saying that we have come up with the point of view which the universal mind took through the eyes of one scribe; we have been that man, and have passed on. First, one, then another, we drain all cisterns,° and waxing greater by all these supplies, we crave a better and more abundant food. The man has never lived that can feed us ever. The human mind cannot be enshrined in a person who shall set a barrier on any one side to this unbounded, unboundable empire. It is one central fire, which, flaming now out of the lips of Etna, lightens the capes of Sicily, and now out of the throat of Vesuvius, illuminates the towers and vineyards of Naples. It is one light which beams out of a thousand stars. It is one soul which animates all men.

. . .

But I have dwelt perhaps tediously upon this abstraction of the Scholar. I ought not delay longer to add what I have to say of nearer reference to the time and to this country.

Historically, there is thought to be a difference in the ideas which predominate over successive epochs, and there are data for marking the genius of the Classic, of the Romantic, and now of Reflective or Philosophical age. With the views I have intimated of the oneness or the identity of the mind through all individuals, I do not much dwell on these differences. In fact, I believe each individual passes through all three. The boy is a Greek; the youth, romantic; the adult, reflective. I deny not, however, that a revolution in the leading idea may be distinctly enough traced.

Our age is bewailed as the age of Introversion. Must that needs be evil? We, it seems, are critical; we are embarrassed with second thoughts; we cannot enjoy any thing for hankering to know whereof the pleasure consists; we are lined with eyes; we see with our feet; the time is infected with Hamlet's unhappiness,—

> "Sicklied o'er with the pale cast of thought."°

Is it so bad then? Sight is the last thing to be pitied. Would we be blind? Do we fear lest we should outsee nature and God, and drink truth dry? I look upon the discontent of the literary class as a mere announcement of the fact that 40

---

cisterns: tanks for storing water

"Sicklied . . . thought": from the "To be or not to be" soliloquy in Shakespeare's *Hamlet*, Act 3, Scene 1

they find themselves not in the state of mind of their fathers, and regret the coming state as untried; as a boy dreads the water before he has learned that he can swim. If there is any period one would desire to be born in, is it not the age of Revolution; when the old and the new stand side by side and admit of being compared; when the energies of all men are searched by fear and by hope; when the historic glories of the old can be compensated by the rich possibilities of the new era? This time, like all times, is a very good one, if we but know what to do with it.

I read with some joy of the auspicious signs of the coming days, as they glimmer already through poetry and art, through philosophy and science, through church and state.

One of these signs is the fact that the same movement which effected the elevation of what was called the lowest class in the state, assumed in literature a very marked and as benign an aspect. Instead of the sublime and beautiful, the near, the low, the common, was explored and poetized. That which had been negligently trodden under foot by those who were harnessing and provisioning themselves for long journeys into far countries, is suddenly found to be richer than all foreign parts. The literature of the poor, the feelings of the child, the philosophy of the street, the meaning of household life, are the topics of the time. It is a great stride. It is a sign—is it not?—of new vigor when the extremities are made active, when currents of warm life run into the hands and the feet. I ask not for the great, the remote, the romantic; what is doing in Italy or Arabia; what is Greek art, or Provençal° minstrelsy; I embrace the common, I explore and sit at the feet of the familiar, the low. Give me insight into to-day, and you may have the antique° and future worlds. What would we really know the meaning of? The meal in the firkin;° the milk in the pan; the ballad in the street; the news of the boat; the glance of the eye; the form and the gait of the body;—show me the ultimate reason of these matters; show me the sublime presence of the highest spiritual cause lurking, as always it does lurk, in these suburbs and extremities of nature; let me see every trifle bristling with the polarity that ranges it instantly on an eternal law; and the shop, the plough, and the ledger referred to the like cause by which light undulates and poets sing;—and the world lies no longer a dull miscellany and lumber-room,° but has form and order; there is no trifle, there is no puzzle, but one design unites and animates the farthest pinnacle and the lowest trench.

Provençal: pertaining to the region of Provence in southeastern France, where the medieval troubadours flourished

antique: ancient

firkin: small wooden barrel or tub

lumber-room: storeroom

This idea has inspired the genius of Goldsmith,° Burns,° Cowper,° and, in a newer time, of Goethe,° Wordsworth,° and Carlyle.° This idea they have differently followed and with various success. In contrast with their writing, the style of Pope,° of Johnson,° of Gibbon,° looks cold and pedantic. This writing is blood-warm. Man is surprised to find that things near are not less beautiful and wondrous than things remote. The near explains the far. The drop is a small ocean. A man is related to all nature. This perception of the worth of the vulgar is fruitful in discoveries. Goethe, in this very thing the most modern of the moderns, has shown us, as none ever did, the genius of the ancients.

There is one man of genius who has done much for this philosophy of life, whose literary value has never yet been rightly estimated;—I mean Emanuel Swedenborg.° The most imaginative of men, yet writing with the precision of a mathematician, he endeavored to engraft a purely philosophical Ethics on the popular Christianity of his time. Such an attempt of course must have difficulty which no genius could surmount. But he saw and showed the connection between nature and the affections of the soul. He pierced the emblematic or spiritual character of the visible, audible, tangible world. Especially did his shade-loving muse hover over and interpret the lower parts of nature; he showed the mysterious bond that allies moral evil to the foul material forms, and has given in epical parables a theory of insanity, of beasts, of unclean and fearful things.

Another sign of our times, also marked by an analogous political movement, is the new importance given to the single person. Every thing that tends to insulate the individual,—to surround him with barriers of natural respect, so that each man shall feel the world is his, and man shall treat with man as a sovereign state with a sovereign state,—tends to true union as well as greatness. "I learned," said the melancholy Pestalozzi,° "that no man in God's wide earth is either willing or able to help any other man." Help must come from the bosom alone. The scholar is that man who must take up into himself all the ability of the time, all the contributions of the past, all the hopes of the future. He must 45

Goldsmith: Oliver Goldsmith (1728–1774), English dramatist, novelist, and poet

Burns: Robert Burns (1759–1796), Scottish poet

Cowper: William Cowper (1731–1800), English poet

Goethe: Johann Wolfgang von Goethe (1749–1832), German dramatist, novelist, and poet

Wordsworth: William Wordsworth (1770–1850), English poet

Carlyle: Thomas Carlyle (1795–1881), English essayist and historian; friend and colleague of Emerson

Pope: Alexander Pope (1688–1744), English poet

Johnson: Samuel Johnson (1709–1784), English essayist and literary figure

Gibbon: Edward Gibbon (1737–1794), English historian, author of *The Decline and Fall of the Roman Empire*

Emanuel Swedenborg: (1688–1772), Swedish scientist and theologian

Pestalozzi: Johann Heinrich Pestalozzi (1746–1827), Swiss educational reformer

be an university of knowledges. If there be one lesson more than another which should pierce his ear, it is, The world is nothing, the man is all; in yourself is the law of all nature, and you know not yet how a globule of sap ascends; in yourself slumbers the whole of Reason; it is for you to know all; it is for you to dare all. Mr. President and Gentlemen, this confidence in the unsearched might of man belongs, by all motives, by all prophecy, by all preparation, to the American Scholar. We have listened too long to the courtly muses of Europe. The spirit of the American freeman is already suspected to be timid, imitative, tame. Public and private avarice make the air we breathe thick and fat. The scholar is decent, indolent, complaisant. See already the tragic consequence. The mind of this country, taught to aim at low objects, eats upon itself. There is no work for any but the decorous and the complaisant. Young men of the fairest promise, who begin life upon our shores, inflated by the mountain winds, shined upon by all the stars of God, find the earth below not in unison with these, but are hindered from action by the disgust which the principles on which business is managed inspire, and turn drudges, or die of disgust, some of them suicides. What is the remedy? They did not yet see, and thousands of young men as hopeful now crowding to the barriers for the career do not yet see, that if the single man plant himself indomitably° on his instincts, and there abide, the huge world will come round to him. Patience,—patience; with the shades of all the good and great for company; and for solace the perspective of your own infinite life; and for work the study and the communication of principles, the making those instincts prevalent, the conversion of the world. Is it not the chief disgrace in the world, not to be an unit;—not to be reckoned one character;—not to yield that peculiar fruit which each man was created to bear, but to be reckoned in the gross, in the hundred, or the thousand, or the party, the section, to which we belong; and our opinion predicted geographically, as the north, or the south? Not so, brothers and friends—please God, ours shall not be so. We will walk on our own feet; we will work with our own hands; we will speak our own minds. The study of letters shall be no longer a name for pity, for doubt, and for sensual indulgence. The dread of man and the love of man shall be a wall of defence and a wreath of joy around all. A nation of men will for the first time exist, because each believes himself inspired by the Divine Soul which also inspires all men.

[1837]

Read

1. Who is the audience for Emerson's speech? How is the audience significant to the message?
2. What is the purpose of the allusion to the Greek myth at the beginning of the essay?
3. How does Emerson define "man thinking"?
4. What strikes you most about Emerson's attitude toward reading?

---

indomitably: unconquerably

Write

1. How would you describe Emerson's style? Consider his choice of images and words, as well as his syntax.
2. Reflect on why this speech was so appealing when it was delivered.
3. How does Emerson emphasize the importance of experience?
4. Write a paragraph about what you think Emerson is urging his hearers to do.

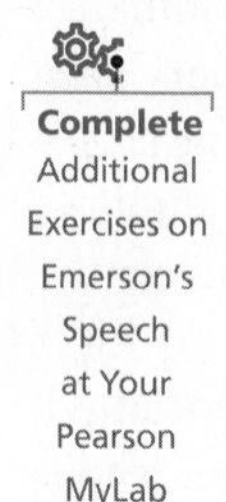

Complete Additional Exercises on Emerson's Speech at Your Pearson MyLab

Connect

1. How does Emerson's appeal to his audience affect you as a twenty-first-century reader?
2. How do you see Emerson's ideas about creativity, experiment, or experience suggested in the writing of any thinkers you read in Unit 1?
3. Write a reflection about any time you think you have been "man [or woman] thinking."

James Diamond, Samuel Dobie, Stephen Hallet, and William Thornton

James Diamond, Samuel Hobie and Stephen Hallet were three of the competitors who submitted designs for the new U.S. Capitol Building. They were all architects interested in Greek revival style and Hallet, a respected architect from France, had recently arrived in the country. The winner of the competition, Dr. William Thornton, was an amateur designer, the only amateur architect in the group. The cornerstone of the Capitol was laid in 1793. The building was finally completed in 1826.

Four Designs for the Capitol Building, 1792

James Diamond's Design

Samuel Dobie's Design

Stephen Hallet's Design

William Thornton's Design

Read

1. What similarities are most striking in the four designs for the Capitol Building?
2. What differences seem most clear?
3. The Capitol Building is in the Greek or Classical style. What characteristics would you think are important to that style based on these designs?

Write

1. Why do you think Thornton's design was chosen?
2. What does the building's design suggest about American government and beliefs?

Connect

1. Find another country's main governmental building to compare with the U.S. Capitol in terms of its physical details and its rhetorical effects.

Contemporary Works

Ethel Stephens Arnett

Ethel Stephens Arnett was a history professor at the University of North Carolina Greensboro, where she taught North Carolina and United States history for over twenty years. Besides her biography of Greensboro native and first lady Dolley Madison, Arnett wrote a history of the last days of the Civil War in North Carolina, a biography of short fiction writer O. Henry, and several other histories of famous North Carolinians.

From *Mrs. James Madison: The Incomparable Dolley*

The world might never have known where Dolley Madison was or what she was doing while the Americans forces were being defeated at the Battle of Bladensburg,° had she not written to her sister Lucy a detailed account of the unusual experience she was undergoing at the President's House. Alone, except for the presence of a few servants, she was waiting for news of the outcome of the military developments. It is somewhat surprising that she did not ask her sister Anna, who was at her near-by home, to come to the President's House and wait with her for whatever might happen, because she and Anna were accustomed to sharing their lives with one another. Available records show that the First Lady at this crucial time wished to present no appearance of anxiety. Since the situation called for utmost calm, she desired that no one should think that she was overly excited. Verily, she was calm enough to realize the importance of keeping a record of what was happening around her, and the letter which she wrote to Lucy was the beginning of her report. As it has turned out, she was writing an important document, which presents the

the Battle of Bladensburg: British victory at Bladensburg, Maryland, on August 24, 1814

most graphic and dramatic description that has yet been released about the situation in Washington at that time. A reproduction of that letter therefore has a place in this account:

Tuesday Augt. 23d 1814

Dear Sister,—My husband left me yesterday morning to join Gen. Winder. He inquired seriously whether I had courage, or firmness to remain in the President's house until his return, on the morrow, or succeeding day, and on my assurance that I had no fear but for him and the success of our army, he left me, beseeching me to take care of myself, and of the cabinet papers, public and private. I have since recd two dispatches from him, written with a pencil; the last is alarming, because he desires I should be ready at a moment's warning to enter my carriage and leave the city; that the army seemed stronger than had been reported, and that it might happen that they would reach the city, with intention to destroy it. x x x x x x I am accordingly ready; I have pressed as many cabinet papers into trunks as to fill one carriage; our private property must be sacrificed, as it is impossible to procure wagons for its transportation. I am determined not to go myself until I see Mr. Madison safe, and he can accompany me,—as I hear of much hostility towards him. x x x Disaffection stalks around us. x x x x My friends and acquaintances are all gone; even Col. C—, with his hundred men, who were stationed as a guard in the enclosure x x French John (a faithful domestic) with his usual activity and resolution, offers to spike the cannon at the gate, and to lay a train of powder which would blow up the British, should they enter the house. To the last proposition I positively object, without being able, however, to make him understand why all advantages in war may not be taken.

Wednesday morn.g, twelve o'clock.—Since sunrise I have been turning my spy glass in every direction and watching with unwearied anxiety, hoping to discern the approach of my dear husband and his friends; but, alas, I can descry° only groups of military wandering in all directions, as if there was a lack of arms, or of spirit to fight for their own firesides!

Three o'clock.—Will you believe it, my Sister? We have had a battle or skirmish near Bladensburg, and I am still here within sound of the cannon! Mr. Madison comes not; may God protect him! Two messengers covered with dust, come to bid me fly; but I wait for him. x x x At this late hour a wagon had been procured; I have had it filled with the plate° and most valuable

---

descry: discern, perceive

plate: metal dishes and utensils plated with gold or silver

portable articles belonging to the house; whether it will reach its destination, the Bank of Maryland, or fall into the hands of British soldiery, events must determine.

Our kind friend, Mr. Carroll, has come to hasten my departure, and is in a very bad humor with me because I insist on waiting until the large picture of Gen. Washington is secured, and it requires to be unscrewed from the wall. This process was found too tedious for these perilous moments; I have ordered the frame to be broken, and the canvas taken out; it is done,—and the precious portrait placed in the hands of two gentlemen of New York, for safe keeping, And now, dear Sister, I must leave this house, or the retreating army will make me a prisoner in it, by filling up the road I am directed to take. When I shall again write you, or where I shall be tomorrow, I cannot tell!!

On the day of August 24, 1814, while Pleasanton° was journeying to Leesburg with his consignment of public records, Dolley was still at the President's House, anxiously waiting for her husband and his friends to return from the army. From the letter she wrote to Lucy, one can almost see her as she went from top window to window, turning her spyglass in every direction and watching with unwearied anxiety, hoping to discern the approach of "my dear husband and his friends." And one can almost feel her distress, as she watched undirected "groups of the military wandering in all directions as if there was a lack of arms, or of spirit to fight for their own firesides." It was a long and lonely vigil she was keeping, but she was never infirm of purpose.

Twice during the day Mayor Blake° went to the President's House to warn Mrs. Madison of the peril of her situation and to urge her immediate departure; still she lingered there for news of the President. As time wore on, she decided to have the full-length portrait of General Washington, which hung in the President's House, removed to a place of safety. That task was so difficult that she asked two of her servants to cut away the large outside frame, in order that they might be able to lift the portrait down from the wall.

At that time it was approximately three o'clock in the afternoon. All at once, "as Sukey, the house-servant, was lolling out of a chamber window, James Smith, a free colored man who had accompanied Mr. Madison to Bladensburg, galloped up to the house, waving his hat, and cried out, 'Clear out, clear out! General Armstrong° has ordered a retreat!' All then was confusion.

Pleasanton: Stephen Pleasanton, a clerk in the State Department

Mayor Blake: James H. Blake (1768–1819), mayor of Washington, DC (1813–1817)

General Armstrong: John Armstrong, Jr. (1758–1843), Madison's Secretary of War, whose failure to defend Washington forced his resignation in September 1814

Mrs. Madison ordered her carriage, and passing through the dining-room, caught up what silver she could crowd into her old-fashioned reticule,° and then jumped into the chariot with her servant girl Sukey, and Daniel Carroll, who took charge of them; Jo Bolin drove them over to Georgetown Heights; the British were expected in a few minutes." This story was told by Paul Jennings, President Madison's valet. He added to his account the comment that "People were running in every direction. John Freeman (the colored butler) drove off in the coachee° with his wife, child, and servant; also a feather bed lashed on behind the coachee, which was all the furniture saved, except part of the silver and the portrait of Washington."

There are extant several somewhat dissimilar narratives concerning the rescue of the famous portrait of George Washington. In her letter to Lucy, Dolley herself clearly described how she had ordered the outside frame broken and the canvas taken out. Charles J. Ingersoll, an intimate friend of the Madisons, in his *Historical Sketch of the Second War between the United States and Great Britain,* gave firsthand information on additional details. He stated that Dolley stood by with a carving knife in her hand while John Sioussat, her First Master of Ceremonies, and Thomas McGaw, her Irish gardner, labored with a hatchet to cut the heavy external gilt frame away from the picture, while preserving it uninjured on the inner wooden frame by which it was kept distended.° 5

In this story's retelling there is a difference of opinion about exactly what each one did, when the men were getting the picture from the wall. It is generally agreed, however, that Jacob Barker and Robert De Peyster were the "two gentlemen of New York" who came in at the last minute to help with the difficult task. "Save that picture," Dolley said to them. "Save that picture, if possible; if not possible, destroy it." Incredibly, the portrait was saved and hastily carried away to its hiding place. Ingersoll concluded:

Carried off, upheld whole in the inner wooden frame, beyond Georgetown, the picture was deposited by Mr. Barker in a place of safety. The presidential household god, the image of the father of his country–by whom its chief city was fixed near his home, and by whose name it was called—was thus snatched from the clutch or torch of the barbarian captors. Such, as near as it can be ascertained, is the truth of its rescue.

Ingersoll's account mentioned Barker only in connection with hiding the portrait. Benson Lossing in his *Pictorial Field-Book of the War of 1812* stated that Barker wrote to him, Lossing, that he, Barker, returned the picture to the President's House. De Peyster, however, was definitely connected with the

---

reticule: small purse or handbag

coachee: a coachlike carriage, but longer and open in front

distended: stretched

rescue, for in 1848 when the Charles Carroll family tried to claim the honor of saving the portrait, De Peyster declared in a letter to Mrs. Madison that he himself had witnessed the dismantling under Mrs. Madison's directions. In the meantime, some one had accused Dolley of trying to get credit for her patriotic act, because in the Library of Congress there is a letter which she wrote to De Peyster, in which she stated; "I acted thus because of my respect for General Washington—not that I felt a desire to gain laurels; but should there be a merit in remaining an hour in danger of life and liberty to save the likeness of anything, the merit in this case belongs to me."

A few months later, as Dolley thought about her demolished home, she summarized for her dear friend Mrs. Latrobe something of her feelings. She wrote that she had been able to save nearly all the silver, the crimson velvet curtains in the Oval Room, General Washington's portrait, the Cabinet papers, a few books, and a small clock. "Everything else belonging to the publick, our own valuable stores of every description, a part of my clothers," burned with the President's House:

.... in short, it would fatigue you to read the list of my losses, or an account of the general dismay, or particular distresses of your acquaintance... I confess that I was so unfeminine as to be free from fear, and willing to remain in the Castle. If I could have had a cannon through every window, but alas! those who should have placed them there, fled before me, and my whole heart mourned for my country! I remained nearly three days out of town, but I cannot tell you what I felt on re-entering it—such destruction—such confusion! The fleet full in view and in the act of robbing Alexandria! The citizens expecting another visit—and at night the rockets were seen flying near us!

[1972]

Read

1. What is the purpose of the biographer's inclusion of the letter from Dolley?
2. How does the writer build suspense as the attack on Washington progresses?
3. How does the story of the painting of George Washington help create a portrait of Dolley Madison?
4. From this excerpt, how would you describe the biographer's purpose?

Write

1. How does Arnett appear to feel about Dolley Madison? What words or details reveal her attitude?
2. Write a short speculation about early nineteenth-century life in America based on this excerpt.

3. What does this piece indicate about the role of women and presidential power at the time?

Connect

1. Find information on the War of 1812 and the invasion of Washington, DC, to give a context to this excerpt of Dolley Madison's escape.
2. Looking at the portrait of George Washington earlier in this unit, why do you think Dolley Madison felt it so important to save it?

Stewart Udall

Stewart Udall (1920–2010) was a politician and pioneer in the modern conservation movement. Born in Arizona, Udall grew up near open land and formed an appreciation for nature and for the American Indian tribes who lived in harmony with it. He was appointed by President John F. Kennedy as Secretary of the Interior in 1960 and served in that post for eight years. Udall was instrumental in creating the Environmental Protection Agency and the federal Wilderness Act.

The Land Wisdom of the Indians

In the dust where we have buried the silent races and their abominations we have buried so much of the delicate magic of life.

—D. H. Lawrence (at Taos)

There are, today, a few wilderness reaches on the North American continent—in Alaska, in Canada, and in the high places of the Rocky Mountains—where the early-morning mantle of primeval America can be seen in its pristine glory, where one can gaze with wonder on the land as it was when the Indians first came. Geologically and geographically this continent was, and is, a masterpiece. With its ideal latitude and rich resources, the two-billion-acre expanse that became the United States was the promised land for active men.

The American continent was in a state of climax at the time of the first Indian intrusions ten millennia or more ago. Superlatives alone could describe the bewildering abundance of flora and fauna that enlivened its landscapes: the towering redwoods, the giant saguaro cacti, the teeming herds of buffalo, the beaver, and the grass were, of their kind, unsurpassed.

The most common trait of all primitive peoples is a reverence for the life-giving earth, and the native American shared this elemental ethic; the land was alive to his loving touch, and he, its son, was brother to all creatures. His feelings were made visible in medicine bundles and dance rhythms for rain, and all of his religious rites and land attitudes savored the inseparable world of nature and God, the Master of Life. During the long Indian tenure the land remained undefiled save for scars no deeper than the scratches of cornfield clearings or the farming canals of the Hohokams on the Arizona desert.

There was skill in gardening along with this respect for the earth, and when Sir Walter Raleigh's colonists came warily ashore on the Atlantic Coast, Indians brought them gifts of melons and grapes. In Massachusetts, too, Indians not only schooled the Pilgrims in the culture of maize and squashes, but taught them how to fertilize the hills with alewives° from the tidal creeks. The Five Nations and the Algonquians of the Northeast; the Creeks, Choctaws, Chickasaws, Cherokees, and Seminoles of the South; the village-dwelling Mandans of the Missouri River country; the Pueblos of Hopi, Zuni, and the Rio Grande; and the Pima of the Southwest, all put the earth to use and made it bring forth fruit. Their implements were Stone Age, but most tribes were acquiring the rudiments of a higher civilization. They were learning how to secure a surplus from the earth, and were beginning to invest it in goods, tools, and buildings, and to devote their leisure hours to craft and art work and to the creation of religious rites and political systems.

The idea has long been implanted in our thinking that all American Indians belonged to nomadic bands that developed neither title to, nor ties with, the land. This is misconceived history, for even the tribes that were not village dwellers, tending garden plots of corn, beans, or cotton, had stretches of land they regarded as their own. But there was a subtle qualification. The land and the Indians were bound together by the ties of kinship and nature, rather than by an understanding of property ownership. "The land is our mother," said Iroquois tradition, said the Midwest Sauk and Foxes, said the Northwest Nez Perces of Chief Joseph. The corn, fruits, roots, fish, and game were to all tribes the gifts which the Earth Mother gave freely to her children. And with that conception, the Indian's emotional attachment for his woods, valleys, and prairies were the very essence of life. 5

The depth of this feeling is reflected in the Navajos, who scorned the rich Oklahoma prairie country offered them by the government, and chose to live in their own arid and rugged deserts. It is reflected also in the Cherokees who, in the space of one generation, changed their whole way of life, established schools and libraries, produced an alphabet, planned a constitution and a legislature, and went to work in their own mills and blacksmith shops—all with the purpose of becoming so civilized that the whites would allow them to stay on their own lands and not ship them west to the Territories.

alewives: small shad-like fish

To the Indian, the homeland was the center of the universe. No member of a civilized people ever spoke of his native land with more pride than is apparent in the speech of the Crow Chief, Arapooish: "The Crow country," he said, "is exactly in the right place. It has snowy mountains and sunny plains; all kinds of climates and good things for every season. When the summer heat scorches the prairies, you can draw up under the mountains, where the air is sweet and cool, the grass fresh, and the bright streams come tumbling out of the snowbanks. There you can hunt the elk, the deer, and the antelope, when their skins are fit for dressing; there you will find plenty of white bears and mountain sheep.

"In the autumn, when your horses are fat and strong from the mountain pastures, you can go down into the plains and hunt the buffalo, or trap beaver in the streams. And when winter comes on, you can take shelter in the woody bottoms along the rivers; there you will find buffalo meat for yourselves, and cottonwood bark for your horses; or you may winter in the Wind River Valley where there is salt weed in abundance.

"The Crow country is exactly in the right place. Everything good is to be found there. There is no country like the Crow country."

Here is affection for the land, but no notion of private ownership. The idea that land could be bought and sold was an alien concept to the Indians of America. They clung possessively to certain chattels,° but lands were nearly always held in common. An individual might have the use of a farm plot, but at his death it reverted back to the community. 10

The confrontation of Indians and whites had in it the seeds of hopeless misunderstanding from the start. The two cultures had produced irreconcilable concepts of landownership, and once the first white man set foot on American soil, the drama unfolded with all the certain sweep of a Greek tragedy.

Englishmen, especially, coveted land. It was something to be owned outright. Had not the English King given the charter deeds? The sixteenth-century Spaniard, by contrast, was not primarily interested in seizing land: the soldier wanted personal plunder; the priest came with his seeds and livestock to save Indian souls.

To the joint-stock° companies of Virginia, intent on commercial profits, and to the colonizing Pilgrims, exclusive possession was the be-all and end-all of landownership. But the Indian's "title," based on the idea that he belonged to the land and was its son, was a charter to use—to use in common with his clan or fellow tribesmen, and not to *use up*. Neither white nor Indian fully grasped the concept of the other. The Indian wanted to live not just in the world, but with it; the white man, who thought in terms of estates and baronies, wanted land he alone could cultivate and use.

---

chattels: movable articles of personal property

joint-stock: stock divided into shares or held in common

In the beginning, friendship and co-operation with the Indians were essential if the colonists were to gain a foothold in America, for the white man was badly outnumbered. To be unneighborly was to risk violence, and respect for Indian rights was the better part of wisdom. The upright conduct of the first colonists in Massachusetts and Virginia drew generous response from powerful chiefs who helped the settlements survive.

Live and let live was the inevitable opening keynote, for muskets could neither cut trees nor keep the peace. In the meeting of alien worlds both Indians and whites had something to learn from each other, and if the newcomers borrowed the idea of a feast of thanksgiving from a harvest celebration of neighboring Indians, so much the better. 15

But the first phase ended quickly, and as stockades were completed and new colonists swelled the ranks of the invaders, conciliation became superfluous. As one historian put it, "The Indians were pressed remorselessly when their friendship became of less value than their land." In Virginia, the Indians watched with consternation and alarm as the white men planted tobacco, used up the soil, and every few years moved on to clear new fields. The planters took the Indians' land, first by cajolery° and trade, then by force. So swiftly did events move that, within forty years of the founding of Jamestown, the mighty Powhatans were landless and in beggary at the edge of their former homes. Elsewhere the details were different, but white expansion followed the same general pattern.

The barrier of misunderstanding that arose when advancing whites encountered Indians was too high for either people to scale. Some weak and venal° chiefs bargained away the rights of their people, but for most tribes the sale of large tracts to the settlers was not a solution to their problems, for they had no land to sell. The warrior chief, Tecumseh, stated the Indian philosophy of nearly all tribes with his reply to the demands of white buyers: "Sell the country? . . . Why not sell the air, the clouds, the great sea?"

To the Indian mind, even after two centuries of acquaintance with the whites, land belonged collectively to the people who used it. The notion of private ownership of land, of land as a commodity to be bought and sold, was still alien to their thinking, and tribe after tribe resisted the idea to the death. Land belonged, they said again and again—in the hills of New York, in the Pennsylvania Alleghenies, and in the Ohio Valley—to their ancestors whose bones were buried in it, to the present generation which used it, and to their children who would inherit it. "The land we live on, our fathers received from God," said the Iroquois Cornplanter to George Washington in 1790, "and they transmitted it to us, for our children, and we cannot part with it. . . . Where is the land on which our children and their children after them are to lie down?"

---

cajolery: wheedling; coaxing; insincere promises

venal: open to bribery, corruptible

Had the Indians lacked leaders of integrity, or been less emotionally tied to their hills and valleys, a compromise might have been arranged, but life and land were so intertwined in the Indian scheme of existence that retreat meant surrender of self—and that was unthinkable.

Before the moments of climax came, weaker tribes in all parts of the country made peace, and some of the stronger ones delayed the inevitable by selling parts of their domain. There were fierce chiefs, too, who would not bargain; men repeating the defiance of Canasatego who, representing the Six Nations in Philadelphia in 1742, spoke with contempt of the money and goods acquired in exchange for land. They were gone in a day or an hour, he said, but land was "everlasting." 20

Yet to many another red man, the new goods had an irresistible allure. Contact with the higher technology of Europeans began to make most of what the Indians had known obsolete, and created needs which they could satisfy only by making increased demands upon the bank of the earth. Once seen, a musket became essential to an Indian warrior; and once an Indian woman had used a steel needle or a woven blanket, she could never again be satisfied with a bone awl or a skin robe. The white man was the only source of the new essentials, and the only way to get them was by trade for things the white man wanted—meat, beaver—and later and farther west, pemmican and buffalo robes. So the Indian, too, became a raider of the American earth, and at the same time was himself raided for his lands by the superior technology and increasingly superior numbers of the white man.

The settlers' demand for new territory was insatiable, and what money could not buy, muskets, deceit, and official ruthlessness could win. Worse, as the bloody thrust and counterthrust went on, hatreds deepened and demagogues argued for a "final" solution of the Indian problem. They coined a slogan that became the byword of the American frontier: "The only good Indian is a dead Indian."

In the westward push, new land became the key to progress, and Indian policy was guided solely by economic expediency. A spokesman for the Ottawa, Sioux, Iowa, Winnebago, and other tribes made this sad and unsuccessful appeal at the Council of Drummond Island in 1816: "The Master of Life has given us lands for the support of our men, women, and children. He has given us fish, deer, buffalo, and every kind of birds and animals for our use. . . . When the Master of Life, or Great Spirit, put us on this land, it was for the purpose of enjoying the use of the animals and fishes, but certain it was never intended that we should sell it or any part thereof which gives us wood, grass and everything."

He got his answer the following year when President James Monroe wrote: "The hunter or savage state requires a greater extent of territory to sustain it than is compatible with the progress and just claims of civilized life . . . and must yield to it."

There was a continent to be redeemed from the wilderness, and the Indians' way of life had to be sacrificed. Thus the policy of forced removal was established, and the Five Civilized Tribes were sent, with scant civility and, in the end, scant humanity, on a thousand-mile "trail of tears" to Oklahoma. 25

In its latter stages the land war moved into its cruelest phase in California, the Southwest, and the Upper Great Plains. Most of the California Indians were neither as warlike nor as land-conscious as the Eastern tribes. But even this did not spare them, and the most pitiless chapters of the struggle were written by frustrated gold-seekers who organized vigilante raids, killed helpless natives, and subsequently collected from the government for their deeds of slaughter.

After the Civil War the "clear the redskins out" policy approached its dramatic climax. The mounted Indians of the Upper Great Plains and the Apaches of the Southwest were fierce warriors who would not be cornered. It took regiments of trained cavalrymen over twenty years to drive them from their sacred hills and hunting grounds. Outarmed and outmanned, these warriors made fierce counter-attacks, and our American pride was dealt a grim blow when the hundredth anniversary of the Declaration of Independence was interrupted by the news of the Custer massacre. The undeclared racial war did not end until the final tragic chapters were written in the Pyrrhic victory° of Sitting Bull at the Little Bighorn, and in the last stands of Crazy Horse, Chief Joseph, and Geronimo.

With the final triumphs of the cavalry, and the uneasy settlement of tribes on reservations, the old slogans gradually disappeared, and the new conscience expressed itself in the saying, "It's cheaper to feed 'em than to fight 'em."

The 1887 Allotment Act, which broke up parts of some reservations and gave individual title to some Indians, further stripped away Indian rights by forcing unprepared tribesmen to deal with unscrupulous land swindlers.

With the passage of time and the steady attrition of old ideas and beliefs, we are at last, hopefully, entering a final phase of the Indian saga. The present generation of Indians accepts the system their fathers could not comprehend. The national government strives to provide the Indian people with adequate health and education programs and to aid them in developing the potential of their human and natural resources. As a singular gesture of atonement, which no civilized country has ever matched, the Congress has established a tribunal, the Indians Claims Commission, through which tribes may be compensated for losses suffered when their lands were forcibly taken from them. 30

After long years of peace, we now have an opportunity to measure the influence of the Indians and their culture on the American way of life. They have left with us much more than the magic of place names that identify our rivers and forests and cities and mountains. They have made a contribution to

Pyrrhic victory: one achieved at too great a cost

our agriculture and to a better understanding of how to live in harmony with the land.

It is ironical that today the conservation movement finds itself turning back to ancient Indian land ideas, to the Indian understanding that we are not outside of nature, but of it. From this wisdom we can learn how to conserve the best parts of our continent.

In recent decades we have slowly come back to some of the truths that the Indians knew from the beginning: that unborn generations have a claim on the land equal to our own; that men need to learn from nature, to keep an ear to the earth, and to replenish their spirits in frequent contacts with animals and wild land. And most important of all, we are recovering a sense of reverence for the land.

But the settlers found the Indians' continent too natural and too wild. Though within a generation that wildness would begin to convert some of their sons, and though reverence for the natural world and its forces would eventually sound in much of our literature, finding its prophets in Thoreau and Muir, those first Europeans, even while looking upon the New World with wonder and hope, were determined to subjugate it.

[1963]

Read

1. How does Udall set the tone for his essay in his *exordium* in the first paragraph?
2. What characteristics of the American Indian does Udall emphasize and why?
3. How does Udall demonstrate his credibility as a writer?
4. How does Udall make comparisons between European colonists and Indian people?

Write

1. Write a description of the persona Udall creates in his essay.
2. Do you find Udall persuasive? What are some details from the text that account for your response?
3. Reflect on Udall's attitude toward "progress" as it is implied in his discussion of Indian and white inhabitants.

Connect

1. Find another text in this unit that anticipates the argument Udall is making about tribal people's rights to land.
2. Compare Udall's use of evidence and detail to Andrew Jackson's use of evidence in his essay in this unit.

Harold Bloom

Writer, literary critic, and professor of English at Yale University, Harold Bloom (b. 1930) was born in New York City and educated at Yale. He is a prolific critic of a wide range of authors and literary movements, as well as studies of religion. His perspectives have made him both celebrated and criticized. He writes from what he calls an aesthetic rather than a cultural position on topics ranging from Shakespeare to the poetic impulse to gender and the Bible. Works such as *The Western Canon* and *Anxiety of Influence* have made him a prominent voice in current literary study. This piece was published in the *New York Times*.

Out of Panic, Self-Reliance

In the spring of 1837, a great depression afflicted the northeastern United States. All the banks in New York City, Philadelphia and Baltimore suspended cash payments, as did many in Boston. Of the 850 banks in the United States, nearly half closed or partly failed. If the crisis of 2008 was caused by poor lending, the Panic of 1837, too, featured speculation and inflation.

The bank failures of 1837 were followed by high unemployment that lasted into 1843. Foreign over-investment (chiefly British) had augmented the bubble, which burst when the wily English pulled their money out. President Martin Van Buren, a Jacksonian Democrat, refused any government involvement in a bailout, and so was widely blamed for the panic. Van Buren was defeated in his re-election bid in 1840 by his Whig opponent, William Henry Harrison.

The similarities between the crashes of 1837 and 1929 are evident again today. I am not an economist or a political scientist, but having been born in 1930, I retain poignant early memories of the impact of the Great Depression upon my father, a working man who struggled to maintain a family with five children in a very hard time. I am a scholar of literature and religion, and would advise whoever becomes president to turn to Ralph Waldo Emerson, whose influential vision of America was deeply informed by the crisis of 1837:

> *I see a good in such emphatic and universal calamity as the times bring, that they dissatisfy me with society. Under common burdens we say there is much virtue in the world, and what evil co-exists is inevitable. I am not aroused to say, "I have sinned: I am in a gall of bitterness, and a bond of iniquity"; but when these full measures come, it then stands confessed—society has played out its last stake; it is checkmated. Young men have no hope. Adults stand like day laborers, idle on the streets. None calleth us to labor. The old wear no crown of warm life on their gray hairs. The present*

generation is bankrupt of principles and hope, as of property. I see man is not what man should be. He is the treadle° of a wheel. He is a tassel at the apron string of society. He is a money chest. He is the servant of his belly. This is the causal bankruptcy, this is the cruel oppression, that the ideal should serve the actual, that the head should serve the feet. Then first, I am forced to inquire if the ideal might not also be tried. Is it to be taken for granted that it is impracticable? Behold the boasted world has come to nothing. Prudence itself is at her wits' end.

Pride, and Thrift, and Expediency, who jeered and chirped and were so well pleased with themselves, and made merry with the dream, as they termed it, of Philosophy and Love,— behold they are all flat, and here is the Soul erect and unconquered still. What answer is it now to say, "It has always been so?" I acknowledge that, as far back as I can see the widening procession of humanity, the marchers are lame and blind and deaf; but to the soul that whole past is but one finite series in its infinite scope. Deteriorating ever and now desperate. Let me begin anew. Let me teach the finite to know its master. Let me ascend above my fate and work down upon my world.

It may shock that the Sage of Concord should react to catastrophe with such idealistic glee. Most Americans—the governor of Alaska,° who never blinks, doubtless among them—would be startled by the admonition to begin anew and ascend above our fate.

There is little disagreement that Emerson was the most influential writer of 19th-century America, though these days he is largely the concern of scholars. Walt Whitman, Henry David Thoreau and William James were all positive Emersonians, while Herman Melville, Nathaniel Hawthorne and Henry James were Emersonians in denial—while they set themselves in opposition to the sage, there was no escaping his influence. To T. S. Eliot, Emerson's essays were an "encumbrance." Waldo the Sage was eclipsed from 1914 until 1965, when he returned to shine, after surviving in the work of major American poets like Robert Frost, Wallace Stevens and Hart Crane.

Beyond literary tradition, Emerson has maintained an effect upon American politics and sociology. The oddity of Emerson in the public sphere is that he has the power to foster fresh versions of the two camps he termed the Party of Memory and the Party of Hope. The political right appropriates his values of remembering private interests as part of the public good, while the left follows his exaltation of the American Adam, a New Man in a New World of hope. The rivalry between these polarized camps is very much apparent in this election.

---

treadle: foot-operated lever that drives a machine
governor of Alaska: Sarah Palin, then the Republican vice-presidential nominee

Emerson was electrified by financial storms. The depression beginning in 1837 spurred his famous oration at Harvard, "The American Scholar":

> *The literature of the poor, the feelings of the child, the philosophy of the street, the meaning of the household life, are the topics of the time. It is a great stride. It is a sign—is it not?—of new vigor, when the extremities are made active, when currents of warm life run into the hands and feet. . . . Let me see every trifle bristling with the polarity that ranges it instantly on an eternal law; and the shop, the plow and the ledger referred to the like cause by which light undulates and poets sing.*

Emerson would have understood our current raging polarities. That American cultural nationalism should have been stimulated by a banking disaster is a wholly Emersonian paradox. Another enigma is the direct link between the lingering financial crisis and Emerson's formulation of his mature religious stance, crucially in his essay, "Self-Reliance," of 1839–40:

> *Life only avails, not the having lived. Power ceases in the instant of repose; it resides in the moment of transition from a past to a new state, in the shooting° of the gulf, in the darting to an aim. . . . Why then do we prate of self-reliance? Inasmuch as the soul is present there will be power not confident but agent.° To talk of reliance is a poor external way of speaking. Speak rather of that which relies because it works and it is. Who has more obedience than I masters me, though he should not raise his finger. Round him I must revolve by the gravitation of spirits. We fancy it rhetoric when we speak of eminent value. We do not yet see that virtue is height, and that a man or a company of men, plastic° and permeable to principles, by the law of nature must overpower and ride all cities, nations, kings, rich men, poets, who are not.*

By "self-reliance" Emerson meant the recognition of the god within us, rather than the worship of the Christian godhead (a deity that some Americans cannot always distinguish from themselves). Whether they know it or not, John McCain and Barack Obama seek power in just this ultimately serious sense, although that marvelous passage means one thing to Emersonians of the right and something very different to Emersonians of the left. Senator Obama's mantra of "change" celebrates the shooting of the gulf, the darting to an aim, setting aside "the having lived." Senator McCain's "change" reflects what remains most authentic about him, the nostalgia of the Party of Memory.

---

shooting: passing quickly over
agent: acting, exerting power
plastic: pliant, flexible

Barack Obama emanates from the tradition of the black church, where "the little me within the big me" is part or particle of God, just as the Emersonian self was. But he is a subtle intellectual and will not mistake himself for the Divine, and he has the curbing influence of Senator Joseph Biden, a conventional Roman Catholic, at his side. John McCain's religiosity is at one with the Party of Memory, but he has aligned himself with Gov. Sarah Palin, who, as an Assemblies of God Pentecostalist,° presumably enjoys closer encounters with the comforting Holy Spirit.

Regardless of these differences, whoever is elected will have to forge a solution to today's panic through his own understanding of self-reliance. As Emerson knew in his glory and sorrow, both of himself and all Americans: "The wealth of the universe is for me. Every thing is explicable and practical for me. . . . I am defeated all the time; yet to victory I am born."

[October 11, 2008]

Read

1. In what ways does Bloom compare the economic crisis of 2008 to the Panic of 1837?
2. How does Bloom suggest that Emerson might be helpful to thinking about the economic crisis?
3. How would you describe the Emersonian Parties of Memory and Hope?
4. How does Bloom use those two "parties" to characterize the 2008 presidential election?

Write

1. Write a brief description characterizing Bloom's use of appeals in this piece.
2. Bloom indicates that Emerson believed that adversity might be a good thing. Write a paragraph using this piece and your own observation and experience to comment on Bloom's claim.
3. How do you think the Parties of Memory and Hope might be reconciled or mediated?

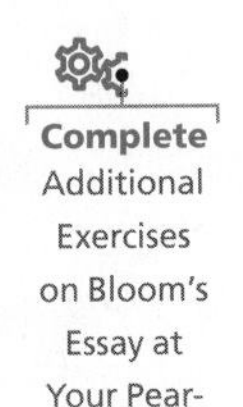

Complete Additional Exercises on Bloom's Essay at Your Pearson MyLab

Connect

1. Use Bloom to examine Emerson's "The American Scholar" in this unit. How might you read Emerson's piece as a challenge to confront and weather adversity? Choose statements and details that help reinforce your ideas.

Pentecostalist: a member of any of various Christian congregations that seek to be filled with the Holy Spirit

UNIT ACTIVITIES

Rhetorical Analysis

1. Choose several lines of speech from two or three writers or characters in Unit 2 and analyze their use of dialect and diction as a way to create a persona. Consider Cooper, Irving, Rowson, or Red Jacket as possibilities.
2. Using one male and one female writer, or one American Indian and one European or American writer, compare the use of rhetorical strategies of openings (*exordium*) and appeals to establish the speaker's authority.

Argument

1. Emerson proposes a plan for Americans to become thinkers and doers in the new country. Using your own experience, observation, and Emerson's ideas, create an argument that suggests how workable his plan might or might not be in twenty-first-century America.
2. Use two writers to establish conflicting claims in favor of exploration and development on the one hand, and preservation and the wilderness on the other. Then, using their claims and your own understanding of the needs of individuals and communities, create an argument that defends, opposes, or works toward compromise on those claims.

Synthesis

Using the arguments, evidence, and opinions advanced by American Indian writers and at least one European or American writer who championed their cause, create a proposal for building the nation that might have been more to the liking of those who were here before the arrival of European settlers.

Red Jacket, "Then I Must Worship the Spirit in My Own Way"
William Apess, from *A Son of the Forest*
George Catlin, "Letter from the Yellowstone River"
Benjamin Franklin, "Notes Concerning the Savages"; "The Speech of Polly Baker"
Stewart Udall, "The Land Wisdom of the Indians"
Samson Occom, "A Short Narrative of My Life"

UNIT 3

AUGUST 29, 2007—LOWER 9TH WARD, NEW ORLEANS, LOUISIANA
Second anniversary of Hurricane Katrina. A deserted, empty church remains derelict and decimated in the Lower 9th Ward. The area remains mostly abandoned and overgrown, ghostly reminders of lives that once were.

Read

1. How does the camera angle in the photograph contribute to its effect on you as a viewer?
2. A critic noted that photos of post-Katrina New Orleans made it look like a "modern Pompeii" (Pompeii was destroyed by a volcanic eruption in the year 79). Looking at this image or images of Hurricane Sandy's destruction, do you think this comparison is a valid one?

Connect

1. How do the texts in the unit demonstrate how we respond to crisis as individuals and communities?
2. How do art and literature promote healing after traumatic events?

How Do We Preserve a Nation?
1837–1865

Human Rights and the Civil War During the period leading up to the Civil War, issues of economics, human rights, freedom, and law grew increasingly important. Human rights for the African slaves brought to the United States in chains were related to other calls for rights. American Indian tribes who were being pushed further and further west, new immigrants, and women all called for freedom. They echoed the language of the revolutionary colonial period and of the abolitionists, both white and black.

The American Renaissance in Arts The time was also marked by a great wave of literary art in New England that critic F. O. Mattheissen called the "American Renaissance." At the same time that former slaves like Frederick Douglass and abolitionists like Wendell Phillips were speaking out against an institution that violated human rights—slavery—Emerson was urging Americans to create a new literature. Artists from Nathaniel Hawthorne to Walt Whitman were responding to his call. This double move—toward the political disintegration of the nation and its cultural integration through a new American literature—characterized the mid-nineteenth century.

GUIDING QUESTIONS

- How do we preserve a nation?
- How do the ideals of the country match its realities?
- How might American ideas and beliefs shape an American literature?
- How do we deal with differences of belief?
- What difference does region make?
- What kind of leaders do we need for the nation?

Texts and Visuals

Wendell Phillips

Wendell Phillips (1811–1884) was born to a distinguished Boston family. He was a friend of many literary figures, especially Henry David Thoreau. Before the Civil War, Phillips toured the country with William Lloyd Garrison, the editor of the abolitionist newspaper *The Liberator*, lecturing against slavery. From all accounts, he was a superb speaker. Although he kept a "commonplace book" with notes, he usually spoke from memory. Phillips supported racial equality. His speech about the black Revolutionary War patriot Crispus Attucks and this speech about Haitian leader Toussaint L'Ouverture show his commitment. The speech was delivered in 1863 as the debate about enlisting black soldiers in the Union Army was raging.

From *Toussaint L'Ouverture*

. . . If I stood here tonight to tell the story of Napoleon, I should take it from the lips of Frenchmen, who find no language rich enough to paint the great captain of the nineteenth century. Were I here to tell you the story of Washington, I should take it from your hearts—you, who think no marble white enough on which to carve the name of the Father of His Country. [Applause.] I am about to tell you the story of a Negro who has left hardly one written line. I am to glean° it from the reluctant testimony of Britons, Frenchmen, Spaniards—men who despised him as a Negro and a slave, and hated him because he had beaten them in many a battle. All the materials for his biography are from the lips of his enemies.

The second story told of him is this. About the time he reached the camp, the army had been subjected to two insults. First, their commissioners, summoned to meet the French Committee, were ignominiously and insultingly dismissed; and when, afterward, François, their general, was summoned to a second conference, and went to it on horseback, accompanied by two officers; a young lieutenant, who had known him as a slave, angered at seeing him in the uniform of an officer, raised his riding whip and struck him over the shoulders. If he had been the savage which the Negro is painted to us, he had only to breathe the insult to his twenty-five thousand soldiers, and they would have trodden out° the Frenchmen in blood.

---

glean: gather
trodden out: trampled, crushed

But the indignant chief rode back in silence to his tent, and it was twenty-four hours before his troops heard of this insult to their general. Then the word went forth, "Death to every white man!" They had fifteen hundred prisoners. Ranged in front of the camp, they were about to be shot. Toussaint, who had a vein of religious fanaticism, like most great leaders—like Mohammed, like Napoleon, like Cromwell,° like John Brown [cheers], he could preach as well as fight—mounting a hillock, and getting the ear of the crowd, exclaimed: "Brothers, this blood will not wipe out the insult to our chief; only the blood in yonder French camp can wipe it out. To shed that is courage; to shed this is cowardice and cruelty besides"; and he saved fifteen hundred lives. [Applause.] . . .

I cannot stop to give in detail every one of his efforts. This was in 1793. Leap with me over seven years; come to 1800; what has he achieved? He has driven the Spaniard back into his own cities, conquered him there, and put the French banner over every Spanish town; and for the first time, and almost the last, the island obeys one law. He has put the mulatto° under his feet. He has attacked Maitland,° defeated him in pitched battles, and permitted him to retreat to Jamaica; and when the French army rose upon Laveaux, their general, and put him in chains, Toussaint defeated them, took Laveaux out of prison, and put him at the head of his own troops. The grateful French in return named him General in Chief. "*Cet homme fait l'ouvertùre partout,*" said one—"This man makes an opening everywhere,"—hence his soldiers named him L'Ouverture, *the opening*.

5 This was the work of seven years. Let us pause a moment, and find something to measure him by. You remember Macaulay° says, comparing Cromwell with Napoleon, that Cromwell showed the greater military genius, if we consider that he never saw an army till he was forty; while Napoleon was educated from a boy in the best military schools in Europe. Cromwell manufactured his own army; Napoleon at the age of twenty-seven was placed at the head of the best troops Europe ever saw. They were both successful; but, says Macaulay, with such disadvantages, the Englishman showed the greater genius. Whether you allow the inference or not, you will at least grant that it is a fair mode of measurement. Apply it to Toussaint. Cromwell never saw an army till he was forty; this man never saw a soldier till he was fifty. Cromwell manufactured his own army—out of what? Englishmen, the best blood in Europe. Out of

---

Cromwell: Oliver Cromwell (1599–1658), military leader and Lord Protector of England following the overthrow of the monarchy

mulatto: person with one white and one black parent

Maitland: Frederick Maitland (1763–1848), English general

Macauley: Thomas Babington Macauley (1800–1859), English historian

the middle class of Englishmen, the best blood of the island. And with it he conquered what? Englishmen, their equals. This man manufactured his army out of what? Out of what you call the despicable race of Negroes, debased, demoralized by two hundred years of slavery, one hundred thousand of them imported into the island within four years, unable to speak a dialect intelligible even to each other. Yet out of this mixed, and, as you say, despicable mass, he forged a thunder-bolt and hurled it at what? At the proudest blood in Europe, the Spaniard, and sent him home conquered [cheers]; at the most warlike blood in Europe, the French, and put them under his feet; at the pluckiest° blood in Europe, the English, and they skulked home to Jamaica. [Applause.] Now if Cromwell was a general, at least this man was a soldier. I know it was a small territory; it was not as large as the continent; but it was as large as that Attica,° which, with Athens for a capital, has filled the earth with its fame for two thousand years. We measure genius by quality, not by quantity.

Further—Cromwell was only a soldier; his fame stops there. Not one line in the statute book of Britain can be traced to Cromwell; not one step in the social life of England finds its motive power in his brain. The state he founded went down with him to his grave. But this man no sooner put his hand on the helm of state than the ship steadied with an upright keel, and he began to evince a statesmanship as marvelous as his military genius. History says that the most statesmanlike act of Napoleon was his proclamation of 1802, at the Peace of Amiens,° when, believing that the indelible loyalty of a native-born heart is always a sufficient basis on which to found an empire, he said: "Frenchmen, come home. I pardon the crimes of the last twelve years; I blot out its parties; I found my throne on the hearts of all Frenchmen,"—and twelve years of unclouded success showed how wisely he judged. That was in 1802. In 1800 this Negro made a proclamation; it runs thus: "Sons of St. Domingo,° come home. We never meant to take your houses or your lands. The Negro only asked that liberty which God gave him. Your houses wait for you; your lands are ready; come and cultivate them"; and from Madrid and Paris, from Baltimore and New Orleans, the emigrant planters crowded home to enjoy their estates, under the pledged word that was never broken of a victorious slave. [Cheers.]

---

pluckiest: bravest, most determined

Attica: a region of Greece

Peace of Amiens: 1802 treaty that established a brief period of peace between England and France

St. Domingo: the French colony in the western part of the island of Hispaniola that became Haiti with its declaration of independence in 1804

Again, Carlyle° has said, "The natural king is one who melts all wills into his own." At this moment he turned to his armies—poor, ill-clad, and half-starved—and said to them: Go back and work on these estates you have conquered; for an empire can be founded only on order and industry, and you can learn these virtues only there. And they went. The French admiral, who witnessed the scene, said that in a week his army melted back into peasants.

It was 1800. The world waited fifty years before, in 1846, Robert Peel° dared to venture, as a matter of practical statesmanship, the theory of free trade. Adam Smith° theorized, the French statesmen dreamed, but no man at the head of affairs had ever dared to risk it as a practical measure. Europe waited till 1846 before the most practical intellect in the world, the English, adopted the great economic formula of unfettered trade. But in 1800 this black, with the instinct of statesmanship, said to the committee who were drafting for him a Constitution: "Put at the head of the chapter of commerce that the ports of St. Domingo are open to the trade of the world." [Cheers.] With lofty indifference to race, superior to all envy or prejudice, Toussaint had formed this committee of eight white proprietors° and one mulatto—not a soldier nor a Negro on the list, although Haitian history proves that, with the exception of Rigaud,° the rarest genius has always been shown by pure Negroes.

Again, it was 1800, at a time when England was poisoned on every page of her statute book with religious intolerance, when a man could not enter the House of Commons without taking an Episcopal communion, when every State in the Union, except Rhode Island, was full of the intensest religious bigotry. This man was a Negro. You say that is a superstitious blood. He was uneducated. You say that makes a man narrow-minded. He was a Catholic. Many say that is but another name for intolerance. And yet—Negro, Catholic, slave—he took his place by the side of Roger Williams,° and said to his committee: "Make it the first line of my Constitution that I know no difference between religious beliefs." [Applause.]

10 Now, blue-eyed Saxon, proud of your race, go back with me to the commencement of the century, and select what statesman you please. Let him be either

---

Carlyle: Thomas Carlyle (1795–1881), Scottish essayist and historian
Robert Peel: Sir Robert Peel (1788–1850), prime minister of Great Britain (1834–1835, 1841–1846)
Adam Smith: (1723–1790), Scottish political economist, author of *The Wealth of Nations* (1776)
proprietors: landowners
Rigaud: André Rigaud (1761–1811), a military commander in the Haitian Revolution
Roger Williams: (1603?–1683), English religious reformer, founder of Rhode Island

American or European; let him have a brain the result of six generations of culture; let him have the ripest training of university routine; let him add to it the better education of practical life; crown his temples with the silver° of seventy years; and show me the man of Saxon lineage for whom his most sanguine° admirer will wreathe a laurel° rich as embittered foes have placed on the brow of this Negro—rare military skill, profound knowledge of human nature, content to blot out all party distinctions, and trust a state to the blood of its sons—anticipating Sir Robert Peel fifty years, and taking his station by the side of Roger Williams before any Englishman or American had won the right; and yet this is the record which the history of rival states makes up for this inspired black of St. Domingo. [Cheers.] . . .

It was 1801. The Frenchmen who lingered on the island described its prosperity and order as almost incredible. You might trust a child with a bag of gold to go from Samana to Port-au-Prince° without risk. Peace was in every household; the valleys laughed with fertility; culture climbed the mountains; the commerce of the world was represented in its harbors. At this time Europe concluded the Peace of Amiens, and Napoleon took his seat on the throne of France. He glanced his eyes across the Atlantic, and, with a single stroke of his pen, reduced Cayenne° and Martinique° back into chains. He then said to his Council, "What shall I do with St. Domingo?" The slaveholders said, "Give it to us." Napoleon turned to the Abbé Gregoire,° "What is your opinion?" "I think those men would change their opinions, if they changed their skins." Colonel Vincent, who had been private secretary to Toussaint, wrote a letter to Napoleon, in which he said: "Sire, leave it alone; it is the happiest spot in your dominions; God raised this man to govern; races melt under his hand. He has saved you this island; for I know of my own knowledge that, when the Republic could not have lifted a finger to prevent it, George III offered him any title and any revenue if he would hold the island under the British crown. He refused, and saved it for France." Napoleon turned away from his Council, and is said to have remarked, "I have sixty thousand idle troops; I must find them something to do." He meant to say, "I am about to seize the crown; I dare not do it in the faces of sixty thousand republican soldiers: I must give them work at a distance to do." The

---

silver: gray hair

sanguine: confident, assured

laurel: In ancient times, a laurel wreath was bestowed as a mark of honor.

Samana to Port-au-Prince: from the eastern tip to the far west of the island, a distance of some 200 miles

Cayenne: capital of French Guiana, on the northern coast of South America

Martinique: an island in the Caribbean

Abbé Gregoire: Henri Grégoire (1750–1831), French priest and abolitionist

gossip of Paris gives another reason for his expedition against St. Domingo. It is said that the satirists of Paris had christened Toussaint, the Black Napoleon; and Bonaparte hated his black shadow. Toussaint had unfortunately once addressed him a letter, "The first of the blacks to the first of the whites." He did not like the comparison. You would think it too slight a motive. But let me remind you of the present Napoleon,° that when the epigrammatists° of Paris christened his wasteful and tasteless expense at Versailles,° *Soulouquerie*, from the name of Soulouque,° the Black Emperor, he deigned to issue a specific order forbidding the use of the word. The Napoleon blood is very sensitive. So Napoleon resolved to crush Toussaint from one motive or another, from the prompting of ambition, or dislike of this resemblance, which was very close. If either imitated the other, it must have been the white, since the Negro preceded him several years. They were very much alike, and they were very French—French even in vanity, common to both. You remember Bonaparte's vainglorious words to his soldiers at the Pyramids:° "Forty centuries look down upon us." In the same mood, Toussaint said to the French captain who urged him to go to France in his frigate, "Sir, your ship is not large enough to carry me." Napoleon, you know, could never bear the military uniform. He hated the restraint of his rank; he loved to put on the gray coat of the Little Corporal, and wander in the camp. Toussaint also never could bear a uniform. He wore a plain coat, and often the yellow Madras handkerchief of the slaves. A French lieutenant once called him a maggot in a yellow handkerchief. Toussaint took him prisoner next day, and sent him home to his mother. Like Napoleon, he could fast many days; could dictate to three secretaries at once; could wear out four or five horses. Like Napoleon, no man ever divined° his purpose or penetrated his plan. He was only a Negro, and so, in him, they called it hypocrisy. In Bonaparte we style it diplomacy. For instance, three attempts made to assassinate him all failed, from not firing at the right spot. If they thought he was in the north in a carriage, he would be in the south on horseback; if they thought he was in the city in a house, he would be in the field in a tent. They once riddled his carriage with bullets; he was on horseback on the other side. The seven Frenchmen who did it were arrested. They expected to be shot. The next day was

the present Napoleon: Louis-Napoléon Bonaparte (1808–1873), nephew and heir of Napoleon I; Emperor Napoleon III (1852–1870)

epigrammatists: satirists, wits

Versailles: lavish French royal chateau

Soulouque: Faustin-Élie Soulouque (1782–1867), Emperor Faustin I of Haïti (1849–1859)

at the Pyramids: during Napoleon's Egyptian campaign of 1798

divined: discovered

some saint's day; he ordered them to be placed before the high altar, and, when the priest reached the prayer for forgiveness, came down from his high seat, repeated it with him, and permitted them to go unpunished. [Cheers.] He had that wit° common to all great commanders, which makes its way in a camp. His soldiers getting disheartened, he filled a large vase with powder, and, scattering six grains of rice in it, shook them up, and said: "See, there is the white, there is the black; what are you afraid of?" So when people came to him in great numbers for office,° as it is reported they do sometimes even in Washington, he learned the first words of a Catholic prayer in Latin, and repeating it, would say, "Do you understand that?" "No, sir." "What! want an office, and not know Latin? Go home and learn it!"

Then, again, like Napoleon—like genius always—he had confidence in his power to rule men. You remember when Bonaparte returned from Elba,° and Louis XVIII° sent an army against him, Bonaparte descended from his carriage, opened his coat, offering his breast to their muskets and saying, "Frenchmen, it is the Emperor!" and they ranged themselves behind him, *his* soldiers, shouting, "*Vive l'Empereur!*" That was in 1815. Twelve years before, Toussaint, finding that four of his regiments had deserted and gone to Leclerc,° drew his sword, flung it on the grass, went across the field to them, folded his arms, and said, "Children, can you point a bayonet at me?" The blacks fell on their knees, praying his pardon. His bitterest enemies watched him, and none of them charged him with love of money, sensuality, or cruel use of power. The only instance in which his sternest critic has charged him with severity is this. During a tumult,° a few white proprietors who had returned, trusting his proclamation, were killed. His nephew, General Moise, was accused of indecision in quelling the riot. He assembled a court-martial, and, on its verdict, ordered his own nephew to be shot, sternly Roman in thus keeping his promise of protection to the whites. Above the lust of gold, pure in private life, generous in the use of his power, it was against such a man that Napoleon sent his army, giving to General Leclerc, the husband of his beautiful sister Pauline, thirty thousand of his best troops, with orders to reintroduce slavery. Among these soldiers came all of Toussaint's old mulatto rivals and foes.

Holland lent sixty ships. England promised by special message to be neutral; and you know neutrality means sneering at freedom and sending arms to ty-

---

wit: understanding, perception

office: position, appointment

Elba: Mediterranean island to which Napoleon was exiled in 1814

Louis XVIII: (1755–1824), king of France (1814–1824)

Leclerc: Charles Leclerc (1772–1802), French general

tumult: agitation, disturbance

rants. [Loud and long-continued applause.] England promised neutrality, and the black looked out on the whole civilized world marshaled against him. America, full of slaves, of course was hostile. Only the Yankee sold him poor muskets at a very high price. [Laughter.] Mounting his horse, and riding to the eastern end of the island, Samana, he looked out on a sight such as no native had ever seen before. Sixty ships of the line,° crowded by the best soldiers of Europe, rounded the point. They were soldiers who had never yet met an equal, whose tread, like Caesar's, had shaken Europe—soldiers who had scaled the Pyramids, and planted the French banners on the walls of Rome. He looked a moment, counted the flotilla, let the reins fall on the neck of his horse, and, turning to Christophe,° exclaimed: "All France is come to Haiti; they can only come to make us slaves; and we are lost!" He then recognized the only mistake of his life—his confidence in Bonaparte, which had led him to disband his army.

Returning to the hills, he issued the only proclamation which bears his name and breathes vengeance: "My children, France comes to make us slaves. God gave us liberty; France has no right to take it away. Burn the cities, destroy the harvests, tear up the roads with cannon, poison the wells, show the white man the hell he comes to make"; and he was obeyed. [Applause.] When the great William of Orange° saw Louis XIV° cover Holland with troops, he said, "Break down the dikes, give Holland back to ocean"; and Europe said, "Sublime!" When Alexander° saw the armies of France descend upon Russia, he said, "Burn Moscow, starve back the invaders"; and Europe said, "Sublime!" This black saw all Europe marshaled to crush him, and gave to his people the same heroic example of defiance.

15 It is true, the scene grows bloodier as we proceed. But, remember, the white man fitly accompanied his infamous attempt to *reduce freemen to slavery* with every bloody and cruel device° that bitter and shameless hate could invent. Aristocracy is always cruel. The black man met the attempt, as every such attempt should be met, with war to the hilt. In his first struggle to gain his freedom, he had been generous and merciful, saved lives and pardoned enemies, as the people in every age and clime have always done when rising

ships of the line: combat vessels

Christophe: Henri Christophe (1767–1820), former slave and one of the leaders of the Haitian Revolution

William of Orange: (1650–1702), Stadtholder of the Dutch Republic (1672–1702), King William III of England (1689–1702)

Louis XIV: (1638–1715), king of France (1643–1715)

Alexander: (1777–1825), Czar Alexander I of Russia (1801–1825)

device: scheme

against aristocrats. Now, to save his liberty, the Negro exhausted every means, seized every weapon, and turned back the hateful invaders with a vengeance as terrible as their own, though even now he refused to be cruel.

Leclerc sent word to Christophe that he was about to land at Cape City. Christophe said, "Toussaint is governor of the island. I will send to him for permission. If without it a French soldier sets foot on shore, I will burn the town, and fight over its ashes."

Leclerc landed. Christophe took two thousand *white* men, women, and children, and carried them to the mountains in safety, then with his own hands set fire to the splendid palace which French architects had just finished for him, and in forty hours the place was in ashes. The battle was fought in its streets, and the French driven back to their boats. [Cheers.] Wherever they went, they were met with fire and sword. Once, resisting an attack, the blacks, Frenchmen born, shouted the "Marseilles Hymn,"° and the French soldiers stood still; they could not fight the "Marseillaise." And it was not till their officers sabered them on that they advanced, and then they were beaten. Beaten in the field, the French then took to lies. They issued proclamations, saying, "We do not come to make you slaves; this man Toussaint tells you lies. Join us, and you shall have the rights you claim." They cheated every one of his officers, except Christophe and Dessalines,° and his own brother Pierre, and finally these also deserted him, and he was left alone. He then sent word to Leclerc, "I will submit. I could continue the struggle for years—could prevent a single Frenchman from safely quitting° your camp. But I hate bloodshed. I have fought only for the liberty of my race. Guarantee that, I will submit and come in." He took the oath to be a faithful citizen; and on the same crucifix Leclerc swore that he should be faithfully protected, and that the island should be free. As the French general glanced along the line of his splendidly equipped troops, and saw, opposite, Toussaint's ragged, ill-armed followers, he said to him, "l'Ouverture, had you continued the war, where could you have got arms?" "I would have taken yours," was the Spartan° reply. [Cheers.] He went down to his house in peace; it was summer. Leclerc remembered that the fever months were coming, when his army would be in hospitals, and when one motion of that royal hand would sweep his troops into the sea. He was too dangerous to be left at large. So they summoned him to attend a council; and here is the only charge made against him—the only charge. They say he was fool enough to go. Grant it; what was the record? The white man lies shrewdly

---

"Marseilles Hymn," "Marsellaise": French national anthem (written 1792)

Dessalines: Jean-Jacques Dessalines (1758–1806), a leader of the Haitian Revolution; self-styled Emperor Jacques I of Haiti (1804–1806)

quitting: leaving

Spartan: simple, terse

to cheat the Negro. Knight-errantry° was truth. The foulest insult you can offer a man since the Crusades is, you lie. Of Toussaint, Hermona, the Spanish general, who knew him well, said, "He was the purest soul God ever put into a body." Of him history bears witness, "He never broke his word." Maitland was traveling in the depths of the woods to meet Toussaint, when he was met by a messenger, and told that he was betrayed. He went on, and met Toussaint, who showed him two letters—one from the French general, offering him any rank if he would put Maitland in his power, and the other his reply. It was, "Sir, I have promised the Englishman that he shall go back." [Cheers.] Let it stand, therefore, that the Negro, truthful as a knight of old, was cheated by his lying foe. Which race has reason to be proud of such record?

But he was not cheated. He was under espionage. Suppose he had refused: the government would have doubted him—would have found some cause to arrest him. He probably reasoned thus: "If I go willingly, I shall be treated accordingly"; and he went. The moment he entered the room, the officers drew their swords, and told him he was prisoner; and one young lieutenant who was present says, "He was not at all surprised, but seemed very sad." They put him on shipboard, and weighed anchor for France. As the island faded from his sight, he turned to the captain, and said, "You think you have rooted up the tree of liberty, but I am only a branch; I have planted the tree so deep that all of France can never root it up." [Cheers.] Arrived in Paris, he was flung into jail, and Napoleon sent his secretary, Caffarelli, to him, supposing he had buried large treasures. He listened awhile, then replied, "Young man, it is true I have lost treasures, but they are not such as you come to seek." He was then sent to the Castle of St. Joux, to a dungeon twelve feet by twenty, built wholly of stone, with a narrow window, high up on the side, looking out on the snows of Switzerland. In winter, ice covers the floor; in summer, it is damp and wet. In this living tomb the child of the sunny tropic was left to die. From this dungeon he wrote two letters to Napoleon. One of them ran thus:— "Sire, I am a French citizen. I never broke a law. By the grace of God, I have saved for you the best island of your realm. Sire, of your mercy grant me justice." Napoleon never answered the letters. The commandant allowed him five francs a day for food and fuel. Napoleon heard of it, and reduced the sum to three. The luxurious usurper, who complained that the English government was stingy because it allowed him only six thousand dollars a month, stooped from his throne to cut down a dollar to a half, and still Toussaint did not die quick enough.

This dungeon was a tomb. The story told is that, in Josephine's time, a young French marquis was placed there, and the girl to whom he was betrothed went to the Empress and prayed for his release.

Knight-errantry: i.e., a code of bravery and honor

Said Josephine to her, "Have a model of it made, and bring it to me." Josephine placed it near Napoleon. He said, "Take it away—it is horrible!" She put it on his footstool, and he kicked it from him. She held it to him the third time, and said, "Sire, in this horrible dungeon you have put a man to die." "Take him out," said Napoleon, and the girl saved her lover. In this tomb Toussaint was buried, but he did not die fast enough. Finally, the commandant was told to go into Switzerland, to carry the keys of the dungeon with him, and to stay four days; when he returned, Toussaint was found starved to death. That imperial assassin was taken twelve years after to his prison at St. Helena,° planned for a tomb, as he had planned that of Toussaint, and there he whined away his dying hours in pitiful complaints of curtains and titles, of dishes and rides. God grant that when some future Plutarch shall weigh the great men of our epoch, the whites against the blacks, he do not put that whining child of St. Helena into one scale, and into the other the Negro meeting death like a Roman, without a murmur, in the solitude of his icy dungeon! 20

From the moment he was betrayed, the Negroes began to doubt the French, and rushed to arms. Soon every Negro but Maurepas° deserted the French. Leclerc summoned Maurepas to his side. He came, loyally bringing with him five hundred soldiers. Leclerc spiked his epaulettes to his shoulders, shot him, and flung him into the sea. He took his five hundred soldiers on shore, shot them on the edge of a pit, and tumbled then in. Dessalines from the mountain saw it, and, selecting five hundred French officers from his prisons, hung then on separate trees in sight of Leclerc's camp; and born, as I was, not far from Bunker Hill, I have yet found no reason to think he did wrong. They murdered Pierre Toussaint's wife at his own door, and after such treatment that it was mercy when they killed her. The maddened husband, who had but a year before saved the lives of twelve hundred white men, carried his next thousand prisoners and sacrificed them on her grave.

The French exhausted every form of torture. The Negroes were bound together and thrown into the sea; any one who floated was shot—others sunk with cannon balls tied to their feet; some smothered with sulphur fumes—others strangled, scourged to death, gibbeted;° sixteen of Toussaint's officers were chained to rocks in desert islands—others in marshes, and left to be devoured by poisonous reptiles and insects. Rochambeau° sent to Cuba for bloodhounds. When they arrived, the young girls went down to the wharf, decked the hounds with ribbons and flowers, kissed their necks, and, seated in the amphitheatre,

---

St. Helena: island in the South Atlantic, site of Napoleon's final exile and death (1815–1821)
Maurepas: Jacques Maurepas, commander of the northeastern town of Port-de-Paix
gibbeted: hanged
Rochambeau: Donatien-Marie-Joseph de Vimeur, vicomte de Rochambeau (1755–1813), French general

the women clapped their hands to see the Negro thrown to these dogs, previously starved to rage. But the Negroes besieged this very city so closely that these same girls, in their misery, ate the very hounds they had welcomed.

Then flashed forth that defying courage and sublime endurance which show how alike all races are when tried in the same furnace. The Roman wife,° whose husband faltered when Nero ordered him to kill himself, seized the dagger, and, mortally wounding her own body, cried, "Poetus, it is not hard to die." The world records it with proud tears. Just in the same spirit, when a Negro colonel was ordered to execution, and trembled, his wife seized his sword, and, giving herself a death-wound, said, "Husband, death is sweet when liberty is gone."

The war went on. Napoleon sent over thirty thousand more soldiers. But disaster still followed his efforts. What the sword did not devour, the fever ate up. Leclerc died. Pauline carried his body back to France. Napoleon met her at Bordeaux, saying, "Sister, I gave you an army—you bring me back ashes." Rochambeau—the Rochambeau of our history—left in command of eight thousand troops, sent word to Dessalines: "When I take you, I will not shoot you like a soldier, or hang you like a white man; I will whip you to death like a slave." Dessalines chased him from the battlefield, from fort to fort, and finally shut him up° in Samana. Heating cannon balls to destroy his fleet, Dessalines learned that Rochambeau had begged of the British admiral to cover his troops with the English flag, and the generous Negro suffered the boaster to embark undisturbed.

25 Some doubt the courage of the Negro. Go to Haiti, and stand on those fifty thousand graves of the best soldiers France ever had, and ask them what they think of the Negro's sword. And if that does not satisfy you, go to France, to the splendid mausoleum of the Counts of Rochambeau, and to the eight thousand graves of Frenchmen who skulked home under the English flag, and ask them. And if that does not satisfy you, come home, and if it had been October 1859,° you might have come by way of quaking Virginia, and asked her what she thought of Negro courage.

You may also remember this—that we Saxons were slaves about four hundred years, sold with the land, and our fathers never raised a finger to end that slavery. They waited till Christianity and civilization, till commerce and the discovery of America, melted away their chains. Spartacus° in Italy led

---

The Roman wife: Arria, wife of Caecina Paetus; he was ordered to commit suicide by the Emperor Claudius after taking part in a rebellion in 42 A.D.

shut him up: confined him

October 1859: John Brown's raid on the federal armory at Harpers Ferry, Virginia, occurred on October 16, 1859; the eighteen men with him included several blacks.

Spartacus: (c. 109–71 B.C.), leader of a slave uprising against the Roman Republic; in fact, believed to have died in battle

the slaves of Rome against the empress of the world. She murdered him, and crucified them. There never was a slave rebellion successful but once, and that was in St. Domingo. Every race has been, some time or other, in chains. But there never was a race that, weakened and degraded by such chattel slavery, unaided, tore off its own fetters,° forged them into swords, and won its liberty on the battlefield, but one, and that was the black race of St. Domingo. God grant that the wise vigor of our government may avert that necessity from our land, may raise into peaceful liberty the four million committed to our care, and show under democratic institutions a statesmanship as farsighted as that of England, as brave as the Negro of Haiti!

So much for the courage of the Negro. Now look at his endurance. In 1805 he said to the white men, "This island is ours; not a white foot shall touch it." Side by side with him stood the South American republics, planted by the best blood of the countrymen of Lope de Vega° and Cervantes.° They topple over so often that you could no more daguerreotype their crumbling fragments than you could the waves of the ocean. And yet, at their side, the Negro has kept his island sacredly to himself. It is said that at first, with rare patriotism, the Haitian government ordered the destruction of all the sugar plantations remaining, and discouraged its culture, deeming that the temptation which lured the French back again to attempt their enslavement. Burn over New York tonight, fill up her canals, sink every ship, destroy her railroads, blot out every remnant of education from her sons, let her be ignorant and penniless, with nothing but her hands to begin the world again—how much could she do in sixty years? And Europe, too, would lend you money, but she will not lend Haiti a dollar. Haiti, from the ruins of her colonial dependence, is become a civilized state, the seventh nation in the catalogue of commerce with this country, inferior in morals and education to none of the West Indian isles. Foreign merchants trust her courts as willingly as they do our own. Thus far, she has foiled the ambition of Spain, the greed of England, and the malicious statesmanship of Calhoun.° Toussaint made her what she is. In this work there was grouped around him a score of men, mostly of pure Negro blood, who ably seconded his efforts. They were able in war and skillful in civil affairs, but not, like him, remarkable for that rare mingling of high qualities which alone makes true greatness, and insures a man leadership among those otherwise almost his equals. Toussaint was indisputably their chief. Courage, purpose, endurance—these are the tests. He did plant a state so deep that all the world has not been able to root it up.

---

fetters: shackles

Lope de Vega: Félix Arturo Lope de Vega y Carpio (1562–1635), immensely prolific Spanish playwright

Cervantes: Miguel de Cervantes Saavedra (1547–1616), Spanish novelist, author of *Don Quixote* (1605–1615)

Calhoun: John C. Calhoun (1782–1850), South Carolina senator and vice president of the United States, leading defender of slavery and states' rights

I would call him Napoleon, but Napoleon made his way to empire over broken oaths and through a sea of blood. This man never broke his word. "NO RETALIATION" was his great motto and the rule of his life; and the last words uttered to his son in France were these: "My boy, you will one day go back to St. Domingo; forget that France murdered your father." I would call him Cromwell, but Cromwell was only a soldier, and the state he founded went down with him into his grave. I would call him Washington, but the great Virginian held slaves. This man risked his empire rather than permit the slave trade in the humblest village of his dominions.

You think me a fanatic tonight, for you read history, not with your eyes, but with your prejudices. But fifty years hence, when Truth gets a hearing, the Muse of History will put Phocion° for the Greek, and Brutus° for the Roman, Hampden° for England, Fayette° for France, choose Washington as the bright, consummate flower of our earlier civilization, and John Brown the ripe fruit of our noonday [thunders of applause], then, dipping her pen in the sunlight, will write in the clear blue, above them all, the name of the soldier, the statesman, the martyr, TOUSSAINT L'OUVERTURE. [Long-continued applause.]

[1863]

Read

1. What is Phillips's purpose in making the comparison between Toussaint and Napoleon?
2. How would you characterize Phillips's approach to his audience? What does he demonstrate that he believes about the audience he addresses?
3. How does Phillips provide evidence that Toussaint should be classified as a hero? How does this characterization work to further Phillips's claim about racial equality?
4. Given the context for this speech, why is this a timely moment for a discussion of the Haitian leader?

Write

1. Write a brief description of the persona Phillips creates for himself as a speaker using a few statements from the text to strengthen your description.

Phocion: called "the "Good" (c. 402–c. 318 B.C.), Athenian statesman

Brutus: Lucius Junius Brutus, founder of the Roman republic (c. 509 B.C.) and ancestor of Caesar's assassin

Hampden: John Hampden (c. 1595–1643), statesman and soldier, leader of the forces opposing King Charles I in the English Civil War

Fayette: Marie-Joseph Paul Yves Roch Gilbert du Motier, Marquis de La Fayette (1757–1834), French aristocrat and military officer, general in the American Revolution

2. What do you believe is the primary appeal Phillips uses in his talk? Find an example of its use.
3. How might an unconvinced audience member answer Phillips's claims in his speech?

Connect

1. Phillips was known as a great speaker. Compare Phillips's style—diction, details and attention to audience—to Ralph Waldo Emerson or to William Cullen Bryant and discuss any elements that make both speakers effective.

Frederick Douglass

Frederick Douglass (1818–1895) was born a slave in Talbot County, Maryland, and learned to read and write despite the prohibition on literacy for slaves. He escaped from bondage in 1838. He first traveled to New York, where he met and married a free black woman. He then moved to New Bedford, Massachusetts, where he had a long and illustrious career as an orator and writer, social reformer, and editor. Lecturing throughout the Northeast on slavery and its abolition, often accompanied by William Lloyd Garrison, the editor of the abolitionist paper *The Liberator,* Douglass quickly became well known. His *Narrative of the Life of a Slave,* published in 1845, was such a strong indictment of slavery that he fled to England to avoid being captured and re-enslaved. Douglass purchased his freedom in 1847 and began his own abolitionist newspaper, *The North Star.* After the Civil War began, he urged President Lincoln to enlist black troops and urged blacks to fight for their freedom. His long record of activism for freedom included support for women. He spoke at the first Women's Rights Convention in Seneca Falls, New York, in 1848 and many women's gatherings throughout the post-Civil War period. A strong critic of American policies that allowed slavery to flourish, he was also a believer in America's promise of freedom. His work holds the country to account for its actions and make good on those promises.

What to the Slave Is the Fourth of July?

(Extract from an Oration, at Rochester, July 5, 1852)

Fellow-Citizens—Pardon me, and allow me to ask, why am I called upon to speak here today? What have I, or those I represent, to do with your national independence? Are the great principles of political freedom and of natural justice, embodied in that Declaration of Independence, extended to us? and am I, therefore, called upon to bring our humble offering to the national altar, and to confess° the benefits, and express devout gratitude for the blessings, resulting from your independence to us?

Would to God, both for your sakes and ours, that an affirmative answer could be truthfully returned to these questions! Then would my task be light, and my burden easy and delightful. For who is there so cold that a nation's sympathy could not warm him? Who so obdurate° and dead to the claims of gratitude, that would not thankfully acknowledge such priceless benefits? Who so stolid° and selfish, that would not give his voice to swell the hallelujahs of a nation's jubilee, when the chains of servitude had been torn from his limbs? I am not that man. In a case like that, the dumb° might eloquently speak, and the "lame man leap as an hart."°

But, such is not the state of the case. I say it with a sad sense of the disparity° between us. I am not included within the pale° of this glorious anniversary! Your high independence only reveals the immeasurable distance between us. The blessings in which you this day rejoice, are not enjoyed in common. The rich inheritance of justice, liberty, prosperity, and independence, bequeathed by your fathers, is shared by you, not by me. The sunlight that brought life and healing to you, has brought stripes° and death to me. This Fourth of July is yours, not mine. You may rejoice, I must mourn. To drag a man in fetters° into the grand illuminated temple of liberty, and call upon him to join you in joyous anthems, were° inhuman mockery and sacrilegious irony. Do you mean, citizens, to mock me, by asking me to speak today? If so, there is a parallel to your conduct. And let me warn you that it is dangerous to copy the example of a nation whose crimes, towering up to heaven, were thrown down by the breath of the Almighty, burying that nation in irrecoverable ruin! I can today take up the plaintive° lament of a peeled and woe-smitten people.

> "By the rivers of Babylon, there we sat down. Yea! we wept when we remembered Zion. We hanged our harps upon the willows in the midst thereof. For there, they that carried us away captive, required of us a

---

confess: acknowledge, admit
obdurate: unyielding
stolid: apathetic, unfeeling
dumb: mute
hart: male deer
disparity: difference, inequality
pale: limits, bounds
stripes: strokes with a whip
fetters: shackles
were: would be
plaintive: mournful

> song; and they who wasted us required of us mirth, saying, Sing us one of the songs of Zion. How can we sing the Lord's song in a strange land? If I forget thee, O Jerusalem, let my right hand forget her cunning. If I do not remember thee, let my tongue cleave to the roof of my mouth."°

Fellow-citizens, above your national, tumultuous joy, I hear the mournful wail of millions, whose chains, heavy and grievous yesterday, are to-day rendered more intolerable by the jubilant shouts that reach them. If I do forget, if I do not faithfully remember those bleeding children of sorrow this day, "may my right hand forget her cunning, and may my tongue cleave to the roof of my mouth!" To forget them, to pass lightly over their wrongs, and to chime in with the popular theme, would be treason most scandalous and shocking, and would make me a reproach° before God and the world. My subject, then, fellow-citizens, is AMERICAN SLAVERY. I shall see this day and its popular characteristics from the slave's point of view. Standing there, identified with the American bondman,° making his wrongs mine, I do not hesitate to declare, with all my soul, that the character and conduct of this nation never looked blacker to me than on this Fourth of July. Whether we turn to the declarations of the past, or to the professions° of the present, the conduct of the nation seems equally hideous and revolting. America is false to the past, false to the present, and solemnly binds herself to be false to the future. Standing with God and the crushed and bleeding slave on this occasion, I will, in the name of humanity which is outraged, in the name of liberty which is fettered, in the name of the constitution and the bible, which are disregarded and trampled upon, dare to call in question and to denounce, with all the emphasis I can command, everything that serves to perpetuate slavery—the great sin and shame of America! "I will not equivocate;° I will not excuse;"° I will use the severest language I can command; and yet not one word shall escape me that any man, whose judgment is not blinded by prejudice, or who is not at heart a slaveholder, shall not confess to be right and just.

5 But I fancy I hear some one of my audience say, it is just in this circumstance that you and your brother abolitionists fail to make a favorable impression on the public mind. Would you argue more, and denounce less, would you persuade more and rebuke less, your cause would be much more likely to succeed. But, I submit, where all is plain there is nothing to be argued. What

---

"By the rivers . . . my mouth": from Psalm 137

reproach: blame or censure conveyed in disapproval

bondman: slave

professions: assertions

equivocate: be evasive, hedge

"I will not . . . excuse": quotation from the first issue (1831) of William Lloyd Garrison's abolitionist newspaper *The Liberator*

point in the anti-slavery creed would you have me argue? On what branch of the subject do the people of this country need light? Must I undertake to prove that the slave is a man? That point is conceded already. Nobody doubts it. The slaveholders themselves acknowledge it in the enactment of laws for their government. They acknowledge it when they punish disobedience on the part of the slave. There are seventy-two crimes in the state of Virginia, which, if committed by a black man (no matter how ignorant he be), subject him to the punishment of death; while only two of these same crimes will subject a white man to the like punishment. What is this but the acknowledgement that the slave is a moral, intellectual, and responsible being. The manhood of the slave is conceded. It is admitted in the fact that southern statute books are covered with enactments° forbidding, under severe fines and penalties, the teaching of the slave to read or write. When you can point to any such laws, in reference to the beasts of the field, then I may consent to argue° the manhood of the slave. When the dogs in your streets, when the fowls of the air, when the cattle on your hills, when the fish of the sea, and the reptiles that crawl, shall be unable to distinguish the slave from a brute, then will I argue with you that the slave is a man!

For the present, it is enough to affirm the equal manhood of the Negro race. Is it not astonishing that, while we are plowing, planting, and reaping, using all kinds of mechanical tools, erecting houses, constructing bridges, building ships, working in metals of brass, iron, copper, silver, and gold; that, while we are reading, writing, and ciphering,° acting as clerks, merchants, and secretaries, having among us lawyers, doctors, ministers, poets, authors, editors, orators, and teachers; that, while we are engaged in all manner of enterprises common to other men—digging gold in California, capturing the whale in the Pacific, feeding sheep and cattle on the hillside, living, moving, acting, thinking, planning, living in families as husbands, wives, and children, and, above all, confessing and worshiping the Christian's God, and looking hopefully for life and immortality beyond the grave—we are called upon to prove that we are men!

Would you have me argue that man is entitled to liberty? that he is the rightful owner of his own body? You have already declared it. Must I argue the wrongfulness of slavery? Is that a question for republicans?°

Is it to be settled by the rules of logic and argumentation, as a matter beset with great difficulty, involving a doubtful application of the principle of justice, hard to be understood? How should I look to-day in the presence of

---

enactments: laws

argue: debate, discuss

ciphering: calculating, solving by arithmetic

republicans: supporters of a republican form of government

Americans, dividing and subdividing a discourse,° to show that men have a natural right to freedom, speaking of it relatively and positively, negatively and affirmatively? To do so, would be to make myself ridiculous, and to offer an insult to your understanding. There is not a man beneath the canopy of heaven that does not know that slavery is wrong for him.

What! am I to argue that it is wrong to make men brutes, to rob them of their liberty, to work them without wages, to keep them ignorant of their relations to their fellow-men, to beat them with sticks, to flay their flesh with the lash, to load their limbs with irons, to hunt them with dogs, to sell them at auction, to sunder° their families, to knock out their teeth, to burn their flesh, to starve them into obedience and submission to their masters? Must I argue that a system, thus marked with blood and stained with pollution, is wrong? No; I will not. I have better employment for my time and strength than such arguments would imply.

What, then, remains to be argued? Is it that slavery is not divine; that God did not establish it; that our doctors of divinity are mistaken? There is blasphemy in the thought. That which is inhuman cannot be divine. Who can reason on such a proposition! They that can, may! I cannot. The time for such argument is past. 10

At a time like this, scorching irony, not convincing argument, is needed. Oh! had I the ability, and could I reach the nation's ear, I would to-day pour out a fiery stream of biting ridicule, blasting reproach, withering sarcasm, and stern rebuke. For it is not light that is needed, but fire; it is not the gentle shower, but thunder. We need the storm, the whirlwind, and the earthquake. The feeling of the nation must be quickened;° the conscience of the nation must be roused; the propriety° of the nation must be startled; the hypocrisy of the nation must be exposed; and its crimes against God and man must be proclaimed and denounced.

What to the American slave is your Fourth of July? I answer, a day that reveals to him, more than all other days in the year, the gross injustice and cruelty to which he is the constant victim. To him, your celebration is a sham; your boasted liberty, an unholy license;° your national greatness, swelling vanity; your sounds of rejoicing are empty and heartless; your denunciations of tyrants, brass-fronted impudence; your shouts of liberty and equality, hollow mockery; your prayers and hymns, your sermons and thanksgivings, with all

---

discourse: formal discussion

sunder: divide, separate

quickened: stirred, stimulated

propriety: decorum, delicacy

license: excessive freedom, lack of proper restraint

your religious parade and solemnity, are to him mere bombast, fraud, deception, impiety, and hypocrisy—a thin veil to cover up crimes which would disgrace a nation of savages. There is not a nation on the earth guilty of practices more shocking and bloody, than are the people of these United States, at this very hour.

Go where you may, search where you will, roam through all the monarchies and despotisms° of the old world, travel through South America, search out every abuse, and when you have found the last, lay your facts by the side of the every-day practices of this nation, and you will say with me, that, for revolting barbarity and shameless hypocrisy, America reigns without a rival.

[1852]

Read

1. How does Douglass use rhetorical questions in the first two pages? (A rhetorical question is asked for effect, when no answer is expected because the answer is obvious, or when the answer will be immediately provided by the speaker.)
2. How do you characterize Douglass's audience for the speech?
3. What images and particular word choices suggest Douglass's state of mind as he delivers his talk?
4. What is Douglass's purpose in suggesting that he is not making an argument?
5. How does Douglass expose irony in the Fourth of July celebration?

Write

1. The title of the essay is a rhetorical question. In a paragraph, write an answer to the question.
2. Use lines from the text to write a description of Douglass's tone.
3. Write a paragraph that responds to Douglass's claims about American history and the Fourth of July.

Connect

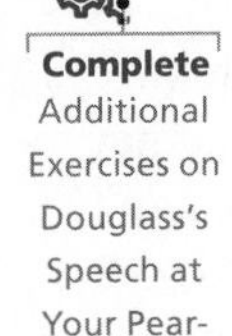

Complete Additional Exercises on Douglass's Speech at Your Pearson MyLab

1. Other writers hold Americans to account for the gap between actions and ideals. Compare Douglass's discussion of American hypocrisy to one other piece in this or a previous unit.
2. How does Douglass's speech echo or differ from Maria Stewart's (Unit 2) in tone and use of appeals?
3. Douglass was a strong supporter of women's rights. How does this essay suggest why he might have been such an advocate for women?

---

despotisms: tyrannies

Sojourner Truth

Sojourner Truth (c. 1797–1883), born Isabella Bomefree, was illiterate. Thus our knowledge of her life and work is wholly dependent on the recording abilities of those who wrote down her speeches and her memories of family and work. This has generated much controversy about what is authentic and what is fictionalized. Much of the information about the life of Sojourner Truth comes from her autobiography, *Narrative of Sojourner Truth,* written by an abolitionist, Olive Gilbert, in 1850. Truth was born into slavery in Ulster County, New York. Sold away from her parents at the age of nine, she had a series of other owners. She married in 1815, had five children, and eventually escaped bondage. In 1843, she changed her name to Sojourner Truth, saying that God had called her to travel and teach. She was a popular speaker at antislavery and women's rights meetings, including the Women's Rights Convention in Akron, Ohio, where she delivered her *Arn't I a Woman?* speech in 1851. She continued to speak and work for women's rights and civil rights until her death in 1883.

Speech to the Women's Rights Convention

Version 1

One of the most unique and interesting speeches of the Convention was made by Sojourner Truth, an emancipated slave. It is impossible to transfer it to paper, or convey any adequate idea of the effect it produced upon the audience. Those only can appreciate it who saw her powerful form, her whole-souled, earnest gesture, and listened to her strong and truthful tones. She came forward to the platform and addressing the President said with great simplicity: "May I say a few words?" Receiving an affirmative answer, she proceeded:

I want to say a few words about this matter. I am a woman's rights. I have as much muscle as any man, and can do as much work as any man. I have plowed and reaped and husked° and chopped and mowed, and can any man do more than that? I have heard much about the sexes being equal. I can carry as much as any man, and can eat as much too, if I can get it. I am as strong as any man that is now. As for intellect, all I can say is, if woman have a pint, and man a quart—why can't she have her little pint full? You need not be afraid to give us our rights for fear we will take too much,—for we can't take more than our pint'll hold. The poor men seem to be all in confusion, and don't know what to do. Why children, if you have woman's rights, give it to her and you will feel better. You will have your own rights, and they won't

husked: removed the husks or shells of corn, nuts, or grain

be so much trouble. I can't read, but I can hear. I have heard the Bible and have learned that Eve caused man to sin. Well, if woman upset the world, do give her a chance to set it right side up again. The Lady has spoken about Jesus, how he never spurned woman from him, and she was right. When Lazarus died, Mary and Martha came to him with faith and love and besought him to raise their brother. And Jesus wept and Lazarus came forth.° And how came Jesus into the world? Through God who created him and a woman who bore him. Man, where is your part? But the women are coming up blessed be God and a few of the men are coming up with them. But man is in a tight place, the poor slave is on him, woman is coming on him, he is surely between a hawk and a buzzard.

[1851]

Version 2
Reminiscences by Frances D. Gage of Sojourner Truth, for May 28–29, 1851

The leaders of the movement trembled on seeing a tall, gaunt black woman in a gray dress and white turban, surmounted° with an uncouth sun-bonnet, march deliberately into the church, walk with the air of a queen up the aisle, and take her seat upon the pulpit steps. A buzz of disapprobation° was heard all over the house, and there fell on the listening ear, "An abolition affair!" "Woman's rights and niggers!" "I told you so!" "Go it, darkey!"

I chanced on that occasion to wear my first laurels° in public life as president of the meeting. At my request order was restored, and the business of the Convention went on. Morning, afternoon, and evening exercises came and went. Through all these sessions old Sojourner, quiet and reticent as the "Lybian Statue,"° sat crouched against the wall on the corner of the pulpit stairs, her sun-bonnet shading her eyes, her elbows on her knees, her chin resting upon her broad, hard palms. At intermission she was busy selling the "Life of Sojourner Truth," a narrative of her own strange and adventurous life. Again and again, timorous° and trembling ones came to me and said, with earnestness, "Don't let her speak, Mrs. Gage, it will ruin us. Every

---

Lazarus came forth: as told in Chapter 11 of the Gospel of John

surmounted: topped

disapprobation: disapproval

laurels: i.e., mark of honor or distinction

the "Lybian Statue": the Libyan Sibyl (1868), a sculpture by American artist William Wetmore Story (1819–1895)

timorous: fearful

newspaper in the land will have our cause mixed up with abolition and niggers, and we shall be utterly denounced." My only answer was, "We shall see when the time comes."

The second day the work waxed warm. Methodist, Baptist, Episcopal, Presbyterian, and Universalist ministers came in to hear and discuss the resolutions presented. One claimed superior rights and privileges for man, on the ground of "superior intellect"; another, because of the "manhood of Christ; if God had desired the equality of woman, He would have given some token of His will through the birth, life, and death of the Saviour." Another gave us a theological view of the "sin of our first mother."

There were very few women in those days who dared to "speak in meeting"; and the august° teachers of the people were seemingly getting the better of us, while the boys in the galleries, and the sneerers among the pews, were hugely enjoying the discomfiture,° as they supposed, of the "strong-minded." Some of the tender-skinned friends were on the point of losing dignity, and the atmosphere betokened a storm. When, slowly from her seat in the corner rose Sojourner Truth, who, till now, had scarcely lifted her head. "Don't let her speak!" gasped half a dozen in my ear. She moved slowly and solemnly to the front, laid her old bonnet at her feet, and turned her great speaking eyes to me. There was a hissing sound of disapprobation above and below. I rose and announced "Sojourner Truth," and begged the audience to keep silence for a few moments.

The tumult subsided at once, and every eye was fixed on this almost Amazon form, which stood nearly six feet high, head erect, and eyes piercing the upper air like one in a dream. At her first word there was a profound hush. She spoke in deep tones, which, though not loud, reached every ear in the house, and away through the throng at the doors and windows. 5

"Wall, chilern, whar dar is so much racket dar must be somethin' out o' kilter. I tink dat 'twixt de niggers of de Souf and de womin at de Norf, all talkin' 'bout rights, de white men will be in a fix pretty soon. But what's all dis here talkin' 'bout?

"Dat man ober dar say dat womin needs to be helped into carriages, and lifted ober ditches, and to hab de best place everywhat. Nobody eber helps me into carriages, or ober mud-puddles, or gibs me any best place!" And raising herself to her full height, and voice to a pitch like rolling thunder, she asked. "And a'n't I a woman? Look at me! Look at my arm! (and she bared her right arm to the shoulder, showing her tremendous muscular power). I have ploughed,

august: eminent, dignified
discomfiture: uneasiness

and planted, and gathered into barns, and no man could head° me! And a'n't I a woman? I could work as much and eat as much as a man—when I could get it—and bear de lash as well! And a'n't I a woman? I have borne thirteen chilern, and seen 'em mos' all sold off to slavery, and when I cried out with my mother's grief, none but Jesus heard me! And a'n't I a woman?

"Den dey talks 'bout dis ting in de head; what dis dey call it?" ("Intellect," whispered some one near.) "Dat's it, honey. What's dat got to do wid womin's rights or nigger's rights? If my cup won't hold but a pint, and yourn holds a quart, wouldn't ye be mean not to let me have my little half-measure full?" And she pointed her significant finger, and sent a keen glance at the minister who had made the argument. The cheering was long and loud.

"Den dat little man in black dar, he say women can't have as much rights as men, 'cause Christ wasn't a woman! Whar did your Christ come from?" Rolling thunder couldn't have stilled that crowd, as did those deep, wonderful tones, as she stood there with outstretched arms and eyes of fire. Raising her voice still louder, she repeated, "What did your Christ come from? From God and a woman! Man had nothin' to do wid Him." Oh, what a rebuke that was to that little man.

Turning again to another objector, she took up the defense of Mother Eve. I can not follow her through it all. It was pointed, and witty, and solemn; eliciting at almost every sentence deafening applause; and she ended by asserting: "If de fust woman God ever made was strong enough to turn de world upside down all alone, dese women togedder (and she glanced her eye over the platform) ought to be able to turn it back, and get it right side up again! And now dey is asking to do it, de men better let 'em." Long-continued cheering greeted this. "'Bleeged° to ye for hearin' on me, and now ole Sojourner han't got nothin' more to say." 10

Amid roars of applause, she returned to her corner, leaving more than one of us with streaming eyes, and hearts beating with gratitude. She had taken us up in her strong arms and carried us safely over the slough° of difficulty turning the whole tide in our favor. I have never in my life seen anything like the magical influence that subdued the mobbish spirit of the day, and turned the sneers and jeers of an excited crowd into notes of respect and admiration. Hundreds rushed up to shake hands with her, and congratulate the glorious old mother, and bid her God-speed on her mission of "testifyin' agin concerning the wickedness of this 'ere people."

[1881]

head: go ahead of; i.e., outdo
'Bleeged: obliged
slough: swamp

Read

1. How do the two versions suggest rhetorical relationships between speaker, writer, and audience?
2. What are the effects of dialect speech in version 2 on you as a reader and your reading of Truth's persona?
3. How does Truth use metaphor or analogy to convey her message?
4. Where do you find *logos* working in the speech?
5. In your opinion, what is the most important evidence that Truth offers?

Write

1. In a paragraph, analyze how Truth creates authority for herself as a speaker.
2. Comment on several places where Truth's attention to the audience is most evident. What is the effect of this deliberate attention?
3. How does Truth connect rights for women and for black people in her speech?
4. Write a brief analysis of Truth's *exordium* (introduction) and of the concluding paragraph.

Additional Exercises on Truth's Speech at Your Pearson MyLab

Connect

1. Compare one rhetorical strategy used by Truth to a similar strategy used by Frederick Douglass or by Henry David Thoreau.
2. Find another speech and examine how the speakers use oral techniques to convey aim and to establish a relationship with their audiences.

Henry David Thoreau

Henry David Thoreau (1817–1862) spent most of his life in Concord, Massachusetts. There he became friends with Ralph Waldo Emerson, who deeply influenced his thinking. Thoreau lived for two years with the Emerson family, working as a handyman, and in 1843 he built a cabin on land owned by Emerson at Walden Pond. He lived there for two years, observing and writing about the world around the pond. *A Week on the Concord and Merrimack Rivers* was published in 1849 and *Walden* in 1854. Thoreau was not well-known during his lifetime, but his words have spoken to generations of readers since then. His themes include the power of nature, the need to "simplify, simplify!" life, and the paths toward social activism. "Civil Disobedience," about the night he spent in jail for refusing to pay taxes in protest of the Mexican American War, became an inspirational guide for social justice workers from Gandhi to Martin Luther King, Jr.

from *Walden*

Where I Lived, and What I Lived For

At a certain season of our life we are accustomed to consider every spot as the possible site of a house. I have thus surveyed the country on every side within a dozen miles of where I live. In imagination I have bought all the farms in succession, for all were to be bought, and I knew their price. I walked over each farmer's premises, tasted his wild apples, discoursed on husbandry° with him, took his farm at his price, at any price, mortgaging it to him in my mind; even put a higher price on it,—took everything but a deed of it,—took his word for his deed, for I dearly love to talk,—cultivated it, and him too to some extent, I trust, and withdrew when I had enjoyed it long enough, leaving him to carry it on. This experience entitled me to be regarded as a sort of real-estate broker by my friends. Wherever I sat, there I might live, and the landscape radiated from me accordingly. What is a house but a *sedes,* a seat?—better if a country seat. I discovered many a site for a house not likely to be soon improved, which some might have thought too far from the village, but to my eyes the village was too far from it. Well, there I might live, I said; and there I did live, for an hour, a summer and a winter life; saw how I could let the years run off, buffet° the winter through, and see the spring come in. The future inhabitants of this region, wherever they may place their houses, may be sure that they have been anticipated. An afternoon sufficed to lay out the land into orchard, wood-lot, and pasture, and to decide what fine oaks or pines should be left to stand before the door, and whence each blasted° tree could be seen to the best advantage; and then I let it lie, fallow° perchance, for a man is rich in proportion to the number of things which he can afford to let alone.

My imagination carried me so far that I even had the refusal of several farms,—the refusal was all I wanted,—but I never got my fingers burned by actual possession. The nearest that I came to actual possession was when I bought the Hollowell Place, and had begun to sort my seeds, and collected materials with which to make a wheelbarrow to carry it on or off with; but before the owner gave me a deed of it, his wife—every man has such a wife—changed her mind and wished to keep it, and he offered me ten dollars to release him. Now, to speak the truth, I had but ten cents in the world, and it surpassed my arithmetic to tell, if I was that man who had ten cents, or who had a farm, or ten dollars, or all together. However, I let him keep the ten dollars and the farm too, for I had carried it far enough; or rather, to be generous, I sold him the farm for just what I gave for it, and, as he was not a rich man, made him a present of ten dollars, and still had my ten cents, and seeds, and materials for a wheelbarrow left. I found thus that I had been a rich man without any damage to my poverty. But I retained the landscape, and I have since annually carried off what it yielded without a wheelbarrow. With respect to landscapes,—

"I am monarch of all I *survey,*
My right there is none to dispute."

. . .

---

husbandry: farming; cultivation and animal breeding
buffet: make one's way through with difficulty
blasted: ruined; blighted or withered
fallow: plowed but unseeded

The present was my next experiment of this kind, which I purpose to describe more at length, for convenience putting the experience of two years into one. As I have said, I do not propose to write an ode to dejection,° but to brag as lustily as chanticleer° in the morning, standing on his roost, if only to wake my neighbors up.

When I first took up my abode in the woods, that is, began to spend my nights as well as days there, which, by accident, was on Independence Day, or the Fourth of July, 1845, my house was not finished for winter, but was merely a defence against the rain, without plastering or chimney, the walls being of rough, weather-stained boards, with wide chinks, which made it cool at night. The upright white hewn° studs° and freshly planed door and window casings gave it a clean and airy look, especially in the morning, when its timbers were saturated with dew, so that I fancied that by noon some sweet gum would exude from them. To my imagination it retained throughout the day more or less of this auroral° character, reminding me of a certain house on a mountain which I had visited a year before. This was an airy and unplastered cabin, fit to entertain a travelling god, and where a goddess might trail her garments. The winds which passed over my dwelling were such as sweep over the ridges of mountains, bearing the broken strains,° or celestial parts only, of terrestrial° music. The morning wind forever blows, the poem of creation is uninterrupted; but few are the ears that hear it. Olympus° is but the outside of the earth everywhere.

5 The only house I had been the owner of before, if I except a boat, was a tent, which I used occasionally when making excursions in the summer, and this is still rolled up in my garret; but the boat, after passing from hand to hand, has gone down the stream of time. With this more substantial shelter about me, I had made some progress toward settling in the world. This frame, so slightly clad, was a sort of crystallization° around me, and reacted on the builder. It was suggestive somewhat as a picture in outlines. I did not need to go outdoors to take the air, for the atmosphere within had lost none of its freshness. It was not so much within-doors as behind a door where I sat, even in the rainiest weather. The Harivansa° says, "An abode without birds is like a meat without seasoning." Such was not my abode, for I found myself suddenly neighbor to the birds; not by having imprisoned one, but having caged myself near them.

---

ode to dejection: the title of an 1802 poem by English author Samuel Taylor Coleridge (1772–1834)

chanticleer: the rooster

hewn: cut

studs: posts in the framework of a wall for supporting sheets of lath, wallboard, or similar material

auroral: morning

strains: passages of music; tunes or airs

terrestrial: earthly

Olympus: mountain home of the Greek gods

crystallization: process of assuming a definite, usually permanent form

Harivansa: epic poem (fifth century A.D.) about the Hindu god Krishna

I was not only nearer to some of those which commonly frequent the garden and the orchard, but to those wilder and more thrilling songsters of the forest which never, or rarely, serenade a villager,—the wood thrush, the veery, the scarlet tanager, the field sparrow, the whip-poor-will, and many others.

I was seated by the shore of a small pond, about a mile and a half south of the village of Concord and somewhat higher than it, in the midst of an extensive wood between that town and Lincoln, and about two miles south of that our only field known to fame, Concord Battle Ground;° but I was so low in the woods that the opposite shore, half a mile off, like the rest, covered with wood, was my most distant horizon. For the first week, whenever I looked out on the pond it impressed me like a tarn° high up on the side of a mountain, its bottom far above the surface of other lakes, and, as the sun arose, I saw it throwing off its nightly clothing of mist, and here and there, by degrees, its soft ripples or its smooth reflecting surface was revealed, while the mists, like ghosts, were stealthily withdrawing in every direction into the woods, as at the breaking up of some nocturnal conventicle.° The very dew seemed to hang upon the trees later into the day than usual, as on the sides of mountains.

. . .

Every morning was a cheerful invitation to make my life of equal simplicity, and I may say innocence, with Nature herself. I have been as sincere a worshipper of Aurora° as the Greeks. I got up early and bathed in the pond; that was a religious exercise, and one of the best things which I did. They say that characters were engraven on the bathing tub of King Tching-thang° to this effect: "Renew thyself completely each day; do it again, and again, and forever again." I can understand that. Morning brings back the heroic ages. I was as much affected by the faint hum of a mosquito making its invisible and unimaginable tour through my apartment at earliest dawn, when I was sitting with door and windows open, as I could be by any trumpet that ever sang of fame. It was Homer's requiem; itself an Iliad and Odyssey in the air, singing its own wrath and wanderings. There was something cosmical about it; a standing advertisement, till forbidden,° of the everlasting vigor and fertility of the world. The morning, which is the most memorable season of the day, is the awakening hour. Then there is least somnolence° in us; and for

---

Concord Battle Ground: site, with neighboring Lexington, of the start of the American Revolution on April 19, 1775

tarn: small mountain lake

conventicle: religious meeting held in secret

Aurora: Roman goddess of the dawn

King Tching-thang: Cheng Tang (c. 1675–1646 B.C.), founder of the Shang dynasty in China

till forbidden: phrase used in nineteenth-century newspapers to indicate that an advertisement would run in each successive issue until it was canceled

somnolence: drowsiness, sleepiness

an hour, at least, some part of us awakes which slumbers all the rest of the day and night. Little is to be expected of that day, if it can be called a day, to which we are not awakened by our Genius,° but by the mechanical nudgings of some servitor,° are not awakened by our own newly acquired force and aspirations from within, accompanied by the undulations of celestial music, instead of factory bells, and fragrance filling the air—to a higher life than we fell asleep from; and thus the darkness bear its fruit, and prove itself to be good, no less than the light. That man who does not believe that each day contains an earlier, more sacred, and auroral hour than he has yet profaned,° has despaired of life, and is pursuing a descending and darkening way. After a partial cessation° of his sensuous life,° the soul of man, or its organs rather, are reinvigorated each day, and his Genius tries again what noble life it can make. All memorable events, I should say, transpire in morning time and in a morning atmosphere. The Vedas° say, "All intelligences awake with the morning." Poetry and art, and the fairest and most memorable of the actions of men, date from such an hour. All poets and heroes, like Memnon,° are the children of Aurora, and emit their music at sunrise. To him whose elastic and vigorous thought keeps pace with the sun, the day is a perpetual morning. It matters not what the clocks say or the attitudes and labors of men. Morning is when I am awake and there is a dawn in me. Moral reform is the effort to throw off sleep. Why is it that men give so poor an account of their day if they have not been slumbering? They are not such poor calculators. If they had not been overcome with drowsiness, they would have performed something. The millions are awake enough for physical labor; but only one in a million is awake enough for effective intellectual exertion, only one in a hundred millions to a poetic or divine life. To be awake is to be alive. I have never yet met a man who was quite awake. How could I have looked him in the face?

We must learn to reawaken and keep ourselves awake, not by mechanical aids, but by an infinite expectation of the dawn, which does not forsake us in our soundest sleep. I know of no more encouraging fact than the unquestionable ability of man to elevate his life by a conscious endeavor. It is something to be able to paint a particular picture, or to carve a statue, and so to make a few objects beautiful; but it is far more glorious to carve and paint the very atmosphere and medium through which we look, which morally we can do. To affect the quality

---

Genius: guiding spirit

servitor: attendant

profaned: abused, treated with irreverence

cessation: pause, halt

sensuous life: the life of the five senses

Vedas: the oldest scriptures of Hinduism

Memnon: Egyptian pharaoh Amenhotep III (114th century B.C.); a huge, earthquake-damaged statue of him was reputed to make musical sounds at about dawn

of the day, that is the highest of arts. Every man is tasked to make his life, even in its details, worthy of the contemplation of his most elevated and critical hour. If we refused, or rather used up, such paltry information as we get, the oracles would distinctly inform us how this might be done.

I went to the woods because I wished to live deliberately, to front° only the essential facts of life, and see if I could not learn what it had to teach, and not, when I came to die, discover that I had not lived. I did not wish to live what was not life, living is so dear; nor did I wish to practise resignation, unless it was quite necessary. I wanted to live deep and suck out all the marrow° of life, to live so sturdily and Spartan-like° as to put to rout all that was not life, to cut a broad swath and shave close, to drive life into a corner, and reduce it to its lowest terms, and, if it proved to be mean,° why then to get the whole and genuine meanness of it, and publish its meanness to the world; or if it were sublime,° to know it by experience, and be able to give a true account of it in my next excursion. For most men, it appears to me, are in a strange uncertainty about it, whether it is of the devil or of God, and have *somewhat hastily* concluded that it is the chief end of man here to "glorify God and enjoy him forever."

10 Still we live meanly, like ants; though the fable tells us that we were long ago changed into men,° like pygmies we fight with cranes;° it is error upon error, and clout° upon clout, and our best virtue has for its occasion a superfluous and evitable° wretchedness. Our life is frittered away by detail. An honest man has hardly need to count more than his ten fingers, or in extreme cases he may add his ten toes, and lump° the rest. Simplicity, simplicity, simplicity! I say, let your affairs be as two or three, and not a hundred or a thousand; instead of a million count half a dozen, and keep your accounts on your thumbnail. In the midst of this chopping sea of civilized life, such are the clouds and storms and quicksands and thousand-and-one items to be allowed for, that a man has to live, if he would not founder and go to the bottom and not make his port at all, by dead reckoning,° and he must be a great calculator indeed who succeeds. Simplify, simplify. Instead of three meals a day, if it be necessary eat but one;

---

front: face, confront

marrow: inmost and choicest part

Spartan-like: with a rigor characteristic of the warrior city-state of Sparta in ancient Greece

mean: inferior, low

sublime: glorious, majestic

fable . . . men: In Greek myth, Zeus turned ants into men to increase the population of the island of Aegina after a plague.

pygmies . . . cranes: According to Homer's *Iliad,* the tribe of Pygmies were constantly at war with a flock of herons, or cranes.

clout: piece or fragment

evitable: avoidable

lump: lump together into an uncounted mass

dead reckoning: method of estimating a ship's position without astronomical observations

ead of a hundred dishes, five; and reduce other things in proportion. Our is like a German Confederacy,° made up of petty states, with its boundary forever fluctuating, so that even a German cannot tell you how it is bounded at any moment. The nation itself, with all its so-called internal improvements, which, by the way are all external and superficial, is just such an unwieldy and overgrown establishment, cluttered with furniture and tripped up by its own traps, ruined by luxury and heedless° expense, by want of calculation and a worthy aim, as the million households in the land; and the only cure for it, as for them, is in a rigid economy, a stern and more than Spartan simplicity of life and elevation of purpose. It lives too fast. Men think that it is essential that the *Nation* have commerce, and export ice, and talk through a telegraph, and ride thirty miles an hour, without a doubt, whether *they* do or not; but whether we should live like baboons or like men, is a little uncertain. If we do not get out sleepers,° and forge rails, and devote days and nights to the work, but go to tinkering upon our *lives* to improve *them,* who will build railroads? And if railroads are not built, how shall we get to heaven in season? But if we stay at home and mind our business, who will want railroads? We do not ride on the railroad; it rides upon us. Did you ever think what those sleepers are that underlie the railroad? Each one is a man, an Irishman, or a Yankee man. The rails are laid on them, and they are covered with sand, and the cars run smoothly over them. They are sound sleepers, I assure you. And every few years a new lot is laid down and run over; so that, if some have the pleasure of riding on a rail, others have the misfortune to be ridden upon. And when they run over a man that is walking in his sleep, a supernumerary° sleeper in the wrong position, and wake him up, they suddenly stop the cars, and make a hue and cry about it, as if this were an exception. I am glad to know that it takes a gang of men for every five miles to keep the sleepers down and level in their beds as it is, for this is a sign that they may sometime get up again.

Why should we live with such hurry and waste of life? We are determined to be starved before we are hungry. Men say that a stitch in time saves nine, and so they take a thousand stitches to-day to save nine to-morrow. As for *work,* we haven't any of any consequence. We have the Saint Vitus' dance,° and *cannot* possibly keep our heads still. If I should only give a few pulls at the parish bellrope, as for a fire, that is, without setting the bell,° there is hardly a man on his farm in the outskirts of Concord, notwithstanding that press° of

---

German Confederacy: an alliance of numerous, small Central European states

heedless: reckless

sleepers: wooden ties on which railroad tracks are laid

supernumerary: more than is needed

Saint Vitus' dance: a nerve condition that produces spasmodic movements

setting the bell: pulling the rope with enough force to make the bell stand mouth upright

press: pressure, urgency

engagements° which was his excuse so many times this morning, nor a boy, nor a woman, I might almost say, but would forsake all and follow that sound, not mainly to save property from the flames, but, if we will confess the truth, much more to see it burn, since burn it must, and we, be it known, did not set it on fire,—or to see it put out, and have a hand in it, if that is done as handsomely;° yes, even if it were the parish church itself. Hardly a man takes a half-hour's nap after dinner, but when he wakes he holds up his head and asks, "What's the news?" as if the rest of mankind had stood his sentinels. Some give directions to be waked every half-hour, doubtless for no other purpose; and then, to pay for it, they tell what they have dreamed. After a night's sleep the news is as indispensable as the breakfast. "Pray tell me anything new that has happened to a man anywhere on this globe,"—and he reads it over his coffee and rolls, that a man has had his eyes gouged out this morning on the Wachito River;° never dreaming the while that he lives in the dark unfathomed mammoth cave° of this world, and has but the rudiment of an eye himself.

For my part, I could easily do without the post-office. I think that there are very few important communications made through it. To speak critically, I never received more than one or two letters in my life—I wrote this some years ago—that were worth the postage. The penny-post° is, commonly, an institution through which you seriously offer a man that penny for his thoughts which is so often safely offered in jest. And I am sure that I never read any memorable news in a newspaper. If we read of one man robbed, or murdered, or killed by accident, or one house burned, or one vessel wrecked, or one steamboat blown up, or one cow run over on the Western Railroad, or one mad dog killed, or one lot of grasshoppers in the winter,—we never need read of another. One is enough. If you are acquainted with the principle, what do you care for a myriad° instances and applications? To a philosopher all *news,* as it is called, is gossip, and they who edit and read it are old women over their tea. Yet not a few are greedy after this gossip. There was such a rush, as I hear, the other day at one of the offices to learn the foreign news by the last arrival, that several large squares of plate glass belonging to the establishment were broken by the pressure,—news which I seriously think a ready wit might write a twelvemonth, or twelve years, beforehand with sufficient accuracy. As for Spain, for instance, if you know how to throw in Don Carlos and the Infanta, and Don Pedro and Seville and Granada,° from time to time in the right proportions,—they may

---

engagements: appointments, arrangements

handsomely: well, appropriately

Wachito River: the Ouachita, in southern Arkansas

mammoth cave: Mammoth Cave in Kentucky has blind fish living in its waters.

penny-post: In the 1840s, letters could be mailed locally for three cents.

myriad: innumerable

Don Carlos . . . Granada: references to political upheavals of the 1830s and '40s, which were already old news when Thoreau was writing this

changed the names a little since I saw the papers,—and serve up a bullfight when other entertainments fail, it will be true to the letter, and give us as good an idea of the exact state or ruin of things in Spain as the most succinct° and lucid reports under this head in the newspapers: and as for England, almost the last significant scrap of news from that quarter was the revolution of 1649;° and if you have learned the history of her crops for an average year, you never need attend to that thing again, unless your speculations are of a merely pecuniary° character. If one may judge who rarely looks into the newspapers, nothing new does ever happen in foreign parts, a French revolution not excepted.

What news! how much more important to know what that is which was never old! "Kieou-pe-yu (great dignitary of the state of Wei) sent a man to Khoungtseu° to know his news. Khoungtseu caused the messenger to be seated near him, and questioned him in these terms: What is your master doing? The messenger answered with respect: My master desires to diminish the number of his faults, but he cannot come to the end of them. The messenger being gone, the philosopher remarked: What a worthy messenger! What a worthy messenger!" The preacher, instead of vexing the ears of drowsy farmers on their day of rest at the end of the week,—for Sunday is the fit conclusion of an ill-spent week, and not the fresh and brave beginning of a new one,—with this one other draggle-tail of a sermon, should shout with thundering voice, "Pause! Avast!° Why so seeming fast, but deadly slow?"

Shams and delusions are esteemed for° soundest truths, while reality is fabulous. If men would steadily observe realities only, and not allow themselves to be deluded, life, to compare it with such things as we know, would be like a fairy tale and the Arabian Nights' Entertainments. If we respected only what is inevitable and has a right to be, music and poetry would resound along the streets. When we are unhurried and wise, we perceive that only great and worthy things have any permanent and absolute existence, that petty fears and petty pleasures are but the shadow of the reality. This is always exhilarating and sublime. By closing the eyes and slumbering, and consenting to be deceived by shows,° men establish and confirm their daily life of routine and habit everywhere, which still is built on purely illusory foundations. Children, who play life, discern its true law and relations more clearly than men, who fail to live it worthily, but who think that they are wiser by experience, that is, by failure.

---

succinct: concise

revolution of 1649: In that year, King Charles I was beheaded and the Puritan Commonwealth was established.

pecuniary: financial

Khoungtseu: Confucius

Avast: stop

esteemed for: regarded as, taken for

shows: appearances

I have read in a Hindoo book, that "there was a king's son, who, being expelled in infancy from his native city, was brought up by a forester, and, growing up to maturity in that state, imagined himself to belong to the barbarous° race with which he lived. One of his father's ministers having discovered him, revealed to him what he was, and the misconception of his character was removed, and he knew himself to be a prince. So soul," continues the Hindoo philosopher, "from the circumstances in which it is placed, mistakes its own character, until the truth is revealed to it by some holy teacher, and then it knows itself to be *Brahme*."° I perceive that we inhabitants of New England live this mean life that we do because our vision does not penetrate the surface of things. We think that that *is* which *appears* to be. If a man should walk through this town and see only the reality, where, think you, would the "Mill-dam"° go to? If he should give us an account of the realities he beheld there, we should not recognize the place in his description. Look at a meeting-house, or a court-house, or a jail, or a shop, or a dwelling-house, and say what that thing really is before a true gaze, and they would all go to pieces in your account of them. Men esteem truth remote, in the outskirts of the system, behind the farthest star, before Adam and after the last man. In eternity there is indeed something true and sublime. But all these times and places and occasions are now and here. God himself culminates° in the present moment, and will never be more divine in the lapse of all the ages. And we are enabled to apprehend° at all what is sublime and noble only by the perpetual instilling and drenching of the reality that surrounds us. The universe constantly and obediently answers to our conceptions; whether we travel fast or slow, the track is laid for us. Let us spend our lives in conceiving then. The poet or the artist never yet had so fair and noble a design but some of his posterity at least could accomplish it.

15 Let us spend one day as deliberately as Nature, and not be thrown off the track by every nutshell and mosquito's wing that falls on the rails. Let us rise early and fast, or break fast, gently and without perturbation;° let company come and let company go, let the bells ring and the children cry,—determined to make a day of it. Why should we knock under° and go with the stream? Let us not be upset and overwhelmed in that terrible rapid and whirlpool called a dinner, situated in the meridian° shallows. Weather this danger and you are safe, for the rest of the way is downhill. With unrelaxed nerves, with

---

barbarous: primitive, unrefined

Brahme: Brahma, the supreme soul and essence of all being

"Mill-dam": a short street in the heart of Concord village, named for an actual local mill-dam

culminates: comes to completion

apprehend: perceive

perturbation: disturbance, upset

knock under: submit, knuckle under

meridian: midday, noonday

ing vigor, sail by it, looking another way, tied to the mast like Ulysses.° If gine whistles, let it whistle till it is hoarse for its pains. If the bell rings, why should we run? We will consider what kind of music they are like. Let us settle ourselves, and work and wedge our feet downward through the mud and slush of opinion, and prejudice, and tradition, and delusion, and appearance, that alluvion° which covers the globe, through Paris and London, through New York and Boston and Concord, through Church and State, through poetry and philosophy and religion, till we come to a hard bottom and rocks in place, which we can call *reality,* and say, This is, and no mistake; and then begin, having a *point d'appui,*° below freshet° and frost and fire, a place where you might found a wall or a state, or set a lamp-post safely, or perhaps a gauge, not a Nilometer,° but a Realometer, that future ages might know how deep a freshet of shams and appearances had gathered from time to time. If you stand right fronting and face to face to a fact, you will see the sun glimmer on both its surfaces, as if it were a cimeter,° and feel its sweet edge dividing you through the heart and marrow, and so you will happily conclude your mortal career. Be it life or death, we crave only reality. If we are really dying, let us hear the rattle in our throats and feel cold in the extremities; if we are alive, let us go about our business.

Time is but the stream I go a-fishing in. I drink at it; but while I drink I see the sandy bottom and detect how shallow it is. Its thin current slides away, but eternity remains. I would drink deeper; fish in the sky, whose bottom is pebbly with stars. I cannot count one. I know not the first letter of the alphabet. I have always been regretting that I was not as wise as the day I was born. The intellect is a cleaver;° it discerns and rifts° its way into the secret of things. I do not wish to be any more busy with my hands than is necessary. My head is hands and feet. I feel all my best faculties concentrated in it. My instinct tells me that my head is an organ for burrowing, as some creatures use their snout and fore paws, and with it I would mine and burrow my way through these hills. I think that the richest vein is somewhere hereabouts; so by the divining-rod° and thin rising vapors I judge; and here I will begin to mine.

[1854]

---

tied . . . Ulysses: In the *Odyssey,* Odysseus (Ulysses) had himself tied to the mast so that he could hear the sirens' song without giving in to their lure.

alluvion: clay, slit, or gravel deposited by streams

point d'appui: French for "base" (i.e., of operations)

freshet: sudden overflow of a stream after a thaw or heavy rain

Nilometer: gauge in ancient times for measuring the rise of the Nile as it approached its flood stage

cimeter: scimitar, a saber with a curved blade

cleaver: heavy, broad-bladed knife used especially by butchers

rifts: breaks, splits

divining-rod: forked stick used to detect underground water or minerals

Read

1. How does Thoreau define "rich" in the first section of the chapter?
2. Why does Thoreau advocate being disconnected from "the news"?
3. How do the descriptive details of the pond and surroundings show what Thoreau values?
4. What does the analogy between human life and ants suggest about Thoreau's argument?
5. How does Thoreau indicate what lessons he believes the woods are there to teach him?

Write

1. Reflect on Thoreau's argument for the simple life. Is it possible to "live deliberately"?
2. Discuss some of the observational details Thoreau includes and what they contribute to his argument.
3. How would you characterize Thoreau's style? Use several lines or images from the text to aid your characterization.
4. Is Thoreau's position persuasive to you? Why or why not?

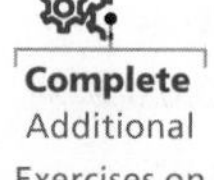

Complete Additional Exercises on Thoreau's Essay at Your Pearson MyLab

Connect

1. How does Thoreau seem to live out Emerson's plan for "man thinking"?
2. Compare Margaret Fuller's and Thoreau's use of the natural world and their descriptions of it.
3. Many writers consider Thoreau a symbol for the environmental movement. What elements in this excerpt suggest why these writers represent Thoreau in this way?

Margaret Fuller

Born in Cambridge, Massachusetts, Margaret Fuller (1810–1850) was part of the Concord Circle that included Ralph Waldo Emerson and Louisa May Alcott. She wrote on equality, abolition, nature and women's rights. Her most famous book, *Woman in the Nineteenth Century,* argued in logical terms for equality of opportunity for women. Fuller became the first American woman to edit a major literary journal, the transcendental *The Dial,* and she was the first woman foreign correspondent when she wrote from Europe for the New York *Daily Tribune.* Fuller had a good education in language, rhetoric, and the classics, much as any young man would receive. Her scholarship and knowledge made her both influential and threatening. After her tragic death in a ship accident, friends edited and rewrote large sections of her journals that were thought too radical. Fuller was rediscovered in the twentieth century as a pioneer for women's rights. *Summer on the Lakes, in 1843* written in 1844, brought her recognition and shows her interest in nature, in the growing country west of New York, and in the indigenous people who lived in unspoiled territory.

From *Summer on the Lakes, in 1843*

The only really rustic feature was of the many coops of poultry near the house, which I understood it to be one of the chief pleasures of the master to feed.

Leaving this place,° we proceeded a day's journey along the beautiful stream, to a little town named Oregon. We called at a cabin, from whose door looked out one of those faces which, once seen, are never forgotten; young, yet touched with many traces of feeling, not only possible, but endured; spirited, too, like the gleam of a finely tempered blade. It was a face that suggested a history, and many histories, but whose scene would have been in courts and camps.° At this moment their circles are dull for want of that life which is waning unexcited in this solitary recess.°

The master of the house proposed to show us a "short cut," by which we might, to especial advantage, pursue our journey. This proved to be almost perpendicular down a hill, studded with young trees and stumps. From these he proposed, with a hospitality of service worthy an Oriental, to free our wheels whenever they should get entangled, also, to be himself the drag, to prevent our too rapid descent. Such generosity deserved trust; however, we women could not be persuaded to render it. We got out and admired, from afar, the process. Left by our guide—and prop! we found ourselves in a wide field, where, by playful quips and turns,° an endless "creek," seemed to divert° itself with our attempts to cross it. Failing in this, the next best was to whirl down a steep bank, which feat our charioteer performed with an air not unlike that of Rhesus,° had he but been as suitably furnished with chariot and steeds!

At last, after wasting some two or three hours on the "short cut," we got out by following an Indian trail,—Black Hawk's!° How fair the scene through which it led! How could they let themselves be conquered, with such a country to fight for!

Afterwards, in the wide prairie, we saw a lively picture of nonchalance, (to speak in the fashion of dear Ireland.) There, in the wide sunny field, with neither tree nor umbrella above his head, sat a pedler, with his pack, waiting apparently for customers. He was not disappointed. We bought, what hold in 5

---

this place: a house on the Rock River in northern Illinois

courts and camps: royal courts and military camps

recess: remote area

quips and turns: Fuller is playing on two meanings of *divert*: "turn aside" and "amuse."

Rhesus: in Greek myth, a king of Thrace who fought for Troy in the Trojan War

Black Hawk: (1767–1838), leader of the Sauk and Fox warriors in the Black Hawk War of 1832

regard to the human world, as unmarked, as mysterious, and as important an existence, as the infusoria° to the natural, to wit, pins. This incident would have delighted those modern sages, who, in imitation of the sitting philosophers° of ancient Ind,° prefer silence to speech, waiting to going, and scornfully smile in answer to the motions of earnest life,

"Of itself will nothing come, That ye must still be seeking?"

However, it seemed to me to-day, as formerly on these sublime occasions, obvious that nothing would come, unless something would go; now, if we had been as sublimely still as the pedler, his pins would have tarried in the pack, and his pockets sustained an aching void of pence!°

Passing through one of the fine, park-like woods, almost clear from underbrush and carpeted with thick grasses and flowers, we met, (for it was Sunday,) a little congregation just returning from their service, which had been performed in a rude° house in its midst. It had a sweet and peaceful air, as if such words and thoughts were very dear to them. The parents had with them all their little children; but we saw no old people; that charm was wanting,° which exists in such scenes in older settlements, of seeing the silver° bent in reverence beside the flaxen° head.

At Oregon, the beauty of the scene was of even a more sumptuous character than at our former "stopping place." Here swelled the river in its boldest course, interspersed by halcyon° isles on which nature had lavished all her prodigality° in tree, vine, and flower, banked by noble bluffs, three hundred feet high, their sharp ridges as exquisitely definite as the edge of a shell; their summits adorned with those same beautiful trees, and with buttresses° of rich rock, crested with old hemlocks, which wore a touching and antique grace amid the softer and more luxuriant vegetation. Lofty natural mounds rose amidst the rest, with the same lovely and sweeping outline, showing everywhere the

---

infusoria: microscopic protozoa
sitting philosophers: especially Buddhists, with their emphasis on meditation and contemplation
Ind: India
pence: pennies, coins
rude: plain, simple
wanting: lacking
silver: gray-haired
flaxen: yellow
halcyon: peaceful
prodigality: extravagance, lavishness
buttresses: supports

plastic° power of water,—water, mother of beauty, which, by its sweet and eager flow, had left such lineaments° as human genius never dreamt of.

Not far from the river was a high crag, called the Pine Rock, which looks out, as our guide observed, like a helmet above the brow of the country. It seems as if the water left here and there a vestige of forms and materials that preceded its course, just to set off its new and richer designs.

The aspect of this country was to me enchanting, beyond any I have ever seen, from its fullness of expression, its bold and impassioned sweetness. Here the flood of emotion has passed over and marked everywhere its course by a smile. The fragments of rock touch it with a wildness and liberality which give just the needed relief. I should never be tired here, though I have elsewhere seen country of more secret and alluring charms, better calculated to stimulate and suggest. Here the eye and heart are filled. 10

How happy the Indians must have been here! It is not long since they were driven away, and the ground, above and below, is full of their traces.

"The earth is full of men."

You have only to turn up the sod to find arrowheads and Indian pottery. On an island, belonging to our host, and nearly opposite his house, they loved to stay, and, no doubt, enjoyed its lavish beauty as much as the myriad° wild pigeons that now haunt its flower-filled shades. Here are still the marks of their tomahawks, the troughs in which they prepared their corn, their caches.°

A little way down the river is the site of an ancient Indian village, with its regularly arranged mounds. As usual, they had chosen with the finest taste. It was one of those soft shadowy afternoons when we went there, when nature seems ready to weep, not from grief, but from an overfull heart. Two prattling,° lovely little girls, and an African boy, with glittering eye and ready grin, made our party gay;° but all were still as we entered their little inlet and trod those flowery paths. They may blacken Indian life as they will, talk of its dirt, its brutality, I will ever believe that the men who chose that dwelling-place were able to feel emotions of noble happiness as they returned to it, and so were the women that received them. Neither were the

---

plastic: pliant, flexible
lineaments: shapes, contours
myriad: innumerable
caches: hidden storage places
prattling: chattering childishly
gay: lively, merry

children sad or dull, who lived so familiarly with the deer and the birds, and swam that clear wave in the shadow of the Seven Sisters.° The whole scene suggested to me a Greek splendor, a Greek sweetness, and I can believe that an Indian brave, accustomed to ramble in such paths, and be bathed by such sunbeams, might be mistaken for Apollo, as Apollo was for him by West.° Two of the boldest bluffs are called the Deer's Walk, (not because deer do *not* walk there,) and the Eagle's Nest. The latter I visited one glorious morning; it was that, of the fourth of July, and certainly I think I had never felt so happy that I was born in America. Wo° to all country folks that never saw this spot, never swept an enraptured gaze over the prospect° that stretched beneath. I do believe Rome and Florence are suburbs compared to this capital of nature's art.

The bluff was decked with great bunches of a scarlet variety of the milkweed, like cut coral, and all starred with a mysterious-looking dark flower, whose cup rose lonely on a tall stem. This had, for two or three days, disputed the ground with the lupine and phlox. My companions disliked, I liked it. 15

. . .

The afternoon was spent in a very different manner. The family, whose guests we were, possessed a gay and graceful hospitality that gave zest to each moment. They possessed that rare politeness which, while fertile in pleasant expedients° to vary the enjoyment of a friend, leaves him perfectly free the moment he wishes to be so. With such hosts, pleasure may be combined with repose. They lived on the bank opposite the town, and, as their house was full, we slept in the town, and passed three days with them, passing to and fro morning and evening in their boats. (To one of these, called the Fairy, in which a sweet little daughter of the house moved about lighter than any Scotch Ellen ever sung, I should indite° a poem, if I had not been guilty of rhyme on the very last page.)° At morning this was very pleasant; at evening, I confess I was generally too tired with the excitements of the day to think it so.

---

the Seven Sisters: the Pleiades, a star cluster in the constellation of Taurus

West: Anglo-American artist Benjamin West (1738–1820) painted Apollo's Enchantment in 1807.

Wo: woe

prospect: scene, view

expedients: stratagems, methods

indite: write

if I had not . . . page: Fuller had inserted a hundred-line poem of hers (omitted here) just before this paragraph.

Their house—a double log cabin—was, to my eye, the model of a Western villa. Nature had laid out before it grounds which could not be improved. Within, female taste had veiled every rudeness°—availed itself of every sylvan° grace.

In this charming abode what laughter, what sweet thoughts, what pleasing fancies, did we not enjoy! May such never desert those who reared it and made us so kindly welcome to all its pleasures!

Fragments of city life were dexterously crumbled into the dish prepared for general entertainment. Ice creams followed the dinner drawn by the gentlemen from the river, and music and fireworks wound up the evening of days spent on the Eagle's Nest. Now they had prepared a little fleet to pass over to the Fourth of July celebration, which some queer° drumming and fifing, from the opposite bank, had announced to be "on hand."

We found the free and independent citizens there collected beneath the trees, among whom many a round Irish visage° dimpled at the usual puffs° of Ameriky.° 20

The orator was a New Englander, and the speech smacked loudly of Boston, but was received with much applause, and followed by a plentiful dinner, provided by and for the Sovereign People, to which Hail Columbia served as grace.

Log Cabin at Rock River

Returning, the gay flotilla hailed the little flag which the children had raised from a log-cabin, prettier than any president ever saw, and drank the health of their country and all mankind, with a clear conscience.

Dance and song wound up the day. I know not when the mere local habitation° has seemed to me to afford so fair a chance of happiness as this. To a person of unspoiled tastes, the beauty alone would afford stimulus enough. But with it would be naturally associated all kinds of wild sports, experiments, and the studies of natural history. In these regards, the poet, the sportsman, the naturalist, would alike rejoice in this wide range of untouched loveliness.

---

rudeness: primitiveness
sylvan: woodland
queer: odd, strange
visage: face
puffs: praises
Ameriky: Fuller's rendering of the Irish pronunciation of *America*
local habitation: an allusion to a speech in Shakespeare's *A Midsummer Night's Dream*; another phrase from this speech, "The lunatic, the lover, and the poet" may be echoed at the end of this paragraph.

Then, with a very little money, a ducal° estate may be purchased, and by a very little more, and moderate labor, a family be maintained upon it with raiment,° food and shelter. The luxurious and minute° comforts of a city life are not yet to be had without effort disproportionate to their value. But, where there is so great, a counterpoise,° cannot these be given up once for all? If the houses are imperfectly built, they can afford immense fires and plenty of covering; if they are small, who cares?—with such fields to roam in. In winter, it may be borne; in summer, is of no consequence. With plenty of fish, and game, and wheat, can they not dispense with a baker to bring "muffins hot" every morning to the door for their breakfast?

Here a man need not take a small slice from the landscape, and fence it in from the obtrusions° of an uncongenial neighbor, and there cut down his fancies to miniature improvements which a chicken could run over in ten minutes. He may have water and wood and land enough, to dread no incursions on his prospect from some chance Vandal that may enter his neighborhood. He need not painfully economise and manage how he may use it all; he can afford to leave some of it wild, and to carry out his own plans without obliterating those of nature. 25

Here, whole families might live together, if they would. The sons might return from their pilgrimages to settle near the parent hearth;° the daughters might find room near their mother. Those painful separations, which already desecrate° and desolate the Atlantic coast, are not enforced here by the stern need of seeking bread; and where they are voluntary, it is no matter. To me, too, used to the feelings which haunt a society of struggling men, it was delightful to look upon a scene where nature still wore her motherly smile and seemed to promise room not only for those favored or cursed with the qualities best adapting for the strifes of competition, but for the delicate, the thoughtful, even the indolent° or eccentric. She did not say, Fight or starve; nor even, Work or cease to exist; but, merely showing that the apple was a finer fruit than the wild crab,° gave both room to grow in the garden.

---

ducal: of or relating to a duke or duchy

raiment: clothing

minute: small, insignificant

counterpoise: state or force that balances or counteracts another

obtrusions: impositions

hearth: floor of a fireplace (familiar symbol for the warmth and coziness of home)

desecrate: violate

indolent: lazy, lethargic

crab: crab apple

A pleasant society is formed of the families who live along the banks of this stream upon farms. They are from various parts of the world, and have much to communicate to one another. Many have cultivated minds and refined manners, all a varied experience, while they have in common the interests of a new country and a new life. They must traverse some space to get at° one another, but the journey is through scenes that make it a separate pleasure. They must bear inconveniences to stay in one another's houses; but these, to the well-disposed, are only a source of amusement and adventure.

The great drawback upon the lives of these settlers, at present, is the unfitness of the women for their new lot.° It has generally been the choice of the men, and the women follow, as women will, doing their best for affection's sake, but too often in heart-sickness and weariness. Beside it frequently not being a choice or conviction of their own minds that it is best to be here, their part is the hardest, and they are least fitted for it. The men can find assistance in field labor, and recreation with the gun and fishing-rod. Their bodily strength is greater, and enables them to bear and enjoy both these forms of life.

The women can rarely find any aid in domestic labor. All its various and careful tasks must often be performed, sick or well, by the mother and daughters, to whom a city education has imparted neither the strength nor skill now demanded.

The wives of the poorer settlers, having more hard work to do than before, very frequently become slatterns;° but the ladies, accustomed to a refined neatness, feel that they cannot degrade themselves by its absence, and struggle under every disadvantage to keep up the necessary routine of small arrangements. 30

With all these disadvantages for work, their resources for pleasure are fewer. When they can leave the housework, they have not learnt to ride, to drive, to row, alone. Their culture has too generally been that given to women to make them "the ornaments of society." They can dance, but not draw; talk French, but know nothing of the language of flowers; neither in childhood were allowed to cultivate them, lest they should tan their complexions. Accustomed to the pavement of Broadway, they dare not tread the wild-wood paths for fear of rattlesnakes!

Seeing much of this joylessness, and inaptitude,° both of body and mind, for a lot which would be full of blessings for those prepared for it, we could

---

get at: reach, get to
lot: fate, fortune in life
slatterns: untidy or slovenly women
inaptitude: lack of ability

not but look with deep interest on the little girls, and hope they would grow up with the strength of body, dexterity, simple tastes, and resources that would fit them to enjoy and refine the western farmer's life.

But they have a great deal to war with in the habits of thought acquired by their mothers from their own early life. Everywhere the fatal spirit of imitation, of reference to European standards, penetrates, and threatens to blight whatever of original growth might adorn the soil.

If the little girls grow up strong, resolute, able to exert their faculties, their mothers mourn over their want of fashionable delicacy. Are they gay, enterprising, ready to fly about in the various ways that teach them so much, these ladies lament that "they cannot go to school, where they might learn to be quiet." They lament the want of "education" for their daughters, as if the thousand needs which call out their young energies, and the language of nature around, yielded no education.

Their grand ambition for their children, is to send them to school in some eastern city, the measure most likely to make them useless and unhappy at home. I earnestly hope that, ere° long, the existence of good schools near themselves, planned by persons of sufficient thought to meet the wants° of the place and time, instead of copying New York or Boston, will correct this mania. Instruction the children want to enable them to profit by the great natural advantages of their position;° but methods copied from the education of some English Lady Augusta, are as ill suited to the daughter of an Illinois farmer, as satin shoes to climb the Indian mounds. An elegance she would diffuse° around her, if her mind were opened to appreciate elegance; it might be of a kind new, original, enchanting, as different from that of the city belle as that of the prairie torch-flower from the shopworn article that touches the cheek of that lady within her bonnet.

To a girl really skilled to make home beautiful and comfortable, with bodily strength to enjoy plenty of exercise, the woods, the streams, a few studies, music, and the sincere and familiar intercourse,° far more easily to be met here than elsewhere, would afford happiness enough. Her eyes would not grow dim, nor her cheeks sunken, in the absence of parties, morning visits, and milliner's shops.

35

---

ere: before

wants: needs

position: situation, place

diffuse: spread

intercourse: interaction, communication

As to music, I wish I could see in such places the guitar rather than the piano, and good vocal more than instrumental music.

The piano many carry with them, because it is the fashionable instrument in the eastern cities. Even there, it is so merely from the habit of imitating Europe, for not one in a thousand is willing to give the labor requisite° to ensure any valuable use of the instrument.

But, out here, where the ladies have so much less leisure, it is still less desirable. Add to this, they never know how to tune their own instruments, and as persons seldom visit them who can do so, these pianos are constantly out of tune, and would spoil the ear of one who began by having any.°

[1844]

Read

1. How does Fuller demonstrate understanding of the American Indians who had lived where she visited?
2. How does Fuller's word choice and sentence structure convey her attitude toward the natural world?
3. What is her aim in the detailed descriptions of the scene in the American Indian village?
4. How does her attitude toward women's role and education get revealed in the last part of the excerpt?
5. How might the piano serve as a symbol for Fuller's criticism?

Write

1. Travel journals were popular during the nineteenth century. What observations do you read that seem typical of a travel journal? Are there any observations that seem atypical?
2. How would you describe Fuller's persona based on this excerpt? Use a line or two from the passage to aid your description.
3. Write a paragraph describing what actions Fuller would recommend to improve women's circumstances.
4. Comment on Fuller's attitude toward the land and use details or scenes to support your thinking.

Connect

1. How do Fuller and Thoreau use similar rhetorical strategies—observations, images—to convey their ideas?
2. How is Fuller's attitude toward the American Indians she encounters similar to that of other writers?
3. Using the passage, speculate on some of the advantages of travel to new places.

---

requisite: necessary

any: any ear for music

Asher Durand

Asher Durand (1796–1881) was born in New Jersey and was apprenticed early to an engraver, where he learned the trade and secured his reputation with an engraving of the Declaration of Independence. He was a part of several arts organizations in New York City, moving from engraving to oil painting. His friendship with artist Thomas Cole led him to concentrate on landscape painting, and he painted scenes of the Adirondacks, the Catskills, and other sites familiar to the Hudson River School painters.

Interior of a Wood

Study of a Wood Interior (c. 1855), Asher Brown Durand. Oil on canvas mounted on panel, 16 3/4 in. x 24 in. (42.55 cm x 60.96 cm). Gift Mrs. Frederic F. Durand, 1932. 1. Addison Gallery of American Art, Phillips Academy, Andover, Massachusetts.

[c. 1855]

Read

1. How does angle contribute to the effect of the painting?
2. Does the painting strike you as realistic or romantic?
3. What is the role of light in the effect of the painting?
4. How would you describe the painting's tone?

Write

1. Write a paragraph reflecting on what the painting suggests about the painter's view of the wilderness and the environment of the woods.
2. If you were using this painting as a cover illustration for a text in this unit or an earlier unit, which text would you choose? Explain your choice.

Connect

1. Compare Cole's painting in Unit 2 to Durand's painting. How does each painter depict the land?

Edgar Allan Poe

Edgar Allan Poe (1809–1849) is one of the best-known American authors, writing macabre tales, literary criticism, poetry, and detective fiction. He was born in Boston and orphaned early in his life. Poe was taken in by a wealthy Virginia family, the Allans, who later quarreled with him over debts and sent him to Baltimore. There, he became editor of a literary magazine, published his first poetry, and married his young cousin, Virginia, in 1836. The poem "The Raven" and a favorable review of his works by poet James Russell Lowell made him famous. In his personal life, he was haunted by debt, ill health, and continuing struggles with alcoholism. "The Purloined Letter" (1844) is one of the earliest detective stories. Poe's famous detective Dupin solves the crime with careful logic and reasoning, celebrated by Poe as "ratiocination." Poe's detective story was imitated by many writers, including Conan Doyle, who created Sherlock Holmes.

The Purloined° Letter

Nil sapientiae odiosius acumine nimio.

—Seneca.°

At Paris, just after dark one gusty evening in the autumn of 18—, I was enjoying the twofold luxury of meditation and a meerschaum,° in company with my friend C. August Dupin, in his little back library, or book-closet, *au troisième,*° *No. 33, Rue Dunôt, Faubourg St. Germain.* For one hour at least we had maintained a profound silence; while each, to any casual observer, might have seemed intently and exclusively occupied with the curling eddies° of smoke that oppressed the atmosphere of the chamber. For myself, however, I was mentally discussing certain topics which had formed matter for conversation between us at an earlier period of the evening; I mean the affair of the Rue Morgue, and the mystery attending the murder of Marie Rogêt.° I looked upon it, therefore, as something of a coincidence, when the door of our apartment was thrown open and

---

Purloined: stolen

epigraph: Latin for "Nothing is more hateful to wisdom than excessive cunning." Seneca (c. 4 B.C.–65 A.D.) was a Roman philosopher and playwright.

meerschaum: a tobacco pipe with a bowl made of meerschaum, a white, claylike mineral

au troisième: French for "on the third floor"

eddies: circular currents

the affair . . . Marie Rogêt: cases solved by Dupin in two earlier Poe stories, "The Murders in the Rue Morgue" and "The Mystery of Marie Rogêt"

admitted our old acquaintance, Monsieur G——, the Prefect° of the Parisian police.

We gave him a hearty welcome; for there was nearly half as much of the entertaining as of the contemptible about the man, and we had not seen him for several years. We had been sitting in the dark, and Dupin now arose for the purpose of lighting a lamp, but sat down again, without doing so, upon G.'s saying that he had called to consult us, or rather to ask the opinion of my friend, about some official business which had occasioned a great deal of trouble.

"If it is any point requiring reflection," observed Dupin, as he forebore to° enkindle° the wick, "we shall examine it to better purpose in the dark."

"That is another of your odd notions," said the Prefect, who had a fashion of calling every thing "odd" that was beyond his comprehension, and thus lived amid an absolute legion of "oddities."

"Very true," said Dupin, as he supplied his visiter with a pipe, and rolled towards him a comfortable chair. 5

"And what is the difficulty now?" I asked. "Nothing more in the assassination way, I hope?"

"Oh no; nothing of that nature. The fact is, the business is *very* simple indeed, and I make no doubt that we can manage it sufficiently well ourselves; but then I thought Dupin would like to hear the details of it, because it is so excessively *odd*."

"Simple and odd," said Dupin.

"Why, yes; and not exactly that, either. The fact is, we have all been a good deal puzzled because the affair *is* so simple, and yet baffles us altogether."

"Perhaps it is the very simplicity of the thing which puts you at fault," said my friend. 10

"What nonsense you *do* talk!" replied the Prefect, laughing heartily.

"Perhaps the mystery is a little *too* plain," said Dupin.

"Oh, good heavens! who ever heard of such an idea?"

"A little *too* self-evident."

"Ha! ha! ha!—ha! ha! ha!—ho! ho! ho!"—roared our visiter, profoundly amused, "oh, Dupin, you will be the death of me yet!" 15

"And what, after all, *is* the matter on hand?" I asked.

"Why, I will tell you," replied the Prefect, as he gave a long, steady, and contemplative puff, and settled himself in his chair. "I will tell

---

Prefect: head, chief administrative official

forebore to: refrained from, held back from

enkindle: light

you in a few words; but, before I begin, let me caution you that this is an affair demanding the greatest secrecy, and that I should most probably lose the position I now hold, were it known that I confided it to any one."

"Proceed," said I.

"Or not," said Dupin.

"Well, then; I have received personal information, from a very high quarter, that a certain document of the last° importance, has been purloined from the royal apartments. The individual who purloined it is known; this beyond a doubt; he was seen to take it. It is known, also, that it still remains in his possession." 20

"How is this known?" asked Dupin.

"It is clearly inferred,"° replied the Prefect, "from the nature of the document, and from the non-appearance of certain results which would at once arise from its passing *out* of the robber's possession;—that is to say, from his employing it as he must design in the end to employ it."

"Be a little more explicit," I said.

"Well, I may venture so far as to say that the paper gives its holder a certain power in a certain quarter where such power is immensely valuable." The Prefect was fond of the cant° of diplomacy.

"Still I do not quite understand," said Dupin. 25

"No? Well; the disclosure of the document to a third person, who shall be nameless, would bring in question the honor of a personage of most exalted station; and this fact gives the holder of the document an ascendancy° over the illustrious personage whose honor and peace are so jeopardized."

"But this ascendancy," I interposed, "would depend upon the robber's knowledge of the loser's knowledge of the robber. Who would dare—"

"The thief," said G., "is the Minister° D——, who dares all things, those unbecoming as well as those becoming a man. The method of the theft was not less ingenious than bold. The document in question—a letter, to be frank—had been received by the personage robbed while alone in the royal *boudoir.* During its perusal° she was suddenly interrupted by the entrance of the other exalted personage

---

last: utmost

inferred: deduced from evidence

cant: jargon

ascendancy: domination, upper hand

Minister: of the government, not the church

perusal: reading, scrutiny

from whom especially it was her wish to conceal it. After a hurried and vain endeavor to thrust it in a drawer, she was forced to place it, open as it was, upon a table. The address, however, was uppermost, and, the contents thus unexposed, the letter escaped notice. At this juncture enters the Minister D——. His lynx° eye immediately perceives the paper, recognises the handwriting of the address, observes the confusion of the personage addressed, and fathoms° her secret. After some business transactions, hurried through in his ordinary manner, he produces a letter somewhat similar to the one in question, opens it, pretends to read it, and then places it in close juxtaposition to the other. Again he converses, for some fifteen minutes, upon the public affairs. At length, in taking leave, he takes also from the table the letter to which he had no claim. Its rightful owner saw, but, of course, dared not call attention to the act, in the presence of the third personage who stood at her elbow. The minister decamped;° leaving his own letter—one of no importance—upon the table."

"Here, then," said Dupin to me, "you have precisely what you demand° to make the ascendancy complete—the robber's knowledge of the loser's knowledge of the robber."

"Yes," replied the Prefect; "and the power thus attained has, for some months past, been wielded, for political purposes, to a very dangerous extent. The personage robbed is more thoroughly convinced, every day, of the necessity of reclaiming her letter. But this, of course, cannot be done openly. In fine,° driven to despair, she has committed° the matter to me." 30

"Than whom," said Dupin, amid a perfect whirlwind of smoke, "no more sagacious° agent could, I suppose, be desired, or even imagined."

"You flatter me," replied the Prefect; "but it is possible that some such opinion may have been entertained."

"It is clear," said I, "as you observe, that the letter is still in possession of the minister; since it is this possession, and not any employment of the letter, which bestows the power. With the employment the power departs."

---

lynx: short-tailed wildcat of Europe and North America

fathoms: comprehends

decamped: left quickly

demand: require

In fine: in short

committed: turned over, entrusted

sagacious: wise, shrewd

"True," said G.; "and upon this conviction I proceeded. My first care was to make thorough search of the minister's hotel;° and here my chief embarrassment lay in the necessity of searching without his knowledge. Beyond all things, I have been warned of the danger which would result from giving him reason to suspect our design."°

"But," said I, "you are quite *au fait*° in these investigations. The Parisian police have done this thing often before." 35

"O yes; and for this reason I did not despair. The habits of the minister gave me, too, a great advantage. He is frequently absent from home all night. His servants are by no means numerous. They sleep at a distance from their master's apartment,° and, being chiefly Neapolitans, are readily made drunk. I have keys, as you know, with which I can open any chamber or cabinet in Paris. For three months a night has not passed, during the greater part of which I have not been engaged, personally, in ransacking the D—— Hôtel. My honor is interested,° and, to mention a great secret, the reward is enormous. So I did not abandon the search until I had become fully satisfied that the thief is a more astute° man than myself. I fancy that I have investigated every nook and corner of the premises in which it's possible that the paper can be concealed."

"But is it not possible," I suggested, "that although the letter may be in possession of the minister, as it unquestionably is, he may have concealed it elsewhere than upon his own premises?"

"This is barely possible," said Dupin. "The present peculiar condition of affairs at court, and especially of those intrigues° in which D—— is known to be involved, would render the instant availability of the document—its susceptibility of being produced at a moment's notice—a point of nearly equal importance with its possession."

"Its susceptibility of being produced?" said I.

"That is to say, of being *destroyed,*" said Dupin. 40

"True," I observed; "the paper is clearly then upon the premises. As for its being upon the person of the minister, we may consider that as out of the question."

---

hotel: in France, the mansion or town residence of a person of rank or wealth

design: intention, plan

au fait: French idiom for "knowledgeable, up to speed"

apartment: part of the house—bedroom, etc.—that is his private living quarters

interested: involved

astute: smart, crafty

intrigues: secret schemes, plots

"Entirely," said the Prefect. "He has been twice waylaid,° as if by footpads,° and his person rigorously searched under my own inspection."

"You might have spared yourself this trouble," said Dupin. "D——, I presume, is not altogether a fool, and, if not, must have anticipated these waylayings, as a matter of course."

"Not *altogether* a fool," said G., "but then he's a poet, which I take to be only one remove from a fool."

"True," said Dupin, after a long and thoughtful whiff from his meerschaum, "although I have been guilty of certain doggerel° myself." 45

"Suppose you detail," said I, "the particulars of your search."

"Why the fact is, we took our time, and we searched *every where.* I have had long experience in these affairs. I took the entire building, room by room; devoting the nights of a whole week to each. We examined, first, the furniture of each apartment. We opened every possible drawer; and I presume you know that, to a properly trained police agent, such a thing as a *secret* drawer is impossible. Any man is a dolt who permits a 'secret' drawer to escape him in a search of this kind. The thing is *so* plain. There is a certain amount of bulk—of space—to be accounted for in every cabinet. Then we have accurate rules. The fiftieth part° of a line° could not escape us. After the cabinets we took the chairs. The cushions we probed with the fine long needles you have seen me employ. From the tables we removed the tops."

"Why so?"

"Sometimes the top of a table, or other similarly arranged piece of furniture, is removed by the person wishing to conceal an article; then the leg is excavated, the article deposited within the cavity, and the top replaced. The bottoms and tops of bed-posts are employed in the same way."

"But could not the cavity be detected by sounding?" I asked. 50

"By no means, if, when the article is deposited, a sufficient wadding of cotton be placed around it. Besides, in our case, we were obliged to proceed without noise."

"But you could not have removed—you could not have taken to pieces *all* articles of furniture in which it would have been possible to make a deposit in the manner you mention. A letter may be

---

waylaid: attacked from ambush

footpads: i.e., muggers

doggerel: verse, usually of poor quality

The fiftieth part: one-fiftieth

line: string or cord

compressed into a thin spiral roll, not differing much in shape or bulk from a large knitting-needle, and in this form it might be inserted into the rung of a chair, for example. You did not take to pieces all the chairs?"

"Certainly not; but we did better—we examined the rungs of every chair in the hotel, and, indeed, the jointings of every description of furniture, by the aid of a most powerful microscope.° Had there been any traces of recent disturbance we should not have failed to detect it instantly. A single grain of gimlet-dust,° for example, would have been as obvious as an apple. And disorder in the glueing—any unusual gaping in the joints—would have sufficed to insure detection."

"I presume you looked to the mirrors, between the boards and the plates, and you probed the beds and the bed-clothes, as well as the curtains and carpets."

"That of course; and when we had absolutely completed every particle of the furniture in this way, then we examined the house itself. We divided its entire surface into compartments, which we numbered, so that none might be missed; then we scrutinized each individual square inch throughout the premises, including the two houses immediately adjoining, with the microscope, as before." 55

"The two houses adjoining!" I exclaimed; "you must have had a great deal of trouble."

"We had; but the reward offered is prodigious."°

"You include the *grounds* about the houses?"

"All the grounds are paved with brick. They gave us comparatively little trouble. We examined the moss between the bricks, and found it undisturbed."

"You looked among D——'s papers, of course, and into the books of the library?" 60

"Certainly; we opened every package and parcel; we not only opened every book, but we turned over every leaf° in each volume, not contenting ourselves with a mere shake, according to the fashion of some of our police officers. We also measured the thickness of every book-*cover*, with the most accurate admeasurement, and applied to each the most jealous° scrutiny of the microscope. Had any of the bindings been recently meddled with, it would have been utterly impossible that the fact should have escaped observation. Some five

---

microscope: magnifying glass

gimlet-dust: sawdust produced by a gimlet, a small tool for boring into wood

prodigious: extraordinarily large, extremely impressive

leaf: page

jealous: vigilant

or six volumes, just from the hands of the binder, we carefully probed, longitudinally, with the needles."

"You explored the floors beneath the carpets?"

"Beyond doubt. We removed every carpet, and examined the boards with the microscope."

"And the paper on the walls?"

"Yes." 65

"You looked into the cellars?"

"We did."

"Then," I said, "you have been making a miscalculation, and the letter is *not* upon the premises, as you suppose."

"I fear you are right there," said the Prefect. "And now, Dupin, what would you advise me to do?"

"To make a thorough re-search of the premises." 70

"That is absolutely needless," replied G——. "I am not more sure that I breathe than I am that the letter is not at the Hôtel."

"I have no better advice to give you," said Dupin. "You have, of course, an accurate description of the letter?"

"Oh yes!"—And here the Prefect, producing a memorandum-book, proceeded to read aloud a minute° account of the internal, and especially of the external appearance of the missing document. Soon after finishing the perusal of this description, he took his departure, more entirely depressed in spirits than I had ever known the good gentleman before.

In about a month afterwards he paid us another visit, and found us occupied very nearly as before. He took a pipe and a chair and entered into some ordinary conversation. At length I said—

"Well, but G——, what of the purloined letter? I presume you have at last made up your mind that there is no such thing as over-reaching° the Minister?" 75

"Confound° him, say I—yes; I made the re-examination, however, as Dupin suggested—but it was all labor lost, as I knew it would be."

"How much was the reward offered, did you say?" asked Dupin.

"Why, a very great deal—a *very* liberal reward—I don't like to say how much, precisely; but one thing I *will* say, that I wouldn't mind giving my individual check for fifty thousand francs to any one who could obtain me that letter. The fact is, it is becoming of more and more importance every day; and the reward has been lately doubled. If it were trebled,° however, I could do no more than I have done."

---

minute: thorough, attentive to even the smallest details

over-reaching: outdoing, getting the better of

Confound: damn

trebled: tripled

"Why, yes," said Dupin, drawlingly, between the whiffs° of his meerschaum, "I really—think, G——, you have not exerted yourself—to the utmost in this matter. You might—do a little more, I think, eh?"

"How?—in what way?" 80

"Why—puff, puff—you might—puff, puff—employ counsel in the matter, eh?—puff, puff, puff. Do you remember the story they tell of Abernethy?"°

"No; hang Abernethy!"

"To be sure! hang him and welcome. But, once upon a time, a certain rich miser conceived the design of spunging upon this Abernethy for a medical opinion. Getting up, for this purpose, an ordinary conversation in a private company, he insinuated° his case to the physician, as that of an imaginary individual.

"'We will suppose,' said the miser, 'that his symptoms are such and such; now, doctor, what would *you* have directed him to take?'

"'Take!' said Abernethy, 'why take *advice,* to be sure.'" 85

"But," said the Prefect, a little discomposed,° "I am *perfectly* willing to take advice, and to pay for it. I would *really* give fifty thousand francs to any one who would aid me in the matter."

"In that case," replied Dupin, opening a drawer, and producing a check-book, "you may as well fill me up° a check for the amount mentioned. When you have signed it, I will hand you the letter."

I was astounded. The Prefect appeared absolutely thunderstricken. For some minutes he remained speechless and motionless, looking incredulously° at my friend with open mouth, and eyes that seemed starting from their sockets; then, apparently recovering himself in some measure, he seized a pen, and after several pauses and vacant stares, finally filled up and signed a check for fifty thousand francs, and handed it across the table to Dupin. The latter examined it carefully and deposited it in his pocket-book; then, unlocking an *escritoire,*° took thence° a letter and gave it to the Prefect. This functionary grasped it in a perfect agony of joy, opened it with a

---

whiffs: puffs

Abernethy: John Abernethy (1764–1831), English surgeon, who had the reputation of being brusque and even rude with his patients

insinuated: hinted, subtly suggested

discomposed: agitated, unsettled

fill me up: write me out

incredulously: disbelievingly

escritoire: French for "writing desk"

thence: from there

trembling hand, cast a rapid glance at its contents, and then, scrambling and struggling to the door, rushed at length unceremoniously from the room and from the house, without having uttered a syllable since Dupin had requested him to fill up the check.

When he had gone, my friend entered into some explanations.

"The Parisian police," he said, "are exceedingly able in their way. They are persevering, ingenious, cunning, and thoroughly versed in the knowledge which their duties seem chiefly to demand. Thus, when G—— detailed to us his mode of searching the premises at the Hôtel D——, I felt entire confidence in his having made a satisfactory investigation—so far as his labors extended." 90

"So far as his labors extended?" said I.

"Yes," said Dupin. "The measures adopted were not only the best of their kind, but carried out to absolute perfection. Had the letter been deposited within the range of their search, these fellows would, beyond a question, have found it."

I merely laughed—but he seemed quite serious in all that he said.

"The measures, then," he continued, "were good in their kind, and well executed; but their defect lay in their being inapplicable to the case, and to the man. A certain set of highly ingenious resources are, with the Prefect, a sort of Procrustean bed,° to which he forcibly adapts his designs. But he perpetually errs by being too deep or too shallow, for the matter in hand; and many a schoolboy is a better reasoner than he. I knew one about eight years of age, whose success at guessing in the game of 'even and odd' attracted universal admiration. This game is simple; and is played with marbles. One player holds in his hand a number of these toys, and demands of another whether that number is even or odd. If the guess is right, the guesser wins one; if wrong, he loses one. The boy to whom I allude won all the marbles of the school. Of course he had some principle of guessing; and this lay in mere observation and admeasurement° of the astuteness of his opponents. For example, an arrant° simpleton is his opponent, and, holding up his closed hand, asks, 'are they even or odd?' Our schoolboy replies, 'odd,' and loses; but upon the second trial he wins, for he then says to himself, 'the simpleton had them even upon the first trial, and his amount of cunning is just sufficient to make him have them odd upon the second; I will therefore guess odd;'—he guesses odd, and wins. Now, with a simpleton a degree above the

---

Procrustean bed: an arbitrary standard; in Greek myth, Procrustes would either stretch people out or cut off part of their legs to force them to fit an iron bed

admeasurement: determination

arrant: downright, thoroughgoing

first, he would have reasoned thus: 'This fellow finds that in the first instance I guessed odd, and, in the second, he will propose to himself upon the first impulse, a simple variation from even to odd, as did the first simpleton; but then a second thought will suggest that this is too simple a variation, and finally he will decide upon putting it even as before. I will therefore guess even;'—he guesses even, and wins. Now this mode of reasoning in the schoolboy, whom his fellows term 'lucky,'—what, in its last analysis, is it?"

"It is merely," I said, "an identification of the reasoner's intellect with that of his opponent." 95

"It is," said Dupin; "and, upon inquiring of the boy by what means he effected° the *thorough* identification in which his success consisted, I received answer as follows: 'When I wish to find out how wise, or how stupid, or how good, or how wicked is any one, or what are his thoughts at the moment, I fashion the expression of my face, as accurately as possible, in accordance with the expression of his, and then wait to see what thoughts or sentiments arise in my mind or heart, as if to match or correspond with the expression.' This response of the schoolboy lies at the bottom of all the spurious° profundity which has been attributed to Rochefoucauld,° to La Bruyere,° to Machiavelli,° and to Campanella."°

"And the identification," I said, "of the reasoner's intellect with that of his opponent, depends, if I understand you aright, upon the accuracy with which the opponent's intellect is admeasured."

"For its practical value it depends upon this," replied Dupin; "and the Prefect and his cohort° fail so frequently, first, by default of this identification, and, secondly, by ill-admeasurement, or rather through nonadmeasurement, of the intellect with which they are engaged. They consider only their *own* ideas of ingenuity; and, in searching for anything hidden, advert only to the modes in which *they* would have hidden it. They are right in this much—that their own ingenuity is a faithful representative of *the mass;* but when the cunning of the individual felon is diverse in character from their own, the felon foils them, of course. This always happens when it is above their own, and very usually when it is below. They have no

---

effected: achieved

spurious: false, counterfeit

Rochefoucauld: François de La Rochefoucauld (1613–1680), French author of maxims

La Bruyere: Jean de La Bruyère (1645–1696), French essayist

Machiavelli: Niccolò Machiavelli (1469–1527), Italian political theorist, author of *The Prince* (1532)

Campanella: Tommaso Campanella (1568–1639), Italian philosopher and poet

cohort: force, group

variation of principle in their investigations; at best, when urged by some unusual emergency—by some extraordinary reward—they extend or exaggerate their old modes of *practice,* without touching their principles. What, for example, in this case of D——, has been done to vary the principle of action? What is all this boring, and probing, and sounding, and scrutinizing with the microscope, and dividing the surface of the building into registered° square inches—what is it all but an exaggeration *of the application* of the one principle or set of principles of search, which are based upon the one set of notions regarding human ingenuity, to which the Prefect, in the long routine of his duty, has been accustomed? Do you not see he has taken it for granted that *all* men proceed to conceal a letter,—not exactly in a gimlet-hole bored in a chair-leg—but, at least, in *some* out-of-the-way hole or corner suggested by the same tenor° of thought which would urge a man to secrete a letter in a gimlet-hole bored in a chair-leg? And do you not see also, that such *recherchés*° nooks for concealment are adapted only for ordinary occasions, and would be adopted only by ordinary intellects; for, in all cases of concealment, a disposal of the article concealed—a disposal of it in this *recherché* manner,—is, in the very first instance, presumable and presumed; and thus its discovery depends, not at all upon the acumen,° but altogether upon the mere care, patience, and determination of the seekers; and where the case is of importance—or, what amounts to the same thing in the political eyes, when the reward is of magnitude,—the qualities in question have *never* been known to fail. You will now understand what I meant in suggesting that, had the purloined letter been hidden any where within the limits of the Prefect's examination—in other words, had the principle of its concealment been comprehended within the principles of the Prefect—its discovery would have been a matter altogether beyond question. This functionary, however, has been thoroughly mystified; and the remote source of his defeat lies in the supposition that the Minister is a fool, because he has acquired renown as a poet. All fools are poets; this the Prefect *feels;* and he is merely guilty of a *non distributio medii*° in thence inferring that all poets are fools."

"But is this really the poet?" I asked. "There are two brothers, I know; and both have attained reputation in letters. The Minister

---

registered: documented

tenor: general tendency

recherchés: French for "obscure or sought out with care"

acumen: insight, shrewdness

non distributio medii: Latin for "undistributed middle," a logical fallacy

I believe has written learnedly on the Differential Calculus. He is a mathematician, and no poet."

"You are mistaken; I know him well; he is both. As poet *and* mathematician, he would reason well; as mere mathematician, he could not have reasoned at all, and thus would have been at the mercy of the Prefect." 100

"You surprise me," I said, "by these opinions, which have been contradicted by the voice of the world. You do not mean to set at naught° the well-digested idea of centuries. The mathematical reason has long been regarded as *the* reason *par excellence.*"

"'*Il y a à parier,*'" replied Dupin, quoting from Chamfort,° "'*que toute idée publique, toute convention reçue, est une sottise, car elle a convenu au plus grand nombre.*'° The mathematicians, I grant you, have done their best to promulgate° the popular error to which you allude, and which is none the less an error for its promulgation as truth. With an art worthy a better cause, for example, they have insinuated the term 'analysis' into application to algebra. The French are the originators of this particular deception; but if a term is of any importance—if words derive any value from applicability—then 'analysis' conveys 'algebra' about as much as, in Latin, '*ambitus*'° implies 'ambition,' '*religio*'° 'religion,' or '*homines honesti,*'° a set of *honorable* men."

"You have a quarrel on hand, I see," said I, "with some of the algebraists of Paris; but proceed."

"I dispute the availability, and thus the value, of that reason° which is cultivated in any especial form other than the abstractly logical. I dispute, in particular, the reason educed° by mathematical study. The mathematics are the science of form and quantity; mathematical reasoning is merely logic applied to observation upon form and quantity. The great error lies in supposing that even the truths of

---

set at naught: disregard, treat as of no account

Chamfort: Sébastien-Roch Nicolas, known as Chamfort (1741–1794), French writer of epigrams and aphorisms

'Il y a . . . nombre': French for "It's safe to bet that every public idea, every accepted convention, is a piece of stupidity, because it was agreeable to the majority."

promulgate: announce, declare

ambitus: Latin for "going around;" with reference to persons, it implies bribery or office seeking

religio: Latin for "scrupulousness, conscientious exactness;" can also suggest superstition

homines honesti: the Roman orator and senator Cicero used this term to refer to those of his own party

reason: here meaning "process of logical thinking," not "motive" or "justification"

educed: developed

what is called *pure* algebra, are abstract or general truths. And this error is so egregious° that I am confounded at° the universality with which it has been received. Mathematical axioms are *not* axioms of general truth. What is true of *relation*—of form and quantity—is often grossly false in regard to morals, for example. In this latter science it is very usually *un*true that the aggregated° parts are equal to the whole. In chemistry also the axiom fails. In the consideration of motive it fails; for two motives, each of a given value, have not, necessarily, a value when united, equal to the sum of their values apart. There are numerous other mathematical truths which are only truths within the limits of *relation.* But the mathematician argues, from his *finite truths,* through habit, as if they were of an absolutely general applicability—as the world indeed imagines them to be. Bryant,° in his very learned 'Mythology,' mentions an analogous source of error, when he says that 'although the Pagan fables are not believed, yet we forget ourselves continually, and make inferences from them as existing realities.' With the algebraists, however, who are Pagans themselves, the 'Pagan fables' *are* believed, and the inferences are made, not so much through lapse of memory, as through an unaccountable° addling° of the brains. In short, I never yet encountered the mere mathematician who could be trusted out of equal roots, or one who did not clandestinely hold it as a point of his faith that $x2 + px$ was absolutely and unconditionally equal to q. Say to one of these gentlemen, by way of experiment, if you please, that you believe occasions may occur where $x2 + px$ is *not* altogether equal to q, and, having made him understand what you mean, get out of his reach as speedily as convenient, for, beyond doubt, he will endeavor to knock you down.

"I mean to say," continued Dupin, while I merely laughed at his last observations, "that if the Minister had been no more than a mathematician, the Prefect would have been under no necessity of giving me this check. I knew him, however, as both mathematician and poet, and my measures were adapted to his capacity, with reference to the circumstances by which he was surrounded. 105

egregious: glaring, flagrant
confounded at: amazed by
aggregated: assembled, gathered
Bryant: Jacob Bryant (1715–1804), English scholar; the first edition of his *A New System or Analysis of Ancient Mythology* appeared in 1774.
unaccountable: inexplicable
addling: muddling

I knew him as a courtier,° too, and as a bold *intriguant.*° Such a man, I considered, could not fail to be aware of the ordinary political modes of action. He could not have failed to anticipate—and events have proved that he did not fail to anticipate—the waylayings to which he was subjected. He must have foreseen, I reflected, the secret investigations of his premises. His frequent absences from home at night, which were hailed by the Prefect as certain aids to his success, I regarded only as *ruses,* to afford opportunity for thorough search to the police, and thus the sooner to impress them with the conviction to which G——, in fact, did finally arrive—the conviction that the letter was not upon the premises. I felt, also, that the whole train of thought, which I was at some pains in detailing to you just now, concerning the invariable principle of political action in searches for articles concealed—I felt that this whole train of thought would necessarily pass through the mind of the Minister. It would imperatively lead him to despise all the ordinary *nooks* of concealment. *He* could not, I reflected, be so weak as not to see that the most intricate and remote recess of his hotel would be as open as his commonest closets to the eyes, to the probes, to the gimlets, and to the microscopes of the Prefect. I saw, in fine, that he would be driven, as a matter of course, to *simplicity,* if not deliberately induced to it as a matter of choice. You will remember, perhaps, how desperately the Prefect laughed when I suggested, upon our first interview, that it was just possible this mystery troubled him so much on account of its being so *very* self-evident."

"Yes," said I, "I remember his merriment well. I really thought he would have fallen into convulsions."

"The material world," continued Dupin, "abounds with very strict analogies to the immaterial; and thus some color of truth has been given to the rhetorical dogma,° that metaphor, or simile, may be made to strengthen an argument, as well as to embellish a description. The principle of the *vis inertiæ,*° for example, seems to be identical in physics and metaphysics. It is not more true in the former, that a large body is with more difficulty set in motion than a smaller one, and that its subsequent *momentum* is commensurate with° this difficulty, than it is, in the latter, that intellects of the vaster capacity, while more forcible, more constant, and more eventful in their move-

---

courtier: person in attendance at a royal court; one seeking favor by flattery or charm

intriguant: French for "plotter, schemer"

dogma: doctrine, principle

vis inertiæ: Latin for "force of inertia"

commensurate with: proportionate to

ments than those of inferior grade, are yet the less readily moved, and more embarrassed and full of hesitation in the first few steps of their progress. Again: have you ever noticed which of the street signs, over the shop doors, are the most attractive of attention?"

"I have never given the matter a thought," I said.

"There is a game of puzzles," he resumed, "which is played upon a map. One party playing requires another to find a given word—the name of town, river, state or empire—any word, in short, upon the motley° and perplexed surface of the chart. A novice in the game generally seeks to embarrass his opponents by giving them the most minutely lettered names; but the adept° selects such words as stretch, in large characters, from one end of the chart to the other. These, like the over-largely lettered signs and placards of the street, escape observation by dint of being excessively obvious; and here the physical oversight is precisely analogous with the moral inapprehension° by which the intellect suffers to pass unnoticed those considerations which are too obtrusively° and too palpably° self-evident. But this is a point, it appears, somewhat above or beneath the understanding of the Prefect. He never once thought it probable, or possible, that the Minister had deposited the letter immediately beneath the nose of the whole world, by way of best preventing any portion of that world from perceiving it.

"But the more I reflected upon the daring, dashing, and discriminating ingenuity of D——; upon the fact that the document must always have been *at hand,* if he intended to use it to good purpose; and upon the decisive evidence, obtained by the Prefect, that it was not hidden within the limits of that dignitary's ordinary search—the more satisfied I became that, to conceal this letter, the Minister had resorted to the comprehensive and sagacious expedient° of not attempting to conceal it at all. 110

"Full of these ideas, I prepared myself with a pair of green spectacles, and called one fine morning, quite by accident, at the Ministerial hotel. I found D—— at home, yawning, lounging, and dawdling, as usual, and pretending to be in the last extremity of *ennui.*° He is, perhaps, the most really energetic human being now alive—but that is only when nobody sees him.

---

motley: multicolored, jumbled
adept: expert
inapprehension: lack of perception or awareness
obtrusively: blatantly
palpably: obviously
expedient: stratagem
ennui: French for "listlessness, weariness"

"To be even with him, I complained of my weak eyes, and lamented the necessity of the spectacles, under cover of which I cautiously and thoroughly surveyed the apartment, while seemingly intent only upon the conversation of my host.

"I paid special attention to a large writing-table near which he sat, and upon which lay confusedly, some miscellaneous letters and other papers, with one or two musical instruments and a few books. Here, however, after a long and very deliberate scrutiny, I saw nothing to excite particular suspicion.

"At length my eyes, in going the circuit of the room, fell upon a trumpery° fillagree° card-rack° of paste-board,° that hung dangling by a dirty blue ribbon, from a little brass knob just beneath the middle of the mantelpiece. In this rack, which had three or four compartments, were five or six visiting cards and a solitary letter. This last was much soiled and crumpled. It was torn nearly in two, across the middle—as if a design,° in the first instance, to tear it entirely up as worthless, had been altered, or stayed,° in the second. It had a large black seal, bearing the D—— cipher° *very* conspicuously, and was addressed, in a diminutive° female hand, to D——, the minister, himself. It was thrust carelessly, and even, as it seemed, contemptuously, into one of the upper divisions of the rack.

"No sooner had I glanced at this letter, than I concluded it to be that of which I was in search. To be sure, it was, to all appearance, radically different from the one which the Prefect had read us so minute a description. Here the seal was large and black, with the D—— cipher; there it was small and red, with the ducal° arms of the S—— family. Here, the address, to the Minister, was diminutive and feminine; there the superscription,° to a certain royal personage, was markedly bold and decided; the size alone formed a point of correspondence. But, then, the *radicalness* of these differences, which was excessive; the dirt; the soiled and torn condition of the paper, so inconsistent with the *true* methodical habits of D——, and 115

---

trumpery: trashy
fillagree: (filigree) decorative, ornamental
card-rack: frame rack with pigeon holes for business or visiting cards
paste-board: stiff board made from layers of paper pasted together
design: plan, intention
stayed: suspended
cipher: monogram
diminutive: small, tiny
ducal: of or pertaining to a duke or dukedom
superscription: address on the outside of a letter

so suggestive of a design to delude the beholder into an idea of the worthlessness of the document; these things, together with the hyper-obtrusive° situation of this document, full in the view of every visitor, and thus exactly in accordance with the conclusions to which I had previously arrived; these things, I say, were strongly corroborative of suspicion, in one who came with the intention to suspect.

"I protracted my visit as long as possible, and, while I maintained a most animated discussion with the Minister, on a topic which I knew well had never failed to interest and excite him, I kept my attention really riveted upon the letter. In this examination, I committed to memory its external appearance and arrangement in the rack; and also fell, at length, upon a discovery which set at rest whatever trivial doubt I might have entertained. In scrutinizing the edges of the paper, I observed them to be more *chafed* than seemed necessary. They presented the *broken* appearance which is manifested when a stiff paper, having been once folded and pressed with a folder, is re-folded in a reversed direction, in the same creases or edges which had formed the original fold. This discovery was sufficient. It was clear to me that the letter had been turned, as a glove, inside out, re-directed, and re-sealed. I bade the Minister good morning, and took my departure at once, leaving a gold snuff-box upon the table.

"The next morning I called for the snuff-box, when we resumed, quite eagerly, the conversation of the preceding day. While thus engaged, however, a loud report, as if of a pistol, was heard immediately beneath the windows of the hotel, and was succeeded by a series of fearful screams, and the shoutings of a mob. D—— rushed to a casement,° threw it open, and looked out. In the meantime, I stepped to the card-rack, took the letter, put it in my pocket, and replaced it by a *fac-simile,* (so far as regards externals,) which I had carefully prepared at my lodgings; imitating the D—— cipher, very readily, by means of a seal formed of bread.

"The disturbance in the street had been occasioned by the frantic behavior of a man with a musket. He had fired it among a crowd of women and children. It proved, however, to have been without a ball,° and the fellow was suffered to go his way as a lunatic or a drunkard. When he had gone, D—— came from the window, whither° I had followed him immediately upon securing° the object in view. Soon

---

hyperobtrusive: especially obvious

casement: window with frames hinged at the side, top, or bottom

ball: pellet, shot (i.e., bullet)

whither: to which place

securing: getting hold of

afterwards I bade him farewell. The pretended lunatic was a man in my own pay."

"But what purpose had you," I asked, "in replacing the letter by a *fac-simile?* Would it not have been better, at the first visit, to have seized it openly, and departed?"

"D——," replied Dupin, "is a desperate man, and a man of nerve. His hotel, too, is not without attendants devoted to his interests. Had I made the wild attempt you suggest, I might never have left the Ministerial presence alive. The good people of Paris might have heard of me no more. But I had an object apart from these considerations. In this matter, I act as a partisan° of the lady concerned. For eighteen months the Minister has had her in his power. She has now him in hers; since, being unaware that the letter is not in his possession, he will proceed with his exactions° as if it was. Thus will he inevitably commit himself, at once, to his political destruction. His downfall, too, will not be more precipitate° than awkward. It is all very well to talk about the *facilis descensus Averni;*° but in all kinds of climbing, as Catalini° said of singing, it is far more easy to get up than to come down. In the present instance I have no sympathy—at least no pity—for him who descends. He is that *monstrum horrendum,*° an unprincipled man of genius. I confess, however, that I should like very well to know the precise character of his thoughts, when, being defied by her whom the Prefect terms 'a certain personage,' he is reduced to opening the letter which I left for him in the card-rack."

120

"How? did you put any thing particular in it?"

"Why—it did not seem altogether right to leave the interior blank—that would have been insulting. D——, at Vienna once, did me an evil turn, which I told him, quite good-humoredly, that I should remember. So, as I knew he would feel some curiosity in regard to the identity of the person who had outwitted him, I thought it a pity not to give him a clue. He is well acquainted with my MS.,° and I just copied into the middle of the blank sheet the words—

---

partisan: supporter

exactions: extortions

precipitate: extremely sudden or abrupt

facilis . . . Averni: Latin for "easy the descent to Avernus," a phrase from Virgil's *Aeneid*; Avernus, a lake within a crater in Italy; was believed to be the entrance to the underworld

Catalani: Angelica Catalani (1780–1849), Italian opera singer

monstrum horrendum: Latin for "horrible monster," also a phrase from the *Aeneid*

MS: common abbreviation for *manuscript*; i.e., handwriting

—Un dessein si funeste,
S'il n'est digne d'Atrée, est digne de Thyeste.°

They are to be found in Crébillon's 'Atrée.'"°

[1844]

Read

1. What do you think the purpose might be of masking the dates (18—) and names (Monsieur G—) in the short story?
2. How does Poe use the narrator to give a portrait of the detective M. Dupin?
3. What is the "moral" of this tale?
4. How does Poe suggest the importance of logic in this story?
5. What clues in the story suggest the relationship between the narrator and M. Dupin?

Write

1. Write about how this story is similar or not to other Poe tales.
2. Reflect on Poe's choice of diction in the story and how diction creates the mood—or feeling—you get as a reader.
3. Write a paragraph about Dupin's use of logic. Do you think his conclusions are simply logical?

Connect

1. How is Dupin like or unlike other detectives you've seen or have read? Consider television detectives, Sherlock Holmes, or others.
2. How do Poe's ideas about solving problems link to other writers you've read in this text? Consider Benjamin Franklin, Thomas Jefferson, and Sojourner Truth as possible comparisons.

Elizabeth Cady Stanton

When Elizabeth Cady (1815–1902) was born, her father openly wished she had been a boy. Her career as a feminist and abolitionist no doubt stemmed from the inequities she experienced working in her father's law office in New York. A fervent abolitionist, she and her husband attended an anti-slavery convention in England during their honeymoon. When women were denied seats at the convention, she and Quaker minister Lucretia Mott decided to host a women's rights convention in New York State; the Seneca Falls Convention was held there in 1848. The Declaration of Sentiments was an ironic rendering of the Declaration of Independence, and it was signed by one hundred people, including

---

quotation: French for "A plan so deadly, if it is not worthy of Atreus, is worthy of Thyestes."

Crébillon's 'Atrée': *Atrée et Thyeste* (1707) is a tragedy by French playwright Prosper Jolyot de Crébillon (1674–1762). In Greek myth, Atreus is cuckolded by his brother Thyestes, and takes revenge by killing Thyestes's sons and serving them to him at a banquet.

thirty-two men, Frederick Douglass among them. The Declaration of Sentiments used abolitionist sensibilities to stake its claims. Women were finally granted the right to vote seventy-two years later, in 1920. Stanton remained a tireless supporter of suffrage until her death, writing a letter the day before she died to the wife of President Theodore Roosevelt, seeking his support for a constitutional amendment.

Declaration of Sentiments

When, in the course of human events, it becomes necessary for one portion of the family of man to assume among the people of the earth a position different from that which they have hitherto° occupied, but one to which the laws of nature and of nature's God entitle them, a decent respect to the opinions of mankind requires that they should declare the causes that impel them to such a course.

We hold these truths to be self-evident: that all men and women are created equal; that they are endowed by their Creator with certain inalienable rights; that among these are life, liberty, and the pursuit of happiness; that to secure these rights governments are instituted, deriving their just powers from the consent of the governed. Whenever any form of government becomes destructive of these ends, it is the right of those who suffer from it to refuse allegiance to it, and to insist upon the institution of a new government, laying its foundation on such principles, and organizing its powers in such form, as to them shall seem most likely to effect° their safety and happiness. Prudence, indeed, will dictate that governments long established should not be changed for light and transient causes; and accordingly all experience hath shown that mankind are more disposed to suffer, while evils are sufferable, than to right themselves by abolishing the forms to which they were accustomed. But when a long train of abuses and usurpations,° pursuing invariably the same object, evinces° a design to reduce them under absolute despotism, it is their duty to throw off such government, and to provide new guards for their future security. Such has been the patient sufferance of the women under this government, and such is now the necessity which constrains° them to demand the equal station to which they are entitled.

The history of mankind is a history of repeated injuries and usurpations on the part of man toward woman, having in direct object° the establishment of an absolute tyranny over her. To prove this, let facts be submitted to a candid° world.

---

hitherto: until now
effect: bring about
usurpations: infringements, seizures
evinces: makes evident
constrains: compels
object: intention
candid: honest, impartial

He has never permitted her to exercise her inalienable right to the elective franchise.°

He has compelled her to submit to laws, in the formation of which she had no voice. 5

He has withheld from her rights which are given to the most ignorant and degraded men—both natives and foreigners.

Having deprived her of this first right of a citizen, the elective franchise, thereby leaving her without representation in the halls of legislation, he has oppressed her on all sides.

He has made her, if married, in the eye of the law, civilly dead.

He has taken from her all right in property, even to the wages she earns.

He has made her, morally, an irresponsible being, as she can commit many crimes with impunity° provided they be done in the presence of her husband. In the covenant of marriage, she is compelled to promise obedience to her husband, he becoming, to all intents and purposes, her master—the law giving him power to deprive her of her liberty, and to administer chastisement.° 10

He has so framed the laws of divorce, as to what shall be the proper causes, and in case of separation, to whom the guardianship of the children shall be given, as to be wholly regardless of° the happiness of women—the law, in all cases, going upon a false supposition of the supremacy of man, and giving all power into his hands.

After depriving her of all rights as a married woman, if single, and the owner of property, he has taxed her to support a government which recognizes her only when her property can be made profitable to it.

He has monopolized nearly all the profitable employments, and from those she is permitted to follow, she receives but a scanty remuneration. He closes against her all the avenues to wealth and distinction which he considers most honorable to himself. As a teacher of theology, medicine, or law, she is not known.

He has denied her the facilities for obtaining a thorough education, all colleges being closed against her.

---

the elective franchise: the vote

impunity: freedom from consequences

chastisement: punishment

regardless of: indifferent to, unconcerned with

He allows her in Church, as well as State, but° a subordinate position, claiming Apostolic° authority for her exclusion from the ministry, and, with some exceptions, from any public participation in the affairs of the Church. 15

He has created a false public sentiment by giving to the world a different code of morals for men and women, by which moral delinquencies° which exclude women from society, are not only tolerated, but deemed of little account° in man.

He has usurped the prerogative of Jehovah himself, claiming it as his right to assign for her a sphere of action, when that belongs to her conscience and to her God.

He has endeavored, in every way that he could, to destroy her confidence in her own powers, to lessen her self-respect, and to make her willing to lead a dependent and abject° life.

Now, in view of this entire disfranchisement° of one-half the people of this country, their social and religious degradation—in view of the unjust laws above mentioned, and because women do feel themselves aggrieved, oppressed, and fraudulently deprived of their most sacred rights, we insist that they have immediate admission to all the rights and privileges which belong to them as citizens of the United States.

In entering upon the great work before us, we anticipate no small amount of misconception, misrepresentation, and ridicule; but we shall use every instrumentality within our power to effect our object. We shall employ agents, circulate tracts,° petition the State and National legislatures, and endeavor to enlist the pulpit and the press in our behalf. We hope this Convention will be followed by a series of Conventions embracing every part of the country. 20

Firmly relying upon the final triumph of the Right and the True, we do this day affix our signatures to this declaration.

[1848]

Read

1. How does the use of the language of the Declaration of Independence in this document suggest the aim of the Declaration of Sentiments?
2. What kinds of proofs are offered for the claims made in the document?
3. How would you characterize the voice of the speaker?
4. Do you think that the declaration is successful in conveying its intentions?

---

but: only, merely
Apostolic: derived from the Apostles
delinquencies: offenses, misdeeds
account: importance
abject: miserable, degrading
disfranchisement: deprival of rights
tracts: pamphlets

Write

1. Why is the 1848 Declaration ironic? Write a paragraph that examines the conscious irony you find at work in the Declaration.
2. Look up the definition and then comment on the use of the word "sentiments" in the title.
3. Respond to any of the charges made in the Declaration of Sentiments from your position as a twenty-first-century reader.
4. Respond as a nineteenth-century reader—male or female.

Complete Additional Exercises on Stanton's Declaration at Your Pearson MyLab

Connect

1. Compare one or two points in the Declaration of Independence to similar points made in the Declaration of Sentiments. How does the diction or intention shift from one to the other?
2. What intentions do the writers have for the culture and for other women as evidenced in the declaration? Do you think these intentions would solve the problems Fuller identifies in her writing?

A. E. Ted Aub

Sculptor A. E. Ted Aub (b. 1955) teaches art at Hobart and William Smith Colleges in Geneva, New York. He has won awards for his sculptures, which often depict historical figures. *When Anthony Met Stanton* was commissioned by Governor George Pataki of New York as a tribute to women's suffrage. It was erected in 1998 as a commemoration of the 150th anniversary of the Seneca Falls Women's Rights Convention. The statue shows early feminists Elizabeth Cady Stanton, Susan B. Anthony, and Amelia Bloomer.

When Anthony Met Stanton

When Anthony Met Stanton (1998), A. E. Ted Aub. Bronze sculptures. Seneca Falls, New York. Photo by Dennis MacDonald/Alamy

[1998]

Read

1. Amelia Bloomer was a feminist and dress reformer. How does the depiction of her suggest her preoccupation?
2. How do the expressions and stances of the women give you an idea of their personalities?
3. What seems to be the sculptor's intention with this sculpture?
4. How do you react to the arrangement of figures?

Write

1. Create a conversation among the women, using what you've learned of women's roles and the suffrage movement.
2. What details in the sculpture suggest the attitude of the figures toward one another and of the sculptor toward the figures?

Connect

1. How does the sculpture reflect the sentiments found in the Declaration of Sentiments?
2. How is this sculpture similar to or different from the statue of Massasoit in Unit 1 in terms of attitude, expression, detail and aim?

Nathaniel Hawthorne

Nathaniel Hawthorne (1804–1864) was born in Salem, Massachusetts, which became the setting for his greatest work *The Scarlet Letter.* The novel has many of the themes that dominated all of Hawthorne's work: sin and redemption, guilt, obsession with the past, and fears about the future. Hawthorne's father, a ship captain, died at sea when he was four, and Hawthorne was raised by his reclusive mother and three sisters. He spent a solitary childhood reading and studying. He worked at the Custom House in Boston for a time, joined a communal experiment at Brook Farm, and finally moved with his wife to the Old Manse in Concord. There he wrote his collection of short stories, *Mosses from an Old Manse,* which gave him some financial security. With the publication of *The Scarlet Letter* in 1850, Hawthorne began to be called the "greatest living American writer," but he was never as popular or financially secure as other writers of the time. He wrote four novels, a parody of life at Brook Farm, *The Blithedale Romance,* a tale of his European sojourn, *The Marble Faun,* and *The House of the Seven Gables,* published in 1851.

The Minister's Black Veil

A Parable

The sexton° stood in the porch of Milford° meeting-house, pulling busily at the bell-rope. The old people of the village came stooping along the street. Children, with bright faces, tripped° merrily beside their parents, or mimicked a graver° gait, in the conscious dignity of their Sunday clothes. Spruce° bachelors looked sidelong at the pretty maidens, and fancied that the Sabbath sunshine made them prettier than on week days. When the throng had mostly streamed into the porch, the sexton began to toll the bell, keeping his eye on the Reverend Mr. Hooper's door. The first glimpse of the clergyman's figures was the signal for the bell to cease its summons.

"But what has good Parson Hooper got upon his face?" cried the sexton in astonishment.

All within hearing immediately turned about, and beheld the semblance of Mr. Hooper, pacing slowly his meditative way towards the meeting-house. With one accord they started,° expressing more wonder than if some strange minister were coming to dust the cushions of Mr. Hooper's pulpit.

"Are you sure it is our parson?" inquired Goodman° Gray of the sexton.

"Of a certainty it is good Mr. Hooper," replied the sexton. "He was to have exchanged pulpits with Parson Shute, of Westbury; but Parson Shute sent to excuse himself yesterday, being to preach a funeral sermon."

5

The cause of so much amazement may appear sufficiently slight. Mr. Hooper, a gentlemanly person, of about thirty, though still a bachelor, was dressed with due clerical neatness, as if a careful wife had starched his band,° and brushed the weekly dust from his Sunday's garb. There was but one thing remarkable in his appearance.

---

sexton: caretaker of a church

Milford: a town in Massachusetts

tripped: skipped

graver: more serious

Spruce: neat and trim

started: made a startled movement

Goodman: Puritan term of address to a male head of a household

band: collar

Swathed° about his forehead, and hanging down over his face, so low as to be shaken by his breath, Mr. Hooper had on a black veil. On a nearer view it seemed to consist of two folds of crape, which entirely concealed his features, except the mouth and chin, but probably did not intercept his sight, further than to give a darkened aspect° to all living and inanimate things. With this gloomy shade before him, good Mr. Hooper walked onward, at a slow and quiet pace, stooping somewhat, and looking on the ground, as is customary with abstracted° men, yet nodding kindly to those of his parishioners who still waited on the meeting-house steps. But so wonder-struck were they that his greeting hardly met with a return.

"I can't really feel as if good Mr. Hooper's face was behind that piece of crape," said the sexton.

"I don't like it," muttered an old woman, as she hobbled into the meeting-house. "He has changed himself into something awful, only by hiding his face."

"Our parson has gone mad!" cried Goodman Gray, following him across the threshold.

10 A rumor of some unaccountable phenomenon had preceded Mr. Hooper into the meeting-house, and set all the congregation astir. Few could refrain from twisting their heads towards the door; many stood upright, and turned directly about; while several little boys clambered upon the seats, and came down again with a terrible racket. There was a general bustle, a rustling of the women's gowns and shuffling of the mens' feet, greatly at variance with that hushed repose which should attend the entrance of the minister. But Mr. Hooper appeared not to notice the perturbation° of his people. He entered with an almost noiseless step, bent his head mildly to the pews on each side, and bowed as he passed his oldest parishioner, a white-haired great-grandsire, who occupied an arm-chair in the centre of the aisle. It was strange to observe how slowly this venerable° man became conscious of something singular° in the appearance of his pastor. He seemed not fully to partake of the prevailing wonder,° till Mr. Hooper had ascended the stairs, and showed himself in the pulpit, face to face with his congregation, except for the black veil. That mysterious emblem was never once withdrawn. It shook with his

---

Swathed: wrapped
aspect: appearance
abstracted: preoccupied, lost in thought
perturbation: agitation
venerable: impressive or worthy of respect because of age
singular: odd, unusual
wonder: astonishment

measured breath, as he gave out the psalm; it threw its obscurity between him and the holy page, as he read the Scriptures; and while he prayed, the veil lay heavily on his uplifted countenance. Did he seek to hide it from the dread° Being whom he was addressing?

Such was the effect of this simple piece of crape, that more than one woman of delicate nerves was forced to leave the meeting-house. Yet perhaps the pale-faced congregation was almost as fearful a sight to the minister, as his black veil to them.

Mr. Hooper had the reputation of a good preacher, but not an energetic one: he strove to win his people heavenward by mild, persuasive influences, rather than to drive them thither° by the thunders of the Word. The sermon which he now delivered was marked by the same characteristics of style and manner as the general series of his pulpit oratory. But there was something, either in the sentiment of the discourse itself, or in the imagination of the auditors,° which made it greatly the most powerful effort that they had ever heard from their pastor's lips. It was tinged, rather more darkly than usual, with the gentle gloom of Mr. Hooper's temperament. The subject had reference to secret sin, and those sad mysteries which we hide from our nearest and dearest, and would fain° conceal from our own consciousness, even forgetting that the Omniscient can detect them. A subtle power was breathed into his words. Each member of the congregation, the most innocent girl, and the man of hardened breast, felt as if the preacher had crept upon them, behind his awful° veil, and discovered their hoarded iniquity° of deed or thought. Many spread their clasped hands on their bosoms. There was nothing terrible° in what Mr. Hooper said, at least, no violence; and yet, with every tremor of his melancholy voice, the hearers quaked. An unsought pathos came hand in hand with awe. So sensible° were the audience of some unwonted° attribute in their minister, that they longed for a breath of wind to blow aside the veil, almost believing that a stranger's visage° would be discovered, though the form, gesture, and voice were those of Mr. Hooper.

---

dread: awe-inspiring, to be feared
thither: there, in that direction
auditors: listeners
fain: willingly, gladly
awful: frightening
iniquity: wickedness
terrible: causing fear or alarm
sensible: aware
unwonted: unaccustomed
visage: face

At the close of the services, the people hurried out with indecorous° confusion, eager to communicate their pent-up amazement, and conscious of lighter spirits the moment they lost sight of the black veil. Some gathered in little circles, huddled closely together, with their mouths all whispering in the centre; some went homeward alone, wrapt in silent meditation; some talked loudly, and profaned the Sabbath day with ostentatious laughter. A few shook their sagacious° heads, intimating that they could penetrate the mystery; while one or two affirmed that there was no mystery at all, but only that Mr. Hooper's eyes were so weakened by the midnight lamp,° as to require a shade. After a brief interval, forth came good Mr. Hooper also, in the rear of his flock. Turning his veiled face from one group to another, he paid due reverence to the hoary° heads, saluted the middle aged with kind dignity as their friend and spiritual guide, greeted the young with mingled authority and love, and laid his hands on the little children's heads to bless them. Such was always his custom on the Sabbath day. Strange and bewildered looks repaid him for his courtesy. None, as on former occasions, aspired to the honor of walking by their pastor's side. Old Squire Saunders, doubtless by an accidental lapse of memory, neglected to invite Mr. Hooper to his table, where the good clergyman had been wont° to bless the food, almost every Sunday since his settlement.° He returned, therefore, to the parsonage, and, at the moment of closing the door, was observed to look back upon the people, all of whom had their eyes fixed upon the minister. A sad smile gleamed faintly from beneath the black veil, and flickered about his mouth, glimmering as he disappeared.

"How strange," said a lady, "that a simple black veil, such as any woman might wear on her bonnet, should become such a terrible thing on Mr. Hooper's face!"

15 "Something must surely be amiss with Mr. Hooper's intellects," observed her husband, the physician of the village. "But the strangest part of the affair is the effect of this vagary,° even on a sober-minded man like myself. The black veil, though it covers only our pastor's face, throws its influence over his whole person, and makes him ghostlike from head to foot. Do you not feel it so?"

---

indecorous: offensive, improper
sagacious: wise
the midnight lamp: suggesting long hours of late-night study
hoary: white with age, ancient
wont: accustomed
settlement: i.e., in Milford
vagary: whim, quirk

"Truly do I," replied the lady; "and I would not be alone with him for the world. I wonder° he is not afraid to be alone with himself!"

"Men sometimes are so," said her husband.

The afternoon service was attended° with similar circumstances. At its conclusion, the bell tolled for the funeral of a young lady. The relatives and friends were assembled in the house, and the more distant acquaintances stood about the door, speaking of the good qualities of the decreased, when their talk was interrupted by the appearance of Mr. Hooper, still covered with his black veil. It was now an appropriate emblem. The clergyman stepped into the room where the corpse was laid, and bent over the coffin, to take a last farewell of his deceased parishioner. As he stooped, the veil hung straight down from his forehead, so that, if her eyelids had not been closed forever, the dead maiden might have seen his face. Could Mr. Hooper be fearful of her glance, that he so hastily caught back the black veil? A person who watched the interview between the dead and living, scrupled° not to affirm, that, at the instant when the clergyman's features were disclosed,° the corpse had slightly shuddered, rustling the shroud and muslin° cap, though the countenance retained the composure of death. A superstitious old woman was the only witness of this prodigy.° From the coffin Mr. Hooper passed into the chamber of the mourners, and thence° to the head of the staircase, to make the funeral prayer. It was a tender and heart-dissolving prayer, full of sorrow, yet so imbued with celestial hopes, that the music of a heavenly harp, swept by the fingers of the dead, seemed faintly to be heard among the saddest accents° of the minister. The people trembled, though they but darkly understood him when he prayed that they, and himself, and all of mortal race, might be ready, as he trusted this young maiden had been, for the dreadful hour that should snatch the veil from their faces. The bearers went heavily forth, and the mourners followed, saddening all the street, with the dead before them, and Mr. Hooper in his black veil behind.

"Why do you look back?" said one in the procession to his partner.

I wonder: I'm surprised
attended: accompanied
scrupled: hesitated
disclosed: revealed
muslin: cotton fabric
prodigy: something causing wonder or amazement
thence: from there
accents: inflections, emphases

"I had a fancy," replied she, "that the minister and the maiden's spirit were walking hand in hand." 20

"And so had I, at the same moment," said the other.

That night, the handsomest couple in Milford village were to be joined in wedlock. Though reckoned a melancholy man, Mr. Hooper had a placid° cheerfulness for such occasions, which often excited a sympathetic smile where livelier merriment would have been thrown away. There was no quality of his disposition which made him more beloved than this. The company at the wedding awaited his arrival with impatience, trusting that the strange awe, which had gathered over him throughout the day, would now be dispelled. But such was not the result. When Mr. Hooper came, the first thing that their eyes rested on was the same horrible black veil, which had added deeper gloom to the funeral, and could portend nothing but evil to the wedding. Such was its immediate effect on the guests that a cloud seemed to have rolled duskily from beneath the black crape, and dimmed the light of the candles. The bridal pair stood up before the minister. But the bride's cold fingers quivered in the tremulous° hand of the bridegroom, and her deathlike paleness caused a whisper that the maiden who had been buried a few hours before was come from her grave to be married. If ever another wedding were so dismal, it was that famous one where they tolled the wedding knell.° After performing the ceremony, Mr. Hooper raised a glass of wine to his lips, wishing happiness to the new-married couple in a strain of mild pleasantry that ought to have brightened the features of the guests, like a cheerful gleam from the hearth.° At that instant, catching a glimpse of his figure in the looking-glass, the black veil involved his own spirit in the horror with which it overwhelmed all others. His frame shuddered, his lips grew white, he spilt the untasted wine upon the carpet, and rushed forth into the darkness. For the Earth, too, had on her Black Veil.

The next day, the whole village of Milford talked of little else than Parson Hooper's black veil. That, and the mystery concealed behind it, supplied a topic for discussion between acquaintances meeting in the street, and good women gossiping at their open windows. It was the first item of news that the tavernkeeper told to his guests. The children babbled of it on their way to school. One imitative little imp

---

placid: calm, even-tempered

tremulous: trembling

that famous one. . . the wedding knell: Hawthorne is alluding to his own story "The Wedding Knell," in which a woman dies at her wedding. It appears just before "The Minister's Black Veil" in his 1837 collection *Twice-Told Tales*.

hearth: fireside

covered his face with an old black handkerchief, thereby so affrighting his playmates that the panic seized himself, and he well-nigh lost his wits by his own waggery.°

It was remarkable that of all the busybodies and impertinent people in the parish, not one ventured to put the plain question to Mr. Hooper, wherefore° he did this thing. Hitherto,° whenever there appeared the slightest call for such interference, he had never lacked advisers, nor shown himself averse to be guided by their judgment. If he erred at all, it was by so painful a degree of self-distrust, that even the mildest censure would lead him to consider an indifferent° action as a crime. Yet, though so well acquainted with this amiable weakness, no individual among his parishioners chose to make the black veil a subject of friendly remonstrance.° There was a feeling of dread, neither plainly confessed nor carefully concealed, which caused each to shift the responsibility upon another, till at length it was found expedient° to send a deputation of the church, in order to deal with Mr. Hooper about the mystery, before it should grow into a scandal. Never did an embassy° so ill discharge its duties. The minister received them with friendly courtesy, but became silent, after they were seated, leaving to his visitors the whole burden of introducing their important business. The topic, it might be supposed, was obvious enough. There was the black veil swathed round Mr. Hooper's forehead, and concealing every feature above his placid mouth, on which, at times, they could perceive the glimmering of a melancholy smile. But that piece of crape, to their imagination, seemed to hang down before his heart, the symbol of a fearful secret between him and them. Were the veil but cast aside, they might speak freely of it, but not till then. Thus they sat a considerable time, speechless, confused, and shrinking uneasily from Mr. Hooper's eye, which they felt to be fixed upon them with an invisible glance. Finally, the deputies returned abashed° to their constituents, pronouncing the matter too weighty to be handled, except by a council of the churches, if, indeed, it might not require a general synod.°

---

waggery: joking
wherefore: why, for what reason
Hitherto: previously
indifferent: ordinary, insignificant
remonstrance: protest
expedient: appropriate
embassy: mission, delegation
abashed: embarrassed
synod: council or assembly

But there was one person in the village unappalled by the awe with which the black veil had impressed all beside herself. When the deputies returned without an explanation, or even venturing to demand one, she, with the calm energy of her character, determined to chase away the strange cloud that appeared to be settling round Mr. Hooper, every moment more darkly than before. As his plighted° wife, it should be her privilege to know what the black veil concealed. At the minister's first visit, therefore, she entered upon the subject with a direct simplicity, which made the task easier both for him and her. After he had seated himself, she fixed her eyes steadfastly upon the veil, but could discern nothing of the dreadful gloom that had so overawed the multitude: it was but a double fold of crape, hanging down from his forehead to his mouth, and slightly stirring with his breath. 25

"No," said she aloud, and smiling, "there is nothing terrible in this piece of crape, except that it hides a face which I am always glad to look upon. Come, good sir, let the sun shine from behind the cloud. First lay aside your black veil: then tell me why you put it on."

Mr. Hooper's smile glimmered faintly.

"There is an hour to come," said he, "when all of us shall cast aside our veils. Take it not amiss, beloved friend, if I wear this piece of crape till then."

"Your words are a mystery, too," returned the young lady. "Take away the veil from them, at least."

"Elizabeth, I will," said he, "so far as my vow may suffer° me. Know, then, this veil is a type° and a symbol, and I am bound to wear it ever, both in light and darkness, in solitude and before the gaze of multitudes, and as with strangers, so with my familiar friends. No mortal eye will see it withdrawn. This dismal shade must separate me from the world: even you, Elizabeth, can never come behind it!" 30

"What grievous affliction hath befallen you," she earnestly inquired, "that you should thus darken your eyes forever?"

"If it be a sign of mourning," replied Mr. Hooper, "I, perhaps, like most other mortals, have sorrows dark enough to be typified° by a black veil."

"But what if the world will not believe that it is the type of an innocent sorrow?" urged Elizabeth. "Beloved and respected as you are, there may be whispers that you hide your face under the

plighted: pledged, engaged
suffer: permit
type: example
typified: represented

consciousness of secret sin. For the sake of your holy office, do away this scandal!"

The color rose into her cheeks as she intimated° the nature of the rumors that were already abroad in the village. But Mr. Hooper's mildness did not forsake him. He even smiled again—that same sad smile, which always appeared like a faint glimmering of light, proceeding from the obscurity beneath of the veil.

"If I hide my face for sorrow, there is cause enough," he merely replied; "and if I cover it for secret sin, what mortal might not do the same?" 35

And with this gentle, but unconquerable obstinacy did he resist all her entreaties. At length Elizabeth sat silent. For a few moments she appeared lost in thought, considering, probably, what new methods might be tried to withdraw her lover from so dark a fantasy, which, if it had no other meaning, was perhaps a symptom of mental disease. Though of a firmer character than his own, the tears rolled down her cheeks. But, in an instant, as it were, a new feeling took the place of sorrow: her eyes were fixed insensibly° on the black veil, when, like a sudden twilight in the air, its terrors fell around her. She arose, and stood trembling before him.

"And do you feel it then, at last?" said he mournfully.

She made no reply, but covered her eyes with her hand, and turned to leave the room. He rushed forward and caught her arm.

"Have patience with me, Elizabeth!" cried he, passionately. "Do not desert me, though this veil must be between us here on earth. Be mine, and hereafter there shall be no veil over my face, no darkness between our souls! It is but a mortal veil—it is not for eternity! O! you know not how lonely I am, and how frightened, to be alone behind my black veil. Do not leave me in this miserable obscurity forever!"

"Lift the veil but once, and look me in the face," said she. 40

"Never! It cannot be!" replied Mr. Hooper.

"Then farewell!" said Elizabeth.

She withdrew her arm from his grasp, and slowly departed, pausing at the door, to give one long shuddering gaze, that seemed almost to penetrate the mystery of the black veil. But, even amid his grief, Mr. Hooper smiled to think that only a material emblem had separated him from happiness, though the horrors, which it shadowed forth, must be drawn darkly between the fondest of lovers.

From that time no attempts were made to remove Mr. Hooper's black veil, or, by a direct appeal, to discover the secret which it was

---

intimated: made known

insensibly: without awareness

supposed to hide. By persons who claimed a superiority to popular prejudice, it was reckoned merely an eccentric whim, such as often mingles with the sober actions of men otherwise rational, and tinges them all with its own semblance of insanity. But with the multitude, good Mr. Hooper was irreparably a bugbear.° He could not walk the street with any peace of mind, so conscious was he that the gentle and timid would turn aside to avoid him, and that others would make it a point of hardihood° to throw themselves in his way. The impertinence of the latter class compelled him to give up his customary walk at sunset to the burial ground; for when he leaned pensively over the gate, there would always be faces behind the gravestones, peeping at his black veil. A fable° went the rounds that the stare of the dead people drove him thence. It grieved him, to the very depth of his kind heart, to observe how the children fled from his approach, breaking up their merriest sports, while his melancholy figure was yet afar off. Their instinctive dread caused him to feel more strongly than aught° else, that a preternatural° horror was interwoven with the threads of the black crape. In truth, his own antipathy to the veil was known to be so great, that he never willingly passed before a mirror, not stooped to drink at a still fountain, lest, in its peaceful bosom, he should be affrighted by himself. This was what gave plausibility to the whispers, that Mr. Hooper's conscience tortured him for some great crime too horrible to be entirely concealed, or otherwise than so obscurely intimated. Thus, from beneath the black veil, there rolled a cloud into the sunshine, an ambiguity of sin or sorrow, which enveloped the poor minister, so that love or sympathy could never reach him. It was said that ghost and fiend consorted with him there. With self-shudderings, and outward terrors, he walked continually in its shadow, groping darkly within his own soul, or gazing through a medium° that saddened the whole world.° Even the lawless wind, it was believed, respected his dreadful secret, and never blew aside the veil. But still good Mr. Hooper sadly smiled at the pale visages of the worldly throng as he passed by.

45 Among all its bad influences, the black veil had the one desirable effect, of making its wearer a very efficient clergyman. By the aid of his mysterious emblem—for there was no other apparent cause—he

---

bugbear: horror, bogeyman

hardihood: boldness, insolence

fable: falsehood

aught: anything

preternatural: supernatural, abnormal

medium: intervening or filtering substance

saddened the world: made the world look sad

became a man of awful power over souls that were in agony for sin. His converts always regarded him with a dread peculiar° to themselves, affirming, though but figuratively, that, before he brought them to celestial light, they had been with him behind that black veil. Its gloom, indeed, enabled him to sympathize with all dark affections. Dying sinners cried aloud for Mr. Hooper, and would not yield their breath till he appeared: though ever, as he stooped to whisper consolation, they shuddered at the veiled face so near their own. Such were the terrors of the black veil, even when Death had bared his visage! Strangers came long distances to attend service at his church, with the mere idle purpose of gazing at his figure, because it was forbidden them to behold his face. But many were made to quake ere they departed! Once, during Governor Belcher's administration,° Mr. Hooper was appointed to preach the election sermon.° Covered with his black veil, he stood before the chief magistrate, the council, and the representatives, and wrought so deep an impression, that the legislative measures of that year were characterized by all the gloom and piety of our earliest ancestral sway.°

In this manner Mr. Hooper spent a long life, irreproachable in outward act, yet shrouded in dismal suspicions; kind and loving, though unloved, and dimly feared; a man apart from men, shunned in their health and joy, but ever summoned to their aid in mortal anguish. As years wore on, shedding their snows above his sable° veil, he acquired a name throughout the New England churches, and they called him Father Hooper. Nearly all his parishioners, who were of mature age when he was settled, had been borne away by many a funeral: he had one congregation in the church, and a more crowded one in the churchyard; and having wrought so late into the evening, and done his work so well, it was now good Father Hooper's turn to rest.

Several persons were visible by the shaded candlelight, in the death chamber of the old clergyman. Natural connections° he had none. But there was the decorously grave, though unmoved physician, seeking only to mitigate° the last pangs of the patient whom he could

---

peculiar: unique

Governor Belcher's administration: Jonathan Belcher (1682–1757) was colonial governor of Massachusetts from 1730 to 1741.

the election sermon: The election sermon, preached to the members of the newly elected government, was a Massachusetts tradition from 1634 to 1884. It was a great honor to be invited to deliver the sermon.

sway: power, control; the allusion is to the Puritan founders of the Massachusetts Bay Colony.

sable: black

Natural connections: blood relatives

mitigate: soften

not save. There were the deacons, and other eminently pious members of his church. There, also, was the Reverend Mr. Clark, of Westbury, a young and zealous divine, who had ridden in haste to pray by the bedside of the expiring minister. There was the nurse, no hired handmaiden of death, but one whose calm affection had endured thus long in secrecy, in solitude, amid the chill of age, and would not perish, even at the dying hour. Who, but Elizabeth! And there lay the hoary head of good Father Hooper upon the death pillow, with the black veil still swathed about his brow, and reaching down over his face, so that each more difficult gasp of his faint breath caused it to stir. All through life that piece of crape had hung between him and the world: it had separated him from cheerful brotherhood and woman's love, and kept him in that saddest of all prisons, his own heart: and still it lay upon his face, as if to deepen the gloom of his darksome chamber, and shade him from the sunshine of eternity.

For some time previous, his mind had been confused, wavering doubtfully between the past and the present, and hovering forward, as it were, at intervals, into the indistinctness of the world to come. There had been feverish turns, which tossed him from side to side, and wore away what little strength he had. But in his most convulsive struggles, and in the wildest vagaries° of his intellect, when no other thought retained its sober influence, he still showed an awful solicitude lest the black veil should slip aside. Even if his bewildered soul could have forgotten, there was a faithful woman at his pillow, who, with averted eyes, would have covered that aged face, which she had last beheld in the comeliness of manhood. At length the death-stricken old man lay quietly in the torpor° of mental and bodily exhaustion, with an imperceptible pulse, and breath that grew fainter and fainter, except when a long, deep, and irregular inspiration° seemed to preclude° the flight of his spirit.

The minister of Westbury approached the bedside.

"Venerable Father Hooper," said he, "the moment of your release is at hand. Are you ready for the lifting of the veil that shuts in time from eternity?" 50

Father Hooper at first replied merely by a feeble motion of his head; then, apprehensive, perhaps, that his meaning might be doubtful, he exerted himself to speak.

"Yea," said he, in faint accents, "my soul hath a patient weariness until that veil be lifted."

---

vagaries: whims, caprices

torpor: lethargy, listlessness

inspirations: inhalations

preclude: prevent, rule out

"And is it fitting," resumed the Reverend Mr. Clark, "that a man so given to prayer, of such a blameless example, holy in deed and thought, so far as mortal judgment may pronounce; is it fitting that a father in the church should leave a shadow on his memory, that may seem to blacken a life so pure? I pray you, my venerable brother, let not this thing be! Suffer us to be gladdened by your triumphant aspect as you go to your reward. Before the veil of eternity be lifted, let me cast aside this black veil from your face!"

And thus speaking, the Reverend Mr. Clark bent forward to reveal the mystery of so many years. But, exerting a sudden energy, that made all the beholders stand aghast, Father Hooper snatched both his hands from beneath the bedclothes, and pressed them strongly on the black veil, resolute to struggle, if the minister of Westbury would contend with a dying man.

"Never!" cried the veiled clergyman. "On earth, never!" 55

"Dark old man!" exclaimed the affrighted minister, "with what horrible crime upon your soul are you now passing to the judgment?"

Father Hooper's breath heaved; it rattled in his throat; but, with a mighty effort, grasping forward with his hands, he caught hold of life, and held it back till he should speak. He even raised himself in bed; and there he sat, shivering with the arms of death around him, while the black veil hung down, awful, at that last moment, in the gathered terrors of a lifetime. And yet the faint, sad smile, so often there, now seemed to glimmer from its obscurity, and linger on Father Hooper's lips.

"Why do you tremble at me alone?" cried he, turning his veiled face round the circle of pale spectators. "Tremble also at each other! Have men avoided me, and women shown no pity, and children screamed and fled, only for my black veil? What, but the mystery which it obscurely typifies, has made this piece of crape so awful? When the friend shows his inmost heart to his friend; the lover to his best beloved; when man does not vainly shrink from the eye of his Creator, loathsomely treasuring up the secret of his sin; then deem me a monster for the symbol beneath which I have lived, and die! I look around me, and, lo! on every visage a Black Veil!"

While his auditors shrank from one another, in mutual affright, Father Hooper fell back upon his pillow, a veiled corpse, with a faint smile lingering on the lips. Still veiled, they laid him in his coffin, and a veiled corpse they bore him to the grave. The grass of many years has sprung up and withered on that grave, the burial stone is moss-grown, and good Mr. Hooper's face is dust; but awful is still the thought that it mouldered beneath the Black Veil!

[1836]

Read

1. How does the veil work to suggest an aim of the story?
2. Where do you find irony in the story or in the narrator's voice?
3. Some critics accused Hawthorne of being too "allegorical." Is there an allegory in this story?

Write

1. What is your attitude toward the minister and his actions throughout the story? Write about how your attitude develops from the beginning of the tale to the end.
2. Reflect on the conflict between individual and community as you see it in this story.
3. Write one sentence that explains what you believe to be Hawthorne's aim in using the image of the black veil. Find a detail or episode that reveals the aim to you.

Connect

1. How does the story connect to some of the preoccupations of the Puritans as you studied them in Unit 1?
2. How does the concept of legend play into the story? Do you find similarities to the use of legend in Irving?
3. Find an essay or speech where the attitude toward human nature is similar to the attitude you find in this story, and compare the two.

From *The House of the Seven Gables*

The Flight of Two Owls

Summer as it was, the east wind set poor Hepzibah's few remaining teeth chattering in her head, as she and Clifford faced it, on their way up Pyncheon Street, and towards the centre of the town. Not merely was it the shiver which this pitiless blast brought to her frame (although her feet and hands, especially, had never seemed so death-a-cold as now), but there was a moral sensation, mingling itself with the physical chill, and causing her to shake more in spirit than in body. The world's broad, bleak atmosphere was all so comfortless! Such, indeed, is the impression which it makes on every new adventurer, even if he plunge into it while the warmest tide of life is bubbling through his veins. What, then, must it have been to Hepzibah and Clifford,—so time-stricken° as they were, yet so like children in their inexperience,—as they left the doorstep, and passed from

time-stricken: i.e., old

beneath the wide shelter of the Pyncheon Elm! They were wandering all abroad, on precisely such a pilgrimage as a child often meditates, to the world's end, with perhaps a sixpence and a biscuit in his pocket. In Hepzibah's mind, there was the wretched consciousness of being adrift. She had lost the faculty of self-guidance; but, in view of the difficulties around her, felt it hardly worth an effort to regain it, and was, moreover, incapable of making one.

As they proceeded on their strange expedition, she now and then cast a look sidelong at Clifford, and could not but observe that he was possessed and swayed by a powerful excitement. It was this, indeed, that gave him the control which he had at once, and so irresistibly, established over his movements. It not a little resembled the exhilaration of wine. Or, it might more fancifully be compared to a joyous piece of music, played with wild vivacity, but upon a disordered instrument. As the cracked jarring note might always be heard, and as it jarred loudest amidst the loftiest exultation of the melody, so was there a continual quake through Clifford, causing him most to quiver while he wore a triumphant smile, and seemed almost under a necessity to skip in his gait.

They met few people abroad,° even on passing from the retired° neighborhood of the House of the Seven Gables into what was ordinarily the more thronged and busier portion of the town. Glistening sidewalks, with little pools of rain, here and there, along their unequal surface; umbrellas displayed ostentatiously in the shop-windows, as if the life of trade had concentrated itself in that one article; wet leaves of the horse-chestnut or elm-trees, torn off untimely by the blast and scattered along the public way; an unsightly accumulation of mud in the middle of the street, which perversely grew the more unclean for its long and laborious washing,—these were the more definable points of a very somber picture. In the way of movement and human life, there was the hasty rattle of a cab or coach, its driver protected by a waterproof cap over his head and shoulders; the forlorn figure of an old man, who seemed to have crept out of some subterranean sewer, and was stooping along the kennel,° and poking the wet rubbish with a stick, in quest of rusty nails; a merchant or two, at the door of the post-office, together with an editor and a miscellaneous politician, awaiting a dilatory° mail; a few visages° of retired sea-captains at the window of an insurance office, looking out

---

abroad: out of doors
retired: withdrawn, secluded
kennel: gutter
dilatory: slow, tardy
visages: faces

vacantly at the vacant street, blaspheming at the weather, and fretting at the dearth° as well of public news as local gossip. What a treasure-trove to these venerable quidnuncs,° could they have guessed the secret which Hepzibah and Clifford were carrying along with them! But their two figures attracted hardly so much notice as that of a young girl, who passed at the same instant, and happened to raise her skirt a trifle too high above her ankles. Had it been a sunny and cheerful day, they could hardly have gone through the streets without making themselves obnoxious to remark.° Now, probably, they were felt to be in keeping with the dismal and bitter weather, and therefore did not stand out in strong relief,° as if the sun were shining on them, but melted into the gray gloom and were forgotten as soon as gone.

Poor Hepzibah! Could she have understood this fact, it would have brought her some little comfort; for, to all her other troubles,—strange to say!—there was added the womanish and old-maiden-like misery arising from a sense of unseemliness in her attire. Thus, she was fain° to shrink deeper into herself, as it were, as if in the hope of making people suppose that here was only a cloak and hood, threadbare and woefully faded, taking an airing in the midst of the storm, without any wearer!

5 As they went on, the feeling of indistinctness and unreality kept dimly hovering round about her, and so diffusing° itself into her system that one of her hands was hardly palpable° to the touch of the other. Any certainty would have been preferable to this. She whispered to herself, again and again, "Am I awake?—Am I awake?" and sometimes exposed her face to the chill spatter of the wind, for the sake of its rude assurance that she was. Whether it was Clifford's purpose, or only chance, had led them thither,° they now found themselves passing beneath the arched entrance of a large structure of gray stone. Within, there was a spacious breadth, and an airy height from floor to roof, now partially filled with smoke and steam, which eddied° voluminously upward and formed a mimic cloud-region over their heads. A train of cars was just ready for a start; the locomotive was

---

dearth: scarcity, lack
quidnuncs: busybodies, gossips (from the Latin for "what now")
obnoxious to remark: objectionable to observers
relief: contrast to their surroundings
fain: disposed
diffusing: spreading
palpable: perceptible
thither: in that direction
eddied: swirled

fretting and fuming, like a steed impatient for a headlong rush; and the bell rang out its hasty peal, so well expressing the brief summons which life vouchsafes° to us in its hurried career. Without question or delay,—with the irresistible decision, if not rather to be called recklessness, which had so strangely taken possession of him, and through him of Hepzibah,—Clifford impelled her towards the cars, and assisted her to enter. The signal was given; the engine puffed forth its short, quick breaths; the train began its movement; and, along with a hundred other passengers, these two unwonted° travelers sped onward like the wind.

At last, therefore, and after so long estrangement from everything that the world acted or enjoyed, they had been drawn into the great current of human life, and were swept away with it, as by the suction of fate itself.

Still haunted with the idea that not one of the past incidents, inclusive of Judge Pyncheon's visit, could be real, the recluse of the Seven Gables murmured in her brother's ear,—

"Clifford! Clifford! Is not this a dream?"

"A dream, Hepzibah!" repeated he, almost laughing in her face. "On the contrary, I have never been awake before!"

10

Meanwhile, looking from the window, they could see the world racing past them. At one moment, they were rattling through a solitude;° the next, a village had grown up around them; a few breaths more, and it had vanished, as if swallowed by an earthquake. The spires of meeting-houses° seemed set adrift from their foundations; the broad-based hills glided away. Everything was unfixed from its age-long rest, and moving at whirlwind speed in a direction opposite to their own.

Within the car there was the usual interior life of the railroad, offering little to the observation of other passengers, but full of novelty for this pair of strangely enfranchised° prisoners. It was novelty enough, indeed, that there were fifty human beings in close relation with them, under one long and narrow roof, and drawn onward by the same mighty influence that had taken their two selves into its grasp. It seemed marvelous° how all these people could remain so quietly in their seats, while so much noisy strength was at work in their behalf.

---

vouchsafes: grants, yields
unwonted: unaccustomed
solitude: solitary place
meeting-houses: houses of worship
enfranchised: freed
marvelous: astonishing

Some, with tickets in their hats (long travelers these, before whom lay a hundred miles of railroad), had plunged into the English scenery and adventures of pamphlet novels, and were keeping company with dukes and earls. Others, whose briefer span forbade their devoting themselves to studies so abstruse,° beguiled° the little tedium of the way with penny-papers.° A party of girls, and one young man, on opposite sides of the car, found huge amusement in a game of ball. They tossed it to and fro, with peals of laughter that might be measured by mile-lengths; for, faster than the nimble ball could fly, the merry players fled unconsciously along, leaving the trail of their mirth afar behind, and ending their game under another sky than had witnessed its commencement. Boys, with apples, cakes, candy, and rolls of variously tinctured° lozenges,°—merchandise that reminded Hepzibah of her deserted shop,—appeared at each momentary stopping-place, doing up their business in a hurry, or breaking it short off, lest the market should ravish° them away with it. New people continually entered. Old acquaintances—for such they soon grew to be, in this rapid current of affairs—continually departed. Here and there, amid the rumble and the tumult, sat one asleep. Sleep; sport; business; graver° or lighter study; and the common and inevitable movement onward! It was life itself!

Clifford's naturally poignant sympathies were all aroused. He caught the color of what was passing about him, and threw it back more vividly than he received it, but mixed, nevertheless, with a lurid and portentous° hue. Hepzibah, on the other hand, felt herself more apart from human kind than even in the seclusion which she had just quitted.

"You are not happy, Hepzibah!" said Clifford apart, in a tone of reproach. "You are thinking of that dismal old house, and of Cousin Jaffrey"—here came the quake through him,—"and of Cousin Jaffrey sitting there, all by himself! Take my advice,—follow my example,—and let such things slip aside. Here we are, in the world, Hepzibah!—in the midst of life!—in the throng of our fellow beings! Let you and I be happy! As happy as that youth and those pretty girls, at their game of ball!"

---

abstruse: esoteric, difficult to understand
beguiled: whiled away
penny-papers: cheap, mass-circulation newspapers
tinctured: tinted; suffused with a solution
lozenges: cough tablets
ravish: carry away by force
graver: more serious
portentous: ominous, foreboding

"Happy—" thought Hepzibah, bitterly conscious, at the word, of her dull and heavy heart, with the frozen pain in it,—"happy. He is mad° already; and, if I could once feel myself broad° awake, I should go mad too!"

If a fixed idea be madness, she was perhaps not remote° from it. Fast and far as they had rattled and clattered along the iron track, they might just as well, as regarded Hepzibah's mental images, have been passing up and down Pyncheon Street. With miles and miles of varied scenery between, there was no scene for her save° the seven old gable-peaks, with their moss, and the tuft of weeds in one of the angles, and the shop-window, and a customer shaking the door, and compelling the little bell to jingle fiercely, but without disturbing Judge Pyncheon! This one old house was everywhere! It transported its great, lumbering° bulk with more than railroad speed, and set itself phlegmatically° down on whatever spot she glanced at. The quality of Hepzibah's mind was too unmalleable° to take new impressions so readily as Clifford's. He had a winged nature; she was rather of the vegetable kind, and could hardly be kept long alive, if drawn up by the roots. Thus it happened that the relation heretofore° existing between her brother and herself was changed. At home, she was his guardian; here, Clifford had become hers, and seemed to comprehend whatever belonged to their new position with a singular rapidity of intelligence. He had been startled into manhood and intellectual vigor; or, at least, into a condition that resembled them, though it might be both diseased and transitory.°

15

The conductor now applied for their tickets; and Clifford, who had made himself the purse-bearer, put a bank-note° into his hand, as he had observed others do.

"For the lady and yourself?" asked the conductor. "And how far?"

"As far as that will carry us," said Clifford. "It is no great matter. We are riding for pleasure merely."

"You choose a strange day for it, sir!" remarked a gimlet°-eyed old gentleman on the other side of the car, looking at Clifford and

mad: insane
broad: wide
remote: far
save: except
lumbering: awkward, clumsy
phlegmatically: dully, sluggishly
unmalleable: inflexible
heretofore: previously, up till now
transitory: fleeting
bank-note: paper currency, bill
gimlet: piercing, penetrating

his companion, as if curious to make them out. "The best chance of pleasure, in an easterly rain, I take it, is in a man's own house, with a nice little fire in the chimney."

"I cannot precisely agree with you," said Clifford, courteously bowing to the old gentleman, and at once taking up the clew° of conversation which the latter had proffered. "It had just occurred to me, on the contrary, that this admirable invention of the railroad—with the vast and inevitable improvements to be looked for, both as to speed and convenience—is destined to do away with those stale ideas of home and fireside, and substitute something better." 20

"In the name of common-sense," asked the old gentleman rather testily, "what can be better for a man than his own parlor and chimney-corner?"

"These things have not the merit which many good people attribute to them," replied Clifford. "They may be said, in few and pithy° words, to have ill served a poor purpose. My impression is, that our wonderfully increased and still increasing facilities of locomotion are destined to bring us around again to the nomadic° state. You are aware, my dear sir,—you must have observed it in your own experience,—that all human progress is in a circle; or, to use a more accurate and beautiful figure, in an ascending spiral curve. While we fancy ourselves going straight forward, and attaining, at every step, an entirely new position of affairs, we do actually return to something long ago tried and abandoned, but which we now find etherealized,° refined, and perfected to its ideal. The past is but a coarse and sensual prophecy of the present and the future. To apply this truth to the topic now under discussion. In the early epochs of our race, men dwelt in temporary huts, of bowers of branches, as easily constructed as a bird's-nest, and which they built,—if it should be called building, when such sweet homes of a summer solstice rather grew than were made with hands,—which Nature, we will say, assisted them to rear where fruit abounded, where fish and game were plentiful, or, most especially, where the sense of beauty was to be gratified by a lovelier shade than elsewhere, and a more exquisite arrangement of lake, wood, and hill. This life possessed a charm which, ever since man quitted it, has vanished from existence. And it typified something better than itself. It had its drawbacks; such as hunger and thirst, inclement weather, hot sunshine, and weary and foot-blistering marches over barren and ugly tracts, that lay between the sites desirable

---

clew: clue, hint
pithy: brief and forceful
nomadic: wandering, roving
etherealized: made insubstantial

for their fertility and beauty. But in our ascending spiral, we escape all this. These railroads—could but the whistle be made musical, and the rumble and the jar° got rid of—are positively the greatest blessing that the ages have wrought out for us. They give us wings; they annihilate the toil and dust of pilgrimage; they spiritualize travel! Transition° being so facile,° what can be any man's inducement to tarry in one spot? Why, therefore, should he build a more cumbrous° habitation than can readily be carried off with him? Why should he make himself a prisoner for life in brick, and stone, and old worm-eaten timber, when he may just as easily dwell, in one sense, nowhere,—in a better sense, wherever the fit and beautiful shall offer him a home?"

Clifford's countenance° glowed, as he divulged this theory; a youthful character shone out from within, converting the wrinkles and pallid duskiness of age into an almost transparent mask. The merry girls let their ball drop upon the floor, and gazed at him. They said to themselves, perhaps, that, before his hair was gray and the crow's-feet tracked his temples, this now decaying man must have stamped the impress of his features on many a woman's heart. But, alas! no woman's eye had seen his face while it was beautiful.

"I should scarcely call it an improved state of things," observed Clifford's new acquaintance, "to live everywhere and nowhere!"

"Would you not?" exclaimed Clifford, with singular° energy. "It is as clear to me as sunshine,—were there any in the sky,—that the greatest possible stumbling-blocks in the path of human happiness and improvement are these heaps of bricks and stones, consolidated with mortar, or hewn timber, fastened together with spike-nails, which men painfully contrive for their own torment, and call them house and home! The soul needs air; a wide sweep and frequent change of it. Morbid influences, in a thousand-fold variety, gather about hearths, and pollute the life of households. There is no such unwholesome atmosphere as that of an old home, rendered poisonous by one's defunct forefathers and relatives. I speak of what I know. There is a certain house within my familiar recollection,—one of those peaked-gable (there are seven of them), projecting-storied edifices, such as you occasionally see in our older towns,—a rusty, crazy, creaky, dry-rotted, dingy, dark, and miserable old dungeon, with an arched window over the porch, and a little

25

jar: jarring motion

Transition: movement, passage from one place to another

facile: easy

cumbrous: cumbersome, unwieldy

countenance: face

singular: unusual, remarkable

shop-door on one side, and a great, melancholy elm before it! Now, sir, whenever my thoughts recur to this seven-gabled mansion (the fact is so very curious that I must needs mention it), immediately I have a vision or image of an elderly man, of remarkably stern countenance, sitting in an oaken elbow-chair, dead, stone-dead, with an ugly flow of blood upon his shirt-bosom! Dead, but with open eyes! He taints the whole house, as I remember it. I could never flourish there, nor be happy, nor do nor enjoy what God meant me to do and enjoy."

His face darkened, and seemed to contract, and shrivel itself up, and wither into age.

"Never, sir!" he repeated. "I could never draw cheerful breath there!"

"I should think not," said the old gentleman, eyeing Clifford earnestly, and rather apprehensively. "I should conceive not, sir, with that notion in your head!"

"Surely not," continued Clifford; "and it were a relief to me if that house could be torn down, or burnt up, and so the earth be rid of it, and grass be sown abundantly over its foundation. Not that I should ever visit its site again! for, sir, the farther I get away from it, the more does the joy, the lightsome freshness, the heart-leap, the intellectual dance, the youth, in short,—yes, my youth, my youth!—the more does it come back to me. No longer ago than this morning, I was old. I remember looking in the glass, and wondering° at my own gray hair, and the wrinkles, many and deep, right across my brow, and the furrows down my cheeks, and the prodigious° trampling of crow's-feet about my temples! It was too soon! I could not bear it! Age had no right to come! I had not lived! But now do I look old? If so, my aspect° belies° me strangely; for—a great weight being off my mind—I feel in the very heyday of my youth, with the world and my best days before me!"

"I trust you may find it so," said the old gentleman, who seemed rather embarrassed, and desirous of avoiding the observation° which Clifford's wild talk drew on them both. "You have my best wishes for it." 30

"For Heaven's sake, dear Clifford, be quiet!" whispered his sister. "They think you mad."

"Be quiet yourself, Hepzibah!" returned her brother. "No matter what they think! I am not mad. For the first time in thirty years my thoughts gush up and find words ready for them. I must talk, and I will!"

---

wondering: being amazed

prodigious: extraordinary

aspect: appearance

belies: misrepresents

observation: notice, attention

He turned again towards the old gentleman, and renewed the conversation.

"Yes, my dear sir," said he, "it is my firm belief and hope that these terms of roof and hearth-stone, which have so long been held to embody something sacred, are soon to pass out of men's daily use, and be forgotten. Just imagine, for a moment, how much of human evil will crumble away, with this one change! What we call real estate—the solid ground to build a house on—is the broad foundation on which nearly all the guilt of this world rests."

[1851]

Read

1. How does the language convey the emotions of the two characters in this scene?
2. How does the writer change the pace—the speed of events—in this excerpt? Why is this change of pace important?
3. What is Clifford's attitude toward the train? How does the narrator suggest a different view?

Write

1. How might this excerpt serve as an example of the opportunities or perils of technology?
2. What does the passage suggest about American attitudes toward change?
3. Write a brief description of how you see the relationship between Clifford and Hepzibah in the excerpt.

Connect

1. Find another text in this unit or an earlier unit that you think compares to the attitude expressed by Clifford about progress. Write a brief analysis of the similarities you find.
2. Rewrite the passage as an argument in favor of or opposing the kind of progress the train represents.

Louisa May Alcott

Louisa May Alcott (1832–1888) is one of the most famous of American authors. She wrote a classic of children's fiction, *Little Women,* published in 1868. *Little Women* and the books that followed, *Little Men, Aunt Jo's Boys, An Old Fashioned Girl,* and others, made Alcott both beloved and wealthy. However, she grew up in poverty with a father whose strict principles and impractical schemes often had the family near starvation. Alcott spent much of her youth in Concord, Massachusetts, where she and her family were befriended by Ralph Waldo Emerson and knew Nathaniel Hawthorne and Henry David Thoreau and others of the Concord circle well. Margaret Fuller taught for a time in her father's school. Alcott's family were fervent abolitionists and Union supporters, and Alcott volunteered for service as a hospital nurse until illness forced her to return home. *Hospital Sketches,* a thinly veiled autobiographical account of her time in the Union Hospital in Washington, DC, was published in 1863. It received much acclaim and launched her career as a successful writer.

From *Hospital Sketches*

CHAPTER 3

A Day

"They've come! they've come! hurry up, ladies—you're wanted."

"Who have come? the rebels?"

This sudden summons in the gray dawn was somewhat startling to a three days' nurse like myself, and, as the thundering knock came at our door, I sprang up in my bed, prepared

> "To gird my woman's form,
> And on the ramparts die,"

if necessary; but my room-mate took it more coolly, and, as she began a rapid toilet,° answered my bewildered question,—

"Bless you, no child; it's the wounded from Fredericksburg;° forty ambulances are at the door, and we shall have our hands full in fifteen minutes." 5

"What shall we have to do?"

"Wash, dress, feed, warm and nurse them for the next three months, I dare say. Eighty beds are ready, and we were getting impatient for the men to come. Now you will begin to see hospital life in earnest, for you won't probably find time to sit down all day, and may think yourself fortunate if you get to bed by midnight. Come to me in the ball-room when you are ready; the worst cases are always carried there, and I shall need your help."

So saying, the energetic little woman twirled her hair into a button at the back of her head, in a "cleared for action" sort of style, and vanished, wrestling her way into a feminine kind of pea-jacket as she went.

I am free to confess that I had a realizing sense of the fact that my hospital bed was not a bed of roses just then, or the prospect before me one of unmingled rapture. My three days' experiences had begun with a death, and,

---

toilet: process of dressing or grooming oneself

Fredericksburg: a battle fought at Fredericksburg, Virginia, December 11–15, 1862, in which the defeated Union forces suffered heavy casualties when repeatedly ordered by Major General Ambrose Burnside to directly charge heavily entrenched Confederate positions

owing to the defalcation° of another nurse, a somewhat abrupt plunge into the superintendence of a ward containing forty beds, where I spent my shining hours washing faces, serving rations, giving medicine, and sitting in a very hard chair, with pneumonia on one side, diphtheria on the other, five typhoids on the opposite, and a dozen dilapidated patriots, hopping, lying, and lounging about, all staring more or less at the new "nuss," who suffered untold agonies, but concealed them under as matronly° an aspect° as a spinster° could assume, and blundered through her trying labors with a Spartan firmness,° which I hope they appreciated, but am afraid they didn't. Having a taste for "ghastliness," I had rather longed for the wounded to arrive, for rheumatism wasn't heroic, neither was liver complaint, or measles; even fever had lost its charms since "bathing burning brows" had been used up in romances, real and ideal; but when I peeped into the dusky street lined with what I at first had innocently called market carts, now unloading their sad freight at our door, I recalled sundry° reminiscences I had heard from nurses of longer standing, my ardor experienced a sudden chill, and I indulged in a most unpatriotic wish that I was safe at home again, with a quiet day before me, and no necessity for being hustled up, as if I were a hen and had only to hop off my roost, give my plumage a peck, and be ready for action. A second bang at the door sent this recreant° desire to the right about,° as a little woolly head popped in, and Joey, (a six years' old contraband,°) announced—

"Miss Blank is jes' wild fer ye, and says fly round right away. They's comin' in, I tell yer, heaps on 'em—one was took out dead, and I see him,—hi! warn't he a goner!" 10

With which cheerful intelligence° the imp scuttled away, singing like a blackbird, and I followed, feeling that Richard was not himself again, and wouldn't be for a long time to come.

The first thing I met was a regiment of the vilest odors that ever assaulted the human nose, and took it by storm. Cologne, with its seven and seventy evil savors, was a posy-bed to it; and the worst of this affliction was, every one had assured me that it was a chronic weakness of all hospitals, and I must bear

---

defalcation: embezzlement

matronly: in the manner of a mature (usually married) woman

aspect: appearance

spinster: woman who has never been married

Spartan firmness: the kind of iron self-control practiced in the warrior city-state of Sparta in ancient Greece

sundry: various

recreant: cowardly, disloyal

right about: 180-degree turn

contraband: escaped slave

intelligence: news, information

it. I did, armed with lavender water, with which I so besprinkled myself and premises, that, like my friend Sairy, I was soon known among my patients as "the nurse with the bottle." Having been run over by three excited surgeons, bumped against by migratory coal-hods,° water-pails, and small boys, nearly scalded by an avalanche of newly-filled tea-pots, and hopelessly entangled in a knot of colored sisters coming to wash, I progressed by slow stages up stairs and down, till the main hall was reached, and I paused to take breath and a survey. There they were! "our brave boys," as the papers justly call them, for cowards could hardly have been so riddled with shot and shell, so torn and shattered, nor have borne suffering for which we have no name, with an uncomplaining fortitude, which made one glad to cherish each as a brother. In they came, some on stretchers, some in men's arms, some feebly staggering along propped on rude crutches, and one lay stark and still with covered face, as a comrade gave his name to be recorded before they carried him away to the dead house. All was hurry and confusion; the hall was full of these wrecks of humanity, for the most exhausted could not reach a bed till duly ticketed and registered; the walls were lined with rows of such as could sit, the floor covered with the more disabled, the steps and doorways filled with helpers and lookers on; the sound of many feet and voices made that usually quiet hour as noisy as noon; and, in the midst of it all, the matron's motherly face brought more comfort to many a poor soul, than the cordial° draughts° she administered, or the cheery words that welcomed all, making of the hospital a home.

The sight of several stretchers, each with its legless, armless, or desperately wounded occupant, entering my ward, admonished me that I was there to work, not to wonder or weep; so I corked up my feelings, and returned to the path of duty, which was rather "a hard road to travel" just then. The house had been a hotel before hospitals were needed, and many of the doors still bore their old names; some not so inappropriate as might be imagined, for my ward was in truth a ball-room, if gun-shot wounds could christen it. Forty beds were prepared, many already tenanted° by tired men who fell down anywhere, and drowsed till the smell of food roused them. Round the great stove was gathered the dreariest group I ever saw—ragged, gaunt and pale, mud to the knees, with bloody bandages untouched since put on days before; many bundled up in blankets, coats being lost or useless; and all wearing that disheartened look which proclaimed defeat, more plainly than any telegram of the Burnside blunder. I pitied them so much, I dared not speak to them, though, remembering all they had been through since the route° at

---

coal-hods: coal-filled open boxes attached to long poles to be carried over the shoulder

cordial: stimulant, liqueur

draughts: drinks

tenanted: occupied

route: rout

Fredericksburg, I yearned to serve the dreariest of them all. Presently, Miss Blank tore me from my refuge behind piles of one-sleeved shirts, odd socks, bandages and lint; put basin, sponge, towels, and a block of brown soap into my hands, with these appalling directions:

"Come, my dear, begin to wash as fast as you can. Tell them to take off socks, coats and shirts, scrub them well, put on clean shirts, and the attendants will finish them off, and lay them in bed."

If she had requested me to shave them all, or dance a hornpipe on the stove funnel, I should have been less staggered; but to scrub some dozen lords of creation at a moment's notice, was really—really—. However, there was no time for nonsense, and, having resolved when I came to do everything I was bid, I drowned my scruples in my wash-bowl, clutched my soap manfully, and, assuming a business-like air, made a dab at the first dirty specimen I saw, bent on performing my task *vi et armis*° if necessary. I chanced to light on a withered old Irishman, wounded in the head, which caused that portion of his frame to be tastefully laid out like a garden, the bandages being the walks, his hair the shrubbery. He was so overpowered by the honor of having a lady wash him, as he expressed it, that he did nothing but roll up his eyes, and bless me, in an irresistible style which was too much for my sense of the ludicrous; so we laughed together, and when I knelt down to take off his shoes, he "flopped" also, and wouldn't hear of my touching "them dirty craters. May your bed above be aisy darlin', for the day's work ye ar doon!—Whoosh! there ye are, and bedad, it's hard tellin' which is the dirtiest, the fut or the shoe." It was; and if he hadn't been to the fore, I should have gone on pulling, under the impression that the "fut" was a boot, for trousers, socks, shoes and legs were a mass of mud. This comical tableau produced a general grin, at which propitious° beginning I took heart and scrubbed away like any tidy parent on a Saturday night. Some of them took the performance like sleepy children, leaning their tired heads against me as I worked, others looked grimly scandalized, and several of the roughest colored like bashful girls. One wore a soiled little bag about his neck, and, as I moved it, to bathe his wounded breast, I said,

15

"Your talisman° didn't save you, did it?"

"Well, I reckon it did, marm, for that shot would a gone a couple a inches deeper but for my old mammy's camphor bag," answered the cheerful philosopher.

Another, with a gun-shot wound through the cheek, asked for a looking-glass, and when I brought one, regarded his swollen face with a dolorous° expression, as he muttered—

---

vi et armis: Latin for "by force and arms"

propitious: favorable, auspicious

talisman: good luck charm, amulet

dolorous: sorrowful

"I vow to gosh, that's too bad! I warn't a bad looking chap before, and now I'm done for; won't there be a thunderin' scar? and what on earth will Josephine Skinner say?"

He looked up at me with his one eye so appealingly, that I controlled my risibles,° and assured him that if Josephine was a girl of sense, she would admire the honorable scar, as a lasting proof that he had faced the enemy, for all women thought a wound the best decoration a brave soldier could wear. I hope Miss Skinner verified the good opinion I so rashly expressed of her, but I shall never know. 20

The next scrubbee was a nice looking lad, with a curly brown mane, and a budding trace of gingerbread over the lip, which he called his beard, and defended stoutly, when the barber jocosely° suggested its immolation.° He lay on a bed, with one leg gone, and the right arm so shattered that it must evidently follow: yet the little Sergeant was as merry as if his afflictions were not worth lamenting over; and when a drop or two of salt water mingled with my suds at the sight of this strong young body, so marred and maimed, the boy looked up, with a brave smile, though there was a little quiver of the lips, as he said,

"Now don't you fret yourself about me, miss; I'm first rate here, for it's nuts to lie still on this bed, after knocking about in those confounded ambulances, that shake what there is left of a fellow to jelly. I never was in one of these places before, and think this cleaning up a jolly thing for us, though I'm afraid it isn't for you ladies."

"Is this your first battle, Sergeant?"

"No, miss; I've been in six scrimmages, and never got a scratch till this last one; but it's done the business pretty thoroughly for me, I should say. Lord! what a scramble there'll be for arms and legs, when we old boys come out of our graves, on the Judgment Day: wonder if we shall get our own again? If we do, my leg will have to tramp from Fredericksburg, my arm from here, I suppose, and meet my body, wherever it may be."

The fancy seemed to tickle him mightily, for he laughed blithely,° and so did I; which, no doubt, caused the new nurse to be regarded as a light-minded sinner by the Chaplain, who roamed vaguely about, informing the men that they were all worms, corrupt of heart, with perishable bodies, and souls only to be saved by a diligent perusal of certain tracts,° and other equally cheering bits of spiritual consolation, when spirituous° ditto° would have been preferred. 25

---

risibles: urge to laugh
jocosely: humorously
immolation: sacrifice, ritual killing
blithely: lightheartedly
tracts: pamphlets, often of a religious nature
spirituous: alcoholic
ditto: likewise (here with reference to *consolation*)

"I say, Mrs.!" called a voice behind me; and, turning, I saw a rough Michigander, with an arm blown off at the shoulder, and two or three bullets still in him—as he afterwards mentioned, as carelessly as if gentlemen were in the habit of carrying such trifles about with them. I went to him, and, while administering a dose of soap and water, he whispered, irefully:

"That red-headed devil, over yonder, is a reb, damn him! You'll agree to that, I'll bet? He's got shet° of a foot, or he'd a cut° like the rest of the lot. Don't you wash him, nor feed him, but jest let him holler till he's tired. It's a blasted shame to fetch them fellers in here, along side of us; and so I'll tell the chap that bosses this concern; cuss me if I don't."

I regret to say that I did not deliver a moral sermon upon the duty of forgiving our enemies, and the sin of profanity, then and there; but, being a red-hot Abolitionist, stared fixedly at the tall rebel, who was a copperhead,° in every sense of the word, and privately resolved to put soap in his eyes, rub his nose the wrong way, and excoriate° his cuticle° generally, if I had the washing of him.

My amiable intentions, however, were frustrated; for, when I approached, with as Christian an expression as my principles would allow, and asked the question—"Shall I try to make you more comfortable, sir?" all I got for my pains was a gruff—

"No; I'll do it myself." 30

"Here's your Southern chivalry, with a witness," thought I, dumping the basin down before him, thereby quenching a strong desire to give him a summary baptism, in return for his ungraciousness; for my angry passions rose, at this rebuff, in a way that would have scandalized good Dr. Watts.° He was a disappointment in all respects, (the rebel, not the blessed Doctor,) for he was neither fiendish, romantic, pathetic, or anything interesting; but a long, fat man, with a head like a burning bush, and a perfectly expressionless face: so I could dislike him without the slightest drawback, and ignored his existence from that day forth. One redeeming trait he certainly did possess, as the floor speedily testified; for his ablutions° were so vigorously performed, that his bed soon stood like an isolated island, in a sea of soap-suds, and he resembled a dripping merman, suffering from the loss of a fin. If cleanliness is a near neighbor to godliness, then was the big rebel the godliest man in my ward that day.

---

shet: shot

cut: cut and run

copperhead: Northerner with Secessionist sympathies

excoriate: abrade, flay, wear away the skin of

cuticle: epidermis, outermost skin layer

Dr. Watts: Isaac Watts (1674–1748), English writer of hymns, including "Joy to the World" and "O God, Our Help in Ages Past"

ablutions: washing, bathing

Having done up our human wash, and laid it out to dry, the second syllable of our version of the word war-fare was enacted with much success. Great trays of bread, meat, soup and coffee appeared; and both nurses and attendants turned waiters, serving bountiful rations to all who could eat. I can call my pinafore° to testify to my good will in the work, for in ten minutes it was reduced to a perambulating bill of fare, presenting samples of all the refreshments going or gone. It was a lively scene; the long room lined with rows of beds, each filled by an occupant, whom water, shears, and clean raiment,° had transformed from a dismal ragamuffin into a recumbent° hero, with a cropped head. To and fro rushed matrons, maids, and convalescent "boys," skirmishing with knives and forks; retreating with empty plates; marching and counter-marching, with unvaried success, while the clash of busy spoons made most inspiring music for the charge of our Light Brigade:

"Beds to the front of them,
Beds to the right of them,
Beds to the left of them,
    Nobody blundered.
Beamed at by hungry souls,
Screamed at with brimming bowls,
Steamed at by army rolls,
    Buttered and sundered.
With coffee not cannon plied,
Each must be satisfied,
Whether they lived or died;
    All the men wondered."

Very welcome seemed the generous meal, after a week of suffering, exposure, and short commons;° soon the brown faces began to smile, as food, warmth, and rest, did their pleasant work; and the grateful "Thankee's" were followed by more graphic accounts of the battle and retreat, than any paid reporter could have given us. Curious contrasts of the tragic and comic met one everywhere; and some touching as well as ludicrous episodes, might have been recorded that day. A six foot New Hampshire man, with a leg broken and perforated by a piece of shell, so large that, had I not seen the wound,

---

pinafore: sleeveless apronlike overdress
raiment: clothing
recumbent: reclining, resting
commons: rations

I should have regarded the story as a Munchausenism,° beckoned me to come and help him, as he could not sit up, and both his bed and beard were getting plentifully anointed with soup. As I fed my big nestling with corresponding mouthfuls, I asked him how he felt during the battle.

"Well, 'twas my fust, you see, so I aint ashamed to say I was a trifle flustered in the beginnin', there was such an allfired racket; for ef there's anything I do spleen° agin, it's noise. But when my mate, Eph Sylvester, caved, with a bullet through his head, I got mad, and pitched in, licketty cut. Our part of the fight didn't last long; so a lot of us larked round Fredericksburg, and give some of them houses a pretty consid'able of a rummage, till we was ordered out of the mess. Some of our fellows cut like time; but I warn't a-goin' to run for nobody; and, fust thing I knew, a shell bust, right in front of us, and I keeled over, feelin' as if I was blowed higher'n a kite. I sung out, and the boys come back for me, double quick; but the way they chucked me over them fences was a caution, I tell you. Next day I was most as black as that darkey yonder, lickin' plates on the sly. This is bully coffee, ain't it? Give us another pull at it, and I'll be obleeged to you."

I did; and, as the last gulp subsided, he said, with a rub of his old handkerchief over eyes as well as mouth: 35

"Look a here; I've got a pair a earbobs and a handkercher pin I'm a goin' to give you, if you'll have them; for you're the very moral° o' Lizy Sylvester, poor Eph's wife: that's why I signalled you to come over here. They aint much, I guess, but they'll do to memorize the rebs by."

Burrowing under his pillow, he produced a little bundle of what he called "truck," and gallantly presented me with a pair of earrings, each representing a cluster of corpulent grapes, and the pin a basket of astonishing fruit, the whole large and coppery enough for a small warming-pan.° Feeling delicate about depriving him of such valuable relics, I accepted the earrings alone, and was obliged to depart, somewhat abruptly, when my friend stuck the warming-pan in the bosom of his night-gown, viewing it with much complacency, and, perhaps, some tender memory, in that rough heart of his, for the comrade he had lost.

Observing that the man next him had left his meal untouched, I offered the same service I had performed for his neighbor, but he shook his head.

"Thank you, ma'am; I don't think I'll ever eat again, for I'm shot in the stomach. But I'd like a drink of water, if you aint too busy."

Munchausenisms: wild exaggerations (after Karl Friedrich Hieronymus, Freiherr von Münchhausen [1720–1797], usually known as Baron Münchhausen, who reputedly told extremely fanciful stories about his military adventures)

spleen: hate

moral: image

warming-pan: metal pan with a cover and long handle designed to hold hot water or coals and used to warm a bed

I rushed away, but the water-pails were gone to be refilled, and it was some time before they reappeared. I did not forget my patient patient, meanwhile, and, with the first mugful, hurried back to him. He seemed asleep; but something in the tired white face caused me to listen at his lips for a breath. None came. I touched his forehead; it was cold: and then I knew that, while he waited, a better nurse than I had given him a cooler draught, and healed him with a touch. I laid the sheet over the quiet sleeper, whom no noise could now disturb; and, half an hour later, the bed was empty. It seemed a poor requital° for all he had sacrificed and suffered,—that hospital bed, lonely even in a crowd; for there was no familiar face for him to look his last upon; no friendly voice to say, Good bye; no hand to lead him gently down into the Valley of the Shadow; and he vanished, like a drop in that red sea upon whose shores so many women stand lamenting. For a moment I felt bitterly indignant at this seeming carelessness of the value of life, the sanctity of death; then consoled myself with the thought that, when the great muster roll was called, these nameless men might be promoted above many whose tall monuments record the barren honors they have won. 40

All having eaten, drank, and rested, the surgeons began their rounds; and I took my first lesson in the art of dressing wounds. It wasn't a festive scene, by any means; for Dr P., whose Aid I constituted myself, fell to work with a vigor which soon convinced me that I was a weaker vessel, though nothing would have induced me to confess it then. He had served in the Crimea,° and seemed to regard a dilapidated body very much as I should have regarded a damaged garment; and, turning up his cuffs, whipped out a very unpleasant looking housewife,° cutting, sawing, patching and piecing, with the enthusiasm of an accomplished surgical seamstress; explaining the process, in scientific terms, to the patient, meantime; which, of course, was immensely cheering and comfortable. There was an uncanny sort of fascination in watching him, as he peered and probed into the mechanism of those wonderful bodies, whose mysteries he understood so well. The more intricate the wound, the better he liked it. A poor private, with both legs off, and shot through the lungs, possessed more attractions for him than a dozen generals, slightly scratched in some "masterly retreat;" and had any one appeared in small pieces, requesting to be put together again, he would have considered it a special dispensation.°

---

requital: repayment

Crimea: The Crimean War (1853–1856) was fought by Britain, France, and their allies against the Russian Empire, for influence in Eastern Europe and the Middle East; an incident of this war was celebrated by Alfred, Lord Tennyson, in "The Charge of the Light Brigade," parodied earlier in this chapter.

housewife: small case for household articles such as needle and thread

special dispensation: exemption from some rule or authority

The amputations were reserved° till the morrow, and the merciful magic of ether was not thought necessary that day, so the poor souls had to bear their pains as best they might. It is all very well to talk of the patience of woman; and far be it from me to pluck that feather from her cap, for, heaven knows, she isn't allowed to wear many; but the patient endurance of these men, under trials of the flesh, was truly wonderful. Their fortitude seemed contagious, and scarcely a cry escaped them, though I often longed to groan for them, when pride kept their white lips shut, while great drops stood upon their foreheads, and the bed shook with the irrepressible tremor of their tortured bodies. One or two Irishmen anathematized° the doctors with the frankness of their nation, and ordered the Virgin to stand by them, as if she had been the wedded Biddy° to whom they could administer the poker, if she didn't; but, as a general thing, the work went on in silence, broken only by some quiet request for roller,° instruments, or plaster, a sigh from the patient, or a sympathizing murmur from the nurse.

It was long past noon before these repairs were even partially made; and, having got the bodies of my boys into something like order, the next task was to minister to their minds, by writing letters to the anxious souls at home; answering questions, reading papers, taking possession of money and valuables; for the eighth commandment was reduced to a very fragmentary condition, both by the blacks and whites, who ornamented our hospital with their presence. Pocket books, purses, miniatures, and watches, were sealed up, labelled, and handed over to the matron, till such times as the owners thereof were ready to depart homeward or campward again. The letters dictated to me, and revised by me, that afternoon, would have made an excellent chapter for some future history of the war; for, like that which Thackeray's "Ensign Spooney"° wrote his mother just before Waterloo, they were "full of affection, pluck, and bad spelling;" nearly all giving lively accounts of the battle, and ending with a somewhat sudden plunge from patriotism to provender,° desiring "Marm," "Mary Ann," or "Aunt Peters," to send along some pies, pickles, sweet stuff, and apples, "to yourn in haste," Joe, Sam, or Ned, as the case might be.

My little Sergeant insisted on trying to scribble something with his left hand, and patiently accomplished some half dozen lines of hieroglyphics, which he gave me to fold and direct, with a boyish blush, that rendered a glimpse of "My Dearest Jane," unnecessary, to assure me that the heroic lad

---

reserved: postponed

anathematized: cursed

Biddy: nickname for the Irish name Bridget

roller: a long, rolled bandage

Thackeray's "Ensign Spooney": a character in *Vanity Fair* (1847–1848) by English novelist William Makepeace Thackeray (1811–1863)

provender: food, provisions

had been more successful in the service of Commander-in-Chief Cupid than that of Gen. Mars;° and a charming little romance blossomed instanter° in Nurse Periwinkle's romantic fancy, though no further confidences were made that day, for Sergeant fell asleep, and, judging from his tranquil face, visited his absent sweetheart in the pleasant land of dreams.

At five o'clock a great bell rang, and the attendants flew, not to arms, but to their trays, to bring up supper, when a second uproar announced that it was ready. The new comers woke at the sound; and I presently discovered that it took a very bad wound to incapacitate the defenders of the faith for the consumption of their rations; the amount that some of them sequestered° was amazing; but when I suggested the probability of a famine hereafter, to the matron, that motherly lady cried out: "Bless their hearts, why shouldn't they eat? It's their only amusement; so fill every one, and, if there's not enough ready to-night, I'll lend my share to the Lord by giving it to the boys." And, whipping up her coffee-pot and plate of toast, she gladdened the eyes and stomachs of two or three dissatisfied heroes, by serving them with a liberal hand; and I haven't the slightest doubt that, having cast her bread upon the waters, it came back buttered, as another large-hearted old lady was wont to say. 45

Then came the doctor's evening visit; the administration of medicines; washing feverish faces; smoothing tumbled beds; wetting wounds; singing lullabies; and preparations for the night. By twelve, the last labor of love was done; the last "good night" spoken; and, if any needed a reward for that day's work, they surely received it, in the silent eloquence of those long lines of faces, showing pale and peaceful in the shaded rooms, as we quitted them, followed by grateful glances that lighted us to bed, where rest, the sweetest, made our pillows soft, while Night and Nature took our places, filling that great house of pain with the healing miracles of Sleep, and his diviner brother, Death.

CHAPTER IV

A Night

Being fond of the night side of nature, I was soon promoted to the post of night nurse, with every facility for indulging in my favorite pastime of "owling." My colleague, a black-eyed widow, relieved me at dawn, we two taking care of the ward, between us, like the immortal Sairy and Betsey,° "turn and turn about." I usually found my boys in the jolliest state of mind their condition

---

Mars: Roman god of war

instanter: instantly

sequestered: requisitioned and confiscated

Sairy and Betsey: Sairy Gamp is an elderly (and alcoholic) nurse and Betsey Prig is her friend, in the novel *Martin Chuzzlewit* (1844) by Charles Dickens (1812–1870).

allowed; for it was a known fact that Nurse Periwinkle objected to blue devils,° and entertained a belief that he who laughed most was surest of recovery. At the beginning of my reign, dumps and dismals° prevailed; the nurses looked anxious and tired, the men gloomy or sad; and a general "Hark!-from-the-tombs-a-doleful-sound" style of conversation seemed to be the fashion: a state of things which caused one coming from a merry, social New England town, to feel as if she had got into an exhausted receiver;° and the instinct of self-preservation, to say nothing of a philanthropic° desire to serve the race, caused a speedy change in Ward No. 1.

More flattering than the most gracefully turned compliment, more grateful than the most admiring glance, was the sight of those rows of faces, all strange to me a little while ago, now lighting up, with smiles of welcome, as I came among them, enjoying that moment heartily, with a womanly pride in their regard, a motherly affection for them all. The evenings were spent in reading aloud, writing letters, waiting on and amusing the men, going the rounds with Dr. P., as he made his second daily survey, dressing my dozen wounds afresh, giving last doses, and making them cozy for the long hours to come, till the nine o'clock bell rang, the gas was turned down, the day nurses went off duty, the night watch came on, and my nocturnal adventure began.

My ward was now divided into three rooms; and, under favor of the matron, I had managed to sort out the patients in such a way that I had what I called, "my duty room," my "pleasure room," and my "pathetic room," and worked for each in a different way. One, I visited, armed with a dressing tray, full of rollers, plasters,° and pins; another, with books, flowers, games, and gossip; a third, with teapots, lullabies, consolation, and sometimes, a shroud.

Wherever the sickest or most helpless man chanced to be, there I held my watch, often visiting the other rooms, to see that the general watchman of the ward did his duty by the fires and the wounds, the latter needing constant wetting. Not only on this account did I meander, but also to get fresher air than the close rooms afforded; for, owing to the stupidity of that mysterious "somebody" who does all the damage in the world, the windows had been carefully nailed down above, and the lower sashes could only be raised in the mildest weather, for the men lay just below. I had suggested a summary° smashing of a few panes here and there, when frequent appeals to headquarters had proved unavailing, and daily orders to lazy attendants had come to nothing. No one seconded the motion, however, and the nails were 50

---

blue devils: fits of depression or melancholy

dumps and dismals: depressions

receiver: receptacle

philanthropic: charitable, humanitarian

plasters: adhesive strips of material for dressing wounds

summary: done quickly and without ceremony

far beyond my reach; for, though belonging to the sisterhood of "ministering angels," I had no wings, and might as well have asked for Jacob's ladder,° as a pair of steps, in that charitable chaos.

One of the harmless ghosts who bore me company during the haunted hours, was Dan, the watchman, whom I regarded with a certain awe; for, though so much together, I never fairly saw his face, and, but for his legs, should never have recognized him, as we seldom met by day. These legs were remarkable, as was his whole figure, for his body was short, rotund, and done up in a big jacket, and muffler;° his beard hid the lower part of his face, his hat-brim the upper; and all I ever discovered was a pair of sleepy eyes, and a very mild voice. But the legs!—very long, very thin, very crooked and feeble, looking like grey sausages in their tight coverings, without a ray of pegtopishness° about them, and finished off with a pair of expansive, green cloth shoes, very like Chinese junks,° with the sails down. This figure, gliding noiselessly about the dimly lighted rooms, was strongly suggestive of the spirit of a beer barrel mounted on cork-screws, haunting the old hotel in search of its lost mates, emptied and staved in long ago.

Another goblin who frequently appeared to me, was the attendant of the pathetic room, who, being a faithful soul, was often up to tend two or three men, weak and wandering as babies, after the fever had gone. The amiable creature beguiled° the watches of the night by brewing jorums° of a fearful beverage, which he called coffee, and insisted on sharing with me; coming in with a great bowl of something like mud soup, scalding hot, guiltless of cream, rich in an all-pervading flavor of molasses, scorch and tin pot. Such an amount of good will and neighborly kindness also went into the mess, that I never could find the heart to refuse, but always received it with thanks, sipped it with hypocritical relish while he remained, and whipped it into the slop-jar the instant he departed, thereby gratifying him, securing one rousing laugh in the doziest hour of the night, and no one was the worse for the transaction but the pigs. Whether they were "cut off untimely in their sins," or not, I carefully abstained from inquiring.

It was a strange life—asleep half the day, exploring Washington the other half, and all night hovering, like a massive cherubim,° in a red rigolette,° over

---

Jacob's ladder: In the Book of Genesis, Jacob has a dream about a ladder to heaven while fleeing from his brother, Esau.

muffler: heavy scarf worn around the neck

pegtopishness: a humorous coinage of Alcott's, signifying the state of being peg-topped (wide at the waist and tapering toward the ankles)

junks: flat-bottomed ships

beguiled: passed pleasantly

jorums: large drinking bowls

cherubim: small, often chubby angel

rigolette: a woman's light, scarflike head covering

the slumbering sons of man. I liked it, and found many things to amuse, instruct, and interest me. The snores alone were quite a study, varying from the mild sniff to the stentorian° snort, which startled the echoes and hoisted the performer erect to accuse his neighbor of the deed, magnanimously forgive him, and wrapping the drapery of his couch about him, lie down to vocal slumber. After listening for a week to this band of wind instruments, I indulged in the belief that I could recognize each by the snore alone, and was tempted to join the chorus by breaking out with John Brown's favorite hymn:

"Blow ye the trumpet, blow!"

I would have given much to have possessed the art of sketching, for many of the faces became wonderfully interesting when unconscious. Some grew stern and grim, the men evidently dreaming of war, as they gave orders, groaned over their wounds, or damned the rebels vigorously; some grew sad and infinitely pathetic, as if the pain borne silently all day, revenged itself by now betraying what the man's pride had concealed so well. Often the roughest grew young and pleasant when sleep smoothed the hard lines away, letting the real nature assert itself; many almost seemed to speak, and I learned to know these men better by night than through any intercourse° by day. Sometimes they disappointed me, for faces that looked merry and good in the light, grew bad and sly when the shadows came; and though they made no confidences in words, I read their lives, leaving them to wonder at the change of manner this midnight magic wrought in their nurse. A few talked busily; one drummer boy sang sweetly, though no persuasions could win a note from him by day; and several depended on being told what they had talked of in the morning. Even my constitutionals° in the chilly halls, possessed a certain charm, for the house was never still. Sentinels tramped round it all night long, their muskets glittering in the wintry moonlight as they walked, or stood before the doors, straight and silent, as figures of stone, causing one to conjure up romantic visions of guarded forts, sudden surprises, and daring deeds; for in these war times the hum drum life of Yankeedom had vanished, and the most prosaic° feel some thrill of that excitement which stirs the nation's heart, and makes its capital a camp of hospitals. Wandering up and down these lower halls, I often heard cries from above, steps hurrying to and fro, saw surgeons passing up, or men coming down carrying a stretcher, where lay a long white figure whose face was shrouded and whose fight was done. Sometimes I stopped to watch the passers in the street, the moonlight shining on the spire opposite, or the

---

stentorian: very loud, booming

intercourse: interaction, communication

constitutionals: walks for one's health

prosaic: dull, unimaginative

gleam of some vessel floating, like a white-winged sea-gull, down the broad Potomac, whose fullest flow can never wash away the red stain of the land.

The night whose events I have a fancy to record, opened with a little comedy, 55 and closed with a great tragedy; for a virtuous and useful life untimely ended is always tragical to those who see not as God sees. My headquarters were beside the bed of a New Jersey boy, crazed by the horrors of that dreadful Saturday. A slight wound in the knee brought him there; but his mind had suffered more than his body; some string of that delicate machine was over strained, and, for days, he had been reliving in imagination, the scenes he could not forget, till his distress broke out in incoherent ravings, pitiful to hear. As I sat by him, endeavoring to soothe his poor distracted° brain by the constant touch of wet hands over his hot forehead, he lay cheering his comrades on, hurrying them back, then counting them as they fell around him, often clutching my arm, to drag me from the vicinity of a bursting shell, or covering up his head to screen himself from a shower of shot; his face brilliant with fever; his eyes restless; his head never still; every muscle strained and rigid; while an incessant stream of defiant shouts, whispered warnings, and broken laments, poured from his lips with that forceful bewilderment which makes such wanderings so hard to overhear.

It was past eleven, and my patient was slowly wearying himself into fitful intervals of quietude, when, in one of these pauses, a curious sound arrested my attention. Looking over my shoulder, I saw a one-legged phantom hopping nimbly down the room; and, going to meet it, recognized a certain Pennsylvania gentleman, whose wound-fever had taken a turn for the worse, and, depriving him of the few wits a drunken campaign had left him, set him literally tripping on the light, fantastic toe "toward home," as he blandly informed me, touching the military cap which formed a striking contrast to the severe simplicity of the rest of his decidedly undress uniform. When sane, the least movement produced a roar of pain or a volley of oaths; but the departure of reason seemed to have wrought an agreeable change, both in the man and his manners; for, balancing himself on one leg, like a meditative stork, he plunged into an animated discussion of the war, the President, lager beer, and Enfield rifles, regardless of any suggestions of mine as to the propriety of returning to bed, lest he be court-martialed for desertion.

Any thing more supremely ridiculous can hardly be imagined than this figure, scantily draped in white, its one foot covered with a big blue sock, a dingy cap set rakingly askew on its shaven head, and placid satisfaction beaming in its broad red face, as it flourished a mug in one hand, an old boot in the other, calling them canteen and knapsack, while it skipped and fluttered in the most unearthly fashion. What to do with the creature I didn't know;

---

distracted: confused, distraught

Dan was absent, and if I went to find him, the perambulator° might festoon° himself out of the window, set his toga on fire, or do some of his neighbors a mischief. The attendant of the room was sleeping like a near relative of the celebrated Seven, and nothing short of pins would rouse him; for he had been out that day, and whiskey asserted its supremacy in balmy whiffs. Still declaiming, in a fine flow of eloquence, the demented gentleman hopped on, blind and deaf to my graspings and entreaties; and I was about to slam the door in his face, and run for help, when a second and saner phantom, "all in white," came to the rescue, in the likeness of a big Prussian, who spoke no English, but divined the crisis, and put an end to it, by bundling the lively monoped° into his bed, like a baby, with an authoritative command to "stay put," which received added weight from being delivered in an odd conglomeration of French and German, accompanied by warning wags of a head decorated with a yellow cotton night cap, rendered most imposing by a tassel like a bell-pull. Rather exhausted by his excursion, the member from Pennsylvania subsided; and, after an irrepressible laugh together, my Prussian ally and myself were returning to our places, when the echo of a sob caused us to glance along the beds. It came from one in the corner—such a little bed!—and such a tearful little face looked up at us, as we stopped beside it! The twelve years old drummer boy was not singing now, but sobbing, with a manly effort all the while to stifle the distressful sounds that would break out.

"What is it, Teddy?" I asked, as he rubbed the tears away, and checked himself in the middle of a great sob to answer plaintively:

"I've got a chill, ma'am, but I aint cryin' for that, 'cause I'm used to it. I dreamed Kit was here, and when I waked up he wasn't, and I couldn't help it, then."

The boy came in with the rest, and the man who was taken dead from the ambulance was the Kit he mourned. Well he might; for, when the wounded were brought from Fredericksburg, the child lay in one of the camps thereabout, and this good friend, though sorely hurt himself, would not leave him to the exposure and neglect of such a time and place; but, wrapping him in his own blanket, carried him in his arms to the transport, tended him during the passage, and only yielded up his charge when Death met him at the door of the hospital which promised care and comfort for the boy. For ten days, Teddy had shivered or burned with fever and ague,° pining the while for Kit, and refusing to be comforted, because he had not been able to thank him for the generous protection, which, perhaps, had cost the giver's life. The vivid dream had wrung the childish heart with a fresh pang, and when I tried the solace fitted for his 60

perambulator: walker
festoon: hang, as a decoration
monoped: one-footed creature
ague: a chill or fit of shivering

years, the remorseful fear that haunted him found vent in a fresh burst of tears, as he looked at the wasted hands I was endeavoring to warm:

"Oh! if I'd only been as thin when Kit carried me as I am now, maybe he wouldn't have died; but I was heavy, he was hurt worser than we knew, and so it killed him; and I didn't see him, to say good bye."

This thought had troubled him in secret; and my assurances that his friend would probably have died at all events, hardly assuaged the bitterness of his regretful grief.

At this juncture, the delirious man began to shout; the one-legged rose up in his bed, as if preparing for another dart,° Teddy bewailed himself more piteously than before: and if ever a woman was at her wit's end, that distracted female was Nurse Periwinkle, during the space of two or three minutes, as she vibrated between the three beds, like an agitated pendulum. Like a most opportune reinforcement, Dan, the bandy, appeared, and devoted himself to the lively party, leaving me free to return to my post; for the Prussian, with a nod and a smile, took the lad away to his own bed, and lulled him to sleep with a soothing murmur, like a mammoth humble bee. I liked that in Fritz, and if he ever wondered afterward at the dainties° which sometimes found their way into his rations, or the extra comforts of his bed, he might have found a solution of the mystery in sundry persons' knowledge of the fatherly action of that night.

Hardly was I settled again, when the inevitable bowl appeared, and its bearer delivered a message I had expected, yet dreaded to receive:

"John is going, ma'am, and wants to see you, if you can come." 65

"The moment this boy is asleep; tell him so, and let me know if I am in danger of being too late."

My Ganymede° departed, and while I quieted poor Shaw, I thought of John. He came in a day or two after the others; and, one evening, when I entered my "pathetic room," I found a lately emptied bed occupied by a large, fair man, with a fine face, and the serenest eyes I ever met. One of the earlier comers had often spoken of a friend, who had remained behind, that those apparently worse wounded than himself might reach a shelter first. It seemed a David and Jonathan° sort of friendship. The man fretted for his mate, and was never tired of praising John—his courage, sobriety, self-denial, and unfailing kindliness of heart; always winding up with: "He's an out an' out fine feller, ma'am; you see if he aint."

---

dart: sudden, rapid movement

dainties: delicacies

Ganymede: In Greek myth, Ganymede is a Trojan prince abducted by Zeus to serve as cupbearer on Mt. Olympus.

David and Jonathan: King David of Israel and Jonathan, the son of his predecessor King Saul, are close friends in the Book of Samuel.

I had some curiosity to behold this piece of excellence, and when he came, watched him for a night or two, before I made friends with him; for, to tell the truth, I was a little afraid of the stately looking man, whose bed had to be lengthened to accommodate his commanding stature; who seldom spoke, uttered no complaint, asked no sympathy, but tranquilly observed what went on about him; and, as he lay high upon his pillows, no picture of dying stateman or warrior was ever fuller of real dignity than this Virginia blacksmith. A most attractive face he had, framed in brown hair and beard, comely featured and full of vigor, as yet unsubdued by pain; thoughtful and often beautifully mild while watching the afflictions of others, as if entirely forgetful of his own. His mouth was grave and firm, with plenty of will and courage in its lines, but a smile could make it as sweet as any woman's; and his eyes were child's eyes, looking one fairly in the face, with a clear, straightforward glance, which promised well for such as placed their faith in him. He seemed to cling to life, as if it were rich in duties and delights, and he had learned the secret of content.° The only time I saw his composure disturbed, was when my surgeon brought another to examine John, who scrutinized their faces with an anxious look, asking of the elder: "Do you think I shall pull through, sir?" "I hope so, my man." And, as the two passed on, John's eye still followed them, with an intentness which would have won a clearer answer from them, had they seen it. A momentary shadow flitted over his face; then came the usual serenity, as if, in that brief eclipse, he had acknowledged the existence of some hard possibility, and, asking nothing yet hoping all things, left the issue in God's hands, with that submission which is true piety.

The next night, as I went my rounds with Dr. P., I happened to ask which man in the room probably suffered most; and, to my great surprise, he glanced at John:

"Every breath he draws is like a stab; for the ball pierced the left lung, broke a rib, and did no end of damage here and there; so the poor lad can find neither forgetfulness nor ease, because he must lie on his wounded back or suffocate. It will be a hard struggle, and a long one, for he possesses great vitality; but even his temperate° life can't save him; I wish it could." 70

"You don't mean he must die, Doctor?"

"Bless you there's not the slightest hope for him; and you'd better tell him so before long; women have a way of doing such things comfortably, so I leave it to you. He won't last more than a day or two, at furthest."

I could have sat down on the spot and cried heartily, if I had not learned the wisdom of bottling up one's tears for leisure moments. Such an end seemed very hard for such a man, when half a dozen worn out, worthless bodies round him, were gathering up the remnants of wasted lives, to linger on for years

---

content: contentment

temperate: moderate

perhaps, burdens to others, daily reproaches to themselves. The army needed men like John, earnest, brave, and faithful; fighting for liberty and justice with both heart and hand, true soldiers of the Lord. I could not give him up so soon, or think with any patience of so excellent a nature robbed of its fulfillment, and blundered into eternity by the rashness or stupidity of those at whose hands so many lives may be required. It was an easy thing for Dr. P. to say: "Tell him he must die," but a cruelly hard thing to do, and by no means as "comfortable" as he politely suggested. I had not the heart to do it then, and privately indulged the hope that some change for the better might take place, in spite of gloomy prophesies; so, rendering my task unnecessary. A few minutes later, as I came in again, with fresh rollers, I saw John sitting erect, with no one to support him, while the surgeon dressed his back. I had never hitherto seen it done; for, having simpler wounds to attend to, and knowing the fidelity of the attendant, I had left John to him, thinking it might be more agreeable and safe; for both strength and experience were needed in his case. I had forgotten that the strong man might long for the gentle tendance of a woman's hands, the sympathetic magnetism of a woman's presence, as well as the feebler souls about him. The Doctor's words caused me to reproach myself with neglect, not of any real duty perhaps, but of those little cares and kindnesses that solace° homesick spirits, and make the heavy hours pass easier. John looked lonely and forsaken just then, as he sat with bent head, hands folded on his knee, and no outward sign of suffering, till, looking nearer, I saw great tears roll down and drop upon the floor. It was a new sight there; for, though I had seen many suffer, some swore, some groaned, most endured silently, but none wept. Yet it did not seem weak, only very touching, and straightway my fear vanished, my heart opened wide and took him in, as, gathering the bent head in my arms, as freely as if he had been a little child, I said, "Let me help you bear it, John."

Never, on any human countenance, have I seen so swift and beautiful a look of gratitude, surprise and comfort, as that which answered me more eloquently than the whispered—

"Thank you, ma'am, this is right good! this is what I wanted!" 75

"Then why not ask for it before?"

"I didn't like to be a trouble; you seemed so busy, and I could manage to get on alone."

"You shall not want° it any more, John."

Nor did he; for now I understood the wistful look that sometimes followed me, as I went out, after a brief pause beside his bed, or merely a passing nod, while busied with those who seemed to need me more than he, because more urgent in their demands; now I knew that to him, as to so many, I was the

---

solace: console

want: lack, do without

poor substitute for mother, wife, or sister, and in his eyes no stranger, but a friend who hitherto° had seemed neglectful; for, in his modesty, he had never guessed the truth. This was changed now; and, through the tedious operation of probing, bathing, and dressing his wounds, he leaned against me, holding my hand fast, and, if pain wrung further tears from him, no one saw them fall but me. When he was laid down again, I hovered about him, in a remorseful state of mind that would not let me rest, till I had bathed his face, brushed his "bonny brown hair," set all things smooth about him, and laid a knot of heath and heliotrope° on his clean pollow. While doing this, he watched me with the satisfied expression I so liked to see; and when I offered the little nosegay, held it carefully in his great hand, smoothed a ruffled leaf or two, surveyed and smelt it with an air of genuine delight, and lay contentedly regarding the glimmer of the sunshine on the green. Although the manliest man among my forty, he said, "Yes, ma'am," like a little boy; received suggestions for his comfort with the quick smile that brightened his whole face; and now and then, as I stood tidying the table by his bed, I felt him softly touch my gown, as if to assure himself that I was there. Anything more natural and frank I never saw, and found this brave John as bashful as brave, yet full of excellencies and fine aspirations, which, having no power to express themselves in words, seemed to have bloomed into his character and made him what he was.

After that night, an hour of each evening that remained to him was devoted to his ease or pleasure. He could not talk much, for breath was precious, and he spoke in whispers; but from occasional conversations, I gleaned° scraps of private history which only added to the affection and respect I felt for him. Once he asked me to write a letter, and as I settled pen and paper, I said, with an irrepressible glimmer of feminine curiosity, "Shall it be addressed to wife, or mother, John?" 80

"Neither, ma'am; I've got no wife, and will write to mother myself when I get better. Did you think I was married because of this?" he asked, touching a plain ring he wore, and often turned thoughtfully on his finger when he lay alone.

"Partly that, but more from a settled sort of look you have; a look which young men seldom get until they marry."

"I didn't know that; but I'm not so very young, ma'am, thirty in May, and have been what you might call settled this ten years; for mother's a widow, I'm the oldest child she has, and it wouldn't do for me to marry until Lizzy has a home of her own, and Laurie's learned his trade; for we're not rich, and I must be father to the children and husband to the dear old woman, if I can."

"No doubt but you are both, John; yet how came you to go to war, if you felt so? Wasn't enlisting as bad as marrying?"

---

hitherto: previously

heath and heliotrope: plants, flowers

gleaned: gathered

"No, ma'am, not as I see it, for one is helping my neighbor, the other pleasing myself. I went because I couldn't help it. I didn't want the glory or the pay; I wanted the right thing done, and people kept saying the men who were in earnest ought to fight. I was in earnest, the Lord knows! but I held off as long as I could, not knowing which was my duty; mother saw the case, gave me her ring to keep me steady, and said 'Go:' so I went." 85

A short story and a simple one, but the man and the mother were portrayed better than pages of fine writing could have done it.

"Do you ever regret that you came, when you lie here suffering so much?"

"Never, ma'am; I haven't helped a great deal, but I've shown I was willing to give my life, and perhaps I've got to; but I don't blame anybody, and if it was to do over again, I'd do it. I'm a little sorry I wasn't wounded in front; it looks cowardly to be hit in the back, but I obeyed orders, and it don't matter in the end, I know."

Poor John! it did not matter now, except that a shot in the front might have spared the long agony in store for him. He seemed to read the thought that troubled me, as he spoke so hopefully when there was no hope, for he suddenly added:

"This is my first battle; do they think it's going to be my last?" 90

"I'm afraid they do, John."

It was the hardest question I had ever been called upon to answer; doubly hard with those clear eyes fixed on mine, forcing a truthful answer by their own truth. He seemed a little startled at first, pondered over the fateful fact a moment, then shook his head, with a glance at the broad chest and muscular limbs stretched out before him:

"I'm not afraid, but it's difficult to believe all at once. I'm so strong it don't seem possible for such a little wound to kill me."

Merry Mercutio's° dying words glanced through my memory as he spoke: "'Tis not so deep as a well, nor so wide as a church door, but 'tis enough." And John would have said the same could he have seen the ominous black holes between his shoulders; he never had; and, seeing the ghastly sights about him, could not believe his own wound more fatal than these, for all the suffering it caused him.

"Shall I write to your mother, now?" I asked, thinking that these sudden tidings° might change all plans and purposes; but they did not; for the man received the order of the Divine Commander to march with the same unquestioning obedience with which the soldier had received that of the human one; doubtless remembering that the first led him to life, and the last to death. 95

Mercutio's: in Shakespeare's *Romeo and Juliet*

tidings: reports, news

"No, ma'am; to Laurie just the same; he'll break it to her best, and I'll add a line to her myself when you get done."

So I wrote the letter which he dictated, finding it better than any I had sent; for, though here and there a little ungrammatical or inelegant, each sentence came to me briefly worded, but most expressive; full of excellent counsel to the boy, tenderly bequeathing "mother and Lizzie" to his care, and bidding him good bye in words the sadder for their simplicity. He added a few lines, with steady hand, and, as I sealed it, said, with a patient sort of sigh, "I hope the answer will come in time for me to see it;" then, turning away his face, laid the flowers against his lips, as if to hide some quiver of emotion at the thought of such a sudden sundering° of all the dear home ties.

These things had happened two days before; now John was dying, and the letter had not come. I had been summoned to many death beds in my life, but to none that made my heart ache as it did then, since my mother called me to watch the departure of a spirit akin to this in its gentleness and patient strength. As I went in, John stretched out both hands:

"I knew you'd come! I guess I'm moving on, ma'am."

He was; and so rapidly that, even while he spoke, over his face I saw the grey veil falling that no human hand can lift. I sat down by him, wiped the drops from his forehead, stirred the air about him with the slow wave of a fan, and waited to help him die. He stood in sore need of help—and I could do so little; for, as the doctor had foretold, the strong body rebelled against death, and fought every inch of the way, forcing him to draw each breath with a spasm, and clench his hands with an imploring look, as if he asked, "How long must I endure this, and be still!" For hours he suffered dumbly,° without a moment's respite, or a moment's murmuring; his limbs grew cold, his face damp, his lips white, and, again and again, he tore the covering off his breast, as if the lightest weight added to his agony; yet through it all, his eyes never lost their perfect serenity, and the man's soul seemed to sit therein, undaunted by the ills that vexed his flesh. 100

One by one, the men woke, and round the room appeared a circle of pale faces and watchful eyes, full of awe and pity; for, though a stranger, John was beloved by all. Each man there had wondered° at his patience, respected his piety, admired his fortitude, and now lamented his hard death; for the influence of an upright nature had made itself deeply felt, even in one little week. Presently, the Jonathan who so loved this comely David, came creeping from his bed for a last look and word. The kind soul was full of trouble, as the choke in his voice, the grasp of his hand, betrayed; but there were no tears, and the farewell of the friends was the more touching for its brevity.

---

sundering: breaking off
dumbly: mutely, wordlessly
wondered: marveled

"Old boy, how are you?" faltered the one.

"Most° through, thank heaven!" whispered the other.

"Can I say or do anything for you anywheres?"

"Take my things home, and tell them that I did my best." 105

"I will! I will!"

"Good bye, Ned."

"Good bye, John, good bye!"

They kissed each other, tenderly as women, and so parted, for poor Ned could not stay to see his comrade die. For a little while, there was no sound in the room but the drip of water, from a stump or two, and John's distressful gasps, as he slowly beathed his life away. I thought him nearly gone, and had just laid down the fan, believing its help to be no longer needed, when suddenly he rose up in his bed, and cried out with a bitter cry that broke the silence, sharply startling every one with its agonized appeal:

"For God's sake, give me air!" 110

It was the only cry pain or death had wrung from him, the only boon° he had asked; and none of us could grant it, for all the airs that blew were useless now. Dan flung up the window. The first red streak of dawn was warming the grey east, a herald of the coming sun; John saw it, and with the love of light which lingers in us to the end, seemed to read in it a sign of hope of help, for, over his whole face there broke that mysterious expression, brighter than any smile, which often comes to eyes that look their last. He laid himself gently down; and, stretching out his strong right arm, as if to grasp and bring the blessed air to his lips in a fuller flow, lapsed into a merciful unconsciousness, which assured us that for him suffering was forever past. He died then; for, though the heavy breaths still tore their way up for a little longer, they were but the waves of an ebbing tide that beat unfelt against the wreck, which an immortal voyager had deserted with a smile. He never spoke again, but to the end held my hand close, so close that when he was asleep at last, I could not draw it away. Dan helped me, warning me as he did so that it was unsafe for dead and living flesh to lie so long together; but though my hand was strangely cold and stiff, and four white marks remained across its back, even when warmth and color had returned elsewhere, I could not but be glad that, through its touch, the presence of human sympathy, perhaps, had lightened that hard hour.

When they had made him ready for the grave, John lay in state for half an hour, a thing which seldom happened in that busy place; but a universal sentiment of reverence and affection seemed to fill the hearts of all who had known or heard of him; and when the rumor of his death went through the house, always astir, many came to see him, and I felt a tender sort of pride

---

Most: almost, mostly

boon: benefit

in my lost patient; for he looked a most heroic figure, lying there stately and still as the statue of some young knight asleep upon his tomb. The lovely expression which so often beautifies dead faces, soon replaced the marks of pain, and I longed for those who loved him best to see him when half an hour's acquaintance with Death had made them friends. As we stood looking at him, the ward master handed me a letter, saying it had been forgotten the night before. It was John's letter, come just an hour too late to gladden the eyes that had longed and looked for it so eagerly! yet he had it; for, after I had cut some brown locks° for his mother, and taken off the ring to send her, telling how well the talisman had done its work, I kissed this good son for her sake, and laid the letter in his hand, still folded as when I drew my own away, feeling that its place was there, and making myself happy with the thought, that, even in his solitary place in the "Government Lot," he would not be without some token of the love which makes life beautiful and outlives death. Then I left him, glad to have known so genuine a man, and carrying with me an enduring memory of the brave Virginia blacksmith, as he lay serenely waiting for the dawn of that long day which knows no night.

[1863]

Read

1. Where do you find humor in language or situation in this chapter?
2. What is the effect of the use of humor on you as a reader?
3. What do you think is the writer's aim in telling this story of the hospital ward?
4. How does dialogue reveal the nurse/narrator's relationship to her patients? How does it suggest the author's relationship to her readers?

Write

1. How would you describe the narrator's attitude toward war?
2. Describe how that attitude is like or unlike the author's.
3. Write a paragraph that explains the appeals Alcott makes use of in this passage.

Connect

1. Discuss how Mathew Brady's photograph in this unit compares with Alcott's piece in tone and detail.
2. How might Margaret Fuller view the nurse's actions and her commentary?

---

locks: tresses, hairs

Mathew Brady

Mathew Brady (c. 1822–1896) was a celebrated photographer who introduced new techniques to the art of photography. With over two thousand photos of the Civil War, he was the first to establish photojournalism as a field. Brady was born in New York to immigrant parents and began working with daguerreotypes. He photographed celebrities and political figures, such as an aging Andrew Jackson. His photographs of the Civil War, beginning in 1861 with the First Battle of Bull Run, provide historians much of what is known about that conflict. He photographed Lincoln many times, including a photograph that is the basis for the five dollar bill. After the war, Brady lost popularity as people tired of seeing images of the conflict. He died penniless.

Wounded Soldiers in Hospital

Wounded Soldiers in Hospital (ca. 1860–ca. 1865), Mathew Brady. War Department. Office of the Chief Signal Officer. (08/01/1866–09/18/1947)/Still Picture Records Section, NARA [ARC ID: 524705/Local ID: 111-B-286]

[c. 1860–c. 1865]

Read

1. Why does the photographer shoot a distant shot rather than a close up?
2. What tone does the photo convey to you?
3. What elements in the photograph reveal something of Brady's intention?

Write

1. Using your own background knowledge and reading, write a paragraph that describes the effect of the photograph on you as a viewer.
2. Comment on the conditions of the hospital ward as if you were a visitor.

Connect

1. How does the photo of the hospital scene compare with Alcott's version of the Civil War hospital?
2. Compare this photograph to Winslow Homer's painting in terms of their aims.

Lydia Howard Huntley Sigourney

Born in Connecticut, Lydia Sigourney (1791–1865) showed an early talent for writing. She was given an excellent education by a wealthy family friend who helped her publish her first book, *Moral Pieces,* in 1815. After she married in 1819, her publications declined for a few years until she resumed writing to supplement the family income. Sigourney published over sixty volumes of poetry and prose, and became a popular writer. Although critics claimed she was derivative and overly sentimental, her reputation has grown with the recovery of women's writing by feminist scholars.

Indian Names

Ye shall say they all have passed away,
    That noble race and brave,
That their light canoes have vanish'd
    From off the crested wave.
That 'mid the forests where they roam'd   5
    There rings no hunter's shout;
But their name is on your waters,
    Ye may not wash it out.

'Tis where Ontario's billow°
    Like Ocean's surge is curled;   10
Where strong Niagara's thunders wake
    The echo of the world;
Where red Missouri bringeth
    Rich tributes from the west,
And Rappahannock sweetly sleeps   15
    On green Virginia's breast.

Ye say, their cone-like cabins,
    That cluster'd o'er the vale,
Have fled away like wither'd leaves
    Before the autumn gale: 20

---

billow: great wave or swell of the sea

But their memory liveth on your hills,
    Their baptism° on your shore;
Your everlasting rivers speak
    Their dialect of yore.°

Old Massachusetts wears it 25
    Within her lordly crown,
And broad Ohio bears it
    'mid all her young renown;
Connecticut hath wreathed it
    Where her quiet foliage waves, 30
And bold Kentucky breathed it hoarse
    Through all her ancient caves.

Wachuset hides its lingering voice
    Within its rocky heart,
And Alleghany graves° its tone 35
    Throughout his lofty chart:°
Monadnock on his forehead hoar°
    Doth seal the sacred trust;°
Your mountains build their monument,
    Though ye destroy their dust. 40

Ye call these red-browned brethren
    The insects of an hour,
Crushed like the noteless° worm amid
    The regions of their power;
Ye drive them from their father's lands, 45
    Ye break of faith the seal,
But can ye from the court of Heaven
    Exclude their last appeal?

---

baptism: i.e., bestowing of names
yore: time past; long ago
graves: engraves
chart: map
hoar: hoary (covered with icy white frost)
trust: consignment for care or custody
noteless: not drawing notice, inconspicuous

Ye see their unresisting tribes,
With toilsome° step and slow, 50
On through the trackless desert pass
A caravan of woe;
Think ye the Eternal's° ear is deaf?
His sleepless vision dim?
Think ye the *soul's blood* may not cry 55
From that far land to him?

[1838]

Read

1. What is the speaker's aim in this poem?
2. How does the use of names help convey the aim?
3. Who do you think is the "you" the speaker addresses?
4. How can you infer the speaker's attitude toward the Indians whom people say "have all passed away"?

Write

1. Write a reflection responding to this poem.
2. Choose a few images or details to help you characterize the speaker's tone in this poem.

Connect

1. How does Sigourney's poem underscore or comment on Andrew Jackson's essay in Unit 2?
2. Do you think Sigourney is critical of the displacement of Indians here? Why or why not?

Harriet Beecher Stowe

Harriet Beecher Stowe (1811–1896) was raised in New England in a family dominated by her Calvinist preacher father, Lyman Beecher. She married a clergyman and, while tending her own family, wrote her most famous book, *Uncle Tom's Cabin.* It became an immediate sensation, drawing on Biblical references, slave narratives, and her experience with the Underground Railroad in Ohio and visits to slave plantations in Kentucky. Full of *pathos* and sensational scenes, the book became a manifesto for the cause of abolition. Stowe also wrote journalistic accounts of New England, and fifteen other novels.

---

toilsome: laborious, wearisome
the Eternal's: God's

From *Uncle Tom's Cabin, or Life Among the Lowly*

The scenes of this story, as its title indicates, lie among a race hitherto° ignored by the associations of polite and refined society; an exotic race, whose ancestors, born beneath a tropic sun, brought with them, and perpetuated to their descendants, a character so essentially unlike the hard and dominant Anglo-Saxon race, as for many years to have won from it only misunderstanding and contempt.

But, another and better day is dawning; every influence of literature, of poetry and of art, in our times, is becoming more and more in unison with the great master chord of Christianity, "good will to man."

The poet, the painter, and the artist, now seek out and embellish the common and gentler humanities of life, and, under the allurements of fiction, breathe a humanizing and subduing influence, favorable to the development of the great principles of Christian brotherhood.

The hand of benevolence is everywhere stretched out, searching into abuses, righting wrongs, alleviating distresses, and bringing to the knowledge and sympathies of the world the lowly, the oppressed, and the forgotten.

In this general movement, unhappy Africa at last is remembered; 5
Africa, who began the race of civilization and human progress in the dim, gray dawn of early time, but who, for centuries, has lain bound and bleeding at the foot of civilized and Christianized humanity, imploring compassion in vain.

But the heart of the dominant race, who have been her conquerors, her hard masters, has at length been turned towards her in mercy; and it has been seen how far nobler it is in nations to protect the feeble than to oppress them. Thanks be to God, the world has at last outlived the slave-trade!

The object of these sketches° is to awaken sympathy and feeling for the African race, as they exist among us; to show their wrongs and sorrows, under a system so necessarily cruel and unjust as to defeat and do away the good effects of all that can be attempted for them, by their best friends, under it.

In doing this, the author can sincerely disclaim any invidious° feeling towards those individuals who, often without any fault of their

---

hitherto: previously
sketches: informal writings
invidious: resentful, hateful

own, are involved in the trials and embarrassments of the legal relations of slavery.

Experience has shown her that some of the noblest of minds and hearts are often thus involved; and no one knows better than they do, that what may be gathered of the evils of slavery from sketches like these, is not the half that could be told, of the unspeakable whole.

In the northern states, these representations may, perhaps, be thought caricatures; in the southern states are witnesses who know their fidelity.° What personal knowledge the author has had, of the truth of incidents such as here are related, will appear in its time. 10

It is a comfort to hope, as so many of the world's sorrows and wrongs have, from age to age, been lived down, so a time shall come when sketches similar to these shall be valuable only as memorials of what has long ceased to be.

When an enlightened and Christianized community shall have, on the shores of Africa, laws, language and literature drawn from among us, may then the scenes of the house of bondage be to them like the remembrance of Egypt to the Israelite,—a motive of thankfulness to Him who hath redeemed them!

For, while politicians contend, and men are swerved this way and that by conflicting tides of interest and passion, the great cause of human liberty is in the hands of one, of whom it is said:

> "He shall not fail nor be discouraged
> Till He have set judgment in the earth."
> "He shall deliver the needy when he crieth,
> The poor, and him that hath no helper."
> "He shall redeem their soul from deceit and violence,
> And precious shall their blood be in His sight."

CHAPTER I

In which the Reader is Introduced to a Man of Humanity

Late in the afternoon of a chilly day in February, two gentlemen were sitting alone over their wine, in a well-furnished dining parlor, in the town of P——, in Kentucky. There were no servants present, and the gentlemen, with chairs closely approaching, seemed to be discussing some subject with great earnestness.

For convenience sake, we have said, hitherto, two *gentlemen*. 15
One of the parties, however, when critically examined, did not seem,

---

fidelity: to the truth; i.e., accuracy

strictly speaking, to come under the species. He was a short, thick-set man, with coarse, commonplace features and that swaggering air of pretension which marks a low man who is trying to elbow his way upward in the world. He was much over-dressed, in a gaudy vest of many colors, a blue neckerchief, bedropped gayly with yellow spots and arranged with a flaunting tie, quite in keeping with the general air of the man. His hands, large and coarse, were plentifully bedecked with rings; and he wore a heavy gold watch-chain, with a bundle of seals° of portentous size, and a great variety of colors, attached to it,—which, in the ardor of conversation, he was in the habit of flourishing and jingling with evident satisfaction. His conversation was in free and easy defiance of Murray's Grammar,° and was garnished at convenient intervals with various profane expressions, which not even the desire to be graphic in our account shall induce us to transcribe.

His companion, Mr. Shelby, had the appearance of a gentleman; and the arrangements of the house, and the general air of the housekeeping, indicated easy, and even opulent° circumstances. As we before stated, the two were in the midst of an earnest conversation.

"That is the way I should arrange the matter," said Mr. Shelby.

"I can't make trade that way—I positively can't, Mr. Shelby," said the other, holding up a glass of wine between his eye and the light.

"Why, the fact is, Haley, Tom is an uncommon fellow; he is certainly worth that sum anywhere,—steady, honest, capable, manages my whole farm like a clock."

"You mean honest, as niggers go," said Haley, helping himself to a glass of brandy. 20

"No; I mean, really, Tom is a good, steady, sensible, pious fellow. He got religion at a camp-meeting, four years ago; and I believe he really *did* get it. I've trusted him, since then, with everything I have,—money, house, horses,—and let him come and go round the country; and I always found him true and square in everything."

"Some folks don't believe there is pious niggers, Shelby," said Haley, with a candid flourish of his hand, "but *I do.* I had a fellow, now, in this yer° last lot I took to Orleans—'t was as good as a meetin',° now, really, to hear that critter pray; and he was quite gentle and quiet like. He fetched me a good sum, too, for I bought him cheap of a man

seals: dies or signets used to stamp impressions in soft substances such as wax

Murray's Grammar: *English Grammar Adapted to the Different Classes of Learners,* first published in 1795, by American grammarian Lindley Murray (1745–1826)

opulent: affluent

yer: corruption of *here*

meetin': religious service

that was 'bliged to sell out; so I realized six hundred on him. Yes, I consider religion a valeyable thing in a nigger, when it's the genuine article, and no mistake."

"Well, Tom's got the real article, if ever a fellow had," rejoined the other. "Why, last fall, I let him go to Cincinnati alone, to do business for me, and bring home five hundred dollars. 'Tom,' says I to him, 'I trust you, because I think you're a Christian—I know you wouldn't cheat.' Tom comes back, sure enough; I knew he would. Some low fellows, they say, said to him—'Tom, why don't you make tracks for Canada?' 'Ah, master trusted me, and I could n't,'—they told me about it. I am sorry to part with Tom, I must say. You ought to let him cover the whole balance of the debt; and you would, Haley, if you had any conscience."

"Well, I've got just as much conscience as any man in business can afford to keep,—just a little, you know, to swear by, as 't were," said the trader, jocularly;° "and, then, I 'm ready to do anything in reason to 'blige friends; but this yer, you see, is a leetle too hard on a fellow—a leetle too hard." The trader sighed contemplatively, and poured out some more brandy.

"Well, then, Haley, how will you trade?" said Mr. Shelby, after an uneasy interval of silence. 25

"Well, have n't you a boy or gal that you could throw in with Tom?"

"Hum!—none that I could well spare; to tell the truth, it 's only hard necessity makes me willing to sell at all. I don't like parting with any of my hands, that's a fact."

Here the door opened, and a small quadroon° boy, between four and five years of age, entered the room. There was something in his appearance remarkably beautiful and engaging. His black hair, fine as floss silk, hung in glossy curls about his round, dimpled face, while a pair of large dark eyes, full of fire and softness, looked out from beneath the rich, long lashes, as he peered curiously into the apartment. A gay° robe of scarlet and yellow plaid, carefully made and neatly fitted, set off to advantage the dark and rich style of his beauty; and a certain comic air of assurance, blended with bashfulness, showed that he had been not unused to being petted and noticed by his master.

"Hulloa, Jim Crow!" said Mr. Shelby, whistling, and snapping a bunch of raisins towards him, "pick that up, now!"

The child scampered, with all his little strength, after the prize, while his master laughed. 30

---

jocularly: lightly, jokingly

quadroon: some who is one-quarter black

gay: brightly colored

"Come here, Jim Crow," said he. The child came up, and the master patted the curly head, and chucked him under the chin.

"Now, Jim, show this gentleman how you can dance and sing." The boy commenced one of those wild, grotesque songs common among the negroes, in a rich, clear voice, accompanying his singing with many comic evolutions of the hands, feet, and whole body, all in perfect time to the music.

"Bravo!" said Haley, throwing him a quarter of an orange.

"Now, Jim, walk like old Uncle Cudjoe, when he has the rheumatism," said his master.

35 Instantly the flexible limbs of the child assumed the appearance of deformity and distortion, as, with his back humped up, and his master's stick in his hand, he hobbled about the room, his childish face drawn into a doleful pucker, and spitting from right to left, in imitation of an old man.

Both gentlemen laughed uproariously.

"Now, Jim," said his master, "show us how old Elder Robbins leads the psalm." The boy drew his chubby face down to a formidable length, and commenced toning a psalm tune through his nose, with imperturbable° gravity.°

"Hurrah! bravo! what a young 'un!" said Haley; "that chap's a case, I'll promise. Tell you what," said he, suddenly clapping his hand on Mr. Shelby's shoulder, "fling in that chap, and I'll settle the business—I will. Come, now, if that ain't doing the thing up about the rightest!"

At this moment, the door was pushed gently open, and a young quadroon woman, apparently about twenty-five, entered the room.

40 There needed only a glance from the child to her, to identify her as its mother. There was the same rich, full, dark eye, with its long lashes; the same ripples of silky black hair. The brown of her complexion gave way on the cheek to a perceptible flush, which deepened as she saw the gaze of the strange man fixed upon her in bold and undisguised admiration. Her dress was of the neatest possible fit, and set off to advantage her finely moulded shape;—a delicately formed hand and a trim foot and ankle were items of appearance that did not escape the quick eye of the trader, well used to run up at a glance the points of a fine female article.

"Well, Eliza?" said her master, as she stopped and looked hesitatingly at him.

"I was looking for Harry, please, sir;" and the boy bounded toward her, showing his spoils,° which he had gathered in the skirt of his robe.

---

imperturbable: calm, unexcitable

gravity: seriousness

spoils: goods won or seized

"Well, take him away, then," said Mr. Shelby; and hastily she withdrew, carrying the child on her arm.

"By Jupiter," said the trader, turning to him in admiration, "there's an article, now! You might make your fortune on that ar° gal in Orleans, any day. I've seen over a thousand, in my day, paid down for gals not a bit handsomer."

"I don't want to make my fortune on her," said Mr. Shelby, dryly;° and, seeking to turn the conversation, he uncorked a bottle of fresh wine, and asked his companion's opinion of it. 45

"Capital, sir—first chop!" said the trader; then turning, and slapping his hand familiarly on Shelby's shoulder, he added—

"Come, how will you trade about the gal?—what shall I say for her—what'll you take?"

"Mr. Haley, she is not to be sold," said Shelby. "My wife would not part with her for her weight in gold."

"Ay, ay! women always say such things, cause they ha'nt no sort of calculation. Just show 'em how many watches, feathers, and trinkets, one's weight in gold would buy, and that alters the case, *I* reckon."

"I tell you, Haley, this must not be spoken of; I say no, and I mean no," said Shelby, decidedly. 50

"Well, you 'll let me have the boy, though," said the trader; "you must own I've come down pretty handsomely for him."

"What on earth can you want with the child?" said Shelby.

"Why, I've got a friend that's going into this yer branch of the business—wants to buy up handsome boys to raise for the market. Fancy articles sentirely—sell for waiters, and so on, to rich 'uns, that can pay for handsome 'uns. It sets off one of yer great places—a real handsome boy to open door, wait, and tend. They fetch a good sum; and this little devil is such a comical, musical concern, he's just the article."

"I would rather not sell him," said Mr. Shelby, thoughtfully; "the fact is, sir, I 'm a humane man, and I hate to take the boy from his mother, sir."

"O, you do?—La! yes—something of that ar natur. I understand, perfectly. It is mighty onpleasant getting on with women, sometimes. I al'ays hates these yer screachin', screamin' times. They are *mighty* onpleasant; but, as I manages business, I generally avoids 'em, sir. Now, what if you get the girl off for a day, or a week, or so; then the thing's done quietly,—all over before she comes home. Your wife might get her some ear-rings, or a new gown, or some such truck,° to make up with her." 55

ar: corruption of *there*

dryly: in a lightly humorous or sarcastic manner

truck: stuff

"I'm afraid not."

"Lor bless ye, yes! These critters an't like white folks, you know; they gets over things, only manage right. Now, they say," said Haley, assuming a candid and confidential air, "that this kind o' trade is hardening to the feelings; but I never found it so. Fact is, I never could do things up the way some fellers manage the business. I 've seen 'em as would pull a woman's child out of her arms, and set him up to sell, and she screechin' like mad all the time;—very bad policy—damages the article—makes 'em quite unfit for service sometimes. I knew a real handsome gal once, in Orleans, as was entirely ruined by this sort o' handling. The fellow that was trading for her did n't want° her baby; and she was one of your real high sort, when her blood was up. I tell you, she squeezed up her child in her arms, and talked, and went on real awful. It kinder makes my blood run cold to think on 't; and when they carried off the child, and locked her up, she jest went ravin' mad and died in a week. Clear waste, sir, of a thousand dollars, just for want of management,—there 's where 't is. It's always best to do the humane thing, sir; that's been *my* experience." And the trader leaned back in his chair, and folded his arm, with an air of virtuous decision, apparently considering himself a second Wilberforce.°

The subject appeared to interest the gentleman deeply; for while Mr. Shelby was thoughtfully peeling an orange, Haley broke out afresh, with becoming° diffidence,° but as if actually driven by the force of truth to say a few words more.

"It don't look well, now, for a feller to be praisin' himself; but I say it jest because it's the truth. I believe I'm reckoned to bring in about the finest droves of niggers that is brought in,—at least, I've been told so; if I have once, I reckon I have a hundred times,—all in good case,—fat and likely, and I lose as few as any man in the business. And I lays it all to my management, sir; and humanity, sir, I may say, is the great pillar of *my* management."

Mr. Shelby did not know what to say, and so he said, "Indeed!" 60

"Now, I've been laughed at for my notions, sir, and I've been talked to. They an't pop'lar, and they an't common; but I stuck to 'em, sir; I've stuck to 'em, and realized° well on 'em; yes, sir, they have paid their passage, I may say," and the trader laughed at his joke.

---

want: lack

Wilberforce: William Wilberforce (1759–1833), British leader of the movement to abolish the slave trade

becoming: pleasing

diffidence: unassertiveness

realized: profited

There was something so piquant° and original in these elucidations° of humanity, that Mr. Shelby could not help laughing in company. Perhaps you laugh too, dear reader; but you know humanity comes out in a variety of strange forms now-a-days, and there is no end to the odd things that humane people will say and do.

Mr. Shelby's laugh encouraged the trader to proceed.

"It's strange now, but I never could beat this into people's heads. Now, there was Tom Loker, my old partner, down in Natchez; he was a clever fellow, Tom was, only the very devil with niggers,—on principle 't was, you see, for a better hearted feller never broke bread; 't was his *system,* sir. I used to talk to Tom. 'Why, Tom,' I used to say, 'when your gals takes on and cry, what's the use o' crackin on 'em over the head, and knockin' on 'em round? It's ridiculous,' says I, 'and don't do no sort o' good. Why, I don't see no harm in their cryin',' says I; 'it's natur,' says I, 'and if natur can't blow off one way, it will another. Besides, Tom,' says I, 'it jest spiles° your gals; they get sickly, and down in the mouth; and sometimes they gets ugly,—particular yallow° gals do,—and it's the devil and all gettin' on 'em broke in. Now,' says I, 'why can't you kinder coax 'em up, and speak 'em fair? Depend on it, Tom, a little humanity, thrown in along, goes a heap further than all your jawin' and crackin'; and it pays better,' says I, 'depend on 't.' But Tom could n't get the hang on 't; and he spiled so many for me, that I had to break off with him, though he was a good-hearted fellow, and as fair a business hand as is goin'."

"And do you find your ways of managing do the business better than Tom's?" said Mr. Shelby. 65

"Why, yes, sir, I may say so. You see, when I any ways can, I takes a leetle care about the onpleasant parts like selling young uns and that,—get the gals out of the way—out of sight, out of mind, you know,—and when it's clean done, and can't be helped, they naturally gets used to it. 'Tan't,° you know, as if it was white folks, that 's brought up in the way of 'spectin' to keep their children and wives, and all that. Niggers, you know, that's fetched up° properly, ha'n't no kind of 'spectations of no kind; so all these things comes easier."

"I 'm afraid mine are not properly brought up, then," said Mr. Shelby.

---

piquant: spicy, stimulating
elucidations: explanations, clarifications
spiles: spoils
yallow: yellow; a light-skinned, mixed-race black person
'T an't: It ain't
fetched up: brought up, raised

"S'pose not; you Kentucky folks spile your niggers. You mean well by 'em, but 'tan't no real kindness, arter all. Now, a nigger, you see, what's got to be hacked and tumbled round the world, and sold to Tom, and Dick, and the Lord knows who, 'tan't no kindness to be givin' on him notions and expectations, and bringin' on him up too well, for the rough and tumble comes all the harder on him arter. Now, I venture to say, your niggers would be quite chop-fallen° in a place where some of your plantation niggers would be singing and whooping like all possessed. Every man, you know, Mr. Shelby, naturally thinks well of his own ways; and I think I treat niggers just about as well as it's ever worth while to treat 'em."

"It 's a happy thing to be satisfied," said Mr. Shelby, with a slight shrug, and some perceptible feelings of a disagreeable nature.

"Well," said Haley, after they had both silently picked their nuts for a season,° "what do you say?" 70

"I'll think the matter over, and talk with my wife," said Mr. Shelby. "Meantime, Haley, if you want the matter carried on in the quiet way you speak of, you'd best not let your business in this neighborhood be known. It will get out among my boys, and it will not be a particularly quiet business getting away any of my fellows, if they know it, I'll promise you."

"O! certainly, by all means, mum! of course. But I'll tell you, I'm in a devil of a hurry, and shall want to know, as soon as possible, what I may depend on," said he, rising and putting on his overcoat.

"Well, call up° this evening, between six and seven, and you shall have my answer," said Mr. Shelby, and the trader bowed himself out of the apartment.

"I'd like to have been able to kick the fellow down the steps," said he to himself, as he saw the door fairly closed, "with his impudent° assurance; but he knows how much he has me at advantage. If anybody had ever said to me that I should sell Tom down South to one of those rascally traders, I should have said, 'Is thy servant a dog, that he should do this thing?'° And now it must come, for aught I see.

---

chop-fallen: downcast, dejected (variant of *chapfallen*)

picked their nuts for a season: Critic Jay Parini explains this curious phrase as follows: "Stowe often writes metaphorically, as when Haley and Shelby finish the initial conversation and Shelby mulls over his options . . . . (They eat nuts, quite literally; but to pick one's nuts for a season was figurative as well as literal.) A momentous decision is taken, and 'a season' was necessary to make it, in the form of a long pause for thinking" (*Promised Land: Thirteen Books That Changed America*, New York: Doubleday, 2008).

call up: come round

impudent: bold, insolent

"Is thy servant . . . such a thing": from the Second Book of Kings (Bible)

And Eliza's child, too! I know that I shall have some fuss with wife about that; and, for that matter, about Tom, too. So much for being in debt,—heigho! The fellow sees his advantage, and means to push it."

75

Perhaps the mildest form of the system of slavery is to be seen in the State of Kentucky. The general prevalence of agricultural pursuits of a quiet and gradual nature, not requiring those periodic seasons of hurry and pressure that are called for in the business of more southern districts, makes the task of the negro a more healthful and reasonable one; while the master, content with a more gradual style of acquisition, has not those temptations to hardheartedness which always overcome frail human nature when the prospect of sudden and rapid gain is weighed in the balance, with no heavier counterpoise° than the interests of the helpless and unprotected.

Whoever visits some estates there, and witnesses the good-humored indulgence of some masters and mistresses, and the affectionate loyalty of some slaves, might be tempted to dream the oft-fabled poetic legend of a patriarchal° institution, and all that; but over and above the scene there broods a portentous° shadow—the shadow of *law*. So long as the law considers all these human beings, with beating hearts and living affections, only as so many *things* belonging to a master,—so long as the failure, or misfortune, or imprudence, or death of the kindest owner, may cause them any day to exchange a life of kind protection and indulgence for one of hopeless misery and toil,—so long it is impossible to make anything beautiful or desirable in the best regulated administration of slavery.

Mr. Shelby was a fair average kind of man, good-natured and kindly, and disposed to easy indulgence of those around him, and there had never been a lack of anything which might contribute to the physical comfort of the negroes on his estate. He had, however, speculated largely and quite loosely; had involved himself deeply, and his notes° to a large amount had come into the hands of Haley; and this small piece of information is the key to the preceding conversation.

Now, it had so happened that, in approaching the door, Eliza had caught enough of the conversation to know that a trader was making offers to her master for somebody.

She would gladly have stopped at the door to listen, as she came out; but her mistress just then calling, she was obliged to hasten away.

---

counterpoise: counterbalance

patriarchal: implying here a sort of familial arrangement, in which a wise and benevolent father figure takes proper care of those under his authority

portentous: ominous

notes: promissory notes

Still she thought she heard the trader make an offer for her boy;—could she be mistaken? Her heart swelled and throbbed, and she involuntarily strained him so tight that the little fellow looked up into her face in astonishment. 80

"Eliza, girl, what ails you to-day?" said her mistress, when Eliza had upset the wash-pitcher, knocked down the work-stand, and finally was abstractedly° offering her mistress a long night-gown in place of the silk dress she had ordered her to bring from the wardrobe.

Eliza started. "O, missis!" she said, raising her eyes; then, bursting into tears, she sat down in a chair, and began sobbing.

"Why, Eliza, child! what ails you?" said her mistress.

"O! missis, missis," said Eliza, "there's been a trader talking with master in the parlor! I heard him."

"Well, silly child, suppose there has." 85

"O, missis, *do* you suppose mas'r would sell my Harry?" And the poor creature threw herself into a chair, and sobbed convulsively.

"Sell him! No, you foolish girl! You know your master never deals with those southern traders, and never means to sell any of his servants, as long as they behave well. Why, you silly child, who do you think would want to buy your Harry? Do you think all the world are set on him as you are, you goosie? Come, cheer up, and hook my dress. There now, put my back hair up in that pretty braid you learnt the other day, and don't go listening at doors any more."

"Well, but, missis, *you* never would give your consent—to—to—"

"Nonsense, child! to be sure, I should n't. What do you talk so for? I would as soon have one of my own children sold. But really, Eliza, you are getting altogether too proud of that little fellow. A man can't put his nose into the door, but you think he must be coming to buy him."

Reässured by her mistress' confident tone, Eliza proceeded nimbly and adroitly with her toilet,° laughing at her own fears, as she proceeded. 90

Mrs. Shelby was a woman of a high class, both intellectually and morally. To that natural magnanimity° and generosity of mind which one often marks as characteristic of the women of Kentucky, she added high moral and religious sensibility and principle, carried out with great energy and ability into practical results. Her husband, who made no professions° to any particular religious character,°

---

abstractedly: inattentively, absentmindedly
toilet: business of dressing or grooming oneself
magnanimity: benevolence, charitableness
professions: affirmations, declarations
character: nature

nevertheless reverenced and respected the consistency of hers, and stood, perhaps, a little in awe of her opinion. Certain it was that he gave her unlimited scope in all her benevolent efforts for the comfort, instruction, and improvement of her servants, though he never took any decided° part in them himself. In fact, if not exactly a believer in the doctrine of the efficiency of the extra good works of saints, he really seemed somehow or other to fancy that his wife had piety and benevolence enough for two—to indulge a shadowy expectation of getting into heaven through her superabundance of qualities to which he made no particular pretension.

The heaviest load on his mind, after his conversation with the trader, lay in the foreseen necessity of breaking to his wife the arrangement contemplated, meeting the importunities° and opposition which he knew he should have reason to encounter.

Mrs. Shelby, being entirely ignorant of her husband's embarrassments,° and knowing only the general kindliness of his temper, had been quite sincere in the entire incredulity° with which she had met Eliza's suspicions. In fact, she dismissed the matter from her mind, without a second thought; and being occupied in preparations for an evening visit, it passed out of her thoughts entirely.

CHAPTER VII

The Mother's Struggle

It is impossible to conceive of a human creature more wholly desolate and forlorn than Eliza, when she turned her footsteps from Uncle Tom's cabin.

Her husband's suffering and dangers, and the danger of her child, all blended in her mind, with a confused and stunning sense of the risk she was running, in leaving the only home she had ever known, and cutting loose from the protection of a friend whom she loved and revered. Then there was the parting from every familiar object,—the place where she had grown up, the trees under which she had played, the groves where she had walked many an evening in happier days, by the side of her young husband,—everything, as it lay in the clear, frosty starlight, seemed to speak reproachfully to her, and ask her whither° could she go from a home like that?

95

decided: definite
importunities: pleadings
embarrassments: financial difficulties
incredulity: disbelief
whither: where

But stronger than all was maternal love, wrought into a paroxysm of frenzy by the near approach of a fearful danger. Her boy was old enough to have walked by her side, and, in an indifferent case,° she would only have led him by the hand; but now the bare thought of putting him out of her arms made her shudder, and she strained him to her bosom with a convulsive grasp, as she went rapidly forward.

The frosty ground creaked beneath her feet, and she trembled at the sound; every quaking leaf and fluttering shadow sent the blood backward to her heart, and quickened her footsteps. She wondered° within herself at the strength that seemed to be come upon her; for she felt the weight of her boy as if it had been a feather, and every flutter of fear seemed to increase the supernatural power that bore her on, while from her pale lips burst forth, in frequent ejaculations,° the prayer to a Friend above—"Lord, help! Lord, save me!"

If it were *your* Harry, mother, or your Willie, that were going to be torn from you by a brutal trader, to-morrow morning,—if you had seen the man, and heard that the papers were signed and delivered, and you had only from twelve o'clock till morning to make good your escape,—how fast could *you* walk? How many miles could you make in those few brief hours, with the darling at your bosom,—the little sleepy head on your shoulder,—the small, soft arms trustingly holding on to your neck?

For the child slept. At first, the novelty and alarm kept him waking; but his mother so hurriedly repressed every breath or sound, and so assured him that if he were only still she would certainly save him, that he clung quietly round her neck, only asking, as he found himself sinking to sleep,

"Mother, I don't need to keep awake, do I?" 100

"No, my darling; sleep, if you want to."

"But, mother, if I do get asleep, you won't let him get me?"

"No! so may God help me!" said his mother, with a paler cheek, and a brighter light in her large dark eyes.

"You 're *sure*, an't you, mother?"

"Yes, *sure*!" said the mother, in a voice that startled herself; for 105 it seemed to her to come from a spirit within, that was no part of her; and the boy dropped his little weary head on her shoulder, and was soon asleep. How the touch of those warm arms, the gentle breathings that came in her neck, seemed to add fire and spirit to her movements! It seemed to her as if strength poured into her in

---

indifferent case: unimportant situation
wondered: marveled
ejaculations: exclamations

electric streams, from every gentle touch and movement of the sleeping, confiding child. Sublime° is the dominion of the mind over the body, that, for a time, can make flesh and nerve impregnable,° and string the sinews° like steel, so that the weak become so mighty.

The boundaries of the farm, the grove, the wood-lot, passed by her dizzily, as she walked on; and still she went, leaving one familiar object after another, slacking not, pausing not, till reddening daylight found her many a long mile from all traces of any familiar objects upon the open highway.

She had often been, with her mistress, to visit some connections, in the little village of T——, not far from the Ohio river, and knew the road well. To go thither,° to escape across the Ohio river, were the first hurried outlines of her plan of escape; beyond that, she could only hope in God.

When horses and vehicles began to move along the highway, with that alert perception peculiar to a state of excitement, and which seems to be a sort of inspiration, she became aware that her headlong pace and distracted air might bring on her remark° and suspicion. She therefore put the boy on the ground, and, adjusting her dress and bonnet, she walked on at as rapid a pace as she thought consistent with the preservation of appearances. In her little bundle she had provided a store of cakes and apples, which she used as expedients° for quickening the speed of the child, rolling the apple some yards before them, when the boy would run with all his might after it; and this ruse, often repeated, carried them over many a half-mile.

After a while, they came to a thick patch of woodland, through which murmured a clear brook. As the child complained of hunger and thirst, she climbed over the fence with him; and, sitting down behind a large rock which concealed them from the road, she gave him a breakfast out of her little package. The boy wondered and grieved that she could not eat; and when, putting his arms round her neck, he tried to wedge some of his cake into her mouth, it seemed to her that the rising in her throat would choke her.

"No, no, Harry darling! mother can't eat till you are safe! We must go on—on—till we come to the river!" And she hurried again

110

Sublime: glorious, inspiring
impregnable: unassailable, invincible
sinews: tendons
thither: there
remark: notice
expedients: means, devices

into the road, and again constrained herself to walk regularly and composedly forward.

She was many miles past any neighborhood where she was personally known. If she should chance to meet any who knew her, she reflected that the well-known kindness of the family would be of itself a blind° to suspicion, as making it an unlikely supposition that she could be a fugitive. As she was also so white as not to be known as of colored lineage, without a critical survey,° and her child was white also, it was much easier for her to pass on unsuspected.

On this presumption, she stopped at noon at a neat farm-house, to rest herself, and buy some dinner for her child and self; for, as the danger decreased with the distance, the supernatural tension of the nervous system lessened, and she found herself both weary and hungry.

The good woman, kindly and gossipping, seemed rather pleased than otherwise with having somebody come in to talk with; and accepted, without examination, Eliza's statement, that she "was going on a little piece, to spend a week with her friends,"—all which she hoped in her heart might prove strictly true.

An hour before sunset, she entered the village of T——, by the Ohio river, weary and foot-sore, but still strong in heart. Her first glance was at the river, which lay, like Jordan, between her and the Canaan of liberty on the other side.

115 It was now early spring, and the river was swollen and turbulent; great cakes of floating ice were swinging heavily to and fro in the turbid waters. Owing to the peculiar form of the shore on the Kentucky side, the land bending far out into the water, the ice had been lodged and detained in great quantities, and the narrow channel which swept round the bend was full of ice, piled one cake over another, thus forming a temporary barrier to the descending ice, which lodged, and formed a great, undulating raft, filling up the whole river, and extending almost to the Kentucky shore.

Eliza stood, for a moment, contemplating this unfavorable aspect of things, which she saw at once must prevent the usual ferry-boat from running, and then turned into a small public house° on the bank, to make a few inquiries.

The hostess, who was busy in various fizzing and stewing operations over the fire, preparatory to the evening meal, stopped, with a fork in her hand, as Eliza's sweet and plaintive° voice arrested her.

---

blind: obstruction
critical survey: careful examination
public house: inn, tavern
plaintive: sorrowful

"What is it?" she said.

"Is n't there any ferry or boat, that takes people over to B——, now?" she said.

"No, indeed!" said the woman; "the boats has stopped running." 120

Eliza's look of dismay and disappointment struck the woman, and she said, inquiringly,

"May be you're wanting to get over?—anybody sick? Ye seem mighty anxious?"

"I 've got a child that 's very dangerous,"° said Eliza. "I never heard of it till last night, and I 've walked quite a piece to-day, in hopes to get to the ferry."

"Well, now, that 's onlucky," said the woman, whose motherly sympathies were much aroused; "I 'm re'lly consarned for ye. Solomon!" she called, from the window towards a small back building. A man, in leather apron and very dirty hands, appeared at the door.

"I say, Sol," said the woman, "is that ar man going to tote them bar'ls over to-night?" 125

"He said he should try, if't was any way prudent," said the man.

"There 's a man a piece down here, that 's going over with some truck this evening, if he durs' to; he 'll be in here to supper to-night, so you 'd better set down and wait. That 's a sweet little fellow," added the woman, offering him a cake.

But the child, wholly exhausted, cried with weariness.

"Poor fellow! he is n't used to walking, and I 've hurried him on so," said Eliza.

"Well, take him into this room," said the woman, opening into a small bedroom, where stood a comfortable bed. Eliza laid the weary boy upon it, and held his hands in hers till he was fast asleep. For her there was no rest. As a fire in her bones, the thought of the pursuer urged her on; and she gazed with longing eyes on the sullen, surging waters that lay between her and liberty. 130

Here we must take our leave of her for the present, to follow the course of her pursuers.

Though Mrs. Shelby had promised that the dinner should be hurried on table, yet it was soon seen, as the thing has often been seen before, that it required more than one to make a bargain. So, although the order was fairly given out in Haley's hearing, and carried to Aunt Chloe by at least half a dozen juvenile messengers, that dignitary only gave certain very gruff snorts, and tosses of her head, and went on with every operation in an unusually leisurely and circumstantial manner.

---

dangerous: dangerously ill

For some singular reason, an impression seemed to reign among the servants generally that Missis would not be particularly disobliged by delay; and it was wonderful what a number of counter accidents occurred constantly, to retard the course of things. One luckless wight contrived to upset the gravy; and then gravy had to be got up *de novo,* with due care and formality, Aunt Chloe watching and stirring with dogged precision, answering shortly, to all suggestions of haste, that she "warn't a going to have raw gravy on the table, to help nobody's catchings." One tumbled down with the water, and had to go to the spring for more; and another precipitated the butter into the path of events; and there was from time to time giggling news brought into the kitchen that "Mas'r Haley was mighty oneasy, and that he could n't sit in his cheer no ways, but was a walkin' and stalkin' to the winders and through the porch."

"Sarves him right!" said Aunt Chloe, indignantly. "He'll get wus nor oneasy, one of these days, if he don't mend his ways. *His* master 'll be sending for him, and then see how he 'll look!"

"He 'll go to torment, and no mistake," said little Jake. 135

"He desarves it!" said Aunt Chloe, grimly; "he 's broke a many, many, many hearts,—I tell ye all!" she said, stopping, with a fork uplifted in her hands; "it 's like what Mas'r George reads in Ravelations,—souls a callin' under the altar! and a callin' on the Lord for vengeance on sich!—and by and by the Lord he 'll hear 'em—so he will!"

Aunt Chloe, who was much revered in the kitchen, was listened to with open mouth; and, the dinner being now fairly sent in, the whole kitchen was at leisure to gossip with her, and to listen to her remarks.

"Sich 'll be burnt up forever, and no mistake; won't ther?" said Andy.

"I 'd be glad to see it, I 'll be boun'," said little Jake.

"Chil'en!" said a voice, that made them all start. It was Uncle Tom, who had come in, and stood listening to the conversation at the door. 140

"Chil'en!" he said. "I 'm afeard you don't know what ye 're sayin'. Forever is a *dre'ful* word, chil'en; it 's awful to think on 't. You oughtenter wish that ar to any human crittur."

"We would n't to anybody but the soul-drivers," said Andy; "nobody can help wishing it to them, they's so awful wicked."

"Don't natur herself kinder cry out on 'em?" said Aunt Chloe. "Don't dey tear der suckin' baby right off his mother's breast, and sell him, and der little children as is crying and holding on by her clothes,—don't dey pull 'em off and sells 'em? Don't dey tear wife and husband apart?" said Aunt Chloe, beginning to cry, "when it 's jest takin' the very life on 'em?—and all the while does they feel one bit,—don't dey drink and smoke, and take it oncommon easy? Lor, if the devil don't get them, what 's he good for?" And Aunt Chloe covered her face with her checked apron, and began to sob in good earnest.

"Pray for them that 'spitefully use you, the good book says," says Tom.

"Pray for 'em!" said Aunt Chloe; "Lor, it 's too tough! I can't pray for 'em." 145

"It 's natur, Chloe, and natur 's strong," said Tom, "but the Lord's grace is stronger; besides, you oughter think what an awful state a poor crittur's soul 's in that 'll do them ar things,—you oughter thank God that you an't *like* him, Chloe. I 'm sure I 'd rather be sold, ten thousand times over, than to have all that ar poor crittur 's got to answer for."

"So 'd I, a heap," said Jake. "Lor, *should n't* we cotch it, Andy?"

Andy shrugged his shoulders, and gave an acquiescent whistle.

"I 'm glad Mas'r did n't go off this morning, as he looked to," said Tom; "that ar hurt me more than sellin', it did. Mebbe it might have been natural for him, but 't would have come desp't hard on me, as has known him from a baby; but I 've seen Mas'r, and I begin ter feel sort o' reconciled to the Lord's will now. Mas'r could n't help hisself; he did right, but I 'm feared things will be kinder goin' to rack, when I 'm gone. Mas'r can't be spected to be a pryin' round everywhar, as I 've done, a keepin' up all the ends. The boys all means well, but they 's powerful car'less. That ar troubles me."

The bell here rang, and Tom was summoned to the parlor. 150

"Tom," said his master, kindly, "I want you to notice that I give this gentleman bonds to forfeit a thousand dollars if you are not on the spot when he wants you; he's going to-day to look after his other business, and you can have the day to yourself. Go anywhere you like, boy."

"Thank you, Mas'r," said Tom.

"And mind yerself," said the trader, "and don't come it over your master with any o' yer nigger tricks; for I 'll take every cent out of him, if you an't thar. If he 'd hear to me, he would n't trust any on ye—slippery as eels!"

"Mas'r," said Tom,—and he stood very straight,—"I was jist eight years old when ole Missis put you into my arms, and you was n't a year old. 'Thar,' says she, 'Tom, that 's to be *your* young Mas'r; take good care on him,' says she. And now I jist ask you, Mas'r, have I ever broke word to you, or gone contrary to you, 'specially since I was a Christian?"

Mr. Shelby was fairly overcome, and the tears rose to his eyes. 155

"My good boy," said he, "the Lord knows you say but the truth; and if I was able to help it, all the world should n't buy you."

"And sure as I am a Christian woman," said Mrs. Shelby, "you shall be redeemed as soon as I can any way bring together means. Sir," she said to Haley, "take good account of who you sell him to, and let me know."

"Lor, yes, for that matter," said the trader, "I may bring him up in a year, not much the wuss for wear, and trade him back."

"I'll trade with you then, and make it for your advantage," said Mrs. Shelby.

"Of course," said the trader, "all 's equal with me; lives trade 'em up as down, so I does a good business. All I want is a livin', you know, ma'am; that 's all any on us wants, I s'pose." 160

Mr. and Mrs. Shelby both felt annoyed and degraded by the familiar impudence of the trader, and yet both saw the absolute necessity of putting a constraint on their feelings. The more hopelessly sordid and insensible he appeared, the greater became Mrs. Shelby's dread of his succeeding in re-capturing Eliza and her child, and of course the greater her motive for detaining him by every female artifice. She therefore graciously smiled, assented, chatted familiarly, and did all she could to make time pass imperceptibly.

At two o'clock Sam and Andy brought the horses up to the posts, apparently greatly refreshed and invigorated by the scamper of the morning.

Sam was there new oiled from dinner, with an abundance of zealous and ready officiousness. As Haley approached, he was boasting, in flourishing style, to Andy, of the evident and eminent success of the operation, now that he had "farly come to it."

"Your master, I s'pose, don't keep no dogs," said Haley, thoughtfully, as he prepared to mount.

"Heaps on 'em," said Sam, triumphantly; "thar's Bruno—he 's a roarer! and, besides that, 'bout every nigger of us keeps a pup of some natur or uther." 165

"Poh!" said Haley,—and he said something else, too, with regard to the said dogs, at which Sam muttered,

"I don't see no use cussin' on 'em, no way."

"But your master don't keep no dogs (I pretty much know he don't) for trackin' out niggers."

Sam knew exactly what he meant, but he kept on a look of earnest and desperate simplicity.

"Our dogs all smells round considable sharp. I spect they 's the kind, though they han't never had no practice. They 's *far* dogs, 170 though, at most anything, if you 'd get 'em started. Here, Bruno," he called, whistling to the lumbering Newfoundland, who came pitching tumultuously toward them.

"You go hang!" said Haley, getting up. "Come, tumble up now."

Sam tumbled up accordingly, dexterously contriving to tickle Andy as he did so, which occasioned Andy to split out into a laugh, greatly to Haley's indignation, who made a cut at him with his riding-whip.

"I 's 'stonished at yer, Andy," said Sam, with awful gravity. "This yer 's a seris bisness, Andy. Yer must n't be a makin' game. This yer an't no way to help Mas'r."

"I shall take the straight road to the river," said Haley, decidedly, after they had come to the boundaries of the estate. "I know the way of all of 'em,—they makes tracks for the underground."

"Sartin," said Sam, "dat 's de idee. Mas'r Haley hits de thing right in de middle. Now, der 's two roads to de river,—de dirt road and der pike,—which Mas'r mean to take?"

Andy looked up innocently at Sam, surprised at hearing this new geographical fact, but instantly confirmed what he said, by a vehement reiteration.

"Cause," said Sam. "I 'd rather be 'clined to 'magine that Lizy 'd take de dirt road, bein' it 's the least travelled."

Haley, notwithstanding that he was a very old bird, and naturally inclined to be suspicious of chaff, was rather brought up by this view of the case.

"If yer warn't both on yer such cussed liars, now!" he said, contemplatively, as he pondered a moment.

The pensive, reflective tone in which this was spoken appeared to amuse Andy prodigiously, and he drew a little behind, and shook so as apparently to run a great risk of falling off his horse, while Sam's face was immovably composed into the most doleful gravity.

"Course," said Sam, "Mas'r can do as he 'd ruther; go de straight road, if Mas'r thinks best,—it 's all one to us. Now, when I study 'pon it, I think de straight road de best, *decidedly*."

"She would naturally go a lonesome way," said Haley, thinking aloud, and not minding Sam's remark.

"Dar an't no sayin," said Sam; "gals is pecular; they never does nothin' ye thinks they will; mose gen'lly the contrar. Gals is nat'lly made contrary; and so, if you thinks they 've gone one road, it is sartin you 'd better go t' other, and then you 'll be sure to find 'em. Now, my private 'pinion is, Lizy took der dirt road; so I think we 'd better take de straight one."

This profound generic view of the female sex did not seem to dispose Haley particularly to the straight road; and he announced decidedly that he should go the other, and asked Sam when they should come to it.

"A little piece ahead," said Sam, giving a wink to Andy with the eye which was on Andy's side of the head; and he added, gravely, "but I 've studded on de matter, and I 'm quite clar we ought not to go dat ar way. I nebber been over it no way. It 's despit lonesome, and we might lose our way,—whar we 'd come to, de Lord only knows." 185

"Nevertheless," said Haley, "I shall go that way."

"Now I think on 't, I think I hearn 'em tell that dat ar road was all fenced up and down by der creek, and thar, an't it, Andy?"

Andy was n't certain; he 'd only "hearn tell" about that road, but never been over it. In short, he was strictly noncommittal.

Haley, accustomed to strike the balance of probabilities between lies of greater or lesser magnitude, thought that it lay in favor of the dirt road aforesaid. The mention of the thing he thought he perceived was involuntary on Sam's part at first, and his confused attempts to dissuade him he set down to a desperate lying on second thoughts, as being unwilling to implicate Eliza.

When, therefore, Sam indicated the road, Haley plunged briskly into it, followed by Sam and Andy. 190

Now, the road, in fact, was an old one, that had formerly been a thoroughfare to the river, but abandoned for many years after the laying of the new pike. It was open for about an hour's ride, and after that it was cut across by various farms and fences. Sam knew this fact perfectly well,—indeed, the road had been so long closed up, that Andy had never heard of it. He therefore rode along with an air of dutiful submission, only groaning and vociferating occasionally that 't was "desp't rough, and bad for Jerry's foot."

"Now, I jest give yer warning," said Haley, "I know yer; yer won't get me to turn off this yer road, with all yer fussin'—so you shet up!"

"Mas'r will go his own way!" said Sam, with rueful submission, at the same time winking most portentously to Andy, whose delight was now very near the explosive point.

Sam was in wonderful spirits,—professed to keep a very brisk look-out,—at one time exclaiming that he saw "a gal's bonnet" on the top of some distant eminence, or calling to Andy "if that thar was n't 'Lizy' down in the hollow;" always making these exclamations in some rough or craggy part of the road, where the sudden quickening of speed was a special inconvenience to all parties concerned, and thus keeping Haley in a state of constant commotion.

After riding about an hour in this way, the whole party made a precipitate and tumultuous descent into a barn-yard belonging to a large farming establishment. Not a soul was in sight, all the hands being employed in the fields; but, as the barn stood conspicuously and plainly square across the road, it was evident that their journey in that direction had reached a decided finale. 195

"Wan't dat ar what I telled Mas'r?" said Sam, with an air of injured innocence. "How does strange gentleman spect to know more about a country dan de natives born and raised?"

"You rascal!" said Haley, "you knew all about this."

"Did n't I tell yer I *know'd,* and yer would n't believe me? I telled Mas'r 't was all shet up, and fenced up, and I did n't spect we could get through,—Andy heard me."

It was all too true to be disputed, and the unlucky man had to pocket his wrath with the best grace he was able, and all three faced to the right about, and took up their line of march for the highway.

In consequence of all the various delays, it was about three-quarters of an hour after Eliza had laid her child to sleep in the village tavern that the party came riding into the same place. Eliza was standing by the window, looking out in another direction, when Sam's quick eye caught a glimpse of her. Haley and Andy were two yards behind. At this crisis, Sam contrived to have his hat blown off, and uttered a loud and characteristic ejaculation, which startled her at once; she drew suddenly back; the whole train swept by the window, round to the front door. 200

A thousand lives seemed to be concentrated in that one moment to Eliza. Her room opened by a side door to the river. She caught her child, and sprang down the steps towards it. The trader caught a full glimpse of her, just as she was disappearing down the bank; and throwing himself from his horse, and calling loudly on Sam and Andy, he was after her like a hound after a deer. In that dizzy moment her feet to her scarce seemed to touch the ground, and a moment brought her to the water's edge. Right on behind they came; and, nerved with strength such as God gives only to the desperate, with one wild cry and flying leap, she vaulted sheer over the turbid current by the shore, on to the raft of ice beyond. It was a desperate leap—impossible to anything but madness and despair; and Haley, Sam, and Andy, instinctively cried out, and lifted up their hands, as she did it.

The huge green fragment of ice on which she alighted pitched and creaked as her weight came on it, but she staid there not a moment. With wild cries and desperate energy she leaped to another and still another cake;—stumbling—leaping—slipping—springing upwards again! Her shoes are gone—her stockings cut from her feet—while blood marked every step; but she saw nothing, felt nothing, till dimly, as in a dream, she saw the Ohio side, and a man helping her up the bank.

"Yer a brave gal, now, whoever ye ar!" said the man, with an oath.

Eliza recognized the voice and face of a man who owned a farm not far from her old home.

"O, Mr. Symmes!—save me—do save me—do hide me!" said Eliza. 205

"Why, what 's this?" said the man. "Why, if 'tan't Shelby's gal!"

"My child!—this boy!—he 'd sold him! There is his Mas'r," said she, pointing to the Kentucky shore. "O, Mr. Symmes, you 've got a little boy!"

"So I have," said the man, as he roughly, but kindly, drew her up the steep bank. "Besides, you 're a right brave gal. I like grit, wherever I see it."

When they had gained the top of the bank, the man paused.

"I 'd be glad to do something for ye," said he; "but then there 's nowhar I could take ye. The best I can do is to tell ye to go *thar,*" said he, pointing to a large white house which stood by itself, off the main street of the village. "Go thar; they 're kind folks. Thar 's no kind o' danger but they 'll help you,—they 're up to all that sort o' thing." 210

"The Lord bless you!" said Eliza, earnestly.

"No 'casion, no 'casion in the world," said the man. "What I 've done 's of no 'count."

"And, oh, surely, sir, you won't tell any one!"

"Go to thunder, gal! What do you take a feller for? In course not," said the man. "Come, now, go along like a likely, sensible gal, as you are. You 've arnt your liberty, and you shall have it, for all me."

The woman folded her child to her bosom, and walked firmly and swiftly away. The man stood and looked after her. 215

"Shelby, now, mebbe won't think this yer the most neighborly thing in the world; but what 's a feller to do? If he catches one of my gals in the same fix, he 's welcome to pay back. Somehow I never could see no kind o' critter a strivin' and pantin', and trying to clar theirselves, with the dogs arter 'em, and go agin 'em. Besides, I don't see no kind of 'casion for me to be hunter and catcher for other folks, neither."

So spoke this poor, heathenish Kentuckian, who had not been instructed in his constitutional relations, and consequently was betrayed into acting in a sort of Christianized manner, which, if he had been better situated and more enlightened, he would not have been left to do.

Haley had stood a perfectly amazed spectator of the scene, till Eliza had disappeared up the bank, when he turned a blank, inquiring look on Sam and Andy.

"That ar was a tolable fair stroke of business," said Sam.

"The gal 's got seven devils in her, I believe!" said Haley. "How like a wildcat she jumped!" 220

"Wal, now," said Sam, scratching his head, "I hope Mas'r 'll 'scuse us tryin' dat ar road. Don't think I feel spry enough for dat ar, no way!" and Sam gave a hoarse chuckle.

"*You* laugh!" said the trader, with a growl.

"Lord bless you, Mas'r, I could n't help it, now," said Sam, giving way to the long pent-up delight of his soul. "She looked so curi's, a leapin' and springin'—ice a crackin'—and only to hear her,—plump! ker chunk! ker splash! Spring! Lord! how she goes it!" and Sam and Andy laughed till the tears rolled down their cheeks.

"I 'll make ye laugh t' other side yer mouths!" said the trader, laying about their heads with his riding-whip.

Both ducked, and ran shouting up the bank, and were on their horses before he was up. 225

"Good-evening, Mas'r!" said Sam, with much gravity. "I berry much spect Missis be anxious 'bout Jerry. Mas'r Haley won't want us no longer. Missis would n't hear of our ridin the critters over Lizy's bridge to-night;" and, with a facetious poke into Andy's ribs, he started off, followed by the latter, at full speed,—their shouts of laughter coming faintly on the wind.

[1852]

Read

1. How does Stowe use sarcasm to convey her attitude toward characters and situations?
2. What is the purpose of the Preface?
3. How is the difference between Shelby and Haley demonstrated by the diction in the dialogue?
4. How does Stowe heighten sympathy for Eliza through descriptive details?
5. How can the reader infer Stowe's attitude toward slavery in this excerpt?

Write

1. Critics have called Stowe's writing sentimental and didactic. How do you see those characteristics in the passage? Do you think that the criticism is valid?
2. How does a dialect work to get across Stowe's aim?
3. Write a brief character description of Mr. Shelby, including what you see as his sense of ethics and propriety.

Connect

1. Abraham Lincoln famously called Harriet Beecher Stowe the "little lady who started this big war." Does this excerpt suggest why he called her that?
2. How does Stowe's description reflect arguments made by African American writers in Unit 2?

Harriet Ann Jacobs

Harriet Ann Jacobs (1813–1897) was born a slave in North Carolina. In her early years she was treated well and taught to read and write by her white mistress. When her mistress died, Harriet was willed to the daughter of a local doctor who mistreated and terrified her. She hid in her grandmother's attic for several years until she escaped into the North and freedom. She worked as a nurse and her employer bought her and set her free. In 1861 she published *Incidents in the Life of a Slave Girl* under the name Linda Brent. The book was nearly forgotten until the civil rights movement and the women's movement gave it renewed attention and interest as a document of literary power and historical accuracy.

From *Incidents in the Life of a Slave Girl*

I

Childhood

I was born a slave; but I never knew it till six years of happy childhood had passed away. My father was a carpenter, and considered so intelligent and skilful in his trade, that, when buildings out of the common line were to be erected, he was sent for from long distances, to be head workman. On condition of paying his mistress two hundred dollars a year, and supporting himself, he was allowed to work at his trade and manage his own affairs. His strongest wish was to purchase his children; but, though he several times offered his hard earnings for that purpose, he never succeeded. In complexion my parents were a light shade of brownish yellow, and were termed mulattoes.° They lived together in a comfortable home; and, though we were all slaves, I was so fondly shielded that I never dreamed I was a piece of merchandise, trusted to them for safe keeping, and liable° to be demanded of them at any moment. I had one brother, William, who was two years younger than myself—a bright, affectionate child. I had also a great treasure in my maternal grandmother, who was a remarkable woman in many respects. She was the daughter of a planter in South Carolina, who, at his death, left her mother and his three children free, with money to go to St. Augustine, where they had relatives. It was during the Revolutionary War; and they were captured on their passage, carried back, and sold to different purchasers. Such was the story my grandmother used to tell me; but I do not remember all the particulars. She was a little girl when she was captured and sold to the keeper of a large hotel. I have often heard her tell how hard she fared during childhood. But as she grew older she evinced° so much intelligence, and was so faithful, that her master and mistress could not help seeing it was for their interest to take care of such a valuable piece of property. She became an indispensable personage in the household, officiating in all capacities, from cook and wet nurse° to seamstress. She was much praised for her cooking; and her nice crackers became so famous in the neighborhood that many people were desirous of obtaining them. In consequence of numerous requests of this kind, she asked permission of her mistress to bake crackers at night, after all the household work was done; and she obtained leave to do it, provided she would clothe herself and her children from the profits. Upon these terms, after working hard all day for her mistress, she began her midnight bakings, assisted by her two oldest children. The business proved profitable; and each year she laid by a little which was saved for a fund to purchase her children. Her master died, and the property was divided among his heirs. The widow had her dower° in the hotel, which she continued to

---

mulattoes: people with one white and one black parent
liable: at risk, vulnerable
evinced: showed
wet nurse: woman who breastfeeds other women's children
dower: that part of her husband's estate allotted to a widow by law

keep open. My grandmother remained in her service as a slave; but her children were divided among her master's children. As she had five, Benjamin, the youngest one, was sold, in order that each heir might have an equal portion of dollars and cents. There was so little difference in our ages that he seemed more like my brother than my uncle. He was a bright, handsome lad, nearly white; for he inherited the complexion my grandmother had derived from Anglo-Saxon ancestors. Though [he was] only ten years old, seven hundred and twenty dollars were paid for him. His sale was a terrible blow to my grandmother; but she was naturally hopeful, and she went to work with renewed energy, trusting in time to be able to purchase some of her children. She had laid up three hundred dollars, which her mistress one day begged as a loan, promising to pay her soon. The reader probably knows that no promise or writing given to a slave is legally binding; for, according to Southern laws, a slave, *being* property, can *hold* no property. When my grandmother lent her hard earnings to her mistress, she trusted solely to her honor. The honor of a slaveholder to a slave!

To this good grandmother I was indebted for many comforts. My brother Willie and I often received portions of the crackers, cakes, and preserves, she made to sell; and after we ceased to be children we were indebted to her for many more important services.

Such were the unusually fortunate circumstances of my early childhood. When I was six years old, my mother died; and then, for the first time, I learned, by the talk around me, that I was a slave. My mother's mistress was the daughter of my grandmother's mistress. She was the foster sister of my mother; they were both nourished at my grandmother's breast. In fact, my mother had been weaned at three months old, that the babe of the mistress might obtain sufficient food. They played together as children; and, when they became women, my mother was a most faithful servant to her whiter foster sister. On her death-bed her mistress promised that her children should never suffer for any thing;° and during her lifetime she kept her word. They all spoke kindly of my dead mother, who had been a slave merely in name, but in nature was noble and womanly. I grieved for her, and my young mind was troubled with the thought who would now take care of me and my little brother.

---

for any thing: i.e., for the lack of any thing

I was told that my home was now to be with her mistress; and I found it a happy one. No toilsome or disagreeable duties were imposed upon me. My mistress was so kind to me that I was always glad to do her bidding and proud to labor for her as much as my young years would permit. I would sit by her side for hours, sewing diligently, with a heart as free from care as that of any free-born white child. When she thought I was tired, she would send me out to run and jump; and away I bounded, to gather berries or flowers to decorate her room. Those were happy days—too happy to last. The slave child had no thought for the morrow; but there came that blight, which too surely waits on every human being born to be a chattel.°

When I was nearly twelve years old, my kind mistress sickened and died. As I saw the cheek grow paler, and the eye more glassy, how earnestly I prayed in my heart that she might live! I loved her; for she had been almost like a mother to me. My prayers were not answered. She died, and they buried her in the little churchyard, where, day after day, my tears fell upon her grave.

I was sent to spend a week with my grandmother. I was now old enough to begin to think of the future; and again and again I asked myself what they would do with me. I felt sure I should never find another mistress so kind as the one who was gone. She had promised my dying mother that her children should never suffer for any thing; and when I remembered that, and recalled her many proofs of attachment to me, I could not help having some hopes that she had left me free. My friends were almost certain it would be so. They thought she would be sure to do it, on account of my mother's love and faithful service. But, alas! we all know that the memory of a faithful slave does not avail much to save her children from the auction block. 5

After a brief period of suspense, the will of my mistress was read, and we learned that she had bequeathed me to her sister's daughter, a child of five years old. So vanished our hopes. My mistress had taught me the precepts of God's Word: "Thou shalt love thy neighbor as thyself." "Whatsoever ye would that men should do unto you, do ye even so unto them." But I was her slave, and I suppose she did not recognize me as her neighbor. I would

chattel: piece of property

give much to blot out from my memory that one great wrong. As a child, I loved my mistress; and, looking back on the happy days I spent with her, I try to think with less bitterness of this act of injustice. While I was with her, she taught me to read and spell; and for this privilege, which so rarely falls to the lot of a slave, I bless her memory.

She possessed but few slaves; and at her death those were all distributed among her relatives. Five of them were my grandmother's children, and had shared the same milk that nourished her mother's children. Notwithstanding° my grandmother's long and faithful service to her owners, not one of her children escaped the auction block. These God-breathing machines are no more, in the sight of their masters, than the cotton they plant, or the horses they tend.

V

The Trials of Girlhood

During the first years of my service in Dr. Flint's family, I was accustomed to share some indulgences with the children of my mistress. Though this seemed to me no more than right, I was grateful for it and tried to merit the kindness by the faithful discharge of my duties. But I now entered on my fifteenth year—a sad epoch in the life of a slave girl. My master began to whisper foul words in my ear. Young as I was, I could not remain ignorant of their import. I tried to treat them with indifference or contempt. The master's age, my extreme youth, and the fear that his conduct would be reported to my grandmother, made him bear this treatment for many months. He was a crafty man and resorted to many means to accomplish his purposes. Sometimes he had stormy, terrific ways that made his victims tremble; sometimes he assumed a gentleness that he thought must surely subdue. Of the two, I preferred his stormy moods, although they left me trembling. He tried his utmost to corrupt the pure principles my grandmother had instilled. He peopled my young mind with unclean images, such as only a vile monster could think of. I turned from him with disgust and hatred. But he was my master. I was compelled to live under the same roof with him—where I saw a man forty years my senior daily violating

---

Notwithstanding: In spite of

the most sacred commandments of nature. He told me I was his property; that I must be subject to his will in all things. My soul revolted against the mean tyranny. But where could I turn for protection? No matter whether the slave girl be as black as ebony or as fair as her mistress. In either case, there is no shadow of law to protect her from insult, from violence, or even from death; all these are inflicted by fiends who bear the shape of men. The mistress, who ought to protect the helpless victim, has no other feelings towards her but those of jealousy and rage. The degradation, the wrongs, the vices, that grow out of slavery, are more than I can describe. They are greater than you would willingly believe. Surely, if you credited one half the truths that are told you concerning the helpless millions suffering in this cruel bondage, you at the North would not help to tighten the yoke. You surely would refuse to do for the master, on your own soil, the mean and cruel work which trained bloodhounds and the lowest class of whites do for him at the South.

Everywhere the years bring to all enough of sin and sorrow; but in slavery the very dawn of life is darkened by these shadows. Even the little child, who is accustomed to wait on her mistress and her children, will learn, before she is twelve years old, why it is that her mistress hates such and such a one among the slaves. Perhaps the child's own mother is among those hated ones. She listens to violent outbreaks of jealous passion and cannot help understanding what is the cause. She will become prematurely knowing in evil things. Soon she will learn to tremble when she hears her master's footfall. She will be compelled to realize that she is no longer a child. If God has bestowed beauty upon her, it will prove her greatest curse. That which commands admiration in the white woman only hastens the degradation of the female slave. I know that some are too much brutalized by slavery to feel the humiliation of their position; but many slaves feel it most acutely and shrink from the memory of it. I cannot tell how much I suffered in the presence of these wrongs nor how I am still pained by the retrospect.° My master met me at every turn, reminding me that I belonged to him and swearing by heaven and earth that he would compel me to submit to him. If I went out for a breath of fresh air, after a day of unwearied toil, his footsteps dogged me. If I knelt by my mother's grave, his dark shadow fell on

---

retrospect: recollection, looking back

me even there. The light heart which nature had given me became heavy with sad forebodings. The other slaves in my master's house noticed the change. Many of them pitied me; but none dared to ask the cause. They had no need to inquire. They knew too well the guilty practices under that roof; and they were aware that to speak of them was an offence that never went unpunished.

10 I longed for some one to confide in. I would have given the world to have laid my head on my grandmother's faithful bosom, and told her all my troubles. But Dr. Flint swore he would kill me, if I was not as silent as the grave. Then, although my grandmother was all in all to me, I feared her as well as loved her. I had been accustomed to look up to her with a respect bordering upon awe. I was very young, and felt shamefaced about telling her such impure things, especially as I knew her to be very strict on such subjects. Moreover, she was a woman of a high spirit. She was usually very quiet in her demeanor; but if her indignation was once roused, it was not very easily quelled. I had been told that she once chased a white gentleman with a loaded pistol because he insulted one of her daughters. I dreaded the consequences of a violent outbreak; and both pride and fear kept me silent. But though I did not confide in my grandmother, and even evaded her vigilant watchfulness and inquiry, her presence in the neighborhood was some protection to me. Though she had been a slave, Dr. Flint was afraid of her. He dreaded her scorching rebukes. Moreover, she was known and patronized by many people; and he did not wish to have his villainy made public. It was lucky for me that I did not live on a distant plantation but in a town not so large that the inhabitants were ignorant of each other's affairs. Bad as are the laws and customs in a slaveholding community, the doctor, as a professional man, deemed it prudent to keep up some outward show of decency.

O, what days and nights of fear and sorrow that man caused me! Reader, it is not to awaken sympathy for myself that I am telling you truthfully what I suffered in slavery. I do it to kindle a flame of compassion in your hearts for my sisters who are still in bondage, suffering as I once suffered.

I once saw two beautiful children playing together. One was a fair white child; the other was her slave and also her sister. When I saw them embracing each other and heard their joyous laughter,

I turned sadly away from the lovely sight. I foresaw the inevitable blight that would fall on the little slave's heart. I knew how soon her laughter would be changed to sighs. The fair child grew up to be a still fairer woman. From childhood to womanhood her pathway was blooming with flowers and overarched by a sunny sky. Scarcely one day of her life had been clouded when the sun rose on her happy bridal morning.

How had those years dealt with her slave sister, the little playmate of her childhood? She, also, was very beautiful; but the flowers and sunshine of love were not for her. She drank the cup of sin, and shame, and misery, whereof° her persecuted race are compelled to drink.

In view of these things, why are ye silent, ye free men and women of the North? Why do your tongues falter in maintenance of the right? Would that I had more ability! But my heart is so full, and my pen is so weak! There are noble men and women who plead for us, striving to help those who cannot help themselves. God bless them! God give them strength and courage to go on! God bless those, everywhere, who are laboring to advance the cause of humanity!

. . .

XXI

The Loophole of Retreat

A small shed had been added to my grandmother's house years ago. 15 Some boards were laid across the joists° at the top, and between these boards and the roof was a very small garret,° never occupied by any thing but rats and mice. It was a pent roof,° covered with nothing but shingles, according to the Southern custom for such buildings. The garret was only nine feet long and seven wide. The highest part was three feet high and sloped down abruptly to the loose board floor. There was no admission° for either light or air. My uncle Philip, who was a carpenter, had very skilfully

whereof: of which
joists: support beams
garret: loft, attic
pent roof: shed roof, flat roof that slopes in one direction
admission: opening

made a concealed trap-door, which communicated with the storeroom . . . The storeroom opened upon a piazza. To this hole I was conveyed as soon as I entered the house. The air was stifling, the darkness total. A bed had been spread on the floor. I could sleep quite comfortably on one side; but the slope was so sudden that I could not turn on the other without hitting the roof. The rats and mice ran over my bed; but I was weary, and I slept such sleep as the wretched may, when a tempest has passed over them. Morning came. I knew it only by the noises I heard, for in my small den day and night were all the same. I suffered for air even more than for light. But I was not comfortless. I heard the voices of my children. There was joy and there was sadness in the sound. It made my tears flow. How I longed to speak to them! I was eager to look on their faces; but there was no hole, no crack, through which I could peep. This continued darkness was oppressive. It seemed horrible to sit or lie in a cramped position day after day, without one gleam of light. Yet I would have chosen this rather than my lot as a slave, though white people considered it an easy one; and it was so compared with the fate of others. I was never cruelly over-worked; I was never lacerated with the whip from head to foot; I was never so beaten and bruised that I could not turn from one side to the other; I never had my heel-strings° cut to prevent my running away; I was never chained to a log and forced to drag it about, while I toiled in the fields from morning till night; I was never branded with hot iron or torn by bloodhounds. On the contrary, I had always been kindly treated and tenderly cared for, until I came into the hands of Dr. Flint. I had never wished for freedom till then. But though my life in slavery was comparatively devoid of hardships, God pity the woman who is compelled to lead such a life!

My food was passed up to me through the trap-door my uncle had contrived; and my grandmother, my uncle Philip, and aunt Nancy would seize such opportunities as they could, to mount up there and chat with me at the opening. But of course this was not safe in the daytime. It must all be done in darkness. It was impossible for me to move in an erect position, but I crawled about my den for exercise. One day I hit my head against something, and found it was a gimlet.° My uncle had left it sticking there when he

---

heel-strings: Achilles tendons

made the trap-door. I was as rejoiced as Robinson Crusoe could have been at finding such a treasure. It put a lucky thought into my head. I said to myself, "Now I will have some light. Now I will see my children." I did not dare to begin my work during the daytime for fear of attracting attention. But I groped round; and having found the side next to the street, where I could frequently see my children, I stuck the gimlet in and waited for evening. I bored three rows of holes, one above another; then I bored out the interstices° between. I thus succeeded in making one hole about an inch long and an inch broad. I sat by it till late into the night, to enjoy the little whiff of air that floated in. In the morning I watched for my children. The first person I saw in the street was Dr. Flint. I had a shuddering, superstitious feeling that it was a bad omen. Several familiar faces passed by. At last I heard the merry laugh of children, and presently two sweet little faces were looking up at me, as though they knew I was there and were conscious of the joy they imparted. How I longed to *tell* them I was there!

My condition was now a little improved. But for weeks I was tormented by hundreds of little red insects, fine as a needle's point, that pierced through my skin and produced an intolerable burning. The good grandmother gave me herb teas and cooling medicines, and finally I got rid of them. The heat of my den was intense, for nothing but thin shingles protected me from the scorching summer's sun. But I had my consolations. Through my peeping-hole I could watch the children, and when they were near enough, I could hear their talk. Aunt Nancy brought me all the news she could hear at Dr. Flint's. From her I learned that the doctor had written to New York to a colored woman, who had been born and raised in our neighborhood and had breathed his contaminating atmosphere. He offered her a reward if she could find out any thing about me. I know not what was the nature of her reply; but he soon after started for New York in haste, saying to his family that he had business of importance to transact. I peeped at him as he passed on his way to the steamboat. It was a satisfaction to have miles of land and water between us, even for a little while; and it was still greater satisfaction to know that he believed me to be in the Free States. My little den

---

gimlet: small tool for boring holes in wood
interstices: openings between things

seemed less dreary than it had done. He returned . . . without obtaining any satisfactory information. When he passed our house next morning, Benny was standing at the gate. He had heard them say that he had gone to find me, and he called out, "Dr. Flint, did you bring my mother home? I want to see her." The doctor stamped his foot at him in a rage, and exclaimed, "Get out of the way, you little damned rascal! If you don't, I'll cut off your head."

Benny ran terrified into the house, saying "You can't put me in jail again. I don't belong to you now." It was well that the wind carried the words away from the doctor's ear. I told my grandmother of it, when we had our next conference at the trap-door, and begged of her not to allow the children to be impertinent° to the irascible° old man.

Autumn came, with a pleasant abatement of heat. My eyes had become accustomed to the dim light, and by holding my book or work in a certain position near the aperture° I contrived to read and sew. That was a great relief to the tedious monotony of my life. But when winter came, the cold penetrated through the thin shingle roof, and I was dreadfully chilled. The winters there are not so long, or so severe as in northern latitudes; but the houses are not built to shelter from cold, and my little den was peculiarly° comfortless. The kind grandmother brought me bed-clothes and warm drinks. Often I was obliged to lie in bed all day to keep comfortable; but with all my precautions, my shoulders and feet were frostbitten. O, those long, gloomy days, with no object for my eye to rest upon and no thoughts to occupy my mind except the dreary past and the uncertain future! I was thankful when there came a day sufficiently mild for me to wrap myself up and sit at the loophole to watch the passers by. Southerners have the habit of stopping and talking in the streets, and I heard many conversations not intended to meet my ears. I heard slave-hunters planning how to catch some poor fugitive. Several times I heard allusions to Dr. Flint, myself, and the history of my children, who, perhaps, were playing near the gate. One would say, "I wouldn't move my little finger to catch her, as

---

impertinent: rude, insolent
irascible: irritable
aperture: opening
peculiarly: particularly

old Flint's property." Another would say, "I'll catch *any* nigger for the reward. A man ought to have what belongs to him, if° he *is* a damned brute." The opinion was often expressed that I was in the Free States. Very rarely did any one suggest that I might be in the vicinity. Had the least suspicion rested on my grandmother's house, it would have been burned to the ground. But it was the last place they thought of. Yet there was no place, where slavery existed, that could have afforded me so good a place of concealment.

Dr. Flint and his family repeatedly tried to coax and bribe my children to tell something they had heard said about me. One day the doctor took them into a shop and offered them some bright little silver pieces and gay° handkerchiefs if they would tell where their mother was. Ellen shrank away from him and would not speak; but Benny spoke up and said, "Dr. Flint, I don't know where my mother is. I guess she's in New York; and when you go there again, I wish you'd ask her to come home, for I want to see her; but if you put her in jail or tell her you'll cut her head off, I'll tell her to go right back."

20

XLI

Free at Last

Mrs. Bruce and every member of her family were exceedingly kind to me. I was thankful for the blessings of my lot, yet I could not always wear a cheerful countenance. I was doing harm to no one; on the contrary, I was doing all the good I could in my small way; yet I could never go out to breathe God's free air without trepidation at my heart. This seemed hard; and I could not think it was a right state of things for any civilized country.

From time to time I received news from my good old grandmother. She could not write; but she employed others to write for her. The following is an extract from one of her last letters:—

> "Dear Daughter: I cannot hope to see you again on earth; but I pray to God to unite us above, where pain will no more rack this feeble body of mine; where sorrow and parting from my children will be no more. God has promised these things if we are faith-

if: even if
gay: brightly colored

ful unto the end. My age and feeble health deprive me of going to church now; but God is with me here at home. Thank your brother for his kindness. Give much love to him, and tell him to remember the Creator in the days of his youth, and strive to meet me in the Father's kingdom. Love to Ellen and Benjamin. Don't neglect him. Tell him for me, to be a good boy. Strive, my child, to train them for God's children. May he protect and provide for you, is the prayer of your loving old mother."

These letters both cheered and saddened me. I was always glad to have tidings° from the kind, faithful old friend of my unhappy youth; but her messages of love made my heart yearn to see her before she died, and I mourned over the fact that it was impossible. Some months after I returned from my flight to New England, I received a letter from her, in which she wrote, "Dr. Flint is dead. He has left a distressed family. Poor old man! I hope he made his peace with God."

I remembered how he had defrauded my grandmother of the hard earnings she had loaned, how he had tried to cheat her out of the freedom her mistress had promised her, and how he had persecuted her children; and I thought to myself that she was a better Christian than I was, if she could entirely forgive him. I cannot say, with truth, that the news of my old master's death softened my feelings towards him. There are wrongs which even the grave does not bury. The man was odious to me while he lived, and his memory is odious now.

His departure from this world did not diminish my danger. 25
He had threatened my grandmother that his heirs should hold me in slavery after he was gone, that I never should be free so long as a child of his survived. As for Mrs. Flint, I had seen her in deeper afflictions than I supposed the loss of her husband would be, for she had buried several children; yet I never saw any signs of softening in her heart. The doctor had died in embarrassed circumstances° and had little to will to his heirs, except such property as he was unable to grasp. I was well aware what I had to expect from the family of Flints; and my fears were confirmed by a letter from the South,

tidings: news, information
embarrassed circumstances: poverty

warning me to be on my guard, because Mrs. Flint openly declared that her daughter could not afford to lose so valuable a slave as I was.

I kept close watch of the newspapers for arrivals;° but one Saturday night, being much occupied, I forgot to examine the Evening Express as usual. I went down into the parlor for it, early in the morning, and found the boy about to kindle a fire with it. I took it from him and examined the list of arrivals. Reader, if you have never been a slave, you cannot imagine the acute sensation of suffering at my heart, when I read the names of Mrs. and Mrs. Dodge, at a hotel in Courtland Street. It was a third-rate hotel, and that circumstance convinced me of the truth of what I had heard, that they were short of funds and had need of my value, as *they* valued me; and that was by dollars and cents. I hastened with the paper to Mrs. Bruce. Her heart and hand were always open to everyone in distress, and she always warmly sympathized with mine. It was impossible to tell how near the enemy was. He might have passed and repassed the house while we were sleeping. He might at that moment be waiting to pounce upon me if I ventured out of doors. I had never seen the husband of my young mistress, and therefore I could not distinguish him from any other stranger. A carriage was hastily ordered; and, closely veiled, I followed Mrs. Bruce, taking the baby again with me into exile. After various turnings and crossings, and returnings, the carriage stopped at the house of one of Mrs. Bruce's friends, where I was kindly received. Mrs. Bruce returned immediately, to instruct the domestics° what to say if any one came to inquire for me.

It was lucky for me that the evening paper was not burned up before I had a chance to examine the list of arrivals. It was not long after Mrs. Bruce's return to her house, before several people came to inquire for me. One inquired for me, another asked for my daughter Ellen, and another said he had a letter from my grandmother, which he was requested to deliver in person.

They were told, "She *has* lived here, but she has left."

"How long ago?"

"I don't know, sir." 30

"Do you know where she went?"

arrivals: of visitors to the city
domestics: household servants

"I do not, sir." And the door was closed.

This Mr. Dodge, who claimed me as his property, was originally a Yankee pedler in the South; then he became a merchant and finally a slaveholder. He managed to get introduced into what was called the first society and married Miss Emily Flint. A quarrel arose between him and her brother, and the brother cowhided him.° This led to a family feud, and he proposed to remove to Virginia. Dr. Flint left him no property, and his own means had become circumscribed,° while a wife and children depended upon him for support. Under these circumstances, it was very natural that he should make an effort to put me into his pocket.

I had a colored friend, a man from my native place, in whom I had the most implicit confidence. I sent for him and told him that Mr. and Mrs. Dodge had arrived in New York. I proposed that he should call upon them to make inquiries about his friends at the South, with whom Dr. Flint's family were well acquainted. He thought there was no impropriety in his doing so, and he consented. He went to the hotel and knocked at the door of Mr. Dodge's room, which was opened by the gentleman himself, who gruffly inquired, "What brought you here? How came you to know I was in the city?"

"Your arrival was published in the evening papers, sir; and I called to ask Mrs. Dodge about my friends at home. I didn't suppose it would give any offence." 35

"Where's that negro girl, that belongs to my wife?"

"What girl, sir?"

"You know well enough. I mean Linda, that ran away from Dr. Flint's plantation, some years ago. I dare say you've seen her, and know where she is."

"Yes sir, I've seen her, and know where she is. She is out of your reach, sir."

"Tell me where she is, or bring her to me, and I will give her a chance to buy her freedom." 40

"I don't think it would be of any use, sir. I have heard her say she would go to the ends of the earth rather than pay any man or woman for her freedom, because she thinks she has a right to

cowhided him: beat him with a whip made of cowhide

circumscribed: limited, restricted

it. Besides, she couldn't do it, if° she would, for she has spent her earnings to educate her children."

This made Mr. Dodge very angry, and some high words passed between them. My friend was afraid to come where I was; but in the course of the day I received a note from him. I supposed they had not come from the South, in the winter, for a pleasure excursion; and now the nature of their business was very plain.

Mrs. Bruce came to me and entreated me to leave the city the next morning. She said her house was watched, and it was possible that some clew° to me might be obtained. I refused to take her advice. She pleaded with an earnest tenderness, that ought to have moved me; but I was in a bitter, disheartened mood. I was weary of flying from pillar to post. I had been chased during half my life, and it seemed as if the chase was never to end. There I sat, in that great city, guiltless of crime yet not daring to worship God in any of the churches. I heard the bells ringing for afternoon service, and, with contemptuous sarcasm, I said, "Will the preachers take for their text, 'Proclaim liberty to the captive, and the opening of prison doors to them that are bound'? or will they preach from the text, 'Do unto others as ye would they should do unto you'?" Oppressed Poles and Hungarians could find a safe refuge in that city; John Mitchell° was free to proclaim in the City Hall his desire for "a plantation well stocked with slaves," but there I sat, an oppressed American, not daring to show my face. God forgive the black and bitter thoughts I indulged on that Sabbath day! The Scripture says, "Oppression makes even a wise man mad," and I was not wise.

I had been told that Mr. Dodge said his wife had never signed away her right to my children, and if he could not get me, he would take them. This it was, more than anything else, that roused such a tempest in my soul. Benjamin was with his uncle William in California, but my innocent young daughter had come to spend a vacation with me. I thought of what I had suffered in slavery at her age, and my heart was like a tiger's when a hunter tries to seize her young.

---

if: even if

clew: clue

John Mitchell: (1815–1875), Irish nationalist and editor whose New York newspaper *The Citizen* was explicitly racist and proslavery

Dear Mrs. Bruce! I seem to see the expression of her face, as she turned away discouraged by my obstinate mood. Finding her expostulations° unavailing, she sent Ellen to entreat me. When ten o'clock in the evening arrived and Ellen had not returned, this watchful and unwearied friend became anxious. She came to us in a carriage, bringing a well-filled trunk for my journey—trusting that by this time I would listen to reason. I yielded to her, as I ought to have done before. 45

The next day, baby and I set out in a heavy snow storm, bound for New England again. I received letters from the City of Iniquity,° addressed to me under an assumed name. In a few days one came from Mrs. Bruce, informing me that my new master was still searching for me and that she intended to put an end to this persecution by buying my freedom. I felt grateful for the kindness that prompted this offer, but the idea was not so pleasant to me as might have been expected. The more my mind had become enlightened, the more difficult it was for me to consider myself an article of property; and to pay money to those who had so grievously oppressed me seemed like taking from my sufferings the glory of triumph. I wrote to Mrs. Bruce, thanking her, but saying that being sold from one owner to another seemed too much like slavery, that such a great obligation could not be easily cancelled and that I preferred to go to my brother in California.

Without my knowledge, Mrs. Bruce employed a gentleman in New York to enter into negotiations with Mr. Dodge. He proposed to pay three hundred dollars down, if Mr. Dodge would sell me, and enter into obligations to relinquish all claim to me or my children forever after. He who called himself my master said he scorned so small an offer for such a valuable servant. The gentleman replied, "You can do as you choose, sir. If you reject this offer you will never get anything; for the woman has friends who will convey her and her children out of the country."

Mr. Dodge concluded that "half a loaf was better than no bread," and he agreed to the proffered° terms. By the next mail I received this brief letter from Mrs. Bruce: "I am rejoiced to tell you that the

---

expostulations: protests, objections
Iniquity: wickedness, gross immorality
proffered: offered, tendered

money for your freedom has been paid to Mr. Dodge. Come home to-morrow. I long to see you and my sweet babe."

My brain reeled as I read these lines. A gentleman near me said, "It's true; I have seen the bill of sale." "The bill of sale!" Those words struck me like a blow. So I was *sold* at last! A human being *sold* in the free city of New York! The bill of sale is on record, and future generations will learn from it that women were articles of traffic in New York, late in the nineteenth century of the Christian religion. It may hereafter prove a useful document to antiquaries,° who are seeking to measure the progress of civilization in the United States. I well know the value of that bit of paper; but much as I love freedom, I do not like to look upon it. I am deeply grateful to the generous friend who procured it, but I despise the miscreant° who demanded payment for what never rightfully belonged to him or his.

50

I had objected to having my freedom bought, yet I must confess that when it was done I felt as if a heavy load had been lifted from my weary shoulders. When I rode home in the cars° I was no longer afraid to unveil my face and look at people as they passed. I should have been glad to have met Daniel Dodge himself, to have had him see me and know me, that he might have mourned over the untoward° circumstances which compelled him to sell me for three hundred dollars.

When I reached home, the arms of my benefactress were thrown round me, and our tears mingled. As soon as she could speak, she said, "O Linda, I'm *so* glad it's all over! You wrote to me as if you thought you were going to be transferred from one owner to another. But I did not buy you for your services. I should have done just the same if you had been going to sail for California tomorrow. I should, at least, have the satisfaction of knowing that you left me a free woman."

My heart was exceedingly full. I remembered how my poor father had tried to buy me, when I was a small child, and how he had been disappointed. I hoped his spirit was rejoicing over me now. I remembered how my good old grandmother had laid up her earnings to purchase me in later years and how often her plans

---

antiquaries: antique dealers or collectors
miscreant: wrongdoer, villain
cars: railroad or streetcars
untoward: adverse, unfavorable

had been frustrated. How that faithful, loving old heart would leap for joy, if she could look on me and my children now that we were free! My relatives had been foiled in all their efforts, but God had raised me up a friend among strangers, who had bestowed on me the precious, long-desired boon.° Friend! It is a common word, often lightly used. Like other good and beautiful things, it may be tarnished by careless handling; but when I speak of Mrs. Bruce as my friend, the word is sacred.

My grandmother lived to rejoice in my freedom; but not long after, a letter came with a black seal. She had gone "where the wicked cease from troubling, and the weary are at rest."

Time passed on, and a paper came to me from the South, containing an obituary notice of my uncle Phillip. It was the only case I ever knew of such an honor conferred upon a colored person. It was written by one of his friends and contained these words: "Now that death has laid him low, they call him a good man and a useful citizen; but what are eulogies to the black man, when the world has faded from his vision? It does not require man's praise to obtain rest in God's kingdom." So they called a colored man a *citizen*! Strange words to be uttered in that region!

Reader, my story ends with freedom, not in the usual way, with marriage. I and my children are now free! We are as free from the power of slaveholders as are the white people of the North; and though that, according to my ideas, is not saying a great deal, it is a vast improvement in *my* condition. The dream of my life is not yet realized. I do not sit with my children in a home of my own. I still long for a hearthstone of my own, however humble. I wish it for my children's sake far more than for my own. But God so orders circumstances as to keep me with my friend Mrs. Bruce. Love, duty, gratitude, also bind me to her side. It is a privilege to serve her who pities my oppressed people and who has bestowed the inestimable boon of freedom on me and my children. 55

It has been painful to me, in many ways, to recall the dreary years I passed in bondage. I would gladly forget them if I could. Yet the retrospection is not altogether without solace; for with those gloomy recollections come tender memories of my good old grandmother, like light, fleecy clouds floating over a dark and troubled sea.

[1861]

---

boon: benefit, blessing

Read

1. How does the speaker use contrast to heighten her reader's sympathy at the beginning of her story?
2. Why does Brent allude to the abuse she suffers rather than state it outright?
3. Where are indications of who Brent believes her readers are?
4. What elements of language suggest the speaker is an educated person?
5. Where do you see Brent's persuasive intention most clearly?

Write

1. Speculate on the use of the alias Linda Brent. Why might Jacobs have created that persona?
2. Find places where Brent omits a detail or a piece of an event and analyze her use of silence as a strategy in the passage.
3. Write a brief analysis of what the passage reveals about slavery and relationships between whites and blacks in that system.

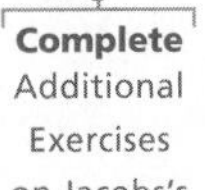

Complete Additional Exercises on Jacobs's Memoir at Your Pearson MyLab

Connect

1. How does the passage suggest the reality or falseness of Stowe's scene in *Uncle Tom's Cabin*?
2. Analyze the use of language and appeal in this passage and compare it with either Frederick Douglass or Wendell Phillips.

Frances Ellen Watkins Harper

Over her long life, Frances Harper (1825–1911) was involved with most of the social justice movements of her time: abolition, the Underground Railroad, the black education movement, anti-lynching laws, and woman's suffrage. Born in Baltimore as a free black, Harper published a book of poetry while still in her teens, and early took a teaching job in the free state of Ohio. She lectured throughout New England on abolition and education, usually without notes. She was a highly successful orator. In 1859, she published what is likely the first short story published by a black person in the United States. Harper was a prolific and popular poet, publishing four volumes of poetry about many topics, focused on black characters and experiences. Her poetry often aimed to challenge and to provoke an emotional response. After the Civil War, she continued to work for education and suffrage, writing poetry, essays, and fiction.

An Appeal to the American People

When a dark and fearful strife
Raged around the nation's life,
And the traitor plunged his steel
Where your quivering hearts could feel,

When your cause did need a friend, 5
We were faithful to the end.

When we stood with bated breath,
Facing fiery storms of death,
And the war-cloud, red with wrath,
Fiercely swept around our path, 10
Did our hearts with terror quail?
Or our courage ever fail?

When the captive, wanting bread,
Sought our poor and lowly shed,
And the blood-hounds missed his way, 15
Did we e'er his path betray?
Filled we not his heart with trust
As we shared with him our crust?

With your soldiers, side by side,
Helped we turn the battle's tide, 20
Till o'er ocean, stream and shore,
Waved the rebel flag no more,
And above the rescued sod
Praises rose to freedom's God.

But to-day the traitor stands 25
With the crimson° on his hands,
Scowling 'neath his brow of hate,
On our weak and desolate,
With the blood-rust on the knife
Aimed at the nation's life. 30

Asking you to weakly yield
All we won upon the field,
To ignore, on land and flood,°
All the offerings of our blood,
And to write above our slain 35
"They have fought and died in vain."

---

crimson: i.e., blood
flood: sea

To your manhood we appeal,
Lest the traitor's iron heel
Grind and trample in the dust
All our new-born hope and trust, 40
And the name of freedom be
Linked with bitter mockery.

[1858]

Read

1. What is the rhetorical effect of the repetition of the first word in the first three stanzas of the poem?
2. How does the poet use rhetorical questions to make connections to her audience?
3. Which appeals seem to be most prominent in the poem?

Write

1. How would you describe the persona Harper creates in the poem?
2. Rewrite the poem in prose, imitating Harper's language and reflecting her aim.
3. Write a reflection on Harper's appeal from your twenty-first-century perspective.

Connect

1. How does Harper's tone echo earlier African American speakers in Unit 1 or 2?
2. How does the poem work as an argument? Find another poem that creates an argument and compare the two.

Walt Whitman

Walt Whitman (1819–1892) is one of the most famous of American poets, called by some the "father of free verse" for his innovations in rhythm, rhyme, line, and image. Born in poverty in New York, he dropped out of school to support his family. His job as a printer taught him a love for language. He later taught school, was a journalist, and served as an Army nurse during the Civil War. *Leaves of Grass,* his signature book of poems, was first published in 1855, and he revised it again and again over the years.

Whitman wrote of the common people and of their leader, Lincoln, whom he eulogized in his poem "When Lilacs Last in the Dooryard Bloom'd" and "Oh Captain, My Captain." He saw the poet as the speaker for the people and as such an arm of democracy, the "great poem" that was America itself.

From *Song of Myself*

1

I CELEBRATE myself, and sing myself,
And what I assume you shall assume,
For every atom belonging to me as good belongs to you.

I loaf and invite my soul,
I lean and loaf at my ease observing a spear of summer grass. 5

My tongue, every atom of my blood, formed from this soil, this air,
Born here of parents born here from parents the same, and their
parents the same,
I, now thirty-seven years old in perfect health begin,
Hoping to cease not till death.

Creeds and schools in abeyance,° 10
Retiring° back a while sufficed at what they are, but never forgotten,
I harbor° for good or bad, I permit to speak at every hazard,°
Nature without check with original energy.

2

Houses and rooms are full of perfumes, the shelves are crowded with perfumes,
I breathe the fragrance myself and know it and like it, 15
The distillation would intoxicate me also, but I shall not let it.

The atmosphere is not a perfume, it has no taste of the distillation, it is odorless,
It is for my mouth forever, I am in love with it,
I will go to the bank° by the wood and become undisguised and naked,
I am mad for it to be in contact with me. 20
The smoke of my own breath,
Echoes, ripples, buzzed whispers, love-root, silk-thread, crotch and vine,
My respiration and inspiration, the beating of my heart, the passing of blood
and air through my lungs,

---

abeyance: temporary inactivity, suspension
Retiring: withdrawing, going away
harbor: contain
hazard: chance
bank: of a river or stream

The sniff of green leaves and dry leaves, and of the shore and dark-colored
 sea-rocks, and of hay in the barn,

The sound of the belched words of my voice loosed to the eddies° of
 the wind, 25
A few light kisses, a few embraces, a reaching around of arms,
The play of shine and shade on the trees as the supple boughs° wag,°
The delight alone or in the rush of the streets, or along the fields and hill-sides,
The feeling of health, the full-noon trill,° the song of me rising from bed and
 meeting the sun.

Have you reckoned° a thousand acres much? have you reckoned the earth much? 30
Have you practiced so long to learn to read?
Have you felt so proud to get at the meaning of poems?

Stop this day and night with me and you shall possess the origin of all poems,
You shall possess the good of the earth and sun, (there are millions of suns left,)
You shall no longer take things at second or third hand, nor look through the
 eyes of the dead, nor feed on the spectres° in books, 35
You shall not look through my eyes either, nor take things from me,
You shall listen to all sides and filter them from your self.

. . .

6

A child said What is the grass? fetching it to me with full hands;
How could I answer the child? I do not know what it is any more than he.

I guess it must be the flag of my disposition, out of hopeful green stuff woven. 40

Or I guess it is the handkerchief of the Lord,
A scented gift and remembrancer° designedly dropt,
Bearing the owner's name someway° in the corners, that we may see and
 remark, and say Whose?

---

eddies: movements, often swirling, that run counter to the main current
boughs: tree limbs
wag: wave or shake
trill: rapid vibrating melody
reckoned: considered
spectres: phantoms, apparitions
remembrancer: memento, souvenir
someway: in some way

Or I guess the grass is itself a child, the produced babe of the vegetation.

Or I guess it is a uniform hieroglyphic, 45
And it means, Sprouting alike in broad zones and narrow zones,
Growing among black folks as among white,
Kanuck,° Tuckahoe,° Congressman, Cuff,° I give them the same, I receive them the same.

And now it seems to me the beautiful uncut hair of graves.

Tenderly will I use you curling grass, 50
It may be you transpire from the breasts of young men,
It may be if I had known them I would have loved them,
It may be you are from old people, or from offspring taken soon out of their mothers' laps,
And here you are the mothers' laps.

This grass is very dark to be from the white heads of old mothers, 55
Darker than the colorless beards of old men,
Dark to come from under the faint red roofs of mouths.

O I perceive after all so many uttering tongues,
And I perceive they do not come from the roofs of mouths for nothing.

I wish I could translate the hints about the dead young men and women, 60
And the hints about old men and mothers, and the offspring taken soon out of their laps.
What do you think has become of the young and old men?
And what do you think has become of the women and children?

They are alive and well somewhere,
The smallest sprout shows there is really no death, 65
And if ever there was it led forward life, and does not wait at the end to arrest° it,
And ceased the moment life appeared.

Kanuck: Canuck (a French Canadian; often derogatory)
Tuckahoe: a Virginian
Cuff: a name for a black man (from *Cuffy*, or *Kofi*, a slave who led a revolt in 1763)
arrest: stop

All goes onward and outward, nothing collapses,
And to die is different from what any one supposed, and luckier.

[1855]

Read

1. What images does the speaker use to draw connections between himself and his audience?
2. What does the speaker want the audience to experience?
3. Whitman announces his intention to "begin." What do you think he is beginning?
4. How do the meanings for the grass change in part 6?
5. Why does the speaker suggest alternate meanings? Is there a final suggestion about what the grass might signify?

Write

1. Write a response to Whitman's passage. What affects you most? Confuses you?
2. How do details contribute to the emotional effect of the poem?
3. How would you describe the persona Whitman creates? Write a paragraph that uses details and language from the poem to contribute to your description.

Connect

1. Why might "graves" be an important image in the poem? What connections might you make to the context of the time?
2. Compare Whitman's intention or argument in the poem with another poet in this unit or an earlier unit.
3. Whitman was an innovator in poetry. Compare this poem with other earlier poems or with others in this unit and list some differences between Whitman's poetry and the others.
4. How does this poem seem to attempt to do the work Emerson suggests for the "American Scholar"?

Abraham Lincoln

As one of the most revered presidents of the United States, Abraham Lincoln's life (1809–1865) has become legendary. Born in a one-room log cabin in the Kentucky wilderness, learning to read by candlelight the tales and histories that were to fire his ambition and success, Lincoln was a laborer, then a lawyer in Illinois, a congressman, and finally president. His words carried such eloquence and power that they are still memorized today. Lincoln's presidency was dominated by the Civil War, and his campaign for that office focused not on the abolition of slavery but on preserving the Union. He was a good politician, a skillful speaker, and an independent thinker. His stand against slavery when he issued the Emancipation Proclamation in 1863 showed his belief that the Union he worked so tirelessly to keep could not be preserved with slavery as a part of it. His rhetoric, using allusions form classical works and from the Bible, colloquial and timely, helped unite people spiritually though they were politically divided.

Gettysburg Address

Address Delivered at the Dedication of the Cemetery at Gettysburg

Four score and seven years ago our fathers brought forth on this continent, a new nation, conceived in Liberty, and dedicated to the proposition that all men are created equal.

Now we are engaged in a great civil war, testing whether that nation, or any nation so conceived and so dedicated, can long endure. We are met on a great battle-field of that war. We have come to dedicate a portion of that field, as a final resting place for those who here gave their lives that that nation might live. It is altogether fitting and proper that we should do this.

But, in a larger sense, we can not dedicate—we can not consecrate—we can not hallow—this ground. The brave men, living and dead, who struggled here, have consecrated it, far above our poor power to add or detract. The world will little note, nor long remember what we say here, but it can never forget what they did here. It is for us the living, rather, to be dedicated here to the unfinished work which they who fought here have thus far so nobly advanced. It is rather for us to be here dedicated to the great task remaining before us—that from these honored dead we take increased devotion to that cause for which they gave the last full measure of devotion—that we here highly resolve that these dead shall not have died in vain—that this nation, under God, shall have a new birth of freedom—and that government of the people, by the people, for the people, shall not perish from the earth.

[November 19, 1863]

Read

1. The battle at Gettysburg was fought in July, 1863. What does the date of this speech suggest about the setting for Lincoln's speech?
2. How does Lincoln use history in his speech?
3. What is the effect of punctuation in the speech?
4. What words indicate the level of diction Lincoln uses?

Write

1. Write a sentence or two that describes the effect of the speech on you as a reader in the twenty-first century.
2. This kind of speech—a dedication and a eulogy—is called *epideictic,* or ceremonial, supposedly without a persuasive aim. Do you agree? If there is an argument, what do you think it is?

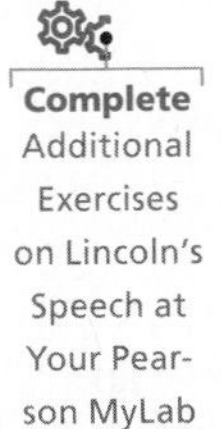
Complete Additional Exercises on Lincoln's Speech at Your Pearson MyLab

3. Write a paragraph on the appeal you believe Lincoln employs most often.
4. Describe the *ethos* Lincoln creates for himself as a speaker in the speech, using lines from the speech itself to aid your description.

Connect

1. How might you have felt as a part of the audience at the battlefield after hearing Lincoln's speech? Choose details from the speech to explain your reaction.
2. How is this speech similar to Lincoln's Second Inaugural in Chapter 4?

Winslow Homer

Winslow Homer (1836–1910) was born in Boston and became one of the foremost painters in the nineteenth century, painting scenes of New England life and work. He often painted children at play and seascapes. He became a lithographer and an illustrator for magazines, including *Harper's Weekly*. *Harper's* sent him to sketch scenes of the Civil War as it was waning. He sketched battlefields and scenes of camp life. *Near Andersonville* depicts a scene outside the notorious prison for Union soldiers near Andersonville, Georgia. Union soldiers are being led to freedom as a freed woman looks out from her cabin.

Near Andersonville

Near Andersonville (1865–1866), Winslow Homer. Oil on canvas, 23" x 18". Newark Museum, Newark, New Jersey/Licensed by Art Resource, NY

[1865–1866]

Read

1. How does the painter use symbols to suggest his aim?
2. What is the relationship between foreground and background?
3. How would you describe the tone the painter evokes in the painting?

Write

1. Write a few sentences that describe the facial expression of the woman in the foreground, using details of her gaze, stance, and position in the painting.
2. How does her expression reveal the painter's aim?
3. Reflect on your response to the painting, in its details and the overall effect.

Connect

1. Write a paragraph that suggests links between this painting and Lincoln's Gettysburg Address.
2. Compare Homer's painting with another painting in an earlier unit in terms of several techniques used by both—light, detail, and effect.

Contemporary Works

Lucille Clifton

Lucille Clifton (1936–2010) was born in upstate New York and educated at Howard University and at the State University of New York at Fredonia. Her first collection of poetry, *Good Times,* was named one of the best books of the year by the *New York Times* in 1969. She published over eight poetry collections, as well as essays and children's books. Her themes concern working lives of African Americans, family relationships, and racial histories. Clifton served as poet laureate of Maryland from 1979–1985.

at the cemetery, walnut grove plantation, south carolina, 1989

among the rocks
at walnut grove
your silence drumming
in my bones,
tell me your names. 5

nobody mentioned slaves
and yet the curious tools

shine with your fingerprints.
nobody mentioned slaves
but somebody did this work 10
who had no guide, no stone,
who moulders under rock.

tell me your names
tell me your bashful names
and i will testify 15
the inventory lists ten slaves
but only men were recognized

among the rocks
at walnut grove
some of these honored dead 20
were dark
some of these dark
were slaves
some of these slaves
were women 25
some of them did this
honored work
tell me your names
foremothers, brothers,
tell me your dishonored names 30
here lies
here lies
here lies
here lies
hear 35

Read

1. What is the importance of using setting as the title of the poem?
2. Who is the speaker addressing in the first stanzas?
3. How does the audience being addressed shift during the poem?
4. How does repetition create rhetorical effects in the poem?

Write

1. Use a line from the poem to explain how the speaker relates to the people she describes in the poem.

2. Discuss how irony or word play heighten the poem's rhetorical message.
3. List a few adjectives that you think characterize the voice of the speaker.

Connect

1. Compare the use of the word "honored" and "dead" in Lincoln's "Gettysburg Address" and Clifton's poem.
2. Locate at least one other text in this unit or an earlier one and discuss the strategies used by the author of the piece and Clifton to describe and honor the lives of ordinary people (LeSueur and Olsen are some examples you might choose).

William Raspberry

William Raspberry (b. 1936) is a journalist and syndicated columnist who wrote for over forty years for *The Washington Post*. He was born in Okolona, Mississippi, and left his small segregated town to begin reporting, covering major events and writing stories on education, race, social justice, and crime. In 1994, he won the Pulitzer Prize for commentary. He taught at Duke University, where he held the Knight Chair in Communication and Journalism. Raspberry retired in 2005. This essay first appeared in his syndicated column in 1982.

The Handicap of Definition

I know all about bad schools, mean politicians, economic deprivation and racism. Still, it occurs to me that one of the heaviest burdens black Americans—and black children in particular—have to bear is the handicap of definition: the question of what it means to be black.

Let me explain quickly what I mean. If a basketball fan says that the Boston Celtics' Larry Bird° plays "black," the fan intends it—and Bird probably accepts it—as a compliment. Tell pop singer Tom Jones° he moves "black" and he might grin in appreciation. Say to Teena Marie° or The Average White Band° that they sound "black" and they'll thank you.

But name one pursuit, aside from athletics, entertainment or sexual performance in which a white practitioner will feel complimented to be told he does it "black." Tell a white broadcaster he talks "black," and he'll sign up for diction lessons.

Larry Bird: (b. 1956), star forward for the Boston Celtics (1979–1992)

Tom Jones: (b. 1940), Welsh pop singer

Teena Marie: (1956–2010), white American R&B and disco singer

The Average White Band: Scottish R&B and funk band of the 1970s

Tell a white reporter he writes "black" and he'll take a writing course. Tell a white lawyer he reasons "black" and he might sue you for slander.

What we have here is a tragically limited definition of blackness, and it isn't only white people who buy it.

Think of all the ways black children can put one another down with charges of "whiteness." For many of these children, hard study and hard work are "white." Trying to please a teacher might be criticized as acting "white." Speaking correct English is "white." Scrimping today in the interest of tomorrow's goals is "white." Educational toys and games are "white."

An incredible array of habits and attitudes that are conducive to success in business, in academia, in the nonentertainment professions are likely to be thought of as somehow "white." Even economic success, unless it involves such "black" undertakings as numbers banking, is defined as "white."

And the results are devastating. I wouldn't deny that blacks often are better entertainers and athletes. My point is the harm that comes from too narrow a definition of what is black.

One reason black youngsters tend to do better at basketball, for instance, is that they assume they can learn to do it well, and so they practice constantly to prove themselves right.

Wouldn't it be wonderful if we could infect black children with the notion that excellence in math is "black" rather than white, or possibly Chinese? Wouldn't it be of enormous value if we could create the myth that morality, strong families, determination, courage and love of learning are traits brought by slaves from Mother Africa and therefore quintessentially° black?

There is no doubt in my mind that most black youngsters could develop their mathematical reasoning, their elocution° and their attitudes the way they develop their jump shots and their dance steps: by the combination of sustained, enthusiastic practice and the unquestioned belief that they can do it.

In one sense, what I am talking about is the importance of developing positive ethnic traditions. Maybe Jews have an innate talent for communication; maybe Chinese are born with a gift for mathematical reasoning; maybe blacks are naturally blessed with athletic grace. I doubt it. What is at work, I suspect, is assumption, inculcated early in their lives, that this is a thing our people do well.

---

quintessentially: most typically
elocution: the art of public speaking

Unfortunately, many of the things about which blacks make this assumption are things that do not contribute to their career success—except for that handful of the truly gifted who can make it as entertainers and athletes. And many of the things we concede to whites are the things that are essential to economic security.

So it is with a number of assumptions black youngsters make about what it is to be a "man": physical aggressiveness, sexual prowess, the refusal to submit to authority. The prisons are full of people who, by this perverted definition, are unmistakably men.

But the real problem is not so much that the things defined as "black" are negative. The problem is that the definition is much too narrow.

Somehow, we have to make our children understand that they are intelligent, competent people, capable of doing whatever they put their minds to and making it in the American mainstream, not just in a black subculture.

What we seem to be doing, instead, is raising up yet another generation of young blacks who will be failures—by definition.

[1982]

Read

1. What kind of evidence does Raspberry use to prove his claim that a big problem for African American children is one of definition?
2. Why does he suggest that limited definition of "black" is such a problem?
3. Why does he believe that so many African American young people are good at basketball, for example?
4. What is Raspberry's aim in comparing African American definitions to the definitions other ethnic groups hold?

Write

1. Respond to Raspberry's claim by agreeing, disagreeing, or qualifying his position based on your experience and reading.
2. Write a brief analysis of Raspberry's primary rhetorical strategies in conveying his idea.

Connect

1. How would Raspberry suggest that slavery and the Civil War continue to have an effect on African Americans' definitions of themselves?
2. Compare Raspberry's argument to Douglass's or to another African American writer in this unit.

Gloria Steinem

Feminist, journalist, and social activist Gloria Steinem (b. 1934) was born in Ohio. Early in her life, her mother became an invalid and her father left the family. She became a writer, an organizer, and a reporter. She worked to establish equal rights for women, helped found the National Women's Political Caucus, and in 1972, founded the feminist magazine *Ms.* As an articulate speaker and writer, Steinem became the face of the women's movement in the 1970s. She continues to work for social justice for women, Hispanics, and African Americans. She is active in politics, especially in the 2008 election, where she supported Democratic nominee Hillary Clinton. This essay was originally published in *The New York Times* as a commentary on the campaign.

Women Are Never Front-Runners

The woman in question became a lawyer after some years as a community organizer, married a corporate lawyer and is the mother of two little girls, ages 9 and 6. Herself the daughter of a white American mother and a black African father — in this race-conscious country, she is considered black — she served as a state legislator for eight years, and became an inspirational voice for national unity.

Be honest: Do you think this is the biography of someone who could be elected to the United States Senate? After less than one term there, do you believe she could be a viable candidate to head the most powerful nation on earth?

If you answered no to either question, you're not alone. Gender is probably the most restricting force in American life, whether the question is who must be in the kitchen or who could be in the White House. This country is way down the list of countries electing women and, according to one study, it polarizes gender roles more than the average democracy.

That's why the Iowa primary was following our historical pattern of making change. Black men were given the vote a half-century before women of any race were allowed to mark a ballot, and generally have ascended to positions of power, from the military to the boardroom, before any women (with the possible exception of obedient family members in the latter).

If the lawyer described above had been just as charismatic but named, say, Achola Obama instead of Barack Obama, her goose would have been cooked long ago. Indeed, neither she nor Hillary Clinton could have used Mr. Obama's public style — or Bill Clinton's either — without being considered too emotional by Washington pundits.

So why is the sex barrier not taken as seriously as the racial one? The reasons are as pervasive as the air we breathe: because sexism is still confused with nature as racism once was; because anything that affects males is seen as more serious than anything that affects "only" the female half of the human race; because children are still raised mostly by women (to put it mildly) so men especially tend to feel they are regressing to childhood when dealing with a powerful woman; because racism stereotyped black men as more "masculine" for so long that some white men find their presence to be masculinity-affirming (as long as there aren't too many of them); and because there is still no "right" way to be a woman in public power without being considered a you-know-what.

I'm not advocating a competition for who has it toughest. The caste systems of sex and race are interdependent and can only be uprooted together. That's why Senators Clinton and Obama have to be careful not to let a healthy debate turn into the kind of hostility that the news media love. Both will need a coalition of outsiders to win a general election. The abolition and suffrage movements progressed when united and were damaged by division; we should remember that.

I'm supporting Senator Clinton because like Senator Obama she has community organizing experience, but she also has more years in the Senate, an unprecedented eight years of on-the-job training in the White House, no masculinity to prove, the potential to tap a huge reservoir of this country's talent by her example, and now even the courage to break the no-tears rule. I'm not opposing Mr. Obama; if he's the nominee, I'll volunteer. Indeed, if you look at votes during their two-year overlap in the Senate, they were the same more than 90 percent of the time. Besides, to clean up the mess left by President Bush, we may need two terms of President Clinton and two of President Obama.

But what worries me is that he is seen as unifying by his race while she is seen as divisive by her sex.

What worries me is that she is accused of "playing the gender card" when citing the old boys' club, while he is seen as unifying by citing civil rights confrontations.

What worries me is that male Iowa voters were seen as gender-free when supporting their own, while female voters were seen as biased if they did and disloyal if they didn't.

What worries me is that reporters ignore Mr. Obama's dependence on the old — for instance, the frequent campaign comparisons to John F. Kennedy — while not challenging the slander that her progressive policies are part of the Washington status quo.

What worries me is that some women, perhaps especially younger ones, hope to deny or escape the sexual caste system; thus Iowa women over 50 and 60, who disproportionately supported Senator Clinton, proved once again that women are the one group that grows more radical with age.

This country can no longer afford to choose our leaders from a talent pool limited by sex, race, money, powerful fathers and paper degrees. It's time to take equal pride in breaking all the barriers. We have to be able to say: "I'm supporting her because she'll be a great president *and* because she's a woman."

[2008]

Read

1. What does Steinem suggest were the reasons for Barack Obama's nomination over Hillary Clinton's?
2. How would you describe the tone of Steinem's article?
3. How does Steinem use history to make her point?
4. The article provoked a fair amount of criticism when it was published. What are the arguments or premises that might provoke criticism from readers?

Write

1. Respond to Steinem's claim about women's struggle to achieve authority in public life.
2. Write a brief paragraph that describes Steinem's persona in this piece. Use lines from the text, her choices of image and diction, to develop your discussion.

Connect

1. How does Steinem's article reinforce or extend any point made by the Declaration of Sentiments?
2. Do you think Steinem's criticism remains valid? Why or why not? For example, Hillary Clinton was secretary of state during the first Obama term. Does this affect Steinem's argument?

N. Scott Momaday

N. Scott Momaday (b. 1934) was born in Lawton, Oklahoma, and spent his first year on the Kiowa Reservation, where his father was raised. His parents were teachers on Indian reservations in Arizona and Oklahoma. Momaday's talent in poetry was recognized early and he won a poetry fellowship to study at Stanford University. His novel, *House Made of Dawn*, won the 1969 Pulitzer Prize for Fiction. The autobiographical work *The Way to Rainy Mountain* is a collection of Kiowa tales. In 2007, President George W. Bush awarded Momaday the National Medal of Arts for his contributions to literature.

From *The Way to Rainy Mountain*

A single knoll° rises out of the plain in Oklahoma, north and west of the Wichita Range. For my people, the Kiowas, it is an old landmark, and they gave it the name Rainy Mountain. The hardest weather in the world is there. Winter brings blizzards, hot tornadic winds arise in the spring, and in summer the prairie is an anvil's edge. The grass turns brittle and brown, and it cracks beneath your feet. There are green belts along the rivers and creeks, linear groves of hickory and pecan, willow and witch hazel. At a distance in July or August the steaming foliage seems almost to writhe in fire. Great green and yellow grasshoppers are everywhere in the tall grass, popping up like corn to sting the flesh, and tortoises crawl about on the red earth, going nowhere in the plenty° of time. Loneliness is an aspect of the land. All things in the plain are isolate; there is no confusion of objects in the eye, but *one* hill or *one* tree or *one* man. To look upon that landscape in the early morning, with the sun at your back, is to lose the sense of proportion. Your imagination comes to life, and this, you think, is where Creation was begun.

I returned to Rainy Mountain in July. My grandmother had died in the spring, and I wanted to be at her grave. She had lived to be very old and at last infirm. Her only living daughter was with her when she died, and I was told that in death her face was that of a child.

I like to think of her as a child. When she was born, the Kiowas were living the last great moment of their history. For more than a hundred years they had controlled the open range from the Smoky Hill River to the Red, from the headwaters of the Canadian to the fork of the Arkansas and Cimarron. In alliance with the Comanches, they had ruled the whole of the southern Plains. War was their sacred business, and they were among the finest horsemen the world has ever known. But warfare for the Kiowas was preeminently a matter of disposition rather than of survival, and they never understood the grim, unrelenting advance of the U.S. Cavalry. When at last, divided and ill-provisioned, they were driven onto the Staked Plains in the cold rains of autumn, they fell into panic. In Palo Duro Canyon they

---

knoll: small, rounded hill

plenty: abundance

abandoned their crucial stores to pillage° and had nothing then but their lives. In order to save themselves, they surrendered to the soldiers at Fort Sill and were imprisoned in the old stone corral that now stands as a military museum. My grandmother was spared the humiliation of those high gray walls by eight or ten years, but she must have known from birth the affliction of defeat, the dark brooding of old warriors.

Her name was Aho, and she belonged to the last culture to evolve in North America. Her forebears came down from the high country in western Montana nearly three centuries ago. They were a mountain people, a mysterious tribe of hunters whose language has never been positively classified in any major group. In the late seventeenth century they began a long migration to the south and east. It was a journey toward the dawn, and it led to a golden age. Along the way the Kiowas were befriended by the Crows, who gave them the culture and religion of the Plains. They acquired horses, and their ancient nomadic° spirit was suddenly free of the ground. They acquired Tai-me, the sacred Sun Dance doll, from that moment the object and symbol of their worship, and so shared in the divinity of the sun. Not least, they acquired the sense of destiny, therefore courage and pride. When they entered upon the southern Plains they had been transformed. No longer were they slaves to the simple necessity of survival; they were a lordly and dangerous society of fighters and thieves, hunters and priests of the sun. According to their origin myth, they entered the world through a hollow log. From one point of view, their migration was the fruit of an old prophecy, for indeed they emerged from a sunless world.

5 Although my grandmother lived out her long life in the shadow of Rainy Mountain, the immense landscape of the continental interior lay like memory in her blood. She could tell of the Crows, whom she had never seen, and of the Black Hills, where she had never been. I wanted to see in reality what she had seen more perfectly in the mind's eye, and traveled fifteen hundred miles to begin my pilgrimage.

Yellowstone, it seemed to me, was the top of the world, a region of deep lakes and dark timber, canyons and waterfalls. But, beautiful as it is, one might have the sense of confinement there. The skyline in all directions is close at hand, the high wall of the woods and deep cleavages of shade. There is a perfect freedom in the mountains, but it belongs to the eagle and

---

pillage: plunder
nomadic: roving, wandering

the elk, the badger and the bear. The Kiowas reckoned their stature by the distance they could see, and they were bent and blind in the wilderness.

Descending eastward, the highland meadows are a stairway to the plain. In July the inland slope of the Rockies is luxuriant with flax and buckwheat, stonecrop and larkspur. The earth unfolds and the limit of the land recedes. Clusters of trees, and animals grazing far in the distance, cause the vision to reach away and wonder to build upon the mind. The sun follows a longer course in the day, and the sky is immense beyond all comparison. The great billowing clouds that sail upon it are the shadows that move upon the grain like water, dividing light. Farther down, in the land of the Crows and Blackfeet, the plain is yellow. Sweet clover takes hold of the hills and bends upon itself to cover and seal the soil. There the Kiowas paused on their way; they had come to the place where they must change their lives. The sun is at home on the plains. Precisely there does it have the certain character of a god. When the Kiowas came to the land of the Crows, they could see the dark lees of the hills at dawn across the Bighorn River, the profusion of light on the grain shelves, the oldest deity ranging after the solstices. Not yet would they veer southward to the caldron° of the land that lay below; they must wean their blood from the northern winter and hold the mountains a while longer in their view. They bore Tai-me in procession to the east.

A dark mist lay over the Black Hills, and the land was like iron. At the top of a ridge I caught sight of Devil's Tower upthrust against the gray sky as if in the birth of time the core of the earth had broken through its crust and the motion of the world was begun. There are things in nature that engender an awful quiet in the heart of man; Devil's Tower is one of them. Two centuries ago, because they could not do otherwise, the Kiowas made a legend at the base of the rock. My grandmother said:

> Eight children were there at play, seven sisters and their brother. Suddenly the boy was struck dumb; he trembled and began to run upon his hands and feet. His fingers became claws, and his body was covered with fur. Directly there was a bear where the boy had been. The sisters were terrified; they ran, and the bear after them. They came to the stump of a great tree, and the tree spoke to them. It bade them climb upon it, and as they did so it began to rise into the air. The bear came to kill them, but they

---

caldron: large pot for boiling

were just beyond its reach. It reared against the tree and scored° the bark all around with its claws. The seven sisters were borne into the sky, and they became the stars of the Big Dipper.

From that moment, and so long as the legend lives, the Kiowas have kinsmen in the night sky. Whatever they were in the mountains, they could be no more. However tenuous° their well-being, however much they had suffered and would suffer again, they had found a way out of the wilderness.

10

My grandmother had a reverence for the sun, a holy regard that now is all but gone out of mankind. There was a wariness in her, and an ancient awe. She was a Christian in her later years, but she had come a long way about, and she never forgot her birthright. As a child she had been to the Sun Dances; she had taken part in those annual rites, and by them she had learned the restoration of her people in the presence of Tai-me. She was about seven when the last Kiowa Sun Dance was held in 1887 on the Washita River above Rainy Mountain Creek. The buffalo were gone. In order to consummate° the ancient sacrifice—to impale the head of a buffalo bull upon the medicine tree—a delegation of old men journeyed into Texas, there to beg and barter for an animal from the Goodnight herd. She was ten when the Kiowas came together for the last time as a living Sun Dance culture. They could find no buffalo; they had to hang an old hide from the sacred tree. Before the dance could begin, a company of soldiers rode out from Fort Sill under orders to disperse the tribe. Forbidden without cause the essential act of their faith, having seen the wild herds slaughtered and left to rot upon the ground, the Kiowas backed away forever from the medicine tree. That was July 20, 1890, at the great bend of the Washita. My grandmother was there. Without bitterness, and for as long as she lived, she bore a vision of deicide.°

Now that I can have her only in memory, I see my grandmother in the several postures that were peculiar to° her: standing at the wood stove on a winter morning and turning meat in a great iron skillet: sitting at the south window, bent above her beadwork, and afterwards, when her vision failed, looking down for a long time into the fold of her hands; going out upon a cane, very slowly as she did when the weight of age came upon her;

---

scored: made cuts or lines in

tenuous: slight, insubstantial

consummate: complete, achieve

deicide: the killing of a god

peculiar to: particular to, characteristic of

praying. I remember her most often at prayer. She made long, rambling prayers out of suffering and hope, having seen many things. I was never sure that I had the right to hear, so exclusive were they of all mere custom and company. The last time I saw her she prayed standing by the side of her bed at night, naked to the waist, the light of a kerosene lamp moving upon her dark skin. Her long, black hair, always drawn and braided in the day, lay upon her shoulders and against her breasts like a shawl. I do not speak Kiowa, and I never understood her prayers, but there was something inherently sad in the sound, some merest hesitation upon the syllables of sorrow. She began in a high and descending pitch, exhausting her breath to silence; then again and again—and always the same intensity of effort, of something that is, and is not, like urgency in the human voice. Transported so in the dancing light among the shadows of her room, she seemed beyond the reach of time. But that was illusion; I think I knew then that I should not see her again.

Houses are like sentinels° in the plain, old keepers of the weather watch. There, in a very little while, wood takes on the appearance of great age. All colors wear soon away in the wind and rain, and then the wood is burned gray and the grain appears and the nails turn red with rust. The windowpanes are black and opaque; you imagine there is nothing within, and indeed there are many ghosts, bones given up to the land. They stand here and there against the sky, and you approach them for a longer time than you expect. They belong in the distance; it is their domain.

Once there was a lot of sound in my grandmother's house, a lot of coming and going, feasting and talk. The summers there were full of excitement and reunion. The Kiowas are a summer people; they abide the cold and keep to themselves, but when the season turns and the land becomes warm and vital they cannot hold still; an old love of going returns upon them. The aged visitors who came to my grandmother's house when I was a child were made of lean° and leather, and they bore themselves upright. They wore great black hats and bright ample shirts that shook in the wind. They rubbed fat upon their hair and wound their braids with strips of colored cloth. Some of them painted their faces and carried the scars of old and cherished enmities.° They were an old council of warlords, come to remind

---

sentinels: sentries, lookouts

lean: the part of meat with little or no fat

enmities: hostilities, animosities

and be reminded of who they were. Their wives and daughters served them well. The women might indulge themselves; gossip was at once the mark and compensation of their servitude. They made loud and elaborate talk among themselves, full of jest and gesture, fright and false alarm. They went abroad in fringed and flowered shawls, bright beadwork and German silver. They were at home in the kitchen, and they prepared meals that were banquets.

There were frequent prayer meetings, and great nocturnal feasts. When I was a child I played with my cousins outside, where the lamplight fell upon the ground and the singing of the old people rose up around us and carried away into the darkness. There were a lot of good things to eat, a lot of laughter and surprise. And afterwards, when the quiet returned, I lay down with my grandmother and could hear the frogs away by the river and feel the motion of the air.

15 Now there is a funeral silence in the rooms, the endless wake of some final word. The walls have closed in upon my grandmother's house. When I returned to it in mourning, I saw for the first time in my life how small it was. It was late at night, and there was a white moon, nearly full. I sat for a long time on the stone steps by the kitchen door. From there I could see out across the land; I could see the long row of trees by the creek, the low light upon the rolling plains, and the stars of the Big Dipper. Once I looked at the moon and caught sight of a strange thing. A cricket had perched upon the handrail, only a few inches away from me. My line of vision was such that the creature filled the moon like a fossil. It had gone there, I thought, to live and die, for there, of all places, was its small definition made whole and eternal. A warm wind rose up and purled° like the longing within me.

The next morning I awoke at dawn and went out on the dirt road to Rainy Mountain. It was already hot, and the grasshoppers began to fill the air. Still, it was early in the morning, and the birds sang out of the shadows. The long yellow grass on the mountain shone in the bright light, and a scissortail° hied° above the land. There, where it ought to be, at the end of a long and legendary way, was my grandmother's grave. Here and there on the dark stones were ancestral names. Looking back once, I saw the mountain and came away.

[1969]

---

purled: passed by with a murmuring sound
scissortail: a bird with a long, forked tail
hied: hurried

Read

1. What does the use of the word "my" in line 2 of the essay suggest about Momaday's persona?
2. How do physical details of setting contribute to what Momaday calls the "loneliness" of the land?
3. How does Momaday create a link between his grandmother and cultural history?
4. What details suggest Momaday's attitude toward nature and the natural world?

Write

1. Use details from the text to write a paragraph that describes Momaday's feelings about his grandmother.
2. How would you describe the tone of the passage? List a few images that suggest the tone to you.
3. How does figurative language help convey the point Momaday makes about history, progress, and Indian life?

Complete Additional Exercises on Momaday's Essay at Your Pearson MyLab

Connect

1. Find another text in this or an earlier unit that describes what and how the old teach the young and compare its description to Momaday's (Hawthorne, Stowe, Emerson, and Cooper are some possibilities).
2. How do you think nature becomes a character in this essay?
3. Compare the portrayal of the grandmother's spirituality to characterizations of spiritual life in any colonial text.

UNIT ACTIVITIES

Rhetorical Analysis

1. Sojourner Truth was an eloquent, effective speaker, but she was illiterate, and so her speeches were recorded by others. Read the two versions of her speech to the Ohio Convention and write an essay that analyzes how the differences in diction, image, spelling, and detail change the effect of the speech and the persona of the speaker.
2. Emerson argued for a literature that would help establish the character of the new nation in its new forms and its use of American settings and characters. Analyze the work of one writer in this unit who you believe demonstrates some of the characteristics Emerson hoped to see in American literature by examining the choice of diction, setting, and genre. Some good possibilities include Douglass, Hawthorne, and Whitman.

Argument

1. The more things change the more they stay the same, the saying goes. Gloria Steinem makes that argument in her piece on Hillary Clinton's

presidential bid in 2008. Do you agree? Use any nineteenth-century writer and your own experience to take a position on Steinem's assertion.

2. It took nearly seventy years from the time Elizabeth Cady Stanton wrote the Declaration of Sentiments until women were given the right to vote. Rewrite one section of the Declaration and then explain how your revision might have been more immediately successful in the cause of women's suffrage.
3. Mathew Brady's photographs of the Civil War were the first starkly real depictions of war and violence that most people had ever seen. He captured scenes of camp life and horrific images of the dead on battlefields. Using the photo of Wounded Soldiers in Hospital, and any experiences or observations that add to your argument, write an essay that takes a position on the usefulness of graphic images of war and violence and its effects.

Synthesis

How does the past influence the present? How much should a country or community value and preserve tradition? The conflict between old and new, tradition and change, loomed large in the middle years of the nineteenth century in America. Evaluate the positions on this conflict in the work of at least four of the following writers and artists.

Nathaniel Hawthorne
Frederick Douglass
Sojourner Truth
Elizabeth Cady Stanton
Walt Whitman
A. E. Ted Aub

SYNTHESIS PROJECT: UNITS 1, 2, 3

America remains a land of immigrants and a land where people continue to move. Their struggles to move from one place to another and their reasons for migrating depend on the culture and context they are in, who they are, and what control they exercise. Read the texts below and then synthesize at least four of them to evaluate the variety of difficulties people encounter as they enter a new territory. Then write a coherent, well-developed essay that discusses what you believe to be the most important reasons for people's persistence in making perilous journeys. Be sure to use the sources to develop your own position.

Nathaniel Philbrick, from *Mayflower*
John Winthrop, "A Modell of Christian Charity"
Lerone Bennett, from *Before the Mayflower*
William Apess, from *A Son of the Forest*
George Catlin, "Letter from the Yellowstone River"
Harriet Ann Jacobs, from *Diary of a Slave Girl*
N. Scott Momaday, from *The Way to Rainy Mountain*

UNIT 4

Detroit, Michigan, has suffered as much as any city in the United States from recent economic decline. The American automobile industry, which began in Detroit in the early 1900s, lost sales to its competitors from Japan, Korea, and Germany starting in the 1970s. In 2011, in an effort to revitalize American car sales and by extension the economy of the region, the Chrysler Corporation started a new sales campaign that took on its competition. Here, a worker wears a T-shirt with the campaign slogan and a modified Chrysler logo.

Read

1. How does the photo communicate a sense of crisis?
2. What sense do you get about Detroit after considering the image?

Connect

1. How do the means used for recovery in Detroit connect to strategies suggested by earlier writers? What additional strategy is suggested?
2. How is a sense of "American-ness" invoked by the texts during this period and in the photo? How would you define this American-ness?

How Do We Recover a Nation?

1865–1933

The period after the Civil War ended in 1865 was marked by a series of upturns and downward spirals. The country grappled with the consequences of war, technological innovation, tremendous population growth, and social ills in the cities. America's growing stability and promise as a nation attracted immigrants from all over the world.

Growth of American Industry Industrialization meant that cities became centers for culture and work. Machines replaced hand labor as factory work replaced farm work as the way most people made a living. Workers flocked to cities where steady work and high pay were promised. As the twentieth century began, conflicts between workers and employers grew stronger when those promises seemed empty. The rights of immigrants, former slaves, and women increasingly became a part of the continuing cultural conversation and a source of unrest and disagreement.

Westward Expansion The country itself expanded to the western edge of the continent. Indians, already pushed from eastern lands or living quietly in unclaimed territory, were moved to reservations. The train, which sped the growth of Western regions and cities, became a symbol of technology and expansion.

World War I America's entrance into the European war in 1917 made it a dominant world power. America's help in winning that war brought a feeling of optimism. However, the forces of economic instability remained, and Europe continued to suffer the terrible effects of years-long violence. By the end of the 1920s a decade of wild speculation and greed caused an economic collapse—the Great Depression—that lasted another ten years.

GUIDING QUESTIONS

- How do we recover a nation?
- How do we reconcile progress and tradition?
- How do we help immigrants become citizens?
- How do we provide opportunities for economic progress?
- What happens to community in large cities?
- What is America's responsibility to the world?

Walt Whitman

Walt Whitman (1819–1892) is one of the most famous of American poets, called by some the "father of free verse" for his innovations in rhythm, rhyme, line, and image. Born in poverty in New York, he dropped out of school to support his family. His job as a printer taught him a love for language. He later taught school, was a journalist, and served as an Army nurse during the Civil War. *Leaves of Grass,* his signature book of poems, was first published in 1855, and he revised it again and again over the years.

Whitman wrote of the common people and of their leader, Lincoln, whom he eulogized in his poem "When Lilacs Last in the Dooryard Bloom'd" and "Oh Captain, My Captain." He saw the poet as the speaker for the people and as such an arm of democracy, the "great poem" that was America itself.

To a Locomotive in Winter

Thee for my recitative,°
Thee in the driving storm even as now, the snow, the winter-day declining,
Thee in thy panoply,° thy measur'd dual throbbing and thy beat convulsive,
Thy black cylindric body, golden brass and silvery steel,
Thy ponderous,° side-bars, parallel and connecting rods, gyrating, shuttling at thy sides 5
Thy metrical, now swelling pant and roar, now tapering in the distance,
Thy great protruding head-light fix'd in front,
Thy long, pale, floating vapor-pennants, tinged with delicate purple,
The dense and murky clouds out-belching from thy smoke-stack,
Thy knitted frame, thy springs and valves, the tremulous° twinkle of thy wheels, 10
Thy train of cars behind, obedient, merrily following,
Through gale or calm, now swift, now slack, yet steadily careering;°
Type of the modern—emblem of motion and power—pulse of the continent,
For once come serve the Muse° and merge in verse, even as here I see thee,

---

recitative: recital, recitation; in music, a passage of text that a singer delivers with natural rhythms of speech

panoply: full ceremonial dress and equipment

ponderous: slow and heavy

tremulous: shaking, quivering

careering: rushing, speeding

Muse: goddess of poetic inspiration

With storm and buffeting° gusts of wind and falling snow, 15
By day thy warning ringing bell to sound its notes,
By night thy silent signal lamps to swing.

Fierce-throated beauty!
Roll through my chant with all thy lawless° music, thy swinging lamps at night,
Thy madly-whistled laughter, echoing, rumbling like an earth-quake, 20
rousing all,
Law of thyself complete, thine own track firmly holding,
(No sweetness debonair of tearful harp or glib piano thine,)
Thy trills of shrieks by rocks and hills return'd,
Launch'd o'er the prairies wide, across the lakes,
To the free skies unpent° and glad and strong. 25

[1881]

Read

1. What is the effect of the use of the pronoun "thy" on your reading?
2. What images does the speaker use to convey his attitude toward the train?

Write

1. Whitman uses *apostrophe* when he speaks directly to the train. Define *apostrophe* and then write a paragraph that explains what Whitman's aim might be in using it in the poem.
2. Comment on how you think this poem reveals Whitman's attitude toward America.

Connect

1. Speculate about the way the train in Whitman's poem might be compared to the computer in the twenty-first century.

From *Democratic Vistas*

America, filling the present with greatest deeds and problems, cheerfully accepting the past, including feudalism, (as, indeed, the present is but the legitimate birth of the past, including feudalism,) counts, as I reckon, for her justification and success, (for who, as yet, dare claim success?) almost entirely

---

buffeting: beating, battering
lawless: free, not following the laws of musical composition
unpent: unconfined

on the future. Nor is that hope unwarranted. To-day, ahead, though dimly yet, we see, in vistas, a copious, sane, gigantic offspring. For our New World I consider far less important for what it has done, or what it is, than for results to come. Sole° among nationalities, these States have assumed the task to put in forms of lasting power and practicality, on areas of amplitude° rivaling the operations of the physical kosmos, the moral political speculations of ages, long, long deferr'd, the democratic republican principle, and the theory of development and perfection by voluntary standards, and self-reliance. Who else, indeed, except the United States, in history, so far, have accepted in unwitting faith, and, as we now see, stand, act upon, and go security° for, these things?

But preluding° no longer, let me strike the key-note of the following strain.° First premising° that, though the passages of it have been written at widely different times, (it is, in fact, a collection of memoranda, perhaps for future designers, comprehenders,) and though it may be open to the charge of one part contradicting another—for there are opposite sides to the great question of democracy, as to every great question—I feel the parts harmoniously blended in my own realization and convictions, and present them to be read only in such oneness, each page and each claim and assertion modified and temper'd by the others. Bear in mind, too, that they are not the result of studying up in political economy, but of the ordinary sense, observing, wandering among men, these States, these stirring years of war and peace. I will not gloss over° the appalling dangers of universal suffrage° in the United States. In fact, it is to admit and face these dangers I am writing. To him or her within whose thought rages the battle, advancing, retreating, between democracy's convictions, aspirations, and the people's crudeness, vice, caprices, I mainly write this essay. I shall use the words America and democracy as convertible° terms. Not an ordinary one is the issue. The United States are destined either to surmount the gorgeous history of feudalism, or else prove the most tremendous failure of time. Not the least doubtful am I on any prospects of their material success. The triumphant future of their business, geographic and productive departments, on larger scales and in more varieties than ever, is certain. In those respects the republic

---

Sole: alone
amplitude: range, abundance
go security: post bond
preluding: giving the introduction
strain: theme
premising: postulating, assuming
gloss over: whitewash
suffrage: voting rights
convertible: interchangeable

must soon (if she does not already) outstrip all examples hitherto° afforded, and dominate the world.

Admitting all this, with the priceless value of our political institutions, general suffrage, (and fully acknowledging the latest, widest opening of the doors,) I say that, far deeper than these, what finally and only is to make of our western world a nationality superior to any hitherto known, and outtopping the past, must be vigorous, yet unsuspected Literatures, perfect personalities and sociologies, original, transcendental,° and expressing (what, in highest sense, are not yet express'd at all,) democracy and the modern. With these, and out of these, I promulge° new races of Teachers, and of perfect Women, indispensable to endow° the birth-stock of a New World. For feudalism, caste, the ecclesiastic° traditions, though palpably° retreating from political institutions, still hold essentially, by their spirit, even in this country, entire possession of the more important fields, indeed the very subsoil, of education, and of social standards and literature.

I say that democracy can never prove itself beyond cavil,° until it founds and luxuriantly grows its own forms of art, poems, schools, theology, displacing all that exists, or that has been produced anywhere in the past, under opposite influences. It is curious to me that while so many voices, pens, minds, in the press, lecture-rooms, in our Congress, &c., are discussing intellectual topics, pecuniary° dangers, legislative problems, the suffrage, tariff and labor questions, and the various business and benevolent° needs of America, with propositions, remedies, often worth deep attention, there is one need, a hiatus° the profoundest, that no eye seems to perceive, no voice to state. Our fundamental want° to-day in the United States, with closest, amplest reference to present conditions, and to the future, is of a class, and the clear idea of a class, of native authors, literatures, far different, far higher in grade than any yet known, sacerdotal,° modern, fit to cope with our occasions, lands, permeating, the whole mass of American mentality, taste, belief, breathing into

---

hitherto: previously
transcendental: surpassing; idealistic
promulge: promulgate, proclaim
endow: supply
ecclesiastic: churchly, clerical
palpably: manifestly, obviously
cavil: trivial objection, quibble
pecuniary: financial, monetary
benevolent: charitable, philanthropic
hiatus: gap
want: need, lack
sacerdotal: priestly

it a new breath of life, giving it decision, affecting politics far more than the popular superficial suffrage, with results inside and underneath the elections of Presidents or Congresses—radiating, begetting appropriate teachers, schools, manners, and, as its grandest result, accomplishing (what neither the schools nor the churches and their clergy have hitherto accomplish'd, and without which this nation will no more stand, permanently, soundly, than a house will stand without a substratum,°) a religious and moral character beneath the political and productive and intellectual bases of the States. For know you not, dear, earnest reader, that the people of our land may all read and write, and may all possess the right to vote—and yet the main things may be entirely lacking?—(and this to suggest them.)

5 View'd, to-day, from a point of view sufficiently over-arching, the problem of humanity all over the civilized world is social and religious, and is to be finally met and treated by literature. The priest departs, the divine literatus° comes. Never was anything more wanted than, to-day, and here in the States, the poet of the modern is wanted, or the great literatus of the modern. At all times, perhaps, the central point in any nation, and that whence° it is itself really sway'd the most, and whence it sways others, is its national literature, especially its archetypal° poems. Above all previous lands, a great original literature is surely to become the justification and reliance, (in some respects the sole reliance,) of American democracy.

[1876]

Read

1. How does Whitman indicate his faith in America in the first few paragraphs?
2. How would you characterize the tone of this excerpt?
3. How does the context of the piece (written in 1876) affect what you take to be Whitman's aim?
4. What would you say is Whitman's primary rhetorical appeal? Find a line or two that you think demonstrates the use of that appeal.

Write

1. Why does Whitman rely upon art to do the work of democracy? Write a brief explanation.
2. Write a response to Whitman's claims about art, democracy, or progress, agreeing with him, disagreeing, or qualifying his position with your own.

---

substratum: foundation

literatus: intellectual

whence: from which source or cause

archetypal: original, as a prototype; perfect or typical, as a specimen

Connect

1. Whitman looks ahead to future vistas in this piece. Compare his vision with one other writer in Unit 1, 2, or 3 who you think has the same forward-looking stance.
2. How does the context of the Civil War, which ended just eleven years before Whitman wrote this piece, affect his position?

Emily Dickinson

Emily Dickinson (1830–1886) spent her entire life in Amherst, Massachusetts. She was the child of a prominent family but was a quiet, reclusive person in her everyday life. She published little during her lifetime, but in the decades after her death she became well respected and revered for her strikingly modern poetry and her equally striking insights into life. Dickinson often used paradox to make her points. In addition, an unusual blend of Latinate and Anglo-Saxon words made her diction dramatically different from other poets of her time. Dickinson continues to be regarded as the most contemporary of nineteenth-century poets.

I like to see it lap the Miles

I like to see it lap the Miles—
And lick the Valleys up—
And stop to feed itself at Tanks°
And then—prodigious° step

Around a Pile of Mountains— 5
And supercilious° peer
In Shanties—by the sides of Roads—
And then a Quarry pare°

To fit its sides, and crawl between
Complaining all the while 10
In horrid—hooting stanza—
Then chase itself down Hill—

Tanks: water tanks
prodigious: tremendous
supercilious: haughty, disdainful
pare: clip, shave

And neigh like Boanerges°—
Then—prompter than a Star 15
Stop—docile° and omnipotent
At its own stable door—

[c. 1862]

Read

1. How does the speaker characterize the train through personification?
2. How does the diction suggest the speaker's persona in the poem?
3. How do the adjectives in the next to last line seem to be contradictory?

Write

1. Write about Dickinson's use of irony in this poem and how you see it conveying her rhetorical aim.
2. Reflect on the way that personification adds to the effect of the poem as you read it.

Connect

1. How does Dickinson's attitude toward the train compare to Whitman's in "To a Locomotive"?
2. Locate another poet or other writer who you think uses irony and compare that work to Dickinson's poem.

The Brain is wider than the Sky

The Brain—is wider than the Sky—
For—put them side by side—
The one the other will contain
With ease—and You—beside—

Boanerges: a surname, meaning "sons of thunder," given by Jesus to the disciples James and John, in the Gospel of St. Mark; with a singular verb, it signifies a fiery preacher or orator

docile: obedient, manageable

The Brain is deeper than the sea— 5
For—hold them—Blue to Blue—
The one the other will absorb—
As Sponges—Buckets—do—

The Brain is just the weight of God—
For—Heft° them—Pound for Pound— 10
And they will differ—if they do—
As Syllable from Sound—

[1896]

Read

1. What images does the speaker use to emphasize the size of the brain?
2. Why is it important for her to make the brain seem massive?
3. What words suggest her tone of voice most clearly to you?

Write

1. What is the effect of the punctuation on you as a reader?
2. Comment on how this poem suggests Dickinson's attitude toward humans and the imagination.

Connect

1. How might Dickinson's ideas on the imagination be compared to Emerson's in Unit 2?
2. Do you think this poem is difficult to understand? Comment on the process of reading it.

Andrew Melrose

Andrew Melrose (1836–1901) was born in Scotland and emigrated to the United States around 1858. He quickly established himself as a painter of landscapes and harbor scenes. Associated with the Hudson River School of painting, Melrose painted atmospheric landscapes in the South and West. This painting's title is a reference to a painting hanging in the U.S. Capitol, *Westward the* Star of Empire *Takes Its Way Near Council Bluffs, Iowa*. It demonstrates the post–Civil War climate of expansionism.

Heft: test the weight of something by lifting it

Westward the Star of Empire *Takes Its Way—Near Council Bluffs, Iowa*

Westward the Star of Empire *Takes Its Way—Near Council Bluffs, Iowa* (1867), Andrew Melrose. Oil on canvas, 34 3/4 in x 55 3/4 in. Autry National Center; 92.147.1

[1867]

Read

1. How do details in the foreground contribute to the effect of the whole?
2. What is the function of light in the painting?
3. How do the details and their placement suggest the relationship between nature and technological progress?

Write

1. What is the significance of the title, given the train in the painting?
2. Write a reflection on how the painting symbolizes American notions of progress and change.

Connect

1. Do you notice anything that would seem to be a loss in the way the westward expansion is visualized here?

Mark Twain

Mark Twain, born Samuel Clemens (1835–1910), is one of America's most celebrated writers. He grew up in Hannibal, Missouri, where his most famous novels *The Adventures of Tom Sawyer* and its sequel, *Adventures of Huckleberry Finn,* were set. Twain was a river pilot on the Mississippi, a miner in Nevada, a newspaper reporter and a lecturer in California, and a humorist. His novels and essays were often based on his varied experiences. He wrote about the pretensions of newly rich Americans in Europe in *The Gilded Age*. His satire of hypocrisy, literary sentimentalism (as in his essay on James Fenimore Cooper), religion, and politics were very clear in late works like *The Mysterious Stranger*.

Fenimore Cooper's Literary Offenses

The Pathfinder and *The Deerslayer* stand at the head of Cooper's novels as artistic creations. There are others of his works which contain parts as perfect as are to be found in these, and scenes even more thrilling. Not one can be compared with either of them as a finished whole.

The defects in both of these tales are comparatively slight. They were pure works of art.—*Prof. Lounsbury*

The five tales reveal an extraordinary fulness of invention.

. . . One of the very greatest characters in fiction, "Natty Bumppo." . . .

The craft of the woodsman, the tricks of the trapper, all the delicate art of the forest, were familiar to Cooper from his youth up. —*Prof. Brander Matthews*

Cooper is the greatest artist in the domain of romantic fiction yet produced by America.—*Wilkie Collins*°

It seems that it was far from right for the Professor of English Literature in Yale, the Professor of English Literature in Columbia, and Wilkie Collins, to deliver opinions on Cooper's literature without having read some of it. It would have been much more decorous° to keep silent and let persons talk who have read Cooper.

Cooper's art has some defects. In one place in *Deerslayer,* and in the restricted space of two-thirds of a page, Cooper has scored 114 offences against literary art out of a possible 115. It breaks the record.

Willkie Collins: (1824–1889), English novelist, author of *The Moonstone* (1868)

decorous: proper

There are nineteen rules governing literary art in the domain of romantic fiction—some say twenty-two. In *Deerslayer* Cooper violated eighteen of them. These eighteen require:

1. That a tale shall accomplish something and arrive somewhere. But the *Deerslayer* tale accomplishes nothing and arrives in the air.
2. They require that the episodes of a tale shall be necessary parts of the tale, and shall help to develop it. But as the *Deerslayer* tale is not a tale, and accomplishes nothing and arrives nowhere, the episodes have no rightful place in the work, since there was nothing for them to develop.
3. They require that the personages in a tale shall be alive, except in the case of corpses, and that always the reader shall be able to tell the corpses from the others. But this detail has often been overlooked in the *Deerslayer* tale.
4. They require that the personages in a tale, both dead and alive, shall exhibit a sufficient excuse for being there. But this detail also has been overlooked in the *Deerslayer* tale.
5. They require that when the personages of a tale deal in conversation, the talk shall sound like human talk, and be talk such as human beings would be likely to talk in the given circumstances, and have a discoverable meaning, also a discoverable purpose, and a show of relevancy, and remain in the neighborhood of the subject in hand, and be interesting to the reader, and help out the tale, and stop when the people cannot think of anything more to say. But this requirement has been ignored from the beginning of the *Deerslayer* tale to the end of it.
6. They require that when the author describes the character of a personage in his tale, the conduct and conversation of that personage shall justify said description. But this law gets little or no attention in the *Deerslayer* tale, as "Natty Bumppo's" case will amply prove.
7. They require that when a personage talks like an illustrated, gilt-edged, tree-calf,° hand-tooled,° seven-dollar Friendship's Offering° in the beginning of a paragraph, he shall not talk like a negro minstrel in the end of it. But this rule is flung down and danced upon in the *Deerslayer* tale.
8. They require that crass stupidities shall not be played upon the reader as "the craft of the woodsman, the delicate art of the forest," by either the author or the people in the tale. But this rule is persistently violated in the *Deerslayer* tale.
9. They require that the personages of a tale shall confine themselves to possibilities and let miracles alone; or, if they venture a miracle, the

---

tree-calf: polished calfskin binding of a book, stained with a treelike design

hand-tooled: hand-worked by a craftsman

Friendship's Offering: an annual anthology published in the mid-nineteenth century

author must so plausibly set it forth as to make it look possible and reasonable. But these rules are not respected in the *Deerslayer* tale.

10. They require that the author shall make the reader feel a deep interest in the personages of his tale and in their fate; and that he shall make the reader love the good people in the tale and hate the bad ones. But the reader of the *Deerslayer* tale dislikes the good people in it, is indifferent to the others, and wishes they would all get drowned together.
11. They require that the characters in a tale shall be so clearly defined that the reader can tell beforehand what each will do in a given emergency. But in the *Deerslayer* tale this rule is vacated.°

In addition to these large rules there are some little ones. These require that the author shall

12. *Say* what he is proposing to say, not merely come near it.
13. Use the right word, not its second cousin.
14. Eschew° surplusage.°
15. Not omit necessary details.
16. Avoid slovenliness of form.
17. Use good grammar.
18. Employ a simple and straightforward style.

Even these seven are coldly and persistently violated in the *Deerslayer* tale.

Cooper's gift in the way of invention was not a rich endowment: but such as it was he liked to work it, he was pleased with the effects, and indeed he did some quite sweet things with it. In his little box of stage properties he kept six or eight cunning devices, tricks, artifices for his savages and woodsmen to deceive and circumvent each other with, and he was never so happy as when he was working these innocent things and seeing them go. A favorite one was to make a moccasined person tread in the tracks of the moccasined enemy, and thus hide his own trail. Cooper wore out barrels and barrels of moccasins in working that trick. Another stage-property that he pulled out of his box pretty frequently was his broken twig. He prized his broken twig above all the rest of his effects, and worked it the hardest. It is a restful chapter in any book of his when somebody doesn't step on a dry twig and alarm all the reds and whites for two hundred yards around. Every time a Cooper person is in peril, and absolute silence is worth four dollars a minute, he is sure to step on a dry twig. There may be a hundred handier things to step on, but that wouldn't satisfy Cooper. Cooper requires him to turn out and find a dry twig; and if he can't do it, go and borrow one. In fact the Leather Stocking Series ought to have been called the Broken Twig Series.

---

vacated: voided, annulled

Eschew: shun, avoid

surplusage: excess

I am sorry there is not room to put in a few dozen instances of the delicate art of the forest, as practiced by Natty Bumppo and some of the other Cooperian experts. Perhaps we may venture two or three samples. Cooper was a sailor—a naval officer; yet he gravely tells us how a vessel, driving toward a lee° shore in a gale, is steered for a particular spot by her skipper because he knows of an *undertow*° there which will hold her back against the gale and save her. For just pure woodcraft, or sailorcraft, or whatever it is, isn't that neat? For several years Cooper was daily in the society of artillery, and he ought to have noticed that when a cannon ball strikes the ground it either buries itself or skips a hundred feet or so; skips again a hundred feet or so—and so on, till it finally gets tired and rolls. Now in one place he loses some "females"—as he always calls women—in the edge of a wood near a plain at night in a fog, on purpose to give Bumppo a chance to show off the delicate art of the forest before the reader. These mislaid people are hunting for a fort. They hear a cannon-blast, and a cannon-ball presently comes rolling into the wood and stops at their feet. To the females this suggests nothing. The case is very different with the admirable Bumppo. I wish I may never know peace again if he doesn't strike out promptly and *follow the track* of that cannon-ball across the plain through the dense fog and find the fort. Isn't it a daisy? If Cooper had any real knowledge of Nature's ways of doing things, he had a most delicate art in concealing the fact. For instances: one of his acute Indian experts, *Chingachgook* (pronounced Chicago, I think), has lost the trail of a person he is tracking through the forest. Apparently that trail is hopelessly lost. Neither you nor I could ever have guessed out the way to find it. It was very different with Chicago. Chicago was not stumped for long. He turned a running stream out of its course, and there, in the slush in its old bed, were that person's moccasin-tracks. The current did not wash them away, as it would have done in all other like cases—no, even the eternal laws of Nature have to vacate when Cooper wants to put up° a delicate job of woodcraft on the reader. 5

We must be a little wary° when Brander Matthews tells us that Cooper's books "reveal an extraordinary fulness of invention." As a rule, I am quite willing to accept Brander Matthew's literary judgments and applaud his lucid and graceful phrasing of them; but that particular statement needs to be taken with a few tons of salt. Bless your heart, Cooper hadn't any more invention than a horse; and I don't mean a high-class horse, either; I mean a clothes horse. It would be very difficult to find a really clever "situation" in Cooper's books; and still more difficult to find one of any kind which he has failed to render absurd by his handling of it. Look at the episodes of "the caves"; and at the celebrated

lee: sheltered from the wind

undertow: a current below the surface moving in a different direction from the surface current

put up: put over

wary: watchful, suspicious

scuffle between Magua and those others on the table-land a few days later; and at Hurry Harry's queer° water-transit from the castle to the ark; and at Deerslayer's half hour with his first corpse; and at the quarrel between Hurry Harry and Deerslayer later; and at—but choose for yourself; you can't go amiss.

If Cooper had been an observer, his inventive faculty would have worked better, not more interestingly, but more rationally, more plausibly. Cooper's proudest creations in the way of "situations" suffer noticeably from the absence of the observer's protecting gift. Cooper's eye was splendidly inaccurate. Cooper seldom saw anything correctly. He saw nearly all things as through a glass eye, darkly. Of course a man who cannot see the commonest little everyday matters accurately is working at a disadvantage when he is constructing a "situation." In the *Deerslayer* tale Cooper has a stream which is fifty feet wide, where it flows out of a lake; it presently narrows to twenty as it meanders along for no given reason, and yet, when a stream acts like that it ought to be required to explain itself. Fourteen pages later the width of the brook's outlet from the lake has suddenly shrunk thirty feet and become the "narrowest part of the stream." This shrinkage is not accounted for. The stream has bends in it, a sure indication that it has alluvial° banks, and cuts them; yet these bends are only thirty and fifty feet long. If Cooper had been a nice and punctilious° observer he would have noticed that the bends were oftener nine hundred feet long than short of it.

Cooper made the exit of that stream fifty feet wide in the first place, for no particular reason; in the second place, he narrowed it to less than twenty to accommodate some Indians. He bends a "sapling" to the form of an arch over this narrow passage, and conceals six Indians in its foliage. They are "laying" for a settler's scow or ark which is coming up the stream on its way to the lake; it is being hauled against the stiff current by a rope whose stationary end is anchored in the lake; its rate of progress cannot be more than a mile an hour. Cooper describes the ark, but pretty obscurely. In the matter of dimensions "it was little more than a modern canal boat." Let us guess, then, that it was about 140 feet long. It was of "greater breadth than common." Let us guess, then, that it was about sixteen feet wide. This leviathan° had been prowling down bends which were but a third as long as itself, and scraping between banks where it had only two feet of space to spare on each side. We cannot too much admire this miracle. A low-roofed log dwelling occupies "two-thirds of the ark's length"—a dwelling ninety feet long and sixteen feet wide, let us say—a kind of vestibule train.° The dwelling has two rooms—each forty-five

---

queer: peculiar, odd

alluvial: pertaining to alluvium, any sediment deposited by flowing water

punctilious: careful, conscientious

leviathan: any huge marine animal, or something of great size and force

vestibule train: a train of passenger cars with enclosed end doors, so that one may walk from car to car

feet long and sixteen feet wide, let us guess. One of them is the bed-room of the Hutter girls, Judith and Hetty; the other is the parlor, in the day time, at night it is papa's bed chamber. The ark is arriving at the stream's exit, now, whose width has been reduced to less than twenty feet to accommodate the Indians—say to eighteen. There is a foot to spare on each side of the boat. Did the Indians notice that there was going to be a tight squeeze there? Did they notice that they could make money by climbing down out of that arched sapling and just stepping aboard when the ark scraped by? No; other Indians would have noticed these things, but Cooper's Indians never notice anything. Cooper thinks they are marvellous creatures for noticing, but he was almost always in error about his Indians. There was seldom a sane one among them.

The ark is 140 feet long; the dwelling is 90 feet long. The idea of the Indians is to drop softly and secretly from the arched sapling to the dwelling as the ark creeps along under it at the rate of a mile an hour, and butcher the family. It will take the ark a minute and half to pass under. It will take the 90-foot dwelling a minute to pass under. Now, then, what did the six Indians do? It would take you thirty years to guess, and even then you would have to give it up, I believe. Therefore, I will tell you what the Indians did. Their chief, a person of quite extraordinary intellect for a Cooper Indian, warily° watched the canal boat as it squeezed along under him, and when he had got his calculations fined down to exactly the right shade, as he judged, he let go and dropped, and *missed the house!* That is actually what he did. He missed the house, and landed in the stern of the scow. It was not much of a fall, yet it knocked him silly. He lay there unconscious. If the house had been 97 feet long, he would have made the trip. The fault was Cooper's, not his. The error lay in the construction of the house. Cooper was no architect.

10 There still remained in the roost five Indians. The boat has passed under and is now out of their reach. Let me explain what the five did—you would not be able to reason it out for yourself. No. 1 jumped for the boat, but fell in the water astern of it. Then No. 2 jumped for the boat, but fell in the water still further astern of it. Then No. 3 jumped for the boat, and fell a good way astern of it. Then No. 4 jumped for the boat, and fell in the water *away* astern. Then even No. 5 made a jump for the boat—for he was a Cooper Indian. In the matter of intellect, the difference between a Cooper Indian and the Indian that stands in front of the cigar shop is not spacious. The scow episode is really a sublime° burst of invention; but it does not thrill, because the inaccuracy of the details throws a sort of air of fictitiousness and general improbability over it. This comes of Cooper's inadequacy as an observer.

The reader will find some examples of Cooper's high talent for inaccurate observation in the account of the shooting match in *The Pathfinder.* "A

---

warily: vigilantly

sublime: supreme, outstanding

common wrought° nail was driven lightly into the target, its head having been first touched with paint." The color of the paint is not stated—an important omission, but Cooper deals freely in important omissions. No, after all, it was not an important omission; for this nail head is *a hundred yards* from the marksman and could not be seen by them at that distance no matter what its color might be. How far can the best eyes see a common house fly? A hundred yards? It is quite impossible. Very well, eyes that cannot see a house fly that is a hundred yards away cannot see an ordinary nail head at that distance, for the size of the two objects is the same. It takes a keen eye to see a fly or a nail head at fifty yards—one hundred and fifty feet. Can the reader do it?

The nail was lightly driven, its head painted, and game called. Then the Cooper miracles began. The bullet of the first marksman chipped an edge of the nail head; the next man's bullet drove the nail a little way into the target—and removed all the paint. Haven't the miracles gone far enough now? Not to suit Cooper; for the purpose of this whole scheme is to show off his prodigy,° Deerslayer-Hawkeye-Long-Rifle-Leather-Stocking-Pathfinder-Bumppo° before the ladies.

> "Be all ready to clench° it, boys!" cried out Pathfinder, stepping into his friend's tracks the instant they were vacant. "Never mind a new nail; I can see that, though the paint is gone, and what I can see, I can hit at a hundred yards, though it were only a mosquito's eye. Be ready to clench!"
>
> The rifle cracked, the bullet sped its way and the head of the nail was buried in the wood, covered by the piece of flattened lead.

There, you see, is a man who could hunt flies with a rifle, and command a ducal° salary in a Wild West show to-day, if we had him back with us.

The recorded feat is certainly surprising, just as it stands; but it is not surprising enough for Cooper. Cooper adds a touch. He had made Pathfinder do this miracle with another man's rifle, and not only that, but Pathfinder did not have even the advantage of loading it himself. He had everything against him, and yet he made that impossible shot, and not only made it, but did it with absolute confidence, saying, "Be ready to clench." Now a person like that would have undertaken that same feat with a brickbat,° and with Cooper to help he would have achieved it, too.

---

wrought: worked; shaped by beating with a hammer

prodigy: person of extraordinary abilities or talent

Deerslayer-Hawkeye-Long-Rifle-Leather-Stocking-Pathfinder-Bumppo: epithets applied in various of the novels to Natty Bumppo, the protagonist of the Leatherstocking Tales

clench: clinch

ducal: appropriate for a duke

brickbat: piece of broken brick

Pathfinder showed off handsomely that day before the ladies. His very first feat was a thing which no Wild West show can touch. He was standing with the group of marksmen, observing—a hundred yards from the target, mind: one Jasper raised his rifle and drove the centre of the bull's-eye. Then the quartermaster fired. The target exhibited no result this time. There was a laugh. "It's a dead miss," said Major Lundie. Pathfinder waited an impressive moment or two, then said in that calm, indifferent, know-it-all way of his, "No, Major—he has covered Jasper's bullet, as will be seen if any one will take the trouble to examine the target." 15

Wasn't it remarkable! How *could* he see that little pellet fly through the air and enter that distant bullet-hole? Yet that is what he did; for nothing is impossible to a Cooper person. Did any of those people have any deep-seated doubts about this thing? No; for that would imply sanity, and these were all Cooper people.

> The respect for Pathfinder's skill and for his *quickness and accuracy of sight* (the italics are mine) was so profound and general, that the instant he made this declaration the spectators began to distrust their own opinions, and a dozen rushed to the target in order to ascertain the fact. There, sure enough, it was found that the quartermaster's bullet had gone through the hole made by Jasper's, and that, too, so accurately as to require a minute° examination to be certain of the circumstance, which, however, was soon clearly established by discovering one bullet over the other in the stump against which the target was placed.

They made a "minute" examination; but never mind; how could they know that there were two bullets in that hole without digging the latest one out? for neither probe nor eyesight could prove the presence of any more than one bullet. Did they dig? No; as we shall see. It is the Pathfinder's turn now; he steps out before the ladies, takes aim, and fires.

But alas! here is a disappointment; an incredible, an unimaginable disappointment—for the target's aspect° is unchanged; there is nothing there but that same old bullet hole!

> "If one dared to hint at such a thing," cried major Duncan, "I should say that the Pathfinder has also missed the target."

As nobody had missed it yet, the "also" was not necessary; but never mind about that, for the Pathfinder is going to speak.

---

minute: extremely small

aspect: appearance

> "No; no, Major," said he, confidently, "that *would* be a risky declaration. I didn't load the piece, and can't say what was in it, but if it was lead, you will find the bullet driving down those of the Quartermaster and Jasper, else is not my name Pathfinder."

Is the miracle sufficient as it stands? Not for Cooper. The Pathfinder speaks again, as he "now slowly advances towards the stage occupied by the females:" 20

> "That's not all, boys, that's not all; if you find the target touched at all, I'll own to a miss. The Quartermaster cut the wood, but you'll find no wood cut by that last messenger."

The miracle is at last complete. He knew—doubtless *saw*—at the distance of a hundred yards—that his bullet had passed into the hole *without fraying the edges.* There were now three bullets in that one hole—three bullets imbedded processionally° in the body of the stump back of the target. Everybody knew this—somehow or other—and yet nobody had dug any of them out to make sure. Cooper is not a close observer, but he is interesting. He is certainly always that, no matter what happens. And he is more interesting when he is not noticing what he is about than when he is. This is a considerable merit.

The conversations in the Cooper books have a curious sound in our modern ears. To believe that such talk really ever came out of people's mouths would be to believe that there was a time when time was of no value to a person who thought he had something to say; when it was the custom to spread a two-minute remark out to ten; when a man's mouth was a rolling-mill° and busied itself all day long in turning four-foot pigs° of thought into thirty-foot bars of conversational railroad iron by attenuation;° when subjects were seldom faithfully stuck to, but the talk wandered all around and arrived nowhere; when conversations consisted mainly of irrelevancies, with here and there a relevancy, a relevancy with an embarrassed look, as not being able to explain how it got there.

Cooper was certainly not a master in the construction of dialogue. Inaccurate observation defeated him here as it defeated him in so many other enterprises of his. He even failed to notice that the man who talks corrupt English six days in the week must and will talk it on the seventh, and can't help himself. In the *Deerslayer* story he lets Deerslayer talk the showiest kind of book talk sometimes, and at other times the basest of base dialects. For

---

processionally: in procession, in a row

rolling-mill: a factory where molten metal is rolled into bars or other shapes

pigs: crude blocks of metal poured from a smelting furnace in order to be rolled into bars

attenuation: process of making something slender

instance, when some one asks him if he has a sweetheart, and if so, where she abides, this is the majestic answer:

> "She's in the forest—hanging from the boughs of the trees, in a soft rain—in the dew on the open grass—the clouds that float about in the blue heavens—the birds that sing in the woods—the sweet springs where I slake my thirst—and in all the other glorious gifts that come from God's Providence!"

And he preceded that, a little before, with this:

> "It consarns° me as all things that touches a fri'nd consarns a fri'nd."

And this is another of his remarks: 25

> "If I was Injin born, now, I might tell of this, or carry in the scalp and boast of the expl'ite afore the whole tribe; or if my inimy had only been a bear"—and so on.

We cannot imagine such a thing as a veteran Scotch Commander-in-Chief comporting himself in the field like a windy melodramatic actor, but Cooper could. On one occasion Alice and Cora were being chased by the French through a fog in the neighborhood of their father's fort.

> *"Point de quartier aux coquins!"*° cried an eager pursuer, who seemed to direct the operations of the enemy.
>
> "Stand firm and be ready, my gallant 60ths!" suddenly exclaimed a voice above them; "wait to see the enemy; fire low, and sweep the glacis."°
>
> "Father! father!" exclaimed a piercing cry out the mist; "it is I! Alice! thy own Elsie! spare, O! save your daughters!"
>
> "Hold!" shouted the former speaker, in the awful° tones of parental agony, the sound reaching even to the woods, and rolling back in solemn echo. "'Tis she! God has restored me my children! Throw open the sallyport,° to the field, 60ths, to the field; pull not a trigger, lest ye kill my lambs! Drive off these dogs of France with your steel."

---

consarns: concerns

Point de quartier aux coquins!: French for (roughly) "[Show] the bastards no mercy!"

glacis: gentle slope, incline

awful: horrific

sallyport: port, or door, in a fortification, through which a sally, or sudden rush, may be made

Cooper's word-sense was singularly dull. When a person has a poor ear for music he will flat and sharp right along without knowing it. He keeps near the tune, but it is *not* the tune. When a person has a poor ear for words, the result is a literary flatting and sharping; you perceive what he is intending to say, but you also perceive that he doesn't *say* it. This is Cooper. He was not a word-musician. His ear was satisfied with the *approximate* word. I will furnish some circumstantial evidence in support of this charge. My instances are gathered from half a dozen pages of the tale called *Deerslayer.* He uses "verbal," for "oral"; "precision," for "facility"; "phenomena," for "marvels"; "necessary," for "predetermined"; "unsophisticated," for "primitive"; "preparation," for "expectancy"; "rebuked," for "subdued"; "dependent on," for "resulting from"; "fact," for "condition"; "fact," for "conjecture"; "precaution," for "caution"; "explain," for "determine"; "mortified," for "disappointed"; "meretricious,"° for "factitious";° "materially," for "considerably"; "decreasing," for "deepening"; "increasing," for "disappearing"; "embedded," for "enclosed"; "treacherous," for "hostile"; "stood," for "stooped"; "softened," for "replaced"; "rejoined,"° for "remarked"; "situation," for "condition"; "different," for "differing"; "insensible," for "unsentient"; "brevity," for "celerity";° "distrusted," for "suspicious"; "mental imbecility," for "imbecility"; "eyes," for "sight"; "counteracting," for "opposing"; "funeral obsequies," for "obsequies."°

There have been daring people in the world who claimed that Cooper could write English, but they are all dead now—all dead but Lounsbury. I don't remember that Lounsbury makes the claim in so many words, still he makes it, for he says that *Deerslayer* is a "pure work of art." Pure, in that connection, means faultless—faultless in all details—and language is a detail. If Mr. Lounsbury had only compared Cooper's English with the English which he writes himself—but it is plain that he didn't; and so it is likely that he imagines until this day that Cooper's is as clean and compact as his own. Now I feel sure, deep down in my heart, that Cooper wrote about the poorest English that exists in our language, and that the English of *Deerslayer* is the very worst that even Cooper ever wrote.

I may be mistaken, but it does seem to me that *Deerslayer* is not a work of art in any sense; it does seem to me that it is destitute° of every detail that goes

---

meretricious: cheap, vulgar
factitious: artificial
rejoined: replied
celerity: swiftness
obsequies: funeral rites
destitute: devoid

to the making of a work of art; in truth, it seems to me that *Deerslayer* is just simply a literary *delirium tremens.*°

A work of art? It has no invention; it has no order, system, sequence or result; it has no lifelikeness, no thrill, no stir, no seeming of reality; its characters are confusedly drawn, and by their acts and words they prove that they are not the sort of people the author claims that they are; its humor is pathetic;° its pathos° is funny; its conversations are—oh! indescribable; its love-scenes odious;° its English a crime against the language. 30

Counting these out, what is left is Art. I think we must all admit that.

[1895]

Read

1. What is the rhetorical aim of Twain's beginning with three quotations? Is there any significance in the fact that two are designated as "Professors"?
2. How does Twain use understatement to convey his sarcasm?
3. What is the primary criticism Twain has to make of Natty Bumppo?
4. Where does the diction develop the persona of the speaker of this critique?

Write

1. How does Twain use exaggeration to convey his message? Write a comment on Twain's exaggeration and whether you find it effective.
2. Write a paragraph that explains what Twain is criticizing about Cooper's writing. What kind of writing do you think he values, given this criticism?

Complete Additional Exercises on Twain's Essay at Your Pearson MyLab

Connect

1. How do you see Twain taking his own advice in *Adventures of Huckleberry Finn* in the next selection?
2. Do you agree with Twain about Cooper after having read a bit of Cooper's work in Unit 2?

Adventures of Huckleberry Finn has been repeatedly banned, sometimes as too progressive, sometimes as racist, but it remains one of the most widely read books in America. Twain has had a profound effect on American writing. He used popular idiom, portrayed common people as fully human, and used elements of the landscape as characters. Those characteristics have become associated with American fiction, and have influenced generations of writers since his time.

---

delirium tremens: the d.t.'s, withdrawal syndrome

pathetic: causing pity or sadness

pathos: poignancy, tenderness

odious: repulsive, disgusting

From *Adventures of Huckleberry Finn*

(Tom Sawyer's Comrade)

Scene: The Mississippi
Time: Forty to Fifty Years Ago

Notice

Persons attempting to find a motive in this narrative will be prosecuted; persons attempting to find a moral in it will be banished; persons attempting to find a plot in it will be shot.

By Order of the Author
Per G.G., Chief of Ordnance.

Explanatory

In this book a number of dialects are used, to wit: the Missouri negro dialect; the extremest form of the backwoods South-Western dialect; the ordinary "Pike-County" dialect; and four modified varieties of this last. The shadings have not been done in a haphazard fashion, or by guess-work; but painstakingly, and with the trustworthy guidance and support of personal familiarity with these several forms of speech.

I make this explanation for the reason that without it many readers would suppose that all these characters were trying to talk alike and not succeeding.

—The Author

Chapter I

You don't know about me, without° you have read a book by the name of "The Adventures of Tom Sawyer," but that ain't no matter. That book was made by Mr. Mark Twain, and he told the truth, mainly. There was things which he stretched, but mainly he told the truth. That is nothing. I never seen anybody but lied, one time or another, without it was Aunt Polly, or the widow, or maybe Mary. Aunt Polly—Tom's Aunt Polly, she is—and Mary, and the Widow Douglas, is all told about in that book—which is mostly a true book; with some stretchers, as I said before.

---

without: unless

Now the way that the book winds up, is this: Tom and me found the money that the robbers hid in the cave, and it made us rich. We got six thousand dollars apiece—all gold. It was an awful° sight of money when it was piled up. Well, Judge Thatcher, he took it and put it out at interest, and it fetched us a dollar a day apiece, all the year round—more than a body could tell what to do with. The Widow Douglas, she took me for her son, and allowed she would sivilize me; but it was rough living in the house all the time, considering how dismal regular and decent the widow was in all her ways; and so when I couldn't stand it no longer, I lit out. I got into my old rags, and my sugar-hogshead° again, and was free and satisfied. But Tom Sawyer, he hunted me up and said he was going to start a band of robbers, and I might join if I would go back to the widow and be respectable. So I went back. 5

The widow she cried over me, and called me a poor lost lamb, and she called me a lot of other names, too, but she never meant no harm by it. She put me in them new clothes again, and I couldn't do nothing but sweat and sweat, and feel all cramped up. Well, then, the old thing commenced again. The widow rung a bell for supper, and you had to come to time. When you got to the table you couldn't go right to eating, but you had to wait for the widow to tuck down her head and grumble a little over the victuals,° though there warn't really anything the matter with them. That is, nothing only everything was cooked by itself. In a barrel of odds and ends it is different; things get mixed up, and the juice kind of swaps around, and the things go better.

After supper she got out her book and learned me about Moses and the Bulrushers;° and I was in a sweat to find out all about him; but by-and-by she let it out that Moses had been dead a considerable long time; so then I didn't care no more about him; because I don't take no stock in dead people.

Pretty soon I wanted to smoke, and asked the widow to let me. But she wouldn't. She said it was a mean° practice and wasn't clean, and I must try to not do it any more. That is just the way with some people. They get down on a thing when they don't know nothing

---

awful: extraordinary

hogshead: large barrel with a 63-gallon capacity

victuals: food, provisions

Moses and the Bulrushers: In the Book of Exodus, the infant Moses is found by Pharaoh's daughter floating in a basket made of bulrushes and sealed with pitch.

mean: low, base

about it. Here she was a bothering about Moses, which was no kin to her, and no use to anybody, being gone, you see, yet finding a power of fault with me for doing a thing that had some good in it. And she took snuff too; of course that was all right, because she done it herself.

Her sister, Miss Watson, a tolerable° slim old maid, with goggles° on, had just come to live with her, and took a set at me now, with a spelling-book. She worked me middling hard for about an hour, and then the widow made her ease up. I couldn't stood it much longer. Then for an hour it was deadly dull, and I was fidgety. Miss Watson would say, "Don't put your feet up there, Huckleberry;" and "don't scrunch up like that, Huckleberry—set up straight;" and pretty soon she would say, "Don't gap° and stretch like that, Huckleberry—why don't you try to behave?" Then she told me all about the bad place, and I said I wished I was there. She got mad, then, but I didn't mean no harm. All I wanted was to go somewheres; all I wanted was a change, I warn't particular. She said it was wicked to say what I said; said she wouldn't say it for the whole world; *she* was going to live so as to go to the good place. Well, I couldn't see no advantage in going where she was going, so I made up my mind I wouldn't try for it. But I never said so, because it would only make trouble, and wouldn't do no good.

Now she had got a start, and she went on and told me all about the good place. She said all a body would have to do there was to go around all day long with a harp and sing, forever and ever. So I didn't think much of it. But I never said so. I asked her if she reckoned Tom Sawyer would go there, and, she said, not by a considerable sight. I was glad about that, because I wanted him and me to be together. 10

Miss Watson she kept pecking at me, and it got tiresome and lonesome. By-and-by they fetched the niggers in and had prayers, and then everybody was off to bed. I went up to my room with a piece of candle and put it on the table. Then I set down in a chair by the window and tried to think of something cheerful, but it warn't no use. I felt so lonesome I most wished I was dead. The stars was shining, and the leaves rustled in the woods ever so mournful; and I heard an owl, away off, who-whooing about somebody that was dead, and a whippowill and a dog crying about somebody that was

tolerable: fairly, reasonably

goggles: eyeglasses

gap: yawn

going to die; and the wind was trying to whisper something to me and I couldn't make out what it was, and so it made the cold shivers run over me. Then away out in the woods I heard that kind of a sound that a ghost makes when it wants to tell about something that's on its mind and can't make itself understood, and so can't rest easy in its grave and has to go about that way every night grieving. I got so down-hearted and scared, I did wish I had some company. Pretty soon a spider went crawling up my shoulder, and I flipped it off and it lit in the candle; and before I could budge it was all shriveled up. I didn't need anybody to tell me that that was an awful bad sign and would fetch me some bad luck, so I was scared and most shook the clothes off of me. I got up and turned around in my tracks three times and crossed my breast every time; and then I tied up a little lock of my hair with a thread to keep witches away. But I hadn't no confidence. You do that when you've lost a horseshoe that you've found, instead of nailing it up over the door, but I hadn't ever heard anybody say it was any way to keep off bad luck when you'd killed a spider.

I set down again, a shaking all over, and got out my pipe for a smoke; for the house was all as still as death, now, and so the widow wouldn't know. Well, after a long time I heard the clock away off in the town go boom—boom—boom—twelve licks—and all still again—stiller than ever. Pretty soon I heard a twig snap, down in the dark amongst the trees—something was a stirring. I set still and listened. Directly I could just barely hear a "*me-yow me-yow!*" down there. That was good! Says I, "*me-yow me-yow*" as soft as I could, and then I put out the light and scrambled out of the window onto the shed. Then I slipped down to the ground and crawled in amongst the trees, and sure enough there was Tom Sawyer waiting for me.

Chapter II

We went tip-toeing along a path amongst the trees back towards the end of the widow's garden, stooping down so as the branches wouldn't scrape our heads. When we was passing by the kitchen I fell over a root and made a noise. We scrouched down and laid still. Miss Watson's big nigger, named Jim, was setting in the kitchen door; we could see him pretty clear, because there was a light behind him. He got up and stretched his neck out about a minute, listening. Then he says,

"Who dah?"

He listened some more; then he come tip-toeing down and stood right between us; we could a touched him, nearly. Well, likely it was 15 minutes and minutes that there warn't a sound, and we all there so close together. There was a place on my ankle that got to itching; but I dasn't scratch it; and then my ear begun to itch; and next my back, right between my shoulders. Seemed like I'd die if I couldn't scratch. Well, I've noticed that thing plenty of times since. If you are with the quality,° or at a funeral, or trying to go to sleep when you ain't sleepy—if you are anywheres where it won't do for you to scratch, why you will itch all over in upwards of a thousand places. Pretty soon Jim says:

"Say—who is you? Whar is you? Dog my cats ef I didn't hear sumf'n. Well, I knows what I's gwyne to do. I's gwyne to set down here and listen tell I hears it agin."

So he set down on the ground betwixt me and Tom. He leaned his back up against a tree, and stretched his legs out till one of them most° touched one of mine. My nose begun to itch. It itched till the tears come into my eyes. But I dasn't scratch. Then it begun to itch on the inside. Next I got to itching underneath. I didn't know how I was going to set still. This miserableness went on as much as six or seven minutes; but it seemed a sight longer than that. I was itching in eleven different places now. I reckoned I couldn't stand it more'n a minute longer, but I set my teeth hard and got ready to try. Just then Jim begun to breathe heavy; next he begun to snore—and then I was pretty soon comfortable agin.

Tom he made a sign to me—kind of a little noise with his mouth—and we went creeping away on our hands and knees. When we was ten foot off, Tom whispered to me and wanted to tie Jim to the tree for fun; but I said no; he might wake and make a disturbance, and then they'd find out I warn't in. Then Tom said he hadn't got candles enough, and he would slip in the kitchen and get some more. I didn't want him to try. I said Jim might wake up and come. But Tom wanted to resk it; so we slid in there and got three candles, and Tom laid five cents on the table for pay. Then we got out, and I was in a sweat to get away; but nothing would do Tom but he must crawl to where Jim was, on his hands and knees, and play something on him. I waited, and it seemed a good while, everything was so still and lonesome.

As soon as Tom was back, we cut along the path, around the garden fence, and by-and-by fetched up on the steep top of the hill the other side of the house. Tom said he slipped Jim's hat off of his head

---

the quality: upperclass people

most: almost

and hung it on a limb right over him, and Jim stirred a little, but he didn't wake. Afterwards Jim said the witches bewitched him and put him in a trance, and rode him all over the State, and then set him under the trees again and hung his hat on a limb to show who done it. And next time Jim told it he said they rode him down to New Orleans; and after that, every time he told it he spread it more and more, till by-and-by he said they rode him all over the world, and tired him most to death, and his back was all over saddle-boils. Jim was monstrous proud about it, and he got so he wouldn't hardly notice the other niggers. Niggers would come miles to hear Jim tell about it, and he was more looked up to than any nigger in that country. Strange niggers would stand with their mouths open and look him all over, same as if he was a wonder.° Niggers is always talking about witches in the dark by the kitchen fire; but whenever one was talking and letting on to know all about such things, Jim would happen in and say, "H'm! You know 'bout witches?" and that nigger was corked up and had to take a back seat. Jim always kept that five-center piece around his neck with a string and said it was a charm the devil give to him with his own hands and told him he could cure anybody with it and fetch witches whenever he wanted to, just by saying something to it; but he never told what it was he said to it. Niggers would come from all around there and give Jim anything they had, just for a sight of that five-center piece; but they wouldn't touch it, because the devil had had his hands on it. Jim was most ruined, for a servant, because he got so stuck up on account of having seen the devil and been rode by witches.

Well, when Tom and me got to the edge of the hill-top, we looked away down into the village and could see three or four lights twinkling, where there was sick folks, may be; and the stars over us was sparkling ever so fine; and down by the village was the river, a whole mile broad, and awful still and grand. We went down the hill and found Jo Harper, and Ben Rogers, and two or three more of the boys, hid in the old tanyard. So we unhitched a skiff° and pulled down the river two mile and a half, to the big scar° on the hillside, and went ashore. 20

We went to a clump of bushes, and Tom made everybody swear to keep the secret, and then showed them a hole in the hill, right in the thickest part of the bushes. Then we lit the candles and crawled

---

wonder: object of amazement

skiff: small boat

scar: cliff, rocky place

in on our hands and knees. We went about two hundred yards, and then the cave opened up. Tom poked about amongst the passages and pretty soon ducked under a wall where you wouldn't a noticed that there was a hole. We went along a narrow place and got into a kind of room, all damp and sweaty and cold, and there we stopped. Tom says:

"Now we'll start this band of robbers and call it Tom Sawyer's Gang. Everybody that wants to join has got to take an oath, and write his name in blood."

Everybody was willing. So Tom got out a sheet of paper that he had wrote the oath on, and read it. It swore every boy to stick to the band, and never tell any of the secrets; and if anybody done anything to any boy in the band, whichever boy was ordered to kill that person and his family must do it, and he mustn't eat and he mustn't sleep till he had killed them and hacked a cross in their breasts, which was the sign of the band. And nobody that didn't belong to the band could use that mark, and if he did he must be sued; and if he done it again he must be killed. And if anybody that belonged to the band told the secrets, he must have his throat cut, and then have his carcass burnt up and the ashes scattered all around, and his name blotted off the list with blood and never mentioned again by the gang, but have a curse put on it and be forgot, forever.

Everybody said it was a real beautiful oath, and asked Tom if he got it out of his own head. He said, some of it, but the rest was out of pirate books, and robber books, and every gang that was high-toned had it.

Some thought it would be good to kill the *families* of boys that told the secrets. Tom said it was a good idea, so he took a pencil and wrote it in. Then Ben Rogers says: 25

"Here's Huck Finn, he hain't got no family—what you going to do 'bout him?"

"Well, hain't he got a father?" says Tom Sawyer.

"Yes, he's got a father, but you can't never find him, these days. He used to lay drunk with the hogs in the tanyard, but he hain't been seen in these parts for a year or more."

They talked it over, and they was going to rule me out, because they said every boy must have a family or somebody to kill, or else it wouldn't be fair and square for the others. Well, nobody could think of anything to do—everybody was stumped, and set still. I was most ready to cry; but all at once I thought of a way, and so I offered them Miss Watson—they could kill her. Everybody said:

"Oh, she'll do, she'll do. That's all right. Huck can come in." 30

Then they all stuck a pin in their fingers to get blood to sign with, and I made my mark on the paper.

"Now," says Ben Rogers, "what's the line of business of this Gang?"

"Nothing only robbery and murder," Tom said.

"But who are we going to rob? houses—or cattle—or—"

"Stuff! stealing cattle and such things ain't robbery, it's burglary," says Tom Sawyer. "We ain't burglars. That ain't no sort of style. We are highwaymen. We stop stages and carriages on the road, with masks on, and kill the people and take their watches and money." 35

"Must we always kill the people?"

"Oh, certainly. It's best. Some authorities think different, but mostly it's considered best to kill them. Except some that you bring to the cave here and keep them till they're ransomed."

"Ransomed? What's that?"

"I don't know. But that's what they do. I've seen it in books; and so of course that's what we've got to do."

"But how can we do it if we don't know what it is?" 40

"Why blame° it all, we've *got* to do it. Don't I tell you it's in the books? Do you want to go to doing different from what's in the books, and get things all muddled up?"

"Oh, that's all very fine to *say,* Tom Sawyer, but how in the nation° are these fellows going to be ransomed if we don't know how to do it to them? that's the thing *I* want to get at. Now what do you *reckon* it is?"

"Well, I don't know. But per'aps if we keep them till they're ransomed, it means that we keep them till they're dead."

"Now, that's something *like.* That'll answer. Why couldn't you said that before? We'll keep them till they ransomed to death—and a bothersome lot they'll be, too, eating up everything and always trying to get loose."

"How you talk, Ben Rogers. How can they get loose when there's a guard over them, ready to shoot them down if they move a peg?" 45

"A guard! Well that *is* good. So somebody's got to set up all night and never get any sleep, just so as to watch them. I think that's foolishness. Why can't a body take a club and ransom them as soon as they get here?"

"Because it ain't in the books so—that's why. Now Ben Rogers, do you want to do things regular, or don't you?—that's the idea. Don't

blame: damn

the nation: damnation

you reckon that the people that made the books knows what's the correct thing to do? Do you reckon *you* can learn 'em anything? Not by a good deal. No, sir, we'll just go on and ransom them in the regular way."

"All right. I don't mind; but I say it's a fool way, anyhow. Say—do we kill the women, too?"

"Well, Ben Rogers, if I was as ignorant as you I wouldn't let on. Kill the women? No—nobody ever saw anything in the books like that. You fetch them to the cave, and you're always as polite as pie to them; and by-and-by they fall in love with you and never want to go home any more."

"Well, if that's the way, I'm agreed, but I don't take no stock in it. Mighty soon we'll have the cave so cluttered up with women, and fellows waiting to be ransomed, that there won't be no place for the robbers. But go ahead, I ain't got nothing to say." 50

Little Tommy Barnes was asleep, now, and when they waked him up he was scared, and cried, and said he wanted to go home to his ma, and didn't want to be a robber any more.

So they all made fun of him, and called him cry-baby, and that made him mad, and he said he would go straight and tell all the secrets. But Tom give him five cents to keep quiet, and said we would all go home and meet next week and rob somebody and kill some people.

Ben Rogers said he couldn't get out much, only Sundays, and so he wanted to begin next Sunday; but all the boys said it would be wicked to do it on Sunday, and that settled the thing. They agreed to get together and fix a day as soon as they could, and then we elected Tom Sawyer first captain and Jo Harper second captain of the Gang, and so started home.

I clumb up the shed and crept into my window just before day was breaking. My new clothes was all greased up and clayey, and I was dog-tired.

Chapter III

Well, I got a good going-over in the morning, from old Miss Watson, on account of my clothes; but the widow she didn't scold, but only cleaned off the grease and clay and looked so sorry that I thought I would behave a while if I could. Then Miss Watson she took me in the closet and prayed, but nothing come of it. She told me to pray every day, and whatever I asked for I would get it. But it warn't so. I tried it. Once I got a fish-line, but no hooks. It warn't any good to me without hooks. I tried for the hooks three or four times, but somehow 55

I couldn't make it work. By-and-by, one day, I asked Miss Watson to try for me, but she said I was a fool. She never told me why, and I couldn't make it out no way.

I set down, one time, back in the woods, and had a long think about it. I says to myself, if a body can get anything they pray for, why don't Deacon Winn get back the money he lost on pork? Why can't the widow get back her silver snuff-box that was stole? Why can't Miss Watson fat up? No, says I to myself, there ain't nothing in it. I went and told the widow about it, and she said the thing a body could get by praying for it was "spiritual gifts." This was too many for me, but she told me what she meant—I must help other people, and do everything I could for other people, and look out for them all the time, and never think about myself. This was including Miss Watson, as I took it. I went out in the woods and turned it over in my mind a long time, but I couldn't see no advantage about it—except for the other people—so at last I reckoned I wouldn't worry about it any more, but just let it go. Sometimes the widow would take me one side and talk about Providence in a way to make a body's mouth water; but maybe next day Miss Watson would take hold and knock it all down again. I judged I could see that there was two Providences, and a poor chap would stand considerable show° with the widow's Providence, but if Miss Watson's got him there warn't no help for him any more. I thought it all out, and reckoned I would belong to the widow's, if he wanted me, though I couldn't make out how he was agoing to be any better off then than what he was before, seeing I was so ignorant and so kind of low-down and ornery.

Pap he hadn't been seen for more than a year, and that was comfortable for me; I didn't want to see him no more. He used to always whale me when he was sober and could get his hands on me; though I used to take to the woods most of the time when he was around. Well, about this time he was found in the river drowned, about twelve mile above town, so people said. They judged it was him, anyway; said this drowned man was just his size, and was ragged, and had uncommon long hair—which was all like pap—but they couldn't make nothing out of the face, because it had been in the water so long it warn't much like a face at all. They said he was floating on his back in the water. They took him and buried him on the bank. But I warn't comfortable long, because I happened to think of something. I knowed mighty well that a drownded man don't float on his back, but on his face. So I knowed then, that this warn't pap, but a woman dressed up in a man's

---

stand considerable show: have a good chance

clothes. So I was uncomfortable again. I judged the old man would turn up again by-and-by, though I wished he wouldn't.

We played robber now and then about a month, and then I resigned. All the boys did. We hadn't robbed nobody, we hadn't killed any people, but only just pretended. We used to hop out of the woods and go charging down on hogdrovers° and women in carts taking garden stuff to market, but we never hived° any of them. Tom Sawyer called the hogs "ingots,"° and he called the turnips and stuff "julery" and we would go to the cave and pow-wow° over what we had done and how many people we had killed and marked. But I couldn't see no profit in it. One time Tom sent a boy to run about town with a blazing stick, which he called a slogan (which was the sign for the Gang to get together), and then he said he had got secret news by his spies that next day a whole parcel of Spanish merchants and rich A-rabs was going to camp in Cave Hollow with two hundred elephants, and six hundred camels, and over a thousand "sumter"° mules, all loaded down with di'monds, and they didn't have only a guard of four hundred soldiers, and so we would lay in ambuscade,° as he called it, and kill the lot and scoop the things. He said we must slick up our swords and guns, and get ready. He never could go after even a turnip-cart but he must have the swords and guns all scoured up for it; though they was only lath° and broom-sticks, and you might scour at them till you rotted and then they warn't worth a mouthful of ashes more than what they was before. I didn't believe we could lick such a crowd of Spaniards and A-rabs, but I wanted to see the camels and elephants, so I was on hand next day, Saturday, in the ambuscade; and when we got the word, we rushed out of the woods and down the hill. But there warn't no Spaniards and A-rabs, and there warn't no camels nor no elephants. It warn't anything but a Sunday-school picnic, and only a primer-class° at that. We busted it up, and chased the children up the hollow;° but we never got anything but some doughnuts and jam, though Ben Rogers got a rag doll, and Jo Harper got a hymn-book and

---

hogdrovers: herdsmen
hived: collected, stashed away
ingots: gold bars
pow-wow: confer
"sumter": sumpter, pack animal
ambuscade: ambush
lath: thin strips of wood
primer-class: introductory class, composed of very young children
hollow: valley

a tract;° and then the teacher charged in and made us drop everything and cut. I didn't see no di'monds, and I told Tom Sawyer so. He said there was loads of them there, anyway; and he said there was A-rabs there, too, and elephants and things. I said, why couldn't we see them, then? He said if I warn't so ignorant, but had read a book called "Don Quixote," I would know without asking. He said it was all done by enchantment. He said there was hundreds of soldiers there, and elephants and treasure, and so on, but we had enemies which he called magicians, and they had turned the whole thing into an infant Sunday School, just out of spite. I said, all right, then the thing for us to do was to go for the magicians. Tom Sawyer said I was a numskull.

"Why," says he, "a magician could call up a lot of genies, and they would hash you up like nothing before you could say Jack Robinson. They are as tall as a tree and as big around as a church."

"Well," I says, "s'pose we got some genies to help *us*—can't we lick the other crowd then?" 60

"How you going to get them?"

"I don't know. How do *they* get them?"

"Why they rub an old tin lamp or an iron ring, and then the genies come tearing in, with the thunder and lightning a-ripping around and the smoke a-rolling, and everything they're told to do they up and do it. They don't think nothing of pulling a shot tower° up by the roots, and belting a Sunday-school superintendent over the head with it—or any other man."

"Who makes them tear around so?"

"Why, whoever rubs the lamp or the ring. They belong to whoever rubs the lamp or the ring, and they've got to do whatever he says. 65 If he tells them to build a palace forty miles long, out of di'monds, and fill it full of chewing gum, or whatever you want, and fetch an emperor's daughter from China for you to marry, they've got to do it—and they've got to do it before sun-up next morning, too. And more—they've got to waltz that palace around over the country wherever you want it, you understand."

"Well," says I, "I think they are a pack of flatheads for not keeping the palace themselves 'stead of fooling them away like that. And what's more—if I was one of them I would see a man in Jericho° before I would drop my business and come to him for the rubbing of an old tin lamp."

---

tract: pamphlet

shot tower: building in which bits of molten lead are dropped from a great height into water, to form shot

Jericho: an ancient city of Palestine

"How you talk, Huck Finn. Why, you'd *have* to come when he rubbed it, whether you wanted to or not."

"What, and I as high as a tree and as big as a church? All right, then; I *would* come; but I lay° I'd make that man climb the highest tree there was in the country."

"Shucks, it ain't no use to talk to you, Huck Finn. You don't seem to know anything, somehow—perfect sap-head."

I thought all this over for two or three days, and then I reckoned I would see if there was anything in it. I got an old tin lamp and an iron ring and went out in the woods and rubbed and rubbed till I sweat like an Injun, calculating to build a palace and sell it; but it warn't no use, none of the genies come. So then I judged that all that stuff was only just one of Tom Sawyer's lies. I reckoned he believed in the A-rabs and the elephants, but as for me I think different. It had all the marks of a Sunday school. 70

[1885]

Read

1. What is the effect of the Notice and Explanatory on your reading of the first couple of paragraphs?
2. Where do you first get a clear sense of Huck's naïve character? Where do you get a first sense of his ethics?
3. How does Twain's narrator suggest his own attitude toward organized religion?
4. Find a few phrases that convey to you the persona of Twain's narrator.

Write

1. How does the narrator indicate the different values of Tom and Huck? Write a paragraph or two that explores the way Twain helps readers understand the difference between them and how one might be more authentic or more ethical.
2. Write a brief description of the importance of language—word choice, dialect, sentence structure—to the aim of this piece.
3. Write a comment on what the aim of this piece might be.

Connect

1. Judging from this excerpt, why do you think *Adventures of Huckleberry Finn* has been called the most "American" of novels?
2. Find another writer in an earlier unit who makes use of humor in the way that Twain does. How are their images and characters similar?

---

lay: bet, wager

Paul Laurence Dunbar

One of the most important writers of the nineteenth century, Paul Laurence Dunbar (1872–1906) was born in Dayton, Ohio, to ex-slaves. Early recognized for his poetic talent, he published a collection of poems, *Oak and Ivy,* when he was twenty. Throughout his brief career, Dunbar wrote poetry, fiction, essays, and criticism, often about the oppression and discrimination faced by African Americans. Famous literary figures Frederick Douglass and William Dean Howells saw his promise as a poet. Howells, an influential publisher, wrote the introduction to his collection *Lyrics of Lowly Life* in 1896. Dunbar continued to write articles, like the one included here, as well as fiction and poetry, until his death from tuberculosis at age 33.

The Race Question Discussed

Negro and White Man

(Suggested by the Wilmington, N.C. Riots)°

Loud, from the South, Damascan° cries
Fall on our ears, unheeded still.
No helping powers stir or rise.
Hate's opiate numbs the nation's will.
Slumbers the north. (While honor dies!)
Soothed by th' insidious breath of lies!

It would seem that the man who sits at his desk in the North and writes about the troubles in the South is very apt to be like a doctor who prescribes for a case he has no chance to diagnose. It would be true in this instance, also, if it were not that what has happened in Georgia has happened in Ohio and Illinois. The race riots in North Carolina were of a piece with the same proceedings in the state of Lincoln. The men who shoot the Negro in Hogansville° are blood brothers to those who hang him in Urbana,° and the deed is neither better nor worse because it happens in one section of the country or other. The race spirit in the United States is not local but general.

---

the Wilmington, N.C. Riots: On November 10, 1898, white supremacists took over the city by force, killing a number of black residents, and installed their own officials in place of the just-elected biracial city government.

Damascan: perhaps an allusion to the massacre of several thousand Christians in Damascus, Syria, in 1860

Hogansville: city in Georgia, site of an assault against a black postmaster in 1897

Urbana: city in Ohio where Charles Mitchell, a black man, was killed by a lynch mob on June 4, 1897

To the outsider, unacquainted with the vagaries° of our national prejudice, the recent and sudden change of attitude of the American toward the Negro would appear inconsistent, to say the least. We are presented with the spectacle of a people gushing, through glowing headlines, over the bravery of its black heroes.° In an incredibly short space of time—almost too brief, it would seem, for the mental transition of the individual, much less the nation—we find the mouthpieces of this same people chronicling the armed resistance of the community to the Negroes in the exercise of those powers and privileges which are the glory of the country for which the colored men fought. The drama of this sudden change of heart is incongruous° to the point of ghastly humor.

The new attitude may be interpreted as saying: "Negroes, you may fight for us, but you may not vote for us. You may prove a strong bulwark° when the bullets are flying, but you must stand from the line when the ballots are in the air. You may be heroes in war, but you must be cravens° in peace."

It is true, as has been insistently urged, that it would be expedient° for the Negro to forego his suffrage° and climb to worth and to the world's respect by other means. By other means! That is the cry of the miners when they ask him out of the mines. It is the word of the whole commercial world when they ask him out of everything—the American shibboleth.° Relinquish! Relinquish! And from the dust of the very lowest places, the places that grind men's souls and kill ambition, the Negroes seek to climb to places of worth and respect.

5 In order to cool the passions and allay the prejudices of the superior race the entire self-effacement of the Negro would be expedient—as expedient as it would be cowardly; and, say what you will of the American people, their respect is not to be won by cowardice. Let those suffering people relinquish one single right that has been given them and the rapacity° of the other race, encouraged by yielding, will ravage them from every privilege that they possess. Passion and prejudice are not sated° by concession, but grow by what they feed on.

---

vagaries: caprices, whims

the bravery of its black heroes: in the Spanish-American War, especially in the battles of El Caney on July 1 and San Juan Hill on July 2, 1898

incongruous: contradictory

bulwark: fortification, buttress

cravens: cowards

expedient: advisable, appropriate

suffrage: right to vote

shibboleth: commonly held principle or view that is unfounded or out-of-date

rapacity: greed, predatoriness

sated: fully satisfied

The Vaudois,° hiding like wild beasts in their mountain fastnesses,° shot like goats upon their own hills, purpling with their blood the streams of their own valleys, France could hate, but dared not despise. The Indian himself, ground to dust under the heel of civilization, driven to death by the greed of a stronger people, will not be remembered with a sneer. But for the Negro honor is dangerous; only cowardice is safe.

The African is told that he is not yet ready to participate in government, because he has not yet learned to govern himself, and the race which preaches this proves its own right to political domination by the rioting, the rapine° and the slaughter, with which for weeks past the civilized world has been scandalized. Since when was ever a psychological° published with a musket?

After all, the question is not one of the Negro's fitness to rule or to vote, but of the right of the whites to murder him for the sake of instruction. Not a groan that the Romans wrung from the hearts of the conquered Britons, but echoed and re-echoed in the sound of her own fall. Every drop of blood that France drew from her own suffering Huguenots on St. Bartholomew's Day° but called its brother to the hungry sod on that awful 14th day of July.° Rome sated her thirst for blood and called it civilization. France indulged her barbaric fancy° and named it religion. America strides through the ashes of burning homes, over the bodies of murdered men, women and children, holding aloft the banner of progress.

Progress! Necessity! Expedience!

But why is it necessary to excuse these acts of sophistry?° Is not murder murder? Is not rapine rapine? Is not outrage outrage? 10

The whites are stronger than the blacks. Why not then say to them openly: "We don't like you; we do not want you in certain places. Therefore when we please we will kill you. We are strong people; you are weak. What we choose to do we will do; right or no right. There is no one to wage with us a holy war in the cause of humanity."

Even the church has attempted to explain and palliate° and we are told from the pulpit that the Negroes have been taught a salutary° lesson: that the

---

Vaudois: or Waldenses, members of a Protestant sect subjected to a massacre by the French in 1545

fastnesses: strongholds

rapine: seizure by force

psychological: i.e., a psychological analysis or evaluation

St. Bartholemew's Day: a widespread slaughter of French Protestants began on August 23, 1572

14th day of July: of 1789, date of the fall of the Bastille and start of the French Revolution

fancy: whim, caprice

sophistry: faulty reasoning

palliate: mitigate, relieve

salutary: beneficial, healthful

whites must prevail. The murderers of Wilmington are congratulated upon the effort they have made toward civilization and purer government. And some of this within a stone's throw of the nation's capitol: When the reckoning shall come, what shall such ministers say? They have not stoned martyrs but they have burned their shoulders with the coats of those who did; and every such is an accomplice dyed with the same blood of the men who stood redhanded over the murdered blacks. And yet, what else could we expect from the pulpit, when we remember that less than forty years ago with the same smug complacency, it was finding excuses for slavery in tracing out the divine intention?

The passions of the people often need a spiritual backing, and shame to say, we have a clergy always ready and willing to furnish it, whether it be when man restrains his fellow men from the exercise of his national rights or murders him for pursuing his political dues. It is a disgrace to the honor of their calling, a reflection upon the intelligences of their heroes, and an insult to the God they profess° to serve.

The text for better and for different sermons might be found for those divines in Paul's first epistle to the Corinthians. It is as apt to-day as it was then, and it applies to the American people with no less strength than it did to the older race. "Take heed," said the apostle, "lest by any means this liberty of yours become a stumbling block to them that are weak."

15 We are comforted with the statement that the sudden enfranchisement of the Negro was a mistake. Perhaps it was, but the whites made it. The mistakes of life are not corrected in that way. Their effects are eternal. You cannot turn back the years and put ten millions of people into the condition that four millions were thirty years ago. You cannot ignore the effects that have ensued, the changes that have followed, and make the problem of today the problem of 1865. It is a different one. The whole aspect of the case has changed. The Negro has changed. Public opinion has shifted. Try as you will, though it has grown away, you cannot put the plant back into the seed. Of course you can root it up entirely; but beware of its juices.

Thirty years ago the American people told the Negro that he was a man with a man's full powers. They deemed it that important they did what they have done few times in the history of the country—they wrote it down in their constitution. And now they come with the shot gun in the South and sophistry in the North to prove to him that it was all wrong.

For so long a time has the black man believed that he is an American citizen that he will not be easily convinced to the contrary. It will take more than the hangings, the burnings and the lynchings, both North and South, to prove it to his satisfaction. He is not so credulous as he was. He is a different man. The American people cannot turn back the tide of years and make him what he was. And so it was an entirely new people with whom they have to deal. It is an entirely new problem which is presented to them for solution.

---

profess: claim

Why then should it not be met with calmness, justice, breadth and manliness which should characterize a great nation?

If the problem is as much the Negro's as the white man's—and I do not say that it is not—he is doing his best to settle it. He is acquiring property. Yes he even builds churches to the religion whose servants preach his damnation. He is going forward. Such catastrophes as the Southern riots, terrible though they be, are but incidents in his growth, which is inevitable. The principle of manhood is springing to life within him. Every year men are being educated to live for it. Every year to some—to many, it seems—God gives the better grace to die for it.

[1898]

Read

1. What is the effect of the verse that begins the essay?
2. How does Dunbar use the analogy at the beginning of the essay to suggest the argument he will make about race?

Write

1. Write a paragraph or two that discusses how Dunbar's critique calls Americans to task. What strategies does Dunbar use to convey his position to his audience?
2. Comment on Dunbar's use of logic in this piece. Why might it be important to use logic in confronting the subject?

Complete Additional Exercises on Dunbar's Essay at Your Pearson MyLab

Connect

1. What connections can you make between Douglass's *Narrative* in Unit 3 and Dunbar's essay?
2. What is the role of experience in making arguments? Consider this piece and one other in this unit to speculate about experience as evidence for claims.

W. E. B. Du Bois

W. E. B. Du Bois (1868–1963) was born in Massachusetts, attended public school, and then studied at Fisk University in Tennessee. His experience in the South showed him the terrible burden newly freed slaves essays, faced—from oppressive laws and customs to outright danger from lynching. His famous collection of essays, *The Souls of Black Folk,* owes much to his education at a Southern black college, as do his histories of the slave trade and Reconstruction. He later attended Harvard University and became the first African American to receive a Ph.D. there. He taught, wrote nineteen books on African American culture and history, and fought for civil rights until his death at age 95. Du Bois was an influence on generations of young African American writers and thinkers, including those who were part of the Harlem Renaissance.

From *The Souls of Black Folk*

The Forethought

Herein lie buried many things which if read with patience may show the strange meaning of being black here in the dawning of the Twentieth Century. This meaning is not without interest to you, Gentle Reader; for the problem of the Twentieth Century is the problem of the color-line.°

I pray you, then, receive my little book in all charity, studying my words with me, forgiving mistake and foible° for sake of the faith and passion that is in me, and seeking the grain of truth hidden there.

I have sought here to sketch, in vague, uncertain outline, the spiritual world in which ten thousand thousand Americans live and strive. First, in two chapters I have tried to show what Emancipation meant to them, and what was its aftermath. In a third chapter I have pointed out the slow rise of personal leadership, and criticised candidly the leader who bears the chief burden of his race to-day. Then, in two other chapters I have sketched in swift outline the two worlds within and without° the Veil, and thus have come to the central problem of training men for life. Venturing now into deeper detail, I have in two chapters studied the struggles of the massed millions of the black peasantry, and in another have sought to make clear the present relations of the sons of master and man.°

Leaving, then, the world of the white man, I have stepped within the Veil, raising it that you may view faintly its deeper recesses,—the meaning of its religion, the passion of its human sorrow, and the struggle of its greater souls. All this I have ended with a tale twice told but seldom written.

Some of these thoughts of mine have seen the light before in other guise.° 5
For kindly consenting to their republication here, in altered and extended form, I must thank the publishers of *The Atlantic Monthly, The World's Work, The Dial, The New World,* and the *Annals of the American Academy of Political and Social Science.*

Before each chapter, as now printed, stands a bar of the Sorrow Songs,—some echo of haunting melody from the only American music which welled up from black souls in the dark past. And, finally, need I add that I who

---

color-line: barrier preventing blacks from full participation in the rights of American citizens

foible: defect; idiosyncrasy

without: outside

man: worker

guise: form

speak here am bone of the bone and flesh of the flesh of them that live within the Veil?

VII

Of the Black Belt

> I am black but comely,° O ye daughters of Jerusalem,
> As the tents of Kedar, as the curtains of Solomon.
> Look not upon me, because I am black,
> Because the sun hath looked upon me:
> My mother's children were angry with me;
> They made me the keeper of the vineyards;
> But mine own vineyard have I not kept.
>
> —The Song of Solomon

Out of the North the train thundered, and we woke to see the crimson soil of Georgia stretching away bare and monotonous right and left. Here and there lay straggling,° unlovely villages, and lean men loafed leisurely at the depots; then again came the stretch of pines and clay. Yet we did not nod, nor weary of the scene; for this is historic ground. Right across our track, three hundred and sixty years ago, wandered the cavalcade of Hernando de Soto,° looking for gold and the Great Sea; and he and his foot-sore captives disappeared yonder in the grim forests to the west. Here sits Atlanta, the city of a hundred hills, with something Western, something Southern, and something quite its own,

---

comely: attractive, pleasing in appearance

straggling: scattered, disorderly

Hernando de Soto: (1500?–1542), Spanish explorer of North America

in its busy life. And a little past Atlanta, to the southwest, is the land of the Cherokees, and there, not far from where Sam Hose° was crucified, you may stand on a spot which is to-day the centre of the Negro problem,—the centre of those nine million men who are America's dark heritage from slavery and the slave-trade.

Not only is Georgia thus the geographical focus of our Negro population, but in many other respects, both now and yesterday, the Negro problems have seemed to be centered in this State. No other State in the Union can count a million Negroes among its citizens,—a population as large as the slave population of the whole Union in 1800; no other State fought so long and strenuously to gather this host of Africans. Oglethorpe° thought slavery against law and gospel; but the circumstances which gave Georgia its first inhabitants were not calculated to furnish citizens over-nice° in their ideas about rum and slaves. Despite the prohibitions of the trustees,° these Georgians, like some of their descendants, proceeded to take the law into their own hands; and so pliant° were the judges, and so flagrant the smuggling, and so earnest were the prayers of Whitefield, that by the middle of the eighteenth century all restrictions were swept away, and the slave-trade went merrily on for fifty years and more.

Down in Darien, where the Delegal riots° took place some summers ago, there used to come a strong protest against slavery from the Scotch Highlanders;° and the Moravians of Ebenezer° did not like the system. But not till the Haytian Terror of Toussaint was the trade in men even checked;° while the national statute of 1808° did not suffice to stop it. How the Africans poured in!—fifty thousand between 1790 and 1810, and then, from Virginia and from smugglers, two thousand a year for many years more. So the thirty thousand Negroes of

---

Sam Hose: (b. Tom Wilkes, 1875?–1899), a black man who killed his employer under disputed circumstances, was mutilated, flayed, and tied to a tree and burned alive by a lynch mob

Oglethorpe: James Edward Oglethorpe (1696–1785), founder of the Georgia colony in 1733

over-nice: delicate, scrupulous

trustees: the Georgia Trustees, a group responsible for planning the laws and structures of the colony of Georgia

pliant: easily influenced

Delegal riots: Twenty-one black men were convicted of insurrection after a large number of black men assembled in Darien, Georgia, on August 23, 1899, to prevent a black prisoner from being taken from the jail and lynched.

Scotch Highlanders: Large numbers of Scots had settled in Georgia from the eighteenth century on.

Moravians of Ebenezer: Ebenezer was a community in Georgia founded by Moravians, German Protestants who had come to America to escape persecution.

checked: restrained

the national statute of 1808: a law forbidding the importation of slaves into the United States

Georgia in 1790 were doubled in a decade,—were over a hundred thousand in 1810, had reached two hundred thousand in 1820, and half a million at the time of the war.° Thus like a snake the black population writhed upward.

But we must hasten on our journey. This that we pass as we leave Atlanta is the ancient land of the Cherokees,—that brave Indian nation which strove so long for its fatherland, until Fate and the United States Government drove them beyond the Mississippi. If you wish to ride with me you must come into the "Jim Crow Car." There will be no objection,—already four other white men, and a little white girl with her nurse, are in there. Usually the races are mixed in there; but the white coach is all white. Of course this car is not so good as the other, but it is fairly clean and comfortable. The discomfort lies chiefly in the hearts of those four black men yonder—and in mine. 10

We rumble south in quite a business-like way. The bare red clay and pines of Northern Georgia begin to disappear, and in their place appears a rich rolling land, luxuriant, and here and there well tilled. This is the land of the Creek Indians; and a hard time the Georgians had to seize it. The towns grow more frequent and more interesting, and brand-new cotton mills rise on every side. Below Macon the world grows darker; for now we approach the Black Belt,—that strange land of shadows, at which even slaves paled° in the past, and whence° come now only faint and half-intelligible murmurs to the world beyond. The "Jim Crow Car" grows larger and a shade better; three rough field-hands and two or three white loafers accompany us, and the newsboy still spreads his wares at one end. The sun is setting, but we can see the great cotton country as we enter it,—the soil now dark and fertile, now thin and gray, with fruit-trees and dilapidated buildings,—all the way to Albany.

At Albany, in the heart of the Black Belt, we stop. Two hundred miles south of Atlanta, two hundred miles west of the Atlantic, and one hundred miles north of the Great Gulf lies Dougherty County, with ten thousand Negroes and two thousand whites. The Flint River winds down from Andersonville, and, turning suddenly at Albany, the county-seat, hurries on to join the Chattahoochee and the sea. Andrew Jackson knew the Flint well, and marched across it once to avenge the Indian Massacre at Fort Mims.° That was in 1814, not long before the battle of New Orleans; and by the Creek treaty that followed this campaign, all Dougherty County, and much other rich land, was ceded to Georgia. Still, settlers fought shy of° this land, for the Indians were all about, and they were unpleasant neighbors in those days. The panic

---

the war: the Civil War (1861–1865)

paled: turned pale out of fear

whence: from

Indian … Mims: On August 30, 1813, during the Creek Indian War, a force of Creeks captured Fort Mims in Alabama, killing some 500 militia and settlers.

fought shy of: avoided

of 1837,° which Jackson bequeathed to Van Buren, turned the planters from the impoverished lands of Virginia, the Carolinas, and east Georgia, toward the West. The Indians were removed to Indian Territory, and settlers poured into these coveted lands to retrieve their broken fortunes. For a radius of a hundred miles about Albany, stretched a great fertile land, luxuriant with forests of pine, oak, ash, hickory, and poplar; hot with the sun and damp with the rich black swamp-land; and here the corner-stone of the Cotton Kingdom was laid.

Albany is to-day a wide-streeted, placid, Southern town, with a broad sweep of stores and saloons, and flanking rows of homes,—whites usually to the north, and blacks to the south. Six days in the week the town looks decidedly too small for itself, and takes frequent and prolonged naps. But on Saturday suddenly the whole county disgorges itself upon the place, and a perfect flood of black peasantry pours through the streets, fills the stores, blocks the sidewalks, chokes the thoroughfares, and takes full possession of the town. They are black, sturdy, uncouth country folk, good-natured and simple, talkative to a degree, and yet far more silent and brooding than the crowds of the Rhine-pfalz,° or Naples, or Cracow. They drink considerable quantities of whiskey, but do not get very drunk; they talk and laugh loudly at times, but seldom quarrel or fight. They walk up and down the streets, meet and gossip with friends, stare at the shop windows, buy coffee, cheap candy, and clothes, and at dusk drive home—happy? well no, not exactly happy, but much happier than as though° they had not come.

Thus Albany is a real capital,—a typical Southern county town, the centre of the life of ten thousand souls; their point of contact with the outer world, their centre of news and gossip, their market for buying and selling, borrowing and lending, their fountain of justice and law. Once upon a time we knew country life so well and city life so little, that we illustrated° city life as that of a closely crowded country district. Now the world has well-nigh forgotten what the country is, and we must imagine a little city of black people scattered far and wide over three hundred lonesome square miles of land, without train or trolley, in the midst of cotton and corn, and wide patches of sand and gloomy soil.

15 It gets pretty hot in Southern Georgia in July,—a sort of dull, determined heat that seems quite independent of the sun; so it took us some days to muster courage enough to leave the porch and venture out on the long country roads, that we might see this unknown world. Finally we started. It was about ten in

The panic of 1837: financial crisis that created a five-year depression

Rhine-pfalz: a region in southwestern Germany

as though: if

illustrated: depicted

the morning, bright with a faint breeze, and we jogged° leisurely southward in the valley of the Flint. We passed the scattered box-like cabins of the brick-yard hands, and the long tenement-row facetiously called "The Ark," and were soon in the open country, and on the confines of the great plantations, of other days. There is the "Joe Fields place"; a rough old fellow was he, and had killed many a "nigger" in his day. Twelve miles his plantation used to run,—a regular barony.° It is nearly all gone now; only straggling bits belong to the family, and the rest has passed to Jews and Negroes. Even the bits which are left are heavily mortgaged, and, like the rest of the land, tilled by tenants. Here is one of them now,—a tall brown man, a hard worker and a hard drinker, illiterate, but versed in farm-lore, as his nodding crops declare. This distressingly new board house is his, and he has just moved out of yonder moss-grown cabin with its one square room.

From the curtains in Benton's house, down the road, a dark comely face is staring at the strangers; for passing carriages are not every-day occurrences here. Benton is an intelligent yellow man with a good-sized family, and manages a plantation blasted by the war and now the broken staff of the widow. He might be well-to-do, they say; but he carouses too much in Albany. And the half-desolate spirit of neglect born of the very soil seems to have settled on these acres. In times past there were cotton-gins and machinery here; but they have rotted away.

The whole land seems forlorn and forsaken. Here are the remnants of the vast plantations of the Sheldons, the Pellots, and the Rensons; but the souls of them are passed. The houses lie in half ruin, or have wholly disappeared; the fences have flown, and the families are wandering in the world. Strange vicissitudes° have met these whilom° masters. Yonder stretch the wide acres of Bildad Reasor; he died in war-time, but the upstart overseer hastened to wed the widow. Then he went, and his neighbors too, and now only the black tenant remains; but the shadow-hand of the master's grand-nephew or cousin or creditor stretches out of the gray distance to connect the rack-rent° remorselessly, and so the land is uncared-for and poor. Only black tenants can stand such a system, and they only because they must. Ten miles we have ridden to-day and have seen no white face.

A resistless feeling of depression falls slowly upon us, despite the gaudy sunshine and the green cotton-fields. This, then, is the Cotton Kingdom,—the shadow of a marvellous dream. And where is the King? Perhaps this is he,—the

---

jogged: rode in a horse-drawn carriage at a steady trot

barony: estate of a baron

vicissitudes: changing circumstances, ups and downs

whilom: onetime, former

rack-rent: exorbitant rent

sweating ploughman, tilling his eighty acres with two lean mules, and fighting a hard battle with debt. So we sit musing, until, as we turn a corner on the sandy road, there comes a fairer scene suddenly in view,—a neat cottage snugly ensconced° by the road, and near it a little store. A tall bronzed man rises from the porch as we hail him, and comes out to our carriage. He is six feet in height, with a sober face that smiles gravely. He walks too straight to be a tenant,—yes, he owns, two hundred and forty acres. "The land is run down since the boom-days of eighteen hundred and fifty," he explains, and cotton is low. Three black tenants live on his place, and in his little store he keeps a small stock of tobacco, snuff, soap, and soda, for the neighborhood. Here is his gin-house° with new machinery just installed. Three hundred bales of cotton went through it last year. Two children he has sent away to school. Yes, he says sadly, he is getting on, but cotton is down to four cents; I know how Debt sits staring at him.

Wherever the King may be, the parks and palaces of the Cotton Kingdom have not wholly disappeared. We plunge even now into great groves of oak and towering pine, with an undergrowth of myrtle and shrubbery. This was the "home-house" of the Thompsons,—slave-barons who drove their coach and four in the merry past. All is silence now, and ashes, and tangled weeds. The owner put his whole fortune into the rising cotton industry of the fifties, and with the falling prices of the eighties he packed up and stole away. Yonder is another grove, with unkempt lawn, great magnolias, and grass-grown paths. The Big House stands in half-ruin, its great front door staring blankly at the street, and the back part grotesquely restored for its black tenant. A shabby, well-built Negro he is, unlucky and irresolute.° He digs hard to pay rent to the white girl who owns the remnant of the place. She married a policeman, and lives in Savannah.

Now and again we come to churches. Here is one now,—Shepherd's, they call it,—a great whitewashed barn of a thing, perched on stilts of stone, and looking for all the world as though it were just resting here a moment and might be expected to waddle off down the road at almost any time. And yet it is the centre of a hundred cabin homes; and sometimes, of a Sunday, five hundred persons from far and near gather here and talk and eat and sing. There is a school-house near,—a very airy, empty shed; but even this is an improvement, for usually the school is held in the church. The churches vary from log-huts to those like Shepherd's, and the schools from nothing to this little house that sits demurely° on the county line. It is a tiny plank-house, perhaps ten by twenty, and has within a double row of rough unplaned benches, resting mostly on legs, sometimes on boxes. Opposite the door

20

ensconced: settled, nestled

gin-house: building for ginning (removing the seeds from) cotton

irresolute: indecisive, hesitant

demurely: modestly

is a square home-made desk. In one corner are the ruins of a stove, and in the other a dim blackboard. It is the cheerfulest schoolhouse I have seen in Dougherty, save° in town. Back of the schoolhouse is a lodge-house° two stories high and not quite finished. Societies meet there, societies "to care for the sick and bury the dead"; and these societies grow and flourish.

We had come to the boundaries of Dougherty, and were about to turn west along the county-line, when all these sights were pointed out to us by a kindly old man, black, white-haired, and seventy. Forty-five years he had lived here, and now supports himself and his old wife by the help of the steer tethered° yonder and the charity of his black neighbors. He shows us the farm of the Hills just across the county line in Baker,—a widow and two strapping° sons, who raised ten bales (one need not add "cotton" down here) last year. There are fences and pigs and cows, and the soft-voiced, velvet-skinned young Memnon,° who sauntered half-bashfully over to greet the strangers, is proud of his home. We turn now to the west along the county line. Great dismantled trunks of pines tower above the green cotton-fields, cracking their naked gnarled° fingers toward the border of living forest beyond. There is little beauty in this region, only a sort of crude abandon that suggests power,—a naked grandeur, as it were. The houses are bare and straight; there are no hammocks or easy-chairs, and few flowers. So when, as here at Rawdon's, one sees a vine clinging to a little porch, and home-like windows peeping over the fences, one takes a long breath. I think I never before quite realized the place of the Fence in civilization. This is the Land of the Unfenced, where crouch on either hand scores of ugly one-room cabins, cheerless and dirty. Here lies the Negro problem in its naked dirt and penury.° And here are no fences. But now and then the criss-cross rails or straight palings° break into view, and then we know a touch of culture is near. Of course Harrison Gohagen,—a quiet yellow man, young, smooth-faced, and diligent,—of course he is lord of some hundred acres, and we expect to see a vision of well-kept rooms and fat beds and laughing children. For has he not fine fences? And those over yonder, why should they build fences on the rack-rented land? It will only increase their rent.

On we wind, through sand and pines and glimpses of old plantations, till there creeps into sight a cluster of buildings,—wood and brick, mills and

---

save: except

lodge-house: meeting hall for fraternal organizations

tethered: tied to a post or other spot

strapping: large, powerfully built

Memnon: huge statue of Pharaoh Amenhotep III in ancient Egypt

gnarled: twisted, bent

penury: poverty, need

palings: fence pickets

houses, and scattered cabins. It seemed quite a village. As it came nearer and nearer, however, the aspect° changed: the buildings were rotten, the bricks were falling out, the mills were silent, and the store was closed. Only in the cabins appeared now and then a bit of lazy life. I could imagine the place under some weird spell, and was half-minded to search out the princess. An old ragged black man, honest, simple, and improvident,° told us the tale. The Wizard of the North—the Capitalist—had rushed down in the seventies to woo this coy° dark soil. He bought a square mile or more, and for a time the field-hands sang, the gins groaned, and the mills buzzed. Then came a change. The agent's son embezzled the funds and ran off with them. Then the agent himself disappeared. Finally the new agent stole even the books, and the company in wrath closed its business and its houses, refused to sell, and let houses and furniture and machinery rust and rot. So the Waters-Loring plantation was stilled by the spell of dishonesty, and stands like some gaunt rebuke to a scarred land.

Somehow that plantation ended our day's journey; for I could not shake off the influence of that silent scene. Back toward town we glided, past the straight and thread-like pines, past a dark tree-dotted pond where the air was heavy with a dead sweet perfume. White slender-legged curlews° flitted by us, and the garnet blooms of the cotton looked gay° against the green and purple stalks. A peasant girl was hoeing in the field, white-turbaned and black-limbed. All this we saw, but the spell still lay upon us.

How curious a land is this,—how full of untold story, of tragedy and laughter, and the rich legacy of human life; shadowed with a tragic past, and big with future promise! This is the Black Belt of Georgia. Dougherty County is the west end of the Black Belt, and men once called it the Egypt of the Confederacy. It is full of historic interest. First there is the Swamp, to the west, where the Chickasawhatchee flows sullenly southward. The shadow of an old plantation lies at its edge, forlorn and dark. Then comes the pool; pendent° gray moss and brackish° waters appear, and forests filled with wild-fowl. In one place the wood is on fire, smouldering in dull red anger; but nobody minds.° Then the swamp grows beautiful; a raised road, built by chained Negro convicts, dips down into it, and forms a way walled

aspect: appearance, view
improvident: imprudent, unthrifty
coy: reserved, unforthcoming
curlews: large shore birds
gay: bright, festive
pendent: hanging
brackish: salty, briny
minds: takes notice, pays attention

and almost covered in living green. Spreading trees spring from a prodigal° luxuriance of undergrowth; great dark green shadows fade into the black background, until all is one mass of tangled semi-tropical foliage, marvellous in its weird savage splendor. Once we crossed a black silent stream, where the sad trees and writhing creepers,° all glinting fiery yellow and green, seemed like some vast cathedral,—some green Milan° builded of wildwood. And as I crossed, I seemed to see again that fierce tragedy of seventy years ago. Osceola, the Indian-Negro chieftain, had risen in the swamps of Florida, vowing vengeance. His war-cry reached the red Creeks of Dougherty, and their war-cry rang from the Chattahoochee to the sea. Men and women and children fled and fell before them as they swept into Dougherty. In yonder shadows a dark and hideously painted warrior glided stealthily on,—another and another, until three hundred had crept into the treacherous swamp. Then the false slime closing about them called the white men from the east. Waist-deep, they fought beneath the tall trees, until the war-cry was hushed and the Indians glided back into the west. Small wonder the wood is red.

[1903]

Read

1. How does Du Bois create a relationship with the reader at the beginning of the work?
2. What does the speaker mean by the Veil? Why does he use that image?
3. What is the effect of the bars of music at the beginning of the chapter?
4. How does Du Bois use imagery to give a feeling of the landscape he passes?

Write

1. What position does Du Bois ask the reader to occupy in the metaphorical journey he takes south? Write about how that position alters your perspective as you read.
2. Write a brief description of Du Bois's persona in this excerpt. Use lines from the text to support your ideas.
3. Write a brief discussion of how Du Bois uses the ethical appeal in this excerpt. What is he claiming for himself and for his readers?

Complete Additional Exercises on Du Bois's Essay at Your Pearson MyLab

Connect

1. Link Du Bois to Dunbar and any other African American writer in an earlier unit in terms of the use of appeals.
2. How does religion play a part in Du Bois's work? Do you find it similar to or different from the way that Phillis Wheatley or Frederick Douglass portray religion?

---

prodigal: extravagant

creepers: surface plants, such as ivy

Milan: a reference to that city's huge Gothic cathedral

Henry Adams

Henry Adams (1838–1918) was the grandson of John Quincy Adams and the great-grandson of John Adams. His distinguished family made him call himself a "failure" even though he was a professor at Harvard, a writer, and a highly respected historian. Traveling in Europe, he became obsessed with cathedrals and their significance in a wildly changing world. He wrote several books on his travels, most importantly *The Education of Henry Adams* in 1904. This memoir, written in the third person, records his struggle to understand the chaotic experience of America and progress; what he "learns" is that science has not resolved the mysteries of the universe. His "Dynamo and the Virgin," excerpted here, is a chapter from *The Education of Henry Adams.*

From *The Education of Henry Adams*

The Dynamo° and the Virgin (1900)

Until the Great Exposition of 1900° closed its doors in November, Adams° haunted it, aching to absorb knowledge, and helpless to find it. He would have liked to know how much of it could have been grasped by the best-informed man in the world. While he was thus meditating chaos, Langley° came by, and showed it to him. At Langley's behest, the Exhibition dropped its superfluous° rags and stripped itself to the skin, for Langley knew what to study, and why, and how; while Adams might as well have stood outside in the night, staring at the Milky Way. Yet Langley said nothing new, and taught nothing that one might not have learned from Lord Bacon,° three

---

Dynamo: electric generator

Great Exposition of 1900: world's fair held in Paris

Adams: In his autobiography, *The Education of Henry Adams,* the author writes of himself in the third person.

Langley: Samuel Pierpont Langley (1834–1906), American astronomer and physicist

superfluous: excessive, unnecessary

Lord Bacon: (1561–1626), English essayist, statesman, and scientist, author of *Of Proficience and Advancement of Learning Divine and Human* (1605)

hundred years before; but though one should have known the "Advancement of Science" as well as one knew the "Comedy of Errors," the literary knowledge counted for nothing until some teacher should show how to apply it. Bacon took a vast deal of trouble in teaching King James I° and his subjects, American or other, towards the year 1620, that true science was the development or economy° of forces; yet an elderly American in 1900 knew neither the formula nor the forces; or even so much as to say to himself that his historical business in the Exposition concerned only the economies or developments of force since 1893, when he began the study at Chicago.°

Nothing in education is so astonishing as the amount of ignorance it accumulates in the form of inert facts. Adams had looked at most of the accumulations of art in the storehouses called Art Museums; yet he did not know how to look at the art exhibits of 1900. He had studied Karl Marx and his doctrines of history with profound attention, yet he could not apply them at Paris. Langley, with the ease of a great master of experiment, threw out of the field every exhibit that did not reveal a new application of force, and naturally threw out, to begin with, almost the whole art exhibit. Equally, he ignored almost the whole industrial exhibit. He led his pupil directly to the forces. His chief interest was in new motors to make his airship feasible, and he taught Adams the astonishing complexities of the new Daimler° motor, and of the automobile, which, since 1893, had become a nightmare at a hundred kilometres° an hour, almost as destructive as the electric tram which was only ten years older; and threatening to become as terrible as the locomotive steam-engine itself, which was almost exactly Adams's own age.

Then he showed his scholar the great hall of dynamos, and explained how little he knew about electricity or force of any kind, even of his own special sun, which spouted heat in inconceivable volume, but which, as far as he knew, might spout less or more, at any time, for all the certainty he felt in it. To him, the dynamo itself was but an ingenious channel for conveying somewhere the heat latent in a few tons of poor coal hidden in a dirty engine-house carefully kept out of sight; but to Adams the dynamo became a symbol of infinity. As he grew accustomed to the great gallery of machines, he began to feel the forty-foot dynamos as a moral force, much as the early Christians felt the

---

King James I: (1566–1625), king of England (1603–1625)

economy: thrifty management

Chicago: site of the 1893 World's Fair

Daimler: Gottlieb Daimler (1834–1900), German engineer, inventor of an early internal combustion engine

a hundred kilometres: approximately 60 miles

Cross. The planet itself seemed less impressive, in its old-fashioned, deliberate, annual or daily revolution, than this huge wheel, revolving within arm's-length at some vertiginous° speed, and barely murmuring—scarcely humming an audible warning to stand a hair's-breadth further° for respect of power—while it would not wake the baby lying close against its frame. Before the end, one began to pray to it; inherited instinct taught the natural expression of man before silent and infinite force. Among the thousand symbols of ultimate energy, the dynamo was not so human as some, but it was the most expressive.

Yet the dynamo, next to the steam-engine, was the most familiar of exhibits. For Adams's objects° its value lay chiefly in its occult° mechanism. Between the dynamo in the gallery of machines and the engine-house outside, the break of continuity amounted to abysmal° fracture for a historian's objects. No more relation could he discover between the steam and the electric current than between the Cross and the cathedral. The forces were interchangeable if not reversible, but he could see only an absolute *fiat*° in electricity as in faith. Langley could not help him. Indeed, Langley seemed to be worried by the same trouble, for he constantly repeated that the new forces were anarchical,° and specially that he was not responsible for the new rays, that were little short of parricidal° in their wicked spirit towards science. His own rays, with which he had doubled the solar spectrum, were altogether harmless and beneficent; but Radium denied its God—or, what was to Langley the same thing, denied the truths of his Science. The force was wholly new.

A historian who asked only to learn enough to be as futile as Langley or Kelvin,° made rapid progress under this teaching, and mixed himself up in the tangle of ideas until he achieved a sort of Paradise of ignorance vastly consoling to his fatigued senses. He wrapped himself in vibrations and rays which were new, and he would have hugged Marconi° and Branly° had he   5

---

vertiginous: dizzying

further: i.e., further back

objects: goals, intentions

occult: secret, mysterious

abysmal: immeasurable, deep as an abyss

fiat: authoritative decree or order

anarchical: lawless, tending to anarchy

parricidal: from *parricide,* the killing of one's parent

Kelvin: William Thompson, Baron Kelvin (1824–1907), British physicist

Marconi: Guglielmo Marconi (1874–1937), Italian electrical engineer, developer of wireless telegraphy by radio waves

Branly: Édouard Branly (1844–1940), French inventor and physicist

met them, as he hugged the dynamo; while he lost his arithmetic in trying to figure out the equation between the discoveries and the economies of force. The economies, like the discoveries, were absolute, supersensual,° occult; incapable of expression in horse-power. What mathematical equivalent could he suggest as the value of a Branly coherer?° Frozen air, or the electric furnace, had some scale or measurement, no doubt, if somebody could invent a thermometer adequate to the purpose; but X-rays° had played no part whatever in man's consciousness, and the atom itself had figured only as a fiction of thought. In these seven years man had translated himself into a new universe which had no common scale of measurement with the old. He had entered a supersensual world, in which he could measure nothing except by chance collisions of movements imperceptible to his senses, perhaps even imperceptible to his instruments, but perceptible to each other, and so to some known ray at the end of the scale. Langley seemed prepared for anything, even for an indeterminable number of universes interfused—physics stark mad in metaphysics.°

Historians undertake to arrange sequences,—called stories, or histories—assuming in silence a relation of cause and effect. These assumptions, hidden in the depths of dusty libraries, have been astounding, but commonly unconscious and childlike; so much so, that if any captious° critic were to drag them to light, historians would probably reply, with one voice, that they had never supposed themselves required to know what they were talking about. Adams, for one, had toiled in vain to find out what he meant. He had even published a dozen volumes of American history for no other purpose than to satisfy himself whether, by the severest process of stating, with the least possible comment, such facts as seemed sure, in such order as seemed rigorously consequent,° he could fix for a familiar moment a necessary sequence of human movement. The result had satisfied him as little as at Harvard College. Where he saw sequence, other men saw something quite different, and no one saw the same unit of measure. He cared little about his experiments and less about his statesmen, who seemed to him quite as ignorant as himself and, as a rule, no more honest; but he insisted on a relation of sequence, and if he could not reach it by one

---

supersensual: beyond the range of the senses

coherer: radio signal detector

X-rays: detected by German physicist Wilhelm Roentgen (1845–1923) in 1895

metaphysics: theoretical philosophy, abstract reasoning

captious: faultfinding, nitpicking

consequent: logically progressing

method, he would try as many methods as science knew. Satisfied that the sequence of men led to nothing and that the sequence of their society could lead no further, while the mere sequence of time was artificial, and the sequence of thought was chaos, he turned at last to the sequence of force; and thus it happened that, after ten years' pursuit, he found himself lying in the Gallery of Machines at the Great Exposition of 1900, his historical neck broken by the sudden irruption of forces totally new.

Since no one else showed much concern, an elderly person without other cares had no need to betray° alarm. The year 1900 was not the first to upset schoolmasters. Copernicus° and Galileo° had broken many professorial necks about 1600; Columbus had stood the world on its head towards 1500; but the nearest approach to the revolution of 1900 was that of 310, when Constantine set up the Cross.° The rays that Langley disowned, as well as those which he fathered, were occult, supersensual, irrational; they were a revelation of mysterious energy like that of the Cross; they were what, in terms of mediæval science, were called immediate modes of the divine substance.

The historian was thus reduced to his last resources. Clearly if he was bound to reduce all these forces to a common value, this common value could have no measure but that of their attraction on his own mind. He must treat them as they had been felt; as convertible, reversible, interchangeable attractions on thought. He made up his mind to venture it; he would risk translating rays into faith. Such a reversible process would vastly amuse a chemist,° but the chemist could not deny that he, or some of his fellow physicists, could feel the force of both. When Adams was a boy in Boston, the best chemist in the place had probably never heard of Venus except by way of scandal,° or of the Virgin except as idolatry;° neither had he heard of dynamos or automobiles or radium; yet his mind was ready to feel the force of all, though the rays were unborn and the women were dead.

---

betray: display

Copernicus: Nicolaus Copernicus (1473–1543), Polish astronomer who established the heliocentric principle of the universe

Galileo: Galileo Galilei (1564–1642), Italian scientist who affirmed the Copernican theory in opposition to the Church

Constantine . . . Cross: Roman emperor Constantine I (280?–337) converted to Christianity and ended the persecution of Christians within the empire

chemist: pharmacist

scandal: i.e., he would have known of Venus only in connection with the treatment of venereal diseases

idolatry: worship of false gods (which Catholic devotion to the Virgin Mary is regarded as by Protestants)

Here opened another totally new education, which promised to be by far the most hazardous of all. The knife-edge along which he must crawl, like Sir Lancelot in the twelfth century, divided two kingdoms of force which had nothing in common but attraction. They were as different as a magnet is from gravitation, supposing one knew what a magnet was, or gravitation, or love. The force of the Virgin was still felt at Lourdes,° and seemed to be as potent as X-rays; but in America neither Venus nor Virgin ever had value as force—at most as sentiment. No American had ever been truly afraid of either.

This problem in dynamics gravely perplexed an American historian. The Woman had once been supreme; in France she still seemed potent, not merely as a sentiment, but as a force. Why was she unknown in America? For evidently America was ashamed of her, and she was ashamed of herself, otherwise they would not have strewn fig-leaves° so profusely all over her. When she was a true force, she was ignorant of fig-leaves, but the monthly-magazine-made American female had not a feature that would have been recognized by Adam. The trait was notorious, and often humorous, but any one brought up among Puritans knew that sex was sin. In any previous age, sex was strength. Neither art nor beauty was needed. Every one, even among Puritans, knew that neither Diana of the Ephesians° nor any of the Oriental goddesses was worshipped for her beauty. She was goddess because of her force; she was the animated dynamo; she was reproduction—the greatest and most mysterious of all energies; all she needed was to be fecund.° Singularly enough, not one of Adams's many schools of education had ever drawn his attention to the opening lines of Lucretius,° though they were perhaps the finest in all Latin literature, where the poet invoked Venus exactly as Dante invoked the Virgin:— 10

"Quae quoniam rerum naturam *sola* gubernas."°

The Venus of Epicurean philosophy survived in the Virgin of the Schools:°—

Lourdes: town in southwestern France and site of a shrine commemorating an apparition of the Virgin Mary in 1858

fig-leaves: symbols of modesty, or prudery, traditionally used to cover the genitals of naked figures in works of art

Diana of the Ephesians: the Roman goddess of the hunt, of the moon, and of birth

fecund: fertile

Lucretius: Titus Lucretius Carus (96?–55 B.C.), Roman poet and philosopher, author of *De Rerum Natura* (*On the Nature of Things*)

Quae . . . gubernas: from *De Rerum Natura*, Book I, l. 21; Latin for: Latin for "Since therefore you alone govern the nature of things"

Schools: of medieval philosophy and theology

> "Donna, sei tanto grande, e tanto vali,
> Che qual vuol grazia, e a te non ricorre,
> Sua disianza vuol volar senz' ali."°

All this was to American thought as though it had never existed. The true American knew something of the facts, but nothing of the feelings; he read the letter, but he never felt the law. Before this historical chasm, a mind like that of Adams felt itself helpless; he turned from the Virgin to the Dynamo as though he were a Branly coherer. On one side, at the Louvre° and at Chartres,° as he knew by the record of work actually done and still before his eyes, was the highest energy ever known to man, the creator of four-fifths of his noblest art, exercising vastly more attraction over the human mind than all the steam-engines and dynamos ever dreamed of; and yet this energy was unknown to the American mind. An American Virgin would never dare command; an American Venus would never dare exist.

[1904]

Read

1. What is the effect of Adams's use of third person in this autobiography? How did you react as a reader?
2. Why were the dynamos so compelling to Adams?
3. What kind of thinking does Adams suggest his guide Langley represents? How does that kind of thinking differ from that of the historian?

Write

1. Discuss how you find the "virgin" and the "dynamo" metaphorical as well as actual in Adams's essay.
2. Comment on what you think Adams's attitude toward audience is in this piece. Does it seem as though he recognizes an audience? If so, how?

Connect

1. You've read other autobiographical accounts in this anthology. Choose one to compare to Adams in terms of use of detail of experiences and the development of a persona.
2. How does Adams's attitude toward technology reflect any current concerns or ideas about technological change?

Donna . . . ali: from Dante, *Paradiso,* Canto XXXIII, ll. 13–15; Latin for "Lady, so great are you and such is your power, / that any who seeks grace and doesn't apply to you, / his desire seeks to fly without wings."

Louvre: Paris art museum, one of the world's largest, containing many works of art inspired by Christian themes

Chartres: city in northern France, site of a splendid Gothic cathedral

Kate Chopin

Kate Chopin (1851–1904) was born in St. Louis, Missouri, to wealthy parents. She was well educated and well prepared for the life of an upper middle-class matron when she married New Orleans merchant Oscar Chopin. After his business failed, she operated a plantation and store. When she was 30 years old, she was left a widow with six children. Chopin wrote poetry, literary criticism, almost a hundred short stories, and two novels, one of which, *The Awakening,* has become a classic. It is a probing study of culture and of the search for female self-identity. Chopin's stories and novels use elements of local color—dialect, a variety of characters from various classes and ethnicities, local customs—to reveal the constraints that culture places on women and to critique economics and social class. "A Pair of Silk Stockings" is one such story.

A Pair of Silk Stockings

Little Mrs. Sommers one day found herself the unexpected possessor of fifteen dollars. It seemed to her a very large amount of money, and the way in which it stuffed and bulged her worn old porte-monnaie° gave her a feeling of importance such as she had not enjoyed for years.

The question of investment was one that occupied her greatly. For a day or two she walked about apparently in a dreamy state, but really absorbed in speculation and calculation. She did not wish to act hastily, to do anything she might afterward regret. But it was during the still hours of the night when she lay awake revolving plans in her mind that she seemed to see her way clearly toward a proper and judicious use of the money.

A dollar or two should be added to the price usually paid for Janie's shoes, which would insure their lasting an appreciable time longer than they usually did. She would buy so and so many yards of percale° for new shirt waists° for the boys and Janie and Mag. She had intended to make the old ones do by skillful patching. Mag should have another gown. She had seen some beautiful patterns, veritable bargains in the shop windows. And still there would be left enough for new stockings—two pairs apiece—and what darning° that would

---

porte-monnaie: French for *purse*

percale: a woven cotton fabric

shirt waists: (usually one word) tailored blouses or shirts

darning: mending holes or tears in garments by stitching

save for a while! She would get caps for the boys and sailor-hats for the girls. The vision of her little brood looking fresh and dainty and new for once in their lives excited her and made her restless and wakeful with anticipation.

The neighbors sometimes talked of certain "better days" that little Mrs. Sommers had known before she had ever thought of being Mrs. Sommers. She herself indulged in no such morbid retrospection.° She had no time—no second of time to devote to the past. The needs of the present absorbed her every faculty. A vision of the future like some dim, gaunt monster sometimes appalled her, but luckily tomorrow never comes.

5 Mrs. Sommers was one who knew the value of bargains; who could stand for hours making her way inch by inch toward the desired object that was selling below cost. She could elbow her way if need be; she had learned to clutch a piece of goods and hold it and stick to it with persistence and determination till her turn came to be served, no matter when it came.

But that day she was a little faint and tired. She had swallowed a light luncheon—no! when she came to think of it, between getting the children fed and the place righted, and preparing herself for the shopping bout, she had actually forgotten to eat any luncheon at all!

She sat herself upon a revolving stool before a counter that was comparatively deserted, trying to gather strength and courage to charge through an eager multitude that was besieging breastworks° of shirting° and figured° lawn.° An all-gone limp feeling had come over her and she rested her hand aimlessly upon the counter. She wore no gloves. By degrees she grew aware that her hand had encountered something very soothing, very pleasant to touch. She looked down to see that her hand lay upon a pile of silk stockings. A placard near by announced that they had been reduced in price from two dollars and fifty cents to one dollar and ninety-eight cents; and a young girl who stood behind the counter asked her if she wished to examine their line of silk hosiery. She smiled, just as if she had been asked to inspect a tiara of diamonds with the ultimate view of purchasing it. But she went on feeling the soft, sheeny° luxurious things—with both hands

---

retrospection: recollection, looking back

breastworks: fortifications

shirting: any cloth used to make shirts

figured: ornamented or patterned

lawn: thin cotton or linen fabric

sheeny: shiny

now, holding them up to see them glisten, and to feel them glide serpent-like through her fingers.

Two hectic blotches came suddenly into her pale cheeks. She looked up at the girl.

"Do you think there are any eights-and-a-half among these?"

10

There were any number of eights-and-a-half. In fact, there were more of that size than any other. Here was a light-blue pair; there were some lavender, some all black and various shades of tan and gray. Mrs. Sommers selected a black pair and looked at them very long and closely. She pretended to be examining their texture, which the clerk assured her was excellent.

"A dollar and ninety-eight cents," she mused aloud. "Well, I'll take this pair." She handed the girl a five-dollar bill and waited for her change and for her parcel. What a very small parcel it was! It seemed lost in the depths of her shabby old shopping-bag.

Mrs. Sommers after that did not move in the direction of the bargain counter. She took the elevator, which carried her to an upper floor into the region of the ladies' waiting-rooms. Here, in a retired° corner, she exchanged her cotton stockings for the new silk ones which she had just bought. She was not going through any acute° mental process or reasoning with herself, nor was she striving to explain to her satisfaction the motive of her action. She was not thinking at all. She seemed for the time to be taking a rest from that laborious and fatiguing function and to have abandoned herself to some mechanical impulse that directed her actions and freed her of responsibility.

How good was the touch of the raw silk to her flesh! She felt like lying back in the cushioned chair and reveling for a while in the luxury of it. She did for a little while. Then she replaced her shoes, rolled the cotton stockings together and thrust them into her bag. After doing this she crossed straight over to the shoe department and took her seat to be fitted.

She was fastidious.° The clerk could not make° her out; he could not reconcile her shoes with her stockings, and she was not too easily pleased. She held back her skirts and turned her feet one way and her head another way as she glanced down at the polished, pointed-tipped boots. Her foot and ankle looked very pretty. She could not realize that they belonged to her and were a part of herself. She wanted an excellent and stylish fit, she told the young fellow who served her,

---

retired: secluded

acute: sharp, penetrating

fastidious: critical, hard to please

make: figure

and she did not mind the difference of a dollar or two more in the price so long as she got what she desired.

It was a long time since Mrs. Sommers had been fitted with gloves. On rare occasions when she had bought a pair they were always "bargains," so cheap that it would have been preposterous and unreasonable to have expected them to be fitted to the hand. 15

Now she rested her elbow on the cushion of the glove counter, and a pretty, pleasant young creature, delicate and deft of touch, drew a long-wristed "kid"° over Mrs. Sommers's hand. She smoothed it down over the wrist and buttoned it neatly, and both lost themselves for a second or two in admiring contemplation of the little symmetrical gloved hand. But there were other places where money might be spent.

There were books and magazines piled up in the window of a stall a few paces down the street. Mrs. Sommers bought two high-priced magazines such as she had been accustomed to read in the days when she had been accustomed to other pleasant things. She carried them without wrapping. As well as she could she lifted her skirts at the crossings. Her stockings and boots and well fitting gloves had worked marvels in her bearing—had given her a feeling of assurance, a sense of belonging to the well-dressed multitude.

She was very hungry. Another time she would have stilled the cravings for food until reaching her own home, where she would have brewed herself a cup of tea and taken a snack of anything that was available. But the impulse that was guiding her would not suffer° her to entertain any such thought.

There was a restaurant at the corner. She had never entered its doors; from the outside she had sometimes caught glimpses of spotless damask° and shining crystal, and soft-stepping waiters serving people of fashion.

When she entered her appearance created no surprise, no consternation, as she had half feared it might. She seated herself at a small table alone, and an attentive waiter at once approached to take her order. She did not want a profusion;° she craved a nice and tasty bite—a half dozen blue-points,° a plump chop with cress,° a something sweet–a crême-frappée,° for instance; a glass of Rhine wine, and after all a small cup of black coffee. 20

"kid": leather glove made from the skin of a kid or goat

suffer: allow

damask: reversible cloth with a woven pattern

profusion: abundance, great quantity

blue-points: oysters

cress: any of various plants, such as watercress, used as a salad

crême-frappée: either a sherbet-like dessert or a sweet liqueur poured over shaved ice

While waiting to be served she removed her gloves very leisurely and laid them beside her. Then she picked up a magazine and glanced through it, cutting the pages with a blunt edge of her knife. It was all very agreeable. The damask was even more spotless than it had seemed through the window, and the crystal more sparkling. There were quiet ladies and gentlemen, who did not notice her, lunching at the small tables like her own. A soft, pleasing strain of music could be heard, and a gentle breeze, was blowing through the window. She tasted a bite, and she read a word or two, and she sipped the amber wine and wiggled her toes in the silk stockings. The price of it made no difference. She counted the money out to the waiter and left an extra coin on his tray, whereupon he bowed before her as before a princess of royal blood.

There was still money in her purse, and her next temptation presented itself in the shape of a matinée poster.

It was a little later when she entered the theatre, the play had begun and the house seemed to her to be packed. But there were vacant seats here and there, and into one of them she was ushered, between brilliantly dressed women who had gone there to kill time and eat candy and display their gaudy attire. There were many others who were there solely for the play and acting. It is safe to say there was no one present who bore quite the attitude which Mrs. Sommers did to her surroundings. She gathered in the whole—stage and players and people in one wide impression, and absorbed it and enjoyed it. She laughed at the comedy and wept—she and the gaudy woman next to her wept over the tragedy. And they talked a little together over it. And the gaudy woman wiped her eyes and sniffled on a tiny square of filmy, perfumed lace and passed little Mrs. Sommers her box of candy.

The play was over, the music ceased, the crowd filed out. It was like a dream ended. People scattered in all directions. Mrs. Sommers went to the corner and waited for the cable car.

25 A man with keen eyes, who sat opposite to her, seemed to like the study of her small, pale face. It puzzled him to decipher what he saw there. In truth, he saw nothing—unless he were wizard enough to detect a poignant wish, a powerful longing that the cable car would never stop anywhere, but go on and on with her forever.

[1897]

Read

1. What is the effect on you when you read the first word of the story?
2. Why does the narrator emphasize Mrs. Sommers's interest in the present moment?
3. How does the narrator reveal Mrs. Sommers as a mother?

Write

1. How are sensory details used to convey the character's situation?
2. Write a paragraph that explores how the ending of the story reveals Chopin's rhetorical aim.
3. Comment on where you find indications of social class and economic issues in the story.

Connect

1. What do you think Chopin's story suggests about women's roles at the end of the nineteenth century? Where do you find indications of Chopin's attitude toward those roles?
2. How does this story connect with other pieces in this unit in which poverty plays an important role in characters' decisions?

Jane Addams

Jane Addams (1860–1935) was the first American woman to win the Nobel Peace Prize in 1931. She founded the Women's International League for Peace and Freedom, and Hull House, a settlement house where hundreds of immigrants and poor learned skills and received help in their quest for citizenship and stability. Born in a small Illinois town to a wealthy mill owner and state representative, Addams early learned the virtues of community and the importance of service. Lincoln was her father's hero and her own, and she often used Lincoln's work as a touchstone for her own.

Addams wrote dozens of books on her activist work for peace, women's rights, economic justice, and the rights of the disenfranchised. During World War I and its aftermath of anti-Communist hysteria, Addams was often called a naïve pacifist and a Bolshevik traitor. But she never abandoned her commitment to peace and civil rights for all. *The Long Road of Woman's Memory,* excerpted here, is drawn from Addams's experiences with the residents of Hull House and their neighbors.

From *The Long Road of Woman's Memory*

Quite as it would be hard for any one of us to select the summer in which he ceased to live that life, so ardent in childhood and early youth, when all the real happenings are in the future, so it must be difficult for old people to tell at what period they began to regard the present chiefly as a prolongation of the past. There is no doubt, however, that such instinctive shiftings and reversals have taken place for many old people who, under the control of Memory, are actually living much more in the past than in the ephemeral° present.

ephemeral: brief, fleeting

It is most fortunate, therefore, that in some subtle fashion these old people, reviewing the long road they have travelled, are able to transmute° their own untoward° experiences into that which seems to make even the most wretched life acceptable. This may possibly be due to an instinct of self-preservation, which checks the devastating bitterness that would result did they recall over and over again the sordid detail of events long past; it is even possible that those people who were not able thus to inhibit their bitterness have died earlier, for as one old man recently reminded me, "It is a true word that worry can kill a cat."

This permanent and elemental function of Memory was graphically demonstrated at Hull-House during a period of several weeks when we were reported to be harboring within its walls a so-called "Devil Baby."

The knowledge of his existence burst upon the residents of Hull-House one day when three Italian women, with an excited rush through the door, demanded that he be shown to them. No amount of denial convinced them that he was not there, for they knew exactly what he was like with his cloven hoofs, his pointed ears and diminutive° tail; the Devil Baby had, moreover, been able to speak as soon as he was born and was most shockingly profane.

The three women were but the forerunners of a veritable° multitude; for six weeks from every part of the city and suburbs the streams of visitors to this mythical baby poured in all day long and so far into the night that the regular activities of the settlement were almost swamped. 5

The Italian version, with a hundred variations, dealt with a pious Italian girl married to an atheist. Her husband in a rage had torn a holy picture from the bedroom wall saying that he would quite as soon have a devil in the house as such a thing, whereupon the devil incarnated himself in her coming child. As soon as the Devil Baby was born, he ran about the table shaking his finger in deep reproach at his father, who finally caught him and, in fear and trembling, brought him to Hull-House.

When the residents there, in spite of the baby's shocking appearance, wishing to save his soul, took him to church for baptism, they found that the shawl was empty and the Devil Baby, fleeing from the holy water, was running lightly over the backs of the pews.

---

transmute: transform
untoward: unfortunate
diminutive: small, tiny
veritable: regular, genuine

The Jewish version, again with variations, was to the effect that the father of six daughters had said before the birth of a seventh child that he would rather have a devil in the family than another girl, whereupon the Devil Baby promptly appeared.

Save° for a red automobile which occasionally figured in the story and a stray cigar which, in some versions, the new-born child had snatched from his father's lips, the tale might have been fashioned a thousand years ago.

Although the visitors to the Devil Baby included persons of every degree of prosperity and education, even physicians and trained nurses, who assured us of their scientific interest, the story constantly demonstrated the power of an old wives' tale among thousands of men and women in modern society who are living in a corner of their own, their vision fixed, their intelligence held by some iron chain of silent habit. To such primitive people the metaphor apparently is still the very "stuff of life," or rather no other form of statement reaches them; the tremendous tonnage of current writing for them has no existence. It was in keeping with their simple habits that the reputed presence of the Devil Baby should not reach the newspapers until the fifth week of his sojourn° at Hull-House after thousands of people had already been informed of his whereabouts by the old method of passing news from mouth to mouth. 10

For six weeks as I went about the house, I would hear a voice at the telephone repeating for the hundredth time that day, "No, there is no such baby"; "No, we never had it here"; "No, he couldn't have seen it for fifty cents"; "We didn't send it anywhere, because we never had it"; "I don't mean to say that your sister-in-law lied, but there must be some mistake"; "There is no use getting up an excursion from Milwaukee, for there isn't any Devil Baby at Hull-House"; "We can't give reduced rates, because we are not exhibiting anything"; and so on and on. As I came near the front door, I would catch snatches of arguments that were often acrimonious: "Why do you let so many people believe it, if it isn't here?" "We have taken three lines of cars to come and we have as much right to see it as anybody else"; "This is a pretty big place, of course you could hide it easy enough"; "What are you saying that for, are you going to raise the price of admission?"

Save: except

sojourn: temporary stay

We had doubtless struck a case of what the psychologists call the "contagion of emotion" added to that "aesthetic sociability"° which impels any one of us to drag the entire household to the window when a procession comes into the street or a rainbow appears in the sky. The Devil Baby of course was worth many processions and rainbows, and I will confess that, as the empty show went on day after day, I quite revolted against such a vapid° manifestation of even an admirable human trait. There was always one exception, however; whenever I heard the high eager voices of old women, I was irresistibly interested and left anything I might be doing in order to listen to them. As I came down the stairs, long before I could hear what they were saying, implicit in their solemn and portentous° old voices came the admonition:°

"Wilt thou reject the past
Big with deep warnings?"

It was a very serious and genuine matter with the old women, this story so ancient and yet so contemporaneous, and they flocked to Hull-House from every direction; those I had known for many years, others I had never known and some whom I had supposed to be long dead. But they were all alive and eager; something in the story or in its mysterious sequences had aroused one of those active forces in human nature which does not take orders, but insists only upon giving them. We had abruptly come in contact with a living and self-assertive human quality!

During the weeks of excitement it was the old women who really seemed to have come into their own, and perhaps the most significant result of the incident was the reaction of the story upon them. It stirred their minds and memories as with a magic touch, it loosened their tongues and revealed the inner life and thoughts of those who are so often inarticulate. They are accustomed to sit at home and to hear the younger members of the family speak of affairs quite outside their own experiences, sometimes in a language they do not understand, and at best in quick glancing phrases which they cannot follow; "More than half the time I can't tell what they are talking about," is an oft-repeated complaint. The story of the Devil Baby evidently put into their hands the sort of material with which they were accustomed

aesthetic sociability: the idea of the universality of the appreciation of art and beauty
vapid: dull, insipid
portentous: foreboding, solemn
admonition: reprimand, caution

to deal. They had long used such tales in their unremitting° efforts at family discipline, ever since they had frightened their first children into awed silence by tales of bugaboo men who prowled in the darkness.

15 These old women enjoyed a moment of triumph as if they had made good at last and had come into a region of sanctions° and punishments which they understood. Years of living had taught them that recrimination with grown-up children and grandchildren is worse than useless, that punishments are impossible, that domestic instruction is best given through tales and metaphors.

As the old women talked with the new volubility° which the story of the Devil Baby had released in them, going back into their long memories and urging its credibility upon me, the story seemed to condense that mystical wisdom which becomes deposited in the heart of man by unnoticed innumerable experiences.

Perhaps my many conversations with these aged visitors crystallized thoughts and impressions I had been receiving through years, or the tale itself may have ignited a fire, as it were, whose light illumined some of my darkest memories of neglected and uncomfortable old age, of old peasant women who had ruthlessly probed into the ugly depths of human nature in themselves and others. Many of them who came to see the Devil Baby had been forced to face tragic experiences, the powers of brutality and horror had had full scope in their lives and for years they had had acquaintance with disaster and death. Such old women do not shirk° life's misery by feeble idealism, for they are long past the stage of make-believe. They relate without flinching the most hideous experiences: "My face has had this queer twist for now nearly sixty years; I was ten when it got that way, the night after I saw my father do my mother to death with his knife." "Yes, I had fourteen children; only two grew to be men and both of them were killed in the same explosion. I was never sure they brought home the right bodies." But even the most hideous sorrows which the old women related had apparently subsided into the paler emotion of ineffectual° regret, after Memory had long done her work upon them; the old people seemed, in some unaccountable way, to lose all bitterness and resentment against life, or rather to be so completely without it that they must have lost it long since.

---

unremitting: constant, ceaseless

sanctions: restrictions

volubility: talkativeness

shirk: evade

ineffectual: powerless, futile

None of them had a word of blame for undutiful children or heedless grandchildren, because apparently the petty and transitory had fallen away from their austere° old age, the fires were burnt out, resentments, hatreds, and even cherished sorrows had become actually unintelligible.

Perhaps those women, because they had come to expect nothing more from life and had perforce° ceased from grasping and striving, had obtained, if not renunciation, at least that quiet endurance which allows the wounds of the spirit to heal. Through their stored-up habit of acquiescence, they offered a fleeting glimpse of the translucent° wisdom, so often embodied in the old, but so difficult to portray. It is doubtless what Michael Angelo had in mind when he made the Sybils old, what Dante meant by the phrase "those who had learned of life," and the age-worn minstrel who turned into song a Memory which was more that of history and tradition than his own.

In contrast to the visitors to the Devil Baby who spoke only such words of groping wisdom as they were able, were other old women who, although they had already reconciled themselves to much misery, were still enduring more: "You might say it's a disgrace to have your son beat you up for the sake of a bit of money you've earned by scrubbing—your own man is different—but I haven't the heart to blame the boy for doing what he's seen all his life, his father forever went wild when the drink was in him and struck me to the very day of his death. The ugliness was born in the boy as the marks of the Devil was born in the poor child up-stairs." 20

Some of these old women had struggled for weary years with poverty and much childbearing, had known what it was to be bullied and beaten by their husbands, neglected and ignored by their prosperous children, and burdened by the support of the imbecile and the shiftless ones. They had literally gone "Deep written all their days with care."

One old woman actually came from the poorhouse, having heard of the Devil Baby "through a lady from Polk Street visiting an old friend who has a bed in our ward." It was no slight achievement for the penniless and crippled old inmate to make her escape. She had asked "a young bar-keep in a saloon across the road" to lend her ten cents, offering as security the fact that she was an old /acquaintance at Hull-House who could not be refused so slight a loan. She marvelled at some length over the goodness of the young man, for she had

---

austere: lacking in luxury or excess

perforce: of necessity, necessarily

translucent: clear, lucid

not had a dime to spend for a drink for the last six months, and he and the conductor had been obliged to lift her into the street car by main strength. She was naturally much elated over the achievement of her escape. To be sure, from the men's side, they were always walking off in the summer and taking to the road, living like tramps they did, in a way no one from the woman's side would demean herself to do; but to have left in a street car like a lady, with money to pay her own fare, was quite a different matter, although she was, indeed "clean wore out" by the effort. However, it was clear that she would consider herself well repaid by a sight of the Devil Baby and that not only the inmates of her own ward, but those in every other ward in the house would be made to "sit up" when she got back; it would liven them all up a bit, and she hazarded the guess that she would have to tell them about that baby at least a dozen times a day.

As she cheerfully rambled on, we weakly postponed telling her there was no Devil Baby, first that she might have a cup of tea and rest, and then through a sheer desire to withhold a blow from a poor old body who had received so many throughout a long, hard life.

As I recall those unreal weeks, it was in her presence that I found myself for the first time vaguely wishing that I could administer comfort by the simple device of not asserting too dogmatically° that the Devil Baby had never been at Hull-House.

. . .

The vivid interest of so many old women in the story of the Devil Baby may have been an unconscious, although powerful, testimony that tragic experiences gradually become dressed in such trappings in order that their spent agony may prove of some use to a world which learns at the hardest; and that the strivings and sufferings of men and women long since dead, their emotions no longer connected with flesh and blood, are thus transmuted into legendary wisdom. The young are forced to heed the warning in such a tale, although for the most part it is so easy for them to disregard the words of the aged. That the old women who came to visit the Devil Baby believed that the story would secure them a hearing at home was evident, and as they prepared themselves with every detail of it, their old faces shone with a timid satisfaction. Their features, worn and scarred by harsh living, as effigies° built into the floor of an old church become dim and defaced by rough-shod feet, grew poignant and solemn. In the midst of their double bewilderment, both that the younger generation was walking in such

25

---

dogmatically: emphatically, authoritatively

effigies: images or representations of persons

strange paths and that no one would listen to them, for one moment there flickered up the last hope of a disappointed life, that it may at least serve as a warning, while affording material for an exciting narrative.

Sometimes in talking to a woman who was "but a hair's breadth this side of the darkness," I realized that old age has its own expression for the mystic renunciation of the world. Their impatience with all non-essentials, the craving to be free from hampering bonds and soft conditions, recalled Tolstoy's last impetuous journey, and I was once more grateful to his genius for making clear another unintelligible impulse of bewildered humanity.

Often, in the midst of a conversation, one of these touching old women would quietly express a longing for death, as if it were a natural fulfilment of an inmost desire, with a sincerity and anticipation so genuine that I would feel abashed° in her presence, ashamed to "cling to this strange thing that shines in the sunlight and to be sick with love for it." Such impressions were, in their essence, transitory,° but one result from the hypothetical visit of the Devil Baby to Hull-House will, I think, remain: a realization of the sifting and reconciling power inherent in Memory itself. The old women, with much to aggravate and little to soften the habitual bodily discomforts of old age, exhibited an emotional serenity so vast and so reassuring, that I found myself perpetually speculating upon how soon the fleeting and petty emotions which now seem unduly important to us might be thus transmuted; at what moment we might expect the inconsistencies and perplexities of life to be brought under this appeasing Memory with its ultimate power to increase the elements of beauty and significance and to reduce, if not to eliminate, all sense of resentment.

[1916]

Read

1. What does Addams indicate is the function of memory for older people?
2. What was the Devil Baby, and how did it function as a metaphor?
3. What does Addams mean by the "contagion of emotion"?
4. What lines in the text suggest how Addams's ideas about her neighbors change during the incident?

Write

1. How does the Devil Baby story function to increase Addams's understanding of people's experience?

---

abashed: embarrassed, disconcerted

transitory: impermanent

2. Write a brief characterization of Addams's persona in this excerpt. Use language from the narrative to help you frame your description.
3. How does Addams suggest the role of poverty in the creation of the Devil Baby myth?

Connect

1. How is the Devil Baby like an "urban legend"? What urban legends have you heard? Do they have a similar function?
2. What role does Addams play in this story? Is her role similar to Franklin's in the essays in Unit 2? Why or why not?

Jacob Riis

Jacob Riis (1849–1914) emigrated to the United States from Denmark when he was 21. His father, a teacher, helped him learn English by encouraging him to read the novels of James Fenimore Cooper. After working as a carpenter and at other odd jobs, Riis began writing stories about immigrants, political corruption, and poverty for the *New York Herald*. His book of text and photographs, *How the Other Half Lives* (1890), which documented the lives of the poor in the tenements of New York, brought him critical acclaim. Riis was a social reformer and advocate of social justice as well as an innovator in film production. He was one of the first to develop the use of flash photography.

New York: Tenement Yard

Women doing laundry in a tenement courtyard on Elizabeth Street (circa 1890s), Jacob A. Riis. Photograph. The Granger Collection, NY

[c. 1890]

Read

1. How do details in the photo suggest its tone?
2. How does the depiction of the people, buildings, and objects contribute to the photograph's effect?
3. What is the relationship of the camera to the people in the photograph?

Write

1. Describe the effect of light and shadow in the photograph.
2. Write a few sentences that express what you think is the aim of this photograph.

Connect

1. How does this photograph illustrate poverty to you? How can you draw connections to other work that confronts poverty?
2. Compare the photographic techniques used by Riis in this photo to the photo "Steerage" by Steiglitz.

Zitkala Sa

Zitkala Sa (Gertrude Simmons Bonnin; 1876–1938) was born on the Pine River Reservation in South Dakota to a Sioux-Yankton mother and a white father. She left the reservation as a child to attend a Quaker missionary school for Indian children in Indiana. She later taught music at the Carlisle Indian School in Pennsylvania and began writing articles for journals like the *Atlantic Monthly* about her experiences, often questioning the teaching practices of Indian schools. Zitkala Sa wrote several collections of stories in addition to memoir. She worked for Indian rights and political causes that supported social justice.

From *The School Days of an Indian Girl*

I

The Land of Red Apples

There were eight in our party of bronzed children who were going East with the missionaries. Among us were three young braves, two tall girls, and we three little ones, Judéwin, Thowin, and I.

We had been very impatient to start on our journey to the Red Apple Country, which, we were told, lay a little beyond the great circular horizon of the Western prairie. Under a sky of rosy apples we dreamt of roaming as freely and happily as we had chased the cloud shadows on the Dakota plains. We had anticipated much pleasure from a ride on the iron horse, but the throngs of staring palefaces disturbed and troubled us.

On the train, fair women, with tottering babies on each arm, stopped their haste and scrutinized the children of absent mothers. Large men, with heavy bundles in their hands, halted near by, and riveted their glassy blue eyes upon us.

I sank deep into the corner of my seat, for I resented being watched. Directly in front of me, children who were no larger than I hung themselves upon the backs of their seats, with their bold white faces toward me. Sometimes they took their forefingers out of their mouths and pointed at my moccasined feet. Their mothers, instead of reproving° such rude curiosity, looked closely at me, and attracted their children's further notice to my blanket. This embarrassed me, and kept me constantly on the verge of tears.

5 I sat perfectly still, with my eyes downcast, daring only now and then to shoot long glances around me. Chancing to turn to the window at my side, I was quite breathless upon seeing one familiar object. It was the telegraph pole which strode by at short paces. Very near my mother's dwelling, along the edge of a road thickly bordered with wild sunflowers, some poles like these had been planted by white men. Often I had stopped, on my way down the road, to hold my ear against the pole, and, hearing its low moaning, I used to wonder what the paleface had done to hurt it. Now I sat watching for each pole that glided by to be the last one.

In this way I had forgotten my uncomfortable surroundings, when I heard one of my comrades call out my name. I saw the missionary standing very near, tossing candies and gums into our midst. This amused us all, and we tried to see who could catch the most of the sweetmeats.

Though we rode several days inside of the iron horse, I do not recall a single thing about our luncheons.

It was night when we reached the school grounds. The lights from the windows of the large buildings fell upon some of the icicled trees that stood beneath them. We were led toward an open door, where the brightness of the lights within flooded out over the heads of the excited palefaces who blocked our way. My body trembled more from fear than from the snow I trod upon.

---

reproving: criticizing, scolding

Entering the house, I stood close against the wall. The strong glaring light in the large whitewashed room dazzled my eyes. The noisy hurrying of hard shoes upon a bare wooden floor increased the whirring in my ears. My only safety seemed to be in keeping next to the wall. As I was wondering in which direction to escape from all this confusion, two warm hands grasped me firmly, and in the same moment I was tossed high in midair. A rosy-cheeked paleface woman caught me in her arms. I was both frightened and insulted by such trifling.° I stared into her eyes, wishing her to let me stand on my own feet, but she jumped me up and down with increasing enthusiasm. My mother had never made a plaything of her wee daughter. Remembering this I began to cry aloud.

They misunderstood the cause of my tears, and placed me at a white table loaded with food. There our party were united again. As I did not hush my crying, one of the older ones whispered to me, "Wait until you are alone in the night." 10

It was very little I could swallow besides my sobs, that evening.

"Oh, I want my mother and my brother Dawée! I want to go to my aunt!" I pleaded; but the ears of the palefaces could not hear me.

From the table we were taken along an upward incline of wooden boxes, which I learned afterward to call a stairway. At the top was a quiet hall, dimly lighted. Many narrow beds were in one straight line down the entire length of the wall. In them lay sleeping brown faces, which peeped just out of the coverings. I was tucked into bed with one of the tall girls, because she talked to me in my mother tongue and seemed to soothe me.

I had arrived in the wonderful land of rosy skies, but I was not happy, as I had thought I should be. My long travel and the bewildering sights had exhausted me. I fell asleep, heaving deep, tired sobs. My tears were left to dry themselves in streaks, because neither my aunt nor my mother was near to wipe them away.

II

The Cutting of My Long Hair

The first day in the land of apples was a bitter-cold one; for the snow still covered the ground, and the trees were bare. A large bell rang for breakfast, its loud metallic voice crashing through the belfry overhead and into our sensitive ears. The annoying clatter of shoes on bare floors gave us no peace. The constant clash of harsh noises, with an undercurrent of many voices murmuring an unknown tongue, made a bedlam° within which 15

trifling: acting foolishly and disrespectfully

bedlam: chaos, pandemonium

I was securely tied. And though my spirit tore itself in struggling for its lost freedom, all was useless.

A paleface woman, with white hair, came up after us. We were placed in a line of girls who were marching into the dining room. These were Indian girls, in stiff shoes and closely clinging dresses. The small girls wore sleeved aprons and shingled° hair. As I walked noiselessly in my soft moccasins, I felt like sinking to the floor, for my blanket had been stripped from my shoulders. I looked hard at the Indian girls, who seemed not to care that they were even more immodestly dressed than I, in their tightly fitting clothes. While we marched in, the boys entered at an opposite door. I watched for the three young braves who came in our party. I spied them in the rear ranks, looking as uncomfortable as I felt.

A small bell was tapped, and each of the pupils drew a chair from under the table. Supposing this act meant they were to be seated, I pulled out mine and at once slipped into it from one side. But when I turned my head, I saw that I was the only one seated, and all the rest at our table remained standing. Just as I began to rise, looking shyly around to see how chairs were to be used, a second bell was sounded. All were seated at last, and I had to crawl back into my chair again. I heard a man's voice at one end of the hall, and I looked around to see him. But all the others hung their heads over their plates. As I glanced at the long chain of tables, I caught the eyes of a paleface woman upon me. Immediately I dropped my eyes, wondering why I was so keenly watched by the strange woman. The man ceased his mutterings, and then a third bell was tapped. Every one picked up his knife and fork and began eating. I began crying instead, for by this time I was afraid to venture anything more.

But this eating by formula was not the hardest trial in that first day. Late in the morning, my friend Judéwin gave me a terrible warning. Judéwin knew a few words of English; and she had overheard the paleface woman talk about cutting our long, heavy hair. Our mothers had taught us that only unskilled warriors who were captured had their hair shingled by the enemy. Among our people, short hair was worn by mourners, and shingled hair by cowards!

We discussed our fate some moments, and when Judéwin said, "We have to submit, because they are strong," I rebelled.

"No, I will not submit! I will struggle first!" I answered. 20

I watched my chance, and when no one noticed I disappeared. I crept up the stairs as quietly as I could in my squeaking shoes,—my moccasins had

shingled: cut close to the head

been exchanged for shoes. Along the hall I passed, without knowing whither° I was going. Turning aside to an open door, I found a large room with three white beds in it. The windows were covered with dark green curtains, which made the room very dim. Thankful that no one was there, I directed my steps toward the corner farthest from the door. On my hands and knees I crawled under the bed, and cuddled myself in the dark corner.

From my hiding place I peered out, shuddering with fear whenever I heard footsteps near by. Though in the hall loud voices were calling my name, and I knew that even Judéwin was searching for me, I did not open my mouth to answer. Then the steps were quickened and the voices became excited. The sounds came nearer and nearer. Women and girls entered the room. I held my breath and watched them open closet doors and peep behind large trunks. Some one threw up the curtains, and the room was filled with sudden light. What caused them to stoop and look under the bed I do not know. I remember being dragged out, though I resisted by kicking and scratching wildly. In spite of myself, I was carried downstairs and tied fast in a chair.

I cried aloud, shaking my head all the while until I felt the cold blades of the scissors against my neck, and heard them gnaw off one of my thick braids. Then I lost my spirit. Since the day I was taken from my mother I had suffered extreme indignities. People had stared at me. I had been tossed about in the air like a wooden puppet. And now my long hair was shingled like a coward's! In my anguish I moaned for my mother, but no one came to comfort me. Not a soul reasoned quietly with me, as my own mother used to do; for now I was only one of many little animals driven by a herder.

III

The Snow Episode

A short time after our arrival we three Dakotas were playing in the snowdrift. We were all still deaf to the English language, excepting Judéwin, who always heard such puzzling things. One morning we learned through her ears that we were forbidden to fall lengthwise in the snow, as we had been doing, to see our own impressions. However, before many hours we had forgotten the order, and were having great sport in the snow, when a shrill voice called us. Looking up, we saw an imperative° hand beckoning us into the house. We shook the snow off ourselves, and started toward the woman as slowly as we dared.

Judéwin said: "Now the paleface is angry with us. She is going to punish us for falling into the snow. If she looks straight into your eyes and talks 25

---

whither: where

imperative: commanding

loudly, you must wait until she stops. Then, after a tiny pause, say, 'No.'" The rest of the way we practiced upon the little word "no."

As it happened, Thowin was summoned to judgment first. The door shut behind her with a click.

Judéwin and I stood silently listening at the keyhole. The paleface woman talked in very severe tones. Her words fell from her lips like crackling embers,° and her inflection° ran up like the small end of a switch.° I understood her voice better than the things she was saying. I was certain we had made her very impatient with us. Judéwin heard enough of the words to realize all too late that she had taught us the wrong reply.

"Oh, poor Thowin!" she gasped, as she put both hands over her ears.

Just then I heard Thowin's tremulous° answer, "No."

With an angry exclamation, the woman gave her a hard spanking. Then she stopped to say something. Judéwin said it was this: "Are you going to obey my word the next time?" 30

Thowin answered again with the only word at her command, "No."

This time the woman meant her blows to smart,° for the poor frightened girl shrieked at the top of her voice. In the midst of the whipping the blows ceased abruptly, and the woman asked another question: "Are you going to fall in the snow again?"

Thowin gave her bad password another trial. We heard her say feebly, "No! No!"

With this the woman hid away her half-worn slipper, and led the child out, stroking her black shorn head. Perhaps it occurred to her that brute force is not the solution for such a problem. She did nothing to Judéwin nor to me. She only returned to us our unhappy comrade, and left us alone in the room.

During the first two or three seasons misunderstandings as ridiculous as this one of the snow episode frequently took place, bringing unjustifiable frights and punishments into our little lives. 35

Within a year I was able to express myself somewhat in broken English. As soon as I comprehended a part of what was said and done, a mischievous spirit of revenge possessed me. One day I was called in from my play for some misconduct. I had disregarded a rule which seemed to me very needlessly binding. I was sent into the kitchen to mash the turnips for dinner.

---

embers: small pieces of live coal or wood

inflection: tone of voice

switch: thin, flexible rod used for whipping

tremulous: trembling

smart: hurt

It was noon, and steaming dishes were hastily carried into the dining-room. I hated turnips, and their odor which came from the brown jar was offensive to me. With fire in my heart, I took the wooden tool that the paleface woman held out to me. I stood upon a step, and, grasping the handle with both hands, I bent in hot rage over the turnips. I worked my vengeance upon them. All were so busily occupied that no one noticed me. I saw that the turnips were in a pulp, and that further beating could not improve them; but the order was, "Mash these turnips," and mash them I would! I renewed my energy; and as I sent the masher into the bottom of the jar, I felt a satisfying sensation that the weight of my body had gone into it.

Just here a paleface woman came up to my table. As she looked into the jar, she shoved my hands roughly aside. I stood fearless and angry. She placed her red hands upon the rim of the jar. Then she gave one lift and stride away from the table. But lo! the pulpy contents fell through the crumbled bottom to the floor! She spared me no scolding phrases that I had earned. I did not heed them. I felt triumphant in my revenge, though deep within me I was a wee bit sorry to have broken the jar.

As I sat eating my dinner, and saw that no turnips were served, I whooped in my heart for having once asserted the rebellion within me.

IV

The Devil

Among the legends the old warriors used to tell me were many stories of evil spirits. But I was taught to fear them no more than those who stalked about in material guise.° I never knew there was an insolent chieftain among the bad spirits, who dared to array his forces against the Great Spirit, until I heard this white man's legend from a paleface woman.

Out of a large book she showed me a picture of the white man's devil. 40
I looked in horror upon the strong claws that grew out of his fur-covered fingers. His feet were like his hands. Trailing at his heels was a scaly tail tipped with a serpent's open jaws. His face was a patchwork: he had bearded cheeks, like some I had seen palefaces wear; his nose was an eagle's bill, and his sharp-pointed ears were pricked up like those of a sly fox. Above them a pair of cow's horns curved upward. I trembled with awe, and my heart throbbed in my throat, as I looked at the king of evil spirits. Then I heard the paleface woman say that this terrible creature roamed loose in the world, and that little girls who disobeyed school regulations were to be tortured by him.

guise: form, shape

That night I dreamt about this evil divinity. Once again I seemed to be in my mother's cottage. An Indian woman had come to visit my mother. On opposite sides of the kitchen stove, which stood in the center of the small house, my mother and her guest were seated in straight-backed chairs. I played with a train of empty spools hitched together on a string. It was night, and the wick burned feebly. Suddenly I heard some one turn our door-knob from without.°

My mother and the woman hushed their talk, and both looked toward the door. It opened gradually. I waited behind the stove. The hinges squeaked as the door was slowly, very slowly pushed inward.

Then in rushed the devil! He was tall! He looked exactly like the picture I had seen of him in the white man's papers. He did not speak to my mother, because he did not know the Indian language, but his glittering yellow eyes were fastened upon me. He took long strides: around the stove, passing behind the woman's chair. I threw down my spools, and ran to my mother. He did not fear her, but followed closely after me. Then I ran round and round the stove, crying aloud for help. But my mother and the woman seemed not to know my danger. They sat still, looking quietly upon the devil's chase after me. At last I grew dizzy. My head revolved as on a hidden pivot. My knees became numb, and doubled under my weight like a pair of knife blades without a spring. Beside my mother's chair I fell in a heap. Just as the devil stooped over me with outstretched claws my mother awoke from her quiet indifference, and lifted me on her lap. Whereupon the devil vanished, and I was awake.

On the following morning I took my revenge upon the devil. Stealing into the room where a wall of shelves was filled with books, I drew forth The Stories of the Bible. With a broken slate pencil I carried in my apron pocket, I began by scratching out his wicked eyes. A few moments later, when I was ready to leave the room, there was a ragged hole in the page where the picture of the devil had once been.

V

Iron Routine

A loud-clamoring bell awakened us at half-past six in the cold winter mornings. From happy dreams of Western rolling lands and unlassoed freedom we tumbled out upon chilly bare floors back again into a paleface day. We had short time to jump into our shoes and clothes, and wet our eyes with icy water, before a small hand bell was vigorously rung for roll call.

45

without: outside

There were too many drowsy children and too numerous orders for the day to waste a moment in any apology to nature for giving her children such a shock in the early morning. We rushed downstairs, bounding over two high steps at a time, to land in the assembly room.

A paleface woman, with a yellow-covered roll book open on her arm and a gnawed pencil in her hand, appeared at the door. Her small, tired face was coldly lighted with a pair of large gray eyes.

She stood still in a halo of authority, while over the rim of her spectacles her eyes pried nervously about the room. Having glanced at her long list of names and called out the first one, she tossed up her chin and peered through the crystals of her spectacles to make sure of the answer "Here."

Relentlessly her pencil black-marked our daily records if we were not present to respond to our names, and no chum of ours had done it successfully for us. No matter if a dull headache or the painful cough of slow consumption° had delayed the absentee, there was only time enough to mark the tardiness. It was next to impossible to leave the iron routine after the civilizing machine had once begun its day's buzzing; and as it was inbred in me to suffer in silence rather than to appeal to the ears of one whose open eyes could not see my pain, I have many times trudged in the day's harness heavy-footed, like a dumb sick brute.

Once I lost a dear classmate. I remember well how she used to mope along at my side, until one morning she could not raise her head from her pillow. At her deathbed I stood weeping, as the paleface woman sat near her moistening the dry lips. Among the folds of the bedclothes I saw the open pages of the white man's Bible. The dying Indian girl talked disconnectedly of Jesus the Christ and the paleface who was cooling her swollen hands and feet. 50

I grew bitter, and censured° the woman for cruel neglect of our physical ills. I despised the pencils that moved automatically, and the one teaspoon which dealt out, from a large bottle, healing to a row of variously ailing Indian children. I blamed the hard-working, well-meaning, ignorant woman who was inculcating° in our hearts her superstitious ideas. Though I was sullen in all my little troubles, as soon

---

consumption: tuberculosis

censured: blamed, condemned

inculcating: instilling, indoctrinating

as I felt better I was ready again to smile upon the cruel woman. Within a week I was again actively testing the chains which tightly bound my individuality like a mummy for burial.

The melancholy of those black days has left so long a shadow that it darkens the path of years that have since gone by. These sad memories rise above those of smoothly grinding school days. Perhaps my Indian nature is the moaning wind which stirs them now for their present record. But, however tempestuous this is within me, it comes out as the low voice of a curiously colored seashell, which is only for those ears that are bent with compassion to hear it.

[1900]

Read

1. In the first paragraphs, how does the narrator use her experience with the other children to convey cultural difference?
2. What images are used to suggest the narrator's feelings as she begins school?
3. What is the effect of Zitkala Sa's use of the word "animals" in section 2?

Write

1. What is the importance of the story of the devil to your understanding of Zitkala Sa's position?
2. What kinds of appeals does Zitkala Sa make in her narrative? Use examples from the text to explore her use of appeals.
3. Comment on Zitkala Sa's aim in this piece and how she achieves it.

Connect

1. How is Zitkala Sa's experience similar to or different from that of Samson Occam? Phillis Wheatley?
2. Speculate on the motives of the people who founded the Indian schools, based on what you read in Zitkala Sa's account and any research that might help you understand the reasons for the schools.

Carl Sandburg

Carl Sandburg (1878–1967) was enormously popular during his lifetime as a poet of the people and for his anecdotes about his hero, Abraham Lincoln. Born in Illinois, Sandburg never finished school, took odd jobs, and finally moved to Chicago, where he wrote for a newspaper and began publishing poetry. Like Walt Whitman, Sandburg believed in the common man. For him, Lincoln was the embodiment of that belief. His biography of Lincoln won the Pulitzer Prize in 1940.

Chicago

Hog Butcher for the World,
Tool Maker, Stacker of Wheat,
Player with Railroads and the Nation's Freight Handler;
Stormy, husky, brawling,
City of the Big Shoulders: 5
They tell me you are wicked and I believe them, for I have seen your painted women under the gas lamps luring the farm boys.
And they tell me you are crooked and I answer: Yes, it is true I have seen the gunman kill and go free to kill again.
And they tell me you are brutal and my reply is: On the faces of women and children I have seen the marks of wanton° hunger.
And having answered so I turn once more to those who sneer at this my city, and I give them back the sneer and say to them:
Come and show me another city with lifted head singing so proud to be alive and coarse and strong and cunning. 10
Flinging magnetic curses amid the toil of piling job on job, here is a tall bold slugger set vivid against the little soft cities;
Fierce as a dog with tongue lapping for action, cunning as a savage pitted against the wilderness,
Bareheaded,
Shoveling,
Wrecking, 15
Planning,
Building, breaking, rebuilding,
Under the smoke, dust all over his mouth, laughing with white teeth,
Under the terrible burden of destiny laughing as a young man laughs,
Laughing even as an ignorant fighter laughs who has never lost a battle, 20
Bragging and laughing that under his wrist is the pulse, and under his ribs the heart of the people,
Laughing!
Laughing the stormy, husky, brawling laughter of Youth, half-naked, sweating, proud to be Hog Butcher, Tool Maker, Stacker of Wheat, Player with Railroads and Freight Handler to the Nation.

[1916]

---

wanton: cruel, merciless

Read

1. How do the names Sandburg gives the city suggest its character?
2. How does the speaker use verbs in the poem?
3. What is the role of repetition in the poem?

Write

1. After reading this poem, how would you characterize Chicago? If you've been to Chicago, use that experience to help frame your response.
2. Describe Sandburg's attitude toward the city, based on the poem.
3. Write a reflection on how you respond to this poem. Are you attracted by the city? Repelled?

Connect

1. How does this poem suggest the influence of Walt Whitman on the poet?
2. How does "Chicago" illustrate or symbolize the move from rural to urban at the beginning of the twentieth century?

Mary Antin

Mary Antin (1881–1949) emigrated from Russia when she was five. She was educated in public schools in America and studied at Columbia University. She began writing journalistic articles on immigration and education, and her autobiography *The Promised Land,* published in 1912, is the story of the success and difficulty that her family faced when they moved to the United States. "The Promise of Free Education" is a chapter from that work.

The Promise of Free Education

Our initiation into American ways began with the first step on the new soil. My father found occasion to instruct or correct us even on the way from the pier to Wall Street, which journey we made crowded together in a rickety cab. He told us not to lean out of the windows, not to point, and explained the word "greenhorn." We did not want to be "greenhorns," and gave the strictest attention to my father's instructions. . . .

The first meal was an object lesson of much variety. My father produced several kinds of food, ready to eat, without any cooking, from little tin cans that had printing all over them. He attempted to introduce us to a queer, slippery kind of fruit, which he called "banana," but had to give it up for the time being. After the meal, he had better luck with a curious piece of furniture on runners, which he called "rocking-chair." There were five of us newcomers, and we found five different ways of getting into the American machine of perpetual motion, and as many ways of getting out of it. One born and bred to the use of a rocking-chair cannot imagine how ludicrous people can make themselves when attempting to use it for the first time. We laughed immoderately over our various experiments with the novelty, which was a wholesome way of letting off steam after the unusual excitement of the day.

In our flat° we did not think of such a thing as storing the coal in the bathtub. There was no bathtub. So in the evening of the first day my father conducted us to the public baths. As we moved along in a little procession, I was delighted with the illumination of the streets. So many lamps, and they burned until morning, my father said, and so people did not need to carry lanterns. In America, then, everything was free, as we had heard in Russia. Light was free; the streets were as bright as a synagogue on a holy day. Music was free; we had been serenaded, to our gaping delight, by a brass band of many pieces, soon after our installation on Union Place.

Education was free. That subject my father had written about repeatedly, as comprising his chief hope for us children, the essence of American opportunity, the treasure that no thief could touch, not even misfortune or poverty. It was the one thing that he was able to promise us when he sent for us; surer, safer than bread or shelter. On our second day I was thrilled with the realization of what this freedom of education meant. A little girl from across the alley came and offered to conduct us to school. My father was out, but we five between us had a few words of English by this time. We knew the word school. We understood. This child, who had never seen us till yesterday, who could not pronounce our names, who was not much better dressed than we, was able to offer us the freedom of the schools of Boston! No application made, no questions asked, no examinations, rulings, exclusions; no machinations,° no fees. The doors stood open for every one of us. The smallest child could show us the way.

5 This incident impressed me more than anything I had heard in advance of the freedom of education in America. It was a concrete proof—almost the thing itself. One had to experience it to understand it.

---

flat: apartment

machinations: schemes

It was a great disappointment to be told by my father that we were not to enter upon our school career at once. It was too near the end of the term, he said, and we were going to move to Crescent Beach in a week or so. We had to wait until the opening of the schools in September. What a loss of precious time—from May till September! . . .

The apex of my civic pride and personal contentment was reached on the bright September morning when I entered the public school. That day I must always remember, even if I live to be so old that I cannot tell my name. To most people their first day at school is a memorable occasion. In my case the importance of the day was a hundred times magnified, on account of the years I had waited, the road I had come, and the conscious ambitions I entertained.

I am wearily aware that I am speaking in extreme figures, in superlatives. I wish I knew some other way to render the mental life of the immigrant child of reasoning age. I may have been ever so much an exception in acuteness° of observation, powers of comparison, and abnormal self-consciousness; none the less were my thoughts and conduct typical of the attitude of the intelligent immigrant child toward American institutions. And what the child thinks and feels is a reflection of the hopes, desires, and purposes of the parents who brought him overseas, no matter how precocious° and independent the child may be. Your immigrant inspectors will tell you what poverty the foreigner brings in his baggage, what want° in his pockets. Let the overgrown boy of twelve, reverently drawing his letters in the baby class, testify to the noble dreams and high ideals that may be hidden beneath the greasy caftan° of the immigrant. Speaking for the Jews, at least, I know I am safe in inviting such an investigation. . . .

The two of us stood a moment in the doorway of the tenement house on Arlington Street, that wonderful September morning when I first went to school. It was I that ran away, on winged feet of joy and expectation; it was she whose feet were bound in the treadmill of daily toil. And I was so blind that I did not see that the glory lay on her, and not on me.

Father himself conducted us to school. He would not have delegated that mission to the President of the United States. He had awaited the day with impatience equal to mine, and the visions he saw as he hurried us over the sun-flecked pavements transcended all my dreams. Almost his first act on landing on American soil, three years before, had been his application for 10

---

acuteness: sharpness

precocious: prematurely advanced or developed

want: need, destitution

caftan: long robe-like garment

naturalization. He had taken the remaining steps in the process with eager promptness, and at the earliest moment allowed by the law, he became a citizen of the United States. It is true that he had left home in search of bread for his hungry family, but he went blessing the necessity that drove him to America. The boasted freedom of the New World meant to him far more than the right to reside, travel, and work wherever he pleased; it meant the freedom to speak his thoughts, to throw off the shackles of superstition, to test his own fate, unhindered by political or religious tyranny. He was only a young man when he landed—thirty-two; and most of his life he had been held in leading-strings.° He was hungry for his untasted manhood.

Three years passed in sordid° struggle and disappointment. He was not prepared to make a living even in America, where the day laborer eats wheat instead of rye. Apparently the American flag could not protect him against the pursuing Nemesis° of his limitations; he must expiate° the sins of his fathers who slept across the seas. He had been endowed at birth with a poor constitution, a nervous, restless temperament, and an abundance of hindering prejudices. In his boyhood his body was starved, that his mind might be stuffed with useless learning. In his youth this dearly gotten learning was sold, and the price was the bread and salt which he had not been trained to earn for himself. Under the wedding canopy he was bound for life to a girl whose features were still strange to him; and he was bidden to multiply himself, that sacred learning might be perpetuated in his sons, to the glory of the God of his fathers. All this while he had been led about as a creature without a will, a chattel,° an instrument. In his maturity he awoke, and found himself poor in health, poor in purse, poor in useful knowledge, and hampered on all sides. At the first nod of opportunity he broke away from his prison, and strove to atone for his wasted youth by a life of useful labor; while at the same time he sought to lighten the gloom of his narrow scholarship by freely partaking of modern ideas. But his utmost endeavor still left him far from his goal. In business, nothing prospered with him. Some fault of hand or mind or temperament led him to failure where other men found success. Wherever the blame for his disabilities be placed, he reaped their bitter fruit. "Give me bread!" he cried to America. "What will you do to earn it?" the challenge came back. And he found that he was master of no art, of no trade; that even his precious learning was of no avail, because he had only the most antiquated methods of communicating it.

---

leading-strings: strings used to guide and support a child who is learning to walk

sordid: dirty, degraded

Nemesis: in mythology, the spirit of divine retribution

expiate: atone for

chattel: piece of property

So in his primary quest he had failed. There was left him the compensation of intellectual freedom. That he sought to realize in every possible way. He had very little opportunity to prosecute° his education, which, in truth, had never been begun. His struggle for a bare living left him no time to take advantage of the public evening school; but he lost nothing of what was to be learned through reading, through attendance at public meetings, through exercising the rights of citizenship. Even here he was hindered by a natural inability to acquire the English language. In time, indeed, he learned to read, to follow a conversation or lecture; but he never learned to write correctly, and his pronunciation remains extremely foreign to this day.

If education, culture, the higher life were shining things to be worshipped from afar, he had still a means left whereby he could draw one step nearer to them. He could send his children to school, to learn all those things that he knew by fame° to be desirable. The common school, at least, perhaps high school; for one or two, perhaps even college! His children should be students, should fill his house with books and intellectual company; and thus he would walk by proxy in the Elysian Fields° of liberal learning. As for the children themselves, he knew no surer way to their advancement and happiness.

So it was with a heart full of longing and hope that my father led us to school on that first day. He took long strides in his eagerness, the rest of us running and hopping to keep up.

15 At last the four of us stood around the teacher's desk; and my father, in his impossible English, gave us over in her charge, with some broken word of his hopes for us that his swelling heart could no longer contain.

[1912]

Read

1. What details does Antin use to demonstrate the strangeness of her new environment in America?
2. Where do you recognize that the speaker is looking back on an earlier time?
3. How does the writer use a self-conscious awareness of diction? What purpose does her consciousness of language serve?
4. What do you think the significance is of "wheat" not "rye"?

Write

1. Find a few details from the narrative and describe how Antin establishes the importance of education to her.
2. What role does family play in the immigrant experience? Write a paragraph that explains how Antin's family is important to her vision of America.

---

prosecute: pursue

fame: reputation

Elysian Fields: a place of perfect happiness (in mythology, the dwelling place of the blessed after death)

Complete Additional Exercises on Antin's Memoir at Your Pearson MyLab

Connect

1. How do you see family playing a significant role in other texts in this unit?
2. What is your opinion of Antin's belief in education? Is this element of the American dream still alive today?

Alfred Steiglitz

Alfred Steiglitz (1864–1946) is one of the most important of American artists; he elevated photography into an art form. He was born to Jewish-German immigrants and was educated in America and Germany, where he first learned photography. He opened a studio in New York, established the Camera Club for artists and photographers, and promoted the work of young artists, including Georgia O'Keefe, whom he married in 1925. Steiglitz's photographs used light and shadow dramatically. His photos vividly depicted the urban landscape of New York and surrounding areas.

The Steerage

The Steerage (1907), Alfred Stieglitz. Printed 1915. Photogravure on vellum. 32.2 x 25.8 cm (12 11/16 x 10 3/16 in). Alfred Stieglitz Collection, 1933 (33.43.419). Image copyright © The Metropolitan Museum of Art/Licensed by Art Resource, NY

[1907]

Read

1. What particular details draw your eye? Why might they be significant?
2. What is the effect of the image split by the gangplank?
3. How do the details contribute to the whole photograph?

Write

1. How would you describe the tone of the photograph? Account for your choice of words with details from the photograph.
2. Write a paragraph that explains what you think Steiglitz's aim is in the photograph.

Connect

1. How does this photograph compare with Jacob Riis's in terms of use of line?
2. How does this photograph comment on Mary Antin's narrative?

Yung Wing

Born in Guangdong Province in China, Yung Wing (1828–1912) studied in missionary schools before coming to the United States. He received a degree from Yale University in 1852, the first Chinese student to graduate from an American college. Yung returned to China as an interpreter and administrator, and later returned to America to buy machinery for China's antiquated factories. He became a naturalized American citizen in 1852 and married American Mary Kellogg. A believer in reform in his native country, Yung worked for better relations with the West and for modernization. When a reactionary coup in China put him in danger, Yung returned to the United States, but not before learning that his Chinese citizenship had been revoked. He was able to make his way back, see his son graduate from Yale, and write his memoir *My Life in China and America* in 1909. He died in Hartford, Connecticut.

From *My Life in China and America*

Chapter V

My College Days

Before entering Yale, I had not solved the problem of how I was to be carried through the collegiate course without financial backing of a definite and well-assured character. It was an easy matter to talk about getting an education by working for it, and there is a kind of romance in it that captivates the imagination, but it is altogether a different thing to face it in a business and practical way. So it proved to me, after I had put my foot into it. I had no one except Brown, who had already done so much for me in bringing me to this country, and Hammond, who fitted me for college. To them I appealed for advice and counsel. I was advised to avail myself of the contingent fund provided for indigent° students. It was in the hands of the trustees of the academy and so well guarded that it could not be appropriated without the recipient's signing a written pledge that he would study for the ministry and afterwards become a missionary. Such being the case, I made up my mind that it would be utterly useless for me to apply for the fund. However, a day was appointed for me to meet the trustees in the parsonage, to talk over the subject. They said they would be too glad to have me avail myself of the fund, provided I was willing to sign a pledge that after graduation I should° go back to China as a missionary. I gave the trustees to understand that I would never give such a pledge for the following reasons: First, it would handicap and circumscribe° my usefulness. I wanted the utmost freedom of action to avail myself of every opportunity to do the greatest good in China. If necessary, I might be obliged to create new conditions, if I found old ones were not favorable to any plan I might have for promoting her highest welfare.

In the second place, the calling of a missionary is not the only sphere in life where one can do the most good in China or elsewhere. In such a vast empire, there can be hardly any limit put upon one's ambition to do good, if one is possessed of the Christ-spirit; on the other hand, if one has not such a spirit, no pledge in the world could melt his ice-bound soul.

In the third place, a pledge of that character would prevent me from taking advantage of any circumstance or event that might arise in the life of a nation like China, to do her a great service.

"For these reasons," I said, "I must decline to give the pledge and at the same time decline to accept your kind offer to help me. I thank you, gentlemen, very much, for your good wishes."

Both Brown and Hammond afterwards agreed that I took the right view on the subject and sustained me in my position. To be sure, I was poor, but I would not allow my poverty to gain the upper hand and compel me to barter away my inward convictions of duty for a temporary mess of pottage.° 5

---

indigent: needy, poor

should: would

circumscribe: limit

mess of pottage: something of little value; a reference to the Book of Genesis, in which Esau sells his birthright to his brother Jacob for a mess of pottage, or meal of lentil soup

During the summer of 1850, it seems that Brown who had been making a visit in the South to see his sister, while there had occasion to call on some of the members of "The Ladies' Association" in Savannah, Ga., to whom he mentioned my case. He returned home in the nick of time, just after I had the interview with the board of trustees of the academy. I told him of the outcome, when, as stated above, he approved of my position, and told me what he had done. He said that the members of the association agreed to help me in college. On the strength of that I gathered fresh courage, and went down to New Haven to pass my examination for entrance. How I got in, I do not know, as I had had only fifteen months of Latin and twelve months of Greek, and ten months of mathematics. My preparation had been interrupted because the academy had been broken up by the Palmer & New London R. R. that was being built close by. As compared with the college preparations of nine-tenths of my class-mates, I was far behind. However, I passed without condition. But I was convinced I was not sufficiently prepared, as my recitations in the class-room clearly proved. Between the struggle of how to make ends meet financially and how to keep up with the class in my studies, I had a pretty tough time of it. I used to sweat over my studies till twelve o'clock every night the whole Freshman year. I took little or no exercise and my health and strength began to fail and I was obliged to ask for a leave of absence of a week. I went to East Windsor to get rested and came back refreshed.

In the Sophomore year, from my utter aversion to mathematics, especially to differential and integral calculus, which I abhorred and detested, and which did me little or no good in the way of mental discipline, I used to fizzle and flunk so often that I really thought I was going to be dropped from the class, or dismissed from college. But for some unexplained reasons I was saved from such a catastrophe, and I squeezed through the second year in college with so low a mark that I was afraid to ask my division tutor, who happened to be Tutor Blodget, who had me in Greek, about it. The only redeeming feature that saved me as a student in the class of 1854, was the fortunate circumstance that I happened to be a successful competitor on two occasions in English composition in my division. I was awarded the first prize in the second term, and the first prize in the third term of the year. These prizes gave me quite an éclat° in the college as well as in the outside world, but I was not at all elated over them on account of my poor scholarship which I felt keenly through the whole college course.

éclat: acclaim, brilliant reputation

Before the close of my second year, I succeeded in securing the stewardship of a boarding club consisting of sophomores and juniors. There were altogether twenty members. I did all the marketing and served at the table. In this way, I earned my board through the latter half of my college course. In money matters, I was supplied with remittances from "The Ladies' Association" in Savannah, and also contributions from the Olyphant Brothers of New York. In addition to these sources of supply, I was paid for being an assistant librarian to the "Brothers in Unity," which was one of the two college debating societies that owned a library, and of which I was a member.

In my senior year I was again elected librarian to the same Society and got $30.00. These combined sums were large enough to meet all my cash bills, since my wants had to be finely trimmed to suit the cloth. If most of the country parsons of that period could get along with a salary of $200 or $300 a year (supplemented, of course, with an annual donation party, which sometimes carried away more than it donated), having as a general thing a large family to look after, I certainly ought to have been able to get through college with gifts of nearly a like amount, supplemented with donations of shirts and stockings from ladies who took an interest in my education.

10 The class of 1854, to which I had the honor and the good fortune to belong, graduated ninety-eight all told. Being the first Chinaman who had ever been known to go through a first-class American college, I naturally attracted considerable attention; and from the fact that I was librarian for one of the college debating societies (Linonia was the other) for two years, I was known by members of the three classes above, and members of the three classes below me. This fact had contributed toward familiarizing me with the college world at large, and my nationality, of course, added piquancy° to my popularity.

As an undergraduate, I had already acquired a factitious° reputation within the walls of Yale. But that was ephemeral° and soon passed out of existence after graduation.

All through my college course, especially in the closing year, the lamentable condition of China was before my mind constantly and weighed on my spirits. In my despondency, I often wished I had never been educated, as education had unmistakably enlarged my mental and moral horizon, and revealed to me responsibilities which the sealed eye of ignorance can never see, and sufferings and wrongs of humanity to which an uncultivated and

piquancy: pungency, flavor
factitious: artificial, manufactured
ephemeral: fleeting, of short duration

callous nature can never be made sensitive. The more one knows, the more he suffers and is consequently less happy; the less one knows, the less he suffers, and hence is more happy. But this is a low view of life, a cowardly feeling and unworthy of a being bearing the impress° of divinity. I had started out to get an education. By dint° of hard work and self-denial I had finally secured the coveted prize and although it might not be so complete and symmetrical a thing as could be desired, yet I had come right up to the conventional standard and idea of a liberal education. I could, therefore, call myself an educated man and, as such, it behooved° me to ask, "What am I going to do with my education?" Before the close of my last year in college I had already sketched out what I should do. I was determined that the rising generation of China should enjoy the same educational advantages that I had enjoyed; that through western education China might be regenerated, become enlightened and powerful. To accomplish that object became the guiding star of my ambition. Towards such a goal, I directed all my mental resources and energy. Through thick and thin, and the vicissitudes° of a checkered life from 1854 to 1872, I labored and waited for its consummation.°

Chapter VI

Return to China

In entering upon my life's work which to me was so full of meaning and earnestness, the first episode was a voyage back to the old country, which I had not seen for nearly ten years, but which had never escaped my mind's eye nor my heart's yearning for her welfare.

. . .

I lost no time in hastening over to Macao to see my aged and beloved mother, who, I knew, yearned to see her long-absent boy. Our meeting was arranged a day beforehand. I was in citizen's dress and could not conveniently change the same for my Chinese costume. I had also allowed a pair of mustaches to grow, which, according to Chinese custom, was not becoming° for an unmarried young man to do. We met with tears of joy, gratitude and thanksgiving. Our hearts were too full even to speak at first. We gave way to

---

impress: imprint

dint: means

behooved: was appropriate for

vicissitudes: changing fortunes, ups and downs

consummation: fulfillment, completion

becoming: proper

our emotions. As soon as we were fairly composed, she began to stroke me all over, as expressive of her maternal endearment which had been held in patient suspense for at least ten years. As we sat close to each other, I gave her a brief recital of my life in America, for I knew she would be deeply interested in the account. I told her that I had just finished a long and wearisome voyage of five months' duration, but had met with no danger of any kind; that during my eight years of sojourn° in the United States, I was very kindly treated by the good people everywhere; that I had had good health and never been seriously sick, and that my chief object during the eight years was to study and prepare myself for my life work in China. I explained to her that I had to go through a preparatory school before entering college; that the college I entered was Yale—one of the leading colleges of the United States, and that the course was four years, which accounted for my long stay and delayed my return to China. I told her that at the end of four years I had graduated with the degree of A.B., analogous to the Chinese title of Siu Tsai, which is interpreted "Elegant Talent;" that it was inscribed on a parchment of sheep skin and that to graduate from Yale College was considered a great honor, even to a native American, and much more so to a Chinese. She asked me naively how much money it conferred. I said it did not confer any money at once, but it enabled one to make money quicker and easier than one can who has not been educated; that it gave one greater influence and power among men and if he built on his college education, he would be more likely to become the leader of men, especially if he had a well-established character. I told her my college education was worth more to me than money, and that I was confident of making plenty of money.

15 "Knowledge," I said, "is power, and power is greater than riches. I am the first Chinese to graduate from Yale College, and that being the case, you have the honor of being the first and only mother out of the countless millions of mothers in China at this time, who can claim the honor of having a son who is the first Chinese graduate of a first-class American college. Such an honor is a rare thing to possess." I also assured her that as long as I lived all her comforts and wants would be scrupulously and sedulously° looked after, and that nothing would be neglected to make her contented and happy. This interview° seemed to give her great comfort and satisfaction.

. . .

sojourn: temporary stay
sedulously: diligently, tirelessly
interview: conversation

I was about a month in England, and then crossed the Atlantic in one of the Cunard steamers and landed in New York in the early spring of 1864, just ten years after my graduation from Yale and in ample time to be present at the decennial° meeting of my class in July. Haskins and his family had preceded me in another steamer for New York, in order that he might get to work on the drawings and specifications of the shop and machinery and get them completed as soon as possible. In 1864, the last year of the great Civil War, nearly all the machine shops in the country, especially in New England, were preoccupied and busy in executing government orders, and it was very difficult to have my machinery taken up. Finally Haskins succeeded in getting the Putnam Machine Co., Fitchburg, Mass., to fill the order.

While Haskins was given sole charge of superintending the execution of the order, which required at least six months before the machinery could be completed for shipment to China, I took advantage of the interim to run down to New Haven and attend the decennial meeting of my class. It was to me a joyous event and I congratulated myself that I had the good luck to be present at our first re-union. Of course, the event that brought me back to the country was altogether unpretentious and had attracted little or no public attention at the time, because the whole country was completely engrossed in the last year of the great Civil War, yet I personally regarded my commission as an inevitable and preliminary step that would ultimately lead to the realization of my educational scheme,° which had never for a moment escaped my mind. But at the meeting of my class, this subject of my life plan was not brought up. We had a most enjoyable time and parted with nearly the same fraternal feeling that characterized our parting at graduation. After the decennial meeting, I returned to Fitchburg and told Haskins that I was going down to Washington to offer my services to the government as a volunteer for the short period of six months, and that in case anything happened to me during the six months so that I could not come back to attend to the shipping of the machinery to Shanghai, he should attend to it. I left him all the papers—the cost and description of the machinery, the bills of lading,° insurance, and freight, and directed him to send everything to the Viceroy's agent in Shanghai. This precautionary step having been taken, I slipped down to Washington.

---

decennial: ten-year

scheme: project, plan

bills of lading: contracts and receipts for the shipping of goods

Brigadier-General Barnes of Springfield, Mass., happened to be the general in charge of the Volunteer Department. His headquarters were at Willard's Hotel. I called on him and made known to him my object, that I felt as a naturalized citizen of the United States, it was my bounden duty to offer my services as a volunteer courier to carry dispatches between Washington and the nearest Federal camp for at least six months, simply to show my loyalty and patriotism to my adopted country, and that I would furnish my own equipments. He said that he remembered me well, having met me in the Yale Library in New Haven, in 1853, on a visit to his son, William Barnes, who was in the college at the time I was, and who afterwards became a prominent lawyer in San Francisco. General Barnes asked what business I was engaged in. I told him that since my graduation in 1854 I had been in China and had recently returned with an order to purchase machinery for a machine shop ordered by Viceroy and Generalissimo Tsang Kwoh Fan. I told him the machinery was being made to order in Fitchburg, Mass., under the supervision of an American mechanical engineer, and as it would take at least six months before the same could be completed, I was anxious to offer my services to the government in the meantime as an evidence of my loyalty and patriotism to my adopted country. He was quite interested and pleased with what I said.

"Well, my young friend," said he, "I thank you very much for your offer, but since you are charged with a responsible trust to execute for the Chinese government, you had better return to Fitchburg to attend to it. We have plenty of men to serve, both as couriers and as fighting men to go to the front." Against this peremptory° decision, I could urge nothing further, but I felt that I had at least fulfilled my duty to my adopted country.

[1909]

Read

1. How does Yung describe himself as a student? What effect does his description have on you as a reader?
2. What does Yung's reflection about knowledge (the less one knows the happier one is . . .) mean in the context of Yung's own education and ambition?
3. How does Yung convey his feeling toward his mother in the passage?

Write

1. What is the effect on you as a reader of the incident where Yung attempts to volunteer for service in the Army?
2. Comment on Yung's use of American ideals to frame his story.

---

peremptory: decisive

3. How does Yung make an argument? Write a sentence that explains his argument, and then in a paragraph describe the methods he uses to make it.

Connect

1. What is your reaction to the tale Yung tells?
2. How is this autobiographical account similar to the story Mary Antin tells? How does it seem different?

Anonymous

The Last Mile of the Transcontinental Railroad, Utah

Work on the Last Mile of the Central Pacific Railroad in 1869. Wood engraving from a sketch by A. R. Waud. The Granger Collection, NY

[1869]

Read

1. What elements in the illustration catch your eye first?
2. How might those elements be symbolic of the purpose of the illustration?
3. How does the illustration reveal the relationship among workers and who the workers are?

Write

1. Describe the scene the illustration depicts, including as many details as you can.
2. Comment on the difference in the jobs being performed and the attitudes of workers', gestures toward their work.

Connect

1. Compare the illustrator's attitude toward the people in the scene to another piece of art in this or an earlier unit.

Frederick Lewis Allen

Frederick Allen (1890–1954) was born in Boston and had a distinguished career as an editor and historian. He taught briefly at Harvard, became the assistant editor of the *Atlantic Monthly,* and in 1940 assumed the editorship of *Harper's Weekly*. His historical works concentrated on the first half of the twentieth century, what would then have been recent and popular history. *Only Yesterday,* excerpted here, chronicled the twenties in the United States and was published in 1931. A sequel, *Since Yesterday,* analyzed the years of the Great Depression.

From *Only Yesterday: An Informal History of the 1920's*

Early in September the stock market broke. It quickly recovered, however; indeed, on September 19th the averages as compiled by the *New York Times* reached an even higher level than that of September 3rd. Once more it slipped, farther and faster, until by October 4th the prices of a good many stocks had coasted to what seemed first-class bargain levels. Steel, for example, after having touched $261\frac{3}{4}$ a few weeks earlier, had dropped as low as 204; American Can, at the closing on October 4th, was nearly twenty points below its high for the year; General Electric was over fifty points below its high; Radio had gone down from $114\frac{3}{4}$ to $82\frac{1}{2}$.

A bad break, to be sure, but there had been other bad breaks, and the speculators who escaped unscathed° proceeded to take advantage of the lessons they had learned in June and December of 1928 and March and May of 1929: when there was a break it was a good time to buy. In the face of all this tremendous liquidation, brokers' loans as compiled by the Federal Reserve Bank of New York mounted to a new high record on October 2nd, reaching $6,804,000,000—a sure sign that margin buyers were not deserting the market but coming into it in numbers at least undiminished. (Part of the increase in the loan figure was probably due to the piling up of unsold securities in dealers' hands, as the spawning of investment trusts and the issue of new common

---

unscathed: unharmed

stock by every manner of business concern continued unabated.) History, it seemed, was about to repeat itself, and those who picked up Anaconda at $109^3/_4$ or American Telephone at 281 would count themselves wise investors. And sure enough, prices once more began to climb. They had already turned upward before that Sunday in early October when Ramsay MacDonald° sat on a log with Herbert Hoover° at the Rapidan camp° and talked over the prospects for naval limitation and peace.

Something was wrong, however. The decline began once more. The wiseacres of Wall Street, looking about for causes, fixed upon the collapse of the Hatry financial group in England (which had led to much forced selling among foreign investors and speculators), and upon the bold refusal of the Massachusetts Department of Public Utilities to allow the Edison Company of Boston to split up its stock. They pointed, too, to the fact that the steel industry was undoubtedly slipping, and to the accumulation of "undigested" securities. But there was little real alarm until the week of October 21st. The consensus of opinion, in the meantime, was merely that the equinoctial° storm of September had not quite blown over. The market was readjusting itself into a "more secure technical position."

. . .

The expected recovery in the stock market did not come. It seemed to be beginning on Tuesday, October 22nd, but the gains made during the day were largely lost during the last hour. And on Wednesday, the 23rd, there was a perfect Niagara of liquidation. The volume of trading was over 6,000,000 shares, the tape was 104 minutes late when the three-o'clock gong ended trading for the day, and the *New York Times* averages for fifty leading railroad and industrial stocks lost 18.24 points—a loss which made the most abrupt declines in previous breaks look small. Everybody realized that an unprecedented number of margin calls° must be on their way to insecurely margined traders, and that the situation at last was getting serious. But perhaps the turn would come tomorrow. Already the break had carried prices down a good deal farther than the previous breaks of the past two years. Surely it could not go on much longer.

The next day was Thursday, October 24th. 5

On that momentous day stocks opened moderately steady in price, but in enormous volume. Kennecott appeared on the tape in a block of 20,000

Ramsay MacDonald: (1886–1937), British prime minister (1924, 1929–1935)

Herbert Hoover: (1874–1964), American president (1929–1933)

Rapidan camp: Hoover's country retreat in Shenandoah National Park in Madison County, Virginia

equinoctial: pertaining to the equinox; the autumnal equinox occurs around September 21

margin calls: demands by brokers that customers deposit more money in their accounts

shares, General Motors in another of the same amount. Almost at once the ticker tape began to lag behind the trading on the floor. The pressure of selling orders was disconcertingly heavy. Prices were going down. . . . Presently they were going down with some rapidity. . . . Before the first hour of trading was over, it was already apparent that they were going down with an altogether unprecedented and amazing violence. In brokers' offices all over the country, tape-watchers looked at one another in astonishment and perplexity. Where on earth was this torrent of selling orders coming from?

The exact answer to this question will probably never be known. But it seems probable that the principal cause of the break in prices during that first hour on October 24th was not fear. Nor was it short selling. It was forced selling. It was the dumping on the market of hundreds of thousands of shares of stock held in the name of miserable traders whose margins were exhausted or about to be exhausted. The gigantic edifice of prices was honeycombed with speculative credit and was now breaking under its own weight.

Fear, however, did not long delay its coming. As the price structure crumbled there was a sudden stampede to get out from under. By eleven o'clock traders on the floor of the Stock Exchange were in a wild scramble to "sell at the market." Long before the lagging ticker could tell what was happening, word had gone out by telephone and telegraph that the bottom was dropping out of things, and the selling orders redoubled in volume. The leading stocks were going down two, three, and even five points between sales. Down, down, down. . . . Where were the bargain-hunters who were supposed to come to the rescue at times like this? Where were the investment trusts, which were expected to provide a cushion for the market by making new purchases at low prices? Where were the big operators who had declared that they were still bullish? Where were the powerful bankers who were supposed to be able at any moment to support prices? There seemed to be no support whatever. Down, down, down. The roar of voices which rose from the floor of the Exchange had become a roar of panic.

United States Steel had opened at $205\frac{1}{2}$. It crashed through 200 and presently was at $193\frac{1}{2}$. General Electric, which only a few weeks before had been selling above 400, had opened this morning at 315—now it had slid to 283. Things were even worse with Radio: opening at $68\frac{3}{4}$, it had gone dismally down through the sixties and the fifties and the forties to the abysmal price of $44\frac{1}{2}$. And as for Montgomery Ward, vehicle of the hopes of thousands who saw the chain store as the harbinger° of the new economic era, it had dropped headlong from 83 to 50. In the space of two short hours, dozens of stocks lost ground which it had required many months of the bull market to gain.

---

harbinger: omen, precursor

10

Even this sudden decline in values might not have been utterly terrifying if people could have known precisely what was happening at any moment. It is the unknown which causes real panic.

. . .

At seven o'clock that night the tickers in a thousand brokers' offices were still chattering; not till after 7:08 did they finally record the last sale made on the floor at three o'clock. The volume of trading had set a new record—12,894,650 shares. ("The time may come when we shall see a five-million-share day," the wise men of the Street had been saying twenty months before!) Incredible rumors had spread wildly during the early afternoon—that eleven speculators had committed suicide, that the Buffalo and Chicago exchanges had been closed, that troops were guarding the New York Stock Exchange against an angry mob. The country had known the bitter taste of panic. And although the bankers' pool had prevented for the moment an utter collapse, there was no gainsaying° the fact that the economic structure had cracked wide open.

Things looked somewhat better on Friday and Saturday. Trading was still on an enormous scale, but prices for the most part held. At the very moment when the bankers' pool was cautiously disposing of as much as possible of the stock which it had accumulated on Thursday and was thus preparing for future emergencies, traders who had sold out higher up were coming back into the market again with new purchases, in the hope that the bottom had been reached. (Hadn't they often been told that "the time to buy is when things look blackest"?) The newspapers carried a very pretty series of reassuring statements from the occupants of the seats of the mighty; Herbert Hoover himself, in a White House statement, pointed out that "the fundamental business of the country, that is, production and distribution of commodities, is on a sound and prosperous basis." But toward the close of Saturday's session prices began to slip again. And on Monday the rout was under way once more.

The losses registered on Monday were terrific—17½ points for Steel, 47½ for General Electric, 36 for Allied Chemical, 34½ for Westinghouse, and so on down a long and dismal list. All Saturday afternoon and Saturday night and Sunday the brokers had been struggling to post their records and go over their customers' accounts and sent out calls for further margin, and another avalanche of forced selling resulted. The prices at which Mr. Whitney's purchases had steadied the leading stocks on Thursday were so readily broken through that it was immediately clear that the bankers' pool had made a strategic retreat. As a matter of fact, the brokers who represented the pool were having their hands full plugging up the "air-holes" in the list—in other words, buying stocks which were offered for sale without any bids at all in sight. Nothing more than this could have been accomplished, even if it could

---

gainsaying: denying

have been wisely attempted. Even six great banks could hardly stem the flow of liquidation from the entire United States. They could only guide it a little, check it momentarily here and there.

Once more the ticker dropped ridiculously far behind, the lights in the brokers' offices and the banks burned till dawn, and the telegraph companies distributed thousands of margin calls and requests for more collateral to back up loans at the banks. Bankers, brokers, clerks, messengers were almost at the end of their strength; for days and nights they had been driving themselves to keep pace with the most terrific volume of business that had ever descended upon them. It did not seem as if they could stand it much longer. But the worst was still ahead. It came the next day, Tuesday, October 29th.

15 The big gong had hardly sounded in the great hall of the Exchange at ten o'clock Tuesday morning before the storm broke in full force. Huge blocks of stock were thrown upon the market for what they would bring. Five thousand shares, ten thousand shares appeared at a time on the laboring ticker at fearful recessions in price. Not only were innumerable small traders being sold out, but big ones, too, protagonists° of the new economic era who a few weeks before had counted themselves millionaires. Again and again the specialist in a stock would find himself surrounded by brokers fighting to sell—and nobody at all even thinking of buying. To give one single example: during the bull market the common stock of the White Sewing Machine Company had gone as high as 48; on Monday, October 28th, it had closed at 11⅛. On that black Tuesday, somebody—a clever messenger boy for the Exchange, it was rumored—had the bright idea of putting in an order to buy at 1—and in the temporarily complete absence of other bids he actually got his stock for a dollar a share! The scene on the floor was chaotic. Despite the jamming of the communication system, orders to buy and sell—mostly to sell—came in faster than human beings could possibly handle them; it was on that day that an exhausted broker, at the close of the session, found a large waste-basket which he had stuffed with orders to be executed and had carefully set aside for safekeeping—and then had completely forgotten. Within half an hour of the opening the volume of trading had passed 3,000,000 shares, by twelve o'clock it had passed 8,000,000, by half-past one it had passed twelve 12,000,000, and when the closing gong brought the day's madness to an end the gigantic record of 16,410,030 shares had been set. Toward the close there was a rally, but by that time the average prices of fifty leading stocks, as compiled by the *New York Times,* had fallen nearly forty points. Meanwhile there was a near-panic in other markets—the foreign stock exchanges, the lesser American exchanges, the grain market.

So complete was the demoralization of the stock market and so exhausted were the brokers and their staffs and the Stock Exchange employees, that at noon that day, when the panic was at its worst, the Governing Committee

---

protagonists: central figures, leading actors

met quietly to decide whether or not to close the Exchange. To quote from an address made some months later by Richard Whitney:

> In order not to give occasion for alarming rumors, this meeting was not held in the Governing Committee Room, but in the office of the president of the Stock Clearing Corporation directly beneath the Stock Exchange floor. . . . The forty governors came to the meeting in groups of two and three as unobtrusively° as possible. The office they met in was never designed for large meetings of this sort, with the result that most of the governors were compelled to stand, or to sit on tables. As the meeting progressed, panic was raging overhead on the floor. . . . The feeling of those present was revealed by their habit of continually lighting cigarettes, taking a puff or two, putting them out and lighting new ones—a practice which soon made the narrow room blue with smoke. . . .

Two of the Morgan partners were invited to the meeting and, attempting to slip into the building unnoticed so as not to start a new flock of rumors, were refused admittance by one of the guards and had to remain outside until rescued by a member of the Governing Committee. After some deliberation, the governors finally decided not to close the Exchange.

It was a critical day for the banks, that Tuesday the 29th. Many of the corporations which had so cheerfully loaned money to brokers through the banks in order to obtain interest at 8 or 9 per cent were now clamoring to have these loans called—and the banks were faced with a choice between taking over the loans themselves and running the risk of precipitating further ruin. It was no laughing matter to assume the responsibility of millions of dollars' worth of loans secured by collateral which by the end of the day might prove to have dropped to a fraction of its former value. That the call money rate never rose above 6 per cent that day, that a money panic was not added to the stock panic, and that several Wall Street institutions did not go down into immediate bankruptcy, was due largely to the nerve shown by a few bankers in stepping into the breach. The story is told of one banker who went grimly on authorizing the taking over of loan after loan until one of his subordinate officers came in with a white face and told him that the bank was insolvent. "I dare say," said the banker, and went ahead unmoved. He knew that if he did not, more than one concern° would face insolvency.

The next day—Wednesday, October 30th—the outlook suddenly and providentially brightened. The directors of the Steel Corporation had declared an extra dividend; the directors of the American Can Company had not only declared an extra dividend, but had raised the regular dividend. There was another flood of reassuring statements—though by this time a cheerful

---

unobtrusively: inconspicuously

concern: company, commercial enterprise

statement from a financier fell upon somewhat skeptical ears. Julius Klein, Mr. Hoover's Assistant Secretary of Commerce, composed a rhapsody on continued prosperity. John J. Raskob declared that stocks were at bargain prices and that he and his friends were buying. John D. Rockefeller poured Standard Oil upon the waters: "Believing that fundamental conditions of the country are sound and that there is nothing in the business situation to warrant the destruction of values that has taken place on the exchanges during the past week, my son and I have for some days been purchasing sound common stocks." Better still, prices rose—steadily and buoyantly. Now at last the time had come when the strain on the Exchange could be relieved without causing undue alarm. At 1:40 o'clock Vice-President Whitney announced from the rostrum that the Exchange would not open until noon the following day and would remain closed all day Friday and Saturday—and to his immense relief the announcement was greeted, not with renewed panic, but with a cheer.

Throughout Thursday's short session the recovery continued. Prices gyrated wildly—for who could arrive at a reasonable idea of what a given stock was worth, now that all settled standards of value had been upset?—but the worst of the storm seemed to have blown over. The financial community breathed more easily; now they could have a chance to set their houses in order.

It was true that the worst of the panic was past. But not the worst prices. There was too much forced liquidation still to come as brokers' accounts were gradually straightened out, as banks called for more collateral, and terror was renewed. The next week, in a series of short sessions, the tide of prices receded once more—until at last on November 13th the bottom prices for the year 1929 were reached. Beside the figures hung up in the sunny days of September they made a tragic showing:

	High price Sept. 3, 1929	Low price Nov. 13, 1929
American Can	$181\frac{7}{8}$	86
American Telephone & Telegraph	304	$197\frac{1}{4}$
Anaconda Copper	$131\frac{1}{2}$	70
Electric Bond & Share	$186\frac{3}{4}$	$50\frac{1}{4}$
General Electric	$396\frac{1}{4}$	$168\frac{1}{8}$
General Motors	$72\frac{3}{4}$	36
Montgomery Ward	$137\frac{7}{8}$	$49\frac{1}{4}$
New York Central	$256\frac{3}{8}$	160
Radio	101	28
Union Carbide & Carbon	$137\frac{7}{8}$	59
United States Steel	$261\frac{3}{4}$	150
Westinghouse E. & M.	$289\frac{7}{8}$	$102\frac{5}{8}$
Woolworth	$100\frac{3}{8}$	$52\frac{1}{4}$

The *New York Times* averages for fifty leading stocks had been almost cut in half, falling from a high of 311.90 in September to a low of 164.43 on November 13th; and the *Times* averages for twenty-five leading industrials had fared still worse, diving from 469.49 to 220.95.

The Big Bull Market was dead. Billions of dollars' worth of profits—and paper profits—had disappeared. The grocer, the window-cleaner, and the seamstress had lost their capital. In every town there were families which had suddenly dropped from showy affluence into debt. . . .

Coolidge-Hoover Prosperity was not yet dead, but it was dying. Under the impact of the shock of panic, a multitude of ills which hitherto° had passed unnoticed or had been offset by stock-market optimism began to beset the body economic, as poisons seep through the human system when a vital organ has ceased to function normally. Although the liquidation of nearly three billion dollars of brokers' loans contracted credit, and the Reserve Banks lowered the rediscount rate, and the way in which the larger banks and corporations of the country had survived the emergency without a single failure of large proportions offered real encouragement, nevertheless the poisons were there: overproduction of capital; overambitious expansion of business concerns; overproduction of commodities under the stimulus of installment buying and buying with stock-market profits; the maintenance of an artificial price level for many commodities; the depressed condition of European trade. No matter how many soothsayers of high finance proclaimed that all was well, no matter how earnestly the President set to work to repair the damage with soft words and White House conferences, a major depression was inevitably under way.

Nor was that all. Prosperity is more than an economic condition; it is a state of mind. The Big Bull Market had been more than the climax of a business cycle; it had been the climax of a cycle in American mass thinking and mass emotion. There was hardly a man or woman in the country whose attitude toward life had not been affected by it in some degree and was not now affected by the sudden and brutal shattering of hope. With the Big Bull Market gone and prosperity going, Americans were soon to find themselves living in an altered world which called for new adjustments, new ideas, new habits of thought, and a new order of values. The psychological climate was changing; the ever-shifting currents of American life were turning into new channels. 25

The Post-war Decade had come to its close. An era had ended.

[1931]

Read

1. How does Allen use figures and statistics to suggest his aim?

---

hitherto: previously

2. How does Allen heighten the effect of the stock market crash by his use of language?
3. What is Allen's claim about fear in this piece?

Write

1. What is the effect of the last paragraph on you as a reader?
2. Write a brief paragraph about the aim and effect of the title *Only Yesterday* on your reading of the piece.
3. Explain how Allen provides context that helps readers understand the decade of the twenties.

Connect

1. How does Stuart Davis's painting *Super Table* suggest some of the characteristics of the twenties that Allen describes?
2. What does Allen's account suggest about some of the factors that contributed to the Great Depression?

Stuart Davis

Stuart Davis (1890–1954) was a modernist painter of the early twentieth century whose art reflected the Jazz Age of the 1920s. He was born in Philadelphia and received praise early in his painting career. He was influenced by the innovative work of painters like Van Gogh and Picasso.

Super Table

Super Table (1925), Stuart Davis. Oil on canvas, 48 x 34 1/8 in. Daniel J. Terra Collection, 1999.37. Terra Foundation for American Art, Chicago. Art copyright © 2012 Estate of Stuart Davis/Licensed by Art Resource, NY/VAGA, New York, NY

[1925]

Read

1. What is the effect of light on your "reading" of the painting?
2. How is the title significant to the tone of this piece?
3. How would you describe the tone?

Write

1. Davis has been called the painter of the Jazz Age. What details in the painting suggest something to you about that time?
2. Write a paragraph that explains how line and image affect your response to the painting.

Connect

1. Compare Stuart Davis's painting with another painting in an earlier unit in terms of focus on subject. How does the subject of the painting suggest something about the culture of the time period?
2. Would you call this painting abstract? Realistic? Find a term that you think captures the style of the painting and explain your choice.

Contemporary Works

Jaron Lanier

Jaron Lanier (b. 1960) is a computer scientist, musician, and writer. He is credited with coining the phrase "virtual reality" to describe programs and products he developed for the Web, including Second Life. Born in New Mexico to Jewish immigrant parents from Europe, Lanier worked at a variety of jobs before studying computer science. His writing studies the effects of technology on culture, and *You Are Not a Gadget* offers both a critique of programming choices in digital media and practical responses from individuals to the massive effects of the computer age on individual minds and cultural decisions.

From *You Are Not a Gadget*

Chapter 1

Missing Persons

Software expresses ideas about everything from the nature of a musical note to the nature of personhood. Software is also subject to an exceptionally rigid process of "lock-in." Therefore, ideas (in the present era, when human affairs are increasingly software driven) have become more subject to lock-in than in previous eras. Most of the ideas that have been locked in so far are not so bad, but some of the so-called web 2.0 ideas are stinkers, so we ought to reject them while we still can.

Speech is the mirror of the soul; as a man speaks, so is he.

—Publilius Syrus°

Fragments Are Not People

Something started to go wrong with the digital revolution around the turn of the twenty-first century. The World Wide Web was flooded by a torrent of petty designs sometimes called web 2.0. This ideology promotes radical freedom on the surface of the web, but that freedom, ironically, is more for machines than people. Nevertheless, it is sometimes referred to as "open culture."

Anonymous blog comments, vapid° video pranks, and lightweight mashups may seem trivial and harmless, but as a whole, this widespread practice of fragmentary, impersonal communication has demeaned interpersonal interaction.

Communication is now often experienced as a superhuman phenomenon that towers above individuals. A new generation has come of age with a reduced expectation of what a person can be, and of who each person might become.

The Most Important Thing About a Technology Is How It Changes People

5 When I work with experimental digital gadgets, like new variations on virtual reality, in a lab environment, I am always reminded of how small changes in the details of a digital design can have profound unforeseen effects on the experiences of the humans who are playing with it. The slightest change in something as seemingly trivial as the ease of use of a button can sometimes completely alter behavior patterns.

For instance, Stanford University researcher Jeremy Bailenson has demonstrated that changing the height of one's avatar in immersive° virtual reality transforms self-esteem and social self-perception. Technologies are extensions of ourselves, and, like the avatars in Jeremy's lab, our identities can be shifted by the quirks of gadgets. It is impossible to work with information technology without also engaging in social engineering.

One might ask, "If I am blogging, twittering, and wikiing a lot, how does that change who I am?" or "If the 'hive mind'° is my audience, who am I?" We inventors of digital technologies are like stand-up comedians or neurosurgeons, in that our work resonates° with deep philosophical questions; unfortunately, we've proven to be poor philosophers lately.

Publilius Syrus: Syrian author of Latin maxims (first century A.D.)

vapid: dull, tedious

immersive: pertaining to digital images and technology that involve the senses deeply

hive mind: state of conformity

resonates: resounds

When developers of digital technologies design a program that requires you to interact with a computer as if it were a person, they ask you to accept in some corner of your brain that you might also be conceived of as a program. When they design an internet service that is edited by a vast anonymous crowd, they are suggesting that a random crowd of humans is an organism with a legitimate point of view.

Different media designs stimulate different potentials in human nature. We shouldn't seek to make the pack mentality as efficient as possible. We should instead seek to inspire the phenomenon of individual intelligence.

10 "What is a person?" If I knew the answer to that, I might be able to program an artificial person in a computer. But I can't. Being a person is not a pat formula, but a quest, a mystery, a leap of faith.

Optimism

It would be hard for anyone, let alone a technologist, to get up in the morning without the faith that the future can be better than the past.

Back in the 1980s, when the internet was only available to a small number of pioneers, I was often confronted by people who feared that the strange technologies I was working on, like virtual reality, might unleash the demons of human nature. For instance, would people become addicted to virtual reality as if it were a drug? Would they become trapped in it, unable to escape back to the physical world where the rest of us live? Some of the questions were silly, and others were prescient.°

How Politics Influences Information Technology

I was part of a merry band of idealists back then. If you had dropped in on, say, me and John Perry Barlow, who would become a cofounder of the Electronic Frontier Foundation, or Kevin Kelly, who would become the founding editor of *Wired* magazine, for lunch in the 1980s, these are the sorts of ideas we were bouncing around and arguing about. Ideals are important in the world of technology, but the mechanism by which ideals influence events is different than in other spheres of life. Technologists don't use persuasion to influence you—or, at least, we don't do it very well. There are a few master communicators among us (like Steve Jobs), but for the most part we aren't particularly seductive.

We make up extensions to your being, like remote eyes and ears (webcams and mobile phones) and expanded memory (the world of details you can search for online). These become the structures by which you connect to the world and other people. These structures in turn can change how you conceive of yourself and the world. We tinker with your philosophy by direct manipulation of your cognitive° experience, not indirectly, through argument.

prescient: showing foresight or foreknowledge

cognitive: pertaining to mental processes

It takes only a tiny group of engineers to create technology that can shape the entire future of human experience with incredible speed. Therefore, crucial arguments about the human relationship with technology should take place between developers and users before such direct manipulations are designed. This book is about those arguments.

The design of the web as it appears today was not inevitable. In the early 1990s, there were perhaps dozens of credible efforts to come up with a design for presenting networked digital information in a way that would attract more popular use. Companies like General Magic and Xanadu developed alternative designs with fundamentally different qualities that never got out the door. 15

A single person, Tim Berners-Lee, came to invent the particular design of today's web. The web as it was introduced was minimalist, in that it assumed just about as little as possible about what a web page would be like. It was also open, in that no page was preferred by the architecture over another, and all pages were accessible to all. It also emphasized responsibility, because only the owner of a website was able to make sure that their site was available to be visited.

Berners-Lee's initial motivation was to serve a community of physicists, not the whole world. Even so, the atmosphere in which the design of the web was embraced by early adopters was influenced by idealistic discussions. In the period before the web was born, the ideas in play were radically optimistic and gained traction in the community, and then in the world at large.

Since we make up so much from scratch when we build information technologies, how do we think about which ones are best? With the kind of radical freedom we find in digital systems comes a disorienting moral challenge. We make it all up—so what shall we make up? Alas, that dilemma—of having so much freedom—is chimerical.°

As a program grows in size and complexity, the software can become a cruel maze. When other programmers get involved, it can feel like a labyrinth. If you are clever enough, you can write any small program from scratch, but it takes a huge amount of effort (and more than a little luck) to successfully modify a large program, especially if other programs are already depending on it. Even the best software development groups periodically find themselves caught in a swarm of bugs and design conundrums.°

Little programs are delightful to write in isolation, but the process of maintaining large-scale software is always miserable. Because of this, digital technology tempts the programmer's psyche into a kind of schizophrenia. There is constant confusion between real and ideal computers. Technologists wish every program behaved like a brand-new, playful little program, and will 20

chimerical: imaginary

conundrums: puzzling problems or questions

use any available psychological strategy to avoid thinking about computers realistically.

The brittle° character of maturing computer programs can cause digital designs to get frozen into place by a process known as lock-in. This happens when many software programs are designed to work with an existing one. The process of significantly changing software in a situation in which a lot of other software is dependent on it is the hardest thing to do. So it almost never happens.

Occasionally, a Digital Eden Appears

One day in the early 1980s, a music synthesizer designer named Dave Smith casually made up a way to represent musical notes. It was called MIDI. His approach conceived of music from a keyboard player's point of view. MIDI was made of digital patterns that represented keyboard events like "key-down" and "key-up."

That meant it could not describe the curvy, transient expressions a singer or a saxophone player can produce. It could only describe the tile mosaic world of the keyboardist, not the watercolor world of the violin. But there was no reason for MIDI to be concerned with the whole of musical expression, since Dave only wanted to connect some synthesizers together so that he could have a larger palette of sounds while playing a single keyboard.

In spite of its limitations, MIDI became the standard scheme to represent music in software. Music programs and synthesizers were designed to work with it, and it quickly proved impractical to change or dispose of all that software and hardware. MIDI became entrenched, and despite Herculean° efforts to reform it on many occasions by a multi-decade-long parade of powerful international commercial, academic, and professional organizations, it remains so.

25

Standards and their inevitable lack of prescience posed a nuisance before computers, of course. Railroad gauges—the dimensions of the tracks—are one example. The London Tube was designed with narrow tracks and matching tunnels that, on several of the lines, cannot accommodate air-conditioning, because there is no room to ventilate the hot air from the trains. Thus, tens of thousands of modern-day residents in one of the world's richest cities must suffer a stifling commute because of an inflexible design decision made more than one hundred years ago.

But software is worse than railroads, because it must always adhere with absolute perfection to a boundlessly particular, arbitrary,° tangled, intractable°

---

brittle: fragile, easily broken

Herculean: calling for great strength or effort (from *Hercules*)

arbitrary: based on personal feelings or opinions; unsupported

intractable: stubborn, inflexible

messiness. The engineering requirements are so stringent° and perverse that adapting to shifting standards can be an endless struggle. So while lock-in may be a gangster in the world of railroads, it is an absolute tyrant in the digital world.

Life on the Curved Surface of Moore's Law

The fateful, unnerving aspect of information technology is that a particular design will occasionally happen to fill a niche and, once implemented, turn out to be unalterable. It becomes a permanent fixture from then on, even though a better design might just as well have taken its place before the moment of entrenchment. A mere annoyance then explodes into a cataclysmic° challenge because the raw power of computers grows exponentially.° In the world of computers, this is known as Moore's law.

Computers have gotten *millions* of times more powerful, and immensely more common and more connected, since my career began—which was not so very long ago. It's as if you kneel to plant a seed of a tree and it grows so fast that it swallows your whole village before you can even rise to your feet.

So software presents what often feels like an unfair level of responsibility to technologists. Because computers are growing more powerful at an exponential rate, the designers and programmers of technology must be extremely careful when they make design choices. The consequences of tiny, initially inconsequential decisions often are amplified to become defining, unchangeable rules of our lives.

30 MIDI now exists in your phone and in billions of other devices. It is the lattice° on which almost all the popular music you hear is built. Much of the sound around us—the ambient° music and audio beeps, the ringtones and alarms—are conceived in MIDI. The whole of the human auditory experience has become filled with discrete° notes that fit in a grid.

Someday a digital design for describing speech, allowing computers to sound better than they do now when they speak to us, will get locked in. That design might then be adapted to music, and perhaps a more fluid and expressive sort of digital music will be developed. But even if that happens, a thousand years from now, when a descendant of ours is traveling at relativistic speeds to explore a new star system, she will probably be annoyed by some awful beepy MIDI-driven music to alert her that the antimatter filter needs to be recalibrated.

---

stringent: strict, severe

cataclysmic: disastrous

exponentially: very rapidly

lattice: grid

ambient: surrounding

discrete: separate, distinct

Lock-in Turns Thoughts into Facts

Before MIDI, a musical note was a bottomless idea that transcended absolute definition. It was a way for a musician to think, or a way to teach and document music. It was a mental tool distinguishable from the music itself. Different people could make transcriptions of the same musical recording, for instance, and come up with slightly different scores.

After MIDI, a musical note was no longer just an idea, but a rigid, mandatory structure you couldn't avoid in the aspects of life that had gone digital. The process of lock-in is like a wave gradually washing over the rulebook of life, culling° the ambiguities of flexible thoughts as more and more thought structures are solidified into effectively permanent reality.

We can compare lock-in to scientific method. The philosopher Karl Popper was correct when he claimed that science is a process that disqualifies thoughts as it proceeds—one can, for example, no longer reasonably believe in a flat Earth that sprang into being some thousands of years ago. Science removes ideas from play empirically,° for good reason. Lock-in, however, removes design options based on what is easiest to program, what is politically feasible, what is fashionable, or what is created by chance.

Lock-in removes ideas that do not fit into the winning digital representation scheme, but it also reduces or narrows the ideas it immortalizes, by cutting away the unfathomable° penumbra° of meaning that distinguishes a word in natural language from a command in a computer program.

35

The criteria that guide science might be more admirable than those that guide lock-in, but unless we come up with an entirely different way to make software, further lock-ins are guaranteed. Scientific progress, by contrast, always requires determination and can stall because of politics or lack of funding or curiosity. An interesting challenge presents itself: How can a musician cherish the broader, less-defined concept of a note that preceded MIDI, while using MIDI all day long and interacting with other musicians through the filter of MIDI? Is it even worth trying? Should a digital artist just give in to lock-in and accept the infinitely explicit, finite idea of a MIDI note?

If it's important to find the edge of mystery, to ponder the things that can't quite be defined—or rendered into a digital standard—then we will have to perpetually seek out entirely new ideas and objects, abandoning old ones like musical notes. Throughout this book, I'll explore whether people are becoming like MIDI notes—overly defined, and restricted in practice to what can be represented in a computer. This has enormous implications: we can conceivably abandon musical notes, but we can't abandon ourselves.

---

culling: selecting, picking

empirically: based on, or provable by, experience or observation

unfathomable: unmeasurable

penumbra: partial shadow

When Dave made MIDI, I was thrilled. Some friends of mine from the original Macintosh team quickly built a hardware interface so a Mac could use MIDI to control a synthesizer, and I worked up a quick music creation program. We felt so free—but we should have been more thoughtful.

By now, MIDI has become too hard to change, so the culture has changed to make it seem fuller than it was initially intended to be. We have narrowed what we expect from the most commonplace forms of musical sound in order to make the technology adequate. It wasn't Dave's fault. How could he have known?

Digital Reification:° Lock-in Turns Philosophy into Reality

A lot of the locked-in ideas about how software is put together come from an old operating system called UNIX. It has some characteristics that are related to MIDI. 40

While MIDI squeezes musical expression through a limiting model of the actions of keys on a musical keyboard, UNIX does the same for all computation, but using the actions of keys on typewriter-like keyboards. A UNIX program is often similar to a simulation of a person typing quickly.

There's a core design feature in UNIX called a "command line interface." In this system, you type instructions, you hit "return," and the instructions are carried out.* A unifying design principle of UNIX is that a program can't tell if a person hit return or a program did so. Since real people are slower than simulated people at operating keyboards, the importance of precise timing is suppressed by this particular idea. As a result, UNIX is based on discrete events that don't have to happen at a precise moment in time. The human organism, meanwhile, is based on continuous sensory, cognitive, and motor processes that have to be synchronized precisely in time. (MIDI falls somewhere in between the concept of time embodied in UNIX and in the human body, being based on discrete events that happen at particular times.)

UNIX expresses too large a belief in discrete abstract symbols and not enough of a belief in temporal,° continuous, nonabstract reality; it is more like a typewriter than a dance partner. (Perhaps typewriters or word processors ought to always be instantly responsive, like a dance partner—but that is not yet the case.) UNIX tends to "want" to connect to reality as if reality were a network of fast typists.

If you hope for computers to be designed to serve embodied people as well as possible people, UNIX would have to be considered a bad design.

*The style of UNIX commands has, incredibly, become part of pop culture. For instance, the URLs (universal resource locators) that we use to find web pages these days, like http://www.jaronlanier.com/, are examples of the kind of key press sequences that are ubiquitous in UNIX.

Reification: process of making an abstract idea into a concrete object

temporal: pertaining to time, transitory

I discovered this in the 1970s, when I tried to make responsive musical instruments with it. I was trying to do what MIDI does not, which is work with fluid, hard-to-notate aspects of music, and discovered that the underlying philosophy of UNIX was too brittle and clumsy for that.

The arguments in favor of UNIX focused on how computers would get literally millions of times faster in the coming decades. The thinking was that the speed increase would overwhelm the timing problems I was worried about. Indeed, today's computers are millions of times faster, and UNIX has become an ambient part of life. There are some reasonably expressive tools that have UNIX in them, so the speed increase has sufficed to compensate for UNIX's problems in some cases. But not all. 45

I have an iPhone in my pocket, and sure enough, the thing has what is essentially UNIX in it. An unnerving element of this gadget is that it is haunted by a weird set of unpredictable user interface delays. One's mind waits for the response to the press of a virtual button, but it doesn't come for a while. An odd tension builds during that moment, and easy intuition is replaced by nervousness. It is the ghost of UNIX, still refusing to accommodate the rhythms of my body and my mind, after all these years.

I'm not picking in particular on the iPhone (which I'll praise in another context later on). I could just as easily have chosen any contemporary personal computer. Windows isn't UNIX, but it does share UNIX's idea that a symbol is more important than the flow of time and the underlying continuity of experience.

The grudging relationship between UNIX and the temporal world in which the human body moves and the human mind thinks is a disappointing example of lock-in, but not a disastrous one. Maybe it will even help make it easier for people to appreciate the old-fashioned physical world, as virtual reality gets better. If so, it will have turned out to be a blessing in disguise.

Entrenched Software Philosophies Become Invisible Through Ubiquity°

An even deeper locked-in idea is the notion of the file. Once upon a time, not too long ago, plenty of computer scientists thought the idea of the file was not so great.

The first design for something like the World Wide Web, Ted Nelson's Xanadu, conceived of one giant, global file, for instance. The first iteration of the Macintosh, which never shipped, didn't have files. Instead, the whole of a user's productivity accumulated in one big structure, sort of like a singular personal web page. Steve Jobs took the Mac project over from the fellow who started it, the late Jef Raskin, and soon files appeared. 50

UNIX had files; the Mac as it shipped had files; Windows had files. Files are now part of life; we teach the idea of a file to computer science students as if it were part of nature. In fact, our conception of files may be more persistent than our ideas about nature. I can imagine that someday physicists might tell

Ubiquity: state or power of being everywhere at once

us that it is time to stop believing in photons,° because they have discovered a better way to think about light—but the file will likely live on.

The file is a set of philosophical ideas made into eternal flesh. The ideas expressed by the file include the notion that human expression comes in severable chunks that can be organized as leaves on an abstract tree—and that the chunks have versions and need to be matched to compatible applications.

What do files mean to the future of human expression? This is a harder question to answer than the question "How does the English language influence the thoughts of native English speakers?" At least you can compare English speakers to Chinese speakers, but files are universal. The idea of the file has become so big that we are unable to conceive of a frame large enough to fit around it in order to assess it empirically.

What Happened to Trains, Files, and Musical Notes Could Happen Soon to the Definition of a Human Being

It's worth trying to notice when philosophies are congealing into locked-in software. For instance, is pervasive° anonymity or pseudonymity a good thing? It's an important question, because the corresponding philosophies of how humans can express meaning have been so ingrained into the interlocked software designs of the internet that we might never be able to fully get rid of them, or even remember that things could have been different.

55 We ought to at least try to avoid this particularly tricky example of impending lock-in. Lock-in makes us forget the lost freedoms we had in the digital past. That can make it harder to see the freedoms we have in the digital present. Fortunately, difficult as it is, we can still try to change some expressions of philosophy that are on the verge of becoming locked in place in the tools we use to understand one another and the world.

A Happy Surprise

The rise of the web was a rare instance when we learned new, positive information about human potential. Who would have guessed (at least at first) that millions of people would put so much effort into a project without the presence of advertising, commercial motive, threat of punishment, charismatic figures, identity politics, exploitation of the fear of death, or any of the other classic motivators of mankind. In vast numbers, people did something cooperatively, solely because it was a good idea, and it was beautiful.

Some of the more wild-eyed eccentrics in the digital world had guessed that it would happen—but even so it was a shock when it actually did come to pass. It turns out that even an optimistic, idealistic philosophy is realizable. Put a happy philosophy of life in software, and it might very well come true!

. . .

photons: units of electromagnetic radiation

pervasive: spread throughout

Where We Are on the Journey

It's time to take stock. Something amazing happened with the introduction of the World Wide Web. A faith in human goodness was vindicated when a remarkably open and unstructured information tool was made available to large numbers of people. That openness can, at this point, be declared "locked in" to a significant degree. Hurray!

At the same time, some not-so-great ideas about life and meaning were also locked in, like MIDI's nuance-challenged conception of musical sound and UNIX's inability to cope with time as humans experience it.

These are acceptable costs, what I would call aesthetic losses. They are counterbalanced, however, by some aesthetic victories. The digital world looks better than it sounds because a community of digital activists, including folks from Xerox Parc (especially Alan Kay), Apple, Adobe, and the academic world (especially Stanford's Don Knuth) fought the good fight to save us from the rigidly ugly fonts and other visual elements we'd have been stuck with otherwise. 60

Then there are those recently conceived elements of the future of human experience, like the already locked-in idea of the file, that are as fundamental as the air we breathe. The file will henceforth be one of the basic underlying elements of the human story, like genes. We will never know what that means, or what alternatives might have meant.

On balance, we've done wonderfully well! But the challenge on the table now is unlike previous ones. The new designs on the verge of being locked in, the web 2.0 designs, actively demand that people define themselves downward. It's one thing to launch a limited conception of music or time into the contest for what philosophical idea will be locked in. It is another to do that with the very idea of what it is to be a person.

Why It Matters

If you feel fine using the tools you use, who am I to tell you that there is something wrong with what you are doing? But consider these points:

- Emphasizing the crowd means deemphasizing individual humans in the design of society, and when you ask people not to be people, they revert to bad moblike behaviors. This leads not only to empowered trolls, but to a generally unfriendly and unconstructive online world.
- Finance was transformed by computing clouds. Success in finance became increasingly about manipulating the cloud at the expense of sound financial principles.
- There are proposals to transform the conduct of science along similar lines. Scientists would then understand less of what they do.
- Pop culture has entered into a nostalgic malaise.° Online culture is dominated by trivial mashups of the culture that existed before the onset

malaise: uneasiness

of mashups, and by fandom responding to the dwindling outposts of centralized mass media. It is a culture of reaction without action.

- Spirituality is committing suicide. Consciousness is attempting to will itself out of existence.

It might seem as though I'm assembling a catalog of every possible thing that could go wrong with the future of culture as changed by technology, but that is not the case. All of these examples are really just different aspects of one singular, big mistake.

The deep meaning of personhood is being reduced by illusions of bits. Since people will be inexorably° connecting to one another through computers from here on out, we must find an alternative. 65

We have to think about the digital layers we are laying down now in order to benefit future generations. We should be optimistic that civilization will survive this challenging century, and put some effort into creating the best possible world for those who will inherit our efforts.

Next to the many problems the world faces today, debates about online culture may not seem that pressing. We need to address global warming, shift to a new energy cycle, avoid wars of mass destruction, support aging populations, figure out how to benefit from open markets without being disastrously vulnerable to their failures, and take care of other basic business. But digital culture and related topics like the future of privacy and copyrights concern the society we'll have if we can survive these challenges.

Every save-the-world cause has a list of suggestions for "what each of us can do": bike to work, recycle, and so on.

I can propose such a list related to the problems I'm talking about:

- Don't post anonymously unless you really might be in danger.
- If you put effort into Wikipedia articles, put even more effort into using your personal voice and expression outside of the wiki to help attract people who don't yet realize that they are interested in the topics you contributed to.
- Create a website that expresses something about who you are that won't fit into the template available to you on a social networking site.
- Post a video once in a while that took you one hundred times more time to create than it takes to view.
- Write a blog post that took weeks of reflection before you heard the inner voice that needed to come out.
- If you are twittering, innovate in order to find a way to describe your internal state instead of trivial external events, to avoid the creeping

inexorably: unalterably

danger of believing that objectively described events define you, as they would define a machine.

These are some of the things you can do to be a person instead of a source of fragments to be exploited by others. 70

[2010]

Read

1. What is the effect on you as a reader of the format of Lanier's opening chapter?
2. How does Lanier establish his credibility on the issue of technological change?
3. What kinds of appeals does Lanier make to help create his argument?
4. What evidence does Lanier offer for his position?

Write

1. How would you describe the persona the speaker creates? Write a brief description using lines from the text.
2. What is the aim and the effect of the list of "things to do" at the end of the chapter? Comment on the workability of Lanier's suggestions.

Connect

1. Do you agree with Lanier's position as it is outlined in the excerpt? How do you respond to it?
2. How would Lanier define progress?

Cecilia Muñoz

Cecilia Muñoz (b. 1960) has served since 2009 as Director for Intergovernmental Affairs for the White House. She is a civil rights advocate, working for the National Council of La Raza, an organization that aids Hispanic Americans. Born in Detroit, she is the daughter of Bolivian immigrants. Muñoz was awarded a MacArthur Fellowship in 2000, and she has been featured on documentaries and films about civil rights and social justice. This piece was written and delivered for National Public Radio's "This I Believe" series in 2005.

Getting Angry Can Be a Good Thing

I believe that a little outrage can take you a long way.

I remember the exact moment when I discovered outrage as a kind of fuel. It was about 1980. I was 17, the daughter of Bolivian immigrants growing up in suburban Detroit. After a dinner table conversation with my family about the wars going on in Central America and the involvement of the United States (my country by birth and my parents' country by choice), a good friend said the thing that set me off. He told me that he thought the U.S. might someday go to war somewhere in Latin America. He looked me in the eye and told me that if it happens, he believes my parents belong in an internment camp just like the Japanese-Americans during World War II.

Now this was someone who knew us, who had sat at our table and knew how American we are. We are a little exotic maybe, but it never occurred to me that we were anything but an American family. For my friend, as for many others, there will always be doubt as to whether we really belong in this country, which is our home, enough doubt to justify taking away our freedom. My outrage that day became the propellant of my life, driving me straight to the civil rights movement, where I've worked ever since.

I guess outrage got me pretty far. I found jobs in the immigrant rights movement. I moved to Washington to work as an advocate. I found plenty more to be angry about along the way and built something of a reputation for being strident.° Someone once sent my mom an article about my work. She was proud and everything but wanted to know why her baby was described as "ferocious."

5 Anger has a way, though, of hollowing out your insides. In my first job, if we helped 50 immigrant families in a day, the faces of the five who didn't qualify haunted my dreams at night. When I helped pass a bill in Congress to help Americans reunite with their immigrant families, I could only think of my cousin who didn't qualify and who had to wait another decade to get her immigration papers.

It's like that every day. You have victories but your defeats outnumber them by far, and you remember the names and faces of those who lost. I still have the article about the farm worker who took his life after we lost a political fight. I have not forgotten his name—and not just because his last name was the same as mine. His story reminds me of why I do this work and how little I can really do.

I am deeply familiar with that hollow place that outrage carves in your soul. I've fed off of it to sustain my work for many years. But it hasn't eaten me away completely, maybe because the hollow place gets filled with other, more powerful things like compassion, faith, family, music, the goodness of people around me. These things fill me up and temper my outrage with a deep sense of gratitude that I have the privilege of doing my small part to make things better.

[2005]

---

strident: grating, irritatingly shrill

Read

1. How does knowing the context for this piece (the NPR series "This I Believe" in which essays are read aloud on the radio) help you read Muñoz's text?
2. How do you think Muñoz would define "outrage"?
3. How does Muñoz use language to develop her persona?

Write

1. What is the function of the narrative Muñoz uses in her piece? Write a brief discussion of how she uses the story.
2. Does the tone of Muñoz's piece seem different from or connected to her title? Is she angry?

Complete Additional Exercises on Muñoz's Essay at Your Pearson MyLab

Connect

1. How does Muñoz's experience link with other experiences of immigrants you've read about in this unit?
2. How does her experience suggest the continuing viability or continuing problems with living *The* "American dream"?

Paul Krugman

Paul Krugman (b. 1953) was born in New York, the son of Jewish immigrants. He is the Woodrow Wilson Professor of Economics at Princeton University and also an op ed columnist for *The New York Times*. In 2008, Krugman won the Nobel Prize in Economics for his work in international trade. He has written 20 books, over 200 scholarly articles, and over 750 columns in the *Times* on economic and political issues.

Stranded in Suburbia

I have seen the future, and it works.°

O.K., I know that these days you're supposed to see the future in China or India, not in the heart of "old Europe."

But we're living in a world in which oil prices keep setting records, in which the idea that global oil production will soon peak is rapidly moving from fringe belief to mainstream assumption. And Europeans who have achieved a high standard of living in spite of very high energy prices—gas in Germany costs more than $8 a gallon—have a lot to teach us about how to deal with that world.

If Europe's example is any guide, here are the two secrets of coping with expensive oil: own fuel-efficient cars, and don't drive them too much.

I have seen . . . it works: Krugman quotes the famous comment made by American muckraking journalist Lincoln Steffens (1866–1936) after a visit to the Soviet Union in 1919.

Notice that I said that cars should be fuel-efficient—not that people should do without cars altogether. In Germany, as in the United States, the vast majority of families own cars (although German households are less likely than their U.S. counterparts to be multiple-car owners).

But the average German car uses about a quarter less gas per mile than the average American car. By and large, the Germans don't drive itsy-bitsy toy cars, but they do drive modest-sized passenger vehicles rather than S.U.V.'s and pickup trucks.

In the near future I expect we'll see Americans moving down the same path. We've already done it once: over the course of the 1970s and 1980s, the average mileage of U.S. passenger vehicles rose about 50 percent, as Americans switched to smaller, lighter cars.

This improvement stalled with the rise of S.U.V.'s during the cheap-gas 1990s. But now that gas costs more than ever before, even after adjusting for inflation, we can expect to see mileage rise again.

Admittedly, the next few years will be rough for families who bought big vehicles when gas was cheap, and now find themselves the owners of white elephants with little trade-in value. But raising fuel efficiency is something we can and will do.

Can we also drive less? Yes—but getting there will be a lot harder.

There have been many news stories in recent weeks about Americans who are changing their behavior in response to expensive gasoline—they're trying to shop locally, they're canceling vacations that involve a lot of driving, and they're switching to public transit.

But none of it amounts to much. For example, some major public transit systems are excited about ridership gains of 5 or 10 percent. But fewer than 5 percent of Americans take public transit to work, so this surge of riders takes only a relative handful of drivers off the road.

Any serious reduction in American driving will require more than this—it will mean changing how and where many of us live.

To see what I'm talking about, consider where I am at the moment: in a pleasant, middle-class neighborhood consisting mainly of four- or five-story apartment buildings, with easy access to public transit and plenty of local shopping.

It's the kind of neighborhood in which people don't have to drive a lot, but it's also a kind of neighborhood that barely exists in America, even in big metropolitan areas. Greater Atlanta has roughly the same population as Greater Berlin—but Berlin is a city of trains, buses and bikes, while Atlanta is a city of cars, cars and cars.

And in the face of rising oil prices, which have left many Americans stranded in suburbia—utterly dependent on their cars, yet having a hard time affording gas—it's starting to look as if Berlin had the better idea.

Changing the geography of American metropolitan areas will be hard. For one thing, houses last a lot longer than cars. Long after today's S.U.V.'s have become antique collectors' items, millions of people will still be living in subdivisions built when gas was $1.50 or less a gallon.

Infrastructure is another problem. Public transit, in particular, faces a chicken-and-egg problem: it's hard to justify transit systems unless there's sufficient population density, yet it's hard to persuade people to live in denser neighborhoods unless they come with the advantage of transit access.

And there are, as always in America, the issues of race and class. Despite the gentrification° that has taken place in some inner cities, and the plunge in national crime rates to levels not seen in decades, it will be hard to shake the long-standing American association of higher-density living with poverty and personal danger.

Still, if we're heading for a prolonged era of scarce, expensive oil, Americans will face increasingly strong incentives to start living like Europeans—maybe not today, and maybe not tomorrow, but soon, and for the rest of our lives.

[2008]

Read

1. What is the aim of the brief opening to the article?
2. What comparisons does Krugman draw and what is the effect of these comparisons on your reading?
3. How does Krugman use opposing claims to help make his case?

Write

1. Describe Krugman's persona in the article. What primary appeal does he make to establish that persona?
2. Write a response to Krugman's contentions using your own opinions or experience.

Complete Additional Exercises on Krugman's Essay at Your Pearson MyLab

Connect

1. Do you recognize the allusion in the last sentence? (Hint: one of the most famous movies of all time, set in unoccupied Africa at the beginning of World War II.) Why is this reference appropriate or useful to Krugman's argument?
2. Where do you find Krugman's position most convincing? Why?

---

gentrification: restoration of poor urban areas by well-to-do new homeowners, leading to displacement of the original inhabitants

UNIT ACTIVITIES

Rhetorical Analysis

1. Nathaniel Hawthorne's character in *The House of the Seven Gables* sees the advent of train travel as an emblem of progress: "These rails give us wings!" As other texts we've read suggest, however, progress—in the form of the train itself or another emblem—might have negative implications as well. Use poems by Walt Whitman and Emily Dickinson to analyze how the train can be both a positive and a negative symbol for progress.
2. In "The Race Question Discussed," Paul Laurence Dunbar writes of the betrayal he felt after the Civil War. In an essay, analyze how Dunbar uses logic, diction, and example to convey his belief that the country has let his people down.
3. From the earliest days of colonization to the present, American thinkers and writers have struggled both to define the meaning of "progress" and to argue for its importance in discussions of government, education, the economy, and human rights. In an essay, analyze how you believe an educated young adult in the late nineteenth or early twentieth century would have defined progress, and contrast that view with how you believe an educated young adult today would define the term. For the earlier perspective, draw on the excerpt from Adams' *The Education of Henry Adams* or Sandburg's "Chicago" or both. For the contemporary perspective, consider either Lanier's "You are Not a Gadget" or Krugman's "Stranded in Suburbia" or both. For the contemporary perspective, you may also draw upon your own reading, experiences, and observations.

Argument

1. Mary Antin believes in the power of education in a free society, a power she recognizes clearly as an immigrant. Using Antin's essay, any other piece in this unit, and your own experience, create an argument that claims or takes issue with education as the most powerful means to sustain democracy and freedom.
2. What is the best path toward success and citizenship in this country? Using at least one text from an immigrant writer in this unit, write an argument that explains how you think newcomers to America can best succeed. Possible authors include Antin, Yung, Steiglitz, Riis, Addams, and Muñoz.

Synthesis

Discuss the idea of progress by evaluating the claims made about how progress is defined and achieved. Use at least four of the following texts:

Lanier, from *You Are Not a Gadget*

Paul Krugman, "Lost in Suburbia"

Walt Whitman, from *Democratic Vistas*

W. E. B. Du Bois, from *The Souls of Black Folk*

Paul Dunbar, "The Race Question Discussed"

Frederick Lewis Allen, from *Only Yesterday*

Analyze the writers' definitions of progress and their evidence in order to define and evaluate progress for yourself.

UNIT 5

This poster by artist and cartoonist Lalo Alcaraz comments on the 2011 Occupy Wall Street protests about the economy.

Read

1. What allusions do you see in the cartoon?
2. What does the statement "We are the 99 Percent" suggest about the importance of community?
3. How does contrast work to dramatize the intention of the cartoon?

Connect

1. What methods for change are suggested by the image that are reinforced in the texts in this unit?
2. What's the role of protest in a democracy?
3. How do the texts in the unit make use of cultural symbols to strengthen their message?

How Should a Nation Change?
1933–1970

The New Deal By 1933, with millions of people still unemployed and a lingering economic collapse, it became clear that the nation needed to change. Innovative ideas for recovery were needed. To meet these needs, President Franklin Roosevelt initiated government programs that spurred economic recovery, created jobs, and helped rebuild confidence in the American economy and way of life.

The Post-War Period After World War II, America emerged as the most powerful nation in the world. Communist countries vied with the United States for influence on developing nations in the Cold War, which lasted until near the end of the twentieth century. Technological growth created economic rewards and challenges. The voices of minorities and women became more insistent, calling on the government to ensure that all citizens received equal rights.

Nation at Risk Depression, war, and cultural change created an environment in which people questioned their beliefs. Many recognized the need to change with the times but felt unready to part with the past. Unparalleled economic growth in the post-war period fueled belief in the American dream, yet the needs of the dispossessed and the poor, as well as global unrest, were felt even in a time of plenty. By 1970, with the country embedded in another war, this one so deeply unpopular that it would mobilize a generation and cause a president to decline to run for a second term, the ideals of the nation and its belief in itself seemed to be at risk.

GUIDING QUESTIONS

- What approaches are most effective to challenge old ideas with new ones?
- How can people mobilize to act for the good of the community?
- What might we hold onto from the past and why?
- Should we use law to shape people's attitudes?
- How do we negotiate a conflict between responsibility to self and country?

Franklin Delano Roosevelt

Franklin Delano Roosevelt (1882–1945) was the 32nd president of the United States from 1933 to 1945. Known as FDR, he was a central figure in national and world events, leading the country through a massive depression and a world war. The legislation he initiated to lift the country out of its devastating economic condition, called the New Deal, reformed financial institutions through regulation and created jobs programs that put people back to work. Roosevelt was born into one of the oldest families in New York, attended Harvard, and married his distant relation Eleanor in 1905. He was a New York senator and governor and Assistant Secretary of the Navy before defeating Herbert Hoover in 1932 to become president. Although he was crippled by polio, most of the country never knew it because he was always photographed standing, supported by a podium. For his work and confident persona during troubled times, FDR is widely regarded by historians as one of the most important presidents. In his speech to the Congress during World War II, FDR emphasized the need for continued sacrifice to finish the war. He also affirmed new principles that he believed would secure a lasting peace. These principles he called a "second Bill of Rights."

From *State of the Union Address*

January 11, 1944

To the Congress:

This Nation in the past two years has become an active partner in the world's greatest war against human slavery.

We have joined with like-minded people in order to defend ourselves in a world that has been gravely threatened with gangster rule.

But I do not think that any of us Americans can be content with mere survival. Sacrifices that we and our allies are making impose upon us all a sacred obligation to see to it that out of this war we and our children will gain something better than mere survival.

We are united in determination that this war shall not be followed by another interim which leads to new disaster—that we shall not repeat the tragic errors of ostrich isolationism—that we shall not repeat the excesses of the wild twenties when this Nation went for a joy ride on a roller coaster which ended in a tragic crash.

When Mr. Hull° went to Moscow° in October, and when I went to Cairo and Teheran° in November, we knew that we were in agreement with our allies in our common determination to fight and win this war. But there were many vital questions concerning the future peace, and they were discussed in an atmosphere of complete candor and harmony. 5

In the last war such discussions, such meetings, did not even begin until the shooting had stopped and the delegates began to assemble at the peace table. There had been no previous opportunities for man-to-man discussions which lead to meetings of minds. The result was a peace which was not a peace.

That was a mistake which we are not repeating in this war.

And right here I want to address a word or two to some suspicious souls who are fearful that Mr. Hull or I have made "commitments" for the future which might pledge this Nation to secret treaties, or to enacting the role of Santa Claus.

To such suspicious souls—using a polite terminology—I wish to say that Mr. Churchill,° and Marshal Stalin,° and Generalissimo Chiang Kai-shek° are all thoroughly conversant with the provisions of our Constitution. And so is Mr. Hull. And so am I.

Of course we made some commitments. We most certainly committed ourselves to very large and very specific military plans which require the use of all Allied forces to bring about the defeat of our enemies at the earliest possible time. 10

But there were no secret treaties or political or financial commitments.

The one supreme objective for the future, which we discussed for each Nation individually, and for all the United Nations, can be summed up in one word: Security.

And that means not only physical security which provides safety from attacks by aggressors. It means also economic security, social security, moral security—in a family of Nations.

In the plain down-to-earth talks that I had with the Generalissimo and Marshal Stalin and Prime Minister Churchill, it was abundantly clear that they are

---

Hull: Cordell Hull (1871–1955), American Secretary of State (1933–1944)

Moscow: site of a war-aims conference of the foreign ministers of the United States, Great Britain, the Soviet Union, and China in October and November 1943

Cairo and Teheran: sites of strategy meetings of the heads of state of the Allied Powers in November and December 1943

Churchill: Sir Winston Churchill (1874–1965), British Prime Minister (1940–1945, 1951–1955)

Stalin: Joseph Stalin (1879–1953), General Secretary of the Communist Party of the Soviet Union (1922–1953), Soviet premier (1941–1953)

Chiang Kai-shek: (1887–1975), Chairman of the National Government of China (1928–1931, 1943–1948)

all most deeply interested in the resumption of peaceful progress by their own peoples—progress toward a better life. All our allies want freedom to develop their lands and resources, to build up industry, to increase education and individual opportunity, and to raise standards of living.

All our allies have learned by bitter experience that real development will not be possible if they are to be diverted from their purpose by repeated wars—or even threats of war. 15

China and Russia are truly united with Britain and America in recognition of this essential fact:

The best interests of each Nation, large and small, demand that all freedom-loving Nations shall join together in a just and durable system of peace. In the present world situation, evidenced by the actions of Germany, Italy, and Japan, unquestioned military control over disturbers of the peace is as necessary among Nations as it is among citizens in a community. And an equally basic essential to peace is a decent standard of living for all individual men and women and children in all Nations. Freedom from fear is eternally linked with freedom from want.°

There are people who burrow through our Nation like unseeing moles, and attempt to spread the suspicion that if other Nations are encouraged to raise their standards of living, our own American standard of living must of necessity be depressed.

The fact is the very contrary. It has been shown time and again that if the standard of living of any country goes up, so does its purchasing power—and that such a rise encourages a better standard of living in neighboring countries with whom it trades. That is just plain common sense—and it is the kind of plain common sense that provided the basis for our discussions at Moscow, Cairo, and Teheran.

Returning from my journeyings, I must confess to a sense of "let-down" when I found many evidences of faulty perspective here in Washington. The faulty perspective consists in overemphasizing lesser problems and thereby underemphasizing the first and greatest problem. 20

The overwhelming majority of our people have met the demands of this war with magnificent courage and understanding. They have accepted inconveniences; they have accepted hardships; they have accepted tragic sacrifices. And they are ready and eager to make whatever further contributions are needed to win the war as quickly as possible—if only they are given the chance to know what is required of them.

---

want: destitution, poverty

However, while the majority goes on about its great work without complaint, a noisy minority maintains an uproar of demands for special favors for special groups. There are pests who swarm through the lobbies of the Congress and the cocktail bars of Washington, representing these special groups as opposed to the basic interests of the Nation as a whole. They have come to look upon the war primarily as a chance to make profits for themselves at the expense of their neighbors—profits in money or in terms of political or social preferment.

Such selfish agitation can be highly dangerous in wartime. It creates confusion. It damages morale. It hampers our national effort. It muddies the waters and therefore prolongs the war.

If we analyze American history impartially, we cannot escape the fact that in our past we have not always forgotten individual and selfish and partisan interests in time of war—we have not always been united in purpose and direction. We cannot overlook the serious dissensions and the lack of unity in our war of the Revolution, in our War of 1812, or in our War Between the States, when the survival of the Union itself was at stake.

25

In the first World War we came closer to national unity than in any previous war. But that war lasted only a year and a half, and increasing signs of disunity began to appear during the final months of the conflict.

In this war, we have been compelled to learn how interdependent upon each other are all groups and sections of the population of America.

Increased food costs, for example, will bring new demands for wage increases from all war workers, which will in turn raise all prices of all things including those things which the farmers themselves have to buy. Increased wages or prices will each in turn produce the same results. They all have a particularly disastrous result on all fixed income groups.

And I hope you will remember that all of us in this Government represent the fixed income group just as much as we represent business owners, workers, and farmers. This group of fixed income people includes: teachers, clergy, policemen, firemen, widows and minors on fixed incomes, wives and dependents of our soldiers and sailors, and old-age pensioners. They and their families add up to one-quarter of our one hundred and thirty million people. They have few or no high pressure representatives at the Capitol. In a period of gross inflation they would be the worst sufferers.

If ever there was a time to subordinate individual or group selfishness to the national good, that time is now. Disunity at home—bickerings, self-seeking partisanship, stoppages of work, inflation, business as usual, politics as usual, luxury as usual—these are the influences which can undermine the morale of the brave men ready to die at the front for us here.

Those who are doing most of the complaining are not deliberately striving to sabotage the national war effort. They are laboring under the delusion that the time is past when we must make prodigious° sacrifices—that the war is already won and we can begin to slacken off. But the dangerous folly of that point of view can be measured by the distance that separates our troops from their ultimate objectives in Berlin and Tokyo—and by the sum of all the perils that lie along the way. 30

Overconfidence and complacency are among our deadliest enemies. Last spring—after notable victories at Stalingrad and in Tunisia and against the U-boats on the high seas—overconfidence became so pronounced that war production fell off. In two months, June and July, 1943, more than a thousand airplanes that could have been made and should have been made were not made. Those who failed to make them were not on strike. They were merely saying, "The war's in the bag—so let's relax."

That attitude on the part of anyone—Government or management or labor—can lengthen this war. It can kill American boys.

Let us remember the lessons of 1918. In the summer of that year the tide turned in favor of the allies. But this Government did not relax. In fact, our national effort was stepped up. In August, 1918, the draft age limits were broadened from 21–31 to 18–45. The President called for "force to the utmost," and his call was heeded. And in November, only three months later, Germany surrendered.

That is the way to fight and win a war—all out—and not with half-an-eye on the battlefronts abroad and the other eye-and-a-half on personal, selfish, or political interests here at home.

Therefore, in order to concentrate all our energies and resources on winning the war, and to maintain a fair and stable economy at home, I recommend that the Congress adopt: 35

1. A realistic tax law—which will tax all unreasonable profits, both individual and corporate, and reduce the ultimate cost of the war to our sons and daughters. The tax bill now under consideration by the Congress does not begin to meet this test.

2. A continuation of the law for the renegotiation of war contracts—which will prevent exorbitant profits and assure fair prices to the Government. For two long years I have pleaded with the Congress to take undue profits out of war.

3. A cost of food law—which will enable the Government (a) to place a reasonable floor under the prices the farmer may expect for his produc-

prodigious: extraordinary, enormous

tion; and (b) to place a ceiling on the prices a consumer will have to pay for the food he buys. This should apply to necessities only; and will require public funds to carry out. It will cost in appropriations about one percent of the present annual cost of the war.

4. Early reenactment of the stabilization statute of October, 1942. This expires June 30, 1944, and if it is not extended well in advance, the country might just as well expect price chaos by summer.

   We cannot have stabilization by wishful thinking. We must take positive action to maintain the integrity of the American dollar.

5. A national service law—which, for the duration of the war, will prevent strikes, and, with certain appropriate exceptions, will make available for war production or for any other essential services every able-bodied adult in this Nation.

These five measures together form a just and equitable whole. I would not recommend a national service law unless the other laws were passed to keep down the cost of living, to share equitably the burdens of taxation, to hold the stabilization line, and to prevent undue profits.

The Federal Government already has the basic power to draft capital and property of all kinds for war purposes on a basis of just compensation.

As you know, I have for three years hesitated to recommend a national service act. Today, however, I am convinced of its necessity. Although I believe that we and our allies can win the war without such a measure, I am certain that nothing less than total mobilization of all our resources of manpower and capital will guarantee an earlier victory, and reduce the toll of suffering and sorrow and blood.

I have received a joint recommendation for this law from the heads of the War Department, the Navy Department, and the Maritime Commission. These are the men who bear responsibility for the procurement of the necessary arms and equipment, and for the successful prosecution of the war in the field. They say:

"When the very life of the Nation is in peril the responsibility for service is common to all men and women. In such a time there can be no discrimination between the men and women who are assigned by the Government to its defense at the battlefront and the men and women assigned to producing the vital materials essential to successful military operations. A prompt enactment of a National Service Law would be merely an expression of the universality of this responsibility." 40

I believe the country will agree that those statements are the solemn truth.

National service is the most democratic way to wage a war. Like selective service for the armed forces, it rests on the obligation of each citizen to serve his Nation to his utmost where he is best qualified.

It does not mean reduction in wages. It does not mean loss of retirement and seniority rights and benefits. It does not mean that any substantial numbers of war workers will be disturbed in their present jobs. Let these facts be wholly clear.

Experience in other democratic Nations at war—Britain, Canada, Australia, and New Zealand—has shown that the very existence of national service makes unnecessary the widespread use of compulsory power. National service has proven to be a unifying moral force based on an equal and comprehensive legal obligation of all people in a Nation at war.

There are millions of American men and women who are not in this war at all. It is not because they do not want to be in it. But they want to know where they can best do their share. National service provides that direction. It will be a means by which every man and woman can find that inner satisfaction which comes from making the fullest possible contribution to victory. 45

I know that all civilian war workers will be glad to be able to say many years hence to their grandchildren: "Yes, I, too, was in service in the great war. I was on duty in an airplane factory, and I helped make hundreds of fighting planes. The Government told me that in doing that I was performing my most useful work in the service of my country."

It is argued that we have passed the stage in the war where national service is necessary. But our soldiers and sailors know that this is not true. We are going forward on a long, rough road—and, in all journeys, the last miles are the hardest. And it is for that final effort—for the total defeat of our enemies—that we must mobilize our total resources. The national war program calls for the employment of more people in 1944 than in 1943.

It is my conviction that the American people will welcome this win-the-war measure which is based on the eternally just principle of "fair for one, fair for all."

It will give our people at home the assurance that they are standing four-square behind our soldiers and sailors. And it will give our enemies demoralizing assurance that we mean business—that we, 130,000,000 Americans, are on the march to Rome, Berlin, and Tokyo.

I hope that the Congress will recognize that, although this is a political year,° national service is an issue which transcends politics. Great power must be used for great purposes. 50

As to the machinery for this measure, the Congress itself should determine its nature—but it should be wholly nonpartisan in its make-up.

---

a political year: an election year

Our armed forces are valiantly fulfilling their responsibilities to our country and our people. Now the Congress faces the responsibility for taking those measures which are essential to national security in this the most decisive phase of the Nation's greatest war.

Several alleged reasons have prevented the enactment of legislation which would preserve for our soldiers and sailors and marines the fundamental prerogative of citizenship—the right to vote. No amount of legalistic argument can becloud this issue in the eyes of these ten million American citizens. Surely the signers of the Constitution did not intend a document which, even in wartime, would be construed to take away the franchise° of any of those who are fighting to preserve the Constitution itself.

Our soldiers and sailors and marines know that the overwhelming majority of them will be deprived of the opportunity to vote, if the voting machinery is left exclusively to the States under existing State laws—and that there is no likelihood of these laws being changed in time to enable them to vote at the next election. The Army and Navy have reported that it will be impossible effectively to administer forty-eight different soldier voting laws. It is the duty of the Congress to remove this unjustifiable discrimination against the men and women in our armed forces—and to do it as quickly as possible.

55

It is our duty now to begin to lay the plans and determine the strategy for the winning of a lasting peace and the establishment of an American standard of living higher than ever before known. We cannot be content, no matter how high that general standard of living may be, if some fraction of our people—whether it be one-third or one-fifth or one-tenth—is ill-fed, ill-clothed, ill-housed, and insecure.

This Republic had its beginning, and grew to its present strength, under the protection of certain inalienable° political rights—among them the right of free speech, free press, free worship, trial by jury, freedom from unreasonable searches and seizures. They were our rights to life and liberty.

As our Nation has grown in size and stature, however—as our industrial economy expanded—these political rights proved inadequate to assure us equality in the pursuit of happiness.

We have come to a clear realization of the fact that true individual freedom cannot exist without economic security and independence. "Necessitous° men are not free men." People who are hungry and out of a job are the stuff of which dictatorships are made.

---

franchise: right to vote

inalienable: inviolable; i.e., incapable of being taken away

Necessitous: needy, poverty-stricken

In our day these economic truths have become accepted as self-evident. We have accepted, so to speak, a second Bill of Rights under which a new basis of security and prosperity can be established for all regardless of station, race, or creed.

Among these are:

60

The right to a useful and remunerative° job in the industries or shops or farms or mines of the Nation;

The right to earn enough to provide adequate food and clothing and recreation;

The right of every farmer to raise and sell his products at a return which will give him and his family a decent living;

The right of every businessman, large and small, to trade in an atmosphere of freedom from unfair competition and domination by monopolies at home or abroad;

The right of every family to a decent home;

The right to adequate medical care and the opportunity to achieve and enjoy good health;

The right to adequate protection from the economic fears of old age, sickness, accident, and unemployment;

The right to a good education.

All of these rights spell security. And after this war is won we must be prepared to move forward, in the implementation of these rights, to new goals of human happiness and well-being.

America's own rightful place in the world depends in large part upon how fully these and similar rights have been carried into practice for our citizens. For unless there is security here at home there cannot be lasting peace in the world.

One of the great American industrialists of our day—a man who has rendered yeoman° service to his country in this crisis—recently emphasized the grave dangers of "rightist reaction" in this Nation. All clear-thinking businessmen share his concern. Indeed, if such reaction should develop—if history were to repeat itself and we were to return to the so-called "normalcy" of the 1920's—then it is certain that even though we shall have conquered our enemies on the battlefields abroad, we shall have yielded to the spirit of Fascism here at home.

I ask the Congress to explore the means for implementing this economic bill of rights—for it is definitely the responsibility of the Congress so to do. Many of these problems are already before committees of the Congress in the form of proposed

---

remunerative: profitable

yeoman: staunch; in a loyal and industrious manner

legislation. I shall from time to time communicate with the Congress with respect to these and further proposals. In the event that no adequate program of progress is evolved, I am certain that the Nation will be conscious of the fact.

Our fighting men abroad—and their families at home—expect such a program and have the right to insist upon it. It is to their demands that this Government should pay heed rather than to the whining demands of selfish pressure groups who seek to feather their nests while young Americans are dying. 65

The foreign policy that we have been following—the policy that guided us at Moscow, Cairo, and Teheran—is based on the common sense principle which was best expressed by Benjamin Franklin on July 4, 1776: "We must all hang together, or assuredly we shall all hang separately."

I have often said that there are no two fronts for America in this war. There is only one front. There is one line of unity which extends from the hearts of the people at home to the men of our attacking forces in our farthest outposts. When we speak of our total effort, we speak of the factory and the field, and the mine as well as of the battleground—we speak of the soldier and the civilian, the citizen and his Government.

Each and every one of us has a solemn obligation under God to serve this Nation in its most critical hour—to keep this Nation great—to make this Nation greater in a better world.

Read

1. Why does FDR believe in the need for a second Bill of Rights?
2. What does FDR mean when he says that people "who are hungry . . . are the stuff of which dictatorships are made?"
3. Who is the "we" the speech refers to?
4. Why are the paragraphs so brief? How does the arrangement affect your reading?

Write

1. Write about which of the rights FDR spells out seems guaranteed to Americans now.
2. Which rights seem not to be secured yet? Should they be?
3. Write a paragraph about what you see as the connection between security and democracy.
4. Add one more right you'd like to see in a new bill of rights.

Complete Additional Exercises on Roosevelt's Speech at Your Pearson MyLab

Connect

1. At the end of his speech, FDR cites Benjamin Franklin. How does the second Bill of Rights connect to either or both of the essays of Franklin's you read in Unit 1?
2. How does the second Bill of Rights extend and affirm the Declaration of Independence?

Eleanor Roosevelt

Eleanor Roosevelt (1884–1962) was the wife of Franklin Delano Roosevelt and a writer, speaker, and activist in her own right. She was born in New York City and raised by a grandmother after being orphaned early in life. Her social conscience developed early. While engaged to FDR, she took him on a tour of New York tenements to deepen his understanding of the problems of the poor. She helped promote FDR's recovery plan by giving speeches and meeting with women's groups across the country and remained in public life until her death. Her column *My Day,* which ran for over twenty years in many newspapers, documented her life in the White House and beyond.

Her support for women, for African Americans, and for oppressed people in the world was unwavering. She was an initiator of the United Nations and its early document, *The Universal Declaration of Human Rights*. President John F. Kennedy called her "the first lady of the world."

My Day

May 9, 1945

NEW YORK, Tuesday—All day yesterday, as I went about New York City, the words "V-E Day"° were on everybody's lips. Part of the time, paper fluttered through the air until the gutters of the streets were filled with it. At Times Square crowds gathered—but that first report the other night had taken the edge off this celebration. No word came through from Washington and everybody still waited for official confirmation. Today it has come.

Over the radio this morning President Truman, Prime Minister Churchill and Marshal Stalin have all spoken—the war in Europe is over. Unconditional surrender has been accepted by the Germans. I can almost hear my husband's voice make that announcement,° for I heard him repeat it so often. The German leaders were not willing to accept defeat, even when they knew it was inevitable, until they had made their people drink the last dregs in the cup of complete conquest by the Allies.

* * *

Europe is in ruins and the weary work of reconstruction must now begin. There must be joy, of course, in the hearts of the peoples whom the Nazis conquered and who are now free again. Freedom without bread, however, has little meaning.

V-E Day: for Victory in Europe; celebrated in the United States on May 8, 1945

I can . . . announcement: President Franklin Delano Roosevelt had died suddenly, of a cerebral hemorrhage, on April 12, 1945.

My husband always said that freedom from want° and freedom from aggression were twin freedoms which had to go hand in hand.

The necessity to share with our brothers, even though it means hardship for ourselves, will now face all of us who live in the fortunate countries which war has not devastated.

I cannot feel a spirit of celebration today. I am glad that our men are no longer going to be shot at and killed in Europe, but the war in the Pacific still goes on. Men are dying there, even as I write. It is far more a day of dedication for us, a day on which to promise that we will do our utmost to end war and build peace. Some of my own sons,° with millions of others, are still in danger.

I can but pray that the Japanese leaders will not force their people to complete destruction too. The ultimate end is sure, but in the hands of the Japanese leaders lies the decision° of how many people will have to suffer before ultimate peace comes.

* * *

What are our ultimate objectives now? Do we want our Allies in Europe, and later in the Far East, to have the opportunity to rebuild quickly? Looked at selfishly, we will probably gain materially if they do. That cannot be our only responsibility, however. The men who fought this war are entitled to a chance to build a lasting peace. What we do in the next months may give them that chance or lose it for them. If we give people bread, we may build friendship among the peoples of the world; and we will never have peace without friendship around the world. This is the time for a long look ahead. This is the time for us all to decide where we go from here.

E. R.

[1945]

Read

1. How does Eleanor Roosevelt's diction suggest her attitude toward the end of the war?
2. What kinds of changes does Eleanor Roosevelt envision now that the war in Europe is ended?
3. How does she characterize the post-war responsibilities of the United States?
4. What is the effect of the rhetorical questions at the end of the column?

---

want: need, destitution

Some of my own sons: all four of the Roosevelts' sons were on active military duty during World War II.

In the hands . . . decision: Japan surrendered on August 14, 1945, after the dropping of atomic bombs on the cities of Hiroshima (August 6) and Nagasaki (August 9).

Write

1. Write your own "My Day" column, reflecting, like Eleanor Roosevelt, on the conclusion of a serious time, personal or public. See how closely you can imitate in style or arrangement.
2. In a paragraph and with at least one specific example, comment on how you see Eleanor Roosevelt's plan for peace as workable or unworkable.

Complete Additional Exercises on Roosevelt's Essay at Your Pearson MyLab

Connect

1. Consider the links between Eleanor Roosevelt and Jane Addams, tracing some similarities in style as well as in approach to world events.
2. How do you see this column affirming Franklin D. Roosevelt's speech? How is the rhetoric different?

Alfred Eisenstaedt

This photo was widely printed in newspapers on VJ Day—August 14, 1945, the day the Japanese surrendered in World War II.

Happy Sailor Kissing Nurse, Times Square

[1945]

Read

1. How does the placement of the figures suggest emotion to the viewer?
2. How does knowing the year tell the "story" of the photograph?

Write

1. This photo was widely printed in newspapers on VJ Day, August 14, 1945. That was the day the Japanese surrendered in World War II. Using the photo and your experience or knowledge, write a small human interest story that might accompany it.
2. If you had to put a one-word title to the photo, what would it be? Explain your choice.

Connect

1. Compare the photo to Eleanor Roosevelt's column, written on VE Day (May 9, 1945, the day the Germans surrendered). How do they suggest similar emotions? How do they differ?

Huey P. Long

Huey Pierce Long (1893–1935) was born in Louisiana. A lawyer, the governor of Louisiana, and a U.S. Senator from 1932–1935, Long was known as a champion of the common people and an enemy of corporations and big business. He established public works programs, built roads and schools, and attempted to create tax structures that would favor the working class. He supported FDR for president, but later criticized many New Deal programs. In 1934, he created the Share Our Wealth Society, whose motto was "Every man a king" and whose aim was to tax corporations to curb the poverty and homelessness of the Great Depression. He was assassinated in 1935.

Sharing Our Wealth

President Roosevelt was elected on November 8, 1932. People look upon an elected President as the President. This is January 1935. We are in our third year of the Roosevelt depression, with the conditions growing worse. . . .

We must now become awakened! We must know the truth and speak the truth.

There is no use to wait three more years. It is not Roosevelt or ruin; it is Roosevelt's ruin.

Now, my friends, it makes no difference who is President or who is senator. America is for 125 million people and the unborn to come. We ran

Mr. Roosevelt for the presidency of the United States because he promised to us by word of mouth and in writing:

1. That the size of the big man's fortune would be reduced so as to give the masses at the bottom enough to wipe out all poverty; and
2. That the hours of labor would be so reduced that all would share in the work to be done and in consuming the abundance mankind produced.

Hundreds of words were used by Mr. Roosevelt to make these promises to the people, but they were made over and over again. He reiterated these pledges even after he took his oath as President. Summed up, what these promises meant was: "Share our wealth." 5

When I saw him spending all his time of ease and recreation with the business partners of Mr. John D. Rockefeller, Jr.,° with such men as the Astors,° etc., maybe I ought to have had better sense than to have believed he would ever break down their big fortunes to give enough to the masses to end poverty—maybe some will think me weak for ever believing it all, but millions of other people were fooled the same as myself. I was like a drowning man grabbing at a straw, I guess. The face and eyes, the hungry forms of mothers and children, the aching hearts of students denied education were before our eyes, and when Roosevelt promised, we jumped for that ray of hope.

. . .

So therefore I call upon the men and women of America to immediately join in our work and movement to share our wealth.

There are thousands of share-our-wealth societies organized in the United States now. We want 100,000 such societies formed for every nook and corner of this country—societies that will meet, talk, and work, all for the purpose that the great wealth and abundance of this great land that belongs to us may be shared and enjoyed by all of us.

We have nothing more for which we should ask the Lord. He has allowed this land to have too much of everything that humanity needs.

So in this land of God's abundance we propose laws, viz.°: 10

1. The fortunes of the multimillionaires and billionaires shall be reduced so that no one person shall own more than a few million dollars to the

---

John D. Rockefeller, Jr.: (1874–1960), son of the founder of Standard Oil (the predecessor of ExxonMobil), was reviled by many because of the violence used in breaking a coal miners' strike in Ludlow, Colorado, in 1914

the Astors: the descendants of the original John Jacob Astor (1763–1848), a fur trader who became the first American multimillionaire

viz.: abbreviation of the Latin term *videlicet,* meaning "namely, that is to say"

person. We would do this by a capital levy tax.° On the first million that a man was worth, we would not impose any tax. We would say, "All right for your first million dollars, but after you get that rich you will have to start helping the balance of us." So we would not levy any capital levy tax on the first million one owned. But on the second million a man owns, we would tax that 1 percent, so that every year the man owned the second million dollars he would be taxed $10,000. On the third million we would impose a tax of 2 percent. On the fourth million we would impose a tax of 4 percent. On the fifth million we would impose a tax of 8 percent. On the sixth million we would impose a tax of 16 percent. On the seventh million we would impose a tax of 32 percent. On the eighth million we would impose a tax of 64 percent; and on all over the eighth million we would impose a tax of 100 percent.

What this would mean is that the annual tax would bring the biggest fortune down to $3 or $4 million to the person because no one could pay taxes very long in the higher brackets. But $3 to $4 million is enough for any one person and his children and his children's children. We cannot allow one to have more than that because it would not leave enough for the balance to have something.

2. We propose to limit the amount any one man can earn in one year or inherit to $1 million to the person.
3. Now, by limiting the size of the fortunes and incomes of the big men, we will throw into the government Treasury the money and property from which we will care for the millions of people who have nothing; and with this money we will provide a home and the comforts of home, with such common conveniences as radio and automobile, for every family in America, free of debt.
4. We guarantee food and clothing and employment for everyone who should work by shortening the hours of labor to thirty hours per week, maybe less, and to eleven months per year, maybe less. We would have the hours shortened just so much as would give work to everybody to produce enough for everybody; and if we were to get them down to where they were too short, then we would lengthen them again.

   As long as all the people working can produce enough of automobiles, radios, homes, schools, and theaters for everyone to have that kind of comfort and convenience, then let us all have work to do and have that much of heaven on earth.
5. We would provide education at the expense of the states and the United States for every child, not only through grammar school and high school but through to a college and vocational education. We would

---

capital levy tax: a tax on capital or property, as opposed to income

simply extend the Louisiana plan° to apply to colleges and all people. Yes; we would have to build thousands of more colleges and employ 100,000 more teachers; but we have materials, men, and women who are ready and available for the work. Why have the right to a college education depend upon whether the father or mother is so well-to-do as to send a boy or girl to college?

We would give every child the right to education and a living at birth.

6. We would give a pension to all persons above sixty years of age in an amount sufficient to support them in comfortable circumstances, excepting those who earn $1,000 per year or who are worth $10,000.
7. Until we could straighten things out—and we can straighten things out in two months under our program—we would grant a moratorium on all debts which people owe that they cannot pay.

And now you have our program, none too big, none too little, but every man a king.

We owe debts in America today, public and private, amounting to $252 billion.

That means that every child is born with a $2,000 debt tied around his neck to hold him down before he gets started. Then, on top of that, the wealth is locked in a vise owned by a few people. We propose that children shall be born in a land of opportunity, guaranteed a home, food, clothes, and the other things that make for living, including the right to education.

Our plan would injure no one. It would not stop us from having millionaires—it would increase them tenfold, because so many more people could make $1 million if they had the chance our plan gives them. Our plan would not break up big concerns.° The only difference would be that maybe 10,000 people would own a concern instead of 10 people owning it. But, my friends, unless we do share our wealth, unless we limit the size of the big man so as to give something to the little man, we can never have a happy or free people. God said so! He ordered it.

We have everything our people need. Too much of food, clothes, and houses—why not let all have their fill and lie down in the ease and comfort God has given us? Why not? Because a few own everything—the masses own nothing. 15

I wonder if any of you people who are listening to me were ever at a barbecue! We used to go there—sometimes 1,000 people or more. If there were 1,000 people, we would put enough meat and bread and everything else on the table for 1,000 people. Then everybody would be called and everyone would eat all

---

the Louisiana plan: Among Long's reforms as governor of Louisiana had been the provision of free textbooks, expansion of literacy programs, and increased access to higher education.

concerns: commercial or manufacturing companies

they wanted. But suppose at one of these barbecues for 1,000 people that one man took 90 percent of the food and ran off with it and ate until he got sick and let the balance rot. Then 999 people would have only enough for 100 to eat and there would be many to starve because of the greed of just one person for something he couldn't eat himself.

Well, ladies and gentlemen, America, all the people of America, have been invited to a barbecue. God invited us all to come and eat and drink all we wanted. He smiled on our land and we grew crops of plenty to eat and wear. He showed us in the earth the iron and other things to make everything we wanted. He unfolded to us the secrets of science so that our work might be easy. God called: "Come to my feast."

Then what happened? Rockefeller, Morgan, and their crowd stepped up and took enough for 120 million people and left only enough for 5 million for all the other 125 million to eat. And so many millions must go hungry and without these good things God gave us unless we call on them to put some of it back.

[1935]

Read

1. How do you know from the first three paragraphs that Long's text is a speech rather than an essay?
2. How would you describe the relationship Long creates with his readers?
3. What are Long's feelings about FDR? Why does he have those feelings?
4. What is the aim of the numbered list Long offers?

Write

1. Long is famous for his phrase "every man a king." Write a paragraph that explains how Long hopes to make that ideal happen.
2. Analyze the kinds of appeals Long uses to connect to and persuade his audience.
3. Write a brief description of the persona Long creates in his diction and imagery.
4. How do you feel about Long's plan? What seems reasonable? What seems unworkable?

Connect

1. How do the images used by FDR in his talk and Huey Long in his speech convey their writer's approach to and understanding of audience?
2. Reflect on how this speech compares with current events or conversations in Congress.
3. Compare the attitudes about the "common man" implied in Long's speech with another writer in this or an earlier unit who speaks for that group. (Riis, Twain, Bryant, Franklin, Steinem are some possible choices).

Brown Brothers

This cartoon was first published in the Cleveland *Plain Dealer* in 1933, during the Great Depression.

An Old Idea

[1933]

Read

1. This cartoon was titled “An Old Idea.” What does that suggest about the cartoonist’s feeling about the issue the cartoon characterizes?
2. How does the dress and movement of the Employer (and the location of his identification) suggest the cartoonist’s perspective on the issue?
3. What is the cliché that fits this cartoon’s message?
4. What are other details that seem significant to you in reading the cartoonist’s aim?

Write

1. Write a paragraph describing the situation as the picture reveals it.
2. Identify each of the players in the scene and describe the part each one plays in the design of the cartoon.
3. How would you describe the wrong headedness of the solution the Employer seems to be offering?

Connect

1. How does the solution proposed by the Employer link to the "solution" offered by internment of the Japanese during World War II?
2. Can you draw connections to the situation of Native Americans as described by writers in Units 1–4?

John Dos Passos

John Dos Passos (1896–1970) was born to a wealthy New York family, attended Harvard, and joined the Army when the country entered World War 1 in 1917. His shock at the violence and waste he witnessed stayed with him throughout his life, and he became a vocal critic of war and a crusader for social justice. His novels, especially *U.S.A.*, are written in an experimental style that combined newsreels, biography, narratives, and descriptive scenes. *U.S.A.* attempts to characterize the history of the country and its need for change.

From *U.S.A.*

Preface

The young man walks fast by himself through the crowd that thins into the night streets; feet are tired from hours of walking; eyes greedy for warm curve of faces, answering flicker of eyes, the set of a head, the lift of a shoulder, the way hands spread and clench; blood tingles with wants; mind is a beehive of hopes buzzing and stinging; muscles ache for the knowledge of jobs, for the roadmender's pick and shovel work, the fisherman's knack with a hook when he hauls on the slithery net from the rail of the lurching trawler, the swing of the bridgeman's arm as he slings down the whitehot rivet, the engineer's slow grip wise on the throttle, the dirtfarmer's use of his whole body when, whoaing the mules, he yanks the plow from the furrow. The young man walks by himself searching through the crowd with greedy eyes, greedy ears taut to hear, by himself, alone.

The streets are empty. People have packed into subways, climbed into streetcars and buses; in the stations they've scampered for suburban trains; they've filtered into lodgings and tenements, gone up in elevators into apartment-houses. In a show-window two sallow° window-dressers in their shirtsleeves are bringing out a dummy girl in a red evening dress, at a corner welders in masks lean into sheets of

sallow: of an unhealthy pale or yellow complexion

blue flame repairing a cartrack,° a few drunk bums shamble along, a sad streetwalker fidgets under an arclight. From the river comes the deep rumbling whistle of a steamboat leaving dock. A tug° hoots far away.

The young man walks by himself, fast but not fast enough, far but not far enough (faces slide out of sight, talk trails into tattered scraps, footsteps tap fainter in alleys); he must catch the last subway, the streetcar, the bus, run up the gangplanks of all the steamboats, register at all the hotels, work in the cities, answer the want-ads, learn the trades, take up the jobs, live in all the boardinghouses, sleep in all the beds. One bed is not enough, one job is not enough, one life is not enough. At night, head swimming with wants, he walks by himself alone.

No job, no woman, no house, no city.

Only the ears busy to catch the speech are not alone; the ears are caught tight, linked tight by the tendrils° of phrased words, the turn of a joke, the singsong fade of a story, the gruff fall of a sentence; linking tendrils of speech twine through the city blocks, spread over pavements, grow out along broad parked avenues, speed with the trucks leaving on their long night runs over roaring highways, whisper down sandy byroads past wornout farms, joining up cities and fillingstations, roundhouses,° steamboats, planes groping along airways; words call out on mountain pastures, drift slow down rivers widening to the sea and the hushed beaches. 5

It was not in the long walks through jostling crowds at night that he was less alone, or in the training camp at Allentown,° or in the day on the docks at Seattle, or in the empty reek of Washington City hot boyhood summer nights, or in the meal on Market Street,° or in the swim off the red rocks at San Diego, or in the bed full of fleas in New Orleans, or in the cold razor-wind off the lake, or in the gray faces trembling in the grind of gears in the street under Michigan Avenue,° or in the smokers° of limited expresstrains, or walking across country, or riding up the dry mountain canyons, or the night without a sleepingbag among frozen bear-tracks in the Yellowstone, or canoeing Sundays in the Quinnipiac;°

---

cartrack: for a streetcar

tug: tugboat

tendrils: threadlike parts by which twining plants and vines attach themselves to other objects

roundhouses: large buildings where locomotives are serviced and repaired

Allentown: A volunteer ambulance driver during World War I, Dos Passos was stationed for a time at Camp Crane in Allentown, Pennsylvania.

Market Street: name of a major street in both Philadelphia and San Francisco

Michigan Avenue: in Chicago

smokers: smoking cars

Quinnipiac: a river in Connecticut

but in his mother's words telling about long ago, in his father's telling about when I was a boy, in the kidding stories of uncles, in the lies the kids told at school, the hired man's yarns, the tall tales the doughboys told after taps;

it was the speech that clung to the ears, the link that tingled in the blood; U.S.A.

U.S.A. is the slice of a continent. U.S.A. is a group of holding companies,° some aggregations° of trade unions, a set of laws bound in calf,° a radio network, a chain of moving picture theatres, a column of stock-quotations rubbed out and written in by a Western Union boy on a blackboard, a public-library full of old newspapers and dog-eared° historybooks with protests scrawled on the margins in pencil. U.S.A. is the world's greatest rivervalley fringed with mountains and hills, U.S.A. is a set of bigmouthed officials with too many bank accounts. U.S.A. is a lot of men buried in their uniforms in Arlington Cemetery. U.S.A. is the letters at the end of an address when you are away from home. But mostly U.S.A. is the speech of the people.

[1938]

Read

1. What is the effect of the first paragraph on your reading? What do you think its aim might be?
2. How does Dos Passos use jargon and other word choice to convey a message about Americans?
3. Who is John Doe?
4. How does arrangement help convey Dos Passos's argument?
5. What is the effect of the violent imagery near the end of the passage?

Write

1. Using any topic from current events, imitate Dos Passos's style: punctuation, arrangement, typeface, syntax, or other elements that seem significant to you.
2. Write a paragraph that analyzes the irony you find in the passage, quoting lines of words that seem especially important to the ironic message.

Connect

1. Find other characters in earlier literature (Huck Finn, Samson Occom are two) that you find similar to John Doe. Consider how they might be alike. Is there a female character who is like John Doe?
2. Consider one visual that provokes the ironic response evoked by this piece and compare the two.

---

holding companies: companies that hold silent controlling stock in other companies

aggregations: groups

calf: calfskin, the customary binding of lawbooks

dogeared: with corners of pages turned down

Meridel LeSueur

Meridel LeSueur (1900–1996) was a respected and prolific journalist and fiction writer whose career spanned over sixty years. Born in Iowa, LeSueur was the daughter of a politically active mother who introduced her to popular reform movements in the Midwest such as populism and the Industrial Workers of the World. During the Great Depression, LeSueur chronicled the hardships of working people, especially women, whose struggles were often overlooked. In addition to newspaper columns, she wrote a memoir and history of the Midwest, *North Star,* published in 1945. Her last volume, a collection of poetry published in 1975, shows the influence on her of American Indian traditions and culture.

Women on the Breadlines

I am sitting in the city free employment bureau. It's the women's section. We have been sitting here now for four hours. We sit here every day, waiting for a job. There are no jobs. Most of us have had no breakfast. Some have had scant rations for over a year. Hunger makes a human being lapse into a state of lethargy, especially city hunger. Is there any place else in the world where a human being is supposed to go hungry amidst plenty without an outcry, without protest, where only the boldest steal or kill for bread, and the timid crawl the streets, hunger like the beak of a terrible bird at the vitals?

We sit looking at the floor. No one dares think of the coming winter. There are only a few more days of the summer. Everyone is anxious to get work to lay up something for that long siege of bitter cold. But there is no work. Sitting in the room we all know it. That is why we don't talk much. We look at the floor dreading to see that knowledge in each other's eyes. There is a kind of humiliation in it. We look away from each other. We look at the floor. It's too terrible to see this animal terror in each other's eyes.

So we sit hour after hour, day after day, waiting for a job to come in. There are many women for a single job. A thin sharp woman sits inside a wire cage looking at a book. For four hours we have watched her looking at that book. She has a hard little eye. In the small bare room there are half a dozen women sitting on the benches waiting. Many come and go. Our faces are all familiar to each other, for we wait here every day.

This is a domestic employment bureau. Most of the women who come here are middle-aged, some have families, some have raised their families and are now alone, some have men who are out of work. Hard times and the man leaves to hunt for work. He doesn't find it. He drifts on. The woman probably doesn't hear from him for a long time. She expects it. She isn't surprised. She struggles alone to feed the many mouths. Sometimes she gets help from the charities. If she's clever she can get herself a good living from the charities, if she's naturally a lick spittle, naturally a little docile and cunning. If she's proud then she starves silently, leaving her children to find work, coming home after a day's searching to wrestle with her house, her children.

Some such story is written on the faces of all these women. There are young girls, too, fresh from the country. Some are made brazen too soon by the city. There is a great exodus of girls from the farms into the city now. Thousands of farms have been vacated completely in Minnesota. The girls are trying to get work. The prettier ones can get jobs in the stores when there are any, or waiting on table, but these jobs are only for the attractive and the adroit. The others, the real peasants, have a more difficult time.

* * *

Bernice sits next to me. She is a Polish woman of thirty-five. She has been working in people's kitchens for fifteen years or more. She is large, her great body in mounds, her face brightly scrubbed. She has a peasant mind and finds it hard even yet to understand the maze of the city where trickery is worth more than brawn. Her blue eyes are not clever but slow and trusting. She suffers from loneliness and lack of talk. When you speak to her, her face lifts and brightens as if you had spoken through a great darkness, and she talks magically of little things as if the weather were magic, or tells some crazy tale of her adventures on the city streets, embellishing them in bright colors until they hang heavy and thick like embroidery. She loves the city anyhow. It's exciting to her, like a bazaar. She loves to go shopping and get a bargain, hunting out the places where stale bread and cakes can be had for a few cents. She likes walking the streets looking for men to take her to a picture show. Sometimes she goes to five picture shows in one day, or she sits through one the entire day until she knows all the dialog by heart.

She came to the city a young girl from a Wisconsin farm. The first thing that happened to her, a charlatan dentist took out all her good shining teeth and the fifty dollars she had saved working in a canning factory. After that she met men in the park who told her how to look out for herself, corrupting her peasant mind, teaching her to mistrust everyone. Sometimes now she forgets to mistrust everyone and gets taken in. They taught her to get what she could for nothing, to count her change, to go back if she found herself cheated, to demand her rights.

She lives alone in little rooms. She bought seven dollars' worth of second-hand furniture eight years ago. She rents a room for perhaps three dollars a month in an attic, sometimes in a cold house. Once the house where she stayed was condemned and everyone else moved out and she lived there all winter alone on the top floor. She spent only twenty-five dollars all winter.

She wants to get married but she sees what happens to her married friends, left with children to support, worn out before their time. So she stays single. She is virtuous. She is slightly deaf from hanging out clothes in winter. She had done people's washing and cooking for fifteen years and in that time saved thirty dollars. Now she hasn't worked steady for a year and she has spent the thirty dollars. She had dreamed of having a little house or a houseboat perhaps with a spot of ground for a few chickens. This dream she will never realize.

She has lost all her furniture now along with the dream. A married friend whose husband is gone gives her a bed for which she pays by doing a great deal of work for the woman. She comes here every day now sitting bewildered, her pudgy hands folded in her lap, She is hungry. Her great flesh has begun to hang in folds. She has been living on crackers. Sometimes a box of crackers lasts a week. She has a friend who's a baker and he sometimes steals the stale loaves and brings them to her.

* * *

A girl we have seen every day all summer went crazy yesterday at the YW. She went into hysterics, stamping her feet and screaming.

She hadn't had work for eight months. "You've got to give me something," she kept saying. The woman in charge flew into a rage that probably came from days and days of suffering on her part, because she is unable to give jobs, having none. She flew into a rage at the girl and there they were facing each other in a rage both helpless, helpless. This woman told me once that she could hardly bear the suffering she saw, hardly hear it, that she couldn't eat sometimes and had nightmares at night.

So they stood there, the two women, in a rage, the girl weeping and the woman shouting at her. In the eight months of unemployment she had gotten ragged, and the woman was shouting that she would not send her out like that. "Why don't you shine your shoes?" she kept scolding the girl, and the girl kept sobbing and sobbing because she was starving.

"We can't recommend you like that," the harassed YWCA woman said, knowing she was starving, unable to do anything. And the girls and the women sat docilely, their eyes on the ground, ashamed to look at each other, ashamed of something.

Sitting here waiting for a job, the women have been talking in low voices about the girl Ellen. They talk in low voices with not too much pity for her, unable to see through the mist of their own torment.

"What happened to Ellen?" one of them asks. She knows the answer already. We all know it.

A young girl who went around with Ellen tells about seeing her last evening back of a café downtown, outside the kitchen door, kicking, showing her legs so that the cook came out and gave her some food and some men gathered in the alley and threw small coin on the ground for a look at her legs. And the girl says enviously that Ellen had a swell breakfast and treated her to one too, that cost two dollars.

A scrub woman whose hips are bent forward from stooping with hands gnarled like water-soaked branches clicks her tongue in disgust. No one saves their money, she says, a little money and these foolish young things buy a hat, a dollar for breakfast, a bright scarf. And they do. If you've ever been without money, or food, something very strange happens when you get a bit of money, a kind of madness. You don't care. You can't remember that you had no money before, that the money will be gone. You can remember nothing but that there is the money for which you have been suffering. Now here it is. A lust takes hold of you. You see food in the windows. In imagination you eat hugely; you taste a thousand meals. You look in windows. Colors are brighter; you buy something to dress up in. An excitement takes hold of you. You know it is suicide but you can't help it. You must have food, dainty, splendid food, and a bright hat so once again you feel blithe, rid of that ratty gnawing shame.

* * *

"I guess she'll go on the street now," a thin woman says faintly, and no one takes the trouble to comment further. Like every commodity now the body is difficult to sell and the girls say you're lucky if you get fifty cents.

It's very difficult and humiliating to sell one's body.

Perhaps it would make it clear if one were to imagine having to go out on the street to sell, say, one's overcoat. Suppose you have to sell your coat so you can have breakfast and a place to sleep, say, for fifty cents. You decide to sell your only coat. You take it off and put it on your arm. The street, that has before been just a street, now becomes a mart, something entirely different. You must approach someone now and admit you are destitute and are now selling your clothes, your most intimate possessions. Everyone will watch you talking to the stranger showing him your overcoat, what a good coat it is. People will stop and watch curiously. You will be quite naked on the street. It is even harder to try to sell one's self, more humiliating. It is even humiliating to try to sell one's labor. When there is no buyer.

The thin woman opens the wire cage. There's a job for a nursemaid, she says. The old gnarled women, like old horses, know that no one will have them walk the streets with the young so they don't move. Ellen's friend gets up and goes to the window. She is unbelievably jaunty. I know she hasn't had work since last January. But she has a flare of life in her that glows like a tiny red flame and some tenacious thing, perhaps only youth, keeps it burning bright. Her legs are thin but the runs in her old stockings are neatly mended clear down her flat shank. Two bright spots of rouge conceal her pallor. A narrow belt is drawn tightly around her thin waist, her long shoulder's stoop and the blades show. She runs wild as a colt hunting pleasure, hunting sustenance.

It's one of the great mysteries of the city where women go when they are out of work and hungry. There are not many women in the bread line. There are no flop houses for women as there are for men, where a bed can be had for a quarter or less. You don't see women lying on the floor at the mission in the free flops. They obviously don't sleep in the jungle or under newspapers in the park. There is no law I suppose against their being in these places but the fact is they rarely are.

Yet there must be as many women out of jobs in cities and suffering extreme poverty as there are men. What happens to them? Where do they go? Try to get into the YW without any money or looking down at heel. Charities take care of very few and only those that are tailed "deserving." The lone girl is under suspicion by the virgin women who dispense charity.

I've lived in cities for many months broke, without help, too timid to get in bread lines. I've known many women to live like this until they simply faint on the street from privations, without saying a word to anyone. A woman will shut herself up in a room until it is taken away from her, and eat a cracker a day and be as quiet as a mouse so there are no social statistics concerning her.

I don't know why it is, but a woman will do this unless she has dependents, will go for weeks verging on starvation, crawling in some hole, going through the streets ashamed, sitting in libraries, parks, going for days without speaking to a living soul like some exiled beast, keeping the runs mended in her stockings, shut up in terror in her own misery, until she becomes too super-sensitive and timid to even ask for a job.

Bernice says even strange men she has met in the park have sometimes, that is in better days, given her a loan to pay her room rent. She has always paid them back.

In the afternoon the young girls, to forget the hunger and the deathly torture and fear of being jobless, try to pick up a man to take them to a ten-cent show. They never go to more expensive ones, but they can always find a man willing to spend a dime to have the company of a girl for the afternoon.

Sometimes a girl facing the night without shelter will approach a man for lodging. A woman always asks a man for help. Rarely another woman. I have known girls to sleep in men's rooms for the night on a pallet without molestation and be given breakfast in the morning.

It's no wonder these young girls refuse to marry, refuse to rear children. They are like certain savage tribes, who, when they have been conquered, refuse to breed.

Not one of them but looks forward to starvation for the coming winter. We are in a jungle and know it. We are beaten, entrapped. There is no way out. Even if there were a job, even if that thin acrid woman came and gave everyone in the room a job for a few days, a few hours, at thirty cents an hour, this would all be repeated tomorrow, the next day and the next.

Not one of these women but knows that despite years of labor there is only starvation, humiliation in front of them.

* * *

Mrs. Gray, sitting across from me, is a living spokeman for the futility of labor. She is a warning. Her hands are scarred with labor. Her body is a great puckered scar. She has given birth to six children, buried three, supported them all alive and dead, bearing them, burying them, feeding them. Bred in hunger they have been spare, susceptible to disease. For seven years she tried to save her boy's arm from amputation, diseased from tuberculosis of the bone. It is almost too suffocating to think of that long close horror of years of child-bearing, child-feeding, rearing, with the bare suffering of providing a meal and shelter.

Now she is fifty. Her children, economically insecure, are drifters. She never hears of them. She doesn't know if they are alive. She doesn't know if she is alive. Such subtleties of suffering are not for her. For her the brutality of hunger and cold. Not until these are done away with can those subtle feelings that make a human being be indulged.

She is lucky to have five dollars ahead of her. That is her security. She has a tumor that she will die of. She is thin as a worn dime with her tumor sticking out of her side. She is brittle and bitter. Her face is not the face of a human being. She has borne more than it is possible for a human being to bear. She is reduced to the least possible denominator of human feelings.

It is terrible to see her little bloodshot eyes like a beaten hound's, fearful in terror.

We cannot meet her eyes. When she looks at any of us we look away. She is like a woman drowning and we turn away. We must ignore those eyes that are surely the eyes of a person drowning, doomed. She doesn't cry out. She goes down decently. And we all look away.

The young ones know though. I don't want to marry. I don't want any children. So they all say. No children. No marriage. They arm themselves alone, keep up alone. The man is helpless now. He cannot provide. If he propagates he cannot take care of his young. The means are not in his hands. So they live alone. Get what fun they can. The life risk is too horrible now. Defeat is too clearly written on it.

So we sit in this room like cattle, waiting for a nonexistent job, willing to work to the farthest atom of energy, unable to work, unable to get food and lodging, unable to bear children—here we must sit in this shame looking at the floor, worse than beasts at slaughter.

It is appalling to think that these women sitting so listless in the room may work as hard as it is possible for a human being to work, may labor night and day, like Mrs. Gray, wash streetcars from midnight to dawn and offices in the early evening, scrub for fourteen and fifteen hours a day, sleep only five hours or so, do this their whole lives, and never earn one day of security, having always before them the pit of the future. The endless labor, the bending back, the water-soaked hands, earning never more than a week's wages, never having in their hands more life than that.

It's not the suffering of birth, death, love that the young reject, but the suffering of endless labor without dream, eating the spare bread in bitterness, being a slave without the security of a slave.

[1932]

Read

1. How does the narrator establish the setting of her piece?
2. Who is the "we" the narrator talks about?
3. How does the speaker suggest tension in the first few paragraphs of the essay?
4. Identify any examples of irony you find in the text.

Write

1. Write a paragraph or so that describes the speaker's attitude toward the people she is describing. Use a phrase or line from the text to help your description.
2. In a sentence, write what you consider to be the aim in the essay.
3. In a paragraph, describe how stories are used by the speaker.
4. List a few adjectives that you think characterize the tone of the essay.

Connect

1. How does LeSueur's discussion of the plight of women compare to Jane Addams's narrative in Unit 4?
2. Consider how LeSueur's description of economic difficulties connects to other time periods in the literature you've read or in the culture today.

Langston Hughes

One of the most versatile and original twentieth-century writers, Langston Hughes (1902–1967) was born in Missouri and moved to Kansas and then Ohio when his parents divorced. He attended Columbia University for a year, worked on a freighter headed for Africa, and began writing poems. By 1925, he was being celebrated as a rising talent in what was to be called the Harlem Renaissance. His work was influenced by Paul Laurence Dunbar, Carl Sandburg, and W. E. B. Du Bois.

Hughes portrayed the life, humor, wit, and endurance of African Americans in short stories, essays, poetry, and history. He wrote 12 volumes of poetry. Hughes has been compared to Whitman in his love for the sweep of humanity and the possibility of transformation within democracy.

Freedom Train°

I read in the papers about the
    Freedom Train.
I heard on the radio about the
    Freedom Train.
I seen folks talkin' about the   5
    Freedom Train.
Lord, I been a-waitin' for the
    Freedom Train!
Down South in Dixie only train I see's
Got a Jim Crow car set aside for me.   10
I hope there ain't no Jim Crow on the Freedom Train,
No back door entrance to the Freedom Train,
No signs FOR COLORED on the Freedom Train,
No WHITE FOLKS ONLY on the Freedom Train.

I'm gonna check up on this   15
    Freedom Train.

Freedom Train: The poem was inspired by the Freedom Train, which toured all of the then forty-eight states between 1947 and 1949. Painted red, white, and blue, it was a traveling exhibit that displayed originals of the Declaration of Independence, the Bill of Rights, and the United States Constitution.

Who's the engineer on the Freedom Train?
Can a coal black man drive the Freedom Train?
Or am I still a porter on the Freedom Train?
Is there ballot boxes on the Freedom Train? 20
When it stops in Mississippi will it be made plain
Everybody's got a right to board the Freedom Train?

Somebody tell me about this
Freedom Train!

The Birmingham station's marked COLORED and WHITE. 25
The white folks go left, the colored go right—
They even got a segregated lane.
Is that the way to get aboard the Freedom Train?

I got to know about this
Freedom Train! 30

If my children ask me, *Daddy, please explain*
Why there's Jim Crow stations for the Freedom Train?
What shall I tell my children? . . . *You* tell me—
'Cause freedom ain't freedom when a man ain't free.

But maybe they explains it on the 35
Freedom Train.

When my grandmother in Atlanta, 83 and black,
Gets in line to see the Freedom,
Will some white man yell, *Get back!*
A Negro's got no business on tbe Freedom Track! 40

Mister, I thought it were the
Freedom Train!

Her grandson's name was Jimmy. He died at Anzio.°
He died for real. It warn't no show.

Anzio: a city on the west coast of Italy, about 35 miles south of Rome, was the site of a combined British and American landing on January 22, 1944 (several months before D-Day), followed by much fighting, many casualties, and, on June 4, the entry of American troops into Rome.

The freedom that they carryin' on this Freedom Train, 45
Is it for real—or just a show again?

Jimmy wants to know about the
Freedom Train.

Will *his* Freedom Train come zoomin' down the track
Gleamin' in the sunlight for white and black? 50
Not stoppin' at no stations marked COLORED nor WHITE
Just stoppin' in the fields in the broad daylight,
Stoppin' in the country in the wide-open air
Where there never was no Jim Crow signs nowhere,
No Welcomin' Committees, nor Politicians of note, 55
No Mayors and such for which colored can't vote
And nary a sign of a color line—
For the Freedom Train will be yours and mine!

Then maybe from their graves in Anzio
The G.I.'s who fought will say, *We wanted it so!* 60
Black men and white will say, *Ain't it fine?*
At home they got a train that's yours and mine!

Then I'll shout, *Glory for the*
Freedom Train!
I'll holler, *Blow your whistle,* 65
Freedom Train!
Thank God-A-Mighty! Here's the
Freedom Train!
Get on board our Freedom Train!

[1947]

Read

1. How does repetition affect your reading of the poem?
2. How does Hughes establish irony in the first stanza?
3. What's the purpose of the ALL CAPS in the poem?
4. How does Hughes use World War II to help convey his purpose?
5. Do you sense a shift in tone in the poem anywhere? How might you account for it?

Write

1. This poem sounds like a song. Write a paragraph that explores techniques in the poem that make it seem musical and speculate on why Hughes would use those techniques.
2. Write about how Hughes uses other people to convey the difference between the "Freedom Train" and the society he lives in.

Connect

1. What similarities do you see between this poem and Antin's essay (Unit 4) or another text in this unit?
2. Hughes has been compared to Whitman. Find places in Whitman's work (Unit 3) where you see diction, syntax, voice, or place that show Whitman's influence on Hughes.

Tomás Rivera

Tomás Rivera (1935–1984) was born in Crystal City, Texas, the child of Mexican American migrant farm workers. He received a Ph.D. from the University Oklahoma in 1969 and served as Chancellor at University of California, Riverside, from 1979 until his death. Rivera was a pioneer in Mexican American literature, writing stories and poems about the lives of Chicano men and women and of the plight of migrant farm workers. His work depicts Mexican American culture linked to traditional Mexican values and to the English-speaking world in North America.

. . . And the Earth Did Not Part

The first time he felt hate and anger was when he saw his mother cry for his uncle and for his aunt. They had both gotten tuberculosis and each of them had been sent to different sanitoriums.° The children had then been parceled out among their aunts and uncles and they had taken care of them as best they could. His aunt had later died and shortly afterward his uncle had been brought home from the sanitorium, but he was already spitting blood every time he coughed. It was then that he saw his mother crying all the time. He had become angry because he couldn't strike back at anyone. He felt the same way now. But this time it was on account of his father.

"You should have left right away, son. Couldn't you see that your father was sick? All of you knew very well that he had been sunstruck before. Why didn't you come home?"

---

sanitoriums: places for long-term treatment of illness

"Well, I don't know. Since the rest of us were soaking wet with sweat we didn't realize it was so hot, but I guess when one has been sunstruck it's different. Anyway, I told him to sit under the tree that's at the end of the rows but he didn't want to. It was then that he started to vomit. Then we saw that he couldn't hoe and we had to drag him to get him under the tree. He didn't struggle anymore. He simply let us take him. He didn't put up a fuss or anything.

"Poor man, my poor husband. He hardly slept last night. Didn't you hear him outside the house? He was twisting and turning all night; it must be painful. God, how I pray he gets well. I've been giving him cool lemonade all day but his eyes are still glassy. If I had been in the field yesterday I assure you that he would not have had a sunstroke. Poor man, he'll have spasms all over his body for at least three days and three nights. Now all of you take care of yourselves. If it gets too hot, rest. Don't overwork yourselves. Don't pay attention to the boss if he hurries you. Since he is not the one breaking his back, he thinks it's easy."

He became angrier when he heard his father moan outside the shack. His father didn't stay inside because he said that he was overcome with anxiety whenever he did. He had to be outside where he could get fresh air. There he could stretch out on the grass and roll around when the spasms hit him. Then he thought about whether his father was going to die from the sunstroke. From time to time he would hear his father pray and ask God for help. At first he had hoped that he would get well soon but the following day he felt his anger increase. And he felt it increase more when his mother or his father clamored for the mercy of God. And their father's moans had awakened them that night and also at dawn and their mother had gotten up and had taken off his scapularies° from around his neck and had washed them for him. She had then lighted some small candles. But to no avail. It was the same as with his uncle and his aunt.

"What do you gain by doing that, mother? Don't tell me that you believe that sort of thing helped my uncle and my aunt? Why is it that we are here on earth as though buried alive? Either the germs eat us from the inside or the sun from the outside. Always some illness. And work, work, day in and day out. And for what? Poor father, he works just as hard as the rest of us, perhaps harder. He was born working, as he says. Barely five

---

scapularies: a pair of cloth squares worn under the clothing for religious purposes

years old and he was already out there planting corn with his father. After feeding the earth and the sun for such a long time, . . . one day unexpectedly he is felled by the sun. And powerless to do anything. And to top it off, praying to God. God doesn't even remember us . . . There must not be a God. . . . No, better not to say it, what if father should worsen? Poor man, at least that must give him some hope."

His mother noticed how furious he was and in the morning she told him to calm down, that everything was in the hands of God and that his father would get well with God's help.

"Come now, do you really believe that? God, I am sure, doesn't give a damn about us. Look, can you tell me if father is mean or without love? You tell me if he has ever hurt anyone?"

"Well, no."

"There you are. See? And my uncle and my aunt? You tell me. And now their poor children not knowing their parents. Why did He have to take them? So you see, God doesn't give a damn about us poor people. Look, why do we have to live under these conditions? Are we hurting anybody? You're such a good person and yet you have to suffer so much. Can't you see? Tell me!"

"Oh, son, don't talk like that. Don't question the will of God. The ground might open up and devour you for talking like that. One must resign oneself to the will of God. Please don't talk like that, son. You frighten me. It seems that already the devil is in your very blood."

"Well, perhaps. At least that way I could release my anger. I'm tired of asking, why? Why you? Why father? Why my uncle? Why my aunt? Why their children? Can you tell me why? Why should we always be tied to the dirt, half buried in the earth like animals without any hope of any kind? You know that the only thing we can look forward to is coming over here every year. And as you yourself say, one does not rest until one dies. I guess that is the way my uncle and my aunt felt, and that's the way father will eventually feel!"

"That's the way it is, son. Only death can bring us rest."

"But, why us?"

"Well, it is said that. . . ."

"Don't say it! Don't tell me anything! I know what you're going to tell me!—that the poor will go to heaven."

The day started out cloudy and he felt the cool morning breeze brush his eyelashes as he and his brothers and sisters started to work.

His mother had had to stay at home to take care of her husband. Thus he felt responsible for encouraging his brothers and sisters. In the morning, at least during the early hours, they were able to withstand the sun, but by ten-thirty the sun had suddenly completely cleared the sky and penetrated everything and everyone. They worked much slower because they would feel weakness and suffocation overcome them if they worked at a hurried pace. They then had to wipe the sweat from their eyes every few minutes because their eyes would become blurry.

"When you kids see blurry, stop working or slow down. When we get to the end of the rows we'll rest awhile to regain our strength. It's going to be hot today. I wish it would remain cloudy, as it was this morning. No one would complain then. But no, once the sun bears down not even a tiny cloud dares show itself out of sheer fright. The hell of it is, we'll be finished here by two and then we have to go to that field that is nothing but hills. It's ok on the top of the hill but when we're in the low parts it's suffocating. Not even the slightest breeze blows through there. Air almost doesn't enter. Remember?

"Yes."

"That's where we'll spend the hottest part of the day. Just drink a lot of water every few minutes even if the boss gets angry. If not you'll get sick. And if you can't take it any longer, tell me right away, ok? We'll go home. You saw what happened to father for holding out. The sun can suck the life out of you."

Just as they had thought, they had had to move to the other field by early afternoon. By three o'clock they were already sopping wet with sweat. Not a single part of their clothing remained dry. Every few minutes they stopped. Sometimes they gasped for breath, then everything became blurred and the fear of sunstroke creeped into them, but they continued. 5

"How do you feel?"

"Man, it's hot! But we have to keep going. At least until six. Only thing is that the water we have is no longer good for our thirst. How I wish I had a glass of cool water, real cold, just pulled up from the well, or an icy coke."

"You're crazy, you'd sure get sunstroke that way. Just don't work too fast. Let's see if we can hold up until six. Can you take it?"

At four o'clock the youngest became sick. He was only nine years old but since he was paid as an adult he tried to keep up with the others. He started to vomit and sat down, then he lay down. Fear stricken they all rushed over to him. He appeared to have fainted and when they opened his eyelids they found his eyes turned around. The one next to him in age started to cry but he told him immediately to shut up and help take him home. Spasms were moving over his small body. He then threw him on his back and carried him by himself. Once again he began asking why?

> "Why my father, and now my little brother? He is barely nine years old. Why? He has to work like an animal, tied to the ground. Father, Mother, and he, my little brother, how could they possibly be guilty of anything?"

Each step that he took toward the house brought forth the echo of the question "why?" Half way down the road he became furious and then he started to cry out of despair. His other brothers and sisters didn't know what to do and they also started to cry, but out of fear. He then began to swear. And he didn't know when, but what he said he had been wanting to say for a long time. He cursed God. Upon doing it he felt the fear instilled in him by time and by his parents. For a split second he saw the earth open up to devour him. But, although he didn't look down, he then felt himself walking on very solid ground; *it was harder than he had ever felt it.* Anger swelled up in him again and he released it by cursing God. Then he noticed that his little brother no longer appeared quite so ill. He didn't know if his other little brothers and sisters realized how serious his curse had been.

That evening he didn't go to sleep until very late. He was experiencing a peace that he had never known before. It seemed to him that he had completely detached himself from everything. He was no longer worried about his father nor about his brother. All that he looked forward to was the new day, the coolness of the morning. By dawn his father was better. He was on his way to recovery. His little brother was also almost completely free of spasms. Time after time he felt surprised at what he had done the previous afternoon. He had cursed God and the earth had not parted. He was going to tell his mother but he decided to keep it a secret. He only told her that the earth didn't devour anyone, and that the sun didn't destroy anyone either.

He left for work and he was faced with a very cool morning. There were clouds and for the first time he felt himself capable of doing and undoing whatever he chose. He looked toward the ground and he kicked it and said to it,

> "Not yet, you can't eat me yet. Someday. But I won't know."

[1971]

Read

1. What is the reaction of the narrator to his mother's tears?
2. How does the first exchange between the narrator and his mother reveal their relationship?
3. Who does the passage suggest the narrator is really angry at? Where do you see it?

Write

1. How does the writer provoke sympathy for the plight of his characters?
2. Write a comment about the significance of the title. Find a line in the text that helps you explain the significance.
3. Analyze the relationship between the narrator's anger and the peace he describes at the end of the passage.

Connect

1. How is Rivera's piece similar in its aim to another piece in the unit?
2. Write about the beneficial or the destructive effects of anger in this story and/or in your own experience.

William Faulkner

"I'm just a farmer who likes to tell stories," William Faulkner (1897–1962) once said to an interviewer. And, if not farming, the stories he told were almost all about the people who lived in the rural South. Faulkner grew up in Oxford, Mississippi, and spent most of his life there, except for his service in the British Royal Air Service during World War I and some work in California after the war. He created a fictional county in Mississippi, Yoknapatawpha County, to place characters and situations that delineated the racial politics, degeneration of the old South, and cultural change in the rural South.

Faulkner's style is often dreamlike and distorts time and space, a form described as "stream of consciousness." His novels have been praised for their style as well as depictions of racial insecurity and prejudice and Southern life. They include *The Sound and the Fury, Light in August,* and his last novel, *The Rivers,* which has been compared to *Adventures of Huckleberry Finn.* His style has been influential to many writers, including Toni Morrison. Faulkner won the Nobel Prize in Literature in 1950, the first American to win after World War II.

Nobel Prize Acceptance Speech, 1950

I feel that this award was not made to me as a man, but to my work—a life's work in the agony and sweat of the human spirit, not for glory and least of all for profit, but to create out of the materials of the human spirit something which did not exist before. So this award is only mine in trust. It will not be difficult to find a dedication for the money part of it commensurate° with the purpose and significance of its origin.° But I would like to do the same with the acclaim too, by using this moment as a pinnacle° from which I might be listened to by the young men and women already dedicated to the same anguish and travail,° among whom is already that one who will some day stand here where I am standing.

Our tragedy today is a general and universal physical fear so long sustained by now that we can even bear it. There are no longer problems of the spirit. There is only the question: When will I be blown up? Because of this, the young man or woman writing today has forgotten the problems of the human heart in conflict with itself which alone can make good writing because only that is worth writing about, worth the agony and the sweat.

He must learn them again. He must teach himself that the basest of all things is to be afraid; and, teaching himself that, forget it forever, leaving no room in his workshop for anything but the old verities° and truths of the heart, the old universal truths lacking which any story is ephemeral° and doomed—love and honor and pity and pride and compassion and sacrifice. Until he does so, he labors under a curse. He writes not of love but of lust, of defeats in which nobody loses anything of value, of victories without hope and, worst of all, without pity or compassion. His griefs grieve on no universal bones, leaving no scars. He writes not of the heart but of the glands.

Until he relearns these things, he will write as though he stood among and watched the end of man. I decline to accept the end of man. It is easy enough to say that man is immortal simply because he will endure: that when the last ding-dong of doom has clanged and faded from the last worthless rock hanging tideless in the last red and dying evening, that even then there will still be one more sound: that of his puny inexhaustible voice, still talking. I refuse to accept this. I believe that man will not merely endure: he will prevail. He is immortal, not because he alone among creatures has an inexhaustible voice, but because he has a soul, a spirit capable of compassion and sacrifice and endurance. The poet's, the writer's, duty is to write about these things. It is his privilege to help man endure by lifting his heart, by reminding him of the

---

commensurate: proportionate, corresponding

purpose . . . origin: In his will, Alfred Nobel had stipulated that the literature prize be awarded for "the most outstanding [body of] work of an idealistic tendency."

pinnacle: summit, peak

travail: labor, toil; agony

verities: true principles or ideas

ephemeral: fleeting, impermanent

courage and honor and hope and pride and compassion and pity and sacrifice which have been the glory of his past. The poet's voice need not merely be the record of man, it can be one of the props, the pillars to help him endure and prevail.

[1950]

Read

1. What does Faulkner suggest is the purpose of literature?
2. What is the reason for the fear Faulkner addresses in paragraph 2?
3. What does Faulkner advise young writers to take as their subjects?
4. What does he suggest they need to change about the subjects of fiction?
5. Why does Faulkner believe that "man is immortal"?

Write

1. Pick a topic that Faulkner would approve of for a young writer. Write a few paragraphs defending your choice.
2. Look back at the Introduction to the unit and consider how Faulkner reflects the sensibilities of the times in his speech.
3. Write four or five words or lines that you think capture Faulkner's persona in the speech.

Complete Additional Exercises on Faulkner's Speech at Your Pearson MyLab

Connect

1. Compare this speech with one other speech in terms of approach to audience, use of techniques.
2. How is Faulkner's idea to write about "the human heart" reflected in the writing of Twain, Hawthorne, Jacobs, Olsen, or others?

Jack Kerouac

Jack Kerouac (1922–1969), novelist and poet, was a pioneer in the Beat movement, a group of young writers whose post-war sensibilities led them to question authority, tradition, and the cultural norms. Instead, the Beats embraced new forms of expression, including improvisational jazz. Kerouac was born in Massachusetts, and his novel, *On the Road,* is the story of his journey west to find new experience and a new spirituality.

Kerouac wrote essays and produced 10 novels in draft. *On the Road*'s experimental autobiographical style influenced many writers in the sixties.

From *On the Road*

I first met Neal not long after my father died . . . I had just gotten over a serious illness that I won't bother to talk about except that it really had something to do with my father's death and my awful feeling that everything was dead. With the coming of Neal there really began for me that part of my life that you could call my life on the road. Prior to that I'd always dreamed of going west, seeing the country, always vaguely planning and never specifically taking off and so on. Neal is the perfect guy for the road because he actually was born on the road, when his parents were passing through Salt Lake City in 1926, in a jalopy, on their way to Los Angeles. First reports of Neal came to me through Hal Chase, who'd shown me a few letters from him written in Colorado reform school. I was tremendously interested in these letters because they so naively and sweetly asked for Hal to teach him all about Nietzsche° and all the wonderful intellectual things that Hal was so justly famous for. At one point Allen Ginsberg and I talked about these letters and wondered if we would ever meet the strange Neal Cassady. This is all far back, when Neal was not the way he is today, when he was a young jailkid shrouded in mystery. Then news came that Neal was out of reform school and was coming to New York for the first time; also there was talk that he had just married a 16 year old girl called Louanne. One day I was hanging around the Columbia campus and Hal and Ed White told me Neal had just arrived and was living in a guy called Bob Malkin's cold water pad in East Harlem, the Spanish Harlem. Neal had arrived the night before, the first time in NY, with his beautiful little sharp chick Louanne; they got off the Greyhound bus at 50 St. and cut around the corner looking for a place to eat and went right in Hector's, and since then Hector's cafeteria has always been a big symbol of NY for Neal. They spent money on beautiful big glazed cakes and creampuffs. All this time Neal was telling Louanne things like this, "Now darling here we are in Ny and although I haven't quite told you everything that I was thinking about when we crossed Missouri and especially at the point when we passed the Bonneville reformatory which reminded me of my jail problem it is absolutely necessary now to postpone all those leftover things concerning our personal lovethings and at once begin thinking of specific worklife plans . . ." and so on in the way that he had in his early days. I went to the coldwater flat° with the boys and Neal came to the door in his shorts. Louanne was jumping off quickly from the bed; apparently he was fucking with her. He always was doing so. This other guy who

---

Nietzsche: Friedrich Wilhelm Nietzsche (1844–1900), German philosopher
coldwater flat: an apartment lacking in modern conveniences

owned the place Bob Malkin was there but Neal had apparently dispatched him to the kitchen, probably to make coffee while he proceeded with his loveproblems. . . . for to him sex was the one and only holy and important thing in life, although he had to sweat and curse to make a living, and so on. My first impression of Neal was of a young Gene Autry°—trim, thin-hipped, blue eyes, with a real Oklahoma accent. In fact he'd just been working on a ranch, Ed Uhl's in Sterling Colo. before marrying L. and coming East. Louanne was a pretty, sweet little thing, but awfully dumb and capable of doing horrible things, as she proved a while later. I only mention this first meeting of Neal because of what he did. That night we all drank beer and I got drunk and blah-blahed somewhat, slept on the other couch, and in the morning, while we sat around dumbly smoking butts from ashtrays in the gray light of a gloomy day Neal got up nervously, paced around thinking, and decided the thing to do was have Louanne making breakfast and sweeping the floor. Then I went away. That was all I knew of Neal at the outset. During the following week however he confided in Hal Chase that he absolutely had to learn how to write from him; Hal said I was a writer and he should come to me for advice. Meanwhile Neal had gotten a job in a parking lot, had a fight with Louanne in their Hoboken° apartment God knows why they went there and she was so mad and so vindictive down deep that she reported him to the police, some false trumped up hysterical crazy charge, and Neal had to lam from Hoboken. So he had no place to live. Neal came right out to Ozone Park where I was living with my mother, and one night while I was working on my book or my painting or whatever you want to call it there was a knock on the door and there was Neal, bowing, shuffling obsequiously° in the dark of the hall, and saying "Hello, you remember me, Neal Cassady? I've come to ask you to show me how to write." "And where's Louanne?" I asked, and Neal said she'd apparently whored a few dollars together or something of that nature and gone back to Denver . . . "the whore!" So we went out to have a few beers because we couldn't talk like we wanted to in front of my mother, who sat in the livingroom reading her paper. She took one look at Neal and decided from the very beginning that he was a madman. She never dreamed she too'd be driving across the mad American night with him more than once. In the bar I told Neal, "For krissakes man I know very well you didn't come to me only to want to become a writer and after all what do I really know about it except you've got to stick to it with the energy of a benny° addict," and he said, "Yes of course, I

Gene Autry: (1907–1998), singer and actor, star of many movie Westerns
Hoboken: city in northeastern New Jersey, directly across the Hudson River from lower Manhattan
obsequiously: submissively, deferentially
benny: benzedrine

know exactly what you mean and in fact those problems have occurred to me but the thing that I want is the realization of those factors that should one depend on Schopenhauer's° dichotomy° for any inwardly realized . . ." and on and on in that way, things I understood not a bit and he himself didn't, and what I mean is, in those days he really didn't know what he was talking about, that is to say, he was a young jailkid all hung up on the wonderful possibilities of becoming a real intellectual and he liked to talk in the tone and using the words but in a jumbled way that he had heard "real intellectuals" talk altho mind you he wasn't so naive as that in all other things, and it took him just a few months with Leon Levinsky to become completely in there with all the terms and the jargon and the style of intellectuality. Nonetheless I loved him for his madness and we got drunk together in the Linden bar behind my house and I agreed that he could stay at my house till he found a job and we furthermore agreed to go out west sometime. That was the winter of 1947. Shortly after meeting Neal I began writing or painting my huge Town and City, and I was about four chapters on when one night, when Neal ate supper at my house, and he already had a new parkinglot job in New York, the hotel NYorker lot on 34 st., he leaned over my shoulder as I typed rapidly away and said "Come on man, those girls won't wait, make it fast," and I said "Hold on just a minute, I'll be right with you soon as I finish this chapter," and I did and it was one of the best chapters in the whole book. Then I dressed and off we flew to NY to meet some girls. As you know to go from Ozone Park to New York takes an hour by elevated and subway, and as we rode in the El over the rooftops of Brooklyn we leaned on each other with fingers waving and yelled and talked excitedly and I was beginning to get the bug like Neal. In all, what Neal was, simply, was tremendously excited with life, and though he was a con-man he was only conning because he wanted so much to live and also to get involved with people that would otherwise pay no attention to him. He was conning me, so-called, and I knew it, and he knew I knew (this has been the basis of our relation) but I didn't care and we got along fine. I began to learn from him as much as he probably learned from me. As far as my work was concerned he said, "Go ahead, everything you do is great." We went to New York, I forget what the situation was, two girls—there were no girls there, they were supposed to meet him or some such thing and they weren't there. We went to his parkinglot where he had a few things to do—change his clothes in the shack in back and spruce up a bit in front of a cracked shack mirror

Schopenhauer: Arthur Schopenhauer (1788–1860), German philosopher
dichotomy: division into two parts, groups, or classifications

and so on, and then we took off. And that was the night Neal met Leon Levinsky. A tremendous thing happened when Neal met Leon Levinsky . . . I mean of course Allen Ginsberg. Two keen minds that they are they took to each other at the drop of a hat. Two piercing eyes glanced into two piercing eyes . . . the holy con-man and the great sorrowful poetic con-man that is Allen Ginsberg. From that moment on I saw very little of Neal and I was a little sorry too . . . Their energies met head-on. I was a lout° compared; I couldn't keep up with them. The whole mad swirl of everything that was to come then began which would mix up all my friends and all I had left of my family in a big dust cloud over the American night—they talked of Burroughs, Hunkey, Vicki, . . . Burroughs in Texas, Hunkey on Riker's Island,° Vicki hung up with Norman Schnall at the time . . . and Neal told Allen of people in the west like Jim Holmes the hunchbacked poolhall rotation shark° and cardplayer and queer saint . . . he told him of Bill Tomson, Al Hinkle, his boyhood buddies, his street buddies . . . they rushed down the street together digging everything in the early way they had which has later now become so much sadder and perceptive.. but then they danced down the street like dingledodies° and I shambled after as usual as I've been doing all my life after people that interest me, because the only people that interest me are the mad ones, the ones who are mad to live, mad to talk, desirous of everything at the same time, the ones that never yawn or say a commonplace thing, but burn, burn, burn like roman candles across the night. Allen was queer in those days, experimenting with himself to the hilt, and Neal saw that, and a former boyhood hustler himself in the Denver night, and wanting dearly to learn how to write poetry like Allen, the first thing you know he was attacking Allen with a great amorous soul such as only a con-man can have. I was in the same room, I heard them across the darkness and I mused and said to myself "Hmm, now something's started, but I don't want anything to do with it." So I didn't see them for about two weeks during which time they cemented their relationship to mad proportions. Then came the great time of traveling, Spring, and everybody in the scattered gang was getting ready to take one trip or another. I was busily at work on my novel and when I came to the halfway mark, after a trip down South with my mother to visit my sister, I got ready to travel west for the very first time. Neal had already left. Allen and I saw him off at the 34th street Greyhound station. Upstairs they

120 125 130 135 140 145 150 155

---

lout: crude person, oaf, boor

Riker's Island: Rikers Island, in the East River, site of New York City's main jail

shark: hustler

dingledodies: a word invented by Kerouac

have a place where you can make pictures for a quarter. Allen took off his glasses and looked sinister. Neal made a profile shot and looked coyly around. I took a straight picture that made me look, as Lucien said, like a 30 year old Italian who'd kill anybody who said anything against his mother. This picture Allen and Neal neatly cut down the middle with a razor and saved a half each in their wallets. I saw those halves later on. Neal was wearing a real western business suit for his big trip back to Denver; he'd finished his first fling in New York. I say fling but he only worked like a dog in parkinglots, the most fantastic parkinglot attendant in the world, he can back a car forty miles an hour into a tight squeeze and stop on a dime at the brickwall, and jump out, snake his way out of close fenders, leap into another car, circle it fifty miles an hour in a narrow space, shift, and back again into a tight spot with a few inches each side and come to a bouncing stop the same moment he's jamming in the emergency brake; then run clear to the ticket shack like a track star, hand a ticket, leap into a newly arrived car before the owner is hardly out, leap literally under him as he steps out, start the car with the door flapping and roar off to the next available parking spot: working like that without pause eight hours a night, evening rush hours and after theater rush hours, in greasy wino pants with a frayed furlined jacket and beat shoes that flap. Now he'd bought a new suit to go back home in; blue with pencil stripes, vest and all, with a watch and watch chain, and a portable typewriter with which he was going to start writing in a Denver roominghouse as soon as he got a job there. We had a farewell meal of franks and beans in a 7th avenue Riker's° and then Neal got on the bus that said Chicago on it and roared off into the night. I promised myself to go the same way when Spring really bloomed and opened up the land. There went our wrangler.° And this was really the way that my whole road experience began and the things that were to come are too fantastic not to tell. I've only spoken of Neal in a preliminary way because I didn't know any more than this about him then. His relation with Allen I'm not in on and as it turned out later, Neal got tired of that, specifically of queerness and reverted to his natural ways, but that's no matter. In the month of July, 1947, having finished a good half of my novel and having saved about fifty dollars from old veteran benefits I got ready to go to the West Coast. My friend Henri Cru had written me a letter from San Francisco saying I should come out there and ship out with him on an around the world liner. He swore he could get me into the engine room. I wrote back and said I'd be satisfied with

Riker's: now-defunct chain of cafeterias, with no connection to the jail

wrangler: cowboy; one who quarrels or brawls

any old freighter so long as I could take a few long Pacific trips and come back with enough money to support myself in my mother's house while I finished my book. He said he had a shack in Marin City and I would have all the time in the world to write there while we went through the rigmarole of getting a ship. He was living with a girl called Diane, he said she was a marvellous cook and everything would jump. Henri was an old prep school friend, a Frenchman brought up in Paris and France and a really mad guy—I never knew how mad and so mad at this time. So he expected me to arrive in ten days. I wrote and confirmed this. . . . in innocence of how much I'd get involved on the road. My mother was all in accord with my trip to the west, she said it would do me good, I'd been working so hard all winter and staying in too much; she even didn't say too much when I told her I'd have to hitch hike some, ordinarily it frightened her, she thought this would do me good. All she wanted was for me to come back in one piece. So leaving my big half-manuscript sitting on top of my desk, and folding back my comfortable home sheets for the last time one morning, I left with my canvas bag in which a few fundamental things were packed, left a note to my mother, who was at work, and took off for the Pacific Ocean like a veritable Ishmael with fifty dollars in my pocket. What a hang up I got into at once! As I look back on it it's incredible that I could have been so damned dumb. I'd been poring over maps of the U. S. in Ozone Park for months, even reading books about the pioneers and savoring names like Platte and Cimarron and so on, and on the road-map was one long red line called Route Six that led from the tip of Cape Cod clear to Ely Nevada and there dipped down to Los Angeles. "I'll just stay on six all the way to Ely," I said to myself and confidently started. To get to six I had to go up to Bear Mtn. New York. Filled with dreams of what I'd do in Chicago, in Denver, and then finally in San Fran, I took the 7th avenue subway to the end of the line at 242nd street, right near Horace Mann the prep school where I had actually met Henri Cru who I was going to see, and there took a trolley into Yonkers; downtown Yonkers I transferred on an outgoing trolley and went to the city limits on the east bank of the Hudson river. If you drop a rose in the Hudson river at its mysterious mouth up near Saratoga think of all the places it journeys by as it goes out to sea forever. . . think of that wonderful Hudson valley. I started hitching up the thing. Five scattered shot rides took me to the desired Bear Mtn. bridge where Route 6 arched in from New England. I had visions of it, I never dreamed it would look like it did. In the first place it began to rain in torrents when I was left off there. It was mountainous. Six came from the wilderness, wound around a traffic circle (after crossing the bridge that is) and disappeared again into the wilderness. Not only was there

200 205 210 215 220 225 230 235 240

no traffic but the rain came down in buckets and I had no shelter. I had to run under some pines to take cover; this did no good; I began crying and swearing and socking myself on the head for being such a damn fool. I was forty miles North of New York, all the way up I'd been worried about the fact that on this, my big opening day, I was only moving north instead of the desired, the so-longed for west. Now I was stuck on my northernmost hangup. I ran a quarter mile to an abandoned cute English style filling station and stood under the dripping eaves. High up over my head the great hairy Bear Mtn. sent down thunderclaps that put the fear of God in me. All I could see were smoky trees and dismal wilderness rising to the skies. "What the hell am I doing up here?" I cursed I cried for Chicago . . . "Even now they're all having a big time, they're doing things, I'm not there, when will I get there!" and so on. . . . Finally a car stopped at the empty filling station, the man and the two women in it wanted to study a map. I stepped right up and gestured in the rain; they consulted; I looked like a maniac of course with my hair all wet my shoes sopping . . . my shoes, damn fool that I am, were Mexican huaraches that, as a fellow later said to me in Wyoming, would certainly grow something if you planted them—plantlike sieves not fit for the rainy night of America and the whole raw road night. But they let me in, and rode me back to Newburgh which I accepted as a better alternative than being trapped in the Bear Mtn wilderness all night. "Besides said the man there's no traffic passes through six . . . if you want to go to Chicago you'd do better going across the Holland tunnel in NY and head for Pittsburgh" and I knew he was right. It was my dream that screwed up, the stupid hearthside idea that it would be wonderful to follow one great red line across America instead of trying various roads and routes. That's my tragic route Six—more to come of it, too. In Newburgh it had stopped raining, I walked down to the river, and among all things I had to ride back to NY in a bus with a delegation of schoolteachers coming back from a weekend in the Mtns.—chatter chatter blah-blah and me swearing for all the time and the money I'd wasted, and telling myself "I wanted to go west and here I've been all day and into the night going up and down, north and south, like something that can't get started." And I swore I'd be in Chicago tomorrow; and made sure of that, taking a bus to Chicago, spending most of my money, and didn't give a damn, just as long as I'd be in that damned Chicago tomorrow. The bus left at 2 o'clock in the morning from the 34 St. bus station sixteen hours after I'd more or less passed it on my way up to Route Six. Sheepishly my foolish ass was carried west. But at least I was headed there at last. I won't describe the trip to Chicago, it was an ordinary bus trip with crying babies and sometimes hot sun and countryfolk getting on at one Penn town after another, and so on, till we got on the plain of Ohio and really rolled, up by Ashtabula and straight across Indiana in the night for Chicago. I arrived in Chicago quite early in the morning, got a room in the Y and went to bed with a very few dollars in my pocket as a consequence of my foolishness. I dug Chicago after a good day's sleep. The wind from Lake Michigan, the beans, bop at the Loop, long walks around So. Halsted and No. Clark and one long walk after midnight into the jungles where a cruising car followed me as a suspicious character. At this time, 1947, bop was going like mad all over America, but it hadn't developed to what it is now. The fellows at the Loop blew, but with a tired air, because bop was somewhere between its Charley Parker Ornithology period and another period that really began with Miles Davis. And as I sat there listening to that sound of the night which it has come to represent for all of us, I thought of all my friends from one end of the country to the other and how they were really all in the same vast backyard doing something so frantic and rushing-about beneath. And for the first time in my life, the following afternoon, I went into the west. It was a warm and beautiful day for hitch-hiking.

[1957]

Read

1. To begin *en medias res* is to start a story in the middle. Why does Kerouac use that technique and what is the effect on you as a reader?
2. How does the description of Neal Cassady suggest the narrator's attitude toward him?
3. What is the effect of the lack of paragraphs in this excerpt (and in the novel as a whole)? Does it aid or distract your reading?
4. How does the narrator describe himself? What words does he use? What words would you use to describe him?
5. What is the purpose of the detailed description of the route out of the city?

Write

1. Imitate Kerouac's style by writing a one-page reflection about the beginning of a trip you've taken (or might take).
2. Reflect on the restlessness that characterizes this passage, using lines from the text and your own experience.

Connect

1. Choose another writer in this unit to compare with Kerouac in terms of style—especially voice and syntax.
2. How might you consider Kerouac's narrator a twentieth-century Huck Finn? Natty Bumppo? Another character?

Father Knows Best

In the early decades of the twentieth century, movies and radio were primary forms of both entertainment and news. As now, situation comedies were highly popular. *Father Knows Best* was a successful radio show beginning in 1949 and in 1954 became one of the most popular television series for over a decade. It starred film actor Robert Young, with Jane Wyatt as his wife. The couple, the Andersons, had three children.

A still from the 1950s television show *Father Knows Best*.

[1956]

Read

1. How do the positions of each of the characters in the television still photo suggest their roles in the family?
2. What details give you clues about the time period of the photo?
3. Who do you think is speaking? Who is listening?

Write

1. Write the conversation that might be taking place at the table.
2. Comment on how the scene depicts family life for the Andersons.

Connect

1. Design a photo for a television show on family life today. How does it differ? How is it the same?
2. Locate an article on suburban life after World War II. How does this scene connect to the description?

John Okada

Born in Seattle, Washington, John Okada (1923–1971) was educated at the University of Washington and Columbia University and served in the Air Force during World War II. He was an obscure writer during his lifetime, and when his most important novel, *No-No Boy,* came out, it received little attention. The novel was rediscovered during the 1970s by a group of Asian American writers, and since then it has found much acclaim.

No-No Boy is one of the first Japanese American novels. Okada wrote about the Japanese internment camps and the adjustment soldiers faced returning from war, as well as the struggles within Japanese communities. This excerpt is the preface to the novel and provides the backdrop for the struggles of Okada's character, Ichiro, and his family.

From *No-No Boy*

Preface

December the Seventh of the year 1941 was the day when the Japanese bombs fell on Pearl Harbor.

As of that moment, the Japanese in the United States became, by virtue of their ineradicable brownness and the slant eyes which, upon close inspection, will seldom appear slanty, animals of a different breed. The moment the impact of the words solemnly being transmitted over the several million radios of the nation struck home, everything Japanese and everyone Japanese became despicable.

The college professor, finding it suddenly impossible to meet squarely the gaze of his polite, serious, but now too Japanese-ish star pupil, coughed on his pipe and assured the lad that things were a mess. Conviction lacking, he failed at his attempt to be worldly and assuring. He mumbled something about things turning out one way or the other sooner or later and sighed with relief when the little fellow, who hardly ever smiled and, now, probably never would, stood up and left the room.

In a tavern, a drunk, irrigating the sponge in his belly, let it be known to the world that he never thought much about° the sneaky Japs and that this proved he was right. It did not matter that he owed

about: of

his Japanese landlord three-weeks' rent, nor that that industrious° Japanese had often picked him off the sidewalk and deposited him on his bed. Someone set up a round of beer for the boys in the place and, further fortified, he announced with patriotic tremor in his alcoholic tones that he would be first in line at the recruiting office the very next morning. That night the Japanese landlord picked him off the sidewalk and put him to bed.

Jackie was a whore and the news made her unhappy because she got two bucks a head and the Japanese boys were clean and considerate and hot and fast. Aside from her professional interest in them, she really liked them. She was sorry and, in her sorrow, she suffered a little with them. 5

A truck and a keen sense of horse-trading had provided a good living for Herman Fine. He bought from and sold primarily to Japanese hotel-keepers and grocers. No transaction was made without considerable haggling and clever maneuvering, for the Japanese could be and often were a shifty lot whose solemn promises frequently turned out to be groundwork for more extended and complex stratagems to cheat him out of his rightful profit. Herman Fine listened to the radio and cried without tears for the Japanese, who, in an instant of time that was not even a speck on the big calendar, had taken their place beside the Jew. The Jew was used to suffering. The writing for them was etched in caked and dried blood over countless generations upon countless generations. The Japanese did not know. They were proud, too proud, and they were ambitious, too ambitious. Bombs had fallen and, in less time than it takes a Japanese farmer's wife in California to run from the fields into the house and give birth to a child, the writing was scrawled for them. The Jap-Jew would look in the mirror this Sunday night and see a Jap-Jew.

The indignation, the hatred, the patriotism of the American people shifted into full-throated condemnation of the Japanese who blotted their land. The Japanese who were born Americans and remained Japanese because biology does not know the meaning of patriotism no longer worried about whether they were Japanese-Americans or American-Japanese. They were Japanese, just as were their Japanese mothers and Japanese fathers and Japanese brothers and sisters. The radio had said as much.

First, the real Japanese-Japanese were rounded up. These real Japanese-Japanese were Japanese nationals who had the misfortune to be diplomats and businessmen and visiting professors. They were put on a boat and sent back to Japan.

---

industrious: hardworking

Then the alien Japanese, the ones who had been in America for two, three, or even four decades, were screened, and those found to be too actively Japanese were transported to the hinterlands° and put in a camp.

The security screen was sifted once more and, this time, the lesser lights were similarly plucked and deposited. An old man, too old, too feeble, and too scared, was caught in the net. In his pocket was a little, black book. He had been a collector for the Japan-Help-the-Poor-and-Starving-and-Flooded-Out-and-Homeless-and-Crippled-and-What-Have-You Fund. "Yamada-san, 50 American cents; Okada-san, two American dollars; Watanabe-san, 24 American cents; Takizaki-san, skip this month because boy broke leg"; and so on down the page. Yamada-san, Okada-san, Watanabe-san, Takizaki-san, and so on down the page were whisked away from their homes while weeping families wept until the tears must surely have been wept dry, and then wept some more. 10

By now, the snowball was big enough to wipe out the rising sun. The big rising sun would take a little more time, but the little rising sun which was the Japanese in countless Japanese communities in the coastal states of Washington, Oregon, and California presented no problem. The whisking and transporting of Japanese and the construction of camps with barbed wire and ominous towers supporting fully armed soldiers in places like Idaho and Wyoming and Arizona, places which even Hollywood scorned for background, had become skills which demanded the utmost of America's great organizing ability.

And so, a few months after the seventh day of December of the year nineteen forty-one, the only Japanese left on the west coast of the United States was Matsusaburo Inabukuro who, while it has been forgotten whether he was Japanese-American or American-Japanese, picked up an "I am Chinese"—not American or American-Chinese or Chinese-American but "I am Chinese"—button and got a job in a California shipyard.

Two years later a good Japanese-American who had volunteered for the army sat smoking in the belly of a B-24 on his way back to Guam from a reconnaissance flight to Japan. His job was to listen through his earphones, which were attached to a high-frequency set, and jot down air-ground messages spoken by Japanese-Japanese in Japanese planes and in Japanese radio shacks.

The lieutenant who operated the radar-detection equipment was a blond giant from Nebraska.

The lieutenant from Nebraska said: "Where you from?" 15

hinterlands: back country, remote areas

The Japanese-American who was an American soldier answered: "No place in particular."

"You got folks?"

"Yeah, I got folks."

"Where at?"

"Wyoming, out in the desert." 20

"Farmers, huh?"

"Not quite."

"What's that mean?"

"Well, it's this way . . . " And then the Japanese-American whose folks were still Japanese-Japanese, or else they would not be in a camp with barbed wire and watchtowers with soldiers holding rifles, told the blond giant from Nebraska about the removal of the Japanese from the Coast, which was called the evacuation, and about the concentration camps, which were called relocation centers.

The lieutenant listened and he didn't believe it. He said: "That's funny. Now, tell me again." 25

The Japanese-American soldier of the American army told it again, and didn't change a word.

The lieutenant believed him this time. "Hell's bells," he exclaimed, "if they'd done that to me, I wouldn't be sitting in the belly of a broken-down B-24 going back to Guam from a reconnaissance mission to Japan."

"I got reasons," said the Japanese-American soldier soberly.

"They could kiss my ass," said the lieutenant from Nebraska.

"I got reasons," said the Japanese-American soldier soberly, and he was thinking about a lot of things but mostly about his friend who didn't volunteer for the army because his father had been picked up in the second screening and was in a different camp from the one he and his mother and two sisters were in. Later on, the army tried to draft his friend out of the relocation camp into the army and the friend had stood before the judge and said let my father out of that other camp and come back to my mother who is an old woman but misses him enough to want to sleep with him and I'll try on the uniform. The judge said he couldn't do that and the friend said he wouldn't be drafted and they sent him to the federal prison where he now was. 30

"What the hell are we fighting for?" said the lieutenant from Nebraska.

"I got reasons," said the Japanese-American soldier soberly and thought some more about his friend who was in another kind of uniform because they wouldn't let his father go to the same camp with his mother and sisters.

[1957]

Read

1. How does Okada use irony in the first few paragraphs to suggest the relationship between Anglo Americans and their Japanese American neighbors?
2. How does Okada suggest that decisions were made regarding the fate of the Japanese after the Pearl Harbor invasion?
3. What is the purpose of the conversation between the Japanese American soldier and the one from Nebraska?

Write

1. The Japanese soldier repeats "I got reasons" several times. Write a paragraph that explains what you think his "reasons" might be.
2. Write about your reaction to the story the Japanese American soldier tells about internment and deportation.

Connect

1. Choose a text from another unit to discuss how fear alters people's actions and causes community breakdown. (Think of Hawthorne, Addams, Du Bois as possibilities).

Tillie Olsen

Tillie Olsen (1913–2007) published only a few works, but she has become known for her prose style, as well as for her ability to describe the lives of the poor, immigrants, and women. She was born in Nebraska to Russian immigrants and began writing early in her life, although she worked as a waitress, domestic worker, and union organizer as well. She married longshoreman and union leader Jack Olsen in 1944. She wrote fiction as well as journalistic accounts. Her autobiographical work *Silences* describes the way women's careers are interrupted by their traditional roles. Her story "I Stand Here Ironing" was published in her most famous collection *Tell Me A Riddle,* first published in 1956. The novella *Tell Me A Riddle* was awarded the O. Henry Prize in 1961 for best American short story.

I Stand Here Ironing

I stand here ironing, and what you asked me moves tormented back and forth with the iron.

"I wish you would manage the time to come in and talk with me about your daughter. I'm sure you can help me understand her. She's a youngster who needs help and whom I'm deeply interested in helping."

"Who needs help." . . . Even if I came, what good would it do? You think because I am her mother I have a key, or that in some way you could use me as a key? She has lived for nineteen years. There is all that life that has happened outside of me, beyond me.

And when is there time to remember, to sift,° to weigh, to estimate, to total? I will start and there will be an interruption and I will have to gather it all together again. Or I will become engulfed with all I did or did not do, with what should have been and what cannot be helped.

5 She was a beautiful baby. The first and only one of our five that was beautiful at birth. You do not guess how new and uneasy her tenancy° in her now-loveliness. You did not know her all those years she was thought homely, or see her poring over her baby pictures, making me tell her over and over how beautiful she had been—and would be, I would tell her—and was now, to the seeing eye. But the seeing eyes were few or nonexistent. Including mine.

I nursed her. They feel that's important nowadays. I nursed all the children, but with her, with all the fierce rigidity of first motherhood, I did like the books then said. Though her cries battered me to trembling and my breasts ached with swollenness, I waited till the clock decreed.

Why do I put that first? I do not even know if it matters, or if it explains anything.

She was a beautiful baby. She blew shining bubbles of sound. She loved motion, loved light, loved color and music and textures. She would lie on the floor in her blue overalls patting the surface so hard in ecstasy her hands and feet would blur. She was a miracle to me, but when she was eight months old I had to leave her daytimes with the woman downstairs to whom she was no miracle at all, for I worked or looked for work and for Emily's father, who "could no longer endure" (he wrote in his good-bye note) "sharing want° with us."

I was nineteen. It was the pre-relief,° pre-WPA° world of the depression. I would start running as soon as I got off the streetcar, running up the stairs, the place smelling sour, and awake or asleep to startle awake, when she saw me she would break into a clogged weeping that could not be comforted, a weeping I can hear yet.

10 After a while I found a job hashing° at night so I could be with her days, and it was better. But it came to where I had to bring her to his family and leave her.

---

sift: examine, scrutinize

tenancy: occupancy

want: need, poverty

relief: government assistance, welfare

WPA: Works Progress Administration, a New Deal project that provided employment in public works projects to millions of Americans between 1935 and 1943

hashing: working as waitress at a hash-house (a cheap restaurant or lunch counter)

It took a long time to raise the money for her fare back. Then she got chicken pox and I had to wait longer. When she finally came, I hardly knew her, walking quick and nervous like her father, looking like her father, thin, and dressed in a shoddy red that yellowed her skin and glared at the pockmarks. All the baby loveliness gone.

She was two. Old enough for nursery school they said, and I did not know then what I know now—the fatigue of the long day, and the lacerations of group life in the kinds of nurseries that are only parking places for children.

Except that it would have made no difference if I had known. It was the only place there was. It was the only way we could be together, the only way I could hold a job.

And even without knowing, I knew. I knew the teacher that was evil because all these years it has curdled into my memory, the little boy hunched in the corner, her rasp, "why aren't you outside, because Alvin hits you? that's no reason, go out, scaredy." I knew Emily hated it even if she did not clutch and implore "don't go Mommy" like the other children, mornings.

15 She always had a reason why we should stay home. Momma, you look sick. Momma, I feel sick. Momma, the teachers aren't there today, they're sick. Momma, we can't go, there was a fire there last night. Momma, it's a holiday today, no school, they told me.

But never a direct protest, never rebellion. I think of our others in their three-, four-year-oldness—the explosions, the tempers, the denunciations, the demands—and I feel suddenly ill. I put the iron down. What in me demanded that goodness in her? And what was the cost, the cost to her of such goodness?

The old man living in the back once said in his gentle way: "You should smile at Emily more when you look at her." What *was* in my face when I looked at her? I loved her. There were all the acts of love.

It was only with the others I remembered what he said, and it was the face of joy, and not of care or tightness or worry I turned to them—too late for Emily. She does not smile easily, let alone almost always as her brothers and sisters do. Her face is closed and sombre,° but when she wants, how fluid. You must have seen it in her pantomimes, you spoke of her rare gift for comedy on the stage that rouses a laughter out of the audience so dear they applaud and applaud and do not want to let her go.

Where does it come from, that comedy? There was none of it in her when she came back to me that second time, after I had had to send her away again. She had a new daddy now to learn to love, and I think perhaps it was a better time.

---

sombre: (usually *somber*), serious, gloomy

Except when we left her alone nights, telling ourselves she was old enough. 20

"Can't you go some other time, Mommy, like tomorrow?" she would ask. "Will it be just a little while you'll be gone? Do you promise?"

The time we came back, the front door open, the clock on the floor in the hall. She rigid awake. "It wasn't just a little while. I didn't cry. Three times I called you, just three times, and then I ran downstairs to open the door so you could come faster. The clock talked loud. I threw it away, it scared me what it talked."

She said the clock talked loud again that night I went to the hospital to have Susan. She was delirious with the fever that comes before red measles, but she was fully conscious all the week I was gone and the week after we were home when she could not come near the new baby or me.

She did not get well. She stayed skeleton thin, not wanting to eat, and night after night she had nightmares. She would call for me, and I would rouse from exhaustion to sleepily call back: "You're all right, darling, go to sleep, it's just a dream," and if she still called, in a sterner voice, "now go to sleep, Emily, there's nothing to hurt you." Twice, only twice, when I had to get up for Susan anyhow, I went in to sit with her.

Now when it is too late (as if she would let me hold and comfort her like I do the others) I get up and go to her at once at her moan or restless stirring. "Are you awake, Emily? Can I get you something?" And the answer is always the same: "No, I'm all right, go back to sleep, Mother." 25

They persuaded me at the clinic to send her away to a convalescent home in the country where "she can have the kind of food and care you can't manage for her, and you'll be free to concentrate on the new baby." They still send children to that place. I see pictures on the society page of sleek young women planning affairs to raise money for it, or dancing at the affairs, or decorating Easter eggs or filling Christmas stockings for the children.

They never have a picture of the children so I do not know if the girls still wear those gigantic red bows and the ravaged looks on the every other Sunday when parents can come to visit "unless otherwise notified"—as we were notified the first six weeks.

Oh it is a handsome place, green lawns and tall trees and fluted° flower beds. High up on the balconies of each cottage the children

---

fluted: grooved, furrowed

stand, the girls in their red bows and white dresses, the boys in white suits and giant red ties. The parents stand below shrieking up to be heard and the children shriek down to be heard, and between them the invisible wall "Not To Be Contaminated by Parental Germs or Physical Affection."

There was a tiny girl who always stood hand in hand with Emily. Her parents never came. One visit she was gone. "They moved her to Rose Cottage" Emily shouted in explanation. "They don't like you to love anybody here."

30 She wrote once a week, the labored writing of a seven-year-old. "I am fine. How is the baby. If I write my leter nicly I will have a star. Love." There never was a star. We wrote every other day, letters she could never hold or keep but only hear read—once. "We simply do not have room for children to keep any personal possessions," they patiently explained when we pieced one Sunday's shrieking together to plead how much it would mean to Emily, who loved so to keep things, to be allowed to keep her letters and cards.

Each visit she looked frailer. "She isn't eating," they told us.

(They had runny eggs for breakfast or mush with lumps, Emily said later, I'd hold it in my mouth and not swallow. Nothing ever tasted good, just when they had chicken.)

It took us eight months to get her released home, and only the fact that she gained back so little of her seven lost pounds convinced the social worker.

I used to try to hold and love her after she came back, but her body would stay stiff, and after a while she'd push away. She ate little. Food sickened her, and I think much of life too. Oh she had physical lightness and brightness, twinkling by on skates, bouncing like a ball up and down up and down over the jump rope, skimming over the hill; but these were momentary.

35 She fretted about her appearance, thin and dark and foreign-looking at a time when every little girl was supposed to look or thought she should look a chubby blonde replica of Shirley Temple.° The doorbell sometimes rang for her, but no one seemed to come and play in the house or be a best friend. Maybe because we moved so much.

There was a boy she loved painfully through two school semesters. Months later she told me how she had taken pennies from my purse to buy him candy. "Licorice was his favorite and I brought him some every day, but he still liked Jennifer better'n me. Why, Mommy?" The kind of question for which there is no answer.

Shirley Temple: (b. 1928), enormously popular child movie star of the 1930s

School was a worry to her. She was not glib or quick in a world where glibness and quickness were easily confused with ability to learn. To her overworked and exasperated teachers she was an over-conscientious "slow learner" who kept trying to catch up and was absent entirely too often.

I let her be absent, though sometimes the illness was imaginary. How different from my now-strictness about attendance with the others. I wasn't working. We had a new baby, I was home anyhow. Sometimes, after Susan grew old enough, I would keep her home from school, too, to have them all together.

Mostly Emily had asthma, and her breathing, harsh and labored, would fill the house with a curiously tranquil sound. I would bring the two old dresser mirrors and her boxes of collections to her bed. She would select beads and single earrings, bottle tops and shells, dried flowers and pebbles, old postcards and scraps, all sorts of oddments; then she and Susan would play Kingdom, setting up landscapes and furniture, peopling them with action.

Those were the only times of peaceful companionship between her and Susan. I have edged away from it, that poisonous feeling between them, that terrible balancing of hurts and needs I had to do between the two, and did so badly, those earlier years. 40

Oh there are conflicts between the others too, each one human, needing, demanding, hurting, taking—but only between Emily and Susan, no, Emily toward Susan that corroding° resentment. It seems so obvious on the surface, yet it is not obvious. Susan, the second child, Susan, golden- and curly-haired and chubby, quick and articulate and assured, everything in appearance and manner Emily was not; Susan, not able to resist Emily's precious things, losing or sometimes clumsily breaking them; Susan telling jokes and riddles to company for applause while Emily sat silent (to say to me later: that was *my* riddle, Mother, I told it to Susan); Susan, who for all the five years' difference in age was just a year behind Emily in developing physically.

I am glad for that slow physical development that widened the difference between her and her contemporaries, though she suffered over it. She was too vulnerable for that terrible world of youthful competition, of preening° and parading, of constant measuring of yourself against every other, of envy, "If I had that copper hair," "If I had that skin. . . ." She tormented herself enough about not looking

corroding: eating or wearing away

preening: primping

like the others, there was enough of the unsureness, the having to be conscious of words before you speak, the constant caring—what are they thinking of me? without having it all magnified by the merciless physical drives.

Ronnie is calling. He is wet and I change him. It is rare there is such a cry now. That time of motherhood is almost behind me when the ear is not one's own but must always be racked° and listening for the child cry, the child call. We sit for a while and I hold him, looking out over the city spread in charcoal with its soft aisles of light. "*Shoogily,*" he breathes and curls closer. I carry him back to bed, asleep. *Shoogily.* A funny word, a family word, inherited from Emily, invented by her to say: *comfort.*

In this and other ways she leaves her seal,° I say aloud. And startle at my saying it. What do I mean? What did I start to gather together, to try and make coherent? I was at the terrible, growing years. War years. I do not remember them well. I was working, there were four smaller ones now, there was not time for her. She had to help be a mother, and housekeeper, and shopper. She had to set her seal. Mornings of crisis and near hysteria trying to get lunches packed, hair combed, coats and shoes found, everyone to school or Child Care on time, the baby ready for transportation. And always the paper scribbled on by a smaller one, the book looked at by Susan then mislaid, the homework not done. Running out to that huge school where she was one, she was lost, she was a drop; suffering over the unpreparedness, stammering and unsure in her classes.

45

There was so little time left at night after the kids were bedded down. She would struggle over books, always eating (it was in those years she developed her enormous appetite that is legendary in our family) and I would be ironing, or preparing food for the next day, or writing V-mail° to Bill, or tending the baby. Sometimes, to make me laugh, or out of her despair, she would imitate happenings or types at school.

I think I said once: "Why don't you do something like this in the school amateur show?" One morning she phoned me at work, hardly understandable through the weeping: "Mother, I did it. I won, I won; they gave me first prize; they clapped and clapped and wouldn't let me go."

Now suddenly she was Somebody, and as imprisoned in her difference as she had been in anonymity.

---

racked: distressed, tormented

seal: mark, stamp

V-mail: a system of microfilming and air transport by which letters could be quickly exchanged between U.S. overseas military personnel and their families during World War II

She began to be asked to perform at other high schools, even in colleges, then at city and statewide affairs. The first one we went to, I only recognized her that first moment when thin, shy, she almost drowned herself into the curtains. Then: Was this Emily? The control, the command, the convulsing and deadly clowning, the spell, then the roaring, stamping audience, unwilling to let this rare and precious laughter out of their lives.

Afterwards: You ought to do something about her with a gift like that—but without money or knowing how, what does one do? We have left it all to her, and the gift has as often eddied° inside, clogged and clotted, as been used and growing.

She is coming. She runs up the stairs two at a time with her light graceful step, and I know she is happy tonight. Whatever it was that occasioned your call did not happen today. 50

"Aren't you ever going to finish the ironing, Mother? Whistler painted his mother in a rocker. I'd have to paint mine standing over an ironing board." This is one of her communicative nights and she tells me everything and nothing as she fixes herself a plate of food out of the icebox.

She is so lovely. Why did you want me to come in at all? Why were you concerned? She will find her way.

She starts up the stairs to bed. "Don't get me up with the rest in the morning." "But I thought you were having midterms." "Oh, those," she comes back in, kisses me, and says quite lightly, "in a couple of years when we'll all be atom-dead° they won't matter a bit."

She has said it before. She *believes* it. But because I have been dredging the past, and all that compounds a human being is so heavily and meaningful in me, I cannot endure it tonight.

I will never total it all. I will never come in to say: She was a child seldom smiled at. Her father left me before she was a year old. I had to work her first six years when there was work, or I sent her home and to his relatives. There were years she had care she hated. She was dark and thin and foreign-looking in a world where the prestige went to blondeness and curly hair and dimples, she was slow where glibness° was prized. She was a child of anxious, not proud, love. We were poor and could not afford for her the soil of easy growth. I was a young mother, I was a distracted mother. There were the other children pushing up, demanding. Her younger sister seemed all that she was not. There were years she did not want me to touch her. She kept too 55

---

eddied: swirled

atom-dead: as a result of an atomic or nuclear war

glibness: fluency or facility in speech

much in herself, her life was such she had to keep too much in herself. My wisdom came too late. She has much to her and probably little will come of it. She is a child of her age, of depression, of war, of fear.

Let her be. So all that is in her will not bloom—but in how many does it? There is still enough left to live by. Only help her to know—help make it so there is cause for her to know—that she is more than this dress on the ironing board, helpless before the iron.

[1954]

Read

1. How does Olsen use "talking to herself" to air her worries?
2. Why do you think she talks to herself rather than to a counselor?
3. Where does the speaker place blame for her daughter's problems?
4. What images does Olsen use to provoke emotion in the reader?
5. How would you describe the mother's attitude toward her daughter?

Write

1. Write an internal monologue like the talking to herself the mother does from the perspective of Emily, the daughter.
2. Reflect on your reactions to the story the mother tells of her life and her daughter's.

Complete Additional Exercises on Olsen's Story at Your Pearson MyLab

Connect

1. Use works by Rowlandson, Bradstreet, Chopin, Rowson, or another woman to compare attitudes and actions between mother and child with the actions in this story.
2. How does first-person narration of a life story affect the reader's attitude toward the narrator? Find a narrative that tells a life story (Zitkala Sa in Unit 4, for example) and consider your reaction to both narratives.

James Baldwin

James Baldwin (1924–1987) was born in Harlem, New York City, to a single mother. He had a troubled childhood with a difficult stepfather. In his later works, he often wrote about familial relationships. His debut novel, *Go Tell It on the Mountain,* in 1953, was well received. After its publication, he continued to write essays, autobiographical works, and criticism that dealt with racial and sexual identities, the civil rights movement, religion, and community. Baldwin emigrated to France in 1948, returning in the 1960s to aid in the civil rights movement. He traveled back and forth between the two continents for the rest of his life.

Baldwin's belief and faith in the experiment of democracy made his critiques and descriptions of American life both poignant and persuasive.

My Dungeon Shook

Letter to My Nephew on the One Hundredth Anniversary of the Emancipation

Dear James:

I have begun this letter five times and torn it up five times. I keep seeing your face, which is also the face of your father and my brother. Like him, you are tough, dark, vulnerable, moody—with a very definite tendency to sound truculent° because you want no one to think you are soft. You may be like your grandfather in this, I don't know, but certainly both you and your father resemble him very much physically. Well, he is dead, he never saw you, and he had a terrible life; he was defeated long before he died because, at the bottom of his heart, he really believed what white people said about him. This is one of the reasons that he became so holy. I am sure that your father has told you something about all that. Neither you nor your father exhibit any tendency towards holiness: you really are of another era, part of what happened when the late E. Franklin Frazier called "the cities of destruction." You can only be destroyed by believing that you really are what the white world calls a nigger. I tell you this because I love you, and please don't forget it.

I have known both of you all your lives, have carried your Daddy in my arms and on my shoulders, kissed and spanked him and watched him learn to walk. I don't know if you've known anybody from that far back; if you've loved anybody that long, first as an infant, then as a child, then as a man, you gain a strange perspective on time and human pain and effort. Other people cannot see what I see whenever I look into your father's face as it is today are all those other faces which were his. Let him laugh and I see a cellar your father does not remember and a house he does not remember and I hear in his present laughter his laughter as a child. Let him curse and I remember him falling down the cellar steps, and howling, and I remember, with pain, his tears, which my hand or your grandmother's so easily wiped away. But no one's hand can wipe away those tears he sheds invisibly today, which one hears in his laughter and in his speech and in his songs. I know what the world has done to my brother and how narrowly he has survived it. And I know, which is much worse, and this is the crime of which I accuse my

---

truculent: hostile, belligerent

country and my countrymen, and for which neither I nor time nor history will ever forgive them, that they have destroyed and are destroying hundreds of thousands of lives and do not know it and do not want to know it. One can be, indeed one must strive to become, tough and philosophical concerning destruction and death, for this is what most of mankind has been best at since we have heard of man. (But remember: most of mankind is not all of mankind.) But it is not permissible that the authors of devastation should also be innocent. It is the innocence which constitutes the crime.

Now, my dear namesake, these innocent and well-meaning people, your countrymen, have caused you to be born under conditions not very far removed from those described for us by Charles Dickens in the London of more than a hundred years ago. (I hear the chorus of the innocents screaming, "No! This is not true! How bitter you are!"—but I am writing this letter to you, to try to tell you something about how to handle them, for most of them do not yet really know that you exist. I know the conditions, under which you were born, for I was there. Your countrymen were not there, and haven't made it yet. Your grandmother was also there, and no one has ever accused her of being bitter. I suggest that the innocents check with her. She isn't hard to find. Your countrymen don't know that she exists, either, though she has been working for them all their lives.)

Well, you were born, here you came, something like fourteen years ago: and though your father and mother and grandmother, looking about the streets through which they were carrying you, staring at the walls into which they brought you, had every reason to be heavyhearted, yet they were not. For here you were, Big James, named for me—you were a big baby, I was not—here you were: to be loved. To be loved, baby, hard, at once, and forever, to strengthen you against the loveless world. Remember that: I know how black it looks today, for you. It looked bad that day, too, yes, we were trembling. We have not stopped trembling yet, but if we had not loved each other none of us would have survived. And now you must survive because we love you, and for the sake of your children and your children's children.

5 This innocent country set you down in a ghetto in which, in fact, it intended that you should perish. Let me spell out precisely what I mean by that, for the heart of the matter is here, and the root of my dispute with my country. You were born where you were born, and faced the future that you faced because you were black and for no other reason. The limits of your ambition were, thus, expected to be set forever. You were born into a society

which spelled out with brutal clarity, and in as many ways as possible, that you were a worthless human being. You were not expected to aspire to excellence: you were expected to make peace with mediocrity. Wherever you have turned, James, in your short time on this earth, you have been told where you could go and what you could do (and how you could do it) and where you could do it and whom you could marry. I know that your countrymen do not agree with me about this, and I hear them saying "You exaggerate." They do not know Harlem, and I do. So do you. Take no one's word for anything, including mine—but trust your experience. Know whence° you came. If you know whence you came, there is really no limit to where you can go. The details and symbols of your life have been deliberately constructed to make you believe what white people say about you.

Please try to remember that what they believe, as well as what they do and cause you to endure, does not testify to your inferiority but to their inhumanity and fear. Please try to be clear, dear James, though the storm which rages about your youthful head today, about the reality which lies behind the words acceptance and integration. There is no reason for you to try to become like white people and there is no basis whatever for their impertinent° assumption that they must accept you. The really terrible thing, old buddy, is that you must accept them. And I mean that very seriously. You must accept them and accept them with love. For these innocent people have no other hope. They are, in effect, still trapped in a history which they do not understand; and until they understand it, they cannot be released from it. They have had to believe for so many years, and for innumerable reasons, that black men are inferior to white men. Many of them, indeed, know better, but, as you will discover, people find it very difficult to act on what they know. To act is to be committed, and to be committed is to be in danger. In this case, the danger, in the minds of most white Americans, is the loss of identity. Try to imagine how you would feel if you woke up one morning to find the sun shinning and all the stars aflame. You would be frightened because it is out of the order of nature. Any upheaval in the universe is terrifying because it so profoundly attacks one's sense of one's own reality. Well, the black man has functioned in the white man's world as a fixed star, as an immovable pillar: and as he

---

whence: from where

impertinent: insolent, rude

moves out of his place, heaven and earth are shaken to their foundations. You, don't be afraid. I said that it was intended that you should perish in the ghetto, perish by never being allowed to go behind the white man's definitions, by never being allowed to spell your proper name. You have, and many of us have, defeated this intention; and, by a terrible law, a terrible paradox, those innocents who believed that your imprisonment made them safe are losing their grasp of reality. But these men are your brothers—your lost, younger brothers. And if the word integration means anything, this is what it means: that we, with love, shall force our brothers to see themselves as they are, to cease fleeing from reality and begin to change it. For this is your home, my friend, do not be driven from it; great men have done great things here, and will again, and we can make America what America must become. It will be hard, James, but you come from sturdy, peasant stock, men who picked cotton and dammed rivers and built railroads, and in the teeth of the most terrifying odds, achieved an unassailable° and monumental dignity. You come from a long line of poets, some of the greatest poets since Homer. One of them° said, The very time I thought I was lost, My dungeon shook and my chains fell off.

You know, and I know, that the country is celebrating one hundred years of freedom one hundred years too soon. We cannot be free until they are free. God bless you, James, and Godspeed.

Your uncle,
James

[1962]

Read

1. How does the genre of the letter affect your reading of the text?
2. What do you think Baldwin's reason is for establishing his nephew's likeness to family members at the beginning of the letter?
3. Why does he describe in detail his relationship to James's father and to James himself?
4. Where do you hear irony in Baldwin's voice?

---

unassailable: invulnerable, indisputable

One of them: the anonymous author of the spiritual "Free at Last" (the same spiritual so famously cited by Martin Luther King, Jr., in his "I Have a Dream" speech), from which Baldwin's quotation is drawn

Write

1. In a line or two, describe Baldwin's purpose in writing to James.
2. Explain what you think Baldwin means by saying "it is the innocence that constitutes the crime."
3. Describe the purpose of the title.

Connect

1. Baldwin's anger is directed at hypocrisy and its consequences. Find other texts in this unit that use anger to create arguments and persuade.
2. Link Baldwin's letter to other letters in this and other units and compare how the genre uses language, arrangement, and detail.

Gwendolyn Brooks

Gwendolyn Brooks (1917–2000) was the first African American writer to receive a Pulitzer Prize, which was awarded for her poetry collection *Annie Allen* in 1949. Brooks spent most of her life in Chicago, and many of her poems have urban settings and working class lives as their themes. As she matured as a writer, her forms became more experimental in diction and rhythm.

Brooks was instrumental in helping young African American poets throughout her career. In 1985, she was named Consultant in Poetry to the Library of Congress.

We Real Cool

The Pool Players
Seven at the Golden Shovel°

We real cool. We
Left school. We

Lurk late. We
Strike straight. We 5

Sing sin. We
Thin gin. We

Jazz° June. We
Die soon.

[1960]

---

the Golden Shovel: apparently a pool hall

Jazz: Two more or less relevant meanings of *jazz* as a verb are "to exaggerate or lie to," and "to give great pleasure to; excite."

Read

1. What is the purpose of setting the scene at the beginning of the poem? What's the importance of the line placement of the setting?
2. How does the reader identify who the "we" is in the poem?
3. What's the importance of the use of dialect in the poem?
4. Where do you find irony in the poem?

Write

1. Write about the purpose of this poem by taking the voice of the "we" and writing a paragraph in prose.
2. Write about the use of repetition in, and how it affects your reading of, the poem.

Connect

1. How does Brooks's vision make a link to Du Bois's ideas in the *Souls of Black Folk*?
2. Find another text (*Adventures of Huckleberry Finn* is an example) that uses dialect speech and compare how the diction helps the writers convey their messages.

Rachel Carson

Born on a small farm in rural Pennsylvania, Rachel Carson (1907–1964) credited her mother with teaching her to love the natural world. Carson was a journalist, naturalist, and environmentalist. She was the first woman to pass the Civil Service Examination, and she got a job with the Federal Bureau of Fisheries. Carson's first book, on underwater life, was the result of her work there. She wrote about her observations of sea life and the habits of land animals. In 1962, she published her most famous book, *Silent Spring,* which documented the disastrous effects of chemicals like DDT on animals and birds. After reading the book, President John F. Kennedy called for testing of chemicals, and ultimately many toxic chemicals were banned. Carson has been called the mother of the modern environmental movement because of her clear observations and her urgent calls to regulate toxic chemicals in the environment.

A Fable for Tomorrow

From *Silent Spring*

There was once a town in the heart of America where all life seemed to live in harmony with its surroundings. The town lay in the midst of a checkerboard of prosperous farms, with fields of grain and hillsides of orchards where, in spring, white clouds of bloom drifted above the green fields. In autumn, oak and maple and birch set up a blaze of color that flamed and flickered across a backdrop of pines. Then foxes barked in the hills and deer silently crossed the fields, half hidden in the mists of the fall mornings.

Along the roads, laurel, viburnum° and alder, great ferns and wildflowers delighted the traveler's eye through much of the year. Even in winter the roadsides were places of beauty, where countless birds came to feed on the berries and on the seed heads of the dried weeds rising above the snow. The countryside was, in fact, famous for the abundance and variety of its bird life, and when the flood of migrants was pouring through in spring and fall people traveled from great distances to observe them. Others came to fish the streams, which flowed clear and cold out of the hills and contained shady pools where trout lay. So it had been from the days many years ago when the first settlers raised their houses, sank their wells, and built their barns.

Then a strange blight crept over the area and everything began to change. Some evil spell had settled on the community: mysterious maladies swept the flocks of chickens; the cattle and sheep sickened and died. Everywhere was a shadow of death. The farmers spoke of much illness among their families. In the town the doctors had become more and more puzzled by new kinds of sickness appearing among their patients. There had been several sudden and unexplained deaths, not only among adults but even among children, who would be stricken suddenly while at play and die within a few hours.

There was a strange stillness. The birds, for example—where had they gone? Many people spoke of them, puzzled and disturbed. The feeding stations in the backyards were deserted. The few birds seen anywhere were moribund;° they trembled violently and could not fly. It was a spring without voices. On the mornings that had once throbbed with the dawn chorus of robins, catbirds, doves, jays, wrens, and scores of other bird voices there was now no sound; only silence lay over the fields and woods and marsh.

5 On the farms the hens brooded, but no chicks hatched. The farmers complained that they were unable to raise any pigs—the litters were small and the young survived only a few days. The apple trees were coming into bloom but no bees droned among the blossoms, so there was no pollination and there would be no fruit.

The roadsides, once so attractive, were now lined with browned and withered vegetation as though swept by fire. These, too, were silent, deserted by all living things. Even the streams were now lifeless. Anglers° no longer visited them, for all the fish had died.

In the gutters under the eaves and between the shingles of the roofs, a white granular° powder still showed a few patches; some weeks before it had fallen like snow upon the roofs and the lawns, the fields and streams.

---

viburnum: any of various trees or shrubs, including the snowball and the cranberry bush

moribund: near death

Anglers: fishermen

granular: grainy

No witchcraft, no enemy action had silenced the rebirth of new life in this stricken world. The people had done it themselves.

This town does not actually exist, but it might easily have a thousand counterparts in America or elsewhere in the world. I know of no community that has experienced all the misfortunes I describe. Yet every one of these disasters has actually happened somewhere, and many real communities have already suffered a substantial number of them. A grim specter has crept upon us almost unnoticed, and this imagined tragedy may easily become a stark reality we all shall know.

What has already silenced the voices of spring in countless towns in America? This book is an attempt to explain. 10

[1962]

Read

1. Why does Carson begin her essay "There was once. . ."?
2. What is the effect of the genre on your reading of the piece?
3. How does Carson use detail to convey her point about the land?
4. What is the "strange blight"?

Write

1. A fable always has a moral. Write a line or two that describes the moral you take from this essay.
2. Does the future Carson describes seem possible? Use an example from a current event or a situation in your community to help you frame your response.
3. Write a fable of your own about the environment. Remember it should be short and with a clear moral at the end.

Connect

1. How does Carson's argument and her diction reflect the ideas or sensibilities of any of the other writers you've read?

Martin Luther King, Jr.

Martin Luther King, Jr. (1929–1968) was a minister, social activist, and the central figure in the civil rights movement. He was born in Atlanta, where his father was a clergyman. He was educated at Morehouse College and received a Ph.D. in 1955 from Boston University. He was minister at a Baptist church in Montgomery when he began organizing peaceful protests against segregation, ultimately leading dozens of marches for equality and an end to segregation, including the 250,000-strong march on Washington in 1963 where his "I Have a Dream" speech was delivered at the Lincoln Memorial.

In 1964, King became the youngest person to receive the Nobel Peace Prize for his work for nonviolent protests and passive resistance. Heavily influenced by Indian leader Mahatma Gandhi, King organized peaceful protests across the South, was jailed 20 times, and was assaulted several times as well. In April, 1968, he was shot and killed. At the time of his death, King had begun to refocus his energies on ending poverty and the Vietnam War. The day of King's birth was established as a national holiday in 1986.

Letter from Birmingham Jail

April 16, 1963

My Dear Fellow Clergymen:

While confined° here in the Birmingham city jail, I came across your recent statement calling my present activities "unwise and untimely." Seldom do I pause to answer criticism of my work and ideas. If I sought to answer all the criticisms that cross my desk, my secretaries would have little time for anything other than such correspondence in the course of the day, and I would have no time for constructive work. But since I feel that you are men of genuine good will and that your criticisms are sincerely set forth, I want to try to answer your statement in what I hope will be patient and reasonable terms.

I think I should indicate why I am here in Birmingham, since you have been influenced by the view which argues against "outsiders coming in." I have the honor of serving as president of the Southern Christian Leadership Conference, an organization operating in every southern state, with headquarters in Atlanta, Georgia. We have some eighty-five affiliated organizations across the South, and one of them is the Alabama Christian Movement for Human Rights. Frequently we share staff, educational and financial resources with our affiliates. Several months ago the affiliate here in Birmingham asked us to be on call to engage in a nonviolent direct-action program if such were deemed necessary. We readily consented, and when the hour came we lived up to our promise. So I, along with several members of my staff, am here because I was invited here. I am here because I have organizational ties here.

But more basically, I am in Birmingham because injustice is here. Just as the prophets of the eighth century B.C. left their villages and carried their "thus saith the Lord" far beyond the boundaries of their home towns,

---

confined: King had been arrested on Good Friday, April 12, 1963, for his involvement in a public civil rights protest in defiance of a court injunction forbidding such actions. He spent eight days in the Birmingham Jail.

and just as the Apostle Paul° left his village of Tarsus and carried the gospel of Jesus Christ to the far corners of the Greco-Roman world, so am I compelled to carry the gospel of freedom beyond my own home town. Like Paul, I must constantly respond to the Macedonian call for aid.

Moreover, I am cognizant° of the interrelatedness of all communities and states. I cannot sit idly by in Atlanta and not be concerned about what happens in Birmingham. Injustice anywhere is a threat to justice everywhere. We are caught in an inescapable network of mutuality, tied in a single garment of destiny. Whatever affects one directly, affects all indirectly. Never again can we afford to live with the narrow, provincial "outside agitator"° idea. Anyone who lives inside the United States can never be considered an outsider anywhere within its bounds.

5

You deplore° the demonstrations taking place in Birmingham. But your statement, I am sorry to say, fails to express a similar concern for the conditions that brought about the demonstrations. I am sure that none of you would want to rest content with the superficial kind of social analysis that deals merely with effects and does not grapple with underlying causes. It is unfortunate that demonstrations are taking place in Birmingham, but it is even more unfortunate that the city's white power structure left the Negro community with no alternative.

In any nonviolent campaign there are four basic steps: collection of the facts to determine whether injustices exist; negotiation; self-purification; and direct action. We have gone through all these steps in Birmingham. There can be no gainsaying° the fact that racial injustice engulfs this community. Birmingham is probably the most thoroughly segregated city in the United States. Its ugly record of brutality is widely known. Negroes have experienced grossly unjust treatment in the courts. There have been more unsolved bombings of Negro homes and churches in Birmingham than in any other city in the nation. These are the hard, brutal facts of the case.

---

the Apostle Paul: Paul had gone to Macedonia after having a vision of a man from Macedonia imploring him to come and help his people. (Acts 16:9–10 in the Bible)

cognizant: aware

"outside agitator": Community leaders frequently blame civil unrest on "outside agitators," suggesting thereby that their own citizens are perfectly content with the way they are treated.

deplore: regret, disapprove of

gainsaying: denying

On the basis of these conditions, Negro leaders sought to negotiate with the city fathers. But the latter consistently refused to engage in good-faith negotiation.

Then, last September, came the opportunity to talk with leaders of Birmingham's economic community. In the course of the negotiations, certain promises were made by the merchants—for example, to remove the stores' humiliating racial signs. On the basis of these promises, the Reverend Fred Shuttlesworth and the leaders of the Alabama Christian Movement for Human Rights agreed to a moratorium° on all demonstrations. As the weeks and months went by, we realized that we were the victims of a broken promise. A few signs, briefly removed, returned; the others remained.

As in so many past experiences, our hopes had been blasted, and the shadow of deep disappointment settled upon us. We had no alternative except to prepare for direct action, whereby we would present our very bodies as a means of laying our case before the conscience of the local and the national community. Mindful of the difficulties involved, we decided to undertake a process of self-purification. We began a series of workshops on nonviolence, and we repeatedly asked ourselves: "Are you able to accept blows without retaliating?" "Are you able to endure the ordeal of jail?" We decided to schedule our direct-action program for the Easter season, realizing that except for Christmas, this is the main shopping period of the year. Knowing that a strong economic-withdrawal program would be the by-product of direct action, we felt that this would be the best time to bring pressure to bear on the merchants for the needed change.

Then it occurred to us that Birmingham's mayoral election was coming up in March, and we speedily decided to postpone action until after election day. When we discovered that the Commissioner of Public Safety, Eugene "Bull" Connor,° had piled up enough votes to be in the run-off, we decided again to postpone action until the day after the run-off so that the demonstrations could not be used to cloud the issues. Like many others, we waited to see Mr. Connor defeated, and to this end we endured

---

moratorium: suspension; authorized delay

Eugene "Bull" Connor: As Birmingham Commissioner of Public Safety, became notorious for ordering the police to turn attack dogs and fire hoses on peaceful demonstrators, including women and children; nationally broadcast television news film of these brutal scenes helped win public support for King's cause

postponement after postponement. Having aided in this community need, we felt that our direct action program could be delayed no longer.

10

You may well ask: "Why direct action? Why sit-ins, marches and so forth? Isn't negotiation a better path?" You are quite right in calling for negotiation. Indeed, this is the very purpose of direct action. Nonviolent direct action seeks to create such a crisis and foster° such a tension that a community which has constantly refused to negotiate is forced to confront the issue. It seeks so to dramatize the issue that it can no longer be ignored. My citing the creation of tension as part of the work of the nonviolent-resister may sound rather shocking. But I must confess that I am not afraid of the word "tension." I have earnestly opposed violent tension, but there is a type of constructive, nonviolent tension which is necessary for growth. Just as Socrates° felt that it was necessary to create a tension in the mind so that individuals could rise from the bondage of myths and half-truths to the unfettered° realm of creative analysis and objective appraisal, so must we see the need for nonviolent gadflies° to create the kind of tension in society that will help men rise from the dark depths of prejudice and racism to the majestic heights of understanding and brotherhood.

The purpose of our direct-action program is to create a situation so crisis-packed that it will inevitably open the door to negotiation. I therefore concur° with you in your call for negotiation. Too long has our beloved Southland been bogged down in a tragic effort to live in monologue rather than dialogue.

One of the basic points in your statements is that the action that I and my associates have taken in Birmingham is untimely. Some have asked: "Why didn't you give the new city administration time to act?" The only answer that I can give to this query is that the new Birmingham administration must be prodded about as much as the outgoing one, before it will act. We are sadly mistaken if we feel that the election of Albert Boutwell as mayor will bring the millennium° to Birmingham. While Mr.

---

foster: encourage, promote

Socrates: Athenian philosopher (fourth century B.C.) who used a technique of probing questions to force his followers to logically examine their most deeply held beliefs

unfettered: unrestrained

gadflies: term used colloquially to describe people who continually provoke or harass

concur: agree

millennium: time of happiness and peace

Boutwell is a much more gentle person than Mr. Connor, they are both segregationists, dedicated to maintenance of the status quo. I have hope that Mr. Boutwell will be reasonable enough to see the futility of massive resistance to desegregation. But he will not see this without pressure from devotees° of civil rights. My friends, I must say to you that we have not made a single gain in civil rights without determined legal and nonviolent pressure. Lamentably,° it is an historical fact that privileged groups seldom give up their privileges voluntarily. Individuals may see the moral light and voluntarily give up their unjust posture; but, as Reinhold Niebuhr° has reminded us, groups tend to be more immoral than individuals.

We know through painful experience that freedom is never voluntarily given by the oppressor; it must be demanded by the oppressed. Frankly, I have yet to engage in a direct-action campaign that was "well timed" in the view of those who have not suffered unduly° from the disease of segregation. For years now I have heard the word "Wait!" It rings in the ear of every Negro with piercing familiarity. This "Wait" has almost always meant "Never." We must come to see, with one of our distinguished jurists,° that "justice too long delayed is justice denied."

We have waited for more than 340 years° for our constitutional and God-given rights. The nations of Asia and Africa are moving with jetlike speed toward gaining political independence, but we still creep at horse-and-buggy pace toward gaining a cup of coffee at a lunch counter. Perhaps it is easy for those who have never felt the stinging darts of segregation to say, "Wait." But when you have seen vicious mobs lynch your mothers and fathers at will and drown your sisters and brothers at whim; when you have seen hate-filled policemen curse, kick and even kill your black brothers and sisters; when you see the vast majority of your twenty million Negro brothers smothering in an airtight cage of poverty in the midst of an affluent society; when you suddenly find your tongue twisted

---

devotees: followers

Lamentably: regrettably, unfortunately

Reinhold Niebuhr: (1892–1971), American theologian

unduly: excessively, inappropriately

one of our distinguished jurists: The quotation is often attributed to British prime minister William Ewart Gladstone (1809–1898), but no verifiable source for it has been found.

more than 340 years: King is alluding to the transportation of the first African slaves to Jamestown, Virginia, in 1619.

and your speech stammering as you seek to explain to your six-year-old daughter why she can't go to the public amusement park that has just been advertised on television, and see tears welling up in her eyes when she is told that Funtown is closed to colored children, and see ominous clouds of inferiority beginning to form in her little mental sky, and see her beginning to distort her personality by developing an unconscious bitterness toward white people; when you have to concoct an answer for a five-year-old son who is asking: "Daddy, why do white people treat colored people so mean?"; when you take a cross-country drive and find it necessary to sleep night after night in the uncomfortable corners of your automobile because no motel will accept you; when you are humiliated day in and day out by nagging signs reading "white" and "colored"; when your first name becomes "nigger," your middle name becomes "boy" (however old you are) and your last name becomes "John," and your wife and mother are never given the respected title "Mrs."; when you are harried by day and haunted by night by the fact that you are a Negro, living constantly at tiptoe stance, never quite knowing what to expect next, and are plagued with inner fears and outer resentments; when you are forever fighting a degenerating sense of "nobodiness"—then you will understand why we find it difficult to wait. There comes a time when the cup of endurance runs over, and men are no longer willing to be plunged into the abyss of despair. I hope, sirs, you can understand our legitimate and unavoidable impatience.

15 *You express a great deal of anxiety over our willingness to break laws. This is certainly a legitimate concern. Since we so diligently urge people to obey the Supreme Court's decision of 1954 outlawing segregation in the public schools, at first glance it may seem rather paradoxical° for us consciously to break laws. One may well ask: "How can you advocate breaking some laws and obeying others?" The answer lies in the fact that there are two types of laws: just and unjust. I would be the first to advocate obeying just laws. One has not only a legal but a moral responsibility to obey just laws. Conversely, one has a moral responsibility to disobey unjust laws. I would agree with St. Augustine° that "an unjust law is no law at all."*

Now, what is the difference between the two? How does one determine whether a law is just or unjust? A just law is a man-made code that

---

paradoxical: seemingly contradictory

St. Augustine: (354–430), philosopher, theologian, and bishop of Hippo Regius (in present-day Algeria)

squares with the moral law or the law of God. An unjust law is a code that is out of harmony with the moral law. To put it in the terms of St. Thomas Aquinas:° An unjust law is a human law that is not rooted in eternal law and natural law. Any law that uplifts human personality is just. Any law that degrades human personality is unjust. All segregation statutes are unjust because segregation distorts the soul and damages the personality. It gives the segregator a false sense of superiority and the segregated a false sense of inferiority. Segregation, to use the terminology of the Jewish philosopher Martin Buber,° substitutes an "I-it" relationship for an "I-thou" relationship and ends up relegating° persons to the status of things. Hence segregation is not only politically, economically and sociologically unsound, it is morally wrong and sinful. Paul Tillich° has said that sin is separation. Is not segregation an existential expression of man's tragic separation, his awful estrangement, his terrible sinfulness? Thus it is that I can urge men to obey the 1954 decision of the Supreme Court, for it is morally right; and I can urge them to disobey segregation ordinances,° for they are morally wrong.

Let us consider a more concrete example of just and unjust laws. An unjust law is a code that a numerical or power majority group compels a minority group to obey but does not make binding on itself. This is difference made legal. By the same token, a just law is a code that a majority compels a minority to follow and that it is willing to follow itself. This is sameness made legal.

Let me give another explanation. A law is unjust if it is inflicted on a minority that, as a result of being denied the right to vote, had no part in enacting or devising the law. Who can say that the legislature of Alabama which set up that state's segregation laws was democratically elected? Throughout Alabama all sorts of devious methods are used to prevent Negroes from becoming registered voters, and there are some counties in which, even though Negroes constitute a majority of the population, not a single Negro is registered. Can any law enacted under such circumstances be considered democratically structured?

St. Thomas Aquinas: (1225–1274), Italian philosopher and theologian
Martin Buber: (1878–1965), Austrian-born Israeli philosopher
relegating: assigning, referring (often, to an inferior status)
Paul Tillich: (1886–1965), German-American philosopher and theologian
ordinances: laws, regulations

Sometimes a law is just on its face and unjust in its application. For instance, I have been arrested on a charge of parading without a permit. Now, there is nothing wrong in having an ordinance which requires a permit for a parade. But such an ordinance becomes unjust when it is used to maintain segregation and to deny citizens the First-Amendment privilege of peaceful assembly and protest.

20

I hope you are able to see the distinction I am trying to point out. In no sense do I advocate evading or defying the law, as would the rabid segregationist. That would lead to anarchy. One who breaks an unjust law must do so openly, lovingly, and with a willingness to accept the penalty. I submit that an individual who breaks a law that conscience tells him is unjust, and who willingly accepts the penalty of imprisonment in order to arouse the conscience of the community over its injustice, is in reality expressing the highest respect for law.

Of course, there is nothing new about this kind of civil disobedience. It was evidenced sublimely° in the refusal of Shadrach, Meshach and Abednego° to obey the laws of Nebuchadnezzar, on the ground that a higher moral law was at stake. It was practiced superbly by the early Christians, who were willing to face hungry lions and the excruciating pain of chopping blocks rather than submit to certain unjust laws of the Roman Empire. To a degree, academic freedom is a reality today because Socrates practiced civil disobedience. In our own nation, the Boston Tea Party represented a massive act of civil disobedience.

We should never forget that everything Adolf Hitler did in Germany was "legal" and everything the Hungarian freedom fighters° did in Hungary was "illegal." It was "illegal" to aid and comfort a Jew in Hitler's Germany. Even so, I am sure that, had I lived in Germany at the time, I would have aided and comforted my Jewish brothers. If today I lived in a Communist country where certain principles dear to the Christian faith are suppressed, I would openly advocate disobeying that country's antireligious laws.

---

sublimely: outstandingly, awe-inspiringly

Shadrach, Meshach and Abednego: three young Jews thrown into a fiery furnace (where they were miraculously preserved) for disobeying the order of King Nebuchadnezzar of Babylon that they bow to a golden idol, in the Book of Daniel (Bible)

Hungarian freedom fighters: In October 1956, thousands of Hungarians began a spontaneous revolt against their Russian-dominated government; the uprising, which lasted for nearly three weeks, was crushed by Soviet forces with great loss of life on both sides.

I must make two honest confessions to you, my Christian and Jewish brothers. First, I must confess that over the past few years I have been gravely disappointed with the white moderate. I have almost reached the regrettable conclusion that the Negro's great stumbling block in his stride toward freedom is not the White Citizen's Councilerº or the Ku Klux Klanner, but the white moderate, who is more devoted to "order" than to justice; who prefers a negative peace which is the absence of tension to a positive peace which is the presence of justice; who constantly says: "I agree with you in the goal you seek, but I cannot agree with your methods of direct action"; who paternalisticallyº believes he can set the timetable for another man's freedom; who lives by a mythical concept of time and who constantly advises the Negro to wait for a "more convenient season." Shallow understanding from people of good will is more frustrating than absolute misunderstanding from people of ill will. Lukewarm acceptance is much more bewildering than outright rejection.

I had hoped that the white moderate would understand that law and order exist for the purpose of establishing justice and that when they fail in this purpose they become the dangerously structured dams that block the flow of social progress. I had hoped that the white moderate would understand that the present tension in the South is a necessary phase of the transition from an obnoxiousº negative peace, in which the Negro passively accepted his unjust plight, to a substantiveº and positive peace, in which all men will respect the dignity and worth of human personality. Actually, we who engage in nonviolent direct action are not the creators of tension. We merely bring to the surface the hidden tension that is already alive. We bring it out in the open, where it can be seen and dealt with. Like a boil that can never be cured so long as it is covered up but must be opened with all its ugliness to the natural medicines of air and light, injustice must be exposed, with all the tension its exposure creates, to the light of human conscience and the air of national opinion before it can be cured.

In your statement you assert that our actions, even though peaceful, must be condemned because they precipitateº violence. But is this a 25

White Citizen's Counciler: The White Citizens' Council was formed in Mississippi in 1954 in opposition to racial integration; it was succeeded by the Council of Conservative Citizens in 1985.
paternalistically: in the manner of a father dealing with his children
obnoxious: highly offensive, objectionable
substantive: solid, real
precipitate: hasten, accelerate

logical assertion? Isn't this like condemning a robbed man because his possession of money precipitated the evil act of robbery? Isn't this like condemning Socrates because his unswerving commitment to truth and his philosophical inquiries precipitated the act by the misguided populace in which they made him drink hemlock?° Isn't this like condemning Jesus because his unique God-consciousness and never-ceasing devotion to God's will precipitated the evil act of crucifixion? We must come to see that, as the federal courts have consistently affirmed, it is wrong to urge an individual to cease his efforts to gain his basic constitutional rights because the quest may precipitate violence. Society must protect the robbed and punish the robber.

I had also hoped that the white moderate would reject the myth concerning time in relation to the struggle for freedom. I have just received a letter from a white brother in Texas. He writes: "All Christians know that the colored people will receive equal rights eventually, but it is possible that you are in too great a religious hurry. It has taken Christianity almost two thousand years to accomplish what it has. The teachings of Christ take time to come to earth." Such an attitude stems from a tragic misconception of time, from the strangely irrational notion that there is something in the very flow of time that will inevitably cure all ills. Actually, time itself is neutral; it can be used either destructively or constructively. More and more I feel that the people of ill will have used time much more effectively than have the people of good will. We will have to repent in this generation not merely for the hateful words and actions of the bad people but for the appalling silence of the good people. Human progress never rolls in on wheels of inevitability; it comes through the tireless efforts of men willing to be co-workers with God, and without this hard work, time itself becomes an ally of the forces of social stagnation. We must use time creatively, in the knowledge that time is always ripe to do right. Now is the time to make real the promise of democracy and transform our pending national elegy° into a creative psalm of brotherhood. Now is the time to lift our national policy from the quicksand of racial injustice to the solid rock of human dignity.

You speak of our activity in Birmingham as extreme. At first I was rather disappointed that fellow clergymen would see my nonviolent efforts

---

hemlock: poisonous drink distilled from the hemlock plant; the means by which Socrates was executed in 399 B.C.

elegy: mournful poem or song; lament for the dead

as those of an extremist. I began thinking about the fact that I stand in the middle of two opposing forces in the Negro community. One is a force of complacency, made up in part of Negroes who, as a result of long years of oppression, are so drained of self-respect and a sense of "somebodiness" that they have adjusted to segregation; and in part of a few middle-class Negroes who, because of a degree of academic and economic security and because in some ways they profit by segregation, have become insensitive to the problems of the masses. The other force is one of bitterness and hatred, and it comes perilously close to advocating violence. It is expressed in the various black nationalist groups that are springing up across the nation, the largest and best-known being Elijah Muhammad's° Muslim movement. Nourished by the Negro's frustration over the continued existence of racial discrimination, this movement is made up of people who have lost faith in America, who have absolutely repudiated° Christianity, and who have concluded that the white man is an incorrigible "devil."

I have tried to stand between these two forces, saying that we need emulate° neither the "do-nothingism" of the complacent nor the hatred and despair of the black nationalist. For there is the more excellent way of love and nonviolent protest. I am grateful to God that, through the influence of the Negro church, the way of nonviolence became an integral part of our struggle.

If this philosophy had not emerged, by now many streets of the South would, I am convinced, be flowing with blood. And I am further convinced that if our white brothers dismiss as "rabble-rousers" and "outside agitators" those of us who employ nonviolent direct action, and if they refuse to support our nonviolent efforts, millions of Negroes will, out of frustration and despair, seek solace° and security in black nationalist ideologies—a development that would inevitably lead to a frightening racial nightmare.

30 *Oppressed people cannot remain oppressed forever. The yearning for freedom eventually manifests itself, and that is what has happened to the American Negro. Something within has reminded him of his birthright of*

Elijah Muhammad: (born Elijah Robert Poole, 1897–1975), leader of the African American separatist Nation of Islam

repudiated: rejected, cast aside

emulate: imitate, attempt to equal

solace: comfort, consolation

freedom, and something without° has reminded him that it can be gained. Consciously or unconsciously, he has been caught up by the Zeitgeist,° and with his black brothers of Africa and his brown and yellow brothers of Asia, South America and the Caribbean, the United States Negro is moving with a sense of great urgency toward the promised land of racial justice. If one recognizes this vital urge that has engulfed the Negro community, one should readily understand why public demonstrations are taking place. The Negro has many pent-up° resentments and latent° frustrations, and he must release them. So let him march; let him make prayer pilgrimages to the city hall; let him go on freedom rides°—and try to understand why he must do so. If his repressed emotions are not released in nonviolent ways, they will seek expression through violence; this is not a threat but a fact of history. So I have not said to my people: "Get rid of your discontent." Rather, I have tried to say that this normal and healthy discontent can be channeled into the creative outlet of nonviolent direct action. And now this approach is being termed extremist.

But though I was initially disappointed at being categorized as an extremist, as I continued to think about the matter I gradually gained a measure of satisfaction from the label. Was not Jesus an extremist for love: "Love your enemies, bless them that curse you, do good to them that hate you, and pray for them which despitefully use you, and persecute you." Was not Amos° an extremist for justice: "Let justice roll down like waters and righteousness like an ever-flowing stream." Was not Paul an extremist for the Christian gospel: "I bear in my body the marks of the Lord Jesus." Was not Martin Luther° an extremist: "Here I stand; I cannot do otherwise, so help me God." And John Bunyan:° "I will stay in jail to the end of my days before I make a butchery of my conscience." And Abraham Lincoln: "This

---

without: outside of

Zeitgeist: German for "spirit of the time"

pent-up: suppressed, not vented

latent: inactive, dormant; existing as potential

freedom rides: "Freedom riders" were civil rights activists in the early 1960s who rode buses from the north to the south to test a 1960 Supreme Court ruling outlawing segregation on buses and in bus stations and facilities involved in interstate commerce.

Amos: Old Testament prophet, author of the Book of Amos

Martin Luther: (1483–1546), German Catholic priest whose *95 Theses* (1517) sparked the Protestant Reformation

John Bunyan: (1628–1688), English writer and preacher, author of *The Pilgrim's Progress* (1678)

nation cannot survive half slave and half free." And Thomas Jefferson: "We hold these truths to be self-evident, that all men are created equal . . ." So the question is not whether we will be extremists, but what kind of extremists we will be. Will we be extremists for hate or for love? Will we be extremists for the preservation of injustice or for the extension of justice? In that dramatic scene on Calvary's hill three men were crucified. We must never forget that all three were crucified for the same crime—the crime of extremism. Two were extremists for immorality, and thus fell below their environment. The other, Jesus Christ, was an extremist for love, truth and goodness, and thereby rose above his environment. Perhaps the South, the nation and the world are in dire need of creative extremists.

I had hoped that the white moderate would see this need. Perhaps I was too optimistic; perhaps I expected too much. I suppose I should have realized that few members of the oppressor race can understand the deep groans and passionate yearnings of the oppressed race, and still fewer have the vision to see that injustice must be rooted out by strong, persistent and determined action. I am thankful, however, that some of our white brothers in the South have grasped the meaning of this social revolution and committed themselves to it. They are still all too few in quantity, but they are big in quality. Some—such as Ralph McGill, Lillian Smith, Harry Golden, James McBride Dabbs, Ann Braden and Sarah Patton Boyle—have written about our struggle in eloquent and prophetic terms. Others have marched with us down nameless streets of the South. They have languished° in filthy, roach-infested jails, suffering the abuse and brutality of policemen who view them as "dirty nigger-lovers." Unlike so many of their moderate brothers and sisters, they have recognized the urgency of the moment and sensed the need for powerful "action" antidotes to combat the disease of segregation.

Let me take note of my other major disappointment. I have been so greatly disappointed with the white church and its leadership. Of course, there are some notable exceptions. I am not unmindful of the fact that each of you has taken some significant stands on this issue. I commend you, Reverend Stallings, for your Christian stand on this past Sunday, in welcoming Negroes to your worship service on a nonsegregated basis. I commend the Catholic leaders of this state for integrating Spring Hill College several years ago.

---

languished: withered, faded

But despite these notable exceptions, I must honestly reiterate that I have been disappointed with the church. I do not say this as one of those negative critics who can always find something wrong with the church. I say this as a minister of the gospel, who loves the church; who was nurtured in its bosom; who has been sustained by its spiritual blessings and who will remain true to it as long as the cord of life shall lengthen.

35

When I was suddenly catapulted into the leadership of the bus protest in Montgomery, Alabama, a few years ago, I felt we would be supported by the white church. I felt that the white ministers, priests and rabbis of the South would be among our strongest allies. Instead, some have been outright opponents, refusing to understand the freedom movement and misrepresenting its leaders; all too many others have been more cautious than courageous and have remained silent behind the anesthetizing° security of stained-glass windows.

In spite of my shattered dreams, I came to Birmingham with the hope that the white religious leadership of this community would see the justice of our cause and, with deep moral concern, would serve as the channel through which our just grievances could reach the power structure. I had hoped that each of you would understand. But again I have been disappointed.

I have heard numerous southern religious leaders admonish° their worshipers to comply with a desegregation decision because it is the law, but I have longed to hear white ministers declare: "Follow this decree because integration is morally right and because the Negro is your brother." In the midst of blatant° injustices inflicted upon the Negro, I have watched white churchmen stand on the sideline and mouth pious irrelevancies and sanctimonious trivialities. In the midst of a mighty struggle to rid our nation of racial and economic injustice, I have heard many ministers say: "Those are social issues, with which the gospel has no real concern." And I have watched many churches commit themselves to a completely otherworldly religion which makes a strange, unbiblical distinction between body and soul, between the sacred and the secular.

I have traveled the length and breadth of Alabama, Mississippi and all the other southern states. On sweltering summer days and crisp autumn

---

anesthetizing: rendering insensible to feeling
admonish: advise
blatant: flagrant, brazenly obvious

mornings I have looked at the South's beautiful churches with their lofty spires pointing heavenward. I have beheld the impressive outlines of her massive religious-education buildings. Over and over I have found myself asking: "What kind of people worship here? Who is their God? Where were their voices when the lips of Governor Barnett° dripped with words of interposition and nullification? Where were they when Governor Wallace° gave a clarion call for defiance and hatred? Where were their voices of support when bruised and weary Negro men and women decided to rise from the dark dungeons of complacency to the bright hills of creative protest?"

Yes, these questions are still in my mind. In deep disappointment I have wept over the laxity° of the church. But be assured that my tears have been tears of love. There can be no deep disappointment where there is not deep love. Yes, I love the church. How could I do otherwise? I am in the rather unique position of being the son, the grandson and the great-grandson of preachers. Yes, I see the church as the body of Christ. But, oh! How we have blemished and scarred that body through social neglect and through fear of being nonconformists.

40 *There was a time when the church was very powerful—in the time when the early Christians rejoiced at being deemed° worthy to suffer for what they believed. In those days the church was not merely a thermometer that recorded the ideas and principles of popular opinion; it was a thermostat that transformed the mores° of society. Whenever the early Christians entered a town, the people in power became disturbed and immediately sought to convict the Christians for being "disturbers of the peace" and "outside agitators." But the Christians pressed on, in the conviction that they were "a colony of heaven," called to obey God rather than man. Small in number, they were big in commitment. They were too God-intoxicated to be "astronomically intimidated." By their effort and example they brought an end to such ancient evils as infanticide° and gladiatorial contests.*

Governor Barnett: (1898–1987), governor of Mississippi (1960–1964)

Governor Wallace: (1919–1998), governor of Alabama (1963–1967, 1971–1979, 1983–1987)

laxity: lack of firmness or strictness

deemed: considered

mores: (pronounced *morays*) customs, social practices

infanticide: the killing of an infant

Things are different now. So often the contemporary church is a weak, ineffectual° voice with an uncertain sound. So often it is an arch-defender of the status quo. Far from being disturbed by the presence of the church, the power structure of the average community is consoled by the church's silent—and often even vocal—sanction° of things as they are.

But the judgment of God is upon the church as never before. If today's church does not recapture the sacrificial spirit of the early church, it will lose its authenticity, forfeit the loyalty of millions, and be dismissed as an irrelevant social club with no meaning for the twentieth century. Every day I meet young people whose disappointment with the church has turned into outright disgust.

Perhaps I have once again been too optimistic. Is organized religion too inextricably° bound to the status quo to save our nation and the world? Perhaps I must turn my faith to the inner spiritual church, the church within the church, as the true ekklesia° and the hope of the world. But again I am thankful to God that some noble souls from the ranks of organized religion have broken loose from the paralyzing chains of conformity and joined us as active partners in the struggle for freedom. They have left their secure congregations and walked the streets of Albany, Georgia, with us. They have gone down the highways of the South on tortuous rides for freedom. Yes, they have gone to jail with us. Some have been dismissed from their churches, have lost the support of their bishops and fellow ministers. But they have acted in the faith that right defeated is stronger than evil triumphant. Their witness° has been the spiritual salt that has preserved the true meaning of the gospel in these troubled times. They have carved a tunnel of hope through the dark mountain of disappointment.

I hope the church as a whole will meet the challenge of this decisive hour. But even if the church does not come to the aid of justice, I have no despair about the future. I have no fear about the outcome of our struggle in Birmingham, even if our motives are at present misunderstood. We will

---

ineffectual: powerless, futile
sanction: approval, permission
inextricably: without the capability of being disentangled
ekklesia: body of the church, congregation of believers (from the Greek)
witness: testimony, bearing of witness

reach the goal of freedom in Birmingham and all over the nation, because the goal of America is freedom. Abused and scorned though we may be, our destiny is tied up with America's destiny. Before the pilgrims landed at Plymouth, we were here. Before the pen of Jefferson etched the majestic words of the Declaration of Independence across the pages of history, we were here. For more than two centuries our forebears labored in this country without wages; they made cotton king; they built the homes of their masters while suffering gross injustice and shameful humiliation—and yet out of a bottomless vitality they continued to thrive and develop. If the inexpressible cruelties of slavery could not stop us, the opposition we now face will surely fail. We will win our freedom because the sacred heritage of our nation and the eternal will of God are embodied in our echoing demands.

45 *Before closing I feel impelled to mention one other point in your statement that has troubled me profoundly. You warmly commended the Birmingham police force for keeping "order" and "preventing violence." I doubt that you would have so warmly commended the police force if you had seen its dogs sinking their teeth into unarmed, nonviolent Negroes. I doubt that you would so quickly commend the policemen if you were to observe their ugly and inhumane treatment of Negroes here in the city jail; if you were to watch them push and curse old Negro women and young Negro girls; if you were to see them slap and kick old Negro men and young boys; if you were to observe them, as they did on two occasions, refuse to give us food because we wanted to sing our grace together. I cannot join you in your praise of the Birmingham Police Department.*

It is true that the police have exercised a degree of discipline in handling the demonstrators. In this sense they have conducted themselves rather "nonviolently" in public. But for what purpose? To preserve the evil system of segregation. Over the past few years I have consistently preached that nonviolence demands that the means we use must be as pure as the ends we seek. I have tried to make clear that it is wrong to use immoral means to attain moral ends. But now I must affirm that it is just as wrong, or perhaps even more so, to use moral means to preserve immoral ends. Perhaps Mr. Connor and his policemen have been rather nonviolent in public, as was Chief Pritchett in Albany, Georgia, but they have used the moral means of nonviolence to maintain the immoral end° of racial

---

end: in the sense of *goal* or *intention*

injustice. As T. S. Eliot° has said: "The last temptation is the greatest treason: To do the right deed for the wrong reason."

I wish you had commended the Negro sit-inners and demonstrators of Birmingham for their sublime courage, their willingness to suffer and their amazing discipline in the midst of great provocation. One day the South will recognize its real heroes. They will be the James Merediths,° with the noble sense of purpose that enables them to face jeering and hostile mobs, and with the agonizing loneliness that characterizes the life of the pioneer. They will be old, oppressed, battered Negro women, symbolized in a seventy-two-year-old woman in Montgomery, Alabama, who rose up with a sense of dignity and with her people decided not to ride segregated buses, and who responded with ungrammatical profundity° to one who inquired about her weariness: "My feets is tired, but my soul is at rest." They will be the young high school and college students, the young ministers of the gospel and a host of their elders, courageously and nonviolently sitting in at lunch counters and willingly going to jail for conscience sake. One day the South will know that when these disinherited children of God sat down at lunch counters, they were in reality standing up for what is best in the American dream and for the most sacred values in our Judaeo-Christian heritage, thereby bringing our nation back to those great wells of democracy which were dug deep by the founding fathers in their formulation of the Constitution and the Declaration of Independence.

Never before have I written so long a letter. I'm afraid it is much too long to take your precious time. I can assure you that it would have been much shorter if I had been writing from a comfortable desk, but what else can one do when he is alone in a narrow jail cell, other than write long letters, think long thoughts and pray long prayers?

If I have said anything in this letter that overstates the truth and indicates an unreasonable impatience, I beg you to forgive me. If I have said anything that understates the truth and indicates my having a patience

---

T. S. Eliot: American poet and critic (1888–1965) who immigrated to England in 1914; the quoted lines are from his verse drama *Murder in the Cathedral* (1935)

James Merediths: James Meredith (b. 1933) was the first African American to be admitted to the University of Mississippi law school; his attempt to enroll, in October 1962, provoked campus rioting. On June 6, 1966, Meredith was shot and wounded while leading a civil rights march from Memphis, Tennessee, to Jackson, Mississippi.

profundity: depth

that allows me to settle for anything less than brotherhood, I beg God to forgive me.

I hope this letter finds you strong in the faith. I also hope that circumstances will soon make it possible for me to meet each of you, not as an integrationist or a civil-rights leader but as a fellow clergyman and a Christian brother. Let us all hope that the dark clouds of racial prejudice will soon pass away and the deep fog of misunderstanding will be lifted from our fear-drenched communities, and in some not too distant tomorrow the radiant stars of love and brotherhood will shine over our great nation with all their scintillating beauty. 50

Yours for the cause of Peace and Brotherhood,
Martin Luther King, Jr.

Read

1. How does the genre of the letter affect the way you read King's piece?
2. How does King use the setting for his writing of the letter as a rhetorical strategy?
3. How does King approach his audience? Where do you see his answering their objections?
4. How does the narrative of events help establish King's persona?

Write

1. Comment on King's contention that "freedom is never freely given by the oppressor."
2. Find an example of metaphor and explain in a line or two how it works as a rhetorical strategy.
3. What kinds of evidence might be most persuasive to his audience? Explain why you think so.
4. In a paragraph, explain how you think King uses the three appeals. How does he show awareness of his audience in his use of these appeals?
5. Write a sentence or two that describes what you think is King's message to his audience.

Complete Additional Exercises on King's Letter at Your Pearson MyLab

Connect

1. How does King's use of appeals compare to the way other civil rights speakers in earlier times used them? Consider Stanton, Stewart, Apess, or others.
2. Find a newspaper article from 1961 about the civil rights protests in Birmingham. How does the background information give context to King's letter?

Robert F. Kennedy

The brother of President John F. Kennedy, Robert Kennedy (1925–1968) was born to a prominent Boston family. He was one of eleven children. He was a lawyer, and when John entered the race for president, Robert served as his campaign manager. As Kennedy's attorney general, Robert began working on civil rights issues and supported the Freedom Riders, who sought an end to racial segregation. In 1964, Kennedy was elected as U.S. Senator from New York.

He ran his own presidential campaign in 1968 for the Democratic nomination, and was on a campaign stop when the news came that Martin Luther King had been assassinated. He broke the news to the audience who was waiting to hear him speak. While celebrating his win in the California primary in June of 1968, Robert Kennedy was murdered by Sirhan Sirhan.

On the Death of Martin Luther King

Ladies and Gentlemen—I'm only going to talk to you just for a minute or so this evening. Because . . .

I have some very sad news for all of you, and I think sad news for all of our fellow citizens, and people who love peace all over the world, and that is that Martin Luther King was shot and was killed tonight in Memphis, Tennessee.

Martin Luther King dedicated his life to love and to justice between fellow human beings. He died in the cause of that effort. In this difficult day, in this difficult time for the United States, it's perhaps well to ask what kind of a nation we are and what direction we want to move in.

For those of you who are black—considering the evidence evidently is that there were white people who were responsible—you can be filled with bitterness, and with hatred, and a desire for revenge.

We can move in that direction as a country, in greater polarization—black people amongst blacks, and white amongst whites, filled with hatred toward one another. Or we can make an effort, as Martin Luther King did, to understand and to comprehend, and replace that violence, that stain of bloodshed that has spread across our land, with an effort to understand, compassion and love. 5

For those of you who are black and are tempted to be filled with hatred and mistrust of the injustice of such an act, against all white people, I would only say that I can also feel in my own heart the same kind of feeling. I had a member of my family killed, but he was killed by a white man.

But we have to make an effort in the United States, we have to make an effort to understand, to get beyond these rather difficult times.

My favorite poet was Aeschylus.° He once wrote: "Even in our sleep, pain which cannot forget falls drop by drop upon the heart, until, in our own despair, against our will, comes wisdom through the awful grace of God."

What we need in the United States is not division; what we need in the United States is not hatred; what we need in the United States is not violence and lawlessness, but is love and wisdom, and compassion toward one another, and a feeling of justice toward those who still suffer within our country, whether they be white or whether they be black.

[Interrupted by applause] 10

So I ask you tonight to return home, to say a prayer for the family of Martin Luther King, yeah that's true, but more importantly to say a prayer for our own country, which all of us love—a prayer for understanding and that compassion of which I spoke. We can do well in this country. We will have difficult times. We've had difficult times in the past. And we will have difficult times in the future. It is not the end of violence; it is not the end of lawlessness; and it's not the end of disorder.

But the vast majority of white people and the vast majority of black people in this country want to live together, want to improve the quality of our life, and want justice for all human beings that abide in our land.

[*Interrupted by applause*]

Let us dedicate ourselves to what the Greeks wrote so many years ago: to tame the savageness of man and make gentle the life of this world.

Let us dedicate ourselves to that, and say a prayer for our country and for our people. Thank you very much. [*Applause*] 15

[1968]

Read

1. What is the effect of the pause at the end of line 1?
2. What do you think the reasons for it are?
3. What details in the speech suggest Robert Kennedy's feelings about Martin Luther King, Jr.?
4. How does Kennedy demonstrate his understanding of audience and the differences among members of his audience?

Write

1. Explain how Kennedy uses this tragic moment to locate something positive that might come from the tragedy.

Aeschylus: (525–456 B.C.), Greek tragic playwright; the lines are slightly misquoted (*despair* for *despite*) from *Agamemnon,* the first play of the Oresteia trilogy (458 B.C.)

Complete Additional Exercises on Kennedy's Speech at Your Pearson MyLab

2. Write a paragraph reflecting on the quote by Aeschylus near the end of the speech.

Connect

1. Compare this speech to Abraham Lincoln's Gettysburg Address, especially in terms of its use of context or occasion and its aims.

John Filo

Troops from the Ohio National Guard killed four students and injured nine when they opened fire on a crowd of protesters at Kent State University in Kent, Ohio, on May 4, 1970.

The protestors were gathering in the University's Commons area in response to an announcement from President Richard Nixon that the United States would send troops into Cambodia, essentially widening the scale and scope of the Vietnam War.

The May 4 demonstration was the culmination of four days of protests. On May 2, demonstrators burned the University's Army Reserve Officer Training Corps (ROTC) building to the ground. In the days following what became known as the Kent State Massacre, over 450 campuses closed because of protests. Five days later in Washington, DC, nearly 100,000 people gathered outside the White House to demand the removal of American troops from Southeast Asia.

John Filo (b. 1948) was a student at Kent State studying photojournalism and a staffer for the Philadelphia *Tribune-Review* when he took this photograph during the shootings at Kent State. He won a Pulitzer Prize for this photograph. Filo later worked as pictorial editor for the *Baltimore Sun* before moving to *Newsweek.* He now is on the communications staff at CBS.

Kent State Massacre

Fourteen-year-old Mary Ann Vecchio kneels over the body of Jeffrey Miller after he was killed by Ohio National Guard troops on the campus of Kent State University on May 4, 1970.

[1970]

Read

1. The photo depicts the shootings at Kent State University in Ohio, which occurred when the National Guard was called in to quell a student protest against the Vietnam War. Four students were killed. What details stand out in the photo, knowing its context?
2. How do the central figures relate to the figures surrounding them?
3. How do you read the expression on the face of the woman in the center?

Write

1. Locate some background information on the student protests of the sixties, and then write a short analysis piece that uses the photograph as part of the discussion of the role students played in the war.
2. After reading, write a short paragraph that speculates on what the young woman might be saying as she looks toward the camera.

Connect

1. Contrast this photo with the VJ Day Happy Sailor Kissing Nurse photograph in terms of central and background characters, contrast, motion, and effect.

Contemporary Works

Alice Yang Murray

Alice Yang Murray (b. 1959) is an associate professor of History at the University of California, Santa Cruz, where she teaches courses in Asian American history, twentieth-century America, and race and gender. She has written four books on Japanese and Asian American life, two on the Japanese internment during World War II.

Dillon S. Myer and the WRA's History of "Relocation, Reintegration, and Rehabilitation"

From Historical Memories of Japanese American Internment and the Struggle for Redress

On March 19, 1942, exactly one month after President Roosevelt signed Executive Order 9066, the Tolan° Committee issued a preliminary report that endorsed the mass removal of Japanese Americans from the West Coast but

Tolan: John H. Tolan (1877–1947); Democratic congressman from California (1935–1947)

opposed proposals for mass incarceration. Although the congressional committee members condoned Secretary of the Navy Frank Knox's false reports of a fifth column° at Pearl Harbor and General John L. DeWitt's portrayal of potential West Coast spies and saboteurs, they also expressed concern about the rights of uprooted Japanese Americans. "Serious constitutional questions," the committee warned, "are raised by the forced detention of citizens against whom no individual charges are lodged." Therefore, the committee recommended that Japanese Americans be given loyalty hearings at "assembly centers" close to their homes, "followed by arrangements for job placement outside of the prohibited areas of all persons certified." Providing an astute prediction of problems later experienced in the camps, the committee proclaimed:

> The incarceration of the Japanese for the duration of the war can only end in wholesale deportation. The maintenance of all Japanese, alien and citizen, in enforced idleness will prove not only a costly waste of the taxpayer's money, but it automatically implies deportation, since we cannot expect this group to be loyal to our Government or sympathetic to our way of life thereafter.

Nevertheless, West Coast Japanese Americans were forcibly removed from their homes and imprisoned in barbed wire compounds guarded by the military and administered by the War Relocation Authority (WRA), a civilian government agency. Yet in 1946, just four years after these camps were established, the head of the WRA, Dillon S. Myer, received from President Harry S. Truman a Medal for Merit for having "won for American democracy a great and significant victory." Conspicuously omitting any reference to an incarceration, the citation praised Myer's "program for the readjustment" of Japanese Americans. Crediting Myer with avoiding the "threat of progressive disaffection,° disloyalty and deportation," the citation celebrated the WRA's program of "progressive relocation, reintegration and rehabilitation of this racial minority." The camps, according to the award, became "an affirmation of American faith in the validity of democratic processes."

Myer's citation for "outstanding service" was quoted verbatim from a WRA recommendation for the award, written by WRA historian Ruth E. McKee. This glowing recommendation, which also offered a whitewashed history of the WRA, denied that the mass removal was motivated by racism. Acknowledging that the federal government had sanctioned a "mass evacuation on the basis of race and ancestry," the WRA feebly maintained that this "unintentionally gave apparent support to the doctrines of the racists" on the West Coast

---

fifth column: group secretly sympathetic to its nation's enemies
disaffection: alienation, estrangement

who had harassed Japanese Americans for forty years. A "war-shaken, misinformed public was increasingly inclined to support the racists' demand that all Japanese Americans should be held in concentration camps for the duration of the war and then be deported to Japan." Resisting these calls, Myer initiated a program "to replace misinformation and vicious invention with factual information and to win for the loyal evacuees public recognition of their right to be fully accepted as Americans."

The WRA director, according to McKee's history, "battled ignorance and intolerance in America" outside the camps by issuing press releases, disseminating pamphlets, and giving lectures on Japanese American loyalty and patriotism. Within the camps, Myer was portrayed as an administrator who drew up WRA policies only after meeting and consulting with Japanese Americans in the camps' barrack communities. McKee further wrote that even though "bewildered young Americans with Japanese faces were obliged to wait behind barbed wire and under armed guard for their country to grant them the right to work and live and die with other Americans, Mr. Myer never allowed them to forget that they had friends who believed in them and who were working for them." Consequently, he "kept alive their faith in the American way of life."

5

One month later McKee sent Myer a report expressing her "complete enthusiasm" for her role in penning the recommendation that helped the director win his Medal for Merit. Also she detailed, however, her serious reservations about the way she had been employed to frame history according to the receiving audience. Entitled "Reflections on the Proper Care and Treatment of Historians," McKee's report declared the "proper function of the Historian is recording in detail and evaluating what happened; the Historian is writing for the benefit of serious students who need a full picture of what happened and why." After only one month on the job, McKee was asked to write the agency's quarterly report to Congress and the president. The division chief unsuccessfully tried to persuade McKee that preparing official agency reports "was a logical and helpful step toward the preparation of the overall history of the agency." But as McKee explained to Myer:

> The writer of official reports to Congress, telling of current and controversial happenings must be careful to tell nothing but the truth, but he must be equally careful to select his truths with discretion. The difference in substance between the two kinds of reporting is the difference between cream and skim milk. It is bad for any writer to be expected to be thorough and scholarly half the time and disingenuously° selective and superficial the rest of the time.

---

disingenuously: insincerely; without candor or frankness

Myer never acknowledged McKee's misgivings about selecting his truths with discretion. As McKee's citation recommendation had noted, Myer and the WRA disseminated "factual information" to defend the WRA's programs and to improve the image of Japanese Americans. Yet the particular set of facts Myer and his staff presented varied with different audiences. While dealing with groups sympathetic to Japanese Americans, Myer portrayed the camps as "normal communities" filled with cheerful Nisei° going to school or playing sports, as their parents attended church or took English language classes. After Congress investigated charges the WRA "pampered" Japanese Americans, Myer emphasized the harsh conditions of the camps and the restrictions imposed upon those deemed disloyal. During WRA campaigns to gain community acceptance of "resettlers" released from the camps, Myer depicted Americans with "Japanese faces" eager to assimilate and to prove their love of democracy by volunteering for military service and by helping the war effort from within the camps. When confronted with Japanese Americans disillusioned by wartime losses, camp policies, and anti-Japanese agitation outside the camps, Myer gave another version of the WRA's history. Acknowledging an "abnormal" life in camp, he nevertheless celebrated WRA "public relations" successes and urged distrustful Japanese Americans to leave camp for "normal" communities.

Myer's History of "Relocation"

The WRA director wasn't always consistent. His public views of mass exclusion and incarceration changed over time. In 1943 Myer told a congressional subcommittee suspicious he might be a reluctant jailer that he believed "the evacuation was within the constitutional power of the National Government." The danger of an invasion on the West Coast; "the possibility that an unknown and unrecognizable minority" of a group "not wholly assimilated" might have greater allegiance to Japan than to the United States; and "the need for speed created the unfortunate necessity for evacuating the whole group instead of attempting to determine who were dangerous among them, so that only those might be evacuated." Myer agreed: "That same need made it impossible to hold adequate investigations or to grant hearings to the evacuees before evacuation." In 1971, however, Myer contradicted this account in a memoir that clearly recognized the civil rights movement had changed many Americans' views of internment. "As director of the WRA," he wrote, "I believed, and still believe, that a selective evacuation of people of Japanese descent from the West Coast military area may have been justified and feasible in early 1942, but I do not believe that a mass evacuation was ever justified."

Nisei: native-born Americans of Japanese descent

In the same memoir, Myer declared the WRA's triumph in "overcoming bitterness, ignorance, and discrimination" had "something important to contribute to the civil rights programs of today." Myer boasted, "The results of the effort to correct what has sometimes been referred to as our worst wartime mistake have proved that a democracy such as ours can correct its mistakes, if there is a will to do so." He went on to say:

> The "Yellow Peril"° propaganda of more than forty years appears to be dead. Through the cooperation of American people of good will with the Japanese American population, the United States was able to prove to the world through loyalty, courage, sacrifice, and positive action that we can rise above the sordid hate and bitterness of racial antipathy and the discriminatory practices stemming there from.

Myer's rose-tinted history of the WRA conveniently left out much of the suffering Japanese Americans experienced during and after the war as a direct result of his administration. Nevertheless, there is evidence Myer wanted to be viewed as the true friend and advocate of Japanese Americans. Richard Nishimoto, an internee at Poston, Arizona, who worked for researchers studying Japanese Americans within the camps, recalled during a visit in 1945 that Myer asked him "how he was received by the evacuees here":

> I said, "You're old enough to take a compliment without getting conceited. So I'll tell you." I said the reactions could be summarized in one sentence. I placed the fingernails of my right hand to my teeth and made a lovelorn look. I said in an adoring tone, "Gee, what a man!" He smiled genuinely. He liked it . . . He said he enjoy[ed] playing politics with members of the Congress. He spends every Saturday afternoon on "the Hill."

10 Nishimoto's reassurance might have helped Myer forget a history of demonstrations and riots within the camps. Perhaps it bolstered° him to continue his "public relations" campaign with an often-hostile Congress. One month later Myer had drinks with Nishimoto's boss, Dorothy Thomas, the director of the research study on the camps. Thomas recalled Myer giving a lengthy account of "what a great man and what a martyr" he considered himself.

Apparently confident that Thomas and other scholars in her study also would see him in this light, Myer gave them access to a wealth of documents on WRA policies after receiving assurance no publications would be issued during the war. For an administrator who was very careful about the way he presented WRA history in wartime, Myer displayed remarkably little concern

---

"Yellow Peril": alleged threat to Western or white civilization by an influx of Asian immigrants

bolstered: supported

about the historical records he made available to the public. After the war, the WRA deposited at the Bancroft Library, at the University of California, Berkeley, a complete set of its files that revealed how the reality of camp life differed from the images projected by Myer and the WRA.

Myer probably assumed his accounts of a benevolent administration would never be challenged. Unlike his predecessor, Milton S. Eisenhower,° Myer never expressed any misgivings about his role as the director of the WRA. In contrast to Myer, Eisenhower depicted the camps in his memoirs as "illustrative of how an entire society can somehow plunge off course." Summoned to the White House in March 1942, Eisenhower was told by Roosevelt "to set up a War Relocation Authority to move the Japanese-Americans off the Pacific Coast." At first Eisenhower confessed he spent "little time pondering the moral implications of the President's decision." A few weeks later, however, he wrote Agriculture Secretary Claude Wickard that after the war "we as Americans are going to regret the avoidable injustices that may have been done." Two months later Interior Secretary Harold Ickes informed Roosevelt, "I have it from several sources that Eisenhower is sick of the job." Just three months after receiving his appointment, Eisenhower left the WRA and accepted an offer to become a deputy in the Office of War Information. Before assuming his new position, Eisenhower asked Myer whether he was interested in the director's post. This was not the first time Eisenhower had advanced Myer's career as a government bureaucrat. Earlier he helped Myer become assistant chief of the Soil Conservation Service and acting administrator of the Agricultural Conservation and Adjustment Administration. Myer remembered being approached by his old friend:

> I asked Milton if he really thought I should take the job. He replied, "Yes, if you can do the job and sleep at night." He said that he had been unable to do so. I was sure that I could sleep, and so agreed to accept the position if he felt that I was the one to do it, although it was not something that I would have chosen for myself.

After being recommended by Eisenhower, Myer was appointed by Roosevelt on June 17, 1942. Myer would later recall that throughout his four years at the WRA, "with very few exceptions I went to bed at night and slept soundly."

Even before the process of removing Japanese Americans from the West Coast had been completed, Myer tried to drum up support for the WRA with a public relations campaign. He wrote an article entitled "Democracy in Relocation" for *Common Ground,* a magazine to promote diversity that was founded by the Common Council for American Unity. In its Democracy Begins at

---

Milton S. Eisenhower: (1899–1985), brother of President Dwight D. Eisenhower

Home issue, the magazine presented the Langston Hughes essay "What Shall We Do about the South?" Hughes wrote about the discrimination African Americans endured. Myer's article presented the WRA as an agency devoted to improving the status of Japanese Americans. Acknowledging Japanese Americans had experienced an "involuntary migration," he nevertheless defined the mass removal and incarceration as an "evacuation." He employed other euphemisms° to describe the compounds that confined Japanese Americans. After "temporary residence in assembly centers" located near their homes, Myer explained, Japanese Americans "now are living in ten relocation centers between the Mississippi River and the high Sierras."

Since *Common Ground* readers tended to share Langston Hughes's critical views of racism, Myer took great pains to defend the mass removal and incarceration. "Evacuation," according to Myer, "seemed necessary to help insure the safety of our western shore against an enemy who looked like these people and who had taken advantage of the situation to infiltrate the Japanese population of our West Coast with his agents." At first, Myer noted, Japanese Americans were simply ordered to leave the western regions of Washington, Oregon, southern Arizona, and California. Yet, he insisted, this "voluntary evacuation" was "doomed to failure, not only because of [the] reluctance to go but because the movement of more than 100,000 people into new communities was bound to cause trouble." Officials in other western states "refused to be responsible for law and order if the evacuees came into their states as unrestricted residents." "This combination of situations pointed to two things," Myer explained, "first, evacuation must be placed on an orderly basis; and second, the evacuated persons must be provided with homes which would offer security and opportunities for work until orderly processes of relocation could be made effective." 15

Consequently, at the end of March, "voluntary evacuation" was replaced with a "planned and systematic evacuation" to an "assembly center" run by the military and then to a WRA "relocation center" in eastern California, Arizona, Utah, Idaho, Wyoming, Colorado, or Arkansas. Describing these sites as "publicly owned land which has possibilities of development for agriculture and other enterprises," Myer vowed to help Japanese Americans "live in a manner as nearly normal as possible, with responsibility for the management of the communities in which they live, with educational opportunities, with a chance to develop initiative, and with reason to look forward to a better day."

Myer was pleased to report to *Common Ground* readers concerned about the violation of Japanese American rights that democracy was alive and well in the camps. The WRA had put families' household goods "in storage at government expense at the time of evacuation" and was sending these goods "as rapidly as possible." The WRA provided all evacuees with food, lodging, and medical care.

---

euphemisms: mild or vague terms in place of harsher or more direct descriptions

And they could earn money by performing tasks for the community as a whole. Community stores, newspapers, churches, and schools further testified to the WRA's concern about the evacuees' welfare. The community government, however, "represented best," in Myer's eyes, "the extent to which democracy is practiced in the relocation centers." After touting the success of a temporary leave program that supplied evacuee workers to sugar beet growers suffering from the wartime labor shortage, Myer anticipated the "great majority" of evacuees "will be available for employment if needed and desired" outside the West Coast.

Few if any Japanese Americans could have endorsed such a sanguine° appraisal of the process of internment. Myer omitted any reference to the role racism had played in motivating mass exclusion and mass incarceration. He made no mention of DeWitt's calls to remove treacherous "Japs" from the Western Defense Command, or statements by public officials in the mountain states condemning the prospect of their states becoming a "dumping ground" for California "Japs." Idaho governor Chase Clark gave a speech suggesting that

> a good solution to the Jap problem in Idaho and the Nation would be to send them all back to Japan, then sink the island. They live like rats, breed like rats and act like rats. We don't want them buying or leasing land and becoming permanently located in our state.

With the exception of Colorado governor Ralph Carr, governors of these western states unanimously opposed voluntary migration and urged that the "enemy aliens" be placed in "concentration camps." Congressman John Rankin, from Mississippi, and Senator Tom Stewart, from Tennessee, also championed imprisoning the "Japs" in concentration camps for the duration of the war. Far from being concerned about Japanese American constitutional rights, both proposed stripping the Nisei of their citizenship. Rankin even entered into the congressional record an article that called for separating the sexes during the detention to prevent an "incubating period" that would allow each family to "emerge with five more children" and "in two generations 25 times as many Japanese."

Also, Myer gave no indication of the hardship exacted by the evacuation. Most Japanese Americans had less than a week's notice before being uprooted from their homes and community. Internment disrupted and altered educational and career plans. But the loss of liberty and the stigma of suspected disloyalty inflicted the deepest wounds. One internee recalled: "On May 16, 1942, my mother, two sisters, niece, nephew, and I left . . . by train. Father joined us later. Brother left earlier by bus. We took whatever we could carry. So much we left behind, but the most valuable thing I lost was my freedom." 20

Instead of providing a custodial service for Japanese Americans' belongings, the government directed the Federal Reserve Board to help "evacuees"

---

sanguine: confident, enthusiastic

dispose of their property. Shortly after Japanese Americans were removed from Bainbridge Island, Washington, Tom G. Rathbone, a field supervisor for the U.S. Employment Service, filed a report exemplifying° the way the government handled property concerns:

> We received tentative information late Friday afternoon to the effect that it was presumed that the Government would pay the transportation costs of such personal belongings and equipment to the point of relocation upon proper notice. When this word was given to the evacuees, many complained bitterly because they had not been given such information prior to that time and had, therefore, sold, at considerable loss, many such properties which they would have retained had they known that it would be shipped to them upon relocation. Saturday morning we received additional word through the Federal Reserve Bank that the question had not been answered and that probably no such transportation costs would be paid. Between the time on Friday afternoon and Saturday morning some Japanese had arranged to repossess belongings which they had already sold and were in a greater turmoil than ever upon getting the latter information.

Ultimately, most of the interned were permitted to bring only what they could carry. They were forced to sell a lifetime of property for a fraction of its true value. Homes, businesses, and prized possessions were lost. Studies estimate total property and income losses, adjusted for inflation and lost interest, at between $1.2 billion and $3.1 billion in 1983 dollars.

Few of those evacuated had any idea of their destination when they appeared at the designated departure point in March 1942. Most of the assembly centers were located at nearby racetracks and fairgrounds. Many families were forced to live in hastily converted horse stalls that still reeked of manure. Then at the end of May, Japanese Americans were labeled, like luggage, with numbered identification tags and sent to WRA camps across the country. Barbed wire, watchtowers, and military police provided stark reminders that they were prisoners who could not leave without WRA approval. Beginning in the summer of 1942, some Japanese Americans received permission to leave camp to join the Military Intelligence Service. Other Japanese Americans who received permission to leave the camps could not return to the West until exclusion was lifted in December 1944. Myer implied camps were on land ripe for agricultural production, when in fact most were located on desert or swamplike terrain. In some camps, winter temperatures dropped to minus 35 degrees and summer temperatures soared as high as 115 degrees. Japanese Americans confined in the Arkansas camps had to contend with swarms of

---

exemplifying: showing by example

chiggers° and mosquitoes during the hot and humid summers. Minidoka's assistant project director described the camp's location in Idaho as "flat land, nothing growing but sagebrush, not a tree in sight." Frequent dust storms made life difficult in almost all the camps. A young Nisei described the dust storms at the Poston, Arizona, camp:

> Our mouths are always gritty, and the rooms including the mess halls cannot be kept clean even by closing all the doors and windows because there are so many cracks in the walls and floors. From about 1:30 p.m. daily, the wind rises, and often we can't see half mile ahead due to the dust cloud. Each step we take we stir up dust. Dust settles on the typewriter and is noticeable even while writing a letter.

The primitive conditions also belied° Myer's image of normal communities. Internees lived in a block that consisted of fourteen barracks subdivided into four or six rooms. Most families shared a single barren room, typically measuring twenty by twenty-five feet. There was little privacy within many barracks because room partitions fell short of the roof. Dust constantly seeped through cracks in the buildings' planks. The WRA supplied only canvas cots, a pot-bellied stove, and a light bulb hanging from the ceiling, but resourceful internees later constructed makeshift furniture from scrap lumber. Also, many internees cultivated their own gardens to supplement the starchy, unappetizing food served in the mess halls, each of which provided for an entire block of approximately 250 people.

Figure 1 **War Relocation Authority sites. Public domain. U.S. War Department, *Final Report: Japanese Evacuation from the West Coast, 1942* (Washington, DC: GPO, 1943), *256–57.***

Central Utah: Capacity: 10,000
Abraham, Millard County, Utah
140 miles southwest of Salt Lake City
4 miles northwest of Delta

Colorado River: Capacity: 20,000
Poston, Yuma County, Arizona
12 miles south of Parker
Halfway between Needles and Yuma

Gila River: Capacity: 15,000
Sacaton, Pinal County, Arizona
50 miles south of Phoenix
3 miles west of Sacaton

Granada: Capacity: 8,000
Granada, Prowers County, Colorado
140 miles east of Pueblo
1½ miles southeast of Granada

(*continued*)

chiggers: parasitic mites whose bite causes severe itching
belied: showed to be false, contradicted

Heart Mountain: Capacity: 11,000
Vocation, Park County, Wyoming
13 miles northeast of Cody
8 miles south of Ralston

Jerome: Capacity: 10,000
Jerome, Chicot and Drew Counties, Arkansas
30 miles southwest of Arkansas City
8 miles south of Dermott

Manzanar: Capacity: 10,000
Manzanar, Inyo County, California
225 miles north of Los Angeles
5 miles south of Independence

Minidoka: Capacity: 10,000
Gooding, Jerome County, Idaho
25 miles northeast of Twin Falls
8 miles north of Eden

Rohwer: Capacity: 10,000
Rohwer, Desha County, Arkansas
25 miles northwest of Arkansas City
8 miles south of Watson

Tule Lake: Capacity: 16,000
Newell, Modoc County, California
35 miles southeast of Klamath Falls
2 miles south of Stronghold

Figure 2 Typical layout of WRA housing block. U.S. War Department, *Final Report: Japanese Evacuation from the West Coast, 1942* (Washington, DC: GPO, 1943), 267.

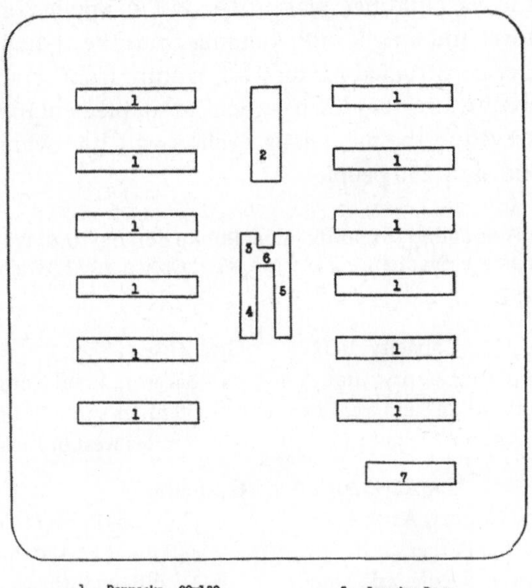

Map of War Relocation Project Sites

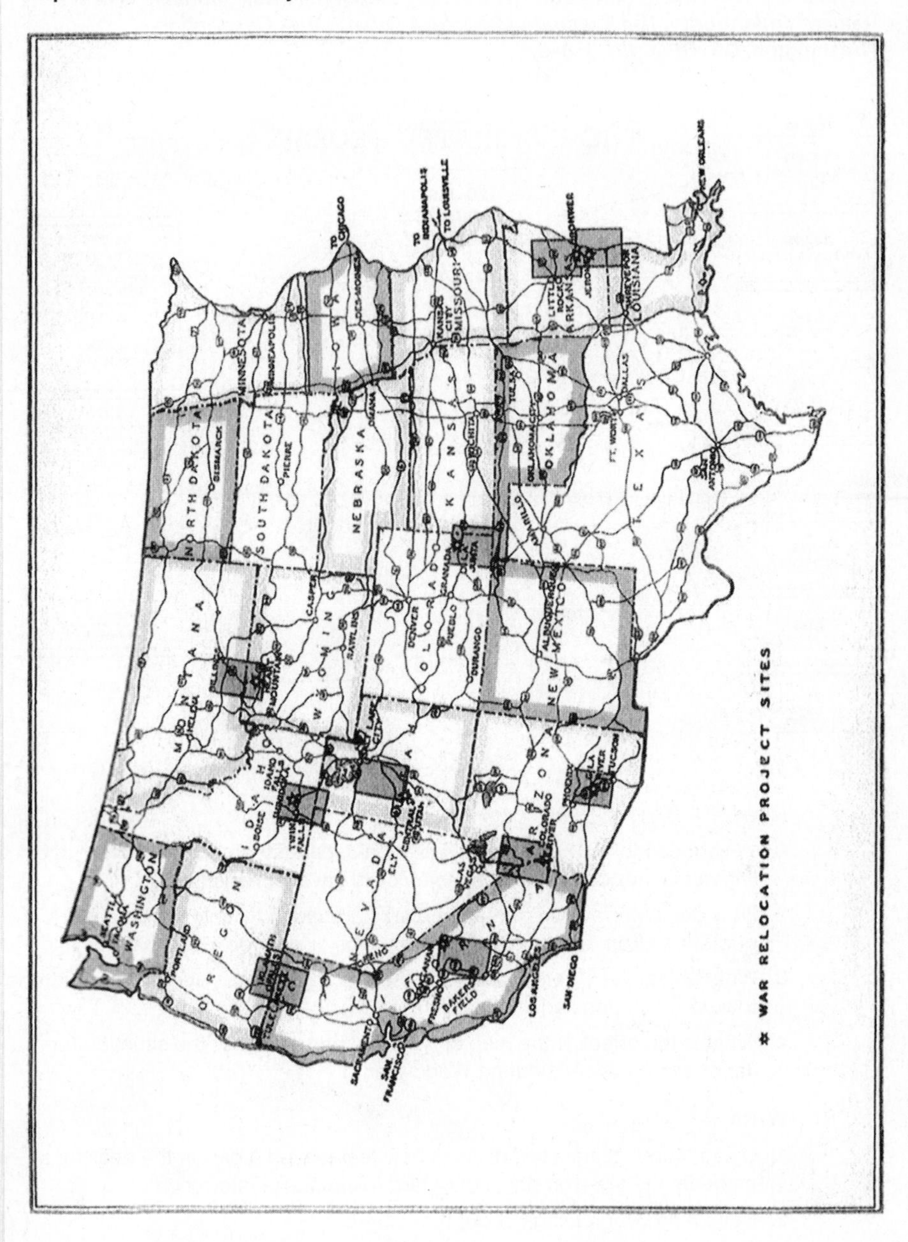

Figure 3 War Relocation Authority Custody statistics. Public domain. U.S. War Relocation Authority, *The Evacuated People: A Quantitative Description* (Washington, DC: GPO. *1946), 8–9.*

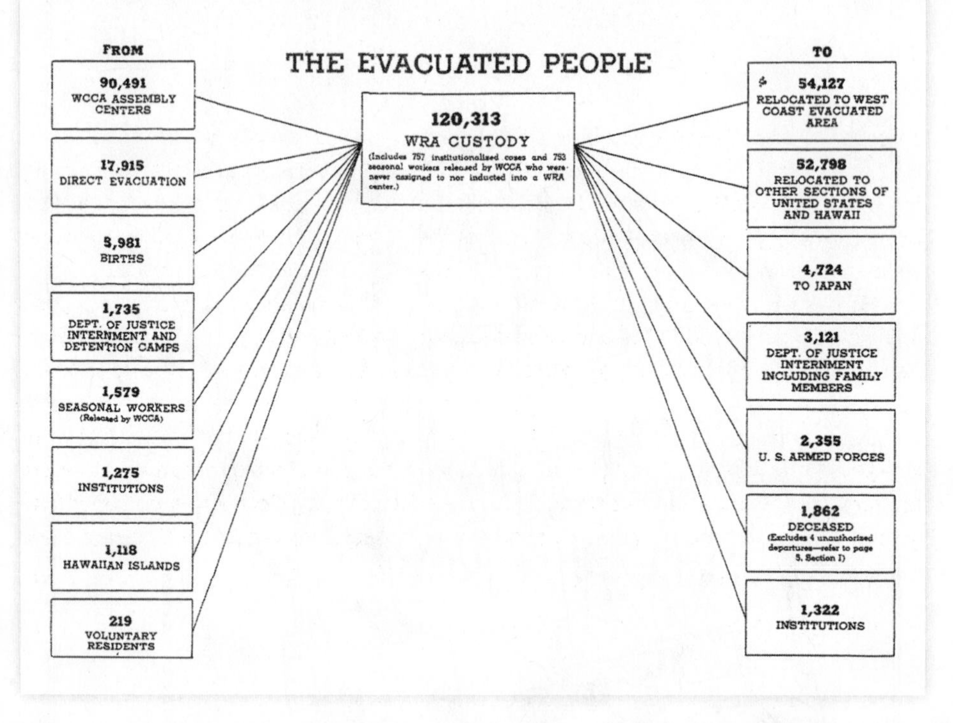

Read

1. Why does Murray begin this chapter on Japanese American imprisonment with a discussion of the reasons officials gave for resisting it?
2. How does Murray use quotation marks around individual words and quotations from others to indicate motives or provide evidence?
3. What adjectives or other details in the first three pages suggest her attitude toward the actions against Japanese Americans?
4. What is the effect of the map on your understanding of the situation for Japanese Americans during World War II?

Write

1. Using Murray's analysis, discuss how fear played a part in the decisions made by the government with regard to Japanese internment.
2. Reflect on your feelings about the decisions.
3. What do you think Murray's strongest evidence is? Why?

Connect

1. Use Andrew Jackson's order in "On Indian Removal" to compare governmental decisions regarding the American Indians in the nineteenth century and the Japanese in World War II.

2. Looking at Langston Hughes's poem "Freedom Train" in this unit, what do you make of the reference to him and his work in the essay?

Thomas Friedman and Michael Mandelbaum

Thomas Friedman (b. 1953) was born and grew up in a middle-class suburb of Minneapolis. He began reporting first on the Middle East and foreign affairs and served as bureau chief for Beirut, Lebanon and for Israel. He has been a writer for *The New York Times* since 1981. While a White House correspondent, Friedman began writing on domestic affairs, and now concentrates on economics, foreign and trade policy, and environmental matters.

He has won three Pulitzer Prizes for reporting. His book on the environmental crisis and global warming, *Hot, Flat, and Crowded,* became a national best seller. *That Used to Be Us* (2011), written with his friend Michael Mandelbaum, explores solutions to what the authors see as this country's biggest challenges in the twenty-first century.

Michael Mandelbaum (b. 1945) is a professor of International Studies at Johns Hopkins University. He grew up in Berkeley, California, the son of a teacher and a professor at Stanford. He has written 12 books, including *The Case for Goliath,* a study of and argument for the dominance of the United States in world affairs, and *Democracy's Good Name* in 2007.

From *That Used to Be Us*

If You See Something, Say Something

This is a book about America that begins in China.

In September 2010, Tom attended the World Economic Forum's summer conference in Tianjin, China. Five years earlier, getting to Tianjin had involved a three-and-a-half-hour car ride from Beijing to a polluted, crowded Chinese version of Detroit, but things had changed. Now, to get to Tianjin, you head to the Beijing South Railway Station—an ultramodern flying saucer of a building with glass walls and an oval roof covered with 3,246 solar panels—buy a ticket from an electronic kiosk° offering choices in Chinese and English, and board a world-class high-speed train that goes right to another roomy, modern train station in downtown Tianjin. Said to be the fastest in the world when it began operating in 2008, the Chinese bullet train covers 115 kilometers, or 72 miles, in a mere twenty-nine minutes.

kiosk: stand or booth

The conference itself took place at the Tianjin Meijiang Convention and Exhibition Center—a massive, beautifully appointed structure, the like of which exists in few American cities. As if the convention center wasn't impressive enough, the conference's co-sponsors in Tianjin gave some facts and figures about it (www.tj-summerdavos.cn). They noted that it contained a total floor area of 230,000 square meters (almost 2.5 million square feet) and that "construction of the Meijiang Convention Center started on September 15, 2009, and was completed in May, 2010." Reading that line, Tom started counting on his fingers: Let's see—September, October, November, December, January . . .

Eight months.

Returning home to Maryland from that trip, Tom was describing the Tianjin complex and how quickly it was built to Michael and his wife, Anne. At one point Anne asked: "Excuse me, Tom. Have you been to our subway stop lately?" We all live in Bethesda° and often use the Washington Metrorail subway to get to work in downtown Washington, D.C. Tom had just been at the Bethesda station and knew exactly what Anne was talking about: The two short escalators had been under repair for nearly six months. While the one being fixed was closed, the other had to be shut off and converted into a two-way staircase. At rush hour, this was creating a huge mess. Everyone trying to get on or off the platform had to squeeze single file up and down one frozen escalator. It sometimes took ten minutes just to get out of the station. A sign on the closed escalator said that its repairs were part of a massive escalator "modernization" project. 5

What was taking this "modernization" project so long? We investigated. Cathy Asato, a spokeswoman for the Washington Metropolitan Transit Authority, had told the *Maryland Community News* (October 20, 2010) that "the repairs were scheduled to take about six months and are on schedule. Mechanics need 10 to 12 weeks to fix each escalator."

A simple comparison made a startling point: It took China's Teda Construction Group thirty-two weeks to build a world-class convention center from the ground up—including giant escalators in every corner—and it was taking the Washington Metro crew twenty-four weeks to repair two tiny escalators of twenty-one steps each. We searched a little further and found that WTOP, a local news radio station, had interviewed the Metro interim general manager, Richard Sarles, on July 20, 2010. Sure, these escalators are old, he said, but "they have not been kept in a state of good repair. We're behind the curve on that, so we have to catch up . . . Just last week, smoke began pouring out of the escalators at the Dupont Circle station during rush hour."

Bethesda: community in Maryland, just outside Washington, DC

On November 14, 2010, *The Washington Post* ran a letter to the editor from Mark Thompson of Kensington, Maryland, who wrote:

> I have noted with interest your reporting on the $225,000 study that Metro hired Vertical Transportation Excellence to conduct into the sorry state of the system's escalators and elevators . . . I am sure that the study has merit. But as someone who has ridden Metro for more than 30 years, I can think of an easier way to assess the health of the escalators. For decades they ran silently and efficiently. But over the past several years—when the escalators are running—aging or ill-fitting parts have generated horrific noises that sound to me like a Tyrannosaurus Rex trapped in a tar pit screeching its dying screams.

The quote we found most disturbing, though, came from a *Maryland Community News* story about the long lines at rush hour caused by the seemingly endless Metro repairs: "'My impression, standing on line there, is people have sort of gotten used to it,' said Benjamin Ross, who lives in Bethesda and commutes every day from the downtown station."

The National Watercooler

People have sort of gotten used to it. Indeed, that sense of resignation, that sense that, well, this is just how things are in America today, that sense that America's best days are behind it and China's best days are ahead of it, have become the subject of watercooler, dinner-party, grocery-line, and classroom conversations all across America today. We hear the doubts from children, who haven't been to China. Tom took part in the September 2010 Council of Educational Facility Planners International (CEFPI) meeting in San Jose, California. As part of the program, there was a "School of the Future Design Competition," which called for junior high school students to design their own ideal green school. He met with the finalists on the last morning of the convention, and they talked about global trends. At one point, Tom asked them what they thought about China. A young blond-haired junior high school student, Isabelle Foster, from Old Lyme Middle School in Connecticut, remarked, "It seems like they have more ambition and will than we do." Tom asked her, "Where did you get that thought?" She couldn't really explain it, she said. She had never visited China. But it was just how she felt. It's in the air. 10

. . .

The goal is for America to remain a great country. This means that while reducing our deficits, we must also invest in education, infrastructure, and research and development, as well as open our society more widely to talented immigrants and fix the regulations that govern our economy. Immigration, education, and sensible regulation are traditional ingredients of the American formula for greatness. They are more vital than ever if we hope to realize the full potential of the American people in the coming decades, to generate the resources to sustain our prosperity, and to remain the global leader that we have been and that the world needs us to be. We, the authors of this book, don't want simply to restore American solvency. We want to maintain American greatness. We are not green-eyeshade guys. We're Fourth of July guys.

China, Again

And to maintain American greatness, the right option for us is not to become more like China. It is to become more like ourselves. Certainly, China has made extraordinary strides in lifting tens of millions of its people out of poverty and in modernizing its infrastructure—from convention centers, to highways, to airports, to housing. China's relentless focus on economic development and its willingness to search the world for the best practices, experiment with them, and then scale those that work is truly impressive.

But the Chinese still suffer from large and potentially debilitating° problems: a lack of freedom, rampant corruption, horrible pollution, and an education system that historically has stifled creativity. China does not have better political or economic systems than the United States. In order to sustain its remarkable economic progress, we believe, China will ultimately have to adopt more features of the American system, particularly the political and economic liberty that are fundamental to our success. China cannot go on relying heavily on its ability to mobilize cheap labor and cheap capital and on copying and assembling the innovations of others.

Still, right now, we believe that China is getting 90 percent of the potential benefits from its second-rate political system. It is getting the most out of its authoritarianism. But here is the shortcoming that Americans should be focused on: We are getting only 50 percent of the potential benefits from our first-rate system. We are getting so much less than we can, should, and must get out of our democracy.

15 In short, our biggest problem is not that we're failing to keep up with China's best practices but that we've strayed so far from our own best practices. America's future depends not on our adopting features of the Chinese system, but on our making our own democratic system work with the kind of focus, moral authority, seriousness, collective action, and stick-to-itiveness that China has managed to generate by authoritarian means for the last several decades.

In our view, all of the comparisons between China and the United States that you hear around American watercoolers these days aren't about China at all. They are about us. China is just a mirror. We're really talking about ourselves and

---

debilitating: weakening

our own loss of self-confidence. We see in the Chinese some character traits that we once had—that once defined us as a nation—but that we seem to have lost.

Orville Schell heads up the Asia Society's Center on U.S.–China Relations in New York City. He is one of America's most experienced China-watchers. He also attended the Tianjin conference, and one afternoon, after a particularly powerful presentation there about China's latest economic leap forward, Tom asked Schell why he thought China's rise has come to unnerve and obsess Americans.

"Because we have recently begun to find ourselves so unable to get things done, we tend to look with a certain over-idealistic yearning when it comes to China," Schell answered. "We see what they have done and project onto them something we miss, fearfully miss, in ourselves"—that "can-do, get-it-done, everyone-pull-together, whatever-it-takes" attitude that built our highways and dams and put a man on the moon. "These were hallmarks of our childhood culture," said Schell. "But now we view our country turning into the opposite, even as we see China becoming animated by these same kinds of energies . . . China desperately wants to prove itself to the world, while at the same time America seems to be losing its hunger to demonstrate its excellence." The Chinese are motivated, Schell continued, by a "deep yearning to restore China to greatness, and, sadly, one all too often feels that we are losing that very motor force in America."

The two of us do feel that, but we do not advocate policies and practices to sustain American greatness out of arrogance or a spirit of chauvinism.° We do it out of a love for our country and a powerful belief in what a force for good America can be—for its own citizens and for the world—at its best. We are well aware of America's imperfections, past and present. We know that every week in America a politician takes a bribe; someone gets convicted of a crime he or she did not commit; public money gets wasted that should have gone for a new bridge, a new school, or pathbreaking research; many young people drop out of school; young women get pregnant without committed fathers; and people unfairly lose their jobs or their houses. The cynic says, "Look at the gap between our ideals and our reality. Any talk of American greatness is a lie." The partisan says, "Ignore the gap. We're still 'exceptional.'" Our view is that the gaps do matter, and this book will have a lot to say about them. But America is not defined by its gaps. Our greatness as a country—what truly defines us—is and always has been our never-ending effort to close these gaps, our constant struggle to form a more perfect union. The gaps simply show us the work we still have to do.

To repeat: Our problem is not China, and our solution is not China. Our problem is us—what we are doing and not doing, how our political system is functioning and not functioning, which values we are and are not living by. 20

---

chauvinism: ultranationalism, superpatriotism

And our solution is us—the people, the society, and the government that we used to be, and can be again. That is why this book is meant as both a wake-up call and a pep talk—unstinting° in its critique of where we are and unwavering in its optimism about what we can achieve if we act together.

Ours is "no longer a question of sacrificing or not sacrificing—we gave up that choice a long time ago," notes Michael Maniates, a professor of political science and environmental science at Allegheny College in Pennsylvania, who writes on this theme. We cannot choose whether or not Americans will sacrifice, but only who will bear the brunt of it. The more the present generation shrinks from the nation's challenges now, the longer sacrifice is deferred, the higher will be the cost to the next generation of the decline in America's power and Americans' wealth.

Fifty years ago, at his inauguration, John F. Kennedy urged his fellow citizens, "Ask not what your country can do for you. Ask what you can do for your country." That idea resonated° with most of the Americans to whom he spoke because they had personal memories of an era of supreme and successful sacrifice, which earned them the name "the Greatest Generation."

Unfortunately, today's challenges differ in an important way from those of the last century. The problems the Greatest Generation faced were inescapable, immediate, and existential:° the Great Depression, German and Japanese fascism, and Soviet communism. The enemies they had to confront were terrifying, tangible, and obvious: long unemployment lines, soup kitchens, heartless bankers evicting families from their homes, the twisted wreckage of Pearl Harbor, the maniacal countenance° and braying voice of Adolf Hitler, the ballistic missiles decorating the May Day parades in Red Square in Moscow—missiles that one day were dispatched to Cuba, just ninety miles from America's shores. When the Soviets weren't putting up a wall topped with barbed wire, slicing through the heart of Berlin like a jagged knife, they were invading Hungary and Czechoslovakia to stomp out a few wildflowers of freedom that had broken through the asphalt layer of communism the Soviet Union had laid down on those two countries. These challenges were impossible to ignore.

Whether or not the public and the politicians all agreed on the strategies for dealing with those challenges—and often they didn't—they recognized that decisions had to be made, endless wrangling had to stop, and denying the existence of such threats or postponing dealing with them was unthinkable. Most Americans understood the world they were living in. They understood, too, that in confronting these problems they had to pull together—they had to

---

unstinting: unrestrained
resonated: resounded
existential: based in experience
countenance: appearance, face

act collectively—in a unified, serious, and determined way. Confronting those challenges meant bringing to bear the full weight and power of the American people. It also meant that leaders could not avoid asking for sacrifice. Kennedy also summoned his countrymen to "pay any price, bear any burden, meet any hardship, support any friend, oppose any foe." Everyone had to contribute something—time, money, energy, and, in many cases, lives. Losing was not an option, nor were delay, denial, dithering, or despair.

Today's major challenges are different. All four—globalization, the IT revolution, out-of-control deficits and debt, and rising energy demand and climate change—are occurring incrementally.° Some of their most troubling features are difficult to detect, at least until they have reached crisis proportions. Save° for the occasional category-5 hurricane or major oil spill, these challenges offer up no Hitler or Pearl Harbor to shock the nation into action. They provide no Berlin Wall to symbolize the threat to America and the world, no Sputnik circling the Earth proclaiming with every cricket-like chirp of its orbiting signal that we are falling behind in a crucial arena of geopolitical competition. We don't see the rushing river of dollars we send abroad every month—about $28 billion—to sustain our oil addiction. The carbon dioxide that mankind has been pumping into the atmosphere since the Industrial Revolution, and at rising rates over the past two decades, is a gas that cannot be seen, touched, or smelled. 25

To be sure, the four great challenges have scarcely gone unnoticed. But in the last few years the country was distracted, indeed preoccupied, by the worst economic crisis in eight decades. It is no wonder that Americans became fixated on their immediate economic circumstances. Those circumstances were grim: American households lost an estimated $10 trillion in the crisis. For more than a year the American economy contracted. Unemployment rose to 9 percent (and if people too discouraged to seek jobs were included, the figure would be significantly higher).

There is an important difference between the challenge of the economic crisis and the four long-term challenges that America faces. The deep recession of late 2007 to 2009 was what economists call a "cyclical event." A recession reduces economic growth to a point below its potential level. But the economy, and the country, eventually recover. By contrast, the four great challenges will determine our overall economic potential. A recession is like an illness, which can ruin a person's week, month, or even year. The four challenges we face are more like chronic conditions. Ultimately, these determine the length and the quality of a person's life. Similarly, how we respond to these major challenges will determine the quality of American life for decades to come. And it is later than we think.

---

incrementally: by continuing increase
Save: except

A few years ago, fans of the Chicago Cubs baseball team, which last won the World Series in 1908, took to wearing T-shirts bearing the slogan "Any team can have a bad century." Countries, too, can have bad centuries. China had three of them between 1644 and 1980. If we do not master the four major challenges we now face, we risk a bad twenty-first century.

Failure is by no means inevitable. Coming back, thriving in this century, preserving the American dream and the American role in the world, will require adopting policies appropriate to confronting the four great challenges. For this there are two preconditions. One is recognizing those challenges—which we have clearly been slow to do. The other is remembering how we developed the strength to face similar challenges in the past. As Bill Gates put it to us: "What was all that good stuff we had that other people copied?"

[2011]

Read

1. Why do the authors begin with the story about China? How is it rhetorically effective?
2. How would you describe the tone in the excerpt you've read?
3. Why do the authors use the Homeland Security phrase "If you see something, say something" to advance their argument?
4. What are the four challenges the authors pose? (Hint: See paragraph that begins "Today's major challenges are different.") How are they different from challenges posed in earlier times in the country?
5. Why is the example of China that begins the text a telling bit of evidence for the claims the text makes?

Write

1. Choose one of the four challenges that you identified above and reflect on what you think it would take to meet it.
2. Friedman and Mandelbaum suggest that Americans have gotten unused to sacrifice. Do you think that's so? Where do you see sacrifice or the unwillingness to sacrifice in everyday life?
3. Write about your reaction to the problems the authors set out and the challenges they pose for young people.

Connect

1. The text strikes a note of urgency in its insistence on the need for change. Find another text in the unit that you think has a similar quality of immediacy and compare the diction, contextual situation, and proposed solutions to this excerpt.
2. Compare the definitions of America implied in this piece to Baldwin's implied definition.

Brent Staples

Brent Staples (b. 1951) was born in Chester, Pennsylvania, to a blue-collar family and was one of nine children. He received his Ph.D. from the University of Chicago and became a reporter for the Chicago *Sun-Times.* He has been a writer for *The New York Times* since 1983.

In 1994, Staples published a book on his family and on African American life in the United States, *Parallel Time: Growing Up in Black and White.* His subjects range across the spectrum of American life and culture.

Black Men and Public Spaces

My first victim was a woman—white, well-dressed, probably in her early twenties. I came upon her late one evening on a deserted street in Hyde Park, a relatively affluent neighborhood in an otherwise mean,° impoverished section of Chicago. As I swung onto the avenue behind her, there seemed to be a discreet, uninflammatory distance between us. Not so. She cast back a worried glance. To her, the youngish black man—a broad 6 feet 2 inches with a beard and billowing hair, both hands shoved into the pockets of a bulky military jacket—seemed menacingly close. After a few more quick glimpses, she picked up her pace and was soon running in earnest. Within seconds she disappeared into a cross street.

That was more than a decade ago. I was 22 years old, a graduate student newly arrived at the University of Chicago. It was in the echo of that terrified woman's footfalls that I first began to know the unwieldy° inheritance I'd come into—the ability to alter public space in ugly ways. It was clear that she thought herself the quarry of a mugger, a rapist, or worse. Suffering a bout of insomnia, however, I was stalking sleep, not defenseless wayfarers. As a softy who is scarcely able to take a knife to a raw chicken—let alone hold one to a person's throat—I was surprised, embarrassed, and dismayed all at once. Her flight made me feel like an accomplice in tyranny. It also made it clear that I was indistinguishable from the muggers who occasionally seeped into the area from the surrounding ghetto. That first encounter, and those that followed, signified that a vast, unnerving gulf lay between nighttime pedestrians—particularly women—and me. And I soon gathered that being perceived as dangerous is a hazard in itself. I only needed to turn a corner into a dicey situation, or crowd

---

mean: poor, shabby

unwieldy: heavy, awkward, difficult to manage

some frightened, armed person in a foyer somewhere, or make an errant° move after being pulled over by a policeman. Where fear and weapons meet—and they often do in urban America—there is always the possibility of death.

In that first year, my first away from my hometown, I was to become thoroughly familiar with the language of fear. At dark, shadowy intersections, I could cross in front of a car stopped at a traffic light and elicit the *thunk, thunk, thunk, thunk* of the driver—black, white, male, or female—hammering down the door locks. On less traveled streets after dark, I grew accustomed to but never comfortable with people crossing to the other side of the street rather than pass me. Then there were the standard unpleasantries with policemen, doormen, bouncers, cabdrivers, and others whose business it is to screen out troublesome individuals *before* there is any nastiness.

I moved to New York nearly two years ago and I have remained an avid night walker. In central Manhattan, the near-constant crowd cover minimizes tense one-on-one street encounters. Elsewhere—in SoHo,° for example, where sidewalks are narrow and tightly spaced buildings shut out the sky—things can get very taut indeed.

5 After dark, on the warrenlike° streets of Brooklyn where I live, I often see women who fear the worst from me. They seem to have set their faces on neutral, and with their purse straps strung across their chests bandolier°-style, they forge ahead as though bracing themselves against being tackled. I understand, of course, that the danger they perceive is not a hallucination. Women are particularly vulnerable to street violence, and young black males are drastically overrepresented among the perpetrators of that violence. Yet these truths are no solace° against the kind of alienation that comes of being ever the suspect, a fearsome entity with whom pedestrians avoid making eye contact.

It is not altogether clear to me how I reached the ripe old age of 22 without being conscious of the lethality nighttime pedestrians attributed to me. Perhaps it was because in Chester, Pennsylvania, the small, angry industrial town where I came of age in the 1960s, I was scarcely noticeable against a backdrop of gang warfare, street knifings, and murders. I grew up one of the good boys, had perhaps a half-dozen fistfights. In retrospect, my shyness of combat has clear sources.

As a boy, I saw countless tough guys locked away; I have since buried several, too. They were babies, really—a teenage cousin, a brother of 22, a childhood friend in his mid-twenties—all gone down in episodes of bravado

---

errant: straying from the proper course

SoHo: (from *South of Houston Street*), neighborhood in lower Manhattan

warrenlike: pertaining to an area or building with many tenants in crowded quarters, in the manner of a rabbit warren

bandolier: broad belt with loops to contain cartridges, worn over the shoulder

solace: consolation

played out in the streets. I came to doubt the virtues of intimidation early on. I chose, perhaps unconsciously, to remain a shadow—timid, but a survivor.

The fearsomeness mistakenly attributed to me in public places often has a perilous flavor. The most frightening of these confusions occurred in the late 1970s and early 1980s, when I worked as a journalist in Chicago. One day, rushing into the office of a magazine I was writing for with a deadline story in hand, I was mistaken for a burglar. The office manager called security and, with an ad hoc° posse, pursued me through the labyrinthine° halls, nearly to my editor's door. I had no way of proving who I was. I could only move briskly toward the company of someone who knew me.

Another time I was on assignment for a local paper and killing time before an interview. I entered a jewelry store on the city's affluent Near North Side. The proprietor excused herself and returned with an enormous red Doberman pinscher straining at the end of a leash. She stood, the dog extended toward me, silent to my questions, her eyes bulging nearly out of her head. I took a cursory° look around, nodded, and bade her good night.

10 Relatively speaking, however, I never fared as badly as another black male journalist. He went to nearby Waukegan, Illinois, a couple of summers ago to work on a story about a murderer who was born there. Mistaking the reporter for the killer, police officers hauled him from his car at gunpoint and but for his press credentials would probably have tried to book him. Such episodes are not uncommon. Black men trade tales like this all the time.

Over the years, I learned to smother the rage I felt at so often being taken for a criminal. Not to do so would surely have led to madness. I now take precautions to make myself less threatening. I move about with care, particularly late in the evening. I give a wide berth to nervous people on subway platforms during the wee hours, particularly when I have exchanged business clothes for jeans. If I happen to be entering a building behind some people who appear skittish,° I may walk by, letting them clear the lobby before I return, so as not to seem to be following them. I have been calm and extremely congenial on those rare occasions when I've been pulled over by the police.

And on late-evening constitutionals° I employ what has proved to be an excellent tension-reducing measure: I whistle melodies from Beethoven and Vivaldi and the more popular classical composers. Even steely New Yorkers hunching toward nighttime destinations seem to relax, and occasionally they even join in the tune. Virtually everybody seems to sense that a mugger

---

ad hoc: (Latin for "for this"), for a specific purpose
labyrinthine: mazelike
cursory: hasty, superficial
skittish: jumpy, likely to flinch or shy away
constitutionals: walks taken for one's health

wouldn't be warbling bright, sunny selections from Vivaldi's *Four Seasons*. It is my equivalent of the cowbell that hikers wear when they know they are in bear country.

[1987]

Read

1. What is your reaction to the word "victim"?
2. How does Staples's diction suggest the irony of the situation he describes?
3. How does he describe the reaction from the people he meets on the street in New York?
4. What do you think of his solution to the problem?
5. How does Staples use personal anecdote to help convey his aim?

Write

1. Write about the feeling a person has when he or she has been wrongly accused. Use some of Staples's language as you write.
2. Explain the metaphorical connection of the image of the cowbell at the end of the piece.

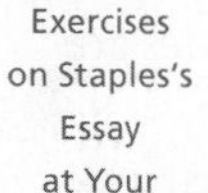

Complete Additional Exercises on Staples's Essay at Your Pearson MyLab

Connect

1. Discuss Staples's essay as a way of explaining Du Bois's contention about double consciousness in *The Souls of Black Folk*.
2. How might you compare Staples's tone to Baldwin's in "My Dungeon Shook"?

UNIT ACTIVITIES

Rhetorical Analysis

1. Choose two writers in this unit and examine the rhetorical strategies they use to convey their message and to persuade their readers. Writers who have a similar aim but use varying genres or choices in diction make good comparisons. Consider as well how effective you believe their choices are in persuading audiences of their position.

   Some possible pairs: Robert Kennedy–Rachel Carson; Robert Kennedy–Martin Luther King, Jr.; Langston Hughes–Huey P. Long; Franklin Roosevelt–Eleanor Roosevelt.
2. Analyze the use of extended example to make a point about the need for change in essays by Staples, Long, or another in this unit.

Argument

1. Using any of the texts in this unit (Okada, Long are examples), argue for the role of the community in making positive changes toward equality and access. Consider issues of power and responsibility—individual, social, governmental—as you frame your argument.
2. Using Franklin D. Roosevelt's speech to the Congress, create an argument for or against one of the items he lists in his second Bill of Rights. To strengthen your argument, use evidence from research, current events, or your own experience. You might select other texts from this unit to help you create and sustain your position.

Synthesis

1. Select any three of the following texts and evaluate their proposals for civic or social change in the country, including the way they use evidence, language, and context to persuade audiences.

   Franklin Delano Roosevelt, "State of the Union Address, January 11, 1944"

   Huey P. Long, "Sharing Our Wealth"

   John Okada, from *No-No Boy*

   Brent Staples, "Black Men in Public Spaces"

   Tillie Olsen, "I Stand Here Ironing"

   Martin Luther King, Jr., "Letter from Birmingham Jail"

2. Many of the texts in this unit speak to change in terms of new ways of determining responsibilities to self and to community or country. Select three texts from the following list or others that seem appropriate, and analyze how each conceives of the dual responsibility to self and other. Then evaluate the claims made by the writers and suggest what citizens need to consider as they make decisions about individual choice and civic responsibility.

   Possible texts:

   John Okada, from *No-No Boy*

   Eleanor Roosevelt, "My Day"

   Rachel Carson, "A Fable for Our Time"

   Robert F. Kennedy, "Speech on the Death of Martin Luther King"

   Photo of Kent State Massacre

UNIT 6

Established in 2006 by U.S. entrepreneur Blake Mycaskie, TOMS Shoes' motto "One for One" describes their practice of donating a pair of shoes to a needy person for every pair of shoes the company sells. The humanitarian effort has been highly successful. TOMS has factories in three countries and gives away shoes in twenty-three countries, including the United States.

Read

1. How can you tell that this photo is an advertisement?
2. How does the photo suggest TOMS Shoes' business ethic?

Connect

1. How do other texts in this unit demonstrate an awareness of global concerns?
2. How do the TOMS material and the literature in the unit suggest a change in American attitudes toward people in other parts of the world?

How Does a Nation Learn to Live in the World?

1970–Present

Economic Globalization In the 1970s, the Vietnam War, the resignation of President Nixon, and an economic crisis created fears about the future of America. However, in the following two decades, the explosion of technology and the breakup of the communist Soviet Union fostered economic expansion and confidence across the globe. In recent years, businesses have increasingly moved their factories outside the United States to hire cheaper labor. At the same time, waves of immigrants and refugees have arrived here looking for opportunity. Both shifts have tested national resources.

Cultural Globalization From immigrants, global trade, foreign travel, and global media, Americans have learned about a wide variety of customs and cultures. The Internet, in particular, has accelerated the recognition that we live in a "global village." As a result, recent literature reflects our diversity and new forms have emerged. Fiction and nonfiction blend in the memoir, visual and linguistic elements combine in graphic novels, oral elements appear in written documents, and dialects change within speeches or essays. People's concerns about facing the challenges of environmental damage, economic decline, cultural differences, and other problems are explored in a wide array of genres and styles of writing and art. We may never have faced as many potential problems as a nation, but we have never had so many looking for solutions.

"Back to the Future" Each of the previous units ends with a few selections by contemporary writers who examine the issues explored by writers of the time. In this last unit, we look back to a writer who examined the future of the country. This "back to the future" essay, an excerpt from Alexis de Tocqueville's *Democracy in America*, was written in 1835. But he has much to say about the United States to Americans today.

GUIDING QUESTIONS

- How does a nation learn to live in the world?
- How do we reconcile the needs of many with individual needs?
- What is the connection between rights and responsibilities?
- How are concepts of ethnic background and race changing?
- How do we balance progress in industry and business with progress in environmental protection?
- What are new needs—and continuing ones—in the twenty-first century?

Simon Ortiz

Simon Ortiz (b. 1941) was born in Albuquerque, New Mexico, and raised in a Pueblo community, speaking a tribal language as his first language. He was sent away to a school where attachment to Indian traditions was discouraged. After serving in the Army, Ortiz received a master's of fine arts degree at the University of Iowa's Writers' Workshop. His first collection of poems, *Naked in the Wind,* was published in 1971. Ortiz has published more than a dozen books of poetry, as well as fiction, essays, and children's literature. He writes about his cultural heritage, the importance of the land, history, and community.

A Designated National Park

Montezuma Castle° in the Verde Valley, Arizona.

DESIGNATED FEDERAL RECREATION FEE AREA
ENTREE FEES
$1.00 FOR 1 DAY PERMIT
MONTEZUMA CASTLE ONLY INCLUDES PURCHASER
OR OTHERS WITH HIM IN PRIVATE NON-COMMERCIAL VEHICLE
$0.50 FOR 1 DAY PERMIT
MONTEZUMA CASTLE ONLY INCLUDES PURCHASER
IN COMMERCIAL VEHICLE

AUTHORIZED
BY THE LAND AND WATER
CONSERVATION FUND ACT OF 1965

This morning,
I have to buy a permit to get back home.
Birds,
they must have been,
these people, 5
"Thank you for letting me come to see you."
I tell them that.

Montezuma Castle: an elaborate castle carved out of a limestone cliff, unrelated to Montezuma and the Aztec Empire

Secreted in my cave,
look at the sun.
Shadows on sycamore, 10
a strange bird and a familiar bird.
River, hear the river.
What it must be,
that pigeon sound.
Hear 15
in my cave, sacred song.
Morning feeling, sacred song.
We shall plant today.

PRESS BUTTON

(on a wooden booth)

"For a glimpse into the lives
of these people who lived here."

Pressing the button, I find
painted sticks and cloth fragments 20
in a child's hand,
her eyelashes still intact.
Girl, my daughter, my mother,
softly asleep.
They have unearthed you. 25

59TH CONGRESS OF THE UNITED STATES OF AMERICA
AT THE FIRST SESSION,
BEGUN AND HELD AT THE CITY OF WASHINGTON
ON MONDAY, THE FOURTH DAY OF DECEMBER,
ONE THOUSAND, NINE HUNDRED AND FIVE.

AN ACT
FOR THE PRESERVATION OF AMERICAN ANTIQUITIES.°

And a last sign post quote:

BUILT SOMETIME BETWEEN
1200 AD AND 1350 AD
ABANDONED BY AD 1450.

AN ACT . . . ANTIQUITIES: signed into law by President Theodore Roosevelt in June 1906; intended to stop looting of historic sites, it allowed the government to restrict use of public lands

s/ The Sinagua Indians°

SEE MUSEUM FOR MORE INFORMATION

[1977]

Read

1. How does your reading change when you read lines written in all capitals?
2. Where do you hear irony in the speaker's voice?
3. What does he think of the birds he describes?
4. What is the effect of the phrase "Press Button"?
5. Who is "they" in the poem?

Write

1. Rewrite this poem as an argument written by the speaker.
2. Describe the choice of diction and syntax as strategies to convey the speaker's aim.
3. Write a reflection on the last line of the poem as a concluding argument.

Connect

1. Reflect on a time you've been to a historical site and consider that occasion in terms of Ortiz's poem.
2. Compare the way this poet deals with ancestors to Joy Harjo's depiction of elders later in this unit.

Andy Warhol

Artist and filmmaker Andy Warhol (1928–1987) was born in Pittsburgh, Pennsylvania, and attended the Carnegie Institute of Technology. He moved to New York where he became a commercial illustrator. His paintings of Campbell's soup cans in the early 1960s brought him fame, and he became a leader of the pop art movement.

Warhol's work celebrated and satirized American commercial culture and mass production. His subjects were products, advertisements, celebrities, and political leaders. Warhol often used silkscreen, which lent itself well to reproduction. In 1972, Andy Warhol included China's chairman Mao Zedong in his famous series of silkscreen paintings. Warhol made films in the 1960s and 1970s as well as art. He comments both on the emptiness of culture and the emotional distance of the artist from the subject. His work is still imitated today.

Sinagua Indians: ancestors of the Hopi, the Sinagua lived in central Arizona from the mid-sixth century A.D. to the early fifteenth century

Mao

Mao (1972), Andy Warhol. Portfolio of 10 screenprints on Beckett High White Paper, 36 x 36 in. Copyright © 2012 The Andy Warhol Foundation for the Visual Arts, Inc./Artists Rights Society (ARS), New York. Photo by Oli Scarff/Getty Images

[1972]

Read

1. Look for a color image of this series of silk-screens on the Internet. How does the effect vary with change in color?
2. What does the change indicate about the viewer? About Mao?
3. What do you know about Mao Zedong that contributes to your reading of this art?

Write

1. Write a speculation about Warhol's aim in painting Mao and about the change in color for each print.
2. Speculate about the tone of these prints. Does the tone shift with the color?
3. Based on this series, what do you think an aim of pop art might be?

Connect

1. Consider the context of 1972 and the Vietnam War and comment on the aim and effect of this piece.
2. How does this painting differ or make connections to other art of famous people? Consider the painting of George Washington in Unit 2, for example.

Gloria Anzaldúa

Gloria Anzaldúa (1942–2004) was born in South Texas in the ranch settlement of Jesus Maria near the Mexican border. She received her master's degree in English at the University of Texas and taught Chicano literature, creative writing, and feminist studies in California, where she also began a career writing essays, poems, fiction, and autobiography about Chicana/Chicano culture. In her work, Anzaldúa explores both the limits of Chicana culture and feeling marginalized by the dominant culture. She often slides between English and Spanish, making a point about language as a border. Her most famous book, *Borderlands/La Frontera,* suggests the power of language and the way that bilingual speakers inhabit both cultures.

How to Tame a Wild Tongue

"We're going to have to control your tongue," the dentist says, pulling out all the metal from my mouth. Silver bits plop and tinkle into the basin. My mouth is a motherlode.

The dentist is cleaning out my roots. I get a whiff of the stench when I gasp. "I can't cap that tooth yet, you're still draining," he says.

"We're going to have to do something about your tongue," I hear the anger rising in his voice. My tongue keeps pushing out the wads of cotton, pushing back the drills, the long thin needles. "I've never seen anything as strong or as stubborn," he says. And I think, how do you tame a wild tongue, train it to be quiet, how do you bridle and saddle it? How do you make it lie down?

Who is to say that robbing a people of its language is less violent than war?

—Ray Gwyn Smith

I remember being caught speaking Spanish at recess—that was good for three licks on the knuckles with a sharp ruler. I remember being sent to the corner of the classroom for "talking back" to the Anglo teacher when all I was trying to do was tell her how to pronounce my name. "If you want to be American, speak 'American.' If you don't like it, go back to Mexico where you belong."

"I want you to speak English. *Pa'hallar buen trabajo tienes que saber hablar el inglés bien. Qué vale toda tu educación si todavía hablas inglés con un 'accent',*"° my mother would say, mortified that I spoke English like a Mexican.

Pa'hallar . . . 'accent': To get a good job you have to be able to speak English well. What good is all your education if you speak English with an accent?

At Pan American University,° I and all Chicano° students were required to take two speech classes. Their purpose: to get rid of our accents.

Attacks on one's form of expression with the intent to censor are a violation of the First Amendment. *El Anglo con cara de inocente nos arrancó la lengua.*° Wild tongues can't be tamed, they can only be cut out.

Overcoming the Tradition of Silence

> Ahogadas, escupimos el oscuro.
> Peleando con nuestra propia sombra
> el silencio nos sepulta.°

En boca cerrada no entran moscas. "Flies don't enter a closed mouth" is a saying I kept hearing when I was a child. *Ser habladora* was to be a gossip and a liar, to talk too much. *Muchachitas bien criadas,* well-bred girls don't answer back. *Es una falta° de respeto* to talk back to one's mother or father. I remember one of the sins I'd recite to the priest in the confession box the few times I went to confession: talking back to my mother, *hablar pa' 'tras, repelar. Hocicona, repelona, chismosa,* having a big mouth, questioning, carrying tales are all signs of being *mal criada.* In my culture they are all words that are derogatory if applied to women—I've never heard them applied to men.

5 The first time I heard two women, a Puerto Rican and a Cuban, say the word "*nosotras,*" I was shocked. I had not known the word existed. Chicanas use *nosotros°* whether we're male or female. We are robbed of our female being by the masculine plural. Language is a male discourse.

> And our tongues have become
> dry the wilderness has
> dried out our tongues and
> we have forgotten speech.
>
> —Irena Klepfisz

Even our own people, other Spanish speakers *nos quieren poner candados en la boca.*° They would hold us back with their bag of *reglas°* *de academia.*

Pan American University: a component of the University of Texas, located in Edinburg

Chicano: native-born American of Mexican ancestry

El Anglo . . . lengua: The innocent-faced Anglo has torn out our tongue.

Ahogadas . . . sepulta: Smothered, we spit out darkness. / Fighting with our own shadow / we're buried in silence.

falta: lack

nosotros: us

nos . . . boca: want to put locks on our mouths.

reglas: rules

Oyé como ladra:
el lenguaje de la frontera

Quien tiene boca se equivoca.°
—Mexican saying

"*Pocho,* cultural traitor, you're speaking the oppressor's language by speaking English, you're ruining the Spanish language," I have been accused by various Latinos and Latinas. Chicano Spanish is considered by the purist and by most Latinos deficient, a mutilation of Spanish.

But Chicano Spanish is a border tongue which developed naturally. Change, *evolución, enriquecimiento° de palabras° nuevas por invencióno adopción* have created variants of Chicano Spanish, *un nuevo lenguaje. Un lenguaje que corresponde a un modo de vivir.°* Chicano Spanish is not incorrect, it is a living language.

For a people who are neither Spanish nor live in a country in which Spanish is the first language; for a people who live in a country in which English is the reigning tongue but who are not Anglo; for a people who cannot entirely identify with either standard (formal, Castilian°) Spanish nor standard English, what recourse is left to them but to create their own language? A language which they can connect their identity to, one capable of communicating the realities and values true to themselves—a language with terms that are neither *español ni inglés,* but both. We speak a patois,° a forked tongue, a variation of two languages.

10 Chicano Spanish sprang out of the Chicanos' need to identify ourselves as a distinct people. We needed a language with which we could communicate with ourselves, a secret language. For some of us, language is a homeland closer than the Southwest—for many Chicanos today live in the Midwest and the East. And because we are a complex, heterogeneous° people, we speak many languages. Some of the languages we speak are

1. Standard English
2. Working class and slang English
3. Standard Spanish
4. Standard Mexican Spanish
5. North Mexican Spanish dialect

Oyé . . . equivoca: It sounds like barking: / the border tongue / Whoever has a mouth makes mistakes.
enriquecimiento: enrichment
palabras: words
modo de vivir: way of life
Castilian: from the Spanish region and former kingdom of Castile
patois: regional or provincial form of a language
heterogeneous: varied, diverse

6. Chicano Spanish (Texas, New Mexico, Arizona, and California have regional variations)
7. Tex-Mex
8. *Pachuco* (called *caló*)

My "home" tongues are the languages I speak with my sister and brothers, with my friends. They are the last five listed, with 6 and 7 being closest to my heart. From school, the media, and job situations, I've picked up standard and working class English. From Mamagrande Locha and from reading Spanish and Mexican literature, I've picked up Standard Spanish and Standard Mexican Spanish. From *los recién llegados,* Mexican immigrants, and *braceros,*° I learned the North Mexican dialect. With Mexicans I'll try to speak either Standard Mexican Spanish or the North Mexican dialect. From my parents and Chicanos living in the Valley,° I picked up Chicano Texas Spanish, and I speak it with my mom, younger brother (who married a Mexican and who rarely mixes Spanish with English), aunts, and older relatives.

With Chicanas from *Nuevo México* or *Arizona* I will speak Chicano Spanish a little, but often they don't understand what I'm saying. With most California Chicanas I speak entirely in English (unless I forget). When I first moved to San Francisco, I'd rattle off something in Spanish, unintentionally embarrassing them. Often it is only with another Chicana *tejano*° that I can talk freely.

Words distorted by English are known as anglicisms or *pochismos.* The *pocho* is an anglicized Mexican or American of Mexican origin who speaks Spanish with an accent characteristic of North Americans and who distorts and reconstructs the language according to the influence of English. Tex-Mex, or Spanglish, comes most naturally to me. I may switch back and forth from English to Spanish in the same sentence or in the same word. With my sister and my brother Nune and with Chicano *tejano* contemporaries I speak in Tex-Mex.

From kids and people my own age I picked up *Pachuco. Pachuco* (the language of the zoot suiters)° is a language of rebellion, both against Standard Spanish and Standard English. It is a secret language. Adults of the culture and outsiders cannot understand it. It is made up of slang words from both English and Spanish. *Ruca* means girl or woman, *vato* means guy or dude, *chale* means no, *simón* means yes, *churro* is sure, talk is *periquiar, pigionear* means petting, *que gacho* means how nerdy, *ponte águila* means watch out,

---

braceros: Mexican laborers temporarily admitted to the United States

the Valley: the Lower Rio Grande Valley, in southernmost Texas, near the Mexican border

tejano: Texan

zoot suiters: Zoot suits were a distinctive style of men's clothing that became very popular with young Mexican Americans, especially in Los Angeles, in the 1940s.

death is called *la pelona.* Through lack of practice and not having others who can speak it, I've lost most of the *Pachuco* tongue.

Chicano Spanish

Chicanos, after 250 years of Spanish/Anglo colonization, have developed significant differences in the Spanish we speak. We collapse two adjacent vowels into a single syllable and sometimes shift the stress in certain words such as *maíz/maiz, cohete/cuete.* We leave out certain consonants when they appear between vowels: *lado/lao, mojado/mojao.* Chicanos from South Texas pronounce *f* as *j* as in *jue (fue).* Chicanos use "archaisms," words that are no longer in the Spanish language, words that have been evolved out. We say *semos, truje, haiga, ansina,* and *naiden.* We retain the "archaic" *j,* as in *jalar,* that derives from an earlier *h* (the French *halar* or the Germanic *halon,* which was lost to standard Spanish in the sixteenth century), but which is still found in several regional dialects such as the one spoken in South Texas. (Due to geography, Chicanos from the Valley of South Texas were cut off linguistically from other Spanish speakers. We tend to use words that the Spaniards brought over from Medieval Spain. The majority of the Spanish colonizers in Mexico and the Southwest came from Extremadura°—Hernán Cortés° was one of them—and Andalucía.° Andalucians pronounce *ll* like a *y,* and their *d's* tend to be absorbed by adjacent vowels: *tirado* becomes *tirao.* They brought *el lenguaje popular, dialectos y regionalismos.*) 15

Chicanos and other Spanish speakers also shift *ll* to *y* and *z* to *s.* We leave out initial syllables, saying *tar* for *estar, toy* for *estoy, hora* for *ahora* (*cubanos* and *puertorriqueños* also leave out initial letters of some words). We also leave out the final syllable such as *pa* for *para.* The intervocalic° *y,* the *ll* as in *tortilla, ella, botella,* gets replaced by *tortia* or *tortiya, ea, botea.* We add an additional syllable at the beginning of certain words: *atocar* for *tocar, agastar* for *gastar.* Sometimes we'll say *lavaste las vacijas,* other times *lavates* (substituting the *ates* verb endings for the *aste*).

We used anglicisms, words borrowed from English: *bola* from ball, *carpeta* from carpet, *máchina de lavar* (instead of *lavadora*) from washing machine. Tex-Mex argot,° created by adding a Spanish sound at the beginning or end of an English word, such as *cookiar* for cook, *watchar* for watch, *parkiar* for park, and *rapiar* for rape, is the result of the pressures on Spanish speakers to adapt to English.

Extremadura: a region of western Spain, bordering Portugal
Hernán Cortés: (1485–1547), Spanish conquistador, colonizer of Mexico
Andalucía: large region of southernmost Spain
intervocalic: (a consonant) placed between two vowels
argot: specialized vocabulary of a particular group

We don't use the word *vosotros/as* or its accompanying verb form. We don't say *claro* (to mean *yes*), *imaginate,* or *me emociona,* unless we picked up Spanish from Latinas, out of a book, or in a classroom. Other Spanish-speaking groups are going through the same, or similar, development in their Spanish.

Linguistic Terrorism

> *Deslenguadas.*° *Somos los del español deficiente.* We are your linguistic nightmare, your linguistic aberration, your linguistic *mestisaje,*° the subject of your *burla.*° Because we speak with tongues of fire we are culturally crucified. Racially, culturally, and linguistically *somos huérfanos*—we speak an orphan tongue.

Chicanas who grew up speaking Chicano Spanish have internalized the belief that we speak poor Spanish. It is illegitimate, a bastard language. And because we internalize how our language has been used against us by the dominant culture, we use our language differences against each other.

20 Chicana feminists often skirt around each other with suspicion and hesitation. For the longest time I couldn't figure it out. Then it dawned on me. To be close to another Chicana is like looking into the mirror. We are afraid of what we'll see there. *Pena.* Shame. Low estimation of self. In childhood we are told that our language is wrong. Repeated attacks on our native tongue diminish our sense of self. The attacks continue throughout our lives.

Chicanas feel uncomfortable talking in Spanish to Latinas, afraid of their censure. Their language was not outlawed in their countries. They had a whole lifetime of being immersed in their native tongue; generations, centuries in which Spanish was a first language, taught in school, heard on radio and TV, and read in the newspaper.

If a person, Chicana or Latina, has a low estimation of my native tongue, she also has a low estimation of me. Often with *mexicanas y latinas* we'll speak English as a neutral language. Even among Chicanas we tend to speak English at parties or conferences. Yet, at the same time, we're afraid the other will think we're *agringadas*° because we don't speak Chicano Spanish. We oppress each other trying to out-Chicano each other, vying to be the "real" Chicanas, to speak like Chicanos. There is no one Chicano language just as there is no one Chicano experience. A monolingual Chicana whose first language is English or Spanish is just as much a Chicana as one who speaks

---

Deslenguadas: foulmouthed women
mestisaje: crossbreeding, miscegenation
burla: mockery
agringadas: Americanized (literally *gringo-ized*) women

several variants of Spanish. A Chicana from Michigan or Chicago or Detroit is just as much a Chicana as one from the Southwest. Chicano Spanish is as diverse linguistically as it is regionally.

By the end of this century, Spanish speakers will comprise the biggest minority group in the United States, a country where students in high schools and colleges are encouraged to take French classes because French is considered more "cultured." But for a language to remain alive it must be used. By the end of this century English, and not Spanish, will be the mother tongue of most Chicanos and Latinos.

. . .

So, if you want to really hurt me, talk badly about my language. Ethnic identity is twin skin to linguistic identity—I am my language. Until I can take pride in my language, I cannot take pride in myself. Until I can accept as legitimate Chicano Texas Spanish, Tex-Mex, and all the other languages I speak, I cannot accept the legitimacy of myself. Until I am free to write bilingually and to switch codes without having always to translate, while I still have to speak English or Spanish when I would rather speak Spanglish, and as long as I have to accommodate the English speakers rather than having them accommodate me, my tongue will be illegitimate.

I will no longer be made to feel ashamed of existing. I will have my voice: Indian, Spanish, white. I will have my serpent's tongue—my woman's voice, my sexual voice, my poet's voice. I will overcome the tradition of silence. 25

> My fingers
> move sly against your palm
> Like women everywhere, we speak in code.
>
> —Melanie Kaye/Kantrowitz

"Vistas," corridos, y comida:

My Native Tongue

In the 1960s, I read my first Chicano novel. It was *City of Night*° by John Rechy,° a gay Texan, son of a Scottish father and a Mexican mother. For days I walked around in stunned amazement that a Chicano could write and could get published. When I read *I Am Joaquín*° I was surprised to see a bilingual book by a Chicano in print. When I saw poetry written in Tex-Mex for the first time, a feeling of pure joy flashed through me. I felt like we really existed as a people. In 1971, when I started teaching High School English to Chicano students, I tried to supplement the required texts with works by Chicanos, only to be reprimanded and forbidden to do so by the principal. He claimed

---

City of Night: published in 1963

John Rechy: born in 1934 in El Paso, Texas

I Am Joaquín: book-length poem (1967) by Rodolfo Gonzales (1928–2005)

that I was supposed to teach "American" and English literature. At the risk of being fired, I swore my students to secrecy and slipped in Chicano short stories, poems, a play. In graduate school, while working toward a Ph.D., I had to "argue" with one adviser after the other, semester after semester, before I was allowed to make Chicano literature an area of focus.

Even before I read books by Chicanos or Mexicans, it was the Mexican movies I saw at the drive-in—the Thursday night special of $1.00 a carload—that gave me a sense of belonging. "*Vámonos a las vistas,*"° my mother would call out and we'd all—grandmother, brothers, sister, and cousins—squeeze into the car. We'd wolf down cheese and bologna white bread sandwiches while watching Pedro Infante° in melodramatic tearjerkers like *Nosotros los pobres,*° the first "real" Mexican movie (that was not an imitation of European movies). I remember seeing *Cuando los hijos se van*° and surmising that all Mexican movies played up the love a mother has for her children and what ungrateful sons and daughters suffer when they are not devoted to their mothers. I remember the singing-type "westerns" of Jorge Negrete° and Miquel Aceves Mejía.° When watching Mexican movies, I felt a sense of homecoming as well as alienation. People who were to amount to something didn't go to Mexican movies, or *bailes,*° or tune their radios to *bolero, rancherita,* and *corrido* music.

. . .

The whole time I was growing up, there was *norteño* music sometimes called North Mexican border music, or Tex-Mex music, or Chicano music, or *cantina* (bar) music. I grew up listening to *conjuntos,* three- or four-piece bands made up of folk musicians playing guitar, *bajo sexto,*° drums, and button accordion, which Chicanos had borrowed from the German immigrants who had come to Central Texas and Mexico to farm and build breweries. In the Rio Grande Valley, Steve Jordan° and Little Joe Hernández° were popular, and Flaco Jiménez° was the accordion king. The rhythms of Tex-Mex music are those of the polka, also adapted from the Germans, who in turn had borrowed the polka from the Czechs and Bohemians.

Vámonos a las vistas: Let's go to the movies.

Pedro Infante: (1917–1957), Mexican actor and singer

Nosostros los pobres: *We the Poor* (1947)

Cuando . . . van: *When the Children Leave* (1941)

Jorge Negrete: (1911–1953), Mexican actor and singer

Miquel Aceves Mejía: (1915–2006), Mexican actor, singer, and composer

bailes: dances

bajo sexto: twelve-string bass

Steve Jordan: Esteban "Steve" Jordan (1939–2010), American accordionist

Little Joe Hernández: José María De León Hernández (b. 1940), known professionally as Little Joe, American singer and pianist

Flaco Jiménez: Leonardo "Flaco" ("Skinny") Jiménez (b. 1939), American accordionist

I remember the hot, sultry evenings when *corridos*—songs of love and death on the Texas-Mexican borderlands—reverberated out of cheap amplifiers from the local *cantinas* and wafted in through my bedroom window.

Corridos first became widely used along the South Texas/Mexican border during the early conflict between Chicanos and Anglos. The *corridos* are usually about Mexican heroes who do valiant deeds against the Anglo oppressors. Pancho Villa's° song, "*La cucaracha,*" is the most famous one. *Corridos* of John F. Kennedy and his death are still very popular in the Valley. Older Chicanos remember Lydia Mendoza,° one of the great border *corrido* singers who was called *la Gloria de Tejas*. Her "*El tango negro,*" sung during the Great Depression, made her a singer of the people. The ever-present *corridos* narrated one hundred years of border history, bringing news of events as well as entertaining. These folk musicians and folk songs are our chief cultural mythmakers, and they made our hard lives seem bearable. 30

I grew up feeling ambivalent about our music. Country-western and rock-and-roll had more status. In the fifties and sixties, for the slightly educated and *agringado* Chicanos, there existed a sense of shame at being caught listening to our music. Yet I couldn't stop my feet from thumping to the music, could not stop humming the words, nor hide from myself the exhilaration I felt when I heard it.

. . .

There are more subtle ways that we internalize identification, especially in the forms of images and emotions. For me food and certain smells are tied to my identity, to my homeland. Woodsmoke curling up to an immense blue sky; woodsmoke perfuming my grandmother's clothes, her skin. The stench of cow manure and the yellow patches on the ground; the crack of a .22 rifle and the reek of cordite.° Homemade white cheese sizzling in a pan, melting inside a folded *tortilla.* My sister Hilda's hot, spicy *menudo,*° *chile colorado* making it deep red, pieces of *panza*° and hominy° floating on top. My brother Carito barbequing *fajitas* in the backyard. Even now and 3,000 miles away, I can see my mother spicing the ground beef, pork, and venison with *chile.* My mouth salivates at the thought of the hot steaming *tamales* I would be eating if I were home.

Si le preguntas a mi mamá, "¿Qué eres?"

> Identity is the essential core of who
> we are as individuals, the conscious
> experience of the self inside.
>
> —Gershen Kaufman

Pancho Villa: José Doroteo Arango Arámbula (1878–1923), known as Francisco "Pancho" Villa, a leader of the Mexican Revolution

Lydia Mendoza: (1916–2007), American singer and guitarist

cordite: a smokeless gunpowder

menudo: a Mexican soup

panza: tripe, cow stomach

hominy: dried corn kernels soaked in lye

Nosotros los Chicanos straddle the borderlands. On one side of us, we are constantly exposed to the Spanish of the Mexicans, on the other side we hear the Anglos' incessant clamoring so that we forget our language. Among ourselves we don't say *nosotros los americanos, o nosotros los españoles, o nosotros los hispanos.* We say *nosotros los mexicanos* (by *mexicanos* we do not mean citizens of Mexico; we do not mean a national identity, but a racial one). We distinguish between *mexicanos del otro lado*° and *mexicanos de este lado.*° Deep in our hearts we believe that being Mexican has nothing to do with which country one lives in. Being Mexican is a state of soul—not one of mind, not one of citizenship. Neither eagle nor serpent, but both. And like the ocean, neither animal respects borders.

> *Dime con quien and as y te diré quien eres.*
> (Tell me who your friends are and I'll tell you who you are.)
>
> —Mexican saying

Si le preguntas a mi mamá, "¿Qué eres?" te dirá, "Soy mexicana."° My brothers and sister say the same. I sometimes will answer "*soy mexicana*" and at others will say "*soy Chicana*" *o* "*soy tejana.*" But I identified as "*Raza*"° before I ever identified as "*mexicana*" or "*Chicana.*"

35 As a culture, we call ourselves Spanish when referring to ourselves as a linguistic group and when copping out. It is then that we forget our predominant Indian genes. We are 70–80 percent Indian. We call ourselves Hispanic or Spanish-American or Latin American or Latin when linking ourselves to other Spanish-speaking peoples of the Western hemisphere and when copping out. We call ourselves Mexican-American to signify we are neither Mexican nor American, but more the noun "American" than the adjective "Mexican" (and when copping out).

Chicanos and other people of color suffer economically for not acculturating.° This voluntary (yet forced) alienation makes for psychological conflict, a kind of dual identity—we don't identify with the Anglo-American cultural values and we don't totally identify with the Mexican cultural values. We are a synergy° of two cultures with various degrees of Mexicanness or Angloness. I have so internalized the borderland conflict that sometimes I feel like one cancels out the other and we are zero, nothing, no one. *A veces no soy nada ni nadie. Pero hasta cuando no lo soy, lo soy.*°

When not copping out, when we know we are more than nothing, we call ourselves Mexican, referring to race and ancestry; *mestizo* when affirming both

---

otro lado: the other side (of the Rio Grande)

este lado: this side

Si . . . mexicana: If you ask my mother, "What are you?," she'll tell you, "I'm Mexican."

Raza: "the race" or "the people" of the Chicano community

acculturating: adopting the traits and patterns of another culture

synergy: a whole greater than the sum of its parts

A veces . . . lo soy: Sometimes I'm nothing and nobody. But even when I'm not, I am.

our Indian and Spanish (but we hardly ever own our Black) ancestry; Chicano when referring to a politically aware people born and/or raised in the United States; *Raza* when referring to Chicanos; *tejanos* when we are Chicanos from Texas.

Chicanos did not know we were a people until 1965 when Cesar Chavez° and the farmworkers united and *I Am Joaquín* was published and *la Raza Unida*° party was formed in Texas. With that recognition, we became a distinct people. Something momentous happened to the Chicano soul—we became aware of our reality and acquired a name and a language (Chicano Spanish) that reflected that reality. Now that we had a name, some of the fragmented pieces began to fall together—who we were, what we were, how we had evolved. We began to get glimpses of what we might eventually become.

Yet the struggle of identities continues, the struggle of borders is our reality still. One day the inner struggle will cease and a true integration take place. In the meantime, *tenémos que hacer la lucha. ¿Quién está protegiendo los ranchos de mi gente? ¿Quién está tratando de cerrar la fisura entre la india y el blanco en nuestra sangre? El Chicano, si, el Chicano que anda como un ladrón en su propia casa.*°

Los Chicanos, how patient we seem, how very patient. There is the quiet of the Indian about us. We know how to survive. When other races have given up their tongue we've kept ours. We know what it is to live under the hammer blow of the dominant *norteamericano* culture. But more than we count the blows, we count the days the weeks the years the centuries the aeons until the white laws and commerce and customs will rot in the deserts they've created, lie bleached. *Humildes*° yet proud, *quietos* yet wild, *nosotros los mexicanos-Chicanos* will walk by the crumbling ashes as we go about our business. Stubborn, persevering, impenetrable as stone, yet possessing a malleability° that renders us unbreakable, we, the *mestizas* and *mestizos,* will remain. 40

[1987]

Read

1. Why is the opening scene appropriate to Anzaldúa's purpose in the essay?
2. How does the narrator describe her school experience?
3. Where do you first find Anzaldúa's argument?

Cesar Chavez: (1927–1993), American civil rights activist and cofounder of the United Farm Workers union

Raza Unida: "People United," focused on improving the political and social situation of the Chicano community

tenémos . . . . casa: we must carry on the struggle. Who's protecting my people's farms? Who's trying to close the fissure between the Indian and the white in our blood? The Chicano, yes, the Chicano who moves like a thief in his own house.

Humildes: humble

malleability: adaptability

4. How do you react to the switch between English and Spanish?
5. What is the purpose of the list in paragraph 10?
6. Why does Anzaldúa sometimes translate a Spanish phrase and sometimes not?

Write

1. Define what "linguistic terrorism" is.
2. Describe Anzaldúa's persona in this piece, using a line or two from the essay.
3. Reflect on Anzaldúa's style—choice of words, arrangement of ideas, adjectives, and verbs that convey tone—and how the style you describe suggests her aim.

Complete the Exercises on Anzaldua's Essay at Your Pearson MyLab

Connect

1. What other pieces that you've read might agree with Anzaldúa's statement: "If you really want to hurt me, talk badly about my language"?

Joy Harjo

Born in Tulsa, Oklahoma, in the Creek Nation, Joy Harjo (b. 1951) studied at the Writers' Workshop at the University of Iowa. She now teaches creative writing at the University of New Mexico and writes poetry and screenplays. Harjo's poetry has been widely recognized for its voice, imagery, and American Indian traditions and themes. Harjo writes about the importance of landscape, the merging of past and present in contemporary culture, and Indian culture and history.

Anchorage

for Audre Lorde°

This city is made of stone, of blood, and fish.
There are Chugatch Mountains to the east
and whale and seal to the west.
It hasn't always been this way, because glaciers
who are ice ghosts create oceans, carve earth 5
and shape this city here, by the sound.
They swim backwards in time.

Audre Lorde: (1934–1992), Caribbean American poet and activist, New York State Poet Laureate (1991–1992)

Once a storm of boiling earth° cracked open
the streets, threw open the town.
It's quiet now, but underneath the concrete 10
is the cooking earth,
and above that, air
which is another ocean, where spirits we can't see
are dancing joking getting full
on roasted caribou, and the praying 15
goes on, extends out.

Nora and I go walking down 4th Avenue
and know it is all happening.
On a park bench we see someone's Athabascan°
grandmother, folded up, smelling like 200 years 20
of blood and piss, her eyes closed against some
unimagined darkness, where she is buried in an ache
in which nothing makes
sense.
We keep on breathing, walking, but softer now, 25
the clouds whirling in the air above us.
What can we say that would make us understand
better than we do already?
Except to speak of her home and claim her
as our own history, and know that our dreams 30
don't end here, two blocks away from the ocean
where our hearts still batter away at the muddy shore.

And I think of the 6th Avenue jail, of mostly Native
and Black men, where Henry told about being shot at
eight times outside a liquor store in L.A., but when 35
the car sped away he was surprised he was alive,
no bullet holes, man, and eight cartridges strewn
on the sidewalk
all around him.

---

a storm of boiling earth: On March 27, 1964, a four-minute earthquake (at 9.2 magnitude, the second-worst recorded) devastated Anchorage, causing over $300 million in property damage and killing nine people; more than 100 people died in various other places because of resulting tsunamis.
Athabascan: an indigenous North American culture comprising a number of different tribes

Everyone laughed at the impossibility of it, 40
but also the truth. Because who would believe
the fantastic and terrible story of all of our survival
those who were never meant
to survive?

[1983]

Read

1. How does Harjo describe glaciers?
2. How do Harjo's images suggest an attitude toward the natural world?
3. How does the speaker make a connection to the Athabascan grandmother?
4. What is the purpose of naming the characters in the poem?

Write

1. Reflect on the response that Henry's tale of his escape provokes in his listeners.
2. Comment on Harjo's choice of the setting of Anchorage for her poem.
3. Write a paragraph that suggests what the speaker means by saying that she and her friend "know it is all happening" (line 18).

Connect

1. This poem's dedication is to Audre Lorde. Locate a poem or speech by Lorde, and then discuss why Harjo might have dedicated to her poem to Lorde.
2. Find some statistics about race, ethnic groups, poverty, gender, and other factors in Anchorage. Comment on what those statistics suggest about the aim of this poem.

Art Spiegelman

Art Spiegelman (b. 1948) was born in Sweden to Polish Jews who survived the Holocaust during the Nazi occupation of Poland in World War II. He grew up in New York City, attended college, and began drawing comics in the 1960s. Along with his wife, Francoise Mouly, Spiegelman printed early versions of his comic book classic *Maus* from his apartment. Eventually it was published commercially as *Maus I: A Survivor's Tale* in 1986. The story of Spiegelman's parents and friends during the terrors of Hitler's rule in Europe, it was immediately successful. The book was awarded a special Pulitzer Prize in 1992.

Spiegelman worked for *The New Yorker* until shortly after the September 11, 2001, terrorist attacks on the World Trade Center. He helped create the famous *New Yorker* cover that features a completely black page with the shadows of the Twin Towers in deeper black. It was rated one of the top ten magazine covers of the century. Spiegelman is an advocate for the power and uses of the comic genre. He regularly lectures at colleges and public forums on visual rhetoric and the comic.

In *Maus,* the Holocaust is presented through the conversation of a son (Art Spiegelman) and his father (Vladek), a survivor of the Nazi camps during World War II. The son wants to tell his father's story. Jewish citizens are depicted as mice; the Germans as cats; the Poles as pigs. In this scene, Vladek remembers a part of the story as he rides his exercise bike and Art listens.

From *Maus I: A Survivor's Tale*

ILZECKI HAD A SON THE SAME AGE LIKE RICHIEU. IF YOU ONLY COULD SEE HOW THOSE CHILDREN PLAYED TOGETHER.
LISTEN, VLADEK..

WE CAN'T KNOW WHAT'S GOING TO HAPPEN TO US - BUT WE MUST KEEP OUR CHILDREN SAFE.

I HAVE A GOOD FRIEND, A POLE, WHO'S WILLING TO HIDE MY SON UNTIL THE SITUATION GETS BETTER.

...I THINK HE'D TAKE YOUR BOY TOO.
YES, YOU MAY BE RIGHT! LET ME SPEAK WITH MY FAMILY.

BUT, I'M TELLING YOU, IT WAS SOMETHING TERRIBLE GOING ON IN OUR HOUSE WHEN I EVEN MENTIONED IT.
WHAT? HAVE YOU GONE CRAZY?
HOW CAN YOU EVEN THINK OF GIVING RICHIEU UP TO COMPLETE STRANGERS?!

I'LL NEVER GIVE UP MY BABY. NEVER!

ILZECKI AND HIS WIFE DIDN'T COME OUT FROM THE WAR.
...BUT HIS SON REMAINED ALIVE; OURS DID NOT.
...AND ANYWAY WE HAD TO GIVE RICHIEU TO HIDE A YEAR LATER.

Gemeinder: headquarters of the Jewish community organization

Sosnowiec: a city in southern Poland, occupied by the Germans in September 1939

Stara Sosnowiec: Old Sosnowiec, a district at the western end of the city

kilo: kilogram (approximately 2.2 pounds)

Modrzejowska: the main commercial street in Sosnowiec

Zionist: supporter of a Jewish homeland (Israel was not founded until 1948)

---

zlotys: the zloty is the standard Polish monetary unit

FOR A WHILE I HAD ALSO A FOOD BUSINESS THAT I DIDN'T YET TELL YOU...

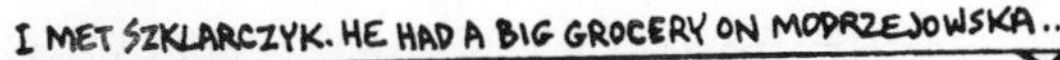
I MET SZKLARCZYK. HE HAD A BIG GROCERY ON MODRZEJOWSKA..

YOU'RE ZYLBERBERG'S SON-IN-LAW, RIGHT? COME INSIDE AND WAIT FOR THE RAIN TO STOP.

SO, TOGETHER WE SAT AND SPOKE, AND HE HELPED, FROM TIME TO TIME, A CUSTOMER...
SORRY- YOU DON'T HAVE ENOUGH COUPONS TO BUY 1/2 KILO OF SUGAR.
STILL... SHE WENT OUT WITH 1/2 KILO. I SMELLED I COULD ARRANGE SOMETHING.

THEN A LITTLE MORE WE SPOKE AND HE MADE TO ME A PROPOSITION...
MAYBE YOU COULD SELL MY "EXTRA" ITEMS TO SMALL SHOPS IN THE AREA ...UNDER THE COUNTER.
IT WAS DANGEROUS TO CARRY THESE THINGS-BUT MAYBE I COULD BE LUCKY.

WHEN SOMEBODY IS HUNGRY HE LOOKS FOR BUSINESS...

ONE TIME I HAD 10 OR 15 KILOS SUGAR TO DELIVER...
HALT, JEW! WHAT ARE YOU CARRYING?

WHAT WAS I SUPPOSED TO SAY? FOR THIS I COULD REALLY HANG!
SUGAR.

...I'M TAKING IT OVER TO MY GROCERY STORE.
OH. YOU HAVE A SHOP?
I MADE SO THEY WOULD THINK IT WAS LEGAL.

I WENT TO THE BACK DOOR WHERE I HAD TO DELIVER...
OPEN UP, POLDEK!

...I'VE GOT OUR SUGAR.
?!
AND THEY LEFT ME GO WITHOUT EVEN CHECKING MY PAPERS!

[1986]

Read

1. What drawing techniques give expression to the characters?
2. How do drawings convey complexity through shadowing, close-ups, use of contrast and line?
3. Where do you "hear" the accent in the father's speech? Why does Spiegelman include it?
4. What do you predict will happen next based on these pages?

Write

1. How do you react to the depiction of Nazi and Jew as cat and mouse?
2. Write a paragraph exploring how the movement back and forth in time affects your reading and the aim.
3. Comment on the relationship of father and son, using one or two panels to illustrate your opinion.
4. Write about the emotional reaction of characters and of you as the reader, and how the graphic contributes to the reaction.

Complete the Exercises on Spiegelman's Graphic Narrative at Your Pearson MyLab

Connect

1. Take one of the pieces you've read in this unit and draw a three-panel cartoon based on it. Consider the rhetorical choices you've made.
2. How is this excerpt like a fable?
3. Look up "black humor." Discuss whether you think Spiegelman makes use of it, and if so, how he does it.

Rita Dove

Rita Dove (b. 1952), named Poet Laureate of the United States in 1993, was the youngest person and the first African American to be awarded this distinction. She grew up in Akron, Ohio, the daughter of a research chemist, and attended Miami University in Ohio and the University of Iowa's Writers' Workshop.

Dove has published more than seven collections of poetry, as well as plays and short stories. She has received numerous awards and distinctions, including the 1987 Pulitzer Prize for her collection *Thomas and Beulah,* which was based on the lives of her grandparents. She often gives readings and lectures.

Banneker°

What did he do except lie
under a pear tree, wrapped in
a great cloak, and meditate

Banneker: Benjamin Banneker (1731–1806), an African American surveyor and astronomer who wrote and published an almanac from 1792 to 1797

on the heavenly bodies?
Venerable,° the good people of Baltimore 5
whispered, shocked and more than
a little afraid. After all it was said
he took to strong drink.
Why else would he stay out
under the stars all night 10
and why hadn't he married?

But who would want him! Neither
Ethiopian nor English, neither
lucky nor crazy, a capacious° bird
humming as he penned in his mind 15
another enflamed letter
to President Jefferson°—he imagined
the reply, polite and rhetorical.°
Those who had been to Philadelphia
reported the statue 20
of Benjamin Franklin
before the library

his very size and likeness.
A wife? No, thank you.
At dawn he milked 25
the cows, then went inside
and put on a pot to stew
while he slept. The clock
he whittled as a boy
still ran.° Neighbors 30
woke him up
with warm bread and quilts.
At nightfall he took out

Venerable: worthy of respect or impressive by virtue of age, character, position, etc.

capacious: roomy, spacious, able to hold a large amount

enflamed . . . Jefferson: On August 19, 1791, Banneker wrote to then-Secretary of State Jefferson, quoting from the Declaration of Independence and calling Jefferson a criminal for keeping and mistreating slaves.

polite and rhetorical: an apt characterization of Jefferson's reply to Banneker's letter

The clock . . . still ran: Using a pocket watch as a model, Banneker carved and assembled a wooden clock that struck the hours; completed when he was 22, it was still working when he died.

his rifle—a white-maned
figure stalking the darkened 35
breast of the Union—and
shot at the stars, and by chance
one went out. Had he killed?
I assure thee, my dear Sir!
Lowering his eyes to fields 40
sweet with the rot of spring, he could see
a government's domed city
rising from the morass° and spreading
in a spiral of lights. . . .

[1983]

Read

1. Why is it so crucial to know who Banneker is when reading this poem?
2. Who seems to be asking the question that begins the poem?
3. What is the significance of the statue of Benjamin Franklin mentioned at the end of the first stanza?
4. How does the reader get a sense of the intellectual accomplishments of Banneker?
5. How does the description of the building of Washington's capital reveal the speaker's attitude?

Write

1. Using Dove's poem, write a short character description of Benjamin Banneker.
2. Comment on what you believe Dove's argument might be in the poem. Find a line or two that suggests the argument.
3. Respond to the lines "At nightfall he took out / his rifle—a white-maned / figure stalking the darkened / breast of the Union—and / shot at the stars."
4. Where do you find irony in the voice of the speaker?

Connect

1. Write a description of the character of Thomas Jefferson as Banneker describes him. Then look back at Thomas Jefferson's work in Unit 1 and compare the persona you hear in Jefferson's *Declaration* to Banneker's characterization.
2. Locate another writer/character in this unit who is an outsider in the larger culture and compare the way the authors depict that marginalization.

---

he could see . . . the morass: In 1791, Banneker assisted in the survey of the land that would become the District of Columbia; contrary to legend, however, he was not involved in the planning of the city of Washington.

Tim O'Brien

Born in Minnesota, Tim O'Brien (b. 1946) attended Macalester College. He served a tour of duty in Vietnam after graduation in 1968. His experiences in the war shaped his writing and thinking; his works have helped define the American experience of Vietnam.

After the war, O'Brien became a journalist and began writing autobiographical stories of his experiences. In 1979, he was awarded the National Book Award for *Going After Cacciato,* and in 1990 he published *The Things They Carried,* a group of short stories about Vietnam. He teaches creative writing at Southwest Texas State University. Often in his work, autobiography and fiction blur, and O'Brien plays with a variety of styles and genres. "On the Rainy River" is the first story in *The Things They Carried.*

On the Rainy River

This is one story I've never told before. Not to anyone. Not to my parents, not to my brother or sister, not even to my wife. To go into it, I've always thought, would only cause embarrassment for all of us, a sudden need to be elsewhere, which is the natural response to a confession. Even now, I'll admit, the story makes me squirm. For more than twenty years I've had to live with it, feeling the shame, trying to push it away, and so by this act of remembrance, by putting the facts down on paper, I'm hoping to relieve at least some of the pressure on my dreams. Still, it's a hard story to tell. All of us, I suppose, like to believe that in a moral emergency we will behave like the heroes of our youth, bravely and forthrightly, without thought of personal loss or discredit. Certainly that was my conviction back in the summer of 1968. Tim O'Brien: a secret hero. The Lone Ranger. If the stakes ever became high enough—if the evil were evil enough, if the good were good enough—I would simply tap a secret reservoir of courage that had been accumulating inside me over the years. Courage, I seemed to think, comes to us in finite quantities, like an inheritance, and by being frugal and stashing it away and letting it earn interest, we steadily increase our moral capital in preparation for that day when the account must be drawn down. It was a comforting theory. It dispensed with all those bothersome little acts of daily courage; it offered hope and grace to the repetitive coward; it justified the past while amortizing° the future.

In June of 1968, a month after graduating from Macalester College,° I was drafted to fight a war I hated. I was twenty-one years old.

amortizing: paying down a mortgage or other debt in regular installments

Macalester College: in St. Paul, Minnesota

Young, yes, and politically naive, but even so the American war in Vietnam seemed to me wrong. Certain blood was being shed for uncertain reasons. I saw no unity of purpose, no consensus on matters of philosophy or history or law. The very facts were shrouded in uncertainty: Was it a civil war? A war of national liberation or simple aggression? Who started it, and when, and why? What really happened to the USS *Maddox* on that dark night in the Gulf of Tonkin?° Was Ho Chi Minh° a Communist stooge, or a nationalist savior, or both, or neither? What about the Geneva Accords?° What about SEATO° and the Cold War? What about dominoes?° America was divided on these and a thousand other issues, and the debate had spilled out across the floor of the United States Senate and into the streets, and smart men in pinstripes could not agree on even the most fundamental matters of public policy. The only certainty that summer was moral confusion. It was my view then, and still is, that you don't make war without knowing why. Knowledge, of course, is always imperfect, but it seemed to me that when a nation goes to war it must have reasonable confidence in the justice and imperative° of its cause. You can't fix your mistakes. Once people are dead, you can't make them undead.

In any case those were my convictions, and back in college I had taken a modest stand against the war. Nothing radical, no hothead stuff, just ringing a few doorbells for Gene McCarthy,° composing a few tedious, uninspired editorials for the campus newspaper. Oddly, though, it was almost entirely an intellectual activity. I brought some energy to it, of course, but it was the energy that accompanies almost any abstract endeavor; I felt no personal danger; I felt no sense of an impending crisis in my life. Stupidly, with a kind of smug removal that I can't begin to fathom,° I assumed that the problems of killing and dying did not fall within my special province.

Gulf of Tonkin: site of an alleged attack on an American destroyer by the North Vietnamese, which became the pretext for a Senate resolution facilitating the escalation of U.S. involvement in Vietnam

Ho Chi Minh: (1890–1969), North Vietnamese president (1945–1969)

Geneva Accords: a negotiated end, in 1954, to the Indochina War, which created the nations of Laos, Cambodia, and Vietnam; Vietnam was temporarily divided pending national elections, which were repeatedly blocked by the Diem government in South Vietnam

SEATO: Southeast Asia Treaty Organization, formed in 1954 and ended in 1977

dominoes: The domino theory, favored by Vietnam War supporters, held that if the Communists took over a nation, neighboring countries would fall to them one after another.

imperative: unavoidable obligation, necessity

Gene McCarthy: Eugene McCarthy (1916–2005), U.S. senator from Minnesota (1959–1971) and antiwar contender for the 1968 Democratic presidential nomination

fathom: comprehend

The draft notice arrived on June 17, 1968. It was a humid afternoon, I remember, cloudy and very quiet, and I'd just come in from a round of golf. My mother and father were having lunch out in the kitchen. I remember opening up the letter, scanning the first few lines, feeling the blood go thick behind my eyes. I remember a sound in my head. It wasn't thinking, just a silent howl. A million things all at once—I was too *good* for this war. Too smart, too compassionate, too everything. It couldn't happen. I was above it. I had the world dicked—Phi Beta Kappa° and summa cum laude and president of the student body and a full-ride scholarship for grad studies at Harvard. A mistake, maybe—a foul-up in the paperwork. I was no soldier. I hated Boy Scouts. I hated camping out. I hated dirt and tents and mosquitoes. The sight of blood made me queasy, and I couldn't tolerate authority, and I didn't know a rifle from a slingshot. I was a *liberal,* for Christ sake: If they needed fresh bodies, why not draft some back-to-the-stone-age hawk? Or some dumb jingo° in his hard hat° and Bomb Hanoi button, or one of LBJ's pretty daughters, or Westmoreland's° whole handsome family—nephews and nieces and baby grandson. There should be a law, I thought. If you support a war, if you think it's worth the price, that's fine, but you have to put your own precious fluids on the line. You have to head for the front and hook up with an infantry unit and help spill the blood. And you have to bring along your wife, or your kids, or your lover. A *law,* I thought.

5 I remember the rage in my stomach. Later it burned down to a smoldering self-pity, then to numbness. At dinner that night my father asked what my plans were.

"Nothing," I said. "Wait."

I spent the summer of 1968 working in an Armour meat-packing plant in my hometown of Worthington, Minnesota. The plant specialized in pork products, and for eight hours a day I stood on a quarter-mile assembly line—more properly, a disassembly line—removing blood clots from the necks of dead pigs. My job title, I believe, was Declotter. After slaughter, the hogs were decapitated, split down the length of the belly, pried open, eviscerated° and strung up

---

Phi Beta Kappa: national honor society whose members are chosen from among undergraduates of high academic ability

jingo: belligerent superpatriot

hard hat: During the Vietnam War, construction workers became associated with strong prowar sentiments and occasional attacks upon antiwar demonstrators.

Westmoreland: General William Westmoreland (1914–2005), U.S. commander in Vietnam (1964–1968), U.S. Army chief of staff (1968–1972)

eviscerated: disemboweled

by the hind hocks on a high conveyer belt. Then gravity took over. By the time a carcass reached my spot on the line, the fluids had mostly drained out, everything except for thick clots of blood in the neck and upper chest cavity. To remove the stuff, I used a kind of water gun. The machine was heavy, maybe eighty pounds, and was suspended from the ceiling by a heavy rubber cord. There was some bounce to it, an elastic up-and-down give, and the trick was to maneuver the gun with your whole body, not lifting with the arms, just letting the rubber cord do the work for you. At one end was a trigger; at the muzzle end was a small nozzle and a steel roller brush. As a carcass passed by, you'd lean forward and swing the gun up against the clots and squeeze the trigger, all in one motion, and the brush would whirl and water would come shooting out and you'd hear a quick splattering sound as the clots dissolved into a fine red mist. It was not pleasant work. Goggles were a necessity, and a rubber apron, but even so it was like standing for eight hours a day under a lukewarm blood-shower. At night I'd go home smelling of pig. It wouldn't go away. Even after a hot bath, scrubbing hard, the stink was always there—like old bacon, or sausage, a dense greasy pig-stink that soaked deep into my skin and hair. Among other things, I remember, it was tough getting dates that summer. I felt isolated; I spent a lot of time alone. And there was also that draft notice tucked away in my wallet.

In the evenings I'd sometimes borrow my father's car and drive aimlessly around town, feeling sorry for myself, thinking about the war and the pig factory and how my life seemed to be collapsing toward slaughter. I felt paralyzed. All around me the options seemed to be narrowing, as if I were hurtling down a huge black funnel, the whole world squeezing in tight. There was no happy way out. The government had ended most graduate school deferments; the waiting lists for the National Guard and Reserves were impossibly long; my health was solid; I didn't qualify for CO° status—no religious grounds, no history as a pacifist. Moreover, I could not claim to be opposed to war as a matter of general principle. There were occasions, I believed, when a nation was justified in using military force to achieve its ends, to stop a Hitler or some comparable evil, and I told myself that in such circumstances I would've willingly marched off to the battle. The problem, though, was that a draft board did not let you choose your war.

Beyond all this, or at the very center, was the raw fact of terror. I did not want to die. Not ever. But certainly not then, not there, not in a wrong war. Driving up Main Street, past the courthouse and the

---

CO: conscientious objector

Ben Franklin store,° I sometimes felt the fear spreading inside me like weeds. I imagined myself dead. I imagined myself doing things I could not do—charging an enemy position, taking aim at another human being.

10 At some point in mid-July I began thinking seriously about Canada. The border lay a few hundred miles north, an eight-hour drive. Both my conscience and my instincts were telling me to make a break for it, just take off and run like hell and never stop. In the beginning the idea seemed purely abstract, the word Canada printing itself out in my head; but after a time I could see particular shapes and images, the sorry details of my own future—a hotel room in Winnipeg,° a battered old suitcase, my father's eyes as I tried to explain myself over the telephone. I could almost hear his voice, and my mother's. Run, I'd think. Then I'd think, Impossible. Then a second later I'd think, *Run*.

It was a kind of schizophrenia. A moral split. I couldn't make up my mind. I feared the war, yes, but I also feared exile. I was afraid of walking away from my own life, my friends and my family, my whole history, everything that mattered to me. I feared losing the respect of my parents. I feared the law. I feared ridicule and censure. My hometown was a conservative little spot on the prairie, a place where tradition counted, and it was easy to imagine people sitting around a table down at the old Gobbler Café on Main Street, coffee cups poised, the conversation slowly zeroing in on the young O'Brien kid, how the damned sissy had taken off for Canada. At night, when I couldn't sleep, I'd sometimes carry on fierce arguments with those people. I'd be screaming at them, telling them how much I detested their blind, thoughtless, automatic acquiescence to it all, their simple-minded patriotism, their prideful ignorance, their love-it-or-leave-it platitudes, how they were sending me off to fight a war they didn't understand and didn't want to understand. I held them responsible. By God, yes, I *did*. All of them—I held them personally and individually responsible—the polyestered Kiwanis boys, the merchants and farmers, the pious churchgoers, the chatty housewives, the PTA and the Lions club° and the Veterans of Foreign Wars and the fine upstanding gentry out at the country club. They didn't know Bao Dai° from the man in the moon. They didn't know history. They didn't

Ben Franklin store: one of a chain of five-and-dime, or discount, stores

Winnipeg: capital city of Manitoba, Canada

Kiwanis . . . Lions club: service organizations of a generally conservative tendency

Bao Dai: (1913–1997), South Vietnamese chief of state (1945–1955), ousted by prime minister Ngo Dinh Diem

know the first thing about Diem's° tyranny, or the nature of Vietnamese nationalism, or the long colonialism of the French—this was all too damned complicated, it required some reading—but no matter, it was a war to stop the Communists, plain and simple, which was how they liked things, and you were a treasonous pussy if you had second thoughts about killing or dying for plain and simple reasons.

I was bitter, sure. But it was so much more than that. The emotions went from outrage to terror to bewilderment to guilt to sorrow and then back again to outrage. I felt a sickness inside me. Real disease.

Most of this I've told before, or at least hinted at, but what I have never told is the full truth. How I cracked. How at work one morning, standing on the pig line, I felt something break open in my chest. I don't know what it was. I'll never know. But it was real, I know that much, it was a physical rupture—a cracking-leaking-popping feeling. I remember dropping my water gun. Quickly, almost without thought, I took off my apron and walked out of the plant and drove home. It was midmorning, I remember, and the house was empty. Down in my chest there was still that leaking sensation, something very warm and precious spilling out, and I was covered with blood and hog-stink, and for a long while I just concentrated on holding myself together. I remember taking a hot shower. I remember packing a suitcase and carrying it out to the kitchen, standing very still for a few minutes, looking carefully at the familiar objects all around me. The old chrome toaster, the telephone, the pink and white Formica on the kitchen counters. The room was full of bright sunshine. Everything sparkled. My house, I thought. My life. I'm not sure how long I stood there, but later I scribbled out a short note to my parents.

What it said, exactly, I don't recall now. Something vague. Taking off, will call, love Tim.

I drove north. 15

It's a blur now, as it was then, and all I remember is a sense of high-velocity and the feel of the steering wheel in my hands. I was riding on adrenaline. A giddy feeling, in a way, except there was the dreamy edge of impossibility to it—like running a dead-end maze—no way out—it couldn't come to a happy conclusion and yet I was doing it anyway because it was all I could think of to do. It was pure flight, fast and mindless. I had no plan. Just hit the border at high speed and crash through and keep on running. Near dusk I passed through

Diem: Ngo Dinh Diem (1901–1963), first president of South Vietnam (1955–1963), assassinated in a coup d'état

Bemidji, then turned northeast toward International Falls. I spent the night in the car behind a closed-down gas station a half mile from the border. In the morning, after gassing up, I headed straight west along the Rainy River, which separates Minnesota from Canada, and which for me separated one life from another. The land was mostly wilderness. Here and there I passed a motel or bait shop, but otherwise the country unfolded in great sweeps of pine and birch and sumac. Though it was still August, the air already had the smell of October, football season, piles of yellow-red leaves, everything crisp and clean. I remember a huge blue sky. Off to my right was the Rainy River, wide as a lake in places, and beyond the Rainy River was Canada.

For a while I just drove, not aiming at anything, then in the late morning I began looking for a place to lie low for a day or two. I was exhausted, and scared sick, and around noon I pulled into an old fishing resort called the Tip Top Lodge. Actually it was not a lodge at all, just eight or nine tiny yellow cabins clustered on a peninsula that jutted northward into the Rainy River. The place was in sorry shape. There was a dangerous wooden dock, an old minnow tank, a flimsy tar paper boathouse along the shore. The main building, which stood in a cluster of pines on high ground, seemed to lean heavily to one side, like a cripple, the roof sagging toward Canada. Briefly, I thought about turning around, just giving up, but then I got out of the car and walked up to the front porch.

The man who opened the door that day is the hero of my life. How do I say this without sounding sappy? Blurt it out—the man saved me. He offered exactly what I needed, without questions, without any words at all. He took me in. He was there at the critical time—a silent, watchful presence. Six days later, when it ended, I was unable to find a proper way to thank him, and I never have, and so, if nothing else, this story represents a small gesture of gratitude twenty years overdue.

Even after two decades I can close my eyes and return to that porch at the Tip Top Lodge. I can see the old guy staring at me. Elroy Berdahl: eighty-one years old, skinny and shrunken and mostly bald. He wore a flannel shirt and brown work pants. In one hand, I remember, he carried a green apple, a small paring knife in the other. His eyes had the bluish gray color of a razor blade, the same polished shine, and as he peered up at me I felt a strange sharpness, almost painful, a cutting sensation, as if his gaze were somehow slicing me open. In part, no doubt, it was my own sense of guilt, but even so I'm absolutely certain that the old man took one look and went right to the heart of things—a kid in trouble. When I asked for a room, Elroy made a little clicking sound with his tongue. He nodded, led me out to one of the cabins, and dropped a key in my hand. I remember smiling at him. I also remember wishing I hadn't. The old man shook his head as if to tell me it wasn't worth the bother.

"Dinner at five-thirty," he said. "You eat fish?" 20

"Anything," I said.

Elroy grunted and said, "I'll bet."

We spent six days together at the Tip Top Lodge. Just the two of us. Tourist season was over, and there were no boats on the river, and the wilderness seemed to withdraw into a great permanent stillness. Over those six days Elroy Berdahl and I took most of our meals together. In the mornings we sometimes went out on long hikes into the woods, and at night we played Scrabble or listened to records or sat reading in front of his big stone fireplace. At times I felt the awkwardness of an intruder, but Elroy accepted me into his quiet routine without fuss or ceremony. He took my presence for granted, the same way he might've sheltered a stray cat—no wasted sighs or pity—and there was never any talk about it. Just the opposite. What I remember more than anything is the man's willful, almost ferocious silence. In all that time together, all those hours, he never asked the obvious questions: Why was I there? Why alone? Why so preoccupied? If Elroy was curious about any of this, he was careful never to put it into words.

My hunch, though, is that he already knew. At least the basics. After all, it was 1968, and guys were burning draft cards, and Canada was just a boat ride away. Elroy Berdahl was no hick. His bedroom, I remember, was cluttered with books and newspapers. He killed me at the Scrabble board, barely concentrating, and on those occasions when speech was necessary he had a way of compressing large thoughts into small, cryptic packets of language. One evening, just at sunset, he pointed up at an owl circling over the violet-lighted forest to the west.

"Hey, O'Brien," he said. "There's Jesus." 25

The man was sharp—he didn't miss much. Those razor eyes. Now and then he'd catch me staring out at the river, at the far shore, and I could almost hear the tumblers° clicking in his head. Maybe I'm wrong, but I doubt it.

One thing for certain, he knew I was in desperate trouble. And he knew I couldn't talk about it. The wrong word—or even the right word—and I would've disappeared. I was wired and jittery. My skin felt too tight. After supper one evening I vomited and went back to my cabin and lay down for a few moments and then vomited again;

---

tumblers: pieces in a lock mechanism that free the bolt

another time, in the middle of the afternoon, I began sweating and couldn't shut it off. I went through whole days feeling dizzy with sorrow. I couldn't sleep; I couldn't lie still. At night I'd toss around in bed, half awake, half dreaming, imagining how I'd sneak down to the beach and quietly push one of the old man's boats out into the river and start paddling my way toward Canada. There were times when I thought I'd gone off the psychic edge. I couldn't tell up from down, I was just falling, and late in the night I'd lie there watching weird pictures spin through my head. Getting chased by the Border Patrol—helicopters and searchlights and barking dogs—I'd be crashing through the woods, I'd be down on my hands and knees—people shouting out my name—the law closing in on all sides—my hometown draft board and the FBI and the Royal Canadian Mounted Police. It all seemed crazy and impossible. Twenty-one years old, an ordinary kid with all the ordinary dreams and ambitions, and all I wanted was to live the life I was born to—a mainstream life—I loved baseball and hamburgers and cherry Cokes—and now I was off on the margins of exile, leaving my country forever, and it seemed so impossible and terrible and sad.

I'm not sure how I made it through those six days. Most of it I can't remember. On two or three afternoons, to pass some time, I helped Elroy get the place ready for winter, sweeping down the cabins and hauling in the boats, little chores that kept my body moving. The days were cool and bright. The nights were very dark. One morning the old man showed me how to split and stack firewood, and for several hours we just worked in silence out behind his house. At one point, I remember, Elroy put down his maul° and looked at me for a long time, his lips drawn as if framing a difficult question, but then he shook his head and went back to work. The man's self-control was amazing. He never pried. He never put me in a position that required lies or denials. To an extent, I suppose, his reticence was typical of that part of Minnesota, where privacy still held value, and even if I'd been walking around with some horrible deformity—four arms and three heads—I'm sure the old man would've talked about everything except those extra arms and heads. Simple politeness was part of it. But even more than that, I think, the man understood that words were insufficient. The problem had gone beyond discussion. During that long summer I'd been over and over the various arguments, all the pros and cons, and it was no longer a question that could be decided by an act of pure reason. Intellect had come up against emotion. My conscience told me to run, but some irrational and powerful

maul: a heavy hammer for driving stakes

force was resisting, like a weight pushing me toward the war. What it came down to, stupidly, was a sense of shame. Hot, stupid shame. I did not want people to think badly of me. Not my parents, not my brother and sister, not even the folks down at the Gobbler Café. I was ashamed to be there at the Tip Top Lodge. I was ashamed of my conscience, ashamed to be doing the right thing.

Some of this Elroy must've understood. Not the details, of course, but the plain fact of crisis.

30 Although the old man never confronted me about it, there was one occasion when he came close to forcing the whole thing out into the open. It was early evening, and we'd just finished supper, and over coffee and dessert I asked him about my bill, how much I owed so far. For a long while the old man squinted down at the tablecloth.

"Well, the basic rate," he said, "is fifty bucks a night. Not counting meals. This makes four nights, right?"

I nodded. I had three hundred and twelve dollars in my wallet.

Elroy kept his eyes on the tablecloth. "Now that's an onseason price. To be fair, I suppose we should knock it down a peg or two." He leaned back in his chair. "What's a reasonable number, you figure?"

"I don't know," I said. "Forty?"

35 "Forty's good. Forty a night. Then we tack on food—say another hundred? Two hundred sixty total?"

"I guess."

He raised his eyebrows. "Too much?"

"No, that's fair. It's fine. Tomorrow, though . . . I think I'd better take off tomorrow."

Elroy shrugged and began clearing the table. For a time he fussed with the dishes, whistling to himself as if the subject had been settled. After a second he slapped his hands together.

40 "You know what we forgot?" he said. "We forgot wages. Those odd jobs you done. What we have to do, we have to figure out what your time's worth. Your last job—how much did you pull in an hour?"

"Not enough," I said.

"A bad one?"

"Yes. Pretty bad."

Slowly then, without intending any long sermon, I told him about my days at the pig plant. It began as a straight recitation of the facts, but before I could stop myself I was talking about the blood clots and the water gun and how the smell had soaked into my skin and how I couldn't wash it away. I went on for a long time. I told him about wild hogs squealing in my dreams, the sounds of butchery, slaughterhouse sounds, and how I'd sometimes wake up with that greasy pig-stink in my throat.

When I was finished, Elroy nodded at me. 45

"Well, to be honest," he said, "when you first showed up here, I wondered about all that. The aroma, I mean. Smelled like you was awful damned fond of pork chops." The old man almost smiled. He made a snuffling sound, then sat down with a pencil and a piece of paper. "So what'd this crud job pay? Ten bucks an hour? Fifteen?"

"Less."

Elroy shook his head. "Let's make it fifteen. You put in twenty-five hours here, easy. That's three hundred seventy-five bucks total wages. We subtract the two hundred sixty for food and lodging, I still owe you a hundred and fifteen."

He took four fifties out of his shirt pocket and laid them on the table.

"Call it even," he said. 50

"No."

"Pick it up. Get yourself a haircut."

The money lay on the table for the rest of the evening. It was still there when I went back to my cabin. In the morning, though, I found an envelope tacked to my door. Inside were the four fifties and a two-word note that said emergency fund.

The man knew.

Looking back after twenty years, I sometimes wonder if the events of that summer didn't happen in some other dimension, a place where your life exists before you've lived it, and where it goes afterward. None of it ever seemed real. During my time at the Tip Top Lodge I had the feeling that I'd slipped out of my own skin, hovering a few feet away while some poor yo-yo with my name and face tried to make his way toward a future he didn't understand and didn't want. Even now I can see myself as I was then. It's like watching an old home movie: I'm young and tan and fit. I've got hair—lots of it. I don't smoke or drink. I'm wearing faded blue jeans and a white polo shirt. I can see myself sitting on Elroy Berdahl's dock near dusk one evening, the sky a bright shimmering pink, and I'm finishing up a letter to my parents that tells what I'm about to do and why I'm doing it and how sorry I am that I'd never found the courage to talk to them about it. I ask them not to be angry. I try to explain some of my feelings, but there aren't enough words, and so I just say that it's a thing that has to be done. At the end of the letter I talk about the vacations we used to take up in this north country, at a place called Whitefish Lake, and how the scenery here reminds me of those good times. I tell them I'm fine. I tell them I'll write again from Winnipeg or Montreal or wherever I end up. 55

On my last full day, the sixth day, the old man took me out fishing on the Rainy River. The afternoon was sunny and cold. A stiff breeze came in from the north, and I remember how the little fourteen-foot boat made sharp rocking motions as we pushed off from the dock. The current was fast. All around us, I remember, there was a vastness to the world, an unpeopled rawness, just the trees and the sky and the water reaching out toward nowhere. The air had the brittle scent of October.

For ten or fifteen minutes Elroy held a course upstream, the river choppy and silver-gray, then he turned straight north and put the engine on full throttle. I felt the bow lift beneath me. I remember the wind in my ears, the sound of the old outboard Evinrude. For a time I didn't pay attention to anything, just feeling the cold spray against my face, but then it occurred to me that at some point we must've passed into Canadian waters, across that dotted line between two different worlds, and I remember a sudden tightness in my chest as I looked up and watched the far shore come at me. This wasn't a daydream. It was tangible and real. As we came in toward land, Elroy cut the engine, letting the boat fishtail lightly about twenty yards off shore. The old man didn't look at me or speak. Bending down, he opened up his tackle box and busied himself with a bobber° and a piece of wire leader,° humming to himself, his eyes down.

It struck me then that he must've planned it. I'll never be certain, of course, but I think he meant to bring me up against the realities, to guide me across the river and to take me to the edge and to stand a kind of vigil as I chose a life for myself.

I remember staring at the old man, then at my hands, then at Canada. The shoreline was dense with brush and timber. I could see tiny red berries on the bushes. I could see a squirrel up in one of the birch trees, a big crow looking at me from a boulder along the river. That close—twenty yards—and I could see the delicate latticework of the leaves, the texture of the soil, the browned needles beneath the pines, the configurations of geology and human history. Twenty yards. I could've done it. I could've jumped and started swimming for my life. Inside me, in my chest, I felt a terrible squeezing pressure. Even now, as I write this, I can still feel that tightness. And I want you to feel it—the wind coming off the river, the waves, the silence, the wooded frontier. You're at the bow of a boat on the Rainy River. You're twenty-one years old, you're scared, and there's a hard squeezing pressure in your chest.

---

bobber: fishing-line float

leader: item that attaches the hook to the fishing line

What would you do?

Would you jump? Would you feel pity for yourself? Would you think about your family and your childhood and your dreams and all you're leaving behind? Would it hurt? Would it feel like dying? Would you cry, as I did?

I tried to swallow it back. I tried to smile, except I was crying.

Now, perhaps, you can understand why I've never told this story before. It's not just the embarrassment of tears. That's part of it, no doubt, but what embarrasses me much more, and always will, is the paralysis that took my heart. A moral freeze: I couldn't decide, I couldn't act, I couldn't comport myself with even a pretense of modest human dignity.

All I could do was cry. Quietly, not bawling, just the chest-chokes.

At the rear of the boat Elroy Berdahl pretended not to notice. He held a fishing rod in his hands, his head bowed to hide his eyes. He kept humming a soft, monotonous little tune. Everywhere, it seemed, in the trees and water and sky, a great worldwide sadness came pressing down on me, a crushing sorrow, sorrow like I had never known it before. And what was so sad, I realized, was that Canada had become a pitiful fantasy. Silly and hopeless. It was no longer a possibility. Right then, with the shore so close, I understood that I would not do what I should do. I would not swim away from my hometown and my country and my life. I would not be brave. That old image of myself as a hero, as a man of conscience and courage, all that was just a threadbare pipe dream. Bobbing there on the Rainy River, looking back at the Minnesota shore, I felt a sudden swell of helplessness come over me, a drowning sensation, as if I had toppled overboard and was being swept away by the silver waves. Chunks of my own history flashed by. I saw a seven-year-old boy in a white cowboy hat and a Lone Ranger mask and a pair of holstered six-shooters; I saw a twelve-year-old Little League shortstop pivoting to turn a double play; I saw a sixteen-year-old kid decked out for his first prom, looking spiffy in a white tux and a black bow tie, his hair cut short and flat, his shoes freshly polished. My whole life seemed to spill out into the river, swirling away from me, everything I had ever been or ever wanted to be. I couldn't get my breath; I couldn't stay afloat; I couldn't tell which way to swim. A hallucination, I suppose, but it was as real as anything I would ever feel. I saw my parents calling to me from the far shoreline. I saw my brother and sister, all the townsfolk, the mayor and the entire Chamber of Commerce and all my old teachers and girlfriends and high school buddies. Like some weird sporting event: everybody screaming from the sidelines, rooting me on—a loud stadium roar. Hotdogs and popcorn—stadium smells, stadium heat. A squad of cheerleaders did cartwheels along the banks of the Rainy River; they had megaphones and pompoms and smooth brown thighs. The crowd swayed left and right. A marching band played fight songs. All my aunts and uncles were there, and Abraham Lincoln, and Saint George, and a nine-year-old girl named Linda who had died of a brain tumor back in fifth grade, and several members of the United States Senate, and a blind poet scribbling notes, and LBJ, and Huck Finn, and Abbie Hoffman,° and all the dead soldiers back from the grave, and the many thousands who were later to die—villagers with terrible burns, little kids without arms or legs—yes, and the Joint Chiefs of Staff were there, and a couple of popes, and a first lieutenant named Jimmy Cross,° and the last surviving veteran of the American Civil War, and Jane Fonda dressed up as Barbarella,° and an old man sprawled beside a pigpen, and my grandfather, and Gary Cooper,° and a kind-faced woman carrying an umbrella and a copy of Plato's *Republic,* and a million ferocious citizens waving flags of all shapes and colors—people in hard hats, people in headbands—they were all whooping and chanting and urging me toward one shore or the other. I saw faces from my distant past and distant future. My wife was there. My unborn daughter waved at me, and my two sons hopped up and down, and a drill sergeant named Blyton sneered and shot up a finger and shook his head. There was a choir in bright purple robes. There was a cabbie from the Bronx. There was a slim young man I would one day kill with a hand grenade along a red clay trail outside the village of My Khe.

The little aluminum boat rocked softly beneath me. There was the wind and the sky.

I tried to will myself overboard.

I gripped the edge of the boat and leaned forward and thought, *Now.*

I did try. It just wasn't possible.

All those eyes on me—the town, the whole universe—and I couldn't risk the embarrassment. It was as if there were an audience to my life, that swirl of faces along the river, and in my head I could hear people screaming at me. Traitor! they yelled. Turncoat! Pussy! 70

Abbie Hoffman: (1936–1989), antiwar activist and writer

a first . . . Cross: a major character in O'Brien's 1990 story collection *The Things They Carried*

Barbarella: title character of a 1968 science-fiction film directed by Fonda's then-husband Roger Vadim

Gary Cooper: (1901–1961), American movie actor noted for playing taciturn, heroic figures

I felt myself blush. I couldn't tolerate it. I couldn't endure the mockery, or the disgrace, or the patriotic ridicule. Even in my imagination, the shore just twenty yards away, I couldn't make myself be brave. It had nothing to do with morality. Embarrassment, that's all it was.

And right then I submitted.

I would go to the war—I would kill and maybe die—because I was embarrassed not to.

That was the sad thing. And so I sat in the bow of the boat and cried.

It was loud now. Loud, hard crying.

75 Elroy Berdahl remained quiet. He kept fishing. He worked his line with the tips of his fingers, patiently, squinting out at his red and white bobber on the Rainy River. His eyes were flat and impassive.° He didn't speak. He was simply there, like the river and the late-summer sun. And yet by his presence, his mute watchfulness, he made it real. He was the true audience. He was a witness, like God, or like the gods, who look on in absolute silence as we live our lives, as we make our choices or fail to make them.

"Ain't biting," he said.

Then after a time the old man pulled in his line and turned the boat back toward Minnesota.

I don't remember saying goodbye. That last night we had dinner together, and I went to bed early, and in the morning Elroy fixed breakfast for me. When I told him I'd be leaving, the old man nodded as if he already knew. He looked down at the table and smiled.

At some point later in the morning it's possible that we shook hands—I just don't remember—but I do know that by the time I'd finished packing the old man had disappeared. Around noon, when I took my suitcase out to the car, I noticed that his old black pickup truck was no longer parked in front of the house. I went inside and waited for a while, but I felt a bone certainty that he wouldn't be back. In a way, I thought, it was appropriate. I washed up the breakfast dishes, left his two hundred dollars on the kitchen counter, got into the car, and drove south toward home.

80 The day was cloudy. I passed through towns with familiar names, through the pine forests and down to the prairie, and then to Vietnam, where I was a soldier, and then home again. I survived, but it's not a happy ending. I was a coward. I went to the war.

[1990]

---

impassive: unemotional

Read

1. What is the purpose of the opening paragraph of the story?
2. How does the narrator use the pig factory as an image?
3. What does the narrator mean by saying he has a kind of "schizophrenia"?
4. What details reveal Elroy's character?
5. Why does the narrator use second person in the paragraph beginning "I remember staring at the old man . . ."?

Write

1. Using the first couple of paragraphs and the end, write a reflection on how the narrator defines courage.
2. In a paragraph, summarize the narrator's dilemma in the story.
3. Describe the relationship of the old man at the Tip Top Lodge and the narrator.
4. How would you describe the purpose of the "hallucination" the narrator has near the end of the story?

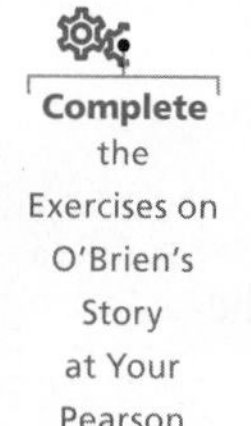

Complete the Exercises on O'Brien's Story at Your Pearson MyLab

Connect

1. Locate information on Vietnam-era student protests and put this story in the context of those protests.
2. How does first person narration work to bring the reader into the world of the story? Find another first person narration in this unit (Anzaldúa or Tan, for example) and compare their use of first person to connect with readers.

Maya Lin

Maya Lin is a sculptor and landscape artist who was born in Ohio in 1959 to parents who had emigrated from China. Her father was the dean of the College of Fine Arts at Ohio University. At the age of 21, Lin won a public design competition for the Vietnam Veterans Memorial. The memorial is of black stone and lists the names of all the fallen service members—over 52,000 names. It was completed in 1982. The sculpture was initially controversial for its nontraditional design and for the choice of the sculptor, whose Asian descent occasioned criticism from some. Viewers of the memorial walk a path that slopes downward as they read names and see themselves reflected in the stone.

Lin has designed other sculptures and landscapes, including the Civil Rights Memorial in Montgomery, Alabama, and Wave Field at the University of Michigan. Lin says she wishes people to be aware of their surroundings, the physical and psychological spaces people occupy.

Vietnam Veterans Memorial, Washington, DC

Vietnam Veterans Memorial (1982), Maya Lin. Stone sculpture. Washington, D.C. Photo by Kumar Sriskandan/ Alamy

[1982]

Read

1. How does this photo suggest the importance of the placement of the memorial?
2. How do the black color of the stone and the texture of the engraving work to create rhetorical effect?
3. What might be the effect of moving down as viewers walk past the sculpture?

Write

1. The memorial is unusual in design and its naming of all armed services members killed in the war. Comment on your reaction to its appearance and to the names on the wall.
2. Speculate on the message this kind of memorial sends about armed services veterans, viewers, and war.

Connect

1. Locate another memorial to veterans of war and compare the two. There is another war memorial at the Vietnam Veterans Memorial site to honor those who served, which would make a good comparison.

Annie Dillard

Annie Dillard (b. 1945) was brought up in Pittsburgh, Pennsylvania, the oldest of three daughters. She grew up loving nature and observing the natural world, and her master's thesis at Hollings College in Virginia was written on Henry David Thoreau. Her book of connected essays, *Pilgrim at Tinker Creek,* won the Pulitzer Prize in 1974. Her writing has been compared to that of Virginia Woolf, as well as to Thoreau. Dillard writes poetry as well as essays and novels, and she has published a memoir of growing up in Pittsburgh, *An American Childhood.* She lives in western Washington.

Living Like Weasels

I

A weasel is wild. Who knows what he thinks? He sleeps in his underground den, his tail draped over his nose. Sometimes he lives in his den for two days without leaving. Outside, he stalks rabbits, mice, muskrats, and birds, killing more bodies than he can eat warm, and often dragging the carcasses home. Obedient to instinct, he bites his prey at the neck, either splitting the jugular vein at the throat or crunching the brain at the base of the skull, and he does not let go. One naturalist refused to kill a weasel who was socketed into his hand deeply as a rattlesnake. The man could in no way pry the tiny weasel off, and he had to walk half a mile to water, the weasel dangling from his palm, and soak him off like a stubborn label.

And once, says Ernest Thompson Seton°—once, a man shot an eagle out of the sky. He examined the eagle and found the dry skull of a weasel fixed by the jaws to his throat. The supposition is that the eagle had pounced on the weasel and the weasel swiveled and bit as instinct taught him, tooth to neck, and nearly won. I would like to have seen that eagle from the air a few weeks or months before he was shot: was the whole weasel still attached to his feathered throat, a fur pendant? Or did the eagle eat what he could reach, gutting the living weasel with his talons before his breast, bending his beak, cleaning the beautiful airborne bones?

II

I have been reading about weasels because I saw one last week. I startled a weasel who startled me, and we exchanged a long glance.

Twenty minutes from my house, through the woods by the quarry and across the highway, is Hollins Pond, a remarkable piece of shallowness, where I like to go at sunset and sit on a tree trunk. Hollins Pond is also called

---

Ernest Thompson Seton: (1860–1946), Canadian-American wildlife writer and artist

Murray's Pond; it covers two acres of bottomland° near Tinker Creek with six inches of water and six thousand lily pads. In winter, brown-and-white steers stand in the middle of it, merely dampening their hooves; from the distant shore they look like miracle itself, complete with miracle's nonchalance.° Now, in summer, the steers are gone. The water lilies have blossomed and spread to a green horizontal plane that is terra firma° to plodding blackbirds, and tremulous° ceiling to black leeches, cray fish, and carp.

This is, mind you, suburbia. It is a five-minute walk in three directions to rows of houses, though none is visible here. There's a 55 mph highway at one end of the pond, and a nesting pair of wood ducks at the other. Under every bush is a muskrat hole or a beer can. The far end is an alternating series of fields and woods, fields and woods, threaded everywhere with motorcycle tracks—in whose bare clay wild turtles lay eggs. 5

So, I had crossed the highway, stepped over two low barbed-wire fences, and traced the motorcycle path in all gratitude through the wild rose and poison ivy of the pond's shoreline up into high grassy fields. Then I cut down through the woods to the mossy fallen tree where I sit. This tree is excellent. It makes a dry, upholstered bench at the upper, marshy end of the pond, a plush jetty° raised from the thorn shore between a shallow blue body of water and a deep blue body of sky.

The sun had just set. I was relaxed on the tree trunk, ensconced° in the lap of lichen,° watching the lily pads at my feet tremble and part dreamily over the thrusting path of a carp. A yellow bird appeared to my right and flew behind me. It caught my eye; I swiveled around—and the next instant, inexplicably, I was looking down at a weasel, who was looking up at me.

III

Weasel! I'd never seen one wild before. He was ten inches long, thin as a curve, a muscled ribbon, brown as fruitwood, soft-furred, alert. His face was fierce, small and pointed as a lizard's; he would have made a good arrowhead. There was just a dot of chin, maybe two brown hairs' worth, and then the pure white fur began that spread down his underside. He had two black eyes I didn't see, any more than you see a window.

The weasel was stunned into stillness as he was emerging from beneath an enormous shaggy wild rose bush four feet away. I was stunned into stillness twisted backward on the tree trunk. Our eyes locked, and someone threw away the key.

---

bottomland: low-lying land close to a river
nonchalance: casual unconcern
terra firma: solid ground
tremulous: quivering, shaking
jetty: dock, pier
ensconced: settled, nestled
lichen: fungus that forms a crustlike growth on tree trunks or rocks

Our look was as if two lovers, or deadly enemies, met unexpectedly on an overgrown path when each had been thinking of something else: a clearing blow to the gut. It was also a bright blow to the brain, or a sudden beating of brains with all the charge and intimate grate of rubbed balloons. It emptied our lungs. It felled the forest, moved the fields, and drained the pond; the world dismantled and tumbled into that black hole of eyes. If you and I looked at each other that way, our skulls would split and drop to our shoulders. But we don't. We keep our skulls. So. 10

He disappeared. This was only last week, and already I don't remember what shattered the enchantment. I think I blinked, I think I retrieved my brain from the weasel's brain, and tried to memorize what I was seeing, and the weasel felt the yank of separation, the careening° splashdown into real life and the urgent current of instinct. He vanished under the wild rose. I waited motionless, my mind suddenly full of data and my spirit with pleadings, but he didn't return.

Please do not tell me about "approach-avoidance conflicts." I tell you I've been in that weasel's brain for sixty seconds, and he was in mine. Brains are private places, muttering through unique and secret tapes—but the weasel and I both plugged into another tape simultaneously, for a sweet and shocking time. Can I help it if it was a blank?

What goes on in his brain the rest of the time? What does a weasel think about? He won't say. His journal is tracks in clay, a spray of feathers, mouse blood and bone: uncollected, unconnected, loose-leaf, and blown.

IV

I would like to learn, or remember, how to live. I come to Hollins Pond not so much to learn how to live as, frankly, to forget about it. That is, I don't think I can learn from a wild animal how to live in particular—shall I suck warm blood, hold my tail high, walk with my footprints precisely over the prints of my hands?—but I might learn something of mindlessness, something of the purity of living in the physical senses and the dignity of living without bias or motive. The weasel lives in necessity and we live in choice, hating necessity and dying at the last ignobly in its talons. I would like to live as I should, as the weasel lives as he should. And I suspect that for me the way is like the weasel's: open to time and death painlessly, noticing everything, remembering nothing, choosing the given with a fierce and pointed will.

V

I missed my chance. I should have gone for the throat. I should have lunged for that streak of white under the weasel's chin and held on, held on through mud and into the wild rose, held on for a dearer life. We could live under the wild rose wild as weasels, mute and uncomprehending. I could very calmly go wild. I could live two days in the den, curled, leaning on mouse fur, sniffing 15

careening: swaying, staggering

bird bones, blinking, licking, breathing musk, my hair tangled in the roots of grasses. Down is a good place to go, where the mind is single. Down is out, out of your ever-loving mind and back to your careless senses. I remember muteness as a prolonged and giddy fast, where every moment is a feast of utterance received. Time and events are merely poured, unremarked, and ingested directly, like blood pulsed into my gut through a jugular vein. Could two live that way? Could two live under the wild rose, and explore by the pond, so that the smooth mind of each is as everywhere present to the other, and as received and as unchallenged, as falling snow?

We could, you know. We can live any way we want. People take vows of poverty, chastity, and obedience—even of silence—by choice. The thing is to stalk your calling in a certain skilled and supple way, to locate the most tender and live spot and plug into that pulse. This is yielding, not fighting. A weasel doesn't "attack" anything; a weasel lives as he's meant to, yielding at every moment to the perfect freedom of single necessity.

VI

I think it would be well, and proper, and obedient, and pure, to grasp your one necessity and not let it go, to dangle from it limp wherever it takes you. Then even death, where you're going no matter how you live, cannot you part. Seize it and let it seize you up aloft even, till your eyes burn out and drop; let your musky flesh fall off in shreds, and let your very bones unhinge and scatter, loosened over fields, over fields and woods, lightly, thoughtless, from any height at all, from as high as eagles.

[1974]

Read

1. How can you tell that Dillard is a keen observer of the world around her from the first two paragraphs?
2. How does Dillard describe the moment of seeing the weasel?
3. How would you characterize Dillard's persona in this essay?
4. What does Dillard say she wants to learn from the weasel?
5. Who is Dillard speaking to? How do you know?

Write

1. Notice that the essay is divided into numbered sections. Write a sentence or two that explains how you think this works in the essay.
2. Comment on the line: "noticing everything, remembering nothing. . ." (paragraph 14).
3. Write down the verbs that are most important to the argument Dillard makes and consider what they contribute to her aim.
4. Find two lines or so that characterize the tone of this essay and comment on how they reveal tone.
5. This essay suggests the need for the wild in life. How would you describe what Dillard means by "wild"?

Complete the Exercises on Dillard's Essay at Your Pearson MyLab

Connect

1. Read Thoreau in Unit 2. Find places in this essay that remind you, in style or meaning, of Thoreau's ideas in *Walden.*
2. How does Dillard's essay speak to environmentalists' concerns for the natural environment? Look up information on environmental protection to make connections to Dillard's essay.

Toni Morrison

Toni Morrison (b. 1931) is an author, critic, teacher, and lecturer. She was born in Ohio to parents who encouraged her love of reading and writing. She graduated from Howard University and received a master's degree from Cornell University. She has written seven novels as well as essays, short stories, and criticism. Her first novel, *The Bluest Eye,* was published in 1970 to great acclaim. Since then, she has been regarded as one of the best living American authors. Morrison has held several teaching positions at Howard, the State University of New York at Albany, Yale, and Princeton. For years, she was an editor at Random House.

Morrison won a Pulitzer Prize for her novel *Beloved* in 1988, and in 1993 she won the Nobel Prize in Literature. The speech below was delivered as she accepted the award.

The Nobel Lecture in Literature

Members of the Swedish Academy, Ladies and Gentlemen:

Narrative has never been merely entertainment for me. It is, I believe, one of the principal ways in which we absorb knowledge. I hope you will understand, then, why I begin these remarks with the opening phrase of what must be the oldest sentence in the world, and the earliest one we remember from childhood: "Once upon a time . . . "

"Once upon a time there was an old woman. Blind but wise." Or was it an old man? A guru, perhaps. Or a *griot*° soothing restless children. I have heard this story, or one exactly like it, in the lore of several cultures.

"Once upon a time there was an old woman. Blind. Wise."

In the version I know the woman is the daughter of slaves, black, American, and lives alone in a small house outside of town. Her reputation for wisdom is without peer° and without question. 5

griot: West African storyteller who preserves and hands down oral traditions
peer: equal

Among her people she is both the law and its transgression. The honor she is paid and the awe in which she is held reach beyond her neighborhood to places far away; to the city where the intelligence of rural prophets is the source of much amusement.

One day the woman is visited by some young people who seem to be bent on disproving her clairvoyance° and showing her up for the fraud they believe she is. Their plan is simple: they enter her house and ask the one question the answer to which rides solely on her difference from them, a difference they regard as a profound disability: her blindness. They stand before her, and one of them says,

"Old woman, I hold in my hand a bird. Tell me whether it is living or dead."

She does not answer, and the question is repeated. "Is the bird I am holding living or dead?"

Still she does not answer. She is blind and cannot see her visitors, let alone what is in their hands. She does not know their color, gender or homeland. She only knows their motive. 10

The old woman's silence is so long, the young people have trouble holding their laughter.

Finally she speaks, and her voice is soft but stern. "I don't know," she says. "I don't know whether the bird you are holding is dead or alive, but what I do know is that it is in your hands. It is in your hands."

Her answer can be taken to mean: if it is dead, you have either found it that way or you have killed it. If it is alive, you can still kill it. Whether it is to stay alive is your decision. Whatever the case, it is your responsibility.

For parading their power and her helplessness, the young visitors are reprimanded, told they are responsible not only for the act of mockery but also for the small bundle of life sacrificed to achieve its aims. The blind woman shifts attention away from assertions of power to the instrument through which that power is exercised.

Speculation on what (other than its own frail body) that bird in the hand might signify has always been attractive to me, but especially so now, thinking as I have been about the work I do that has brought me to this company. So I choose to read the bird as language and the woman as a practiced writer. 15

She is worried about how the language she dreams in, given to her at birth, is handled, put into service, even withheld from her for certain nefarious° purposes. Being a writer, she thinks of language partly as a system, partly as a

---

clairvoyance: ESP, second sight; foreknowledge
nefarious: wicked

living thing over which one has control, but mostly as agency—as an act with consequences. So the question the children put to her, "Is it living or dead?," is not unreal, because she thinks of language as susceptible° to death, erasure; certainly imperiled and salvageable only by an effort of the will. She believes that if the bird in the hands of her visitors is dead, the custodians are responsible for the corpse. For her a dead language is not only one no longer spoken or written, it is unyielding language content to admire its own paralysis. Like statist° language, censored and censoring. Ruthless in its policing duties, it has no desire or purpose other than to maintain the free range of its own narcotic narcissism, its own exclusivity and dominance. However, moribund,° it is not without effect, for it actively thwarts° the intellect, stalls conscience, suppresses human potential. Unreceptive to interrogation, it cannot form or tolerate new ideas, shape other thoughts, tell another story, fill baffling silences. Official language smitheried° to sanction° ignorance and preserve privilege is a suit of armor, polished to shocking glitter, a husk from which the knight departed long ago. Yet there it is; dumb, predatory, sentimental. Exciting reverence in schoolchildren, providing shelter for despots, summoning false memories of stability, harmony among the public.

She is convinced that when language dies, out of carelessness, disuse, indifference, and absence of esteem, or killed by fiat,° not only she herself but all users and makers are accountable for its demise. In her country children have bitten their tongues off and use bullets instead to iterate° the void of speechlessness, of disabled and disabling language, of language adults have abandoned altogether as a device for grappling with meaning, providing guidance, or expressing love. But she knows tongue-suicide is not only the choice of children. It is common among the infantile heads of state and power merchants whose evacuated language leaves them with no access to what is left of their human instincts, for they speak only to those who obey, or in order to force obedience.

The systematic looting of language can be recognized by the tendency of its users to forgo its nuanced, complex, mid-wifery properties, replacing them with menace and subjugation. Oppressive language does more than represent violence; it is violence; does more than represent the limits of knowledge; it limits knowledge. Whether it is obscuring state language or the faux language

---

susceptible: liable, vulnerable
statist: official; in the service of the state
moribund: near death
thwarts: hinders, prevents
smitheried: forged
sanction: approve
fiat: order or decree
iterate: repeat

of mindless media; whether it is the proud but calcified° language of the academy or the commodity-driven language of science; whether it is the malign language of law-without-ethics, or language designed for the estrangement of minorities, hiding its racist plunder in its literary cheek—it must be rejected, altered and exposed. It is the language that drinks blood, laps vulnerabilities, tucks its fascist boots under crinolines° of respectability and patriotism as it moves relentlessly toward the bottom line and the bottomed-out mind. Sexist language, racist language, theistic° language—all are typical of the policing languages of mastery, and cannot, do not, permit new knowledge or encourage the mutual exchange of ideas.

The old woman is keenly aware that no intellectual mercenary or insatiable dictator; no paid-for politician or demagogue,° no counterfeit journalist would be persuaded by her thoughts. There is and will be rousing language to keep citizens armed and arming; slaughtered and slaughtering in the malls, courthouses, post offices, playgrounds, bedrooms and boulevards; stirring, memorializing language to mask the pity and waste of needless death. There will be more diplomatic language to countenance° rape, torture, assassination. There is and will be more seductive, mutant language designed to throttle women, to pack their throats like pâté-producing geese with their own unsayable, transgressive words; there will be more of the language of surveillance disguised as research; of politics and history calculated to render the suffering of millions mute; language glamorized to thrill the dissatisfied and bereft into assaulting their neighbors; arrogant pseudo-empirical° language crafted to lock creative people into cages of inferiority and hopelessness.

Underneath the eloquence, the glamour, the scholarly associations, however stirring or seductive, the heart of such language is languishing,° or perhaps not beating at all—if the bird is already dead. 20

She has thought about what could have been the intellectual history of any discipline if it had not insisted upon, or been forced into, the waste of time and life that rationalizations for and representations of dominance required—lethal discourses of exclusion blocking access to cognition° for both the excluder and the excluded.

---

calcified: hardened, rigidified

crinolines: petticoats

theistic: pertaining to belief in God

demagogue: leader who appeals to emotions and prejudices

countenance: tolerate

empirical: based on observation or experiment

languishing: losing strength, weakening

cognition: perception or knowledge

The conventional wisdom of the Tower of Babel story is that the collapse was a misfortune. That it was the distraction or the weight of many languages that precipitated the tower's failed architecture. That one monolithic° language would have expedited° the building, and heaven would have been reached. Whose heaven, she wonders? And what kind? Perhaps the achievement of Paradise was premature, a little hasty if no one could take the time to understand other languages, other views, other narratives. Had they, the heaven they imagined might have been found at their feet. Complicated, demanding, yes, but a view of heaven as life; not heaven as post-life.

She would not want to leave her young visitors with the impression that language should be forced to stay alive merely to be. The vitality of language lies in its ability to limn° the actual, imagined and possible lives of its speakers, readers, writers. Although its poise is sometimes in displacing experience, it is not a substitute for it. It arcs toward the place where meaning may lie. When a President of the United States thought about the graveyard his country had become, and said, "The world will little note nor long remember what we say here. But it will never forget what they did here," his simple words were exhilarating in their life-sustaining properties because they refused to encapsulate the reality of 600,000 dead men in a cataclysmic race war. Refusing to monumentalize, disdaining the "final word," the precise "summing up," acknowledging their "poor power to add or detract," his words signal deference° to the uncapturability of the life it mourns. It is the deference that moves her, that recognition that language can never live up to life once and for all. Nor should it. Language can never "pin down" slavery, genocide, war. Nor should it yearn for the arrogance to be able to do so. Its force, its felicity, is in its reach toward the ineffable.°

Be it grand or slender, burrowing, blasting or refusing to sanctify; whether it laughs out loud or is a cry without an alphabet, the choice word or the chosen silence, unmolested language surges toward knowledge, not its destruction. But who does not know of literature banned because it is interrogative; discredited because it is critical; erased because alternate?° And how many are outraged by the thought of a self-ravaged° tongue?

---

monolithic: solid, unbroken; huge
expedited: hastened
limn: depict
deference: respectful submission
ineffable: unsayable
alternate: alternative
ravaged: badly damaged

Word-work is sublime,° she thinks, because it is generative;° it makes meaning that secures our difference, our human difference—the way in which we are like no other life. 25

We die. That may be the meaning of life. But we *do* language. That may be the measure of our lives.

"Once upon a time . . ." Visitors ask an old woman a question. Who are they, these children? What did they make of that encounter? What did they hear in those final words: "The bird is in your hands"? A sentence that gestures toward possibility, or one that drops a latch?° Perhaps what the children heard was, "It is not my problem. I am old, female, black, blind. What wisdom I have now is in knowing I cannot help you. The future of language is yours."

They stand there. Suppose nothing was in their hands. Suppose the visit was only a ruse, a trick to get to be spoken to, taken seriously as they have not been before. A chance to interrupt, to violate the adult world, its miasma° of discourse about them. Urgent questions are at stake, including the one they have asked: "Is the bird we hold living or dead?" Perhaps the question meant: "Could someone tell us what is life? What is death?" No trick at all; no silliness. A straightforward question worthy of the attention of a wise one. An old one. And if the old and wise who have lived life and faced death cannot describe either, who can?

But she does not; she keeps her secret, her good opinion of herself, her gnomic° pronouncements, her art without commitment. She keeps her distance, enforces it and retreats into the singularity of isolation, in sophisticated, privileged space.

Nothing, no word follows her declaration of transfer. That silence is deep, deeper than the meaning available in the words she has spoken. It shivers, this silence, and the children, annoyed, fill it with language invented on the spot. 30

"Is there no speech," they ask her, "no words you can give us that help us break through your dossier° of failures? through the education you have just given us that is no education at all because we are paying close attention to what you have done as well as to what you have said? to the barrier you have erected between generosity and wisdom?

---

sublime: exalted, grand
generative: procreative
latch: fastener of a door or gate
miasma: unwholesome or noxious atmosphere
gnomic: aphoristic, tersely expressed
dossier: file, folder

"We have no bird in our hands, living or dead. We have only you and our important question. Is the nothing in our hands something you could not bear to contemplate, to even guess? Don't you remember being young, when language was magic without meaning? When what you could say, could not mean? When the invisible was what imagination strove to see? When questions and demands for answers burned so brightly you trembled with fury at not knowing?

"Do we have to begin consciousness with a battle heroes and heroines like you have already fought and lost, leaving us with nothing in our hands except what you have imagined is there? Your answer is artful,° but its artfulness embarrasses us and ought to embarrass you. Your answer is indecent in its self-congratulation. A made-for-television script that makes no sense if there is nothing in our hands.

"Why didn't you reach out, touch us with your soft fingers, delay the sound bite, the lesson, until you knew who we were? Did you so despise our trick, our modus operandi,° that you could not see that we were baffled about how to get your attention? We are young. Unripe. We have heard all our short lives that we have to be responsible. What could that possibly mean in the catastrophe this world has become; where, as a poet said, "nothing needs to be exposed since it is already barefaced"? Our inheritance is an affront. You want us to have your old, blank eyes and see only cruelty and mediocrity. Do you think we are stupid enough to perjure ourselves again and again with the fiction of nationhood? How dare you talk to us of duty when we stand waist deep in the toxin° of your past?

"You trivialize us and trivialize the bird that is not in our hands. Is there no context for our lives? No song, no literature, no poem full of vitamins, no history connected to experience that you can pass along to help us start strong? You are an adult. The old one, the wise one. Stop thinking about saving your face. Think of our lives and tell us your particularized world. Make up a story. Narrative is radical, creating us at the very moment it is being created. We will not blame you if your reach exceeds your grasp;° if love so ignites your words that they go down in flames and nothing is left but their scald. Or if, with the reticence of a surgeon's hands, your words suture only the places where blood might flow. We know you can never do it properly—once and for all. Passion is never enough; neither is skill. But try. For our sake and yours forget your 35

artful: clever, tricky

modus operandi: Latin for "method of operating"

toxin: poison

reach . . . grasp: an allusion to a passage in "Andrea Del Sarto" by English poet Robert Browning (1812–1889): "Ah, but a man's reach should exceed his grasp, / Or what's a heaven for?"

name in the street; tell us what the world has been to you in the dark places and in the light. Don't tell us what to believe, what to fear. Show us belief's wide skirt and the stitch that unravels fear's caul.° You, old woman, blessed with blindness, can speak the language that tells us what only language can: how to see without pictures. Language alone protects us from the scariness of things with no names. Language alone is meditation.

"Tell us what it is to be a woman so that we may know what it is to be a man. What moves at the margin. What it is to have no home in this place. To be set adrift from the one you knew. What it is to live at the edge of towns that cannot bear your company.

"Tell us about ships turned away from shorelines at Easter, placenta in a field. Tell us about a wagonload of slaves, how they sang so softly their breath was indistinguishable from the falling snow. How they knew from the hunch of the nearest shoulder that the next stop would be their last. How, with hands prayered in their sex, they thought of heat, then sun. Lifting their faces as though it was there for the taking. Turning as though there for the taking. They stop at an inn. The driver and his mate go in with the lamp, leaving them humming in the dark. The horse's void° steams into the snow beneath its hooves and the hiss and melt are the envy of the freezing slaves.

"The inn door opens: a girl and a boy step away from its light. They climb into the wagon bed. The boy will have a gun in three years, but now he carries a lamp and a jug of warm cider. They pass it from mouth to mouth. The girl offers bread, pieces of meat and something more: a glance into the eyes of the one she serves. One helping for each man, two for each woman. And a look. They look back. The next stop will be their last. But not this one. This one is warmed."

It's quiet again when the children finish speaking, until the woman breaks into the silence.

"Finally," she says. "I trust you now. I trust you with the bird that is not in your hands because you have truly caught it. Look. How lovely it is, this thing we have done—together." 40

"The Acceptance Speech"

Your Majesties, Your Highnesses, Ladies and Gentlemen:

I entered this hall pleasantly haunted by those who have entered it before me. That company of laureates is both daunting and welcoming, for among its lists are names of persons whose work has made whole worlds available to me. The

---

caul: embryonic membrane that occasionally covers a baby's head at birth

void: i.e., urine

sweep and specificity of their art have sometimes broken my heart with the courage and clarity of its vision. The astonishing brilliance with which they practiced their craft has challenged and nurtured my own. My debt to them rivals the profound one I owe to the Swedish Academy for having selected me to join that distinguished alumni.

Early in October an artist friend left a message which I kept on the answering service for weeks and played back every once in a while just to hear the trembling pleasure in her voice and the faith in her words. "My dear sister," she said, "the prize that is yours is also ours and could not have been placed in better hands." The spirit of her message with its earned optimism and sublime trust marks this day for me.

I will leave this hall, however, with a new and much more delightful haunting than the one I felt upon entering: that is the company of the laureates yet to come. Those who, even as I speak, are mining, sifting° and polishing languages for illuminations none of us has dreamed of. But whether or not any one of them secures a place in this pantheon,° the gathering of these writers is unmistakable and mounting. Their voices bespeak civilizations gone and yet to be; the precipice from which their imaginations gaze will rivet us; they do not blink or turn away. 45

It is, therefore, mindful of the gifts of my predecessors, the blessing of my sisters, in joyful anticipation of writers to come that I accept the honor the Swedish Academy has done me, and ask you to share what is for me a moment of grace.

[1993]

Read

1. What is the effect on your expectations when you read "Once upon a time?"
2. What do you think the bird represents in the tale when you first read it?
3. How does Morrison move in and out of the tale throughout the essay? Why?
4. What is "tongue-suicide"?
5. How do you read the connection between Morrison and the "old woman"?

Write

1. Write a paragraph that discusses Morrison's attitude toward language.
2. What does the old woman want from the children? What do they want from her? Discuss how those desires change throughout the tale.

---

sifting: examining; sorting

pantheon: group of people celebrated for their achievements in a particular field

3. Do you think the use of the fable within the speech works? Why or why not?
4. Respond to the line "Word-work is sublime" (paragraph 25).

Connect

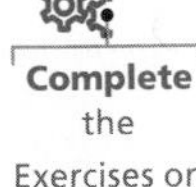

Complete the Exercises on Morrison's Speech at Your Pearson MyLab

1. Anzaldúa speaks strongly about the importance of language, as does Morrison. Do you think their reasons for this belief are the same or different?
2. Find a page or two of one of Morrison's works. Use it to speculate about how Morrison highlights the importance of "word-work."
3. Compare Morrison's Nobel Prize acceptance speech with William Faulkner's in Unit 5. How do you see cultural context making a difference in the aims of the speeches?

David Sedaris

Essayist and humorist David Sedaris (b. 1956) grew up in Raleigh, North Carolina, the oldest of six children. He attended Kent State University and the Art Institute of Chicago. He began reading a diary he had kept on a trip across the United States first to patrons at a Chicago club and then on a local radio station. He continues to do readings for National Public Radio. Sedaris has published several collections of humorous autobiographical essays that reflect on the foibles of everyday life.

Me Talk Pretty One Day, from which the essay that follows was taken, was published in 2000 and explores failed attempts at communication. Sedaris has also written the *SantaLand Diaries,* the tale of his work as a Christmas elf at Macy's in New York City, and *When You Are Engulfed in Flames*. His latest book is a collection of animal fables, *Squirrel Seeks Chipmunk: A Modest Bestiary* (2010).

Go Carolina

Anyone who watches even the slightest amount of TV is familiar with the scene: An agent knocks on the door of some seemingly ordinary home or office. The door opens, and the person holding the knob is asked to identify himself. The agent then says, "I'm going to ask you to come with me."

They're always remarkably calm, these agents. If asked "Why do I need to go anywhere with you?" they'll straighten their shirt cuffs or idly brush stray hairs from the sleeves of their sport coats and say, "Oh, I think we both know why."

The suspect then chooses between doing things the hard way and doing things the easy way, and the scene ends with either gunfire or the gentlemanly application of handcuffs. Occasionally it's a case of mistaken identity, but most often the suspect knows exactly why he's being taken. It seems he's been expecting this to happen. The anticipation has ruled his life, and now, finally, the wait is over. You're sometimes led to believe that this person is actually relieved, but I've never bought it. Though it probably has its moments, the average day spent in hiding is bound to beat the average day spent in prison. When it comes time to decide who gets the bottom bunk, I think anyone would agree that there's a lot to be said for doing things the hard way.

The agent came for me during a geography lesson. She entered the room and nodded at my fifth-grade teacher, who stood frowning at a map of Europe. What would needle me later was the realization that this had all been prearranged. My capture had been scheduled to go down at exactly 2:30 on a Thursday afternoon. The agent would be wearing a dung°-colored blazer over a red knit turtleneck, her heels sensibly low in case the suspect should attempt a quick getaway.

5 "David," the teacher said, "this is Miss Samson, and she'd like you to go with her now."

No one else had been called, so why me? I ran down a list of recent crimes, looking for a conviction that might stick. Setting fire to a reportedly flameproof Halloween costume, stealing a set of barbecue tongs from an unguarded patio, altering the word *hit* on a list of rules posted on the gymnasium door; never did it occur to me that I might be innocent.

"You might want to take your books with you," the teacher said. "And your jacket. You probably won't be back before the bell rings."

Though she seemed old at the time, the agent was most likely fresh out of college. She walked beside me and asked what appeared to be an innocent and unrelated question: "So, which do you like better, State° or Carolina°?"

She was referring to the athletic rivalry between the Triangle area's° two largest universities. Those who cared about such things tended to express their allegiance by wearing either Tar Heel powder blue, or Wolf Pack red, two

dung: excrement, manure

State: North Carolina State University

Carolina: the University of North Carolina

the Triangle area: an eight-county region in central North Carolina, whose three "points" are the cities of Raleigh, Durham, and Chapel Hill

colors that managed to look good on no one. The question of team preference was common in our part of North Carolina, and the answer supposedly spoke volumes about the kind of person you either were or hoped to become. I had no interest in football or basketball but had learned it was best to pretend otherwise. If a boy didn't care for barbecued chicken or potato chips, people would accept it as a matter of personal taste, saying, "Oh well, I guess it takes all kinds." You could turn up your nose at the president or Coke or even God, but there were names for boys who didn't like sports. When the subject came up, I found it best to ask which team my questioner preferred. Then I'd say, "Really? Me, too!"

Asked by the agent which team I supported, I took my cue from her red turtleneck and told her that I was for State. "Definitely State. State all the way." 10

It was an answer I would regret for years to come.

"State, did you say?" the agent asked.

"Yes, State. They're the greatest."

"I see." She led me through an unmarked door near the principal's office, into a small, windowless room furnished with two facing desks. It was the kind of room where you'd grill someone until they snapped, the kind frequently painted so as to cover the bloodstains. She gestured toward what was to become my regular seat, then continued her line of questioning.

"And what exactly are they, State and Carolina?" 15

"Colleges? Universities?"

She opened a file on her desk, saying, "Yes, you're right. Your answers are correct, but you're saying them incorrectly. You're telling me that they're college*th* and univer*thi*tie*th*, when actually they're colleges and universities. You're giving me a *th* sound instead of a nice clear *s*. Can you hear the distinction between the two different sounds?"

I nodded.

"May I please have an actual answer?"

"Uh-huh." 20

"'Uh-huh' is not a word."

"Okay."

"Okay what?"

"Okay," I said. "Sure, I can hear it."

"You can hear what, the distinction? The contrast?" 25

"Yeah, that."

It was the first battle of my war against the letter *s*, and I was determined to dig my foxhole before the sun went down. According to Agent Samson, a "state certified speech therapist," my *s* was sibilate, meaning that I lisped. This was not news to me.

"Our goal is to work together until eventually you can speak correctly," Agent Samson said. She made a great show of enunciating her own sparkling *s*'s, and the effect was profoundly irritating. "I'm trying to help you, but the longer you play these little games the longer this is going to take."

The women spoke with a heavy western North Carolina accent, which I used to discredit her authority. Here was a person for whom the word *pen* had two syllables. Her people undoubtedly drank from clay jugs and hollered for Paw when the vittles were ready—so who was she to advise me on anything? Over the coming years I would find a crack in each of the therapists sent to train what Miss Samson now defined as my lazy tongue. "That's its problem," she said. "It's just plain lazy."

30

My sisters Amy and Gretchen were, at the time, undergoing therapy for their lazy eyes,° while my older sister, Lisa, had been born with a lazy leg that had refused to grow at the same rate as its twin. She'd worn a corrective brace for the first two years of her life, and wherever she roamed she left a trail of scratch marks in the soft pine floor. I liked the idea that a part of one's body might be thought of as lazy—not thoughtless or hostile, just unwilling to extend itself for the betterment of the team. My father often accused my mother of having a lazy mind, while she in turn accused him of having a lazy index finger, unable to dial the phone when he knew damn well he was going to be late.

My therapy sessions were scheduled for every Thursday at 2:30, and with the exception of my mother, I discussed them with no one. The word *therapy* suggested a profound failure on my part. Mental patients had therapy. Normal people did not. I didn't see my sessions as the sort of thing that one would want to advertise, but as my teacher liked to say, "I guess it takes all kinds." Whereas my goal was to keep it a secret, hers was to inform the entire class. If I got up from my seat at 2:25, she'd say, "Sit back down, David. You've still got five minutes before your speech therapy session." If I remained seated until 2:27, she'd say, "David, don't forget you have a speech therapy session at two-thirty." On the days I was absent, I imagined she addressed the room, saying, "David's not here today but if he were, he'd have a speech therapy session at two-thirty."

My sessions varied from week to week. Sometimes I'd spend the half hour parroting whatever Agent Samson had to say. We'd occasionally pass the time examining charts on tongue position or reading childish s-laden

---

lazy eyes: Lazy eye, or amblyopia, is a deficiency of vision in one eye without an apparent physical cause.

texts recounting the adventures of seals or settlers named Sassy or Samuel. On the worst of days she'd haul out a tape recorder and show me just how much progress I was failing to make.

"My speech therapist's name is Miss Chrissy Samson." She'd hand me the microphone and lean back with her arms crossed. "Go ahead, say it. I want you to hear what you sound like."

She was in love with the sound of her own name and seemed to view my speech impediment as a personal assault. If I wanted to spend the rest of my life as David Thedarith, then so be it. She, however, was going to be called Miss Chrissy Samson. Had her name included no s's, she probably would have bypassed a career in therapy and devoted herself to yanking out healthy molars or performing unwanted clitoridectomies° on the schoolgirls of Africa. Such was her personality.

35

"Oh, come on," my mother would say. "I'm sure she's not *that* bad. Give her a break. The girl's just trying to do her job."

I was a few minutes early one week and entered the office to find Agent Samson doing her job on Garth Barclay, a slight, kittenish boy I'd met back in the fourth grade. "You may wait outside in the hallway until it is your turn," she told me. A week or two later my session was interrupted by mincing° Steve Bixler, who popped his head in the door and announced that his parents were taking him out of town for a long weekend, meaning that he would miss his regular Friday session. "Thorry about that," he said.

I started keeping watch over the speech therapy door, taking note of who came and went. Had I seen one popular student leaving the office, I could have believed my mother and viewed my lisp as the sort of thing that might happen to anyone. Unfortunately, I saw no popular students. Chuck Coggins, Sam Shelton, Louis Delucca: obviously, there was some connection between a sibilate s and a complete lack of interest in the State versus Carolina issue.

None of the therapy students were girls. They were all boys like me who kept movie star scrapbooks and made their own curtains. "You don't want to be doing that," the men in our families would say. "That's a girl thing." Baking scones and cupcakes for the school janitors, watching *Guiding Light* with our mothers, collecting rose petals for use in a fragrant potpourri:° anything worth doing turned out to be a girl thing. In order to

---

unwanted clitoridectomies: Forced female genital mutilation is a ritual practice in a number of cultures, especially in Africa.

mincing: affected, dainty

potpourri: jar of dried flower petals and spices used as scent

enjoy ourselves, we learned to be duplicitous.° Our stacks of *Cosmopolitan* were topped with an unread issue of *Boy's Life* or *Sports Illustrated,* and our decoupage° projects were concealed beneath the sporting equipment we never asked for but always received. When asked what we wanted to be when we grew up, we hid the truth and listed who we wanted to sleep with when we grew up. "A policeman or a fireman or one of those guys who works with high-tension wires." Symptoms were feigned, and our mothers wrote notes excusing our absences on the day of the intramural softball tournament. Brian had a stomach virus or Ted suffered from that twenty-four-hour bug that seemed to be going around.

"One of these days I'm going to have to hang a sign on that door," Agent Samson used to say. She was probably thinking along the lines of SPEECH THERAPY LAB, though a more appropriate marker would have read FUTURE HOMOSEXUALS OF AMERICA. We knocked ourselves out trying to fit in but were ultimately betrayed by our tongues. At the beginning of the school year, while we were congratulating ourselves on successfully passing for normal, Agent Samson was taking names as our assembled teachers raised their hands, saying, "I've got one in my homeroom," and "There are two in my fourth-period math class." Were they also able to spot the future drunks and depressives? Did they hope that by eliminating our lisps, they might set us on a different path, or were they trying to prepare us for future stage and choral careers?

Miss Samson instructed me, when forming an s, to position the tip of my tongue against the rear of my top teeth, right up against the gum line. The effect produced a sound not unlike that of a tire releasing air. It was awkward and strange-sounding, and elicited° much more attention than the original lisp. I failed to see the hissy s as a solution to the problem and continued to talk normally, at least at home, where my lazy tongue fell upon equally lazy ears. At school, where every teacher was a potential spy, I tried to avoid an s sound whenever possible. "Yes," became "correct," or a military "affirmative." "Please," became "with your kind permission," and questions were pleaded rather than asked. After a few weeks of what she called "endless pestering" and what I called "repeated badgering," my mother bought me a pocket thesaurus,° which provided me with s-free alternatives to just 40

---

duplicitous: deceitful

decoupage: the art of decorating a surface with pictures or other cutouts and then coating it with lacquer or varnish

elicited: drew, provoked

thesaurus: reference book of synonyms

about everything. I consulted the book both at home in my room and at the daily learning academy other people called our school. Agent Samson was not amused when I began referring to her as an articulation coach, but the majority of my teachers were delighted. "What a nice vocabulary," they said. "My goodness, such big words!"

Plurals presented a considerable problem, but I worked around them as best I could; "rivers," for example, became either "a river or two" or "many a river." Possessives were a similar headache, and it was easier to say nothing than to announce that the left-hand and the right-hand glove of Janet had fallen to the floor. After all the compliments I had received on my improved vocabulary, it seemed prudent to lie low and keep my mouth shut. I didn't want anyone thinking I was trying to be a pet of the teacher.

When I first began my speech therapy, I worried that the Agent Samson plan might work for everyone but me, that the other boys might strengthen their lazy tongues, turn their lives around, and leave me stranded. Luckily my fears were never realized. Despite the woman's best efforts, no one seemed to make any significant improvement. The only difference was that we were all a little quieter. Thanks to Agent Samson's tape recorder, I, along with the others, now had a clear sense of what I actually sounded like. There was the lisp, of course, but more troubling was my voice itself, with its excitable tone and high, girlish pitch. I'd hear myself ordering lunch in the cafeteria, and the sound would turn my stomach. How could anyone stand to listen to me? Whereas those around me might grow up to be lawyers or movie stars, my only option was to take a vow of silence and become a monk. My former classmates would call the abbey, wondering how I was doing, and the priest would answer the phone. "You can't talk to him!" he'd say. "Why, Brother David hasn't spoken to anyone in thirty-five years!"

"Oh, relax," my mother said. "Your voice will change eventually."

"And what if it doesn't?"

She shuddered. "Don't be so morbid." 45

It turned out that Agent Samson was something along the lines of a circuit-court° speech therapist. She spent four months at our school and then moved on to another. Our last meeting was held the day before school let out for Christmas. My classrooms were all decorated, the halls—everything but her office, which remained as bare as ever. I was expecting a regular half hour of Sassy the seal and was delighted to find her packing up her tape recorder.

circuit-court: court that meets at different places within its judicial district

"I thought that this afternoon we might let loose and have a party, you and I. How does that sound?" She reached into her desk drawer and withdrew a festive tin of cookies. "Here, have one. I made them myself from scratch and, boy, was it a mess! Do you ever make cookies?"

I lied, saying that no, I never had.

"Well, it's hard work," she said. "Especially if you don't have a mixer."

It was unlike Agent Samson to speak so casually, and awkward to sit in the hot little room, pretending to have a normal conversation. 50

"So," she said, "what are your plans for the holidays?"

"Well, I usually remain here and, you know, open a gift from my family."

"Only one?" she asked.

"Maybe eight or ten."

"Never six or seven?" 55

"Rarely," I said.

"And what do you do on December thirty-first, New Year's Eve?"

"On the final day of the year we take down the pine tree in our living room and eat marine life."

"You're pretty good at avoiding those s's," she said. "I have to hand it to you, you're tougher than most."

I thought she would continue trying to trip me up, but instead she talked about her own holiday plans. "It's pretty hard with my fiancé in Vietnam," she said. "Last year we went up to see his folks in Roanoke,° but this year I'll spend Christmas with my grandmother outside of Asheville.° My parents will come, and we'll all try our best to have a good time. I'll eat some turkey and go to church, and then, the next day, a friend and I will drive down to Jacksonville to watch Florida play Tennessee in the Gator Bowl." 60

I couldn't imagine anything worse than driving down to Florida to watch a football game, but I pretended to be impressed. "Wow, that ought to be eventful."

"I was in Memphis last year when NC State whooped Georgia fourteen to seven in the Liberty Bowl," she said. "And next year, I don't care who's playing, but I want to be sitting front-row center at the Tangerine Bowl. Have you ever been to Orlando? It's a super fun place. If my future husband can find a job in his field, we're hoping to move down there within a year or two. Me living in Florida. I bet that would make you happy, wouldn't it?"

Roanoke: city in southwestern Virginia
Asheville: city in western North Carolina

I didn't quite know how to respond. Who was this college bowl fanatic with no mixer and a fiancé in Vietnam, and why had she taken so long to reveal herself? Here I'd thought of her as a cold-blooded agent when she was really nothing but a slightly dopey, inexperienced speech teacher. She wasn't a bad person, Miss Samson, but her timing was off. She should have acted friendly at the beginning of the year instead of waiting until now, when all I could do was feel sorry for her.

"I tried my best to work with you and the others, but sometimes a person's best just isn't good enough." She took another cookie and turned it over in her hands. "I really wanted to prove myself and make a difference in people's lives, but it's hard to do your job when you're met with so much resistance. My students don't like me, and I guess that's just the way it is. What can I say? As a speech teacher, I'm a complete failure."

She moved her hands toward her face, and I worried that she might start to cry. "Hey, look," I said. "I'm thorry." 65

"Ha-ha," she said. "I got you." She laughed much more than she needed to and was still at it when she signed the form recommending me for the following year's speech therapy program. "Thorry, indeed. You've got some work ahead of you, mister."

I related the story to my mother, who got a huge kick out of it. "You've got to admit that you really are a sucker," she said.

I agreed but, because none of my speech classes ever made a difference, I still prefer to use the word *chump*.

[2000]

Read

1. Why does Sedaris use a scene from a television crime show to open the essay?
2. When do you first know that the essay is funny rather than completely serious?
3. How does Sedaris poke fun at teachers?
4. How would you describe David's mother?
5. How does Sedaris use diction and punctuation to heighten readers' understanding of his speech problem?

Write

1. Write about what the speech therapy story reveals about school methods. Does it strike you as true?
2. Reflect on how humor is used to get across points that may not be funny.
3. Use a few lines from the essay to characterize Sedaris's tone.

4. Locate a few places where Sedaris uses hyperbole to get across his point. How and why is he using that exaggeration?

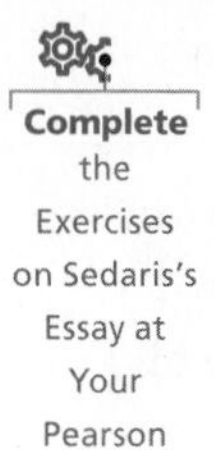

Connect

1. Sedaris writes about his difference from others in his class and the effect it had on him. Compare the techniques of conveying that message with another writer in this section (Rodriguez, for example) who speaks of the effect difference has on a person's ideas about herself or himself.
2. Sedaris has been compared to Mark Twain in his wry approach to the events of life and people's reactions to it. Look back at the Twain passage in Unit 4 and compare the tone and use of character in Sedaris and Twain.

Amy Tan

Amy Tan's parents emigrated from China to California, where Tan was born in 1952 and has spent most of her life. She worked as an editor, a technical writer, and a reporter before writing *The Joy Luck Club* in 1989, which was an immediate success. The novel was an intergenerational tale of four Chinese women and their Chinese American daughters. Later novels like *The Kitchen God's Wife* (1991), *The Hundred Secret Senses* (1995), and *The Bonesetter's Daughter* (2001) also examine family relationships and cultural change. Tan has also written children's books and a collection of autobiographical essays, from which this essay is reprinted.

Mother Tongue

I am not a scholar of English or literature. I cannot give you much more than personal opinions of the English language and its variations in this country or others.

I am a writer. And by that definition, I am someone who has always loved language. I am fascinated by language in daily life. I spend a great deal of my time thinking about the power of language—the way it can evoke an emotion, a visual image, a complex idea, or a simple truth. Language is the tool of my trade. And I use them all—all the Englishes I grew up with.

Recently, I was made keenly aware of the different Englishes I do use. I was giving a talk to a large group of people, the same talk I had already given to half a dozen other groups. The nature of the talk was about my writing, my life, and my book, *The Joy Luck Club*. The talk was going along well enough, until I remembered one major difference that made the whole talk sound wrong. My mother was in the room. And it was perhaps the first time she had heard me give a lengthy speech, using the kind of English I have never used with her. I was saying things like, "The intersection of memory upon imagination" and "There is an aspect of my fiction that relates to thus-and-thus"—a speech filled with carefully wrought grammatical phrases, burdened, it suddenly seemed to me, with nominalized forms,° past perfect tenses, conditional phrases, all the forms of standard English that I had learned in school and through books, the forms of English I did not use at home with my mother.

Just last week, I was walking down the street with my mother, and I again found myself conscious of the English I was using, and the English I do use with her. We were talking about the price of new and used furniture and I heard myself saying this: "Not waste money that way." My husband was with us as well, and he didn't notice any switch in my English. And then I realized why. It's because over the twenty years we've been together I've often used the same kind of English with him, and sometimes he even uses it with me. It has become our language of intimacy, a different sort of English that relates to family talk, the language I grew up with.

5 So you'll have some idea of what this family talk I heard sounds like, I'll quote what my mother said during a recent conversation which I videotaped and then transcribed. During this conversation, my mother was talking about a political gangster in Shanghai° who had the same last name as her family's, Du, and how the gangster in his early years wanted to be adopted by her family, which was rich by comparison. Later, the gangster became more powerful, far richer than my mother's family, and one day showed up at my mother's wedding to pay his respects. Here's what she said in part:

> Du Yusong having business like fruit stand. Like off the street kind. He is Du like Du Zong—but not Tsung-ming Island° people. The local people call putong, the river east side, he belong to that side local people. The man want to ask Du Zong father take him in like become own family. Du Zong father wasn't look down on him, but didn't take seriously, until the man big like become a mafia. Now important person, very hard to inviting him. Chinese way, came only to show respect, don't stay for dinner. Respect for

---

nominalized forms: nouns derived from other parts of speech, such as *infantilization*
Shanghai: most populous city in China and in the world
Tsung-ming Island: or Chongming, island in the Yangtze River Delta, off Shanghai

making big celebration, he shows up. Mean gives lots of respect. Chinese custom. Chinese social life that way. If too important won't have to stay too long. He come to my wedding. I didn't see, I heard it. I gone to boy's side, they have YMCA dinner. Chinese age I was nineteen.

You should know that my mother's expressive command of English belies how much she actually understands. She reads the *Forbes* report,° listens to *Wall Street Week*,° converses daily with her stockbroker, reads all of Shirley MacLaine's books with ease—all kinds of things I can't begin to understand. Yet some of my friends tell me they understand 50 percent of what my mother says. Some say they understand 80 to 90 percent. Some say they understand none of it, as if she were speaking pure Chinese. But to me, my mother's English is perfectly clear, perfectly natural. It's my mother tongue. Her language, as I hear it, vivid, direct, full of observation and imagery. That was the language that helped shape the way I saw things expressed things, made sense of the world.

Lately, I've been giving more thought to the kind of English my mother speaks. Like others, I have described it to people as "broken" or "fractured" English. But I wince when I say that. It has always bothered me that I can think of no way to describe it other than "broken," as if it were damaged and needed to be fixed, as if it lacked a certain wholeness and soundness. I've heard other terms used, "limited English," for example. But they seem just as bad, as if everything is limited, including people's perceptions of the limited English speaker.

I know this for a fact, because when I was growing up, my mother's "limited" English limited *my* perception of her. I was ashamed of her English. I believed that her English reflected the quality of what she had to say. That is, because she expressed them imperfectly her thoughts were imperfect. And I had plenty of empirical° evidence to support me: the fact that people in department stores, at banks, and at restaurants did not take her seriously, did not give her good service, pretended not to understand her, or even acted as if they did not hear her.

My mother has long realized the limitations of her English as well. When I was fifteen, she used to have me call people on the phone to pretend I was she. In this guise, I was forced to ask for information or even to complain

Forbes report: a subscription investment newsletter

Wall Street Week: a weekly public television program (1972–2005) focused on investment news and information

empirical: based on experience or observation

and yell at people who had been rude to her. One time it was a call to her stockbroker in New York. She had cashed out her small portfolio and it just so happened we were going to go to New York the next week, our very first trip outside California. I had to get on the phone and say in an adolescent voice that was not very convincing, "This is Mrs. Tan."

And my mother was standing in back whispering loudly, "Why he don't send me check, already two weeks late. So mad he lie to me, losing me money." 10

And then I said in perfect English, "Yes, I'm getting rather concerned. You had agreed to send the check two weeks ago, but it hasn't arrived."

Then she began to talk more loudly. "What he want, I come to New York tell him front of his boss, you cheating me?" And I was trying to calm her down, make her be quiet, while telling the stockbroker, "I can't tolerate any more excuses. If I don't receive the check immediately, I am going to have to speak to your manager when I'm in New York next week." And sure enough, the following week there we were in front of this astonished stockbroker, and I was sitting there red-faced and quiet, and my mother, the real Mrs. Tan, was shouting at his boss in her impeccable broken English.

We used a similar routine just five days ago, for a situation that was far less humorous. My mother had gone to the hospital for an appointment, to find out about a benign brain tumor a CAT scan had revealed a month ago. She said she had spoken very good English, her best English, no mistakes. Still, she said, the hospital did not apologize when they said they had lost the CAT scan and she had come for nothing. She said they did not seem to have any sympathy when she told them she was anxious to know the exact diagnosis, since her husband and son had both died of brain tumors. She said they would not give her any more information until the next time and she would have to make another appointment for that. So she said she would not leave until the doctor called her daughter. She wouldn't budge. And when the doctor finally called her daughter, me, who spoke in perfect English—lo and behold—we had assurances the CAT scan would be found, promises that a conference call on Monday would be held, and apologies for any suffering my mother had gone through for a most regrettable mistake.

I think my mother's English almost had an effect on limiting my possibilities in life as well. Sociologists and linguists probably will tell you that a person's developing language skills are more influenced by peers. But I do think that the language spoken in the family, especially in immigrant families which are more insular,° plays a large role in shaping the language

---

insular: isolated, separated

of the child. And I believe that it affected my results on achievement tests, IQ tests, and the SAT. While my English skills were never judged as poor, compared to math, English could not be considered my strong suit. In grade school I did moderately well, getting perhaps B's, sometimes B-pluses, in English and scoring perhaps in the sixtieth or seventieth percentile on achievement tests. But those scores were not good enough to override the opinion that my true abilities lay in math and science, because in those areas I achieved A's and scored in the ninetieth percentile or higher.

15 This was understandable. Math is precise; there is only one correct answer. Whereas, for me at least, the answers on English tests were always a judgment call, a matter of opinion and personal experience. Those tests were constructed around items like fill-in-the-blank sentence completion, such as, "Even though Tom was ______, Mary thought he was ______." And the correct answer always seemed to be the most bland combinations of thoughts, for example, "Even though Tom was shy, Mary thought he was charming," with the grammatical structure "even though" limiting the correct answer to some sort of semantic° opposites, so you wouldn't get answers like, "Even though Tom was foolish, Mary thought he was ridiculous." Well, according to my mother, there were very few limitations as to what Tom could have been and what Mary might have thought of him. So I never did well on tests like that.

The same was true with word analogies, pairs of words in which you were supposed to find some sort of logical, semantic relationship—for example, "*Sunset* is to *nightfall* as ______ is to ______." And here you would be presented with a list of four possible pairs, one of which showed the same kind of relationship: *red* is to *stoplight, bus* is to *arrival, chills* is to *fever, yawn* is to *boring.* Well, I could never think that way. I knew what the tests were asking, but I could not block out of my mind the images already created by the first pair, "*sunset* is to *nightfull*"—and I would see a burst of colors against a darkening sky, the moon rising, the lowering of a curtain of stars. And all the other pairs of words—red, bus, stoplight, boring—just threw up a mess of confusing images, making it impossible for me to sort out something as logical as saying: "A sunset precedes nightfall" is the same as "a chill precedes a fever." The only way I would have gotten that answer right would have been to imagine an associative situation, for example, my being disobedient and staying out past sunset, catching a chill at night, which turns into feverish pneumonia as punishment, which indeed did happen to me.

---

semantic: having to do with distinctions in the meanings of words

I have been thinking about all this lately, about my mother's English, about achievement tests. Because lately I've been asked, as a writer, why there are not more Asian Americans represented in American literature. Why are there few Asian Americans enrolled in creative writing programs? Why do so many Chinese students go into engineering? Well, these are broad sociological questions I can't begin to answer. But I have noticed in surveys—in fact, just last week—that Asian students, as a whole, always do significantly better on math achievement tests than in English. And this makes me think that there are other Asian-American students whose English spoken in the home might also be described as "broken" or "limited." And perhaps they also have teachers who are steering them away from writing and into math and science, which is what happened to me.

Fortunately, I happen to be rebellious in nature and enjoy the challenge of disproving assumptions made about me. I became an English major my first year in college, after being enrolled as pre-med. I started writing nonfiction as a freelancer the week after I was told by my former boss that writing was my worst skill and I should hone° my talents toward account management.

But it wasn't until 1985 that I finally began to write fiction. And at first I wrote using what I thought would be wittily crafted sentences, sentences that would finally prove I had mastery over the English language. Here's an example from the first draft of a story that later made its way into *The Joy Luck Club,* but without this line: "That was my mental quandary° in the nascent° state." A terrible line, which I can barely pronounce.

20 Fortunately, for reasons I won't get into today, I later decided I should envision a reader for the stories I would write. And the reader I decided upon was my mother, because these were stories about mothers. So with this reader in mind—and in fact she did read my early drafts—I began to write stories using all the Englishes I grew up with: the English I spoke to my mother, which for lack of a better term might be described as "simple"; the English she used with me, which for lack of a better term might be described as "broken"; my translation of her Chinese, which could certainly be described as "watered down"; and what I imagined to be her translation of her Chinese if she could speak in perfect English, her internal language, and for that I sought to preserve the essence, but neither an English nor a

---

hone: sharpen
quandary: state of uncertainty or perplexity
nascent: being born, starting to develop

Chinese structure. I wanted to capture what language ability tests can never reveal: her intent, her passion, her imagery, the rhythms of her speech and the nature of her thoughts.

Apart from what any critic had to say about my writing, I knew I had succeeded where it counted when my mother finished reading my book and gave me her verdict: "So easy to read."

[2003]

Read

1. What is the effect of Tan's beginning with what she is not?
2. What does Tan mean by "different Englishes"?
3. How do you understand Tan's relationship with her mother?
4. How does Tan understand the differences between math and English?

Write

1. How does Tan use her mother's English to understand her own?
2. Reflect on the way that language affects perceptions of people, using examples from Tan's essay.
3. How would you state Tan's argument in a line or two?

Complete the Exercises on Tan's Essay at Your Pearson MyLab

Connect

1. Find another piece in this unit that suggests the importance of language to success and communication (Rodriguez is an example).
2. How does your language change in formal and informal situations? Compare your own experience with Tan's discussion.

George W. Bush

George Walker Bush (b. 1946) served as the 43rd President of the United States from 2001 to 2009. His father, George Herbert Walker Bush, served as the 41st President. They are the second father-son pair to lead the country; the other pair is John Adams and his son John Quincy Adams. Bush grew up in New Haven, Connecticut, attended Yale and Harvard Business School, and worked in the oil business before becoming governor of Texas in 1995.

After the terrorist attacks on September 11, 2001, President Bush initiated the War on Terror, which sent American military members into Iraq and Afghanistan. Bush also developed education programs, health care initiatives, and economic stimuli to accelerate the nation's recovery from a recession. After serving two terms, Bush moved back to Texas, where he is a public speaker. In 2010 he published a book about his life, *Decision Points.* The speech below was delivered on national television on the evening of September 11, 2001, after the terrorist attacks.

Address to the Nation

Good evening. Today, our fellow citizens, our way of life, our very freedom came under attack in a series of deliberate and deadly terrorist acts. The victims were in airplanes, or in their offices; secretaries, businessmen and women, military and federal workers; moms and dads, friends and neighbors. Thousands of lives were suddenly ended by evil, despicable acts of terror.

The pictures of airplanes flying into buildings, fires burning, huge structures collapsing, have filled us with disbelief, terrible sadness, and a quiet, unyielding anger. These acts of mass murder were intended to frighten our nation into chaos and retreat. But they have failed; our country is strong.

A great people has been moved to defend a great nation. Terrorist attacks can shake the foundations of our biggest buildings, but they cannot touch the foundation of America. These acts shattered steel, but they cannot dent the steel of American resolve.

America was targeted for attack because we're the brightest beacon for freedom and opportunity in the world. And no one will keep that light from shining.

Today, our nation saw evil, the very worst of human nature. And we responded with the best of America—with the daring of our rescue workers, with the caring for strangers and neighbors who came to give blood and help in any way they could. 5

Immediately following the first attack, I implemented our government's emergency response plans. Our military is powerful, and it's prepared. Our emergency teams are working in New York City and Washington, D.C. to help with local rescue efforts.

Our first priority is to get help to those who have been injured, and to take every precaution to protect our citizens at home and around the world from further attacks.

The functions of our government continue without interruption. Federal agencies in Washington which had to be evacuated today are reopening for essential personnel tonight, and will be open for business tomorrow. Our financial institutions remain strong, and the American economy will be open for business, as well.

The search is underway for those who are behind these evil acts. I've directed the full resources of our intelligence and law enforcement communities to find those responsible and to bring them to justice. We will make no distinction between the terrorists who committed these acts and those who harbor them.

I appreciate so very much the members of Congress who have joined me in strongly condemning these attacks. And on behalf of the American people, I thank the many world leaders who have called to offer their condolences and assistance. 10

America and our friends and allies join with all those who want peace and security in the world, and we stand together to win the war against terrorism. Tonight, I ask for your prayers for all those who grieve, for the children whose worlds have been shattered, for all whose sense of safety and security has been threatened. And I pray they will be comforted by a power greater than any of us, spoken through the ages in Psalm 23: "Even though I walk through the valley of the shadow of death, I fear no evil, for You are with me."

This is a day when all Americans from every walk of life unite in our resolve for justice and peace. America has stood down enemies before, and we will do so this time. None of us will ever forget this day. Yet, we go forward to defend freedom and all that is good and just in our world.

Thank you. Good night, and God bless America.

[September 11, 2001]

Read

1. What choices in diction does Bush make to describe the events of September 11 from his perspective?
2. What words or phrases in the first paragraph help you understand his tone?
3. What is the effect of the last sentence of the first paragraph?
4. How are the comparisons Bush makes effective in conveying his aim?
5. What is the rhetorical aim in quoting from the Psalms in the Bible?

Write

1. Use a few lines from the speech to identify its various audiences.
2. Find images or words used to establish authority and control.
3. Reflect on the aim of this speech, remembering its delivery was on national television.

Complete the Exercises on Bush's Speech at Your Pearson MyLab

Connect

1. Compare this speech with a presidential speech in another unit in terms of tone and context (Andrew Jackson, Abraham Lincoln, Franklin Delano Roosevelt).
2. Find responses to Bush's speech in the newspapers and magazines of the time. What was the effect of the speech at the time?

Jean Louis Blondeau

Jean Louis Blondeau is the French photographer who chronicled the famous high-wire stunt between the World Trade Center Twin Towers performed by Phillippe Petit in 1974. Blondeau and Petit were longtime friends who had worked together staging various high-wire acts, often without permission from the authorities. The Twin Tower walk was a clandestine effort. Blondeau's photographs were stunning and resulted in the film *Man on Wire,* which tells the story of the risky adventure. Blondeau lives in Paris, as does Petit.

Philippe Petit Between the Twin Towers

[August 7, 1974]

Read

1. What details do you notice first?
2. As you keep looking at the photo, what details begin to strike you that you missed on first look?
3. How is light important to the effect of the photo?

Write

1. Respond to the emotional effect of the photo.
2. How does the arrangement of the photo suggest its rhetorical aim?
3. Write about what the photo suggests about the walker.

Connect

1. Look at the magazine cover of *The New Yorker* that follows on the next page. How might you consider the two together?
2. Petit said after his walk that many Americans asked him why he wanted to make such a dangerous walk. What do you think motivates people to take such risks?

Ana Juan

Ana Juan (b. 1961) is an illustrator of children's books and a painter whose works have appeared on album covers, promotional material, book jackets, and the cover of *The New Yorker.* She won a national award for the following illustration. She lives and works in Madrid, Spain.

New Yorker Cover

[September 12, 2011]

Read

1. What is the effect of the horizontal line in the drawing?
2. How do dark and light work in the drawing?
3. What is the use of reflection as a rhetorical tool?

Write

1. Write a reflection about the way past and present are depicted in the drawing.

2. Reflect on your response to the drawing.
3. Is this drawing an illustration of a "picture is worth a thousand words"?

Connect

1. Use this drawing and the speech by President Bush above to comment on the effect and response to the terrorist attacks of September 11, 2001.

Sandra Cisneros

Born in Chicago in 1954, Sandra Cisneros traveled back and forth between the United States and her family's home in Mexico City. She attended the Writers' Workshop at the University of Iowa and wrote essays and stories that described her multicultural experience. *The House on Mango Street* (1984) was an immediate success and helped gain attention for other Chicano writers. In much of her writing, Cisneros crosses genre borders, linking stories through continuing themes, blending autobiography and fiction, and using bilingual diction.

A poet as well as a prose writer, Cisneros has published several well-regarded collections, including *My Wicked, Wicked Ways* (1987) and *Woman Hollering Creek* (1991), that explore women's and societal issues. Cisneros lives in Texas.

Eleven

What they don't understand about birthdays and what they never tell you is that when you're eleven, you're also ten, and nine, and eight, and seven, and six, and five, and four, and three, and two, and one. And when you wake up on your eleventh birthday, you expect to feel eleven, but you don't. You open your eyes and everything's just like yesterday, only it's today. And you don't feel eleven at all. You feel like you're still ten. And you are—underneath the year that makes you eleven.

Like some days you might say something stupid, and that's the part of you that's still ten. Or maybe some days you might need to sit on your mama's lap because you're scared, and that's the part of you that's five. And maybe one day when you're all grown up, maybe you will need to cry like if you're three, and that's okay. That's what I tell Mama when she's sad and needs to cry. Maybe she's feeling three.

Because the way you grow old is kind of like an onion or like the rings inside a tree trunk or like my little wooden dolls that fit one inside the other, each year inside the next one. That's how being eleven years old is.

You don't feel eleven. Not right away. It takes a few days, weeks even, sometimes even months before you say eleven when they ask you. And you don't feel smart eleven, not until you're almost twelve. That's the way it is.

5

Only today I wish I didn't have only eleven years rattling inside me like pennies in a tin Band-Aid box. Today I wish I was one hundred and two instead of eleven because if I was one hundred and two I'd have known what to say when Mrs. Price put the red sweater on my desk. I would've known how to tell her it wasn't mine instead of just sitting there with that look on my face and nothing coming out of my mouth.

"Whose is this?" Mrs. Price says, and she holds the red sweater up in the air for all the class to see. "Whose? It's been sitting in the coatroom for a month."

"Not mine," says everybody. "Not me."

"It has to belong to somebody," Mrs. Price keeps saying, but nobody can remember. It's an ugly sweater with red plastic buttons and a collar and sleeves all stretched out like you could use it for a jump rope. It's maybe a thousand years old, and even if it belonged to me I wouldn't say so.

Maybe because I'm skinny, maybe because she doesn't like me, that stupid Sylvia Saldívar says, "I think it belongs to Rachel." An ugly sweater like that, all raggedy and old, but Mrs. Price believes her. Mrs. Price takes the sweater and puts it right on my desk, but when I open my mouth nothing comes out.

10

"That's not, I don't, you're not . . . Not mine," I finally say in a little voice that was maybe me when I was four.

"Of course it's yours," Mrs. Price says. "I remember you wearing it once." Because she's older and the teacher, she's right and I'm not.

Not mine, not mine, not mine, but Mrs. Price is already turning to page thirty-two, and math problem number four. I don't know why, but all of a sudden I'm feeling sick inside, like the part of me that's three wants to come out of my eyes, only I squeeze them shut tight and bite down on my teeth real hard and try to remember today I am eleven, eleven. Mama is making a cake for me for tonight, and when Papa comes home everybody will sing Happy birthday, happy birthday to you.

But when the sick feeling goes away and I open my eyes, the red sweater's still sitting there like a big red mountain. I move the red sweater to the corner of my desk with my ruler. I move my pencil and books and eraser as far from it as possible. I even move my chair a little to the right. Not mine, not mine, not mine.

In my head I'm thinking how long till lunchtime, how long till I can take the red sweater and throw it over the schoolyard fence, or leave it hanging on a parking meter, or bunch it up into a little ball and toss it in the alley. Except when math period ends Mrs. Price says loud and in front of everybody, "Now, Rachel, that's enough," because she sees I've shoved the red sweater to the tippy-tip corner of my desk and it's hanging all over the edge like a waterfall, but I don't care.

"Rachel," Mrs. Price says. She says it like she's getting mad. "You put that sweater on right now and no more nonsense." 15

"But it's not—"

"Now!" Mrs. Price says.

This is when I wish I wasn't eleven, because all the years inside of me—ten, nine, eight, seven, six, five, four, three, two, and one—are pushing at the back of my eyes when I put one arm through one sleeve of the sweater that smells like cottage cheese, and then the other arm through the other and stand there with my arms apart like if the sweater hurts me and it does, all itchy and full of germs that aren't even mine.

That's when everything I've been holding in since this morning, since when Mrs. Price put the sweater on my desk, finally lets go, and all of a sudden I'm crying in front of everybody. I wish I was invisible but I'm not. I'm eleven and it's my birthday today and I'm crying like I'm three in front of everybody. I put my head down on the desk and bury my face in my stupid clown-sweater arms. My face all hot and spit coming out of my mouth because I can't stop the little animal noises from coming out of me, until there aren't any more tears left in my eyes, and it's just my body shaking like when you have the hiccups, and my whole head hurts like when you drink milk too fast.

But the worst part is right before the bell rings for lunch. That stupid Phyllis Lopez, who is even dumber than Sylvia Saldívar, says she remembers the red sweater is hers! I take it off right away and give it to her, only Mrs. Price pretends like everything's okay. 20

Today I'm eleven. There's a cake Mama's making for tonight, and when Papa comes home from work we'll eat it. There'll be candles and presents and everybody will sing Happy birthday, happy birthday to you, Rachel, only it's too late.

I'm eleven today. I'm eleven, ten, nine, eight, seven, six, five, four, three, two, and one, but I wish I was one hundred and two. I wish I was anything but eleven, because I want today to be far away already, far away like a runaway balloon, like a tiny *o* in the sky, so tiny-tiny you have to close your eyes to see it.

[1991]

Read

1. How do you know the voice in the first paragraph is that of a child?
2. What is the effect of beginning paragraphs with the words *Like* and *Because*?
3. How does the narrator feel about the teacher? How does the teacher feel about her?
4. How does the narrator provoke sympathy from the reader?
5. What is the effect of the repetition in the last two paragraphs?

Write

1. Write a short reflection on why the girl in the story cries.
2. Comment on how Cisneros uses the red sweater to suggest a theme for her story.
3. Speculate on why "eleven" is the birthday Cisneros chooses.

Connect

1. Compare Cisneros's attitude toward her teacher and school with David Sedaris's in "Go Carolina."
2. The story uses a lot of dialogue. Find another piece in this unit where dialogue does a lot of work in conveying the conflicts or the aim. Write about how writers use the dialogue for rhetorical effect.

Naomi Shihab Nye

Naomi Shihab Nye is the daughter of a German American mother and a Palestinian American father. Born in St. Louis in 1952, Nye moved with her family to Jordan when she was fourteen. In Jordan her father edited a newspaper and she wrote a column. She became close to her Palestinian relatives, especially her grandmother. When the family moved to Texas just before the Six Day War in 1967, she began to write of her experiences in the Middle East and family stories.

Nye lives in San Antonio, where the borderland culture often figures in her essays, poems, and stories. She writes of suffering and healing, of the pain of displacement and of cultural change, and of the power of family. Nye's collection of essays, *Never in a Hurry,* was published in 1996, and she has published poetry for both adults and children. She conducts workshops for the Texas Commission for the Arts in schools across Texas. Since the World Trade Center terrorist attacks in 2001, she has worked against terrorism and prejudice toward Arab Americans.

One Moment on Top of the Earth

For Palestine and for Israel

In February she was dying again, so he flew across the sea to be with her. Doctors came to the village. They listened and tapped and shook their heads. She's a hundred and five, they said. What can we do? She's leaving now. This is how some act when they're leaving. She would take no food or drink in her mouth. The family swabbed her dry lips with water night and day, and the time between. Nothing else. And the rooster next-door still marked each morning though everything else was changing. Her son wrote three letters saying, Surely she will die tonight. She is so weak. Sometimes she knows who I am and sometimes she calls me by the name of her dead sister. She dreams of the dead ones and shakes her head. Fahima said, Don't you want to go be with them? And she said, I don't want to have anything to do with them. You go be with them if you like. Be my guest. We don't know what is best. We sit by her side all the time because she cries if we walk away. She feels it, even with her eyes shut. Her sight is gone. Surely she will die tonight.

Then someone else who loved her got on an airplane and flew across the sea. When she heard he was landing, she said, Bring me soup. The kind that is broth with nothing in it. They lit the flame. He came and sat behind her on the bed, where she wanted him to sit, so she could lean on him and soak him up. It was cold and they huddled together, everyone in one room, telling any story five times and stretching it. Laughing in places besides ones which had seemed funny before. Laughing more because they were in that time of sadness that is fluid and soft. She who had almost been gone after no eating and drinking for twenty days was even laughing. And then she took the bread that was torn into small triangles, and the pressed oil, and the soft egg. She took the tiny glass of tea between her lips. She took the match and held it, pressing its tiny sulfuric head between her fingers so she could feel the roughness. Something shifted inside her eyes, so the shapes of people's faces came alive again. Who's that? she said about a woman from another village who had entered her room very quietly with someone else. She's lovely, but who is she? I never saw her before. And they were hiding inside themselves a tenderness about someone being so close to gone and then returning.

She wanted her hair to be washed and combed. She wanted no one arguing in her room or the courtyard outside. She wanted a piece of lamb meat grilled with fat dripping crispily out of it. She wanted a blue velvet dress and a black sweater. And they could see how part of being alive was wanting things again. And they sent someone to the store in the next town, which was a difficult thing since you had to pass by many soldiers. And in all these years not one had ever smiled at them yet.

Then the two men from across the sea had to decide what to do next, which was fly away again, as usual. They wished they could take her with them but she, who had not even entered the Holy City° for so long though it was less than an hour away, said yes and no so much about going they knew she meant no. After a hundred and five years. You could not blame her. Even though she wasn't walking anymore, this was definitely her floor. This voice calling from the tower of the little village mosque. This rich damp smell of the stones in the walls.

So they left and I came, on the very next day. We were keeping her busy. 5
She said to me, *Marhabtein*—Hello twice—which is what she always says instead of just Hello and our hands locked tightly together. Her back was still covered with sores, so she did not want to lie down. She wanted to eat whatever I had with me. Pralines° studded with pecans, and chocolate cake. They said, Don't give her too much of that. If it's sweet, she'll just keep eating. She wanted cola, water and tea. She wanted the juice of an orange. She said to me, So how is everybody? Tell me about all of them. And I was stumbling in the tongue° again, but somehow she has always understood me. They were laughing at how badly I stumbled and they were helping me. It was the day which has no seams in it at the end of a long chain of days, the golden charm. They were coming in to welcome me, Abu Ahmad with his black cloak and his cane and his son still in Australia, and my oldest cousin Fowzl the king of smiling, and Ribhia with her flock of children, and the children's children carrying sacks of chips° now, it was the first year I ever saw them carrying chips, and my cousin's husband the teller of jokes who was put in prison for

---

the Holy City: Jerusalem
Pralines: confections of pecans, butter, and brown sugar
the tongue: the language (referring to Arabic here)
chips: pieces of dried animal dung used for fuel

nothing like everybody else, and the ones who always came whose names I pretended to know. We were eating and drinking and telling the stories. My grandmother told of a woman who was so delicate you could see the water trickling down her throat as she drank. I had brought her two new headscarves, but of course she only wanted the one that was around my neck. And I wouldn't give it to her. There was energy in teasing. I still smelled like an airplane and we held hands the whole time except when she was picking up crumbs from her blanket or holding something else to eat.

And then it was late and time for sleep. We would sleep in a room together, my grandmother, my aunt Fahima, my cousin Janan of the rosy cheeks, a strange woman, and I. It reminded me of a slumber party. They were putting on their long nightgowns and rewrapping their heads. I asked about the strange woman and they said she came to sleep here every night. Because sometimes in such an upsetting country when you have no man to sleep in the room with you, it feels safer to have an extra woman. She had a bad cold and was sleeping on the bed next to me. I covered my head against her hundred sneezes. I covered my head as my father covered his head when he was a young man and the bombs were blowing up the houses of his friends. I thought about my father and my husband here in this same room just a few days ago and could still feel them warming the corners. I listened to the women's bedtime talking and laughing from far away, as if it were rushing water, the two sleeping on the floor, my grandmother still sitting up in her bed—Lie down, they said to her, and she said, I'm not ready—and then I remembered how at ten o'clock the evening news comes on in English from Jordan and I asked if we could uncover the television set which had stood all day in the corner like a patient animal no one noticed. It stood there on its four thin legs, waiting.

Janan fiddled with dials, voices crisscrossing borders more easily than people cross in this part of the world, and I heard English rolling by like a raft with its rich *r*'s and I jumped on to it. *Today,* the newscaster said, *in the ravaged*° *West Bank* . . . and my ear stopped. I didn't even hear what had happened in this place where I was. Because I was thinking, Today, in this room full of women. In this village on the lip of a beautiful mountain. Today, between blossoming trees and white sheets. The news couldn't see into this room of glowing coals or the ones drinking tea and fluffing pillows who are invisible. And I, who had felt the violence inside myself many times more than once, though I was brought up not to be violent, though no one was ever violent with me in any way, I could not say what it was we all still had to learn,

---

ravaged: devastated

or how we would do it together. But I could tell of a woman who almost died who by summer would be climbing the steep stairs to her roof to look out over the fields once more. Who said one moment on top of the earth is better than a thousand moments under the earth. Who kept on living, again and again. And maybe an old country with many names could be that lucky too, someday, since at least it should have as much hope as invisible women and men.

[1996]

Read

1. How does the speaker depict the dying grandmother in the first lines?
2. What do you predict is the purpose of the essay from the dedication that begins it?
3. What is the effect of omitting the quotation marks around the lines people speak?
4. Why do you think the speaker details all the things the grandmother wants?
5. What does the television being turned on provoke in the speaker's mind?

Write

1. Describe the "I" in the story and her relationship to the grandmother.
2. Write about the way the title reveals the aim of the essay.
3. Reflect on the effect of the syntax in this essay, especially the use of fragments.

Connect

1. Find another piece in this unit that offers a hope for healing in the way this essay does. Compare the way the authors describe that hope.
2. Consider the role that age plays in this essay. Use your own experience or an essay in this unit to discuss that role.

Richard Rodriguez

Writer and former teacher Richard Rodriguez was born in San Francisco in 1944, the child of Mexican immigrants who had great expectations for their four children. Rodriguez attended Catholic school, where the nuns quickly noticed his abilities and encouraged him to speak only English at home. His autobiographical narrative *Hunger of Memory,* published in 1982, recounts the separation he felt from his home language and his public identity.

Rodriguez writes memoir, essays, and criticism, and his work often discusses the mix of racial, cultural, and ethnic identities in the United States. He has been criticized for his stand against bilingual education. Other books include *Mexico's Children* (1992), *Days of Obligation: An Argument with My Mexican Father* (1993), and *Brown: The Last Discovery of America* (2003), which is about the changing demographics in the United States.

From *Hunger of Memory*

1

Visiting the East Coast or the gray capitals of Europe during the long months of winter, I often meet people at deluxe hotels who comment on my complexion. (In such hotels it appears nowadays a mark of leisure and wealth to have a complexion like mine.) Have I been skiing? In the Swiss Alps? Have I just returned from a Caribbean vacation? No. I say no softly but in a firm voice that intends to explain: My complexion is dark. (My skin is brown. More exactly, terra-cotta° in sunlight, tawny in shade. I do not redden in sunlight. Instead, my skin becomes progressively dark; the sun singes the flesh.)

When I was a boy the white summer sun of Sacramento would darken me so, my T-shirt would seem bleached against my slender dark arms. My mother would see me come up the front steps. She'd wait for the screen door to slam at my back. "You look like a *negrito*" she'd say, angry, sorry to be angry, frustrated almost to laughing, scorn. "You know how important looks are in this country. With *los gringos* looks are all that they judge on. But you! Look at you! You're so careless!" Then she'd start in all over again. "You won't be satisfied till you end up looking like *los pobres* who work in the fields, *los braceros.*"

(Los braceros: Those men who work with their *brazos,* their arms; Mexican nationals who were licensed to work for American farmers in the 1950s. They worked very hard for very little money, my father would tell me. And what money they earned they sent back to Mexico to support their families, my mother would add. *Los pobres*—the poor, the pitiful, the powerless ones. But paradoxically also powerful men. They were the men with brown-muscled arms I stared at in awe on Saturday mornings when they showed up downtown like gypsies to shop at Woolworth's or Penney's. On Monday nights they would gather hours early on the steps of the Memorial

---

terra-cotta: a brownish-red clay often used to make flowerpots

Auditorium for the wrestling matches. Passing by on my bicycle in summer, I would spy them there, clustered in small groups, talking—frightening and fascinating men—some wearing Texas *sombreros* and T-shirts which shone fluorescent in the twilight. I would sit forward in the back seat of our family's '48 Chevy to see them, working alongside Valley highways: dark men on an even horizon, loading a truck amid rows of straight green. Powerful, powerless men. Their fascinating darkness—like mine—to be feared.)

"You'll end up looking just like them." . . .

2

5 Complexion. My first conscious experience of sexual excitement concerns my complexion. One summer weekend, when I was around seven years old, I was at a public swimming pool with the whole family. I remember sitting on the damp pavement next to the pool and seeing my mother, in the spectators' bleachers, holding my younger sister on her lap. My mother, I noticed, was watching my father as he stood on a diving board, waving to her. I watched her wave back. Then saw her radiant, bashful, astonishing smile. In that second I sensed that my mother and father had a relationship I knew nothing about. A nervous excitement encircled my stomach as I saw my mother's eyes follow my father's figure curving into the water. A second or two later, he emerged. I heard him call out. Smiling, his voice sounded, buoyant, calling me to swim to him. But turning to see him, I caught my mother's eyes. I heard her shout over to me. In Spanish she called through the crowd: "Put a towel on over your shoulders." In public, she didn't want to say why. I knew.

That incident anticipates the shame and sexual inferiority I was to feel in later years because of my dark complexion. I was to grow up an ugly child. Or one who thought himself ugly. *(Feo.)* One night when I was eleven or twelve years old, I locked myself in the bathroom and carefully regarded my reflection in the mirror over the sink. Without any pleasure I studied my skin. I turned on the faucet. (In my mind I heard the swirling voices of aunts, and even my mother's voice, whispering; whispering incessantly° about lemon juice solutions and dark, *feo* children.) With a bar of soap, I fashioned a thick ball of lather. I began soaping my arms. I took my father's straight razor out of the medicine cabinet. Slowly, with steady deliberateness, I put the blade against my flesh, pressed it as close as I could without cutting, and moved it up and down across my skin to see if I could get out, somehow lessen, the dark. All I succeeded in doing, however, was in shaving my arms

---

incessantly: unendingly, without ceasing

bare of their hair. For as I noted with disappointment, the dark would not come out. It remained. Trapped. Deep in the cells of my skin.

Throughout adolescence, I felt myself mysteriously marked. Nothing else about my appearance would concern me so much as the fact that my complexion was dark. My mother would say how sorry she was that there was not money enough to get braces to straighten my teeth. But I never bothered about my teeth. In three-way mirrors at department stores, I'd see my profile dramatically defined by a long nose, but it was really only the color of my skin that caught my attention.

I wasn't afraid that I would become a menial laborer because of my skin. Nor did my complexion make me feel especially vulnerable to racial abuse. (I didn't really consider my dark skin to be a racial characteristic. I would have been only too happy to look as Mexican as my light-skinned older brother.) Simply, I judged myself ugly. And, since the women in my family had been the ones who discussed it in such worried tones; I felt my dark skin made me unattractive to women.

Thirteen years old. Fourteen. In a grammar school art class, when the assignment was to draw a self-portrait, I tried and I tried but could not bring myself to shade in the face on the paper to anything like my actual tone. With disgust then I would come face to face with myself in mirrors. With disappointment I located myself in class photographs—my dark face undefined by the camera which had clearly described the white faces of classmates. Or I'd see my dark wrist against my long-sleeved white shirt.

10 I grew divorced from my body. Insecure, overweight, listless. On hot summer days when my rubber-soled shoes soaked up the heat from the sidewalk, I kept my head down. Or walked in the shade. My mother didn't need anymore to tell me to watch out for the sun. I denied myself a sensational° life. The normal, extraordinary, animal excitement of feeling my body alive—riding shirtless on a bicycle in the warm wind created by furious self-propelled motion—the sensations that first had excited in me a sense of my maleness, I denied. I was too ashamed of my body. I wanted to forget that I had a body because I had a brown body. I was grateful that none of my classmates ever mentioned the fact.

I continued to see the *braceros,* those men I resembled in one way and, in another way, didn't resemble at all. On the watery horizon of a Valley afternoon, I'd see them. And though I feared looking like them, it was with

---

sensational: having to do with the senses

silent envy that I regarded them still. I envied them their physical lives, their freedom to violate the taboo of the sun. Closer to home I would notice the shirtless construction workers, the roofers, the sweating men tarring the street in front of the house. And I'd see the Mexican gardeners. I was unwilling to admit the attraction of their lives. I tried to deny it by looking away. But what was denied became strongly desired.

In high school physical education classes, I withdrew, in the regular company of five or six classmates, to a distant corner of a football field where we smoked and talked. Our company was composed of bodies too short or too tall, all graceless and all—except mine—pale. Our conversation was usually witty. (In fact we were intelligent.) If we referred to the athletic contests around us, it was with sarcasm. With savage scorn I'd refer to the "animals," playing football or baseball. It would have been important for me to have joined them. Or for me to have taken off my shirt, to have let the sun burn dark on my skin, and to have run barefoot on the warm wet grass. It would have been very important. Too important. It would have been too telling a gesture to admit the desire for sensation, the body, my body.

Fifteen, sixteen. I was a teenager shy in the presence of girls. Never dated. Barely could talk to a girl without stammering. In high school I went to several dances, but I never managed to ask a girl to dance. So I stopped going. I cannot remember high school years now with the parade of typical images: bright drive-ins or gliding blue shadows of a Junior Prom. At home most weekend nights, I would pass evenings reading. Like those hidden, precocious° adolescents who have no real-life sexual experiences, I read a great deal of romantic fiction. "You won't find it in your books," my brother would playfully taunt me as he prepared to go to a party by freezing the crest of the wave in his hair with sticky pomade. Through my reading, however, I developed a fabulous and sophisticated sexual imagination. At seventeen, I may not have known how to engage a girl in small talk, but I had read *Lady Chatterley's Lover.*°

. . .

It annoyed me to hear my father's teasing: that I would never know what "real work" is; that my hands were so soft. I think I knew it was his way of admitting pleasure and pride in my academic success. But I didn't smile.

---

precocious: unusually mature, prematurely developed

Lady Chatterley's Lover: 1928 novel by British author D. H. Lawrence (1885–1930), banned until 1959 because of its sexual frankness

My mother said she was glad her children were getting their educations and would not be pushed around like *los pobres.* I heard the remark ironically as a reminder of my separation from *los braceros.* At such times I suspected that education was making me effeminate. The odd thing, however, was that I did not judge my classmates so harshly. Nor did I consider my male teachers in high school effeminate. It was only myself I judged against some shadowy, mythical Mexican laborer—dark like me, yet very different.

15 Language was crucial. I knew that I had violated the ideal of the *macho* by becoming such a dedicated student of language and literature. *Machismo* was a word never exactly defined by the persons who used it. (It was best described in the "proper" behavior of men.) Women at home, nevertheless, would repeat the old Mexican dictum that a man should be *feo, fuerte, y formal.* "The three Fs," my mother called them, smiling slyly. *Feo* I took to mean not literally ugly so much as ruggedly handsome. (When my mother and her sisters spent a loud, laughing afternoon determining ideal male good looks, they finally settled on the actor Gilbert Roland,° who was neither too pretty nor ugly but had looks "like a man.") *Fuerte,* "strong," seemed to mean not physical strength as much as inner strength, character. A dependable man is *fuerte. Fuerte* for that reason was a characteristic subsumed° by the last of the three qualities, and the one I most often considered—*formal.* To be *formal* is to be steady. A man of responsibility, a good provider. Someone *formal* is also constant. A person to be relied upon in adversity. A sober man, a man of high seriousness.

I learned a great deal about being *formal* just by listening to the way my father and other male relatives of his generation spoke. A man was not silent necessarily. Nor was he limited in the tones he could sound. For example, he could tell a long, involved, humorous story and laugh at his own humor with high-pitched giggling. But a man was not talkative the way a woman could be. It was permitted a woman to be gossipy and chatty. (When one heard many voices in a room, it was usually women who were talking.) Men spoke much less rapidly, and often men spoke ill monologues. (When one voice sounded in a crowded room, it was most often a man's voice one heard.) More important than any of this was the fact that a man never verbally revealed his emotions. Men did not speak about their unease in moments of crisis or danger. It was the woman who worried aloud when her husband

---

Gilbert Roland: (1905–1994), Mexican-born (as Luis Antonio Dámaso de Alonso) American movie actor

subsumed: included, incorporated

got laid off from work. At times of illness or death in the family, a man was usually quiet, even silent. Women spoke up to voice prayers. In distress, women always sounded quick ejaculations° to God or the Virgin; women prayed in clearly audible voices at a wake held in a funeral parlor. And on the subject of love, a woman was verbally expansive. She spoke of her yearning and delight. A married man, if he spoke publicly about love, usually did so with playful, mischievous irony. Younger, unmarried men more often were quiet. (The *macho* is a silent suitor. *Formal.*)

At home I was quiet, so perhaps I seemed *formal* to my relations and other Spanish-speaking visitors to the house. But outside the house—my God!—I talked. Particularly in class or alone with my teachers, I chattered. (Talking seemed to make teachers think I was bright.) I often was proud of my way with words. Though, on other occasions, for example, when I would hear my mother busily speaking to women, it would occur to me that my attachment to words made me like her. Her son. Not *formal* like my father. At such times I even suspected that my nostalgia for sounds—the noisy, intimate Spanish sounds of my past—was nothing more than effeminate yearning.

High school English teachers encouraged me to describe very personal feelings in words. Poems and short stories I wrote, expressing sorrow and loneliness, were awarded high grades. In my bedroom were books by poets and novelists—books that I loved—in which male writers published feelings the men in my family never revealed or acknowledged in words. And it seemed to me that there was something unmanly about my attachment to literature. Even today, when so much about the myth of the *macho* no longer concerns me, I cannot altogether evade such notions. Writing these pages, admitting my embarrassment or my guilt, admitting my sexual anxieties and my physical insecurity, I have not been able to forget that I am not being *formal.*

So be it.

[1982]

Read

1. How is the first paragraph different from the next one in time? How does that difference influence your reading?
2. How does the speaker's mother use the people termed "los braceros"?
3. What is the effect of the parenthesis that follows paragraph 3?

---

ejaculations: exclamations

4. What is the importance of complexion, according to Rodriguez?
5. How does Rodriguez describe himself as a student?

Write

1. Use statements from the essay to consider Rodriguez's style as a writer.
2. Write a few sentences that explain what the aim of this piece is.
3. Write a few paragraphs that address what Rodriguez thinks about the importance of language. When have you found language to be crucial to understanding or acceptance?
4. Speculate about what the title might mean in the context of this chapter.

Connect

1. How does Rodriguez differ from or seem the same as other writers of color in this unit?
2. What do you think it means to be what Rodriguez calls "not formal"?

Pat Mora

Pat Mora (b. 1942) grew up in El Paso, Texas, and is a poet, essayist, and children's book author. She completed her master's degree in English at the University of Texas, El Paso. Mora writes of working-class women, Chicano culture, and the world of work. She often uses Spanish words to frame her arguments about the power of language.

Mora's collection of poetry, *Borders* (1986), illustrates the way that many Mexicans and other ethnic groups feel forced to choose one culture or the other, one language or the other. Her work suggests the importance of change and movement among cultural traditions.

University Avenue

We are the first
of our people° to walk this path.
We move cautiously
unfamiliar with the sounds,
guides for those who follow. 5
Our people prepared us
with gifts from the land
    fire
        herbs and song

our people: All four of Mora's grandparents immigrated to Texas from Mexico in the early twentieth century.

hierbabuena° soothes us into morning 10
rhythms hum in our blood
abrazos° linger round our bodies
cuentos° whisper lessons *en español.*
We do not travel alone.
Our people burn deep within us. 15

[1986]

Read

1. Who are the "we" Mora's speaker presents?
2. What are the gifts the speaker says "we've" received?
3. What is the importance of those gifts?
4. What is the effect of the words in Spanish on your reading?

Write

1. Write several adjectives that you think describe the tone of the poem.
2. Reflect on your reaction to what you see as the message of the poem.
3. Write a sentence about the purpose of the title.

Connect

1. Like Joy Harjo's poem, Mora's poem has a generational component. What is the importance of the past for both these writers?
2. Compare the use of examples and images in this poem with another poem from this unit.

David Foster Wallace

Short story writer, journalist, and essayist David Foster Wallace (1962–2008) is best known for his over one thousand–page book *Infinite Jest,* published in 1996. Wallace grew up in Chicago, became a writer and a teacher, and was a professor of creative writing at Pomona College in California.

In 2000, he covered the Republican presidential primary and the campaign of John McCain for *Rolling Stone* magazine. He was a frequent writer for *Harper's, The Nation,* and other journals. Wallace often wrote on culture, art, and sports and of the irony of the human condition and the healing power of language. He suffered from depression for most of his life and committed suicide in 2008. An unfinished novel, *The Pale King,* was published in 2011.

---

hierbabuena: mint
abrazos: hugs, embraces
cuentos: stories, tales

The Devil Is a Busy Man

Three weeks ago, I did a nice thing for someone. I can not say more than this, or it will empty what I did of any of its true, ultimate value. I can only say: a nice thing. In a general context, it involved money. It was not a matter of out and out "giving money" to someone. But it was close. It was more classifiable as "diverting" money to someone in "need." For me, this is as specific as I can be.

It was two weeks, six days, ago that the nice thing I did occurred. I can also mention that I was out of town—meaning, in other words, I was not where I live. Explaining why I was out of town, or where I was, or what the overall situation that was going on was, however, unfortunately, would endanger the value of what I did further. Thus, I was explicit with the lady that the person who would receive the money was to in no way know who had diverted it to them. Steps were explicitly taken so that my namelessness was structured into the arrangement which led to the diversion of the money. (Although the money was, technically, not mine, the secretive arrangement by which I diverted it was properly legal. This may lead one to wonder in what way the money was not "mine," but, unfortunately, I am unable to explain in detail. It is, however, true.) This is the reason. A lack of namelessness on my part would destroy the ultimate value of the nice act. Meaning, it would infect the "motivation" for my nice gesture—meaning, in other words, that part of my motivation for it would be, not generosity, but desiring gratitude, affection, and approval towards me to result. Despairingly, this selfish motive would empty the nice gesture of any ultimate value, and cause me to once again fail in my efforts to be classifiable as a nice or "good" person.

Thus, I was very intransigent° about the secrecy of my own name in the arrangement, and the lady, who was the only other person with any knowing part in the arrangement (she, because of her job, could be classified as "the instrument" of the diversion of the money) whatsoever, acquiesced, to the best of my knowledge, in full to this.

Two weeks, five days, later, one of the people I had done the nice thing for (the generous diversion of funds was to two people—more specifically, a common law married couple—but only one of them called) called, and said, "hello," and that did I, by any possible chance, know anything about who was responsible for ______, because he just wanted to tell that person, "thank you!," and what a God-send

---

intransigent: inflexible, obstinant

this ______ dollars that came, seemingly, out of nowhere from the ______ was, etc.

Instantly, having cautiously rehearsed for such a possibility at great lengths, already, I said, coolly, and without emotion, "no," and that they were barking completely up the wrong tree for any knowledge on my part. Internally, however, I was almost dying with temptation. As everyone is well aware, it is so difficult to do something nice for someone and not want them, desperately, to know that the identity of the individual who did it for them was you, and to feel grateful and approving towards you, and to tell myriads° of other people what you "did" for them, so that you can be widely acknowledged as a "good" person. Like the forces of darkness, evil, and hopelessness in the world at large itself, the temptation of this frequently can overwhelm resistance. 5

Therefore, impulsively, during the grateful, but inquisitive, call, unprescient° of any danger, I said, after saying, very coolly, "no," and "the wrong tree," that, although I had no knowledge, I could well imagine that whoever, in fact, was, mysteriously responsible for ______ would be enthusiastic to know how the needed money, which they had received, was going to be utilized—meaning, for example, would they now plan to finally acquire health insurance for their new-born baby, or service the consumer debt in which they were deeply mired, or etc.?

My uttering this, however, was, in a fatal instant, interpreted by the person as an indirect hint from me that I was, despite my prior denials, indeed, the individual responsible for the generous, nice act, and he, throughout the remainder of the call, became lavish in his details on how the money would be applied to their specific needs, underlining what a God-send it was, with the tone of his voice's emotion transmitting both gratitude, approval, and something else (more specifically, something almost hostile, or embarrassed, or both, yet I can not describe the specific tone which brought this emotion to my attention adequately). This flood of emotion, on his part, caused me, sickeningly, too late, to realize, that what I had just done, during the call, was to not only let him know that I was the individual who was responsible for the generous gesture, but to make me do so in a subtle, sly manner that appeared to be, insinuationally,° euphemistic,°

---

myriads: multitudes
unprescient: lacking in foresight or awareness
insinuationally: in a deviously hinting manner
euphemistic: misleadingly mild or indirect

meaning, employing the euphemism: "whoever was responsible for ______," which, combined together with the interest I revealed in the money's "uses" by them, could fool no one about its implying of me as ultimately responsible, and had the effect, insidiously,° of insinuating that, not only was I the one who had done such a generous, nice thing, but also, that I was so "nice"—meaning, in other words, "modest," "unselfish," or "untempted by a desire for their gratitude"—a person, that I did not even want them to know that I was who was responsible. And I had, despairingly, in addition, given off these insinuations so "slyly," that not even I, until afterward—meaning, after the call was over—, knew what I had done. Thus, I showed an unconscious and, seemingly, natural, automatic ability to both deceive myself and other people, which, on the "motivational level," not only completely emptied the generous thing I tried to do of any true value, and caused me to fail, again, in my attempts to sincerely be what someone would classify as truly a "nice" or "good" person, but, despairingly, cast me in a light to myself which could only be classified as "dark," "evil," or "beyond hope of ever sincerely becoming good."

[1999]

Read

1. How does the length of sentences contribute to your reading of this story?
2. How does diction and detail suggest irony in the tone of the speaker?
3. What is the effect of punctuation—parentheses, dash, quotation marks—throughout the story?
4. What is the importance of the word "temptation" in the fourth paragraph?

Write

1. Do you agree with Wallace's claim about the motives for good deeds?
2. What makes a person "good" or not, according to the story?
3. Reflect on the conversation the narrator has with the person he helped. What might the conversation suggest about charity for giver and receiver?
4. Wallace consistently qualifies his comments. Find a place where he qualifies and comment on how that technique contributes to the tone or message of his piece.

Connect

1. Compare the irony in this piece to the irony used by a writer in this unit or in an earlier one. (You might think of Sedaris and Franklin.)
2. Do you agree with Wallace's position on "goodness," and by extension, human nature?

---

insidiously: cunningly; in a falsely harmless-seeming manner

Anchee Min

Anchee Min (b. 1957) was born in Shanghai, China, during the Cultural Revolution of Mao Tse Tung. Her parents were teachers who took laboring jobs after being accused by the Communist government of being "bourgeois intellectuals." Min was sent by the government to work in rural areas, and she worked for a film production company before becoming a writer. She emigrated to the United States to study at the Art Institute of Chicago. She has written six novels, including a historical novel on the life of Madame Mao in 2001. Her memoir *Red Azalea* was a *New York Times* notable book in 1994.

Footprints on the Flag

I arrived in America in 1984 and attended The School of the Art Institute of Chicago. I worked as a gallery attendant. During the 1987 art exhibition, one of the pieces was an American flag laid flat on the floor. About three feet above, mounted from the wall, was the artist's diary. I noticed that the viewers had to step on the flag in order to read the diary. As a result, the flag started to have footprints on it. I thought that I had neglected my duty, so each time after a viewer left I would take off my jacket and wipe the flag clean. I kept thinking if someone did this to our national flag in China, he would have been prosecuted.

I became sick of cleaning the flag. Eventually when a viewer came I would go up to him or her and would say politely, "Please do not step on the flag."

Weeks later the artist came. He was displeased that there were not enough footprints on the flag. He explained that it was his intention to have people step on the flag.

What offended me more was that the artist planned to burn the flag in public when the show ended. I understood that I had no right to stop him. I was emotional because if it were not for America I would not have been alive today. America took me in after I denounced the Communist China.

5 When the artist's admirers told me to get my English straight so that I could have the "right understanding of this evil country," I wished that I could sound out the words that were boiling inside my head. "Twenty years earlier I had done exactly what you are doing now!" As a child, I was taught

to hate Americans. "Long Live Chairman Mao"° was the first phrase I learned to write before my own name. I not only burnt American flags, but also denounced my beloved teacher as an American spy in order to demonstrate my loyalty toward the Communist Party. As a teen, I was given a gun with a knife to practice stabbing a straw dummy wearing a U.S. soldier's uniform. My schoolmates and I watched propaganda films, where American soldiers were shown scooping out the eyes of a young Viet Cong, a girl of my own age.

I was ready to die for my country if Americans dared to set their foot on the soil of China. I couldn't wait to be sent to Vietnam to become a martyr. I wanted to model myself after the hero who tied grenades on his back and jumped into a group of U.S. Marines, blowing them up as well as himself. I dreamed of my remains being shipped back to the homeland wrapped in the Communist red flag—my family and friends sad, but proud.

The American artist protested that he lacked freedom. In my view, he had too much. He took America for granted. If he had been in China twenty years ago, I would have taught him a good lesson.

[2007]

Read

1. How does Min set up the differences between the United States and China in the first paragraph?
2. What is the speaker's reaction to the displeasure of the artist?
3. Why does she have an impulse to clean the flag?
4. How does the speaker's lack of skills with English inhibit her?

Write

1. Do you think it's possible to have "too much freedom," as Min contends at the essay's end?
2. Analyze the rhetorical strategies Anchee Min makes use of in her extended example of the American flag to support her argument about freedom.

Connect

1. Find another text that illustrates the argument that Min makes about immigrants and the United States in this or another unit and discuss the connections between the two.

Chairman Mao: Mao Zedong (1893–1976), communist revolutionary and leader of the People's Republic of China from 1949 to 1976

Billy Collins

Billy Collins was born in 1941 and raised in New York. He received his Ph.D. in romantic poetry from the University of California, Riverside, and began teaching at Lehman College after his graduation. His poems have been published widely. Several of his poetry collections, including *Questions About Angels* (1991) and *The Art of Drowning* (1995), have become popular as well as critical successes, a rarity for poetry books.

Collins writes about what he calls the "serious bits of fluff in our lives" that people experience and that poetry can pay attention to. He often uses humor and commonplace associations to connect with his readers as he writes about the simple and profound moments of everyday life.

Introduction to Poetry

I ask them to take a poem
and hold it up to the light
like a color slide

or press an ear against its hive.

I say drop a mouse into a poem 5
and watch him probe his way out,

or walk inside the poem's room
and feel the walls for a light switch.

I want them to water-ski
across the surface of a poem 10
waving at the author's name on the shore.

But all they want to do
is tie the poem to a chair with rope
and torture a confession out of it.

They begin beating it with a hose 15
to find out what it really means.

[2001]

Read

1. How do you know who the "I" is and who the "them" is?
2. What does the "I" want "them" to do with the poem?
3. Why can't they do it?
4. How does the image of water-skiing suggest how readers should read poems?
5. What is the analogy at the end of the poem?

Write

1. Write about an experience you have had learning poetry in school.
2. Explain one of the images the speaker uses to suggest a method for reading a poem.
3. Comment on the poem's structure, especially its placement of lines and its opening words.

Connect

1. Find another poem in this unit that you think uses personification or other imagery in the way that Collins does and compare the two.
2. How does the speaker imply criticism? Where do you find other critiques of education among writers in this unit?

Edwidge Danticat

Born in Haiti in 1969, Danticat immigrated to the United States when she was twelve. As a young girl in Brooklyn, Danticat had a hard time negotiating the cultural differences between Haiti and America. In college, she began writing about cultural difference and dislocation. Her master's thesis at Brown University became her first novel *Breath, Eyes, Memory* (1994). A collection of short stories *Krik?Krak!* (1995) was also highly successful. Her second novel *The Farming of Bones* (1998) won an American Book Award.

Danticat often writes about the problems immigrants face in new cultures, the customs of her native Haiti, as well as Haitian American politics.

New York Day Women

Today, walking down the street, I see my mother. She is strolling with a happy gait, her body thrust toward the don't walk sign and the yellow taxicabs that make forty-five-degree turns on the corner of Madison and Fifty-seventh Street.

I have never seen her in this kind of neighborhood, peering in Chanel and Tiffany's and gawking at the jewels glowing in the Bulgari windows. My mother never shops outside of Brooklyn. She has never seen the advertising office where I work. She is afraid to take the subway, where you may meet those young black militant street preachers who curse black women for straightening their hair.

Yet, here she is, my mother, who I left at home that morning in her bathrobe, with pieces of newspapers twisted like rollers in her hair. My mother, who accuses me of random offenses as I dash out of the house.

Would you get up and give an old lady like me your subway seat? In this state of mind, I bet you don't even give up your seat to a pregnant lady.

My mother, who is often right about that. Sometimes I get up and give my seat. Other times; I don't. It all depends on how pregnant the woman is and whether or not she is with her boyfriend or husband and whether or not *he* is sitting down.

As my mother stands in front of Carnegie Hall, one taxi driver yells to another, "What do you think this is, a dance floor?"

My mother waits patiently for this dispute to be settled before crossing the street.

In Haiti when you get hit by a car, the owner of the car gets out and kicks you for getting blood on his bumper.

My mother who laughs when she says this and shows the large gap in her mouth where she lost three more molars to the dentist last week. My mother, who at fifty-nine, says dentures are okay.

You can take them out when they bother you. I'll like them. I'll like them fine.

Will it feel empty when Papa kisses you?

Oh no, he doesn't kiss me that way anymore.

My mother, who watches the lottery drawing every night on channel 11 without ever having played the numbers.

A third of that money is all I would need. We would pay the mortgage, and your father could stop driving that taxicab all over Brooklyn.

I follow my mother, mesmerized by the many possibilities of her journey. Even in a flowered dress, she is lost in a sea of pinstripes and gray suits, high heels and elegant short skirts, Reebok sneakers, dashing from building to building.

My mother, who won't go out to dinner with anyone.

If they want to eat with me, let them come to my house, even if I boil water and give it to them.

My mother, who talks to herself when she peels the skin off poultry.

Fat, you know, and cholesterol. Fat and cholesterol killed your aunt Hermine.

My mother, who makes jam with grapefruit peel and then puts in cinnamon bark that I always think is cockroaches in the jam. My mother, whom I have always bought household appliances for, on her birthday. A nice rice cooker, a blender.

20

I trail the red orchids in her dress and the heavy faux leather bag on her shoulders. Realizing the ferocious pace of my pursuit, I stop against a wall to rest. My mother keeps on walking as though she owns the sidewalk under her feet.

As she heads toward the Plaza Hotel, a bicycle messenger swings so close to her that I want to dash forward and rescue her, but she stands dead in her tracks and lets him ride around her and then goes on.

My mother stops at a corner hot-dog stand and asks for something. The vendor hands her a can of soda that she slips into her bag. She stops by another vendor selling sundresses for seven dollars each. I can tell that she is looking at an African print dress, contemplating my size. I think to myself, Please Ma, don't buy it. It would be just another thing that I would bury in the garage or give to Goodwill.

Why should we give to Goodwill when there are so many people back home who need clothes? We save our clothes for the relatives in Haiti.

25

Twenty years we have been saving all kinds of things for the relatives in Haiti. I need the place in the garage for an exercise bike.

You are pretty enough to be a stewardess. Only dogs like bones.

This mother of mine, she stops at another hot-dog vendor's and buys a frankfurter that she eats on the street. I never knew that she ate frankfurters. With her blood pressure, she shouldn't eat anything with sodium. She has to be careful with her heart, this day woman.

I cannot just swallow salt. Salt is heavier than a hundred bags of shame.

She is slowing her pace, and now I am too close. If she turns around, she might see me. I let her walk into the park° before I start to follow.

30

My mother walks toward the sandbox in the middle of the park. There a woman is waiting with a child. The woman is wearing a leotard with biker's shorts and has small weights in her hands. The woman kisses the child good-bye and surrenders him to my mother; then she bolts off, running on the cemented stretches in the park.

The child given to my mother has frizzy blond hair. His hand slips into hers easily, like he's known her for a long time. When he

the park: Central Park, at its southern end

raises his face to look at my mother, it is as though he is looking at the sky.

My mother gives the child the soda that she bought from the vendor on the street corner. The child's face lights up as she puts in a straw in the can for him. This seems to be a conspiracy just between the two of them.

My mother and the child sit and watch the other children play in the sandbox. The child pulls out a comic book from a knapsack with Big Bird on the back. My mother peers into his comic book. My mother, who taught herself to read as a little girl in Haiti from the books that her brothers brought home from school.

My mother, who has now lost six of her seven sisters in Ville Rose° and has never had the strength to return for their funerals.

Many graves to kiss when I go back. Many graves to kiss. 35

She throws away the empty soda can when the child is done with it. I wait and watch from a corner until the woman in the leotard and biker's shorts returns, sweaty and breathless, an hour later. My mother gives the woman her child back and strolls farther into the park.

I turn around and start to walk out of the park before my mother can see me. My lunch hour is long since gone. I have to hurry back to work. I walk through a cluster of joggers, then race to a *Sweden Tours* bus. I stand behind the bus and take a peek at my mother in the park. She is standing in a circle, chatting with a group of women who are taking other people's children on an afternoon outing. They look like a Third World Parent-Teacher Association meeting.

I quickly jump into a cab heading back to the office. Would Ma have said hello had she been the one to see me first?

As the cab races away from the park, it occurs to me that perhaps one day I would chase an old woman down a street by mistake and that old woman would be somebody else's mother, who I would have mistaken for mine.

Day women come out when nobody expects them. 40

Tonight on the subway, I will get up and give my seat to a pregnant woman or a lady about Ma's age.

My mother, who stuffs thimbles in her mouth and then blows up her cheeks like Dizzy Gillespie° while sewing yet another Raggedy Ann doll that she names Suzette after me.

I will have all these little Suzettes in case you never have any babies, which looks more and more like it is going to happen.

My mother who had me when she was thirty-three—*l'âge du Christ*—at the age that Christ died on the cross.

Ville Rose: the mother's (fictional) hometown in Haiti

Dizzy Gillespie: John Birks "Dizzy" Gillespie (1917–1993), American jazz trumpeter and composer

That's a blessing, believe you me, even if American doctors say by that time you can make retarded babies.

My mother, who sews lace collars on my company softball T-shirts when she does my laundry.

Why, you can't you look like a lady playing softball?

My mother, who never went to any of my Parent-Teacher Association meetings when I was in school.

You're so good anyway. What are they going to tell me? I don't want to make you ashamed of this day woman. Shame is heavier than a hundred bags of salt. 45

[1995]

Read

1. Why does the speaker follow her mother?
2. What is the effect on your reading of the lines of text in bold print?
3. Find a couple of lines that help you characterize the speaker in the story.
4. What does the narrator mean by "day women"?
5. Where do you see change in the narrator's attitude from beginning to end of the story?

Write

1. Write a short reflection on the relationship between mother and daughter. Include one phrase or sentence that helps define it for you.
2. Comment on the last line of the story.
3. How does the writer use repetition to help get across her aim?
4. How well does the mother know herself, do you think?

Connect

1. Compare this story with Amy Tan's "Mother Tongue" in terms of the narrator's position and the mother's character.
2. How does the structure of this story contribute to its meaning? Find another piece in this unit or a previous one and comment on how the arrangement of ideas, or structure, affects the message. (Gloria Anzaldúa is an example.)

Dave Barry

Dave Barry (b. 1947) is a humor writer, journalist, and novelist who wrote a syndicated column for *The Miami Herald* for nearly twenty years. Born in New York, Barry began writing humor as a college student. He worked for newspapers and taught writing before his humor columns made him famous. In 1988, he was awarded the Pulitzer Prize for commentary, for his "consistently effective use of humor as a device for presenting fresh insights into serious concerns." A television sitcom *Dave's World* (1993–1997) was based on Barry's life and columns. Barry continues to write humor, children's books, and screenplays. His novel *Lunatics* was published in 2012.

Independence Day

This year, why not hold an old-fashioned Fourth of July picnic?

Food poisoning is one good reason. After a few hours in the sun, ordinary potato salad can develop bacteria the size of raccoons. But don't let the threat of agonizingly painful death prevent you from celebrating the birth of our nation, just as Americans have been doing ever since that historic first July Fourth, when our Founding Fathers—George Washington, Benjamin Franklin, Thomas Jefferson, Bob Dole° and Tony Bennett°—landed on Plymouth Rock

Step one in planning your picnic is to decide on a menu. Martha Stewart has loads of innovative suggestions for unique, imaginative and tasty summer meals. So you can forget about her. "If Martha Stewart comes anywhere near my picnic, she's risking a barbecue fork to the eyeball" should be your patriotic motto. Because you're having a *traditional* Fourth of July picnic, and that means a menu of hot dogs charred into cylinders of industrial-grade carbon, and hamburgers so undercooked that when people try to eat them, they leap off the plate and frolic on the lawn like otters.

Dad should be in charge of the cooking, because only Dad, being a male of the masculine gender, has the mechanical "know-how" to operate a piece of technology as complex as a barbecue grill. To be truly traditional, the grill should be constructed of the following materials:

- 4 percent "rust-resistant" steel;
- 58 percent rust;
- 23 percent hardened black grill scunge from food cooked as far back as 1987 (the scunge should never be scraped off, because it is what is actually holding the grill together);
- 5 percent spiders.

If the grill uses charcoal as a fuel, Dad should remember to start lighting the fire early (no later than April 10) because charcoal, in accordance with federal safety regulations, is a mineral that does not burn. The spiders get a huge kick out of watching Dad attempt to ignite it; they

Bob Dole: U.S. senator from Kansas from 1969 to 1996; he was the Republican candidate for President in 1996

Tony Bennett: American singer of popular music, standards, and show tunes

emit hearty spider chuckles and slap themselves on all eight knees. This is why many dads prefer the modern gas grill, which ignites at the press of a button and burns with a steady, even flame until you put food on it, at which time it runs out of gas.

While Dad is saying traditional bad words to the barbecue grill, Mom can organize the kids for a fun activity: making old-fashioned ice cream by hand, the way our grandparents' generation did. You'll need a hand-cranked ice-cream maker, which you can pick up at any antique store for $1875. All you do is put in the ingredients and start cranking! It makes no difference what specific ingredients you put in, because—I speak from bitter experience here—no matter how long you crank them, they will never, ever turn into ice cream. Scientists laugh at the very concept. "Ice cream is not formed by cranking," they point out. "Ice cream is formed by freezers." Our grandparents' generation wasted millions of man-hours trying to produce ice cream by hand; this is what caused the Great Depression.

When the kids get tired of trying to make ice cream (allow about twenty-five seconds for this) it's time to play some traditional July Fourth games. One of the most popular is the "sack race." All you need is a bunch of old-fashioned burlap sacks, which you can obtain from the J. Peterman catalog for $277.50 apiece. Call the kids outside, have them line up on the lawn and give each one a sack to climb into; then shout "GO!" and watch the hilarious antics begin as, one by one, the kids sneak back indoors and resume trying to locate pornography on the Internet.

Come nightfall, though, everybody will be drawn back outside by the sound of loud, traditional Fourth of July explosions coming from all around the neighborhood. These are caused by the fact that various dads, after consuming a number of traditionally fermented beverages, have given up on conventional charcoal-lighting products and escalated to gasoline. As the spectacular pyrotechnic show lights up the night sky, you begin to truly appreciate the patriotic meaning of the words to *The Star-Spangled Banner,* written by Francis Scott Key to commemorate the fledgling nation's first barbecue:

> And the grill parts' red glare;
> Flaming spiders in air;
> Someone call 911;
> There's burning scunge in Dad's
> hair.

After the traditional visit to the hospital emergency room, it's time to gather 'round and watch Uncle Bill set off the fireworks that he purchased from a roadside stand operated by people who spend way more on tattoos than dental hygiene. As Uncle Bill lights the firework fuse and scurries away, everybody is on pins and needles until, suddenly and dramatically, the fuse goes out. So Uncle Bill relights the fuse and scurries away again, and the fuse goes out again, and so on, with Uncle Bill scurrying back and forth with his Bic lighter like a deranged Olympic torchbearer until, finally, the fuse burns all the way down, and the firework, emitting a smoke puff the size of a grapefruit, makes a noise—"phut"—like a squirrel passing gas. Wow! What a fitting climax for your traditional old-fashioned July Forth picnic!

Next year you'll go out for Chinese food.

[1998]

Read

1. Where in the essay do you first realize that Barry is using humor?
2. How does hyperbole (exaggeration for effect) heighten the comic effect in the essay?
3. What is the purpose of the bulleted list in paragraph 4?
4. Where do you find deliberate inaccuracies?

Write

1. Comment on how Barry uses repetition of words and images in his essay.
2. What is the aim of Barry's piece? Use a line from the text to support your thinking.
3. How does Barry describe the "typical" American family?

Connect

1. Imitate Barry's style by writing a piece on another holiday that uses a family gathering as its context.
2. Compare Barry's piece to a text that makes use of satire or humor to convey its message in this or an earlier unit. How do you find the two compare in tone as well as style?

Back to the Future

Alexis de Tocqueville

French author and politician Alexis de Tocqueville (1805–1859) was born in Paris. His father was a government official, and de Tocqueville studied law as preparation for political life. Believing that monarchy was outdated, de Tocqueville looked to the United States as a model for democratic action. He traveled to America to learn about the political development of the country. *Democracy in America* was published in 1835; a second volume was published in 1840. He returned to France and was in political service until the coup of Louis Napoleon in 1850, which restored the monarchy.

An early work of sociology and political science, *Democracy in America* explored the effects of changes in social conditions on individuals and the state. De Tocqueville believed that democracy balanced liberty and equality, and that equality was "an unstoppable force" in modern life. One key difference he found between Americans and Europeans was in the former's desire to make money, which in his opinion accounted for the different cultures and values. De Tocqueville's work was highly regarded and remains influential in histories and cultural studies of the United States.

From *Democracy in America*

"It is evident," says Hamilton in the *Federalist,* no. 12, "from the state of the country, from the habits of the people, from the experience we have had on the point itself that it is impracticable to raise any very considerable sums by direct taxation." The direct tax is in fact the most visible and burdensome of taxes; but at the same time, it is the only one that can always be resorted to during a war.

A single example will allow the reader to judge.

The Constitution gives Congress the right to call the state militias into active duty when it is a matter of suppressing an insurrection or repelling an invasion. Another article says that in this case the President of the United States is the Commander in Chief of the militia.

At the time of the War of 1812, the President ordered the militias of the North to move toward the national borders; Connecticut and Massachusetts, whose interests were harmed by the war,° refused to send their contingents.

5

The Constitution, they said, authorizes the federal government to use the militias in cases of *insurrection or invasion*; but in the present situation there was neither insurrection nor invasion. They added that the same Constitution that gave the Union the right to call the militias into active service, left the states the right to appoint the officers. It followed, according to them, that even in war, no officer of the Union had the right to command the militias, except the President in person. But this was a matter of serving in an army commanded by someone other than him.

These absurd and destructive doctrines received not only the sanction° of the Governors and the legislature, but also that of the courts of justice of these two states; and the federal government was forced to find elsewhere the troops that it needed.

---

whose interests . . . the war: Since Great Britain was the major trading partner of these states, the disruption of commerce inflicted serious economic damage upon them.

sanction: approval

[A fact of this nature proves, better than all that I could say, the inability the American Union would have to sustain a great war, even with the improved organization that the 1789 Constitution gave it.

Allow for a moment the existence of such a nation in the midst of the aggressive peoples of Europe where sovereignty is unified and omnipotent, and the relative weakness of the American Union will become for you a proven and plain truth.]

So how is it that the American Union, all protected as it is by the relative perfection of its laws, does not dissolve in the middle of a great war? It is because it has no great wars to fear.

[In general, we must give up citing the example of the United States to prove that confederations can sustain great wars, for the Union has never had a single one of this nature. 10

Even that of 1812, which the Americans speak about with such pride, was nothing compared to the smallest of those that the ambition of Louis XIV° or the French Revolution brought about in Europe. The reason is simple.]

Placed in the center of an immense continent, where human industry can expand without limits, the Union is almost as isolated from the world as if it were enclosed on all sides by the ocean.

Canada numbers only a million inhabitants; its population is divided into two enemy nations.° The rigors of climate limit the extent of its territory and close its ports for six months of the year.

From Canada to the Gulf of Mexico, there are still a few, half-destroyed, savage tribes that six thousand soldiers drive before them.

In the South, the Union at one point touches the empire of Mexico; probably great wars will come from there one day [if the Anglo-Americans and the Mexicans each continue to form a single, unified nation. In Mexico, in fact, there is a numerous population that, different from its neighbors by language, religion, habits and interest [broken text (ed.)]]. But, for a long time still, the little developed state of its civilization, the corruption of its mores° and its poverty will prevent Mexico from taking an elevated rank among nations. As for the great powers of Europe, their distance makes them little to be feared. 15

So the great happiness of the United States is not to have found a federal constitution that allows it to sustain great wars, but to be so situated that there are none to fear.

Louis XIV: (1638–1715), King of France (1643–1715)

two enemy nations: In 1831 Canada was still a colony of Great Britain, which by the Constitution Act of 1791 had divided it into two separate political units, Lower Canada (the French) and Upper Canada (the English).

mores: customs

No one can appreciate more than I the advantages of the federal system. There I see one of the most powerful devices favoring prosperity and human liberty. I envy the fate of nations permitted to adopt it. But I refuse, nonetheless, to believe that confederated republics could struggle for long, with equal strength, against a nation where governmental power would be centralized.

The people who, in the presence of the great military monarchies of Europe, would come to divide sovereignty, would seem to me to abdicate, by this fact alone, its power and perhaps its existence and its name.

Admirable position of the New World where man has only himself as an enemy. To be happy and free, he only has to want to be.

[1835]

Read

1. De Tocqueville repeatedly compares European political systems to the democracy of the American system. How does his first example in the excerpt serve to make his case?
2. How do you read the text in the square brackets that follows the example?
3. Why is de Tocqueville sure that war doesn't threaten America?
4. From the benefit of your hindsight, what do you feel de Tocqueville might be leaving out?

Write

Complete the Exercises on de Tocqueville's Essay at Your Pearson MyLab

1. Write a message to de Tocqueville, telling him what you think he got right and what he might have gotten wrong.
2. Reflect on de Tocqueville's statement that America is a place where "human industry can expand without limits."
3. What kind of worry does de Tocqueville admit to concerning the federal system of the United States? What do you think of his worry?

Connect

1. Write about how one of the writers in this unit would respond to de Tocqueville's assertion that Americans are limited only by their desire.

UNIT ACTIVITIES

Rhetorical Analysis

1. Several writers in this unit describe minority experiences in America, discussing the difficulties presented by culture, language, and economics, among other things. Choose two of these pieces and analyze the argument writers make about minority experiences. Support your argument by

analyzing the rhetorical choices each makes in terms of language, use of evidence, and appeals.

2. Use two pieces of different genres but similar arguments to analyze the effect genre has on the approach and the effect of an argument. Two possible pieces are Joy Harjo and Richard Rodriguez.

Argument

1. Using one piece to provide evidence and support for your ideas, discuss what you believe about the balance of individual rights and the rights of the community. The photograph of Phillipe Petit could work as an example.
2. Several writers like Pat Mora claim that humans are part of the land and imply that we need to protect the environment. Use any writer in this unit to create an argument about how humans in the twenty-first century might live in ways that nurture the natural world.

Synthesis

The influx of new citizens, cultures, and languages into communities across the United States has brought challenges and opportunities. In addition, our participation in global matters of war and economics has furthered our desire to live together on a smaller and smaller planet. Using three of the following pieces, evaluate the problems and opportunities presented by our increasingly diverse culture and then discuss what you think are the most important elements the country should consider as it participates in a global environment.

Tim O'Brien, "On the Rainy River"
Gloria Anzaldúa, "How to Tame a Wild Tongue"
Toni Morrison, *The Nobel Lecture in Literature*
Anchee Min, "Footprints on the Flag"
Simon Ortiz, "Designated National Park"
Naomi Shihab Nye, "One Moment on Top of the Earth"
George W. Bush, *Address to the Nation*

SYNTHESIS PROJECT: UNITS 4, 5, 6

In the United States, there has been a long struggle to achieve equal rights for new or disenfranchised citizens. African Americans, immigrants from many countries, women, and others have used their writing to be heard in their communities and in the nation.

Read the texts listed below, and select at least four of them. Evaluate the rhetorical strategies that each writer uses to find voice and audiences. Then write a coherent, well-developed essay that discusses the strategies (such as use of imagery, diction, kinds of proof, and genre) that create an effective voice that will be heard.

Jane Addams, from *The Long Road of Woman's Memory*
W. E. B. Du Bois, from *The Souls of Black Folk*
Zitkala Sa, from *The School Days of an Indian Girl*
Cecilia Muñoz, "Getting Angry Can Be a Good Thing"
James Baldwin, "My Dungeon Shook"
Martin Luther King, Jr., "Letter from Birmingham Jail"
Alfred Steiglitz, "The Steerage"
Gloria Anzaldúa, "How to Tame a Wild Tongue"

Appendix 1

Public Speaking

What You Will Learn

- To plan your speech with audience and purpose in mind
- To develop the central idea and main ideas of your speech
- To gather supporting material
- To organize and draft your speech
- To rehearse and deliver your speech

Public speaking is often crucial to success in school and in a career. People are called upon continually to explain an idea, describe a plan, defend a project, argue a position or suggest a direction in the worlds of education and business. Yet public speaking provokes a fair amount of anxiety for many people. How do I look? Do I know enough? Will the audience pay attention? are all questions that speakers confront when preparing and writing a speech. They are *rhetorical* questions, concerned with the speaker's attitude toward her own **persona,** with her knowledge of **audience,** and with her understanding of her **subject** and **intention**. Just as understanding and practicing rhetoric allows writers to become more skillful and confident, understanding rhetoric aids speakers in developing and delivering speeches.

The difference between speaking and writing is obvious: one is immediate and bound by time constraints; the other distant and without restrictions of time. That difference means that rhetorical strategies such as length and development of persona change. A speech is usually shorter than a written text to accommodate listeners' ability to stay attentive. Furthermore, since a speech is dependent on the physical presence of the speaker, details such as dress and demeanor become part of the performance as well as part of the audience's response. Other features such as the location for the speech and the size of the audience become significant.

But there are significant similarities as well. Gathering ideas, doing research, organizing, and revising are part of the composing processes for both writers and speakers. Writers often use what they've learned as readers to provide ideas for their writing; speakers use what they've learned as listeners to give them ideas for working on oral speech. Much of the material appended here is applicable to writing and research as well as to public speaking.

What follows are some further suggestions for developing experience and expertise in preparing, organizing, and delivering speeches at school, at work, or as part of a community.

Consider Your Audience

Why should the central focus of public speaking be the audience? Why is it not topic selection, outlining, or research? The simple truth is, your audience influences the topic you choose and every later step of the speechmaking process. Your selection of topic, purpose, and even major ideas should be based on a thorough understanding of your listeners. In a very real sense, your audience "writes" the speech.

As Figure A.1 shows, considering your audience is an ongoing activity. The needs, attitudes, beliefs, values, and other characteristics of your audience should

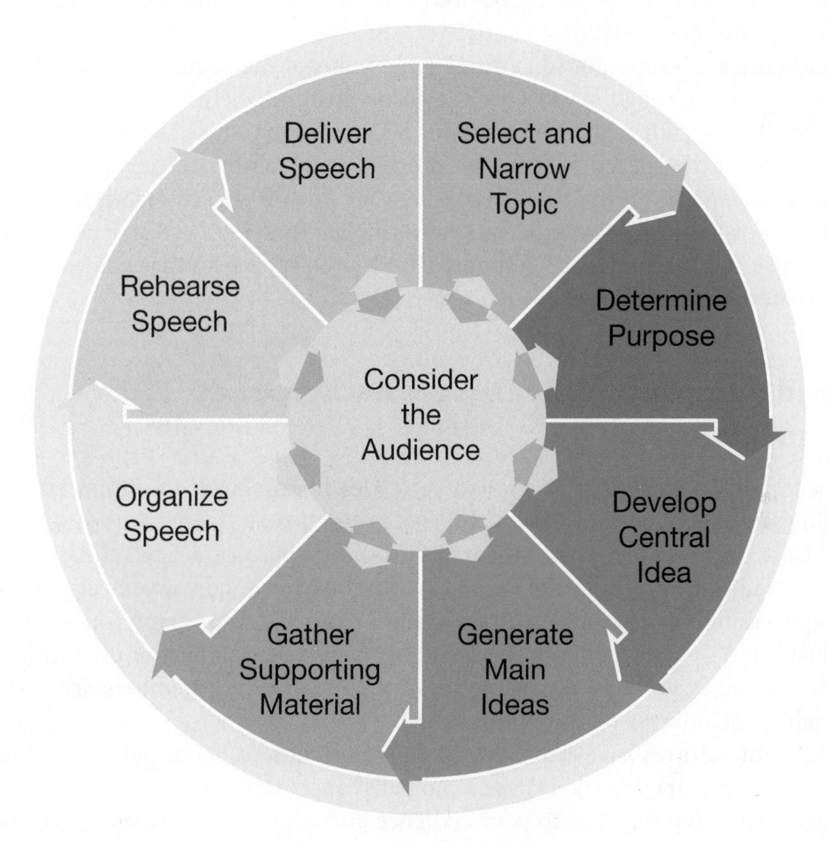

Figure A.1

This model of the speechmaking process emphasizes the importance of considering your audience as you work on each task involved in designing and presenting a speech.

play a leading role at every step. After you select your topic, you need to consider how the audience will respond to your examples, organization, and delivery. That's why, in the model, arrows connect the center of the diagram with each step of the process. At any point during the process, you may need to revise your thinking or your material if you learn new information about your audience. So the arrows from each step in the process also point back into the center.

Gather and Analyze Information About Your Audience

Being audience-centered means keeping your audience in mind at every step of the speechmaking process. To do that, you need to first identify and then analyze information about your listeners. For example, just by looking at members of your class, you will be able to determine such basic information as approximately how old they are and the percentage of males and females; you also know that they are all students. To determine other, less obvious information, you may need to ask them questions or design a short questionnaire.

Audience analysis is not something you do only at the beginning of preparing your speech. It is an ongoing activity. The needs, attitudes, beliefs, values, and other characteristics of your audience influence the choices you make about your speech at every step of the speech-preparation process. Being audience-centered involves making decisions about the content and delivery of your speech *before* you speak, based on knowledge of your audience's values, beliefs, and knowledge. It also means being aware of your audience's responses *during* the speech so that you can make appropriate adjustments.

Consider the Culturally Diverse Backgrounds of Your Audience

You need not give speeches in foreign countries to recognize the importance of adapting to different cultural expectations of individual audience members. People in the United States are highly diverse in terms of their culture, age, ethnicity, and religious tradition. Consider the various cultural backgrounds of your classmates. How many different cultural and ethnic traditions do they represent? You will want to adjust not only your delivery style but also your topic, pattern of organization, and the examples you use, according to who your audience members are and in what subject or subjects they are interested.

Different cultures have radically different expectations about public speaking. In Russia, for example, speakers have a "no frills" approach that emphasizes content over delivery. Being sensitive to your audience and adapting your message accordingly will serve you well, not only when addressing listeners with different cultural backgrounds from your own, but in all types of situations. If you learn to analyze your audience and adapt to their expectations, you can apply these skills in numerous settings: at a job interview, during a business presentation, or at city council election campaign event.

Select and Narrow Your Topic

While keeping your audience foremost in mind, your next task is to determine what you will talk about and to limit your topic to fit the constraints of your speaking assignment.

If your first speech assignment is to introduce yourself, your speech topic has been selected for you—you are the topic. It is not uncommon to be asked to speak on a specific subject. Often, though, you will be asked to speak but will not be given a topic. The task of selecting and narrowing a topic will be yours. Choosing or finding a topic on which to speak can be frustrating. "What should I talk about?" can become a haunting question.

Although there is no single answer to the question of what you should talk about, you may discover a topic by asking three standard questions: "Who is the audience?" "What are my interests, talents, and experiences?" and "What is the occasion?"

It's a good idea to give yourself plenty of time to select and narrow your topic. Don't wait until the last minute to ponder what you might talk about. One of the most important things you can do to be an effective speaker is to start preparing your speech well in advance of your speaking date.

Who Is the Audience?

Your topic may grow from basic knowledge about your audience. For example, if you know that your audience members are primarily between the ages of twenty-five and forty, this information should help you select a topic of interest to people who are probably working and either seeking partners or raising families. An older audience may lead you to other questions or issues: "Will Social Security be there when I need it?" or "The advantages of belonging to the AARP."

What Are Your Interests, Talents, and Experiences?

Rather than wracking your brain for exotic topics and outlandish ideas, examine your own background. Your hobbies and your ancestry are sources for topic ideas. What issues do you feel strongly about? Reflect on jobs you've held, news stories that catch your interest, events in your hometown, your career goals, or interesting people you have met.

Once you have chosen your topic, narrow it to fit the time limits for your talk. If you've been asked to deliver a ten-minute speech, the topic "How to find counseling help in school" would be more manageable than the topic "How to make the most of your high school experience." Of course, as our model suggests, your audience should be foremost in your mind when you work on your topic.

What Is the Occasion?

Besides your audience, you should consider the occasion for the speech when choosing a topic. A commencement address calls for a different topic, for example, than does a speech to a model railroad club. Another aspect of the occasion you'll want to consider is the physical setting of your speech. Will you be speaking to people seated in chairs arranged in a circle, or will you be standing in front of rows of people? The physical surroundings as well as the occasion affect the degree of formality your audience expects in your choice of topics.

Determine Your Purpose

You might think that once you have your topic, you are ready to start the research process. Before you do that, however, you need to decide on both a general and a specific purpose. There are three **general purposes** for speeches: to *inform,* to *persuade,* and to *entertain.*

When you inform, you teach, define, illustrate, clarify, or elaborate on a topic. The primary objective of class lectures and workshops is to inform.

A speech to persuade seeks to change or reinforce listeners' attitudes, beliefs, values, or behavior. Ads on TV, the radio, and the Internet; sermons; political speeches; and sales presentations are examples of speeches designed to persuade. To be a skilled persuader, you need to be sensitive to your audience's attitudes toward you and your topic.

The third general purpose for a speech is to entertain your audience. After-dinner speeches and comic monologues are mainly intended as entertainment. Often the key to an effective entertaining speech lies in your choice of stories, examples, and illustrations, as well as in your delivery.

Your **specific purpose** is a concise statement indicating what you want your listeners to be able to do, remember, or feel when you finish your speech. A specific purpose statement identifies the audience response you desire. Here again, we emphasize the importance of focusing on the audience as you develop your specific purpose. Perhaps you have had the experience of listening to a speaker and wondering, "What's the point? I know he's talking about education, but I'm not sure where he's going with this subject." You may have understood the speaker's general purpose, but the specific one wasn't clear. If you can't figure out what the specific purpose is, it is probably because the speaker does not know, either.

Deciding on a specific purpose is not difficult once you have narrowed your topic: "At the end of my speech, the class will be able to identify three counseling facilities on campus and describe the best way to get help at each one." Notice that this purpose is phrased in terms of what you would like the audience to be able to do by the end of the speech. Your specific purpose should be a fine-tuned, audience-centered goal. For an informative speech, you may simply want your audience to restate an idea; define new words; or identify, describe, or illustrate something. In a persuasive speech, you may try to rouse your listeners to take a class, buy something, or vote for someone.

Once you have formulated your specific purpose, write it down on a piece of paper or note card, and keep it before you as you read and gather ideas for your talk. Your specific purpose should guide your research and help you choose supporting materials that are related to your audience. As you continue to work on your speech, you may even decide to modify your purpose. But if you have an objective in mind at all times as you move through the preparation stage, you will stay on track.

Develop Your Central Idea

You should now be able to write the central idea of your speech. Whereas your statement of a specific purpose indicates what you want your audience to do when you have finished your speech, your central idea identifies the essence of your message. Think of it as a one-sentence summary of your speech. Here is an example:

Topic:	The South Beach Diet
General Purpose:	To inform
Specific Purpose:	At the end of my speech, the audience will be able to identify the three key elements in the South Beach Diet.
Central Idea:	The South Beach Diet is based on reducing the amount of carbohydrates you eat, drinking more water, and increasing the amount of exercise you get.

Generate the Main Ideas

In the words of H. V. Prochnow, "A good many people can make a speech, but saying something is more difficult." Effective speakers are good thinkers; they say something. They know how to play with words and thoughts to develop their **main ideas**. The ancient Romans called this skill **invention**—the ability to develop or discover ideas that result in new insights or new approaches to old problems. The Roman orator Cicero called this aspect of speaking the process of "finding out what [a speaker] should say."

Once you have an appropriate topic, a specific purpose, and a well-worded central idea down on paper, the next task is to identify the major divisions of your speech, or key points that you wish to develop. To determine how to subdivide your central idea into key points, ask these three questions:

1. Does the central idea have logical divisions?
2. Can you think of several reasons why the central idea is true?
3. Can you support the central idea with a series of steps?

Let's look at each of these questions along with examples of how to apply them.

Does the Central Idea Have Logical Divisions?

If the central idea is "There are three ways to interpret the stock market page of your local newspaper," your speech could be organized into three parts. You will simply identify the three ways to interpret the stock market page and use each as a major point. A speech about the art of applying theatrical makeup could also be organized into three parts: eye makeup, face makeup, and hair color. Looking for logical divisions in your speech topic is the simplest way to determine key points.

Can You Think of Several Reasons Why the Central Idea Is True?

If your central idea is "Medicare should be expanded to include additional coverage for individuals of all ages," each major point of your speech could be a reason you think Medicare should be expanded. For example, Medicare should be expanded because (1) not enough people are being served by the present system, (2) the people currently being served receive inadequate medical attention, and (3) the elderly cannot afford to pay what Medicare does not now cover. If your central idea is a statement that something is good or bad, you should focus on the reasons your central idea is true. Use these reasons as the main ideas of the speech.

Can You Support the Central Idea with a Series of Steps?

Suppose your central idea is "Running for a campus office is easy to do." Your speech could be developed around a series of steps, telling your listeners what to do first, second, and third to get elected. Speeches describing a personal experience or explaining how to build or make something can usually be organized in a step-by-step progression.

Your time limit, your topic, and the information gleaned from your research will determine how many major ideas will be in your speech. A three- to five-minute speech might have only two major ideas. In a very short speech, you may develop only one major idea with examples, illustrations, and other forms of support. Don't spend time trying to divide a topic that does not need dividing.

Gather Verbal and Visual Supporting Material

With your main idea or ideas in mind, your next job is to gather material to support them—facts, examples, definitions, and quotations from others that illustrate, amplify, clarify, and provide evidence. Here, as always in preparing your speech, the importance of being an audience-centered speaker cannot be overemphasized. There's a saying that an ounce of illustration is worth a ton of talk. If a speech is boring, it is usually because the speaker has not chosen supporting material that is relevant or interesting to the audience. Don't just give people data; connect facts to their lives. As one sage quipped, "Data is not information any more than 50 tons of cement is a skyscraper."

Criteria for Choosing Supporting Material

Supporting material should be personal and concrete, and it should appeal to your listeners' senses. Tell stories based on your own experiences, and provide vivid descriptions of things that are tangible so that your audience can visualize what you are talking about.

Besides sight, supporting material can appeal to touch, hearing, smell, and taste. The more senses you trigger with words, the more interesting your talk will be. Descriptions such as "the rough, splintery surface of weather-beaten wood" or "the sweet, cool, refreshing flavor of cherry ices" evoke sensory images. In addition, relating abstract statistics to something tangible can help communicate your ideas more clearly. For example, if you say that a company sells 2.6 billion pounds of snack food each year, your listeners will have a hazy idea that 2.6 billion pounds is a lot of potato chips; but if you add that 2.6 billion pounds is triple the weight of the Empire State Building, you've made your point more memorably.

Developing Your Research Skills

How does a public speaker find interesting and relevant supporting material? By developing good research skills. President Woodrow Wilson once admitted, "I use not only all the brains I have, but all that I can borrow." Although it is important to have good ideas, it is equally important to know how to build on existing knowledge. You can probably think of a topic or two about which you consider yourself an expert. Chances are that if you gave a short speech about a sport that you had practiced for years or about a recent trip that you took, you would not need to gather much additional information. But sooner or later, you will need to do some research on a topic in order to speak intelligently about it to an audience.

Besides searching for verbal forms of supporting material, you can also seek visual supporting material. Almost any presentation can be enhanced by reinforcing key ideas with visual aids. Often the most effective visual aids are the simplest: an object, a chart, a graph, a poster, a model, a map, or a person—perhaps you—to demonstrate a process or skill.

Make your visual images large enough to be seen and allow plenty of time to prepare them; look at your audience, not your presentation aid; control your audience's attention by timing your visual displays; and keep your presentation aids simple. Always concentrate on communicating effectively with your audience, not on dazzling your listeners with glitzy presentation displays.

Organize Your Speech

A wise person once said, "If effort is organized, accomplishment follows." A clearly and logically structured speech helps your audience remember what you say. A logical structure also helps you feel more in control of your speech, and greater control helps you feel more comfortable while delivering your message.

Classical rhetoricians—early students of speech—called the process of developing an orderly speech disposition. Speakers need to present ideas, information, examples, illustrations, stories, and statistics in an orderly sequence so that listeners can easily follow what they are saying.

Divide Your Speech

Every well-prepared speech has three major divisions: the introduction, the body, and the conclusion. The introduction helps capture attention, serves as an overview of the speech, and provides your audience with reasons to listen to you. The body presents the main content of your speech. The conclusion summarizes your key ideas. You may have heard this advice on how to organize a speech: "Tell them what you're going to tell them (the introduction), tell them (the body of the speech), and tell them what you told them (the conclusion)."

Because your introduction previews your speech and your conclusion summarizes it, most public-speaking experts recommend that you prepare your introduction and conclusion after you have carefully organized the body of your talk.

Outline Your Speech

If you have already generated your major ideas on the basis of logical divisions, reasons, or steps, you are well on your way to developing an outline. Indicate your major ideas by Roman numerals. Use capital letters for your supporting points. Use Arabic numerals if you need to subdivide your ideas further. Do not write your speech word for word. If you do, you will sound stilted and unnatural. It may be useful, however, to use brief notes—written cues on note cards—instead of a complete manuscript.

Sample Outline

Topic:
How to invest money

To inform, persuade, or entertain.

General Purpose:
To inform

A statement of what your audience should be able to do after hearing your speech

Specific Purpose:
At the end of my speech, the audience should be able to identify two principles that will help them better invest their money.

A one-sentence summary of your talk

Central Idea:
Knowing the source of money, how to invest it, and how money grows can lead to increased income from wise investments.

Attention-catching opening line

Introduction:
Imagine for a moment that it is the year 2050. You are 65 years old. You've just picked up your mail and opened an

envelope that contains a check for $100,000! No, you didn't win the lottery. You smile as you realize your own modest investment strategy over the last fifty years has paid off handsomely.

Preview major ideas

Today I'd like to answer three questions that can help you become a better money manager: First, where does money come from? Second, where do you invest it? And third, how does a little money grow into a lot of money?

Tell the audience why they should listen to you

Knowing the answers to these three questions can literally pay big dividends for you. With only modest investments and a well-disciplined attitude, you could easily have an annual income of $100,000 or more.

I, II, III. Major ideas

A, B, C. Supporting ideas

Body:

I. There are two sources of money.
   A. You already have some money.
   B. You will earn money in the future.
II. You can do three things with a dollar.
   A. You can spend your money.
   B. You can lend your money to others.
   C. You can invest your money.
III. Two principles can help make you rich.
   A. The "magic" of compound interest can transform pennies into millions.
   B. Finding the best rate of return on your money can pay big dividends.

Summarize main ideas and restate central ideas

Conclusion:

Today I've identified three key aspects of effective money management: (1) knowing sources of money, (2) knowing what you can do with money, and (3) understanding money-management principles that can make you rich. Now, let's go "back to the future"! Remember the good feeling you had when you received your check for $100,000? Recall that feeling again when you are depositing your first paycheck. Remember this simple secret for accumulating wealth: Part of all I earn is money to keep. It is within your power to "go for the gold."

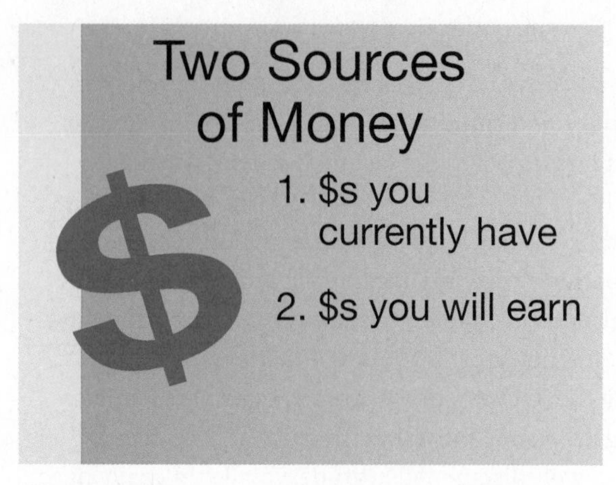

Figure A.2

Presentation Graphic for the First Major Idea in Your Speech

Consider Presentation Aids

In addition to developing a written outline to use as you speak, consider using presentation aids to add structure and clarity to your major ideas. Developing simple visual reinforcers of your key ideas can help your audience retain essential points. For example, the first major idea in the outline just presented could be summarized on a visual aid such as the one in Figure A.2.

Rehearse Your Speech

Remember this joke? One man asks another, "How do you get to Carnegie Hall?" The answer: "Practice, man, practice." The joke may be older than Carnegie Hall itself, but it is still good advice to all beginners, including novice speakers. A speech is a performance. As with any stage performance, whether it is music, dance, or theater, you need to rehearse. Experienced carpenters know to "measure twice, saw once." Rehearsing your speech is a way to "measure" your message so that you get it right when you present it to your audience.

Rehearse Your Speech Aloud

The best way to practice is to stand just as you will when you deliver your speech to your audience. As you rehearse out loud, try to find a comfortable way to phrase your ideas, but don't try to memorize your talk. In fact, if you have rehearsed your speech so many times that you are using exactly the same words every time, you have rehearsed long enough. Rehearse just enough so that you can discuss your ideas and supporting material without leaving out major parts of your speech. It is all right to use notes, but most public-speaking instructors limit the number of notes you may use.

Practice Making Eye Contact

As you rehearse with your imaginary audience, practice making eye contact as often as you can. Also, be aware of the volume of your voice; you will need to practice speaking loudly enough for all in the room to hear. If you are not sure what to do with your hands when you rehearse, just keep them at your side. Focus on your message, rather than worrying about how to gesture. Avoid jingling change with your hand in your pocket or using other gestures that could distract your audience. If you practice your speech as if you were actually delivering it, you will be a more effective speaker when you talk to the audience.

Make Decisions About the Style of Your Speech

Besides rehearsing your physical delivery, you also will decide about the style of your speech. "Style," said novelist Jonathan Swift, "is proper words in proper places." The words you choose and your arrangement of those words make up the style of your speech. As we have said, some audiences respond to a style that is simple and informal. Others prefer a grand and highly poetic style. To be a good speaker, you must become familiar with the language your listeners are used to hearing and must know how to select the right word or phrase to communicate an idea. Work to develop an ear for how words will sound to your audience.

Deliver Your Speech

The time has come, and you're ready to present your speech to your audience. Delivery is the final step in the preparation process. Before you walk to the front of the room, look at your listeners to see if the audience assembled is what you were expecting. Are the people out there of the age, race, and gender that you had predicted? Or do you need to make last-minute changes in your message to adjust to a different mix of audience members?

When you are introduced, walk calmly and confidently to the front of the room, establish eye contact with your audience, smile naturally, and deliver your attentioncatching opening sentence. Concentrate on your message and your audience. Deliver your speech in a conversational style, and try to establish rapport with your listeners. Deliver your speech just as you rehearsed it before your imaginary audience: Maintain eye contact, speak loudly enough to be heard, and use some natural variations in pitch. Finally, remember the advice of columnist Ann Landers: "Be sincere, be brief, and be seated."

Analyze the Sample Presentation at Your Pearson MyLab

Appendix 2

Listening Skills

What You Will Learn

- To use effective listening techniques
- To analyze and evaluate speeches

Are you a good listener? Considerable evidence suggests that your listening skills could be improved. Within hours after listening to a lecture or speech, you will recall only about 50 percent of the message. Forty-eight hours later, you are above average if you remember more than 25 percent of the message. (And in a recent survey of adult listeners, only 15 percent reported that they were above-average listeners.)

You hear billions of words each year. Yet how much information do you retain? In this appendix, we are going to focus on improving your listening skills. If you apply the principles and suggestions we offer, we believe you will become not only a better listener but also a better public speaker. In addition, improving your listening skills will strengthen your ability to think critically and evaluate what you hear and enhance your listening in one-on-one interpersonal interactions.

Effective Listening

Effective listening occurs when we select, attend to, understand, and remember a message.

- **Select.** To **select** a sound is to single out a message from several competing messages. A listener has many competing messages to sort through, including personal thoughts.
- **Attend.** To **attend** to a sound is to focus on it. Most people's average attention span while listening to someone talk is about 8 seconds.
- **Understand.** To **understand** something, people assign meaning to the information that comes their way. Although no single theory explains how people make sense of words, we do know that you understand what you hear by relating it to something you have already seen or heard.

- **Remember.** To **remember** is to recall ideas and information. Most listening experts believe that the main way to determine if audience members have been listening is to determine what they remember.

It is possible to become a more effective listener by listening with your eyes as well as your ears, by listening mindfully, and listening skillfully. The chart "How to Enhance Your Listening Skills" provides detailed suggestions for improving your skills.

Analyzing and Evaluating Speeches

Your critical thinking and listening skills will help you evaluate not only the speeches of others but also your own speeches. When you evaluate something, you judge its value and appropriateness. To make a judgment about the value of something, it's important to use criteria for what is and is not effective or appropriate.

HOW TO: Enhance Your Listening Skills

	The Good Listener . . .	The Poor Listener . . .
Listen with Your Eyes as Well as Your Ears	Looks for nonverbal clues to aid understanding	Focuses only on the words
	Adapts to the speaker's delivery	Is easily distracted by the delivery of the speech
Listen Mindfully	Controls emotions	Erupts emotionally when listening
	Listens before making a judgment about the value of the content	Jumps to conclusions about the value of the content
	Mentally asks, "What's in it for me?"	Does not attempt to relate to the information personally
Listen Skillfully	Identifies a listening goal	Does not have a listening goal in mind
	Listens for major ideas	Listens for isolated facts
	Seeks opportunities to practice listening skills	Avoids listening to difficult information
	Understands and adapts his or her listening style to the speaker	Is not aware of how to capitalize on his or her listening style
	Listens actively by re-sorting, rephrasing, and repeating what is heard	Listens passively, making no effort to engage with the information heard

Here is a checklist of criteria you can use to evaluate the effectiveness of speeches.

A CHECKLIST FOR EVALUATING THE EFFECTIVENESS OF A PRESENTATION

Audience Orientation

- ☐ Did the speaker make a specific effort to adapt to the audience?

Topic Selection

- ☐ Was the topic appropriate for the audience, the occasion, and the speaker?
- ☐ Was the speech narrowed to fit the time limits?

Purpose

- ☐ Was the general purpose clear?
- ☐ Was the specific purpose appropriate for the audience?
- ☐ Was the purpose achieved?

Central Idea

- ☐ Was the central idea clear enough to be summarized in one sentence?

Main Ideas

- ☐ Were the main ideas clearly identified in the introduction of the speech, developed in the body of the speech, and summarized in the conclusion of the speech?

Supporting Material

- ☐ Did the speaker use varied and interesting supporting material?
- ☐ Did the speaker use effective and appropriate evidence to support conclusions?
- ☐ Did the speaker use credible supporting material?

Organization

- ☐ Did the speech have a clear introduction that caught attention, provided a preview of the speech, and established the speaker's credibility?
- ☐ Did the speaker organize the body of the speech in a logical way?
- ☐ Did the speaker use transitions, summaries, and signposts to clarify the organization?
- ☐ Did the speaker appropriately summarize the major ideas and provide closure to the speech during the conclusion?

Speech Rehearsal

- ☐ Did the speech sound as though it was well rehearsed?
- ☐ Did the speaker seem familiar with the speech content?

Speech Delivery

- ☐ Did the speaker make appropriate eye contact with the audience?
- ☐ Did the speaker use appropriate volume and vocal variation?
- ☐ Did the speaker use gestures and posture appropriately?
- ☐ Did the speaker use presentation aids that were easy to see and handled effectively?
- ☐ Did the speaker use presentation aids that were of high quality?

Appendix 3

Conducting Research and Documenting Sources

What You Will Learn

- To distinguish among primary and secondary and scholarly and popular sources
- To use sources including books, periodicals, and Internet sources
- To evaluate sources—print, electronic, and online
- To summarize, paraphrase, synthesize, and quote material
- To recognize and avoid plagiarism
- To cite and document sources properly in your paper

When you write substantial papers for advanced courses in high school and nearly all courses in college, you rarely get the opportunity to write solely from within yourself, drawing on just your own personal thoughts, experiences, and ideas. More often, when you write such papers, you use material from two outwardly directed activities:

- Reading, defined broadly to include reading print and electronic texts and listening to live or recorded sources; and
- Observing, both in controlled situations such as laboratory experiments and field observations and in naturalistic situations such as art museums.

Reading and observing are closely related. Both require more than a simple decoding of words, sounds, or visual images. Both require you, the reader and observer, to

- Draw on your prior knowledge of the ideas and issues being placed before you in the text or the scene
- Hypothesize what the author's or creator's **purpose** was (as we explain in Chapters 3 and 4)
- Work your way through the text or observational experience, simultaneously determining the degree to which the text or experience is matching up with

the hypothesized purpose, and predicting what will come next in the text or experience

- Answer the "so what?" question about the text or scene after you have finished reading or observing: What did this text or scene mean to you, and how do you connect that meaning to yourself, to the world around you, and to other texts and scenes that you have previously encountered?

Collectively, reading and observing, as defined above, are called **research**. While some instructors might specifically assign you to write a **research paper,** in advanced high school and most college courses, instructors more frequently will assign something called simply a major paper, a term paper, an essay, or a project and expect you to **synthesize** and incorporate the research you do in it. As Chapter 6 points out, in such papers, your argument—the main idea or thesis—is central. The research you do must enter into conversation with and support your argument. With the possible exception of a paper for which the primary purpose is simply to review published scholarship on a particular topic, your goal is to write an argument supported by research, not simply to parrot back what you learned from your research.

To engage in successful research, a high school and college student needs to be able to evaluate and document sources.

Primary and Secondary Sources

In the language of academic research, a **primary source** is a document that represents the first evidence of something happening or being thought or said. So, for example, in literature, primary sources are novels, poems, plays, and short stories. In other fields in the arts and humanities, primary sources include diaries, letters, photographs, autobiographies, works of art, maps, videos, films, sound recordings, published interviews, newspaper and magazine articles, and published first-hand accounts. A **secondary source,** on the other hand, is created *after* a primary source and often comments upon or analyzes primary sources. Secondary sources include textbooks, biographies, and scholarly books, articles, chapters, and other media that provide informed opinions on a past event or a primary source.

Many research projects assigned in high school and college courses either are based on a primary source to be considered in the project or assume that you, the writer, have already encountered a primary source. As we explain below, a central task in conducting research is **synthesizing** your reading of secondary sources and incorporating that synthesis in your argument.

Scholarly Sources and Popular Sources

Another important distinction that a successful researcher needs to make is between **scholarly sources** and **popular sources,** a distinction that may be made about books, periodicals, and electronic sources found on the Internet.

Watch the Video on Research Sources at Your Pearson MyLab

The following table, adapted from Mary Kay Mulvaney and David Jolliffe's textbook, *Academic Writing: Genres, Samples, and Resources* (Pearson, 2005), describes the major differences between these two types of source materials.

Scholarly Sources	Popular Sources
Written by experts in the academic discipline or field	Written by professional writers who usually do not have degrees in the subject that the source is about
Often more challenging to read	Usually easier to read
More serious, in-depth coverage of the subject, often with references to other sources that scholars in the field might want to know about	Less in-depth coverage; if research is reported, it is cast in terms for the general reader
Often focuses on narrow subtopics within a field	Usually provides broader overviews of topics
Source is heavily referenced, may have footnotes or endnotes, and has an extensive bibliography or works cited list	Few if any references are provided other than brief quotes from practitioners or participants
Often includes supplementary materials such as appendices, indexes, bibliographies, and detailed charts and graphs	Frequently includes photographs and simplified charts and graphs
Often has little visual appeal; emphasis is on the content	Frequently has high visual appeal, using techniques that allow a reader to get the gist or main idea
Geared to an audience of specialists in a field or novices preparing to enter the field	Geared to a well-educated, curious general public
Frequently published by academic presses that often have the word "university" in their title	Usually published by commercial or not-for-profit presses

Without meaning to diminish the vital role that popular sources—magazine articles, documentary programs on public television, and so on—play in keeping the general public informed about a range of important topics, most instructors would discourage a student from relying solely on popular sources in a research project.

A vital part of learning to become a successful academic writer is becoming aware of scholarly sources and learning to adapt and synthesize material from them.

Conducting Research Using the Internet

Using the Internet to find sources for a research project has an up side and a down side. On the up side: Using the Internet is easy. If you can get to a computer with Internet access, you will probably be able to call up literally thousands of sites by typing your topic into a search engine like Google, Bing, or Ask.com. And the types of materials available on Internet sites are wonderfully varied and abundant: You can find articles, reproductions of primary sources such as newspaper pages, art work, audio recordings, and video files that might be pertinent to your topic.

On the down side: Using the Internet can be a tremendously inefficient way to gather information, and the information itself is potentially inaccurate. First of all, the broader your topic is, the more irrelevant information an Internet search will call up. Second, the Internet is by and large un-refereed—that is, anyone who wants to post something can publish it, no matter whether the author/creator has any credentials to write on the subject or has done any research.

A savvy researcher knows that the first step in conducting Internet research is not simply to type the topic into a search engine and then go fishing through the results. The first thing anyone who is new to Internet research should do is take a bit of time and work with a simple tutorial on the subject. One of the very best ones comes from the Online Writing Lab (OWL) at Purdue University, which has been kind enough to make this resource available to the public. To get to it, go to the OWL Web site and look for "Internet Literacy." Under Internet Literacy, click "Searching the World Wide Web." You will find a great tutorial that covers these topics:

- Searching the World Wide Web: Overview
- How the Internet and Search Engines Work
- Kinds of Search Engines and Directories
- Searching with a Search Engine
- Searching with a Web Directory
- Search Engine and Web Directory List
- Resources to Search the Invisible Web
- Other Useful Sites for Finding Information
- Other Strategies for Web Searching

Once you have worked your way through these sections—and you should plan to spend a couple of hours total on this task—you will be much better equipped to search the Internet for relevant material and to sort through what you find.

Watch the Video on Conducting Online Keyword Searches at Your Pearson MyLab

Evaluating Research Before Using It in a Paper

When you are writing a paper that involves research, it's easy to fall victim to two types of faulty thinking.

The first is the "I-found-it; therefore-it's-going-to-go-in-my-paper" fallacy. Remember that you are not compelled to put every piece of research you find into your project. Some of it may simply not pertain to your argument. Ask yourself this question before deciding whether to synthesize the research into your project: "Can this source *enter in the conversation* that I am having with my sources as I develop *my* argument?" (See Chapter 6 for more explanation of developing your argument by "conversing" with sources.) If the source *can* enter into this conversation, you might be able to incorporate it in your paper.

The other sand trap is the "it's-published-in-print-or-on-the-Internet; therefore-it's-true" fallacy. Scholarly books, book chapters, and journal articles (see above) have generally been reviewed carefully by experts in the field before they are published, and conscientious editors frequently evaluate the material in popular-press books and articles before they go to press. Sites on the Internet are another matter: Some documents have been scrutinized and approved before they have been posted on the Web; others have not. It's always a good idea, therefore, to evaluate every source you use before you decide to incorporate it in your paper.

Writers in many fields use a checklist with the acronym CARS to evaluate sources they find in their research. CARS stands for "Credibility," "Accuracy," "Reasonableness," and "Support." Here is a version of this checklist developed by Robert Harris, an instructor at Southern California College:

CHECKLIST FOR EVALUATING SOURCES

☐ *Credibility.* If a source is credible, it is

- Trustworthy: The quality of evidence and argument is evident; the author's credentials are available; quality control is evident; it is a known or respected authority; it has organizational support.
- Evidence-Based: There is sufficient evidence presented to make the argument persuasive.
- Compelling: There are compelling arguments and reasons given.
- Detailed: There are enough details to draw a reasonable conclusion.

☐ *Accuracy.* If a source is accurate, it is

- Up-to-date, factual, detailed, exact, comprehensive.
- Dated: If there is no date on the document, give it a second look before using it. An old date on information known to change rapidly is also suspect.

Watch the Video on Weighing Evidence at Your Pearson MyLab

- Clear: It does not contain assertions that are vague or otherwise lacking detail.
- Controlled: It is concise and qualified rather than sweeping in its language.
- Open-minded: It acknowledges that other views are possible.

☐ *Reasonableness.* If a source is reasonable, it is fair, balanced, objective, and reasoned; there is no conflict of interest; there is an absence of fallacies or slanted tone.

Here are some clues to a lack of reasonableness:

- Intemperate tone or language ("stupid jerks," "shrill cries of my extremist opponents")
- Exaggerated claims ("Thousands of children are murdered every day in the United States.")
- Sweeping statements of excessive significance ("This is the most important idea ever conceived!")
- Conflict of interest ("Welcome to the Old Stogie Tobacco Company Home Page. To read our report, 'Cigarettes Make You Live Longer,' click here." or "When you buy a stereo, beware of other brands that lack our patented circuitry.")

☐ *Support.* If a source is valid, it will have listed sources, contact information, and available corroboration. Its claims will be supported; documentation will be supplied.

Some source considerations include these:

- Where did this information come from?
- What sources did the information creator use?
- Are the sources listed?
- Is there a bibliography or other documentation?
- Does the author provide contact information in case you wish to discuss an issue or request further clarification?
- What kind of support for the information is given?

Documentation: The Key to Avoiding Plagiarism

Once you decide a source is good enough to include in your paper, you need to document it to avoid plagiarism.

Plagiarism is using someone else's work—words, ideas, or illustrations, published or unpublished—without giving the creator of that work sufficient credit.

Watch the Video on Plagiarism at Your Pearson MyLab

A serious breach of scholarly ethics, plagiarism can have severe consequences. Students risk a failing grade or disciplinary action ranging from suspension to expulsion.

It can be difficult to tell when you have unintentionally plagiarized something. The legal doctrine of **fair use** allows writers to use a limited amount of another's work in their own papers and books. However, to make sure that they are not plagiarizing that work, writers need to take care to credit the source accurately and clearly for *every* use. **Documentation** is the method writers employ to give credit to the creators of material they use. It involves providing essential information about the source of the material, which enables readers to find the material for themselves. It requires two elements: (1) a list of sources used in the paper and (2) citations in the text to items in that list. To use documentation and avoid unintentionally plagiarizing from a source, you need to know how to

- Identify sources and information that need to be documented.
- Document sources in a Works Cited list.
- Use material gathered from sources: in summary, paraphrase, and quotation.
- Create in-text references.
- Use correct grammar and punctuation to blend quotations into a paper.

Identifying Sources and Information That Need to Be Documented

Whenever you use information from **outside sources,** you need to identify the source of that material. Major outside sources include books, newspapers, magazines, government sources, radio and television programs, material from electronic databases, correspondence, films, plays, interviews, speeches, and information from Web sites. Virtually all the information you find in outside sources requires documentation. The one major exception to this guideline is that you do not have to document common knowledge. **Common knowledge** is widely known information about current events, famous people, geographical facts, or familiar history. However, when in doubt, the safest strategy is to provide documentation.

Documenting Sources in a Works Cited List

You need to choose the documentation style that is required by your instructor. Take care to use only one documentation style in any one paper and to follow its documentation formats consistently. The most widely used style manuals are *MLA Handbook for Writers of Research Papers*, published by the Modern Language Association (MLA), which is popular in the fields of English language and literature; the *Publication Manual of the American Psychological Association* (APA), which is favored in the social sciences; and *The Chicago Manual of Style* (CMS), published by the University of Chicago Press, which is preferred in other humanities and sometimes business. Other, more specialized style manuals are used in various fields. Certain information is included in citation formats in all styles:

- Author or other creative individual or entity
- Source of the work
- Relevant identifying numbers or letters
- Title of the work
- Publisher or distributor
- Relevant dates

Constructing a Works Cited List in MLA Style

In an actual Works Cited list, items are not listed separately by type of source. All items are alphabetized by authors' last names. When no author is given, an item can be alphabetized by title, by editor, or by the name of the sponsoring organization. MLA style spells out names in full, inverts only the first author's name, and separates elements with a period. In the MLA Works Cited items below, note the use of punctuation such as commas, colons, and angle brackets to separate and introduce material within elements. All entries include the medium of publication of the source: Prints, Web, Video, and so on.

Books

Bidart, Frank. Introduction. *Collected Poems*. By Robert Lowell. Ed. Frank Bidart and David Gewanter. New York: Farrar, Strauss and Giroux, 2003. vii–xvi. Print.

Chernow, Ron. *Alexander Hamilton*. New York: Penguin, 2004. Print.

Conant, Jennet. *109 East Palace: Robert Oppenheimer and the Secret City of Los Alamos*. New York: Simon, 2005. Print.

—. *Tuxedo Park: A Wall Street Tycoon and the Secret Palace of Science That Changed the Course of World War II*. New York: Simon, 2002. Print.

Maupassant, Guy de. "The Necklace." Trans. Marjorie Laurie. *An Introduction to Fiction*. Ed. X. J. Kennedy and Dana Gioia. 7th ed. New York: Longman, 1999, 160–66. Print.

Periodicals

"Living on Borrowed Time." *Economist* 25 Feb.–3 Mar. 2006: 34–37. Print.

"RomneyCare 2.0." Editorial. *Wall Street Journal*, 6 Aug. 2012, sec. A: 12. Print.

Spinello, Richard A. "The End of Privacy." *America* 4 Jan. 1997: 9–13. Print.

Williams, N. R., M. Davey, and K. Klock-Powell. "Rising from the Ashes: Stories of Recovery, Adaptation, and Resiliency in Burn Survivors." *Social Work Health Care* 36.4 (2003): 53–77. Print.

Zobenica, Jon. "You Might as Well Live." Rev. of *A Long Way Down* by Nick Hornby. *Atlantic* July–Aug. 2005: 148. Print.

Electronic Sources

For sources found on the internet, the first date in the entry is the date of publication or posting. It is followed by the medium of publication, Web, and the date you accessed it.

Glanz, William. "Colleges Offer Students Music Downloads." *Washington Times.* Washington Times, 25 Aug. 2004. Web. 17 Oct. 2012.

Libya: A Threat to Society? Arbitrary Detention of Women and Girls for "Social Rehabilitation." Human Rights Watch. Human Rights Watch, 27 Feb. 2006. Web. 4 Mar. 2010.

McNichol, Elizabeth C., and Iris J. Lav. "State Revenues and Services Remain below Pre-Recession Levels." *Center on Budget & Policy Priorities.* 6 Dec. 2005. Web. 10 Mar. 2006.

"Worldwide Press Freedom Index 2012." *Reporters Without Borders.* Reporters Without Borders, 2012. Web. 28 Feb. 2012.

Using Material Gathered from Sources: Summary, Paraphrase, Quotation

You can integrate material into your paper in three ways—by summarizing, paraphrasing, and quoting. A quotation, paraphrase, or summary must be used in a manner that accurately conveys the meaning of the source.

A **summary** is a brief restatement in your own words of the source's main ideas. Summary is used to convey the general meaning of the ideas in a source, without giving specific details or examples that may appear in the original. A summary is always much shorter than the work it treats. Take care to give the essential information as clearly and succinctly as possible in your own language.

Rules to Remember: Summary

1. Write the summary using your own words.
2. Indicate clearly where the summary begins and ends.
3. Use attribution and parenthetical reference to tell the reader where the material came from.
4. Make sure your summary is an accurate restatement of the source's main ideas.
5. Check that the summary is clearly separated from your own contribution.

A **paraphrase** is a restatement, in your own words and using your own sentence structure, of specific ideas or information from a source. The chief purpose of a paraphrase is *to maintain your own writing style* throughout your paper. A paraphrase can be about as long as the original passage.

Watch the Video on Summarizing at Your Pearson MyLab

Rules to Remember: Paraphrase

1. Use your own words and sentence structure. Do not duplicate the source's words or phrases.
2. Use quotation marks within your paraphrase to indicate words and phrases you do quote.
3. Make sure your readers know where the paraphrase begins and ends.
4. Check that your paraphrase is an accurate and objective restatement of the source's specific ideas.
5. Immediately follow your paraphrase with a parenthetical reference indicating the source.

A **quotation** reproduces an actual part of a source, word for word, to support a statement or idea, to provide an example, to advance an argument, or to add interest or color to a discussion. The length of a quotation can range from a word or a phrase to several paragraphs. In general, quote the least amount possible that gets your point across to the reader.

Rules to Remember: Quotation

1. Copy the words from your source to your paper exactly as they appear in the original. Do not alter the spelling, capitalization, or punctuation of the original. If a quotation contains an obvious error, you may insert [sic], which is Latin for "so" or "thus," to show that the error is in the original.
2. Enclose short quotations (four or fewer lines of text) in quotation marks, and set off longer quotations as block quotations.
3. Immediately follow each quotation with a parenthetical reference that gives the specific source information required.

Creating In-Text References

In-text references need to supply enough information to enable a reader to find the correct source listing in the Works Cited list. To cite a source properly in the text of your report, you generally need to provide some or all of the following information for each use of the source:

- Name of the person or organization that authored the source.
- Title of the source (if there is more than one source by the same author or if no author is given).
- Page, paragraph, or line number, if the source has one.

Watch the Video on Paraphrasing at Your Pearson MyLab

Watch the Video on Quoting at Your Pearson MyLab

These items can appear as an attribution in the text ("According to Smith . . . ") or in a parenthetical reference placed directly after the summary, paraphrase, or quotation. The examples that follow are in MLA style.

Using an Introductory Attribution and a Parenthetical Reference

The author, the publication, or a generalized reference can introduce source material. Remaining identifiers (title, page number) can go in the parenthetical reference at the end, as in the first sentence of the example below. If a source, such as a Web site, does not have page numbers, it may be possible to put all the necessary information into the in-text attribution, as in the second sentence of the example below.

> *The Economist* noted that since 2004, "state tax revenues have come roaring back across the country" ("Living" 34). However, McNichol and Lav, writing for the Center on Budget and Policy Priorities, claim that recent gains are not sufficient to make up for the losses suffered.

Identifying material by an author of more than one work used in your paper

The attribution and the parenthetical reference combined must provide the title of the work, the author, and the page number of the citation.

> Describing the testing of the first atom bomb, Jennet Conant says, "The test had originally been scheduled for 4:00 A.M. on July 16, when most of the surrounding population would be sound asleep and there would be the least number of witnesses" (*109 East Palace* 304–05).

Identifying material that the source is quoting

To use material that has been quoted in your cited source, add *qtd. in,* for "quoted in." Here, only one source by Conant is given in the Works Cited list.

> The weather was worrisome, but procrastination was even more problematic. General Groves was concerned that "every hour of delay would increase the possibility of someone's attempting to sabotage the tests" (qtd. in Conant, 305).

Using Correct Grammar and Punctuation to Blend Quotations into a Paper

Quotations must blend seamlessly into the writer's original sentence, with the proper punctuation, so that the resulting sentence is neither ungrammatical nor awkward.

Watch the Video on Integrating Quotations at Your Pearson MyLab

Using a Full-Sentence Quotation of Fewer Than Four Lines

A quotation of one or more complete sentences can be enclosed in double quotation marks and introduced with a verb, usually in the present tense and followed by a comma. Omit a period at the close of a quoted sentence, but keep any question mark or exclamation mark. Insert the parenthetical reference, then a period.

> One commentator asks, "What accounts for the government's ineptitude in safeguarding our privacy rights?" (Spinello 9).
>
> "What accounts," Spinello asks, "for the government's ineptitude in safeguarding our privacy rights?" (9).

Introducing a Quotation with a Full Sentence

Use a colon after a full sentence that introduces a quotation.

> Spinello asks an important question: "What accounts for the government's ineptitude in safeguarding our privacy rights?" (9).

Introducing a Quotation with "That"

A single complete sentence can be introduced with a *that* construction.

> Chernow suggests that "the creation of New York's first bank was a formative moment in the city's rise as a world financial center" (199–200).

Quoting Part of a Sentence

Make sure that quoted material blends grammatically into the new sentence.

> McNichol and Lav assert that during that period, state governments were helped by "an array of fiscal gimmicks."

Using a Quotation That Contains Another Quotation

Replace the internal double quotation marks with single quotation marks.

> Lowell was "famous as a 'confessional' writer, but he scorned the term," according to Bidart (vii).

Adding Information to a Quotation

Any addition for clarity or any change for grammatical reasons should be placed in square brackets.

> In *109 East Palace*, Conant notes the timing of the first atom bomb test, "The test had originally been scheduled for 4:00 A.M. on July 16,

[1945,] when most of the surrounding population would be sound asleep" (304–05).

Omitting Information from Source Sentences

Indicate an omission with ellipsis marks (three spaced dots).

> In *109 East Palace*, Conant says, "The test had originally been scheduled for 4:00 A.M. on July 16, when . . . there would be the least number of witnesses" (304–05).

Using a Quotation of More Than Four Lines

Begin a long quotation on a new line and set off the quotation by indenting it one inch from the left margin and double spacing it throughout. Do not enclose it in quotation marks. Put the parenthetical reference *after* the period at the end of the quotation.

> One international organization recently documented the repression of women's rights in Libya:
>
> > The government of Libya is arbitrarily detaining women and girls in "social rehabilitation" facilities, . . . locking them up indefinitely without due process. Portrayed as "protective" homes for wayward women and girls, . . . these facilities are de facto prisons . . . [where] the government routinely violates women's and girls' human rights, including those to due process, liberty, freedom of movement, personal dignity, and privacy. (*Libya*)

Is It Plagiarism? Test Yourself on In-Text References

Read the Original Source excerpt. Can you spot the plagiarism in the examples that follow it?

Original Source

> To begin with, language is a system of communication. I make this rather obvious point because to some people nowadays it isn't obvious: they see language as above all a means of "self-expression." Of course, language is one way that we express our personal feelings and thoughts—but so, if it comes to that, are dancing, cooking and making music. Language does much more: it enables us to convey to others what we think, feel

Watch the Video on Tests for Direct Quotations at Your Pearson MyLab

and want. Language-as-communication is the prime means of organizing the cooperative activities that enable us to accomplish as groups things we could not possibly do as individuals. Some other species also engage in cooperative activities, but these are either quite simple (as among baboons and wolves) or exceedingly stereotyped (as among bees, ants and termites). Not surprisingly, the communicative systems used by these animals are also simple or stereotypes. Language, our uniquely flexible and intricate system of communication, makes possible our equally flexible and intricate ways of coping with the words around us: in a very real sense, it is what makes us human. (Claiborne 8)

Works Cited entry:

Claiborne, Robert. *Our Marvelous Native Tongue: The Life and Times of the English Language.* New York: New York Times, 1983. Print.

Plagiarism Example 1

One commentator makes a distinction between language used as **a means of self-expression** and **language-as-communication**. It is the latter that distinguishes human interaction from that of other species and allows humans to work cooperatively on complex tasks (8).

What's wrong? The source's name is not given, and there are no quotation marks around words taken directly from the source (in **boldface** in the example).

Plagiarism Example 2

Claiborne notes that language "is the prime means of organizing the cooperative activities." Without language, we would, consequently, not have civilization.

What's wrong? The page number of the source is missing. A parenthetical reference should immediately follow the material being quoted, paraphrased, or summarized. You may omit a parenthetical reference only if the information that you have included in your attribution is sufficient to identify the source in your Works Cited list and no page number is needed.

Plagiarism Example 3

Other animals also **engage in cooperative activities**. However, these actions are not very complex. Rather they are either the very **simple** activities of, for example, **baboons and wolves** or the **stereotyped** activities of animals such as **bees, ants and termites** (Claiborne 8).

What's wrong? A paraphrase should capture a specific idea from a source but must not duplicate the writer's phrases and words (in **boldface** in the example). In the example, the wording and sentence structure follow the source too closely.

Avoiding Plagiarism: Note-Taking Tips

The most effective way to avoid unintentional plagiarism is to follow a systematic method of note-taking and writing.

- **Keep copies of your documentation information.** For all sources that you use, keep copies of the title and copyright pages and the pages with quotations you need. Save or print online sources and keep those, too. Highlight the relevant citation information in color. Keep these materials until your paper has been graded.
- **Quotation or paraphrase?** Assume that all the material in your notes is direct quotation unless you indicated otherwise. Double-check any paraphrase for quoted phrases, and insert the necessary quotation marks.
- **Create the Works Cited list first**. Before you start writing your paper, your list is a **working bibliography,** a list of possible sources to which you add source entries as you discover them. As you finalize your list, you can delete the items you decided not to use in your paper.

Source of Documentation section: Linda Stern, Publishing School of Continuing and Professional Studies, New York University.

Watch the Video on Note-Taking at Your Pearson MyLab

Glossary of Rhetorical Terms

A

Active voice: In a sentence written in the active voice, the doer of the action is the subject and the receiver of the action is the direct object. (p. 93)
Alliteration: The repetition of consonant sounds at the beginning or in the middle of two or more adjacent words. (p. 99)
Allusion: An indirect reference in a text to a person, place, or thing, fictitious or factual. (p. 95)
Anadiplosis (a-nuh-duh-PLOH-suhs): The repetition of the last word of one clause at the beginning of the following clause. (p. 100)
Analysis: Closely examining elements in a text, such as its subject, style, and/or structure so as to understand the whole entity. (p. 10)
Anglo-Saxon diction: Words that are used in less formal kinds of writing. (p. 90)
Anthimeria (an-thuh-MEER-ee-uh): A figure, specifically a trope, in which one part of speech, usually a verb, substitutes for another, usually a noun. (p. 101)
Antimetabole: A scheme, in which words are repeated in different grammatical structures. (p. 98)
Antithesis: A part of a text in which the content of the clauses, phrases, or words being balanced in the parallel structure offers a striking contrast. Antithesis points out to the reader differences between two juxtaposed ideas rather than similarities. (p. 97)
Appeals: The collective term for the ways a text emphasizes the logical structure of the argument, the credibility and character of the writer or speaker, and the emotions of the audience. (p. 51)
Appositive: A construction, specifically a scheme, in which two coordinating elements are set side by side, and the second explains or modifies the first. (p. 99)
Argument: The central point a text is making; a reason or set of reasons given with the aim of persuading others that an action or idea is right or wrong. (p. 108)
Arrangement: The rhetorical term for the organization and structure of a text. (p. 54)
Assonance: The repetition of vowel sounds in the stressed syllables of two or more adjacent words. (p. 99)
Asyndeton: A figure, specifically a scheme, in which conjunctions that might connect related items are deliberately omitted. (p. 99)
Audience: The readers or listeners to whom a text is directed or who are invoked by the text. (p. 78)

C

Claim: A point or proposition put forward by a writer that then requires development and support. (p. 79)
Climax: In composition, the repetition of words, phrases, or clauses in order of increasing number or importance. (p. 100)
Close reading: A method of paying careful attention to the organization, diction, syntax, imagery, and figurative language of a text in order to understand its meaning. (p. 20)
Cloze test: A technique of removing every seventh word from a text to see if a reader can predict what word should appear in the blank. (p. 23)
Connotation: The implied, suggested meaning of a word; the associations connected to a word. (p. 89)
Context: The time, place, and situation that give rise to a piece of writing. (p. 5)

D

Deductive argument: An argument that begins with general ideas and then develops specific points that follow from the general. (p. 111)
Denotation: The literal definition of a word. (p. 89)
Diction: A collective term for word choice and variety of vocabulary. (p. 32)

E

Ellipsis: Any omission of words, the meaning of which is provided by the overall context of the passage. (p. 99)
Epistrophe (e-PIS-truh-fee): The repetition of the same group of words at the end of successive clauses. (p. 100)
Ethos: The way a text is seen to be effective because it emphasizes the character and credibility of the writer or speaker. (p. 51)

Exordium: The introduction or beginning of any text that draws the reader into its subject matter and central argument. (p. 56)

F

Figurative language: Any words or phrases that stand out because they are constructed using tropes or schemes that sharpen, clarify, and make writing more expressive. (p. 54)
Five-paragraph theme: A genre, frequently taught in American schools, in which the writer offers a "hook" and thesis in the first paragraph, provides three "body" paragraphs developing the thesis, and then produces a conclusion that re-emphasizes the importance of the thesis. (p. 115)

G

Genre: The type, form, or shape of a text; for example the journal, editorial, letter, essay, and poem are all different genres. (p. 29)

H

Haiku: A type of poem that has seventeen syllables arranged in three lines. (p. 34)
Hyperbole: A figure, specifically a trope, in which the writer deliberately overstates or exaggerates. (p. 101)

I

Imagery: The sights, sounds, tastes, smells, and tactile feelings that words or phrases in a text evoke. (p. 94)
Inductive argument: An argument that begins with specific points or details and then develops a general thesis based on them. (p. 111)
Intention: The reaction from readers and listeners the author or creator of a text wants to achieve. See also ***purpose***. (p. 6)
Irony: A figure, specifically a trope, in which words are meant to contradict their literal meaning. (p. 101)

J

Jargon: Diction and syntax used by a specific professional or academic group. (p. 90)
Juxtaposition: The placing of one item next to another one in order to understand both items better. (p. 11)

L

Lament: A type of poem in which the speaker is expressing woe or sorrow. (p. 46)
Latinate diction: Words that are generally more formal. (p. 90)
Litotes: A figure, specifically a trope, in which the writer deliberately understates a point. (p. 101)
***Logos*:** The way a text is seen to be effective because of the logical structure of its central argument. (p. 51)

M

Metaphor: An implied comparison between two things that, on the surface, seem dissimilar but that, upon further examination, share common characteristics. (p. 100)
Metonymy (muh-TAH-nuh-mee): A figure, specifically a trope, in which something is referred to by one of its attributes. (p. 100)

N

Narrative: A story or a story line, generally part of a larger text. (p. 37)
Nestorian order: A method for arranging material, named after the character Nestor in *The Odyssey,* in which the writer begins with material of middle importance, then provides material with the weakest importance, and finishes by offering material of highest importance. (p. 125)

O

Onomatopoeia: A figure, specifically a trope, in which the sound of words suggests their meaning. (p. 101)
Oxymoron: A figure, specifically a trope, in which words that have apparently contradictory meanings are placed near each other in a sentence. (p. 101)

P

Parallel structure, parallelism: The repetition of related words, phrases, or clauses in the same grammatical structure. (p. 97)
Parenthesis: A figure, specifically a scheme, in which additional material is inserted within a sentence. (This is the same spelling as the singular of parentheses, the punctuation marks.) (p. 98)
Passive voice: In a sentence that uses the passive voice, the receiver of the action is the subject, the verb contains some form of *to be* as a helper and a past participle, and the doer of the action is the object of a preposition in a prepositional phrase after the verb. (p. 93)
Pathos: The way a text is seen to be effective because it draws on the emotions of the audience. (p. 51)

Periodic sentence: A sentence structured so that its meaning is not closed or finished until at or near the end of the sentence. (p. 93)
Periphrasis (puh-RI-frah-suhs): A descriptive word or phrase is used to refer to a proper name. (p. 100)
Persona: The type of personality or character a text implies that its writer, speaker, or narrator has. (p. 55)
Personification: A figure, specifically a trope, in which non-human entities are given human characteristics. (p. 100)
Prediction: A central activity in reading comprehension, the act of anticipating what will come next in a text. (p. 23)
Pun: The generic name for a play on words. (p. 100)
Purpose: What the author or creator of a text intends the text to do for the readers or listeners. See also ***intention***. (p. 6)

R

Reader's repertoire: The collection of experiences that a reader can draw upon to make meaning of a text. (p. 7)
Rhetoric: (a) The art of finding all the available means of persuasion in a given case; (b) the art of writing or speaking well; and (c) the ways people produce texts to create and communicate meaning. (p. 6)
Rhetorical analysis: The act of separating any text into its component parts in order to understand how the text forges meaning, achieves a purpose, or creates an effect. (p. 72)
Rhetorical question: A figure, specifically a trope, in which a question is posed not to be answered but simply to move the development of an idea further or suggest a point. (p. 101)
Rhetorical triangle: A graphic depiction of any act of communication, showing the relationships among reader, author, and meaning. (p. 6)
Rogerian argument: A method of creating arguments by establishing common ground with an audience, offering more than one perspective on the idea and working toward mutual action by mediation or compromise. (p. 113)

S

Scheme: Any artful variation in the ways words, phrases, or sentences are constructed. (p. 95)
Simile: A direct comparison of two things, using the word *like* or *as*. (p. 100)
Six-part oration: An argument model, developed by the second-century B.C. Roman orator Marcus Tullius Cicero, containing an exordium, narration, partition, confirmation, refutation, and peroration. (p. 116)
Slang: Diction and syntax that are used by a specific social, age, or ethnic group. (p. 90)
Stance: The interpersonal relationship between the writer or speaker and the audience implied in a text. (p. 55)
Style: The choices a writer makes regarding words and phrases in a text—the language a writer uses. (p. 21)
Synecdoche (suh-NEK-duh-kee): A figure, specifically a trope, in which a part of something represents the whole. (p. 100)
Syntax: A collective term for sentence type, length, and structure. (p. 32)
Synthesis essay: An argumentative essay in which the writer synthesizes insights and information from other sources besides his or her own observations and experiences into the development of the thesis and main points. (p. 128)

T

Thesis: The central point or claim a text makes and develops. (p. 79)
Tone: The attitude of an author or creator of a text to its subject matter. (p. 20)
Toulmin argument: A method of analyzing an argument developed by the twentieth-century British philosopher Stephen Toulmin. Arguments analyzed using the Toulmin method identify an argument's claim, evidence, warrant, backing, rebuttal, and qualifier. (p. 112)
Trope: Any artful variation from the typical expression of ideas or words. (p. 95)

V

Voice: A term used in rhetorical and literary analysis to describe a writer's, speaker's, or narrator's tone and style. A writer's voice often reveals the writer's relationship to the text. (p. 32)

Z

Zeugma: A figure in which more than one item in a sentence is governed by a single word, usually a verb. (p. 97)

Credits

Text Credits

Chapter 1

p. 5: From *The Dumbest Generation* by Mark Bauerlein, copyright © 2008 by Mark Bauerlein. Used by permission of Jeremy P. Tarcher, an imprint of Penguin Group (USA) Inc. **p. 18:** From "The Plastic Pink Flamingo: A Natural History" by Jennifer Price. Reprinted from *The American Scholar,* Volume 68, No. 2, Spring 1999. Copyright © 2004 by the author. Reprinted by permission. **p. 20:** Source: Copyright 2006 The College Board. Reproduced with permission. http://apcentral.collegeboard.com. **p. 22:** (a) Bharati Mukherjee. *Letters of Transit: Reflections on Exile, Identity, Language, and Loss.* New York: The New Press. 2000, pg. 71. (b) David Sedaris, *Me Talk Pretty One Day.* Boston. Little, Brown and Co, 2000, p. 166. (c) Excerpt from "Casa" page 14 is reprinted with permission from publisher of *Silent Dancing: A Partial Remembrance of a Puerto Rican Childhood* by Judith Ortiz Cofer (© 1990 Arte Público Press-University of Houston). (d) Leslie Marmon Silko, *Yellow Woman and a Beauty of the Spirit: Essays on Native American Life Today.* New York: Simon & Schuster, 1996, pg. 26. **p. 23:** Source: Copyright © 2011–2012 The College Board. Reproduced with permission. http://apcentral.collegeboard.com. **p. 24:** Excerpt from *Womenfolks: Growing Up Down South* by Shirley Abbott. Copyright © 1983 by Shirley Abbott. Reprinted by permission of Houghton Mifflin Harcourt Publishing Company. All rights reserved.

Chapter 2

p. 30: Naomi Baron, *Always On,* New York: Oxford, 2009, p. 60. **p. 32:** (1) McMichael, George; Leonard, James S.; Fisher Fishkin, Shelley; Bradley, David; Nelson, Dana D.; Csicsila, Joseph, *Concise Anthology of American Literature, 7th Ed.,* © 2011. Reprinted and Electronically reproduced by permission of Pearson Education, Inc., Upper Saddle River, New Jersey. (2) From *The Dumbest Generation* by Mark Bauerlein, copyright © 2008 by Mark Bauerlein. Used by permission of Jeremy P. Tarcher, an imprint of Penguin Group (USA) Inc. **p. 34:** Bashō *The Complete Haiku,* Matsuo Bashō translated and annotated by Jane Reichhold. Kodansha, Tokyo: 2008. Reprinted by permission of Jane Reichhold. **p. 35:** "My Mother Enters the Work Force," from *On The Bus With Rosa Parks* by Rita Dove. Copyright © 1999 by Rita Dove. Used by permission of W. W. Norton & Company. **p. 36:** "Curtains" by Sandra Cisneros from *My Wicked Wicked Ways.* Copyright © 1987 by Sandra Cisneros, published by Third Woman Press and in hardcover by Alfred A. Knopf. By permission of Third Woman Press and Susan Bergholz Literary Services, New York, NY and Lamy, NM. All rights reserved. **p. 37:** Toni Morrison, *Sula.* New York: Vintage. 2004, pg. 3. **p. 41:** Pages 8 & 9 from *La Perdida* by Jessica Abel, 2006. **p. 43:** Neal Gabler. *Life the Movie: How Entertainment Conquers Reality.* New York: Vintage. 2000, pg. 20. (AP exam prompt) Source: Copyright © 2003 The College Board. Reproduced with permission. http://apcentral.collegeboard.com.

Chapter 3

p. 54: Kyle Jarrard, *Those Were the Books.* New York: International Herald Tribune. 2012. **p. 56:** "Small Change" by Malcolm Gladwell. Copyright © 2010 by Malcolm Gladwell. Originally Published in *The New Yorker.* Reprinted by permission of the author.

Chapter 4

p. 73: "Benjamin Franklin and The Invention of America" reprinted with the permission of Simon & Schuster, Inc. from *Benjamin Franklin: An American Life* by Walter Isaacson. Copyright © 2003 by Walter Isaacson. All rights reserved. **p. 77:** "Indian Boarding School: The Runaways" by Louise Erdrich, currently collected in *Original Fire: Selected and New Poems* by Louise Erdrich. Copyright © 2003 by Louise Erdrich used by permission of The Wylie Agency LLC. **p. 94:** Ernest Gaines, *A Lesson Before Dying.* New York: Vintage, 1993. pg. 16

Chapter 6

p. 130: "Is Light Rail the Answer to Transit Woes?" by Megan Reilly. Reprinted by permission of the author.

Unit 1

p. 255: "In Dark and Dismal Swamp" from *Mayflower* by Nathaniel Philbrick, copyright © 2006 by Nathaniel Philbrick. Used by permission of Viking Penguin, a division of Penguin Group (USA) Inc. **p. 262:** From *Before the Mayflower: A History of Black America,* 2007. Courtesy Johnson Publishing Company, LLC. All rights reserved. **p. 267:** From *The Wordy Shipmates* by Sarah Vowell, copyright © 2008 by Sarah Vowell. Used by permission of Riverhead Books, an imprint of Penguin Group (USA) Inc.

Unit 2

p. 398: From *Mrs. James Madison: The Incomparable Dolley* by Ethel S. Arnett. Reprinted by permission of Georgia Bonds. **p. 403:** "The Land Wisdom of the Indians" by Stewart Udall from *The Quiet Crisis.* Copyright © 1963 by Gibbs Smith. Reprinted by permission of Gibbs Smith. **p. 410:** "Out of Panic, Self-Reliance" by Harold Bloom from *The New York Times,* September 12,

2008. © 2008 The New York Times. All rights reserved. Used by permission and protected by the Copyright Laws of the United States. The printing, copying, redistribution, or retransmission of this Content without express written permission is prohibited. http://www.nytimes.com

Unit 3

p. 592: Lucille Clifton, "at the cemetery, walnut grove plantation, south carolina, 1989" from *The Collected Poems of Lucille Clifton.* Copyright © 1991 by Lucille Clifton. Reprinted with the permission of The Permissions Company, Inc. on behalf of BOA Editions Ltd., www.boaeditions.org. **p. 594:** "The Handicap of Definition" by William Raspberry from *The Washington Post.* © January 6, 1982 The Washington Post. All rights reserved. Used by permission and protected by the Copyright Laws of the United States. The printing, copying, redistribution, or retransmission of this Content without express written permission is prohibited. www.washingtonpost.com. **p. 597:** "Women Are Never Front-Runners" by Gloria Steinem from *The New York Times,* January 8, 2008. Copyright © 2008 The New York Times. All rights reserved. Used by permission and protected by the Copyright Laws of the United States. The printing, copying, redistribution, or retransmission of this Content without express written permission is prohibited. **p. 600:** From *The Way to Rainy Mountain* by N. Scott Momaday. Copyright © 1969 University of New Mexico Press. Reprinted by permission.

Unit 4

p. 715: "Missing Persons" by Jaron Lanier from *You are Not a Gadget*: A Manifesto, 2010, pp. 3–23. **p. 727:** "Getting Angry Can Be a Good Thing" by Cecilia Muñoz from the book *THIS I BELIEVE: The Personal Philosophies of Remarkable Men and Women* edited by Jay Allison and Dan Gediman, copyright © 2006 by This I Believe, Inc. Reprinted by permission of Henry Holt and Company, LLC. **p. 729:** "Stranded in Suburbia" by Paul R. Krugman from *The New York Times,* May 19, 2008. © 2008 The New York Times. All rights reserved. Used by permission and protected by the Copyright Laws of the United States. The printing, copying, redistribution, or retransmission of this Content without express written permission is prohibited. http://www.nytimes.com

Unit 5

p. 746: "May 9, 1945" from *My Day* by Eleanor Roosevelt. Reprinted by permission of The Estate of Eleanor Roosevelt. **p. 755:** "Preface" from *U.S.A.* by John Dos Passos. Copyright 1930, 1932, 1933, 1934, 1935, 1936, 1937 by John Dos Passos. Copyright 1946 by John Dos Passos and Houghton Mifflin Company. Copyright © renewed 1958, 1960 by John Dos Passos. Reprinted by permission of Lucy Dos Passos Coggin. **p. 758:** Meridel LeSueur, "Women of the Breadlines" from *Harvest*: Collected Stories. Reprinted with the permission of The Permissions Company, Inc., on behalf of West End Press, Albuquerque, New Mexico. www.westendpress.org. **p. 765:** "Ballad of the Freedom Train," September 1947 by Langston Hughes, from *The Collected Poems of Langston Hughes*, 1994, p. 323. **p. 768:** . . . And the Earth Did Not Part by Tomas Rivera from . . . *And the Earth Did Not Devour Him,* 1987. **p. 773:** Nobel Prize Acceptance Speech, December 10, 1950 by William Faulkner. © The Nobel Foundation 1950. Reprinted by permission of The Nobel Foundation. **p. 776:** From *On The Road* by Jack Kerouac, copyright © 1955, 1957 by Jack Kerouac; renewed © 1983 by Stella Kerouac, renewed © 1985 by Stella Kerouac and Jan Kerouac. Used by permission of Viking Penguin, a division of Penguin Group (USA) Inc. **p. 785:** Excerpt from "Preface" from *No-No Boy* by John Okada. Reprinted by permission of Washington University Press. **p. 789:** "I Stand Here Ironing" reproduced from *Tell Me a Riddle and Other Works* by Tillie Olsen by permission of the University of Nebraska Press. Copyright 1956, 1957, 1960, 1961 by Tillie Olsen. **p. 798:** "My Dungeon Shook: Letter to My Nephew on the One Hundredth Anniversary of the Emancipation" © 1962 by James Baldwin was originally published in *The New Yorker.* Copyright renewed. Collected in *The Fire Next Time,* published by Vintage Books. Reprinted by arrangement with the James Baldwin Estate. **p. 802:** "We Real Cool" by Gwendolyn Brooks. Reprinted by permission of Brooks Permissions. **p. 803:** "A Fable for Tomorrow" from *Silent Spring* by Rachel Carson. Copyright © 1962 by Rachel L. Carson, renewed 1990 by Roger Christie. Reprinted by permission of Houghton Mifflin Harcourt Publishing Company and Frances Collin, Trustee. All copying, including electronic, or re-distribution of this text, is expressly forbidden. All rights reserved. **p. 806:** "Letter From Birmingham Jail" by Martin Luther King Jr. Reprinted by arrangement with The Heirs to the Estate of Martin Luther King Jr., c/o Writers House as agent for the proprietor New York, NY. Copyright 1963 Dr. Martin Luther King Jr; copyright renewed 1991 Coretta Scott King. **p. 828:** "Dillon S. Myer and the WRA's History of 'Relocation, Reintegration, and Rehabilitation'" from *Historical Memories of the Japanese American Internment and the Struggle for Redress* by Alice Yang Murray. Copyright © 2008 by the Board of Trustees of the Leland Stanford Jr. University. All rights reserved. Used with permission of Stanford University Press, www.sup.org. **p. 841:** Excerpt from *That Use to Be Us* by Thomas L. Friedman and Michael Mandelbaum. Copyright © 2011 by Thomas L. Friedman and Michael Mandelbaum. Reprinted by permission of Picador. **p. 849:** "Black Men and Public Space" by Brent Staples. Reprinted by permission of the author.

Unit 6

p. 856: "Designated National Park" by Simon J. Ortiz. Originally published in *Woven Stone,* University of Arizona Press, Tucson AZ, 1992. Permission granted by author Simon J. Ortiz. **p. 860:** "How to Tame a Wild Tongue" by Gloria Anzaldúa from *Borderlands/La Frontera: The New Mestiza.* Copyright © 1987, 1999, 2007, 2012 by Gloria Anzaldúa. Reprinted by permission of Aunt Lute Books. www.auntlute.com. **p. 871:** "Anchorage", Copyright © 1983 by Joy Harjo, from *She Had Some Horses* by Joy Harjo. Used by permission of W. W. Norton & Company, Inc. **p. 874:** From *The Complete Maus* by Art Spiegelman, copyright Maus, Volume I copyright © 1973, 1980, 1981, 1982, 1983, 1984, 1985, 1986 by Art Spiegelman Maus, Volume II copyright © 1986, 1989, 1990, 1991 by Art Speigelman. Used by permission of Pantheon Books, a division of Random House, Inc. Any third party use of this material, outside of this publication, is prohibited. Interested parties must apply directly to Random House, Inc. for permission. **p. 880:** "Banneker" from *Museum: Poems* by Rita Dove, Carnegie Mellon University Press, Pittsburgh, PA. © 1992 by Rita Dove. Reprinted by permission of the author. **p. 883:** "On the Rainy River" from *The Things They Carried* by Tim O'Brien. Copyright © 1990 by Tim O'Brien. Reprinted by permission of Houghton Mifflin Harcourt Publishing Company. All rights reserved. **p. 900:** "Living Like Weasels" from *Teaching a Stone to Talk: Expeditions and Encounters* by Annie Dillard. Copyright © 1982 by Annie Dillard. Reprinted by permission of HarperCollins Publishers. **p. 904:** Nobel Prize Acceptance Speech by Toni Morrison. © The Nobel Foundation 1993. Reprinted by permission of The Nobel Foundation. **p. 914:** "Go Carolina" from *Me Talk Pretty One Day* by David Sedaris. Copyright © 2000 by David Sedaris. Reprinted by permission of Little, Brown and Company. **p. 922:** "Mother Tongue" by Amy Tan. Copyright © 1990 by Amy Tan. First appeared in *The Three Penny Review.* Reprinted by permission of the author and the Sandra Dijkstra Agency. **p. 933:** "Eleven" from *Woman Hollering Creek.* Copyright © 1991 by Sandra Cisneros. Published by Vintage Books, a division of Random House, Inc., New York and originally in hardcover by Random House, Inc. By permission of Susan Bergholz Literary Services, New York, NY and Lamy, NM. All rights reserved. **p. 937:** "One Moment on Top of the Earth" from *Never in a Hurry, Essays on People and Places* by Naomi Shihab Nye. Copyright 1996 by University of South Carolina Press. Reprinted by permission of University of South Carolina Press. **p. 941:** From *Hungry of Memory* by Richard Rodriguez. Copyright © 1982 by Richard Rodriguez. Reprinted by permission of Georges Borchardt, Inc., on behalf of the author. **p. 947:** "University Avenue" is reprinted with permission from the publisher of "Borders" by Pat Mora (© 1986 Arte Público Press-University of Houston). **p. 949:** "The Devil is a Busy Man" from *Brief Interviews with Hideous Men* by David Foster Wallace. Copyright © 1999 by David Foster Wallace. By permission of Little, Brown and Company. All rights reserved. **p. 952:** From "Footprints on the Flag" by Anchee Min. Copyright © 2007 by Anchee Min. The original version of this essay appeared in *The New Yorker* in 2001. Reprinted by permission of the author and the Sandra Dijkstra Literary Agency. **p. 954:** Billy Collins, "Introduction to Poetry" from *The Apple That Astonished Paris.* Copyright © 1988, 1996 by Billy Collins. Reprinted with the permission of The Permissions Company, Inc., on behalf of the University of Arkansas Press, www.uapress.com **p. 955:** "New York Day Women" from *Krik? Krak!,* copyright © 1995 by Edwidge Danticat, reprinted by permission of Soho Press, Inc. All rights reserved. **p. 960:** "Independence Day" by Dave Barry, from *Dave Barry is Not Taking This Sitting Down.* 2000, pp. 185–188. **p. 963:** From *Democracy in America* by Alexis de Tocqueville edited by James T. Schleifer and Eduardo Nolla, Copyright © 2010. Reprinted by permission of Liberty Fund, Inc. **p. 969:** Beebe, Steven A.; Beebe, Susan J., *Public Speaking Handbook, 3rd Ed.,* © 2012. Reprinted and Electronically reproduced by permission of Pearson Education, Inc., Upper Saddle River, New Jersey.

Photo Credits

FM

p. xxix: (top) Courtesy of Johnathon Williams; (bottom) Courtesy of University Relations, The University of North Carolina at Greensboro

Chapter 1

p. 4: Interfoto/Alamy. **p. 5:** Cover from *The Best American Comics 2011* by Alison Bechdel. Jacket art copyright © 2011 by Jillian Tamaki. Reprinted by permission of Houghton Mifflin Harcourt Publishing Company. All rights reserved. **p. 9:** Image Courtesy of The Advertising Archives. **p. 10:** Splash News/Corbis. **p. 11:** (left) Image Courtesy of The Advertising Archives; (right) Splash News/Corbis. **p. 13:** (top) *From the Back Window, 291* (1915), Alfred Stieglitz. Platinum print, 25.1 × 20.2 cm (9 7/8 × 7 15/16 in.). Alfred Stieglitz Collection, 1949 (49.55.35). Image copyright © The Metropolitan Museum of Art/Licensed by Art Resource, NY; (bottom) *New York, Old house on Bleeker Street, on a back lot between Mercer and Greene Streets* (circa 1890), Jacob A. Riis. Photograph. Museum of the City of New York/Getty Images

Chapter 3

p. 69: Jack Moebes/Corbis. **p. 70:** Andre Jenny Stock Connection Worldwide/Newscom

Chapter 6

p. 131: Richard Cummins/SuperStock

Unit 1

p. 164: Deosum/Fotolia. **p. 170:** Everett Collection Inc/Alamy. **p. 193:** Illustration from *A Narrative of the Captivity, Sufferings and Removes of Mrs. Mary Rowlandson.* Published by Nathaniel Coverly in Boston,

1770. **p. 211:** *Massasoit* (1921), Cyrus E. Dallin. Bronze sculpture. Plymouth, Massachusetts. Photo by Patti McConville/Alamy. **p. 226:** Illustration from *Information respecting the history, condition and prospects of the Indian tribes of the United States.* Part 5 by Henry Rowe Schoolcraft, published in Philadelphia in 1855. Photo by SSPL/The Image Works. **p. 234:** *Watson and the Shark* (1778), John Singleton Copley. Oil on canvas, overall: 182.1 × 229.7 cm (71 11/16 × 90 7/16 in.) framed: 241.3 × 264.2 × 10.1 cm (95 × 104 × 4 in.) Ferdinand Lammot Belin Fund 1963.6.1. Courtesy National Gallery of Art, Washington. **p. 254:** *Portrait of James Badger* (1760), Joseph Badger. Oil on canvas, 42 1/2 × 33 1/8 in. (108 × 84.1 cm). Photo by Peter Horree/Alamy

Unit 2

p. 284: Mandel Ngan/AFP/Getty Images. **p. 289:** *George Washington* (Lansdowne portrait) (1796), Gilbert Stuart. Oil on canvas, 97 1/2 × 62 1/2 inches. National Portrait Gallery, Smithsonian Institution. Photo by AP Images. **p. 336:** (left & right) Jean-Erick Pasquier/Gamma-Rapho/Getty Images. **p. 354:** *Scene from "The Last of the Mohicans," Cora Kneeling at the Feet of Tamenund* (1827), Thomas Cole. Oil on canvas. 25 3/8 × 35 1/16 in. Bequest of Alfred Smith. 1868.31868.3. Wadsworth Atheneum Museum of Art, Hartford, CT/Licensed by Art Resource, NY. **p. 355:** *Self Portrait* (1824), George Catlin. The Granger Collection, NY. **p. 359:** *Portrait of William Apess,* engraved by Illman and Pilbrow (litho), Paradise, John (1783–1833) (after)/American Antiquarian Society, Worcester, Massachusetts/The Bridgeman Art Library. **p. 396:** Universal Images Group Limited/Alamy. **p. 397:** (top, middle, & bottom) Universal Images Group Limited/Alamy

Unit 3

p. 416: Charlie Varley/Sipa Press/Newscom. **p. 463:** *Study of a Wood Interior* (c. 1855), Asher Brown Durand. Oil on canvas mounted on panel, 16 3/4 in. × 24 in. (42.55 cm × 60.96 cm). Gift Mrs. Frederic F. Durand, 1932.1. Addison Gallery of American Art, Phillips Academy, Andover, Massachusetts. All Rights Reserved. **p. 487:** *When Anthony Met Stanton* (1998), A. E. Ted Aub. Bronze sculptures. Seneca Falls, New York. Photo by Dennis MacDonald/Alamy. **p. 536:** *Wounded Soldiers in Hospital* (ca. 1860–ca. 1865), Mathew Brady. War Department. Office of the Chief Signal Officer. (08/01/1886–09/18/1947)/Still Picture Records Section, NARA [ARC ID: 524705/Local ID: 111-B-286]. **p. 564:** Pearson Education, Inc. **p. 591:** *Near Andersonville* (1865–1866), Winslow Homer. Oil on canvas, 23" × 18". Newark Museum, Newark, New Jersey/Licensed by Art Resource, NY. **p. 599:** Jacques Brinon/AP Images

Unit 4

p. 608: Jim West/Alamy. **p. 618:** *Westward the Star of Empire Takes Its Way—Near Council Bluffs, Iowa* (1867), Andrew Melrose. Oil on canvas, 34 3/4 in × 55 3/4 in. Autry National Center; 92.147.1. **p. 659:** *Henry Brooks Adams* (1868), Samuel Laurence. The Granger Collection, NY. **p. 679:** *Women doing laundry in a tenement courtyard on Elizabeth Street* (circa 1890s), Jacob A. Riis. Photograph. The Granger Collection, NY. **p. 680:** Bettmann/Corbis. **p. 691:** Picture History. **p. 696:** *The Steerage* (1907), Alfred Stieglitz. Printed 1915. Photogravure on vellum. 32.2 × 25.8 cm (12 11/16 × 10 3/16 in). Alfred Stieglitz Collection, 1933 (33.43.419). Image copyright © The Metropolitan Museum of Art/Licensed by Art Resource, NY. **p. 697:** *Yung Wing* (1878). Wood engraving. The Granger Collection, NY. **p. 705:** *Work on the Last Mile of the Central Pacific Railroad in 1869.* Wood engraving from a sketch by A. R. Waud. The Granger Collection, NY. **p. 714:** *Super Table* (1925), Stuart Davis. Oil on canvas, 48 × 34 1/8 in. Daniel J. Terra Collection, 1999.37. Terra Foundation for American Art, Chicago. Art copyright © 2012 Estate of Stuart Davis/Licensed by Art Resource, NY/VAGA, New York, NY

Unit 5

p. 734: Copyright © 2012 Lalo Alcaraz, www.laloalcaraz.com. **p. 748:** Alfred Eisenstaedt/Time & Life Pictures/Getty Images. **p. 754:** Brown Brothers. **p. 784:** NBC Television/Getty Images. **p. 827:** John Filo/AP Images

Unit 6

p. 854: PRNewsFoto/TOMS Shoes/AP Images. **p. 859:** *Mao* (1972), Andy Warhol. Portfolio of 10 screenprints on Beckett High White paper, 36 × 36 in. Copyright © 2012 The Andy Warhol Foundation for the Visual Arts, Inc./Artists Rights Society (ARS), New York. Photo by Oli Scarff/Getty Images. **p. 899:** *Vietnam Veterans Memorial* (1982), Maya Lin. Stone sculpture. Washington, DC. Photo by Kumar Sriskandan/Alamy **p. 913:** Pascal Saez/SIPA/Newscom. **p. 922:** European Pressphoto Agency B.V./Alamy **p. 931:** Jean-Louis Blondeau/Polaris. **p. 932:** Ana Juan/Copyright © 2001 The New Yorker Magazine/Conde Nast. **p. 933:** Zuma Press/Newscom. **p. 936:** GL Portrait/Alamy Stock Photo. **p. 940:** Christopher Felver/Corbis

Index